THE HARVARD GUIDE TO
AFRICAN-AMERICAN HISTORY

H HARVARD
UNIVERSITY
PRESS
REFERENCE
LIBRARY

The Harvard Guide to African-American History

Evelyn Brooks Higginbotham
EDITOR-IN-CHIEF

Leon F. Litwack and Darlene Clark Hine
GENERAL EDITORS

Randall K. Burkett
ASSOCIATE EDITOR

Foreword by Henry Louis Gates, Jr.

HARVARD UNIVERSITY PRESS
Cambridge, Massachusetts, and London, England   2001

Library of Congress Cataloging-in-Publication Data

The Harvard guide to African-American History / Evelyn Brooks Higginbotham, editor-in-chief;
Leon F. Litwack and Darlene Clark Hine, general editors; Randall K. Burkett, associate editor;
foreword by Henry Louis Gates, Jr.
    p.   cm.—(Harvard University Press reference library)
  Includes bibliographical references and index.
  ISBN 0-674-00276-8 (alk. paper)
  1. Afro-Americans—History—Handbooks, manuals, etc.
  2. Afro-Americans—History—Bibliography.
  3. Afro-Americans—Historiography.
  I. Higginbotham, Evelyn Brooks, 1945–
  II. Litwack, Leon F.
  III. Hine, Darlene Clark. IV. Series.
  E185.H326 2001
  973'.0496073—dc21   00-053861

To the memory of Nathan I. Huggins (1927–1989)

Contents

Contents viii

Foreword

Henry Louis Gates, Jr.

The Harvard Guide to African-American History is a pivotal publication in the current renaissance of African-American Studies. Drawing upon the research of key experts in the field, it provides carefully selected lists of the most important publications across the whole spectrum of black history. It will shape the future study of African-American history just as the *Harvard Guide to American History* did for U.S. history decades ago.

The history of the people of African descent emerged in the last quarter of the twentieth century as a major academic discipline in its own right, as well as a major influence on American history. While it has now become a cliché to say "African-American history is American history," we are also learning that "American history is African-American history." A sophisticated awareness of the fundamental interplay of what we once naively thought were separate subjects frozen in time is creating new insights, new questions, and, most important, a new vitality in the study and understanding of our inextricably interwoven past.

It is both astonishing and humbling to realize not only how rich the treasure of black history is, but how much more of it remains to be mined. African-American historiography remains a pregnant field. In every one of the divisions of this *Guide,* there is much more to be discovered. The utility of the *Guide* is that it lays out the best of what has been done and so points the researcher to what can be analyzed next. The opportunities are literally unlimited, and I envy the students and scholars who will be led into the new world of ignored, forgotten, and distorted history.

Malcolm X once wrote that "of all our studies, history is the best qualified to reward our research." That has probably always been true, but in the present moment it is a belated but glorious promise to which this book is an illuminating guide.

On the Evolution of Scholarship in Afro-American History

John Hope Franklin

Every generation has the opportunity to write its own history, and indeed it is obliged to do so. Only in that way can it provide its contemporaries with the materials vital to understanding the present and to planning strategies for coping with the future. Only in that way can it fulfill its obligation to pass on to posterity the accumulated knowledge and wisdom of the past, which, after all, give substance and direction for the continuity of civilization.

According to my calculation, there have been four generations of scholarship—of unequal length—in Afro-American history. The first generation began auspiciously with the publication in 1882 of the two-volume *History of the Negro Race in America* by George Washington Williams and ended around 1909 with the publication of Booker T. Washington's *Story of the Negro*. Although it is difficult to characterize this first period of serious scholarship in the field, it is safe to say that the primary concern of the writers was to explain the process of adjustment Afro-Americans made to conditions in the United States. Whether it was the aggressive integrationism of George Washington Williams or the mild accommodationism of Booker T. Washington, the common objective of the writers of this period was to define and describe the role of Afro-Americans in the life of the nation. They by no means shared the same view of the past or the same way of writing history; they delineated the epic of Afro-American history in the manner that their talents and training permitted. They wrought as well as they could; and they wrought well.

There were no trained, professional historians among them, with the exception of W. E. B. Du Bois, who deserted the field shortly after he entered it. As he roamed across the fields of history, sociology, anthropology, political science, education, and literature, Du Bois became one of the few people ever who could be considered truly qualified in the broad field of Afro-American studies. Likewise, it is impossible to confine Du Bois to one generation. His life spanned three generations, and he made contributions to each of them. Others of the first generation were able, industrious, and well focused. They were historians more interested in es-

From Darlene Clark Hine, ed., *The State of Afro-American History: Past, Present, and Future* (Baton Rouge: Louisiana State University Press, 1986).

pousing the causes of human beings than in adhering strictly to the canons of history. They provided panoramic, even pictorial views of Afro-Americans from the earliest times to the present. They wrote of "The Progress of the Race," "A New Negro for a New Century," and "The Remarkable Advancement of the American Negro." As one of them said, in commenting on post–Civil War Afro-Americans, "Starting in the most humble way, with limited intelligence and exceedingly circumscribed knowledge . . . they have gone on from year to year accumulating a little until the savings, as represented by their property, have built churches, erected schools, paid teachers and preachers, and greatly improved the home and home life." Obviously their concern was with adjustment, adaptation, and the compatibility of Afro-Americans with the white world in which they were compelled to live.

The second generation was marked by no special fanfare until the publication of Du Bois's *The Negro* in 1915, the founding of the Association for the Study of Negro Life and History also in 1915, the launching of the *Journal of Negro History* in 1916, and the publication in 1922 of Carter G. Woodson's *The Negro in Our History.* Woodson was the dominant figure of the period. He was not only the leading historian but also the principal founder of the association, editor of the *Journal,* and executive director of the Associated Publishers. He gathered around him a circle of highly trained younger historians whose research he directed and whose writings he published in the *Journal of Negro History* and under the imprint of the Associated Publishers. Monographs on labor, education, Reconstruction, art, music, and other aspects of Afro-American life appeared in steady succession, calling to the attention of the larger community the role of Afro-Americans, more specifically the contributions they had made to the development of the United States. The articles and monographs reflected prodigious research and zeal in pursuing the truth that had *not* been the hallmark of much of the so-called scientific historical writing produced in university seminars in this country some years earlier.

Woodson provided the intellectual and practical leadership of the second generation. With his strong sense of commitment, he offered the spirit and enthusiasm of a pioneer, a discoverer. He even provided the principal theme for the period when he said—in his writings and on numerous occasions—that it was the objective of him and his colleagues "to save and publish the records of the Negro, that the race may not become a negligible factor in the thought of the world." Nor should the record of Afro-Americans become a negligible factor in their own thought, Woodson contended. Thus he began doing everything possible to keep the history of Afro-Americans before them and before the larger community as well. Every annual meeting of the Association for the Study of Negro Life and History had several sessions devoted to the teaching of Afro-American history in the elementary and secondary schools. In 1926 Woodson began the annual observance of Negro History Week to raise the consciousness of Afro-Americans regarding their own worth and to draw the attention of others to what Afro-Americans had contributed to American civilization. Shortly thereafter he launched the *Negro History Bulletin,* a magazine for students, teachers, and the general public. Forty years before this country began to observe History Day, there was Negro History Week. Fifty years after the beginning of the *Negro History Bulletin,* the

American Historical Association was still wrestling with the idea of a popular history magazine for students and the general public.

The second generation of Afro-American historical scholarship was coming to a close some years before Woodson's death in 1950. Perhaps a convenient place to mark the beginning of the third generation is with the appearance in 1935 of W. E. B. Du Bois's *Black Reconstruction*. Although Du Bois had gone to some length to disassociate himself from efforts toward racial integration when he left the NAACP the previous year, *Black Reconstruction* reflected little of the separatist sentiment that characterized some of his other writings in 1934 and 1935. In his book on Reconstruction, as the subtitle indicates, he was interested in "the part which black folk played in the attempt to reconstruct democracy in America." In this attempt Du Bois saw merit in blacks and whites working together, espousing the same causes, voting together, and promoting the same candidates. If his book lacked the scholarship of *The Suppression of the African Slave Trade,* which had appeared forty years earlier in 1896, it achieved a level of original interpretation seldom if ever matched by the most profound students of history.

The third generation of Afro-American historical scholarship spanned, roughly, a twenty-five-year period that ended with the close of the 1960s. Most of the members of this generation were, like Du Bois, interested in the role that Afro-Americans played in the nation's history. Their training was similar to that of the second generation, but their interests were different. They looked less to Afro-American achievements and more to the interactions of blacks with whites, and more to the frequent antagonisms than to the rare moments of genuine cooperation. They tended to see Afro-American history in a larger context, insisting that any event that affected the status of Afro-Americans was a part of Afro-American history even if no Afro-Americans were directly involved. Mississippi's Theodore Bilbo, reading Rayford Logan's *What the Negro Wants* (1944) to his colleagues in the United States Senate and interpreting it for their benefit, was as much a part of Afro-American history as was Heman Sweatt's seeking admission to the University of Texas Law School.

The third generation experienced the fire and brimstone of World War II. Its predicament was not one that Adolf Hitler created but one created by the racial bigotry within their own government and in the American community in general. While all Afro-Americans were exposed to this special brand of racial perversion in the form of eloquent, if shallow, pronouncements against worldwide racism, Afro-American historians were especially sensitive to the persistent hypocrisy of the United States from the colonial years right down to World War II. Small wonder that they had difficulty maintaining a semblance of balance in the face of studied racial discrimination and humiliation. One of them declared that the United States government was "guilty of catering to the ideals of white supremacy." Another called on the United States to "address herself to the unfinished business of democracy," adding somewhat threateningly that "time was of the essence." If anyone doubts the impatience and anger of Afro-American historians during those years, he or she should examine the proceedings of the annual meetings of the Association for the Study of Negro Life and History or follow the activities of the historians themselves.

A salient feature of this generation was the increasing number of white historians working in the field. Some years earlier the second generation of historians
had indicated that there were numerous areas in which work needed to be done.
White historians entered the field to share in the work. One of them published the
first extensive study of slavery in almost forty years and another wrote an elaborate
work on the antislavery movement. Still another presented the first critical examination of Negro thought in the late nineteenth century. Interestingly enough, hostile white critics called these white historians "neo-abolitionists." Others worked
on Afro-Americans in the antebellum North, Afro-American intellectual history,
racial discrimination in education, and Afro-Americans in urban settings. Mean-
while, university professors began to assign dissertation topics in Afro-American
history to white as well as Afro-American students. They also participated in the
annual meetings of the Association for the Study of Negro Life and History and
contributed to the *Journal of Negro History.* By the end of the 1960s Afro-American
history was no longer the exclusive domain of Afro-Americans.

I believe that Carter G. Woodson would have been pleased with this involvement of white historians in the third generation of scholarship. When he founded
the *Journal of Negro History* in 1916, he invited white scholars to sit on the editorial
board and to contribute articles. He was, nevertheless, a man of shrewd insights,
and I am not suggesting for a moment that he would have approved of or even tol-
erated whites of the third generation whose motives were more political than
scholarly. Even so, he would have welcomed papers for publication in the *Journal
of Negro History,* whether submitted by whites or blacks, so long as they were the
product of rigorous scholarship and were not contaminated by the venom of racial bias. I knew him well and spent many hours with him each year between 1940
and 1950, when he died. He would have been appalled at the bickering that envel-
oped the association in the 1960s over the question of whether white historians
should be permitted to participate in the work of the association. He had always
insisted that men and women should be judged strictly on the basis of their work
and not on the basis of their race or the color of their skin.

In the fourth generation, which began around 1970, there emerged the largest
and perhaps the best-trained group of historians of Afro-America that had ever
appeared. The Afro-Americans in the group were trained, as were the white historians, in graduate centers in every part of the country, in contrast to those of the
third generation, who had been trained at three or four universities in the East and
Midwest. No area of inquiry escaped their attention. They worked on the colonial
period, the era of Reconstruction, and the twentieth century. They examined slavery, the Afro-American family, and antebellum free blacks. Their range was wide,
and they brought educational, cultural, and military subjects, among many others,
under their scrutiny.

These new approaches as well as the accelerated intensity in the study of Afro-
American history were greatly stimulated by the drive for equality that had already
begun in the third period. In their insistence that they be accorded equal treatment
in every respect, Afro-Americans summoned the history of the United States to
their side. They had been here from the beginning, they argued, and had done
more than their share in making the country rich and great. Since history vali-

dated their claims, it was important that the entire nation should become familiar with the facts of Afro-American history. Consequently, it should be studied more intensely, written about more extensively, and taught more vigorously. Institutions of higher education came under pressure to add courses in Afro-American history and related fields and to employ specialists in the field. Responses were varied. One dean at a leading predominantly white university said that he had no objection to a course in Afro-American history, but it would be difficult in view of the fact that there was not sufficient subject matter to occupy the teachers and students for a *whole* semester. Another rushed out and persuaded one of the leaders in the black community, who happened to be a Baptist minister, to teach a course in Afro-American history. Despite the intellectual, educational, and political considerations affecting their decisions, many colleges and universities incorporated courses in Afro-American history into their curricula.

It was the frenetic quality of the concerns of university administrators that cast doubts on their interest in maintaining high academic standards in the area of Afro-American studies. As students intensified their demands for courses in this area, university officials seemed more interested in mollifying students than in enriching the curriculum with courses taught by well-trained professors who maintained high standards. The results were that some courses were staffed by persons whose familiarity with what they taught was minimal and whose approach tended to confirm the views of the dean who thought there was not sufficient subject matter in Afro-American history to span an entire semester.

It is nothing short of marvelous that under the circumstances scholarship in Afro-American history moved to a new high level of achievement. Some claimed that those who taught were not doing the researching and writing and, thus, were not adding to the body of knowledge that was needed in order to satisfy our doubting dean. That was true, to some extent, but it was no less true in, say, diplomatic, cultural, intellectual, or economic history. There have always been more purveyors than creators of knowledge in all fields, and there is nothing fundamentally wrong with this, I suppose. We who teach *and* do research and write tend to think that the dual activity is more healthy intellectually, but that is a matter of opinion. What is remarkable in the field of Afro-American history is not that there were so many teachers who did not write but that there were so many who did.

Perhaps it was because scholars in the field of Afro-American history saw so many opportunities to reinterpret their field that such a large number of them were engaged in researching and writing. There was zeal, even passion, in much that they wrote, for they were anxious to correct all the errors and misinterpretations of which earlier historians had been guilty. Thus, they undertook to revise not only the racist historians of an earlier day but the Afro-American historians of an earlier generation as well. There was not always the grace and charity and certainly not the gratitude that one might expect of persons whose work almost invariably rested on the work of their intellectual godfathers. That, however, was relatively unimportant, especially if the work they produced was of the highest quality and made a solid contribution to the scholarship of Afro-American history. This was true often enough that one could blush more often in pride than in sorrow.

Some writing, nevertheless, was stimulated by publishers who were anxious to take advantage of a growing market. Under pressure from their agents and editors, some scholars produced works that had the sole merit of having been written with more than deliberate speed. When the speed was not great enough to produce "instant" books, publishers prevailed on some scholars to anthologize the writings of others. Some of the products were of great merit, bringing together as they did the best writings of some of the leaders in the field. Some of the products, however, were excellent illustrations of how scholars and scholarship can be corrupted by the prospect of monetary gain. Many anthologies were literally thrown together, without any thought being given to arrangement or organization and without any introduction, interpretation, or connective tissue. The only thing that one can say of such works is that they were not alone in the nature and extent of their compromise with intellectual integrity. Lecturers could be just as bad or worse. One recalls how in the early 1970s one of the "authoritative" lecturers in Afro-American history broke an engagement at a leading western university and simply informed them by telegram that he had been offered more money to lecture at another institution. Perhaps more common were "instant" professors, black and white, who rushed into the field to make a quick reputation as well as a quick buck. Unhappily, college and university administrators did not display the same skill in detecting the charlatans in this field that they did in some other fields. Thus, the field often suffered from the presence of so-called authorities whose abilities were no higher than their motives.

At this point one must not dwell on defects of scholarship or even the character of the scholars. Time will take care of such matters, without even so much as a suggestion from us as to how we should like to settle them. Instead, we could better serve the present *and* the future by attempting, as historians, to take lessons from the last century and use them to make certain that this generation will make significant improvements over what preceding generations had to offer.

In his *History of the Negro Race in America* (1882), George Washington Williams was extremely critical of Frederick Douglass for various positions he took on slavery and freedom in the years before the Civil War. We could excoriate Williams, as did his contemporaries, but that would be unfair without at least first understanding Williams' impatience with a political party that had betrayed not only the freedmen but Frederick Douglass, their chosen spokesman, as well. Likewise, one could be extremely critical of Carter G. Woodson's preoccupation with the achievements of Afro-Americans, but one should remember that Woodson was hurling historical brickbats at those who had said that Afro-Americans had achieved nothing at all. One could likewise be extremely critical of the historians of the third generation for their preoccupation with what may be called "mainstream history." In the process, some claim, they neglected some cherished attributes of Afro-American life and history, such as race pride and cultural nationalism. Such claims overlook the important fact that the historians of the third generation were compelled by circumstances to fight for the integration of Afro-American history into the mainstream of the nation's history. Their fight to integrate Afro-American history into the mainstream was a part of the fight by Afro-American students to break into the graduate departments of history in every predominantly white university in the southern states and in very many such institutions outside the South. It was also a part of the fight of Afro-Americans to gain admission to the mainstream of American life—for the vote, for equal treatment, for equal opportunity, for their rights as Americans. They pursued that course in order to be able to refute those, including our favorite dean—our favorite whipping boy, incidentally—who argued that Afro-Americans had little or no history. They also did so in order to support their argument that Afro-American history should be recognized as a centerpiece—an adornment, if you will—of the history of the United States.

The excoriations and strictures heaped on one generation of Afro-American historians by succeeding generations could better be spent on more constructive pursuits. Better trained and with better means of communication, they could, for example, seek to tell us more than we already know about malingering and sabotage among slaves. They could devote more attention to writing vignettes if not full biographies of hundreds of important Afro-Americans, the remembrance and recognition of whom are endangered by neglect and the passage of time. They could devote some of their energies to helping us understand how it is, in a country committed to the dignity of man, that so much energy has been spent throughout its history to maintain the proposition that Afro-Americans have no dignity and, therefore, are not deserving of respect. Thomas Jefferson argued it when he likened Afro-Americans to the orangutan. Fourth generation historians of Afro-America have come close to arguing it by claiming that slaves, as a whole, were not only content but were imbued with the Protestant work ethic that gave them a sense of commitment to what they were doing. No area of intellectual endeavor needs such stumbling blocks to truth, whether it comes out of the eighteenth century or out of the last quarter of the twentieth century.

The implications of all of this for the teaching of Afro-American history are profound, to say the least. As a relatively new field, at least only recently recognized as a respectable field of intellectual endeavor, it is alive and vibrant. This is why it can easily attract and excite a large number of graduate and undergraduate students. It provides, moreover, a very important context in which much, if not the whole, of the history of the United States can be taught and studied. It also provides an important context in which much of the history of the United States can be reexamined and rewritten. In its unique position as one of the most recent areas of intellectual inquiry, it invites the attention of those who genuinely seek new avenues to solve some of the nation's most difficult historical problems. And, if it is a valid area of intellectual inquiry, it cannot be segregated by sex, religion, or race. Historians must be judged by what they do, not by how they look.

I like to think that it was more than opportunism that increased the offerings in Afro-American history in the colleges and universities across the land. I like to believe that it was more than the excitement of the late 1960s that provided new opportunities to teach and learn Afro-American history. I prefer to entertain the thought that in addition to those other considerations there was the valid interconnection between the history of a people and their drive for first-class citizenship. The quest for their history, lost and strayed, was a quest in which black and white alike could and did participate, as both teachers and writers of history. The drive for first-class citizenship was a drive whose immediate benefit could be enjoyed only by those who had been denied it or by those others who at least truly understood the loathsome nature that such denial represented.

Some members of the fourth generation, no doubt, will regard this sentiment as optimistic if not maudlin. I would be the first to say that there is some of both in it. I would only add that when one begins a poem, a hymn, a short story, or even a history, one must be optimistic about its completion and about what it seeks to teach. If one believes in the power of his own words and in the words of others, one must also hope and believe that the world will be a better place by our having spoken or written those words.

Editors' Introduction

In 1896 Harvard University launched its first historical monograph series with the publication of W. E. B. Du Bois's *The Suppression of the African Slave Trade to the United States of America, 1638–1870.* The event was noteworthy. Harvard Historical Studies constituted one of the earliest examples of a university-sponsored series; and the doctoral dissertation of the Harvard history department's first African-American Ph.D. achieved the coveted position of becoming volume one. Most noteworthy, however, was the ironic timing of the publication: in the very year that the Supreme Court sanctioned racial segregation. At the dawn of the 20th century and in an era when African-Americans faced racial inequality in both subtle and terrifying forms, Du Bois entered the historical profession with little assurance of winning respect for the history of his people. It was not simply that most of his peers reinforced prevailing racial attitudes; they helped to create and shape those attitudes, justifying on historical and "scientific" grounds a whole complex of laws, judicial decisions, customs, and creeds that dictated a separate and unequal place for black men and women. It would take a half-century and the civil rights movement for African-American history to gain visibility in the academy, and in the larger society considerably longer.

The Harvard Guide to African-American History debuts at a very different time and to a very different audience. Today an explosion of books and articles attests to the widespread and growing interest in the African-American past. The major historical organizations—the American Historical Association, the Organization of American Historians, and the Southern Historical Association—now devote sessions to black history and publish articles on this subject in their quarterly journals. At the dawn of the 21st century, black history is recognized as a vibrant field of scholarly inquiry—a legitimate part of the American heritage.

In hindsight what seems remarkable is the degree to which research and writing persisted despite the decades-long omission of African-Americans from mainstream historical literature and textbooks. In a nation that embraced so passionately its racial myths and biases, W. E. B. Du Bois produced *A Select Bibliography of the Negro American* (1905), one of the Atlanta University Publications. In 1915 Carter G. Woodson, the second Harvard-trained black historian, founded the Association for the Study of Negro Life and History and one year later established the *Journal of Negro History.* Woodson encouraged black scholars and teachers to preserve and take pride in the history of their people so that "the race may not become a negligible factor in the thought of the world."

Still another indication of the ongoing effort to record the black experience was the *Negro Year Book* (1912), edited by Monroe N. Work, Director of the Department of Records and Research at Tuskegee Normal and Industrial Institute. The final section contained a bibliography, and with each new volume that bibliography expanded. Finally, in 1921 the Carnegie Corporation of New York provided support for a far more ambitious effort by Work, in order to provide "extended and comprehensive references to sources of information relating to all phases of the present day life of the Negro, to the conditions affecting this life and also to the anthropological and historical background of the same." Published in 1928, *A Bibliography of the Negro in Africa and America* offered nearly 700 pages and 37,000 references to published works. It remains to this day a monument not only to the devotion and scholarship of Monroe Work but to the resourcefulness of early scholars of black history. *The Harvard Guide to African-American History* is a basic reference work that builds on their pioneering efforts.

Perhaps no individual is more responsible for the current prominence of African-American history than John Hope Franklin, another Harvard-trained historian. In 1947 Franklin published *From Slavery to Freedom,* an authoritative, comprehensive, and deeply researched text that would over the next half-century introduce more than two million students and nonstudents alike to African-American history and to the idea that African-Americans had a history. Thus we introduce this *Guide* with Franklin's reflections on the evolving character of the field. Although this reprinted article provides a historiographic examination through the 1970s, it is now apparent that a growing number of scholars, white and black, significantly expanded the parameters of historical expression and documentation begun in the 1960s and early 1970s. In the last two decades of the 20th century, scholars have come increasingly to examine people who spent their lives in relative obscurity, who never shared the fruits of affluence, and who never enjoyed power. Through them we hear the new voices of black women in addition to men. We learn of new historical experiences of everyday resistance in addition to familiar forms of political protest. We discover new cultural perspectives on racial and gender identity, profoundly transforming our understanding of individual and collective consciousness.

The *Harvard Guide* speaks to the maturation, complexity, and scholarly integrity of African-American history. It is aimed at the general reader, the research scholar, the teacher, and students preparing papers in high schools and in colleges and universities. In reflecting the new scholarship, it incorporates the varieties of expression and documentation, including the rich oral tradition. A reference guide, it is arranged in thematic and chronological parts. The first focuses on Historical Research Aids and Materials, acquainting readers with reference tools and repositories throughout the United States. In the form of both bibliographic essays and useful source lists, specialists in diverse fields provide a wealth of primary and secondary sources, traditional and nontraditional, to assist the researcher. Topics include Bibliography, Reference Works, Internet Sources, Manuscript Collections,

Primary Sources on Microform, Newspapers and Selected Periodicals, Government Documents, Oral History, Art, Music, Photography, and Film and Television.

The second part, Comprehensive and Chronological Histories, begins with a chapter on comprehensive sources, namely, writings covering a century or more. The next ten chapters represent specific periods in African-American history between 1492 and 1999. Thus the first chronological chapter begins with African society and the slave trade in the year that the New World became known to European explorers. The dispersion of Africans to Europe and the New World colonies is reflected by the diasporic character of the sources in the first two chronological chapters; the subsequent chapters' sources chronicle the history of people of African descent in the United States.

Documenting the breadth of African-American history in bibliographic form has required an interdisciplinary perspective—inclusive of such topics as general studies, historiography, secondary sources on newspapers and periodicals, race relations, government, demography, family, religion, thought and expression, education, work and entrepreneurial activity, medicine, and science and technology. Additionally, the broad topics of race relations, government, society, and thought and expression contain subdivisions that capture an array of issues such as slavery, black/ethnic relations, segregation, law, politics and voting, urban life, leisure and sports, emigration and nationalism, and literature and poetry, to name only a few.

For the most part, the chapters are arranged similarly to assure some uniformity and continuity across the entire spectrum of African-American history. However, the format deviates in a few places, in order to facilitate research. The predominant theme of the slave trade for the period 1492–1690 required a breakdown for Africa, Europe, and countries in the New World, and the preponderance of writings on Brazil necessitated a category distinct from the larger grouping of countries under the heading South America. For the period 1831–1856 the amount of writing on the economics of slavery necessitated a separate subheading under slavery. For general studies of the period 1865–1877, the massive number of sources on Reconstruction required the more efficient categorization by state. Because of the international proliferation of African-American history, the comprehensive and chronological studies include sources in foreign languages. Foreign-language titles are identified by original language and translated into English.

In regard to subject placement, many works do not fit neatly into a single period. Several writings in the chapter on Comprehensive Studies cover a century or more, yet nevertheless focus on a shorter time span. Such writings (studies of slavery, for example) will reappear in one or more period chapters. At times, writings appear under multiple categories in a single chapter because of their range of information. In an effort to reduce too many duplicate citations, we have limited the placement of sources that cover related topics. Accordingly, most publications dealing with school desegregation in the 1950s are listed under the heading Education rather than Segregation/Jim Crow. Likewise, sources concerning the legal framework of slavery are generally included under Law, and not under Slavery. For effective use of this volume, readers should consult several related headings in re-searching a particular topic.

The third part of this volume, Histories of Special Subjects, was developed to provide a more focused look at topics of widespread and growing interest. Sources on African-American women are integrated throughout this volume. However, readers with a particular interest in this subject will be pleased to find the separate section on Women, which adopts the same categorical format as the chronological bibliographies. The Geographical Areas chapter was developed for ease in finding sources devoted to regions, states, and local communities, although such sources appear in other parts of this guide.

For readers in search of specific individuals in history, the Autobiography and Biography chapter provides an alphabetical listing of names with birth and death dates and occupation. Both autobiographies and autobiographical writings (pub-lished memoirs or diaries) are placed together with biographical sources. In most cases, works that focus primarily upon the life of an individual appear in the Auto-biography and Biography chapter rather than in the chronological bibliographies. Exceptions to this practice occur in those cases in which a certain autobiography, biography, or memoir deals significantly with the historical background of a spe-cific time period. Such works are included in both the Autobiography and Biogra-phy chapter and the appropriate chronological bibliography. When consulting the chronological bibliographies, therefore, readers should be aware that many sec-tions—for example, Slavery, Civil Rights, and Music and Performing Arts—in-clude only a portion of the vast number of personal profiles that such topics have inspired. These sections may be augmented significantly by consulting the Autobi-ography and Biography chapter.

Finally, it must be emphasized that *The Harvard Guide to African-American His-tory* is a selective resource. The field of African-American history has grown so rapidly, both in scope and in the sheer number of publications, that we could not possibly hope to include every book and article. No doubt some works deserving of inclusion are not here, and some that are included perhaps should have been omitted. The *Harvard Guide* does not include review essays, very short articles, or theses and Ph.D. dissertations. In the case of revised editions, only the latest edi-tion is recorded. For example, John Hope Franklin's *From Slavery to Freedom* is cited in its 8th edition (2000). Nor did our production time allow for the inclusion of as many studies published in the year 2000 as we would have liked. Although thousands of writings are included in this volume, we recognize the inevitability of inadvertent omissions and sincerely apologize for them.

EVELYN BROOKS HIGGINBOTHAM

LEON F. LITWACK

DARLENE CLARK HINE

Acknowledgments

The Harvard Guide to African-American History owes its existence to many people over time. It was first and foremost the inspiration of Nathan I. Huggins, chairman of the Afro-American Studies Department and director of the W. E. B. Du Bois Institute for Afro-American Research at Harvard University between 1980 and 1989. Huggins envisioned a reference work on the order of the *Harvard Guide to American History*, but with a format reflective of the thematic and chronological categories unique to the black experience. His untimely death in 1989 left the project's actual development to others. A special word of gratitude goes to his successor and current departmental chair Henry Louis Gates, Jr., for keeping Huggins's dream alive through the unfailing and generous support of the W. E. B. Du Bois Institute. Under the direction of Jacqueline Goggin, Richard Newman, and Randall Burkett—all managing editors of the project at different times between 1991 and 1996—the *Harvard Guide* enlisted significant funding support as well as the collaboration of an array of scholars.

In addition to the scholars whose names appear as authors in this volume, special appreciation goes to those who provided citations for specific sections and lent other expertise. Cheryl Greenberg helped to augment our listing of works related to black-ethnic relations, especially black-Jewish relations. Patricia Sullivan offered materials on civil rights and performed other valuable roles in the oversight of the project. Philippe Wamba was critical to organizing the initial data in computer-ready format.

The presentation of foreign-language titles was made possible by a number of international scholars: Maria Diedrich, Sonia Di Loreto, Michel Fabre, Atsuko Furomoto, Dolores Magdalena Gayo, Sandra Grieco, Peter J. Muehlbauer, Hideyuki Otsuka, Carl Pedersen, Alessandro Portelli, Dorra Triki, and Xi Wang. The Collegium for African-American Research (CAAR) in Europe played a significant role in engaging the support of several of the aforementioned individuals.

We are grateful for superb student helpers and other research staff who worked conscientiously in such tasks as data entry, verifying citations, translating foreign-language citations, and searching out additional titles. They include: Kevin Adams, Junko Araki, Daniel Baer, Sylvia Baldwin, Naomi Coquillon, Illya Davis, Dayle Delancey, Barrington Edwards, Camille Forbes, April Garrett, Amma Y. Ghartey-Tagoe, Jamal Kwame Greene, Yolanda Howze, Sarah Jackson, Joseph Kennedy,

Chaundra Candace King, Stephen Marshall, Sharee McKenzie, Jacqueline McLeod, Aaron Myers, Yasuhiro Okada, William Pannapacker, Charles Postel, Gary J. Presto, Pilar Quezzaire-Belle, Sherie Michelle Randolph, Kelena Reid, Sharifa Rhodes-Pitts, Alonford James Robinson, Lisa Robinson, Marveta Ryan, Marcy Sacks, Phillippa M. Scarlett, Carey Elizabeth Schwaber, Kimberly Sims, Darryl Anthony Smith, Pamela Smoot, Nia Charlotte Stephens, Christopher Strain, Shirley E. Thompson, Corey Walker, Matthew Whitaker, Diana I. Williams, and Andre Willis.

At times certain individuals played particularly outstanding roles, indeed critical to the life of the project. Their cumulative efforts over the years gave clarity and structure to an unwieldy and uneven mass of citations. The editors of the *Harvard Guide* offer heartfelt thanks to Adam Biggs and C. Dale Gadsden in the earlier period and later to Mitsi A. Sellers, Lia Miranda Pyne, Kevin R. Amer, Elizabeth A. Herbin, and Shalanda D. Dexter, who brought the book to fruition. They entered and verified enormous amounts of data, answered the editors' and contributors' queries, checked for new work in print, and searched for obscure information. At the very end, the indexing of the many thousands of entries proved to be a formidable task, overcome only by the tireless assistance of several students, whose names have already been mentioned; but a special debt of gratitude is owed to C. Dale Gadsden for her talent and diligence in this process.

We must also give sincere thanks to Harvard University in the persons of Provost Harvey Fineberg, counsel Allan Ryan, and Harvard University Press editors Aida Donald and Jennifer Snodgrass for their wise and patient guidance at points along the way. Finally, the *Harvard Guide* could not have been published without significant funding from the National Endowment for the Humanities, the Ford Foundation, the Mellon Foundation, the Rockefeller Foundation, the W. E. B. Du Bois Institute, and Harvard University Press. We are grateful for your confidence in the merit of this project. We hope that this volume will vindicate your trust.

I

HISTORICAL RESEARCH AIDS AND MATERIALS

1   *Bibliography*

Richard Newman

A bibliography is not simply a list of books but rather a list characterized by particularity: everything written by a certain author, for example, or on a specific subject, or held by a certain repository. The materials relevant to the particularity called African-American history and culture are not entirely under bibliographic control—that is, they have never been fully and systematically collected, organized, and made accessible. This is partly because African-American studies is a relatively new field in the academy. Yet it is owing more to mainstream scholars' having traditionally believed either that people of African descent actually have no history, or, when that was disproved, that their history could not be retrieved and known.

This essay, while listing and describing bibliographies in African-American history, is not meant to be comprehensive. Some fields are omitted here because they are covered in other essays in this book: reference works, art, music, photography, and film and television. Genres intentionally excluded, with the exception of a few items, are indexes, guides, anthologies, exhibition catalogs, dealers' catalogs, handbooks, directories, and works on non-U.S. subjects. The largest category omitted (and often the best place to look for citations) is that of bibliographies at the end of specialized books and monographs.

Bibliography itself has been revolutionized by recent technology. The computer is a master at high-speed searching, selecting, sorting, organizing, and list-making. Cooperative library networks afford researchers a vast universe in which to track subjects or authors or titles. As electronic devices become more sophisticated and widespread, the task will become even simpler. At present, however, not everything has been entered into electronic form. There are still unusual titles to be cataloged, serials to be indexed, even biographies of major figures to be written before the computer alone can suffice as an exhaustive source for bibliographic information.

This essay omits some earlier material because it is dated, and some later material because a novice can find it on a computer. The black consciousness movements of the 1950s and 1960s resulted in a flurry of bibliographic work in the 1970s and 1980s. The African-American renaissance of the 1980s and 1990s, especially the development of academic black studies programs and departments, encouraged bibliographers who realized that scholarship required, at its base, identification of books and articles, manuscripts and reports. This means that many of the bibliographies in this essay date from the 1970s and 1980s, and that most material with later imprints is available online, but it also means that much primary and original research remains to be done.

After a note on black bibliographic historiography, this essay deals with several genres particular to bibliography, and then follows the same order of subjects as the chronological bibliographies in this volume.

HISTORIOGRAPHY

There is not yet a history of African-American bibliography, nor is there any historiographic study of how African-American materials have been gathered, cataloged, and presented over the years. There are reports of the library holdings of Johann Blumenbach (1752–1840) and Henri Grégoire (1750–1831), the first collectors (so far as we know) of books by Africans and people of African descent. Perhaps the first true printed bibliography in the field is the list of twenty-three publications on slavery contained on p. xiv of *Substance of the Debate in the House of Commons, on the 15th of May 1823, on a Motion for the Mitigation and Gradual Abolition of Slavery throughout the British Dominions* . . . (1823), printed in London by Ellerton and Henderson for the Society for the Mitigation and Gradual Abolition of Slavery throughout the British Dominions.

Free Northern African-Americans during the antebellum period established an extraordinary number of men's and women's literary societies and beneficent organizations, whose members met to present papers, conduct formal debates, and socialize. Many of these societies had their own libraries, some with surprisingly extensive holdings. To take one example, a private collection contains the handwritten minute book, bound in floral wallpaper, of the Female Friendly Society of Marietta, Pennsylvania, dated 1819. Along with the club's constitution and accounts of members' dues payments, it catalogs the Society's large library. The number of these black organizations has been underestimated, and their roles have not yet been fully studied. When they are, the significance of their libraries and the bibliographies that were created to catalog them will be better understood. At this point, it can be said that bibliographical lists of books had a far more important place in free black life before Emancipation than has been thought.

The two oldest known printed bibliographies compiled by African-Americans themselves need to be mentioned. One is "A List of Autobiographies (Colored) Traced Back as far as May 5th, 1761," compiled by Levin Tilmon and constituting pp. 31–36 of his *The Consequences of One Important Mis-Step in Life* . . . (1853), which Tilmon, a Congregational minister, self-published in New York. The other is technically not a bibliography: *Catalogue of the Library in the Reading Room of The Institute for Colored Youth* . . . (1853) in Philadelphia. This is a list of more than 1,000 entries (some repeated) in a 36-page pamphlet. The library, interestingly enough, contains no books by black authors, but there are several titles on Africa, dealing with missions and travel. There are a few antislavery titles, mostly British or Quaker, suggesting Quaker support for the library. Both publications are exceedingly rare.

GENERAL BIBLIOGRAPHIES

A number of large, general bibliographies cut broadly across the subfields of African-American studies. Perhaps the best known is Monroe N. Work, *A Bibliography of the Negro in Africa and America* (1928). An outgrowth of the New Negro Movement of the 1920s, this comprehensive compilation was funded by the Carnegie Corporation. Monroe N. Work of the Department of Records and Research at Tuskegee Institute collected statistical information on the Negro for Booker T. Washington and, beginning in 1912, began publishing bibliographies in the *Negro Year Book,* which he edited. Nearly half the citations in Work's *Bibliography* deal with Africa, the Caribbean, and Latin America. The American material is organized chronologically, with an emphasis on slavery, and divided into such subjects as politics, church, military, and education. Social science topics include population, economic conditions, women, health, lynching, and the "race problem." Both books and articles are included. There is a name index of authors identified as "Negro" in the text.

The black activism of the 1960s also produced general bibliographies, notably Dorothy B. Porter, *The Negro in the United States: A Selected Bibliography* (1970). This is organized by subject, then alphabetically by author, and provides Library of Congress call numbers. The diverse subjects span a plethora of areas: cookery, organizations, entertainment, regional studies, and riots. Another study from the period is Elizabeth W. Miller, *The Negro in America: A Bibliography* (rev. ed., 1970). Besides including traditional historical material, this compilation responded to current events by adding sections on the Freedom Movement, Black Nationalism, and Black Power. *The Negro in America* is selectively annotated.

Charles L. Blockson's *Catalogue of the Charles L. Blockson Afro-American Collection, A Unit of the Temple University Libraries* (1990) also serves as a general one-volume bibliography. It is organized by subject and has detailed subject, author, and title indexes. An unusual bibliography is *African and African-American Studies: The* Choice *Ethnic Studies Reviews* (1992). This volume reprints all the relevant reviews from *Choice* magazine from volumes 27 through 29, September 1989 through July 1992. It is organized in broad subject areas: Humanities, Science and Technology, and Social and Behavioral Sciences. It offers author and title indexes but its great value is the succinct descriptive and evaluative signed reviews. Another general compilation, but which has a number of entries on libraries and librarianship, is *Nine Decades of Scholarship: A Bibliography of the Writings, 1892–1983, of the Staff of the Schomburg Center for Research in Black Culture* (1986), by Betty K. Gubert and Richard Newman.

So many relevant titles are published now that it is difficult to keep up with current bibliography. Some serials, however, do list new publications. *The Journal of American History,* a quarterly publication of the Organization of American Historians, includes a regular section called "Recent Scholarship," divided by subject. One subsection is devoted to African-American books, articles, dissertations, and texts, but relevant entries may also show up in other listings, such as "Civil War and Reconstruction" or "Visual and Performing Arts." *The Journal of Southern History* includes an annual bibliography (usually the May issue) with a section entitled "African American." *The Journal of Blacks in Higher Education,* a quarterly, regularly lists recent books under "Black Literary Digest" and new articles and papers under "Scholarly Papers." *The Black Scholar* includes a lengthy current "Books Received" annotated bibliography in each issue. A great many specialized newsletters list new publications in their fields, such as the "Bibliography Update" section of the *Oscar Micheaux Society Newsletter.*

LIBRARY CATALOGS

Especially for older books, there is probably no better place to locate bibliographic citations than in the catalogs of those few major libraries that have specialized over the years in acquiring black material. Although these catalogs are listed in the essay in this volume on general reference tools, they are in fact highly useful bibliographies.

The Schomburg Center for Research in Black Culture, a division of the Research Libraries of the New York Public Library, holds the largest collection of materials (more than 5 million items) in this country specifically devoted to works by and about Africans and people of African descent. For example, the first publication of the *Dictionary Catalogue of the Schomburg Collection of Negro Literature and History* (1962) photographically reproduced the 177,000 cards then in the library's catalog and printed them in book form. The Schomburg Center collects not only books but also pamphlets, photographs, microforms, sound recordings, moving images, periodicals, ephemera, and works of art, from all countries and in all languages. An author-title-subject listing in a single alphabet, the *Catalogue* benefited from the New York Public Library's tradition of strong subject cataloging, facilitating access and, in fact, contributing significantly to the early days of academic black studies. When the book catalogs went out of print, microfilm versions were made available by their commercial publisher.

Multivolume book supplements to the Schomburg *Catalogue* were issued in 1967, 1972, and 1974. The New York Public Library catalog went online in 1972, and acquisitions since that date (including, of course, pre-1972 imprints acquired after 1972) became available on CATNYP, the library's online public access catalog, along with African-American titles on the Machine Readable Cataloguing (MARC) tapes, that is, those acquired by the Library of Congress. In addition to being computerized, these annual acquisitions were also published in book form as the *Bibliographic Guide to Black Studies.*

The New York Public Library has recently issued, through a commercial firm, *Black Studies on Disc,* an annually updated CD-ROM database that collects all the Schomburg catalogs, both retrospectively and post-1972, and adds the *Index to Black Periodicals,* an index to articles in black journals and magazines. The result is more than 150,000 bibliographic records and periodical citations. *Black Studies on Disc,* particularly with the expanded coverage still to be added, probably has become the single most comprehensive place to search for African-American materials.

RARE BOOKS

Because of their special importance in documenting African-American history, as well as their commercial value and interest to collectors as objects, rare books are the subject of significant bibliographies. The most important is Dorothy B. Porter,

"Early American Negro Writings: A Bibliographical Study," *The Papers of the Bibliographical Society of America* 39:3 (1945): 192–268. This pioneering study demonstrates that African-American writing did in fact exist from the earliest days, beginning with the publications of Briton Hammon and Jupiter Hammon, both in 1760, and that "almost the very earliest imprints of Negro writings in this country were declarations or appeals in the cause of freedom." Porter describes in detail 292 titles published up to 1835, listed alphabetically by author. A superb essay introduces the checklist.

Afro-Americana 1553–1906: Author Catalogue of The Library Company of Philadelphia and the Historical Society of Pennsylvania (1973) reports 11,466 books and pamphlets, 4,952 manuscripts, and 180 broadsides in those collections. Each section is organized alphabetically by author. The subject index to books and pamphlets is too broad to be useful, however. The holdings of another rare book library are discussed in a bibliographic essay by Richard Newman, "Words like Freedom: Afro-American Books and Manuscripts in the Henry W. and Albert A. Berg Collection of English and American Literature," in *Words like Freedom: Essays on African-American Culture and History* (1996), 3–27. These rarities in the New York Public Library are described chronologically.

Especially strong in abolitionist literature, Betty K. Gubert's *Early Black Bibliographies, 1863–1918* (1982) photographically reproduces nineteen old, rare, and out-of-print bibliographies. Among the unusual lists are Robert M. Adger's "Catalogue of Rare Books on Slavery and Negro Authors on Science, History, Poetry, Religion, Biography, etc." (1904), and Daniel A. P. Murray's "Preliminary List of Books and Pamphlets by Negro Authors for Paris Exposition and Library of Congress" (1900). A collector's selection of important titles is listed by Charles L. Blockson in *A Commented Bibliography of 100 and 1 Influential Books by and about People of African Descent (1556–1992): A Collector's Choice* (1989). Blockson's selections run from Leo Africanus to Alice Walker. A similar list was created by Edwin Wolf II in "Black Americana: A New World of Books," *AB Bookman's Weekly* 58 (1 Nov. 1976): 2363+. Also chronological, Wolf's list begins with George Keith's *An Exhortation and Caution to Friends concerning Buying or Keeping Negroes* (1693).

HISTORY

Bibliographies that emphasize history include Dwight L. Smith, *Afro-American History: A Bibliography* (1974). This is a list of 2,953 annotated items, drawn from *America: History and Life* and hundreds of professional journals dated 1954 to 1972. It is organized chronologically by large periods, then into subjects, then alphabetically by author. Strong on political and social history, the book also gives citations on race and racial attitudes. It contains author and subject indexes. A second volume (1981) of 4,112 annotated citations is drawn from 48,500 entries in the *America: History and Life* database from 1974 to 1978. The pool for this volume was expanded to cover 1,900 serials in thirty languages. The organizational scheme is the same as in volume one, but the index has been greatly expanded for better access.

The period before 1954 is covered, in part, by Richard Newman in *Black Index: Afro-Americana in Selected Periodicals, 1907–1949* (1981). This work lists articles drawn from 350 periodicals arranged in a single alphabet that combines authors and subjects. Most sources are general historical journals. *The Journal of Negro History* is excluded since it is separately indexed. Researchers should always be aware of bibliographies in *The Journal of Negro History,* for many years the major periodical source in the field. See, for example, Daniel S. Gray's "Bibliographical Essay: Black Views on Reconstruction," *Journal of Negro History* 58:1 (1973): 73–85. James M. McPherson's *Blacks in America: Bibliographic Essays* (1971) lists 4,000 book and serial titles grouped in chronological periods starting with pre-slavery.

It is unusual to have a record of the contents of an African-American's library, but one example is William L. Petrie and Douglas E. Stover, *Bibliography of the Frederick Douglass Library at Cedar Hill* (1995). Although badly designed, organized, and printed, this book lists 2,200 items owned by Douglass or added by the family following his death.

GUIDES

There are several general guides to those African-American resources that include bibliographies: Nathaniel Davis, *An Annotated Bibliography of Selected Resources* (1985) and Rosemary M. Stevenson, *Index to Afro-American Reference Resources* (1988). The most comprehensive listing of separately published bibliographies themselves is Richard Newman, *Black Access: A Bibliography of Afro-American Bibliographies* (1984). More than 3,000 entries cover subject fields including discographies, bibliographic essays, checklists, and exhibition catalogs, as well as bibliographies issued by particular libraries. Entries are organized in a single alphabet by author, but there is a detailed subject index that includes the names of issuing institutions, as well as a chronological index to those bibliographies that cover specific time periods.

AUTOBIOGRAPHY AND BIOGRAPHY

The most useful bibliographic guide to autobiographies is Russell C. Brignano's *Black Americans in Autobiography* (rev. ed., 1984). Part I lists 424 autobiographies, many obscure and little known, alphabetically by author. Library locations are provided, as well as very helpful short annotations. The volume's second part, which Brignano calls "autobiographical books," lists 228 diaries, travelogues, collections of letters, essays, and other publications. Part III consists of fourteen titles Brignano had not seen; and Part IV is a checklist of forty-one post–World War II reprintings of autobiographies and autobiographical titles originally issued before 1865. Accessibility is enhanced by several indexes: titles, year of first publication (from 1789 to 1982), locations and institutions, organizations, activities, and occupations. The revised edition has nearly twice as many entries as the original edition.

In *Autobiographies by Americans of Color, 1980–1994* (1997), Rebecca Stuhr-Rommereim annotates 220 autobiographies published since 1980. The researcher should also consult William L. Andrews, "Annotated Bibliography of Afro-American Biography, Beginnings to 1930," *Resources in American Literature Study* 12 (1982): 119–33.

Apart from literary figures, few African-Americans are the subjects of book-length bibliographic studies. Herbert Aptheker's *Annotated Bibliography of the Published Writings of W. E. B. Du Bois* (1973) is a comprehensive listing of 1,975 entries. It is arranged by format (magazines and newspapers edited by Du Bois and magazines and newspapers edited by others), and then chronologically. Aptheker has provided a running commentary for entries, placing them in historical context. There are name and subject indexes, and a list of books mentioned by Du Bois. Paul G. Partington, in *W. E. B. Du Bois: A Bibliography of His Published Writings* (rev. ed., 1979) lists 2,377 unannotated entries, also organizing them by format. Several later editions or supplements contain additions and corrections. *W. E. B. Du Bois: A Bibliography of Writings about Him* (1989), by Robert W. McDonnell and Paul G. Partington, is highly selective, poorly organized, and not indexed.

William H. Fisher, in *Free at Last: A Bibliography of Martin Luther King, Jr.* (1977), gives material by and about King and lists books, dissertations, periodicals, manuscripts, and book reviews. Sherman E. Pyatt's *Martin Luther King, Jr.: An Annotated Bibliography* (1986) is divided into such sections as biography, Southern Christian Leadership Conference (SCLC), major awards, FBI files, marches, and demonstrations. The staff of the Martin Luther King, Jr., Papers Project, directed at Stanford University by Clayborne Carson, produced *A Guide to Research on Martin Luther King, Jr., and the Modern Black Freedom Struggle* (1989).

Susan Duffy's *Shirley Chisholm: A Bibliography of Writings by and about Her* (1988) includes primary source materials like speeches and videotapes, as well as newspaper articles (but cited only by the titles of the papers). Sister M[ary] Anthony Scally, in *Carter G. Woodson: A Bio-Bibliography* (1985), lists books, periodicals, and dissertations, along with material by and about Woodson in the *Journal of Negro History* and the *Negro History Bulletin*, both of which he edited. Scally also includes references to Woodson in books and serials. Lenwood G. Davis and Janet L. Sims, authors of *Marcus Garvey: An Annotated Bibliography* (1980), have arranged their book alphabetically by author, with an index. Timothy V. Johnson's *Malcolm X: A Comprehensive Bibliography* (1986) covers speeches, interviews, FBI files, book reviews of the *Autobiography,* and news reports from four types of publications: the mainstream press, the African-American press, the left-wing press, and the African press. It includes author and subject indexes. Janet L. Sims-Wood's *Marian Anderson, an Annotated Bibliography and Discography* provides a listing of Anderson's recordings and documents writings about her.

SLAVERY, THE SLAVE TRADE, AND ABOLITIONISM

The literature on slavery, though vast, is largely under bibliographic control. A very brief but useful introduction is printed in James S. Olson's *Slave Life in America: A Historiography and Selected Bibliography* (1983). The interpretive historiographic essay is informative, and the bibliography itself begins with primary sources: slave narratives, memoirs, and travel accounts by white authors. There are citations on slavery's background, its institutions, and the world of the slaves themselves. At the other extreme of inclusiveness is John David Smith's *Black Slavery in the Americas: An Interdisciplinary Bibliography, 1865–1980* (2 vols., 1982). Smith's massive compilation of more than 15,000 items covers the African background, historiography, and the issue of race. The main body of his study is organized by state and region, including the North, Midwest, and West, and also Canada, the Caribbean, and Central and South America. There are unusual sections on black slavery among the Indians, the mind of the slave, resistance, slavery and the Civil War, and topics dealing with everyday slave life like diet and medicine.

Primary materials are emphasized by David Lowell Dumond in *A Bibliography of Antislavery in America* (1961), which includes British abolitionist literature circulated in the United States. Dumond is especially strong in the inclusion of the various acts, addresses, annual reports, almanacs, newspapers and periodicals, minutes, and tracts of the abolitionist organizations, including the African Institution, American Anti-Slavery Society, American and Foreign Anti-Slavery Society, American Colonization Society, American Reform Tract and Book Co., and the Free Produce Association. Publications of state and local organizations are listed, too, particularly the active Massachusetts and Pennsylvania societies. Dumond is strong, also, in citations of the controversial literature of the day, including sermons and church pronouncements.

One of the more interesting and sophisticated bibliographies, because of both its comprehensiveness and its inclusion of many unusual European citations, is Peter C. Hogg's *The African Slave Trade and Its Suppression: A Classified and Annotated Bibliography of Books, Pamphlets, and Periodical Articles* (1973). The book is more inclusive than the title suggests. Hogg organizes Part I, on the trade, geographically, and includes a great deal of its economic and legal aspects. Part II, on abolitionism and suppression, lists controversial literature, materials from the anti-slavery societies, biographies of slaves and abolitionists, and unique material on such topics as the origins of the slaves and the naval blockade.

Best for the contemporary and ongoing bibliography of slavery is Joseph C. Miller's *Slavery and Slaving in World History: A Bibliography, volume I: 1900–1991* (1999), which updates an earlier version of the book. Miller has also edited a second volume, *Slavery and Slaving in World History: A Bibliography, volume II: 1992–1996* (1999). In these works, Miller covers research published on the ancient and medieval worlds as well as the modern period. He organizes his bibliography geographically by region in the United States and by country in Spanish America. Slavery in the Muslim world is also covered. There is an author index and a subject and keyword index. Miller is updated periodically in the journal *Slavery and Abolition*. Much less useful is Lawrence S. Thompson's book, *The Southern Black, Slave and Free: A Bibliography of Anti- and Pro-Slavery Books and Pamphlets and of Social and Economic Conditions in the South from the Beginnings to 1950* (1970). It has only a single alphabet by author and no indexes.

There are several bibliographic guides to important slavery and abolitionist collections in American libraries: *The Birney Anti-Slavery Collection at the John Hopkins University* (1985); Geraldine Hopkins Hubbard, comp., and Julian S.

Fowler, ed., "A Classified Catalogue of the Collection of Anti-Slavery Propaganda in the Oberlin College Library," *Oberlin College Library Bulletin* 2:3 (1932): 1–84; and Crawford B. Lindsay, "The Cornell University Special Collection on Slavery" (1949), an unpublished dissertation. The great Cornell collection was donated by the abolitionist Samuel J. May (1797–1871). His cousin, Samuel May, Jr. (1810–1899), compiled "Catalogue of Anti-Slavery Publications in America, 1750–1853," which was appended to the *Proceedings* of the American Anti-Slavery Society in 1863; it is reprinted in Betty K. Gubert, *Early Black Bibliographies, 1863–1918* (1982).

Researchers can also consult a number of more specialized bibliographies. James S. Olson compiled *Slave Life: A Historiography and Selected Bibliography* (1983). American slavery in specific geographic areas is covered in such lists as F. A. Sampson and W. C. Breckinridge, "Bibliography of Slavery in Missouri," *Missouri Historical Review* 2 (Apr. 1908): 233–44 and George R. Woolfolk, "Sources of the History of the Negro in Texas with Special Reference to Their Implications for Research on Slavery," *Journal of Negro History* 42:1 (Jan. 1957): 38–47.

Edgar T. Thompson, in *The Plantation: An International Bibliography* (1983), deals with pre– and post–Civil War plantation societies in the United States and around the world. Lorenzo Dow Turner's *Anti-Slavery Sentiment in American Literature prior to 1865* is a book-length bibliographic essay in which literature is broadly defined. Turner organizes his material first in large chronological periods, and then divides each period into subjects like "Moral and Religious," "Social and Economic," and "Plans for the Emancipation of the Slave." A specialized bibliography on case law is *Slavery in the Courtroom: An Annotated Bibliography of American Cases* (1985) by Paul Finkelman.

BLACK-WHITE RELATIONS

Meyer Weinberg's *Racism in Contemporary America* (1996) consists of 15,000 entries arranged under eighty-seven subject headings, including "Affirmative Action," "Humor," "Tests," and various states. This work also covers groups other than African-Americans, and there is an author index. Constance E. Obudho's *Black-White Racial Attitudes: An Annotated Bibliography* (1976) is organized by subject, listing books, articles, and dissertations from 1950 to 1974. The Center for Community Group Mental Health Problems issued a *Bibliography on Racism* (1976), consisting of abstracts of journal articles with author and subject indexes.

VIOLENCE AND RACIAL DISTURBANCES

In *Lynching and Vigilantism in the United States: An Annotated Bibliography* (1997), Norton H. Moses cites 4,200 works on collective violence in all genres: books, articles, government documents, and theses. After dealing with general works, the author adopts a basically chronological organization, beginning with the colonial era and running to 1996. A major section is devoted to the lawless American Western frontier, and unusual categories include anti-lynching bills, laws, organizations, leaders, and vigilantism in literature and art.

The *Ku Klux Klan: A Bibliography* (1984), by Lenwood G. Davis and Janet L. Sims-Wood, contains 10,000 citations, three-quarters of which are to newspaper articles. Klan publications and government reports are also included. William Harvey Fisher compiled *The Invisible Empire: A Bibliography of the Ku Klux Klan* (1980). William King edited *Urban Racial Violence in the United States: An Historical and Comparative Bibliography* (1974).

POLITICS

Hanes Walton, Jr.'s *Study and Analysis of Black Politics: A Bibliography* (1973) is updated and supplemented by Rosemary Stevenson's "Black Politics in the U.S.: A Recent Literature," *Black Scholar* (Mar.-Apr. 1988): 58–61.

MILITARY

The black presence and participation in U.S. wars is documented in John J. Slonaker's *African-American Military History: A Bibliography* (1993). Slonaker is Chief of the Historical Reference Branch of the U.S. Army Military History Institute. His bibliography is organized in chronological sections, with a great deal of material on the Civil War, as well as on 20th-century conflicts. He includes citations on the Brownsville Affair and black military service in the Philippines. There are appendixes on Medal of Honor recipients and on Isaiah Dorman, who was with Custer at the Battle of the Little Big Horn. Periodical articles are a special feature of *Black Americans in the Military* (1993), issued by the Pentagon Library and reflecting the library's holdings.

Perhaps the most extensive coverage of blacks in the military is Thomas Truxtun Moebs, *Black Soldiers—Black Sailors—Black Ink: Research Guide on African-Americans in U.S. Military History, 1526–1900* (1994), consisting of 1,737 pages in four volumes with ten appendixes. Volume III is a 250-page bibliography listing books, articles, and archives, organized alphabetically by subject with extensive cross-referencing. Subjects include persons, regiments, conflicts, and such unusual topics as Annapolis, artillery, the Philippine Insurrection, and prisoners of war.

Betty K. Gubert, in *Invisible Wings: An Annotated Bibliography on Blacks in Aviation, 1916–1993* (1994), covers the whole field of aviation, including early pioneers like Bessie Coleman and Eugene Bullard, but a substantial number of the book's citations deal with the armed forces. These, too, are arranged chronologically, with special focus on the Tuskegee Airmen, prisoners of war, Benjamin O. Davis, Jr., Daniel James, Jr., and astronauts. Related bibliographies are Lenwood G. Davis and George Hill, *Blacks in the American Armed Forces, 1776–1983: A Bibliography* (1985), and Colin Cameron and Judith Blackstone, *Minorities in the Armed Forces: A Selective, Occasionally Annotated Bibliography* (1970).

DEMOGRAPHY

Jamshid A. Momeni, *Demography of the Black Population in the United States: An Annotated Bibliography with a Review Essay* (1983) contains 350 heavily annotated entries dealing with fertility, health, migration, urbanization, and vital statistics. Momeni's *Housing and Racial/Ethnic Minority Status in the United States: An Annotated Bibliography with a Review Essay* (1987) is another helpful resource. Frank Alexander Ross and Louise Venable Kennedy, *A Bibliography of Negro Migration* (rpt. 1969), is a classic work covering 1865 to 1932 and organized in two parts: printed material and readily accessible mimeographed material; and manuscripts and inaccessible mimeographed material. Each section is then arranged alphabetically by author. Several appendixes provide access to the entries by chronology, geography, and subject.

Other general studies include Edgar Tristam Thompson and Alma Macy Thompson, *Race and Region: A Descriptive Bibliography* (rpt. 1971); Robert A. Obudho and Jeannine B. Scott, *Afro-American Demography and Urban Issues: A Bibliography* (1985); and *Black Immigration and Ethnicity in the United States: An Annotated Bibliography* (1985), compiled by the Center for Afro-American and African Studies at the University of Michigan.

Regional studies include James de T. Abajian's *Blacks and Their Contributions to the American West: A Bibliography and Union List of Library Holdings through 1970* (1974), an extraordinary compilation of 4,302 citations. They are arranged into sixty-three subject areas, including such unusual topics as armed services, entertainment, cookbooks, miscegenation and passing, and ranch life and cowboys. Under subjects, entries are alphabetical by author. There is a list of regional periodicals and newspapers, and a comprehensive index. Roger D. Hardaway, *A Narrative Bibliography of the African-American Frontier: Blacks in the Rocky Mountain West, 1535–1912* (1996) is another important study, and includes annotations that are particularly useful for photographs and maps.

Donald A. Sinclair, *The Negro and New Jersey: A Checklist of Books, Pamphlets, Official Publications, Broadsides, and Dissertations, 1754–1964, in the Rutgers University Library* (1965) is first divided into before and after slavery (1866), then alphabetically by author. Two other regional compilations are *Southeastern Frontier: Europeans, Africans, and American Indians, 1513–1840: A Critical Bibliography* (1982), by James Howlett O'Donnell III, and "Dissertations and Theses relating to African-American Studies in Texas: A Selected Bibliography," written by Paul M. Lucko and published in *Southwestern Historical Quarterly* 94:6 (1993): 547–73.

FAMILY

Perhaps the earliest bibliography on the African-American family is W. E. B. Du Bois's "A Select Bibliography on the Negro American Family" in *The Negro American Family: Report of a Social Study* . . . (1908), pp. 6–8. More recent compilations include Walter R. Allen, *Black American Families, 1965–1984: A Classified, Selectively Annotated Bibliography* (1986); Lenwood G. Davis and Janet Sims, *The Black Family in the United States: A Selected Bibliography of Annotated Books, Articles, and Dissertations* (1978); and Cleopatra S. Howard, *A Resource Guide on Black Families in America* (1980). Phyllis Rauch Klotman and Wilmer H. Baatz, *The Black Family and the Black Woman: A Bibliography* (1978) is a major compilation, organized chronologically, but limited to the holdings of the Indiana University Library.

Hector F. Myers, Phyllis G. Rana, and Marcia Harris, *Black Child Development in America, 1927–1977: An Annotated Bibliography,* contains 1,274 entries, all citing social science literature from the professional journals. It is organized in sections on the development of language, body, mind, personality, and social behavior, and includes author and subject indexes. Charlotte Dunmore, in *Black Children and Their Families* (1976), includes sections on adoption and mental health. Two other lists featuring children are Valora Washington's *Black Children and American Institutions: An Ecological Review and Resource Guide* (1988), and *Black Adolescence: Current Issues and Annotated Bibliography* (1990) by the Consortium for Research on Black Adolescence with Velma McBride Murry and Georgia Winter.

Two studies in geriatrics are Frieda R. Butler, *A Resource Guide on Black Aging* (1981), and Lenwood G. Davis, *The Black Aged in the U.S.: An Annotated Bibliography* (1980). A bibliography on genealogy is included in Tommie M. Young, *Afro-American Genealogy: A Sourcebook* (1987).

RURAL LIFE

Two bibliographies deal with African-Americans in agriculture: Joel Schor and Cecil Harvey, *A List of References for the History of Black Americans in Agriculture, 1619–1974* (1975); and Irwin Weintraub, *Black Agriculturalists in the United States, 1865–1973: An Annotated Bibliography* (1976).

RELIGION

Despite being error-prone and inconveniently organized, *The Howard University Bibliography of Afro-American Religious Studies, with Locations in American Libraries* (1977), by Ethel L. Williams and Clifton F. Brown, is, with 13,000 sources, the largest and most comprehensive bibliography in religion. It covers Africa, including the ancient kingdoms of Kush and Egypt, modern independent churches, and Christian missions arranged by African country. Major lists then cover Christianity and slavery in the New World organized by denomination; the black church, including storefronts and sects, Black Jews, and Muslims; civil rights; and black identity, including black theology and black power. Appendixes list the manuscripts, autobiographies, and biographies of 6,000 religious figures. There is a name index.

Looking at more specific themes, there is Marilyn Richardson's *Black Women and Religion: A Bibliography* (1980), which cites not only books and articles, but works of art, films, musical compositions, and recordings, along with biographical sketches. *Black Theology: A Critical Assessment and Annotated Bibliography* (1987) by James H. Evans is arranged in three sections: Origin and Development of Black Theology; Liberation, Feminism, and Marxism; and Cultural and Global Discussion. Richard Newman's *Lemuel Haynes, 1753–1833: A Bio-Bibliography* (1986) surveys both primary and secondary sources. The primary bibliography lists Haynes's sermons and speeches organized chronologically, including the seventy editions of his satirical sermon "Universal Salvation."

Pentecostalism is not only the major religious phenomenon of the 20th century, but it is also a movement with strong African-American origins and with a significant international constituency of people of color. The major bibliographic study is Sherry Sherrod Dupree's *African-American Holiness and Pentecostal Movement: A Bibliography* (1996). The book is organized doctrinally by the major Pentecostal groupings: Trinitarian, Apostolic, Evangelical Charismatic, and Holiness. There are many supporting lists: a section on Pentecostal origins, including the Azusa Street Revival and William J. Seymour, as well as citations on Black Jews, leader-centered groups, women founders and leaders, FBI reports, storefront churches, and a geographic index.

The *Newsletter of the Afro-American Religious History Group of the American Academy of Religion*, published twice a year from 1976 to 1996, regularly includes bibliographies. Two examples are Hans A. Baer's "The Black Spiritual Tradition," 9:1 (1984): 9–11, and Judith Weisenfeld and Richard Newman's "African-American Women's Religious Biography," 20:1 (1995): 5–9. Judith Weisenfeld continues the newsletter on the internet as *The North Star: A Journal of African-American Religious History*.

NATIONALISM

Afro-American Nationalism: An Annotated Bibliography of Militant Separatist and Nationalist Literature (1986), by Agustina Herod and Charles C. Herod, is divided into chronological sections—pre–Civil War, post–Civil War, 1945–1965, 1965–1980—and into subjects: Marcus Garvey, religion, black power, and cultural nationalism. Betty Lanier Jenkins and Susan Phillis, *Black Separatism: A Bibliography* (1976), consists of annotated citations on such themes as identity, education, economics, and religion. It is divided into two parts, one on the separation versus integration controversy, the other on institutional and psychological aspects of nationalism. Richard Newman's *Black Power: A Bibliography* (1969) consists of nonannotated citations to periodical literature immediately following the Black Power movement of 1966.

LANGUAGE AND LINGUISTICS

Ila W. Brasch and Walter M. Brasch's *A Comprehensive Annotated Bibliography of American Black English* (1974) is arranged in a single alphabet by author with no subject index, so the book is valuable only if the researcher is looking for a particular author's work. *Black English: An Annotated Bibliography* (1973) by Dolores C. Leffall and James P. Johnson is a brief but helpful guide.

FOLKLORE

A standard source for folklore is John F. Szwed and Roger D. Abrahams, *Afro-American Folk Culture: An Annotated Bibliography of Materials from North, Central and South America, and the West Indies* (1978). Folklore is defined broadly, and in this two-volume work with 3,331 entries devoted to North America alone, there are citations to such subjects as music, dance, religion, funerals, games, jokes, names, vocabulary, slavery, and voodoo. Citations within each geographical area are arranged alphabetically by author. While there is an index, it refers only to numbered entries in the text, and the indexing terms are so general as to be almost without use. Under "city life," for instance, there are some 150 numbers, referring the user back to 150 otherwise unidentified entries. Two other folklore sources are William R. Ferris's *Mississippi Black Folklore: A Research Bibliography and Discography* (1971) and Brett Williams's *John Henry: A Bio-Bibliography* (1983), which covers texts and songs on the legendary character.

LITERATURE AND POETRY

Literature is the field within African-American studies that has received the most bibliographic attention, probably because there is both academic and popular interest in writers and their work. One of the earliest comprehensive studies is Janheinz Jahn's *A Bibliography of Neo-African Literature from Africa, America, and the Caribbean* (1965). Also published in German, this work's great value is its international scope, covering both Africa and the diaspora. African-American writers are listed alphabetically. Jahn was followed in the 1970s by a number of American compilations. One is *Past and Present: A Biographical and Bibliographical Dictionary* (1975), a two-volume work by Theresa Gunnels with portraits.

Other comprehensive collections include Roger Whitlow, *Black American Literature: A Critical History with a 1,520-Title Bibliography of Works Written by and about Black Americans* (1976), and Geraldine O. Matthews, *Black American Writers, 1772–1949: A Bibliography and Union List* (1975), which includes 1,600 authors organized by subject with a name index. M. Thomas Inge, Maurice Duke, and Jackson R. Bryer, *Black American Writers: Bibliographical Essays* (1978), is a two-volume work described as a bio-bibliography. Volume 1 begins with Jupiter Hammon and runs up to Langston Hughes and the Harlem Renaissance, and includes such writers as Frances Ellen Watkins Harper, Booker T. Washington, and Sutton E. Griggs. Volume 2 consists of longer essays on contemporary writers Richard Wright, Ralph Ellison, James Baldwin, and Amiri Baraka (LeRoi Jones).

An early study specializing in novels is Maxwell Whiteman's *Century of Fiction by American Negroes, 1853–1952: A Selective Bibliography* (1955). Arranged alphabetically by author, Whiteman's work is remarkable for its unearthing of obscure titles. He also includes an important introductory essay, a chronological list, and information on publishers. A supplement was issued in 1953. Helen Ruth Houston, *Afro-American Novel, 1965–1975: A Descriptive Bibliography of Primary and Secondary Material,* leaves a gap, but does pick up after Whiteman and emphasizes sociological analysis. For each of fifty-six novelists, Houston presents a biographical sketch and a chronological list of works with plot summaries. She includes critical books and articles on each author. Robert A. Corrigan compiled "Afro-American Fiction: A Checklist 1853–1970," in *Midcontinent American Studies Journal* 11:2 (1970): 114–35. Carol Fairbanks and Eugene A. Engeldinger, *Black American Fiction: A Bibliography* (1978), spans the 20th century up to the book's publication date. The book is organized alphabetically by author and encompasses novels, short fiction, book reviews, biographies, and criticism. Edward Margolies and David Bakish, in *Afro-American Fiction, 1853–1976: A Guide to Information Sources* (1979), list 723 novels. There is also a bibliography of ninety-eight short story collections (both individual authors and anthologies), a chronological list of fiction beginning with William Wells Brown's *Clotel*, and author-title-subject indexes. Short fiction is the subject of Preston M. Yancy's *The Afro-American Short Story: A Comprehensive, Annotated Index with Selected Commentaries* (1986). More recent bibliographies are Robert Fikes, Jr., "The Persistent Allure of Universality: African-American Authors with White Life Novels, 1890–1945," *The Western Journal of Black Studies* 20:4 (1996): 221–26, and D. C. Moore, "Revisiting a Silenced Giant: Alex Haley's *Roots*, a Bibliographic Essay and Research Report on the Haley Archives at the University of Tennessee, Knoxville," *Resources for American Literary Study* 22:2 (1998).

Poetry and drama are surveyed by William P. French, Michel Fabre, Amrijit Singh, and Genevieve Fabre in *Afro-American Poetry and Drama, 1760–1965: A Guide to Information Sources* (1979). This covers poetry from 1760 to 1975 and drama from 1850 to 1975. The poetry citations first list general works, then individual poets, arranged chronologically. The drama section first lists general works, then individual playwrights, arranged alphabetically within chronological periods. Unpublished plays are also included. Frank Deodene and William P. French provide citations for first editions of separately published books and pamphlets from 1944 to 1971 in *Black American Poetry since 1944: A Preliminary Checklist* (1971).

There are a number of important specialized bibliographies in the field of literature. Margaret Perry, *The Harlem Renaissance: An Annotated Bibliography and Commentary* (1982) lists general works, then citations for material by and about nineteen major writers from 1919 to 1980. Martin Olsson compiled *A Selected Bibliography of Black Literature: The Harlem Renaissance* (1973). Sister M. Anthony Scally, in *Negro Catholic Writers, 1900–1943* (1945), provides biographical sketches, many of little-known subjects, followed by an annotated bibliography of books, articles, poems, and reviews. Others include Edward Clar, *Black Writers in New England . . .*(1985); Lorris Elliott, *The Bibliography of Literary Writings by Blacks in Canada* (1986); and Mamie Marie Booth Foster, *Southern Black Creative Writers, 1829–1853: Bibliographies* (1988).

A number of prominent African-American writers are covered in individual bibliographies. Curtis W. Ellison and E. W. Metcalf, Jr., *William Wells Brown and Martin R. Delany: A Reference Guide* (1978), contains writings about these two authors organized chronologically, then arranged by books and shorter writings. *Charles W. Chesnutt: A Reference Guide* (1977) by the same authors covers the secondary literature from 1887 to 1975 in the same format as their Brown-Delany volume. Margaret Perry, *Bio-Bibliography of Countee P. Cullen, 1903–1946* (1971) provides a biographical essay, then lists citations by and about Cullen, including his work that appears in anthologies. While now dated, Fred L. Standley and Nancy Standley, *James Baldwin: A Reference Guide* (1980), is useful for early material.

Michael W. Peplow and Robert S. Bravard, *Samuel R. Delany: A Primary and Secondary Bibliography, 1962–1979* (1980), is organized chronologically and includes a long introduction, excellent annotations, information on editions, and variants. Appendixes include juvenilia, unpublished work, and collections of Delanyana. E. W. Metcalf, Jr., *Paul Laurence Dunbar: A Bibliography* (1975), includes primary and secondary citations, both arranged chronologically. The primary materials cover songs, plays, and letters; the secondary section includes articles and books mentioning Dunbar. Both Dunbar's articles and reviews of his work are annotated.

The perennially popular Langston Hughes is the focus of Donald C. Dickinson, *A Bibliography of Langston Hughes, 1902–1967* (1967). Major sections include books by Hughes, books edited by him, book-length translations, works in non-English languages, drama, poems, and appearances in collections. Entries about Hughes include selected reviews of major books. Despite its later imprint, Thomas A. Mikolyzk, *Langston Hughes: A Bio-Bibliography* (1990), is less useful, partly because it does not adequately discriminate between major and minor works about Hughes, and also because it is inadequate for Hughes's books published in translation. R. Baxter Miller, *Langston Hughes and Gwendolyn Brooks: A Reference Guide* (1978), is well annotated. The works by and about Hughes were published between 1924 and 1977, and those by and about Brooks were published between 1944 and 1977.

Robert E. Fleming, *James Weldon Johnson and Arna Wendell Bontemps: A Reference Guide* (1978), covers writings about these two authors arranged chronologically. David A. Middleton, *Toni Morrison: An Annotated Bibliography* (1987), has useful annotations, but there are an astonishing number of omissions. Irma E. Goldstraw, *Derek Walcott: An Annotated Bibliography of His Work* (1984), includes reviews, interviews, and recordings, as well as books, plays, poems, and articles. Erma Davis Banks and Keith Byerman, *Alice Walker: An Annotated Bibliography, 1968–1986* (1989), doubles the coverage of Louis H. and Darnell D. Pratt, *Alice Malsenior Walker: An Annotated Bibliography, 1968–1986* (1988).

The first published African-American author is the subject of William H. Robinson, *Phillis Wheatley: A Bio-Bibliography* (1981). Entries about Wheatley and her work range from 1761 to 1979 and are organized first by date, then into books and shorter articles. Probably the most extensive bibliographic coverage of any black author is Keneth Kinnamon, *A Richard Wright Bibliography: Fifty Years of Criticism and Commentary, 1933–1982* (1988). Highly detailed and covering literature from fifty-four countries, this list is organized chronologically and then alphabetically by author. Charles T. Davis and Michel Fabre, in *Richard Wright: A Primary Bibliography* (1982), provide references to both published and unpublished works, as well as translations. The arrangement is first chronological, then by genre. An unusual bibliography is Michel Fabre, *Richard Wright: Books and Writers* (1990), a listing of the books in Wright's library. Some are annotated by Fabre with appropriate comments from Wright's own letters and writings. There are, in addition, two unusual appendixes. One is of blurbs, introductions, and reviews written by Wright. The other is a bibliography on the Negro in Chicago compiled by Wright in 1936 when he was working for the Federal Works Progress Administration.

Elizabeth A. Settle and Thomas A. Settle, *Ishmael Reed: A Primary and Secondary Bibliography* (1982), is divided into two parts. Part I, Primary Sources, encompasses books, edited works, excerpts, poetry, and media (video and sound record-ings). Arranged chronologically within these categories, entries run until 1981. The secondary sources, in Part II, are also chronological and cover 1967 to 1980. A title index accesses both sections. Hazel Irvin, *Ann Petry: A Bio-Bibliography* (1993), also covers both primary and secondary materials. An unusual feature is that the section on interviews reproduces the actual texts. Michel Fabre, Robert E. Skinner, and Lester Sullivan, in *Chester Himes: An Annotated Primary and Second-ary Bibliography* (1992), provide citations for Himes's novels, short fiction, non-fiction, manuscripts (with locations), and a filmography. The secondary bibliogra-phy is organized in chronological sections beginning with 1945.

In African-American theater, Esther Spring Arata and Nicholas John Rotoli compiled *Black American Playwrights, 1800 to the Present: A Bibliography* (1976). They list some 1,500 plays by more than 500 playwrights, alphabetically by play-wright; they also give play and filmscript titles, sometimes with the date, but un-fortunately with no other information. Plays published in periodicals are in-cluded, as are citations for reviews. There is a title index. With Marlene J. Erickson, Sandra Dewitz, and Mary Linse Alexander, Arata published *More Black American Playwrights* (1978), which also lists 500 authors. John Gray compiled *Black Theatre and Performance* (1990), organized in three sections: "Cultural History and the Arts," "African Theatre," and "Black Theatre and Performance in the Diaspora." These headings are subdivided into geographical areas, and then arranged by indi-vidual playwright. There are artist, title, subject, and author indexes.

In *Black Playwrights, 1823–1977: An Annotated Bibliography of Plays* (1977), James V. Hatch and Omanii Abdullah list 2,700 plays by 900 authors. Most are plays for the stage, but film, TV, and radio plays are included. A related title is Rob-ert W. Glenn, *Black Rhetoric: A Guide to Afro-American Communication* (1976). Glenn lists anthologies, books, essays, and speeches, but his subject categories (his-tory, literature, education) are too general to be useful.

An early bibliography on poetry is Arthur A. Schomburg, *A Bibliographical Checklist of American Negro Poetry* (1916), published by the book dealer Charles Heartman. Schomburg covers about 200 titles, listed in a single alphabet by poet. Many of these writers are obscure, and their books are rare. With Schomburg's broad interests, it is no surprise that he includes Haitian and Afro-Cuban poets; there is an especially strong listing for Diego Gabriel de la Concepción Valdés (pseud. Plácido). Dorothy B. Porter updates Schomburg with her *North American Negro Poets: A Bibliographical Checklist of Their Writings, 1760–1944* (rpt., 1963).

EDUCATION

Meyer Weinberg, in *The Education of the Minority Child: A Comprehensive Bibliog-raphy of 10,000 Selected Entries* (1970), focuses on African-Americans, including women, and draws on 500 periodicals, covering this subject from the colonial pe-riod to the time of publication. There is an author-title-subject index. Weinberg is also the compiler of *School Integration: A Comprehensive Classified Bibliography of 3,100 References* (1967). This includes school integration's legal aspects, effects, and relationship with the civil rights movement. Richard H. Quay's *In Pursuit of*

Equality of Educational Opportunity: A Selective Bibliography and Guide to the Research Literature (1977) is limited in usefulness because it is organized by author, then by journal article, without annotation, and the articles are not always title-indicative. Its "Bibliography of Bibliographies on Equality of Educational Opportunity and Related Issues" is, however, valuable.

Kathryn Swanson's *Affirmative Action and Preferential Admissions in Higher Education: An Annotated Bibliography* (1981) includes material on law and the courts, the philosophical debate, and academic and community responses. The sources include government publications, court cases, and chapters in collected works. *Black Higher Education in the United States: A Selected Bibliography on Negro Higher Education and Historically Black Colleges and Universities* (1978) by Frederick Chambers is arranged by formats such as dissertations, institutional histories, reports, and government publications. Adult and vocational education is the theme of Leo McGee and Harvey G. Neufeldt's *Education of the Black Adult in the United States: An Annotated Bibliography* (1985).

The Journal of Negro Education, which began in April 1932, regularly runs a section called "Current Literature on Negro Education," which covers the whole range of African-American studies. It consists of book reviews, abstracts, digests, and a bibliography divided in three parts: (1) books, bulletins, pamphlets, and monographs; (2) theses and dissertations, including master's theses; and (3) periodicals.

WORK AND ENTERPRISE

George H. Hill's *Black Business and Economics: A Selected Bibliography* (1985) has 2,668 entries, but is weak because the listed articles, mostly newspaper pieces, are not annotated. Also, the subject areas of banking, capitalism, and consumerism, for example, are too broad. The index is only of proper names. Other bibliographies, such as Thelma Y. Halliday, *The Negro in the Field of Business: An Annotated Bibliography* (1972), and Joseph Wilson and Thomas Weissinger, *Black Labor in America: A Selected Annotated Bibliography* (1986), do not adequately fill the gaps in the field. Janet L. Sims-Wood, *Black Women in the Employment Sector* (1979), does attempt to provide some important missing information.

MEDICINE AND HEALTH

Mitchell F. Rice and Woodrow Jones, Jr., *Health of Black Americans from Post-Reconstruction to Integration, 1871–1960: An Annotated Bibliography of Contemporary Sources* (1990), consists largely of annotated journal articles arranged chronologically. An introduction discusses health and working conditions, disease, and medical care. Other studies in the field are Vinnie M. Danner, *A Bibliography of Published and Unpublished Materials on the Health Status of Blacks, Minorities, and the Poor* (1972), and Lenwood G. Davis, *A History of Public Health, Health Problems, Facilities and Services in the Black Community: A Working Bibliography* (1976). A related subject is covered by Beatrice R. Treiman, Pamela B. Street, and Patricia Shanks, *Blacks and Alcohol: A Selective Annotated Bibliography* (1976).

WOMEN

Interest in the life and work of African-American women, especially in literature, has resulted in the creation of numerous relevant bibliographies. Perhaps the most useful historical source is *The Pen Is Ours: A Listing of Writings by and about African-American Women before 1910; with Secondary Bibliography to the Present* (1991), by Jean Fagan Yellin and Cynthia D. Bond. This compilation lists some 200 women, the lesser as well as the better known, and is organized alphabetically by person-subject within certain larger categories: (1) women who produced separate published writings and whose earliest publications appeared before the end of 1910; (2) women who were held in slavery and whose dictated narratives or biographies were published before the end of 1910; (3) women whose works appeared in periodicals and collections and whose earliest publication appeared before the end of 1910; and (4) women who were not writers, but who were the subjects of published writings before the end of 1910. Papers in collections are noted.

Another comprehensive literary compilation is Casper LeRoy Jordan, *A Bibliographical Guide to African-American Women Writers* (1993), which ranges from Lucy Terry Prince to the well-known writers of the 1990s. Poetry, memoirs, diaries, and privately printed and small press publications are among the genres included. Craig Werner, *Black American Women Novelists* (1989), has a strong introduction, but covers only thirty-three writers. Ronda Gilkin, *Black American Women in Literature: A Bibliography, 1976–1989,* lists works by and about 300 writers including many little-known and less published authors. The main body of the bibliography is alphabetical by subject, then lists by genre. An appendix covers works about black women writers.

Women in other categories are found in Gail Schlachter and Donna Belli, *Minorities and Women: A Guide to Reference Literature in the Social Sciences* (1977). Culinary arts, musical conductors, and college presidents are among the fields in Ora Williams, *American Black Women in the Arts and Social Sciences: A Bibliographical Survey* (rev. ed., 1994), and Andrea Timberlake et al., *Women of Color and Southern Women: A Bibliography of Social Science Research, 1975 to 1988* (1988). A particularly useful compilation is Gayle J. Hardy, *American Women Civil Rights Activists: Bio-Bibliographies of 68 Leaders, 1825–1992* (1993). For each of the sixty-eight subjects, she provides a chronological biography, background information, and an unusually broad bibliography: longer and shorter publications by and about, primary sources, and media materials such as films and recordings.

Another general bibliography dealing with women is Janet L. Sims-Wood, *The Progress of Afro-American Women: A Selected Bibliography and Resource Guide* (1980). This book is organized primarily by occupation, such as "Medicine, Nursing," "Law and Law Enforcement," "Armed Services and Defense Work," but also by such relevant subjects as "Sex and Sexual Discrimination," as well as by format, such as audiovisual materials and magazines. Others are J. R. Roberts, *Black Lesbianism: An Annotated Bibliography* (1981); Bernice Redfern, *Women of Color in the United States: A Guide to the Literature* (1988); and Lenwood G. Davis, *The Black Woman in American Society: A Selected Annotated Bibliography* (1975).

Shorter than book-length bibliographies are Rosalyn M. Terborg-Penn, "The

Historical Treatment in the Women's Suffrage Movement, 1900–1920: A Bibliographic Essay," *A Current Bibliography on African Affairs* 7:3 (Summer 1974), 245–59; Jacqueline Johnson Jackson, "Partial Bibliography on or Related to Black Women," *Journal of Social and Behavioral Sciences* 2:1 (Winter 1975): 90–135; John H. Bracey, Jr., "Afro-American Women: A Brief Guide to Writings from Historical and Feminist Perspectives," *Contributions in Black Studies* 8 (1986–1987): 106–10; Deborah Gray White, "Mining the Forgotten: Manuscript Sources for Black Women's History," *Journal of American History* 74 (Summer 1987): 237–43; and Ruthe Winegarten, "Black Texas Women: A Sourcebook: Documents, Biographies," *Timeline* (1996).

2   *Reference Works*

BARBARA A. BURG AND
RANDALL K. BURKETT

The explosive growth of scholarly work in the field of African-American studies over the past twenty-five years has been accompanied by a dramatic expansion of reference guides, encyclopedias, almanacs, chronologies, bibliographies, indexes, and biographical dictionaries. It is important to recognize, however, that African-American scholars, clergy, antiquarians, and entrepreneurs began publishing reference tools related to the history of their race as early as the 1840s. This essay will highlight the most important reference tools for research in African-American history, exclusive of bibliographies and finding aids for specific genres of materials (art, film, music, manuscripts, photography, serials, government records, and oral history) for which specific essays appear in this volume.

A useful general guide to reference tools for all aspects of African-American studies is Nathaniel Davis, comp. and ed., *Afro-American Reference: An Annotated Bibliography of Selected Resources* (*Bibliographies and Indexes in Afro-American and African Studies* 9), published in 1985. It annotates 642 reference works, mostly in book form, concentrating on bibliographies, bibliographical guides, indexes, dictionaries, almanacs, and directories. The standard comprehensive guide to reference books is Robert Balay, ed., *Guide to Reference Books* (11th ed., 1996).

We have organized reference works into the following categories: Dictionary Catalogs; Biographical Sources; Encyclopedias and Dictionaries; Indexes; Chronologies and Atlases; Directories, Yearbooks, and Annuals; Guides; and Statistical Sources.

DICTIONARY CATALOGS

The printed catalogs of the major African-American research collections, most of which were created over many years at historically black colleges and universities, are more than guides to the holdings of those particular institutions. They are also important bibliographies of African and African-American materials, providing valuable information about the materials (whether the author was of African descent, for example) along with added entries often left out of regular card- and computer-based library catalogs. The nine-volume *Dictionary Catalog of the Jesse E. Moorland Collection of Negro Life and History* (1970), with the two-volume supplement published in 1976, is an outstanding example. Responding to the research needs and queries of students and scholars over a lifetime of work as head of the Moorland-Spingarn Research Center at Howard University, Curator Dorothy Burnett Porter (Wesley) created thousands of entries for periodical articles, speeches published in newspapers, African-American illustrators of books, and other important information. Certain in-house finding aids created by the library staff were published later as appendixes to the printed catalog.

The following list represents published dictionary catalogs by institution.

Amistad Research Center, *Author and Added Entry Catalog of the American Missionary Association Archives* (3 vols., 1970?), with an introduction by Clifton H. Johnson. This catalog forms the core of the manuscript and other collections around which the Amistad Center, now located at Tulane University, built an outstanding African-American archive. References to the many American Missionary Association–supported schools and mission stations are provided in vol. 3, pp. 893–932.

Chicago Public Library, *The Dictionary Catalog of the Vivian G. Harsh Collection of Afro-American History and Literature* (4 vols., 1978). This finding aid catalogs one of the largest African-American research collections of books, periodicals, and manuscript collections. Several noteworthy collections include the Illinois Writers Project papers, Heritage Press archives, and the papers of Horace Cayton, Era Bell Thompson, Marjorie Stewart Joyner, Ben Burns, and Eugene Winslow.

Fisk University, Library, *Dictionary Catalog of the Negro Collection of the Fisk University Library, Nashville, Tennessee* (6 vols., 1974). The catalog identifies more than 35,000 books and pamphlets on African-American life and culture.

Hampton Institute, Collis P. Huntington Library, *A Classified Catalogue of the Negro Collection in the Collis P. Huntington Library, Hampton Institute* (1940), compiled by the Writers' Program of the Works Projects Administration in the state of Virginia. This catalog identifies the Huntington Library's pre-1940 holdings of manuscripts, documents, newspaper clippings, periodicals, and pamphlets on blacks in Africa and America. The history of the Civil War and Reconstruction is a particular strength of the collection.

Hampton University, *Dictionary Catalog of the George Foster Peabody Collection of Negro Literature and History* (2 vols., 1972), with an introduction by Fritz Joseph Malval. Some 15,000 books, pamphlets, journals, newspapers, and documents are identified, constituting a portion of the entire Peabody Collection at Hampton University. The pamphlet collection on slavery includes material from 1705 to the late 1880s. Photographs, vertical file materials, phonograph records, and paintings in the collection are not included in the catalog.

Howard University, Libraries, *Dictionary Catalog of the Arthur B. Spingarn Collection of Negro Authors* (2 vols., 1970). This is perhaps the largest single listing of books and pamphlets by African-American authors. A "Music Catalog of Negro Composers" is included as an appendix to vol. 2, pp. 657–784.

Howard University, Libraries, Moorland Foundation, *Dictionary Catalog of the Jesse E. Moorland Collection of Negro Life and History* (9 vols., 1970) with the two-volume supplement published in 1976. In addition to the printed book and pamphlet collection, Vol. 9 includes an Index to African Periodicals and an Index to American Negro Periodicals. An Index to Biographies also forms part of the volume supplements published in 1976.

Institute of Jamaica, Kingston, West India Reference Library, *The Catalogue of the West India Reference Library* (6 vols., 1980). Part I is arranged by authors and titles, and consists of three volumes. Part II also consists of three volumes and is arranged by subject. This catalog includes printed books, periodicals, and pamphlets from 1547. Although comprehensive, the strength of the collection is in Jamaica and the English-speaking Caribbean.

Library Company of Philadelphia, *Afro-Americana, 1553–1906: Author Catalog of the Library Company of Philadelphia and the Historical Society of Pennsylvania* (1973). Compiled with the assistance of Phillip Lapsansky and others at the Library Company and the Historical Society (HSP), this is an invaluable guide to pre-20th-century material by and about blacks. The core of the HSP materials are papers of the Pennsylvania Abolition Society and the American Negro Historical Society. Substantial additions to the Library Company collections have been made since this catalog was published, and all Afro-American items held by the Library Company have been added to the Research Libraries Group (RLG) Bibliographic File and hence are searchable online.

New York Public Library, Schomburg Collection of Negro Literature and History, *Black Studies on Disc* (1999), the CD-ROM version of the entire *Dictionary Catalog of the Schomburg Collection of Negro Literature and History* (9 vols., 1962), including all published supplementary volumes and the 1989–1993 volumes of the *Index to Black Periodicals*. This CD-ROM offers both direct searching as well as browsing capabilities with these access points: name, title, journal title, subject, material type, contents, country, date, description, publisher, place of publication, and language. Updated annually, this CD-ROM provides unparalleled access to the most comprehensive collection of Afro-Americana in the world.

Schomburg Center for Research in Black Culture, *Bibliographic Guide to Black Studies* (annual publication, 1975–). This annual list of publications serves in part as an annual supplement to the *Dictionary Catalog of the Schomburg Center for Research in Black Culture,* although it represents only those holdings in the New York Public Library. These annual volumes are now superseded by the CD-ROM *Black Studies on Disc.*

Northwestern University, Melville J. Herskovits Library of African Studies, *Catalog of the Melville J. Herskovits Library of African Studies* (8 vols., 1972). This is an expanded edition of the 1962 two-volume Northwestern University publication of the *Catalog of the African Collection.* There is a six-volume supplement, published in 1978, under the same title. Vols. 5 and 6 of the supplement contain the list of works reported by other libraries in the joint acquisitions list of Africana since 1962.

Old Slave Mart Museum and Library, *Catalog of the Old Slave Mart Museum and Library* (2 vols., 1978). Vol. 1 contains books, periodicals, documents, maps, realia, vertical files, and ephemera. Vol. 2 includes audiovisuals, slides, photographs, and flatwork. The collection itself is at present not open to researchers.

Temple University, Libraries, *Catalogue of the Charles L. Blockson Afro-American Collection,* ed. Charles L. Blockson (1990). A descriptive bibliography, arranged by subject, of the holdings of the Charles L. Blockson collection, a unit of the Temple University Libraries Special Collections. This catalog identifies only a portion of the rich materials housed in the Blockson collection.

Texas Southern University, Library, *Heartman Negro Collection: Catalogue* (1956). This collection contains books, pamphlets, periodicals, maps, broadsides, documents, almanacs, lithographs, oil paintings, musical scores, clippings, cartoons, and various "curios" dating from 1655 to 1955. Newspapers date from 1762 to 1900.

University of Miami, Coral Gables, Florida, Cuban and Caribbean Library, *Catalog of the Cuban and Caribbean Library* (6 vols., 1977). This book catalog was created from the holdings of the University of Miami Library. Included are books by Caribbean authors and works published in the Caribbean, here defined as "Cuba, the Greater and Lesser Antilles, the Guyanas, Venezuela, Mexico, Colombia, and Central America except San Salvador."

BIOGRAPHICAL SOURCES

Late 18th- and early 19th-century abolitionists compiled the earliest biographical dictionaries of men and women of African descent. They sought to demonstrate the intellectual, social, and moral accomplishments of slaves as a means of validating their humanity and justifying emancipation. Among the first of this genre was William Dickson's *Letters on Slavery* (London, 1789). The most notable was the French Abbé Henri Grégoire's *De la Litterature des Nègres: Ou, Recherchés sur Leurs Facultés Intellectueles, Leurs Qualités Morales et Leur Litterature: Suiviés des Notices sur la Vie et les Ouvrages des Nègres Qui Se Sont Distingués dans les Sciences, les Lettres et les Arts* (1808), published in English under the title *An Enquiry Concerning the Intellectual and Moral Faculties, and Literature of Negroes* (1810). Other notable early collections include Abigail Field Mott, *Biographical Sketches and Interesting Anecdotes of Persons of Colour* (1826), and Wilson Armistead, *A Tribute for the Negro* (1848).

The first such volume written by an African-American was Robert Benjamin Lewis's *Light and Truth from Ancient and Sacred History*, published in Portland, Maine, in 1836 and reprinted in expanded versions in 1844, 1849, and 1851. These subsequent editions were published in Boston "By a Committee of Colored Men" under the title *Light and Truth: Collected from the Bible and Ancient and Modern History: Containing the Universal History of the Colored and the Indian Race, from the Creation of the World to the Present Time.* The second collective biography by an African-American author was Ann Plato's *Essays: Including Biographies and Miscellaneous Pieces, in Prose and Poetry* (1841). Perhaps the most well known of the mid-19th-century collective biographies were William Cooper Nell's *The Colored Patriots of the American Revolution* (1855) and William Wells Brown's *The Black Man: His Antecedents, His Genius, and His Achievements,* first published by the African-American printer Thomas Hamilton in New York in 1863.

Beginning in the 1880s, such volumes were produced on an almost annual basis and covered members of specific groups (religious, professional, fraternal, or other organizations) as well as general who's whos. Among the most notable are William J. Simmons's *Men of Mark: Eminent, Progressive and Rising* (1887); I. Garland Penn's *The Afro-American Press, and Its Editors* (1891); Lawson A. Scruggs's *Women of Distinction: Remarkable in Works and Invincible in Character* (1892); and Monroe A. Majors's *Noted Negro Women: Their Triumphs and Activities* (1893). These volumes were written and often published by African-Americans and were targeted primarily for a black readership.

By the turn of the century, some white publishers noticed the emergence of an African-American market and began to produce collective biographies and other reference tools. These books were sold both by mail and through sales agents. J. L. Nichols, for example, a publisher of Bibles and other religious books, produced a popular volume by H. F. Kletzing and William H. Crogman entitled *Progress of a Race: Or, the Remarkable Advancement of the Afro-American Negro* (1897), which went through five editions. At least three of these were published with Nichols as coeditor (1920, 1925, and 1929). The most ambitious of the non-black compiler-editors was Arthur B. Caldwell, a publisher from suburban Atlanta who, between 1917 and 1923, produced seven remarkable volumes entitled *History of the American Negro.* These provided detailed biographical sketches with steel-engraved portraits of the subjects, and focused on citizens of Georgia (in two volumes), South Carolina, North Carolina, Virginia, Washington, D.C., and West Virginia.

Frank Lincoln Mather compiled a standard reference, *Who's Who of the Colored Race* (1915). Less famous, but equally valuable, is *The National Cyclopedia of the Colored Race,* for which Clement F. Richardson served as editor-in-chief. That volume was published in 1919 by the National Publishing Company in Montgomery, Alabama, and financed by a group of African-Americans based in New Orleans. In addition to biographies, this volume contains sketches of the history of black schools, fraternal organizations, and local churches. The standard biographical source for the first half of the 20th century is *Who's Who in Colored America,* published in seven volumes between 1927 and 1950.

Nearly 300 collected biographies published prior to 1951 (including all of the above) have been indexed by Randall K. Burkett, Nancy H. Burkett, and Henry Louis Gates, Jr., in *Black Biography, 1790–1950: A Cumulative Index* (3 vols., 1991). The index provides access to biographical sketches and illustrations of nearly 30,000 individuals and supplies birth and death dates, place of birth, occupation, and religious affiliation of subjects. Vol. 3 provides the complete list of all volumes indexed. It also offers access to subjects by place of birth, occupation, and religious affiliation, as well as a list of all women included. The compilers separately published a microfiche edition of the full text of all volumes indexed, under the title *Black Biographical Dictionaries, 1790–1950* (1987). Full-text online access to all volumes is available in *African American Biographical Database* (1998), through Chadwyck-Healey, Inc.

Other more recent collective biographies include:

Contemporary Black Biography: Profiles from the International Black Community (1992–). This ongoing, multivolume biographical encyclopedia offers broad and international coverage of individuals in wide-ranging fields. Although most of the subjects are contemporary, selected individuals from earlier periods who have made an impact on contemporary life are also included. Includes nationality, occupation, and subject and name indexes. Entries are signed and include references.

Dictionary of Literary Biography. This comprehensive series of biographical dictionaries is organized by topic, period, or genre and contains individual articles about persons who contributed to North American literature. Each volume provides a bibliographical guide and overview for a particular area of literature. African-American writers are the subject of six separate volumes, edited by Thadious M. Davis and Trudier Harris: *Afro-American Fiction Writers after 1955* (*Dictionary of Literary Biography,* vol. 33, 1984); *Afro-American Poets since 1955* (vol. 41, 1985); *Afro-American Writers before the Harlem Renaissance* (vol. 50, 1986); *Afro-American Writers, 1940–1955* (vol. 76, 1988); *Afro-American Fiction Writers after 1955: Dramatists and Prose Writers* (vol. 38, 1985). Also see Trudier Harris, ed., *Afro-American Writers from the Harlem Renaissance to 1940* (vol. 51, 1987).

Foner, Eric, *Freedom's Lawmakers: A Directory of Black Officeholders during Reconstruction* (2nd ed., 1996). This biographical dictionary contains some 1,510 descriptive entries about major state officials, members of constitutional conventions, and legislators of the period. Each entry includes bibliographic references. Also included are indexes by state, occupation, office held, birth status, and topic.

Foster, Mamie Marie Booth, comp., *Southern Black Creative Writers, 1829–1953: Biobibliographies* (1988). Brief biographical sketches include schools attended, occupation, honors and awards, and bibliographies of works. Includes a bibliography of references and an index of authors by state and period.

Harris, Sheldon, *Blues Who's Who: A Biographical Dictionary of Blues Singers* (1979). Biographical entries of 571 blues singers who lived between 1900 and 1977 include nicknames and pseudonyms, birth and death dates, instruments played, biographies, influences, quotations, references, and photographs.

Haskins, James, *Distinguished African American Political and Governmental Leaders* (1999). This selective dictionary profiles the lives of 104 notable elected and appointed leaders drawn from U.S. political and governmental life (state, county, and city) from the early 19th century to 1998. The individuals chosen include cabinet members, congressional leaders, ambassadors and diplomats, governors, and mayors. Biographical entries feature education, positions held, early years, career highlights, and a bibliography including Websites. Appendixes include lists of the leaders by birth date, position, state and party affiliation. A bibliography and index complete the volume.

Hodges, Graham Russell, ed., *The Black Loyalist Directory: African Americans in Exile after the American Revolution* (1995). Providing an introduction to the alliances between African-Americans and the British Army during the American Revolution, this directory includes brief descriptions of some 3,000 loyalists.

Kessler, James H., *Distinguished African American Scientists of the 20th Century* (1996). Lengthy articles describe the life and work of one hundred mathematicians, physicists, chemists, biologists, engineers, geologists, anthropologists, and physicians. Also provided are indexes by research area and date of birth.

Logan, Rayford W., and Michael R. Winston, ed., *Dictionary of American Negro Biography* (1982). This compendium of scholarly biographical essays on major figures is an important resource for biographical information. It includes no individual living as of January 1, 1970. Entries are written and signed by well-known scholars and include bibliographical references.

Organ, Claude H., Jr., and Margaret M. Kosiba, ed., *A Century of Black Surgeons: The U.S.A. Experience* (2 vols., 1987). This work deals with institutional and organizational contributions in vol. 1; vol. 2 includes a current profile of black surgeons, individual contributions, and contemporary surgery chairmen.

Peterson, Bernard L., Jr., *Early Black American Playwrights and Dramatic Writers: A Biographical Directory and Catalog of Plays, Films, and Broadcasting Scripts* (1990). This directory includes information on about 218 pioneer African-American playwrights and screenwriters who wrote or produced in the United States and Europe during the 19th century and first half of the 20th century.

Phelps, Shirelle, ed., *Who's Who among African Americans* (10th ed., 1998/99). This title is a continuation of the earlier *Who's Who among Black Americans* series. This volume contains career and biographical information about more than 20,000 individuals and an obituary section noting individuals who had died since the previous edition.

Porters, David L., ed., *African-American Sports Greats: A Biographical Dictionary* (1995). Profiles of 166 African-American athletes, mostly active after World War II and representing eleven different sports, are featured. Each entry includes a bibliography and is signed by one of forty-two contributors.

Ragsdale, Bruce A., and Joel D. Treese, *Black Americans in Congress, 1870–1989* (1990). Sponsored by the U.S. House of Representatives, this biographical dictionary of legislators is arranged alphabetically and includes lengthy biographical entries for some sixty-five African-American members of the United States Congress. Biographical descriptions tend to emphasize information about significant elections and the legislative accomplishments of each legislator. A photographic portrait and bibliographical references are also provided within each entry.

Riley, James A., *The Biographical Encyclopedia of the Negro Baseball Leagues* (1994). Entries for more than 4,000 players, with careers ranging from 1872 through 1950, include full name, nickname, career beginning and ending dates, position played, teams, biographical sketch, statistics, and sources. Also provides individual entries for teams. Includes bibliography and index.

Roses, Lorraine Elena, and Ruth Elizabeth Randolph, *Harlem Renaissance and Beyond: Literary Biographies of 100 Black Women Writers, 1900–1945* (1990). Entries provide a brief literary biography of major figures as well as of a number of women who published relatively little and have been largely neglected in other biographical works. Also included is a bibliography of selected primary and secondary sources.

Salem, Dorothy C., ed., *African American Women: A Biographical Dictionary* (1993). Included are nearly 300 biographies of women who have made significant contributions to social reform, politics, arts and entertainment, religion, business, education, and the professions from the colonial era to the present. Entries offer summaries and critical descriptions of the women, their significance, and their works. Each entry is signed and includes a bibliography.

Sammons, Vivian Ovelton, *Blacks in Science and Medicine* (1990). Biographical information is provided for more than 1,500 men and women in science and medicine, with an index by type of work. Entries give birth and death dates, specialties, education, employment, organization memberships, publications, references in which persons were noted, and dissertation title when available. This volume includes a bibliography.

Smith, J. Clay, Jr., *Emancipation: The Making of the Black Lawyer, 1844–1944* (1993). This is a comprehensive treatment of the first one hundred years of African-Americans in the legal profession, including a chapter on the history of blacks in legal education, national, and state bar associations. The majority of the text recounts the history of black lawyers, organized by regions—New England, Atlantic States, Southeastern States, and Southern States. Appendixes include lists of individual lawyers arranged by state/territory, the number of lawyers in each state/territory, a table of cases, and a lengthy bibliography.

Smith, Jessie Carney, ed., *Notable Black American Men* (1999). This companion volume to *Notable Black American Women* (1992) presents biographies of 500 men from the 18th century to the present. Diverse occupations and areas of activity are represented, and there are more than 400 photographs. Each entry is signed by the author and contains a list of references. The volume is well indexed by geography (state and city), occupation, and subject.

———, *Notable Black American Women* (1992) and *Notable Black American Women,* Book II (1996). The 1992 publication includes 500 biographical essays, with photographs when available, ranging from colonial times to the present. It presents a selective core of prominent women with broad geographic, historical, and professional representation. Each entry is signed and includes bibliographical references. Book II provides information on an additional 300 women and includes occupation, geographic, and subject indexes.

ENCYCLOPEDIAS AND DICTIONARIES

Appiah, Kwame Anthony, and Henry Louis Gates, Jr., ed., *Africana: The Encyclopedia of the African and African American Experience* (1999). This massive single volume surveys Africa, Africans, and people of African descent in Latin America and the Caribbean, North America, and Europe. There are twelve "featured essays" by leading scholars and a total of 233 contributors who sign many but not all of the essays. The volume is well illustrated, with extensive maps (both geopolitical and thematic), tables, and charts. Entries are arranged alphabetically, from Aardvark to Zydeco, and focus on Africa (40 percent), Latin America and the Caribbean (30 percent), and North America (30 percent). A small number of articles deals with Europe and with "Cross Cultural" topics. Extensive attention is devoted to the arts, especially music. Entries contain no citations, but there is a 30-page "select bibliography."

———, *Encarta Africana* (1999). CD-ROM. Inspired by W. E. B. Du Bois's dream of producing the first encyclopedia of Africana, this multimedia encyclopedia includes more than 3,000 articles, 2,500 videos, audio clips, maps and photographs, and an interactive timeline of Africans and people of African descent.

Bradley, David, and Shelley Fisher Fishkin, ed., *The Encyclopedia of Civil Rights in America* (3 vols., 1998). Some 683 articles discuss places, events, historical eras, and individuals, as well as broad issues. Articles are signed and include a list of references; many are illustrated. Appendixes include a "Table of Court Cases, 1833–1996"; a "Guide to Rights Organizations" (arranged by state), a list of museums and memorials, filmography, and bibliography. Entries address Native Americans, Asian Americans, Latinos, and women, as well as African-Americans. All entries are listed in the back of each volume by category and there is a comprehensive index.

Hine, Darlene Clark, Elsa Barkley Brown, and Rosalyn Terborg-Penn, ed., *Black Women in America: An Historical Encyclopedia* (1993). This encyclopedia contains 804 entries, 641 about black women and 163 about general topics and organizations. Articles are signed

and include bibliographies. The volume concentrates on women who played a role na-
tionally or who made national news, including some prominent in local communities. A
chronology of black women in the United States and an index by profession both enhance
the usefulness of this important work.

Jones-Wilson, Faustine C., *Encyclopedia of African-American Education* (1996). Featured are articles about the people, institutions, organizations, policies, laws, and theories that have
had an impact on the education of African-Americans in the United States. Each article
includes a bibliography and is signed.

Joyce, Donald Franklin, *Black Book Publishers in the United States: A Historical Dictionary of the
Presses, 1817–1990* (1991). In-depth profiles of black publishers are included along with
publishing history, comments on publications, sources, selected list of titles, library locations, and officers.

Kellner, Bruce, ed., *The Harlem Renaissance: A Historical Dictionary for the Era* (1984). This
biographical dictionary deals primarily with people, events, and literature between 1917
and 1935. Entries are signed and include bibliographical references. Appendixes include a
chronology of events, a bibliography of books published by or about African-Americans
during the Harlem Renaissance, plays and musicals by or about African-Americans, a listing of newspapers and other serial publications, and a glossary of Harlem slang used in
the 1920s and 1930s.

Low, W. Augustus, and Virgil A. Clift, ed., *Encyclopedia of Black America* (1981). This important historical encyclopedia combines biographical entries and topical articles. Each entry
includes bibliographical references.

Lowery, Charles D., and John F. Marszalek, ed., *Encyclopedia of African-American Civil Rights:
From Emancipation to the Present* (1992). This work contains more than 800 short articles
covering individuals, organizations, events, and court cases. Entries are signed, and each
contains a selected bibliography. A detailed chronology from 1861 to 1990 is included.

Luker, Ralph E., *Historical Dictionary of the Civil Rights Movement* (1997). The emphasis in this
encyclopedic dictionary is on events, organizations, judicial decisions, legislation, and individuals of the post–World War II era. In addition to descriptive entries, this dictionary
also includes a bibliographic essay and a bibliography of both primary and secondary
sources. Although there is no index, most entries include cross-references to related entries in the volume.

Miller, Randall M., and John David Smith, ed., *Dictionary of Afro-American Slavery* (updated
ed., 1997). The period from the first North American English settlement to Reconstruction is covered. Includes entries on regions of the United States, broad topics, and selected
biographies. Entries contain bibliographical references.

Murphy, Larry G., J. Gordon Melton, and Gary L. Ward, ed., *Encyclopedia of African American
Religions* (1993). A treasure trove of information is found in this resource on black religious institutions in the United States. Of its nearly 1,200 entries, 343 are devoted to religious organizations and 773 are biographical sketches. The volume also contains thirty
longer signed essays on major topics and denominations. All entries contain references,
and there is an eighteen-page chronology of African-American history, a bibliography,
and a thorough index.

Nuñez, Benjamin, *Dictionary of Afro-Latin American Civilization* (1980). A historical and descriptive dictionary including more than 4,500 entries dealing with terms, phrases, events,
and selected biographies covers African cultural influence in Latin America. Name and
subject indexes and a bibliography are also included.

Pyatt, Sherman E., and Alan Johns, *A Dictionary and Catalog of African American Folklife of the
South* (1999). The first section of this volume includes alphabetically arranged entries describing a wide range of topics related to African-American folklife in the South. These
entries are based on both interviews and scholarly works. The second section includes an
extensive catalog of books, articles, and other information resources arranged by topic.
The dictionary is indexed by author and keyword.

Rodriguez, Junius P., ed., *The Historical Encyclopedia of World Slavery* (2 vols., 1997). This two-
volume work provides a comprehensive and detailed treatment of the institution of slav-

ery from its origins in the earliest Near Eastern societies. A wide range of topics is covered concerning the practice of slavery, beginning with the ancient world and continuing into contemporary times. Maps and illustrations supplement the entries. Entries are signed and include references for further reading. Vol. 2 contains an extensive index and bibliography divided by continent and time period.

Salzman, Jack, David Lionel Smith, and Cornel West, *Encyclopedia of African-American Culture and History* (5 vols., 1996). This major source includes some 2,200 entries dealing with biographies, events, historical eras, legal cases, music, visual arts, architecture, and professions. All fifty states have entries, as do major cities. Also included are photographs, illustrations, and scholarly essays that examine the legacy of events. Appendixes include a wealth of statistical information regarding awards and honors, business, economics, education, health, politics, population, and sports.

Shavit, Donald, *The United States in Africa: A Historical Dictionary* (1989). African-Americans are well represented among the featured persons, institutions, and events that affected relations between the United States and Africa. Appendixes include chiefs of American diplomatic missions in Africa, 1863–1988, and lists of individuals by occupation.

Walker, Juliet E. K., ed., *Encyclopedia of African American Business History* (1999). The purpose of this encyclopedia, as described by the editor, is "to illuminate the historic continuity of black business in America from colonial times to the post–civil rights era and underscore the diversity of black business activities from slavery to freedom." Included in more than 200 entries are biographies of businesspeople, articles on black business history topics, such as "Great Depression and Black Business Survivors," and articles that survey black business participation in selected industries, such as "Transportation Enterprises." Individual entries include bibliographies for suggested further reading. The volume concludes with a Chronology of Black Business History beginning in 1619, a selected bibliography arranged in six categories, and a subject index.

Wilson, Charles Reagan, and William Ferris, *Encyclopedia of Southern Culture* (1989). Sponsored by the Center for the Study of Southern Culture, University of Mississippi, this work covers the regional cultural achievements and the cultural landscape of the South. Articles identify distinctive regional differences and provide basic facts and bibliographical data about Southern cultural patterns and their historical development. An overview essay is followed by a series of alphabetically arranged themes, and then brief, alphabetically arranged topical and biographical entries.

Wright, Richard Robert, Jr., *Encyclopaedia of the African Methodist Episcopal Church* (2nd ed., 1947). In addition to several thousand biographical sketches, this volume contains much information on the history and organizational structure of the denomination. The first edition of this work, also edited by Richard R. Wright, Jr., was published under the title *Centennial Encyclopedia of the African Methodist Episcopal Church* (1916) and contains very little overlap with the 1947 edition.

INDEXES

Abajian, James de T., *Blacks in Selected Newspapers, Censuses and Other Sources: An Index to Names and Subjects* (3 vols., 1977). See also James de T. Abajian, *Blacks in Selected Newspapers, Censuses and Other Sources: An Index to Names and Subjects: First Supplement* (2 vols., 1985). The volumes provide a name and subject index of more than fifty selected 19th- and 20th-century newspapers and periodicals, 19th-century federal and state census records, 19th-century city directories, and a variety of other published biographies, state and municipal records, lists, directories, and reports. The two-volume supplement indexes additional sources "more narrowly defined in time than in previous volumes."

Burkett, Randall K., Nancy H. Burkett, and Henry Louis Gates, Jr., *Black Biography, 1790–1950: A Cumulative Index* (3 vols., 1991). This work affords access to biographical sketches and illustrations of nearly 30,000 individuals, with birth and death dates, place of birth, occupation, and religious affiliation. Vol. 3 provides access by place of birth, occupation, and religious affiliation.

Chicago Public Library, Omnibus Project, *The Chicago Afro-American Union Analytic Catalog: An Index to Materials on the Afro-American in the Principal Libraries of Chicago* (5 vols., 1972). This catalog indexes 75,000 books, periodicals, theses, yearbooks, and exhibition catalogs, arranging them by author, title, and subject. Articles have been included from more than 1,000 periodicals published between 1890 and 1940.

Frankovich, Nicholas, and David Larzelere, ed., *The Columbia Granger's Index to African-American Poetry* (1999). This index identifies poems contained in some 33 poetry anthologies and in 32 volumes of collected and selected works by individual poets. Each poem is indexed by title, by first line and last line, by author, and by subject.

Jacobs, Donald M., ed., *Index to The American Slave* (1981). This index to *The American Slave*, the forty-volume set of slave narratives compiled by the WPA and edited by George P. Rawick, contains an alphabetically arranged slave identification file, identifying the narratives by location, as well as by the age and occupation of the individual interviewed. An alphabetical name index by state and a general subject index are also provided. The general subject index is very limited in its coverage.

The Kaiser Index to Black Resources, 1948–1986 (5 vols., 1992). This extremely valuable subject guide to 174,000 references to periodical literature, newspaper articles, and ephemera was formerly a card file created and maintained by Ernest Kaiser at the Schomburg Center for Research in Black Culture.

Lawson, Jacqueline A., *An Index of African Americans Identified in Selected Records of the Bureau of Refugees, Freedmen, and Abandoned Lands* (1995). This index to the names of African-Americans identified in the letters and registers of the National Archives, Record Group 105, *Records of the Bureau of Refugees, Freedmen, and Abandoned Lands, 1865–1872* provides names and locations of African-Americans who corresponded with the Freedmen's Bureau or whose names were mentioned in letters to the Commissioner of the Bureau.

Spradling, Mary Mace, ed., *In Black and White: A Guide to Magazine Articles, Newspaper Articles, and Books concerning More Than 15,000 Black Individuals and Groups* (2 vols., 3rd ed., 1980). See also Mary Mace Spradling, ed., *In Black and White: Supplement: A Guide to Magazine Articles, Newspaper Articles, and Books concerning More Than 6,700 Black Individuals and Groups* (1985). This guide provides references to individuals and groups worldwide that are found in magazine and newspaper articles and books. It includes an index to occupations and a bibliography of all the works scanned. A supplement was published in 1985.

CHRONOLOGIES AND ATLASES

Christian, Charles M., *Black Saga: The African American Experience* (1995). Highlighted are significant events pre-1492 to 1994. Includes a bibliography and index.

Cowan, Thomas Dale, and Jack Maguire, *Timelines of African-American History: 500 Years of Black Achievement* (1994). Covering from 1492 to 1993, each year's events are subdivided into headings such as politics and civil rights, business and employment, religion and education, literature and journalism, science and technology, and the performing arts. A bibliography and index are included.

Harley, Sharon, *The Timetables of African-American History: A Chronology of the Most Important People and Events in African-American History* (1995). Covers the period 1492 to 1992 and highlights events in general history, education, laws and legal actions, religion, literature, publications and the black press, the arts, science, technology, and medicine and sports. An index is included.

Jenkins, Everett, Jr., *Pan-African Chronology: A Comprehensive Reference to the Black Quest for Freedom in Africa, the Americas, Europe, and Asia, 1400–1865* (1996). Covering the most significant events in African, African-American, and Pan-African history, this publication is arranged by century and then geographically by Africa, Europe, Asia, the Americas, and the United States. Includes bibliography and index.

Rodriguez, Junius P., *Chronology of World Slavery* (1999). This work is a complementary volume to the author's *Historical Encyclopedia of World Slavery* (see slavery section in this chapter), providing broad coverage of pivotal events during slavery's long history. The chronology is divided into the following sections: Ancient World, Europe, Asia, Africa, Latin America, United States, and Contemporary History. Brief, informative essays (sidebars) supplement the chronological arrangement of events and appear throughout the work on topics such as "Greco-Roman Women as Slaves," "Slavery in Southeast Asia," and "Jayhawkers." The volume ends with a convenient gathering of some eighty representative documents, beginning with excerpts from "The Code of Hammurabi" (ca. 1790 B.C.E.) and ending with "Brazilian Government Recognizes Slave Labor" (1995). An index and bibliography divided by continent and time period are included.

Smallwood, Arwin D., with Jeffrey M. Elliott, *The Atlas of African-American History and Politics: From the Slave Trade to Modern Times* (1998). Some 145 maps illustrate aspects of African-American history, covering the African Slave Trades and Beginnings of African Slavery in the Americas to African-Americans and the Challenges of the 1990s. The book is divided into eleven units or topics, with each unit including lengthy map and text sources. Contains index.

DIRECTORIES, YEARBOOKS, AND ANNUALS

Mabundo, L. Mpho, ed., *The African-American Almanac* (7th ed., 1997). Formerly *The Negro Almanac,* this is a comprehensive work which has been expanded. It includes significant documents in African-American history, a section on Africans in America, 1600 to 1900, and sections on law, politics, population, the family, religion, literature, media, science, and medicine. It includes a bibliography of publications between 1990 and 1992.

Murray, Florence, ed., *The Negro Handbook* (1942, 1944, 1946–47, 1949). These four volumes provide factual information for the years 1942 through 1948. Data include population, vital statistics, civil rights, crime, education, labor, housing, business, farms, government and politics, armed forces, religion, sports, media, theater, and organizations.

National Urban League, *The State of Black America* (1976–). Published annually, each volume contains an overview of events of the past year by the Urban League director and essays by prominent scholars and administrators on current issues. Excellent recent statistical information is found here, with a chronology of events for the year.

Negro Year Book (11 vols., 1912–1952). An irregular annual publication, its title varies slightly. Published editions include: 1912, 1913, 1914–15, 1916–17, 1918–19, 1921–22, 1925–26, 1931–32, 1937–38, 1941–46, 1952. The series was initiated and edited by Monroe Nathan Work, head of the Records and Research Department of Tuskegee Institute from 1908 to 1938, and by Jessie Parkhurst Guzman thereafter. In the early volumes, Work documented achievements of African-Americans; from 1925–26 onward, he also sought to describe and explain conditions. In the 1941–46 and 1952 editions, a variety of specialists authored specific chapters. Work's massive Tuskegee Institute News Clippings File provided the documentary evidence for each *Negro Year Book.* Work subscribed to hundreds of black newspapers (many of which are no longer extant) and organized clippings according to the evolving categories used in the yearbooks. These materials, comprising 362 linear feet of mounted clippings, are available on 252 reels of microfilm and provide extraordinary subject access to black newspapers in the period.

Payne, Wardell J., ed., *Directory of African American Religious Bodies: A Compendium by the Howard University School of Divinity* (2nd ed., 1995). The work includes historical overviews and contemporary listings of African-American religious traditions, bodies, councils and organizations, and educational institutions, followed by a selected bibliography.

Schomburg Center for Research in Black Culture, *The New York Public Library African American Desk Reference* (1999). This handbook can answer questions ranging from Mary McLeod Bethune's recipe for sweet potato pie to lists of African-Americans in the federal judiciary. The volume includes nineteen topical chapters that cover a wide range of historical, cultural, and practical information. Beginning with a timeline of African-American history, the volume utilizes charts, sidebars, reading lists, recipes, glossaries, quotes, and biographical profiles, within topics such as slavery, politics, the African diaspora, family and heritage, religion, education, health, business, literature, performing arts, fine and applied arts, media, and sports. Each chapter concludes with a list of sources for additional information. A comprehensive index is included.

GUIDES

Andrews, William L., Frances Smith Foster, and Trudier Harris, ed., *The Oxford Companion to African American Literature* (1997). This unique encyclopedic guide is devoted to the "texts and the historical and cultural contexts of African American literature." It includes topical essays, biographical articles, analytical and descriptive entries about major novels, poems, dramatic works, autobiographies, essay collections, children's and young adult literature, prominent literary characters, and cultural issues. Articles are signed and include bibliographies.

Byers, Paula K., ed., *African American Genealogical Sourcebook* (1995). This comprehensive guide to historical and genealogical research begins with essays by experts in the field of African-American genealogy, covering immigration and migration patterns in the United States and basic genealogical records. Part II lists information resources, including national, regional, state and foreign organizations, libraries and archives, print, and non-print resources. Extensive bibliographies are included as well as author, title, and organization indexes.

Curtis, Nancy C., *Black Heritage Sites: An African American Odyssey and Finder's Guide* (1996). A variety of historic sites—homes, schools and colleges, churches, cemeteries, and monuments—are described. The guide is organized into five regions: South, Northeast, Midwest, Southwest, and West, including Alaska and Hawaii, and then by state and city. Each region begins with a historical essay by the author. The index provides access by type of structure or by theme, such as women's clubs or the civil rights movement.

Davis, Townsend, *Weary Feet, Rested Souls: A Guided History of the Civil Rights Movement* (1998). This publication is a guide to historically significant sites—churches, houses, schools and colleges, bus stations, stores, jails, etc.—in Alabama, Arkansas, Georgia, Mississippi, North Carolina, South Carolina, and Tennessee, related to the civil rights movement ca. 1954–1968. Arranged alphabetically by state and city, entries include a street map highlighting the sites, an essay outlining the civil rights history of the city, followed by a detailed description of each significant site. Includes photographs. Entries contain lengthy lists of interviewees and bibliographies, including books, articles, audio and video recordings, manuscript collections, and legal cases.

Fuller, Sara, ed., *The Ohio Black History Guide* (1975). This guide to resources documenting Ohio black history represents the holdings of some 200 Ohio libraries, universities, and historical societies, including Ohio materials in the Library of Congress and the National Archives. The guide is arranged by format: printed materials, dissertations and theses, manuscripts, government records, and audiovisual materials.

Ham, Debra Newman, ed., *The African American Mosaic: A Library of Congress Resource Guide for the Study of Black History and Culture* (1993). This is a richly narrated, chronologically arranged guide to materials in the Library of Congress relating to African-American history. Includes reproductions of many illustrations and photographs from the collections.

Moebs, Thomas Truxtun, *Black Soldiers, Black Sailors, Black Ink: Research Guide on African-Americans in U.S. Military History, 1526–1900* (1994). An exhaustive guide to primary and secondary research material about pre-1901 African-American participation in military service, this single-volume work is arranged into four major sections: Writings of African-American Veterans and Military Writings of African-American Civilians; Chronology of Black Soldiers and Sailors; Subject Bibliography; and African-American Unit Histories. It includes data on 12,000 individuals who served before 1901. Women who served as "combatants, nurses, scouts, or spies" are included.

Newman, Richard, *African American Quotations* (1998). This source contains some 2,500 quotations in English by more than 500 individuals from the 18th century to the present.

Subject headings range from "Achievement" to "Victory." Entries are arranged alphabetically by subject. There are indexes to subjects and to authors of quotations, as well as an
occupations index.

Peterson, Bernard L., Jr., *The African American Theatre Directory, 1816–1960: A Comprehensive
Guide to Early Black Theatre Organizations, Companies, Theatres, and Performing Groups*
(1997). This work provides information on some 500 African-American theatrical organizations, companies, and performing groups. Also included are more than 200 black-oriented or black-controlled theaters, halls, and performance spaces. Entries are listed alphabetically. Appendixes include theaters included and those not included in the directory;
theater organizations are classified under eight main types, such as Minstrel Companies,
Touring Musicals, Resident Theatre Companies, Community Little Theatre Groups and
Professional Theatrical Organizations. Includes bibliography and index of names, organizations and theaters, and show titles.

Savage, Beth L., *African American Historic Places* (1994). More than 800 sites, historic districts,
buildings, and objects recognized in the National Register of Historic Places are identified
for their significance to social history, community development, education, science and
medicine, arts, literature, women's history, military events, and civil rights in forty-two
states and two territories. Sites are arranged by state and city. It includes indexes by state
and city, occupation, name of individual, organization, and subject.

Smythe, Mabel M., ed., *The Black American Reference Book* (1976). This is a compendium of
scholarly essays on topics such as "The Black Role in the Economy," "The Black Family,"
"The Black Role in American Politics," and "Black Influences in the American Theater."
Contributors include John Hope Franklin, Constance Baker Motley, Langston Hughes,
and Arna Bontemps. Articles include bibliographies. A previous edition was published by
John Preston Davis, ed., *The American Negro Reference Book* (1966).

Valade, Roger M., III, ed., *The Schomburg Center Guide to Black Literature: From the Eighteenth
Century to the Present* (1996). More than 500 brief biographical essays about novelists, poets, critics, dramatists, journalists, editors, screenwriters, children's writers, and essayists
are highlighted, along with summaries of more than 400 literary works, with essays on literary themes, topics, and movements. Includes definitions of terms and genres.

STATISTICAL SOURCES

Cramer, Clayton E., *Black Demographic Data, 1790–1860: A Sourcebook* (1997). This volume
provides information on the changing population distribution of antebellum African-
Americans, supplying census data by region and state. Tables and graphs offer details on
free and slave black populations prior to the Civil War.

Hornor, Louise L., ed., *Black Americans: A Statistical Sourcebook* (1996). This reference source is
a compendium of statistics from the federal government, especially from the U.S. Bureau
of the Census. Its tables cover demographics, vital statistics, education, government and
elections, crime, labor force, income, and selected special topics. Each table cites the statistical source. The dates of the statistics vary and represent the latest available at the time of
publication.

Smith, Jessie Carney, and Carrell Peterson Horton, comp. and ed., *Historical Statistics of Black
America* (2 vols., 1995). Historical data from the 18th century through 1975 related to agriculture, business and economics, legal justice, education, the family, media, the military,
politics and elections, population, religion, slavery and the slave trade, and vital statistics
are presented. Each table identifies the data source.

Smith, Jessie Carney, and Carrell Peterson Horton, ed., *Statistical Record of Black America* (4th
ed., 1997). The data encompass attitudes, business and economics, crime, law enforcement and legal justice, education, health and medical care, housing, income, spending and
wealth, labor and employment, politics and elections, population, sports and leisure, the
family, and vital statistics. The statistics gathered are through 1995 and each table cites the
original source of the data. A bibliography of all sources utilized is included.

U.S. Bureau of the Census, *Negroes in the United States* (1904–1935). In 1904, the Bureau of the

Census produced the first of several publications designed to bring together in one volume the wide range of previously dispersed census data about the African-American population. These publications are *Negroes in the United States* (Bulletin 8) (1904); *Negroes in the United States* (Bulletin 129) (1915); *Negro Population in the United States, 1790–1915* (1918); and *Negroes in the United States, 1920–1932* (1935). Although some of the data in these volumes was republished from previous census publications, much of the material had never been printed. In addition to numerous tables, these volumes include essays about each category of data providing substantial analysis and evaluation of the data and how it was collected. An essay of particular note in the 1904 edition is W. E. B. Du Bois's "The Negro Farmer."

3 Internet Resources

RAQUEL VON COGELL

The World Wide Web, one part of the Internet, was developed in the late 1980s and has grown phenomenally since the mid-1990s. While some fear the quality of research will diminish if students rely too heavily on it, the Web makes it possible for students and scholars to access an enormous and rapidly growing body of textual, graphical, and interactive material that was previously inaccessible to most researchers.

Using search engines to find good Websites can be a daunting task. However, guides such as the *Britannica Internet Guide (http://www.britannica.com), Internet Scout Project* at the University of Wisconsin, Madison *(http://scout.cs.wisc.edu/ index.html), Librarians' Index to the Internet* in California *(http://lii.org/), African American Internet Resources* at Emory University *(http://info.library.emory.edu/ref/ aair/index.html),* and *Africana.com*'s links make navigating the Web easier and provide Web searchers another route to useful sites.

The Web sources in this essay are arranged in the following categories: Arts; Biography; Dance; Film; History; History (Regional); Literature; Museums; Music; Photographs and Prints; Politics; Theater; Libraries, Institutes, and Research Centers; and Library Catalogs. The sites included were selected because of their exceptional quality and usefulness.

The World Wide Web is a rapidly changing avenue for research, and new sites appear almost daily. Effective use of this medium will be essential for researchers at all levels in the 21st century.

ARTS

I'll Make Me a World. PBS *(http://www.pbs.org/immaw/).* "Celebrates the achievements of 20th-century African-American writers, dancers, painters, actors, filmmakers, musicians, and other artists."

International Index to Black Periodicals (http://iibp.chadwyck.com/). A database available through Chadwyck-Healey indexing scholarly and popular black periodicals.

BIOGRAPHY

African American Biographical Database (http://aabd.chadwyck.com/). A full-text, searchable database of biographies of thousands of African-Americans. The content is drawn from *Black Biographical Dictionaries, 1790–1950.*

African-American Journey—People (http://www.pbs.org/aajourney/people.html). Biographical information on contemporary and historical African-American figures.

American Life Histories: Manuscripts from the Federal Writers' Project, 1936–1940. Library of Congress *(http://lcweb2.loc.gov/wpaintro/wpahome.html)*.

American Slave Narratives. University of Virginia *(http://xroads.virginia.edu/~HYPER/wpa/wpahome.html)*. A sample of slave narratives found in the collection *The American Slave: A Composite Autobiography,* ed. George P. Rawick (Greenwood Press, 1972–1979). The narratives are drawn from WPA interviews of former slaves.

American Visionaries: Frederick Douglass. National Park Service *(http://www.cr.nps.gov/csd/exhibits/douglass/)*.

By Popular Demand: Jackie Robinson and Other Baseball Highlights, 1860s–1960s (http://memory.loc.gov/ammem/jrhtml/jrhome.html).

The Encyclopædia Britannica Guide to Black History. Britannica Online *(http://www.eb.com:180/blackhistory/)*. A source of brief biographical sketches of historical and contemporary black figures.

The Faces of Science: African Americans in the Sciences (http://www.princeton.edu/~mcbrown/display/faces.html).

First-Person Narratives of the American South, 1860–1920. Library of Congress, American Memory Series *(http://memory.loc.gov/ammem/award97/ncuhtml/fpnashome.html)*. Includes a number of narratives by ex-slaves.

North American Slave Narratives, Beginnings to 1920. University of North Carolina, Chapel Hill Libraries *(http://metalab.unc.edu/docsouth/neh/neh.html)*. Full-text narratives including *Incidents in the Life of a Slave Girl* by Harriet Jacobs and Booker T. Washington's *Up from Slavery: An Autobiography.*

Remembering Slavery Web. Smithsonian Institution *(http://www.rememberingslavery.org/)*. Companion to the book *Remembering Slavery: African Americans Talk about Their Personal Experiences of Slavery and Emancipation.*

United States Colored Troops Database. National Park Service *(http://www.itd.nps.gov/cwss/usct.html)*. A database of more than 200,000 names of individuals who served in the USCT. The site also includes regimental histories of the units in which the USCT served.

DANCE

Alvin Ailey American Dance Theater (http://www.alvinailey.org/).

FILM

African-American Studies Videotapes and Audiocassettes. University of California, Berkeley *(http://www.lib.berkeley.edu/MRC/AfricanAmVid.html)*.

Black Film Center/Archive. Indiana University, Bloomington *(http://www.indiana.edu/~bfca/index.html)*.

BlackFilm.com (http://www.blackfilm.com/home/).

BlackFilmMakers.net (http://www.blackfilmmakers.net/).

California Newsreel (http://www.newsreel.org/index.htm). African American Video *(http://www.newsreel.org/aframeri.htm)*.

First Run/Icarus Films (http://www.frif.com/). African American Studies Videos and Films *(http://www.frif.com/subjects/afriamer.html)*.

Separate Cinema (http://www.separatecinema.com/). An "archive of movie posters, lobby cards, stills and assorted ephemera spans the past century of important historic black cinema."

HISTORY

Aboard the Underground Railroad. National Park Service *(http://www.cr.nps.gov/nr/ underground/).*

African American Dates in Time (http://www.igc.apc.org/africanam/dates/).

African American History and Culture. National Park Service *(http://tps.cr.nps.gov/crm/ issue.cfm?volume=20&number=02).* Vol. 20, no. 2 of the journal *Cultural Resource Management.*

African-American Journey. PBS *(http://www.pbs.org/aajourney/).* An index of more than 100 PBS sites related to the African-American experience.

The African-American Mosaic. Library of Congress *(http://lcweb.loc.gov/exhibits/african/ intro.html).* An online exhibit and Web companion to the publication *The African-American Mosaic: A Library of Congress Resource Guide for the Study of Black History and Culture.*

African American Odyssey: A Quest for Full Citizenship. Library of Congress *(http:// lcweb2.loc.gov/ammem/aaohtml/aohome.html). African American Odyssey: A Quest for Full Citizenship* draws from the Library of Congress's extensive collection of "rare books, government documents, manuscripts, maps, musical scores, plays, films, and recordings" about African-American history and culture.

African American Perspectives: Pamphlets from the Daniel A. P. Murray Collection, 1818–1907. Library of Congress *(http://lcweb2.loc.gov/ammem/aap/aaphome.html).* A searchable and browsable site of more than 300 full-text pamphlets. According to the site's introductory notes, the collection includes "sermons on racial pride and political activism; annual reports of charitable, educational, and political organizations; and college catalogs and graduation orations. Also included are biographies, slave narratives, speeches by members of Congress, legal documents, poetry, playbills, dramas, and librettos."

African-Americans in Army History. U.S. Army Center for Military History *(http:// www.army.mil/cmh-pg/topics/afam/afam-usa.htm).*

African American Studies Journals. JSTOR *(http://www.jstor.org).* JSTOR provides full-text access to a journal's backfile. Most journals have a "moving wall" period, which means there is a "gap between the most recently published issue and the date of the most recent issues available in JSTOR." Nonliterary African-American studies journals include *Journal of Black Studies, The Journal of Blacks in Higher Education, The Journal of Negro Education, The Journal of Negro History,* and *Transition.*

African American Theses and Dissertations: 1907–1997. University of California, Berkeley *(http://sunsite.berkeley.edu/Bibliographies/AfricanAmerican/).* A bibliography of theses and dissertations written at the University of California, Berkeley.

Africans in America: America's Journey through Slavery. PBS *(http://www.pbs.org/wgbh/aia/).*

Amistad (http://www.amistad.org/). A listing of diverse historical, legal, and artistic sources related to the *Amistad* slave revolt (1841).

Connections: African-American History and CRM. National Park Service *(http://tps.cr.nps.gov/ crm/issue.cfm?volume=19&number=02).* Vol. 19, no. 2 of the journal *Cultural Resource Management.*

Exploring Amistad: Race and the Boundaries of Freedom in Antebellum Maritime America. Mystic Seaport, the Museum of America and the Sea *(http://amistad.mysticseaport.org/main/ welcome.html).*

From Slavery to Freedom: The African-American Pamphlet Collection, 1824–1909 (http:// memory.loc.gov/ammem/aapchtml/aapchome.html).

H-Afro-Am (http://www.h-net.msu.edu/~afro-am/). H-Afro-Am is a discussion list for scholars and professionals in African-American studies and part of the H-Net, Humanities & Social Sciences On-Line initiative at Michigan State University.

Heroes in the Ships: African Americans in the Whaling Industry. Kendall Whaling Museum, Sharon, Massachusetts *(http://www.kwm.org/collections/exhibits/heroes/home.htm).* A historical overview of blacks in the whaling industry.

History of African-Americans in the Civil War. National Park Service *(http://www.itd.nps.gov/ cwss/africanh.html).*

Homecoming. PBS *(http://www.pbs.org/homecoming/).* Story of African-American farms and farmers.

International Index to Black Periodicals (http://iibp.chadwyck.com/). A database available through Chadwyck-Healey indexing scholarly and popular black periodicals.

Little Rock Central High: The 40th Anniversary (http://www.centralhigh57.org/).

Malcolm X: A Research Site. Africana Studies Program, University of Toledo *(http:// www.brothermalcolm.net/).*

The Marcus Garvey and Universal Negro Improvement Association Papers Project. James S. Coleman African Studies Center, UCLA *(http://www.isop.ucla.edu/mgpp/).* This site provides introductory text and sample documents from each volume of the Marcus Garvey and Universal Negro Improvement Association Papers, edited by Robert A. Hill.

The Martin Luther King, Jr., Papers Project. Stanford University *(http://www.stanford.edu/group/ King/).* Primary and secondary research materials about Martin Luther King, Jr.

The North Star: A Journal of African-American Religious History. Afro-American Religious History group of the American Academy of Religion *(http://cedar.barnard.columbia.edu/ ~north/).*

Our Shared History: Celebrating African American History & Culture. The National Park Service *(http://www.cr.nps.gov/aahistory/).*

Port Chicago Mutiny (http://www.portchicagomutiny.com/). Information about events surrounding the World War II military disaster at Port Chicago Naval Munitions base, located on San Francisco Bay.

Records of Slave Ship Movement between Africa and the Americas, 1817–1843. Data and Program Library Service, University of Wisconsin-Madison *(http://dpls.dacc.wisc.edu/slavedata/ slaintro1.html).* "Provides access to the raw data and documentation which contains information on slave ship movement between Africa and the Americas from 1817–1843. Specifically, the data file contains information on the ship's port of arrival, date of arrival, type of vessel, tonnage, master's name, number of guns, number of crew, national flag, number of slaves, port of departure, number of days of voyage, and mortality."

Slavery and Resistance. National Park Service *(http://tps.cr.nps.gov/crm/ issue.cfm?volume=21&number=04).* Vol. 21, no. 4 of the journal *Cultural Resource Management.*

Soldiers with Swords: The Black Press. PBS *(http://www.pbs.org/blackpress/).* Historical overview of the African-American press.

The Two Nations of Black America. PBS *(http://www.pbs.org/wgbh/pages/frontline/shows/race/).* *Frontline*'s report about the "chasm between the upper and lower classes of black America."

The Underground Railroad. National Geographic *(http://www.nationalgeographic.com/features/ 99/railroad/j1.html).*

HISTORY (REGIONAL)

African American Experience in Ohio: 1850–1920. The Ohio Historical Society *(http:// www.ohiohistory.org/africanam/), (http://memory.loc.gov/ammem/award97/ohshtml/ aaeohome.html).*

African-American Women—Online Archival Exhibits. Special Collections Library, Duke University *(http://scriptorium.lib.duke.edu/collections/african-american-women.html).*

Afro-American Sources in Virginia: A Guide to Manuscripts. University Press of Virginia *(http:// www.upress.virginia.edu/plunkett/mfp.html).*

Black Archives of Mid-America. Black Archives of Mid-America, Inc. and the Kansas City Public Library *(http://www.blackarchives.org/).*

Black History of New Hampshire (http://www.seacoastnh.com/blackhistory/).

Black New York (http://digital.nypl.org/wpa.html). A forthcoming digital collection from the New York Public Library.

The Buffalo Soldiers on the Western Frontier. International Museum of the Horse *(http://www.imh.org/imh/buf/buf1.html).*

The Church in the Southern Black Community. University of North Carolina at Chapel Hill Libraries *(http://metalab.unc.edu/docsouth/church/index.html).*

Getting Word: The Monticello African American Oral History Project (http://www.monticello.org/gettingword/GWhome.html).

Guide to African-American Documentary Resources in North Carolina. University Press of Virginia *(http://www.upress.virginia.edu/epub/pyatt/).*

Harlem 1900–1940: An African American Community. School of Information, University of Michigan *(http://www.si.umich.edu/CHICO/Harlem/).* This site presents a cultural history of Harlem and profiles activists, artists, writers, and leaders who flourished during this period. The images featured are from the Schomburg Center for Research in Black Culture.

In the Steps of Esteban: Tucson's African American Heritage (http://dizzy.library.arizona.edu/images/afamer/homepage.html).

Inventory of African American Historical and Cultural Resources—Maryland. Maryland's Online Public Information Network *(http://www.sailor.lib.md.us/docs/af_am/af_am.html).*

Persistence of the Spirit: African-American Experience in Arkansas. Arkansas Humanities Resource Center *(http://www.aristotle.net/persistence/).*

Race and Place: African American Histories. The Virginia Center for Digital History and the Carter G. Woodson Institute for African and Afro-American Studies, both at University of Virginia *(http://www.vcdh.virginia.edu/afam/home.html).*

Small Towns, Black Lives: African American Communities in Southern New Jersey. Wendel A. White *(http://www.blacktowns.org/).*

LITERATURE

Afam-Lit. A discussion list for all genres of African-American literature. To subscribe, send the message, "subscribe afam-lit *your name*" to listserv@listserv.uic.edu.

African American Studies Literary Journals. JSTOR *(http://www.jstor.org/).* Includes the backfile, excluding the most recent three years, of *African American Review* and its previous titles, *Black American Literature Forum* and *Negro American Literature Forum. Callaloo*'s backfile is also available in JSTOR, and recent issues are available through Johns Hopkins University Press's Project Muse *(http://www.press.jhu.edu/muse.html).*

African American Women Writers of the 19th Century. The New York Public Library Digital Library Collections, Digital Schomburg *(http://digital.nypl.org/schomburg/writers_aa19/).* Full-text works of biography and autobiography, fiction, poetry, and essays.

Givens Collection of African American Literature. University of Minnesota, Special Collections Department of Wilson Library *(http://www.lib.umn.edu/special/rare/givens/).* "The Givens Collection of African American Literature contains more than 6,000 books, pamphlets, manuscripts, letters, and ephemera of African-American literature produced during a span of more than 200 years, from the late eighteenth century to the present." Additional information about the collection can be found at the PBS Website *Literature and Life: The Givens Collection (http://www.pbs.org/ktca/litandlife/).*

Texts by and about African-Americans. University of Virginia *(http://etext.lib.virginia.edu/subjects/African-American.html).*

MUSEUMS

African American Museum in Philadelphia. Philadelphia, Pennsylvania *(http://
    aampmuseum.org/).*
Anacostia Museum. Washington, D.C. *(http://www.si.edu/anacostia/).*
California African American Museum. Los Angeles, California *(http://www.caam.ca.gov/).*
DuSable Museum of African-American History. Chicago, Illinois *(http://
    www.dusablemuseum.org/).*
Hampton University Museum. Hampton, Virginia *(http://ww2.hamptonu.edu/other/museum/
    index.htm).*
Museum of African American History. Detroit, Michigan *(http://maah-detroit.org/).*
Museum of Afro American History. Boston, Massachusetts *(http://www.afroammuseum.org/).*
National Civil Rights Museum. Memphis, Tennessee *(http://www.midsouth.rr.com/civilrights/).*
Studio Museum in Harlem. New York, New York *(http://www.studiomuseuminharlem.org/).*

MUSIC

African-American Sheet Music (1850–1920) from Brown University. Library of Congress, Ameri-
    can Memory Series *(http://memory.loc.gov/ammem/award97/rpbhtml/aasmhome.html).*
Archives of African American Music and Culture. Indiana University, Bloomington *(http://
    www.indiana.edu/~aaamc/index.html).*
The Blue Flame Cafe (http://www.blueflamecafe.com/).
Center for Black Music Research. Columbia College, Chicago *(http://www.cbmr.org/).*
Chicago Jazz Archive. Regenstein Library, University of Chicago *(http://www.lib.uchicago.edu/e/
    su/cja/).*
The Duke Ellington Society (http://duke.fuse.net/duke.html).
Institute of Jazz Studies. John Cotton Dana Library, Rutgers University *(http://
    libraries.rutgers.edu:80/rulib/abtlib/danlib/jazz.htm).*
Louis Armstrong Online. Louis Armstrong House and Archives, Queens College, CUNY *(http://
    www.satchmo.net/).*
National Association of Negro Musicians (http://edtech.morehouse.edu/cgrimes/index.html).
"Now What a Time": Blues, Gospel, and the Fort Valley Music Festivals, 1938–1943. Library of
    Congress *(http://memory.loc.gov/ammem/ftvhtml/).* "Consists of sound recordings, pri-
    marily blues and gospel songs, and related documentation from the folk festival at Fort
    Valley State College (now Fort Valley State University), Fort Valley, Georgia."
*University of Mississippi Libraries Blues Archive (http://www.olemiss.edu/depts/general_library/
    files/music/bluesarc.html).*
William Grant Still Music (http://www.williamgrantstillmusic.com/). Dedicated to preserving
    and promoting the achievements of the Afro-American composer and conductor William
    Grant Still, and minority and women composers.

PHOTOGRAPHS AND PRINTS

African Americans during WWII. National Archives and Records Administration *(http://
    gopher.nara.gov:70/1/inform/dc/audvis/still/aframww2).*
American Colonization Society Daguerreotypes. Library of Congress *(http://lcweb2.loc.gov/
    ammem/daghtml/dagamco1.html).*
Creative Americans: Portraits by Carl Van Vechten, 1932–1964. Library of Congress *(http://
    lcweb2.loc.gov/ammem/vvhome.html).* Includes figures of the Harlem Renaissance.
The Holsinger Studio Collection Image Database. University of Virginia Library, Special Collec-
    tions Department *(http://speccol.lib.virginia.edu/holsinger).* Late 19th- and early 20th-cen-
    tury images of African-Americans taken by Rufus W. Holsinger in and around Charlottes-
    ville.

Images of African Americans from the 19th Century. The New York Public Library Digital Library Collections, Digital Schomburg *(http://digital.nypl.org/schomburg/images_aa19/).*

Jackson Davis Collection of African American Educational Photographs. University of Virginia Library, Special Collections Department *(http://www.lib.virginia.edu/speccol/jdavis/).* Photographs taken in the southern United States from 1915 to 1930.

POLITICS

PoliticallyBlack.com (http://www.politicallyblack.com/).

THEATER

African-American Shakespeare Company (http://www.african-americanshakes.org/).

Black Theatre Companies (http://www.bridgesweb.com/blackcomp.html).

Women of Color, Women of Words. Angela Weaver, Theatre Bibliographer, University of Mississippi *(http://www.scils.rutgers.edu/~cybers/home.html).* A site devoted to African-American women playwrights.

LIBRARIES, INSTITUTES, AND RESEARCH CENTERS

African American History and Culture (http://www.si.edu/resource/faq/nmah/afroam.htm).

Amistad Research Center. Tulane University *(http://www.tulane.edu/~amistad/; http://www.tulane.edu/~amistad/mmenu.html).*

Auburn Avenue Research Library on African-American Culture and History. Atlanta-Fulton Public Library System *(http://aarl.af.public.lib.ga.us/index.html).*

Charles L. Blockson Afro-American Collection. Temple University *(http://www.library.temple.edu/blockson/speccol.htm).*

Collegium for African American Research (CAAR). University of Southern Denmark *(http://www.hum.ou.dk/projekter/CAAR/).*

Frederick D. Patterson Research Institute. United Negro College Fund *(http://www.patterson-uncf.org/).*

John Hope Franklin Research Center for African and African American Documentation. Duke University *(http://scriptorium.lib.duke.edu/franklin/).*

Joint Center for Political and Economic Studies (http://www.jointctr.org/).

Library of Congress (http://lcweb.loc.gov/). African-American History and Culture Manuscript Collection Description (http://lcweb.loc.gov/rr/mss/guide/african.html).

Moorland-Spingarn Research Center. Howard University *(http://www.founders.howard.edu/moorland-spingarn/).*

Schomburg Center for Research in Black Culture. New York Public Library *(http://www.nypl.org/research/sc/sc.html).*

Smithsonian Institution (http://www.si.edu/). African American History and Culture (http://www.si.edu/resource/faq/nmah.afroam.htm).

The Vivian G. Harsh Research Collection of Afro-American History and Literature. Chicago Public Library *(http://www.chipublib.org/002branches/woodson/wnharsh.html).*

W. E. B. Du Bois Institute for Afro-American Research. Harvard University *(http://web-dubois.fas.harvard.edu).*

William Monroe Trotter Institute. University of Massachusetts *(http://www.trotterinst.org/).*

LIBRARY CATALOGS

The sites listed here provide links to library catalogs specializing in African-American history and culture.

African American and/or Black Studies Catalogs. Cornell University *(http://www.library. cornell.edu/africana/Library/Catalogs.html).*

African American Online Catalogs. UCLA *(http://www.library.ucla.edu/libraries/url/colls/ africanamer/cats.htm).*

CITING INTERNET SOURCES

Online! A Reference Guide to Using Internet Resources. Bedford/St. Martin's Press *(http:// www.bedfordstmartins.com/online/).* Authored by Andrew Harnack and Eugene Kleppinger, this book (available online and in print) provides information on citing Internet sources using MLA, APA, and Chicago style manuals, among others.

4   *Manuscript Collections*

Earl Lewis and Marya McQuirter

Manuscript collections in African-American history are located in universities, governmental agencies, public libraries, archives, and historical societies throughout the United States. Such collections include organizational, familial, institutional, and personal papers, consisting of letters, memoranda, accounts, reports, and ephemera.

Researchers should first consult the institutions that primarily focus on collecting materials on African-Americana: the Schomburg Center for Research in Black Culture, New York Public Library; the Moorland-Spingarn Research Center, Howard University; the Amistad Research Center, Tulane University; the Fisk University Library; the Robert W. Woodruff Library, Atlanta University Center; the Hampton University Archives; and the Tuskegee University Archives.

The Schomburg Center for Research in Black Culture has perhaps the world's largest collections of materials on Africa and the African diaspora. Its holdings include more than 450 manuscript collections, totaling more than 5 million items. Among the collections are the papers of Alexander Crummell, John E. Bruce, and the Civil Rights Congress; and manuscripts of the social critic George Schuyler and his daughter, the pianist Philippa Schuyler, the bibliophile Arthur Schomburg, and the author and activist Amiri Baraka. The list of holdings in the Schomburg is available on the Research Libraries Information Network (RLIN), and many items are available on microfilm. It can also be accessed through the Internet at *www.nypl.org/research/sc/sc.html.*

The Moorland-Spingarn Research Center at Howard University contains documents spanning the histories and cultures of people of African descent. The Manuscript Division has more than 160 collections available for researchers to examine. Among the largest and richest collections are the Alain Locke Papers, the records of the Washington Conservatory of Music, and the Jesse E. Moorland Papers. For a more complete guide to MSRC holdings, consult Greta S. Wilson, comp., *The Guide to Processed Collections in the Manuscript Division of the Moorland-Spingarn Research Center* (1983); Sharon Green, Joellen Elbashir, and Helen Rutt, comp., *Update to the Guide to the Processed Collections in the Manuscript Division of the Moorland-Spingarn Research Center* (1993); and *Update (#2) to the Guide to Processed Collections in the Manuscript Division of the Moorland-Spingarn Research Center* (1995).

The Amistad Research Center, at Tulane University, New Orleans, is a historical research library with more than 8 million manuscript pieces. The collection emphasizes the relationship between African-Americans and Native Americans, as well as other topics. Among the larger institutional collections held are the archives and records of the American Missionary Association; among private papers are those of the Harlem Renaissance poet Countee Cullen, and the founder and director of Operation Crossroads Africa, James H. Robinson. The Amistad Research Center has published the following guides to its collections: *Manuscript Holdings/ The Amistad Research Center* (1991); *Author and Added Entry Catalog of the American Missionary Association Archives* (3 vols., 1970); and the *Archives, 1943–1970, Addn., 1942–1976 (Interfiled): Guide to the Collection* of the Race Relations Department, United Church Board for Homeland Ministries (1979). The Amistad Research Center can also be reached via the Internet at *www.arc.tulane.edu.*

The Fisk University Library's Special Collections contain more than 100 archival and manuscript collections. Major holdings include the Julius Rosenwald Archives, which detail the philanthropic activities of the noted businessman. Of general interest are papers of the writer Charles W. Chesnutt as well as papers of the sociologist George Edmund Haynes and the composer J. Rosamond Johnson.

The Division of Special Collections and Archives of the Atlanta University Center, Robert W. Woodruff Library, was established by the consolidation of the Special Collections libraries in the Atlanta University Center: Atlanta University, Clark College, the Interdenominational Theological Center, Morehouse College, Morris Brown College, and Spelman College. Some of its major collections are the Countee Cullen–Harold Jackman Memorial Collection, the Henry P. Slaughter Collection, the University Archives, the Interdenominational Theological Center Library records, and the Trevor Arnett Library. For more on this collection, see *Guide to Manuscripts and Archives in the Negro Collection of Trevor Arnett Library* (1971).

The intersection of industrial education, philanthropy, and politics is documented in materials at Hampton University and Tuskegee University. The Hampton University Archives record the educational aspirations of African-Americans and Native Americans, with some files on interracial relations. See, for example, Fritz J. Malval, comp., *A Guide to the Archives of Hampton Institute* (1985). Holdings include detailed records on Hampton students and faculty, general information on educational experiences and experiments, and materials related to Hampton-initiated publications such as the *Southern Workman*. Tuskegee University's Hollis Burke Frissell Library-Archives houses many papers of Tuskegee founder Booker T. Washington, the bibliographer Monroe Work, and the agronomist George Washington Carver. When combined with the Booker T. Washington Papers in the Library of Congress, these sources give the researcher a broad view of Washington's involvement in politics, business, and education.

Researchers can consult the published guides to these libraries. Many also have more detailed finding aids to specific collections. The only national guide to African-American manuscript collections is Walter Schatz's *Directory of Afro-American Resources* (1970), an updated edition of which is greatly needed. This volume remains, however, an immensely valuable research tool. An important project is the Cooperative HBCU Archival Survey Project, which is surveying historically black colleges and universities for information on their holdings.

To assist the researcher in locating the appropriate repository, there are four excellent national guides to resources on African-American manuscript collections. The National Inventory of Documentary Sources in the United States (NIDS) offers finding aids on microfiche to major repositories in the United States. NIDS is divided into several sections: Federal Records; Manuscript Division, Library of Congress; State Archives, State Libraries and State Historical Societies; and Academic and Research Libraries and other Repositories. Some of the federal repositories include the Smithsonian, the National Archives, the Library of Congress, and the Hoover, Roosevelt, Truman, Eisenhower, Kennedy, Johnson, and Ford Presidential Libraries. Many state libraries have published guides to their manuscript and other holdings. An example is "An Annotated Guide to Sources for the Study of African-American History in the Museum and Library Collections of the Connecticut Historical Society," published as Special Series no. 1 of *The Connecticut Historical Society Bulletin* (1994).

The Library of Congress's *National Union Catalog of Manuscript Collections* (NUCMC, 1994), is an indispensable source with extensive listings under the subject heading "Afro-American." The NUCMC team now catalogs collections in RLIN for those repositories unable to make such information available themselves. A machine-readable NUCMC database will soon be accessible to researchers online or on CD-ROM. Debra Newman Ham edited a valuable sourcebook, *The African-American Mosaic: A Library of Congress Resource Guide for the Study of Black History and Culture* (1993).

Lee Ash and William G. Miner's *Subject Collections* (1993) is a two-volume subject guide to repositories. Although it does not focus solely on manuscript collections, it is a very useful source. It is indexed by subject, then by place, and then by institution. It lists telephone and fax numbers, street and e-mail addresses, and whether there are published guides to collections.

This essay culls from the above sources to provide an overview of manuscript collections from the African past through the civil rights era. The essay also includes a discussion of collections related to labor, education, religion, family, regionalism, architecture, art, business, and science.

AFRICAN BACKGROUND

Substantial materials on Africa can be located in several repositories nationwide. Nongovernmental holdings at Northwestern University's Melville Herskovits Library of African Studies form an important collection. For more information, consult Purnima Mehta Bhatt's *Scholar's Guide to Washington, D.C. for African Studies* (1980) and Aloha South, comp., *Guide to Non-Federal Archives and Manuscripts in the United States relating to Africa* (2 vols., 1988). Those sources include 3,000 Arabic and Hausa manuscripts from Kano, the G. M. Carter–T. Karis collection on South African politics, the Dennis Brutus Papers, the papers of the African Studies Association and the African Literature Association, and the Economic Survey of Liberia Papers. The Boston University African Studies Library and the University of Wisconsin, Madison, also have extensive collections. The University of Wisconsin houses more than 30,000 books, manuscript holdings, sound recordings, and films detailing Africa's history and place in world affairs. A researcher can access the holdings online.

Michigan State University has one of the most comprehensive repositories on Africa. The Michigan State University African Library has archival resources on the slave trade; British Colonial and Foreign Office archival materials; the Kenya National Archives (microfilm); and sources on Ethiopia and the Sahel.

Researchers can also consult religious and colonial manuscripts for materials on Africa. The Records of the African Methodist Episcopal Church, Department of Home and Foreign Missions (1912–1960), which document A.M.E. missionary activities in Africa, are located at the Schomburg Center. The American Colonization Society Records at the Library of Congress provide materials on West African settlements, while the Hall of Records in Annapolis, Md., houses the Maryland in Liberia Papers. Papers of the American Board of Commissions for Foreign Missions, housed in Houghton Library, Harvard University, are rich in material on Africa.

SLAVE TRADE

Pertinent information on the slave trade spans the globe, since slave trading occurred in both international and national contexts. Internationally, few sources rival the papers of the Royal African Company and the South Sea Company, which are housed, respectively, in the Public Records Office Records of the Treasury and the British Museum in London. Additional information on the South Sea Company can be found in the Clements Library at the University of Michigan. A number of state and regional archives document slave trading between Africa and the Americas and within the United States. In addition to the records of large plantations housed in state libraries and historical societies across the American South, one should consult the collections in the Huntington Library in California, the Chicago Historical Society, the Newberry Library in Chicago, the Library of Congress (e.g., papers of the British admiral Sir George Cockburn), as well as the papers of those American presidents who owned slaves, such as George Washington, Thomas Jefferson, and James Madison. The papers of the latter, for example, contain information on the *Amistad* slave mutiny.

The Inter-University Consortium for Political and Social Research at the Institute of Social Research, University of Michigan, maintains a computerized listing of slave sales and appraisals compiled by the economic historians Robert Fogel and Stanley Engerman. The Andrew Hull Foote Papers and the Robert T. Spence Papers at the Library of Congress contain letterbooks and other materials on slave trading. For manuscripts on the slave trade in the mid-18th century, consult the Medford Historical Society Library, Medford, Massachusetts.

SLAVERY AND SLAVE LIFE

The institution of slavery is documented in many sources. Kenneth Stampp has edited a multivolume microfilm collection on antebellum southern plantations for the University Press of America. A comparable effort by Anne Firor Scott and

William Chafe documents the lives, perspectives, and affairs of southern (primarily white) women and their families.

State and regional libraries are enormously important for the study of slavery. Materials on colonial and antebellum slavery in the Chesapeake region and the Upper South can be found in the Maryland Historical Society, the Virginia Historical Society, the Virginia State Library, the Colonial Williamsburg Foundation, the Valentine Museum in Richmond, the Alderman Library at the University of Virginia, the Earl Gregg Swem Library at the College of William and Mary, the Perkins Library at Duke University, and the Southern Historical Collection at the University of North Carolina at Chapel Hill. These libraries contain information on the economics and social structures of slavery, African influences on religion and architecture, and sources detailing the growth of a post–Revolutionary War free black population. For more information on these subjects, see Michael Plunkett's *Afro-American Sources in Virginia: A Guide to Manuscripts* (1990).

The Lower South had a demographic history different from that of the Upper South, which shaped its social and political landscape. A black majority existed in South Carolina long before the colonists instigated the Revolutionary War. In this setting, the Creole language of Gullah emerged and African religious practices blended with those of Christianity and Islam. Researchers who are interested in slavery in the Lower South should examine materials at the South Carolina Historical Society, Charleston; the Special Collections Department at Emory University; the Howard Tilton Library and the Amistad Collection at Tulane University; the Louisiana State Museum Archives as well as those of Louisiana State University; and the Barker Texas History Center at the University of Texas at Austin. Border South collections can be found in the Tennessee State Library and Archives. Xavier University of New Orleans houses the collection of Heartman Manuscripts on Slavery, more than 4,000 manuscripts compiled by the Mississippi book-dealer Charles F. Heartman. Though focusing on slavery in Louisiana, it contains some documents from Virginia, the Carolinas, and elsewhere. The collection has been microfilmed and there is a published guide (1982).

The social and cultural world of enslaved African-Americans was rich and varied. Notable oral history collections are found in the Southern Historical Collection at the University of North Carolina at Chapel Hill. Important collections of slave narratives are located in the Fisk University Library. Information on slave narratives in Virginia can be located in the Roscoe Lewis Papers in the University Archives at Hampton University; the Rare Book Room and the Folklore Collection at the Library of Congress; the files of the Works Project Administration–sponsored Virginia Writers' Project in the Virginia State Library; and the Manuscripts Department at the University of Virginia Library.

Slavery in the North lasted well into the early decades of the 19th century in many locations. Aspects of this history are revealed in the personal papers and memoirs of African-Americans who gained some social prominence, such as Paul Cuffe and Richard Allen. Materials on colonial slavery in the Schomburg Center include bills of sale, information on the 1740s insurrection in New York City, and references to black life in colonial New York and New England. Of equal value are the papers of various Quaker communities scattered throughout the North. Consult, for example, papers in the library of Swarthmore College in Pennsylvania. Legal challenges are equally valuable for what they reveal about the life and expectations of African-Americans. Court challenges in individual northern colonies and states such as Massachusetts also provide rich sources.

For materials on the American Revolution see *Manuscript Sources in the Library of Congress for Research in the American Revolution* (1975). John R. Sellers and his coauthors provide useful information about African-Americans who served on both sides of the conflict and those who became refugees as a result of the war. In addition, the library of the National Society of the Daughters of the American Revolution, located in Washington, D.C., has begun to compile names of African-American Revolutionary War veterans and patriots.

ABOLITIONISM

Scholars conducting research on abolitionists should visit Wichita State University for the Merrill Collection of William Lloyd Garrison Papers; the Peabody Institute Library for the Parker Pillsbury Anti-Slavery Collection; and the Minneapolis Public Library and Information Center for books, pamphlets, broadsides, newspapers, letters, and documents on abolitionist movements. The library of the University of Massachusetts at Amherst contains materials on the antislavery movement in New England, and the Boston Public Library has a substantial collection of records of both black and white abolitionists. The Black Abolitionist Papers (1830–1865), under the general editorship of George E. Carter and C. Peter Ripley, chronicle black involvement in the fight to abolish slavery of 1830–1865, and include on microfilm some 14,000 documents by nearly 300 black men and women. A five-volume letterpress edition of selected documents, with thorough annotation, was edited by C. Peter Ripley et al.

The massive American Colonization Society papers are found at the Library of Congress and are available on microfilm. Researchers should also consult the State Slavery Statutes, UPA microfilm collection, which was filmed from the holdings of the Law Library, Library of Congress. The Bliss Forbush Collection at the Soper Library, Morgan State University, contains original material and a collection of manuscripts, early pamphlets, and books. Of note are fifty-four documents illustrative of Quaker attitudes toward slavery, an original manumission paper, and two documents in the handwriting of famed reformer Elias Hicks. Extant copies of the period's black newspapers that championed abolition can be found in several locations, including the Library of Congress; the American Antiquarian Society in Worcester, Massachusetts; the Schomburg Center; and the Center for Research Libraries in Chicago, a major repository that is supported by and serves many of the country's leading research universities.

A smaller but valuable collection detailing the antislavery campaign is found in the Anti-Slavery Collection in the Carnegie Library at Oberlin College. The result of a gift from the collector William Goodell, the collection contains materials detailing various positions in the debate. Sources include platforms, addresses, proceedings, children's literature, and songs from the period. The Birney Anti-Slavery Collection of The Johns Hopkins University is an important source for the printed

history of abolitionism; it also contains extensive proslavery and African colonization materials, as well as sources for the study of African-American education.

Two repositories that have significant holdings on the Underground Railroad
are the Charles L. Blockson Collection at Temple University and the Proverbs and
Heritage's Underground Railroad Museum in Windsor, Canada. Extensive correspondence of the Philadelphia conductor William Still is found in the Historical
Society of Pennsylvania. The papers of Senator Charles Sumner (available on microfilm and in a letterpress edition) are housed at Houghton Library, Harvard
University. The papers include approximately 26,000 letters, including correspondence from Frances Ellen Watkins Harper, Frederick Douglass, and George T.
Downing, the New York caterer and underground railroad participant. A checklist
of black correspondents in the Sumner Papers is found in the *Newsletter of the
Afro-American Religious History Group* 12:2(1988): 8–9. They include John Cromwell, Alexander Crummell, William Cooper Nell, Joseph H. Rainey (the first black
U.S. Congressman), and John Rock (the first African-American admitted to practice before the U.S. Supreme Court).

CIVIL WAR AND RECONSTRUCTION

All searches should begin with a review of materials in the Bureau of Refugees,
Freedmen, and Abandoned Lands, Record Group 105, in the National Archives.
Elaine Every compiled the *Records of the Bureau of Freedmen, Refugees, and Abandoned Lands: Washington Headquarters* (1973). See also Ira Berlin et al., *Freedom: A
Documentary History of Emancipation* (multiple vols., 1982). Equally valuable for
exploring African-American family history are the records of Civil War Pensions,
also found at the National Archives. These materials should be supplemented by
manuscripts at the Moorland-Spingarn Research Center, such as the Civil War
Collection, which includes 428 clothing account books detailing the debits and
credits of black soldiers. There are also Regimental Consolidated Morning Reports
on daily company statistics. These statistics record, for example, those sick and ar-
rested among enlisted men and officers.

Researchers of the Reconstruction era should consult the South Caroliniana Library at the University of South Carolina, the Elbert Collection at Wellesley College, the Tennessee State Library and Archives, the Historic New Orleans Collection, the William R. Perkins Library at Duke University, the Virginia State Library,
the Southern Historical Collection at the University of North Carolina, and state
archives in each of the former confederate states. One may consult *The Directory of
Afro-American Resources* (1970), edited by Walter Schatz, for the location of the
papers of individual black legislators and politicians of the period, such as Blanche
K. Bruce, Richard H. Cain, and John Mercer. The letter books of William Pledger,
found at Duke University, contain important information on Reconstruction in
Georgia.

The trans-Mississippi West was important to Reconstruction-era African-
Americans. In Oklahoma, Kansas, and California, all-black towns were established. To facilitate research, begin with U.S. Justice Department materials in Record Group 60, the National Archives. Supplement those materials with coverage

from black and white newspapers and papers in the following libraries or collections: the Tennessee State Archives and Library; the Louisiana State University Archives; the Kansas State Historical Society; and the Tulare County Free Library in Visalia, California. A nearly 200-page guide to manuscripts and broadsides at the Historical Society of Pennsylvania and the Library Company of Philadelphia (including papers of the American Negro Historical Society [Penn.]) appears as an appendix to *Afro-Americana, 1553–1906: Author Catalog of the Library Company of Philadelphia and the Historical Society of Pennsylvania* (1973).

LABOR

One of the most notable African-American organizations working for employment and economic justice was the Brotherhood of Sleeping Car Porters, the papers of which are housed in the C. L. Dellums Collection of the Bancroft Library, University of California, Berkeley. The archives of the Pullman Palace Car Company, employer of many porters, are housed at the Newberry Library in Chicago, while the papers of A. Philip Randolph, who headed the union and came to embody the black porters' fight for union recognition, reside at the Library of Congress.

Several collections document union and nonunion efforts to organize workers in domestic service and household employment. The Records of the National Domestic Workers Union, organized in 1968 by Dorothy Lee Bolden, are housed at the Southern Labor Archives, Georgia State University, and at the organization's office in Atlanta. Materials on domestic workers in the South are found in the Federal Writers Project Papers, Southern Historical Collection, University of North Carolina, Chapel Hill. The papers of the National Committee on Household Employment are housed at the National Archives for Black Women's History.

A comprehensive review of the history of African-American labor should include a careful perusal of pertinent slavery-era documents. Governmental records in the National Archives are a font of information, especially the Freedmen's Bureau Records for the 19th century and the Labor Department files for the 20th.

Numerous organizational files and personal papers contain valuable materials on the labor activities and aspirations of African-Americans, especially for the 20th century. A roster of organizational files includes the papers of the Amalgamated Clothing Workers of America (Martin P. Catherwood Library, Cornell University); United Auto Workers (Walter Reuther Library, Wayne State University); and the United Packinghouse Workers (State Historical Society of Wisconsin). Also of value are the papers of prominent labor leaders ranging from Samuel Gompers to John L. Lewis, Sidney Hillman, and Walter Reuther. An important repository for sources on historical and contemporary labor matters is the George Meany Archives in Silver Spring, Md.

RELIGION

Inquiry into the religious beliefs and practices of African-Americans should begin with the Schomburg Center for Research in Black Culture, which has extensive collections on religious institutions and individuals. For twenty years (1976–1996), the biannual *Newsletter of the Afro-American Group of the American Academy of Religion,* edited by Randall K. Burkett, regularly published a section on manuscript sources for the study of African-American religious history. These issues constitute an important source for primary research material.

Many denominational centers as well as local churches maintain their own archives. State-based archives sometimes include such records. In Michigan, for example, the Bentley Historical Library has the records of the Second Baptist Church of Detroit, as well as the papers of A.M.E. Bishop Charles S. Smith. Church materials also appear in the papers of state and national associations and of certain individuals. The North Carolina Baptist Historical Association at Wake Forest University, Winston-Salem, for example, holds the records of the North Carolina Baptist Association. The papers of the Women's Convention, Auxiliary to the National Baptist Convention, are located in the Nannie Helen Burroughs Papers at the Library of Congress. For additional information on black women in religion consult the Research/Resource Center of the Black Women in Church and Society organization at the Interdenominational Theological Center in Atlanta.

In the Records of the Bureau of the Census (RG 29), at the National Archives, there are census schedules of the African Methodist Episcopal Zion Church and the Colored Methodist Episcopal Church. At Wilberforce University's Rembert Stokes Learning Center, Archives and Special Collections, are A.M.E. Church conference minutes (as well as the history of Wilberforce University), and records of A.M.E. leaders such as Bishop Benjamin W. Arnett. Holdings of the Mother Bethel African Methodist Episcopal Church Historical Museum, Philadelphia, are available on microfilm. For autobiographical manuscripts of itinerant preachers consult the Berkshire Athenaeum, Pittsfield, Massachusetts; and the Shaker Manuscript Collection of Western Reserve Historical Society, Cleveland.

Divinity schools and seminaries are also rich repositories. For example, the Howard University School of Divinity Library, Washington, D.C., and the R. C. Ransom Memorial Library of Payne Theological Seminary at Wilberforce have materials on the history of the A.M.E. Church. Carnegie Library at Livingstone College and Hood Theological Seminary's Bishop William J. Walls Center, both in Salisbury, N.C., have excellent collections for A.M.E. Zion Church history.

The Archives and Records Center of the Archdiocese of Chicago houses research materials on black Catholicism. Holdings include the Madaj Collection, consisting of all archdiocesan correspondence from 1852 to 1928. The papers of Albert Cardinal Meyer include personal and official correspondence and material produced and generated by the Chicago Conference on Religion and Race held in 1963. Additional sources at the Center provide information on black parishes, including parish correspondence. The Society of St. Joseph (run by the Josephites) has maintained an active involvement with African-American parishioners. For information on the Josephites and on black Catholics in general, consult the Josephite Archives in Baltimore.

The library of the American Baptist Historical Society in Rochester, N.Y., has a substantial body of materials on black Baptists. Consult Lester B. Scherer, *Afro-American Baptists: A Guide to Materials in the Library of the American Baptist His-*

torical Society (1985) or *American Baptist Quarterly* 4 (Sept. 1985): 82–99. These collections include annual minutes of associations and state conventions, records of regional and denominational bodies, records of educational institutions, and church-related periodicals. Many of these and other black Baptist records are available on microfilm from the Historical Commission of the Southern Baptist Convention in Nashville.

The African Orthodox Church Archives, housed at the Pitts Theology Library, Emory University, contain manuscript and printed materials on the African Orthodox Church of South Africa. Included is an excellent source on Daniel William Alexander, Patriarch of the African Orthodox Church of South Africa, as well as personal papers, correspondence, clergy records, and baptism and marriage records. Most of the documents are written in English; there are also a few in Afrikaans, Sotho, Tswana, and Xhosa. Robert Collins and Peter Duignan's *Americans in Africa: A Preliminary Guide to American Missionary Archives and Library Manuscript Collections on Africa* (1963) provides a valuable guide to manuscript collections documenting African-American missionary activity in Africa generally.

The DuPree African American Pentecostal Collection at the Schomburg Center is one of the first attempts to document the history of black Holiness and Pentecostal churches. The collection includes pamphlets, programs, sermons, biographies, audiotapes, films, gospel sheet music, and women's convention badges. Two other notable collections are housed at the Seymour Center, Archives Section, Washington, D.C. The E. Myron Noble Middle Atlantic Gospel Ministries Collection includes correspondence, mission history, biographical materials, brochures, newsletters reflecting the history of the African American Pentecostal-Holiness Project in Washington, D.C., 1900–1949; and records of Middle Atlantic Regional Gospel Ministries. The Evelyn M. E. Taylor African American Holiness Pentecostal Collection includes correspondence, church histories, reports, clippings, fliers, and other papers reflecting the history of the Holiness-Pentecostal Project in Charleston, W.Va., and Landover, Md., beginning with the founding of the House of Prayer, an early black Holiness-Pentecostal church serving Jefferson County and West Virginia's Eastern Panhandle in the late 1920s. The Billy Graham Center archives at Wheaton College, Illinois, has material on the North American Evangelical Protestant Mission, including documents on African-American religious history. One can also find materials from the 1988 Atlanta Congress on Evangelizing Black America, and Prison Fellowship Ministries records.

Some notable black ministers and theologians have deposited their personal papers in archives. The papers of William H. Sheppard, a Baptist missionary, are at Hampton University. The papers (1902–1933) of William H. Simons (1881–1938), Baptist missionary to Africa and YMCA International Secretary, are part of the Library of Congress manuscript collection. This collection includes diaries, letters, notes, and miscellany such as photographs and copies of African newspapers. The papers of Kelly Miller Smith, pastor of Nashville's First Baptist Church and a civil rights activist, include correspondence, biographical and personal materials, appointment books, writings (primarily sermons), church records, subject files, pamphlets, bulletins, and awards. The private papers and original tapes of Howard Thurman are housed at the Boston University Mugar Memorial Library in Special Collections. Sue Bailey Thurman's papers are also at Boston University, but papers of her parents, Isaac G. and Susie Bailey (Arkansas), are housed in the Special Collections Department, Robert W. Woodruff Library, Emory University. These include extensive correspondence between Susie Bailey and her daughter Sue Bailey Thurman, the personal library of Howard and Sue Bailey Thurman, and nearly a thousand photographs.

The National Archives is also a source for the study of black religion, but the records are scattered and require digging by the researcher. The single richest source comes from Military Reference Branch records of the assistant commissioners of the Freedmen's Bureau (RG 105). Bureau officers were involved in disputes over ownership of antebellum church buildings that pitted white trustees against black congregations. In Record Group 92, *Records of the Office of the Quartermaster General,* for example, researchers can find claims filed by African-Americans for damages sustained by black churches from Union troops during the Civil War. The Civil Reference Branch of the National Archives includes information on religion in the Works Progress Administration files on religious music and in "The Investigative Case Files of the Bureau of Investigation, 1908–1922."

In the central files of the Department of Justice, 1870 to 1933, is material on a newsletter of the African Methodist Church, which allegedly published articles "of an extremely radical nature." The records of the Department of State, particularly the central files records, include materials on the conduct of A.M.E. bishops in South Africa and information regarding churches in other African countries. These are only samples of the wide range of materials on African-American religious history to be found in the National Archives.

The Maryland Diocesan Archive at the Maryland Historical Society comprises approximately 60,000 items, chiefly manuscripts, concerning the history of the Episcopal Church in Maryland and throughout the world. This collection is exceptionally valuable for its holdings from the mid-18th century to the present concerning slavery, emancipation, the condition of blacks, and church work. General Theological Seminary, New York City, also houses important manuscript collections for African-American Episcopal history.

For manuscripts on African-Americans in the Baha'i Faith, consult the National Baha'i Archives, Dorothy Champ Papers, in Wilmette, Ill. Also consult the Hilda Strauss Papers and the Phoebe Apperson Hearst Collection at the Bancroft Library, University of California, Berkeley, and the George William Cook Papers at the Moorland-Spingarn Research Center, Howard University. The national historical libraries for the major predominantly white denominations (e.g., the Presbyterian Historical Society in Philadelphia; the Methodist Archives and History Center, Drew University; and the Archives and Historical Collections of the Episcopal Church, Austin, Tex.) are important sources for the study of African-American participation in their respective institutions.

EDUCATION

Educational opportunities for African-Americans expanded dramatically after emancipation. Invaluable are the American Missionary Association Papers in the

Amistad Research Center at Tulane University. For instance, the papers of John A. Rockwell (Superintendent of the American Missionary Association's Lincoln School in Macon, Ga.) contain 250 letters from the period 1865–1867 and record his efforts on behalf of freed people. The correspondence deals almost exclusively with the problems of administering and supplying a school for Negroes in the heart of the Old Confederacy.

The federal government took an active role in the education of blacks after the Civil War. A great deal of that history is recorded in the Freedmen's Bureau Records (RG 105) in the National Archives. See also the John Preston McConnell Library, Alumni Special Collections, Radford University, Radford, Va., which has a collection on the Christianburg Institute, originally a black freedmen's school.

In addition to papers in the Freedmen's Bureau, files in the National Archives, and the papers of individual black churches and personalities, examine the files of the first generation of black colleges. The Clark-Atlanta University Robert W. Woodruff Library, Division of Special Collections, has archival holdings for academic institutions in the Atlanta University Center consortium: Atlanta University; Clark College; The Interdenominational Theological Seminary; Gammon Theological Seminary (Methodist); Morehouse School of Religion (Baptist); Charles H. Mason Theological Seminary (Church of God in Christ); Phillips School of Theology (Christian Methodist Episcopal); Johnson C. Smith Seminary, Inc. (Presbyterian); Turner Theological Seminary (A.M.E); Morehouse College; Morris Brown College; and Spelman College.

Given the early and far-reaching role of "the Wizard of Tuskegee" in shaping educational opportunities for African-Americans, it is appropriate to begin a study of black education by consulting the Booker T. Washington Papers in the Library of Congress. Supplement that collection with materials in the Tuskegee University Archives and materials in the Archives and Library at Hampton University. One should also consult the papers of the northern field representative for Tuskegee, Frank Chisolm. (The Frank P. and Helen Chisolm Papers are housed in the Special Collections Department, Robert W. Woodruff Library, Emory University.) Of equal value for their breadth and diversity are the papers of Washington's sometime adversary W. E. B. Du Bois, whose papers are held at the University of Massachusetts, Amherst.

Much can be learned about the role of women in education by reviewing the archives at historically black colleges and universities, especially those that trained successive generations of black schoolteachers. For additional information, explore the personal papers of a number of noted educators. The Nannie Helen Burroughs Papers at the Library of Congress are extremely rich for the study of education. Mary E. Branch, the first woman president of Tillotson College, has papers in the Downs-Jones Library at Houston-Tillotson College, Austin, Tex.

Some papers of the prominent 20th-century educator Charlotte Hawkins Brown are at the Schlesinger Library at Harvard University. The most complete collection of Brown's manuscripts are at the Division of Archives and History, North Carolina Department of Cultural Resources, Historical Sites Section, Raleigh, North Carolina. Materials on Brown and the Palmer Institute can also be found at the Schomburg Center; the North Carolina Historical Room at Greensboro Place, Greensboro, N.C.; and the collection of African-American women's materials at Bennett College in Greensboro, N.C. It is also useful to review materials at the W. C. Jackson Library at the University of North Carolina, Greensboro, and at the Amistad Research Center, Tulane University.

A number of other prominent educators have papers in national and regional repositories. The Hallie Quinn Brown Papers are located in the library named in her honor at Central State University in Wilberforce, Ohio. The Anna J. Cooper Papers can be found in the Moorland-Spingarn Research Center. The Fanny Jackson Coppin Papers at the Oberlin College Archives provide materials concerning her Oberlin years. For information on the Institute of Colored Youth, consult the Friends Historical Library, Swarthmore College. Marion Vera Cuthbert, noted educator and organizational leader, has personal papers in the Spelman College Archives, including information on the YWCA Summer Training Institutes. Also see Records Files Collections, YWCA of the USA, National Board Archives, New York City; Mugar Memorial Library, Boston University; and Talladega College Archives. The papers of Sara P. "Sadie" Delaney are in seven bound volumes of letters and clippings at the Schomburg Center for Research in Black Culture. Juliette Derricotte, dean of women at Fisk, has papers in the Thomas Elsa Jones Papers at Fisk University. The collection contains materials on Derricotte during her Fisk tenure. The library at Talladega College in Alabama has material on her undergraduate years.

A number of religious denominations played prominent roles in educating African-Americans. See, for example, the Financial Department of the A.M.E. Church in Washington, D.C., which has the annual budgets of educational institutions supported by the A.M.E. Church: Daniel Payne College, Birmingham, Ala.; Shorter Junior College, North Little Rock, Ark.; Edward Waters College, Jacksonville, Fla.; Paul Quinn College, Waco, Tex. The National Archives of the Episcopal Church, located in Austin, Tex., houses papers of the American Church Institute for Negroes, established to raise funds for historically black colleges and schools supported by the Episcopal Church.

The papers of a number of educational funds and associations are available. The United Negro College Fund (UNCF), New York, houses its own records, including correspondence, minutes, records, photographs, oral history tapes and transcripts, and general information about the history of black education. The Southern Education Fund, Atlanta, has the correspondence, minutes, and related files of the Peabody Fund, Slater Fund, and Jeanes Fund, materials relating to education in the South, and select correspondence with Booker T. Washington. The Phelps-Stokes Fund Archives, New York, has data on education from the 1910s to the present: African student scholarships in the United States, education in Liberia, western Africa and other areas of Africa, U.S. government aid for African scholarships, and the New York State's Colonization Society's educational programs in Liberia since 1822. Perhaps the most important single source for information on black schools is the Rockefeller Archive Center, Tarrytown, N.Y., which maintains files of the General Education Board and its southern programs. Black college officials all over the South wrote to the Rockefellers with detailed information on their schools, and these were often followed up with staff reports that provide additional documentation on school programs and prospects.

The relationship between education and religion is delineated in a number of valuable collections. Talladega College's Slavery Historical Collections, Talladega, Ala., has information about the history of the college, African missions (especially Liberia), and historical developments in education for blacks. See Leon P. Spencer's *Guide to the Archives of Talladega College* (1981). School Sisters of St. Francis Archives, Milwaukee, Wis., has manuscripts relating to rural and urban mission schools, 1866 to the present.

The struggle for equal pay and accreditation dominated educational activities across the South. Black teachers' fight for salaries equal to whites' is most vividly captured in the NAACP Papers, located in the Library of Congress. Also see the papers of individual teacher associations. The uncataloged Virginia Teacher Association Papers are housed at Virginia State University in Petersburg, Va. In addition, the Bishop College Library's Southwest Research Center and Museum of African American Life and Culture has a collection of papers (1929–1952) of Dr. J. J. Rhoads, the first black president of the college and the Texas State Colored Teachers Association. Jackson State University, Henry T. Sampson Library, Special Collections, Jackson, Miss., has manuscript collections of formerly all-black schools seeking accreditation by the Southern Association of Colleges and Schools, 1960–1969.

Like their female counterparts, a number of black male educators who made major contributions left papers. Among this group are the Horace Mann Bond Papers found at the University of Massachusetts, Amherst. See *The Horace Mann Bond Papers, 1830 (1926–1972) 1979: A Guide* (1982) by Barbara S. Meloni et al. The sociologists Charles S. Johnson and Merl Epps have extensive papers at Fisk University. The papers of Rayford Logan, Alain Locke, and Mordecai Wyatt Johnson are housed at the Moorland-Spingarn Research Center, while the papers of Carter G. Woodson are at the Library of Congress.

For a look at contemporary educational debates and their historical underpinnings, see the papers of the American Federation of Teachers (AFT); National Educational Association (NEA); and the files for the Department of Health, Education and Welfare (RG 235) in the National Archives. The AFT papers are housed in the Walter Reuther Library at Wayne State University. The NEA papers can be seen at the NEA headquarters in Washington, D.C.

FAMILY

Scholars can consult local repositories for information on marriages and divorces by reviewing court records and petitions. African-American newspapers are an unequaled source, and the largest collection is found at the State Historical Society of Wisconsin, Madison. Women's Bureau papers, WPA records, Children's Bureau Papers, and Labor Department surveys are also rich sources. See, for example, the general correspondence of the Bureau of Human Nutrition and Home Economics (RG 176), which contains a study pertaining to food consumption of black farm families. The National Archives frequently cataloged both the finished report and the materials that went into the reports.

Social welfare concerns have predominated since W. E. B. Du Bois pioneered the study of black family life in the *Philadelphia Negro* and in his Atlanta University Studies. Therefore, see the Du Bois Papers as well as the papers of the sociologists

E. Franklin Frazier and Charles S. Johnson at the Moorland-Spingarn Research Center and Fisk University Library, respectively. Valuable ethnographic materials are housed in the archives of the University of Chicago; quantitative datasets, such as World War I and Depression-era surveys, can be located at the Institute for Social Research at the University of Michigan. Likewise, the Johns Hopkins Medical Institution, Allan Mason Chesney Medical Archives, has the records of the Colored Orphan's Asylum of Baltimore.

For general information on social welfare, and particularly that of African-Americans, consult the Social Welfare Archives at the University of Minnesota. Records of the Afro-American Family and Community Services Organization, which operated in the Cabrini-Green neighborhood from 1968 to 1982, are available at the Chicago Historical Society. Similar efforts are found in the several community association papers affiliated with settlement houses in cities such as Atlanta.

LITERATURE

The papers of late 19th- and early 20th-century writers are geographically dispersed. Clark-Atlanta's Countee Cullen–Harold Jackman Collection is a large collection on artists and writers, including Georgia Douglas Johnson and Owen Dodson. The papers of the influential 19th-century abolitionist and writer Angelina Grimké can be found in the Angelina Weld Grimké Collection at the Moorland-Spingarn Research Center and the Weld-Grimké Collection at the Clements Library, University of Michigan. The Paul Laurence Dunbar Papers are at the Ohio Historical Society, and Sara Fuller has edited the microfilm collection (1972). Fuller also edited *The Ohio Black History Guide* (1975), which identifies relevant printed matter, theses, manuscripts, government records, and audiovisual materials housed at the Ohio Historical Society. The papers of Dunbar's contemporary Charles W. Chesnutt are located at Fisk University.

No period is more celebrated in African-American literary history than the 1920s, often referred to as the Harlem Renaissance. The James Weldon Johnson Memorial Collection, Beinecke Library, Yale University, contains not only the James Weldon Johnson Papers but also the papers of many of his contemporaries, such as Walter White, Wallace Thurman, and many others. The papers of other key participants have been collected. Gwendolyn Bennett's personal papers and literary effects are at the Schomburg Center for Research in Black Culture. Letters from Bennett are included in the Countee Cullen Papers in the Amistad Research Center, the Woodruff Library at Atlanta University Center, and the Alain Locke Papers, Moorland-Spingarn Research Center. The Countee Cullen Papers at the Amistad Research Center include correspondence, financial records, legal papers, a diary, manuscripts of his writings, and a scrapbook. See, for instance, Florence E. Borders, *Guide to the Microfilm Edition of the Countee Cullen Papers, 1921–1969* (1975). Jessie Redmond Fauset's papers are available in the NAACP Papers, Library of Congress. An important collection of James Weldon Johnson papers, offering insight into his personal and family life, is housed in the Robert W. Woodruff Library, Emory University. This collection includes many photographs as well as books from Johnson's personal library.

Langston Hughes's personal library, with approximately 3,300 items, is held in the Langston Hughes Memorial Library, Lincoln University, Pennsylvania. Many of Hughes's papers are also found in the Johnson Collection at Yale University. The papers of his onetime friend and sometime nemesis Zora Neale Hurston are in a number of locations: see the James Weldon Johnson collection, Beinecke Library, Yale; the Alain Locke Papers, Moorland-Spingarn; the University of Florida, Gainesville; and Fisk University. Georgia Douglas Johnson's papers can be found in several collections: the Library of the Neighborhood Union Collection, Robert W. Woodruff Library, Atlanta University Center; the Oberlin College Archives; the Hammond Foundation Records; and the Library of Congress. More of Johnson's papers are in Miscellaneous Letters and Papers at the Schomburg Center; the Countee Cullen Papers at the Amistad Research Center; and various collections at the Moorland-Spingarn Research Center. Richard Newman published in 1989 a useful guide, *Words Like Freedom: Afro-American Books and Manuscripts in the Henry W. and Albert A. Berg Collection of English and American Literature,* a part of New York Public Library.

A number of authors who gained prominence after World War II have also deposited their papers in libraries. Raymond Andrews's papers are located at Emory University's Robert W. Woodruff Library. Maya Angelou's papers are housed at the Z. Smith Reynolds Library at Wake Forest University. The papers and literary effects of the poet Gwendolyn Brooks are at Chicago State University. Alice Dunbar-Nelson's manuscripts are in Special Collections at the Morris Library, University of Delaware, Newark. Nikki Giovanni's papers reside at the Mugar Memorial Library, Boston University. Naomi Long Madgett's papers are being collected in the Special Collections of Fisk University Library.

PERFORMING ARTS

There are numerous collections on African-Americans and the performing arts. The Hatch-Billops Collection, Inc., created by James V. Hatch and Camille Billops, is one of the most important collections for the study of African-American arts and letters of the 20th century. At present located in New York City, it includes the archives of the Negro Ensemble Theatre; Karamu; and a massive clipping file on theater and the arts. It also contains more than 1,400 interviews with artists, writers, actors, musicians, and other creative figures of the late 20th century, as well as typescripts of the plays of Willis Richardson, thousands of photographs and slides, and printed ephemera.

The Detroit Public Library has the E. Azalia Hackley Collection, concentrating on blacks in the performing arts. The Middle Georgia Historical Society, Inc., Archives and Special Collections has the Douglass Theatre Collection of cinema and burlesque papers, financial records and materials concerning black vaudeville. For research on dance, consult the dance collection of the New York Public Library, and also the Schomburg Center for Research in Black Culture for the Asadata Dafora Papers.

The Free Southern Theater Records, 1963–1978, are housed at the Amistad Research Center. The records of the Negro Actors Guild of America are available at the Schomburg Center. The Billy Rose Theatre Collection, New York Public Library for the Performing Arts, New York City, has a clipping file on the actress and director Osceola Archer. The Howard University Players, under the leadership of Anne Cooke, an innovative director and educator in theater, became the first U.S. undergraduate group invited by the State Department and a foreign government to perform abroad. Manuscript collections that document Cooke's life include the Howard University Channing Pollock Archives, Theatre Collection; the Moorland-Spingarn Research Center, Manuscript Division; the Atlanta University Archives, Manuscript Division; the Spelman College Archives, Atlanta; and the Rockefeller Education Board Archives, Manuscript and Recipients' File Divisions, Rockefeller University, North Tarrytown, N.Y.

A large photographic archive and correspondence with "Bricktop" (Ada Smith) are found in Emory University's Robert W. Woodruff Library, along with the papers of the singer and music publisher Victoria Spivey. Emory also holds papers of the artist Benny Andrews, as well as an extensive collection of film posters, lobby cards, and press books in its Afrrican-American Cinema Collection.

SCIENCE

A section on science invariably begins with the agronomist George Washington Carver. Manuscript collections documenting Carver's life can be found at Clark-Atlanta, Tuskegee University, the U.S. National Park Service, the George Washington Carver National Monument Library, and the National Archives in the Records of the Bureau of Plant Industry, Soils, and Agricultural Engineering (RG 54) in the general correspondence of the Office of the Chief of the Bureau of Plant Industry, 1908–1939.

Historically black colleges and universities with medical institutions are fertile research sites. The Meharry Medical College Library/Black Medical Archives of Meharry Medical College has two important collections: the Black Medical History Collection, with 100 manuscript collections, and the Meharry Archives Collection, with 235 boxes of manuscripts. In addition, the Howard University Health Sciences Library has clippings and pamphlets on sickle cell anemia and files on medicine, dentistry, and psychiatry.

Several repositories document the contributions made by women scientists. Virginia M. Alexander, Caroline Virginia Still Wiley Anderson, Lucy Hughes Brown, and Rebecca Cole were Philadelphia physicians who have a file in the Black Women Physicians Collection, Special Collection on Women in Medicine at the Medical College of Pennsylvania. The papers and personal letters of Caroline Still Anderson are available at Temple University's Charles Blockson Collection and the Oberlin College Archives, Oberlin, Ohio; the Berean Institute, Philadelphia; and the Historical Society of Pennsylvania. Dorothy Brown, surgeon, has papers in the Special Collections at Fisk. Jewell Plummer Cobb has personal papers at the Schomburg Center. Hallie Tanner Dillon, physician, has papers at the University of Pennsylvania Archives. Moreover, the papers of Dorothy Ferebee, found in the Moorland-Spingarn Research Center, include information on the Mississippi Health project.

Black women fought through racial barriers to significantly shape the field of nursing. The papers of Anna de Costa Banks, a nurse who attended the Hampton Institute and worked for the Ladies Benevolent Society in Charleston, S.C., are in the Hampton University Archives and at the Waring Historical Library, Medical University of South Carolina. The papers of the Ladies Benevolent Society of Charleston are at the South Carolina Historical Society, Charleston. Moorland-Spingarn also houses the Mabel Staupers Collection, as does the Amistad Research Center. Hampton University maintains both the M. Elizabeth Carnegie Nursing History Archives and the Dixie Hospital manuscripts. Finally, it is important to review the National Association of Colored Graduate Nurses Collection in the Schomburg Center.

Papers of the Harvard-trained anthropologist Caroline Bond Day are located in the Peabody Museum, Harvard University, while papers of the eminent Chicago-trained anthropologist St. Clair Drake are found at the Schomburg Library.

ARCHITECTURE

For research on architecture, consult Howard University and Tuskegee University. Tuskegee's Architectural Library has a wide array of materials. The Moorland-Spingarn Research Center in conjunction with the Howard University School of Architecture has the papers of Albert I. Cassell, an architect who designed many of Howard's buildings. The collection also includes Cassell's original plans for an interracial suburb in Maryland named Casselton. Howard H. Mackey, Sr. (1901–1987), an architect and educator, joined Howard's architecture faculty in 1924. In 1950 Howard became the first predominantly black school of architecture in the United States to be accredited. Mackey's papers (1925–1975) include reports, articles, and correspondence that document the growth of architectural education; at the same time the papers show Mackey's influence in countries such as Guyana, Suriname, and Trinidad.

When persons seek to have structures designated as historical sites, they are required to complete a significant amount of research; this research is held at the Historic Preservation Review Board. In addition, cities hire architectural firms to survey neighborhoods, which results in very detailed historical information, also stored at the Historic Preservation Review Board.

BUSINESS

The National Business League in Washington, D.C., houses its own records and those of its predecessor organization, the National Negro Business League (NNBL). Holdings include the League's articles of incorporation, its by-laws and constitution, the minutes of its national board of directors' meetings, the correspondence of its founder, Booker T. Washington, and photographs, sound recordings, and a 1928 (and 1940s) survey of black-operated businesses in thirty-three cities. Also consult the Emmett J. Scott Collection at the Morgan State University Soper Library for materials on the NNBL. Scott served as Booker T. Washington's secretary at Tuskegee, and was one of the founders of the National Negro Business League.

Many other umbrella organizations championed the business interests of African-Americans. The National Insurance Association has the correspondence, minutes, and convention proceedings of the National Negro Insurance Association (1921–1954), which became the National Insurance Association (1954–present). These papers were recently designated to go to the Amistad Research Center, New Orleans. Papers of the Atlanta Life Insurance Company are held by the Auburn Avenue Research Library in Black History and Culture, the Herndon Home, and Emory University's Woodruff Library, all in Atlanta. For information on blacks in the media, including the business side of journalism, see the Claude A. Barnett Papers in the Chicago Historical Society; for materials on the relationship between black workers and white businesses consult the National Urban League Papers in the Library of Congress.

Small-business owners often maintained their own files, so it is essential to contact long-established small businesses directly. Lucy Crump Jefferson opened a funeral home in 1894 in Mississippi. The records of the Jefferson business are located in the Jefferson Funeral Home in Vicksburg, Miss. Papers of the Hanley Company, Undertakers, founded in Atlanta in the early 1920s, are located at Emory University. Local historical societies and public libraries often house papers of local businesses: the papers of the Buffalo Cooperative Economic Society (1929–1960), for example, are at the Buffalo and Erie County Public Library.

Businesspeople such as Madam C. J. Walker, Elijah Roberts, and Herbert Heller have manuscript collections at the Indiana Historical Society. For materials on the beauty culture business, consult the Madam C. J. Walker papers at the Indiana Historical Society and the Claude A. Barnett Papers at the Chicago Historical Society. The Warshaw Collection of Business Americana, at the Smithsonian's National Museum of American History, consists of advertising cards, posters, trade catalogs, greeting cards, and business letterheads. The papers of the barber George A. Myers are located at the Ohio Historical Society. The Robert R. Church Family Papers are housed at the John Willard Brister Library, Memphis State University.

Another research angle is the impact of citizens on businesses. The numerous "Don't Buy Where You Can't Work" campaigns throughout the United States greatly affected white businesses. The New Negro Alliance organized the Washington, D.C., campaign; its papers are available at the Moorland-Spingarn Research Center, Howard University. Also consult the papers of the acclaimed jurist William H. Hastie, which are found in the Harvard University Law Library.

CIVIL RIGHTS

The struggle for civil rights, especially that of the civil rights and Black Power eras spanning the 1940s to 1970s, has been one of the more thoroughly researched and documented chapters in African-American history. The Library of Congress has an extensive collection of manuscripts on individuals and organizations. Personal papers held there include those of Lorenzo Johnston Greene, Patricia Roberts Harris, Rayford Logan, Thurgood Marshall, A. Philip Randolph, Bayard Rustin, Arthur Spingarn, Mary Church Terrell, and Roy Wilkins. Organizational papers at the Library of Congress include those of the National Urban League, the Leadership Conference on Civil Rights, the NAACP, the NAACP Legal Defense and Education Fund, and the Southern Christian Leadership Conference (SCLC).

The Martin Luther King, Jr., Center for Non-Violent Social Change, Inc.–King Library and Archives in Atlanta holds significant collections on civil rights organizations. These include the papers of the Mississippi Freedom Democratic Party, 1964–1965; the Student Nonviolent Coordinating Committee; the Southern Christian Leadership Conference; and the Congress of Racial Equality, 1944–1968.

The State Historical Library of Wisconsin is also an important repository for civil rights records. Its manuscript collections include the papers of Daisy Bates, Howard Zinn, and Annie Rankin. Organizational papers at the library include those of the Western and Southern Regional Offices of the Congress of Racial Equality, 1959–1976. It also has the Daniel H. M. Murray Papers, including draft bibliographic sketches, notes, and correspondence, particularly research materials related to Murray's unpublished "Historical and Biographical Encyclopedia of the Colored Race." Consult Jane Wolff and Eleanor Mckay, ed., *The Papers of Daniel Murray: Guide to a Microfilm Edition* (1977).

The personal papers of well-known individuals are housed in repositories throughout the country, often with collections in several places. Researchers should consult two books for help locating collections: Jessie Carney Smith, *Notable Black American Women* (1992), and Darlene Clark Hine, Elsa Barkley Brown, and Rosalyn Terborg-Penn, ed., *Black Women in America: An Historical Encyclopedia* (1993). Some individuals' papers are found in unlikely locations. The papers of the North Carolinian Robert F. Williams, for example, are located in the Bentley Library in Ann Arbor, Mich. The file covers not only Williams's life in North Carolina, but also his activities in Cuba and the People's Republic of China, and his role as President of the Michigan-based Republic of New Africa. Below is listed in alphabetical order a select group of personal papers.

The papers of Charlotta Bass, journalist and political activist, can be found in the California Library for Social Studies in Los Angeles. Some of her letters are also in the Calvin Benham Papers at the University of Iowa. The papers of the noted educator and rights activist Mary McLeod Bethune are found in a number of manuscript collections: the Bethune Foundation, Bethune-Cookman College, Daytona Beach, Fla.; the Amistad Research Center; National Association of Colored Women's Clubs, Washington, D.C.; and Fisk University. See also the National Council of Negro Women Papers at the Bethune Museum and Archives, the Eleanor Roosevelt Papers and the Franklin D. Roosevelt Papers, Franklin D. Roosevelt Library, Hyde Park, N.Y., and the National Youth Administration, RG 109, at the National Archives. Also consult the Mary Church Terrell Papers at the Library of Congress.

Ralph Bunche's Papers at the University of California, Los Angeles, Department of Special Collections, document Bunche's academic and diplomatic careers. This collection is valuable for the correspondence and reports he and others produced for Gunnar Myrdal and the Carnegie Foundation–sponsored project that culminated in *An American Dilemma.*

The papers of the social activist and educator Septima Clark are housed in both the College of Charleston, South Carolina, and the Papers of Highlander Research and Education Center, State Historical Library of Madison, Wisconsin. Materials on Shirley Graham Du Bois are in the Julius Rosenwald Archives, Fisk University. The file spans the years 1939–1946, with particular emphasis on Du Bois's 1939 grant application. The W. E. B. Du Bois Papers are at the University of Massachusetts, Amherst, Library, with a smaller holding at Fisk University. Researchers should consult Robert W. McDonnell, *The Papers of W. E. B. Du Bois, 1803 (1877– 1963) 1979: A Guide* (1981).

The Hoyt Fuller Papers, at the Atlanta University Center, contain correspondence, manuscripts, and memorabilia that document Fuller's relationships with other writers, his career as editor of *Negro Digest* and *Black World,* and his role as the founder-publisher of *First World.* For the flowering of early 20th-century black nationalism and capitalist ventures, no source rivals the Marcus Garvey and UNIA Papers Project, based at the University of California at Los Angeles. This project, directed by Robert A. Hill, has brought together original material and copies of relevant materials from repositories around the world. These document Garvey's early life and rise to prominence, with special focus on the Universal Negro Improvement Association and the African Communities League; they highlight both Garvey's international reach and the scrutiny his prominence engendered.

For the history of black female social activism see the papers of Fannie Lou Hamer, active in the Mississippi Freedom Democratic Party. Her papers are found in the Amistad Research Center and in the Fannie Lou Hamer Collection, Coleman Library, Tougaloo College. Elizabeth Ross Haynes, who worked with the YWCA, has a small collection in the James Weldon Johnson Memorial Collection, Yale University, and in the archives of the National Board of the YWCA in New York City. Dorothy Height's papers are available at the office of the National Council of Negro Women in Washington, D.C., and in the National Council of Negro Women Papers at the National Archives of Black Women's History, Washington, D.C.

The papers of John and Lugenia Burns Hope are housed in the archives of the Woodruff Library, Atlanta University Center, along with the Neighborhood Union Collection, which documents an institution Lugenia Burns Hope founded. Other perspectives on social welfare can be gleaned from the Jane Edna Hunter and the Phillis Wheatley Association Papers, available at the Western Reserve Historical Society, Cleveland.

Among the key collections on black activism are the letters of the social theorist and author C. L. R. James at the Schomburg Center; the Harold Cruse Papers at the Auburn Avenue Research Library on African-American History and Culture, Atlanta; the Rev. Dr. Martin Luther King, Jr., Papers at the King Center, Atlanta, and at Boston University; the Pauli Murray Papers in the Schlesinger Library, Harvard University; the Eslanda Robeson Papers at the Moorland-Spingarn Research Center; and the Paul Robeson Papers at the Schomburg Center. For more information on Paul Robeson, see David H. Werning, comp., *A Guide to the Microfilm Edition to the Paul Robeson Collection* (1991) and the Moorland-Spingarn Research Center's extensive Paul Robeson Collection. The papers of Bayard Rustin, the behind-the-scenes organizer of the March on Washington and numerous other civil rights campaigns, are housed at the A. Philip Randolph Institute, New York City.

Researchers should consult some of the larger collections to find manuscript sources on individuals who may not have their own papers collected. For example, manuscript materials on Henrietta Vinton Davis, the elocutionist and prominent member of the Universal Negro Improvement Association and African Communities League, are found in the Marcus Garvey and UNIA Papers.

Although most African-Americans aligned themselves with the Democratic Party after the 1936 reelection of Franklin D. Roosevelt, some continued to participate in the Republican Party. Roscoe Conkling Simmons, whose papers are at Harvard University, chaired the Colored Speakers' Bureau of the Republican National Committee during the 1920s, and his papers contain materials for the years 1890–1951. Whitney Young, Sr., and Whitney Young, Jr., played an active role in the debates roiling the nation about civil rights. The Whitney M. Young, Jr., Papers are in the Rare Book and Manuscript Library, Columbia University. The Whitney M. Young, Sr., Papers are at the Blazer Library, Kentucky State University.

Organizational papers relating to civil rights and black power are abundant. For manuscripts on black feminist movements, consult the National Archives for Black Women's History for the papers of the National Alliance of Black Feminists and the Third World Women's Alliance, an offshoot of the Student Nonviolent Coordinating Committee (SNCC). The papers of the National Negro Congress are available at the Schomburg Center for Research in Black Culture. Check local repositories for the papers of local chapters. The papers of the Institute of the Black World, 1968–1974, are also available at the Schomburg Center.

A large collection of Black Panther Party Papers is housed at the Stanford University Libraries. Stanford's collection includes legal documents, correspondence, private papers, and photographs. Papers are also available at the African American Historical and Cultural Society at the Library of San Francisco. Materials on local branches can be found at the Bancroft Library at the University of California, Berkeley, the Labadie Collection at the University of Michigan, and in the Martin Luther King, Jr., Papers.

The Atlanta University Archives has, in addition to the administrative records of the university, several major organizational holdings including the Association of Southern Women for the Prevention of Lynching, the Neighborhood Union (a private social welfare agency), the Southern Conference for Human Welfare, and the Southern Regional Council.

State archives and historical societies are also rich repositories for documenting the struggle for civil rights. The Alabama Department of Archives and History in Montgomery, for example, has papers that document the response of Alabama's public officials to the civil rights movement. Equally valuable are the personal papers of former state governors and state commissions.

CONCLUSION

Whether researching individuals, organizations, or cultural forms, manuscript collections are fundamental sources. This essay serves only as an introduction to primary documents in African-American history. As archivists and librarians in repositories throughout the country respond to changing technologies by using microform and the Internet, these materials will become accessible to an even larger number of researchers. Nonetheless, the materials currently available are rich in their variety, complexity, and completeness.

5   *Primary Sources on Microform*

Nathaniel Bunker

The amount of research material in microform relevant to African-American studies is so voluminous that it is often difficult for the student to gain an overview of the important collections held in major research libraries or readily available through interlibrary loan facilities. This checklist identifies the principal microfilmed collections of personal papers, political and religious archives, and printed materials that might be of continuing research value.

The listing for each microfilm collection identifies the library or repository holding the original manuscript or printed material (e.g., the Alexander Crummell Papers, held in the Schomburg Center for Research in Black Culture, the New York Public Library). In those instances where a microfilm publisher has for a particular project brought together materials drawn from a number of repositories, the list below identifies the publisher as the source (e.g., *Black Biographical Dictionaries,* published by Chadwyck-Healey, Inc.). The number of microfilm reels or microfiche in the collection is also identified to give some indication of size or scope.

Several microfilm publishers are actively engaged in filming additional collections of African-American studies material. The latest catalogs of these publishers are good sources of information about new or forthcoming microfilm collections. Among these publishers are:

Adam Matthew Publications
8 Oxford Street
Marlborough, Wiltshire SN8 1AP
England

Chadwyck-Healey Inc.
1101 King Street
Alexandria, VA 22314

Primary Source Media
12 Lunar Drive
Woodbridge, CT 06525

Scholarly Resources, Inc.
104 Greenhill Avenue
Wilmington, DE 19805

UMI
300 North Zeeb Road
Ann Arbor, MI 48106

University Publications of America
4520 East-West Highway
Bethesda, MD 20814

Another reliable source of collection information is *The Guide to Microforms in Print* (1961–), which is periodically updated and identifies the publisher of each microform title.

Abolition and Emancipation: Papers of Thomas Clarkson, William Lloyd Garrison, Zachary Macaulay, Harriet Martineau, Harriet Beecher Stowe and William Wilberforce. 7 microfilm reels. Henry E. Huntington Library and Art Gallery.

African-American Baptist Annual Reports, 1865–1990s. Includes the minutes of 1,039 African-American Baptist associations and conventions in twenty-seven states and regions. 105 microfilm reels. American Baptist Historical Society.

Agricultural and Manufacturing Census Records of Fifteen Southern States for the Years 1850, 1860, 1870, and 1880. 313 microfilm reels. University of North Carolina Library.

Allston, Robert Francis Withers, 1801–1864. *Robert F. W. Allston Papers.* Plantation records. 456 microfiches. South Carolina Historical Society.

American Civil Liberties Union. *American Civil Liberties Union Archives, 1912–1950.* 293 microfilm reels. Princeton University.

American Colonization Society. *Records, 1792–1965.* 323 microfilm reels. Library of Congress.

American Committee on Africa. *Records.* 51 microfilm reels. Amistad Research Center, Tulane University.

American Fund for Public Service. *Records, 1922–1941.* Includes records relating to the American Civil Liberties Union, the NAACP, the Brotherhood of Sleeping Car Porters, and the Southern Tenant Farmers Union. 36 microfilm reels. Rare Books and Manuscripts Division, Center for the Humanities, New York Public Library.

American Home Missionary Society. *Records, 1816–1894.* 385 microfilm reels. Amistad Research Center, Tulane University.

American Negro Historical Society. *Records, 1790–1901.* 12 microfilm reels. Historical Society of Pennsylvania.

Americans for Democratic Action. *Records, 1932–1965.* 142 microfilm reels. State Historical Society of Wisconsin.

Anti-Slavery Propaganda in the Oberlin College Library. Collection contains 2,500 pamphlets. 7,235 microfiches. Oberlin College Library.

Association of Southern Women for the Prevention of Lynching. *Papers, 1930–1942.* 8 microfilm reels. Robert W. Woodruff Library, Atlanta University Center.

Barnett, Claude, 1890–. *The Claude A. Barnett Papers: The Associated Negro Press, 1918–1967.* 198 microfilm reels. Archives and Manuscripts Department, Chicago Historical Society.

Bennett, Gwendolyn, 1902–1981. *Papers.* 2 microfilm reels. Schomburg Center for Research in Black Culture, New York Public Library.

Bethune, Mary McLeod, 1875–1955. *Papers, 1923–1942.* 1 microfilm reel. Amistad Research Center, Tulane University.

Bethune, Mary McLeod, 1875–1955. *The Bethune-Cookman College Collection, 1922–1955.* 13 microfilm reels. Bethune-Cookman College.

Bethune, Mary McLeod, 1875–1955. *The Bethune Foundation Collection: Part 1, Writings, Diaries, Scrapbooks, Biographical Materials and Files on the National Youth Administration and Women's Organizations: Part 2, correspondence files, 1914–1955; and Subject Files, 1939–1955.* 61 microfilm reels. Bethune-Cookman College.

Black Abolitionists Papers, 1830–1865. 17 reels. University Microfilms International.

Black Academy of Arts and Letters. *Records* 1969–1973. 10 microfilm reels. Schomburg Center for Research in Black Culture, New York Public Library.

Black Biographical Dictionaries, 1790–1950. 1,068 microfiches. Chadwyck-Healey, Inc.

Black Culture, a Core Library on the African American Experience. Books, pamphlets, and other sources on many topics. 417 microfilm reels. University Microfilms International.

Black Literature, 1827–1940. Fiction, poetry, book reviews, and literary notices appearing in black periodicals and newspapers. About 2,000 microfiches with cumulative index on CD-ROM. Chadwyck-Healey, Inc.

Black Newspaper Collection, 1896–1993. 1,352 microfilm reels. University Microfilms International.

Black Workers in the Era of the Great Migration, 1916–1929. 25 microfilm reels. U.S. National Archives.

Blacks in the U.S. Armed Forces: Basic Documents, 1639–1973. 5 microfilm reels. Scholarly Resources Inc.

Blackwell family. *Papers.* Includes the papers of abolitionists Lucy Stone and Henry Brown Blackwell. 76 microfilm reels. Library of Congress.

Bond, Horace Mann, 1904–1972. *Papers.* 98 microfilm reels. University of Massachusetts at Amherst Library.

Brotherhood of Sleeping Car Porters. *Records, 1925–1969.* 50 microfilm reels. Chicago Historical Society and the Newberry Library.

Browder, Earl, 1891–1973. *Papers.* Browder was the General Secretary of the Communist Party of America, and the collection contains considerable documentation on the tactics of the Communist Party with regard to African-Americans, particularly in the instances of the Scottsboro Case and the activities of the National Negro Congress. 36 microfilm reels. Arents Research Library, Syracuse University.

Bruce, John Edward, 1856–1924. *Papers.* Bruce was an African-American journalist. 4 microfilm reels. Schomburg Center for Research in Black Culture, New York Public Library.

Bunche, Ralph J., 1904–1971. *Papers,* ca. 1939–ca. 1970. 7 microfilm reels. Special Collections, Research Libraries, University of California at Los Angeles.

Butler, Pierce, 1744–1822. *Butler Plantation Papers.* 21 microfilm reels. Historical Society of Pennsylvania.

California. Governor's Commission on the Los Angeles Riots (Watts). *Transcripts, Descriptions, Consultants' Reports, and Selected Documents.* 6 microfilm reels.

Carver, George Washington, 1864?–1943. *Papers.* 67 microfilm reels. Tuskegee Institute.

Chesnutt, Charles Waddell, 1858–1932. *Papers, 1889–1932.* 1 microfilm reel. Western Reserve Historical Society. Chestnut family. *Chestnut, Miller, and Manning Papers.* Plantation records. 107 microfiches. South Carolina Historical Society.

Cheves, Langdon, 1776–1857. *Langdon Cheves Papers.* Plantation records. 194 microfiches. South Carolina Historical Society.

Child, Lydia Maria Frances, 1802–1880. *The Collected Correspondence of Lydia Maria Child, 1817–1880.* Child was an abolitionist active in the American Anti-Slavery Society. 97 microfiches.

Civil Rights Congress (U.S.). *Papers of the Civil Rights Congress, ca. 1946–1956.* 125 microfilm reels. Schomburg Center for Research in Black Culture, New York Public Library.

Civil Rights during the Johnson Administration, 1963–1969. 69 microfilm reels. Lyndon Baines Johnson Library.

Civil Rights during the Kennedy Administration. 47 microfilm reels. John F. Kennedy Library.

Civil Rights during the Nixon Administration, 1969–1974. 46 microfilm reels. U.S. National Archives.

Columbia University. Oral History Research Office. *Oral History Collection.* Contains transcripts of interviews with various black leaders involved in civil rights activities. 2,690 microfiches.

Commission on Interracial Cooperation. *Papers, 1919–1944.* 55 microfilm reels. Robert W. Woodruff Library, Atlanta University Center.

Congress of Industrial Organizations (U.S.). *Operation Dixie: The C.I.O. Organizing Committee Papers, 1946–1953.* 75 microfilm reels. William R. Perkins Library, Duke University.

Congress of Racial Equality. *Congress of Racial Equality Papers, 1959–1976.* Includes the files of the Western and Southern Regional Offices. 80 microfilm reels. State Historical Society of Wisconsin.

Congress of Racial Equality. *CORE: The Papers of the Congress of Racial Equality: Addendum, 1944–1968.* 25 microfilm reels. Library and Archives, Martin Luther King, Jr., Center for Nonviolent Social Change.

Congress of Racial Equality. *Records, 1941–1967.* 49 microfilm reels. Library and Archives, Martin Luther King, Jr., Center for Nonviolent Social Change.

Conrad, Earl. *Earl Conrad/Harriet Tubman Collection.* 2 microfilm reels. Schomburg Center for Research in Black Culture, New York Public Library.

Cosme y Almanza, Eusebia Adriana. *Papers.* Cosme y Almanza was an actress and CBS radio personality in the 1930s. 2 microfilm reels. Schomburg Center for Research in Black Culture, New York Public Library.

Crummell, Alexander, 1819–1898. *Papers.* 10 microfilm reels. Schomburg Center for Research in Black Culture, New York Public Library.

Cullen, Countee, 1903–1946. *Papers.* 7 microfilm reels. Amistad Research Center, Tulane University.

Davis, Angela, 1944–. *Case Collection.* 13 microfilm reels. Meiklejohn Civil Liberties Institute, Berkeley, California.

Davis, John Preston, 1905–1973. *Papers.* Davis was active in the National Negro Congress and editor of the first edition of the *American Negro Reference Book.* 2 microfilm reels. Schomburg Center for Research in Black Culture, New York Public Library.

Dent, John Horry, d. 1892. *Farm Journals and Account Books, 1840–1892.* 4 microfilm reels. University of Alabama Library.

Detroit Urban League. *Records, 1916–1950.* 35 microfilm reels. University of Michigan Library.

Douglass, Frederick, 1817?–1895. *Papers.* 34 microfilm reels. Library of Congress.

Du Bois, W. E. B. (William Edward Burghardt), 1868–1963. *Papers.* 1 microfilm reel. Fisk University Library.

Du Bois, W. E. B. (William Edward Burghardt), 1868–1963. *Papers.* 89 microfilm reels. University of Massachusetts at Amherst Library.

Dunbar, Paul Laurence, 1872–1906. *Miscellaneous Items.* 1 microfilm reel. Schomburg Center for Research in Black Culture, New York Public Library.

Dunbar, Paul Laurence, 1872–1906. *Papers.* 9 microfilm reels. Ohio Historical Society.

East St. Louis Race Riot of 1917. 8 microfilm reels. Illinois Supreme Court and the U.S. National Archives.

Federal Surveillance of Afro-Americans (1917–1925): The First World War, the Red Scare, and the Garvey Movement. 25 microfilm reels. U.S. National Archives and other federal record centers.

Federal Writers' Project. *Records.* The Federal Writers' Project was a New Deal project designed to collect life histories of rural Southerners, including some interviews with black tenant farmers, laborers, and domestic workers. 220 microfiches. University of North Carolina Library.

Foster, Abigail Kelley, 1811–1887. *Kelley-Foster Papers, ca. 1838–1868.* Includes correspondence relating to the abolition of slavery. 1 microfilm reel. American Antiquarian Society.

Free Southern Theater. *The Free Southern Theater Records, 1963–1978.* 47 microfilm reels. Amistad Research Center, Tulane University.

Garrison, William Lloyd, 1805–1879. *Papers.* 1 microfilm reel. Massachusetts Historical Society.

General Education Board (New York, N.Y.). *The General Education Board Archives: The Early Southern Program.* African-American education, 1901–1967. 159 microfilm reels. Rockefeller Archive Center.

General Education Board (New York, N.Y.). *The General Education Board Archives: The New Southern Program and Related Programs 1931–1961.* 207 microfilm reels. Rockefeller Archive Center.

Green, John Patterson, 1845–1940. *Papers, 1869–1910.* Green was active in the Republican Party. 6 microfilm reels. Western Reserve Historical Society.

Hamer, Fannie Lou, 1917–1977. *Papers, 1966–1978.* 17 microfilm reels. Amistad Research Center, Tulane University.

Hampton University (Va.). *The Hampton University Newspaper Clipping File, 1873–1940.* 790 microfiches. Collis P. Huntington Library, Hampton University.

Hastie, William H., 1904–1974. *The William H. Hastie Papers.* 107 microfilm reels. Harvard University Law School Library.

Hope, John, 1868–1936. *Papers of John and Lugenia Burns Hope.* 21 microfilm reels. Robert W. Woodruff Library, Atlanta University Center.

Hughes, Langston, 1902–1967. *Langston Hughes Collection.* 4 microfilm reels. Schomburg Center for Research in Black Culture, New York Public Library.

International Labor Defense. *Papers of the International Labor Defense, 1927–ca. 1947.* 22 microfilm reels. Schomburg Center for Research in Black Culture, New York Public Library.

Iowa University Libraries. *The Right Wing Collection.* Contains anti-black publications, including those of the KKK and the American White Nationalist Party. 177 microfilm reels.

Johnson, George P. *Negro Film Collection.* 12 microfilm reels. Research Libraries, University of California, Los Angeles.

Johnson, Oakley C. *Papers.* Johnson was a civil rights advocate from 1946–1959, in Alabama, Louisiana, Texas, and New York City. 5 microfilm reels. Schomburg Center for Research in Black Culture, New York Public Library.

Kennedy, Stetson. *The Stetson Kennedy Collection.* Includes material on the Ku Klux Klan during the 1930s and 1940s. 4 microfilm reels. Schomburg Center for Research in Black Culture, New York Public Library.

Laura Spelman Rockefeller Memorial. *Appropriations, 1917–1945.* Includes grants for social welfare, emergency relief, and interracial relations. 89 microfilm reels. Rockefeller Archive Center.

Louisiana State University Library. *Southern Historical Manuscripts.* Plantation records from Louisiana, southwestern Mississippi, and the lower Mississippi Valley, as well as the papers of two families of free blacks in Louisiana, the Atala Chelette Family papers, 1819–1900, and the Norbert Badin Family papers, 1829–1900. 526 microfiches.

Malcolm X, 1925–1965. *Transcripts of the Malcolm X Assassination Trial.* 3 microfilm reels. New York State Supreme Court, New York City.

Manigault Family Papers, 1750–1900. Plantation records. 100 microfiches. South Carolina Historical Society.

Maryland State Colonization Society. *Papers, 1817–1902.* 31 microfilm reels. Maryland State Historical Society.

McCray, John Henry. *Papers, 1929–1989.* Editor of an important black newspaper, *The Lighthouse and Informer.* 18 microfilm reels. South Caroliniana Library.

Miscellaneous Negro Newspapers on Microfilm. 12 microfilm reels. Library of Congress.

Mississippi Oral History Collection. A few of the transcripts are of interviews with black civil rights activists in Mississippi, such as Charles Evers and Fannie Lou Hamer. 163 microfiches. University of Southern Mississippi Library.

Morrison, Allan. *Papers, 1940–1968.* Morrison was the first black war correspondent for *Stars and Stripes;* New York editor of *Ebony.* 3 microfilm reels. Schomburg Center for Research in Black Culture, New York Public Library.

Mother Bethel African Methodist Episcopal Church. *Records, 1760–1972.* Includes all available filmed issues of the *Christian Recorder.* 24 microfilm reels. African Methodist Episcopal Church, Philadelphia, Pennsylvania.

Murray, Daniel Alexander Payne, 1852–1925. *Papers, 1881–1925.* 27 microfilm reels. State Historical Society of Wisconsin.

Myers, George A., 1859–1930. *Papers, 1890–1929.* Myers was a three-time delegate to the Republican National Convention. 8 microfilm reels. Ohio Historical Society.

National Association for the Advancement of Colored People. *Papers of the NAACP.* 1,120 microfilm reels. U.S. National Archives.

National Association of Colored Graduate Nurses. *Records, 1908–1951.* 2 microfilm reels. Schomburg Center for Research in Black Culture, New York Public Library.

National Association of Colored Women's Clubs. *Records, 1895–1992.* 41 microfilm reels. National Headquarters of the NACWC, Washington, D.C.

National Negro Business League. *Records of the National Negro Business League.* 14 microfilm reels. Tuskegee University Archives and the Library of Congress.

National Negro Congress (U.S.). *Papers, 1933–1947.* 94 microfilm reels. Schomburg Center for Research in Black Culture, New York Public Library.

Negro Labor Committee. *Negro Labor Committee Records, 1925–1969.* 17 microfilm reels. Schomburg Center for Research in Black Culture, New York Public Library.

New Deal Agencies and Black America in the 1930s. 25 microfilm reels. University Publications of America.

Papers of the American Slave Trade. 53 microfilm reels. University Publications of America.

Parrish, Richard. *Papers, 1950–1975.* Parrish was a member of the New York Teachers Guild, the National Afro-American Labor Council, and other civil rights and labor groups. 10 microfilm reels. Schomburg Center for Research in Black Culture, New York Public Library.

Pennsylvania Society for Promoting the Abolition of Slavery. *The Pennsylvania Abolition Society Papers, 1775–1975.* 32 microfilm reels. Historical Society of Pennsylvania.

Pickens, William, 1881–1954. *Papers.* Pickens was an NAACP executive and chief of the Interracial Section of the U.S. Treasury. 29 microfilm reels. Schomburg Center for Research in Black Culture, New York Public Library.

Presbyterian Church in the U.S.A. Board of Missions for Freedmen. *Annual Reports, 1866–1923.* 3 microfilm reels. Presbyterian Historical Society, Department of History, Presbyterian Church (U.S.A.).

Race, Slavery, and Free Blacks: Petitions to Southern Legislatures, 1777–1867. 23 microfilm reels. Race and Slavery Petitions Project, University of North Carolina at Greensboro.

Randolph, A. Philip (Asa Philip), 1889–1979. *The Papers of A. Philip Randolph, 1925–1978.* 35 microfilm reels. Library of Congress.

Records of Antebellum Southern Plantations from the Revolution through the Civil War. 1,188 microfilm reels. University Publications of America.

Robeson, Paul, 1898–1976. *The Paul Robeson Collection, 1949–1956.* 9 microfilm reels. Schomburg Center for Research in Black Culture, New York Public Library.

Roosevelt, Eleanor, 1884–1962. *The Papers of Eleanor Roosevelt, 1933–1945.* Correspondents include Walter White, Mary McLeod Bethune, Roy Wilkins, A. Philip Randolph, and Pauli Murray. 20 microfilm reels. Franklin D. Roosevelt Library.

Rustin, Bayard, 1910–. *The Bayard Rustin Papers.* 23 microfilm reels. A. Philip Randolph Institute.

Schomburg, Arthur A., 1874–1938. *Papers.* 12 microfilm reels. Schomburg Center for Research in Black Culture, New York Public Library.

Schomburg Center for Research in Black Culture. *Black Newspapers: Sample Issues, 1845–1966.* 4 microfilm reels.

Schomburg Center for Research in Black Culture. *Blacks in the Railroad Industry, 1946–1954.* 1 microfilm reel.

Schomburg Center for Research in Black Culture. *Problems of the American Negro.* A collection of manuscripts used by Gunnar Myrdal in preparation of his book *American Dilemma.* 13 microfilm reels.

Schomburg Center for Research in Black Culture. *Schomburg Center Clipping File, 1925–1988.* 14,896 microfiches.

Schomburg Center for Research in Black Culture. *A Selection of Titles from the Schomburg Center.* 660 microfilm reels.

Schomburg Center for Research in Black Culture. *The Slavery and Abolition Collections.* 1 microfilm reel.

Schomburg Center for Research in Black Culture. *W. E. B. Du Bois Newspaper Clippings.* 1 microfilm reel.

Slavery and Anti-Slavery Pamphlets from the Libraries of Salmon P. Chase and John P. Hale. 5 microfilm reels. University Microfilms International.

Slavery: Catalyst for Conflict. 6,708 microfiches. About 5,900 historical documents. University Microfilms International.

Slavery in Antebellum Southern Industries. 125 microfilm reels. University Publications of America.

Slavery, Source Material, and Critical Literature. 11,949 microfiches. Primary Source Media.

Smeltzer, Ralph E. *Manuscript Notes and Correspondence.* Relating to the civil rights movement in Selma, Alabama, 1963–1965. 3 microfilm reels. Harvard University Library.

Smith, Gerrit, 1797–1874. *Gerrit Smith Papers.* 77 microfilm reels. Arents Research Library, Syracuse University.

Smythe, Hugh H. *Papers.* Smythe was a U.S. diplomat. 6 microfilm reels. Schomburg Center for Research in Black Culture, New York Public Library.

Socialist Party (U.S.). *Records, 1897–1963.* The Socialist Party and its members were active in furthering civil rights and labor rights, working with sympathetic organizations such as the Southern Tenant Farmers' Union and the American Civil Liberties Union. 142 microfilm reels. William R. Perkins Library, Duke University.

Socialist Party (U.S.). *Records: Addendum, 1919–1976.* 38 microfilm reels. William R. Perkins Library. Duke University.

Southern Christian Leadership Conference. *Records, 1954–1970.* 83 microfilm reels. Library and Archives, Martin Luther King, Jr., Center for Nonviolent Social Change.

Southern Education Reporting Service. *Facts on File, May 1954–December 1973.* SERS desegregation documentary collection, including newspaper editorials, letters to the editor, newspaper and magazine articles, and speeches on race relations. 291 microfilm reels.

Southern Regional Council. *The Southern Regional Council Papers, 1944–1968.* 225 microfilm reels. Robert W. Woodruff Library, Atlanta University Center.

Southern Tenant Farmers' Union. *The Green Rising, 1910–1977: A Supplement to the Southern Tenant Farmers Union Records.* 15 reels. Southern Historical Collection, University of North Carolina Library.

Southern Tenant Farmers' Union. *Records, 1934–1970.* 60 microfilm reels. Southern Historical Collection, University of North Carolina Library.

Southern Women and Their Families in the 19th Century: Papers and Diaries. Includes material on slavery. 419 microfilm reels. University Publications of America.

Stanford University. *Project South Oral History Collection.* Interviews conducted during 1965 with civil rights workers, including representatives of CORE, the Southern Christian Leadership Conference, and the Freedom Democratic Party. 68 microfiches. Stanford University Library.

State Free Negro Capitation Tax Books, Charleston, South Carolina, ca. 1811–1860. 2 microfilm reels. South Carolina Department of Archives and History.

State Slavery Statutes. 354 microfiches. University Publications of America.

Still, William, 1821–1902. *Letterpress Book.* 2 microfilm reels. Historical Society of Pennsylvania.

Student Nonviolent Coordinating Committee (U.S.). *Student Nonviolent Coordinating Committee Papers, 1959–1972.* 73 microfilm reels. Library and Archives, Martin Luther King, Jr., Center for Nonviolent Social Change.

Students for a Democratic Society (U.S.). *Records, 1958–1970.* 41 microfilm reels. State Historical Society of Wisconsin.

Sumner, Charles, 1811–1874. *Papers.* 85 microfilm reels. Harvard University Library.

Tappan, Benjamin, 1773–1857. *Papers.* 11 microfilm reels. Library of Congress.

Tappan, Lewis, 1788–1873. *Papers.* 7 microfilm reels. Library of Congress.

Terrell, Mary Church, 1863–1954. *Papers.* 34 microfilm reels. Library of Congress.

Tourgee, Albion Winegar, 1838–1905. *Papers.* 60 microfilm reels. Chautauqua County Historical Society, Westfield, N.Y.

Tuskegee Institute. *The Tuskegee Institute News Clipping File, 1899–1966.* 252 microfilm reels.

United Church Board for Homeland Ministries. Race Relations Department. *Archives, 1943–1970.* 56 microfilm reels. Amistad Research Center, Tulane University.

United Negro College Fund. *Archives, 1944–1971.* 3,525 microfiches. United Negro College Fund.

U.S. Army. Massachusetts Infantry Regiment, 54th (1863–1865). *Records of the Fifty-Fourth Massachusetts Infantry Regiment (Colored), 1863–1865.* 7 microfilm reels. U.S. National Archives.

U.S. Bureau of Refugees, Freedmen, and Abandoned Lands. *Records of the Bureau of Refugees, Freedmen, and Abandoned Lands.* 763 microfilm reels. U.S. National Archives.

U.S. Committee of Fair Employment Practice. *Selected Documents from the Committee Records, 1941–1946.* 212 microfilm reels. U.S. National Archives.

U.S. Department of Justice. *The Peonage Files of the U.S. Department of Justice, 1901–1945.* 26 microfilm reels. U.S. National Archives.

U.S. Federal Bureau of Investigation. *Centers of the Southern Struggle: FBI Files on Selma, Memphis, Montgomery, Albany, and St. Augustine.* 21 microfilm reels. Collection of Professor David Garrow. University Publications of America.

U.S. Federal Bureau of Investigation. *Communist Infiltration of the Southern Christian Leadership Conference: FBI Investigation File.* 9 microfilm reels. U.S. Federal Bureau of Investigation Central Files.

U.S. Federal Bureau of Investigation. *FBI File: MIBURN (Mississippi Burning), the Investigation of the Murders of Michael Henry Schwerner, Andrew Goodman, and James Earl Chaney, June 21, 1964.* 1 microfilm reel. U.S. Federal Bureau of Investigation Central Files.

U.S. Federal Bureau of Investigation. *FBI File on A. Philip Randolph, 1922–1964.* 1 microfilm reel. U.S. Federal Bureau of Investigation Central Files.

U.S. Federal Bureau of Investigation. *FBI File on Elijah Muhammad.* 3 microfilm reels. U.S. Federal Bureau of Investigation Central Files.

U.S. Federal Bureau of Investigation. *FBI File on Malcolm X.* 10 microfilm reels. U.S. Federal Bureau of Investigation Central Files.

U.S. Federal Bureau of Investigation. *FBI File on Paul Robeson.* 2 microfilm reels. U.S. Federal Bureau of Investigation Central Files.

U.S. Federal Bureau of Investigation. *FBI File on Roy Wilkins.* 1 microfilm reel. U.S. Federal Bureau of Investigation Central Files.

U.S. Federal Bureau of Investigation. *FBI File on the Black Panther Party, North Carolina.* 2 microfilm reels. U.S. Federal Bureau of Investigation Central Files.

U.S. Federal Bureau of Investigation. *FBI File on the KKK Murder of Viola Liuzzo.* 1 microfilm reel. U.S. Federal Bureau of Investigation Central Files.

U.S. Federal Bureau of Investigation. *FBI File on the Moorish Science Temple of America (Noble Drew Ali).* 3 microfilm reels. U.S. Federal Bureau of Investigation Central Files.

U.S. Federal Bureau of Investigation. *FBI File on the Muslim Mosque, Inc.* 3 microfilm reels. U.S. Federal Bureau of Investigation Central Files.

U.S. Federal Bureau of Investigation. *FBI File on the NAACP.* 4 microfilm reels. U.S. Federal Bureau of Investigation Central Files.

U.S. Federal Bureau of Investigation. *FBI File on the National Negro Congress.* 2 microfilm reels. U.S. Federal Bureau of Investigation Central Files.

U.S. Federal Bureau of Investigation. *FBI File on the Organization of Afro-American Unity (OAAU).* 1 microfilm reel. U.S. Federal Bureau of Investigation Central Files.

U.S. Federal Bureau of Investigation. *FBI File on the Reverend Jesse Jackson.* 1 microfilm reel. U.S. Federal Bureau of Investigation Central Files.

U.S. Federal Bureau of Investigation. *FBI File on the Student Nonviolent Coordinating Committee.* 3 microfilm reels. U.S. Federal Bureau of Investigation Central Files.

U.S. Federal Bureau of Investigation. *FBI File on W. E. B. Du Bois.* 1 microfilm reel. U.S. Federal Bureau of Investigation Central Files.

U.S. Federal Bureau of Investigation. *Marcus Garvey: FBI Investigation File.* 1 microfilm reel. U.S. Federal Bureau of Investigation Central Files.

U.S. Federal Bureau of Investigation. *Martin Luther King, Jr.: FBI File.* 25 microfilm reels. Collection of Professor David Garrow. University Publications of America.

U.S. Federal Bureau of Investigation. *Martin Luther King, Jr.: FBI Assassination File.* 25 microfilm reels. U.S. Federal Bureau of Investigation Central Files.

U.S. Federal Bureau of Investigation. Counterintelligence Program. *COINTELPRO: The FBI File.* 1956–1971. 30 microfilm reels. U.S. Federal Bureau of Investigation Central Files.

U.S. President (1963–1969). *Oral Histories of the Johnson Administration, 1963–1969.* Contains transcripts of interviews with leaders active in the civil rights movement and the War on Poverty, including those of Barbara Jordan, Aaron Henry, Thurgood Marshall, A. Philip Randolph, and Andrew Young, Jr. 763 microfiches. Lyndon Baines Johnson Library.

U.S. President's Committee on Civil Rights. *President Truman's Committee on Civil Rights.* 10 microfilm reels. Harry S. Truman Library.

U.S. Women's Bureau. *Records of the Women's Bureau of the Department of Labor, 1918–1965.* Includes documents on the situation of black women in industry and domestic labor. 23 microfilm reels. U.S. National Archives.

Universal Negro Improvement Association. *Records of the Central Division, New York, 1918–1959.* 6 microfilm reels. Schomburg Center for Research in Black Culture, New York Public Library.

University of Oxford. Rhodes House Library. *The Rhodes House Library, Oxford, Anti-Slavery Collection, 1795–1880.* 59 microfilm reels.

War on Poverty, 1964–1968. 16 microfilm reels. Lyndon Baines Johnson Library.

Washington, Booker T., 1856–1915. *Papers, 1864–1960.* 388 microfilm reels. Library of Congress.

Weaver, Robert Clifton. *Papers, 1923–1970.* 5 microfilm reels. Schomburg Center for Research in Black Culture, New York Public Library.

White, Clarence Cameron, 1880–1960. *Papers.* Composer and educator. 10 microfilm reels. Schomburg Center for Research in Black Culture, New York Public Library.

White House Conference "To Fulfill These Rights" (1966: Washington, D.C.). *Records of the White House Conference on Civil Rights, 1965–1966.* 20 microfilm reels. Lyndon Baines Johnson Library.

Williamson, Harry Albro. *Chips from the Quarries, the Harry A. Williamson Collection of Negro Masonry, 1940–1959.* 5 microfilm reels. Schomburg Center for Research in Black Culture, New York Public Library.

Woodson, Carter Godwin, 1875–1950. *The Carter G. Woodson Collection of Negro Papers and Related Documents.* 10 microfilm reels. Library of Congress.

Woodson, Carter Godwin, 1875–1950. *Papers of Carter G. Woodson and the Association for the Study of Negro Life and History, 1915–1950.* 25 microfilm reels. Association for the Study of Afro-American Life and History.

Wright, Richard, 1908–1960. *Richard Wright Collection, 1935–1967.* 2 microfilm reels. Schomburg Center for Research in Black Culture, New York Public Library.

Writers' Program. *Slave Narratives.* 11 microfilm reels. Library of Congress.

Writers' Program. *Slave Narratives: Appraisal Sheets.* 2 microfilm reels. Library of Congress.

Writers' Program (New York). *Negroes of New York, 1936–1941: Research Studies.* 5 microfilm reels. Schomburg Center for Research in Black Culture, New York Public Library.

Xavier University (Louisiana) Library. *The Heartman Manuscript Collection on Slavery.* 7 microfilm reels.

6   Newspapers and Selected Periodicals

James P. Danky

The press, commonly called "the first draft of history," serves as a window to society—a record and almanac that documents the issues and events important to the community it serves. It captures for posterity a community's events and provides a weekly (and occasionally daily) record of news, political debates, literary society programs, athletic accomplishments, club activities, and church meetings in African-American communities. The black press is not a static guide. The editorial page of a newspaper embodies one of the most precious ingredients of American democracy—the First Amendment—as it seeks to explain, guide, and shape public opinion.

The press is an invaluable asset for the history and historiography of the black experience. Through editorial decisions and policies, newspapers synthesize and generate culture even as they document it. Through their reporting, black newspapers have documented facts of African-American history that are often neglected or distorted by the mainstream press, and through their editorial pages, they have fought against injustice and helped shape African-American social movements.

The first African-American newspaper, *Freedom's Journal,* was founded in New York in 1827 by Samuel E. Cornish and John B. Russwurm. Cornish and Russwurm differed in their views on repatriation to Africa, a leading debate in black circles at the time, but they shared a vision of their newspaper as a corrective to the racist coverage of blacks that they saw in other New York papers. They also shared a vision of their paper as a forum for blacks to speak openly to one another and the world about their views on slavery, racism, and other issues that affected their lives as African-Americans. This vision came to be shared by many different black papers in many American cities.

At least forty black papers were published before the Civil War; the most famous was Frederick Douglass's *North Star,* with its staunchly antislavery editorial views. Hundreds of other papers were founded during the 19th century, ranging from small church publications to major urban newspapers such as the *Washington Bee,* Baltimore *Afro-American,* and *Philadelphia Tribune.* The black press also spread beyond its Northeastern roots to include such papers as the Indianapolis *Freeman, Wisconsin Weekly Advocate, Iowa Bystander,* and the Colorado *Statesman.*

The introductory essay of this chapter was adapted from Henry Lewis Suggs's unpublished manuscript "The History and Historiography of the Black Press."

From Douglass on, the black press provided a central platform from which race leaders could speak out. Ida B. Wells used her Memphis paper to denounce lynching, and her press building was destroyed by white supremacists as a result. W. E. B. Du Bois wrote columns for the *New York Globe* (1883–1884), the *New York Freeman* (1884–1885), the *Pittsburgh Courier* (1936–1938), the *Chicago Defender* (1945–1948), and the New York *Amsterdam News* (1944–1949), among others. Herbert Aptheker's *The Complete Works of W. E. B. Du Bois: Newspaper Columns by W. E. B. Du Bois* (1986), Paul G. Partington's *The Rare Periodicals of W. E. B. Du Bois* (1991), and David Levering Lewis's *W. E. B. Du Bois: The Biography of a Race* (1994) together provide excellent access to Du Bois's serial contributions. Booker T. Washington was notorious for his financial and editorial influence over leading papers in several cities, most notably T. Thomas Fortune's New York *Age*.

The papers also provided a useful forum for African-Americans to address international affairs and foreign policy issues. Traditional presses such as the Baltimore *Afro-American, Pittsburgh Courier,* New York *Amsterdam News,* Norfolk *Journal and Guide,* and the *Chicago Defender* used their editorial pages to report, explain, and guide, as well as to direct public opinion on such issues as the Haitian Revolution of 1915, the Liberian forced labor controversy of 1930, and the Italian invasion of Ethiopia in 1935. Correspondents covered in detail the progress of battles and the treatment of black soldiers in World Wars I and II.

The black press played a key role in disseminating information about black cultural and social institutions. Local papers covered the activities of clubs, organizations, and churches, and many of these organizations and churches also published their own journals. The National Association for the Advancement of Colored People's *The Crisis,* the National Urban League's *Opportunity,* and the Universal Negro Improvement Association's *Negro World* are all examples of national publications affiliated with large organizations. The black women's club movement generated several papers, such as the National Association of Colored Women's *Women's Era* and *National Notes,* which are valuable for their documentation of women's activity from the turn of the 20th century. These papers give women's perspectives on domesticity, temperance, education, and social welfare, and they document women's businesses and organizations and the achievements of individual women. Finally, periodicals and papers published by churches, such as the *A.M.E. Church Review, The Christian Recorder* (the oldest black newspaper in America that is still being published), and the National Baptist Convention's *Christian Banner,* published weekly sermons and literary pieces, arbitrated religious and denominational disputes, and functioned as a recorder of churches' efforts in such areas as evangelism, education, and social reform.

Whether produced by a club, a church, or an independent businessperson, all black newspapers share the same specialty: coverage of local and national events that have been often misrepresented or ignored by the mainstream white press. Research on racial violence, voting, civil rights, education, poverty, and social welfare benefits enormously by utilizing black newspapers. Through features and obituaries, the papers document family histories and home, farm, and business ownership, making them also key sources for African-American genealogical research. Through articles, essays, fiction, and advertisements, they chronicle the daily life and culture of their subscribers. Only the black papers announced the marriage of a sharecropper's daughter or the graduation of a Harlem student.

Regional and state libraries, state museums, state archival collections, local historical societies, and the personal papers collections of many editors and contributors are appropriate sites to begin primary research on extant papers, articles, and clipping files. For example, the Schomburg Center for Research in Black Culture of the New York Public Library, the State Historical Society of Wisconsin Library, the Peabody Special Collection in the Huntington Memorial Library at Hampton University, the Tuskegee University Library, the Moorland-Spingarn Research Center at Howard University, the Avery Research Center in Charleston, S.C., the National Afro-American Museum in Wilberforce, Ohio, and the Great Plains Black Museum in Omaha, Neb., house newspapers along with clipping files from the black press.

Since they are organized by subject, the clipping files at the Schomburg Center and at Hampton, Tuskegee, and Howard Universities are particularly useful to researchers, with all but those at Howard available on microfilm or microfiche. The vertical file collection of the Moorland-Spingarn Library at Howard is still in the process of being fully indexed, but it contains clippings and ephemera on a wide variety of black subject matter and provides a particularly rich chronicle of Howard-related materials, especially the accomplishments of its alumni and faculty. The vertical file collection at the Schomburg Center was begun in 1925, although some clippings are older, and includes hundreds of thousands of articles cataloged under 10,000 subject headings. This clipping file includes items from newspapers, as well as typescripts, broadsides, pamphlets, programs, and other ephemera. Contemporary material is preserved in its original form, while older materials are contained on microfiche and microfilm. Another valuable tool associated with the Schomburg is the *Kaiser Index to Black Resources, 1948–1986* (1992). This is an index to serials and other sources created over a lifetime of reference work by the distinguished black bibliographer Ernest Kaiser.

The Hampton University Peabody newspaper clipping file, covering the period 1873–1940, is available on microfiche. The collection catalogs 567 items on 790 microfiches, divided into more than 30 large subject categories such as Business, Education, Health, Labor, Literature, Politics, Professions, Race Problems, Race Progress, Religion, and Voluntary Associations, and then further subdivided within each category. The Tuskegee Institute's news clipping file, covering the period 1899–1960, contains clippings from more than 300 publications, including national and foreign newspapers as well as black newspapers, magazines, religious publications, and special-interest publications. The Tuskegee collection is available on microfilm on 252 reels arranged chronologically by year, then alphabetically by subject within each year. The collection includes an index and provides extraordinary subject access to articles in hundreds of black newspapers no longer extant.

The Miscellaneous Negro Newspapers collection of the Library of Congress has preserved smaller papers on a series of twelve reels, and most of the larger papers are available on separate microfilms. For a detailed listing of the holdings, consult the Library of Congress publication "Negro Newspapers on Microfilm: A Selected

List" (1953). Or the researcher can find a compilation of newspapers in the holdings of the Library of Congress under John Pluge, Jr., comp., *The Black Press* (1991).

More primary materials can be found in the personal papers of W. E. B. Du Bois, Ida B. Wells, and many key publishers, whose papers are located in archival collections and public libraries within their respective cities: Carl Murphy of the Baltimore *Afro-American,* Robert Vann of the *Pittsburgh Courier,* P. B. Young, Sr., of the Norfolk *Journal and Guide,* Chester Franklin of the Kansas City *Call,* Cecil Newman of the *Minneapolis Spokesman,* John McCray of the Columbia, S.C., *Light House and Informer,* Charles Hunter of the Raleigh *Gazette,* and Monroe Trotter of the Boston *Guardian.* Biographies of individual publishers, such as Andrew Buni's *Robert L. Vann of the Pittsburgh Courier: Politics and Black Journalism* (1974) and Henry Lewis Suggs's *P. B. Young, Newspaperman: Race, Politics and Journalism in the New South, 1910–1962* (1988), also contain source information.

Of special importance are the papers of Claude A. Barnett, director of the Associated Negro Press. Barnett's papers, which are housed at the Chicago Historical Society, include press releases sent by the Associated Negro Press to African-American newspapers from 1928 to 1964, press releases sent by the World News Service to African newspapers from 1960 to 1963, and clippings from many black publications. The extensive correspondence in the Barnett Papers is especially rich, since participants in major controversies within the African-American community sought to make certain that ANP press releases reflected "their" side of the issues being contested. Barnett was well aware of the power he wielded, and he exploited this for the benefit of his press service. Barnett was personally interested in the emergence of independent nations in Africa, and the collection is very important for its documentation of African-American perceptions of Africa.

An indispensable guide is *African-American Newspapers and Periodicals: A National Bibliography* (1998), edited by James P. Danky and Maureen E. Hady of the State Historical Society of Wisconsin. This comprehensive list provides full bibliographic citations for more than 6,000 black newspapers and periodicals of all types. They date from 1827 to the present, ranging from scholarly to popular, and including information on editors, frequency of publication, format, price, and publishing organizations. Several indexes to specific papers and periodicals also exist. For example, Donald M. Jacobs's *Antebellum Black Newspapers: Indices to New York's Freedom's Journal (1827–1829), The Rights of All (1829), The Weekly Advocate (1837) and the Colored American (1837–1841)* (1976); Georgetta Merritt Campbell's *Extant Collections of Early Black Newspapers: A Research Guide to the Black Press, 1880–1915, with an Index to the Boston Guardian, 1902–1904* (1981); and the Rose Bibliography Project's *Analytical Guide and Indexes to the Colored American Magazine 1900–1909* (1974) are key tools for researching a topic that may have been covered in one of these publications.

SECONDARY SOURCES

There are a number of important secondary sources on the black press. I. Garland Penn's classic *The Afro-American Press and Its Editors* (1891) has been helpful to researchers on the subject for more than a century. More recently published reference works include Martin Dann's *The Black Press, 1827–1890* (1971); Henry La Brie's *The Black Newspaper in America: A Guide* (1973); Penelope Bullock's *The Afro-American Periodical Press, 1838–1909* (1981); Henry Lewis Suggs's *The Black Press in the South, 1865–1979* (1983) and *The Black Press in the Middle West, 1865–1985* (1996); Frankie Hutton's *The Early Black Press in America, 1827–1860* (1993); and Barbara K. Henritze's *Bibliographic Checklist of African-American Newspapers* (1995).

The following list provides both specialized and general sources for conducting research on black serials.

Alexander, Ann Field, "Between Two Worlds: John Mitchell's Richmond Childhood," *Virginia Cavalcade* 40:3 (1991): 120–31.

Anderson, Charles E., "Blacks in the New York News Community," *Harvard Journal of Afro-American Affairs* 2:2 (1971): 52–73.

Anderson, Talmadge, "An Ideological Treatise on Black Publications and Black Writers: The Evolvement of the *Western Journal of Black Studies,*" *Serials Librarian* 9:1 (1984): 7–15.

Bayton, James A., and Ernestine Bell, "An Exploratory Study of the Role of the Negro Press," *Journal of Negro Education* (Dec. 1951): 8–15.

Beard, Richard L., and Cyril E. Zoerner II, "Associated Negro Press: Its Founding, Ascendancy and Demise," *Journalism Quarterly* (Mar. 1969): 47–52.

Berkman, Dave, "Advertising in *Ebony* and *Life:* Negro Aspirations vs. Reality," *Journalism Quarterly* (Dec. 1963): 53–64.

Bernardi, Gayle K., and Thomas W. Segady, "The Development of African-American Newspapers in the American West: A Sociohistorical Perspective," *Journal of Negro History* 75:3–4 (1990): 96–111.

"Black Publishers Today," *Harvard Journal of Afro-American Affairs* 2:2 (1971): 46–51.

Brooks, Maxwell R., *The Negro Press Re-examined: Political Content of Leading Negro Newspapers* (1959).

Browne, Robert S., "The Origin, Birth and Adolescence of the *Review of Black Political Economy* and the Black Economic Research Center," *Review of Black Political Economy* 21:3 (1993): 9–23.

Brundage, Fitzhugh, "'To Howl Loudly': John Mitchell, Jr. and His Campaign against Lynching in Virginia," *Canadian Review of American Studies* 22:3 (1991): 325–41.

Bryan, Carter R., *Negro Journalism in America before Emancipation* (1969).

Bullock, Penelope, *The Afro-American Periodical Press, 1838–1909* (1981).

Buni, Andrew, *Robert L. Vann of the Pittsburgh Courier: Politics and Black Journalism* (1974).

Campbell, Georgetta Merritt, *Extant Collections of Early Black Newspapers: A Research Guide to the Black Press, 1880–1915, with an Index to the Boston Guardian, 1902–1904* (1981).

Connor, William P., "Reconstruction Rebels: *The New Orleans Tribune* in Post-War Louisiana," *Louisiana History* 21:2 (1980): 159–81.

Cooper, Arnold, "'Protection to All, Discrimination to None': *The Parsons Weekly Blade,* 1892–1900," *Kansas History* (1986): 58–71.

Cornish, Lori, "Samuel Cornish: Co-founder of the Nation's First Black Newspaper," *Media History* 7:1 (Mar. 1987): 25–28.

Dann, Martin E., ed., *The Black Press, 1827–1890: The Quest for National Identity* (1971).

Davis, Henry Vance, *The Black Press: From Mission to Commercialism, 1827–1927* (1990).

Davis, Thomas J., "Three Dark Centuries around Albany: A Survey of Black Life in New York's Capital City Area before World War I," *Afro-Americans in New York Life and History* 7:1 (1983): 7–23.

Detweiler, Frederick German, *The Negro Press in the United States* (1922).

——— "The Negro Press Today," *American Journal of Sociology* (Nov. 1938): 391–400.

Douglas, Thomas E., *Horace Roscoe Clayton* (1989).

Du Bois, W. E. B., "The American Negro Press," *Negro Digest* (Apr. 1943): 33–36.

————— "Editing *The Crisis*," *The Crisis* (Mar. 1951): 147–51.

Ellis, Mark, "America's Black Press, 1914–18," *History Today* 41 (Sept. 1991): 20–27.

Finkle, Lee, *Forum for Protest: The Black Press during World War II* (1975).

Fishel, Leslie H., Jr., "Carte de Visite: T. Thomas Fortune, Race Leader," *Hayes Historical Journal* 7:2 (1988): 58–60.

Fleener, Nickieann, "'Breaking down Buyer Resistance': Marketing the 1935 *Pittsburgh Courier* to Mississippi Blacks," *Journalism History* 13:3–4 (1986): 78–85.

Fox, Stephen R., *The Guardian of Boston: William Monroe Trotter* (1970).

Franklin, V. P., "'Voice of the Black Community': The *Philadelphia Tribune*, 1912–1941," *Pennsylvania History* 51:4 (1984): 261–84.

————— "W. E. B. Du Bois as Journalist," *Journal of Negro Education* 56:2 (1987): 240–44.

Frazier, E. Franklin, *The Black Bourgeoisie: The Rise of a Middle Class in the United States* (1957).

Fultz, Michael, "'The Morning Cometh': African-American Periodicals, Education, and the Black Middle Class, 1900–1930," in James P. Danky and Wayne A. Wiegand, ed., *Print Culture in a Diverse America* (1998).

Gavins, Raymond, *The Perils and Prospects of Southern Black Leadership: Gordon Blaine Hancock, 1884–1970* (1977).

Gibbons, R. Arnold, and Dana R. Ulloth, "The Role of the *Amsterdam News* in New York City's Media Environment," *Journalism Quarterly* 59:3 (1982): 451–55.

Gordon, Eugene, "The Negro Press," *American Mercury* (June 1926): 207–15.

Gordon-Lyles, Dianne, "Early Black Religious Press: *Christian Recorder*," *Media History Digest* 9:1 (1989): 53–59.

Gorham, Thelma Thurston, *The Negro Press: Past, Present, and Future: A Documentary Research Report 1827–1967* (1968).

Grossman, Charles R., "Blowing the Trumpet: The *Chicago Defender* and Black Migration during World War I," *Illinois Historical Journal* 78:2 (1985): 82–96.

Hatchett, David, "The Black Press," *The Crisis* 94:1 (1987): 14–19.

Hellwig, David J., "The Afro-American Press and United States Involvement in Cuba, 1902–1912," *Mid-America* 72:2 (1990): 135–45.

————— "The Afro-American Press and Woodrow Wilson's Mexican Policy, 1913–1917," *Phylon* 48:4 (1987): 261–70.

Henritze, Barbara K., *Bibliographic Checklist of African-American Newspapers* (1995).

Hill, George H., ed., "Robert Abbott: Defender of the Black Press," *Bulletin of Bibliography* 42:2 (1985): 53–55.

Hill, Roy L., *Who's Who in the American Negro Press* (1960).

Hogan, Lawrence D., *A Black National News Service: Claude Barnett, the Associated Negro Press and Afro-American Newspapers, 1919–1945* (1984).

Honey, Michael, "One View of Black Life in the South during the 'Nadir': The *Richmond Planet*, 1885–1900," *Potomac Review* 21 (1981): 28–38.

Howard-Pitney, David, "Calvin Chase's *Washington Bee* and Black Middle-Class Ideology," *Journalism Quarterly* 63:1 (1986): 89–97.

Humrich, Shauna L., "Ida B. Wells-Barnett: The Making of a Public Reputation," *Purview Southwest* (1989): 1–20.

Hutton, Frankie, *The Early Black Press in America, 1827 to 1860* (1993).

Johnson, Ben, and Mary Ballard-Johnson, *Who's What and Where* (1985).

Johnson, Violet, "Pan-Africanism in Print: The *Boston Chronicle* and the Struggle for Black Liberation and Advancement, 1930–50," in James P. Danky and Wayne A. Wiegand, ed., *Print Culture in a Diverse America* (1998).

Jones, Allen W., "Voice for Improving Rural Life: Alabama's Black Agricultural Press," *Agricultural History* 58:3 (1984): 209–20.

Jones, Lester M., "The Editorial Policy of Negro Newspapers of 1917–1918 as Compared with That of 1941–1942," *Journal of Negro History* (Jan. 1944): 24–31.

Jones, Wendell Primus, *The Negro Press and the Higher Education of Negroes, 1933–1952: A Study of News and Opinion on Higher Education in the Three Leading Negro Newspapers* (1954).

Kerlin, Robert T., *The Voice of the Negro* (1920).

King, William, "'Our Men in Vietnam': Black Media as a Source of the Afro-American Experience in Southeast Asia," *Vietnam Generation* 1:2 (1989): 94–117.

Klassen, Teresa C., and Owen V. Johnson, "Sharpening of the Blade: Black Consciousness in Kansas, 1892–1897," *Journalism Quarterly* 63:2 (1986): 298–304.

Kobre, Sidney, and Reva H., *A Gallery of Leading Black Journalists Who Advanced Their Race and Our Nation* (1993).

Kountze, Mabe, *A History of the Early Colored Press in Massachusetts and a Second Sketch of the Boston Guardian Weekly* (1967).

Krieling, Albert, "The Rise of the Black Press in Chicago," *Journalism History* 4:4 (Dec. 1977): 132–36, 156.

La Brie, Henry G., *The Black Press: A Bibliography* (1973).

——— *A Profile of the Black Newspaper: Old Guard Black Journalists Reflect on the Past, Present, and Future* (1973).

——— *A Survey of Black Newspapers* (1979).

La Brie, Henry G., ed., *Perspectives of the Black Press, 1974* (1974).

La Brie, Henry III, and William J. Zima, "Directional Quandaries of the Black Press in the United States," *Journalism Quarterly* 48:4 (Dec. 1971): 640–44, 651.

Loupe, Diane E., "Storming and Defending the Color Barrier at the University of Missouri School of Journalism: The Lucile Bluford Case," *Journalism History* 16:1–2 (1989): 20–31.

Marks, Carole, "Lines of Communication, Recruitment Mechanisms, and the Great Migration of 1916–1918," *Social Problems* 31:1 (1983): 73–83.

Marks, George P., comp. and ed., *The Black Press Views American Imperialism (1898–1900)* (1971).

Mathews, Basil, *Booker T. Washington: Educator and Interracial Interpreter* (1948).

Matthews, John M., "Black Newspapermen and the Black Community in Georgia, 1890–1930," *Georgia History Quarterly* 68:3 (1984): 356–81.

Matthews, Victoria Earle, "The Value of Race Literature," *Massachusetts Review* 27:2 (1986): 169–91.

McCall, Nathan, *Makes Me Wanna Holler: A Young Black Man in America* (1994).

McMillen, Neil R., "Black Journalism in Mississippi: The Jim Crow Years," *Journal of Mississippi History* 49:2 (1987): 129–38.

Meier, August, *Booker T. Washington and the Negro Press: With Special Reference to the Colored American Magazine* (1953?).

Myrdal, Gunnar, *An American Dilemma: The Negro Problem and Modern Democracy* (1944).

Neal, Diane, "Seduction, Accommodation, or Realism? Tabs Gross and the *Arkansas Freeman*," *Arkansas Historical Quarterly* 48:1 (1989): 57–64.

Nordin, Kenneth D., "In Search of Black Unity: An Interpretation of the Content and Function of *Freedom's Journal*," *Journalism History* 4:4 (Dec. 1977): 123–28.

Oak, Vishnu V., *The Negro Newspaper* (1948).

O'Kelly, Charlotte G., "Black Newspapers and the Black Protest Movement," *Phylon* 43:1 (1982): 1–14.

——— "The Black Press: Conservative or Radical, Reformist or Revolutionary?" *Journalism History* 4:4 (Dec. 1977): 114–16.

Painter, Nell, "Black Journalism: The First Hundred Years," *Harvard Journal of Afro-American Affairs* 2:2: 30–42.

Paz, D. G., "John Albert Williams and Black Journalism in Omaha," *Midwest Review* 10 (1988): 14–32.

Penn, I. Garland, *The Afro-American Press and Its Editors* (1891).

Perry, Clay, "John P. Mitchell, Virginia's Journalist of Reform," *Journalism History* 4:4 (1977): 142–56.

Potter, Vilma Raskin, *A Reference Guide of Afro-American Publications and Editors: 1827–1946* (1993).

Prattis, P. L., "Racial Segregation and Negro Journalism," *Phylon* 8:4 (1947): 305–14.

Pride, Armistead Scott, *The Black Press: A Bibliography* (1968).

———— "Rights of All: Second Step in Development of Black Journalism," *Journalism History* 4:4 (1977): 129–31.

Pride, Armistead Scott, and Clint C. Wilson II, *A History of the Black Press* (1997).

Samuels, Wilfred D., "Hubert H. Harrison and 'The New Negro Manhood Movement,'" *Afro-Americans in New York Life and History* 5:1 (1981): 29–41.

Schneider, Richard C., comp., *African American History in the Press, 1851–1899: From the Coming of the Civil War to the Rise of Jim Crow as Reported and Illustrated in Selected Newspapers of the Time* (1996).

Schuyler, George Samuel, *Our Press a Flaming Sword in Fight for Race Progress: Its Unifying Role Brought Negroes Closer Together* (1950).

Sentman, Mary Alice, and Patrick S. Washburn, "How Excess Profits Tax Brought Ads to Black Newspapers in World War II," *Journalism Quarterly* 64:4 (1987): 769–74, 867.

Smith, C. Calvin, "From 'Separate but Equal to Desegregation': The Changing Philosophy of L. C. Bates," *Arkansas Historical Quarterly* 42:3 (1983): 254–70.

Smoot, James S., "The Negro Press: Voice for Civil Rights," *Freedomways* (Mar. 1963): 202–14.

Snorgrass, J. William, "The Black Press in the San Francisco Bay Area, 1856–1900," *California History* 60:4 (1981): 306–17.

Stevens, Charles, "J. A. (Billboard) Jackson and the News: Pioneer in Black Musical Entertainment and Journalism," *The Western Journal of Black Studies* 16:1 (1992): 30.

Stevens, John D., "The Black Press Looks at 1920's Journalism," *Journalism History* 7:3–4 (1980): 109–13.

———— "From the Back of the Foxhole: Black Correspondents in World War II," *Journalism Monographs* 27 (Feb. 1973): 61.

Stevens, Summer E., and Owen V. Johnson, "From Black Politics to Black Community: Harry C. Smith and the Cleveland Gazette," *Journalism Quarterly* 67:4 (1990): 1090–1102.

Stovall, Mary E., "The *Chicago Defender* in the Progressive Era," *Illinois Historical Journal* 83:3 (1990): 159–72.

Streator, George, "Working on 'The Crisis,'" *The Crisis* (Mar. 1951): 158–61.

Streitmatter, Rodger, "African-American Women Journalists and Their Male Editors: A Tradition of Support," *Journalism Quarterly* 70:2 (1993): 276.

———— "No Taste for Fluff: Ethel L. Payne, African-American Journalist," *Journalism Quarterly* 68:3 (1991): 528–40.

Streitmatter, Rodger, and Barbara Diggs-Brown, "Marvel Cooke: An African-American Woman Journalist Who Agitated for Social Reform," *Afro-American in New York Life and History* 16:2 (1992): 47–68.

Strother, T. Ella, "The Black Image in the *Chicago Defender*, 1905–1975," *Journalism History* 4:4 (1977): 137–56.

Suggs, Henry Lewis, *P. B. Young, Newspaperman: Race, Politics, and Journalism in the New South, 1910–1962* (1988).

———— "The Response of the African-American Press to the United States Occupation of Haiti, 1915–1934," *Journal of Negro History* 73.1–4 (1988): 33–45.

Suggs, Henry Lewis, ed., *The Black Press in the Middle West, 1865–1985* (1996).

———— *The Black Press in the South, 1865–1979* (1983).

Sullins, William S., and Paul Parsons, "Roscoe Dunjee: Crusading Editor of Oklahoma's *Black Dispatch*, 1915–1955," *Journalism Quarterly* 69:1 (1992): 204–13.

Thompson, Julius E., *The Black Press in Mississippi, 1865–1985* (1993).

Thornbrough, Emma Lou, "American Negro Newspapers, 1880–1914," *Business History Review* 40 (1966): 467–90.

——— *T. Thomas Fortune: Militant Journalist* (1972).

Tinney, James S., and Justine J. Rector, ed., *Issues and Trends in Afro-American Journalism* (1980).

Tripp, Bernell, *Origins of the Black Press: New York, 1827–1847* (1992).

——— *The Search for Unity: The Importance of the Black Press in the Emigration/Colonization Issues of the 1880's* (1992).

Vaughn-Roberson, Courtney, and Brenda Hill, "*The Brownies' Book* and *Ebony Jr.!* Literature as a Mirror of the Afro-American Experience," *Journal of Negro Education* 58:4 (1989): 494–510.

Ward, Jerry, "Southern Black Aesthetics: The Case of *Nkombo Magazine*," *Mississippi Quarterly* 44:2 (1991): 143–50.

Washburn, Patrick S., "J. Edgar Hoover and the Black Press in World War II," *Journalism History* 13:1 (1986): 26–33.

Weaver, Bill, and Oscar C. Page, "The Black Press and the Drive for Integrated Graduate and Professional Schools," *Phylon* 43:1 (1982): 15–28.

Williams, James D., "Is the Black Press Needed?" *Civil Rights Digest* (Dec. 1970): 8–15.

Williams, Nudie, "The Black Press in Oklahoma: The Formative Years, 1889–1907," *Chronicles of Oklahoma* 61:3 (1983): 309–19.

Wolseley, Roland Edgar, *The Black Press, U.S.A.* (1990).

NEWSPAPERS AND SELECTED PERIODICALS

The following list represents the most important serials published during their respective time periods and should be read with the accompanying key:

?   Publishing dates are uncertain.
*   Title published beyond specific time frame.
**   Title repeated from previous time frame(s). For a full publication history of these serials, consult James P. Danky and Maureen E. Hady, ed., *African-American Newspapers and Periodicals: A National Bibliography* (1998).
mf   Available on microfilm.

1827–1877

The Aliened American (Cleveland, Ohio) 1852–1854 mf

The Anglo-African Magazine (New York) 1859–1865 mf

The Christian Index (Memphis, Tenn.) 1867–present* mf

The Christian Recorder (Philadelphia) 1852–present* mf (Variant titles: *A.M.E. Christian Recorder, Christian Recorder of the African Methodist Episcopal Church;* also published in Nashville, Tenn.)

The Colored American (Augusta, Ga.) 1865–1866 mf

The Colored American (New York) 1837–1842 mf

The Colored Citizen (Cincinnati, Ohio) 1863–1869 mf

The Elevator (San Francisco) 1865–1904* mf

Frederick Douglass' Paper (Rochester, N.Y.) 1851–1860 mf

Freedom's Journal (New York) 1827–1829 mf

The Genius of Freedom (New York) 1845–1847

Le Union: Journal Politique, Litteraire et Progressiste (New Orleans) 1862–1864 mf

The Loyal Georgian (Augusta, Ga.) 1867–1867 mf (Variant title: *Weekly Loyal Georgian*)

Maryville Republican (Maryville, Tenn.) 1867–1878* mf

Mirror of the Times (San Francisco) 1857–1862 mf

Missionary Record (Charleston, S.C.) 1868–1879* mf

The Mystery (Pittsburgh, Pa.) 1843–1847

New National Era and Citizen (Washington, D.C.) 1870–1874 mf (Variant titles: *New Era, New National Era*)

New Orleans Tribune (New Orleans, La.) 1864–1870? mf (Variant titles: *La Tribune de la Nouvelle-Orleans*)

Pacific Appeal (San Francisco) 1862–1880* mf

The People's Advocate (Washington, D.C.) 1876–1880* mf

The Ram's Horn (New York) 1847–1848 mf

Rights of All (New York) 1829–1830 mf

Savannah Tribune (Savannah, Ga.) 1875–present* mf (Variant title: *Colored Tribune*, 1875–1876)

Southern Workman (Hampton, Va.) 1872–1910* mf (Variant title: *Southern Workman and Hampton School Record*, 1885–1900)

Southwestern Christian Advocate (Philadelphia) 1866–1909* mf (Variant title: *Southwestern Advocate*, 1866–1876)

The Virginia Star (Richmond, Va.) 1877–1888* mf

Weekly Louisianian (New Orleans, La.) 1870–1882* mf (Variant title: *Louisianian*, 1870–1871)

1878–1915

A.M.E. Church Review (Philadelphia) 1884–present* mf (Also published in Nashville, 1919–1972, and in Atlanta, 1972–1984)

Advance (Wilmington, Del.) 1889–1901 mf

Afro-American (Baltimore) 1892–present* mf

Afro-American Presbyterian (Charlotte, N.C.) 1879–1939* mf

Alexander's Magazine (Boston) 1904–1909 mf (Variant title: *Alexander's Magazine and the National Domestic*)

The Appeal (St. Paul, Minn.) 1885–1923* mf (Variant title: *Western Appeal*)

Atlanta Independent (Atlanta) 1903–1928* mf

Baptist Vanguard (Little Rock, Ark.) 1894–1981* mf

The Black Dispatch (Oklahoma City, Okla.) 1915–1982* mf

Boley Progress (Muskogee, Okla.) 1905–1926 mf (Variant title: *Weekly Progress*)

The Boston Advance (Boston) 1896–1907 mf

Boston Chronicle (Boston) 1915–1966?* mf

Broad Ax (Chicago) 1895–1927?* mf (Also published in Salt Lake City, Utah, 1895–1899)

California Eagle (Los Angeles) 1879–1966* mf

Chicago Defender (Chicago) 1905–present* mf (Variant title: *Chicago Daily Defender*)

The Christian Index (Memphis, Tenn.) 1867–present ** mf

The Christian Recorder (Philadelphia) 1852–present** mf (Variant titles: *A.M.E. Christian Recorder, Christian Recorder of the African Methodist Episcopal Church;* also published in Nashville, Tenn.)

Christian Review (Philadelphia) 1913–1952* mf

The Church Advocate (Baltimore) 1892–1923*

Cleveland Gazette (Cleveland, Ohio) 1883–1945* mf (Variant title: *Gazette*)

Colorado Statesman (Denver, Colo.) 1895–1961* mf

Colored American (Washington, D.C.) 1893–1904 mf

Colored American Magazine (New York) 1900–1909 mf (Also published in Boston, 1900–1904)

The Conservator (Chicago) 1878–1912 mf

The Crisis (Baltimore) 1910–present* mf

Dayton Forum (Dayton, Ohio) 1913–1949* mf (Variant title: *The Forum*)

The Defender (Philadelphia) 1897–1909? mf

Denver Star (Denver, Colo.) 1913–1963* mf

The Detroit Informer (Detroit) 1897–1916* mf

The Elevator (San Francisco) 1865–1904** mf

Florida Sentinel (Pensacola, Fla.) 1887–1918* mf

Gary Sun (Gary, Ind.) 1905–1929* mf (Variant title: *National Defender and Sun*)

The Guardian (Boston) 1901–1960?*

Horizon (Washington, D.C.) 1907–1910 mf

Howard's Negro American Magazine (Harrisburg, Pa.) 1889–? (Variant title: *Howard's Negro American Monthly Magazine*)

Huntsville Gazette (Huntsville, Ala.) 1879–1894 mf (Variant title: *Weekly Gazette*)

Indianapolis Recorder (Indianapolis, Ind.) 1897–present* mf (Variant title: *Recorder*)

Indianapolis World (Indianapolis, Ind.) 1883?–1932* mf

Iowa Bystander (Des Moines, Iowa) 1894–1986* mf (Variant titles: *Iowa State Bystander,* 1894–1896; *Bystander,* 1916–1922; *New Iowa Bystander,* 1972–1986)

Journal and Guide (Norfolk, Va.) 1901–present* mf (Variant titles: *Norfolk Journal and Guide,* 1922–1973; *New Journal and Guide,* 1975–1977)

Kansas City Advocate (Kansas City, Kans.) 1914–1926 (Variant titles: *Kansas City Independent, Kansas City Advocate and Independent*)

The Langston City Herald (Langston City, Okla.) 1891–1902 mf

The Lexington Standard (Lexington, Ky.) 1892–1912 mf

Liberia (Washington, D.C.) 1892–1909 mf

The Light (Vicksburg, Miss.) 1891–1922* mf (Variant title: *Vicksburg Light*)

Maryville Republican (Maryville, Tenn.) 1867–1878** mf

McDowell Times (Keystone, W.V.) 1904–1941* mf

Missionary Record (Charleston, S.C.) 1868–1879** mf

Missionary Seer (New York) 1900–present* mf

The Mulhall Enterprise (Mulhall, Okla.) 1894–1911 mf

Muskogee Cimeter (Muskogee, Okla.) 1899–1930* mf

National Baptist Union Review (Nashville, Tenn.) 1899?–present* mf (Variant titles: *National Baptist Union, National Baptist Review*)

Negro Star (Wichita, Kans.) 1908–1953* mf

Negro World (St. Paul, Minn.) 1892–? mf (Also published in Minneapolis)

New Age Dispatch (Los Angeles) 1907–1949* mf (Variant title: *New Age*)

New Jersey Trumpet (Newark, N.J.) 1887–1953* mf

Oakland Sunshine (Oakland, Calif.) 1897–1922* mf

Pacific Appeal (San Francisco) 1862–1880** mf

The Parsons Weekly Blade (Parson, Kans.) 1892–1901 mf (Variant titles: *Parsons Blade, Blade*)

The People's Advocate (Washington, D.C.) 1876–1880** mf

The People's Elevator (Independence, Kans.) 1892–1931* mf (Variant title: *Oklahoma Guide,* 1892–1922)

People's Recorder (Columbia, S.C.) 1893–1905 mf

Philadelphia Tribune (Philadelphia) 1884–present* mf

The Pioneer Press (Martinsburg, W.V.) 1882–1918* mf

Pittsburgh Courier (Pittsburgh, Pa.) 1910–present* (Variant titles: *Courier, Pittsburgh New Courier*)

The Portland New Age (Portland, Ore.) 1896–1907 mf

Richmond Planet (Richmond, Va.) 1883–1945* mf

The Rising Son (Kansas City, Mo.) 1896–1918* mf

The Rock Hill Messenger (Rock Hill, S.C.) 1896–1919* mf

St. Louis Argus (St. Louis, Mo.) 1912–present* mf

San Francisco Vindicator (San Francisco) 1884–1900 mf

Savannah Tribune (Savannah, Ga.) 1875–present** mf (Variant title: *Colored Tribune,* 1875–1876)

The Seattle Republican (Seattle, Wash.) 1894–1915 mf
The Sedalia Times (Sedalia, Mo.) 1893–1905 mf
Southern Republican (New Orleans, La.) 1898–1907 mf
Southern Workman (Hampton, Va.) 1872–1910** mf (Variant title: *Southern Workman and
    Hampton School Record*, 1885–1900)
Southwestern Christian Advocate (Philadelphia) 1866–1929** mf (Variant title: *Southwestern
    Advocate*, 1866–1876)
The State Capitol (Springfield, Ill.) 1886–1910 mf
The Union (Cincinnati, Ohio) 1907–1952* mf
The Virginia Star (Richmond, Va.) 1877–1888** mf
Voice of Missions (New York) 1893–present* mf
Voice of the Negro (Atlanta) 1904–1907 mf
Washington Bee (Washington, D.C.) 1882–1922* mf (Variant title: *The Bee*, 1882–1884)
Weekly Louisianian (New Orleans, La.) 1870–1882** mf (Variant title: *Louisianian*, 1870–1871)
Western Outlook (San Francisco) 1894–1928* mf
Wichita Searchlight (Wichita, Kans.) 1900–1912 mf (Variant title: *The Searchlight*)
Wisconsin Weekly Advocate (Milwaukee) 1893–1915 mf
Woman's Era (Boston) 1894–1897 mf

1916–1945

Abbott's Monthly (Chicago) 1930–1933
Africo-American Presbyterian (Charlotte, N.C.) 1879–1939** mf
Afro-American (Baltimore) 1892–present** mf
Age (New York) 1887–1953** mf
A.M.E. Church Review (Philadelphia) 1884–1919** mf (Also published in Nashville, 1919–
    1972, and in Atlanta, 1972–1984)
American Unity: A Monthly Education Guide (New York) 1942–1961*
Amsterdam News (New York) 1943–present* mf
The Appeal (St. Paul, Minn.) 1885–1923** mf (Variant title: *Western Appeal*)
Arkansas Survey (Little Rock, Ark.) 1923–1935 mf
Atlanta Independent (Atlanta) 1903–1928** mf
Atlanta World (Atlanta) 1928–present (Variant title: *Atlanta Daily World*)
Baptist Vanguard (Little Rock, Ark.) 1894–1981** mf
The Black Dispatch (Oklahoma City, Okla.) 1915–1982** mf
Black Secrets (New York) 1936–present* (Variant title: *Secrets*)
Black World (Chicago) 1942–1976* (Variant title: *Negro Digest*, 1942–1970)
Boley Progress (Muskogee, Okla.) 1905–1926** mf (Variant title: *Weekly Progress*)
Boston Chronicle (Boston) 1915–1960?** mf
Broad Ax (Chicago) 1895–1927?** mf (Also published in Salt Lake City, Utah, 1895–1899)
The Brown American (Philadelphia) 1936–1945 mf
California Eagle (Los Angeles) 1879–1966** mf
California Voice (San Francisco) 1919–present* mf
Cayton's Monthly (Seattle, Wash.) 1916–1921 mf (Variant title: *Cayton's Weekly*)
Chicago Defender (Chicago) 1905–present** mf (Variant title: *Chicago Daily Defender*)
The Christian Index (Memphis, Tenn.) 1867–present** mf
The Christian Recorder (Philadelphia) 1852–present** mf (Variant titles: *A.M.E. Christian Re-
    corder, Christian Recorder of the African Methodist Episcopal Church;* also published in
    Nashville, Tenn.)
Christian Review (Philadelphia) 1913–1952** mf
The Church Advocate (Baltimore) 1892–1923**
Cleveland Call and Post (Cleveland, Ohio) 1919–present* (Variant title: *Call and Post*)
Cleveland Gazette (Cleveland, Ohio) 1883–1945** mf (Variant title: *Gazette*)

Colorado Statesman (Denver, Colo.) 1895–1961** mf

Commonwealth (Gary, Ind.) 1924–1934 mf

The Crisis (Baltimore) 1910–present** mf

Dayton Forum (Dayton, Ohio) 1913–1949** mf

Denver Star (Denver, Colo.) 1913–1963** mf

The Detroit Informer (Detroit) 1897–1916** mf

Detroit Tribune (Detroit) 1922–1966* mf (Variant titles: *Tribune Independent, New Tribune*)

Ebony (Chicago) 1945–present*

The Evening Whirl (St. Louis) 1938–present* mf (Variant title: *St. Louis Whirl-Examiner,* 1991–
    1993)

Florida Sentinel (Pensacola, Fla.) 1887–1918** mf

Gary American (Gary, Ind.) 1927–present* mf (Variant title: *Gary Colored American*)

Gary Sun (Gary, Ind.) 1905–1929** mf (Variant title: *National Defender and Sun*)

The Guardian (Boston) 1901–1960?**

Half Century Magazine: A Colored Magazine for the Home and the Homemaker (Chicago)
    1916–1925 mf

Houston Defender (Houston, Tex.) 1930–present* mf

Indianapolis Recorder (Indianapolis, Ind.) 1897–present** mf (Variant title: *Recorder*)

Indianapolis World (Indianapolis, Ind.) 1883?–1932** mf

Informer and Texas Freeman (Houston, Tex.) 1919–1973?* mf (Variant titles: *Houston Informer
    and the Texas Freeman,* 1930–1934; *Informer,* 1934–1941)

Inglewood Hawthorne Wave (Los Angeles) 1918–1981*

Iowa Bystander (Des Moines, Iowa) 1894–1980** mf (Variant titles: *Iowa State Bystander,*
    1894–1896; *Bystander,* 1916–1922; *New Iowa Bystander,* 1972–1986)

Journal of Negro History (Washington, D.C.) 1916–present* mf

Kansas City Advocate (Kansas City, Kans.) 1914–1926** mf (Variant titles: *Kansas City Inde-
    pendent, Kansas City Advocate and Independent*)

The Liberator (New York) 1929–1932 mf (Variant title: *Negro Champion*)

The Light (Vicksburg, Miss.) 1891–1922** mf (Variant title: *Vicksburg Light*)

Los Angeles Sentinel (Los Angeles) 1934–present* mf

Louisiana Weekly (New Orleans, La.) 1925–present* mf (Variant title: *New Orleans Herald,*
    1925)

Louisville Leader (Louisville, Ky.) 1917–1950* mf

McDowell Times (Keystone, W.V.) 1904–1941** mf

Messenger: New Opinion of the Negro (New York) 1917–1928 mf

The Miami Times (Miami, Fla.) 1923–present** mf

Missionary Lutheran (St. Louis, Mo.) 1923–1961*

Missionary Seer (New York) 1900–present** mf

The Morehouse Journal of Science (Atlanta) 1926–1945

Muskogee Cimeter (Muskogee, Okla.) 1899–1930** mf

NAACP Bulletin (New York) 1940–1949?* mf

National Baptist Union Review (Nashville, Tenn.) 1899?–present** mf (Variant titles: *National
    Baptist Union, National Baptist Review*)

National Bar Journal (St. Louis, Mo.) 1941–1951*

The National Medical News (New York) 1924–1941? (Variant title: *Howard Medical News*)

National Negro Health News (Washington, D.C.) 1933–1950* mf

The Negro Churchman (New York) 1923–1931

The Negro College Quarterly (Wilberforce, Ohio) 1943–1947* mf

Negro Digest (New York) 1940–1940 (Variant title: *Negro World Digest*)

Negro History Bulletin (Washington, D.C.) 1937–present* mf

The Negro Quarterly: A Review of Negro Life and Culture (New York) 1942–1943 mf

Negro Star (Wichita, Kans.) 1908–1953** mf

The Negro World (New York) 1917–1933 mf

The New Advance (Charlotte, N.C.) 1938–1948*

New Age Dispatch (Los Angeles) 1907–1949** mf (Variant title: *New Age*)

New Day (Philadelphia) 1936–present* mf

New Jersey Herald News (Newark, N.J.) 1938–1966*

Oakland Sunshine (Oakland, Calif.) 1897–1922** mf

The Ohio State News (Columbus, Ohio) 1935–1952* mf

Opportunity: Journal of Negro Life (New York) 1923–1949* mf

The People's Elevator (Independence, Kans.) 1892–1931** mf (Variant title: *Oklahoma Guide,* 1892–1922)

The People's Voice (New York) 1942–1948* mf

Philadelphia Tribune (Philadelphia) 1884–present** mf

The Pilot (Kansas City, Mo.) 1927–1939? mf (Variant titles: *Urban League Pilot, Pilot of the Urban League*)

The Pioneer Press (Martinsburg, W.V.) 1882–1918** mf

Pittsburgh Courier (Pittsburgh, Pa.) 1910–present** (Variant titles: *Courier, Pittsburgh New Courier*)

Quarterly Review of Higher Education among Negroes (Charlotte, N.C.) 1933–1969* mf

Race (New York) 1935–1936

Richmond Planet (Richmond, Va.) 1883–1945** mf

The Rising Son (Kansas City, Mo.) 1896–1918** mf

The Rock Hill Messenger (Rock Hill, S.C.) 1896–1919** mf

The Rural Messenger (Tuskegee, Ala.) 1924–1936

St. Louis American (St. Louis, Mo.) 1927–present*

St. Louis Argus (St. Louis, Mo.) 1912–present** mf

Saint Paul Sun (St. Paul, Minn.) 1941–1976* mf

Savannah Tribune (Savannah, Ga.) 1875–present** mf (Variant title: *Colored Tribune,* 1875–1876)

The Sepia Socialite (New Orleans, La.) 1937–1945

Southwestern Christian Advocate (Philadelphia) 1866–1929** mf (Variant title: *Southwestern Advocate,* 1866–1876)

Twin-City Herald (Minneapolis, Minn.) 1927–1940 mf

The Union (Cincinnati, Ohio) 1907–1952** mf

Voice of Missions (New York) 1893–present** mf

The Waco Messenger (Waco, Tex.) 1929–present mf

Washington Bee (Washington, D.C.) 1882–1922** mf (Variant title: *The Bee,* 1882–1884)

Washington Tribune (Washington, D.C.) 1921–1946* mf

Western Outlook (San Francisco) 1894–1928** mf (Also published in Oakland, Calif.)

Wisconsin Enterprise-Blade (Milwaukee, Wis.) 1916–1943? mf (Variant title: *Wisconsin Weekly Blade*)

1946–present

About . . . Time (Rochester, N.Y.) 1972–

Africa Speaks: The Voice of the Colored Man in Canada (Toronto, Ontario) 1950–1975

African American Review (Terre Haute, Ind.) 1967–present mf (Variant titles: *Negro American Literature Forum, Black American Literature Forum*)

Afro-American (Baltimore) 1892–present** mf

Age (New York) 1887–1953** mf

Alabama Tribune (Montgomery, Ala.) 1951–1964? mf

AME Church Review (Philadelphia) 1884–present** mf (Also published in Nashville, 1919–1972, and in Atlanta, 1972–1984)

American Legacy (New York) 1995–

American Unity: A Monthly Education Guide (New York) 1942–1961**

American Visions (Washington, D.C.) 1986–

Amsterdam News (New York) 1943–present** mf

Arkansas State Press (Little Rock, Ark.) 1984–present mf

Atlanta World (Atlanta) 1928–present** (Variant title: *Atlanta Daily World*)

Baptist Vanguard (Little Rock, Ark.) 1894–1981** mf

Bay State Banner (Dorchester, Mass.) 1965–present mf

Bible Way News Voice (Washington, D.C.) 1948?–1980? mf

Black Beat (New York) 1970–present mf (Variant title: *Soul Teen*)

Black Books Bulletin (Chicago) 1971–1981

Black Careers (Philadelphia) 1965–1982 mf

Black Dispatch (Oklahoma City, Okla.) 1915–1982** mf

The Black Panther (Oakland, Calif.) 1967–1980 mf (Also published in San Francisco, 1968–
     1969)

The Black Scholar: Journal of Black Studies and Research (Oakland, Calif.) 1969–present mf

Black Secrets (New York) 1936–present** (Variant title: *Secrets*)

Black World (Chicago) 1942–1976** (Variant title: *Negro Digest,* 1942–1970)

Boston Chronicle (Boston) 1915–1960?** mf

The Bulletin (Sarasota, Fla.) 1959–present mf

California Eagle (Los Angeles) 1879–1966** mf

California Voice (San Francisco) 1919–present** mf

Campus Chats (Tuskegee, Ala.) 1946–1973

Catawba Synod Argus (Charlotte, N.C.) 1956–1970

Charlotte Post (Charlotte, N.C.) 1975–present mf

Chicago Defender (Chicago) 1905–present** mf (Variant title: *Chicago Daily Defender*)

The Chicago Gazette (Chicago) 1949–present

The Christian Index (Memphis, Tenn.) 1867–present** mf

The Christian Recorder (Philadelphia) 1852–present** mf (Variant titles: *A.M.E. Christian Re-
     corder, Christian Recorder of the African Methodist Episcopal Church;* also published in
     Nashville, Tenn.)

Christian Review (Philadelphia) 1913–1952** mf

Cleveland Call and Post (Cleveland, Ohio) 1919–present** (Variant title: *Call and Post*)

Colorado Statesman (Denver, Colo.) 1895–1961** mf (Variant title: *Challenger,* 1963–1964)

The Columbus Challenger (Columbus, Ohio) 1963–1975 mf (Variant title: *Challenger,* 1963–
     1964)

Columbus Times (Columbus, Ga.) 1961–present* mf

The Crisis (Baltimore) 1910–present** mf

Dance Herald: A Journal of Black Dance (New York) 1975–1981

Dayton Forum (Dayton, Ohio) 1913–1949** mf (Variant title: *The Forum*)

The Dental Search-Light (Nashville, Tenn.) 1947–1959

Denver Star (Denver, Colo.) 1913–1963** mf

Detroit Tribune (Detroit) 1922–1966** mf (Variant titles: *Tribune Independent, New Tribune*)

Ebony (Chicago) 1945–present

Emerge (Washington, D.C.) 1989–

The Evening Whirl (St Louis, Mo.) 1938–present** mf (Variant title: *St. Louis Whirl Examiner,*
     1991–1993)

Final Call (Chicago) 1979–

Freedom Call (Milwaukee, Wis.) 1948?–1967 mf

Gary American (Gary, Ind.) 1977–present** mf (Variant title: *Gary Colored American*)

The Guardian (Boston) 1901–1960?** mf

Harlem Quarterly (New York) 1949–1950 mf

Harvard Journal of Afro-American Affairs (Cambridge, Mass.) 1965–1971 (Variant title: *Har-
     vard Journal of Negro Affairs,* 1968)

Houston Defender (Houston, Tex.) 1930–present** mf

Indianapolis Recorder (Indianapolis, Ind.) 1897–present** mf (Variant title: *Recorder*)

Informer and Texas Freeman (Houston, Tex.) 1919–1973?** mf (Variant titles: *Houston In-
     former and the Texas Freeman,* 1930–1934; *Informer,* 1934–1941)

Inglewood Hawthorne Wave (Los Angeles) 1918–1981**

Iowa Bystander (Des Moines, Iowa) 1894–1986** mf (Variant titles: *Iowa State Bystander,*
   1894–1896; *Bystander,* 1916–1922; *New Iowa Bystander,* 1972–1986)

Jet (Chicago) 1951–present mf

Journal and Guide (Norfolk, Va.) 1901–present** mf (Variant titles: *Norfolk Journal and Guide,*
   1922–1973; *New Journal and Guide,* 1975–1977)

Journal of Black Studies (Newbury Park, Calif.) 1970–present mf

Journal of Human Relations (Wilberforce, Ohio) 1952–1973

The Journal of Negro History (Washington, D.C.) 1916–present** mf

The Kansas City Globe (Kansas City, Mo.) 1972–present mf

The Lamp (Miami, Fla.)1966–1986?

Liberator (New York) 1961–1971

Los Angeles Sentinel (Los Angeles) 1934–present** mf

Louisiana Weekly (New Orleans, La.) 1925–present** mf (Variant title: *New Orleans Herald,*
   1925)

Louisville Leader (Louisville, Ky.) 1917–1950** mf

Madison Times (Madison, Wis.) 1990–

The Miami Times (Miami, Fla.) 1923–present** mf

The Midwest Journal: A Magazine of Research and Creative Writing (Jefferson City, Mo.) 1948–
   1956

Missionary Lutheran (St. Louis, Mo.) 1923–1961**

Missionary Seer (New York) 1900–present** mf

NAACP Bulletin (New York) 1940–1949?**

National Baptist Union Review (Nashville, Tenn.) 1899?–present** mf (Variant titles: *National
   Baptist Union, National Baptist Review*)

National Bar Journal (St. Louis, Mo.) 1941–1951**

National Negro Health News (Washington, D.C.) 1933–1950** mf

Negro College Quarterly (Wilberforce, Ohio) 1943–1947** mf

Negro History Bulletin (Washington, D.C.) 1937–present** mf

Negro Star (Wichita, Kans.) 1908–1953** mf

The New Advance (Charlotte, N.C.) 1938–1948**

The New Age Dispatch (Los Angeles) 1907–1949** mf (Variant title: *New Age*)

New Day (Philadelphia) 1936–present** mf

New Dayton Express (Dayton, Ohio) 1964–1971 mf (Variant titles: *Dayton Express, Dayton Express Urban Weekly*)

New Jersey Herald News (Newark, N.J.) 1938–1966**

New South (Atlanta) 1946–1973 mf

New York Recorder (Brooklyn, N.Y.) 1953–1987 mf

North American Informant (Washington, D.C.) 1946–1978

Obsidian II: Black Literature in Review (Raleigh, N.C.) 1986–present mf

Ohio Sentinel (Columbus, Ohio) 1949–1963 mf

The Ohio State News (Columbus, Ohio) 1935–1952** mf

Opportunity: Journal of Negro Life (New York) 1923–1949** mf

The People's Voice (New York) 1942–1948** mf

Philadelphia Tribune (Philadelphia) 1884–present** mf

Pittsburgh Courier (Pittsburgh, Pa.) 1910–present** (Variant titles: *Courier, Pittsburgh New
   Courier*)

Quarterly Review of Higher Education among Negroes (Charlotte, N.C.) 1933–1969** mf

Saint Paul Sun (St. Paul, Minn.) 1941–1976** mf

Savannah Tribune (Savannah, Ga.) 1875–present** mf (Variant title: *Colored Tribune,* 1875–
   1876)

Shreveport Sun (Shreveport, La.) 1966–present mf

St. Louis American (St. Louis, Mo.) 1927–present** (Variant title: *St. Louis AM*)

St. Louis Argus (St. Louis, Mo.) 1912–present** mf

Transition (Durham, N.C.) 1963–

Tri-State Defender (Memphis, Tenn.) 1951–present mf
Twin Cities Courier (Minneapolis, Minn.) 1966–1986 mf
The Union (Cincinnati, Ohio) 1907–1952** mf
Voice of Missions (New York) 1893–present** mf
The Waco Messenger (Waco, Tex.) 1929–present** mf
Washington Tribune (Washington, D.C.) 1921–1946** mf
West Virgina Beacon Digest (Charleston, W.V.) 1957–present mf
Western Journal of Black Studies (Pullman, Wash.) 1977–present

7 *Government Documents*

Debra Newman Ham

Whether searching for individual service records of African-American Revolutionary War soldiers, analyzing the relationship between blacks and the United States Congress, or investigating the assassination of Martin Luther King, Jr., the researcher will find federal records indispensable for a thorough study of African-American history and culture. The largest repository of federal records is the National Archives and Records Administration (NARA, formerly called the National Archives and Records Service, NARS), and its federal records centers and presidential libraries.

NARA has published a number of finding aids to assist researchers in the use of its collections. African-American history resources among federal records are rich and varied. Created by blacks or about them, these records provide both group and individual perspectives on the role of African-Americans in United States history.

Additionally, there are numerous papers of individuals—both black and white—who have served the federal government over the past two hundred years; their papers provide important information documenting the relationship between African-Americans and the government. These papers are among the holdings of various repositories throughout the United States. Although this essay concentrates on federal records that are held by NARA, it also suggests some tools for locating personal papers of federal officeholders who were instrumental in African-American affairs. One of the most useful is the *National Union Catalog of Manuscript Collections* (NUCMC), issued annually from 1959 to 1984 by the Library of Congress. A useful aid in using NUCMC is the *Index to Personal Names in the National Union Catalog of Manuscript Collections, 1959–1984* (1988, 2 vols.). More recent information about manuscript collections can be accessed online through the Archival Manuscript Control (AMC) file of RLIN (Research Libraries Information Network) and OCLC (Online Computer Library Center). Retrospective online cataloging is still in the discussion stage.

NARA records are divided into more than four hundred numbered record groups. A record group (RG) usually consists of the records of a single agency or, if it is a large agency, its component bureaus. For example, the General Records of the Department of Labor comprise RG 174, while its bureaus such as the Women's Bureau and the Bureau of Employment Security are RGs 86 and 183, respectively. To preserve the integrity and interrelationship of these records, NARA endeavors to keep them in the same order as that maintained by their creating agencies.

Only a very few record groups include concentrated information for African-American history; most materials are interspersed throughout the holdings. Because of the large number of documents, each record group is controlled by a narrative index known as an inventory. If an agency still exists, its inventory is called "preliminary," while the finding aid for a defunct agency is called "final." Regulations or restrictions for the use of these records vary by agency, so it is necessary for the researcher to contact NARA before visiting. In addition, NARA houses only non-current federal records. For access to recent records, the researcher should write directly to the individual agency. If the agency denies access, a second letter, citing the Freedom of Information Act, will prompt the agency to review its decision. Yet keep in mind that the Privacy Act restricts research for seventy years on many federal records with personal information, such as census data.

Because several hundred record groups present a great deal of difficulty with subject access even with the aid of inventories, NARA has periodically issued subject guides, special lists, essays, conference papers, and name or subject indexes to facilitate the use of the collections by researchers. These finding aids are usually available at the National Archives and its regional offices or at government document depository libraries. Many of the finding aids are also available in a microfiche publication entitled *The National Inventory of Documentary Sources* (1983) and a NARA publication entitled *The National Archives on Microfilm* (M248).

Some of the more recent guides are available for sale at NARA, and published inventories and special lists are usually available from the agency. However, only unpublished inventories or folder lists are available for some record groups, and these finding aids are usually accessible only at the location where the record groups are housed.

A particularly useful 32-page NARA brochure, *Select List of Publications of the National Archives and Records Administration* (1989), provides an extensive list of guides, microfilm catalogs, reference information papers, inventories, and special lists. Leaflets with addresses and phone numbers of regional archives and presidential libraries are also available at no cost from NARA by writing to the National Archives and Records Administration, Washington, D.C. 20408. Many of these finding aids are also available online *(gopher.nara.gov)* or through the World Wide Web *(http://www.nara.gov)*.

USEFUL GUIDES FOR AFRICAN-AMERICAN HISTORY

Some finding aids provide subject access to African-American history materials from the early years of the formation of the federal government through the late 20th century, while others are geared only to a specific period, record group, or subject. In 1984, the Archives published *Black History: A Guide to Civilian Records in the National Archives,* by Debra L. Newman. This 369-page narrative guide is arranged by record group number and includes a description of African-American records among the files of civilian agencies. *Black History* includes an extensive index, numerous illustrations, and information about NARA's audiovisual collection. It describes records of agencies from the Continental Congresses (RG 360) of the 18th century through the American Revolution Bicentennial Administration (RG 452) of the 20th century.

Black History does not include descriptions of the files of military agencies, but does describe materials generated by civilian war agencies, such as the Office of War Information (RG 208) and the War Manpower Commission (RG 211). Many pay and claims records for United States Colored Troops are among the files of the General Accounting Office (RG 217). A proposed companion guide to black history materials among the records of military agencies has not been completed by NARA, but several finding aids, which are described below, do provide helpful information about African-American military records. The chronological overview below provides a brief synopsis of the materials in *Black History* and some other useful guides.

A National Archives conference volume edited by Robert L. Clark, *Afro-American History: Sources for Research* (1981), includes essays that describe the variety of ways creative scholars have located and used NARA black history resources. Among the contributions are "Genealogy of Afro-Americans," by Alex Haley; "Familial Values of Freedmen and Women," by Herbert Gutman; "Presidential Libraries as Sources for Research on Afro-Americans," by J. C. James; "Saving Federal Records for Research," by Harold T. Pinkett; "Using Federal Archives: Some Problems in Doing Research," by Okon Edet Uya; "Federal Appointment Papers and Black History," by James Dent Walker; "Military Records for Nonmilitary History," by Preston Amos; and "Freedmen's Bureau Records: Texas, A Case Study," by Barry A. Crouch.

An entire issue of *Prologue: Quarterly of the National Archives and Records Administration* 29:2 (Summer 1997) is dedicated to African-American history. It includes articles such as "The Freedmen's Savings and Trust Company and African American Genealogical Research," by Reginald Washington; "Institutions of Memory and the Documentation of African Americans in Federal Records," by Walter B. Hill, Jr.; "Preserving the Legacy of the United States Colored Troops," by Budge Weidman; and "The USIA Motion Picture Collection and African American History," by Donald Roe. The issue is divided into six sections: Civil War and Reconstruction, Labor Issues, Civil Rights, Pictorial Records, Research Aids, and Genealogy.

Aloha South's *Guide to Federal Archives Relating to Africa* (1977) includes a number of topics relevant to African-American history. It provides researchers with numerous references to the African slave trade and its suppression, African colonization, back-to-Africa movements, the role of African-American diplomats in Africa, and political, social, and cultural relations between Africans and African-Americans.

Chapter 12 of *The Guide to Genealogical Research in the National Archives* (rev. ed., 1983) is entitled "Records of Black Americans." The chapter covers a variety of record groups that include vital statistics, as well as military service and pension information. The chapter is particularly useful for locating records relating to African-American participation in various wars.

The records of the presidents of the United States and the U.S. Congress include many documents that chronicle the status of African-Americans throughout

United States history. Before the establishment of presidential libraries by Franklin Delano Roosevelt, most—but not all—of the papers of U.S. Presidents were housed at the Library of Congress. The majority of the Library's presidential papers are microfilmed and item-indexed. Many of the presidents' papers have also been published in volumes with extensive indexes that facilitate location of resources for African-American history.

Presidential libraries, built with private funds raised for each President, are subsequently donated to the National Archives for staffing and management. Two useful guides for locating presidential papers are *Records of the Presidency: Presidential Papers and Libraries from Washington to Reagan,* by Frank I. Schick with Renee Schick and Mark Carroll (1989), and *A Guide to Manuscripts in the Presidential Libraries,* by Dennis A. Burton, James B. Rhoads, and Raymond W. Smock (1985). The Burton guide, which includes information for about fifty years of American history beginning in the 1930s, includes a number of sources about the modern civil rights struggle.

A volume spanning the American experience is *Guide to the Records of the United States Senate at the National Archives* (Senate Doc. 100-42, U.S. Senate Bicentennial Publication no. 7, 1989), by Robert W. Coren, Mary Rephlo, David Kepley, and Charles South. A few of the many black history topics addressed are pro- and antislavery activities, Liberian colonization, the sectional controversy, the Civil War and Reconstruction, black military service, freedmen's rights, civil rights, voting rights legislation, education of blacks, expositions, discrimination, integration and segregation, and various incidents of racial violence (RG 46). The indexes of the Senate *Journals of Legislative Proceedings* provide a Congress-by-Congress synopsis of African-American issues addressed by that body.

The *Guide to the Records of the United States House of Representatives at the National Archives* by Charles E. Schamel, Mary Rephlo, Rodney Ross, David Kepley, Robert W. Coren, and James Gregory Bradsher (100th Congress, 2nd session, House of Representatives Doc. No. 100-245, 100th Congress, 2nd session, 1989) includes several topics relevant to African-American studies, including slavery, free blacks, civil rights, destitution, relief, education, Washington, D.C., schools, employment and labor conditions, expositions, housing, military service, racial discrimination, desegregation, and racial violence (RG 233).

Published papers of the Congress, which are a part of the Publications of the U.S. Government (RG 287), including both the *American State Papers* (1832–1861, 38 vols.) and the *Serial Set,* have been indexed in the *CIS U.S. Serial Set Index, 1789–1969* (1979–, 36 vols.). The *American State Papers* is an official reprint edition of the documents of the first fourteen Congresses. Later records are included in the *Serial Set,* which begins with the 15th Congress in 1817 and continues to the present. References to black history materials in the CIS index appear under headings such as Negro, colored, Africa, colonization, freedmen, slavery, race, discrimination, fugitives, Missouri Compromise, servitude, and others.

There are several guides that are useful for finding papers of individual Congressional representatives, some of which include black history materials: John J. McDonough, *Members of Congress: A Checklist of Their Papers in the Manuscript Division, Library of Congress* (1980); *Guide to Research Collections of Former United*

States Senators, 1789–1982 (1983; Supplement, 1985, 1987); and *A Guide to Research Collections of Former Members of the United States House of Representatives, 1789–1987,* prepared under the direction of Raymond W. Smock (1988).

THE PRE-FEDERAL PERIOD

Records relating to African-American service in colonial militias are described in *A Guide to Pre-Federal Records in the National Archives,* compiled by Howard H. Wehmann and revised by Benjamin L. DeWhitt (1989). Other topics described in the guide are slavery, the slave trade, free blacks, and laws affecting African-Americans. *The Negro in the Military Service of the United States, 1639–1886* (M858) is a microfilm publication that includes materials from the Records of the Adjutant General's Office (RG 94), some of which relate to service in the pre-federal period. The *Guide to Records in the National Archives Relating to American Indians,* compiled by Edward Hill (1981), provides information about the presence of runaway slaves among Indians from the earliest period of American history.

THE REVOLUTIONARY ERA

Extensive indexes available for the Records of the Continental and Confederation Congresses and the Constitutional Convention are *Index: Journals of the Continental Congress, 1774–1789,* compiled by Kenneth Harris and Steven D. Tilley (1976), and *Index: The Papers of the Continental Congress, 1774–1789* (1978, 5 vols.). In the *Index* to the Journals, records for black history are found under headings such as Negroes, mulattoes, slaves, slavery, and slave trade. The records pertain to the enlistment of free blacks for service in the Revolutionary War, petitions and addresses for the abolition of slavery and the slave trade, ways to enumerate blacks and mulattoes in the population, slave revolts, British-instigated slave insurrections, the disposition of captured fugitive slaves and blacks taken by U.S. vessels, attempts to get South Carolina and Georgia to raise 1,000 able-bodied black troops, the return of slaves captured by the British, taxes on slaves, slavery in the Northwest Territory, and calls for Indians—particularly Seminoles—to return fugitive slaves.

The *Index* to the Papers includes the following headings for black history: Africa, mulattoes, Negroes, slaves, slavery and the slave trade. In addition, the names of various individuals are identified as "Negro" in the *Index.* Much of the material for black history concerns the evacuation of blacks by the British in 1783. Lists of those who left with the British are called "Inspection Rolls" and are dated June 13 and 25; July 8, 10–16, and 29–31; August 13–22; September 5–13 and 22; and November 19, 1783. These inspection rolls were created so that reparations could be made to the owners of the slaves at a later date. Consequently, careful information about each evacuee was kept, such as age, description, former owner's name and address, and the name of the persons (if any) in whose custody they were traveling.

The *List of Black Servicemen Compiled from the War Department Collection of Revolutionary War Records* by Debra L. Newman (Special List 36, 1974) includes names of soldiers who are identified as African-American in the service records or whose names seem to indicate that they were of African descent (Cudjoe, Cuffe, Quok, etc.). The *Guide to Genealogical Research* describes military service files for blacks who served in the Revolutionary and Civil Wars, naval service records, and materials about Indian freedmen. The guide instructs researchers in the use of pension applications (RG 15, Records of the Veterans Administration) and claims records, both of which often provide valuable biographical information about black servicemen. Other references to African-American history are interspersed through the guide.

Black History describes the General Records of the United States Government (RG 11)—the enrolled acts and resolutions of Congress 1789–1962—which are arranged by Congress. They consist of the original engrossed copies of the laws of the United States and of joint resolutions signed by the Speaker of the House, the President of the Senate, and the President of the United States. Many of these laws pertain to matters directly affecting black Americans. (Examples from the post-Revolutionary period include the Act to Prohibit the Importation of Slaves, 1807; the Missouri Compromise, 1819–1821; and the Compromise of 1850.) The Constitution, Bill of Rights, ratified and unratified amendments, presidential proclamations, Executive Orders, and perfected treaties are also a part of this record group.

List of Free Black Heads of Families in the First Census of the United States, 1790 (1974), by Debra L. Newman; *Free Negro Heads of Families in the United States in 1830*, by Carter G. Woodson (1925); and U.S. Bureau of the Census, *Negro Population in the United States, 1790–1915* (1968), provide specific information about black citizens. Chapter 12 of the *Guide to Genealogical Research in the National Archives* discusses information contained in the decennial population schedules of the Census Bureau. Census data became progressively more detailed with each succeeding census. The 1790 schedules contain the names of the heads of families and, for each household, the number of white males sixteen years of age and above, the number under sixteen years, the number of white females, the names of other free persons (most of whom were free blacks), the number in their families, and the number of slaves. A further breakdown of the black population did not begin until the census of 1820, which enumerated male and female slaves and free colored persons.

Schedules for the censuses before 1850 give only the name of each head of family, followed by such family information as the number of dependents by age and sex. Beginning with the 1850 census, the schedules contain the name of each individual, as well as age, sex, state or country of birth, and occupation. The censuses of 1850 and 1860 include separate schedules of the slave population.

THE ANTEBELLUM PERIOD

Senate records from the 1st (1789–1791) through the 35th Congresses (1857–1859) also include information about claims for slaves seized by the British during the Revolutionary War and the War of 1812, as well as claims for slaves captured or lost in wars with Native Americans, particularly with the Seminoles.

The Negro in the Military Service of the United States, 1639–1886 (1963) includes materials from the Records of the Adjutant General's Office (RG 94) relating to blacks during the War of 1812. Claims commissions detail an extremely interesting aspect of African-American history, particularly after the War of 1812. Although some records relating to claims are among the Congressional and Treasury Department records, others are included in the records of Boundary and Claims Commissions and Arbitrations (RG 76). This is a collective record group established from segregated files relating to international boundaries, claims, and arbitrations received from the Department of State and international commissions. Following each war, citizens or foreign nationals make claims to the federal government to pay for items that were lost or destroyed during the combat. For example, following the War of 1812, the United States was a party in a dispute with Great Britain over property and slaves lost during the war. Some of the slaves were voluntary fugitives, while others were taken by force. Some of the provisions of the Treaty of Ghent, signed on December 24, 1814, called for the restoration of "all territory, places, and possessions." A dispute arose as to how these provisions should apply to slaves. The dispute was referred to the Emperor of Russia for arbitration, and he decided in 1822 in favor of the United States. A mixed claims commission was established on June 30, 1822, to determine the average amount to be paid as compensation for each slave and to determine the validity of property claims. These records are among Records of the Boundary and Claims Commissions and Arbitrations (RG 76). The miscellaneous records of the Mixed Claims Commission, 1814–1828 (7 vols.), include documents in support of the claims of some individuals, correspondence, reports about slaves and property taken away by the British, papers regarding the sale of slaves carried off by the British, depositions and other documents regarding the value of slaves in Louisiana in 1815, a list of slave owners showing place of residence, a list of blacks said to be freed, a list of refugee slaves in Nova Scotia, 1815–1818, and other documents.

The earliest agitation against slavery recorded in the Senate *Journals* was generated by Quaker groups. Most Congresses during the antebellum period include memorials and petitions from Quakers. During the 16th Congress (1818–1821), the question of the admission of slave and free states into the Union was temporarily settled by the Missouri Compromise. In spite of the Compromise, the number of petitions for the abolition of slavery continued to increase. During the 24th and 25th Congresses (1835–1839), many petitions from citizens, including some signed only by women, protested against slavery in general, the slave trade, slavery in the District of Columbia and in the territories, and the kidnapping of free blacks. In addition to these concerns, petitions from the 27th through the 29th Congresses (1841–1846) protested against the admission of Texas as a slave state. Resolutions and memorials relating to slavery were also sent by various state legislatures. During the 18th Congress (1823–1825), for example, the General Assembly of Ohio recommended that Congress consider the gradual emancipation of all slaves.

Before the Civil War, African-American history materials among the records of the House of Representatives generally pertain to slavery, abolition, the slave trade, the colonization of blacks in Africa, the status of free blacks, and fugitive slaves.

During the 6th Congress (1799–1801), for example, there was a Select Committee on Fugitive Slave Laws. Questions pertaining to these laws or their repeal were also considered by the Committee on the Judiciary during the 28th, 32nd, and 33rd Congresses (1843–1845, 1851–1853, and 1853–1855, respectively). The Committee of the Whole House during the 33rd Congress (1853–1855) also considered the repeal of the Fugitive Slave Law and the exclusion of the slave trade in the Territories.

The House Committee on the District of Columbia discussed slavery, the slave trade, and abolition in the District from the 20th (1827–1829) through the 34th (1855–1857) Congresses. Other committees that debated the question of slavery in the District include two Committees of the Whole House, one in the 20th Congress (1827–1829) and another in the 33rd (1853–1855), and the Select Committee on the Abolition of Slavery in the District of Columbia in the 23rd and 24th Congresses (1833–1837). The Committee of the Whole House considered abolition in the entire United States during the 29th Congress (1845–1847).

Many other aspects of the slavery question were addressed by House committees from the 27th to the 36th Congresses (1841–1861), such as abolition, suppression of the slave trade, the sale of slaves for debts due the United States, slavery in the territories, and freedom for the Africans on the *Amistad*. The *Amistad* was a Spanish schooner that was commandeered in 1839 by the Africans on board. The Africans ordered the crew to steer the schooner for Africa. Instead, they steered it to the vicinity of Long Island, where it was seized by a U.S. brig.

Of special interest is a petition to the 13th Congress (1813–1815) from the African-American merchant and shipbuilder Paul Cuffee, a Quaker, who transported thirty-eight blacks to settle in Sierra Leone at his own expense. Many federal records address the difficulties faced by black Americans who emigrated to Liberia, blacks who served as diplomats in Africa, and back-to-Africa movements in the 20th century.

Colonization has been a recurring theme in the history of blacks in America. The American Colonization Society, founded in December 1816, attempted to encourage free blacks to move to Liberia. The influential members of the society regularly urged the Congress and private citizens to donate financial support for the resettlement of African-Americans. The members of the society were able to attract the support of a number of state legislatures during many Congresses that sent resolutions favoring colonization, but a few states sent resolutions urging that no federal monies be used for colonizing blacks. During the 20th Congress (1827–1829), for example, the legislature of South Carolina resolved "to oppose all appropriations in favor of the Colonization Society."

The Guide to Federal Archives Relating to Africa and *Black History* also describes resources for other aspects of the colonization movement documented through Congressional records. When slave ships were seized, the Africans (called "recaptives") on board were freed and subsequently sent, in most cases, by the U.S. government to the Colonization Society's Liberian colony. The records of various Congresses include deliberations about annual appropriations for the transport (and a short period of maintenance) of the recaptives, U.S. naval vessels that patrolled the Liberian coast from time to time, and the support of ships that were used in the suppression of the African slave trade. In the exceptional case of the *Amistad,* the Senate, during the 33rd (1853–1855) and 35th (1857–1859) Congresses, received a number of petitions about the disposition of these Africans. Records pertaining to colonization and the suppression of the slave trade are among the records of the Department of the Interior (RG 48), Records of the District Courts of the United States (RG 21), Naval Records Collection of the Office of Naval Records and Library (RG 45), General Records of the Department of State (RG 59), Records of the Foreign Service Posts of the Department of State (RG 84), and Records of U.S. Attorneys and Marshals (RG 8).

Black History describes records concerning the capture of several slaving vessels. For example, the General Records of the Department of the Treasury (RG 56) include a series of letters received from the Navy Department, 1823–1909. These pertain to the capture of slavers by U.S. Navy vessels, especially during the years 1860 and 1861. The ships involved include the *Storm King, Erie, Bogota,* and *Wildfire.* Lists of the crews of the U.S. vessels are given along with some information about the number of Africans on each ship and the amount of bounty to be paid.

Slavery documents among the Records of the U.S. Customs Service (RG 36) are also discussed in *Black History.* An 1807 law prohibited the transportation of slaves in any vessel under forty tons except on the rivers of the United States. Section 8 of the same act required that all vessels of forty tons or more carrying slaves in the coastal trade file duplicate manifests (at the port of origin and at the port of destination) showing the name of each slave, the names and residences of the exporter and consignee, the age and description of the slave, and a pledge that the slaves had not been imported after 1807. The records of custom houses include slave manifests for four ports: Philadelphia, 1790–1840; New Orleans, 1819–1852 and 1860–1861; Mobile, 1822–1860; and Savannah, 1801–1860. The manifests include dates of arrival and the names of the vessel. They show tonnage and nationality of the vessel, and name (usually first name only), age, and sex of the slave. Crew lists and shipping articles among the Customs Bureau records indicate that some of the crew were African-Americans.

Black History describes several series among the Department of Justice Records (RG 60) that include sources for African-American history. *Opinions on Legal Questions, 1790–1870,* contains materials relating to slavery and the slave trade, citizenship status of free black people, service of African-American men in the Armed Forces, treatment of black sailors in various ports, black servants' legal status, petitions of African-American prisoners for pardons, American Colonization Society activities, testimony of blacks in court, and the right of African-Americans to own property. Letters received, 1813–1870, concern subjects such as the African slave trade and domestic slavery. Even after the African slave trade was declared illegal, many ships continued to engage in the trade. Records relating to the *Amistad* and other slavers—such as the *Antelope,* captured in 1819; the *Wildflower,* 1860; the *Susan,* 1861; the *Emily and Caroline,* 1814; and the *Nicaragua,* 1858—are among the letters received.

Black History provides information about the General Records of the Department of the Treasury—Letters received from the Navy Department, 1823–1909.

This series includes more information pertaining to the capture of slavers by U.S. Navy vessels, especially from 1860 and 1861. The ships involved include the slavers *Storm King, Erie, Bogota,* and *Wildfire.* Lists of the crews of the U.S. vessels are given along with some information about the number of Africans on each ship and the amount of bounty to be paid.

THE CIVIL WAR

The Union: Guide to Federal Archives Relating to the Civil War by Kenneth W. Munden and Henry Putney Beers (1962), is more than 700 pages long and covers hundreds of topics about African-Americans in the period just before, during, and immediately after the war. Some of the numerous black history topics covered are recruitment and military action of United States Colored Troops, conditions and rights of freedmen, riots, racial violence, education, emancipation, colonization, and race relations among blacks, whites, and Native Americans.

Tabular Analysis of the Records of the U.S. Colored Troops and Their Predecessor Units in the National Archives of the United States, by Joseph B. Ross (1973), describes regimental records, including correspondence, orders, descriptive books, and morning reports. The *Guide to the Archives of the Government of the Confederate States of America* (1968) discusses records relating to black civilian laborers and other aspects of the African-American population in the South.

The *Guide to Records in the National Archives Relating to American Indians* discusses the records of the Office of the Secretary of the Interior, Indian Territory Division. This source includes information about the members of the Five Civilized Tribes, who held slaves and participated along with other Indians in the Civil War. During the war, the Creeks and Seminoles had divided loyalties, but the Chickasaws and Choctaws and some of the Cherokees became Confederate allies. Some loyal Indians were enlisted in Confederate and Union military forces and participated in campaigns in the Indian Territory. After the war, the government aided Indian refugees in Kansas to return to their homes in Indian Territory, and punitive measures were imposed on the principal tribes that had remained there. As a result of treaties negotiated in 1866, the tribes were obliged to make numerous concessions, including the freeing of black slaves held by them, the extension of the rights enjoyed by the Indians to the freedmen, and the allotment to freedmen of a share of tribal lands. Government action in subsequent years to obtain for freedmen their share of the land, and Indian resistance to this provision in the treaties, resulted in records that are valuable for genealogy and the history of slavery among the Indians at the time of the Civil War. The Records of the Bureau of Indian Affairs (RG 75), Civilization Division, document the Civil War claims of loyal Creeks relative to individual claims of free Indians and freedmen who were loyal to the Union during the Civil War.

Many, including President Abraham Lincoln, believed that whites and blacks would have difficulty living in the same nation and envisioned the colonization of African-Americans somewhere outside the United States. In 1862, Congress passed several acts to aid in the colonization of free blacks. On August 4, 1862, Rev. James Mitchell was appointed by President Lincoln as an agent to assist in the execution of these laws on colonization. Several colonization projects were started in places such as Haiti, New Granada, British Honduras, and the British and Danish West Indies. None, however, was successful, and on July 2, 1864, Congress repealed the appropriations for colonization projects except such money as was needed to meet previously incurred expenses and existing commitments. Records relating to postwar colonization are among the records of the Department of the Interior.

During the Civil War, many Senate discussions involved slavery, freedom, and the use and treatment of black troops. Some of the slavery issues during the 37th and 38th Congresses (1861–1865) were the right of slaves or former slaves to file claims for property used or destroyed by Union troops, the abolition of slavery, and the suppression of the slave trade. Several important Congressional hearings about the use and treatment of African-American troops took place during this period.

Some of the many issues involving freedmen debated by the Senate were the plight of black refugees, the franchise, civil rights, employment of freedmen, establishment of the Freedmen's Bureau, establishment and operation of the Freedmen's Savings and Trust Company, freedmen's hospitals, Freedmen's Village, the activities of various Freedmen's Aid Societies, and the removal of the "disqualification of color" for carrying U.S. mail.

To obtain money to carry on the Civil War, new taxes were levied on many articles, and the Office of the Commissioner of Internal Revenue was established to collect them. Files relating to these taxes are among the Records of the Internal Revenue Service (RG 58). An act of August 5, 1861, provided for a direct tax and an income tax. The most complete records relating to the direct tax in the National Archives are those for South Carolina. These records give details about the transition of blacks in the Beaufort area from slavery to freedom. The files include information about land sales to "heads of families of the African race," land plots, claims of former owners, use of proceeds from farmlands to support schools, and files for African-American collectors of internal revenue, such as Henry A. Rucker, Joseph E. Lee, J. E. Shephard, and Charles W. Anderson.

Black Studies: A Select Catalog of National Archives Microfilm Publications, compiled by Susan P. Garro (1984), describes major concentrations of black history records that NARA has microfilmed. About sixty pages of the hundred-page guide provide a detailed description of the microfilmed edition of the Records of the Bureau of Refugees, Freedmen, and Abandoned Lands (RG 105). This agency, popularly known as the Freedmen's Bureau, was administered by the War Department. Microfilmed records relating to the United States Colored Troops (a segment of the Records of the Adjutant General's Office) are also described at length in *Black Studies.* Census, Congressional, Army, Navy, Agricultural, and Interior Department and other microfilmed records relating to African-American history are described in this guide. Other microfilm publications relate to the Freedmen's Savings and Trust Company and black Congressional Medal of Honor recipients.

RECONSTRUCTION AND ITS AFTERMATH

Much of the legislation during the Reconstruction period involved the rights of black Americans. The Senate *Journals* give information about the ratification of the 13th, 14th, and 15th Amendments to the Constitution. Civil rights, political rights, and equal protection under the law were all important considerations of the Senate. Many petitions were received from blacks asking for equal rights with white Americans. There was much violence against African-Americans during this period. During the 41st and 42nd Congresses (1869–1873), the Select Committee on Alleged Outrages in Southern States was active. During the 42nd Congress, for example, African-American citizens of Frankfort, Kentucky, petitioned for "enaction of laws for the better protection of life in that State."

During and after the Civil War, Senate and House committees addressed slavery and emancipation, black troops in the war effort, the plight of freedmen, civil rights for blacks, and contested elections that involved black congressmen-elect. In the Reconstruction period, from the 39th through the 44th Congresses (1865–1877), a variety of black history issues were included in the Senate *Journals*. The Freedmen's Bureau was continued until 1872. The Freedmen's Savings and Trust Company failed in 1874. Many of the duties, problems, and investigations of the Freedmen's Bureau were reviewed by the Senate. As a result of the failure of the Freedman's Savings and Trust Company, petitions and claims were filed and appear among the records until after the turn of the century. Institutions such as Freedmen's Hospital and Howard University, both in Washington, D.C., were established during this period, and various matters pertaining to them appear in the Senate records into the 20th century. There are petitions and claims from freedmen who lived among the Five Civilized Tribes. Many records concern the welfare of freedmen in matters such as homes for the aged, education, employment, care of orphans, and protection of life.

At the end of the Reconstruction period and up to the turn of the 20th century, the Senate *Journals* reflect the continuation of many African-American concerns, such as colonization, migration to the North and West, treatment of black soldiers and sailors and claims made by them, agitation for civil and political rights and for equal protection under the laws, claims against the Freedman's Savings and Trust Company, relief of aged and poor African-Americans, and land and employment for blacks. There were petitions from black citizens on each of these matters. The *Report and Testimony of the Select Committee of the United States Senate to Investigate the Causes of the Removal of the Negroes from the Southern States to the Northern States,* 46th Congress, 2nd Session, Senate Report 693 (3 vols., 1880), is an incomparable source for economic, social, and political conditions in the South during this period. Also of great value is the *Report of the Committee of the Senate upon the Relations between Labor and Capital, and Testimony Taken by the Committee* (5 vols., 1885), which contains substantial testimony by both blacks and whites on labor conditions in the South. During the 52nd Congress (1891–1893), Frederick Douglass and others petitioned "for a hearing in respect to lawless outrages upon colored people in certain southern states."

During Reconstruction, several House of Representatives committees dealt with issues relating to civil and political rights for African-Americans. The Committee on the Judiciary handled matters pertaining to civil rights legislation during the 43rd and 45th Congresses (1873–1875 and 1877–1879). During the postwar period many blacks were voting and running for public office. The Committee on Elections dealt with contested elections, some of which involved blacks.

Many records relating to the appointment of African-Americans to political positions during the Reconstruction period are among the Treasury, Customs, and State Department records. Treasury Department—Records of Presidential appointments, 1833–1945, include information for the following black officials: for Register of the Treasury, James C. Napier, William T. Vernon, and Blanche K. Bruce; for customs officials, P. B. S. Pinchback, William D. Crum, and Robert Smalls; and for collectors of internal revenue, Charles W. Anderson and Joseph E. Lee. Included in the files are recommendations, petitions, oaths of office, notices of promotions and dismissals, letters received and copies of letters sent relating to charges and investigations, and unsuccessful as well as successful applications. Applications for appointments as Customs Service officials, 1833–1910, in the Treasury records include files for African-Americans such as John C. Dancy, James B. Dudley, and Robert Smalls. The Records of the U.S. Customs Service includes correspondence with some black collectors of customs, including Robert Smalls.

The Treasury Department Biography of Treasury Employees, 1835–1912, can serve as a partial index to employment applications and recommendations. For each employee, the biography gives position, grade, age, date of appointment, state of residence, congressional district, relatives in office, military service, and the names of persons who submitted recommendations. The biography includes racial designations in some volumes in the form of a small letter "c" for colored, usually in red ink. Most information about African-American employees is from the post–Civil War period.

Letters received, 1813–1870, in the Attorney General's Office in the Department of Justice, provide information about African-Americans during and after the Civil War, including subjects such as the confiscation of slaves during the war, employment of freed slaves, racial violence and riots, the right of blacks to own land, political rights, the Enforcement Act, the Civil Rights Act of 1866, suffrage, whites' attempts to reclaim ownership of former slaves by force, the Freedmen's Bureau, and nonprosecution of whites for crimes against blacks. Justice Department, Letters received, 1871–1884, provide sources, especially for the southern states, about election outrages and riots, race riots, the rise of white terrorist organizations such as the Ku Klux Klan, the administration of the 14th Amendment, the Enforcement Act, the civil rights acts, arrests without due process, taxation of black people, intermarriage of blacks and whites, Indians and freedmen, abduction of African-American people, bounty frauds in cases of black troops, and education. Of special interest is a group of reports on the activities of the Ku Klux Klan, 1871–1872, prepared by a Secret Service agent who infiltrated the group. *The Report of the Joint Select Committee Appointed to Inquire into the Condition of the Affairs in the Late Insurrecting States, so far as Regards the Execution of Laws and the Safety of the Lives and Property of the Citizens of the United States and Testimony Taken* (14 vols., 1872) is not confined to Klan activity. The volumes contain a massive amount of information on black leadership, community life, and politics in the South, organized by state. The last volume is a general index to the set.

Department of Justice year files, 1884–1903, concern similar topics, such as election frauds and violence, racial violence, and peonage. Problems that African-Americans encountered in the post–Civil War South are well documented in this series. Records of U.S. Attorneys and Marshals (RG 118), 1853–1871, for the Reconstruction period include materials relating to election fraud and to racial violence and civil rights. Records of the District Courts of the United States (RG 21) for the Maryland district court, 1790–1911, include cases pertaining to efforts to enforce voting rights for blacks during the Reconstruction era and include some registers of black voters in Richmond, Va., 1886–1892. General Records of the Department of the Treasury include letters received by the Southern Claims Commission between 1871 and 1880. The correspondence indicates that many of the claimants were "colored citizens."

The *Guide to Genealogical Research, Black Studies,* and the *Guide to the Records in the National Archives Relating to American Indians* provide information about sources dealing with the military activities of African-American soldiers in the post–Civil War period, such as the Buffalo Soldiers and Spanish-American War participants.

THE 20TH CENTURY

The vast majority of the African-American population of the United States was engaged in agricultural pursuits before the large-scale migrations to the North during and after the two World Wars. Many issues concerning blacks were raised with the Secretary of Agriculture (RG 16) or other officials in the Department of Agriculture. Some pertain to agricultural education and improved training for black farmers; others concern the political affairs of African-Americans in general. For example, the general correspondence of the office of the Secretary of Agriculture, 1906–1970, includes a number of black history topics such as civil rights, discrimination, farm tenancy, economic opportunity, equal employment, extension work, black staff, sharecropping, lynching, the distribution of the black population, migration, the war, and African-American colleges (especially Tuskegee Institute).

The Federal Extension Service (RG 33) was organized as a part of the Department of Agriculture in 1923 to help farmers carry out new farming and home enterprises through the services of county agricultural and home demonstration agents. Even before this service was organized, the Agriculture Department showed an increasing interest in the development of extension activities among African-American farmers. The Department employed black agricultural and home demonstration agents to work with African-American farm families. The annual narrative and statistical reports of these agents, 1908–1944, kept by the Federal Extension Service, were segregated by race and provide detailed information about the government's efforts with African-American farm families.

During the 57th Congress (1901–1903), black history concerns included in the Senate *Journals* consist of petitions to the Committee on Education and Labor asking for an investigation of conditions in the South, memorials of blacks asking for legislation to see that their rights were enforced, petitions for a home for aged and infirm blacks, and petitions and memorials in support of numerous actions, such as an exposition for blacks, the creation of a commission to inquire into their condition, the establishment of a memorial home in honor of black soldiers, and the creation of pensions for black people who had been enslaved. From the 59th through the 61st Congresses (1905–1911), there are unpublished records, printed hearings, and petitions about the "Affray at Brownsville, Texas," of August 1906, an incident that led to members of the all-black 25th U.S. Infantry being dismissed because of alleged violence against whites in Brownsville. Among the printed records is the *Summary Discharge or Mustering out of Regiments or Companies,* 59th Congress, 2nd Session, Senate Doc. 155 (1907), containing detailed accounts from participants and witnesses to the episode, with military records of each soldier discharged, maps, and photographs of Brownsville. Petitions from blacks protested the government's treatment of the soldiers, and many called for their reenlistment.

The Department of Justice's straight numerical files, 1904–1937, and the classified subject files, 1914–1941 and 1945–1949, provide extensive and detailed information about racial tensions and violence in the South, anti-lynching legislation, peonage, election fraud, inequitable distribution of relief to blacks after the 1912 Mississippi flood, discrimination in education and employment, the terror spread by the Ku Klux Klan, the separatist efforts of Marcus Garvey and his Universal Negro Improvement Association, voting rights struggles, and labor union activities.

African-Americans' dissatisfaction with their political and economic situations was manifested in a number of ways. Urban blacks demonstrated some interest in various nationalist movements. The most publicized endeavor was the black nationalist movement led by the Jamaican-born Marcus Garvey. Garvey's movement was popular during and after World War I. Both South's *Guide* and *Black History* indicate that records about Garvey, his Universal Negro Improvement Association, and his Black Star Steamship Line appear in several record groups. These are the General Records of the Department of State (RG 59), Records of the U.S. Shipping Board (RG 32), Records of the Bureau of Marine Inspection and Navigation (RG 41), General Records of the Department of Justice (RG 60), and Records of the Office of the Pardon Attorney. Other Pan-African activities were also of great interest to the State Department.

To locate information about African-American participation in and agitation during the World Wars, see the *Handbook of Federal World War Agencies and Their Records, 1917–1921* (1943). Records relating to African-American homefront workers during the World Wars and between them can be located by using Debra L. Newman's *Selected Documents Pertaining to Black Workers among the Records of the Department of Labor and Its Component Bureaus, 1902–1969* (Special List 40, 1977). Documents cited in this special list provide information about the role of African-American women in the U.S. workforce, outline strategies utilized by blacks to end discrimination in the workplace, and highlight the pivotal role of organizations such as the National Association for the Advancement of Colored People, the Urban League, and various fraternities and sororities. Many of the documents pertain to the work of the Labor Department's Division of Negro Economics (RG 174), under George E. Haynes and Karl F. Phillips, and the Bureau of Economic Security Division of Negro Labor (RG 183), under Lawrence Oxley. Records of a variety of labor investigation agencies such as the Committee on Fair

Employment Practice (RG 228), the National Labor Relations Board (RG 25), and the War Manpower Commission (RG 211) also include important information about African-American efforts to integrate the labor force.

A variety of record groups supply information about African-Americans during the Depression and the New Deal era. The records of the Agricultural Adjustment Administration (AAA) are a part of RG 145, Records of the Agricultural Stabilization and Conservation Service. The AAA administered aid to African-American farmers through programs and parity payments designed to conserve resources and provide aid for black farmers. Three AAA field offices were directed by African-Americans. Many black youths and some African-American veterans participated in Civilian Conservation Corps (RG 35) programs. Usually, separate camps were established for black enrollees, but in a few cases camps were integrated. CCC correspondence, reports, and photographs include information about blacks. Photographs show African-American enrollees taking part in vocational, academic, and job training programs; performing conservation, reclamation, and reforestation duties; aiding in the restoration of historical buildings and sites; and pursuing recreational activities. The records of other New Deal agencies such as the National Recovery Administration (RG 9), the Works Projects Administration (RG 69), and the National Youth Administration (RG 119), provide extensive documentation about the role of blacks during this period.

Federal Records of World War II (1951), another useful guide, aids the researcher in locating materials about policies relating to blacks in the armed forces, segregated units, racial attitudes of military leaders and personnel, and agitation for desegregation of the military. The records of the Office of War Information (RG 208) and those of the Committee for Congested Production Areas (RG 212) include extensive documentation of black participation in the war effort at home and abroad.

An NARA brochure, *Pictures of African Americans during World War II* (1993), aids the researcher in using NARA photographs. The *Guide to the Holdings of the Still Pictures Branch of the National Archives,* compiled by Barbara Lewis Burger (1990), provides information about photographs of blacks in the military, including Tuskegee Airmen during World War II. Some of the material available online includes photographic reproductions. Information about locating service records for blacks in the military is available in the *Guide to Genealogical Records*.

Military files relating to African-American women's history can be located in *American Women and the U.S. Armed Forces: A Guide to the Records of Military Agencies in the National Archives Relating to American Women,* compiled by Charlotte Palmer Seeley and revised by Virginia C. Purdy and Robert Gruber (1992). A companion NARA guide to women's history resources among the records of civilian agencies is not yet completed, but drafts of it may be available for the researcher's perusal.

Some of the major areas for black history during and after the World Wars listed in the Senate *Journals* are matters relating to blacks in the District of Columbia, discrimination against blacks, denial of civil rights, emigration to the North, and colonization in Africa. The records also concern protests against lynching and mob violence, equal protection under the laws, miscegenation, higher education, African-Americans in the Armed Forces, the establishment of black National Guard units, blacks in industry, blacks in the war effort, the establishment of the Committee on Fair Employment Practice, equal employment, voting rights, and race riots.

House committees addressed themselves to numerous issues concerning black Americans during the 20th century. At the turn of the century, during the 56th Congress (1899–1901), the Committee of Military Affairs examined the case of 2d Lt. Henry O. Flipper, the first black graduate of West Point. During the same Congress, the Committee on the Judiciary discussed legislation against lynching, a subject that repeatedly occupied the Committee's time until the 80th Congress (1947–1948).

Several committees examined problems of violence and discrimination against black people. In the 66th Congress (1919–1921), the members of the House Committee on the Judiciary discussed equal rights and discrimination. During the 67th Congress (1921–1923), they discussed the crimes of the Ku Klux Klan. Racial violence was addressed during the 65th Congress (1917–1919) by the Select Committee to Investigate Conditions in Illinois and Missouri Interfering with Interstate Commerce between the States; the Committee's inquiry is documented under the heading "Race Rioting in East St. Louis, Illinois, 1917." The Committee on Military Affairs investigated the Houston riot during the 67th Congress (1921–1923). In 1917, a battalion of the 24th Infantry, U.S. Colored Troops, fought with white residents of Houston; seventeen whites and two blacks died.

Various matters pertaining to fair employment practices were deliberated by the House Committee on Labor, the Committee on Education and Labor, the Committee on the Civil Service, and the Select Committee to Investigate Acts of Executive Agencies Beyond the Scope of Their Authority, 78th through the 81st Congresses (1943–1950). During the 84th and 85th Congresses (1955–1958), and even in more recent Congresses, questions about rights for black Americans have often come under the umbrella terms "civil rights" and "equal rights." These rights have been discussed by the House Committee on Rules and by the Judiciary Committee. The House Select Committee on Assassinations, 94th and 95th Congresses (1975–1978) investigated the circumstances surrounding the assassinations of President John F. Kennedy and the civil rights activist Dr. Martin Luther King, Jr.

Records of the Supreme Court of the United States (RG 267), 1792–, include famous historical cases such as *Dred Scott v. Sandford* (19 Howard 393) and *Plessy v. Ferguson* (163 U.S. 537), as well as renowned 20th-century cases such as *Brown v. Board of Education of Topeka* (347 U.S. 483). For the 1955 through the 1969 terms, audiotape recordings of oral arguments before the Court are available. These recordings serve as audio documentation of every case argued relating to the legal status of African-Americans in the areas of education, due process, jury service, forced confession, housing, public accommodations, transportation, recreation, and voting rights.

Two useful guides for locating information about presidential policies toward African-Americans, especially in the area of civil rights, are *Records of the Presi-*

dency: Presidential Papers and Libraries from Washington to Reagan (1989); and *A Guide to Manuscripts in the Presidential Libraries* (1985). A few of the many topics relating to African-Americans are labor, education, military service, racial violence, segregation, integration, the Depression, New Deal agencies, civil rights organizations, the civil rights movement, civil rights and voting rights legislation, affirmative action, and busing.

The guides, finding aids, and other materials described in this essay should aid any researcher in the quest for federal records relating to African-American history and culture. The chronological overview barely skims the surface of the ocean of material available on this topic. A researcher who learns to use the tools described in this essay will gain access to more material among these records than almost anyone can imagine. Additionally, new methods of describing and publishing archival materials are being developed annually. Commercial microfilming companies are now offering reproductions of federal records. An ever expanding variety of sources is available online. As new methods facilitating the use of these materials are discovered, the richness of African-American historical resources will become even more appreciated.

8 *Oral History*

ELINOR DES VERNEY SINNETTE

During the last four decades of the 20th century, oral history has become an increasingly important method of corroborating and complementing written historical evidence. Oral history has been particularly useful for recapturing the hidden and elusive strands of African-American history that have, over the course of time, been lost, forgotten, ignored, or distorted. African-Americans preserved much of their history and culture, as had their African forebears, through oral rather than written means. Customs, culture, and knowledge of significant events were handed down by word of mouth from generation to generation and African-American oral history projects and programs have their genesis in that oral tradition.

In the early 1970s, interest in oral tradition and African-American genealogy was furthered when Alex Haley decided to investigate stories that were passed down through several generations of his family about their "furthest-back person—the African." Haley mesmerized his audience at the meeting of the Oral History Association conference in 1972 when he related the reasons for his motivation and early work. His partly fictional book, *Roots: The Saga of an American Family* (1976), became an instant bestseller. Earlier on, Haley's interviews with Malcolm X had served as the basis of *The Autobiography of Malcolm X* (1964). Indeed, the British oral historian Paul Thompson cited Haley's interviews with Malcolm X as an outstanding example of the use of oral history technique. Thompson's *The Voices of the Past: Oral History* (1988) provides a valuable introductory study of the uses of oral sources as well as practical information about designing oral history projects. In addition, his work emphasizes the importance of oral history in the collection and documentation of the experiences of minority populations, where written evidence is often limited. Oral history is valuable to African-American historiography precisely because it provides firsthand, eyewitness accounts of events, thoughts, and reactions of a people whose very history has been ignored or, worse yet, demeaned.

The slave narrative, perhaps the earliest example of African-American oral history, emerged as critical evidence to counter various apologetic accounts of slavery. William Still, an African-American abolitionist, writer, and businessman, interviewed fugitive slaves as they came under his supervision while he served as chair of the Vigilance Committee of Philadelphia's Anti-Slavery Society. The slave stories were published in 1872, under a lengthy title that fully describes their contents: *The Underground Railroad: A Record of Facts, Authentic Narratives, Letters,*

Etc. Narrating the Hardships, Hair-Breadth Escapes and Death Struggles of the Slaves in their Efforts for Freedom as Related by Themselves and Others, or Witnessed by the Author. William Still's interviews provided important insights on the Underground Railroad, and especially the role of slaves in planning and engineering their flight to freedom.

Oral history played an important role in the early works of African-American academics and writers such as W. E. B. Du Bois, Carter G. Woodson, Charles Spurgeon Johnson, and E. Franklin Frazier in the first part of the 20th century. Johnson's work provides an outstanding example of the use of oral history. Johnson, a sociologist at Fisk University in Nashville and founder and head of the Social Science Institute, conducted pioneering research into southern African-American life. Ophelia Settle, later known as Ophelia Settle Egypt, a sociologist who would play a key role in the establishment of Howard University's School of Social Work and in various significant community projects in the Washington, D.C., area, served as one of Charles Johnson's research assistants from 1928 to 1930. She and a stenographer traveled throughout West Tennessee, Georgia, and Kentucky, gathering data for Johnson's study. Ophelia Settle soon realized that the families she was interviewing spoke mostly of their slavery experiences. Charles S. Johnson's book *Shadow of the Plantation* (1934) constitutes a written record of these interviews. This pathbreaking study incorporated the words of those whom Johnson called "the folk people"—some six hundred families in all.

Other researchers and scholars at Fisk University recognized the importance of oral evidence. Andrew Polk Watson, studying for a master's degree in the department of anthropology, visited the homes of ex-slaves and conducted more than one hundred interviews from 1927 to 1929. These autobiographical accounts, focusing mainly on the religious aspects of slave life, were edited by Guy B. Johnson and published by the Social Science Institute in *God Struck Me Dead: Religious Conversion Experiences and Autobiographies of Negro Ex-Slaves* (1945). This book was reissued by Pilgrim Press in 1969, under the editorship of Clifton H. Johnson. In Louisiana in 1929, John B. Cade, head of the Extension Division at Southern University, sent his students, many of whom were mature teachers, to interview former slaves and former slave owners. Eighty-two interviews were conducted, covering such topics as slave housing, family life, religious practices, and working conditions. Cade wrote about the project in the July 1935 issue of the *Journal of Negro History* under the title "Out of the Mouths of Slaves."

In the 1930s the federal government sponsored several projects that entailed interviewing former slaves. Lawrence Reddick, a Fisk University graduate and budding historian at Kentucky State College in 1932, collected reminiscences of the slave experience in Kentucky and Indiana under the auspices of a Federal Emergency Relief Administration Program. In 1937, he interviewed blacks in Georgia for the Federal Writers' Project. Under this government program, former slave narratives were collected and preserved. The folklorist B. A. Botkin, editor of *Lay My Burden Down: A Folk History of Slavery* (1945), was chief editor of the Writers' Unit of the Library of Congress Project from 1939 to 1941; the slave narratives are now deposited in the Library of Congress Manuscript Reading Room. The collection is composed of seven reel-to-reel tapes and forty-two five-inch archival boxes of transcripts. In 1972, the narratives were compiled into a Supplementary Series 1 (19 vols.), *The American Slave: A Complete Autobiography, 1972–1978,* edited by George P. Rawick, as well as a Supplementary Series 2 (9 vols.). In addition, a number of important books came out of the WPA collections, including *The Negro in Virginia: Compiled by Workers of the Writers' Program of the Work Projects Administration in the State of Virginia* (1940); Georgia Writers' Project, *Drums and Shadows: Survival Studies among the Georgia Coastal Negroes* (1940); T. Lindsay Baker and Julie P. Baker, *The WPA Oklahoma Slave Narratives* (1996); Lyle Saxon, *Gumbo Ya-Ya: A Collection of Louisiana Folk Tales* (1945); Ronnie C. Tyler and Lawrence R. Murphy, *The Slave Narratives of Texas* (1974); Charles L. Perdue, Jr., Thomas E. Barden, and Robert K. Philips, ed., *Weevils in the Wheat: Interviews with Virginia Ex-Slaves* (1976); and T. Lindsay Baker and Julie P. Baker, *Till Freedom Cried Out: Memories of Texas Slave Life* (1997). A history of the effort to recapture memories of slavery is found in Jerre Mantione, *The Dream and the Deal: The Federal Writers' Project, 1935–1943* (1972).

Critical reviews and critiques of this vast federal oral history project include C. Vann Woodward, "History from Slave Sources," *American Historical Review* 79 (1974); Eugene Genovese, "Getting to Know the Slaves," *New York Review of Books* (21 Sept. 1972); John W. Blassingame, "Using the Testimony of Ex-Slaves: Approaches and Problems," *Journal of Southern History* 41 (Nov. 1975), as well as the introduction to Blassingame, *Slave Testimony: Two Centuries of Letters, Speeches, Interviews, and Autobiographies* (1977); Leonard Rapport, "How Valid Are the Federal Writers' Project Life Stories: An Iconoclast among the True Believers," in *Oral History Review* (1979), and "A Case Study: The Ex-Slave Narratives" in David Henige, ed., *Oral Historiography* (1982); and Paul D. Escott, ed., *Slavery Remembered: A Record of Twentieth-Century Slave Narratives* (1979).

The historian-folklorist Gladys-Marie Fry began to conduct group interviews concerning the slave experience for her doctoral dissertation at the University of Indiana. At first she was discouraged, since her informants sought to disassociate themselves from their slavery heritage, appearing more enthusiastic about discussing the current status of black people. However, a fortuitous Halloween night thunderstorm provided the dramatic backdrop for an evening meeting during which Fry's narrators began to relate their perceptions of the white slaveholders' and overseers' social and psychological control over the slaves. Fry's informants spoke of the internal devastation of the psyche by the "peculiar institution." Her study was published as *Night Riders in Black Folk History* (1975).

As an organized activity, modern-day oral history dates back to 1948 when the historian Allan Nevins launched an oral history project at Columbia University in New York City. Nevins feared that the vital dimensions of historical events would be lost to scholars and researchers with the death of those persons who played significant roles in such events. Founded by Nevins and continued under the leadership of his successors, the Columbia Oral History Research Office has systematically recorded the experiences and reminiscences of living persons who have contributed significantly to historical events in their society, including African-American leaders.

Its report, *Oral History at Columbia: American Craftspeople Project: Projects and*

Interviews, 1987–1992, lists current holdings and major additions to the collection. The memoir of the Rev. Dr. M. Moran Weston, longtime rector of St. Phillips Episcopal Church in Harlem, is a major addition to African-American religious history. This memoir joins those of such outstanding African-Americans as the psychologist Kenneth B. Clark; the pioneer journalist and political adviser Louis Martin; and civil rights activists Bayard Rustin, Stoney Cooks, Ernest Green, and John Lewis.

The Washington Press Club Foundation's Women in Journalism collection is also housed at Columbia's Oral History Research Office and includes interviews of outstanding African-American women such as Lucille Bluford, Charlayne Hunter-Gault, Ethel Payne, and Frances Murphy, of the Afro-American newspaper dynasty. The Columbia office contains interviews related to the Alabama Civil Rights Project and transcribed interviews with former members of the Black Panther Party, which were conducted by Lewis Cole for his book *This Side of Glory: The Autobiography of David Hilliard and the Story of the Black Panther Party* (1993). The Columbia University Oral History Office has served as consultant to, and provided interviewers for, several important subsidized African-American oral history projects, among them the oral histories of African-American foreign service personnel, including African-American ambassadors to foreign countries.

The Regional Oral History Office in the Bancroft Library at the University of California, Berkeley, was established in 1954. Interviews with African-Americans prominent in 20th-century California history are available to researchers at the Department of Special Collections in the Young Research Library at the University of California, Los Angeles (UCLA), and at other selected repositories. Among the UCLA holdings are the recorded recollections of Frances Mary Albrier (1898–1987), political and civic leader; Willie L. Brown, Jr., Speaker of the California Assembly; C. L. Dellums (1900–1989), civil rights leader and international president of the Brotherhood of Sleeping Car Porters; Allen Broussard, California Supreme Court Justice; and Harry and Marguerite Williams, early black residents of Richmond, California. In 1980, the Bancroft Library published a *Catalogue of the Regional Oral History Office, 1954–1979,* containing entries for more than 300 oral history interviews. Another regional oral history archive is Duke University's Behind the Veil: Documenting African-American Life in the Jim Crow South in the John Hope Franklin Historical Collections, Special Collections Library of the Perkins Library. This is a holding of 1300 interviews. More than fifty graduate students interviewed elderly black men and women living in ten Southern states. The Behind the Veil project captures the racist conditions and black self-help activities of the era of segregation. William H. Chafe utilized these archives in his Presidential Address to the Organization of American Historians on April 23, 1999. His speech was published as "'The Gods Bring Threads to Webs Begun': African-American Life in the Jim Crow South," *Journal of American History* 86 (2000).

In using the resources of any or all of the approximately 400 oral history collections in the United States, Canada, Europe, and elsewhere, researchers will find oral history interviews and memoirs in various formats, including edited and unedited transcripts, reel-to-reel tapes, and cassette tapes. In the more recently organized collections there may be videotaped interviews as well. In recent years, beset by the high cost of conducting interviews and producing transcripts, many oral history repositories have found that preparing an index to each taped interview is sufficient to assist researchers in locating sections of the interview that are of particular interest.

The most recent and comprehensive list of oral history transcripts and interviews is found in *Oral History Index: An International Directory of Oral History,* published in 1990 by the Meckler Company. The volume contains the names and locations of nearly 400 oral history centers, with individual interviews listed alphabetically by name of interviewee and referred by number to the repository in which the interview is deposited or located. Students of African-American history are advised to contact oral history centers listed in this volume, since a considerable number of what might be regarded as predominantly white repositories house valuable collections of African-American oral history resources.

The Archives of American Art, a bureau of the Smithsonian Institution, holds the personal papers and oral history interviews of more than fifty late 19th-century and contemporary African-American artists, among them Romare Bearden, Jacob Lawrence, Faith Ringgold, and Emma Amos. The Amistad Research Center, located at Tulane University, houses more than 500 audio and videotaped interviews, of which two collections are noteworthy: the New Orleans Jazz and Heritage Foundation interviews conducted by the writer Thomas C. Dent, and interviews with New Orleans's black and white civil rights activists conducted by the oral historian Kim Lacy Rogers. Rogers has written two insightful articles concerning these interviews: "Organizational Experience and Personal Narrative: Stories of New Orleans's Civil Rights Leadership," *Oral History Review* 13 (1985), and "Oral History and the History of the Civil Rights Movement," *Journal of American History* (Sept. 1988).

The State Historical Society of Wisconsin at Madison is an important repository of recorded sound materials on black history. They are organized into three broad areas: the history of black citizens of Wisconsin; the history of the civil rights movement of the 1950s, 1960s, and 1970s; and a sizable collection of African-American labor history. Experiences of Wisconsin's black citizens are documented in five collections. The first consists of interviews with black settlers from rural Wisconsin, conducted by the Society's staff in 1973, documenting the establishment of black communities in Wisconsin between 1850 and World War I. Five other projects were conducted in 1975 with African-American residents of Janesville and Beloit, Wis. Finally, two individual memoirs, one of a black woman from Milwaukee, and the other of a black United Auto Workers official, shed light on Wisconsin's African-American social and work life in the 1930s and 1940s. There is a published guide to the Historical Society's civil rights–related materials, *Social Action Collections at the State Historical Society of Wisconsin: A Guide* (1983). The collections listed include individual memoirs as well as tape recordings of meetings, workshop sessions, and selected speeches. There is also a substantial number of recordings related to the activities of the Highlander Research and Education Center in Tennessee, of which the legendary civil rights activist Rosa Parks is an illustrious alumna. It is important to note that the collections of both the State Historical Society of Wisconsin and the African American Artists Archives are described in RLIN (Research Libraries Information Network), thus providing important information to researchers searching that database. The Amistad Collection at Tulane University is described on OCLC (Online Computer Library Center).

Over the years, African-Americans have struggled long and hard for recognition as first-class citizens in the land of their birth, and the black experience in the nation's military service is a revealing and poignant historical episode. A number of the military services have incorporated oral history projects into their historical units: the United States Naval Institute Oral History Program in Annapolis, Md.; the United States Air Force Academy Library at Colorado Springs, Colo.; and the United States Army Military Historical Institute at Carlisle Barracks, Pa. The Senior Officer Oral History Program (SOOHP) of the United States Army War College and Military History Institute at Carlisle Barracks holds 2,000 hours of taped interviews and 100,000 pages of transcribed interviews with army officer personnel. "A History of Blacks in the Armed Forces" lists substantive interviews with Generals Benjamin O. Davis, Frederic E. Davison, and Edward Greer, Vice Admiral S. L. Gravely, Jr., Commander Dennis D. Nelson, James Evans, and former congressman Charles C. Diggs. The army's oral history program now focuses on the history of the institution itself, explicitly recognizing the vital role of African-Americans in the armed forces. All of the interviews are open to researchers except that of General Davis.

Mary Penick Motley, *The Invisible Soldier: The Experience of the Black Soldier in World War II* (1975) is an early oral history study of blacks in the military. In the preface to this landmark work, Motley reports the problems she encountered while interviewing soldiers who found it difficult to discuss their wartime experiences with a woman historian. Two other military oral history studies are worthy of mention: Wallace Terry, *Bloods: An Oral History of the Vietnam War* (1984), and *The Golden Thirteen: Recollections of the First Black Naval Officers* (1993), edited by Paul Stillwell.

With the rise of the women's movement in the last half of the 20th century, interest in the role of women in the history and development of America has led the major oral history centers to include collections of the memoirs of African-American women. One noteworthy center of black women's oral history is located at the Schlesinger Library at Harvard University. The Schlesinger project set out to collect oral memoirs of a select group of older black women (many in their seventies and eighties) who had demonstrated extraordinary ability in their chosen professions. Between 1976 and 1981, seventy-two such women from various parts of the United States were interviewed by black women scholars, historians, and educators. Their transcribed interviews were deposited not only in the Schlesinger Library but in several other repositories nationwide. Among those interviewed was the author Margaret Walker Alexander, whose best-selling novel *Jubilee* (1966), based on her great-grandmother's life, exemplifies the use of family oral tradition. Also included in the Schlesinger collections are interviews with the artist and professor Lois Mailou Jones; the physician to poor migratory workers, Dr. Lena Edwards; the diplomat Zelma George; and the opera singer Etta Moten Barnett. Facsimiles of the transcripts, edited by Ruth Edmond Hill, are in a ten-volume set published as *The Black Women Oral History Project* (1990). In addition, there is a growing literature of oral testimony by black women, including Susan Tucker, *Telling Memories among Southern Women: Domestic Workers and Their Employers in the Segregated South* (1988); Emily Herring Wilson, *Hope and Dignity: Older Black Women of the South* (1983); Audrey Olsen Faulkner et al., ed., *When I Was Comin' Up: An Oral History of Aged Blacks* (1982); and Elizabeth Clark-Lewis, *Living In, Living Out: African American Domestics in Washington, D.C., 1910–1940* (1994).

Important regional studies are represented by two small oral collections, one at the Avery Research Center for African-American History and Culture of the College of Charleston and the other at the Penn Center of the Sea Islanders on St. Helena Island, S.C. The Avery Research Center was established to preserve and document the unique historical and cultural heritage of African-Americans of South Carolina, especially the Gullah culture of the low country island communities of St. John, James Island, and St. Helena, where West African customs and rituals (mainly those from Sierra Leone) have been identified. The Center is located on the site of the former Avery Normal Institute, which was established for the education of slaves in 1865. The Center holds manuscripts, personal papers, organizational records, and photographs of black South Carolinians, a reference collection of books, as well as a collection of video- and audiotaped oral history interviews. The Penn Center on St. Helena Island, South Carolina, is one of the oldest and most historically significant institutions in North America. The Penn Center's museum, library, and outreach programs provide information concerning the rich local history of this community. The memories and recollections of island residents are preserved on reel-to-reel tapes available to researchers, and stories of slavery days have been preserved through oral histories in the Gullah creole language collected from 1971 to 1975. The Center's video collection preserves songs, dances, and general sounds of the islands, and researchers are encouraged to use the resources of this unique and valuable facility. Three noteworthy oral history studies of this area are Mamie Garvin Fields and Karen Fields, *Lemon Swamp and Other Places: A Carolina Memoir* (1983); Guy and Candie Carawan, ed., *"Ain't You Got a Right to the Tree of Life?" The People of Johns Island, S.C.—Their Faces, Their Words and Their Songs* (1966, 1989); Ronald Daisy, *Reminiscences of Sea Island Heritage—Legacy of Freedmen on St. Helena Island* (1986).

The most important collections of African-American oral history resources at traditionally black institutions are housed at Fisk University in Nashville, Tenn., and at the Moorland-Spingarn Research Center at Howard University in Washington, D.C. The black oral history program at Fisk University was established in 1970 by Special Collections librarian Ann Allen Shockley, approximately forty years after Charles S. Johnson's pioneering oral history project. In 1971 the program received a National Endowment for the Humanities (NEH) grant to conduct interviews over a two-year period. Among the interviewees were Shirley Graham Du Bois, author, activist, and widow of W. E. B. Du Bois; the baseball player Henry "Hank" Aaron; the historian John Hope Franklin; the author Alex Haley; and the artist Aaron Douglas. Informants discussed a variety of topics, such as the civil rights movement, the Harlem Renaissance, blacks and the Catholic Church, and everyday life in the nation's all-black towns.

A sizable number of interviews were conducted by individual researchers for their own books or dissertations and later donated to the Fisk collection. Persons interested in the rituals and ceremonies of traditionally black universities or in Fisk University's history will find useful the collection of more than 100 audio-tapes of such campus events as convocations, commencement speeches, lectures, and seminars. Also preserved in the oral history office is an extensive collection of documents, photographs, and artifacts donated by the program's interviewees.

The first and so far only conference on Black Oral History was sponsored by the Fisk program in 1972 in Nashville, Tenn. The program was designed to familiarize librarians, historians, archivists, scholars, and researchers with the merits and methods of oral history in the collection, preservation, and documentation of African-American history.

In 1966, while serving on the Board of Directors of the Fund for the Advancement of Education, the political scientist and former diplomat Ralph J. Bunche proposed that the Fund award one final grant to establish a center of resources to document the history of black Americans. Dr. Bunche's original proposal led to the creation in 1967 of the Civil Rights Documentation Project (CRDP) at the Moorland-Spingarn Research Center at Howard University. The selected project director, Vincent Browne, was a Howard University professor as well as a former student and protégé of Dr. Bunche. The project was financed for the next six years by the Fund for the Advancement of Education and the Ford Foundation.

The interviewees and narrators of the Civil Rights Documentation Project were, for the most part, persons who would never write an autobiography or otherwise record their contributions to social change in the United States. They were selected from participants in a wide range of civil rights activities, among which were the 1954 Supreme Court decision on school desegregation and the Montgomery bus boycott of 1955–1956. Most noteworthy in this historic event is the memoir of Rosa Parks, whose interview revealed her long-term association with civil rights causes and organizations. There are more than one hundred black and white women's oral history memoirs in the collection, presenting an interesting and sometimes poignant view of women's roles in the civil rights struggle.

The late Ella Baker, who may be considered the doyenne of the civil rights movement, contributed a revealing memoir in which she stated her views concerning her role as a woman and non-minister in the Southern Christian Leadership Conference (SCLC). Baker later went on to assist young black activists in founding the Student Nonviolent Coordinating Committee (SNCC). The Civil Rights Documentation Project at Moorland-Spingarn also houses interviews with lawyers and judges who handled civil rights cases and with persons active in the implementation of court decisions in school desegregation cases. Mention must be made of five memoirs, each of considerable length, produced by faculty members of the Howard University Law School regarding their participation in school desegregation cases across the nation and before the Supreme Court. From the oral history transcripts of the participants, a clear picture emerges of the era of judicial and legislative struggle for civil rights originating in the Howard University Law School under the leadership of Charles Hamilton Houston. One interviewee remembered that before each school desegregation case was argued in court, it was argued nights earlier in the law school by the faculty and students.

The collection at Moorland-Spingarn even includes interviews with persons opposed to particular aspects of the civil rights movement. One such interview was with a journalist sympathetic to the cause of the Ku Klux Klan. The journalist described a Klan rally he attended and went on to describe "the ordinary people of the South" as being on the edge of "a collective nervous breakdown composed in equal parts of ignorance, rage, and paranoia." Prominent among these transcripts is a lengthy interview with Calvin Craig, who served as Grand Dragon of the Georgia Realm United Klans of America in Atlanta. Craig was a determined segregationist and ironically a vice chairman of a local Model Cities Program, where he worked, without complaint, under the supervision of a black man. A finding aid to the collection, *Bibliography of the Holdings of the Civil Rights Documentation Project,* was published in 1970. It has been revised and renamed *The Finding Aid to the Ralph J. Bunche Oral History Collection.* Initial research in the collection was done by persons working on the successful *Eyes on the Prize* television series, which was followed by the publication of Henry Hampton et al., ed., *Voices of Freedom: An Oral History of the Civil Rights Movement from the 1950s through the 1980s* (1990). The book incorporates salient parts of individual interviews with participants in the marches and sit-ins.

While continuing to enhance its civil rights material, Moorland-Spingarn also developed several other significant projects in its oral history collection. The memoirs of Howard University alumni, faculty, and staff were collected to further document the history of the university. The recorded recollections of World War II veterans of the 366th Infantry Regiment and the Tuskegee Airmen, who served in segregated units in Italy, document black military history in the United States. A Donors Program exists, wherein those organizations and individuals depositing papers and archives in Moorland's Manuscript Department are encouraged to add a tape-recorded oral history memoir to their donation. The Manuscript Department is also one of several repositories of the transcripts of the Schlesinger Library's Black Women Oral History Project.

Significant and timely modifications have been made over the years in the methods of recording oral interviews. In 1948, the reel-to-reel tape recorder was introduced to American scholars and researchers. Later, small portable tape recorders with highly sensitive microphones proved more efficient and less cumbersome to oral historians, folklorists, and others wishing to capture the spoken word. Now the video camera, with its promise of clear, lifelike sound pictures of the interviewee, competes with older forms of recording. Considerable debate has taken place among oral historians, academics, researchers, and scholars as to the pros and cons of videotaping. A large amount has been written concerning both the latest equipment and the technique and philosophy of the process. Five indispensable sources of information concerning the matter are W. Richard Whittaker, "Why Not Try Videotaping Oral History?" *Oral History Review* 9 (1981); Brad Jolly, *Videotaping Oral History* (1982); Joel Gardner, "Oral History and Video," *Oral History Review* 12 (1984); Dan Snipe, "The Future of Oral History and Moving Images," *Oral History Review* 19 (1991); and Pamela M. Henson and Terri A. Schorzman,

"Videohistory: Focusing on the American Past," *Journal of American History* 78 (1991).

The oral history component of one of the most recognized repositories of worldwide African and African-American resources, the Schomburg Center for Research in Black Culture, has adopted the videotape technique in conducting oral history interviews. The Schomburg Center, a branch of the New York Public Library, was established in 1926, when Arthur Alfonso Schomburg, a black bibliophile and collector, left his considerable private collection of books, documents, and artifacts to form the nucleus of the library's research collection. The Oral History Collection, in the Moving Image and Recorded Sound Division, was established in 1980. The Schomburg holds videotaped interviews with famous and obscure individuals. Outstanding are those with the dancers Katherine Dunham and Pearl Primus, where actual footwork and movements are shown and explained. Interviews are conducted by the curator and by consultants, contracted interviewers, and selected volunteers. The collection consists of approximately 2,000 hours of audiocassette and 300 videocassette interviews, and covers subjects such as "Black Physicians and Health Care in the African American Community," "African American Labor Leaders," "Black Dance Pioneers," "Black Scientists," and "Community Development Corporation Leaders." The collection is accessible on a local database, as well as RLIN and OCLC, and the processed and cataloged tapes are made available to researchers by appointment.

A significant contribution to the oral history documentation of the African-American experience has been the Schomburg Center's oral history department's sponsoring of "The Afro-American Labor Leadership Oral/Video History Series" by Joseph Wilson in 1984. The first series of interviews was conducted in the traditional audio recording format with such labor leaders as Charles Hayes, Jim Bell, Lillian Roberts, James Jackson, and Cleveland Roberts. When the project began using video, ten interviews were conducted, each approximately two hours in length. It was reported that the extra dimensions of video permitted researchers to observe the narrators' facial and body language. Documentaries on African-American labor history include Joseph F. Wilson, comp. and ed., *Black Labor in America 1865–1983* (1986) and Joseph F. Wilson, ed., *Tearing Down the Color Bar: A Documentary History and Analysis of the Brotherhood of Sleeping Car Porters* (1989); and Jack Santino, *Miles of Smiles, Years of Struggle: Stories of Black Pullman Porters* (1989).

Oral historians and oral history aficionados have access to conferences, seminars, and workshops sponsored by the national Oral History Association and the various regional associations such as Oral History in the Mid Atlantic Region (OHMAR), the New England Oral History Association, and others in most areas of the United States. The national association publishes both a newsletter and the *Oral History Review*. Issued annually, the *Review*'s almost 200-page volumes carry a wealth of informative articles, book reviews, and bibliographies. In 1979 the association adopted a set of guidelines to assist in the establishment of new oral history programs and to address problems of ongoing projects. Ten years later, the association revised the guidelines to include and promote multicultural uses of oral history.

By 1990 both the Oral History Association and the American Historical Association had adopted guidelines on the use of interviews and oral sources in historical research. It would be advisable for anyone embarking on an oral history project to read the guidelines and seriously consider the interviewer's responsibilities regarding the confidentiality and ownership of the interview. Whatever the purpose of the interview, whether for a published work or for deposit in a repository, the narrator should sign a statement giving permission for its use. The Oral History Association published John Neuenschwander's *Oral History and the Law* (1985), a volume that addresses many of the questions that arise with regard to the legal aspects of oral history interviewing. The book is now available in a second, revised edition that has been expanded to include results of court cases concerning oral history and legal issues that have been explored since the mid-1980s such as defamation, invasion of privacy, and recommendations for handling interviewees' legal release forms.

Over a ten-year period, with grant and foundation support, Duke University established a Center for the Study of Civil Rights and Race Relations. The University's Oral History Program, using as its motivation the civil rights movement of the 1960s, trained African-American historians in "the rewriting of traditional American historical scholarship" through oral sources. The program's objective was to provide graduate training in oral history research methodology, and its success is attested to in the work of three of its former students. Alphine W. Jefferson, "Echoes from the South: The History and Methodology of the Duke University Oral History Program, 1972–1982," *Oral History Review* 12 (1984), provides a lengthy overview of the Duke project. George C. Wright, interviewing African-Americans of his native Appalachia, documented their positive values and survival strategies in coping with hardship in "Oral History and the Search for the Black Past in Kentucky," *Oral History Review* 10 (1982). Albert S. Broussard, "Oral Recollections and the Historical Reconstruction of Black San Francisco, 1915–1940," *Oral History Review* 12 (1984), prefigures Broussard, *Black San Francisco: The Struggle for Racial Equality in the West, 1900–1954* (1993). Broussard is the first African-American to serve as national president of the Oral History Association.

Utilizing the recollections of participants in historical events, oral history has proved to be an invaluable asset in documenting the African-American experience. With increasing attention being paid to uncovering the African-American past, scholars will need to become more conversant with accepted oral history techniques. Fortunately, there appears to be a growing recognition by scholars of the need to incorporate the discipline as a valid instrument in the academic enterprise and to acquire, preserve, and expand repositories of African-American oral history.

9   *Art*

Betty Kaplan Gubert and John Gennari

The 1990s represented a productive period for the scholarly study of African-American art. A marked increase in monographic studies of individual artists coincided with an enhanced multicultural emphasis in museum exhibition practices, broadening and deepening access to objects and images created by African-Americans as well as to empirical and interpretive information about their producers. The number of titles published in the last decade in which an individual black artist's life and work is examined (roughly fifty, counting both book-length works and catalogs of exhibitions) is almost double the number published from 1940 to 1990. Such a notable outpouring is the cultural fruit of civil rights and black pride struggles, the growth and acceptance of African-American Studies departments (along with the legitimation of African-American subject matter in other humanities disciplines) at colleges and universities, and the recognition by publishers and curators of a diverse book-buying and museum-going public interested in African-American art.

The recent upsurge of interest in African-American art is measurable not just in quantitative output, however, but also in a qualitative shift in scholarly discourse. Art historians traditionally have tended to look at art produced by African-Americans when that art could be classified as "high" (associated with the post-Renaissance tradition of professionally trained production for patrons or the cosmopolitan market), "folk" (domestic and community-oriented objects and images thought to express the indigenous vernacular values of common African-Americans), or "primitive" (embodying the ostensibly "natural" qualities of a pre-civilized people operating outside of markets and educational or cultural institutions).

In recent scholarship and curatorial practice, these categories have been viewed as historically situated cultural constructions rather than as universal and timelessly meaningful descriptions of social reality. This reformulation of the very idea of art, central to the anti-foundationalist turn in cultural studies, has been especially important to the conceptualization of African-American art. It has meant that slave artisans and craftspeople and antebellum free persons of color working in the building, furniture, and decorative arts trades have become the subject of a burgeoning scholarship on African-American material culture (see, for example, John Michael Vlach, *Back of the Big House: The Architecture of Plantation Slavery* [1993]).

In the late 20th century, African-American artists such as Faith Ringgold and

Adrian Piper garnered critical acclaim for multimedia and interdisciplinary work that challenges traditional notions of artistic mastery (e.g., Adrian Piper, *Out of Order, Out of Sight* [1996], a two-volume collection of the philosopher/conceptual artist's notes for her performance pieces and art criticism from 1976 to 1992). Also, the paintings, sculptures, quilts, and other creations of Southern African-American "folk" artists have enjoyed a much-publicized vogue in the 1990s cosmopolitan art world (such as in Glenn Robert Smith and Robert Kenner, *Discovering Ellis Ruley: The Story of an American Outsider Artist* [1993], and Roland L. Freeman, *A Communion of the Spirits: African-American Quilters, Preservers, and Their Stories* [1996]).

It is not just the antihierarchical bent of recent cultural criticism and programming that has invigorated the scholarly study of much African-American art customarily marginalized in the European-centered art-historical discourse. Also important within the broader frame of cultural studies has been the conceptualization of a trans-Atlantic African diasporic culture, a migratory consciousness through which Africans and persons of African descent in Europe, the Caribbean, and South and North America have manifested shared patterns of cultural memory, structures of feeling, and stylistic modes of expression across artistic disciplines. While perhaps most influential in literary and music scholarship, where works such as Henry Louis Gates, Jr., *The Signifying Monkey: A Theory of Afro-American Literary Criticism* (1988), and Paul Gilroy, *The Black Atlantic: Modernity and Double Consciousness* (1993), have assumed paradigmatic significance, transnational frameworks have also structured the study of African-American visual and plastic arts. See Robert Farris Thompson, *Face of the Gods: Art and Altars of Africa and the African Americas* (1993) and *Flash of the Spirit: African and Afro-American Art and Philosophy* (1983).

Increasingly, as well, the creative visions, practices, and products of black artists are being situated within larger cultural histories that trace the evolution of ideas and images of blackness in Western society. Most significant in this regard is "The Image of the Black in Western Art," a photo archive curated by the W. E. B. Du Bois Institute for Afro-American Research at Harvard University. Spanning nearly 5,000 years and documenting virtually all forms of media, this archive is an unprecedented research project devoted to the systematic investigation of how people of African descent have been perceived and represented in art.

STANDARD REFERENCE WORKS

All of these developments in recent studies of African-American art build upon the foundation laid by the scholars who introduced African-Americans into the traditional canon of art history. Early and important surveys are Alain Locke's *The Negro in Art* (1940), James A. Porter's *Modern Negro Art* (1943), Cedric Dover's *American Negro Art* (1960), Judith Wragg Chase's *Afro-American Art & Craft* (1971), Elsa Fine's *The Afro-American Artist: A Search for Identity* (1973), and David Driskell's landmark catalog, *Two Centuries of Black American Art* (1976). Elton Fax, an artist (as is Driskell), wrote two collective biographies, *Seventeen Black Artists* (1971) and *Black Artists of the New Generation* (1977). Two bibliographies make available many scattered and ephemeral sources about artists. They are *Afro-American Artists: A Bio-Bibliographical Directory* (1973) by Theresa Dickason Cederholm, and Lynn Moody Igoe's *250 Years of Afro-American Art: An Annotated Bibliography* (2 vols., 1981).

These reference books influenced scholars who chose one artist whose life should be accorded attention and whose work should receive critical evaluation. The examination of these artists brought to public, or at least academic, attention many artists who had been omitted from standard reference works once thought to be comprehensive. In addition, major public African-American art collections have been cataloged and documented in the important study *To Conserve a Legacy: American Art from Historically Black Colleges and Universities,* by Richard J. Powell and Jock Reynolds (1999).

STUDIES OF INDIVIDUAL ARTISTS

Horace Pippin: A Negro Painter in America (1947), by Selden Rodman, appeared in the year after Pippin's death. A lavish production, it included one of four autobiographical sketches written by Pippin. Rodman briefly mentions "the known artists of his race in the United States"—Jacob Lawrence, Romare Bearden, Charles Sebree, and Eldzier Cortor. Allan Rohan Crite, a Boston artist, illustrated *Were You There When They Crucified My Lord?* (1944), *All Glory: Brush Drawings on the Prayer of Consecration* (1947), and *Three Spirituals from Earth to Heaven* (1948). Not at all autobiographical, they are nonetheless significant for any study of Crite.

Lois Mailou Jones: Peintures, 1937–1951 (1952) was printed in France for the artist in an edition of 500 copies, with 112 prints. The director of the Harmon Foundation, Mary B. Brady, provided biographical information on Jones, while James A. Porter discussed her art in Paris and the French countryside. Ollie Harrington, the cartoonist for the *Pittsburgh Courier* and other newspapers, gathered a selection of his cartoons in *Bootsie and Others* (1958), with an introduction by Langston Hughes.

West Africa Vignettes (1960; the 1963 edition has thirteen additional drawings) records Elton C. Fax's trips to four countries. The text accompanying the sketches is in English and French. John Biggers illustrated his 1957 trip to Ghana in *Ananse: The Web of Life in Africa* (1962). *Images of Dignity: The Drawings of Charles White* (1967) was "the first book printed on a living black artist in U.S. history" (*Freedomways* 20:3 [1980]: 164). One other monograph on a black artist appeared in this decade. *Henry Ossawa Tanner, American Artist* (1969), by Marcia M. Mathews, was the first biographical study of Tanner, who died in 1937.

The Art of Romare Bearden: The Prevalence of Ritual (1972) was the first coffee-table book by one of the country's leading art publishers to feature a black artist. Although short on biographical information, it was a sumptuous publication, in large format, with half of the ninety-one plates in full color. Remaindered some years later, it is now available only in the rare book world. Tom Feeling's *Black Pilgrimage* (1972) was that unusual publication, an artist's autobiography. *Through Black Eyes: Journeys of a Black Artist to East Africa and Russia* (1974) recorded in both words and pictures Elton Fax's continued odyssey. Milton W. Brown wrote

Jacob Lawrence (1974) for the Whitney Museum of American Art. *Beauford Delaney: A Retrospective* (1978) was the catalog for the exhibition of his work at the Studio Museum in Harlem.

The entire issue of *Freedomways* 20:3 (1980) was dedicated to Charles White, who died in 1979, and it includes reminiscences, an interview, and a 22-page bibliography. James D. Parks wrote *Robert S. Duncanson: Nineteenth Century Black Romantic Painter* (1980). Four women artists were recognized in the following books or catalogs: *A Life in Art: Alma Thomas 1891–1978* (1981), by Merry A. Foresta; *The Art of Elizabeth Catlett* (1984), by Samella S. Lewis; *Faith Ringgold: Twenty Years of Painting, Sculpture, and Performance 1963–1983* (1984), by Michele Wallace; and *Clementine Hunter: American Folk Artist* (1988), by James L. Wilson. The Bahamian folk artist Amos Ferguson received wider attention through the exhibition and catalog *Paint by Mr. Amos Ferguson* (1984), by Ute Stebich. *James Lesesne Wells: Sixty Years in Art* (1986), by Richard Powell and Jock Reynolds, and *Jacob Lawrence: American Painter* (1986), by Ellen Harkins Wheat followed. *Joshua Johnson: Freeman and Early American Portrait Painter* (1987), by Carolyn Weekley, surveyed the life of Johnson (or Johnston, as his name is sometimes written). The decade closed with works on Palmer Hayden, James W. Washington, Jr., Norman Lewis, and Raymond Lark. They are *Echoes of Our Past: The Narrative Artistry of Palmer C. Hayden* (1988), by Allan M. Gordon; *The Spirit in the Stone: The Visionary Art of James W. Washington, Jr.* (1989), by Paul J. Karlstrom; *Norman Lewis: From the Harlem Renaissance to Abstraction* (1989), by Ann Gibson; and *Raymond Lark: American Artist of Tradition and Diversity* (1989), by Wilfred D. Samuels.

The 1970s and 1980s witnessed the publication of several works in architecture and material culture studies with a focus on African-American practitioners. Charles A. Brown's *W. A. Rayfield: Pioneer Black Architect of Birmingham, AL* (1972); Rodney Barfield's *Thomas Day, Cabinetmaker* (1975); John Michael Vlach's *The Afro-American Tradition in Decorative Arts* (1978), as well as his *Charleston Blacksmith: The Work of Philip Simmons* (1981); and Rosalind G. Bauchum's *The Black Architect* (1982) are key texts published during this period.

Because so many works on individual black artists were published in the 1990s, this essay will cite only selected titles. The Los Angeles–based architect Paul R. Williams, described as "perhaps the most successful Negro artist in the United States" in *Life* magazine in 1938, is the subject of a biography (*Paul R. Williams, Architect* [1993]) written by his granddaughter Karen E. Hudson. Well-known painters such as Romare Bearden and Henry O. Tanner were the subjects of substantial volumes. Myron Schwartzman wrote *Romare Bearden: His Life and Art* (1990), a work enriched by sound scholarship, personal friendship, and rich visual material. The catalog for the Studio Museum in Harlem's retrospective exhibition, *Memory and Metaphor: The Art of Romare Bearden, 1940–1987* (1991), by Sharon F. Patton, followed. *Henry Ossawa Tanner* (1991), by Dewey F. Mosby, includes an essay by Tanner's grandniece, Rae Alexander-Minter. Minter also wrote *Across Continents and Cultures: The Art and Life of Henry Ossawa Tanner* (1995). A video on Tanner's life and work, Casey King's *Henry Ossawa Tanner: Great American Artist, African-American Legend*, appeared in 1991.

Works on Jacob Lawrence, the third member of the triumvirate of best-known black artists, take close looks at his prints and his series of paintings. *Jacob Lawrence: The Frederick Douglass and Harriet Tubman Series of 1938–40* (1991), by Ellen Harkins Wheat, his biographer; *Jacob Lawrence: The Migration Series* (1992), edited by Elizabeth Hutton Turner; and *Jacob Lawrence: Thirty Years of Prints 1963–1993: A Catalogue Raisonné* (1994), edited by Peter Nesbett, all offer information about the artist as well as aspects of his work.

Recently published catalogs include *Charles Alston, Artist and Teacher* (1990) and Eleanor Flomenhaft's *Faith Ringgold: A 25 Year Survey* (1990). An autobiography, *We Flew Over the Bridge: The Memoirs of Faith Ringgold,* appeared in 1995. Jontyle Theresa Robinson and Wendy Greenhouse coauthored *The Art of Archibald Motley, Jr.* (1991), about the artist known for scenes of black night life during the 1920s in Chicago, New York, the South, and Paris. Richard J. Powell, in *Homecoming: The Art and Life of William H. Johnson* (1991), renewed interest in an artist of great power whose works were rescued from destruction by the Harmon Foundation. *David Hammons: Rousing the Rubble* (1991) highlighted an artist who uses hair, chicken bones, and other found objects as his media. Frank Maresca and Roger Ricco edited *Bill Traylor: His Art, His Life* (1991). Traylor, a folk artist from Alabama, is represented through 152 color illustrations of his work. Biographical information is provided by Charles Shannon, who supported and preserved the works from 1939 to 1947, when Traylor died at 93. Books in this decade that celebrated other folk artists were *Elijah Pierce, Woodcarver* (1992); *Discovering Ellis Ruley: The Story of an American Outsider Artist* (1993), by Glenn Robert Smith and Robert Kenner; *Minnie Evans: Artist* (1993); *I Tell My Heart: The Art of Horace Pippin* (1993), by Judith Stein; and *Thornton Dial: Image of the Tiger* (1993).

Juanita Marie Holland and Corrine Jennings uncovered new information in *Edward Mitchell Bannister, 1828–1901* (1992), a study of a painter about whom little had been known. *James A. Porter, Artist and Art Historian: The Memory of the Legacy* (1992) showed many of the artist's works, and *Jean-Michel Basquiat* (1992), by Richard Marshall, served as a memorial to the young artist. Lucinda H. Gedeon wrote *Melvin Edwards, Sculpture: A Thirty-Year Retrospective, 1963–1993* (1993). Joseph D. Ketner wrote *The Emergence of the African-American Artist: Robert S. Duncanson, 1821–1872* (1993). Ollie Harrington was the subject of two books published in 1993, both edited and with an introduction by M. Thomas Inge. *Dark Laughter: The Satiric Art of Oliver W. Harrington from the Walter O. Evans Collection of African-American Art* consists of Harrington's cartoons from the late 1950s through the 1980s, the years of his expatriation. *Why I Left America and Other Essays* is autobiographical.

"Resonance, Transformation, and Rhyme: The Art of Renée Stout," examines the sculptures of the artist in *Astonishment and Power* (1993). Tritobia Hayes Benjamin wrote *The Life and Art of Lois Mailou Jones* (1994), a catalog for a traveling exhibition. *Aaron Douglas: Art, Race, and the Harlem Renaissance* (1995), by Amy Helene Kirschke, is the first full-length study of the artist known for his graphic partnership with the literary works of the Harlem Renaissance. Douglas's last forty years, however, were beyond the scope of Kirschke's thesis and are treated only briefly. *The Art of John Biggers: View from the Upper Room* (1995), by Alvia J. Wardlow, accompanies the recent traveling exhibition. Biggers, like Jones, Douglas, and Porter, was a professor of art and influenced generations of students as well as artists.

Ernie Barnes, a professional football player for five years, majored in art in college and later wrote an autobiography, *From Pads to Palette* (1995). Robert L. Douglass has examined the work of one of the founders of the Black Arts Movement and Afri-Cobra in *Wadsworth Jarrell: The Artist as Revolutionary* (1996). *Gullah Images: The Art of Jonathan Green* (1996) is a deluxe publication with many reproductions of Green's paintings, but with little biographical information. The life of Beauford Delaney, who lived in France for more than forty years, has been thoroughly explored by David A. Leeming in *Amazing Grace: A Biography of Beauford Delaney* (1997).

THE FUTURE OF AFRICAN-AMERICAN ARTS SCHOLARSHIP

The aforementioned monographs vary in length from fifty to more than three hundred pages, and vary therefore in depth of research as well as number of illustrations. Notwithstanding this recent blossoming of works devoted to a single artist, important symposia collections, exhibition catalogs, and standard reference works with collective biographies should not be overlooked. *People of Color in Architecture* (1991), an exhibition catalog and collection of essays from a symposium held at Yale University, serves as a useful overview of the architecture profession and suggests directions for future study of individual architects. The best of the recent art history reference works is *A History of African-American Artists from 1792 to the Present* (1993), by Romare Bearden and Harry Henderson. There are lengthy essays on major artists, as well as on artists who have not yet been studied sufficiently to be the subjects of entire books. Some of these are Grafton T. Brown, Edmonia Lewis, Richmond Barthe, Hale Woodruff, Sargent Johnson, and Eldzier Cortor. Bearden and Henderson's original research has unearthed new information, especially about Joshua Johnson. The reader will not find anything on Romare Bearden (as an author he thought his inclusion would be inappropriate) or on artists born after 1925. These artists, coming of age in the 1950s, faced a different set of social circumstances—the G.I. Bill, the dismantling of segregation, the opening of art galleries to artists of color, and the civil rights movement—that the authors decided were beyond the scope of their study. Nevertheless, this book stands as a model of research for the history of African-American art. Some of the artists awaiting scholarly attention are Emma Amos, Benny Andrews, Robert Colescott, Richard Hunt, Adrian Piper, and Rose Piper. The newly published *St. James Guide to Black Artists* (1997), with information about 400 artists, should generate the production of other monographs.

In the growing field of historical material culture studies, John Michael Vlach's *Back of the Big House: The Architecture of Plantation Slavery* (1993) will likely define the terms of discussion for the foreseeable future. In this profusely illustrated book, Vlach shifts his focus from African building traditions on American soil to slave appropriation of the world assigned to them for the purpose of creative resistance.

GENERAL REFERENCE

Albany Institute of History and Art, *The Negro Artist Comes of Age: A National Survey of Contemporary American Artists* (1945).

Cederholm, Theresa Dickason, *Afro-American Artists: A Bio-Bibliographic Directory* (1973).

Davis, Lenwood G., *Black Artists in the United States: An Annotated Bibliography of Books, Articles, and Dissertations on Black Artists, 1779–1979* (1980).

Fowler, Carolyn, *Black Arts and Black Aesthetics: A Bibliography* (1981).

Grant, Bradford C., and Dennis Alan Mann, *Directory, African American Architects* (1991).

Henkes, Robert, *The Art of Black American Women: Works of Twenty-Four Artists of the Twentieth Century* (1993).

Holmes, Oakley N., Jr., *The Complete Annotated Resource Guide to Black American Art: Books, Doctoral Dissertations, Exhibition Catalogs, Periodicals, Films, Slides, Large Prints, Speakers, Filmstrips, Videotapes, Black Museums, Art Galleries, and Much More* (1978).

Igoe, Lynn Moody, *250 Years of Afro-American Art: An Annotated Bibliography* (1981).

Louisiana Writers' Project, *Gumbo Ya-Ya: Anthology of Contemporary African-American Women Artists* (1995).

St. Louis Public Library, *An Index to Black American Artists* (1972).

Taha, Halima, *Collecting African American Art: Works on Paper and Canvas* (1998).

Travis, Jack, ed., *African American Architects in Current Practice* (1992).

Weiss, Ellen, *An Annotated Bibliography on African-American Architects and Builders* (1993).

SCHOLARLY STUDIES

Adele, Lynne, *Black History, Black Vision: The Visionary Image in Texas* (1989).

African Americans in Art: Selections from the Art Institute of Chicago (1999).

Afro-American Artists: New York and Boston (1970).

Afro-American Artists: North Carolina, USA (1980).

Anderson, Gennell, *The Call of the Ancestors* (1988).

Another Face of the Diamond: Pathways through the Black Atlantic South (1988).

Atkinson, J. Edward, *Black Dimensions in Contemporary Art* (1971).

Baking in the Sun: Visionary Images from the South (1987).

Barfield, Rodney, *Thomas Day, Cabinetmaker* (1975).

Barnett-Aden Collection (1974).

Bauchum, Rosalind G., *The Black Architect* (1982).

Bearden, Romare, and Harry Henderson, *A History of African-American Artists, from 1792 to the Present* (1993).

——— *Six Black Masters of American Art* (1972).

Bearden, Romare, and Carol Holty, *The Painter's Mind: A Study of the Relations of Structure and Space in Painting* (1969).

Biggers, John Thomas, *Black Art in Houston: The Texas Southern University Experience Presenting the Art of Biggers and [Carroll] Simms and Their Students* (1978).

Black Art Ancestral Legacy: The African Impulse in African-American Art (1989).

Bomani, Asake, and Belvie Rooks, *Paris Connections: African American Artists in Paris* (1992).

Chase, Judith Wragg, *Afro-American Art and Craft* (1971).

Davis, Donald Fred, *Contributions of Four Blacks to Art Education in the South, 1920–1970* (1983).

Deacon, Deborah A., "The Art and Artifacts Collection of the Schomburg Center for Research in Black Culture," in *Bulletin of Research in the Humanities, NYPL* (1981).

Doty, Robert M., *Contemporary Black Artists in America* (1971).

Dover, Cedric, *American Negro Art* (1960).

Driskell, David C., *African American Visual Aesthetics: A Postmodernist View* (1995).

——— *Amistad II: Afro-American Art* (1975).

——— *Contemporary Visual Expressions: The Art of Sam Gilliam, Martha Jackson-Jarvis, Keith Morrison, and William T. Williams* (1987).

——— *Hidden Heritage: Afro-American Art, 1800–1950* (1985).

——— *Two Centuries of Black American Art* (1976).

East/West: Contemporary American Art (1985).

The Evolution of Afro-American Artists, 1800–1950 (1967).

Explorations in the City of Light: African-American Artists in Paris, 1945–1965 (1996).

Fax, Elton C., *Black Artists of the New Generation* (1977).

——— *Seventeen Black Artists* (1971).

Ferguson, Leland, *Uncommon Ground: Archaeology and Early African America, 1650–1800* (1992).

Ferris, William, *Afro-American Folk Art and Craft* (1983).

Fine, Elsa, *The Afro-American Artist: A Search for Identity* (1973).

Forever Free: Art by African-American Women, 1862–1980 (1980).

Freeman, Roland L., *A Communion of the Spirits: African-American Quilters, Preservers, and Their Stories* (1996).

Fry, Gladys-Marie, *Stitched from the Soul: Slave Quilts from the Ante-Bellum South* (1990).

Gaither, Edmund Barry, *Massachusetts Masters: Afro-American Artists* (1988).

Golden, Thelma, *Black Male: Representations of Masculinity in Contemporary American Art* (1994).

Goode-Bryant, Linda, *Contextures* (1978).

Greene, Carroll Jr., *American Visions, Afro-American Art, 1986* (1987).

Hall, Robert L., *Gathered Visions: Selected Works by African-American Women Artists* (1992).

Harlem Renaissance: Art of Black America (1987).

The Harmon and Harriet Kelley Collection of African American Art (1994).

Hartigan, Lynda Roscoe, *Sharing Traditions: Five Black Artists in Nineteenth Century America* (1985).

Herbert F. Johnson Museum of Art, *Directions in Afro-American Art* (1974).

Kraskin, Sandra, *Wrestling with History: A Celebration of African American Self-Taught Artists from the Collection of Ronald and June Shelp* (1996).

Leon, Eli, *Who'd a Thought It: Improvisations in African-American Quilting* (1987).

Lewis, Samella, *Art: African American* (1990).

Livingston, Jane, and John Beardsley, *Black Folk Art in America: 1930–1980* (1982).

Locke, Alain, *Negro Art Past and Present* (1936).

——— *The Negro in Art* (1940).

McElroy, Guy C., *Facing History: The Black Image in American Art, 1710–1940* (1990).

Morrison, Keith, *Art in Washington and Its Afro-American Presence, 1940–1970* (1985).

New Black Artists (1969).

Next Generation: Southern Black Aesthetic (1990).

19 Sixties: A Cultural Awakening Re-Evaluated, 1965–1975 (1989).

Perry, Regenia A., *Free within Ourselves: African-American Artists in the Collection of the National Museum of American Art* (1992).

——— *What It Is: Black American Folk Art from the Collection of Regenia Perry* (1982).

Porter, James A., *Modern Negro Art* (1992).

Powell, Richard J., *Black Art and Culture in the Twentieth Century* (1997).

Reynolds, Gary A., and Beryl J. Wright, *Against the Odds: African-American Artists and the Harmon Foundation* (1989).

Robinson, Jontyle Theresa, *Bearing Witness: Contemporary Works by African-American Women Artists* (1996).

The Search for Freedom: African American Abstract Painting, 1945–1975 (1991).

Since the Harlem Renaissance: 50 Years of Afro-American Art (1985).

The Studio Museum in Harlem: 25 Years of African-American Art (1985).

Taylor, William E., *A Shared Heritage: Art by Four African Americans* (1996).

Teilhet, Jean, *Dimensions of Black* (1970).

Tradition and Conflict: Images of a Turbulent Decade, 1963–1973 (1985).

Uncommon Beauty in Common Objects: The Legacy of African American Craft Art (1993).

Vlach, John Michael, *The Afro-American Tradition in Decorative Arts* (1978).

———— *Back of the Big House: The Architecture of Plantation Slavery* (1993).
Walter O. Evans Collection of African American Art (1991).
Welsh-Asante, Kariamu, *The African Aesthetic: Keeper of the Traditions* (1993).
Willis, John Ralph, *Fragments of American Life: An Exhibition of Paintings* (1976).
Yale School of Architecture, *People of Color in Architecture* (1991).
Yet Still We Rise: African-American Art in Cleveland, 1920–1970 (1996).

INDIVIDUAL ARTISTS

Alston, Charles
Alston, Charles, *Charles Alston: Artist and Teacher* (1990).
Amos, Emma
Emma Amos: Paintings and Prints, 1982–1992 (1993).
Bannister, Edward M.
Holland, Juanita Marie, and Corrine Jennings, *Edward Mitchell Bannister, 1828–1901* (1992).
Barnes, Ernie
Barnes, Ernie, *From Pads to Palette* (1995).
Basquiat, Jean-Michel
Marshall, Richard, *Jean-Michel Basquiat* (2 vols., 1992, 1996).
Bearden, Romare
Gelburd, Gail, *A Graphic Odyssey: Romare Bearden as Printmaker* (1992).
Gelburd, Gail, and Thelma Golden, *Romare Bearden in Black-and-White: Photomontage Projections, 1964* (1997).
Patton, Sharon F., *Memory and Metaphor: The Art of Romare Bearden, 1940–1987* (1991).
Schwartzman, Myron, *Romare Bearden: His Life and Art* (1990).
Washington, M. Bunch, *The Art of Romare Bearden: The Prevalence of Ritual* (1972).
Biggers, John
Biggers, John, *Ananse: The Web of Life in Africa* (1962).
Wardlow, Alvia J., *The Art of John Biggers: View from the Upper Room* (1995).
Blackburn, Bob
Bob Blackburn's Printmaking Workshop: Artists of Color (1992).
Buchanan, Beverly
Beverly Buchanan, Shackworks: A 16-Year Survey (1994).
Catlett, Elizabeth
Catlett, Elizabeth, *Elizabeth Catlett: Works on Paper, 1944–1992,* ed. Jeanne Zeidler (1993).
Lewis, Samella, *The Art of Elizabeth Catlett* (1984).
Crite, Allan Rohan
Crite, Allan Rohan, *All Glory: Brush Drawings on the Prayer of Consecration* (1947).
———— *Three Spirituals from Earth to Heaven* (1948).
———— *Were You There When They Crucified My Lord?* (1944).
Day, Thomas
Barfield, Rodney, *Thomas Day: Cabinetmaker* (1975).
Delaney, Beauford
Delaney, Beauford, *Beauford Delaney: A Retrospective* (1978).
Leeming, David A., *Amazing Grace: A Biography of Beauford Delaney* (1998).
Dial, Thornton
Thornton Dial: Image of the Tiger (1993).
Douglas, Aaron
Kirschke, Amy Helene, *Aaron Douglas: Art, Race, and the Harlem Renaissance* (1995).
Duncanson, Robert S.
Ketner, Joseph D., *The Emergence of the African-American Artist: Robert S. Duncanson, 1821–1872* (1993).
Parks, James D., *Robert S. Duncanson: 19th Century Black Romantic Painter* (1980).

Porter, James A., "Robert S. Duncanson: Midwestern Romantic Realist," *Art in America* (1951).

Edwards, Melvin

Gedeon, Lucinda H., *Melvin Edwards, Sculpture: A Thirty-Year Retrospective, 1963–1993* (1993).

Evans, Minnie

Kenner, Robert, *Minnie Evans: Artist* (1993).

Fax, Elton C.

Fax, Elton C., *Through Black Eyes: Journeys of a Black Artist to East Africa and Russia* (1974).

——— *West Africa Vignettes* (1960).

Feelings, Tom

Feelings, Tom, *Black Pilgrimage* (1972).

——— *The Middle Passage: White Ships, Black Cargo* (1995).

Ferguson, Amos

Stebich, Ute, *Paint by Mr. Amos Ferguson* (1984).

Green, Jonathan

Green, Jonathan, *Gullah Images: The Art of Jonathan Green* (1996).

Hammons, David

Hammons, David, *David Hammons: Rousing the Rubble* (1981).

Sill, Robert, *David Hammons in the Hood* (1994).

Harrington, Ollie

Harrington, Ollie, *Bootsie and Others* (1958).

Inge, M. Thomas, ed., *Why I Left America and Other Essays* (1993).

———, ed., *Dark Laughter: The Satiric Art of Oliver W. Harrington from the Walter O. Evans Collection of African American Art* (1993).

Hayden, Palmer

Gordon, Allan M., *Echoes of Our Past: The Narrative Artistry of Palmer C. Hayden* (1988).

Hunter, Clementine

Wilson, James L., *Clementine Hunter: American Folk Artist* (1988).

Jarrell, Wadsworth

Douglass, Robert L., *Wadsworth Jarrell: The Artist as Revolutionary* (1996).

Johnson, Joshua

Weekley, Carolyn, *Joshua Johnson: Freeman and Early American Portrait Painter* (1987).

Johnson, William H.

Novae: William H. Johnson and Bob Thompson (1990).

Powell, Richard J., *Homecoming: The Art and Life of William H. Johnson* (1991).

Jones, Lois M.

Benjamin, Tritobia Hayes, *The Life and Art of Lois Mailou Jones* (1994).

Brady, Mary B., and James A. Porter, *Lois Mailou Jones: Peintures, 1937–1951* (1952).

Lark, Raymond

Samuels, Wilfred D., *Raymond Lark: American Artist of Tradition and Diversity* (1989).

Lawrence, Jacob

Brown, Milton W., *Jacob Lawrence* (1974).

Lawrence, Jacob, *The Great Migration: An American Story* (1992).

Nesbett, Peter, ed., *Jacob Lawrence: Thirty Years of Prints, 1963–1993: A Catalogue Raisonné* (1994).

Powell, Richard J., *Jacob Lawrence* (1992).

Turner, Elizabeth Hutton, *Jacob Lawrence: The Migration Series* (1993).

Wheat, Ellen Harkins, *Jacob Lawrence: American Painter* (1986).

——— *Jacob Lawrence: The Frederick Douglass and Harriet Tubman Series of 1938–1940* (1991).

Lewis, Norman

Gibson, Ann, *Norman Lewis: From Harlem Renaissance to Abstraction* (1989).

Motley, Archibald, Jr.

Robinson, Jontyle Theresa, and Wendy Greenhouse, *The Art of Archibald Motley, Jr.* (1991).

Norman, Joseph
  Dialogue: John Wilson, Joseph Norman (1995).
Olugebefola, Ademola
  Thomas, Harold A., III, *Ademola Olugebefola: A 25 Year Legacy of Classics in American Art, 1965–1990* (1993).
Overstreet, Joe
  Joe Overstreet: (Re)call and Response (1996).
Pierce, Elijah
  Roberts, Norma, ed., *Elijah Pierce, Woodcarver* (1992).
Pindell, Howardena
  Howardena Pindell, Paintings and Drawings: A Retrospective Exhibition, 1972–1992 (1992).
Pippin, Horace
  Rodman, Selden, *Horace Pippin: A Negro Painter in America* (1947).
  Stein, Judith, *I Tell My Heart: The Art of Horace Pippin* (1993).
Porter, James A.
  James A. Porter, Artist and Art Historian: The Memory of the Legacy (1992).
Rayfield, W. A.
  Brown, Charles A., *W. A. Rayfield: Pioneer Black Architect of Birmingham, AL* (1972).
Ringgold, Faith
  Flomenhaft, Eleanor, *Faith Ringgold: A 25 Year Survey* (1990).
  Ringgold, Faith, *We Flew over the Bridge: The Memoirs of Faith Ringgold* (1995).
  Wallace, Michele, *Faith Ringgold: Twenty Years of Painting, Sculpture, and Performance, 1963–1983* (1984).
Ruley, Ellis
  Smith, Glenn Robert, and Robert Kenner, *Discovering Ellis Ruley: The Story of an American Outsider Artist* (1993).
Simmons, Philip
  Vlach, John Michael, *Charleston Blacksmith: The Work of Philip Simmons* (1981).
Stout, Renée
  Berns, Marla, *Dear Robert, I'll See You in the Crossroads: A Project by Renée Stout* (1995).
  "Resonance, Transformation, and Rhyme: The Art of Renée Stout," in Wyatt MacGaffey and Michael D. Harris, *The Eyes of Understanding* (1993).
Tanner, Henry Ossawa
  Mathews, Marcia M., *Henry Ossawa Tanner, American Artist* (1969).
  Mosby, Dewey F., *Across Continents and Cultures: The Art and Life of Henry Ossawa Tanner* (1995).
  ——— *Henry Ossawa Tanner* (1991).
Thomas, Alma
  Foresta, Merry A., *A Life in Art: Alma Thomas, 1891–1978* (1981).
  Thomas, Alma, *Alma W. Thomas: A Retrospective of the Paintings* (1998).
Thompson, Bob
  Golden, Thelma, *Bob Thompson* (1998).
Traylor, Bill
  Maresca, Frank, and Roger Ricco, ed., *Bill Traylor: His Art, His Life* (1991).
Washington, James W., Jr.
  Karlstrom, Paul J., *The Spirit in the Stone: The Visionary Art of James W. Washington, Jr.* (1989).
Watson, Barrington
  Watson, Barrington, *Barrington* (1993).
Wells, James Lesesne
  Powell, Richard, and Jock Reynolds, *James Lesesne Wells: Sixty Years in Art* (1986).
White, Charles
  White, Charles, *Images of Dignity: The Drawings of Charles White* (1967).
  Freedomways 20:3 (1980). Entire issue.

Williams, Paul R.
  Hudson, Karen E., *Paul R. Williams, Architect* (1993).
Williams, William T.
  Fourteen Paintings [William T. Williams] (1991).
Wilson, John
  Dialogue: John Wilson, Joseph Norman (1995).

UNIVERSITIES AND LIBRARIES

Hampton University, Hampton, Va. Among the 1,500 paintings, graphics, and sculptures are Henry O. Tanner's *Lion's Head* (1892) and *The Banjo Lesson* (1893), and works by major artists of the Harlem Renaissance, including Aaron Douglas, Malvin Gray Johnson, Hale Woodruff, and Richmond Barthe. Other works include those of Augusta Savage, Romare Bearden, John Biggers, Jacob Lawrence, Elizabeth Catlett, Allan Crite, Palmer Hayden, Norman Lewis, James Wells, Charles White, and Ellis Wilson.

Howard University Gallery of Art, Washington, D.C. This is a wide-ranging collection of works by such 19th-century artists as Robert Duncanson, Edward Bannister, and Edmonia Lewis, and by such contemporary artists as Richard Hunt and Sam Gilliam. Also includes Alain Locke's collection of paintings and African sculptures.

Fisk University, Nashville, Tenn. The collection holds 900 paintings, prints, and sculptures by African-American artists, including murals and other works by Aaron Douglas, who taught at Fisk from 1937 to 1966.

The Clark Atlanta University Collection of Afro-American Art, Atlanta, Ga. This major institutional art collection was started in 1942 when Hale Woodruff instituted an annual exhibition for African-American artists. Works by Charles Alston and Lois Mailou Jones were among the winning entries in the inaugural exhibition. The exhibition continued until 1970, accounting for 300 of the collection's acquisitions. This core collection was augmented by gifts and purchases, including works by Romare Bearden, Palmer Hayden, Jacob Lawrence, and Archibald Motley. It also includes *Art of the Negro,* a six-part mural painted by Woodruff in 1950.

Arts and Artifacts Collection of the Schomburg Center for Research in Black Culture, New York Public Library, New York, N.Y. The collection includes works shown during the Harmon Foundation's annual art exhibitions starting in the 1920s, as well as gifts from friends, patrons, and artists. Strong in works from the 1930s Works Progress Administration (WPA) by such artists as Palmer Hayden, Malvin Gray Johnson, and Jacob Lawrence, the collection also includes works by E. Simms Campbell, Barbara Chase-Riboud, Beauford Delaney, Horace Pippin, Charles Sebree, and Bill Traylor.

The Amistad Research Center, Tulane University, New Orleans, La. Holdings include the Aaron Douglas collection of nearly 300 paintings and sculptures by African-American artists. Rich in work from the Harlem Renaissance, including twelve paintings by Douglas and seventeen by Malvin Gray Johnson, there are also seventeen paintings by the 19th-century artist Edward M. Bannister.

MUSEUMS

The National Museum of American Art, Smithsonian Institution, Washington, D.C. The collection contains the works of 105 African-American artists from all periods, including James Hampton's room-sized 180-piece assemblage, *The Throne of the Third Heaven of the Nations Millennium General Assembly.* The museum has acquired many distinguished private and foundation collections, such as those of Alma Thomas, Warren Robbins, and the Harmon Foundation.

The Studio Museum in Harlem, New York, N.Y. Opened in 1968 as a studio and exhibition space for contemporary artists, the museum since 1982 has assembled a collection of

10,000 items in all media. The collection is particularly strong in the politically conscious art of the sixties.

National Center for Afro-American Artists, Elma Lewis School, Boston, Mass. This collection began in 1978 with a donation of more than 200 works by Allan Crite, Richard Yarde, and John Wilson, among others.

The Amistad Foundation African-American Collection, Wadsworth Athenaeum, Hartford, Conn. Six thousand objects have been collected by Randolph Linsly Simpson, documenting the history of blacks in America. Primarily a collection of images and artifacts representing African-Americans, the collection also includes a sculpture by Richmond Barthe and a painting by David Bowser.

The Museum of African American Art, Tampa, Fla. Eighty-one artists from 1860 to 1955 are represented in the Barnett-Aden Collection of 171 paintings, sculpture, and lithographs.

DuSable Museum, Chicago, Ill. The collection includes 800 works from the WPA period and the Black Arts Movement.

Museum of African American Art, Los Angeles, Calif. The museum is home to the Palmer C. Hayden Collection and Archives as well as the works of many contemporary artists.

CORPORATE COLLECTIONS

Golden State Mutual Life Insurance Company, Los Angeles, Calif. With the opening of a new building in 1949, two African-American artists were commissioned to paint murals depicting the history of blacks in California. Charles Alston's mural *Exploration and Colonization* covers the period from 1527 to 1850, while Hale Woodruff's *Settlement and Development* covers 1850 to 1949. The company's art collection includes works by Charles White, John Biggers, Hughie Lee-Smith, Richard Hunt, Beulah Woodard, Betye Saar, Henry O. Tanner, and Richmond Barthe.

Atlanta Life Insurance Company, Atlanta, Ga. The lobby of this corporate headquarters displays work by young and local African-American artists and by historical figures such as Romare Bearden, Elizabeth Catlett, Ed Dwight, Jacob Lawrence, and Hale Woodruff. The annual juried exhibitions continue to augment the collection, which now includes more than 300 pieces in many media.

Johnson Publishing Company, Chicago, Ill. This collection of 250 pieces, including paintings, sculpture, drawings, and lithographs by both internationally known and Chicago-based African-American artists, is displayed in public spaces and in the editorial offices of *Ebony* and *Jet* magazines. The corporate building, opened in 1971, was designed by the African-American architect John Moutoussamy.

10 *Music*

Portia K. Maultsby

The African-American musical tradition consists of several genres representative of both oral and written forms of expression. Each musical genre, which is associated with a specific historical period, social context, and function, mirrors four centuries of cultural evolution and social change. As such, African-American music is an important resource for the study of African-American history and culture. Song lyrics can be used to examine the responses of African-Americans to their position as a marginalized group in society, song interpretations to identify aesthetic ideals of an African heritage that establish African-American music as part of an African cultural continuum, and the works of African-American composers to examine how musicians trained in European traditions reconcile their dual musical and national identities. African-American music provides a window into the worldviews and experiences of a people who have used music to express their innermost feelings, preserve their cultural identity, and record their history.

This essay, which is organized around musical genres and traditions, identifies major collections of African-American music housed in various repositories throughout the country, describes finding aids and other tools available to access collections, and lists selected historical studies, bibliographies, discographies, and filmographies on African-American music.

EARLY REPOSITORIES

In the decades following the Civil War, proponents of African-American culture and history recognized the need to document and preserve the musical tradition. A small number of repositories—at Fisk University, Hampton Institute, Howard University (Moorland-Spingarn Research Center), the Library of Congress, and the Schomburg Center for Research in Black Culture (a branch of the New York Public Library)—began collecting music-related materials during the late 19th and early 20th centuries.

References to these and other collections are found in D. W. Krummel and Jean Geil et al., *Resources of American Music History: A Directory of Source Materials from Colonial Times to World War II* (1981); Jon Michael Spencer, *As the Black School Sings: Black Music Collections at Black Universities and Colleges with a Union List of Book Holdings* (1988); Jessie Carney Smith, *Black Academic Libraries and Research Collections: An Historical Survey* (1977); Deborra Richardson, "The Music Collections at the Schomburg Center for Research in Black Culture," *Black Music*

Research Newsletter 8:3 (1986): 6, and "The Music Department at the Moorland-Spingarn Research Center," *Black Music Research Newsletter* 8:1 (1985): 7, 10; and Suzanne Flandreau, "Black Music Collections," in Jack Salzman, David Lionel Smith, and Cornel West, ed., *Encyclopedia of African-American Culture and History*, vol. 4, 1907–1013 (1996).

Since the early 20th century, during the growth of public interest in African-American culture and history, other public libraries and universities such as the Detroit Public Library (E. Azalia Hackley Collection), Rutgers University (Institute of Jazz Studies), the University of Mississippi (Blues Archive), and Columbia College in Chicago (Center for Black Music Research), have established divisions devoted exclusively to African-American music.

Materials exist in all formats, including sound and video recordings, motion pictures, handwritten musical manuscripts, published scores, sheet music, photographs, oral histories, manuscripts, printed materials, musical instruments, realia, and ephemera. In some repositories, materials form part of larger African-American history and culture collections; in others, they are found in general or specialized African-American music holdings. Many collections contain materials related to two or more musical genres and traditions. In such cases, only those collections with substantial materials in one or more areas have been described in this essay.

Many collections are available through national library databases such as the Online Computer Library Center (OCLC), the Research Libraries Information Network (RLIN), and those listed on the Internet. Most repositories have finding aids such as in-house databases, inventory lists, published catalogs and guides, collection descriptions, and indexes. At the Schomburg Center for Research in Black Culture, for example, noncirculating research collections are accessible through a number of online bibliographic resources, including the New York Public Library's Research Libraries Online Public Catalog (CATNYP), OCLC, RLIN, and the Internet. The Center's catalog is also available in a CD-ROM format, and many of its holdings are listed in *The Kaiser Index to Black Resources, 1948–1986, from the Schomburg Center for Research in Black Culture of the New York Public Library* (1992).

Collections housed at the National Museum of American History, Smithsonian Institution, are accessible through the Institution's Research Information System (SIRIS), an online database. A brief description of manuscripts is found in the *Guide to Manuscript Collections in the National Museum of History and Technology* (1978). Registers and other finding aids are also available for collections in the Archives Center of the National Museum of American History.

The Center for Black Music Research (CBMR) at Columbia College, Chicago, maintains an in-house CBMR Database that serves as a union catalog to the black music holdings of six Chicago-area libraries, including Roosevelt University, the University of Chicago, Northwestern University, the Carter G. Woodson Regional Library of the Chicago Public Library, and the Newberry Library. This database also provides an index to the complete library holdings (including vertical file materials) of the Center; its specialized thesaurus allows for detailed searching of the collections.

SELECTED HISTORICAL SURVEYS

Collections from the nation's repositories, combined with other resources, provide materials for collectors, musicians, critics, and scholars to conduct research on African-American music. The first works were published in a variety of journals and magazines beginning in the late 19th century, including *Dwight's Journal of Music* (1852–1881), *Lippincott's Magazine* (1868–1915), *Putnam's Monthly* (1853–1857, 1868–1870), *Century Magazine* (1882–1930), *Atlantic Monthly* (1857–1932), *Southern Workman* (1872–1939), *Popular Science Monthly* (1872–1895; 1900–1950), *Musical Observer* (1907–1931), and *Negro Music Journal* (1902–1903). The monthly *Negro Music Journal* (rpt., 1970), established by black musicians in Washington, D.C., was the first journal to be devoted exclusively to African-American music. William E. Terry discusses the *Journal's* content in "The Negro Music Journal: An Appraisal," *The Black Perspective in Music* 5:2 (1977): 146–60.

Another early source that includes general references to African-American music and musicians is *The Negro Yearbook: An Annual Encyclopedia of the Negro* (1912–1952) published by the Tuskegee Institute Department of Records and Research. Similarly, seven decades after *The Negro Yearbook* was first published, Eileen Southern began publishing *The Black Perspective in Music* (1973–1991) through the Foundation for Research in the Afro-American Creative Arts, Inc., which was followed by several publications established by Samuel Floyd through the Center for Black Research at Columbia College: *Black Music Research Bulletin* (1988–1990), first titled *Black Music Research Newsletter* (1977–1987); *Black Music Research Journal* (1980–); *CBMR Digest* (1988–); *Lenox Avenue: A Journal of Interartistic Inquiry* (1995–1999); and a monograph series. These publications cover a wide range of topics on various musical genres, traditions, and musicians. Journals devoted to specific musical genres are identified within that category in the narrative.

The first historical survey published on African-American music was James M. Trotter's *Music and Some Highly Musical People* (1879). Jennifer DeLapp provides an index to Trotter's book in *Black Music Research Journal* 15:1 (1995): 109–36. Trotter's work provided the foundation for subsequent surveys published in the 20th century, including Maud Cuney-Hare, *Negro Musicians and Their Music* (1936); Alain Locke, *The Negro and His Music: Negro Art Past and Present* (1936); and Eileen Southern, *The Music of Black America: A History* (3rd ed., 1997). Studies that survey African-American music within a sociocultural context include LeRoi Jones [Amiri Baraka], *Blues People: The Negro Experience in White America and the Music that Developed from It* (1963); Ben Sidran, *Black Talk* (1971); Ortiz M. Walton, *Music: Black, White and Blue; A Sociological Survey of the Use and Misuse of Afro-American Music* (1972); Christopher Small, *Music of the Common Tongue: Survival and Celebration in Afro-American Music* (1987); and Samuel Floyd, *The Power of Black Music: Interpreting Its History from Africa to the United States* (1995).

The first published works that examined various issues related to black music research, study, and curricular development are the proceedings from the first two summer seminars (1969 and 1971) on African-American music organized by the now defunct Black Music Center at Indiana University. These works, *Black Music in Our Culture: Curricular Ideas on the Subjects, Materials and Problems* (1970) and *Reflections on Afro-American Music in Music* (1973), edited by Dominique-Rene de Lerma, brought greater recognition to the importance of 20th-century genre studies and the need for reference tools to identify the growing body of literature on African-American music and related traditions.

Since the 1960s, many bibliographies, encyclopedias, biographical dictionaries, indexes, registers, catalogs, discographies, and filmographies, either general in scope or specific to a musical tradition or historical period, have been published. The most comprehensive reference guide for printed materials on African-American music is the four-volume series *Bibliography of Black Music,* by Dominique-Rene de Lerma. Vol. 1, subtitled *Reference Materials* (1981), identifies libraries, museums and collections, encyclopedias, lexicons, etymologies, bibliographies of the music, bibliographies of the literature, discographies, iconographies, directories of organizations, dissertations and theses, and periodicals. Vol. 2, *Afro-American Idioms* (1981), covers general histories, minstrelsy, spirituals and earlier folk music, ragtime, musical theater, concert music, band music, blues, gospel music, rhythm and blues and other popular music, and jazz. Vol. 3, *Geographical Studies* (1982), includes forty-three African countries and culture groups, twenty-nine countries in South America and the Caribbean, and twenty states in the United States in addition to Washington, D.C., and Mexico. Vol. 4, subtitled *Theory, Education, and Related Studies* (1984), focuses on topics related to instruments, performance practice, improvisation, the oral tradition, notation, musical elements, compositional techniques, dance, aesthetics, and cultural histories, along with social and cultural issues.

Two other excellent references are Jo Ann Skowronski, *Black Music in America: A Bibliography* (1981), and Samuel A. Floyd, Jr., and Marsha J. Reisser, *Black Music in the United States: An Annotated Bibliography of Selected Reference and Research Materials* (1983). Skowronski's work is divided into three sections: Selected Musicians and Singers, General References, and Reference Works (organized by decade). Unique features of Floyd and Reisser's selected bibliography are the inclusion of discographic and iconographic references, anthologies and collections of printed music, record companies, and repositories and archives.

Another important resource for printed materials is Dominique-Rene de Lerma and Marsha J. Reisser, *Black Music and Musicians in* The New Grove Dictionary of American Music *and* The New Harvard Dictionary of Music (1989). This book extracts African-American musical references from *The New Grove Dictionary of American Music* (1986) and *The New Harvard Dictionary of Music* (1986). Other such resources are Bernhard Hefele, *Jazz-Bibliography: International Literature on Jazz, Blues, Spirituals, Gospels, and Ragtime with a Selected List of Works on the Social and Cultural Background from the Beginning to the Present* (1981); Kimberly R. Vann, *Black Music in* Ebony: *An Annotated Guide to the Articles on Music in* Ebony *Magazine, 1945–1985* (1990); and Eddie S. Meadows, *Theses and Dissertations on Black American Music* (1980).

General bibliographic references that include African-American citations are David Horn and R. Jackson, *The Literature of American Music in Books and Folk*

Music Collections: A Fully Annotated Bibliography (1977), Supplement I (1988); and Guy A. Marco, *Literature of American Music in Books and Folk Music Collections, 1983–1993* (1996). Biographical sources are Lemuel Berry, Jr., *Biographical Dictionary of Black Musicians and Music Educators* (1978); Eileen Southern, *Biographical Dictionary of Afro-American and African Musicians* (1982); and Ellistine Perkins Holly, *Biographies of Black Composers and Songwriters: A Supplementary Textbook* (1990).

Other useful references for the study of African-American music are Mary Mace Spradling, ed., *In Black and White: A Guide to Magazine Articles, Newspaper Articles, and Books concerning More Than 15,000 Black Individuals and Groups* (3rd ed., 1985); *In Black and White, Supplement: A Guide to Magazine Articles, Newspaper Articles, and Books concerning More Than 6,700 Black Individuals and Groups* (3rd ed., 1985); Josephine Wright, "A Preliminary Bibliographical Guide to Periodical Literature for Black Music Research," *Black Music Research Newsletter* 8:2 (1986): 3–4, which identifies a range of 19th- and early 20th-century periodicals containing primary information about black music; Jack Salzman, David Lionel Smith, and Cornel West, ed., *The Encyclopedia of African-American Culture and History* (5 vols., 1996); Darlene Clark Hine, ed., *Black Women in America: An Historical Encyclopedia* (2 vols., 1993); and Ellen Koskoff, gen. ed., and Portia K. Maultsby, sub-ed., "African-American Music," in *Garland Encyclopedia of World Music: United States and Canada*, vol. 3 (2000). The latter three publications include many important entries on African-American music genres and traditions, performers, composers, educators, and organizations, among other topics.

Discographies that cover three or more African-American musical genres are David Edwin Cooper, *International Bibliography of Discographies: Classical Music and Jazz and Blues, 1962–1972: A Reference Book for Record Collectors, Dealers, and Libraries* (1975), and Dean Tudor and Nancy Tudor, *Black Music* (1979). The latter provides an annotated guide to approximately 1,300 important LP recordings of blues, rhythm and blues, gospel, soul, and reggae. *Black Music* also includes a brief history of each of these genres and an index of book and periodical citations, directory of labels and selected record companies, specialist record stores, and an artists index.

References to black music in films by and about blacks are found in *Frame by Frame: A Black Filmography* (1979), by Phyllis Klotman, and *Frame by Frame II: A Filmography of the African American Image, 1978–1996* (1997), by Phyllis Klotman and Gloria Gibson.

FOLK MUSIC

Major repositories collect recordings and other related materials, including sheet music, to preserve folk and popular forms of African-American expression and to provide references for musical performance. African-American music exists primarily as oral expression. Therefore, sound recordings are particularly important to studies of this tradition. While transcriptions and published scores are useful to the study of folk idioms, many provide only a skeletal outline of the melody, omitting nuances central to African-American musical performance. The aesthetic and oral traditions allow for spontaneous, improvisatory, and interactive expression that cannot be conveyed on the written score. Therefore, recordings, especially field recordings, provide the most authentic renditions of African-American musical performance.

Field recordings are primary to the preservation and documentation of African-American folk idioms—field hollers, work songs, protest songs, recreational and social songs (including dance music), spirituals, rural blues, and early gospel music. The folk idioms, along with popular and classical traditions, are well documented in various formats by the Library of Congress, the Schomburg Center for Research in Black Culture, and the Archives of Traditional Music at Indiana University.

The Archive of Folk Culture at the American Folklife Center at the Library of Congress has the largest collection of field and commercial recordings related to African-American folk music and culture. Many field recordings and related print materials were collected or written by the folklorists Robert Winslow Gordon, John Lomax, Alan Lomax, Herbert Halpert, and Zora Neale Hurston. From this material, the Archive of Folk Culture has issued cassette, disc, and compact disc recordings (accompanied by extensive liner notes) of field hollers, work songs, blues, spirituals, hymns, ballads, game songs, and religious services, among other folk styles. Finding aids to these field recordings include *Principal Collections of Field Recordings in the Archive of Folk Songs Which Contain Negro Spirituals* (1970); *Folk Recordings Selected from the Archive of Folk Culture* (1989), which are available from the American Folklife Center; *Publications in Print* (1991), a general reference; and *An Inventory of the Bibliographies and Other References and Finding Aids Prepared by the Archive of Folksong, Library of Congress* (n.d.).

Collections of the Archive of Folk Culture also include books, periodicals, sheet music, songbooks, photographs, recordings, manuscripts, moving-image materials, and ephemera on the African-American folk tradition. These and other materials are described in a guide to the general holdings of the Library of Congress, *The African-American Mosaic: A Library of Congress Resource Guide for the Study of Black History and Culture* (1993), edited by Debra Newman Ham and published by the Library of Congress. The discussion on music covers a variety of African-American forms: minstrel songs, religious music (hymns, Negro spirituals, and gospel music), protest songs, work songs, blues, ragtime, jazz, musicals, popular, and concert traditions in historical context. Another useful reference is Walter Rose Whittlesey, *Negro Music: Catalog of Negro Music Actually Composed by Members of that Race* (1918), on microfilm.

The Archives of Traditional Music at Indiana University is another repository containing important collections on African-American folk and related traditions (Africa, Latin America, and the Caribbean). The Archives hold approximately 200 field collections of spirituals, gospel music, protest songs, blues, work songs and other secular genres, religious services, and folktales; 425 piano rolls including popular music; and 50,000 commercial ragtime, jazz, and blues recordings. Holdings include collections of the folklorists Natalie Curtis Burlin; Guy B. Johnson; Alan, John, and Elizabeth Lomax; Herbert Halpert; Harold Courlander; Richard Dorson; and Lorenzo Turner.

The Folkways field recordings, reissued by the Smithsonian Institution, complement the holdings of the Archives of Traditional Music at Indiana University and the Archive of Folk Culture at the Library of Congress. These recordings contain spirituals, game songs, work songs, folk songs, gospel, blues, freedom songs, and concert music and are accompanied by updated liner notes.

Other repositories that have noteworthy African-American folk collections are the Hampton University Archives (notes about spirituals recorded by the folklorist Natalie Curtis Burlin), the Moorland-Spingarn Research Center at Howard University (transcriptions of spirituals from Saint Helena Island published by Nicholas George J. Ballanta-Taylor and Natalie Curtis Burlin, and arrangements of Creole folk songs by Camille Nickerson and Maude Cuney-Hare), the Black Arts Research Center in Nyack, New York (commercial recordings, manuscripts, print materials, and photographs), the Center for Popular Culture at Middle Tennessee State University (commercial recordings and photographs), the Folk Music Archives at University of North Carolina at Chapel Hill (field recordings), the Center for Southern Folklore in Memphis (field and commercial recordings and films), the Avery Research Center for African-American History and Culture in Charleston, S.C. (field recordings made in the Sea Islands), and the Southern Folklife Collection at the University of North Carolina at Chapel Hill (field and commercial recordings). Materials in the Tom Dent Collection of the Amistad Research Center at Tulane University represent a variety of folk and popular musical styles, such as blues, protest songs, brass bands, New Orleans jazz and rhythm and blues, and zydeco.

The folk music tradition has received a great deal of attention from collectors, travelers, critics, and scholars, among others. Their observations, creative works, and publications are referenced in *African-American Traditions in Song, Sermon, Tale, and Dance, 1600s–1920: An Annotated Bibliography of Literature, Collections, and Artworks* (1990), compiled by Eileen Southern and Josephine Wright. This comprehensive work is organized around historical periods, and it draws from a broad range of primary source material such as missionary reports, travel accounts, diaries, local histories, literary works (fiction and nonfiction), slave narratives, legal documents, popular magazines, and artwork.

Citations on African-American music are listed in some reference works on American folk music and Afro-American folk culture: Charles Haywood, *A Bibliography of North American Folklore and Folksong* (2nd ed., 1961); John F. Szwed and Roger D. Abrahams, *Afro-American Folk Culture: An Annotated Bibliography of Materials from North, Central, and South America and the West Indies* (1978); Terry E. Miller, *Folk Music in America: A Reference Guide* (1986); and Robert Sacre, "Negro Spirituals and Gospel Songs: Indexes to Selected Periodicals," *Black Music Research Journal* 15:2 (1995): 143–243.

Important historical studies on the folk tradition include Henry Edward Krehbiel, *Afro-American Folksongs: A Study in Racial and National Music* (1914); John W. Work, *Folk Song of the American Negro* (1915); Natalie Curtis Burlin, *Negro Folk Songs* (1918); Howard Odum and Guy B. Johnson, *The Negro and His Songs: A Study of Typical Negro Songs in the South* (1925); Dorothy Scarborough, *On the Trail of Negro Folk-Songs* (1925); Guy B. Johnson, *Folk Culture on St. Helena Island*

South Carolina (1930); Miles Mark Fisher, *Negro Slave Songs in the United States* (1953); Harold Courlander, *Negro Folk Music, U.S.A.* (1963); John Lovell, Jr., *Black Song: The Forge and the Flame: The Story of How the Afro-American Spiritual Was Hammered Out* (1972); Mary Allen Grissom, *The Negro Sings a New Heaven: A Collection of Songs with Melodies* (1930); Bessie Jones and Bess Lomax Hawes, *Step It Down: Games, Plays, and Stories from the Afro-American Heritage* (1972); Dena J. Epstein, *Sinful Tunes and Spirituals: Black Folk Music to the Civil War* (1977); and Howard W. Odum and Guy B. Johnson, *Negro Workaday Songs* (1926). Another important reference is Paul Oliver, *Songsters and Saints: Vocal Traditions on Race Records* (1984).

The first major collections published are William Francis Allen et al., *Slave Songs of the United States* (1867); M. F. Armstrong and Helen W. Ludlow, *Hampton and Its Students* (1874); J. B. T. Marsh, *The Story of the Jubilee Singers: With Their Songs* (1876); William Barton, *Old Plantation Hymns* (1899); Samuel Coleridge-Taylor, *Twenty-Four Negro Melodies* (1905); Nicholas Ballanta, *Saint Helena Island Spirituals: Recorded and Transcribed at Penn Normal Industrial and Agricultural School . . . South Carolina* (1924); James Weldon Johnson and J. Rosamond Johnson, *The Books of American Negro Spirituals, Including the Book of American Negro Spirituals [1925] and The Second Book of Negro Spirituals [1926]* (1942); R. Nathaniel Dett, ed., *Religious Folk-Songs of the Negro: As Sung at Hampton Institute* (1927); John W. Work, ed., *American Negro Songs and Spirituals* (1940); and Lydia A. Parrish, *Slave Songs of the Georgia Sea Islands* (1942). The *Index to Negro Spirituals* (1937), compiled by the Cleveland Public Library, identifies spirituals and their variations listed under the same or different titles from thirty-one collections.

Beginning in the 19th century, many aspects of the African-American folk tradition (music, language, and dance) were transformed into popular forms of expression on the minstrel stage. Inspired by this tradition, the professional songwriters Daniel D. Emmett, Stephen Foster, and James Bland created and popularized a body of music known as minstrel or Ethiopian songs. In the late 19th and early 20th centuries, professional songwriters such as W. C. Handy, Perry Bradford, Scott Joplin, and Eubie Blake continued this tradition, writing original compositions based on vernacular forms like the blues, folk versions of instrumental dance music, and other folk idioms. The publication of these compositions as sheet music provides another resource for the study and performance of commercial versions of African-American folk traditions.

SHEET MUSIC AND SONGBOOKS

The Library of Congress and the Schomburg Center have vast sheet music holdings of folk, popular, and classical traditions. However, one of the largest sheet music and songbook collections related to African-American popular forms is housed at the John Hay Library at Brown University. Of the approximately 500,000 titles, African-American materials constitute approximately 7,000 items, including songs by James Bland, Ernest Hogan, Cole and Johnson, Williams and Walker, Duke Ellington, and Stevie Wonder, among others. This collection also contains songs about African-Americans (dialect songs and songs from the minstrel stage). Some songs are fully cataloged, with bibliographic records in local and national databases.

Housed in the Smithsonian's Archives Center at the National Museum of American History is the Sam DeVincent Collection of Illustrated American Sheet Music, ca. 1790–1980. This collection holds about 130,000 pieces of sheet music (many with lithographs), of which about 7,800 items represent various African-American genres. Even though vocal and instrumental ragtime compositions predominate, this collection includes minstrel songs, folk songs and spirituals, blues, jazz, and concert music. A finding aid, *Register of the Sam DeVincent Collection of Illustrated American Sheet Music, ca. 1790–1980, Series 3: African-American Music, ca. 1828–1980* (1989), by Karen Linn, accompanies the collection.

One of the few collections devoted exclusively to compositions by and about African-Americans is the Nation's Bank Black Sheet Music Collection, located in the Library Special Collections at the University of South Florida. This collection contains more than 5,000 items representative of jazz, blues, ragtime, minstrelsy, cakewalks, two-steps, spirituals, rock, and boogie-woogie. Another sheet music collection is the J. Francis Driscoll Collection of American Sheet Music. Of the 84,000 titles, more than 339 pieces are by approximately 47 black composers spanning ca. 1818 through 1954. An article by Samuel A. Floyd, Jr., "Black Music in the Driscoll Collection," *Black Perspective in Music* 2:2 (1974): 158–171, describes the representation of African-American songwriters in this collection.

The collections discussed above are complemented by smaller but noteworthy holdings containing a substantial amount of African-American sheet music from minstrelsy, ragtime, blues, jazz, and gospel: the Center for Popular Music at Middle Tennessee State University; the Archive of Popular Music at UCLA; the Barnard A. and Morris N. Young Library of Early American Popular Music at the University of Illinois, Urbana-Champaign; the Corning Sheet Music Collection at the University of Michigan; the American Music Collection of the New York Public Library for the Performing Arts (which also houses first edition imprints of thousands of piano ragtime compositions); the E. Azalia Hackley Collection at the Detroit Public Library; the Buffalo and Erie County Public Library; and the Duke University Library. The latter collection is described in Charles Herbert Bowling, "Bibliography of Negro Antebellum Songs as Found in the Sheet Music Collection of the Duke University Library, Durham, North Carolina" (M.A. Thesis, North Carolina Central College, Durham, 1960).

The Music Department of the Moorland-Spingarn Research Center at Howard University has an impressive array of sheet music and unpublished manuscripts of blues, gospel, and popular music, including songs from black musicals. This collection is described in the Music Catalog section of *The Dictionary Catalog of the Arthur B. Spingarn Collection of Negro Authors* (2 vols., 1970), by Dorothy Porter, and in an unpublished in-house "Guide to the Sheet Music in the Moorland-Spingarn Research Center" (1988) compiled by Deborra A. Richardson, with a foreword (which gives a historical overview of the development of black music) by the musicologist Doris McGinty.

A collection that complements sheet music and songbooks on popular music is the John Rosamond Johnson Papers (1879–1975). These papers, housed in the Music Library at Yale University, include musical manuscripts, published works, lyrics, vaudeville sketches, radio sketches, diaries, photographs, programs, clippings, advertisements, and biographical notes. A register accompanies the collection.

Historical studies on the 19th- and early 20th-century popular musical tradition are Hans Nathan, *Dan Emmett and the Rise of Early Negro Minstrelsy* (1962); Robert C. Toll, *Blacking Up: The Minstrel Show in Nineteenth-Century America* (1974) and *On with the Show: The First Century of Show Business in America* (1976); Thomas Riis, *More Than Just Minstrel Shows: The Rise of Black Musical Theatre at the Turn of the Century* (1992); Annemarie Bean et al., ed., *Inside the Minstrel Mask: Readings in Nineteenth Century Blackface Minstrelsy* (1996); Tom Fletcher, *100 Years of the Negro in Show Business* (1954); Allen Woll, *Black Musical Theatre from* Coontown *to* Dreamgirls (1989); Charles Hamm, *Yesterdays: Popular Song in America* (1979); Sam Dennison, *Scandalize My Name: Black Imagery in American Popular Music* (1982); and Reid Badger, *A Life in Ragtime: A Biography of James Reese Europe* (1995).

Other valuable references are Henry T. Sampson, *Blacks in Blackface: A Source Book on Early Black Musical Shows* (1980); W. T. Lhamon, Jr., *Raising Cain: Blackface Performance from Jim Crow to Hip Hop* (1998); Mark W. Booth, *American Popular Music: A Reference Guide* (1983); Allen L. Woll, *Dictionary of the Black Theatre: Broadway, Off-Broadway, and Selected Harlem Theatre* (1983); and Ken Bloom, *American Song: The Complete Musical Theatre Companion [1877–1995]* (2 vols., 2nd ed., 1996).

Although popular music dominates most sheet music and songbook collections, some contain sacred idioms. For example, the Harris Collection at Brown University includes hymnals associated with the African Methodist Episcopal Church and other African-American denominations of the 19th and 20th centuries. Similar materials, an assortment of religious songbooks and hymnals published mainly by black companies, are found in the Religious Songbook and Hymnal Collection, 1900–1963, at the Archives of the John B. Cade Library at Southern University. Related collections are found at the Black Music Archive at Hampton University; the Popular Culture Collection of the Special Collections Department at Michigan State University; and the Center for Popular Music at Middle Tennessee State University. The latter also has a collection of gospel songbooks with some material relating to jubilee groups. The Archives Center at the Smithsonian Institution's National Museum of American History houses the Martin and Morris Music Company Records (ca. 1930–1985), the largest sheet music and songbook collection of gospel music.

20TH-CENTURY POPULAR MUSIC

Popular music provides an invaluable resource for documenting the complex and diverse nature of post–World War II African-American culture. Prior to the 1990s, only a few libraries and archives collected materials on this tradition. One of the first repositories to do so systematically was the Popular Culture Library and Audio Center at Bowling Green State University. Among its vast collection of more than 600,000 items (recordings, sheet music, song files and lists, catalogs of recording dealers and manufacturers, periodicals, and ephemera), many are devoted to African-American music.

The Center for Popular Music located at Middle Tennessee State University also has a significant amount of African-American material. Of the more than 55,000 published sound recordings, an estimated 30 to 40 percent are of black music genres (blues, jazz, spirituals, gospel, rhythm and blues, soul, and contemporary popular). The Center also has posters, photographs of black artists, sheet music by African-American songwriters, and printed materials. Its vertical files contain biographical information on many black artists, representing a variety of musical styles. The Center's collections are listed in several in-house finding aids, including a database. Cataloged sound recordings are available on OCLC and are accessible through the university's online catalog; a printed finding aid accompanies special collections of books and scores; and several photograph collections are described in an unpublished manuscript.

The John Edwards Memorial Foundation, located at the University of North Carolina at Chapel Hill, and the Archive of Popular American Music, at the University of California, Los Angeles, have significant collections on popular music. Rhythm and blues is included in the Foundation's 27,000 commercial recordings, 1,500 tape recordings, and 150 transcriptions. The Archive of Popular American Music has large collections of recordings, sheet music, and photographs related to music for film, stage (minstrelsy, vaudeville, burlesque, Broadway, etc.), radio, television, Tin Pan Alley, ragtime, blues, gospel, jazz, reggae, rhythm and blues, and rap. The Archive's collections are only partially accessible.

Other significant holdings are found in the Archives of African-American Music and Culture (AAAMC) and the Archives of Traditional Music (ATM) at Indiana University, and the Center for Black Music Research at Columbia College in Chicago. AAAMC specializes in post–World War II styles of popular music (rhythm and blues, soul, funk, disco, and rap). Holdings include sound and video recordings, oral histories (including taped interviews and transcriptions), radio programs, photographs, air-check tapes of African-American disc jockeys, posters, and vertical files of clippings. Highlights of the collections are Lee Bailey's radio productions of "Radioscope" and "Hip Hop Countdown," consisting of music, narration, and sound bites from artists of the 1980s and 1990s; the complete catalog of Mr. R&B Records (including rhythm and blues, big bands, rock and roll, and vocal group recordings from the 1930s through the 1950s); program transcripts and production materials from Radio Smithsonian's thirteen-part radio series, "Black Radio: Telling It Like It Was"; and production materials from the video *Music as Metaphor,* produced for the National Afro-American Museum in Wilberforce, Ohio.

Other major collections housed in the Archives of African American Music and Culture (also found in the Archives of Traditional Music at Indiana University) are the Johnny Otis Collection of 780 radio programs of black popular music and interviews with musicians from the 1950s and 1960s; and the complete Westwood One "Special Edition" radio programs (numbering 315), which consist of music, narration, and interviews with popular music artists from the 1970s and 1980s (available through OCLC and IUCAT, Indiana University). The holdings of the

Archives of African American Music and Culture are accessible through its Web-site *(http://www.indiana.edu/~aaamc)*, and inventories for several collections are available.

Among the varied holdings at the Center for Black Music Research at Columbia College, Chicago, are the Sue Cassidy Clark Papers, which contain 109 taped interviews, interview transcriptions, typescripts and published articles, photographs, and clippings on popular musicians. The Chuck Berry Project Research Papers, 1958–1984, consisting of news clippings, articles, trial transcripts, and interviews with Berry's daughter and with his guitarist, Billy Peek, are located at the Western Historical Manuscript Collection in St. Louis.

The Archives Center at the National Museum for American History, Smithsonian Institution, houses video- and audiotapes and other materials from the symposium "Rhythm and Blues, 1945–1955." This forum, organized by the Program in African-American Culture, features performers, record company executives, disc jockeys, and other music industry personnel. Materials for studies on black record companies are the focus of the Leon T. Rene Papers, 1920–1979 (songwriter and owner of Excelsior/Exclusive Records, Los Angeles), at the John B. Cade Library at Southern University. Oral histories related to the rhythm and blues tradition are found in the Central Avenue Sounds Oral History Project in the Oral History Program at the University of California, Los Angeles; the Archives of the Rhythm and Blues Foundation in Washington, D.C.; and the Archives of African-American Music and Culture at Indiana University.

Photographs and other general materials on African-American popular music are located at the Library of Congress, the Afro-American Historical and Cultural Museum in Philadelphia, the Schomburg Center for Research in Black Culture, the Moorland-Spingarn Research Center at Howard University, the E. Azalia Hackley Collection of the Detroit Public Library, and the Black Arts Research Center in Nyack, N.Y. The latter has numerous materials related to popular music of the African diaspora, which are accessible through a database.

Of the many histories of post–World War II American popular music, only a few have been devoted exclusively to the African-American tradition. They include the following: Arnold Shaw, *Honkers and Shouters: The Golden Years of Rhythm & Blues* (1978); Johnny Otis, *Upside Your Head! Rhythm and Blues on Central Avenue* (1993); John Broven, *Walking to New Orleans: The Story of New Orleans Rhythm & Blues* (1974); Jeff Hannusch, *I Hear You Knockin': The Sound of New Orleans Rhythm and Blues* (1985); Charlie Gillett, *The Sound of the City: The Rise of Rock and Roll* (rev. and expanded ed., 1984); Phyl Garland, *The Sound of Soul* (1969); Michael Haralambos, *Right On: From Blues to Soul in Black America* (1974); Gerri Hirshey, *Nowhere to Run: The Story of Soul Music* (1984); Peter Guralnick, *Sweet Soul Music: Rhythm & Blues and the Southern Dream of Freedom* (1986); Robert Pruter, *Chicago Soul* (1991); Nelson George, *The Death of Rhythm & Blues* (1988); Gerald Lyn Early, *One Nation under a Groove: Motown and American Culture* (1995); Radcliffe A. Joe, *This Business of Disco* (1980); Rickey Vincent, *Funk: The Music, the People, and the Rhythm of the One* (1995); Rob Bowman, *Soulsville U.S.A.: The Story of Stax Records* (1997); Nelson George, *Hip-Hop America* (1998); and Brian Ward, *Just My Soul Responding: Rhythm and Blues, Black Consciousness, and Race Relations* (1998).

Studies on rap music dominate recent African-American popular music stud-ies. Noteworthy are David Toop, *Rap Attack 2: African Rap to Global Hip Hop* (1991); Brian Cross, *It's Not about a Salary: Rap, Race, and Resistance in Los Angeles* (1993); Tricia Rose, *Black Noise: Rap Music and Black Culture in Contemporary America* (1994); Russell Potter, *Spectacular Vernaculars: Hip-Hop and the Politics of Postmodernism* (1995); Michael Eric Dyson, *Between God and Gangsta Rap: Bear-ing Witness to Black Culture* (1996); William Eric Perkins, ed., *Droppin' Science: Critical Essays on Music and Hip Hop Culture* (1996); and Adam Krims, *Rap Music and the Poetics of Identity* (2000). The only bibliographies and discographies de-voted exclusively to an African-American popular style are on rap music: Judy Mc-Coy, *Rap Music in the 1980s: A Reference Guide* (1992), and Havelock Nelson and Michael A. Gonzales, *Bring the Noise: A Guide to Rap Music and Hip-Hop Culture* (1991). *Rap Music* includes a guide to the literature, a selected discography, and date, subject, artist, and title indexes. *Bring the Noise* provides a descriptive analysis of recordings by various rap artists.

Other historical studies that include substantial material on African-American popular music are Peter Wicke, *Rock Music: Culture, Aesthetics and Sociology* (1990), Philip Ennis, *The Seventh Stream: The Emergence of Rock 'n' Roll in Ameri-can Popular Music* (1992), and Reebee Garofalo, *Rockin' Out: Popular Music in the USA* (1996). Biographical sketches of African-American musicians and disco-graphic references are included in Irwin Stambler, *Encyclopedia of Pop, Rock and Soul* (1974); Norm N. Nite, *Rock On: The Illustrated Encyclopedia of Rock 'n' Roll*, vol. 1: *The Solid Gold Years* (1985), vol. 2: *The Years of Change, 1964–1978* (1985), vol. 3: *The Video Revolution, 1978–Present* (1985); Arnold Shaw, *Dictionary of American Pop/Rock* (1982); Jay Warner, *The Billboard Book of American Singing Groups: A History, 1940–1990* (1992); and Patricia Romanowski and Holly George-Warren, ed., *The New Rolling Stone Encyclopedia of Rock & Roll* (rev. and updated ed., 1995).

The major discographic references on popular music include Joel Whitburn, *Top Rhythm & Blues Singles, 1942–1988* (1988), with supplements issued each year; Steve Propes, *Those Oldies But Goodies: A Guide to 50's Record Collecting* (1973) and *Golden Oldies: A Guide to 60's Record Collecting* (1974); Fernando L. Gonzalez, *Disco-File: The Discographical Catalog of American Rock & Roll and Rhythm & Blues Vocal Harmony Groups; Race, Rhythm & Blues, Rock & Roll, Soul, 1902–1976* (2nd ed., 1977); Robert Pruter, ed., *The Blackwell Guide to Soul Record-ings* (1993); Stewart Goldstein, *Oldies But Goodies: The Rock 'n' Roll Years* (1977); George Albert et al., *The Cash Box: Black Contemporary Singles Charts, 1960–1984* (1986); Frank Hoffmann and George Albert, *The Cash Box: Black Contemporary Album Charts, 1975–1984* (1986); and Paul C. Mawhinney, *Musicmaster: The 45 RPM Record Directory: 1947 to 1982* (1983), plus supplements.

GOSPEL MUSIC

Materials on gospel music (excluding sound recordings) were scarce in the na-tion's repository centers prior to the presentation of scholarly programs by the Program in African-American Culture (PAAC) of the National Museum of Amer-ican History (NMAH) in collaboration with the Smithsonian Division of Performing Arts. Beginning in 1977, and through the systematic programming of gospel music symposia and live performances, the Smithsonian Institution has become a major repository for this tradition. Materials (video- and audiotapes, program booklets, etc.) from scholarly forums sponsored by PAAC, in addition to those of Bishop Eugene Smallwood and the Martin and Morris Music Company Records, ca. 1930–1985, are preserved in NMAH's Archives Center.

The Martin and Morris Music Company (1940–ca. 1988), established in Chicago by Sallie Martin and Kenneth Morris, is the oldest continuously operating black gospel music publishing company. The Martin and Morris Music Company Records include music and songbooks published and distributed by Martin and Morris and other companies, advertising photographs and ephemera, correspondence between the company and composers, business and financial records, and a list of publishers and copyright owners distributed by the company.

Gospel music collections at other repositories include the Ira Tucker Collection (singer with the Dixie Hummingbirds) at the National Afro-American Museum and Cultural Center in Wilberforce, Ohio; papers, sheet music, and recordings from the Gospel Light Music Store of Philadelphia at the Southern Folklife Collection at the University of North Carolina at Chapel Hill; the Thomas A. Dorsey Collection at Fisk University; radio shows of interviews with Moses Asch (collector and record producer) and the gospel music scholar George Ricks at the Ethnomusicology Archives, University of Washington; 100 television programs of the Emmy award–winning gospel music series *Jubilee Showcase* (1963–1984), more than 15,000 gospel compositions published by the Martin and Morris Publishing Company of Chicago, and gospel music recordings at the Music Information Center of the Chicago Public Library. Finding aids accompany the *Jubilee Showcase* programs.

Smaller gospel music collections (sheet music, songbooks, and recordings) are housed at the Library of Congress; the Schomburg Center for Research in Black Culture; the Archives of Traditional Music at Indiana University; the Archive of Popular American Music at the University of California, Los Angeles; the Center for Popular Music at Middle Tennessee University; the Center for Black Music Research at Columbia College in Chicago; the New York Library for the Performing Arts; and the Music Library at Yale University.

Photographs are valuable resources in the study of gospel music, and they can be found in the Rev. L. O. Taylor Collection (1928–1960s) at the Center for Southern Folklore Archives in Memphis; the Fred and Rose Plaut Archives located in the Music Library at Yale University (a register accompanies this collection); the Museum of African-American History in Detroit; and the Jack T. Franklin Collection of the Afro-American Historical and Cultural Museum in Philadelphia. Photographs of gospel performers are also found in general collections at the Center for Popular Music, Middle Tennessee State University; the Schomburg Center for Research in Black Culture; the Library of Congress; and the Archives Center of the National Museum of American History, Smithsonian Institution. The John Baker Jazz Film Collection at the 18th & Vine Historical Jazz District, Kansas City, is another visual resource for gospel music performers.

Prior to the 1980s and with few exceptions, scholars excluded gospel music from their research agenda. Among the few scholarly works that are devoted to or include material on this tradition are George R. Ricks, *Some Aspects of the Religious Music of the United States Negro: An Ethnomusicological Study with Special Emphasis on the Gospel Tradition* (1977); Bernice Johnson Reagon, ed., *We'll Understand It Better By and By: Pioneering African American Gospel Composers* (1992); Michael W. Harris, *The Rise of Gospel Blues: The Music of Thomas Andrew Dorsey in the Urban Church* (1992); Kip Lornell, *Happy in the Service of the Lord: Afro-American Gospel Music Quartets in Memphis* (2nd ed., 1995); Anthony Heilbut, *The Gospel Sound: Good News and Bad News* (rev. ed., 1985); Daniel Wolff, *You Send Me: The Life and Times of Sam Cooke* (1995); and Ray Allen, *Singing in the Spirit: African-American Sacred Quartets in New York City* (1991). Much of the research on gospel music by Pearl Williams-Jones, Horace Boyer, and Mellonee Burnim, which explores the cultural significance of this tradition and provides theoretical models for analysis, appears in journals and edited works.

Irene Jackson's compilation, *Afro-American Religious Music: A Bibliography and a Catalogue of Gospel Music* (1979), identifies literature related to the development of gospel music (sources on African traditions, African-American culture and history, folk songs, spirituals, church histories, and black religion) and lists gospel composers and their compositions. The omission of a gospel music bibliographic category and the lack of annotations for bibliographic citations limit the scholarly use of this source as a reference on gospel music. Horace Boyer's *How Sweet the Sound: The Golden Age of Gospel Music* (1995) is the only source that provides lengthy biographical and general information on more than 100 gospel singers. The *Gospel Music Encyclopedia* (1979), compiled by Robert Anderson and Gail North, includes information on selected African-American gospel performers. Another valuable reference is Robert Sacre's "Negro Spirituals and Gospel Songs: Indexes to Selected Periodicals," *Black Music Research Journal* 15:2 (1995): 143–243. The only journal devoted to African-American religious music is *Black Sacred Music: A Journal of Theomusicology* (1987–1995), founded and edited by Jon Michael Spencer. The strength of this journal is its special issues, which consist largely of reprinted articles. Other issues should be consulted with caution since most are flawed in some critical ways.

Important discographies are Cedric J. Hayes and Robert Laughton, comp., *Gospel Records, 1943–1969: A Black Music Discography* (1992), and Robert M. W. Dixon and John Godrich, comp., *Blues and Gospel Records, 1902–1943* (3rd rev. ed., 1982).

BLUES

The blues tradition has had wide appeal among collectors for many decades and is represented in the holdings of several repositories. The largest and most comprehensive blues collection is located at the University of Mississippi Blues Archive. It contains more than 20,000 recordings of blues (including B. B. King's entire record collection) and related genres, photographs, major blues periodicals, files of *Living Blues* magazine, papers of Trumpet Records, and collections on various blues performers such as Gertrude "Ma" Rainey and B. B. King.

Blues oral histories are a major part of the holdings at the University of Mississippi Blues Archive and other repositories. The Oral History, American Music Project at Yale University has in its holdings the Robert Neff and Anthony Connor Blues Collection of more than sixty interviews with artists such as Roosevelt Sykes, James Cotton, Willie Dixon, John Lee Hooker, J. B. Hutto, Esther Phillips, Koko Taylor, Big Momma Thornton, Sippie Wallace, Junior Wells, and Brownie McGhee. The North Carolina Department of Cultural Resources, Division of Archives and History, in Raleigh, houses the Bull City Project, which includes performances and interviews of artists including Odell Johnson, Arthur Lyons, Thomas and Pauline Burt, Jules Sellers, Salina McMillon, and Charles Russell.

The Central Avenue Sounds Oral History Project of the University of California, Los Angeles, includes blues musicians. The Regional Oral History Office of the Bancroft Library at the University of California, Berkeley, has initiated the Oakland Blues project; and the University of Washington Ethnomusicology Archives has sound tracks to film footage produced at the university of blues artists such as Furry Lewis, Son House, Booker White, Lightnin' Hopkins, Johnny Shines, Sonny Terry and Brownie McGhee, Fred McDowell, Mance Lipscomb, and the Rev. Gary Davis.

The Chicago Blues Archive at the Information Center of the Harold Washington Library has approximately 2,000 sound recordings, tapes of club performances, radio programs, videos, photographs, manuscripts, and papers and recordings from annual blues festivals. An inventory is available for this archive and materials are accessible through a database inventory. The W. C. Handy Home and Museum in Florence, Ala., is a repository for the sheet music of Handy and his associates, 1,000 uncataloged items, the holograph text of Handy's book, *Father of the Blues* (1941), visual works, photographs, and recordings from Handy's personal collection. Handy's papers (1873–1958) and those related to the Handy Brothers' Music Co. also form part of the Countee Cullen Memorial Collection at Atlanta University. W. C. Handy is also represented in the Jesse E. Moorland and the Arthur B. Spingarn Collections in the Moorland-Spingarn Research Center at Howard University, in the Amistad Research Center at Tulane University, in the Special Collections at Fisk University, and in the James Weldon Johnson Memorial Collection in the Beinecke Rare Book and Manuscript Library at Yale University.

Other significant blues collections are held in the Library of Congress; the Schomburg Center for Black History and Culture; the Archives of Traditional Music at Indiana University; the Archives Center of the Smithsonian's National Museum of American History; the Center for Popular Music at Middle Tennessee State University; the Center for Southern Folklore Archives; the Delta Blues Museum of the Carnegie Public Library in Clarksdale, Miss.; the John Edwards Memorial Foundation at the University of North Carolina at Chapel Hill; the Archive of Popular American Music at the University of California; and the Jesse E. Moorland and the Arthur Spingarn Collections at the Moorland-Spingarn Research Center at Howard University.

The Fred Reif Collection in the Museum of African-American History in Detroit includes 109 photographs of renowned blues singers. Blues musicians are also represented in the Jack T. Franklin Collection of photographs at the Afro-

American Historical and Cultural Museum in Philadelphia, and in the John Baker Jazz Film Collection at the 18th & Vine Historical Jazz District, Kansas City.

The first studies on the blues were written primarily by music critics. Since the 1970s, more scholars have engaged in research on this tradition. Their works, which explore the blues within a sociocultural context, provide a more comprehensive examination of the music and its performers. Important publications are Charles Keil, *Urban Blues* (1966); Paul Oliver, *The Story of the Blues* (1969); James Cone, *The Spirituals and the Blues: An Interpretation* (1972); Albert Murray, *Stomping the Blues* (1976); William Ferris, *Blues from the Delta* (rev. ed., 1978); Jeff Titon, *Early Downhome Blues: A Musical and Cultural Analysis* (2nd ed., 1994); Robert Palmer, *Deep Blues* (1981); Mike Rowe, *Chicago Blues: The City and the Music* (1981); David Evans, *Big Road Blues: Tradition and Creativity in the Folk Blues* (1982); Bruce Bastin, *Red River Blues: The Blues Tradition in the Southeast* (1986); Julio Finn, *The Bluesman: The Musical Heritage of Black Men and Women in the Americas* (1986); Daphne Duval Harrison, *Black Pearls: Blues Queens of the 1920s* (1988); William Barlow, *"Looking Up at Down": The Emergence of Blues Culture* (1989); Peter J. Silvester, *A Left Hand Like God: A History of Boogie-Woogie Piano* (1989); Alan Lomax, *The Land Where the Blues Began* (1993); Lawrence Cohn, ed., *Nothing but the Blues: The Music and the Musicians* (1993); and Gerhard Kubik, *Africa and the Blues* (1999). Other useful sources are Paul Oliver, *Conversations with the Blues* (1965); Francis Davis, *The History of the Blues: The Roots, the Music, the People, from Charley Patton to Robert Cray* (1995); Samuel B. Charters, *The Bluesmen* (1967); Harry Oster, *Living Country Blues* (1969); Giles Oakley, *The Devil's Music: A History of the Blues* (1976); Stanley Booth, *Rhythm Oil: A Journey through the Music of the American South* (1991); and Barry Lee Pearson, *Virginia Piedmont Blues: The Lives and Art of Two Virginia Bluesmen* (1990).

A major reference for lyrics is Michael Taft, *Blues Lyric Poetry: A Concordance* (3 vols., 1984). Other sources for blues lyrics are Paul Oliver, *Blues Fell This Morning: Meaning in the Blues* (2nd ed., 1990); Eric Sackheim, *The Blues Line: A Collection of Blues Lyrics* (1969); Paul Garon, *Blues and the Poetic Spirit* (1975); and Jeff Titon, *Downhome Blues Lyrics: An Anthology from the Post–World War II Era* (1981).

Important blues anthologies are W. C. Handy, ed., *Blues: An Anthology: Complete Words and Music of 53 Great Songs,* rev. Jerry Silverman (1972); Moses Asch and Alan Lomax, ed., *The Leadbelly Songbook; The Ballads, Blues, and Folksongs of Huddie Ledbetter* (1962); and Jerry Silverman, comp. and ed., *Folk Blues: 110 American Folk Blues* (2nd ed., 1968).

The most comprehensive bibliography of printed materials, which includes a filmography, is Mary L. Hart, Brenda M. Eagles, and Lisa N. Howorth, *The Blues: A Bibliographical Guide* (1989). The two most valuable biographical dictionaries are Sheldon Harris, *Blues Who's Who: A Biographical Dictionary of Blues Singers* (expanded ed., 1993), and Gerard Herzhaft, *Encyclopedia of the Blues,* trans. Brigitte Debord (1992).

Important discographies are Robert M. W. Dixon and John Godrich, comp., *Blues and Gospel Records, 1902–1943* (3rd ed., 1982); Mike Leadbitter et al., *Blues Records, 1943–1970: A Selective Discography* (2 vols., 1987); and Paul Oliver, ed., *The Blackwell Guide to Blues Records: Revised Edition with CD Supplement* (1991).

The journals *Living Blues* (1970–), published by the Center for Southern Culture, University of Mississippi, and *Blues Unlimited* (1963–1987), published in the United Kingdom, are other valuable sources for information (articles, bibliographies, and other discographies) on various blues traditions and performers.

RAGTIME

Ragtime was the first improvisatory form of African-American instrumental music published as written compositions. While materials on this genre are included in both general and specialized collections on African-American music, some repositories are devoted exclusively to this tradition. The Central Missouri Ragtime Collection of State Fair Community College in Sedalia has sheet music, piano rolls, interviews with Eubie Blake, scrapbooks of performances of Scott Joplin's opera *Treemonisha,* contracts between Joplin and Stark, and paper and architectural memorabilia. The piano rolls recorded by Joplin are found at the Scott Joplin House State Historic Site in St. Louis, and correspondence by and about Joplin is among the holdings at Fisk University. The latter materials are described in an unpublished in-house finding aid, "A Guide to the Scott Joplin Collection in the Fisk University Library" (1961). The Arthur B. Spingarn Collection at the Moorland-Spingarn Research Center at Howard University also houses sheet music by Joplin.

The Eubie Blake Papers (correspondence and related documents, photographs, music manuscripts, and ephemera from 1918 through 1983) are located at the Maryland Historical Society. Two unpublished guides accompany the collection. Materials on Blake can also be found in the Jesse E. Moorland Collection at the Moorland-Spingarn Research Center.

Another ragtime collection is the Blind Boone Memorial Foundation, Inc., Papers, 1886–1976, located in the Western Historical Manuscript Collection at Columbia, Mo. Included in this collection are compositions by John William "Blind" Boone, orchestrations, choral arrangements of his music, correspondence, programs, and posters from a memorial concert in 1961.

Only a few major histories on ragtime have been published; they include Rudi Blesh and Harriet Janis, *They All Played Ragtime* (rev. ed., 1971); William John Schafer and Johannes Riedel, *The Art of Ragtime: Form and Meaning of an Original Black American Music* (1973); Peter Gammond, *Scott Joplin and the Ragtime Era* (1975); Terry Waldo, *This Is Ragtime: A Musical History* (1976); David A. Jasen and Trebor Jay Tichenor, *Rags and Ragtime* (1978); Edward A. Berlin, *Ragtime: A Musical and Cultural History* (1980); John Edward Hasse, ed., *Ragtime: Its History, Composers, and Music* (1985); Edward A. Berlin, *King of Ragtime: Scott Joplin and His Era* (1994); and Susan Curtis, *Dancing to a Black Man's Tune: A Life of Scott Joplin* (1994).

Journals and magazines devoted to ragtime are *The Ragtimer* (1962–), originally titled *Ragtime Society; The Mississippi Rag* (1973–); *Rag Times* (1982–1987); and *Ragtime Review* (1914–1918).

Other major references are David A. Jasen, *Recorded Ragtime, 1897–1958* (1973); Trebor J. Tichenor, comp., *Ragtime Rarities: Complete Original Music for 63 Piano Rags* (1975); and Vera Brodsky Lawrence, *The Complete Works of Scott Joplin* (2 vols., 1981).

JAZZ

Jazz was the first form of African-American music to be adapted and adopted into the mainstream of American music in the 20th century. Therefore, it has received more attention from both music critics and scholars than any other form of African-American music. The national and international status of jazz is apparent from the numerous repositories and collections devoted exclusively to this tradition.

The Institute of Jazz Studies at Rutgers University has one of the largest jazz collections in the country. It encompasses more than 100,000 commercial and noncommercial sound recordings, more than 3,000 books, national and international periodicals, vertical files, sheet music, arrangements, instruments, oral histories (audiotapes and written transcripts), and realia. The finding aid *Institute for Jazz Studies Register and Indexes,* produced on microfiche, lists the 78s, LPs, CDs, and audiotapes that have been cataloged by the Institute for Jazz Studies on the RLIN database from 1978 to 1991.

A large number of jazz resources are also found in the William Ransom Hogan Jazz Archive at Tulane University. While the primary emphasis of this archive is the New Orleans jazz style as played by New Orleans musicians (such as Buddy Bolden, King Oliver, Jelly Roll Morton, and Louis Armstrong), its collections include a variety of related styles such as ragtime, blues, gospel, and Cajun, as well as African and West Indian forms. Materials number approximately 1,500 oral histories, 35,000 phonodiscs, 130 phonocylinders, 38,000 pieces of popular sheet music from the mid-19th century through the 1950s, more than 7,000 photographs, posters, rare films, videos, vertical files, serials, and artifacts. The Archive also has several special holdings such as the Dominic LaRocca, Robichaux, Al Rose, and William Russell collections. These and other collections contain correspondence, photographs, scrapbooks, interview material, posters, film, contracts, phonorecords, notes, oral histories, manuscripts (compositions and special arrangements), sheet music, and piano-vocal lead sheets, among other items. Finding aids include an Oral History Index and *The Collection of 78 RPM Phonograph Recordings: Catalog of the William Ransom Hogan Jazz Archive* (2 vols., 1984).

The most comprehensive collection on Louis Armstrong is found at Queens College in New York. It contains Armstrong's personal collection of papers, photographs, scrapbooks, commercial and private recordings, memorabilia, musical instruments, the 200-page handwritten manuscript for Armstrong's autobiography, *Satchmo: My Life in New Orleans* (1954), thousands of unpublished photographs of Armstrong and his contemporaries, and more than 500 reel-to-reel tape boxes decorated by Armstrong.

Materials on several other New Orleans jazz musicians are located in the New Orleans Jazz Club Collections of the Louisiana State Museum and in the Amistad Research Center at Tulane University. The New Orleans Jazz Collections contain more than 12,000 photographs, 2,500 tapes, 7,500 phonograph recordings, sheet music, posters, correspondence, films, books, periodicals, and files on 1,200 musicians, artwork, special collections, and memorabilia. Materials from this collection make up a permanent exhibit (located in the Old U.S. Mint building in New Orleans) that features the actual instruments played by New Orleans musicians such as Louis Armstrong, Kid Ory, Sidney Bechet, and Freddie Keppard. The Amistad Research Center holds the papers of the jazz arranger and bandleader Fletcher Henderson. More than forty arrangements by Henderson also form part of the Benny Goodman Collection at the American Music Collection of the New York Public Library for the Performing Arts. Other jazz materials in the Performing Arts division include manuscripts and scores of Charles Mingus and correspondence of various jazz musicians.

The Duke Ellington Collection is the largest of the African-American music manuscript holdings at the Archives Center of Smithsonian's National Museum of American History. It contains original manuscripts, commercial and noncommercial recordings (test pressings, air-checks, live performances, auditions, outtakes, and interviews), photographs, correspondence, scrapbooks, news clippings, concert programs, and posters. In-house finding aids are available for this collection. Other major jazz collections are found at the Library of Congress, the Schomburg Center, the Detroit Public Library, the Center for Popular Music at Middle Tennessee State University, and the Archive of Popular American Music at the University of California, Los Angeles.

Smaller but noteworthy collections are in the Jazz Institute of Chicago Archive at the University of Chicago; the Dance Archives at Yale University (not yet cataloged); the Center for Black Music Research at Columbia College, Chicago; the Archives of Traditional Music at Indiana University; the Jazz-Blues-Gospel Hall of Fame Repository at the Music Information Center of the Chicago Public Library; the E. Azalia Hackley Collection of the Detroit Public Library; and the Black Arts Research Center in Nyack, N.Y.

Over the last two decades, various institutions have conducted jazz oral history projects, which are important to the study of African-American music. Oral histories provide personal accounts of the lives and experiences of musicians as well as recording their unique perspectives on the music. Such projects include the Oral History Project at Rutgers University; the Jazz Oral History Collection at the Smithsonian Institution's National Museum of American History; the Oral History American Music Project and the Duke Ellington Project, both at Yale University; the Kansas City Jazz Oral History Collection at the Western Historical Manuscript Collection; the St. Louis Jazzmen Project at the Western Historical Manuscript Collection; the New Orleans Jazz and Heritage Foundation Oral History Collection of the Amistad Research Center; the Norma Teagarden Oral History at the Bancroft Library, University of California, Berkeley; and the Central Avenue Sounds Oral History Project of UCLA's Oral History Program. The Standifer Video Archives in the African-American Music Collection at the University of Michigan and the Schomburg Center for Black History and Culture include video interviews with jazz musicians.

Photographs of jazz musicians can be found in the Fred and Rose Plaut Archives located in the Music Library at Yale University (a register accompanies this collection); the Otto Hess Collection at the American Music Collection of the New York Public Library for the Performing Arts; the Ed McKenzie Collection at the Museum of African-American History in Detroit; the Jack T. Franklin Collection at the Afro-American Historical and Cultural Museum in Philadelphia; the Archives Center of the Smithsonian's National Museum of American History; the

Library of Congress; the Schomburg Center for Black History and Culture; the Museum of African-American History in Detroit; and the Center for Southern Folklore in Memphis.

The two most important jazz film collections are the John Baker Jazz Film Collection at the 18th & Vine Historical Jazz District, Kansas City, and the Ernie Smith Jazz Film Collection at the Archives Center of the Smithsonian's National Museum of American History.

Most of the early jazz publications were written by European music critics, who drew most of their data from commercial recordings, published reviews, and anecdotes. Even though many of these works have been revised, they should be consulted with caution because of their flawed research methodologies and analytical models, and the lack of substantial documentation. The publications cited below represent divergent approaches to jazz scholarship and the perspectives of both European and American music critics and jazz scholars.

Among the studies published from the 1920s to the 1950s are Hugues Panassié, *Hot Jazz: The Guide to Swing Music* (rpt., 1970) and *The Real Jazz* (rev. ed., 1973); Winthrop Sargeant, *Jazz: Hot and Hybrid* (3rd ed., 1975); André Hodeir, *Jazz: Its Evolution and Essence* (1956); Alan Lomax, *Mister Jelly Roll: The Fortunes of Jelly Roll Morton, New Orleans Creole and "Inventor of Jazz"* (2nd ed., 1973); Joachim E. Berendt, *The Jazz Book: From Ragtime to Fusion and Beyond* (6th ed., 1991); Nat Shapiro and Nat Hentoff, *Hear Me Talkin' to Ya: The Story of Jazz as Told by the Men Who Made It* (2nd ed., 1966); Marshall Stearns, *The Story of Jazz* (1956); and Nat Hentoff and Albert J. McCarthy, ed., *Jazz: New Perspectives on the History of Jazz by Twelve of the World's Foremost Jazz Critics and Scholars* (2nd ed., 1974).

Several influential jazz studies were published during the 1960s and 1970s, including Leroy Ostransky, *The Anatomy of Jazz* (1960); Nat Hentoff, *The Jazz Life* (1961); Samuel B. Charters and Leonard Kunstadt, *Jazz: A History of the New York Scene* (1962); Ira Gitler, *Jazz Masters of the Forties* (2nd ed., 1983); Gunther Schuller, *Early Jazz: Its Roots and Musical Development* (1968); LeRoi Jones [Amiri Baraka], *Black Music* (1968); Frank Kofsky, *Black Nationalism and the Revolution in Music* (1970); Martin Williams, *The Jazz Tradition* (2nd rev. ed., 1993); Duke Ellington, *Music Is My Mistress* (1973); Albert McCarthy, *Big Band Jazz* (1974); Arthur Taylor, *Notes and Tones: Musician-to-Musician Interviews* (1977); and Dizzy Gillespie with Al Fraser, *To Be or Not . . . to Bop: Memoirs* (1979).

Major jazz publications from the 1980s and 1990s include Nathan W. Pearson, Jr., *Goin' to Kansas City* (1987); Gunther Schuller, *The Swing Era: The Development of Jazz, 1930–1945* (1989); Ira Gitler, *Swing to Bop: An Oral History of the Tradition in Jazz in the 1940s* (1985); David N. Baker, ed., *New Perspectives on Jazz* (1990); Burton W. Peretti, *The Creation of Jazz: Music, Race, and Culture in Urban America* (1992); David H. Rosenthal, *Hard Bop: Jazz and Black Music, 1955–1965* (1992); William H. Kenney, *Chicago Jazz: A Cultural History, 1904–1930* (1993); Mark Tucker, ed., *The Duke Ellington Reader* (1993); David Stowe, *Swing Changes: Big Band Jazz in New Deal America* (1994); Paul Berliner, *Thinking in Jazz: The Infinite Art of Improvisation* (1994); Ben Sidran, *Talking Jazz: An Oral History* (expanded ed., 1995); and Ingrid Monson, *Saying Something: Jazz Improvisation and Interaction* (1996).

Noteworthy studies that include African-American women in jazz are Sally

Placksin, *American Women in Jazz: 1900 to the Present: Their Words, Lives, and Music* (1982); Linda Dahl, *Stormy Weather: The Music and Lives of a Century of Jazzwomen* (1984); and Jan Leder, *Women in Jazz: A Discography of Instrumentalists, 1913–1968* (1985).

Several comprehensive guides are available on jazz. Major bibliographies are Carl Gregor, Duke of Mecklenburg, *International Jazz Bibliography; Jazz Books from 1919 to 1968* (1969); John Gray, comp., *Fire Music: A Bibliography of the New Jazz: 1959–1990* (1991); Eddie S. Meadows, *Jazz Research and Performance Materials: A Selected and Annotated Bibliography* (2nd ed., 1995); and Donald Kennington and Danny L. Read, *The Literature of Jazz: A Critical Guide* (rev. ed., 1980). The latter two sources cover several areas including jazz histories; biographies; analysis, theory, and criticism; reference sources; periodical literature; jazz and literature; organizations; and jazz on film.

The most comprehensive jazz encyclopedias are Barry Kernfeld, ed., *The New Grove Dictionary of Jazz* (1988), and Leonard Feather, *The Encyclopedia of Jazz in the Sixties* (1966) and *The Encyclopedia of Jazz in the Seventies* (1976). Consult also Brian Case and Stan Britt, *The Harmony Illustrated Encyclopedia of Jazz*, rev. and updated by Chrissie Murray (1987), originally published as *The Illustrated Encyclopedia of Jazz* (1978). Another useful jazz reference tool is Samuel Barclay Charters, *Jazz: New Orleans, 1885–1963: An Index to the Musicians of New Orleans* (rev. ed., 1963).

Several important discographies have been published on jazz, such as Pete Moon, *A Bibliography of Jazz Discographies Published since 1960* (rev. ed., 1972); Daniel Allen, *Bibliography of Discographies, Vol. 2: Jazz* (1981); Brian Rust, *Jazz Records, 1897–1942* (2 vols., 5th rev. and enlarged ed., 1982); Albert J. McCarthy et al., *Jazz on Record: A Critical Guide to the First 50 Years, 1917–1967* (1968); Richard Cook and Brian Morton, *The Penguin Guide to Jazz on CD, LP, and Cassette* (new ed., 1994); and Barry Kernfeld, ed., *The Blackwell Guide to Recorded Jazz* (2nd ed., 1995). Walter Bruyninckx has published several discographies on jazz: *Jazz: Modern Jazz, Be-Bop, Hard Bop, West Coast* (1985); *Jazz: Traditional Jazz, 1897–1985: Origins, New Orleans, Dixieland, Chicago Styles* (1985); *Progressive Jazz: Free–Third Stream Fusion* (1984); *Swing, 1920–1985: Swing Dance Bands and Combos* (1985); *The Vocalists, 1917–1986: Singers and Crooners* (1990); and *60 Years of Recorded Jazz, 1917–1977* (1979).

Jazz recordings since 1945 are the focus of Max Harrison et al., comp., *Modern Jazz, 1945–1970: The Essential Records: A Critical Selection* (1975), and Erik Raben, *Jazz Records, 1942–80, A Discography* (1987). The most comprehensive jazz filmography is Jean-Roland Hippenmeyer, *Jazz sur Films: Ou, 55 Années de Rapports Jazz-Cinema Vue a Travers Plus de 800 Films Tournés entre 1917 et 1972* (1973). A related work is David Meeker, *Jazz in the Movies* (1981).

The leading jazz journals and magazines are published in the United States and Europe. The three published in the United States are *Metronome* (1885–1961), *Downbeat* (1934–), and the *Annual Review of Jazz Studies* (1982–). Originally titled *Journal of Jazz Studies* (1973–1981), *Jazzforschung* (1969–) is published in Austria, and *Jazz Monthly* (1954–1971) and *Jazz Journal* (1948–1966) in England.

CLASSICAL MUSIC

Vernacular and popular forms of African-American expression often inspired African-American composers trained in the Western European school of composition. In some compositions, they based their thematic materials on or borrowed the formal, melodic, and harmonic structures, rhythmic patterns, and aesthetic qualities from various idioms including spirituals, work songs, blues, ragtime, jazz, gospel, and rap music. Using Western European models, African-American composers transformed the folk spiritual into choral works and art songs (solo voice) for performance on the concert stage during the first decades of the 20th century. Also, many performers who were trained in the techniques of Western European vocal and instrumental performance incorporated the original and arranged works of African-American composers into their repertoires. Therefore, the following discussion of classical music and composers includes arrangers of folk spirituals for the concert stage as well as performers whose repertoire encompasses the arranged spiritual.

Many African-American composers and performers either taught or were students at historically black universities. Several small but important collections are located at these institutions, including Fisk University (Fisk Jubilee Singers Archives and the Arthur Cunningham and Scott Joplin Collections), Hampton Institute (Hampton Quartet Collection, 1889–1938, and the Roland Marvin Carter Collection, 1963–1986), and Jackson State University (Opera/South Collection). The larger repositories that have holdings on composers and performers are the Schomburg Center, the Moorland-Spingarn Research Center at Howard University, the Library of Congress, the Center for Black Music Research, the Amistad Research Center, and the E. Azalia Hackley Collection at the Detroit Public Library.

The Manuscripts, Archives and Rare Books, and Moving Image and Recorded Sound Divisions of the Schomburg Center contain papers, correspondence, programs, music manuscripts, clippings, recorded and printed interviews, scrapbooks, legal contracts, financial records, photographs, and recordings of various African-American composers, performers, and music organizations. Represented in the collections are the cellist Marion W. Cumbo; the concert and opera singers Jules Bledsoe and Paul Robeson; the accompanist Lawrence Brown; the composers Blind Tom, Edward Boatner, Philippa Duke Schuyler, and Clarence Cameron White; and performing groups and organizations such as the National Association of Negro Musicians, the National Negro Opera Company, the Negro String Quartet, and the Symphony of the New World.

The Moorland-Spingarn Research Center at Howard University houses several important collections on African-American composers. Highlights are the Jesse E. Moorland Collection, the Arthur Spingarn Collection, and the Washington Conservatory of Music Records. The Jesse E. Moorland Collection includes information on more than 180 composers, such as Will Marion Cook, William Dawson, R. Nathaniel Dett, Samuel Coleridge-Taylor, William Grant Still, James Weldon Johnson, and John Rosamond Johnson.

The Arthur B. Spingarn Collection has impressive print materials, songbook collections, sheet music, scores, and musical manuscripts (some of which are autographed by the composer) of more than 200 African-American, Afro-Cuban, and Afro-Brazilian composers, including Will Marion Cook, William L. Dawson, R. Nathaniel Dett, James Reese Europe, Harry T. Burleigh, Samuel Coleridge-Taylor, and Florence B. Price.

The Washington Conservatory of Music Records has more than 5,619 items, including correspondence, organization and student records, financial papers, notebooks, programs, photographs, clippings, periodicals, memorabilia, and documents related to the Conservatory's founder, Harriet Gibbs Marshall, and her husband, Napoleon Bonaparte. Among the holdings of the Manuscript Department are the materials of several musicians, such as Marian Anderson and Samuel Coleridge-Taylor.

The above and other holdings of the Center are listed in the Music Catalog section of the *Dictionary Catalog of the Arthur B. Spingarn Collection of Negro Authors* (2 vols., 1970), compiled by Dorothy Porter; "The Guide to the Music Department Collections at the Moorland-Spingarn Research Center" (unpublished), compiled by Deborra A. Richardson; and the *Guide to Processed Collections in the Manuscript Division of the Moorland-Spingarn Research Center* (1983), compiled by Greta S. Wilson and published by the Center.

The Library of Congress also has several important collections consisting of correspondence, musical manuscripts, and recordings of and related to several African-American composers. Among those represented are Ulysses Kay, William Grant Still, and Francis Johnson.

The Center for Black Music Research houses several collections of important materials on African-American composers and concert music in general. General collections include the recordings, manuscripts, and scores of the composers Talib Rasul Hakim, Leslie Adams, Edmund Thornton Jenkins, Olly Wilson, Hale Smith, William Grant Still, David Baker, William Banfield, Michael Woods, Lee Cloud, Jeffery Mumford, Ed Bland, and Daniel Roumain, among others. Special collections donated by Dominique-Rene de Lerma and William Duncan Allen augment these materials. De Lerma's collection, for example, contains correspondence, scores, ephemera concerning black composers and performers, and approximately 600 commercial recordings of performances by black performers and compositions by black composers. It also has papers of the black scholar and composer James Furman and music manuscripts of Richard C. Moffatt.

The Amistad Research Center at Tulane University is another major repository for materials on African-American composers, including Roger Dickerson, Loretta Cessor Manggrum, Hale Smith, and Howard Swanson, as well as on two local chapters of the National Association of Negro Musicians, the B-Sharp Music Club of New Orleans, and the Chicago Music Association. The collections consist of correspondence, personal papers, newspaper clippings, programs, sheet music, and original manuscripts.

The Beinecke Rare Book and Manuscript Library at Yale University houses the James Weldon Johnson Memorial Collection, which contains musical manuscripts (sixty-two are autographed), anthologies of black songs, editions of music with texts by blacks, editions with music by blacks, recordings, and a large quantity of correspondence among Harlem Renaissance writers and artists and their musician friends, representative of both classical and nonclassical traditions.

Musical manuscripts are by Hall Johnson, Ulysses Kay, Howard Swanson, Harry Burleigh, William Dawson, Clarence Cameroon White, J. Rosamond Johnson, Florence B. Price, Philippa Schuyler, Margaret Bonds, and William Grant Still. Some manuscripts are complete works and others consist of only a few bars. The library's printed music collection contains scores by John Rosamond Johnson and Samuel Coleridge-Taylor. A published catalog, *Music, Printed and Manuscript, in the James Weldon Johnson Collection of Negro Arts and Letters: An Annotated Catalog* (1982), by Ray Linda Brown, accompanies the James Weldon Johnson Collection.

Other important holdings on African-American composers are found in the Music Department at Fisk University (John Wesley Work III Collection, 1915–1967), the Robert W. Woodruff Library at Atlanta University (Maud Cuney-Hare Collection, 1900–1936), the Music Library and the Archives of African-American Music and Culture at Indiana University (Undine Smith Moore Collection of Original Manuscripts and Scores and the General Art Music Collection), and the Archives Center at Smithsonian's National Museum of American History (video collection from symposia on black American composers).

Although many collections contain materials on several musicians, others are devoted to specific individuals. Therefore, materials on individual musicians are found in both general and specialized collections. For example, the largest collection devoted exclusively to Harry Burleigh is the Harry Thacker Burleigh Collection, 1884–1981, at the Erie County Historical Society in Erie, Pennsylvania. He is also represented in the general collections of several other repositories noted elsewhere in this discussion.

Similarly, one of the largest, if not the largest, specialized collection on R. Nathaniel Dett and William Grant Still (the William Grant Still and Verna Arvey Papers) are in the University Archives and Historical Collections at Michigan State University and the University of Arkansas–Fayetteville, respectively. Like Burleigh, Dett and Still are also represented in other repositories. The Hampton University Archives and the Niagara Falls (N.Y.) Public Library, among other repositories, have materials on Dett. Papers, manuscripts, and scores of Still are represented in the holdings of the Library of Congress; the Manuscript Department at Duke University; the Center for Black Music Research at Columbia College, Chicago; the Henry T. Sampson Library at Jackson State University in Jackson, Miss.; the Archives of the Hollis Burke Fissell Library at Tuskegee Institute in Tuskegee, Ala.; and Fisk University.

Collections on African-American women composers are scarce in the nation's repositories. The most comprehensive is the Helen Walker-Hill Collection at the American Music Research Center at the University of Colorado at Boulder. It consists of some 600 published or photocopied works by approximately eighty composers from the late 19th and 20th centuries, the majority representative of the 20th century. A 21-page inventory of these materials is available.

Other significant holdings on African-American women composers are the Julia Perry Papers at Fisk University, the Florence Smith Price Papers located at the University of Arkansas–Fayetteville, and musical manuscripts by Margaret Bonds in the Maud Cuney-Hare Collection, 1900–1936, in the Special Collections and Archives Division at Atlanta University. The Price Papers contain correspondence, published and unpublished music manuscripts, photographs, and other records created or received by the composer. Two original manuscripts by Florence Price are in the Center for Black Music Research at Columbia College and one is at the Library of Congress. The General Art Music Collection and the Undine Smith Moore Collection in the Archives of African-American Music and Culture at Indiana University include original compositions by Undine Smith Moore, Regina Harris Baiocchi, Lettie Beckon Alson, Lena McLin, and Dorothy Rudd Moore. Scores by Zenobia Perry, Rachel Eubanks, Margaret Bonds, and Tania Leon are also found in the collections of the Center for Black Music Research.

Most collections on African-American concert music are devoted to composers. Even though performers are included in a number of repositories, they are better represented in some repositories than others. For example, the focus of materials in the E. Azalia Hackley Collection at the Detroit Public Library, established through the efforts of the Detroit chapter of the National Association of Negro Musicians, is the careers of concert and opera singers, as represented by Marian Anderson and Roland Hayes. Materials of these and other artists are indexed in the *Catalog of the E. Azalia Hackley Memorial Collection of Negro Music, Dance, and Drama* (1979), which is divided into four parts: books and musical scores, sheet music, broadsides and posters, and photographs.

African-American performers predominate in several other repositories. The papers of the concert singer Marian Anderson are housed in the Rare Book Collections at the University of Pennsylvania. This collection is described in *Marian Anderson: A Catalog of the Collection at the University of Pennsylvania Library* (1981), by Neda M. Westlake and Otto Edwin Albrecht. The Amistad Research Center has collections that are devoted to or include materials on the concert and opera singers Carol Lovette Brice, Ann Wiggins Brown, Albert Walker and Jessie Covington Dent, Eva Jessye, Paul Robeson, William Warfield and Camilla Williams, Leontyne Price, and Mattiwilda Dobbs. The Fisk Jubilee Singers are well documented at Fisk University, as are the Hampton Institute Choir, the Hampton Folk Singers, the Crusaders Male Chorus, and alumni Dorothy Maynor and Roland Carter at Hampton University. The University Archives at Hampton University has photographs, music programs, program and biographical notes, and concert reviews of visiting artists.

A collection devoted to the Wings over Jordan Choir is located at the National Afro-American Museum and Cultural Center in Wilberforce, Ohio, and materials on Eva Jessye are found in several repositories, including the African-American Music Collection at the University of Michigan, the Special Collections Department at Pittsburgh State University in Kansas, and the Manuscript Collections at the Amistad Research Center. Materials on the concert pianist Natalie Hinderas, the violinist Charles McCabe, the Philadelphia Concert Orchestra, and the vocalists Marian Anderson and Ethel De Preist, among others, are found in collections at the Afro-American Historical and Cultural Museum in Philadelphia. Repositories with holdings related to opera productions, such as *Porgy and Bess,* are found in the African-American Music Collection at the University of Michigan; the Robert A. Wachsman and the Robert Breen Collections at the Jerome Lawrence and Robert E. Lee Theater Research Institute at Ohio State University; the

Opera/South Collection (1969–1984) in Special Collections at Jackson State University; the Manuscripts, Archives and Rare Books Division of the Schomburg Center; and the Moorland-Spingarn Research Center and the Channing Pollock Theatre Collection, both at Howard University. The Music Division of the Library of Congress houses the Negro Opera Company Collection.

The Standifer Video Archive in the African-American Collection at the University of Michigan includes interviews of African-American composers. Videotapes of symposia on and performances of black concert music organized by the Program in African-American Culture at the Smithsonian Institution are located in the Archives Center at the National Museum of American History.

Since the 1970s, several reference works have been published on black concert music (performers and composers). Devoted exclusively to musicians of the pre–Civil War era is Arthur R. LaBrew's *Black Musicians of the Colonial Period, 1700–1800: A Preliminary Index* (rev. ed., 1981). Musicians from the 18th through the 20th century are identified or discussed in James M. Trotter, *Music and Some Highly Musical People* (1881); Maud Cuney-Hare, *Negro Musicians and Their Music* (1936); Raoul Abdul, *Blacks in Classical Music: A Personal History* (1977); David Baker et al., *The Black Composer Speaks* (1977); D. Antoinette Handy, *Black Women in American Bands and Orchestras* (1980); Mildred Denby Green, *Black Women Composers: A Genesis* (1983); Samuel Floyd, ed., *Black Music in the Harlem Renaissance: A Collection of Essays* (1990); and John Gray, comp., *Blacks in Classical Music: A Bibliographical Guide to Composers, Performers, and Ensembles* (1988). Another useful reference on 20th-century composers is Alice Tischler, *Fifteen Black American Composers: A Bibliography of Their Works* (1981).

Publications that identify composers and their works are Evelyn Davidson White, *Choral Music by African-American Composers: A Selected, Annotated Bibliography* (2nd ed., 1996); Helen Walker-Hill, *Music by Black Women Composers: A Bibliography of Available Scores* (1995), *Piano Music by Black Women Composers: A Catalog of Solo and Ensemble Works* (1992), and *Music by Black Women Composers: A Bibliography of Their Works* (1995); Linda Nell Phillips, "Piano Music by Black Composers: A Computer-Based Bibliography" (D.M.A. diss., Ohio State University, 1977); and Zelma George, "A Guide to Negro Music: An Annotated Bibliography of Negro Folk Music, and Art Music by Negro Composers or Based on Negro Thematic Material" (Ed.D. diss., New York University, 1954). Aaron Horne has compiled several excellent bibliographies: *Woodwind Music of Black Composers: A Bibliography* (1990), *String Music of Black Composers: A Bibliography* (1991), *Keyboard Music of Black Composers: A Bibliography* (1992), and *Brass Music of Black Composers: A Bibliography* (1996). Most of the publications above include biographical sketches, descriptions of works, and a selected bibliography.

The only collections of the concert works of African-American composers are R. Nathaniel Dett, *The Collected Piano Works of R. Nathaniel Dett* (1973) and Willis Patterson, *Anthology of Art Songs by Black American Composers* (1977). Similarly, the only discographic guide to recordings of concert music by African-American performers is Patricia Turner, *Dictionary of Afro-American Performers: 78 RPM and Cylinder Recordings of Opera, Choral Music, and Song, c. 1900–1949* (1990).

The proliferation of reference works on African-American music since the early

1970s reflects a sustained and ongoing interest in this tradition. Since the first seminars held at Indiana University, many musicologists, ethnomusicologists, music educators, and performers now include this music in their research agendas, classroom and public lectures, recitals, and concerts. Established and budding African-American composers continue to draw from vernacular traditions (including popular idioms) for creative inspiration. The reference and archival materials developed and made accessible by dedicated researchers, librarians, and museum curators have contributed immensely to the diversity that has always defined the musical landscape of the American society.

11 *Photography*

Deborah Willis

The photograph is an important but often overlooked research tool for historians. Curators, filmmakers, and journalists regularly use photographs to illustrate ideas and events, as well as to document the lives of individuals. Indeed, as John Berger observes, "photography has been used for police filing, war reporting, military reconnaissance, pornography, encyclopedic documentation, family albums, postcards, anthropological records, sentimental moralizing, inquisitive probing (the wrongly named 'candid camera'), aesthetic effects, news reporting, and formal portraiture." Yet few historians have realized the extent to which photographs might serve as the basis for analysis and interpretation of the past. This essay invites scholars to view the photograph as a rewarding medium for historical research while also identifying the major repositories where photographic collections of African-American life and culture can be found.

Photographs are variously categorized as portraits, art photography, photojournalism, documentary, and social documentary photography. They are also categorized by their physical characteristics, which are identified by the following techniques and applications:

1. Direct positives: daguerreotype (1839–1855), ambrotype (1852–1870), and tintype (1854–1900).

2. Negatives on paper: calotype (ca. 1841–1855) and Eastman (ca. 1884–1895); negatives on glass: collodion (ca. 1851–1880) and gelatin dry plate (1878–1920); negatives on gelatin: Eastman film (ca. 1884–1890); negatives on clear plastic: nitro-cellulose (1889–1903) and cellulose acetate (1939–).

3. Prints: salt print or salted paper print (ca. 1839–1860); albumen print (1850–1895); stereograph (1850–1890); platinum print (1873–1937); postcard (1880–); and silver gelatin or gelatin silver print (1883–).

Experimentation with daguerreotype processing began in the late 1830s. By August 1839 newspapers in Paris and London described Louis Mandé Daguerre's process in detail. Thus, anyone interested in the process could obtain details of the techniques involved. In brief, the daguerreotype is a positive image that is formed on a silver plate. Typical exposures were as long as twenty minutes. Special vises were placed on chairs to hold human subjects' necks in place—thus the relatively stiff appearance of portraits in daguerreotypes. Later chemical developments would shorten the length of time of exposure. Although this process was rapidly overtaken by negative-to-positive photographic techniques, the daguerreotype actually offered the clearest, most detailed resolution of all photographic processes.

At the same time as the invention of the daguerreotype, in England, Henry Fox Talbot, a scholar, scientist, and inventor, created the negative/positive process of photography. Talbot's method is the foundation for the way photography is practiced today. The first negative was made from a piece of paper treated with photosensitive chemicals. Objects were placed on the paper and the paper was exposed to sunlight. The resulting exposure left a negative image on the paper, in which the tonal values are the opposite of those of the subject. (Modern photography uses a camera to make an exposure of a negative on film or acetate.) Talbot made the first successful negative in 1835. However, he did not exhibit the photographic results until four years later, on the heels of Daguerre's announcement, which overshadowed his achievement. In 1841, Talbot patented the calotype process (the name derives from the Greek *kalos*, which means beautiful). It utilized a negative paper that was prepared with silver iodide, which had better light sensitivity and the fastest exposure time of all photo processes, at one minute.

With the opening of commercial photography studios in America, portraits of African-Americans were commissioned for personal and commercial purposes. By 1840, thousands of Americans (including African-Americans) were producing daguerreotypes. In northern cities that had a growing free black population, the demand for daguerreotypes grew with the rise of a black middle class of clergymen, orators, entrepreneurs, inventors, educators, abolitionists, artisans, and artists. Images of the black elite of this period survive in repositories around the country. Photographs of well-known black personalities were also bought and sold as art, traded as *cartes de visite* (calling cards), sold as a fund-raising technique (Sojourner Truth's famous *carte de visite* declared "I sell the shadow to support the substance"), and published in books and periodicals. Although there are several books and articles about the early advancements made in the art of photography, few records exist concerning the value of the medium to African-Americans as subjects. One of the exceptions is Jeanne Moutoussamy-Ashe's *Viewfinders: Black Women Photographers* (1986).

It was not only the social elite whose images survive from the mid- and late 19th century. Many enslaved Africans were photographed as property of their owners, along with livestock, homes, and other "possessions." Scientists and anthropologists also photographed some enslaved Africans. Such is the case of the much-discussed daguerreotypes (fifteen in number) housed in Harvard University's Peabody Museum. The Harvard scientist Louis Agassiz commissioned these well-preserved daguerreotypes in 1850, which were made by Joseph T. Zealy, a white photographer based in Columbia, S.C. Zealy photographed African-born enslaved men and women (reported to be from the Congo) who lived on a plantation owned by B. F. Taylor of South Carolina. The daguerreotypes provide anatomical studies of the faces and the nude upper bodies of both male and female subjects, and reveal mid-19th-century scientific and political theories about race and difference.

Both black-owned and white-owned photography studios produced portraits of African-Americans. White studios found it commercially profitable to create negative and satirical photographs of black subjects. These images, often printed as postcards, proliferated throughout the United States, provoking hostile criticism from the African-American community. For those African-American families able to avail themselves of photography studios in the 19th and early 20th centuries, the medium afforded the commemoration of a special occasion in the sitter's life, such as the achievement of social or political status in the community, courtship, marriage, birth, or death. As photography became popular and more accessible to the general public, images made by documentary and studio photographers included those of families, military servicemen and -women, dances, banquets, private parties, and participants in conventions and large rallies. These photographs have become vital sources for understanding African-American cultural history. Like any other historical source, however, photographs do not speak for themselves. As Lawrence Levine writes, "The importance of photography as a source is precisely this: it can freeze conflicting realities, ambiguities, paradoxes, so that we can see them, examine them, recognize the larger, more complex, and often less palatable truths they direct us to . . . Photographs, then, are a source that needs to be interpreted and supplemented by other evidence."

In the last ten years, a growing number of libraries, historical societies, museums, and picture agencies have begun to collect photographs as social and community history. Scholars have focused on the ways in which one looks at and interprets photographs and how identity and representation are constructed in photographs of African-Americans. Nell Irvin Painter's *Sojourner Truth: A Life, a Symbol* (1996) is a model for the creative use of photographic evidence, providing useful analysis of a subject's efforts to define her own identity in the minds of her "readers." Photographs enable us visually to read historical moments through fashion, architecture, and landscape, as well as through constructed poses and candid situations.

Deborah Willis has authored three comprehensive books on the work of black photographers: *Black Photographers, 1840–1940: An Illustrated Bio-Bibliography* (1985), *An Illustrated Bio-Bibliography of Black Photographers, 1940–1988* (1989), and *Reflections in Black: A History of Black Photographers, 1840 to the Present* (2000). Based on detailed research in city directories, newspapers, books, and photographs of black subjects by white and black photographers found in public collections, these are the only reference works that provide a national overview of African-American photography. A valuable resource for identifying photographic imagery and information about individual photographers is James de T. Abajian's *Blacks in Selected Newspapers, Censuses, and Other Sources: An Index to Names and Subjects* (1974). The social historian Douglas Daniels, in *Pioneer Urbanites: A Social and Cultural History of Black San Francisco* (1980), provides an excellent study, making creative use of photographs in his research. He chronicles the books, repositories, and primary source materials for scholars interested in researching obscure or hard-to-find photographic materials of blacks in one northern California community. Daniel's work serves as a model for research on the African-American urban experience.

The Prints and Photographs Division of the Library of Congress in Washington, D.C., is the most important photographic collection in this country. Unique in its scope and richness, this collection contains more than 14 million images. They range from watercolor views, portraits, and master prints and photographs to architectural renderings and working drawings, mass-produced propaganda posters, news photographs, and printed ephemera. The collection comprises magazine and newspaper archives (such as the *Look Magazine* and the *U.S. News and World Report* collections); portraits, stereographs, and 19th-century images of blacks; and photographs from federal agencies (such as the Farm Security Administration, Office of War Information, and Works Progress Administration).

The Library of Congress also houses photographs from the archives of the National Association for the Advancement of Colored People and the Harmon Foundation. Subject headings related to these archives include Civil Rights Activities, World's Fairs (for example, the Paris Exposition of 1900), World War I and World War II, Reconstruction, Slavery, Colleges and Universities (including black land-grant colleges), and Ku Klux Klan Activity. A significant number of movie stills and photographs from television programs are included in the collection, as are images of black subjects by such notable photographers as Carl Van Vechten, Gordon Parks, Russell Lee, Frances Benjamin Johnston, Danny Lyon, and W. Eugene Smith. In the Portrait Collection are a variety of images by occupation: musicians and singers, such as Julian "Cannonball" Adderly, Pearl Bailey, Count Basie, and Thomas "Blind Tom" Bethune; sports figures Muhammad Ali, Jackie Robinson, and Wilt Chamberlain; authors James Baldwin and Maya Angelou; and political figures Frederick Douglass, Mary Church Terrell, Ralph Bunche, Thurgood Marshall, and Shirley Chisholm.

The National Archives and Records Administration's Still Picture Branch, also in Washington, D.C., houses original photographs and negatives, as well as machine-readable images. To be found here are photographs of the Civil War, western exploration, the Office of War Information, the Harmon Foundation, the United States Information Agency, Federal Art Project, National Youth Administration, and portraits of black legislators, entertainers, and agricultural workers.

The Schomburg Center for Research in Black Culture, part of the Research Libraries of the New York Public Library, houses one of the country's finest collections of photography. The Center's Photographic Collection of more than 300,000 prints and negatives forms the most complete description of the black experience through studio portraits, news photographs, and family albums. Items range from mid-18th-century slavery prints to present-day photographic images. Subject headings include Africa, Art, Authors, Civil War, Civil Rights, Entertainment, Military, Organizations, Slavery, Reconstruction, Street Scenes, and Weddings. There are also portraits of personalities and legendary figures representing all aspects of African-American life and culture. Photographs from federal agencies such as the Farm Security Administration, Office of War Information, Works Progress Administration, and the National Youth Agency are well represented, as are individual photographers' collections, such as those of Morgan and Marvin Smith, Austin Hansen, James VanDerZee, Aaron Siskind, Doris Ulmann, and Carl Van Vechten. The collection is open to the public on a walk-in basis; however, there is limited seating, and researchers should write in advance to schedule an appointment to ensure accommodation.

The Afro-American Historical and Cultural Museum (Philadelphia) houses family photographic collections dating from the mid-1800s to the present. Its most significant collection is the Jack T. Franklin Collection (early 1950s to the present), a valuable selection of more than 300,000 important photographs. Franklin worked as a freelance photographer for the black *Philadelphia Tribune,* photographing political, religious, and social groups, as well as the major community leaders in the Philadelphia area. These included Cecil Moore, Leon Sullivan, Marian Anderson, Sadie T. M. Alexander, Raymond Pace Alexander, Stokely Carmichael, Ralph Abernathy, Roy Wilkins, John Lewis, and the activist disc jockey Georgie Woods. Franklin's photographs of civil rights activities in the Philadelphia area and documentation of the visits of Malcolm X, Martin Luther King, and Dick Gregory are important records. Other key subjects by Franklin are fraternal and Masonic groups, the National Association for the Advancement of Colored People, the Congress of Racial Equality, the Southern Christian Leadership Conference, and the Student Nonviolent Coordinating Committee.

The University of South Carolina's Caroliniana Library (Columbia, S.C.) houses the Richard Samuel Roberts collection. This collection centers on blacks in the South during the 1920s and 1930s. More than 3,000 glass-plate negatives and thousands of prints depict black families, businesses, church activities, men and women at work, birthday parties, graduations, and funerals. The studio portraits provide visual documentation of the families who visited the studios, as do the images taken in the homes of families in the rural South. The library's collection is also enhanced with photographs of rural scenes, chain-gang work sites, burial sites, and genre scenes dating back to the 1840s.

The prints and photographs collection of the Charles L. Blockson Afro-American Collection, Temple University (Philadelphia), consists of diverse subject matter from portraits and family collections to documentary photographs by John W. Mosley, a Philadelphia-based photographer working from the mid-1930s through the 1960s. The collection consists of more than 500,000 photographic prints and negatives that provide a visual history of notable black entertainers, social and political personalities, and the social, cultural, religious, and family life of Philadelphia's African-Americans. The collection has a significant number of sports images, including track meets, basketball players, and Negro League baseball players and teams such as the Homestead Grays, Philadelphia Stars, Cubans, Baltimore Elite Giants, and Birmingham Black Barons. Major league black players such as Jackie Robinson and Roy Campanella also appear. Charles L. Blockson, *The Journey of John W. Mosley* (1992), provides an excellent sample of the photographs in this rich collection.

The Moorland-Spingarn Research Center, Howard University, acquires photographs through its manuscript division. The extensive photographic archive focuses on the intellectual life of Howard University and the Washington, D.C., African-American community. Of paramount importance is the collection of the Scurlock Studio. Founded by Addison N. Scurlock and his sons, Robert and George, it was Washington's leading African-American portrait studio, and its work is dominant among Howard's portrait collection. The photographs include subjects such as Mordecai Wyatt Johnson, W. E. B. Du Bois, Rayford Logan, Alain Locke, Anna Julia Cooper, Mary McLeod Bethune, Madame Lillian Evanti, Sterling Brown, Charles S. Johnson, and the presidents of land grant black colleges, among others. Papers of Paul Robeson and Alain Locke, also at the Moorland-Spingarn Research Center, include photographs of their activities.

The James Weldon Johnson Collection at the Beinecke Library, Yale University, includes works by the writer and photographer Carl Van Vechten. His photographs of Pearl Bailey, Lena Horne, Langston Hughes, Zora Neale Hurston, James Weldon Johnson, James Earl Jones, Leontyne Price, and Paul Robeson are among the hundreds of images produced by Van Vechten from the 1930s through the late 1950s. Within this special manuscript collection are photographs culled from the personal papers of Countee Cullen, W. C. Handy, Langston Hughes, James Weldon Johnson, Claude McKay, and Walter White.

Other significant university archives with distinctive African-American photographic collections include the Harry Ranson Humanities Research Center at the University of Texas–Austin; Harvard University Libraries; Hampton University; Tuskegee University; University of Virginia; Fisk University; Florida A & M University; Duke University's Center for Documentary Studies; Clark Atlanta University; University of Mississippi; the Center for Creative Photography at the University of Arizona; the Amistad Research Center at Tulane University; and Coppin State College, which houses a photographic archive of African-American newspapers. These repositories include rare historical and contemporary collections of black subjects and their communities.

Some curators and librarians have bought photographic collections from dealers or families, while other collections have found their way to repositories by chance (donated, for example, by neighbors or by the photographers themselves). The Auburn Avenue Research Library on African American Culture and History in Atlanta collects broadly. A recent acquisition of the photographic collection of the Jacksonville, Fla., photographer Ellis Weems is a clear indication of the future direction of this library. This collection consists of more than 10,000 prints and negatives of the African-American community in Jacksonville. The library is also acquiring photographs of prominent black Atlantans and their family collections.

The Atlanta History Center is the largest repository in the Atlanta area of photographic materials. The collection of African-American history includes photographs from the Herndon family. Alonzo F. Herndon became a national figure as founder of the Atlanta Life Insurance Company. The collection also contains unidentified portraits of laborers and their families.

The National African American Museum and Cultural Center in Wilberforce, Ohio; the Chicago Historical Society; the Wadsworth Athenaeum's Simpson African-American Collection in Hartford, Conn.; and the Oakland Public Library each have well-rounded study collections ranging from the daguerreotype era to the present. The National Civil Rights Museum in Memphis, Tenn., offers a collection of photographs from the Memphis community, and collects a breadth of photographic material relating to the modern civil rights era. The Museum of African American Life and Culture in Dallas, Tex., was founded in 1974 as part of Bishop

College Library and is now dedicated to the research, identification, selection, acquisition, presentation, and preservation of visual art forms and documents that relate to the life and culture of the African-American community. The Museum houses the *Sepia* magazine photographic archive of more than 50,000 images.

The largest private collection of photographic materials is the Bettmann Archives (now part of Corbis Images). It is noted for being among the world's most diverse image libraries. Located in New York City, it houses more than 16 million films and digital images. The Bettmann image library was founded in the 1930s, and its scope today ranges from portraits and the arts to photojournalism, historical events, and sports. Corbis, founded in 1989 by Bill Gates, acquired the world-renowned Bettmann Archive in 1995, offering researchers digital images and access to its extensive archive by electronic searches.

Many of the collections cited consist of daguerreotypes, ambrotypes, tintypes, and albumen prints on cabinet cards, mounted on *cartes de visite.* Later in the 19th century, collections expanded the range of the photographic medium through the preservation of glass negatives, lantern slides, stereographs, and postcards. Documentary and portrait photographs of black subjects, as well as photographs produced by photo-artists working in the 20th century, are being actively acquired.

INDIVIDUAL PHOTOGRAPHERS

Ball, J. P.
  Willis, Deborah, *J. P. Ball: Daguerrean and Studio Photographer* (1993).
Bey, Dawoud
  Bey, Dawoud, *Dawoud Bey: Portraits, 1975–1995* (1995).
DeCarava, Roy
  Alinder, James, *Roy DeCarava: Photographs* (1981).
  Dawson, Danny, *The Sound I Saw: Jazz Photographs of Roy DeCarava* (1983).
  DeCarava, Roy, and James Alinder, ed., *Roy DeCarava: Photographs* (1981).
  DeCarava, Roy, and Langston Hughes, *The Sweet Flypaper of Life* (1957).
  Galassi, Peter, *Roy DeCarava: A Retrospective* (1996).
Freeman, Roland
  Freeman, Roland, *Southern Roads, City Pavements: Photographs of Black Americans* (1981).
Friedlander, Lee
  Friedlander, Lee, *The Jazz People of New Orleans* (1992).
Higgins, Chester, Jr.
  Higgins, Chester, Jr., *Drums of Life* (1974).
  ——— *Feeling the Spirit* (1995).
Hinton, Milt
  Hinton, Milt, and David Berger, *Bass Line: The Stories and Photographs of Milt Hinton* (1988).
Imes, Birney
  Imes, Birney, *Juke Joint: Photographs* (1990).
Johnston, Frances Benjamin
  Johnston, Frances Benjamin, *The Hampton Album* (1966).
Kanaga, Consuelo
  Millstein, Barbara H., and Sarah M. Lowe, *Consuelo Kanaga: An American Photographer* (1992).
Lanker, Brian
  Lanker, Brian, *I Dream a World: Portraits of Black Women Who Changed America* (1989).
Levitt, Helen
  Levitt, Helen, *A Way of Seeing* (1965).

Lewis, Harvey James

The Photographs of Harvey James Lewis, 1878–1968: The Lewis Studio, McDonald, Pennsylvania (1981).

Light, Ken

Light, Ken, *Delta Time: Mississippi Photographs by Ken Light* (1995).

Lyon, Danny

Lyon, Danny, *Memories of the Southern Civil Rights Movement* (1992).

Mauskopf, Norman

Mauskopf, Norman, *A Time Not Here: The Mississippi Delta* (1996).

Miner, Leigh Richmond

Dabbs, Edith M., *Face of an Island: Leigh Richmond Miner's Photographs of Saint Helena Island* (1971).

Moore, Charles

Durham, Michael S., *Powerful Days: The Civil Rights Photography of Charles Moore* (1991).

Mosley, John W.

Blockson, Charles L., *The Journey of John W. Mosley* (1992).

Norberg, Marc

Norberg, Marc, *Black & White Blues* (1995).

Parks, Gordon

Parks, Gordon, *Born Black* (1971).

Polk, P. H.

Lomax, Pearl Cleage, *P. H. Polk: Photographer* (1980).

Roberts, Richard Samuel

Johnson, Thomas L., and Phillip C. Dunn, *A True Likeness: The Black South of Richard Samuel Roberts, 1920–1936* (1986).

Roma, Thomas

Roma, Thomas, *Come Sunday: Photographs by Thomas Roma* (1996).

Scurlock, Addison N.

The Historic Photographs of Addison N. Scurlock (1974).

Simpson, Lorna

Fusco, Coco, *Uncanny Dissonance: The Work of Lorna Simpson* (1991).

Willis, Deborah, *Lorna Simpson* (1993).

Siskind, Aaron

Siskind, Aaron, *Harlem Document: Photographs, 1932–1940* (1981).

Smith, Morgan and Marvin

Smith, Morgan, and Marvin Smith, *Harlem: The Vision of Morgan and Marvin Smith* (1998).

Ulmann, Doris

Featherstone, David, *Doris Ulmann: American Portraits* (1985).

Ulmann, Doris, *The Darkness and the Light: Photographs by Doris Ulmann* (1974).

VanDerZee, James

Billops, Camille, and Owen Dodson, *The Harlem Book of the Dead: Photographs by James Van Der Zee* (1978).

De Cock, Liliane, and Reginald McGhee, *James Van Der Zee* (1973).

Haskins, Jim, *James Van DerZee: The Picture-Takin' Man* (1979).

McGhee, Reginald, *The World of James Van DerZee* (1969).

Willis, Deborah, *VanDerZee: Photographer, 1886–1983* (1993).

Van Vechten, Carl

Byrd, Rudolph P., ed., *Generations in Black & White: Photographs by Carl Van Vechten from the James Weldon Johnson Memorial Collection* (1993).

Davis, Keith F., ed., *The Passionate Observer: Photographs by Carl Van Vechten* (1993).

Mauriber, Saul, comp., *Portraits: The Photographs of Carl Van Vechten* (1978).

Weems, Carrie Mae

Kirsch, Andrea, and Susan Fisher Sterling, *Carrie Mae Weems* (1993).

Welty, Eudora

Welty, Eudora, *Photographs* (1989).

GENERAL WORKS

Andrews, Bert, and Paul Carter Harrison, *In the Shadow of the Great White Way: Black Theatre in Photographs* (1989).

Balch Institute, *Philadelphia African Americans: Color, Class & Style, 1840–1940* (1988).

Baldwin, Frederick C., *"We Ain't What We Used to Be": Photographs by Frederick C. Baldwin* (1983).

Baraka, Amiri, and Bill Abernathy, *In Our Terribleness* (1970).

Battle, Thomas, and Marcia Bracey Battle, *For Women Only: An Exhibition of Local Black Women Photographers* (1983).

Bearden, Romare, and Harry Henderson, *A History of African-American Artists from 1792 to the Present* (1993).

Bogle, Donald, *Brown Sugar: Eighty Years of America's Black Female Superstars* (1980).

Bunch, Lonnie, *California Black Photographers: The Tradition Continues* (1983).

Campbell, Mary Schmidt, *Tradition and Conflict: Images of a Turbulent Decade, 1963–1973* (1985).

Coar, Valencia Hollins, *A Century of Black Photographers: 1840–1960* (1983).

Cole, Carolyn Koso, and Kathy Kobayashi, *Shades of L.A.: Pictures from Ethnic Family Albums* (1996).

Collins, Charles, and David Cohen, ed., *The African Americans* (1993).

Cottman, Michael, *The Million Man March* (1995).

Cottman, Michael, and Deborah Willis, *The Family of Black America* (1996).

Crawford, Joe, *The Black Photographer's Annual,* vols. 1–4 (1972–1980).

Darrah, William Culp, *Stereoviews: A History of Stereographs in America and Their Collections* (1977).

Davis, Thulani, *Malcolm: The Great Photographs* (1993).

Driskell, David, *Two Centuries of Black American Art* (1976).

Dugan, Ellen, ed., *Picturing the South: 1860 to the Present* (1996).

Featherstone, David, *Doris Ulmann: American Portraits* (1985).

Freeman, Roland, *Southern Roads/City Pavements: Photographs of Black Americans* (1981).

Freed, Leonard, *Black in White America* (1969).

Gernsheim, Helmut, and Allison Gernsheim, *A Concise History of Photography* (1965).

Golden, Thelma, ed., *Black Male: Representations of Masculinity in Contemporary American Art* (1994).

Grabowski, John J., and Olivia Martin, *Somebody Somewhere Wants Your Photograph* (1980).

Hansberry, Lorraine, *The Movement: Documentary of a Struggle for Equality* (1964).

Higgins, Chester, Jr., *Drums of Life* (1974).

——— *Feeling the Spirit* (1995).

Higgins, Chester, Jr., and Orde Coombs, *Some Time Ago: A Historical Portrait of Black Americans, 1850–1950* (1980).

Higgins, Chester, Jr., and Harold McDougall, *Black Women* (1970).

Hoobler, Dorothy, and Thomas Hoobler, *The African American Family Album* (1995).

Huches, Michael, *"Don't Grieve after Me": The Black Experience in Virginia, 1619–1986* (1986).

Hughes, Langston, and Milton Meltzer, *A Pictorial History of Black America* (1957).

Johnston, Frances Benjamin, *The Hampton Album* (1966).

Jones, Kellie, *Dawoud Bey* (1996).

Let This Be Your Home: The African American Migration to Philadelphia, 1900–1940 (1991).

Levitt, Helen, *A Way of Seeing* (1965, 1981).

Litwack, Leon F., and Hilton Als, *Without Sanctuary* (1999).

McQuaid, James, *An Index to American Photographic Collections* (1982).

Marc, Stephen, *The Black Trans-Atlantic Experience: Street Life and Culture in Ghana, Jamaica, England, and the United States* (1992).

Mayer, Robert A., *Blacks in America: A Photographic Record* (1986).

Merritt, Carole, *Homecoming: African-American Family History in Georgia* (1982).

Metropolitan Museum of Art, *The Waking Dream: Photography's First Century* (1993).

Miller, Fredric M., Morris J. Vogel, and Allen F. Davis, *Philadelphia Stories: A Photographic History, 1920–1960* (1988).

Moore, Charles, *Powerful Days: The Civil Rights Photography of Charles Moore* (1991).

Moore, Joe Louis, *The Legacy of the Panthers: A Photographic Exhibition* (1995).

Moutoussamy-Ashe, Jeanne, *Daufuskie Island: A Photographic Essay* (1982).

———— *Viewfinders: Black Women Photographers* (1986).

Natanson, Nicholas, *The Black Image in the New Deal: The Politics of FSA Photography* (1992).

O'Neal, Hank, *A Vision Shared: A Classic Portrait of America and Its People* (1976).

Parker, Chad, and Francis Paudras, *To Bird with Love* (1980).

Parks, Gordon, *Born Black* (1971).

———— *A Choice of Weapons* (1966).

Powell, Richard J., et al., *Rhapsodies in Black: Art of the Harlem Renaissance* (1997).

Reagon, Bernice Johnson, and Worth Long, *We'll Never Turn Back* (1980).

Reynolds, Gary A., and Beryl J. Wright, *Against the Odds: African-American Artists and the Harmon Foundation* (1990).

Robinson, Jontyle Theresa, *Bearing Witness: Contemporary Works by African American Women Artists* (1996).

Rosenblum, Naomi, *A World History of Photography* (1989).

Rudisill, Richard, *Mirror Image: The Influence of the Daguerreotype in American Society* (1971).

Schoener, Allon, *Harlem on My Mind: Cultural Capital of Black America: 1900–1968* (1968).

Stewart, Charles, and Paul Carter Harrison, *Jazz Files* (1985).

Stryker, Roy Emerson, and Nancy Wood, *In This Proud Land: America, 1935–1943, As Seen in the FSA Photographs* (1973).

Sullivan, George, *Black Artists in Photography, 1840–1940* (1996).

Walker, Rosalyn, *A Resource Guide to the Visual Arts of Afro-Americans* (1971).

Willis, Deborah, *Picturing Us: African American Identity in Photography* (1994).

———— *Reflections in Black: A History of Black Photographers, 1840 to the Present* (2000).

Willis, Deborah, and Howard Dodson, *Black Photographers Bear Witness: 100 Years of Social Protest* (1989).

Willis, Deborah, and Jane Lusaka, *Visual Journal: Harlem and D.C. in the Thirties and Forties* (1996).

Willis-Thomas, Deborah, *Black Photographers, 1840–1940: A Bio-Bibliography* (1985).

———— *An Illustrated Bio-Bibliography of Black Photographers: 1940–1988* (1989).

Wright, Richard, and Edwin Rosskam, *12 Million Black Voices: A Folk History of the Negro in the United States* (1941).

12   *Film and Television*

Thomas Cripps

The study of African-Americans as both creators and subjects of motion pictures has made rapid strides in recent years. Books and articles that once seemed seminal or definitive are now regarded as almost quaint in their naïveté. Thus, I have framed this essay as a historiography, a chronicle of a maturing sophistication. What has made this development possible is the rediscovery of a large number of movies, the primary sources of film history, and their increasing availability as formerly inaccessible archives throw open their doors to an ever larger public. The opening of this visual record and its documentation constitute nothing less than a revolution in the writing of the history of American visual culture and the role of African-Americans in it.

ACCESSING FILMS

Published inventories of films or filmographies are of uneven quality. Many of these books were generated as marketing tools for vendors who come and go; their addresses frequently change and therefore will not be listed here. Sometimes films are also rendered elusive by the practice of marketing them as videocassettes rather than in the costlier celluloid format. As a result, films of historical importance but limited market value often have slipped from canonical memory.

The best filmographies are those least market driven—that is, those published by libraries and universities rather than commercial firms. The best general work remains Kenneth W. Munden, ed., *The American Film Institute Catalog of Motion Pictures Produced in the United States* (1971–). Its value for scholars of African-American life is that it is indexed by topic and each title is accompanied by a fairly faithful synopsis.

The best black-oriented work is still Phyllis Rauch Klotman, ed., *Frame by Frame: A Black Filmography* (1979), followed by *Frame by Frame II: A Filmography of the African American Image, 1978–1994* (1997), edited by Klotman and Gloria J. Gibson, and providing substantial information on more recent films. Other works include Marshall Hyatt, ed., *The Afro-American Cinematic Experience: An Annotated Bibliography and Filmography* (1983), a less ambitious collection that focuses only on "major films." Harry Alleyn Johnson, ed., *Multimedia Materials for Afro-American Studies: A Curriculum Orientation and Annotated Bibliography of Resources* (1971), remains useful despite its age and pedagogical tone. Library catalogs are useful because of their documentary focus. Two good, if brief, sources are

Nancy C. Quade, ed., *The Black Man in Films: African Heritage and American History* (1977), and Cecily Garver and David Raizman, ed., *Race Relations: A Feature and Documentary Filmography* (1984). Still useful despite its attention to only the film format is James L. Limbacher, ed., *Feature Films on 8 mm and 16 mm* (7th ed., 1985). Filmographies may be augmented by culling film titles and their sources from the endnotes of such scholarly monographs as Thomas Cripps, *Slow Fade to Black: The Negro in American Film, 1900–1942* (1977). An ongoing labor of love that exists in several forms—at once an anthology, a filmography, a monograph, and a catalog—is Gerald O'Grady's sometimes self-published *The Films of the Civil Rights [Movement]* (ca. 1989), a definitive list of a documentary genre. The latest and perhaps the most thorough of the filmographies is Alan Gevinson, ed., *Within Our Gates: Ethnicity in American Feature Films, 1911–1960* (1997). Only its self-imposed limits to feature films released before 1960 circumscribe its use.

The first step toward research is often closest to home. Rentals or purchases from chain stores such as Blockbuster or Sun Coast, each of which maintains an in-store catalog, are useful resources for researchers. In many markets, local specialty stores, such as Video American in Baltimore, Md., offer a stock of historical, often specifically black movies. Mail order clubs come and go, among them currently Fubutu in Stone Mountain, Ga., which bills itself as "The Premiere Black Video Club" and offers a catalog, similar to *Proud to Be . . . A Black Video Collection* [sic] (1991) of Charlotte, N.C. Mail order dealers also offer catalogs. Facets Multimedia (Chicago), for example, has published an African-American list and a *100 Best Documentaries* list that includes Lionel Rogosin's *Come Back Africa*, Bert Stern's *Jazz on a Summer's Day*, and Helen Levitt and Janice Loeb's *The Quiet One*. See also *The Library of African Cinema*, offered by California Newsreel of San Francisco, and the Black Filmmakers' Foundation *Catalogue*, which features its members' work. Firms with different agendas handle black material under other rubrics. See, for example, the catalog of Third World Newsreel, *In Color: 60 Years of Minority Women in Film . . . 1921–1981;* the catalog of Viewfinders, Inc., *Uncommon Video*, which includes blacks under "Other Music"; and the Documentary Resources and Filmmakers Library, which lists blacks under "Africa" and "Multiculturalism."

Catalogs of posters, of either exhibits or sales offerings, provide another access to moving-image data. Three varied examples of the genre include the Schomburg Center's *Black Images in Film* (1984), with an essay by Donald Bogle and an interview with the collector Ernie Smith; the William Grant Still Community Center (Los Angeles), *A History of Blacks in Film* (1981); and John Kish and Edward Mapp, *A Separate Cinema: Fifty Years of Black Cast Films* (1992 et seq.); the last two issues are exquisitely colored.

Researchers should also know of the data banks that have come online. The old National Information Center for Educational Media index (NICEM) has been subsumed by *A-V On Line* on the *Dialog* net, where a title search will locate many fugitive audiovisual documents, mostly in university libraries. These Internet resources are increasingly indexed in periodicals such as *PCNovice Guide to the Web: How to Find Anything on the Web* and *Harvey Hahn's Internet and Web Yellow Pages* (15th ed., 1998).

Websites, while offering few specifically "black" databases, can be helpful through using aptly chosen keywords or titles to instigate searches. Among these Websites, usually generated by libraries or universities, are the Division of Motion Pictures, Broadcasting and Recorded Sound of the Library of Congress; *Cinema-Space,* by the Film Studies Program of the University of California, Berkeley; the *CineMedia Directory* of Griffith University, Brisbane, Australia; and *Screensite* of the College of Communications of the University of Alabama. Other sites are more purely products of the Internet itself. Many search engines, such as Yahoo, Lycos, Excite, Alta Vista, and Magellan, provide hyperlinks to Websites that address a scholar's queries. Other creations inspired by the Internet are Stewart M. Clamen's *Movie Information Collection* and *The Internet Movie DataBase (IMDb).*

Pointedly "black" Websites must begin with that of the Black Film Center/Archive at Indiana University. It not only informs with respect to its own holdings but also provides links to other sources. A similar site is the Media Resources Center of Moffitt Library at the University of California, Berkeley, a project of the African-American Studies Program. Some more personal Websites come and go. Among the more persistently surviving of these less institutional sites are Julie Dash's *Geechee Girls Multimedia,* Ashley Marcelline's *Black Film & Video Guide,* the *Black Cultural Studies Website* (sponsored by a community of scholars), and commercial sites such as *California Newsreel* and *Best Video.*

Finally, several print reference works have been transferred to CD-ROM databases. *Bowker's Complete Video Directory* (1995), for example, has become *Variety's Video Directory Plus;* NICEM's printed version, easily superseded by Bowker, has become *The Film & Video Finder;* and a popular reference, *The Video Source Book* (17th ed., 1996), has reappeared as *Videohound Multimedia,* complete with graphics, movie star biographies, and other data.

FILM ARCHIVES

The next level of inquiry entails a visit to the half-dozen American film archives. Although offering catalog access only on their premises, their staffs are unfailingly helpful in replying to written and telephoned queries. The George Eastman House Museum of Photography in Rochester, N.Y., a relatively small repository, houses not only a sampling of Hollywood portrayals of blacks, but also prints of Paul Robeson's first movie, Oscar Micheaux's *Body and Soul* (1924), and Robeson's Swiss-made avant-garde film *Borderline* (1930). The holdings range from Edison's topical reportage, *A West Indian Woman Bathing a Baby* (ca. 1895), through such Hollywood movies as Jim Tully's chronicle of hobo life, *Beggars of Life* (1928), with its black nomad played by Edgar "Blue" Washington.

Of equal stature is the Museum of Modern Art Film Study Center in New York City, with holdings that range over the history of the motion picture medium. Beginning with D. W. Griffith's early Biograph films as well as his racist epic *The Birth of a Nation* (1915), the collection includes Hollywood fare such as Samuel Goldwyn's *Jubilo* (1919), with its sentimental hobo's role (played by Will Rogers as an homage to black wit). It also holds Griffith's *One Exciting Night* (1922) and his *Abraham Lincoln* (1930); MGM's African yarn *West of Zanzibar* (1929); and Preston Sturges's *Sullivan's Travels* (1941), with its neatly rendered black church sequence. Particularly strong in Warner Brothers, United Artists, and RKO films, the Wisconsin Center for Theatre Research at the Wisconsin Historical Society helps scholars to understand Warner's social-problem films of the 1930s with their socially conscious black bit parts, along with *Casablanca* (1942) and other films of World War II that hint of changing racial ideology. As for the Division of Motion Pictures, Broadcasting, and Recorded Sound in the Library of Congress, no brief citation could do justice to its vast and increasing holdings, save to say that it spans the entire history of moviemaking, beginning with its prehistory in the 1890s. Growing at a great pace is the Film and Television Archive of UCLA, which is particularly strong in Hollywood products, evidence of its close relationship with the movie industry.

In addition to these major archives, several smaller repositories offer possibilities to shrewd researchers. Major universities have increasingly developed film study centers mainly for the use of their students (one of the best being the Harvard Film Archive), but because they are meant for the use of their constituencies, access is limited. Many television stations hold stocks of worn 16-millimeter relics of the days when Hollywood sold off its films to TV. Thus, of equal interest to university archives but as restrictive of access are such stations as KDKA-TV (Pittsburgh), flagships of small groups of local stations, in this case Westinghouse Group W. There are also regional archives, not all of which survive; for example, the Southwestern Film and Television Archive in Southern Methodist University in Dallas has closed. But the city of Kansas City, hoping to promote itself as a historic center of jazz, has bought the huge John H. Baker collection of jazz on film as the core of its hoped-for jazz museum. Two specifically African-American centers are the Schomburg Center for the Study of Black Culture in New York, which has embarked on an ambitious program of acquisitions including the Ernie Smith collection of jazz on film, and the Black Film Center/Archive at Indiana University, which has focused on acquiring artifacts of the "race movie" industry such as the films of the Norman Studio.

Many of these same repositories contain rich veins of the ephemera of moviemaking—scripts, production records, clippings, reviews, and fan mail—preserved both as primary sources of motion picture history and as a contribution to African-American history. The Eastman House, for example, holds a fine collection of reviews drawn from the earliest (and scarcest) movie trade paper, while the Museum of Modern Art holds a similar "living" file of contemporary reviews in both popular and trade paper serials. The Library of Congress is an excellent resource. Its collections are augmented by unique papers such as the records of the George Kleine importing firm, the staff reports of wartime movies kept by the Office of War Information (OWI), and material filed in compliance with copyright law. To take only one instance of the importance of such sources for black film history, the OWI routinely recorded liberalized racial portrayals in its evaluations of wartime theatrical movies, both for their value as domestic propaganda and as suitable fare for formerly enemy-occupied countries.

On the Pacific Coast are relatively younger archives, each with its particular emphasis. The Pacific Film Archive at the University of California, Berkeley, leans toward avant-garde, radical, and alternative film companies, many of them regional in focus. The two archives with the closest links to the Hollywood movie industry, those at the University of California at Los Angeles and the University of Southern California, owe much to the generosity of both the corporations and the persons who have formed Hollywood. The collections reflect this in the prolific holdings of local trade paper clippings from *Daily Variety,* the *Hollywood Reporter,* and the local daily press. In addition, the Margaret Herrick Library of the Academy of Motion Picture Arts and Sciences draws frequent contributions of serial ephemera from the collections of former moviemakers and actors. Predictably, there are few African-Americans in their ranks, but there are occasional "finds" such as the campaign of the gossip columnist Hedda Hopper on behalf of a posthumous special Oscar for James Baskette, whose performance as Uncle Remus in *The Song of the South* had profoundly affected her. Proximity to the Hollywood industry has also led to a much greater emphasis on acquiring copies of scripts; in the cases of the Cinema and Television Library and Archives of USC and the Film and Television Archive and Theatre Library of UCLA they now total in the thousands.

MANUSCRIPTS AND RECORDS

Written sources are found in all these widely scattered libraries. One of the earliest records of black concern with moviemaking is the Emmett J. Scott Papers in the Soper Library of Morgan State University in Baltimore, a trail of documents that begins in the Library of Congress with the papers of Booker T. Washington, whom Scott served as secretary. Together with the Julius Rosenwald Papers in the Regenstein Library of the University of Chicago, they reveal much about the production of *The Birth of a Race* (1918), a black-produced attempt to rebut the slanders of D. W. Griffith's *The Birth of a Nation* (1915). Parallel to this project, the National Association for the Advancement of Colored People (NAACP) conducted a nationwide campaign to suppress or censor Griffith's movie. Elements of both endeavors, *The Birth of a Race* and the drive to quash *The Birth of a Nation,* are revealed in the NAACP records in the Library of Congress, and to a lesser extent in the W. E. B. Du Bois Papers at the University of Massachusetts at Amherst. Griffith's own papers in the Museum of Modern Art are also informative, not only for *The Birth of a Nation,* but for his earlier work at the Biograph studio.

The largest body of personal papers related to moviemaking by blacks is the George P. Johnson Collection in the Arts Library Special Collections of the UCLA Research Library. Johnson and his brother, Noble, an actor at Universal, saved not only the records of their own firm, the Lincoln Motion Picture Company, but also several file drawers of the ephemera of other "race movie" firms such as Douglass, Sidney Dones, Gate City, Norman, and the longest-lived of them all, Oscar Micheaux, as well as clippings from the black and white press. The papers of Micheaux's occasional star, Lorenzo Tucker, are in the Schomburg Center. And the paper record of yet another "race movie" company, the Norman Studio of Florida, are in the Black Film Center/Archive at Indiana University.

From the late 1920s through the 1940s—the classical Hollywood era—the bulk of paper documents shifts to the corporate records of the studios themselves.

Thousands of feet of these records have been given to university archives by the studios, eager either to claim their places in history or to write off their contributions against their federal taxes. Free access to this material has been impeded by recent court decisions tightening the doctrine of "fair use" as it applies to quoting from unpublished manuscripts.

Of all the studio archives, the most imposing in both bulk and relevance are the corporate records of 20th Century Fox and RKO at UCLA; the Warner Brothers Archives at USC and the Wisconsin State Historical Library; and United Artists records, also in Wisconsin. Filed according to various requirements of management, the most useful are the actual production records of individual films. But finding aids lead the researcher through every aspect of corporate life from script to screen. The researcher need only check titles to find information. For example, in the 20th Century Fox records under *Pinky* appear all of the many drafts of the script through which a conservative novel, Cid Ricketts Sumner's *Quality,* became a liberal "message movie" of 1949. Accompanying the scripts are the interoffice memoranda of Darryl F. Zanuck and his writers. Similarly, in the Warner Brothers archive, a researcher can follow the casting decisions that eventually placed Sam the piano player in *Casablanca* (1942) or the debates that resulted in a fully rounded black character rather than a stereotype in Howard Koch's script for John Huston's movie made from Ellen Glasgow's Pulitzer Prize–winning novel, *In This Our Life* (1941).

Other corporate records are disappointing. Those of Paramount in the Herrick Library of the Academy of Motion Picture Arts and Sciences seem small by comparison, while those of the Metro-Goldwyn-Mayer Legal Department have been removed to Atlanta by their new owner, Turner Entertainment, where they now seem indefinitely warehoused. Access to the records at the Walt Disney Archive in Burbank is slowed by the archive's request to know in advance the research's approach and to read the results of the research before publication. And quoting from the documents is made all but impossible. Yet despite the difficulties of accessibility while working there, the archive is invaluable for learning the circumstances of the production of many movies.

While not, strictly speaking, a corporate archive, the files of the Production Code Administration—the so-called Breen Office—of the Motion Picture Association of America, housed in the Herrick Library of the Academy, are a treasure for the data they provide on Hollywood's racial practices. Organized by film title, these PCA records provide a running historical account of the various ways of handling such politically charged issues as miscegenation, equality of the races, and challenges to Southern racial etiquette. Along with the PCA files, a thorough scholar will wish to consult several state and city censors for their own local customs in dealing with racial material. The archives of the states of New York, Pennsylvania, Maryland, and Virginia, as well as the city of Chicago, possess records of local censors.

Collections of personal papers are smaller and more scattered, but rewarding to the scholar able to reach them. Sometimes they can be researched by telephone, mail, or fax, but the necessity of using locally generated finding aids generally obliges the serious scholar to visit libraries in person.

Several useful collections range from the onset of the sound film era to World War II. A small group of letters and clippings in the Norman Holmes Pearson Collection in the Beinecke Library at Yale University is essential for the study of Paul Robeson's part in the Swiss-made film *Borderline* (1930). A larger collection of Robeson's papers is in the Moorland-Spingarn Research Center at Howard University. In the Beinecke Library's James Weldon Johnson Collection are papers of Walter White of the NAACP, reflecting his lifelong interest in Hollywood; Langston Hughes, revealing his work on the ill-fated Soviet film *Black and White,* his screenwriting for Sol Lesser's *Way Down South* (1939), and several film ideas that were never produced; and Johnson's own peripheral interest in movies.

The papers of other figures of the 1930s include small holdings of Leigh Whipper and Hattie McDaniel in the Moorland-Spingarn Research Center. Some of McDaniel's papers can also be found in the possession of Ruby Berkeley Goodwin, of North Hollywood. The papers of Claude A. Barnett, the black journalist who most aggressively tried to change Hollywood attitudes toward African-American performance in movies, are in the Chicago Historical Society. They are particularly important for his efforts to energize black reporting on Hollywood by recruiting Fay Jackson as correspondent, and for his work during World War II and afterward on behalf of improved portrayals of blacks in government propaganda films. The papers of Fredi Washington, who enjoyed a brief spate of good roles in the 1930s, are in the Amistad Center at Tulane University.

The paper record of the making of the 1930s capstone of Hollywood achievement, *Gone with the Wind,* is scattered. Its entry in the PCA files seems lost. The record of its progress from the best-selling book of 1936 to the Oscar winner of 1939 lies in several manuscript collections, among them the David O. Selznick Papers in the Humanities Research Center of the University of Texas; the papers of Selznick's first of several screenwriters, Sidney Howard, at the Bancroft Library, University of California, Berkeley; the papers of Margaret Mitchell and her Hollywood liaison, Susan Myrick of the *Macon Telegraph,* both in the Hargrett Library of the University of Georgia in Athens; and the diary of Victor Shapiro, at UCLA.

The onset of World War II brought a new dimension to the movie portrayal of African-Americans. A federal agency, the Office of War Information, was formed to serve as a sort of PCA for propaganda matters. In addition to consulting the OWI records in the National Archives in Suitland, Md., the scholar will wish to examine several collections of personal papers for data on the making and civilian distribution of such propaganda films as *The Negro Soldier* (1944) and *Teamwork* (1945). See, for example, the papers of Philleo Nash in the Harry S. Truman Library in Independence, Mo.; the papers of General Lyman Munson in the American Heritage Center of the University of Wyo.; the papers of Lowell Mellett in the Franklin D. Roosevelt Library in Hyde Park, N.Y.; the Nelson Poynter Papers in the Poynter Memorial Library of the University of South Florida in St. Petersburg; and the papers of Judge William Hastie in the National Archives in Washington, D.C.

The Wisconsin Center for Film and Theatre Research holds several useful collections that reflect the impact of World War II on American racial arrangements. Walter Wanger's collection is pertinent because of the paper record of his movie, *Sundown* (1941), which, in the course of the struggle for Africa between the British

8th Army and the Afrika Korps, grew from a mere *Saturday Evening Post* African "yarn" into the more racially liberal final cut of the film, in which a character asserts that "the England that's going to win this war is going to do away with a lot of that [racist] nonsense." Also of interest is Albert Maltz's script for the Oscar-winning short *The House I Live In,* which he wrote as an essay on "race." Dore Schary, the producer of *Bataan* (1943), *Crossfire* (1947), and *The Boy with the Green Hair* (1948), all of which carry a message about racism, is represented with a large holding. Abraham Polonsky, writer of the racial allegory *Body and Soul* (1947) and *Odds against Tomorrow* (1959), which he wrote while blacklisted, is represented by papers, script pages, and a diary. Edward Dmytryk, director of *Crossfire,* also has papers in the Center. David Susskind, who produced the integrationist *A Man Is Ten Feet Tall* for television and, with Sidney Poitier in the lead, brought it to the movie screen as *Edge of the City,* also has a large collection. Last, in a much later and grittier style, Shirley Clarke, maker of *The Cool World* (1963) and *The Connection* (1961), is also represented in the papers at the Wisconsin Center for Film and Theatre Research.

The Mugar Library at Boston University holds several collections that touch upon specific events in the history of blacks in the movies of the 1940s and after. The papers of Robert Hardy Andrews, together with the Schary papers (in the Wisconsin Center), reveal the complex provenance of the racially integrated propaganda movie *Bataan* (1943). The persistent evolution of postwar racial material may be seen in the papers of Michael Blankfort, screenwriter of *Lydia Bailey* (1952), a romance of the Haitian revolution, and *Broken Arrow* (1950), in which Indians act as surrogates for all racial minorities. Also of value are the papers of Sal Lobino (working name Evan Hunter), author of *Blackboard Jungle,* from which yet another Poitier movie was derived. The entire roster of contributors to the Twentieth Century Collection, as it is called, warrants scanning for continually added collections as well as augmentations of already deposited papers. For example, at present the papers of the novelist John Oliver Killens shed no light on *Odds against Tomorrow,* for which he is the credited writer.

Other repositories hold papers of a small number of moviemakers. The papers of King Vidor, director of *Hallelujah!,* and those of Stanley Kramer, producer of *Home of the Brave* and *The Defiant Ones,* are at UCLA. Hedda Hopper's campaign for a posthumous Oscar for James Baskette's Uncle Remus in *Song of the South* is reflected in her papers in the Herrick Library, while the production records of the Disney film are in the Walt Disney Archive in Burbank. David O. Selznick's papers at the Humanities Research Center at the University of Texas shed light on the ambivalent racial politics of *Since You Went Away* (1944) and *Duel in the Sun* (1946). Some of the pressure against MGM to change the racial angle of *Tennessee Johnson* (1942) may be found in the papers of its writer, John L. Balderston, in the Library of Congress and in the Performing Arts Branch of the New York Public Library. Clarence Brown's papers at the University of Tennessee tell us much about the making and reception of the film of William Faulkner's *Intruder in the Dust* (1949). The American Heritage Center of the University of Wyoming holds the papers of Louis DeRochemont, producer of the "message movie" *Lost Boundaries* (1949) and other racial projects, as well as the papers of General Lyman Munson, an advocate of the release of *The Negro Soldier* in 1944.

In the Special Collections of the Morris Library of Southern Illinois University in Carbondale are the papers of John Howard Lawson, screenwriter of *Sahara* (1943) and *Cry, the Beloved Country* (1951), written while Lawson was blacklisted. In the same library, Katherine Dunham's papers reveal her choreographic work in several films in the war years and the ensuing decade. A large body of Carl Lerner's papers in the Museum of Modern Art, including audience-response preview cards, are informative about the making and reception of *Black Like Me* (1964), a movie in the liberal spirit of wartime propaganda (if not actual policy). The Moorland-Spingarn Research Center at Howard University contains the large Paul Robeson Archive, which records some of his filmmaking career both in Europe and America. In addition, there are the previously cited small holdings, mainly of ephemera, under the names of Hattie McDaniel and Leigh Whipper.

The Arthur Schomburg Center for Research in Black Culture in New York City has sought to augment its manuscript holdings in recent years. Of particular value are several volumes of clippings concerning moviemaking and reception as well as a vertical file of reviews. There is also a growing inventory of motion picture stills. In addition to the Ernie Smith Collection, which includes both paper ephemera and films, a few smaller manuscript collections are also held. Among them are the notebooks of the comedian Bert Williams, a selection of Paul Robeson's papers, and the papers of Leigh Whipper.

Here it should be said that in most of the foregoing repositories there are deposits of scripts, hundreds of them in the case of the California centers such as the Charles Feldman and Louis B. Mayer Libraries of the American Film Institute. And the Thalberg Collection in the William B. Meredith Library of Dartmouth College holds several scripts that are informatively marked with censors' marginalia. Mail-order dealers in nostalgia and memorabilia also sell scripts, advertising mainly in their own trade papers, most extensively in *Big Reel*.

REFERENCE WORKS

Although monographs—whether books or articles—have been few until recently, a boom in writing about black movies obliges the reader to consult guides to such literature. The two best of these are Allen L. Woll and Randall M. Miller, ed., *Ethnic and Racial Images in American Film and Television: Historical Essays* (1987), and Marshall Hyatt, ed., *The Afro-American Cinematic Experience: An Annotated Bibliography and Filmography* (1983). More selective and less useful are J. William Snorgrass and Gloria T. Woody, ed., *Blacks and the Media: A Selected, Annotated Bibliography* (1985); John Gray, ed., *Blacks in Film and Television: A Pan-African Bibliography of Films, Filmmakers, and Performers* (1990); and Mary Mace Spradling, ed., *In Black and White: Afro-Americans in Print* (3rd ed., 1985), a useful text that takes in many fields of African-American activity.

Among the most useful indexes of motion picture materials apart from the general guides to periodical literature are volumes that include both original reviews and later critical and historical writing. For an index to reviews, see Patricia King Hansen and Stephen L. Hansen, ed., *Film Review Index* (2 vols., 1986). For both historical and current reviews, see Jay Robert Nash and Stanley Ralph Ross, ed., *The Motion Picture Guide 1927–1983* (1985, et seq.); the *New York Times Motion*

Picture Reviews (1970); *Variety Motion Picture Reviews* (1983); Max Joseph Alvarez, ed., *Index to Motion Pictures Reviewed by Variety, 1907–1980* (1982); and *Magill's Cinema Annual* (1980, et seq.).

The several indexes to serial literature often duplicate each other, but each has an emphasis that compels scanning them all. The oldest is the Work Progress Administration's *Film Index* (1941) and its sequel, Richard Dyer MacCann and Ted Perry, ed., *The New Film Index: 1930–1970* (1975). Linda Batty, ed., *Retrospective Index to Film Periodicals, 1930–1971* (1971), covers similar ground but with a tighter focus. John C. Gerlach and Lana Gerlach, ed., *The Critical Index: A Bibliography of Articles on Film in English, 1946–1973* (1974) casts a wider net. And two annual works, Vincent Aceto et al., ed., *Film Literature Index* (1973, et seq.), and Karen Jones, ed., *The International Index to Film Periodicals* (1974, et seq.) cover the current literature.

SURVEYS

As for the literature itself, the three earliest scholarly surveys are now more than two decades old and yet still serve as primers. They are Daniel J. Leab, *From Sambo to Superspade: The Black Experience in Motion Pictures* (1975); Donald Bogle, *Toms, Coons, Mulattoes, Mammies & Bucks: An Interpretive History of Blacks in American Films* (2nd ed., 1993); and Thomas Cripps, *Slow Fade to Black: The Negro in American Film, 1900–1942* (1977), the latter followed by an extension, *Making Movies Black: The Hollywood Message Movie from World War II to the Civil Rights Era* (1993). In addition to these books, many scholars are indebted to two venerable works that defined the field for many years: the British journalist Peter Noble's *The Negro in Film* (1948); and a well-researched Communist Party tract by V. J. Jerome, *The Negro in Hollywood* (1950). The British magazine *Sight and Sound* (March 1948) ran Noble's filmography, *The Cinema and the Negro, 1905–1948*, as a "special supplement."

For a time, a narrative mode dominated the literature, whether scholarly, popular, or polemical, as though in search of "progress" in the treatment of black subjects in the movies. For three decades after World War II the formula was set. See, for example, Carlton Moss, "The Negro in American Films," *Freedomways* (Spring 1963): 134–42, and Thomas Cripps, "The Death of Rastus: The Negro in American Films since 1945," *Phylon* 28 (Fall 1967): 267–75, for depictions of slim progress. Gary Null, *Black Hollywood: The Negro in American Film* (1975), adopted the form to the photographic essay. James P. Murray, Jr., *To Find an Image: Black Film from Uncle Tom's Cabin to Super Fly* (1973), amended the formula to sound an early plea for an eventually indigenous black cinema. Albert Johnson, the first postwar academic chronicler of black movies, focused on new releases in "Beige, Brown, or Black," *Film Quarterly* 13 (Fall 1959): 38–43, and his "The Negro in American Films: Some Recent Works," *Film Quarterly* 18 (Summer 1965): 14–30. Abroad, an expatriate, Jim Pines, weighed in with a polemic, *Blacks in Film: A Survey of Racial Themes and Images in American Film* (1975).

From the onset of the era of survey historians in the 1970s, Leab, Bogle, and Cripps utilized the handiest means of reaching for a new and as yet ill-defined readership by creating an anthology of classic but fugitive pieces mixed with schol-arly essays drawn from works in progress. Uneven in quality, these pieces nonethe-less introduced the work of specialists to general readers. Among the first were Lindsay Patterson, ed., *Black Films and Film-makers: A Comprehensive Anthology from Stereotype to Superhero* (1975); Richard A. Maynard, ed., *Myth and Reality: Africa on Film* (1974) and *Black Man on Film: Racial Stereotyping* (1974); and Adelaide M. Cromwell, ed., *Black Images in Films: Stereotyping and Self-Perception As Viewed by Black Actresses* (1974), the proceedings of a Boston University con-ference.

More recently, anthologies have grown more reflective, theoretical, and ideolog-ical. See, for example, Manthia Diawara, ed., *Black American Cinema* (1993); Mbye B. Cham and Claire Andrade-Watkins, ed., *Blackframes: Critical Perspectives on Black Independent Cinema* (1988); Gladstone L. Yearwood, ed., *Black Cinema Aes-thetics: Issues in Independent Black Filmmaking* (1982), the proceedings of a con-ference at Ohio University; and Valerie Smith, ed., *Representing Blackness: Issues in Film and Video* (1997). Taken together, these works erect a scaffolding for an emerging black aesthetic that rests not on the Hollywood movie but on a romanti-cally pristine "black independent film." Of them all, Michael T. Martin, ed., *Cin-ema of the Black Diaspora: Diversity, Dependence, and Oppositionality* (1996), seeks a catholic position arising from both history and a multivariate black world cul-ture rather than merely adapting Hollywood style to fit black aesthetics.

Accompanying the spate of anthologies has come a cycle of special issues of journals, a nearly full list of which is in Diawara, *Black American Cinema* (p. 310). At their best, they span a range of topics—aesthetics, polemical journalism, inter-views, and, more rarely, history. They include "The Black Image in the Mass Me-dia," *Freedomways* (3rd quarter, 1974); a "dossier" on "Le Cinema Noir Americain" in *CinemAction* 46 (1988); and the wide-ranging, uneven, mainly theoretical "Black Cinema," *Wide Angle* 13:3–4 (Oct. 1991). While not precisely a "black" is-sue, *Film History* 6:3 (1994), on "exploitation film," devoted space to race and gen-der in 1930s "jungle movies" and to "the trope of blaxploitation" inspired by *Sweet Sweetback's Baad Asssss Song*. In one way or another, their contribution is in their insistence on a "rebirth of the aesthetic in cinema" (which is also the title of Clyde Taylor's essay in *Wide Angle* 13:3–4 [Oct. 1991]: 12–34).

CRITICISM

The most thoughtful African-American criticism of motion pictures has arisen out of a few defining moments of renewed black group consciousness, the most important eras being the Harlem Renaissance of the 1920s, the era of World War II with its shifting racial ideologies expressed in the "conscience liberalism" of Amer-ican propaganda, and the age of the civil rights movement. From this historical perspective the serious reader will see the social context of the history of a popular art as "the cultural performance inside oppression," as Diawara so aptly describes it in his essay in *Wide Angle*.

Consult, for example, the August 1929 number of *Close Up*, devoted entirely to "Aframerican Cinema." Following on the rage for black culture in the Harlem Re-

naissance, *Close Up*, a short-lived, earnestly bohemian journal produced in Ter-
ritet, Switzerland, by the expatriates Kenneth Macpherson and Winifred Bryher as
the organ of their avant-garde studio, Pool Films, presciently sensed the rising tide
of racism in the world and challenged it by standing against the popular culture
stereotypes that fed it. *Close Up* amounted to a manifesto that in 1929 urged upon
blacks the simultaneous needs for direct protest against Hollywood, the forming
of a cadre of black filmmakers, and a formulation of a black aesthetic against
which to test movies. Geraldyn Dismond, for example, surveyed "The Negro Actor
in the American Movies" from *The Birth of a Nation* to *Hallelujah!*, while noting
the rise of makers of "race movies." Elmer Carter, editor of the Urban League's *Opportunity*, complained in his "Of Negro Motion Pictures" of the movies' succumb-
ing to "racial antagonism." Macpherson, in his own editorial, called for an autono-
mous black cinema because "authentic Negro films can be produced only by
Negroes," a stance affirmed in Harry Alan Potamkin's "The Aframerican Cinema,"
which demanded "a formulation of aesthetic principles" grounded in "primitive
African sculpture and dance." Even Walter White of the biracial NAACP wrote of
"anticipating" an "honest" black cinema in his "Letter."

Not only had *Close Up* asserted an early black politics of movie art, but it also
gave focus to an inchoate critical canon. In the years between the world wars, African-American commentary on movies appeared only erratically, mainly in the
columns of Billy Rowe, Pittsburgh *Courier;* D. Ireland Thomas, *Chicago Defender;*
Lester Walton, New York *Age;* Fay Jackson, Associated Negro Press; Ralph
Mathews, Baltimore *Afro-American;* and A. S. "Doc" Young, Leon Hardwick,
Charlotta Bass, Harry Levette, Ruby Berkeley Goodwin, and Lawrence LaMar in
the West Coast papers *California Eagle* and *Los Angeles Sentinel.* Apart from these
newspaper critics, black commentary on movies appeared only occasionally. See,
for example, "Moving Pictures of Tuskegee," *Tuskegee Student* (25 Jan. 1913): 2;
and NAACP, "Fighting a Vicious Film" (1915), a broadside against *The Birth of a
Nation.* Few scholar-critics joined in. Herman G. Weinberg (a legendary art house
manager and critic), "The Emperor Jones," *Close Up* (Dec. 1933): 351–52; the
Howard University scholars Alain Locke and Sterling Brown, "Folk Values in a
New Medium," in *Folk-Say: A Regional Miscellany* (1930), appraising Hollywood's
version of folk culture in *Uncle Tom's Cabin* and *Hallelujah!*; and Brown's "*Imitation of Life*: Once a Pancake," *Opportunity* 13 (March 1935): 87–88, are among
the few.

Both the pace and thrust of critical writing picked up during World War II,
partly because American propaganda promoted a sort of liberalism of conscience
and partly because black rhetoric took up a cry for a "Double V" over both foreign
fascism and domestic racism. The resulting integrationist ideology coupled with
the Allied victory over fascism gave African-Americans an access to federal power
that had been unavailable to them since Reconstruction. The ideology was
grounded in three principles: first, that indicators of race—skin color and such—
were mere biological trivia upon which no sensible public policy could be based;
second, that racism was only misinformation correctable through reeducation or
"social engineering," as it was called; and third, as the historian Kenneth M.
Stampp wrote in *The Peculiar Institution* (1956), "that innately Negroes *are*, after

all, only white men with black skins" (viii). With respect to movies, this three-pronged sensibility was shared, almost as a war prize, among the Hollywood leftist and Marxist survivors of the prewar popular front; black activists such as Walter White of the NAACP, whose agency made plans for a Hollywood bureau; and the liberal cell within OWI, some of whom hoped for a peacetime extension of their agency.

The resulting shift of racial liberalism toward the center of national attention (if not political action) was reflected in both wartime and postwar literature, as, for example, in a page-one *Variety* headline of March 25, 1942: "Better Breaks for Negroes in H'wood." The next year, *The Proceedings of the [Hollywood] Writers' Congress Held at UCLA in October 1943* (1944) contained no less than three essays on race: William Grant Still, "The Negro and His Music in Films," 277–79; Dalton Trumbo, "Minorities and the Screen," 495–501; and Walter White, "Address," on the urgency of using movies to raise black morale, 14–18. A year later, Lawrence D. Reddick, curator of the Schomburg Collection, formulated a prescriptive essay, "Educational Programs for the Improvement of Race Relations: Motion Pictures, the Press, and Libraries," in the *Journal of Negro Education* 13 (Summer 1944): 367–89.

By the war's end, such commentary kept alive the notion of the "Double V" by invoking the catchwords *tolerance, brotherhood,* and *teamwork* that had leavened both government and civil propaganda. At the same time, Marxist and overseas voices informed some of the writings of the times. As early as February 1940, David Platt began his sharply worded history of blacks in Hollywood in the *Daily Worker.* His thesis was vigorously taken up in postwar essays such as Victor Jeremy Jerome's *The Negro in Hollywood Films* (1950), Peter Noble's *The Negro in Films* (1948), and Leon Hardwick's "Negro Stereotypes on the Screen," *Hollywood Quarterly* 1 (Jan. 1946): 234–36.

The most astonishing carryover of wartime racial politics was in the personal, almost confessional, essays of white Hollywoodians in black serials. An informed reader might have expected to see the black composer William Grant Still ask "How Do We Stand in Hollywood?" in *Opportunity* (Spring 1945): 74–77; or Canada Lee's "Our Part in 'Body and Soul,'" *Opportunity* (Winter 1948): 21. But along with their essays came a flurry by white liberals. See, for example, John Garfield (who played opposite Lee in *Body and Soul*), "How Hollywood Can Better Race Relations," *Negro Digest* (Nov. 1947): 4–8; Marsha Hunt, "A Hollywood Actress Looks at the Negro," *Negro Digest* (Sept. 1947): 10–14; Samuel Goldwyn, "How I Became Interested in Social Justice," *Opportunity* (Summer 1948): 100–101; David O. Selznick, "Negro Lobby in Hollywood," *Negro Digest* (Aug. 1946): 27–28; Dore Schary, "Minorities in the Movies," *Negro Digest* (Feb. 1948): 23–24, the latter advocating boycotting of his own industry, a point taken up in "Needed: A Negro Legion of Decency," *Ebony* (Feb. 1947): 36–37, and in Charles R. Metzger, "Pressure Groups and the Motion Picture Industry," *Annals of the American Academy of Political and Social Science* 254 (Nov. 1947): 110–15, in an issue devoted entirely to postwar moviemaking and society.

With the onset of an age of self-consciously political "message movies" in 1949, the wartime "Double V" was pressed into service as a weapon in the Cold War.

Each movie seemed weighed not only on its merits but also on its effect upon the ideological conflict with the Soviet Union. Quality was also often measured in terms of the movies' impact on juvenile delinquency or other "social problems." See, for example, Richard Winnington, "Negro Films [Message Movies]," *Sight and Sound* (Jan. 1950): 27–30; Gerald Weales, "Pro-Negro Films in Atlanta," *Films in Review* (Nov. 1952): 455–62, finding their impact "nil"; and Ralph Ellison, "The Shadow and the Act [on *Intruder in the Dust*]," *Reporter* (6 Dec. 1949): 17–19.

Scholars resumed the empirical study of audience reception much in the manner of the 1930s "Payne Fund Studies" such as L. L. Thurstone, "The Influence of Motion Pictures on Children's Attitudes," *Journal of Social Psychology* 2 (Aug. 1931): 291–305. See, for example, a run of essays on a cycle of movies about anti-Semitism that anticipated the coming racial message movies: Eunice Cooper and Helen Dinerman, "Analysis of the Film 'Don't Be a Sucker': A Study in Communication," *Public Opinion Quarterly* 15 (Summer 1951): 243–64; Samuel H. Flowerman, "Mass Propaganda in the War against Bigotry," *Journal of Abnormal and Social Psychology* 42 (Oct. 1942): 429–39; Louis E. Raths and Frank N. Trager, "Public Opinion and *Crossfire*," *Journal of Educational Sociology* 21 (Feb. 1948): 345–68; I. C. Rosen, "The Effect of the Motion Picture 'Gentleman's Agreement' on Attitudes toward Jews," *Journal of Psychology* 26 (Oct. 1948): 525–36; and Martha Wolfenstein and Nathan Leites, "Two Social Scientists View 'No Way Out,' The Unconscious vs. the Message in an Anti-Bias Film," *Commentary* (Nov. 1950): 389–91.

Despite an erratic pace, the flow of literature on African-Americans in movies persisted, seemingly driven by the twin engines of black and liberal hopes for the spoils of the "Double V" and a national wish to be on the good side of the Cold War. Indeed, World War II came to be regarded as a seedbed of subsequent racial activism even as the Cold War came to be the arena in which the movement was acted out. The strongest argument for an ideological link between World War II and later racial politics is to be found in the work of Thomas Cripps. See, for example, "Winds of Change: *Gone with the Wind* and Racism as a National Issue," in Darden Ashbury Pyron, ed., *Recasting:* Gone with the Wind *in American Culture* (1983): 137–52; "Movies, Race, and World War II: *Tennessee Johnson* as an Anticipation of the Strategies of the Civil Rights Movement," *Prologue* 14:2 (Summer 1982): 49–67; "*Casablanca, Tennessee Johnson,* and *The Negro Soldier:* Hollywood Liberals and World War II," in K. R. M. Short, ed., *Feature Films As History* (1981): 138–56; "Racial Ambiguities in American Propaganda Movies," in Short, ed., *Film and Radio Propaganda in World War II* (1983): 125–45; and, with David Culbert, "*The Negro Soldier* (1944): Film Propaganda in Black and White," *American Quarterly* 31:5 (Winter 1979): 616–40.

Not all historians agreed in seeing World War II as a triumph of racial liberalism. For the most carefully asserted counterargument, see Clayton R. Koppes and Gregory D. Black, "Blacks, Loyalty, and Motion Picture Propaganda in World War II," *Journal of American History* 73 (1986): 383–406, and *Hollywood Goes to War: How Politics, Profits & Propaganda Shaped World War II Movies* (1987), chaps. 4 and 6. For other angles on the era and its racial ideology, see John D. Stevens, "The Black Reaction to *Gone with the Wind*," *Journal of Popular Film* 2 (Fall 1973):

366–71; Leonard J. Leff, "David O. Selznick: *Gone with the Wind:* 'The Negro Problem,'" *Georgia Review* 38 (1984): 146–64; Robert Morseberger, "Adrift in Steinbeck's *Lifeboat*," *Literature/Film Quarterly* 4 (Fall 1976): 325–38; Morseberger, "Slavery and *The Santa Fe Trail*, or John Brown on Hollywood's Sour Apple Tree," *American Studies* 18 (Fall 1971): 87–98; Bruce M. Tyler, *From Harlem to Hollywood: The Struggle for Racial and Cultural Democracy, 1920–1943* (1992), in which he sees black culture itself at stake in this era; and Virginia Warner, "*The Negro Soldier:* A Challenge to Hollywood," in Lewis Jacobs, ed., *The Documentary Tradition from Nanook of the North to Woodstock* (1971): 224–26.

From the heyday of the civil rights movement onward, critical response to the postwar era remained strong, driven by new levels of theory, ideology, racial politics, and measures of audience receptivity. See, for example, Vinicius De Moraes, "The Making of a Documentary: *The Quiet One* [1947]," *Hollywood Quarterly* 4 (Summer 1950): 375–84; Thomas Cripps, "*Native Son* in the Movies," *New Letters* 38 (Winter 1972): 49–63; and Michelle Wallace, "Race, Gender, and Psychoanalysis in Forties Film: *Lost Boundaries, Home of the Brave,* and *The Quiet One*," in Diawara, *Black American Cinema,* all of which carried the interest in black film onto a more complex plane. See also Regina K. Fadiman, *Faulkner's Intruder in the Dust: Novel into Film* (1978).

In the light of the civil rights movement, it was but a short step to reexamine the notion of "progress" in movies. Beginning with James Baldwin's "Life Straight in de Eye [on *Carmen Jones*]," *Commentary* (Jan. 1955): 74–77, and through the 1960s, critics sought a reckoning of change against what had gone before. See, for example, Robert Hunter, "Hollywood and the Negro," *Negro Digest* (May 1966): 37–41; and Martin S. Dworkin, "The New Negro on the Screen," *Progressive* (Oct. 1960): 39–41; (Nov. 1960): 33–36; (Dec. 1960): 34–36; (Jan. 1961): 36–38; (Feb. 1961): 38–41. Generally, Dworkin finds more "progress" than met "de eye" of Baldwin. William J. Sloan, "The Documentary Film and the Negro: The Evolution of the Integration Film," *Cinema Journal* 5 (1965): 66–69, makes a tentative link between "reality" film and the politics of black portrayal. Carlton Moss, "The Negro in American Film," *Freedomways* (Spring 1963): 134–42, following Noble's example, traces progress from the era of "primitive" film at the turn of the century, a path also taken by Anne K. and Hart M. Nelsen, "The Prejudicial Film: Progress and Stalemate, 1915–1967," *Phylon* 31 (Summer 1967): 142–47. Like Sloan, Thomas Cripps in "The Death of Rastus: Negroes in American Films since 1945," *Phylon* 28 (Fall 1967): 267–75, links postwar movies to the goals asserted by the "Double V" rhetoric of World War II.

Throughout the ensuing quarter-century, much critical comment was driven by a simmering rage at Hollywood's indifference to racial injustice. Writings about the most unambiguous icon of racism, D. W. Griffith's *The Birth of a Nation* (1915), helped define a new politics of criticism. No anthology seemed complete without a polemic aimed at this easy target; no other film thereafter was safe from similar scrutiny. Among many, see particularly Everett Carter, "Cultural History Written with Lightning: The Significance of *Birth of a Nation*," *American Quarterly* 12 (Fall 1960): 347–57; Thomas Cripps, "The Reaction of the Negro to the Motion Picture 'The Birth of a Nation,'" *Historian* 25 (May 1963): 344–62; Russell Merritt,

"Dixon, Griffith, and the Southern Legend," *Cinema Journal* 12 (Fall 1972): 26–45; Maxim Simcovich, "The Impact of Griffith's *The Birth of a Nation* on the Modern Ku Klux Klan," *Journal of Popular Film* 1 (Winter 1972): 45–55; and Russell Merritt, "D. W. Griffith's *The Birth of a Nation:* Going after Little Sister," in Peter Lehman, ed., *Close Viewings: An Anthology of New Film Criticism* (1990): 215–37. See also Nickie Fleener, "Answering Film with Film: The Hampton Epilogue, A Positive Alternative to the Negative Black Stereotypes Presented in *Birth of a Nation*," *Journal of Popular Film* 7 (1980): 400–25, an account of Griffith's attempt to placate black protest by means of a short film on Negro "progress" since Reconstruction. The distinguished historian of the South John Hope Franklin, in "*Birth of a Nation:* Propaganda as History," *Massachusetts Review* 20 (Autumn 1979): 417–34, rejects all analyses that appear to allow art and racism to coexist. A highly informative, often perceptive, heavily documented albeit querulous jeremiad is Seymour Stern, ed., "Griffith: I—*The Birth of a Nation*," *Film Culture* (Spring/ Summer 1965). And for an apologia by a backer of the movie, see Roy E. Aitken, *The Birth of a Nation Story* (1965).

The preceding list is meant to suggest not only that one political film could rivet the attention of scholars and critics but also that less self-consciously (or even unconsciously) political films received similar treatment. See, for example, the largely index-accessible social and political commentary on such films as *Gone with the Wind, Imitation of Life,* and *The Scar of Shame.*

BIOGRAPHY

Coincident with the growth of a canon of movie criticism, there emerged a cycle of biographies of movie stars and a parallel run of biographies and autobiographies of directors and producers and, in lesser volume, screenwriters. Far from scholarly, they were mainly sagas of "getting over," beating the system, winning the game on its own terms. Among them were Arnold Shaw, *Belafonte* (1960); Sammy Davis, Jr., with Burt and Jane Boyar, *Yes I Can: The Story of Sammy Davis, Jr.* (1965); Lena Horne and Richard Schickel, *Lena* (1965), one of several Horne books; Carolyn Ewers, *Sidney Poitier: The Long Journey* (1969); William Hoffman, *Sidney* (1971); Alvin H. Marill, *The Films of Sidney Poitier* (1978); and Ethel Waters with Charles Samuels, *His Eye on the Sparrow* (1951). The rare tragedies were recounted in Dorothy Dandridge and Earl Conrad, *Everything and Nothing: The Dorothy Dandridge Tragedy* (1970); Earl Mills, *Dorothy Dandridge* (1970); and Carlton Jackson, *Hattie: The Life of Hattie McDaniel* (1988).

Books about musical performers who made forays into moviemaking often include a chapter that takes up their struggles with the Hollywood system. See, for example, the many books by and about Paul Robeson, particularly Martin Bauml Duberman, *Paul Robeson* (1988); and Thomas Cripps, "Paul Robeson and Black Identity in American Movies," *Massachusetts Review* 11 (Summer 1970): 468–85. Other musical figures often appearing in movies about whom biographies were written include Duke Ellington, Louis Armstrong, Bessie Smith, Billie Holiday, and Nat "King" Cole.

More recently, biographical and autobiographical essays have grown more scholarly and more reflective. Early on, the poet Langston Hughes's *I Wonder as I Wander* (1956) included an uncommonly complex political chapter on *Black and White,* an aborted African-American political melodrama to be shot in Odessa at Stalin's behest. Much later, Sidney Poitier, in *This Life* (1980) and *The Measure of a Man* (2000), probed his own motives far more deeply than most show-business autobiographies. The rare scholarly treatments reached for similar seriousness of purpose. See, for example, Phyllis Rauch Klotman, "The Black Writer in Hollywood circa 1930: The Case of Wallace Thurman" and Houston A. Baker, Jr., "Spike Lee and the Commerce of Culture," both in Manthia Diawara, ed., *Black American Cinema;* and Donald Bogle, *Dorothy Dandridge: A Biography* (1997). For a life of a "race movie" actor, see Richard Grupenhoff, *The Black Valentino: The Career of Lorenzo Tucker* (1988), one of Oscar Micheaux's actors.

DOCUMENTARY FILMS

Only a few thoughtfully researched and written documentaries have taken up the subject of African-Americans in movies. Following from CBS-TV's *Black History: Lost, Stolen, or Strayed* (1968), with its damning narrative of the black experience in Hollywood focused on the comedian Stepin Fetchit, a few useful films and videos emerged. The low-budget *The Black Image in Film* (1970), though syndicated, is seldom seen. James Limbacher and Barbara Bryant's three-part *Minorities in Film* (1975), while somewhat more accessible, also suffers from poor production values and weak historical consulting. Until recently, *Black Shadows on a Silver Screen* (1976), in the "American Documents" series, stood alone in the complexity of its historical argument and its visual imagery, which show Hollywood movies and "race movies" in parallel courses. Then Marlon Riggs's *Ethnic Notions* (1986) extended the analysis into 19th-century American graphic art and advertising, which he linked to African-American cinema performance. The most recent of these productions, *Midnight Ramble* (1993), used Oscar Micheaux's life in "race movies" as a window onto the entire genre. Less useful is *That's Black Entertainment* (1989), which limited its visual documents to a single trove of recently rediscovered "race movies" in Tyler, Texas. In February 1998 the AMC cable channel ran its own compilation, *The Black Experience in Hollywood.*

BLAXPLOITATION MOVIES

Regrouping within black circles followed disillusionment at the death of Martin Luther King. This sentiment manifested itself in a spate of so-called blaxploitation movies in the 1970s that targeted young, black, urban audiences. The seemingly gratuitous violence of the genre inspired yet another cycle of black movie criticism, first in journalism, then in the scholarly quarterlies. *Newsweek,* for example, ran three major stories within a year: "The Black Movie Boom" (Sept. 6, 1971): 66; "Blacks vs. Shaft" (Aug. 28, 1972): 87–88; and Charles Michener, "Black Movies" (Oct. 23, 1972): 74–82. By the end of 1972 Pauline Kael's often-cited "Notes on Black Movies" had appeared in the *New Yorker* (Dec. 2, 1972): 159–65.

As in the case of *The Birth of a Nation,* a single movie stirred the debate about "blaxploitation" films. *Sweet Sweetback's Baad Asssss Song* (1971) became an icon of the age with Huey P. Newton's "He Won't Bleed Me: A Revolutionary Analysis of *Sweet Sweetback's Baad Asssss Song*" in *Black Panther* (June 19, 1971): A–L [*sic*]. On the other side, the film seemed mere fantasy to the *Ebony* editor Lerone Bennett in "The Emancipation Orgasm: *Sweet Sweetback* in Wonderland," *Ebony* (Sept. 1971): 106–108, a notion shared by Kuumba Workshop, a Chicago community drama group, in its pamphlet *From a Black Perspective: . . . Sweet Sweetback's Baad Asssss Song* [1972?]. The first scholarly treatment, albeit in interview form, Horace W. Coleman, "Melvin Van Peebles," *Journal of Popular Film* 5 (Fall 1971): 368–84, took Newton's point of view.

In academic circles *Sweetback* enjoyed considerable attention as a seminal work, though other less strident pictures had also contributed to the "blaxploitation" cycle. Gladstone L. Yearwood, ed., *Black Cinema Aesthetics: Issues in Black Independent Filmmaking* (1982), the proceedings of an Ohio University conference, features a "colloquy" in which Van Peebles himself testified. As late as the 1990s, the film still carried its age well, enjoying a place in academic conferences and in the scholarly literature. See Thomas Cripps, "*Sweet Sweetback's Baad Asssss Song* and the Changing Politics of Genre Film," in Peter Lehman, ed., *Close Viewings: An Anthology of New Film Criticism* (1990): 238–61; references to it in Ed Guerrero, *Framing Blackness: The African American Image in Film* (1993); and Michael T. Martin, ed., *Cinema of the Black Diaspora: Diversity, Dependence, Oppositionality* (1995). See also Jon Hartmann, "The Trope of Blaxploitation in Critical Responses to *Sweetback*," *Film History* 6 (1994): 382–404.

Sweetback not only generated its own round of journalistic commentary, but also stimulated the "blaxploitation" cycle and its canon of criticism. See, for example, James Robert Parish and George H. Hill, ed., *Black Action Films: Plots, Critiques, Casts, and Credits for 235 Theatrical Releases and Made-for-Television Releases* (1989); and on specific titles, see Donald Bogle, "*Uptown Saturday Night:* A Look at Its Place in Film History," *Freedomways* (4th quarter, 1974): 320–30; Loyle Hairston, "The Black Film: 'Supernigger' as Folk Hero," *Freedomways* (3rd quarter, 1974): 218–22; Richard Dyer, "Is *Car Wash* a Musical?" in Diawara, *Black American Cinema:* 93–106; and Maurice Peterson, "*The Book of Numbers*," *Essence* (Jan. 1973): 26. For a whimsical history that includes interviews, credits, and synopses, all phrased in hyperbolic jive talk, see Darius James, *That's Blaxploitation! Roots of the Baadasssss 'Tude* [sic] (1995).

RACE MOVIES

Of all the genres of movies, "race movies" have faced the most problematic fate at the hands of critics and historians, although in recent years they have begun to find readier acceptance. Almost all of the early writers—Noble, Leab, Bogle—gave them only passing attention or found them merely "imitation" Hollywood. Between the world wars they were often reviled in the black press and turned up in the serials only in Harry Alan Potamkin, "The Aframerican Film," *Close Up* (Aug. 1929): 107–17; James Asendio, "The History of Negro Motion Pictures," *International Photographer* (Jan. 1940): 16–17; and Herb Golden, "Negro and Yiddish

Film Boom," *Variety* (Jan. 3, 1940). See particularly Leab, "All Colored, But Not Much Different: Films Made for Negro Ghetto Audiences, 1913–1928," *Phylon* 36 (Sept. 1975): 321–39; and Leab, "A Pale Black Imitation: All Colored Films, 1930–1960," *Journal of Popular Film* 4 (1975), 56–76.

Before 1975 only one essay suggested that the genre of race movies merited study, if only as documents of social history. See Thomas Cripps, "Movies in the Ghetto, B.P.—Before Poitier," *Negro Digest* (Feb. 1969): 21–27, 45–48. It was not until 1975 that "race movies" made it into the mainstream. See for example J. Hoberman, "A Forgotten Black Cinema Surfaces," *Village Voice* (Nov. 17, 1975): 1 ff. Then, in 1977, Henry T. Sampson, *Blacks in Black and White: A Source Book on Black Films (1904–1950)* (1977) revealed both the rich fund of paper documentation of "race movies" and also guessed at their numbers and helped anticipate a critical school devoted to them. In the same year, Cripps, *Slow Fade to Black: The Negro in American Film, 1900–1942* (1977), gave them two chapters, one on silent and one on sound films, finding them a genuine black cultural achievement, albeit one that daunted critics because of low production budgets that made them seem wanting in cinematic values.

Scarcity of surviving prints precluded any author from writing the definitive essay on a "race movie." The first writings on *The Birth of a Race* (1918), for example, appeared long before any critic had seen the film. It earned a mention in the early literature and turned up in *Black Shadows on a Silver Screen* (1976), but only as seen through its posters and some paste-ups of the *Tampa Tribune* (where some of it was shot). Much of the film remains lost, but its production may be traced in Cripps, "*The Birth of a Race* Company: An Early Stride toward a Black Cinema," *Journal of Negro History* 59 (Jan. 1974): 28–37. When the film itself was discovered in Texas, it reappeared in print in a "quest" piece: Cripps, "*The Birth of a Race*: A Lost Film Rediscovered in Texas," *Texas Humanist* (March-April 1983): 10–11. A belated premiere was held at the Kennedy Center in Washington in 1980. Almost a decade later, when a sheaf of music cues to the silent film turned up, yet another piece attempted to assess its new place in history: Cripps, "The Making of *The Birth of a Race*: The Emerging Politics of Identity in Silent Movies," in Daniel Bernardi, ed., *The Birth of Whiteness: Race and the Emergence of U.S. Cinema* (1996): 38–55. Altogether more than a half-dozen articles appeared, each one analyzing a new film of which, since 1918 or so, no one has seen a complete print. The quarter-century-long story suggests the ongoing nature of writing African-American film history, as new sources are revealed.

Each new recovery of a lost shard of film invites new assessments and revisions of revisions. Indeed, the long career of the beau ideal of makers of "race movies," Oscar Micheaux, has inspired such revisionism as each recaptured film from his formerly lost corpus is examined. He has grown from a derided naïf into the namesake of an annual award given by the Directors Guild of America. His revisionists begin with Jane Gaines, "Fire and Desire: Race, Melodrama, and Oscar Micheaux," in Diawara, *Black American Cinema*: 49–70, a fresh appraisal of *Within Our Gates* (1919), a film discovered by Cripps only in 1979 in the Cineteca España in Madrid. See also J. Ronald Green and Horace Neal, Jr., "Oscar Micheaux and the Racial Slur: A Response to the Rediscovery of Oscar Micheaux," *Journal of Film and Video* 40 (Fall 1988): 66–71; and Green's "'Twoness' in the Style of Oscar Micheaux," in Diawara, *Black American Cinema*: 26–48, the latter a cavil that appraised earlier work on Micheaux as "ill-founded." For a full accounting of work on Micheaux, see Charlene Regester, "The Misreading and Rereading of African American Filmmaker Oscar Micheaux," *Film History* 7 (1995): 426–49. Among recent books are Betti Carol VanEpps-Taylor's *Oscar Micheaux: Dakota Homesteader, Author, Pioneer Film Maker: A Biography* (1998); J. Ronald Green's *Straight Lick: The Cinema of Oscar Micheaux* (2000); and Pearl Bowser and Louise Spence, *Writing Himself into History: Oscar Micheaux, His Silent Films, and His Audiences* (2000).

Revisionism arises not only from new discoveries but also from fresh considerations, which in film historiography might derive from theories of feminism, linguistics, anthropology, or the work of Freud and Marx. See, for example, three views of a Colored Players production of 1927: Ronald Goldwyn, "*The Scar of Shame*," *Discover* [Philadelphia *Sunday Bulletin*] (Nov. 17, 1974): 14–23; Thomas Cripps, "Race Movies as Voices of the Black Bourgeoisie: *The Scar of Shame*," in John E. O'Connor and Martin A. Jackson, eds., *American History/American Film* (1979): 39–56; and Jane Gaines, "*The Scar of Shame*: Skin Color and Caste in Black Silent Melodrama," *Cinema Journal* 21 (Summer 1987): 3–21.

More than any other aspect of film study, the apprehending of the viewer's reception has enchanted the student of African-Americans and movies, partly because the data seem so tantalizingly at hand. They range from tabular data such as opinion samplings to gleanings from newspaper advertising, letters to editors, and the opinions expressed in preview cards—much of it given systematic meaning by the authors' uses of theorists of group behavior such as Jürgen Habermas, Stuart Hall, Elias Canetti, and Jacques Lacan. Essentially, this sort of formulation has superseded the empirical viewer-samplings that dominated the 1930s and 1940s, thereby giving free rein to inference and sociological imagination by including the theorists among the primary sources, and by treating the audience as a credible witness rather than merely as a passive, statistically derived subject.

All such sketches rest upon some form of "counting the house," through scanning trade papers or ethnic newspapers or studio account books. A good sampling of such literature includes the following: Thomas Cripps, "The Myth of the Southern Box Office: A Factor in Racial Stereotyping in American Movies, 1920–1940," in James C. Curtis and Lewis L. Gould, ed., *The Black Experience in America: Selected Essays* (1970); Gregory A. Waller, "Another Audience: Black Moviegoing, 1907–1916 [in Lexington, Ky.]," *Cinema Journal* (Winter 1992): 3–25; Mary Carbine, "'The Finest outside the Loop': Motion Picture Exhibition in Chicago's Black Metropolis, 1905–1928," *Camera Obscura* 23 [1990]: 9–42; Dan Streible, "The Harlem Theatre: Black Film Exhibition in Austin, Texas, 1920–1973," in Diawara, *Black American Cinema*: 221–36; Renee Ward, "Black Films, White Profits," *Black Scholar* 7 (May 1976): 12–25; and Jesse Algeron Rhines, *Black Film/White Money* (1996), a history of distribution of movies to blacks. For a more personal angle, see Nelson George, *Blackface: Reflections on African Americans and the Movies* (1994).

Students of audience reception have attempted to define the prospective audience for an emerging "black independent cinema" that stands apart from the classical Hollywood model. This audience seems focused, political, self-conscious, and far from passive. Its chroniclers include Charles W. Peavy, "Black Consciousness and the Contemporary Cinema," in Ray B. Browne, ed., *Popular Culture and the Expanding Consciousness* (1973): 178–200, and James Baldwin's polemic, *The Devil Finds Work* (1976). Movie critics became cultural critics in Diawara, "Black Spectatorship: Problems of Identification and Resistance," *Screen* 29 (Autumn 1988): 67–70 (and in his *Black American Cinema*); Jacqueline Bobo, "The Subject Is Money: Recreating the Black Film Audience as a Theoretical Paradigm," *Black American Literature Forum* 25 (Summer 1991): 421–31; Tommy L. Lott, "A No-Theory Theory of Contemporary Black Cinema," in Martin, *Cinemas of the Black Diaspora:* 40–55; and Wahneema Lubiano, "But Compared to What? Reading, Realism, Representation, and Essentialism in *School Daze, Do the Right Thing,* and the Spike Lee Discourse," *Black American Literature Forum* 25 (Summer 1991): 253–82.

Running through the literature is a thread that traces back to the prison notebooks of Antonio Gramsci, one of the founders of the Italian Communist Party, who spent many years in Mussolini's jails. His ideas influenced the American Left, perhaps because his work—at least as it appears in English—holds out the hope for minorities of cultivating an indigenous resistant culture while also promising an alternative to the ever more remote likelihood of a Marxist rising of the workers against their capitalist masters. This alternative allows a minority to bargain for enhanced status during times of crisis within the dominant culture.

The earliest such writing was Stuart Hall's widely read piece, "Gramsci's Relevance for the Study of Race and Ethnicity," *Journal of Communications Inquiry* 10 (Summer 1966): 5–27. James Snead, "Recording Blackness: The Visual Rhetoric of the Black Independent Film," program notes, Whitney Museum New American Filmmakers series 23 (n.d.): 1–2, and Clyde Taylor, "The Ironies of Palace-Subaltern Discourse," in Diawara, *Black American Cinema:* 177–99, were other contributors to this politics of movie art. Snead, a promising scholar, died while writing a book eventually completed by Colin McCabe and Cornel West, ed., *White Screens Black Images: Hollywood from the Dark Side* (1994). His hope had been to construct on ground cleared by Gramsci and others an "oppositional aesthetic" that might be adapted to mass marketing. This notion of an oppositional aesthetic grounded in reception as well as in production may be seen in several of the essays in Gina Dent, ed., *Black Popular Culture: A Project by Michele Wallace* (1992).

Yet another parallel line of critical argument emerged in the form of a feminist canon, also grounded in oppositional and alternative readings. See, for example, bell hooks, "The Oppositional Gaze: Black Female Spectators," and Jacqueline Bobo, "Reading through the Text: The Black Woman as Audience," in Diawara, *Black American Cinema:* 272–302; and Sharon Alile Larkin, "Black Women Filmmakers Defining Ourselves: Feminism in Our Own Voice," in Deidre Pribam, ed., *Female Spectators: Looking at Film and Television* (1988); and Gloria Gibson-Hudson, "African American Literature as a Model for Analysis of Films by African American Women," *Wide Angle* 13 (1991): 44–54. Three book-length formulations of a "womanist" aesthetic are Mark A. Reid, *Redefining Black Film* (1993);

Lisa M. Anderson, *Mammies No More: The Changing Image of Black Women on Stage and Screen* (1997); and Part II of Sharon Willis, *High Contrast: Race and Gender in Contemporary Hollywood Films* (1997). In addition, a lively school of journalism has been stirred by specific releases. See, for example, "The Deltas Go to Hollywood [*Countdown at Kusini*]," *Essence* (May 1975): 30–32; Cheryl B. Butler, "*The Color Purple* Controversy: The Black and White Spectator," *Wide Angle* 13 (1991): 62–71; Toni Cade Bambara, "Reading the Signs, Empowering the Eye: *Daughters of the Dust* and the Black Independent Film Movement," in Diawara, *Black American Cinema*: 118–44; Karen Alexander, "*Daughters of the Dust*: Julie Dash Talks about African American Women's Cinema and Images from Her Film," *Sight and Sound* (Sept. 1993): 20–22; Joel Brouwer, "Repositioning: Center and Margin in Julie Dash's 'Daughters of the Dust,'" *African American Review* 29 (Spring 1995): 5–16; and "Exhaling and Inhaling: Was the Movie Fair to Black Men and Black Women?" [panel discussion of *Waiting to Exhale*], *Ebony* (April 1996): 116–20.

Sometimes essays on genres in which Africans or African-Americans have been historically treated pejoratively are informative. See, for example, two books on the South in the media: Jack Temple Kirby, *Media-Made Dixie: The South in the American Imagination* (1978), and Edward D. C. Campbell, *The Celluloid South: Hollywood and the Southern Myth* (1981). Colonialist genres such as Tarzan movies have also generated a body of literature. See, for example, Gabe T. Essoe, *Tarzan of the Movies: A Pictorial History of More Than Fifty Years of ERB's Legendary Hero* (1973), and Robert W. Fenton, *The Big Swingers: A Biography, Edgar Rice Burroughs, 1875–1950; Tarzan, 1912–* (1967).

Black music on film has almost never been treated as the basis for a politics, perhaps because music has most often been used incidentally as background in films. A glance at David Meeker, *Jazz in the Movies: A Guide to Jazz Musicians 1917–1977* (1977), suggests the critical result of this ancillary role of music—the truism that if one hears the music then the movie has failed. A few jazz shorts and set pieces within musicals are the exceptions. The literature includes Krin Gabbard, *Jammin' the Margins: Jazz and the American Cinema* (1996); Allen L. Woll, "Separate But Equal: Blacks in Wartime Musicals," in *The Hollywood Musical Goes to War* (1983); parts of Jane Feuer, *The Hollywood Musical* (1993); a few articles such as James Naremore, "Uptown Folk: Blackness and Entertainment in *Cabin in the Sky*," *Arizona Quarterly* 48:4 (1992): 99–124, and Barry Keith Grant, "Jungle Nights in Harlem: Jazz, Ideology, and the Animated Cartoon," *University of Hartford Studies in Literature* 21:3 (1989): 3–12; and two essays in Gabbard, ed., *Representing Jazz* (1995), Arthur Knight's closely worked piece, "*Jammin' the Blues* or the Sight of Jazz," and Adam Knee, "Doubling, Music, and Race in *Cabin in the Sky*." More recently this linkage between African-American and popular culture and movies has been explored as a subtheme in Jeffrey Melnick's *A Right to Sing the Blues: African Americans, Jews, and American Popular Song* (1999).

An emerging field of inquiry is blackface performance on film, a genre derived from one of American culture's oldest forms. Only recently has the literature begun to take up the racial politics embedded in blackface performance. Early works were mainly descriptive. See, for example, Carl Wittke, *Tambo and Bones: A History of the American Minstrel Stage* (1930); Hans Nathan, *Dan Emmett and the Rise of Early Negro Minstrelsy* (1962); and Robert Toll, *Blacking Up: The Minstrel Show in the Nineteenth Century* (1974); and, somewhat more socially analytical, Joseph Boskin, *Sambo: The Rise & Demise of an American Jester* (1986). Recent literature has linked minstrelsy to white gains from it, the purposes it served for the white working class, and its entanglement with Jewish culture. See particularly Eric Lott, *Love & Theft: Blackface Minstrelsy and the American Working Class* (1993). W. T. Lhamon, Jr., has carried this theme "from Jim Crow to Hip Hop" (with considerable attention to movies such as those of Al Jolson) in his *Raising Cain: Blackface Performance from Jim Crow to Hip Hop* (1998).

For the place of minstrelsy in movies, see Robert L. Carringer's annotated script, *The Jazz Singer* (1979); Michael Rogin's trial essays, "Blackface, White Noise: The Jewish Jazz Singer Finds His Voice," *Critical Inquiry* 18 (Spring 1992): 417–53, and "Making America Home: Racial Masquerade and Ethnic Assimilation in the Transition to Talking Pictures," *Journal of American History* 79 (Dec. 1992): 1050–77; and his book, *Blackface, White Noise: Jewish Immigrants and the Hollywood Melting Pot* (1996). See also Doug McClelland, *Blackface to Blacklist: Al Jolson, Larry Parks, and 'The Jolson Story'* (1987). A valuable visual source for the genre and its history is Marlon Riggs's film *Ethnic Notions*.

The flow of scholarly writing on African-Americans in movies shows no sign of abating. Current releases inspire rigorously theoretical essays grounded in the literature. Thus the reader will wish to consult each newly published guide to periodical writing, new editions of older anthologies, and newly minted electronic versions of various guides. For examples of recent work, see Jacqueline Jones, "The Ghetto Aesthetic," *Wide Angle* 13:3–4 (1991): 32–43, on macho posturing in *Boyz in the Hood*; Paula J. Massood, "Mapping the Hood: The Genealogy of City Space in *Boyz in the Hood* and *Menace II Society*," *Cinema Journal* 35:2 (Winter 1996): 85–97; and essays cited herein by Cheryl B. Butler on *The Color Purple* and Toni Cade Bambara on *Daughters of the Dust*. Among the most imaginative pieces in this ongoing literature is Judith Weisenfeld's "For Rent, 'Cabin in the Sky': Race, Religion, and Representational Quagmires in American Film," *Semeia* 74 (1996): 147–165, for its attention to religion as treated in two key race movies, with an analysis deepened by contrast with Hollywood portrayals of black folk religion.

Another source for the study of recent movies is one largely unavailable for older works. Journals and memoirs of the making and reception of a movie provide valuable insight into the particulars of black films. Only Van Peebles's paperback on the making of *Sweetback* speaks for older filmmakers. For recent examples, see Spike Lee's books, which include not only accounts of filmmaking but also scripts and stills: *Uplift the Race: The Construction of School Daze* (with Lisa Jones) (1988); and the two editions, British and American, of *Malcolm X: The Trials and Tribulations of the Making of Malcolm X* (1992, 1993). See also Terry McMillan et al., *Five for Five: The Films of Spike Lee* (1991).

A peripheral but sometimes informative source is the journalism in the newsletters and journals of teachers and counselors. Each new and seemingly threatening movie cycle has led educators to reflect on the effects of movies on their pupils. To cite only two examples of the genre, see Edward Hayes et al., *"Superfly, The Mack,* and Black Youth Counselors," *School Counselor* (Jan. 1975): 174–79, and James S. Weeks, "Roles, Goals, and Values: The Cinematic Experience," *Personnel and Guidance Journal* 49 (May 1971): 769–74. A sidebar to this form of analysis focused on accuracy and impact has arisen concerning the genre of "docudrama," a derivative of the older "biopic" form. Whether television fare such as *Roots* or theatrical films such as Oliver Stone's *JFK* and *Nixon* and Steven Spielberg's *Amistad,* the genre has stirred historians to challenge its accuracy and demand restraint on artistic license. For a sampling of such writing, see Mark C. Carnes, ed., *Past Imperfect: History According to the Movies* (1995), which includes essays on *Glory* (James M. McPherson), *Gone with the Wind* (Catherine Clinton), *The Birth of a Nation* (Leon F. Litwack), *Matewan* (Eric Foner), *Mississippi Burning* (William H. Chafe), and *Malcolm X* (Clayborne Carson).

The history of the black 54th Massachusetts Regiment as dramatized in the movie *Glory* has attracted particular attention, ranging from its making to its reception. See particularly C. Peter Jorgensen, "The Making of *Glory*," *Civil War Times Illustrated* 28 (1989): 52–59; Jim Cullen, *The Civil War in Popular Culture: A Reusable Past* (1995); Robert Burgoyne, *Film Nation: Hollywood Looks at U.S. History* (1997); and Thomas Cripps, "The Absent Presence in *Glory*," *Historical Journal of Film, Radio and Television* 14 (1994): 367–376. Also see Martin H. Blatt, "*Glory*: Hollywood History, Popular Culture, and the 54th Massachusetts Regiment," and Thomas Cripps, "*Glory* as a Meditation on the Saint-Gaudens Monument," in Martin H. Blatt, Thomas J. Brown, and Donald Yacovone, ed., *Hope and Glory: Essays on the Legacy of the 54th Massachusetts Regiment* (2000). For a continuing updating of the literature, see *African Americans in Film and Television: A Short Bibliography of Materials in the UC Berkeley Libraries* (1996, et seq.), *http:// www.lib.berkeley.edu/by.*

TELEVISION

Television has replaced movies as the preferred American mass medium for conveying the moving image. Particularly this is so with respect to the B movie, the former bread-and-butter fare for exhibitors of Hollywood's classical era. The two media share a common reliance on unsubtle melodrama, often offering a piously reformist message. The audiences for TV and B movies are also remarkably the same: habitual, loyal to certain genres and formulas and familiar characters, and, to an extent, measurable. B-movie audiences seemed so predictable that *Variety* referred to them as "sure-seaters," a trait more precisely measured in television by means of ratings systems that tell broadcasters how many viewers there are for each show and what percentage of the viewing audience they represent.

VIEWING TELEVISION PROGRAMS

African-American programming, or any television artifacts for that matter, remain unsystematically accessible to scholars. Early American television was recorded, if at all, on "kinescopes," or films shot directly from often snowy and indistinct television screens. The first generation of tape recording allowed data storage only on costly and bulky two-inch tapes. Under these conditions, only the occasionally noteworthy show or documentary would be preserved. The rare exceptions were made possible by shooting a TV program on motion picture film with an eye toward eventual syndication, or repeat broadcasting in local markets. In a cost-conscious, market-driven enterprise like commercial television, a filmed show might be saved not for its archival value but for its income-earning potential, while an important event on tape might be erased so the tape could be reused for tomorrow's news.

Gradually, this tendency is changing. Local television stations have begun depositing archival news and documentary videotapes in university libraries for preservation and research. Independent producers and freelance personnel often carry off some material evidence—tapes, scripts, and correspondence—from projects they work on. As these workers reach the end of their careers, they seek a place in the history of the medium by depositing their work in archives. Thus the very archives already listed as troves of moviemaking information have also begun to accumulate television materials. Indeed, the Library of Congress and the libraries of USC, UCLA, and other universities have added either the term "broadcasting" or "television" to their archives dedicated to the moving image.

Repositories dedicated specifically to broadcasting are marked by the widest range of mission. One-dimensional archives such as the Museum of Advertising in Portland, Oreg., and the Julian Cantor Archive at the University of Oklahoma devoted to political "spots," as well as small libraries such as the broadcasting museum of the Thousand Oaks Public Library in California, nonetheless intersect with the interests of black film research. A good example is the Vanderbilt Television News Archive in Nashville, Tenn., which since the late 1960s has preserved almost all network news broadcasts, many documentaries, and additional products of local and cable news outlets. The tapes are carefully indexed in a staple-bound catalog and made available to teachers and scholars as off-air teaching aids and research sources. Another such service is the Southern Telenews Library of ARIQ Footage in East Hampton, N.Y.

The most useful of these dedicated museums is the Museum of Television and Radio in New York City. Established by William S. Paley, founder of CBS, it has maintained the closest of relationships with network broadcasters. In addition to both video- and audiotapes that can be viewed on the 53rd Street premises, the holdings also include a large collection of scripts and other paper materials. The taped programs range from incidental black appearances such as Joe Walcott's role in *Playhouse 90: Requiem for a Heavyweight* and the black performers doing their five-minute bits on *Toast of the Town* and other vaudeville hours, to such black-centered fare as *In the First Person: Langston Hughes; See It Now: The Lady from Philadelphia* [Marian Anderson]; *Roots: An ABC Novel for Television;* network coverage of the civil rights movement; and episodes of *The Amos 'n' Andy Show.* At this writing, a West Coast affiliate of the Museum of Television and Radio in New York has opened in Beverly Hills, which also offers research facilities to scholars. A similar Museum of Broadcasting in Chicago offers an imposing array of actual operating equipment through which visitors see and hear programs—a public mission that the museum seems more dedicated to than to scholarly research.

Unlike the medium of motion pictures, television has not drawn the attention of African-American librarians and archivists. However, the venerable Arthur A. Schomburg Center in New York has embarked upon a program to create a publicly accessible holding of representative television programming that has featured black journalism, documentary subjects, and performance art, both musical and dramatic.

As in the case of movie research, the Library of Congress and the Film and Television Archive of UCLA offer the largest group of holdings not specifically devoted to African-American subjects but which include them as part of their larger inventories. They both include a full range of television genres—sitcoms, drama, cop shows, quiz shows, and documentary programming, all of which are accessible by title in electronic databases. Of the private collections that provide stock footage to documentary producers, Sherman Grinberg and the Prelinger Collection in New York City, the ARIQ Southern Telenews Library, and J. Fred MacDonald Associates of Chicago are among the largest. Their research practices and fees vary, as do their cataloging methods. The most dedicated to black material and the most accessible by telephone or fax is MacDonald Associates. Another source for videotapes of television programming are commercial rental stores, which have inventories of both documentaries and genre shows with ongoing African-American characters such as *Heroes, Star Trek,* and *I Spy.*

MANUSCRIPTS AND RECORDS

The Wisconsin Center for Film and Theatre Research in Madison, Wis., holds a solid collection of television materials that a student of African-American moving images would find useful. The massive records of NBC, running to hundreds of boxes as well as numerous reels, disks, tapes, and microfilm are augmented regularly. Their use is limited only by the keywords that a diligent researcher's interests can devise. The personal papers include those of Ernest Kinoy, coauthor of *Roots,* a TV version of Edna Ferber's *Showboat,* and a proposed serial entitled *Change at 125th Street.* The producer David Susskind is represented by the production records of a TV remake of *Body and Soul* (1947), a boxing story featuring Bernie Hamilton; *A Man Is Ten Feet Tall,* a Sidney Poitier vehicle; a drama about the lynching of Emmett Till in Mississippi; and *East Side/West Side,* a primetime urban drama with Cicely Tyson in a continuing role.

Smaller collections include papers related to other specific projects. The Perry Wolff Papers contain documents on CBS's *Black History: Lost, Stolen, or Strayed,* an early attempt at a history of the African-American moving image. In the papers of both Rod Serling and John Frankenheimer there are papers and scripts documenting *A Town Has Turned to Dust,* a *Playhouse 90* program on the lynching of a black man that its makers were obliged to soften into a general treatment of lynching in the American West. A few collections, such as that of Bruce Geller, shed light on the genre of cop show with one black regular cast member, as in Geller's *Mannix* and *Mission Impossible.* In a reflection of how TV adapts to its market, the Hal Kanter Papers document the career of a writer-producer who helped create *Amos 'n' Andy, The Beulah Show, Julia,* and *Chico and the Man* as American racial politics changed.

Among the informative holdings of the UCLA Theatre Arts Library are similar personal collections related to television. For example, scripts of shows featuring continuing black roles appear in several inventories. See Bruce Geller's papers on *Mannix*; Robert Mintz's on *Room 222*; Michael Rhodes's on *Mod Squad*; Steve Binder's papers for his work on *The Flip Wilson Show*; Gene Roddenberry's *Star Trek* archive; and the *Room 222* archive of fifty scripts. Robert L. Shayon's papers reflect his interest in the work of the United Council of Churches and its monitoring of Southern regional programming in order to ascertain service to black communities. The Cinema-Television Library of USC holds similar collections by various practitioners, but particularly the Charles Gosden and Freemen Correll *Amos 'n' Andy* collection of scripts, tapes, and other ephemera.

REFERENCE WORKS

The literature of television history is more elusive than that of movies, mainly because the bibliographies are fewer, and so the dutiful reader must rely on bibliographies in monographs. A useful bibliography is George H. Hill and Sylvia Hill, ed., *Blacks on Television: A Selectively Annotated Bibliography* (1985). Among the monographic literature three books stand out with respect to bibliography: J. Fred MacDonald, *Blacks and White TV: Afro-Americans in Television since 1948* (1983); Jannette L. Dates and William Barlow, ed., *Split Image: Afro-Americans in the Mass Media* (2nd ed., 1993), which contains endnotes following each of its essays; and for African-Americans in broadcast commercials, Marilyn Kern-Foxworth, *Aunt Jemima, Uncle Ben, and Rastus: Blacks in Advertising, Yesterday, Today, and Tomorrow* (1994). The latter two focus on media, broadly defined, so that in Kern-Foxworth data on broadcasting must be culled. In Dates and Barlow, although there is a general bibliographical essay on all media, more specialized bibliographies may be found in Dates's own essays in part 4, "The Television Industry." Another such bibliography within a reference anthology is Nagueyalti Warren, "From Uncle Tom to Cliff Huxtable, Aunt Jemima to Aunt Nell: Images of Blacks in Film and Television Industry," in Jessie Carney Smith, ed., *Images of Blacks in American Culture: A Reference Guide to Information Sources* (1988). See also Paula M. Poindexter and Carolyn A. Stroman, "Blacks and Television: A Review of Research Literature," *Journal of Broadcasting* 25 (Spring 1981): 103–22, for empirical work.

Here we should also note that bibliographies appear in a few references that index both film and television scholarship. Among those previously cited under "Reference Works" are Woll and Miller, *Ethnic and Racial Images in American Film and Television*; Snorgrass and Woody, *Blacks and the Media*; Gray, *Blacks in Film and Television*; and Spradling, *In Black and White*.

Television, unlike motion pictures, has taken some of its shape and direction from various federal regulators and plaintiffs who have pled for racial justice in broadcasting. Not only are the records of, say, the Federal Communications Commission (FCC) open to public scrutiny, but local television stations are obliged to open their "ascertainment records" (records of their meeting community "needs") to the public. Many of the policies reflected in these records have in turn been monitored by private agencies such as the United Council of Churches, the Citizens Communications Center, and the National Black Media Coalition, some of whom have kept records of their activities. The files of the FCC itself are open to scrutiny in its Dockets Branch and Public Information Office in Washington, D.C. Of particular interest are cases of petitions to deny licenses on grounds of failure to meet community needs. One such widely influential case was that of WLBT-TV (Jackson, Miss.), in which the FCC found in favor of plaintiffs in a 1964 plea in which citizens' groups, among them the United Council of Churches (which was awarded legal standing in the case), kept logs of denial of access to TV by blacks, censorship of racially challenging network programs, and other violations. Another instance of federal intervention in broadcasting is the United States Commission on Civil Rights report *Window Dressing on the Set: Women and Minorities in Television* (1977; updated, 1979), which studied everything from racial content analysis of current and past programming, to the impact of such cases as WLBT on policy-making, to the need for stronger federal intervention in the medium of broadcasting.

GENRES

In broadcasting, genres have typically been regarded as means of communicating—news, documentary, commercials, drama, sports, sitcoms, and so on—rather than as formal types of performance such as the western, the musical, and the women's melodramas. Thus criticism and scholarship have tended to take the form of social rather than artistic analysis and have inquired into television's effects on audiences far longer than such empirical studies had drawn the attention of movie scholars. The literature has persisted in its focus on black images and their impact on audiences rather than borrowing from the aesthetic canons of literature and drama.

In the field of news broadcasting, for example, see Paul L. Fisher and Ralph Lowenstein, ed., *Race and the News Media* (1967), particularly essays on blacks in broadcasting by Don Farmer, William B. Monroe, Jr., Joseph L. Brechner, and William Peters; James S. Tinney and Justine J. Rector, ed., *Issues and Trends in Afro-American Journalism* (1980); and Charles U. Daly, ed., *The Media and the Cities* (1968), a report by the University of Chicago Center for Policy Study that takes up the coverage of cities by "white media." For a treatment of "image" as transformed by coverage of both sports and news, see Thomas Cripps, "The Noble Black Savage: A Problem in the Politics of Television Art," *Journal of Popular Culture* 8 (Spring 1975): 687–95. For coverage of a specific event, see Justin Wren-Lewis, "TV Coverage of the Riots," *Screen Education* 40 (1981–1982): 15–33. On a specific documentary series, see Paula Matabane and Oscar Gandy, Jr., "Through the Prism of Race and Controversy: Did Viewers Learn Anything from 'The Africans'?" *Journal of Black Studies* 19 (Sept. 1988): 3–16. And on the news from local stations, see Robert Entman, "Modern Racism and the Images of Blacks in Local News," *Critical Studies in Mass Communication* 7 (Dec. 1990). A pioneering autobiography is Gil Noble, *Black Is the Color of My TV Tube* (1981).

One genre ubiquitous in broadcast television is the commercial message. Among the most useful essays on the treatment of blacks in TV advertising, particularly for bibliography, is R. F. Bush et al., "There Are More Blacks in TV Commercials," *Journal of Advertising Research* 17 (Feb. 1977): 21–25; Chester M. Pierce, Jean V. Carew, Diane Pierce-Gonzales, and Deborah Willis, "An Experiment in Racism: TV Commercials," *Education and Urban Society* 10 (1977): 61–87; Robert E. Pitts, D. Joel Whelan, Robert O'Keefe, Vernon Murray, "Black and White Response to Culturally Targeted Television Commercials: A Value Based Approach," *Psychology and Marketing* 6 (Winter 1989): 311–28; Robert E. Wilkes and Humberto Valencia, "Hispanics and Blacks in Television Commercials," *Journal of Advertising* 18 (1989): 19–25; and Thomas R. Donohue, "Effects of Commercials on Black Children," *Journal of Advertising Research* 15 (Dec. 1975): 41–47.

In addition to these forms of address unique to television, the medium has assimilated genres from older performance media. For example, critics have identified a symbiotic new idiom, the made-for-TV movie. For a monographic scholarly inquiry into its race angles, see Elayne Rapping, *The Movie of the Week: Private Stories, Public Events* (1992), especially chap. 5, "TV Movies as History: Class, Race, and the Past." For a study of a single movie, see Douglas Gomery, "*Brian's Song*: Television, Hollywood, and the Evolution of the Movie Made for Television," in John E. O'Connor, ed., *American History/American Television: Interpreting the Video Past* (1983).

The precursors of the sitcom—the comedy of manners, the farce, and the social satire—followed a highly visual, rapidly paced, glib formula that lent itself to the tightly compressed medium of television. Critics have found in both the genre and its specific programs a profoundly affecting ideology of race that manages to evolve beyond the overt racism of the 19th century while at the same time embodying half-hidden racial encodings. See, for example, Darryl Y. Hammamoto, *Nervous Laughter: The Television Sitcom and Liberal Democratic Ideology* (1989); Herman Gray, "Television and the New Black Man: Black Male Images in Prime-Time Situation Comedy," *Media, Culture, and Society* 8 (1986): 223–42; and Janet Sims-Wood, "The Black Female: Mammy, Jemima, Sapphire, and Other Images," in Smith, *Images of Blacks in American Culture.*

Several critics have analyzed specific television sitcoms by asking what message the shows sent and what was received. See, for example, John C. Brigham and Linda W. Giesbrecht, "All in the Family: Racial Attitudes," *Journal of Communication* 26 (1976): 69–74; John Downing, "*The Cosby Show* and American Racial Discourse," in Geneva Smitherman-Donaldson and T. van Dijk, ed., *Discourse and Discrimination* (1988); Sut Jhally and Justin Lewis, *Enlightened Racism: The Cosby Show, Audiences, and the Myth of the American Dream* (1992); and most recently, Leslie B. Inniss and Joe R. Feagin, "'The Cosby Show': The View from the Black Middle Class," *Journal of Black Studies* 25 (July 1995): 692–710.

Other genres have received attention from critics but at a lesser volume than the sitcoms, which seemed to probe racism more deeply than did self-consciously "serious" programming. In addition to Rapping's and Gomery's work on made-for-TV movies, see also Richard Carpenter, "*I Spy* and *Mission Impossible*: Gimmicks and a Fairy Tale," *Journal of Popular Culture* 1 (1967): 286–90, and Carl Gardner and Margaret Henry, "Racism, Anti-Racism and Access Television: The Making of *Open Door*," *Screen Education* 31 (1979): 69–81. On the changing face of black music on television, see J. Fred MacDonald, "Black Perimeters: Paul Robeson, Nat

Cole, and the Roles of Blacks in American TV," *Journal of Popular Film and Television* 7 (1979): 246–64; Pat Aufderheide, "Music Videos: The Look of the Sound," *Journal of Communication* 36 (Winter 1986): 57–78; and Marsha Kinder, "Music Video and the Spectator: Television, Ideology, and the Dream," *Film Quarterly* 38 (Feb. 1984): 3–15. An emerging field of inquiry is science fiction. See, for example, Micheal [sic] Pounds, *Race in Space: The Representation of Ethnicity in Star Trek and Star Trek: The Next Generation* (1997).

Perhaps because commercial television is only a half-century old and seems such a personal medium, usually viewed in the home and lending itself to statistical measurement, many critics regard television as a social organism that changes America even as it is changed in the process. See, for example, chapter 10 of S. Robert Lichter, Linda S. Lichter, and Stanley Rothman, *Watching America: What Television Tells Us about Our Lives* (1991), a sampling of program content that focuses on the sitcom *Diff'rent Strokes*. Other such studies include Paula Matabane, "Television and the Black Audience: Cultivating Moderate Perspectives on Racial Integration," *Journal of Communication* 38 (Autumn 1988): 21–38; Thomas R. Donohue, "Black Children's Perceptions of Favorite TV Characters as Models of Anti-Social Behavior," *Journal of Broadcasting* 19 (Spring 1975): 153–67; R. L. Allen and D. E. Clarke, "Ethnicity and Media Behavior: A Study of Blacks and Latinos," *Journal of Broadcasting* 24 (Winter 1980): 23–34; and Bradley S. Greenberg, the most prolific of these students of audience measurement, "Children's Reactions to TV Blacks," *Journalism Quarterly* 49 (Spring 1972): 5–14, an essay based on interviews with fourth and fifth graders. Sometimes performance itself is studied as a form of behavior, as in P. T. Reid, "Racial Stereotyping on Television: A Comparison of the Behavior of Both Black and White Television Characters," *Journal of Applied Psychology* 64 (Oct. 1979): 465–71.

One strain of this study of television as behavior is overtly political in intent, portraying the "image" of blacks as stereotyped and therefore unreal in its reflection of American social life, an ignominy for which a political solution is suggested. Among the most thorough of these are reports commissioned by federal agencies. See, for example, David L. Lange, Robert K. Baker, and Sandra Ball, *Mass Media and Violence: A Report to the National Commission on the Causes and Prevention of Violence,* particularly chap. 4, "Intergroup Communication": 43–66; Donald E. Ledwig, *To Know Ourselves: A Report to the 101st Congress on Public Broadcasting and the Needs of Minorities and Other Groups* (1989); and the previously cited *Window Dressing on the Set*. Such reports often inspired journalistic pleas for action. See, for example, Milan D. Meeske, "Black Ownership of Broadcast Stations: A FCC Licensing Problem," *Journal of Broadcasting* 20 (Spring 1976: 261–71), a report on three specific Southern stations. Another such essay, Clint C. Wilson II and Felix Guitierrez, *Minorities and the Media: Diversity and the End of Mass Communications* (1985), evokes another agency, the Equal Employment Opportunity Commission, as a possible agent of change.

As cited in *The Media and the Cities* (1968), academic institutes such as the University of Chicago Center for Policy Study sometimes took up the racial politics of broadcasting. One such report is Andrew W. Jackson, ed., *Black Families and the Medium of Television* (1982), a study by the Rush Program in Child Development and Social Policy of the University of Michigan.

Implicit in the literature of the scholarly and critical quarterlies is a similar call for change. See, for example, John F. Seggar, "Television's Portrayal of Minorities and Women, 1971–1975," *Journal of Broadcasting* 21 (Fall 1977): 435–46, one of several pieces by this author; Churchill Roberts, "The Portrayal of Blacks on Network Television," *Journal of Broadcasting* 15 (Winter 1970–71): 45–53; Sheila Smith Hobson, "The Rise and Fall of Blacks in Serious Television," *Freedomways* (3rd quarter, 1974): 185–99, one of a group of essays in a special issue, "The Black Image in the Mass Media"; Mary Ellison, "The Manipulating Eye: Black Images in Non-Documentary TV," *Journal of Popular Culture* 18 (1985): 73–80; Jannette L. Dates, "Thoughts on Black Stereotypes in Television," in Randall M. Miller, ed., *Ethnic Images in American Film and Television* (1978), proceedings of a lecture series sponsored by the Balch Institute of Philadelphia; Charlotte G. O'Kelly and Linda Edwards Bloomquist, "Women and Blacks on TV," *Journal of Communication* 26 (Aug. 1976): 179–84, a commentary on similar studies; and David Berkman, "Minorities in Public Broadcasting," *Journal of Communication* 30 (Summer 1980): 179–88. A broadly cast book on the subject is Bernard Rubin, ed., *Small Voices and Great Trumpets: Minorities and the Media* (1980).

Television, like movies, has produced an occasional cause célèbre that has focused and even defined the politics of the art of mass media. Two such products are *Amos 'n' Andy* and *Roots,* each for different reasons. The former program stirred a decades-long debate over the issue of bringing broad racial comedy to television while other forms of black performance were denied airtime. The definitive work on the show is Melvin Patrick Ely, *The Adventures of Amos 'n' Andy: A Social History of an American Phenomenon* (1991). Other scholarly works include Frank Wertheim, *Radio Comedy* (1979), for *Sam 'n' Henry,* a radio precursor of the show; Thomas Cripps, "Amos 'n' Andy and the Debate over American Racial Integration," in O'Connor, *American History/American Television;* and Arnold M. Shankman, "Black Pride and Protest: The Amos 'n' Andy Crusade," *Journal of Popular Culture* 12 (Fall 1978): 236–52. See also Norman Kagan, "Amos 'n' Andy: Twenty Years Late or Two Decades Early?" *Journal of Popular Culture* 9 (1975): 71–76.

Roots stirred debate over the achievement and effect of a long fictional tale rooted in part in the documents of slave times and in part in oral histories taken down by its author, Alex Haley. Apart from its mixed pedigree, *Roots* was the most celebrated event in the chronicle of the racial politics of the medium and is more richly documented than most broadcasting history. Primary sources for *Roots* may be found in the proceedings of several court trials, Haley's own papers at the University of Tennessee, and a firsthand account, David L. Wolper and Quincy Troupe, *The Inside Story of TV's Roots* (1978). The best essay on its history remains Leslie Fishbein, "*Roots:* Docudrama and the Interpretation of History," in O'Connor, *American History, American Television: Interpreting the Video Past* (1983). See also two essays on *Roots* taken from the *New York Times* and an original piece by Virginia B. Platt, "Authentic Sources and the Media," in which she invokes the German classicist Leopold von Ranke as a model for making "true" TV, all in James Monaco, ed., *Media Culture* (1978). And for a survey of research up to 1978, see Stuart S. Sulin, "'Roots' Research: A Sum of Findings," *Journal of Broadcasting* 22 (Summer 1978): 309–20.

What did *Roots* mean to America? The literature reflects a wish that the series might profoundly affect American racial arrangements. See, for example, David A. Gerber, "Haley's *Roots* and Our Own: Inquiry into the Nature of a Popular Phenomenon," *Journal of Ethnic Studies* 5 (Fall 1977): 87–111; a celebratory essay, Howard F. Stein, "In Search of *Roots:* An Epic of Origins and Destiny," *Journal of Popular Culture* 11 (Summer 1977): 11–17; Phillip Vandor, "On the Meaning of *Roots,*" *Journal of Communication* 27 (Autumn 1977): 64–69; and for a sample of appraisals, Horace Newcomb, ed., *Television: The Critical View* (2nd ed., 1979), "*Roots:* Eight Points of View."

Empirical studies of audience samples proliferated following the splash made by *Roots*. For a sample of the genre, see Robert E. Balon, "The Impact of *Roots* on a Racially Heterogeneous Southern Community [Austin, Texas]," *Journal of Broadcasting* 22 (Summer 1978): 299–307; John Rothbart Howard and Lee Sloan, "The Response to *Roots:* A National Survey," *Journal of Broadcasting* 22 (Summer 1978): 279–87; and Ken K. Hur and John B. Robinson, "The Social Impact of 'Roots,'" *Journalism Quarterly* 55 (Spring 1978): 19–24.

At the top of this essay I referred to the rapidly opening access to the visual and written record of African-Americans—as both creative agents and as subjects of the media of the moving image—as "nothing less than a revolution." After reviewing the available materials we can reaffirm this phenomenon and also predict its continued acceleration into as yet unimagined research sources. This means not only a future of ever more sophisticated inquiry, much of it probably increasingly interactive, but also an ever quickening rate of obsolescence of finding aids, guides to research, and other compendia. Thus, for instance, a resourceful user will wish to develop personal research tools that will take into account rapidly changing Internet addresses. Each new resource will make for even greater access to the primary records that make the writing of history and criticism possible.

II

COMPREHENSIVE AND CHRONOLOGICAL HISTORIES

13 *Comprehensive Studies*

13.1 GENERAL STUDIES

Adler, Mortimer J., Charles Van Doren, and George Ducas, ed., *The Negro in American History* (3 vols., 1969).

Altman, Susan, *The Encyclopedia of African-American Heritage* (1997).

Appiah, Kwame Anthony, and Henry Louis Gates, Jr., ed., *Africana: The Encylopedia of the African and African American Experience* (1999).

Aptheker, Herbert, ed., *A Documentary History of the Negro People in the United States* (7 vols., 1951–1994).

——— *Essays in the History of the American Negro* (1945).

Bardolph, Richard, *The Negro Vanguard* (1959).

Bennett, Lerone, Jr., *Before the Mayflower: A History of Black America* (6th ed., 1993).

Bergman, Peter M., and Mort M. Bergman, comp., *The Chronological History of the Negro in America* (1969).

Berry, Mary Frances, and John W. Blassingame, *Long Memory: The Black Experience in America* (1982).

"Black Popular Culture," *Journal of Popular Culture* 4 [special issue] (1971).

Boles, John B., *Black Southerners, 1619–1869* (1983).

Brawley, Benjamin Griffith, *A Social History of the American Negro: Being a History of the Negro Problem in the United States, Including a History and Study of the Republic of Liberia* (1921).

Broom, Leonard, and Norval D. Glenn, *Transformation of the American Negro* (1965).

Christian, Charles M., and Sari J. Bennett, *Black Saga: The African American Experience* (1995).

Collins, Charles, and David Cohen, ed., *The African Americans* (1993).

Coombs, Norman, *The Black Experience in America* (1972).

Cromwell, John Wesley, *The Negro in American History: Men and Women Eminent in the Evolution of the American of African Descent* (1914).

Curtis, Nancy C., *Black Heritage Sites: An African-American Odyssey and Finder's Guide* (1996).

Diggs, Irene, "The Biological and Cultural Impact of Blacks on the United States," *Phylon* 41 (1980): 153–66.

Dormon, James H., *The Afro-American Experience: A Cultural History through Emancipation* (1974).

Du Bois, William Edward Burghardt, *The Gift of Black Folk: The Negroes in the Making of America* (1924).

Ellison, Mary, *The Black Experience: American Blacks since 1865* (1974).

Fabre, Geneviève, and Robert O'Meally, ed., *History and Memory in African-American Culture* (1994).

Field, Ron, *African Peoples of the Americas: From Slavery to Civil Rights* (1995).

Fishel, Leslie H., Jr., and Benjamin Quarles, ed., *The Black American: A Documentary History* (1970).

Foner, Philip S., *Essays in Afro-American History* (1978).

Franklin, John Hope, and Alfred A. Moss, *From Slavery to Freedom: A History of African Americans* (8th ed., 1999).

211

Frazier, E. Franklin, *The Negro in the United States* (rev. ed., 1957).

Fredrickson, George M., *Black Liberation: A Comparative History of Black Ideologies in the United States and South Africa* (1995).

Gaines, Kevin K., *Uplifting the Race: Black Leadership, Politics, and Culture in the Twentieth Century* (1996).

Goode, Kenneth G., *From Africa to the United States and Then . . . : A Concise Afro-American History* (2d ed., 1976).

Grant, Joanne, ed., *Black Protest: History, Documents, and Analyses, 1619 to the Present* (1968).

Green, Fletcher M., and J. Isaac Copeland, comp., *The Old South* (1980).

Harding, Vincent, *The Other American Revolution* (1980).

Harris, Middleton, *The Black Book* (1974).

Hay, Frederick J., *African-American Community Studies from North America: A Classified, Annotated Bibliography* (1991).

Henderson, Alexa Benson, and Janice Sumler-Edmund, *Freedom's Odyssey: African American History Essays from* Phylon (1999).

Hine, Darlene Clark, ed., *Black Women in American History: The Twentieth Century* (1990).

Hine, Darlene Clark, Elsa Barkley Brown, and Rosalyn Terborg-Penn, ed., *Black Women in America: An Historical Encyclopedia* (2 vols., 1993).

Hine, Darlene Clark, Wilma King, and Linda Reed, ed., *"We Specialize in the Wholly Impossible": A Reader in Black Women's History* (1995).

Hine, Darlene Clark, and Jacqueline McLeod, ed., *Crossing Boundaries: Comparative History of Black People in Diaspora* (1999).

Hine, Darlene Clark, and Kathleen Thompson, *A Shining Thread of Hope: The History of Black Women in America* (1998).

Horton, James Oliver, and Lois E. Horton, *A History of the African American People: The History, Traditions, and Culture of African Americans* (1997).

Huggins, Nathan I., Martin Kilson, and Daniel M. Fox, ed., *Key Issues in the Afro-American Experience* (2 vols., 1971).

Hughes, Langston, Milton Meltzer, and C. Eric Lincoln, *A Pictorial History of Blackamericans* (5th rev. ed., 1983).

Issacs, Harold R., *The New World of Negro Americans* (1963).

Johnson, Charles S., *The Negro in American Civilization: A Study of Negro Life and Race Relations in the Light of Social Research* (1930).

Kaplan, Sidney, *American Studies in Black and White: Selected Essays, 1949–1989,* ed. Allan D. Austin (1991).

Katz, William Loren, ed., *Eyewitness: A Living Documentary of the African American Contribution to American History* (1995).

Kilson, Marion, "Afro-American Social Structure, 1790–1970," in Martin L. Kilson, and Robert I. Rotberg, ed., *The African Diaspora: Interpretive Essays* (1976): 414–58.

Leonard, William Torbet, *Masquerade in Black* (1986).

Levine, Lawrence W., *Black Culture and Black Consciousness: Afro-American Folk Thought from Slavery to Freedom* (1977).

Lincoln, C. Eric, *The Negro Pilgrimage in America: The Coming of Age of the Black Americans* (rev. ed., 1969).

Marable, Manning, and Leith Mullings, ed., *Let Nobody Turn Us Around: Voices of Resistance, Reform, and Renewal: An African American Anthology* (2000).

Meier, August, and Elliott M. Rudwick, *Along the Color Line: Explorations in the Black Experience* (1976).

———— *From Plantation to Ghetto: An Interpretive History of American Negroes* (3d ed., 1976).

————, ed., *The Making of Black America: Essays in Negro Life and History* (2 vols., 1969).

Meltzer, Milton, ed., *In Their Own Words: A History of the American Negro, 1618–1865* (1964).

Newby, I. A., *The South: A History* (1978).

Newman, Richard, and Marcia Sawyer, *Everybody Say Freedom: Everything You Need to Know about African-American History* (1996).

Ottley, Roi, *Black Odyssey: The Story of the Negro in America* (1948).

Parsons, Talcott, and Kenneth B. Clark, ed., *The Negro American* (1966).

Patterson, Orlando, *Rituals of Blood: Consequences of Slavery in Two American Centuries* (1998).

Piersen, William D., *From Africa to America: African American History from the Colonial Era to the Early Republic, 1526–1790* (1996).

Quarles, Benjamin, *Black Mosaic: Essays in Afro-American History and Historiography* (1988).

———— *The Negro in the Making of America* (2d ed., 1987).

Ravage, John W., *Black Pioneers: Images of the Black Experience on the North American Frontier* (1997).

Redding, J. Saunders, *They Came in Chains: Americans from Africa* (1950).

Riley, Carroll L., "Blacks in the Early Southwest," *Ethnohistory* 19 (1972): 247–60.

Salzman, Jack, David Lionel Smith, and Cornel West, ed., *Encyclopedia of African-American Culture and History* (1996).

Segal, Ronald, *The Black Diaspora* (1995).

Sollors, Werner, and Maria Diedrich, ed., *The Black Columbiad: Defining Moments in African American Literature and Culture* (1994).

Stokes, Melvyn, and Rick Halpern, ed., *Race and Class in the American South since 1890* (1994).

Taylor, Arnold, *Travail and Triumph: Black Life and Culture in the South since the Civil War* (1976).

Taylor, Quintard, *In Search of the Racial Frontier: African Americans in the American West, 1528–1900* (1999).

Thompson, Daniel C., *Sociology of the Black Experience* (1974).

Thompson, V. B., *The Making of the African Diaspora in the Americas, 1441–1900* (1987).

Toppin, Edgar A., *A Biographical History of Blacks in America since 1528* (1971).

Van Deusen, John George, *The Black Man in White America* (1938).

Wesley, Charles H., *In Freedom's Footsteps: From the African Background to the Civil War* (1968).

Weyl, Nathaniel, *The Negro in American Civilization* (1960).

White, John, *Black Leadership in America, 1895–1968* (1985).

Williams, George Washington, *History of the Negro Race in America from 1619 to 1880* (2 vols., 1883).

Williams, Lorraine, ed., *Africa and the Afro-American Experience* (1977).

Woods, N. Frank, *Picturing a People: A History of African Americans from 1619–1900* (1997).

Woodson, Carter G., *The African Background Outlined* (1936).

Woodson, Carter G., and Charles H. Wesley, *The Negro in Our History* (12th ed., rev. and enlarged, 1972).

Wright, Richard, and Edwin Rosskam, *Twelve Million Black Voices: A Folk History of the Negro in the United States* (1941).

13.2   HISTORIOGRAPHY

Axelrod, Stanley, "The Treatment of the Negro in American History School Textbooks," *Negro History Bulletin* 29 (1966): 135–44.

Blassingame, John W., "The Afro-Americans: From Mythology to Reality," in William H. Cartwright and Richard L. Watson, Jr., ed., *The Reinterpretation of American History and Culture* (1973): 53–79.

Blight, David W., "Nathan Irvin Huggins, the Art of History, and the Irony of the American Dream," *Reviews in American History* 22 (1994): 174–90.

Butchart, Ronald E., "'Outthinking and Outflanking the Owners of the World': A Historiography of the African American Struggle for Education," *History of Education Quarterly* 28 (1988): 333–66.

Carpenter, Mary Elizabeth, *The Treatment of the Negro in the American History School Textbooks* (1941).

Carter, Dan T., "From Segregation to Integration," in John B. Boles and Evelyn Thomas Nolen, ed., *Interpreting Southern History: Historiographical Essays in Honor of Sanford W. Higginbotham* (1987): 408–33.

Cimbala, Paul A., and Robert F. Himmelberg, ed., *Historians and Race: Autobiography and the Writing of History* (1996).

Davis, David Brion, "Constructing Race: A Reflection," *William and Mary Quarterly* 54 (1997): 7–18.

——— "Slavery and the Post-World War II Historians," *Daedalus* 103 (1974): 1–16.

de Graaf, Lawrence B., "Recognition, Racism, and Reflections on the Writing of Western Black History," *Pacific Historical Review* 44 (1975): 22–51.

Drimmer, Melvin, *Issues in Black History: Reflections and Commentaries on the Black Historical Experience* (1987).

Du Bois, William Edward Burghardt, *Black Folk, Then and Now: An Essay on the History and Sociology of the Negro Race* (1939).

Fields, Barbara J., "Ideology and Race in American History," in J. Morgan Kousser and James M. McPherson, ed., *Region, Race and Reconstruction: Essays in Honor of C. Vann Woodward* (1982): 143–77.

——— "Slavery, Race, and Ideology in the United States of America," *New Left Review* 181 (1990): 95–118.

Franklin, John Hope, *Race and History: Selected Essays, 1938–1988* (1989).

Franklin, Vincent P., and James D. Anderson, ed., *New Perspectives on Black Educational History* (1978).

Fredrickson, George M., *The Arrogance of Race: Historical Perspectives on Slavery, Racism, and Social Inequality* (1988).

Genovese, Eugene D., *In Red and Black: Marxian Explorations in Southern and Afro-American History* (1971).

Goggin, Jacqueline, "Carter G. Woodson and the Collection of Source Materials for Afro-American History," *American Archivist* 48 (1985): 261–71.

Goings, Kenneth W., and Raymond A. Mohl, ed., *The New African American Urban History* (1996).

Greene, Lorenzo J., *Selling Black History for Carter G. Woodson: A Diary, 1930–1933,* ed. Arvarh E. Strickland (1996).

Harding, Vincent, *Beyond Chaos: Black History and the Search for the New Land* (1970).

Haynes, Robert V., comp., *Blacks in White America before 1865: Issues and Interpretations* (1972).

Hellwig, David J., "Afro-American Views of Immigrants, 1830–1930: An Historiographical-Bibliographical Essay," *Immigration History Newsletter* 13 (1981): 1–5.

Higginbotham, Evelyn Brooks, "Beyond the Sound of Silence: Afro-American Women in History," in Darlene Clark Hine, ed., *Black Women's History: Theory and Practice* (1990): 175–92.

——— "African-American Women's History and the Metalanguage of Race," *Signs* 17 (1992): 251–74.

Hine, Darlene Clark, *Hine Sight: Black Women and the Re-Construction of American History* (1994).

Hine, Darlene Clark, ed., *The State of Afro-American History: Past, Present, and Future* (1986).

Holt, Thomas C., "Explaining Race in American History," in Anthony Molho, and Gordon S. Wood, ed., *Imagined Histories: American Historians Interpret the Past* (1998): 107–19.

——— "Marking: Race, Race-Making, and the Writing of History," *American Historical Review* 100 (1995): 1–19.

Holt, Thomas C., and Elsa Barkley Brown, *Major Problems in African American History* (1999).

Huggins, Nathan I., *Revelations: American History, American Myths,* ed. Brenda Smith Huggins (1995).

Hull, Gloria T., Patricia Bell Scott, and Barbara Smith, ed., *All the Women Are White, All the Blacks Are Men, But Some of Us Are Brave: Black Women's Studies* (1982).

Keita, Maghan, *Race and the Writing of History: Riddling the Sphinx* (2000).

Kelley, Robin D. G., "'But a Local Phase of a World Problem,': Black History's Global Vision, 1883–1950," *Journal of American History* 86 (1999): 1045–77.

Kiple, Kenneth F., "A Survey of Recent Literature on the Biological Past of the Black," in Kenneth F. Kiple, ed., *The African Exchange: Toward a Biological History of Black People* (1987): 7–34.

Kusmer, Kenneth L., "Urban Black History at the Crossroads," *Journal of Urban History* 13 (1987): 460–70.

Lewis, Earl, "To Turn As on a Pivot: Writing African-Americans into a History of Overlapping Diasporas," *American Historical Review* 100 (1995): 765–87.

Meier, August, "Benjamin Quarles and the Historiography of Black America," *Civil War History* 26 (1980): 101–16.

——— "Whither the Black Perspective in Afro-American Historiography?" *Journal of American History* 70 (1983): 101–05.

Meier, August, and Elliott M. Rudwick, *Black History and the Historical Profession, 1915–1980* (1986).

———— "J. Franklin Jameson, Carter G. Woodson, and the Foundations of Black Historiography," *American Historical Review* 89 (1984): 1005–15.

————, ed., *The Making of Black America: Essays in Negro Life and History* (2 vols., 1969).

Morton, Patricia, *Disfigured Images: The Historical Assault on Afro-American Women* (1991).

Moses, Wilson Jeremiah, *Afrotopia: The Roots of African American Popular History* (1998).

Nash, Gary B., "The Hidden History of Mestizo America," *Journal of American History* 82 (1995): 941–64.

Quarles, Benjamin, *Black Mosaic: Essays in Afro-American History and Historiography* (1988).

Ramsey, Guthrie P., Jr., "Cosmopolitan or Provincial? Ideology in Early Black Music Historiography, 1867–1940," *Black Music Research Journal* 16 (1996): 11–42.

Scott, Daryl Michael, *Contempt and Pity: Social Policy and the Image of the Damaged Black Psyche, 1880–1996* (1997).

Scruggs, Otey, "Carter G. Woodson, the Negro History Movement, and Africa," *Pan African Journal* 7 (1974): 37–50.

Sensbach, Jon F., "Charting a Course in Early African-American History," *William and Mary Quarterly* 50 (1993): 394–405.

Shapiro, Herbert, ed., *African American History and Radical Historiography: Essays in Honor of Herbert Aptheker* (1998).

Shepperson, George, "The Afro-American Contribution to African Studies," *Journal of American Studies* 8 (1974): 281–301.

Thorpe, Earl E., *The Central Theme of Black History* (1969).

———— *The Mind of the Negro: An Intellectual History of Afro-Americans* (1961).

Trotter, Joe William, Jr., "African-American Workers: New Directions in United States Labor Historiography," *Labor History* 35 (1994): 495–523.

Walker, Clarence E., "The American Negro as Historical Outsider, 1836–1935," *Canadian Review of American Studies* 17 (1986): 137–54.

———— *Deromanticizing Black History: Critical Essays and Reappraisals* (1991).

Williamson, Joel, "Wounds Not Scars: Lynching, the National Conscience, and the American Historian," with responses by Edward L. Ayers, David W. Blight, George M. Fredrickson, Robin D. G. Kelley, David Levering Lewis, Steven M. Stowe, and Jacqueline Dowd Hall, *Journal of American History* 83 (1997): 1217–72.

Winston, Michael R., "Through the Back Door: Academic Racism and the Negro Scholar in Historical Perspective," *Daedalus*: 678–719.

13.3 SECONDARY SOURCES ON NEWSPAPERS AND PERIODICALS

Belles, A. Gilbert, "The Black Press in Illinois," *Journal of the Illinois State Historical Society* 68 (1975): 344–52.

Bullock, Penelope L., *The Afro-American Periodical Press, 1838–1909* (1981).

Daniel, Walter C., *Black Journals of the United States* (1982).

Danky, James P., and Maureen E. Hady, ed., *African-American Newspapers and Periodicals: A National Bibliography* (1998).

Dann, Martin E., ed., *The Black Press, 1827–1890: The Quest for National Identity* (1971).

Detweiler, Frederick German, *The Negro Press in the United States* (1922).

Doreski, C. K., *Writing America Black: Race Rhetoric in the Public Sphere* (1998).

Farrar, Hayward, *The Baltimore Afro-American, 1892–1950* (1998).

Johnson, Abby Arthur, and Ronald Maberry Johnson, *Propaganda and Aesthetics: The Literary Politics of Afro-American Magazines in the Twentieth Century* (1979).

Kimbrough, Marvin G., *Black Magazines: An Exploratory Study* (1973).

North Carolina Central University, School of Library Science, African American Materials Project, *Newspapers and Periodicals by and about Black People: Southeastern Library Holdings* (1978).

Oak, Vishnu Vitthal, *The Negro Newspaper* (1948).

O'Kelly, Charlotte G., "Black Newspapers and the Black Protest Movement: Their Historical Relationship, 1827–1945," *Phylon* 43 (1982): 1–14.

Partington, Paul G., *The* Moon Illustrated Weekly: *Black America's First Weekly Magazine* (1986).

Penn, I. Garland, *The Afro-American Press and Its Editors* (1891).

Shaw, Donald Lewis, "News about Slavery from 1820–1860 in Newspapers of South, North, and West," *Journalism Quarterly* 61 (1984): 483–92.

Simmons, Charles A., *The African American Press: A History of News Coverage during National Crises, with Special Reference to Four Black Newspapers, 1827–1965* (1998).

Snorgrass, J. William, "Pioneer Black Women Journalists from the 1850s to the 1950s," *Western Journal of Black Studies* 6 (1982): 150–58.

Stevens, John D., "Reflections in a Dark Mirror: Comic Strips in Black Newspapers," *Journal of Popular Culture* 10 (1976): 239–44.

Streitmatter, Rodger, *Raising Her Voice: African-American Women Journalists Who Changed History* (1994).

Suggs, Henry Lewis, ed., *The Black Press in the South, 1865–1979* (1983).

———, ed., *The Black Press in the Middle West, 1865–1965* (1996).

Thompson, Julius E., *The Black Press in Mississippi, 1865–1985* (1988).

Wolseley, Roland Edgar, *Black Press U.S.A.* (2d ed., 1990).

13.4   RACE RELATIONS

13.4.1   Slave Trade

Berlin, Ira, "The Slave Trade and the Development of Afro-American Society in English Mainland North America, 1619–1775," *Southern Studies* 20 (1981): 122–36.

Curtin, Philip D., *The Atlantic Slave Trade: A Census* (1969).

——— "The Atlantic Slave Trade, 1600–1800," *History of West Africa* 1 (1972): 240–68.

——— *The Rise and Fall of the Plantation Complex: Essays on Atlantic History* (1990).

Donnan, Elizabeth, ed., *Documents Illustrative of the History of the Slave Trade to America* (4 vols., 1930–1935).

Du Bois, William Edward Burghardt, *The Suppression of the African Slave Trade to the United States of America, 1638–1870* (1896).

Duignan, Peter, and Clarence Clendenen, *The United States and the African Slave Trade, 1619–1862* (1963).

Eltis, David, "Free and Coerced Transatlantic Migrations: Some Comparisons," *American Historical Review* 88 (1983): 251–80.

——— *The Rise of African Slavery in the Americas* (2000).

Eltis, David, and Stanley L. Engerman, "Fluctuations in Sex and Age Ratios in the Transatlantic Slave Trade, 1663–1864," *Economic History Review* 46 (1993): 308–23.

Eltis, David, and Norman P. Girvan, "The Economic Impact of the Ending of the African Slave Trade to the Americas," *Social and Economic Studies* 37 (1988): 143–72.

Engerman, Stanley L., "The Atlantic Economy of the Eighteenth Century: Some Speculations on Economic Development in Britain, America, Africa, and Elsewhere," *Journal of European Economic History* 24 (1995): 145–75.

Faber, Eli, *Jews, Slaves, and the Slave Trade: Setting the Record Straight* (1998).

Inikori, Joseph E., "Measuring the Atlantic Slave Trade: An Assessment of Curtin and Anstey," *Journal of African History* 17 (1976): 197–223.

——— "The Slave Trade and the Atlantic Economies, 1451–1870," in Unesco, *The African Slave Trade from the Fifteenth to the Nineteenth Century* (1979): 56–87.

Klein, Herbert S., *The Atlantic Slave Trade* (1999).

——— "Slaves and Shipping in Eighteenth-Century Virginia," *Journal of Interdisciplinary History* 5 (1975): 383–412.

Mannix, Daniel P., and Malcolm Cowley, *Black Cargoes: A History of the Atlantic Slave Trade, 1518–1865* (1962).

Miller, Joseph C., "Mortality in the Atlantic Slave Trade: Statistical Evidence on Causality," *Journal of Interdisciplinary History* 11 (1981): 385–423.

Minchinton, W. E., "Western Europe and the Atlantic Economy in the Eighteenth Century," *Bijdragen en Mededelingen Betreffende de Geschiedenis der Nederlanden* 91 (1976): 273–92.

Piersen, William D., "White Cannibals, Black Martyrs: Fear, Depression, and Religious Faith as Causes of Suicide among New Slaves," *Journal of Negro History* 62 (1977): 147–51.

Richardson, David, "Across the Desert and the Sea: Trans-Saharan and Atlantic Slavery, 1500–1900," *Historical Journal* 38 (1995): 195–204.

Thomas, Hugh, *The Slave Trade: The Story of the Atlantic Slave Trade: 1440–1870* (1999).

13.4.2   Slavery

Abzug, Robert H., and Stephen E. Maizlish, ed., *New Perspectives on Race and Slavery in America: Essays in Honor of Kenneth M. Stampp* (1986).

Azevedo, Celia M., *Abolitionism in the United States and Brazil: A Comparative Perspective* (1995).

Beckles, Hilary, and Verene Shepherd, ed., *Caribbean Slave Society and Economy* (1991).

Berlin, Ira, *Many Thousands Gone: The First Two Centuries of Slavery in North America* (1998).

Blassingame, John W., *The Slave Community: Plantation Life in the Antebellum South* (rev. and enlarged ed., 1979).

———, ed., *Slave Testimony: Two Centuries of Letters, Speeches, Interviews, and Autobiographies* (1977).

Catterall, Helen Tunnicliff, ed., *Judicial Cases Concerning American Slavery and the Negro* (5 vols., 1926–1937).

David, Paul A., Herbert G. Gutman, Richard Sutch, Peter Temin, and Gavin Wright, *Reckoning With Slavery: A Critical Study in the Quantitative History of American Negro Slavery* (1976).

Davis, David Brion, *From Homicide to Slavery: Studies in American Culture* (1986).

——— *The Problem of Slavery in Western Culture* (1966).

——— *Slavery and Human Progress* (1984).

——— "Slavery and the Post-World War II Historians," *Daedalus* 103 (1974): 1–16.

Davis, T. R., "Negro Servitude in the United States," *Journal of Negro History* 8 (1923): 247–83.

Degler, Carl N., *Neither Black nor White: Slavery and Race Relations in Brazil and the United States* (1971).

Dillon, Merton Lynn, *Slavery Attacked: Southern Slaves and Their Allies, 1619–1865* (1990).

Drescher, Seymour, and Stanley L. Engerman, ed., *A Historical Guide to World Slavery* (1998).

Elkins, Stanley, *Slavery: A Problem in American Institutional and Intellectual Life* (3d ed., 1976).

Eltis, David, "Labour and Coercion in the English Atlantic World from the Seventeenth to the Early Twentieth Century," *Slavery and Abolition* 14 (1993): 207–26.

Engerman, Stanley L., and Eugene D. Genovese, ed., *Race and Slavery in the Western Hemisphere: Quantitative Studies* (1975).

Federal Writers' Project, *Lay My Burden Down: A Folk History of Slavery* (1945).

Finkelman, Paul, ed., *Slavery and the Law* (1996).

———, ed., *Slavery, Race, and the American Legal System, 1700–1872* (7 series, 1988).

Fogel, Robert W., and Stanley L. Engerman, *Time on the Cross: The Economics of American Negro Slavery* (1974).

——— *Time on the Cross: Evidence and Methods: A Supplement* (1974).

Fogel, Robert W., *Without Consent or Contract: The Rise and Fall of American Slavery* (1989).

Fogel, Robert W., and Stanley L. Engerman, ed., *Without Consent or Contract: The Rise and Fall of American Slavery: Technical Papers* (2 vols., 1992).

Fogel, Robert W., Ralph A. Galantine, and Richard L. Manning, ed., *Without Consent or Contract: The Rise and Fall of American Slavery: Evidence and Methods* (1992).

Gaspar, David Barry, and Darlene Clark Hine, ed., *More Than Chattel: Black Women and Slavery in the Americas* (1996).

Genovese, Eugene D., *From Rebellion to Revolution: Afro-American Slave Revolts in the Making of the Modern World* (1979).

———— *Roll, Jordan, Roll: The World the Slaves Made* (1974).

———— *The World the Slaveholders Made* (1969).

Goodheart, Lawrence B., Richard D. Brown, and Stephen G. Rabe, ed., *Slavery in American Society* (3d ed., 1993).

Greenberg, Kenneth S., *Masters and Statesmen: The Political Culture of American Slavery* (1985).

Gutman, Herbert G., *The Black Family in Slavery and Freedom, 1750–1925* (1976).

Harris, J. William, ed., *Society and Culture in the Slave South* (1992).

Harris, Marvin, *Patterns of Race in the Americas* (1964).

Huggins, Nathan I., *Black Odyssey: The Afro-American Ordeal in Slavery* (1977).

Jordan, Winthrop D., *White Over Black: American Attitudes Toward the Negro, 1550–1812* (1968).

Klein, Herbert S., *Slavery in the Americas: A Comparative Study of Virginia and Cuba* (1967).

Kolchin, Peter, *American Slavery, 1619–1877* (1993).

———— *Unfree Labor: American Slavery and Russian Serfdom* (1987).

Lane, Ann J., ed., *The Debate Over Slavery: Stanley Elkins and His Critics* (1971).

McKenzie, Edna B., *Freedom in the Midst of a Slave Society* (1980).

Mellon, James, ed., *Bullwhip Days: The Slaves Remember* (1988).

Mintz, Sidney, ed., *Slavery, Colonialism, and Racism* (1975).

Morris, Thomas D., *Southern Slavery and the Law, 1619–1860* (1996).

Mullin, Michael, ed., *American Negro Slavery: A Documentary History* (1976).

Parish, Peter J., *Slavery: History and Historians* (1989).

Patterson, Orlando, *Slavery and Social Death: A Comparative Study* (1982).

Price, Richard, ed., *Maroon Societies: Rebel Slave Communities in the Americas* (3d ed., 1996).

Rawick, George P., ed., *The American Slave: A Composite Autobiography* (19 vols., 1973–1976).

————, ed., *The American Slave: A Composite Autobiography: Supplement, Series 1* (12 vols., 1977).

————, ed., *The American Slave: A Composite Autobiography: Supplement, Series 2* (10 vols., 1979).

Rose, Willie Lee, ed., *A Documentary History of Slavery in North America* (1976).

Rubin, Vera, and Arthur Tuden, ed., *Comparative Perspectives on Slavery in New World Plantation Societies* (1977).

Small, Stephen, "Racial Group Boundaries and Identities: People of 'Mixed Race' in Slavery across the Americas," *Slavery and Abolition* 15 (1994): 17–37.

Stampp, Kenneth M., *The Peculiar Institution: Slavery in the Antebellum South* (1956).

Stevenson, Brenda E., *Life in Black and White: Family and Community in the Slave South* (1996).

Stuckey, Sterling, *Slave Culture: Nationalist Theory and the Foundations of Black America* (1987).

Tadman, Michael, *Speculators and Slaves: Masters, Traders, and Slaves in the Old South* (1989).

Tannenbaum, Frank, *Slave and Citizen: The Negro in the Americas* (1946).

Van Deburg, William L., *Slavery and Race in American Popular Culture* (1984).

Walsh, Lorena Seebach, *From Calabar to Carter's Grove: The History of a Virginia Slave Community* (1997).

Watson, Alan D., *Slave Law in the Americas* (1989).

White, Deborah Gray, *Ar'n't I a Woman? Female Slaves in the Plantation South* (1985).

White, Shane, and Graham White, "Slave Clothing and African-American Culture in the Eighteenth and Nineteenth Centuries," *Past and Present* 148 (1995): 149–86.

13.4.3   Black/White Relations

Baker, Lee D., *From Savage to Negro: Anthropology and the Construction of Race, 1896–1954* (1998).

Bay, Mia, *The White Image in the Black Mind: African-American Ideas about White People, 1830–1925* (1999).

Butcher, Margaret Just, *The Negro in American Culture: Based on Materials Left by Alain Locke* (rev. and updated ed., 1971).

Cassity, Michael J., *Chains of Fear: American Race Relations since Reconstruction* (1984).

———— *Legacy of Fear: American Race Relations to 1900* (1985).

Degler, Carl N., *The Other South: Southern Dissenters in the Nineteenth Century* (1974).

Feldstein, Stanley, comp., *The Poisoned Tongue: A Documentary History of American Racism and Prejudice* (1972).

Foner, Philip S., *American Socialism and Black Americans: From the Age of Jackson to World War II* (1977).

Franklin, John Hope, *The Color Line: Legacy for the Twenty-First Century* (1993).

Fredrickson, George M., *The Arrogance of Race: Historical Perspectives on Slavery, Racism, and Social Inequality* (1988).

Frost, Peter, "Fair Women, Dark Men: The Forgotten Roots of Colour Prejudice," *History of European Ideas* 12 (1990): 669–79.

George, Nelson, *Blackface: Reflections on African Americans and the Movies* (1994).

Goings, Kenneth W., *Mammy and Uncle Mose: Black Collectibles and American Stereotyping* (1994).

Gossett, Thomas F., *Race: The History of an Idea in America* (1963).

Grimshaw, Allen D., "Lawlessness and Violence in America and Their Special Manifestations in Changing Negro-White Relationships," *Journal of Negro History* 44 (1959): 52–72.

Gubar, Susan, *Racechanges: White Skin, Black Face in American Culture* (1997).

Hodes, Martha, ed., *Sex, Love, Race: Crossing Boundaries in North American History* (1999).

———— *White Women, Black Men: Illicit Sex in the Nineteenth-Century South* (1997).

Inscoe, John C., ed., *Georgia in Black and White: Explorations in the Race Relations of a Southern State, 1865–1950* (1994).

Iton, Richard, *Solidarity Blues: Race, Culture, and the American Left* (2000).

Jordan, Winthrop D., *White Over Black: American Attitudes Toward the Negro, 1550–1812* (1968).

Kern-Foxworth, Marilyn, *Aunt Jemima, Uncle Ben, and Rastus: Blacks in Advertising, Yesterday, Today, and Tomorrow* (1994).

MacCann, Donnarae, *White Supremacy in Children's Literature: Characterizations of African Americans, 1830–1900* (1998).

Marx, Anthony W., "Contested Citizenship: The Dynamics of Racial Identity and Social Movements," *International Review of Social History* 40 (1995): 159–83.

———— "Race-Making and the Nation-State," *World Politics* 48 (1996): 180–208.

Mercier, John Dennis, *The Evolution of the Black Image in White Consciousness, 1876–1954: A Popular Culture Perspective* (1984).

Myrdal, Gunnar, *An American Dilemma: The Negro Problem and Modern Democracy* (1944).

Osofsky, Gilbert, *The Burden of Race: A Documentary History of Negro-White Relations in America* (1967).

Reimers, David M., *White Protestantism and the Negro* (1965).

Riggs, Marlon, prod., *Ethnic Notions* (videocassette, 1986).

Roediger, David R., ed., *Black on White: Black Writers on What It Means to Be White* (1998).

Sanders, Ronald, *Lost Tribes and Promised Lands: The Origins of American Racism* (1978).

Suthern, Orrin Clayton, "Minstrelsy and Popular Culture," *Journal of Popular Culture* 4 (1971): 658–73.

Takaki, Ronald T., *Iron Cages: Race and Culture in Nineteenth Century America* (1979).

Tillman, James A., Jr., and Mary Norman Tillman, "Black Intellectuals, White Liberals, and Race Relations: An Analytic Overview," *Phylon* 33 (1972): 54–66.

Toll, Robert C., *Blacking Up: The Minstel Show in Nineteenth-Century America* (1974).

Turner, Jonathan H., Royce Singleton, Jr., and David Musick, *Oppression: A Socio-History of Black-White Relations in America* (1984).

Turner, Patricia A., *Ceramic Uncles and Celluloid Mammies: Black Images and Their Influence on Culture* (1994).

Van Deburg, William L., *Slavery and Race in American Popular Culture* (1984).

Williamson, Joel, *The Crucible of Race: Black/White Relations in the American South since Emancipation* (1984).

Wittke, Carl, *Tambo and Bones: A History of the American Minstrel Stage* (1930).

13.4.4 Black/Native American Relations

Cornell, Stephen, "Land, Labour and Group Formation: Blacks and Indians in the United States," *Ethnic and Racial Studies* 13 (1990): 368–88.

Dinnerstein, Leonard, Roger L. Nichols, and David M. Reimers, *Natives and Strangers: Blacks, Indians, and Immigrants in America* (2d ed., 1990).

Forbes, Jack D., *Black Africans and Native Americans: Color, Race, and Caste in the Evolution of Red-Black Peoples* (1988).

———— "Mustees, Half-Breeds, and Zambos in Anglo North America: Aspects of Black-Indian Relations," *American Indian Quarterly* 7 (1983): 57–83.

Littlefield, Daniel F., Jr., *Africans and Seminoles: From Removal to Emancipation* (1977).

———— *Africans and Creeks: From the Colonial Period to the Civil War* (1979).

Mandell, Daniel R., "Shifting Boundaries of Race and Ethnicity: Indian-Black Intermarriage in Southern New England, 1760–1880," *Journal of American History* 85 (1998): 466–501.

May, Katja, *African Americans and Native Americans in the Creek and Cherokee Nations, 1830s to 1920s: Collision and Collusion* (1996).

Nash, Gary B., "The Hidden History of Mestizo America," *Journal of American History* 82 (1995): 941–64.

Parry, Ellwood, *The Image of the Indian and the Black Man in American Arts, 1590–1900* (1974).

Silver, Timothy, *A New Face on the Countryside: Indians, Colonists, and Slaves in South Atlantic Forests, 1500–1800* (1990).

13.4.5 Black/Ethnic Relations

Berson, Lenora E., *The Negroes and the Jews* (1971).

Clark, Dennis, "Urban Blacks and Irishmen: Brothers in Prejudice," in Miriam Ershkowitz and Joseph Zikmund, II, ed., *Black Politics in Philadelphia* (1973): 15–30.

Dinnerstein, Leonard, Roger L. Nichols, and David M. Reimers, *Natives and Strangers: Blacks, Indians, and Immigrants in America* (2d ed., 1990).

Franklin, V. P., Genna Rae McNeil, Nancy L. Grant, and Harold M. Kletnick, ed., *African Americans and Jews in the Twentieth Century: Studies in Convergence and Conflict* (1998).

Fuchs, Lawrence H., *The American Kaleidoscope: Race, Ethnicity, and the Civic Culture* (1990).

Hellwig, David J., "Afro-American Views of Immigrants, 1830–1930: An Historiographical-Bibliographical Essay," *Immigration History Newsletter* 13 (1981): 1–5.

———— "Strangers in Their Own Land: Patterns of Black Nativism, 1830–1930," *American Studies* 23 (1982): 85–98.

Hershberg, Theodore, et al., "A Tale of Three Cities: Blacks and Immigrants in Philadelphia: 1850–1880, 1930 and 1970," *Annals of the American Academy of Political and Social Science* (1979): 55–81.

Heyd, Milly, *Mutual Reflections: Jews and Blacks in American Art* (1999).

Hurvitz, Nathan, "Blacks and Jews in American Folklore," *Western Folklore* 33 (1974): 301–25.

Lieberson, Stanley, *A Piece of the Pie: Blacks and White Immigrants since 1880* (1980).

Light, Ivan Hubert, *Ethnic Enterprise in America: Business and Welfare among Chinese, Japanese, and Blacks* (1972).

Murray, Frank, "The Irish and Afro-Americans in United States History," *Freedomways* 22 (1982): 21–31.

Nash, Gary B., and Richard Weiss, ed., *The Great Fear: Race in the Mind of America* (1970).

Nederveen Pieterse, Jan, *White on Black: Images of Africa and Blacks in Western Popular Culture* (1992).

Salzman, Jack, Adina Back, and Gretchen Sullivan Sorin, *Bridges and Boundaries: African Americans and American Jews* (1992).

Salzman, Jack, and Cornel West, ed., *Struggles in the Promised Land: Toward a History of Black-Jewish Relations in the United States* (1997).

Shankman, Arnold, *Ambivalent Friends: Afro-Americans View the Immigrant* (1982).

———— "Black on Yellow: Afro-Americans View Chinese-Americans, 1850–1935," *Phylon* 39 (1978): 1–17.

———— "Black on Green: Afro-American Editors on Irish Independence, 1840–1921," *Phylon* 41 (1980): 284–99.

Smith, J. Owens, "The Politics of Income and Educational Differences between Blacks and West Indians," *Journal of Ethnic Studies* 13 (1985): 17–30.

Sowell, Thomas, *Ethnic America: A History* (1981).

Toll, William, "Pluralism and Moral Force in the Black-Jewish Dialogue," *American Jewish History* 77 (1987): 87–105.

Weisbord, Robert G., and Arthur Stein, *Bittersweet Encounter: The Afro-American and the American Jew* (1970).

Wytrwal, Joseph A., *Polish-Black Encounters: A History of Polish and Black Relations in America since 1619* (1982).

13.4.6   Segregation/Jim Crow

Chafe, William H., "'The Gods Bring Threads to Webs Begun': African American Life in the Jim Crow South," *Journal of American History* 86 (2000): 1531–51.

Fredrickson, George M., *White Supremacy: A Comparative Study in American and South African History* (1981).

Marx, Anthony W., "Race-Making and the Nation-State," *World Politics* 48 (1996): 180–208.

Rasmussen, R. Kent, *Farewell to Jim Crow: The Rise and Fall of Segregation in America* (1997).

Weinstein, Allen, and Frank Otto Gatell, ed., *The Segregation Era, 1863–1954: A Modern Reader* (1970).

13.4.7   Violence and Racial Disturbances

Bryant, Jerry H., *Victims and Heroes: Racial Violence in the African American Novel* (1997).

Grimshaw, Allen D., "Lawlessness and Violence in America and Their Special Manifestations in Changing Negro-White Relationships," *Journal of Negro History* 44 (1959): 52–72.

Harris, Trudier, *Exorcising Blackness: Historical and Literary Lynching and Burning Rituals* (1984).

Platt, Anthony M., ed., *The Politics of Riot Commissions, 1917–1970: A Collection of Official Reports and Critical Essays* (1971).

Shapiro, Herbert, *White Violence and Black Response: From Reconstruction to Montgomery* (1988).

Takaki, Ronald T., *Violence in the Black Imagination: Essays and Documents* (1972).

13.4.8   Civil Rights

Allen, Robert, and Pamela P. Allen, *Reluctant Reformers: Racism and Social Reform Movements in the United States* (1974).

Baumann, Mark K., and Berkley Kalin, ed., *The Quiet Voices: Southern Rabbis and Black Civil Rights, 1880s to 1990s* (1997).

Blaustein, Albert P., and Robert L. Zangrando, ed., *Civil Rights and the American Negro: A Documentary History* (1968).

Cook, Robert, *Sweet Land of Liberty: The Black Struggle for Civil Rights in Twentieth Century America* (1997).

Franklin, John Hope, *Racial Equality in America* (1976).

Harding, Vincent, *There is a River: The Black Struggle for Freedom in America* (1981).

Haskins, James, *Separate, but Not Equal: The Dream and the Struggle* (1998).

Howard-Pitney, David, *The Afro-Jeremiad: Appeals for Justice in America* (1990).

Hughes, Langston, *Fight for Freedom: The Story of the NAACP* (1962).

Levine, Michael L., *African Americans and Civil Rights: From 1619 to the Present* (1996).

Marable, Manning, *Black Leadership: Four Great American Leaders and the Struggle for Civil Rights* (1998).

Meier, August, Elliott M. Rudwick, and Francis L. Broderick, ed., *Black Protest Thought in the Twentieth Century* (2d ed., 1971).

Okihiro, Gary Y., ed., *In Resistance: Studies in African, Caribbean, and Afro-American History* (1986).

Wilson, Sondra Kathryn, ed., *In Search of Democracy: The NAACP Writings of James Weldon Johnson, Walter White, and Roy Wilkins (1920–1977)* (1999).

13.5 GOVERNMENT

13.5.1 Law

Bardaglio, Peter W., *Reconstructing the Household: Families, Sex, and the Law in the Nineteenth-Century South* (1995).
Bardolph, Richard, ed., *The Civil Rights Record: Black Americans and the Law, 1849–1970* (1970).
Barnes, Catherine A., *Journey from Jim Crow: The Desegregation of Southern Transit* (1983).
Bell, Derrick A., Jr., *Race, Racism and American Law* (4th ed., 2000).
Berry, Mary Frances, *Black Resistance, White Law: A History of Constitutional Racism in America* (rev. ed., 1994).
Catterall, Helen Tunnicliff, ed., *Judicial Cases Concerning American Slavery and the Negro* (5 vols., 1926–1937).
Cornwell, JoAnne, "The United States and South Africa: History, Civil Rights and the Legal and Cultural Vulnerability of Blacks," *Phylon* 47 (1986): 285–93.
Cottrol, Robert J., and Raymond T. Diamond, "The Second Amendment: Toward An Afro-Americanist Reconsideration," *Georgetown Law Journal* 80 (1991): 309–61.
Eastland, Terry, and William J. Bennett, ed., *Counting by Race: Equality from the Founding Fathers to Bakke and Weber* (1979).
Finkelman, Paul, ed., *Slavery and the Law* (1996).
———, ed., *Slavery, Race, and the American Legal System, 1700–1872* (7 series, 1988).
Franklin, John Hope, and Genna Rae McNeil, ed., *African Americans and the Living Constitution* (1995).
Greenberg, Jack, ed., *Blacks and the Law* (1973).
——— *Race Relations and American Law* (1959).
Harris, Paul, *Black Rage Confronts the Law* (1997).
Higginbotham, A. Leon, Jr., "Racism and the Early American Legal Process, 1619–1896," *Annals of the American Academy of Political and Social Science* (1973): 1–17.
——— *Shades of Freedom: Racial Politics and Presumptions of the American Legal Process* (1996).
Howard, John R., *The Shifting Wind: The Supreme Court and Civil Rights from Reconstruction to* Brown (1999).
Konvitz, Milton R., *A Century of Civil Rights: With a Study of State Laws against Discrimination* (1961).
Leonard, Walter J., "The Development of the Black Bar," *Annals of the American Academy of Political and Social Science* (1973): 134–43.
Miller, Loren, *The Petitioners: The Story of the Supreme Court of the United States and the Negro* (1961).
Morris, Thomas D., *Southern Slavery and the Law, 1619–1860* (1996).
Murray, Pauli, ed., *States' Laws on Race and Color* (1950).
Nieman, Donald G., *Promises to Keep: African-Americans and the Constitutional Order, 1776 to the Present* (1991).
Sickels, Robert J., *Race, Marriage and the Law* (1972).
Smith, J. Clay, Jr., *Emancipation: The Making of the Black Lawyer, 1844–1944* (1993).

13.5.2 Crime and Punishment

Hawkins, Darnell F., "Trends in Black-White Imprisonment: Changing Conceptions of Race or Changing Patterns of Social Control?" *Crime and Social Justice* 24 (1985): 187–209.
Rafter, Nicole Hahn, *Partial Justice: Women in State Prisons, 1800–1935* (1985).
Schatzberg, Rufus, and Robert J. Kelly, *African-American Organized Crime: A Social History* (1996).

Wright, A. J., comp., *Criminal Activity in the Deep South, 1700–1930: An Annotated Bibliography* (1989).

13.5.3   Politics and Voting

Bailey, Harry A., Jr., ed., *Negro Politics in America* (1967).

Barnes, Catherine A., *Journey from Jim Crow: The Desegregation of Southern Transit* (1983).

Christopher, Maurine, *Black Americans in Congress* (1976).

Clayton, Sheryl Howard, *Black Members of Congress and Their Speeches and Tributes* (1987).

Foner, Philip S., *American Socialism and Black Americans: From the Age of Jackson to World War II* (1977).

Giddings, Paula, *When and Where I Enter: The Impact of Black Women on Race and Sex in America* (rev. ed., 1996).

Gomes, Ralph C., and Linda Faye Williams, ed., *From Exclusion to Inclusion: The Long Struggle for African American Political Power* (1992).

Gordon, Ann D., with Bettye Collier-Thomas, John H. Bracey, Arlene Voski Avakian, and Joyce Avrech Berkman, ed., *African American Women and the Vote, 1837–1965* (1997).

Hamilton, Charles V., comp., *The Black Experience in American Politics* (1973).

Harris, Robert J., *The Quest for Equality: The Constitution, Congress, and the Supreme Court* (1960).

Hutchinson, Earl Ofari, *Betrayed: A History of Presidential Failure to Protect Black Lives* (1996).

Kilson, Martin L., "The Political Status of American Negroes in the Twentieth Century," in Martin L. Kilson and Robert I. Rotberg, ed., *The African Diaspora: Interpretive Essays* (1976): 459–84.

King, Desmond, *Separate and Unequal: Black Americans and the U.S. Federal Government* (1995).

Ladd, Everett Carll, *Negro Political Leadership in the South* (1966).

Lewinson, Paul, *Race, Class, and Party: A History of Negro Suffrage and White Politics in the South* (1932).

Logan, Rayford W., *The Diplomatic Relations of the United States with Haiti, 1776–1891* (1941).

Lusane, Clarence, *No Easy Victories: Black Americans and the Vote* (1996).

Marable, Manning, "Patterns of Black Political Protest, 1877–1977," *Journal of Ethnic Studies* 7 (1979): 57–64.

Price, Edward, "The Black Voting Rights Issue in Pennsylvania, 1780–1900," *Pennsylvania Magazine of History and Biography* 100 (1976): 356–73.

Ragsdale, Bruce A., and Joel D. Treese, *Black Americans in Congress, 1870–1989* (1990).

Riley, Russell L., *The Presidency and the Politics of Racial Inequality: Nation-Keeping from 1831 to 1965* (1999).

Rustin, Bayard, et al., "The Voting Rights Act—An Historical Perspective," *Journal of Intergroup Relations* 4 (1975): 5–37.

Steele, James, *Freedom's River: The African-American Contribution to Democracy* (1994).

Terborg-Penn, Rosalyn, *African American Women in the Struggle for the Vote, 1850–1920* (1998).

Walton, Hanes, Jr., and C. Vernon Gray, "Black Politics at the National Republican and Democratic Conventions, 1868–1972," *Phylon* 36 (1975): 269–78.

Walton, Hanes, Jr., and Delacy W. Stanford, "Black Governors and Gubernatorial Candidates in the United States of America: 1868–1972," *Political Science Review* 19 (1980): 312–28.

Weston, Rubin F., *Racism in U.S. Imperialism: The Influence of Racial Assumptions on American Foreign Policy, 1893–1946* (1972).

13.5.4   Military

Astor, Gerald, *The Right to Fight: A History of African Americans in the Military* (1998).

Foner, Jack D., *Blacks and the Military in American History: A New Perspective* (1974).

Greene, Robert Ewell, *Black Defenders of America, 1775–1973* (1974).

Lanning, Michael Lee, ed., *The African American Soldier: From Crispus Attucks to Colin Powell* (1997).

MacGregor, Morris J., and Bernard C. Nalty, ed., *Blacks in the United States Armed Forces: Basic Documents* (13 vols., 1977).

McGlone, John D., *Monuments and Memorials to Black Military History, 1775 to 1891* (1985).

Mullen, Robert W., *Blacks in America's Wars: The Shift in Attitudes from the Revolutionary War to Vietnam* (1973).

Nalty, Bernard C., *Strength for the Fight: A History of Black Americans in the Military* (1986).

Nalty, Bernard C., and Morris J. MacGregor, ed., *Blacks in the Military: Essential Documents* (1981).

Nelson, Dennis Denmark, *The Integration of the Negro into the United States Navy, 1776–1947* (1951).

Rackleff, Robert B., "The Black Soldier in Popular American Magazines, 1900–1971," *Negro History Bulletin* 34 (1971): 185–89.

Slonaker, John, comp., *The U.S. Army and the Negro* (1971).

13.6   DEMOGRAPHY

Coale, Ansley, and Norfleet W. Rives, Jr., "A Statistical Reconstruction of the Black Population of the United States, 1880–1970: Estimates of True Numbers by Age and Sex, Birth Rates and Total Fertility," *Population Index* 39 (1973): 3–36.

Davis, Dernoral, "Toward a Socio-Historical and Demographic Portrait of Twentieth-Century African-Americans," in Alferdteen Harrison, ed., *Black Exodus: The Great Migration from the American South* (1991): 1–19.

Farley, Reynolds, *Growth of the Black Population: A Study of Demographic Trends* (1970).

Holmes, S. J., *The Negro's Struggle for Survival: A Study in Human Ecology* (1937).

Johnson, Daniel M., and Rex R. Campbell, *Black Migration in America: A Social Demographic History* (1981).

McFalls, Joseph A., Jr., "Impact of VD on the Fertility of the U.S. Black Population, 1880–1950," *Social Biology* 20 (1973): 2–19.

McFalls, Joseph A., Jr., and George S. Masnick, "Birth Control and the Fertility of the U.S. Black Population, 1880 to 1980," *Journal of Family History* 6 (1981): 89–106.

McKee, Jesse O., "A Geographical Analysis of the Origin, Diffusion, and Spatial Distribution of the Black American in the United States," *Southern Quarterly* 12 (1974): 203–16.

Price, Daniel O., *Changing Characteristics of the Negro Population* (1969).

13.7   FAMILY

Ballard, Allen B., *One More Day's Journey: The Story of a Family and a People* (1984).

Bardaglio, Peter W., *Reconstructing the Household: Families, Sex, and the Law in the Nineteenth-Century South* (1995).

Billingsley, Andrew, *Climbing Jacob's Ladder: The Enduring Legacy of African-American Families* (1992).

Broussard, Albert S., *African-American Odyssey: The Stewarts, 1853–1963* (1998).

Cottman, Michael, Deborah Willis, and Linda Tarrant-Reid, *The Family of Black America* (1996).

Foster, Herbert J., "African Patterns in the Afro-American Family," *Journal of Black Studies* 14 (1983): 201–32.

Frazier, E. Franklin, *The Free Negro Family: A Study of Family Origins before the Civil War* (1932).

——— *The Negro Family in the United States* (rev. and abridged ed., 1966).

Gutman, Herbert G., *The Black Family in Slavery and Freedom, 1750–1925* (1976).

Harris, William G., "Research on the Black Family: Mainstream and Dissenting Perspectives," *Journal of Ethnic Studies* 6 (1979): 45–64.

Hoobler, Dorothy, and Thomas Hoobler, *The African American Family Album* (1995).

Klotter, James C., "Slavery and Race: A Family Perspective," *Southern Studies* 17 (1978): 375–97.

Krech, Shepard, III, "Black Family Organization in the Nineteenth Century: An Ethnological Perspective," *Journal of Interdisciplinary History* 12 (1982): 429–52.

McAdoo, Harriette Pipes, and Rosalyn Terborg-Penn, "Historical Trends and Perspectives of Afro-American Families," *Trends in History* 3 (1985): 97–111.

Merritt, Carole, *Homecoming: African-American Family History in Georgia* (1982).

Moran, Robert E., "The Negro Dependent Child in Louisiana, 1800–1935," *Social Services Review* 45 (1971): 53–61.

Morgan, Kathryn L., *Children of Strangers: The Stories of a Black Family* (1980).

Patterson, Ruth Polk, *The Seed of Sally Good'n: A Black Family of Arkansas, 1833–1953* (1985).

Porterfield, Ernest, *Black and White Mixed Marriages* (1978).

Quander, Rohulamin, "The Quander Family, 1684–1910: Its History and Its Roots," *Journal of the Afro-American Historical and Genealogical Society* 3 (1982): 47–53.

Russell-Wood, A. J. R., "The Black Family in the Americas," *Societas* 8 (1978): 1–38.

Shimkin, Demitri B., and Victor Uchendu, "Persistence, Borrowing, and Adaptive Changes in Black Kinship Systems: Some Issues and Their Significance," in Demitri B. Shimkin, Edith M. Shimkin, and Dennis A. Frate, ed., *The Extended Family in Black Societies* (1978): 391–406.

Sudarkasa, Niara, "African and Afro-American Family Structure: A Comparison," *Black Scholar* 11 (1980): 37–60.

13.8   SOCIETY

13.8.1   Rural Life (Including Black Settlements)

Aiken, Charles S., "New Settlement Pattern of Rural Blacks in the American South," *Geographical Review* 75 (1985): 383–404.

Anderson, Martha E., *Black Pioneers of the Northwest, 1800–1918* (1980).

Crum, Mason, *Gullah: Negro Life in the Carolina Sea Islands* (1940).

Holland, Jacqueline L., "The African-American Presence on Martha's Vineyard," *Dukes County Intelligencer* 33 (1991): 3–26.

Johnson, Charles S., *Shadow of the Plantation* (1934).

Katz, William Loren, *The Black West: A Documentary and Pictorial History of the African American Role in the Westward Expansion of the United States* (1996).

McGee, Leo, and Robert Boone, ed., *The Black Rural Landowner—Endangered Species: Social, Political, and Economic Implications* (1979).

Montell, William L., *The Saga of Coe Ridge: A Study in Oral History* (1970).

Pease, William H., and Jane Pease, *Black Utopia: Negro Communal Experiments in America* (1963).

Porter, Kenneth Wiggins, *The Negro on the American Frontier* (1971).

Schweninger, Loren, "A Vanishing Breed: Black Farm Owners in the South, 1651–1982," *Agricultural History* 63 (1989): 41–60.

Taylor, Quintard, *In Search of the Racial Frontier: African Americans in the American West, 1528–1990* (1999).

Trotti, Michael, "Freedmen and Enslaved Soil: A Case Study of Manumission, Migration, and Land," *Virginia Magazine of History and Biography* 104 (1996): 455–80.

Westmacott, Richard Noble, *African-American Gardens and Yards in the Rural South* (1992).

Woodson, Carter G., *The Rural Negro* (1930).

Works Projects Administration, Georgia Writers' Project, Savannah Unit, *Drums and Shadows: Survival Studies among the Georgia Coastal Negroes* (1940).

13.8.2   Urban Life (Including Migration)

Bethel, Elizabeth Rauh, *Promiseland: A Century of Life in a Negro Community* (1981).

Bontemps, Arna, and Jack Conroy, *Anyplace But Here* (1966).

———— *They Seek a City* (1945).

Borchert, James, *Alley Life in Washington: Family, Community, Religion, and Folklife in the City, 1850–1970* (1980).

Broussard, Albert S., *Black San Francisco: The Struggle for Racial Equality in the West, 1900–1954* (1993).

Carter, Wilmoth Annette, *The Urban Negro in the South* (1961).

Cox, Bette Yarbrough, *Central Avenue—Its Rise and Fall, 1890-c. 1955, Including the Musical Renaissance of Black Los Angeles* (1996).

Devlin, George A., *South Carolina and Black Migration, 1865–1940: In Search of the Promised Land* (1989).

Eisinger, Peter K., *The Politics of Displacement: Racial and Ethnic Transition in Three American Cities* (1980).

Farley, Reynolds, "The Urbanization of Negroes in the United States," *Journal of Social History* 1 (1968): 241–58.

Franklin, Joseph, *All through the Night: The History of Spokane Black Americans, 1860–1940* (1989).

Gill, Flora, *Economics and the Black Exodus: An Analysis of Negro Emigration from the Southern United States, 1910–70* (1979).

Goings, Kenneth W., and Raymond A. Mohl, ed., *The New African American Urban History* (1996).

Graham, Leroy, *Baltimore: The Nineteenth Century Black Capital* (1982).

Green, Constance McLaughlin, *The Secret City: A History of Race Relations in the Nation's Capitol* (1967).

Greenbaum, Susan D., *Afro-Cubans in Ybor City: A Centennial History* (1986).

Groh, George W., *The Black Migration: The Journey to Urban America* (1972).

Hawkins, Homer C., "Trends in Black Migration from 1863 to 1960," *Phylon* 34 (1973): 140–52.

Hershberg, Theodore, et al., "A Tale of Three Cities: Blacks and Immigrants in Philadelphia: 1850–1880, 1930 and 1970," *Annals of the American Academy of Political and Social Science* (1979): 55–81.

Hodges, Graham Russell, *Root and Branch: African Americans in New York and East Jersey, 1613–1863* (1999).

Johnson, Daniel M., and Rex R. Campbell, *Black Migration in America: A Social Demographic History* (1981).

Jones, Faustine C., "Black Americans and the City: A Historical Survey," *Journal of Negro Education* 42 (1973): 261–82.

Kornweibel, Theodore, Jr., ed., *In Search of the Promised Land: Essays in Black Urban History* (1981).

Kusmer, Kenneth L., "Urban Black History at the Crossroads," *Journal of Urban History* 13 (1987): 460–70.

Lovett, Bobby L., *The African-American History of Nashville, Tennessee, 1780–1930: Elites and Dilemmas* (1999).

Lynch, Hollis Ralph, ed., *The Black Urban Condition: A Documentary History, 1866–1971* (1973).

Sernett, Milton C., *Bound for the Promised Land: African American Religion and the Great Migration* (1997).

Taeuber, Karl E., and Alma F. Taeuber, *Negroes in Cities: Residential Segregation and Neighborhood Change* (1965).

Terrell, Lloyd P., and Marguerite Terrell, *Blacks in Augusta: A Chronology, 1741–1977* (1977).

Travis, Dempsey J., *An Autobiography of Black Chicago* (1981).

Trotter, Joe William, Jr., *River Jordan: African American Urban Life in the Ohio Valley* (1998).

Ward, David, *Poverty, Ethnicity, and the American City, 1840–1925: Changing Conceptions of the Slum and the Ghetto* (1989).

Warren, Christian, "Northern Chills, Southern Fevers: Race-Specific Mortality in American Cities, 1730–1900," *Journal of Southern History* 63 (1997): 23–56.

White, Dana F., "The Black Sides of Atlanta: A Geography of Expansion and Containment, 1870–1970," *Atlanta Historical Journal* 26 (1982): 199–225.

Woodson, Carter G., *A Century of Negro Migration* (1918).

13.8.3   Material Culture

Benberry, Cuesta, *Always There: The African-American Presence in American Quilts* (1992).

Ferris, William, ed., *Afro-American Folk Art and Crafts* (1983).

Goings, Kenneth W., *Mammy and Uncle Mose: Black Collectibles and American Stereotyping* (1994).

Lornell, Kip, "Black Material Folk Culture," *Southern Folklore Quarterly* 42 (1978): 287–94.

Turner, Patricia A., *Ceramic Uncles and Celluloid Mammies: Black Images and Their Influence on Culture* (1994).

Vlach, John Michael, *The Afro-American Tradition in Decorative Arts* (1978).

——— *By the Work of Their Hands: Studies in Afro-American Folklife* (1991).

Wahlman, Maude S., *Signs and Symbols: African Images in African American Quilts* (1993).

White, Shane, and Graham White, "Slave Clothing and African-American Culture in the Eighteenth and Nineteenth Centuries," *Past and Present* 148 (1995): 149–86.

13.8.4   Color and Class

Balch Institute for Ethnic Studies, *Philadelphia African Americans: Color, Class and Style, 1840–1940* (1988).

Dorman, James H., ed., *Creoles of Color of the Gulf South* (1996).

Durant, T. J., Jr., and J. S. Louden, "The Black Middle Class in America: Historical and Contemporary Perspectives," *Phylon* 47 (1986): 253–63.

Frazier, E. Franklin, *Black Bourgeoisie: The Rise of a New Middle Class in the United States* (1957).

Kilson, Marion, "Afro-American Social Structure, 1790–1970," in Martin L. Kilson and Robert I. Rotberg, ed., *The African Diaspora: Interpretive Essays* (1976): 414–58.

Muraskin, William A., *Middle-Class Blacks in a White Society: Prince Hall Freemasonry in America* (1975).

Reuter, Edward Byron, *The Mulatto in the United States* (1918).

Schoenberg, Sandra, and Charles Bailey, "The Symbolic Meaning of an Elite Black Community: The Ville in St. Louis," *Missouri Historical Society Bulletin* 33 (1977): 94–102.

Sollors, Werner, *Neither Black nor White yet Both: Thematic Explorations of Interracial Literature* (1997).

——— "'Never Was Born': The Mulatto, An American Tragedy?" *Massachussetts Review* 27 (1986): 293–316.

Williamson, Joel, *New People: Miscegenation and Mulattoes in the United States* (1980).

13.8.5   Associational Life

Davis, Harry E., *A History of Freemasonry among Negroes in America* (1946).

Greene, B. Gwendolyn, "From 'the Chapel' to the Buffalo Urban League," *Afro-Americans in New York Life and History* 21 (1997): 41–45.

Grimshaw, William H., *Official History of Freemasonry among the Colored People of North America* (1903).

Mjagkij, Nina, *Light in the Darkness: African Americans and the YMCA, 1852–1946* (1994).

Muraskin, William A., *Middle-Class Blacks in a White Society: Prince Hall Freemasonry in America* (1975).

Record, Wilson, "Negro Intellectuals and Negro Movements in Historical Perspective," *American Quarterly* 8 (1956): 3–20.

Ross, Edyth L., ed., *Black Heritage in Social Welfare, 1860–1930* (1978).

Voorhis, Harold Van Buren, *Negro Masonry in the United States* (1940).

Wesley, Charles H., *History of the Improved Benevolent and Protective Order of Elks of the World, 1898–1954* (1955).

——— *The History of Alpha Phi Alpha: A Development in College Life, 1906–1979* (1979).

White, Deborah Gray, *Too Heavy a Load: Black Women in Defense of Themselves, 1894–1994* (1999).

Williams, Loretta J., *Black Freemasonry and Middle-Class Realities* (1980).

13.8.6   Leisure and Sports

Chadwick, Bruce, *When the Game Was Black and White: The Illustrated History of the Negro Leagues* (1992).

Fleischer, Nat, *Black Dynamite: The Story of the Negro in the Prize Ring from 1782 to 1938* (5 vols., 1938–47).

Hazzard-Gordon, Katrina, *Jookin': The Rise of Social Dance Formations in African-American Culture* (1990).

Henderson, Edwin Bancroft, *The Negro in Sports* (1939).

Jaher, Frederic Cople, "White America Views Jack Johnson, Joe Louis, and Muhammad Ali," in Donald Spivey, ed., *Sport in America: New Historical Perspectives* (1985): 145–92.

Jones, Bessie, and Bess Lomax Hawes, *Step It Down: Games, Plays, Songs, and Stories from the Afro-American Heritage* (1972).

Miller, Patrick B., "The Anatomy of Scientific Racism: Racialist Responses to Black Athletic Achievement," *Journal of Sport History* 25 (1998): 119–51.

Peterson, Robert, *Only the Ball Was White: A History of Legendary Black Players and All-Black Professional Teams* (1992).

Ribowsky, Mark, *A Complete History of the Negro Leagues, 1884–1955* (1997).

Riley, James A., *The Biographical Encyclopedia of the Negro Baseball Leagues* (1994).

——— *The Negro Leagues* (1996).

Rogosin, Donn, *Invisible Men: Life in Baseball's Negro Leagues* (1983).

Ruck, Rob, *Sandlot Seasons: Sport in Black Pittsburgh* (1987).

Sammons, Jeffrey T., *Beyond the Ring: The Role of Boxing in American Society* (1988).

Sinnette, Calvin H., *Forbidden Fairways: African Americans and the Game of Golf* (1998).

Wiggins, William H., Jr., and Douglas DeNatale, ed., *Jubilation! African American Celebrations in the Southeast* (1993).

13.9   RELIGION

Baer, Hans A., *The Black Spiritual Movement: A Religious Response to Racism* (1984).

——— "Towards a Systematic Typology of Black Folk Healers," *Phylon* 43 (1982): 327–43.

Baer, Hans A., and Merrill Singer, *African-American Religion in the Twentieth Century: Varieties of Protest and Accommodation* (1992).

Baldwin, Lewis V., "'A Home in Dat Rock': Afro-American Folk Sources and Slave Visions of Heaven and Hell," *Journal of Religious Thought* 41 (1984): 38–57.

——— "Black Women and African Union Methodism, 1813–1983," *Methodist History* 21 (1983): 225–37.

——— "Festivity and Celebration in a Black Methodist Tradition, 1813–1981," *Methodist History* 20 (1982): 183–91.

——— *"Invisible" Strands in African Methodism: A History of the African Union Methodist Protestant and Union American Methodist Episcopal Churches, 1805–1980* (1983).

Bastide, Roger, *African Civilisations in the New World* (1971).

Bechler, Le Roy, *The Black Mennonite Church in North America, 1886–1986* (1986).

Beck, Carolyn S., "Our Own Vine and Fig Tree: The Authority of History and Kinship in Mother Bethel," *Review of Religious Research* 29 (1988): 369–84.

Bennett, Robert A., "Black Episcopalians: A History from the Colonial Period to the Present," *Historical Magazine of the Protestant Episcopal Church* 43 (1974): 231–46.

Boles, John B., ed., *Masters and Slaves in the House of the Lord: Race and Religion in the American South, 1740–1870* (1988).

Bragg, George F., *History of the Afro-American Group of the Episcopal Church* (1922).

Brewer, John Mason, *The Word on the Brazos: Negro Preacher Tales from the Brazos Bottoms of Texas* (1953).

Bringhurst, Newell George, *Saints, Slaves, and Blacks: The Changing Place of Black People within Mormonism* (1981).

Brotz, Howard, *The Black Jews of Harlem: Negro Nationalism and the Dilemmas of Negro Leadership* (1964).

Bush, Lester E., Jr., "Mormonism's Negro Doctrine: An Historical Overview," *Dialogue* 8 (1973): 11–68.

Campbell, James T., *Songs of Zion: The African Methodist Episcopal Church in the United States and South Africa* (1995).

Campen, Henry C., Jr., "Black Theology: The Concept and Its Development," *Lutheran Quarterly* 23 (1971): 388–99.

Caravaglios, Maria G., *The American Catholic Church and the Negro Problem in the Eighteenth and Nineteenth Centuries* (1974).

Carpenter, Delores C., "Black Women in Religious Institutions: A Historical Summary from Slavery to the 1960s," *Journal of Religious Thought* 46 (1989): 7–27.

Collier-Thomas, Bettye, *Daughters of Thunder: Black Women Preachers and Their Sermons, 1850–1979* (1997).

Culver, Dwight W., *Negro Segregation in the Methodist Church* (1953).

Davis, Cyprian, *The History of Black Catholics in the United States* (1990).

———— "The Holy See and American Black Catholics: A Forgotten Chapter in the History of the American Church," *U.S. Catholic Historian* 7 (1988): 157–81.

Del Pino, Julius E., "Blacks in the United Methodist Church from Its Beginning to 1968," *Methodist History* 19 (1980): 3–20.

Du Bois, William Edward Burghardt, ed., *The Negro Church* (1903).

DuPree, Sherry Sherrod, *The African-American Holiness Pentecostal Movement: An Annotated Bibliography* (1996).

Earnest, Joseph B., *The Religious Development of the Negro in Virginia* (1914).

Fichter, Joseph H., "American Religion and the Negro," *Daedalus* 94 (1965): 1085–1106.

Fitts, Leroy, *A History of Black Baptists* (1985).

Fordham, Monroe, "Origins of the Michigan Street Baptist Church, Buffalo, New York," *Afro-Americans in New York Life and History* 21 (1997): 7–18.

Frazier, E. Franklin, *The Negro Church in America* (1964).

Fulop, Timothy E., and Albert J. Raboteau, *African American Religion: Interpretive Essays in History and Culture* (1996).

Gillard, John T., *The Catholic Church and the American Negro* (1930).

Glazier, Stephen D., "Mourning in the Afro-Baptist Tradition: A Comparative Study of Religion in the American South and in Trinidad," *Southern Quarterly* 23 (1985): 141–56.

Hayden, Robert C., *Faith, Culture, and Leadership: A History of the Black Church in Boston* (1983).

Haynes, Leonard L., Jr., *The Negro Community within American Protestantism, 1619–1844* (1953).

Holloway, Joseph E., ed., *Africanisms in American Culture* (1990).

Hood, James W., *One Hundred Years of the African Methodist Episcopal Zion Church* (1895).

Hopkins, Leroy, "Bethel African Methodist Church (Lancaster): Prolegomenon to a Social History," *Journal of the Lancaster County Historical Society* 90 (1986): 205–36.

Hubbard, Dolan, *The Sermon and the African-American Literary Imagination* (1996).

Jackson, Irene V., "Music among Blacks in the Episcopal Church: Some Preliminary Considerations," *History Magazine of the Protestant Church* 49 (1980): 21–35.

Jacobs, Claude, and Andrew Kaslow, *The Spiritual Churches of New Orleans: Origins, Beliefs, and Rituals of an African-American Religion* (1991).

Johnson, Alonzo, and Paul Jersild, ed., *Ain't Gonna Lay My 'Ligion Down: African American Religion in the South* (1996).

Johnson, Paul E., ed., *African-American Christianity: Essays in History* (1994).

Johnston, Ruby Funchess, *The Development of Negro Religion* (1954).

———— *The Religion of Negro Protestants: Changing Religious Attitudes and Practices* (1956).

Knighton, A. Stanley, *The Children is Crying: Congregationalism among Black People* (1979).

Lewis, Harold T., *Yet with a Steady Beat: The African American Struggle for Recognition in the Episcopal Church* (1996).

Lincoln, C. Eric, ed., *The Black Experience in Religion* (1974).

Lincoln, C. Eric, and Lawrence H. Mamiya, *The Black Church in the African American Experience* (1990).

Loescher, Frank Samuel, *The Protestant Church and the Negro* (1948).

Mays, Benjamin E., *The Negro's God As Reflected in His Literature* (1938).

Mays, Benjamin E., and Joseph William Nicholson, *The Negro's Church* (1933).

McBeth, Leon, "Images of the Black Church in America," *Baptist History and Heritage* 16 (1981): 19–28, 40.

McCall, Emmanuel L., "Home Mission Board Ministry in the Black Community," *Baptist History and Heritage* 16 (1981): 29–40.

McDonough, Gary W., *Black and Catholic in Savannah, Georgia* (1993).

McNally, Michael J., "A Peculiar Institution: Catholic Parish Life and the Pastoral Mission to the Blacks in the Southeast, 1850–1980," *U.S. Catholic Historian* 5 (1986): 67–80.

Mitchell, Henry H., *Black Belief: Folk Beliefs of Blacks in America and West Africa* (1975).

Moore, LeRoy, Jr., "The Spiritual: Soul of Black Religion," *American Quarterly* 23 (1971): 658–76.

Moses, Wilson Jeremiah, *Black Messiahs and Uncle Toms: Social and Literary Manipulations of a Religious Myth* (rev. ed., 1993).

Murray, Andrew E., *Presbyterians and the Negro: A History* (1966).

Newman, Richard, *Black Power and Black Religion: Essays and Reviews* (1987).

Ochs, Stephen J., *Desegregating the Altar: The Josephites and the Struggle for Black Priests, 1871–1960* (1990).

Osborne, William A., *The Segregated Covenant: Race Relations and American Catholics* (1967).

Parker, Inez Moore, *The Rise and Decline of the Program of Education for Black Presbyterians of the United Presbyterian Church, U.S.A., 1865–1970* (1977).

Payne, Daniel A., *History of the African Methodist Episcopal Church* (1891).

Phillips, Charles H., *The History of the Colored Methodist Episcopal Church in America* (1898).

Phillips, Paul D., "The Interracial Impact of Marshall Keeble, Black Evangelist, 1878–1968," *Tennessee Historical Quarterly* 36 (1977): 62–74.

Pipes, William H., *Say Amen, Brother! Old Time Negro Preaching: A Study in American Frustration* (1951).

Raboteau, Albert J., *A Fire in the Bones: Reflections on African-American Religious History* (1995).

Reid, Stevenson, *History of Colored Baptists in Alabama* (1949).

Reimers, David M., *White Protestantism and the Negro* (1965).

Rosenberg, Bruce A., *The Art of the American Folk Preacher* (1970).

Russell, Lester F., *Black Baptist Secondary Schools in Virginia, 1887–1957* (1981).

Sernett, Milton C., ed., *African American Religious History: A Documentary Witness* (1999).

—— *Bound for the Promised Land: African American Religion and the Great Migration* (1997).

Shaw, James B. F., *The Negro in the History of Methodism* (1954).

Shockley, Grant S., "Methodism, Society, and Black Evangelism in America: Retrospect and Prospect," *Methodist History* 12 (1974): 145–82.

Simms, James Meriles, *The First Colored Baptist Church in North America* (1888).

Simpson, George Eaton, "Black Pentecostalism in the United States, 1906–1970," *Phylon* 35 (1974): 203–11.

—— *Black Religions in the New World* (1978).

Singleton, George A., *The Romance of African Methodism: A Study of the African Methodist Episcopal Church* (1952).

Smith, Charles Spencer, *A History of the African Methodist Episcopal Church, 1856–1922: Being a Volume Supplemental to* A History of the African Methodist Episcopal Church, *by Daniel Alexander Payne* (1922).

Smith, Edward D., *Climbing Jacob's Ladder: The Rise of the Black Churches in Eastern American Cities, 1740–1877* (1988).

Smith, H. Shelton, *In His Image But . . . : Racism in Southern Religion, 1780–1910* (1972).

Taylor, Clarence, *The Black Churches of Brooklyn* (1994).

Thurman, Howard, *Deep River: Reflections on the Religious Insight of Certain of the Negro Spirituals* (rev. and enlarged ed., 1955).

——— *The Negro Spiritual Speaks of Life and Death: Being the Ingersoll Lecture on the Immortality of Man* (1947).

Traxler, Margaret E., "American Catholics and Negroes," *Phylon* 30 (1979): 355–66.

Tucker, David M., *Black Pastors and Leaders: Memphis, 1819–1972* (1975).

Turner, William C., Jr., "Black Evangelicalism: Theology, Politics, and Race," *Journal of Religious Thought* 45 (1989): 40–56.

Unterkoefler, Ernest L., ed., *The American Catholic Church and the Negro Problem in the Eighteenth and Nineteenth Centuries* (1974).

Wahlman, Maude S., "Religious Symbols in Afro-American Folk Art," *New York Folklore* 12 (1986): 1–24.

Walls, William J., *The African Methodist Episcopal Zion Church: Reality of the Black Church* (1974).

Washington, James Melvin, ed., *Conversations with God: Two Centuries of Prayers by African Americans* (1994).

——— *Frustrated Fellowship: The Black Baptist Quest for Social Power* (1986).

Washington, Joseph, *Black Religion: The Negro and Christianity in the United States* (1964).

Weatherford, Willis D., *American Churches and the Negro: An Historical Study from Early Slave Days to the Present* (1957).

Wheeler, Edward L., "An Overview of Black Southern Baptist Involvements," *Baptist History and Heritage* 16 (1981): 3–11, 40.

Wills, David W., and Richard Newman, *Black Apostles at Home and Abroad: Afro-Americans and the Christian Mission from the Revolution to Reconstruction* (1982).

Wilmore, Gayraud S., *Black and Presbyterian: The Heritage and the Hope* (1983).

——— *Black Religion and Black Radicalism: An Interpretation of the Religious History of Afro-American People* (1983).

Wilson, Fallin, Jr., *The African American Church in Birmingham, Alabama, 1815–1963: A Shelter in the Storm* (1997).

Wilson, Frank T., "Living Witnesses: Black Presbyterians in Ministry," *Journal of Presbyterian History* 53 (1975): 187–222.

Wingfield, Harold L., "The Historical and Changing Role of the Black Church: The Social and Political Implications," *Western Journal of Black Studies* 12 (1988): 127–34.

Wood, Forrest G., *The Arrogance of Faith: Christianity and Race in America from the Colonial Era to the Twentieth Century* (1990).

Woodson, Carter G., *The History of the Negro Church* (2d ed., 1945).

Young, Henry J., *Major Black Religious Leaders, 1755–1940* (1977).

13.10   THOUGHT AND EXPRESSION

13.10.1   Race, Gender, and Identity

Baer, Hans A., and Yvonne Jones, ed., *African Americans in the South: Issues of Race, Class, and Gender* (1992).

Banks, William M., *Black Intellectuals: Race and Responsibility in American Life* (1996).

Bolsterli, Margaret Jones, "'The Very Food We Eat': A Speculation on the Nature of Southern Culture," *Southern Humanities* 16 (1982): 119–27.

Boulware, Marcus H., *The Oratory of Negro Leaders, 1900–1968* (1969).

Brotz, Howard, ed., *Negro Social and Political Thought, 1850–1920: Representative Texts* (1966).

Carby, Hazel V., *Race Men* (1998).

Cruse, Harold, *The Crisis of the Negro Intellectual: From Its Origins to the Present* (1967).

Diedrich, Maria, Henry Louis Gates, Jr., and Carl Pedersen, ed., *Black Imagination and the Middle Passage* (1999).

Dunbar-Nelson, Alice Moore, ed., *Masterpieces of Negro Eloquence: The Best Speeches Delivered by the Negro from the Days of Slavery to the Present Time* (1914).

Eisenstadt, Peter R., ed., *Black Conservatism: Essays in Intellectual and Political History* (1999).

Foner, Philip S., comp., *The Voice of Black America: Major Speeches by Negroes in the United States, 1797–1971* (1972).

Foner, Philip S., and Robert J. Branham, ed., *Lift Every Voice: African American Oratory, 1787–1900* (1998).

Franklin, Vincent P., *Black Self-Determination: A Cultural History of African-American Resistance* (2d ed., 1992).

Fullinwider, S. P., *The Mind and Mood of Black America: Twentieth Century Thought* (1969).

Gaines, Kevin K., *Uplifting the Race: Black Leadership, Politics, and Culture in the Twentieth Century* (1996).

Gates, Henry Louis, Jr., *Figures in Black: Words, Signs, and the "Racial" Self* (1987).

Giddings, Paula, *When and Where I Enter: The Impact of Black Women on Race and Sex in America* (rev. ed., 1996).

Gilroy, Paul, *The Black Atlantic: Modernity and Double Consciousness* (1993).

Gomez, Michael A., *Exchanging Our Country Marks: The Transformation of African Identities in the Colonial and Antebellum South* (1998).

Guy-Sheftall, Beverly, ed., *Words of Fire: An Anthology of African-American Feminist Thought* (1995).

Herskovits, Melville Jean, *The Myth of the Negro Past* (1941).

Hine, Darlene Clark, Wilma King, and Linda Reed, ed., *"We Specialize in the Wholly Impossible": A Reader in Black Women's History* (1995).

Howard-Pitney, David, *The Afro-Jeremiad: Appeals for Justice in America* (1990).

James, Joy, *Shadowboxing: Representations of Black Feminist Politics* (1999).

Jones-Jackson, Patricia, *When Roots Die: Endangered Traditions on the Sea Islands* (1987).

Kelley, Robin D. G., *Race Rebels: Culture, Politics, and the Black Working Class* (1996).

Lerner, Gerda, comp., *Black Women in White America: A Documentary History* (1972).

Levine, Lawrence W., *Black Culture and Black Consciousness: Afro-American Folk Thought from Slavery to Freedom* (1977).

Lewis, David Levering, ed., *W. E. B. Du Bois: A Reader* (1995).

Loewenberg, Bert James, and Ruth Bogin, ed., *Black Women in Nineteenth Century American Life: Their Words, Their Thoughts, Their Feelings* (1976).

Mamiya, Lawrence H., and Patricia A. Kaurouma, "You Never Hear about Their Struggles: Black Oral History in Poughkeepsie, New York," *Afro-Americans in New York Life and History* 4 (1980): 55–70.

Marable, Manning, "History and Black Consciousness: The Political Culture of Black America," *Monthly Review: An Independent Socialist Magazine* 47 (1995): 71–88.

Marx, Anthony W., "Contested Citizenship: The Dynamics of Racial Identity and Social Movements," *International Review of Social History* 40 (1995): 159–83.

Meier, August, Elliott M. Rudwick, and Francis L. Broderick, ed., *Black Protest Thought in the Twentieth Century* (2d ed., 1971).

Moses, Wilson Jeremiah, *Black Messiahs and Uncle Toms: Social and Literary Manipulations of a Religious Myth* (rev. ed., 1993).

Newman, Richard, *Words Like Freedom: Essays on African-American Culture and History* (1996).

Ostendorf, Bernhard, "Black Poetry, Blues, and Folklore: Double Consciousness in Afro-American Oral Culture," *Amerikastudien/American Studies* 20 (1975): 209–59.

Pollard, Leslie J., *Complaint to the Lord: Historical Perspectives on the African American Elderly* (1996).

Posnock, Ross, "How It Feels to Be a Problem: Du Bois, Fanon, and the 'Impossible Life' of the Black Intellectual," *Critical Inquiry* 23 (1997): 323–49.

Reid, Ira de Augustine, "The John Canoe Festival: A New World Africanism," *Phylon* 3 (1942): 349–70.

Rooks, Noliwe M., *Hair Raising: Beauty, Culture, and African American Women* (1996).

Sollors, Werner, *Neither Black nor White yet Both: Thematic Explorations of Interracial Literature* (1997).

Sterling, Dorothy, ed., *We Are Your Sisters: Black Women in the Nineteenth Century* (1984).

Thorpe, Earl E., *The Mind of the Negro: An Intellectual History of Afro-Americans* (1961).

White, Deborah Gray, *Too Heavy a Load: Black Women in Defense of Themselves, 1894–1994* (1999).

White, Shane, and Graham White, *Stylin': African American Expressive Culture From Its Beginnings to the Zoot Suit* (1998).

Wiggins, William H., Jr., *O Freedom! Afro-American Emancipation Celebrations* (1987).
Woodson, Carter G., ed., *Negro Orators and Their Orations* (1925).
Works Projects Administration, Georgia Writers' Project, Savannah Unit, *Drums and Shadows: Survival Studies among the Georgia Coastal Negroes* (1940).

13.10.2   Emigration and Nationalism

Akpan, M. B., "Black Imperialism: Americo-Liberian Rule over the African Peoples of Liberia, 1841–1964," *Canadian Journal of African Studies* 7 (1973): 217–36.
Berghahn, Marion, *Images of Africa in Black American Literature* (1977).
Bracey, John H., Jr., August Meier, and Elliott Rudwick, ed., *Black Nationalism in America* (1970).
Bush, Roderick D., *We Are Not What We Seem: Black Nationalism and Class Struggle in the American Century* (1999).
Essien-Udom, E. U., *Black Nationalism: A Search for an Identity in America* (1962).
Fredrickson, George M., *Black Liberation: A Comparative History of Black Ideologies in the United States and South Africa* (1995).
Hill, Adelaide Cromwell, and Martin Kilson, comp. and ed., *Apropos of Africa: Sentiments of Negro American Leaders on Africa from the 1800s to the 1950s* (1969).
Magubane, Bernard, *The Ties That Bind: African-American Consciousness of Africa* (1987).
Moses, Wilson Jeremiah, ed., *Classical Black Nationalism: From the American Revolution to Marcus Garvey* (1996).
——— *The Golden Age of Black Nationalism: 1850–1925* (1978).
——— *The Wings of Ethiopia: Studies in African-American Life and Letters* (1990).
Nzuwah, Mariyawanda, and William King, "Afro-Americans and the U.S. Policy toward Africa: An Overview," *Journal of Southern African Affairs* 2 (1977): 235–44.
Pinkney, Alphonso, *Red, Black, and Green: Black Nationalism in the United States* (1976).
Scott, William R., "'And Ethiopia Shall Stretch Forth Its Hands': The Origins of Ethiopianism in Afro-American Thought, 1767–1896," *Umoja* 2 (1978): 1–14.
Stuckey, Sterling, *Slave Culture: Nationalist Theory and the Foundations of Black America* (1987).
Van Deburg, William L., ed., *Modern Black Nationalism: From Marcus Garvey to Louis Farrakhan* (1997).

13.10.3   Language and Linguistics

Aldon, Lynn Nielsen, *Black Chant: Languages of African-American Postmodernism* (1997).
Bailey, Guy, Natalie Maynor, and Patricia Cukor-Avila, ed., *The Emergence of Black English: Text and Commentary* (1991).
Baugh, John, *Black Street Speech: Its History, Structure, and Survival* (1983).
Boulware, Marcus H., *The Oratory of Negro Leaders, 1900–1968* (1969).
Brasch, Walter M., *Black English and the Mass Media* (1981).
Brown, David H., "Conjure/Doctors: An Explanation of Black Discourse in America, Antebellum to 1940," *Folklore Forum* 23 (1990): 3–46.
Dillard, J. L., *Black English: Its History and Usage in the United States* (1972).
Dunbar-Nelson, Alice Moore, ed., *Masterpieces of Negro Eloquence: The Best Speeches Delivered by the Negro from the Days of Slavery to the Present Time* (1914).
Major, Clarence ed., *Juba to Jive: A Dictionary of African-American Slang* (1994).
Montgomery, Michael B., *The Crucible of Carolina: Essays on the Development of Gullah Language and Culture* (1994).
Montgomery, Michael B., and Guy H. Bailey, *Language Variety in the South: Perspectives in Black and White* (1986).
Rickford, John R., and Angela A. Rickford, "Cut-Eye and Suck-Teeth: African Words and Gestures in New World Guise," *Journal of American Folklore* 89 (1976): 294–309.
Roberts, John Willie, *From Trickster to Badman: The Black Folk Hero in Slavery and Freedom* (1989).
Taylor, Orlando L., "Some Sociolinguistic Concepts of Black Language," *Today's Speech* 19 (1971): 19–26.

Turner, Lorenzo Dow, *Africanisms in the Gullah Dialect* (1949).

Woodson, Carter G., ed., *Negro Orators and Their Orations* (1925).

13.10.4   Folklore and Humor

Abernethy, Francis E., Patrick B. Mullen, and Alan B. Govenar, ed., *Juneteenth Texas: Essays in African-American Folklore* (1996).

Abrahams, Roger D., ed., *Afro-American Folktales: Stories from Black Traditions in the New World* (1985).

Abrahams, Roger D., "The Changing Concept of the Negro Hero," in Mody C. Boatright, Wilson M. Hudson, and Allen Maxwell, ed., *The Golden Log* (1962): 119–34.

———— "Playing the Dozens," *Journal of American Folklore* 75 (1962): 209–20.

Ballowe, Hewitt Leonard, *The Lawd Sayin' the Same: Negro Folk Tales of the Creole Country* (1947).

Brake, Robert, "The Lion Act Is Over: Passive/Aggressive Patterns of Communication in American Negro Humor," *Journal of Popular Culture* 9 (1975): 549–60.

Brewer, John Mason, *American Negro Folklore* (1968).

———— *The Word on the Brazos: Negro Preacher Tales from the Brazos Bottoms of Texas* (1953).

Cook, William W., "Change the Joke and Slip the Yoke: Traditions of Afro-American Satire," *Journal of Ethnic Studies* 13 (1985): 109–34.

Dance, Daryl Cumber, *Shuckin' and Jivin': Folklore from Contemporary Black Americans* (1978).

Dorson, Richard Mercer, ed., *Negro Folktales in Michigan* (1956).

———— *Negro Tales from Pine Bluff, Arkansas, and Calvin, Michigan* (1958).

Dundes, Alan, comp., *Mother Wit from the Laughing Barrel: Readings in the Interpretation of Afro-American Folklore* (1972).

Garner, Thurman, "Black Ethos in Folktales," *Journal of Black Studies* 15 (1984): 53–66.

Goss, Linda, and Marian E. Barnes, *Talk That Talk: An Anthology of African-American Storytelling* (1989).

Harris, Trudier, "Adventures in a 'Foreign Country': African American Humor and the South," *Southern Cultures* 1 (1995): 457–65.

Holloway, Joseph E., ed., *Africanisms in American Culture* (1990).

Hughes, Langston, ed., *The Book of Negro Humor* (1966).

Hughes, Langston, and Arna Bontemps, ed., *The Book of Negro Folklore* (1958).

Hurvitz, Nathan, "Blacks and Jews in American Folklore," *Western Folklore* 33 (1974): 301–25.

Jackson, Bruce, ed., *The Negro and His Folklore in Nineteenth-Century Periodicals* (1967).

Johnson, Guy B., *John Henry: Tracking Down a Negro Legend* (1929).

Puckett, Newbell Niles, *Folk Beliefs of the Southern Negro* (1926).

Roberts, John Willie, *From Trickster to Badman: The Black Folk Hero in Slavery and Freedom* (1989).

Saxon, Lyle, *Gumbo Ya-Ya: A Collection of Louisiana Folk Tales* (1945).

Spaulding, Henry D., ed., *Encyclopedia of Black Folklore and Humor* (1972).

Turner, Patricia A., *I Heard It Through the Grapevine: Rumor in African-American Culture* (1993).

13.10.5   Literature and Poetry

Andrews, William L., Frances Smith Foster, and Trudier Harris, ed., *The Oxford Companion to African American Literature* (1997).

Baker, Houston A., *Long Black Song: Essays in Black American Literature and Culture* (1972).

Bell, Bernard, *The Afro-American Novel and Its Tradition* (1987).

Berghahn, Marion, *Images of Africa in Black American Literature* (1977).

Bloom, Harold, ed., *Black American Women Fiction Writers* (1994).

Bloom, Harold, and William Golding, ed., *Black American Women Poets and Dramatists* (1995).

Bluestein, Gene, "The Blues as a Literary Theme," *Massachusetts Review* 8 (1967): 593–617.

Bone, Robert, *Down Home: A History of Afro-American Short Fiction from Its Beginning to the End of the Harlem Rennaissance* (1975).

———— *The Negro Novel in America* (1958).

235   *Thought and Expression* / **13.10.5**

Bracks, Lean'tin L., *Writings on Black Women of the Diaspora: History, Language, and Identity* (1998).

Brawley, Benjamin Griffith, *Early Negro American Writers* (1935).

———— *The Negro Genius: A New Appraisal of the Achievement of the American Negro in Literature and the Fine Arts* (1937).

———— *The Negro in Literature and Art* (1910).

Brown, Sterling A., "The American Race Problem As Reflected in American Literature," *Journal of Negro Education* 8 (1939): 275–90.

———— "A Century of Negro Portraiture in American Literature," *The Massachusetts Review* 7 (1966): 73–96.

———— *The Negro in American Fiction* (1937).

———— *Negro Poetry and Drama* (1937).

Brown, Sterling A., Arthur Paul Davis, and Ulysses Lee, ed., *The Negro Caravan: Writings by American Negroes* (1941).

Bryant, Jerry H., *Victims and Heroes: Racial Violence in the African American Novel* (1997).

Busacca, Basil, "Checklist of Black Playwrights: 1823–1970," *Black Scholar* 5 (1973): 48–54.

Butcher, Margaret Just, *The Negro in American Culture: Based on Materials Left by Alain Locke* (rev. and updated ed., 1971).

Callahan, John F., *In the American Grain: The Pursuit of Voice in Twentieth-Century Black Fiction* (1988).

Campbell, Jane, *Mythic Black Fiction: The Transformation of History* (1986).

Carby, Hazel V., *Reconstructing Womanhood: The Emergence of the Afro-American Woman Novelist* (1987).

Corrigan, Robert A., "Afro-American Fiction: A Checklist, 1853–1970," *Mid-Continent American Studies Quarterly* 11 (1970): 114–35.

Davis, Arthur P., *From the Dark Tower: Afro-American Writers, 1900 to 1960* (1974).

Fabre, Michel, *From Harlem to Paris: Black American Writers in France, 1840–1980* (1991).

Gates, Henry Louis, Jr., *Figures in Black: Words, Signs, and the "Racial" Self* (1987).

Gates, Henry Louis, Jr., and Nellie Y. McKay, ed., *The Norton Anthology of African-American Literature* (1997).

Gayle, Addison, Jr., *The Way of the New World: The Black Novel in America* (1975).

Gloster, Hugh Morris, *Negro Voices in American Fiction* (1948).

Greene, J. Lee, *Blacks in Eden: The African American Novel's First Century* (1996).

Harris, Trudier, *Exorcising Blackness: Historical and Literary Lynching and Burning Rituals* (1984).

Hatch, James Vernon, and Abdullah Omanii, *Black Playwrights, 1823–1977: An Annotated Bibliography of Plays* (1977).

Jackson, Blyden, *A History of Afro-American Literature: The Long Beginning, 1746–1895* (1989).

Jackson, Blyden, and Louis D. Rubin, Jr., *Black Poetry in America: Two Essays in Historical Interpretation* (1974).

Johnson, James Weldon, ed., *The Book of American Negro Poetry* (rev. ed., 1958).

Jones, Gayl, *Liberating Voices: Oral Tradition in African American Literature* (1991).

Kawash, Samira, *Dislocating the Color Line: Identity, Hybridity, and Singularity in African-American Narrative* (1997).

Kerlin, Robert Thomas, *Negro Poets and Their Poems* (3d ed., rev. and enlarged., 1935).

Kinnamon, Kenneth, "The Political Dimension of Afro-American Literature," *Soundings* 58 (1975): 130–44.

MacCann, Donnarae, *White Supremacy in Children's Literature: Characterizations of African-Americans, 1830–1900* (1998).

Major, Clarence, ed., *The Garden Thrives: Twentieth-Century African-American Poetry* (1996).

Mason, Julian, "Black Writers of the South," *Mississippi Quarterly* 31 (1978): 169–84.

McDowell, Deborah E., *'The Changing Same': Black Women's Literature, Criticism, and Theory* (1995).

Montgomery, Maxine Lavon, *The Apocalypse in African-American Fiction* (1996).

Mullane, Deirdre, ed., *Crossing the Danger Water: Four Hundred Years of African-American Writing* (1993).

Posnock, Ross, *Color and Culture: Black Writers and the Making of the Modern Intellectual* (1998).

Redding, Jay Saunders, *To Make a Poet Black* (1939).

Roediger, David R., ed., *Black on White: Black Writers on What It Means to Be White* (1998).

Scott, Nathan A., Jr., "Black Literature," in Daniel Hoffman, ed., *The Harvard Guide to Contemporary American Writing* (1979): 287–341.

Sherman, Joan R., *Invisible Poets: Afro-Americans of the Nineteenth Century* (1974).

Shockley, Ann Allen, *Afro-American Women Writers, 1746–1933: An Anthology and Critical Guide* (1988).

Silk, Catherine, and John Silk, *Racism and Anti-Racism in American Popular Culture: Portrayals of African Americans in Fiction and Film* (1990).

Sollors, Werner, *Neither Black nor White yet Both: Thematic Explorations of Interracial Literature* (1997).

Sundquist, Eric J., *To Wake the Nations: Race in the Making of American Literature* (1993).

Wagner, Jean, *The Black Poets of the United States from Paul Laurence Dunbar to Langston Hughes* (1973).

Washington, Mary Helen, *Invented Lives: Narratives of Black Women, 1860–1960* (1987).

Zafar, Rafia, *We Wear the Mask: African Americans Write American Literature, 1760–1870* (1997).

13.10.6 Music and Performing Arts

Ames, Russell A., "Implications of Negro Folk Song," *Science and Society* 15 (1951): 163–73.

———— "Protest and Irony in Negro Folksong," *Science and Society* 14 (1950): 193–213.

Anderson, Lisa M., *Mammies No More: The Changing Image of Black Women on Stage and Screen* (1997).

Andrews, Bert, and Paul Carter Harrison, *In the Shadow of the Great White Way: Black Theatre in Photographs* (1989).

Baker, Houston A., Jr., *Blues, Ideology, and Afro-American Literature: A Vernacular Theory* (1984).

Baraka, Imamu Amiri (LeRoi Jones), *Black Music* (1967).

———— *Blues People: Negro Music in White America* (1963).

Baraka, Imamu Amiri (LeRoi Jones), and Amina Baraka, *The Music: Reflections on Jazz and Blues* (1987).

Barlow, William, *"Looking Up At Down": The Emergence of Blues Culture* (1989).

Bastin, Bruce, *Crying for the Carolines* (1971).

———— *Red River Blues: The Blues Tradition in the Southeast* (1986).

Blesh, Rudi, *Shining Trumpets: A History of Jazz* (rev. ed., 1958).

Bluestein, Gene, "The Blues as a Literary Theme," *Massachusetts Review* 8 (1967): 593–617.

Bogle, Donald, *Brown Sugar: Eighty Years of America's Black Female Superstars* (1980).

Brown, Cecilia R., "The Afro-American Contribution to Dance in the United States, 1619–1965," *Negro Heritage* 14 (1975): 63–71.

Brown, Sterling A., "Negro Folk Expression: Spirituals, Seculars, Ballads and Work Songs," *Phylon* 14 (1953): 45–61.

Buckner, Reginald Tyrone, and Steven Weiland, ed., *Jazz in Mind: Essays on the History and Meanings of Jazz* (1991).

Charters, Samuel, *The Bluesmen* (1967).

———— *The Country Blues* (1960).

———— *The Poetry of the Blues* (1963).

Cimbala, Paul A., "Black Musicians from Slavery to Freedom: An Exploration of an African-American Folk Elite and Cultural Continuity in the Nineteenth Century Rural South," *Journal of Negro History* 80 (1995): 15–29.

Cohn, Lawrence, *Nothing but the Blues: The Music and the Musicians* (1993).

Conway, Eugenia C., *The Afro-American Tradition of Folk Banjo* (1980).

Courlander, Harold, *Negro Folk Music, U.S.A.* (1963).

Cox, Bette Yarbrough, *Central Avenue—Its Rise and Fall, 1890-c. 1955, Including the Musical Renaissance of Black Los Angeles* (1996).

Crawford, Scott A. G. M., "The Black Actor as Athlete and Mover: An Historical Analysis of Sterotypes, Distortions and Bravura Performances in American Action Films," *Canadian Journal of History of Sport* 22 (1991): 23–33.

Cuney-Hare, Maud, *Negro Musicians and Their Music* (1936).

Davis, Arthur Kyle, Jr., *Folk-Songs of Virginia: A Descriptive Index and Classification of Material Collected under the Auspices of the Virginia Folklore Society* (1949).

Davis, Francis, *The History of the Blues* (1995).

Dett, R. Nathaniel, ed., *Religious Folk-Songs of the Negro As Sung at Hampton Institute* (1927).

Dunas, Jeff, *State of the Blues* (1998).

Edmonds, Randolph, "The Negro in the American Theater, 1700–1969," *Pan African Journal* 7 (1974): 13–28.

Emery, Lynne Fauley, *Black Dance in the United States from 1619 to 1970* (1972).

Epstein, Dena J., *Sinful Tunes and Spirituals: Black Folk Music to the Civil War* (1977).

Evans, David, *Big Road Blues: Tradition and Creativity in the Folk Blues* (1982).

Fabre, Geneviève, *Drumbeats, Masks, and Metaphor: Contemporary Afro-American Theatre* (1983).

Ferris, William, *Blues from the Delta* (1978).

Finkelstein, Sidney, *Jazz: A People's Music* (1948).

Finn, Julio, *The Bluesman: The Musical Heritage of Black Men and Women in the Americas* (1992).

Fisher, Miles Mark, *Negro Slave Songs in the United States* (1953).

Garon, Paul, *Blues and the Poetic Spirit* (1975).

Giddins, Gary, *Visions of Jazz: The First Century* (1998).

Gioia, Ted, *The History of Jazz* (1997).

Govenar, Alan, *Meeting the Blues* (1988).

Green, Mildred D., *Black Women Composers: A Genesis* (1983).

Handy, D. Antoinette, *Black Women in American Bands and Orchestras* (1981).

Handy, W. C., ed., *Blues: An Anthology* (1926).

Hansen, Chadwick, "Jenny's Toe: Negro Shaking Dances," *American Quarterly* 19 (1967): 554–63.

Hare, Maud Cuney, *Negro Musicians and Their Music* (1936).

Hart, Mary L., Brenda M. Eagles, and Lisa N. Howorth, *The Blues: A Bibliographical Guide* (1989).

Haskins, James, *Black Music in America: A History through Its People* (1987).

Heilbut, Anthony, *The Gospel Sound: Good News and Bad Times* (1971).

Herzhaft, Gerard, *Encyclopedia of the Blues* (1992).

Hill, Errol, "Remarks on Black Theater History," *Massachusetts Review* 28 (1987): 609–14.

Horowitz, Irving Louis, and Charles Nanry, "Ideologies and Theories about American Jazz," *Journal of Jazz Studies* 2 (1975): 24–41.

Hughes, Langston, and Milton Meltzer, *Black Magic: A Pictorial History of the Negro in American Entertainment* (1967).

Issacs, Edith Juliet Rich, *The Negro in the American Theatre* (1947).

Jackson, Bruce, ed., *Wake Up Dead Man: Afro-American Worksongs from Texas Prisons* (1972).

Jackson, George Pullen, *White and Negro Spirituals: Their Life Span and Kinship* (1943).

Johnson, James Weldon, Lawrence Brown, and J. Rosamond Johnson, ed., *The Book of American Negro Spirituals* (1925).

Johnson, James Weldon, and J. Rosamond Johnson, ed., *The Second Book of Negro Spirituals* (1926).

Kennedy, R. Emmet, *Mellows: A Chronicle of Unknown Singers* (1925).

Kofsky, Frank, "Afro-American Innovation and the Folk Tradition in Jazz: Their Historical Significance," *Journal of Ethnic Studies* 7 (1979): 1–12.

Leadbitter, Mike, ed., *Nothing But the Blues: An Illustrated Documentary* (1971).

Leonard, William Torbet, *Masquerade in Black* (1986).

Lhamon, W. T., Jr., *Raising Cain: Blackface Performance from Jim Crow to Hip Hop* (1998).

Lomax, John A. and Alan Lomax, *American Ballads and Folk Songs* (1934).

Long, Richard A., *The Black Tradition in American Dance* (1989).

Lovell, John, Jr., *Black Song: The Forge and the Flame: The Story of How the Afro-American Spiritual Was Hammered Out* (1972).

Metcalfe, Ralph H., Jr., "The Western African Roots of Afro-American Music," *Black Scholar* 1 (1970): 16–25.

Mitchell, Lofton, *Black Drama: The Story of the American Negro in the Theatre* (1967).

Murray, Albert, *The Blue Devils of Nada: A Contemporary American Approach to Aesthetic Statement* (1996).

————— *Stomping the Blues* (1976).

Newman, Richard, *Go Down Moses: A Celebration of the African-American Spiritual* (1998).

Oakley, Giles, *The Devil's Music: A History of the Blues* (1977).

Oliver, Paul, *Blues Fell this Morning: Meaning in the Blues* (2d rev. ed., 1990).

————— *Conversation with the Blues* (2d ed., with CD, 1997).

————— *Savannah Syncopators: African Retentions in the Blues* (1970).

————— *Screening the Blues: Aspects of the Blues Tradition* (1968).

Patterson, Lindsay, comp. and ed., *Anthology of the American Negro in the Theatre: A Critical Approach* (2d ed., 1976).

Ramsey, Guthrie P., Jr., "Cosmopolitan or Provincial? Ideology in Early Black Music Historiography, 1867–1940," *Black Music Research Journal* 16 (1996): 11–42.

Reagon, Bernice Johnson, ed., *We'll Understand It Better By and By: Pioneering African American Gospel Composers* (1992).

Roach, Hildred, *Black American Music: Past and Present* (2d ed., 1992).

Schafer, William J., and Richard B. Allen, *Brass Bands and New Orleans Jazz* (1977).

Schuller, Gunther, *Early Jazz: Its Roots and Musical Development* (1968).

————— *The Swing Era: The Development of Jazz, 1930–1945* (1989).

Skowronski, JoAnn, *Black Music in America: A Bibliography* (1981).

Southern, Eileen, *The Music of Black Americans: A History* (3d ed., 1997).

Stearns, Marshall Winslow, *The Story of Jazz* (expanded ed., 1958).

Stearns, Marshall, and Jean Stearns, *Jazz Dance: The Story of American Vernacular Dance* (1968).

Stewart, Earl L., *African-American Music: An Introduction* (1998).

Stuckey, Sterling, *Going through the Storm: The Influence of African-American Art in History* (1994).

Titon, Jeff Todd, *Early Downhome Blues: A Musical and Cultural Analysis* (2d ed., with CD, 1989).

Tucker, Iantha Elizabeth Lake, *The Role of Afro-Americans in Dance in the United States from Slavery Through 1983: A Slide Presentation* (1984).

Woll, Allen L., *Black Musical Theatre: From* Coontown *to* Dreamgirls (1989).

————— *Dictionary of the Black Theatre: Broadway, Off-Broadway, and Selected Harlem Theatre* (1983).

Work, John W., *American Negro Songs* (1940).

13.10.7 Art (Drawing, Painting, Photography, Printmaking, Sculpture)

Bearden, Romare, and Harry Henderson, *A History of African American Artists: From 1792 to the Present* (1993).

Bunch, Lonnie, *California Black Photographers: The Tradition Continues* (1983).

Coar, Valencia Hollins, ed., *A Century of Black Photographers, 1840–1960* (1983).

Dallas Museum of Art, comp., *Black Art Ancestral Legacy: The African Impulse in African-American Art* (1989).

Davis, Lenwood G., and Janet L. Sims, *Black Artists in the United States: An Annotated Bibliography of Books, Articles, and Dissertations on Black Artists, 1789–1979* (1980).

Dover, Cedric, *American Negro Art* (1960).

Driskell, David C., *Two Centuries of Black American Art* (1976).

Dugan, Ellen, ed., *Picturing the South, 1860 to the Present: Photographers and Writers* (1996).

Ferris, William, ed., *Afro-American Folk Art and Crafts* (1983).

Guillaume, Paul, and Thomas Munro, *Primitive Negro Sculpture* (1926).

Heyd, Milly, *Mutual Reflections: Jews and Blacks in American Art* (1999).

Higgins, Chester, Jr., and Orde Coombs, *Some Time Ago: A Historical Portrait of Black Americans from 1850–1950* (1980).

Honour, Hugh, *The Image of the Black in Western Art: From the American Revolution to World War I* (1989).

Leininger, Theresa, "The Transatlantic Tradition: African American Artists in Paris, 1830–1940," in Asake Bomani, and Belvie Rooks, ed., *Paris Connections: African American Artists in Paris* (1992): 9–23.

Locke, Alain LeRoy, ed., *Negro Art: Past and Present* (1936).

———, ed., *The Negro in Art: A Pictorial Record of the Negro Artist and of the Negro Theme in Art* (1940).

Mayer, Robert A., ed., *Blacks in America: A Photographic Record* (1986).

McElroy, Guy P., *Facing History: The Black Image in American Art, 1710–1940* (1990).

Moutoussamy-Ashe, Jeanne, *Viewfinders: Black Women Photographers* (1986).

Parry, Ellwood, *The Image of the Indian and the Black Man in American Arts, 1590–1900* (1974).

Porter, James Amos, *Modern Negro Art* (1943).

Powell, Richard J., *Black Art and Culture in the Twentieth Century* (1997).

Segy, Ladislas, *African Sculpture Speaks* (4th enlarged ed., 1975).

Sullivan, George, *Black Artists in Photography, 1840–1940* (1996).

Thompson, Robert Farris, *Flash of the Spirit: African and Afro-American Art and Philosophy* (1983).

Vlach, John Michael, *The Afro-American Tradition in Decorative Arts* (1978).

Wahlman, Maude S., "Religious Symbols in Afro-American Folk Art," *New York Folklore* 12 (1986): 1–24.

——— *Signs and Symbols: African Images in African American Quilts* (1993).

Willis, Deborah, ed., *Picturing Us: African American Identity in Photography* (1994).

Willis, Deborah, and Howard Dodson, *Black Photographers Bear Witness: 100 Years of Social Protest* (1989).

Willis-Thomas, Deborah, *Black Photographers, 1840–1940: An Illustrated Bio-Bibliography* (1985).

13.10.8   Film and Broadcasting

Anderson, Lisa M., *Mammies No More: The Changing Image of Black Women on Stage and Screen* (1997).

Baldwin, James, *The Devil Finds Work* (1976).

Bernardi, Daniel, ed., *The Birth of Whiteness: Race and the Emergence of United States Cinema* (1996).

Bogle, Donald, *Brown Sugar: Eighty Years of America's Black Female Superstars* (1980).

——— *Toms, Coons, Mulattoes, Mammies, and Bucks: An Interpretive History of Blacks in American Films* (3d ed., 1994).

Cham, Mbye B., and Claire Andrade-Watkins, ed., *Blackframes: Critical Perspectives on Black Independent Cinema* (1988).

Crawford, Scott A. G. M., "The Black Actor as Athlete and Mover: An Historical Analysis of Stereotypes, Distortions and Bravura Performances in American Action Films," *Canadian Journal of History of Sport* 22 (1991): 23–33.

Dates, Jannette L., and William Barlow, *Split Image: African Americans in the Mass Media* (2d ed., 1993).

Diawara, Manthia, ed., *Black American Cinema* (1993).

George, Nelson, *Blackface: Reflections on African Americans and the Movies* (1994).

Guerrero, Ed, *Framing Blackness: The African American Image in Film* (1993).

Lyman, Stanford M., "Race, Sex, and Servitude: Images of Blacks in American Cinema," *International Journal of Politics, Culture, and Society* 4 (1990): 49–77.

Noble, Peter, *The Negro in Film* (1948).

Null, Gary, *Black Hollywood: The Negro in Motion Pictures* (1975).

Patterson, Lindsay, comp., *Black Films and Film-Makers: A Comprehensive Anthology from Stereotype to Superhero* (1975).

Rhines, Jesse Algeron, *Black Film, White Money* (1996).

Silk, Catherine, and John Silk, *Racism and Anti-Racism in American Popular Culture: Portrayals of African Americans in Fiction and Film* (1990).

Snead, James A., *White Screens, Black Images: Hollywood from the Dark Side,* ed. Colin McCabe and Cornel West (1994).

Woll, Allen L., and Randall M. Miller, ed., *Ethnic and Racial Images in American Film and Television: Historical Essays and Bibliography* (1987).

Yearwood, Gladstone L., ed., *Black Cinema Aesthetics: Issues in Black Independent Filmmaking* (1982).

13.11 EDUCATION

Anderson, James D., *The Education of Blacks in the South, 1860–1935* (1988).

Bacote, Clarence A., *The Story of Atlanta University: A Century of Service, 1865–1965* (1969).

Baker, Liva, *The Second Battle of New Orleans: The Hundred-Year Struggle to Integrate the Schools* (1996).

Ballard, Allen B., *The Education of Black Folk: The Afro-American Struggle for Knowledge in White America* (1973).

Bigglestone, W. E., "Oberlin College and the Negro Student, 1865–1940," *Journal of Negro History* 56 (1971): 198–219.

Bond, Horace Mann, *The Education of the Negro in the American Social Order* (1934).

———— *Education for Freedom: A History of Lincoln University, Pennsylvania* (1976).

Brown, Philip L., *A Century of "Separate but Equal" Education in Anne Arundel County* (1988).

Bullock, Henry Allen, *A History of Negro Education in the South: From 1619 to the Present* (1967).

Butchart, Ronald E., "'Outthinking and Outflanking the Owners of the World': A Historiography of the African American Struggle for Education," *History of Education Quarterly* 28 (1988): 333–66.

Campbell, Clarice T., and Oscar Allan Rogers, *Mississippi: The View from Tougaloo* (1979).

Daniel, Philip T. K., "A History of Discrimination against Black Students in Chicago Secondary Schools," *History of Education Quarterly* 20 (1980): 147–60.

Drago, Edmund L., *Initiative, Paternalism, and Race Relations: Charleston's Avery Normal Institute* (1990).

Drake, St. Clair, "The Black University in the American Social Order," *Daedalus* 100 (1971): 833–97.

Du Bois, William Edward Burghardt, *The Education of Black People: Ten Critiques, 1906–1960,* ed. Herbert Aptheker (1973).

Dyson, Walter, *Howard University, the Capstone of Negro Education, a History: 1867–1940* (1941).

Fleming, John E., *The Lengthening Shadow of Slavery: A Historical Justification for Affirmative Action for Blacks in Higher Education* (1976).

Franklin, Vincent P., *The Education of Black Philadelphia: The Social and Educational History of a Minority Community, 1900–1950* (1979).

Franklin, Vincent P., and James D. Anderson, ed., *New Perspectives on Black Educational History* (1978).

Frost, Olivia Pleasants, "The Journey of Five Generations of a Freedman's Family on Their Quest for Higher Education," *Journal of the Afro-American Historical and Genealogical Society* 3 (1982): 54–64.

Gallagher, Buell G., *American Caste and the Negro College* (1938).

Gleason, Eliza Valeria Atkins, *The Southern Negro and the Public Library: A Study of the Government and Administration of Public Library Service to Negroes in the South* (1941).

Goggins, Lathardus, *Central State University: The First One Hundred Years, 1887–1987* (1987).

Greene, Harry Washington, *Holders of Doctorates among American Negroes: An Educational and Social Study of Negroes Who Have Earned Doctoral Degrees in Course, 1876–1943* (1946).

Hardin, John A., *Fifty Years of Segregation: Black Higher Education in Kentucky, 1904–1954* (1997).

Heintze, Michael R., *Private Black Colleges in Texas, 1865–1954* (1985).

Hill, Susan T., *The Traditionally Black Institutions of Higher Education: Their Development and Status, 1860 to 1982* (1985).

Holmes, Dwight Oliver Wendell, *The Evolution of the Negro College* (1934).

Jackameit, William P., "A Short History of Negro Public Higher Education in West Virginia, 1890–1965," *West Virginia History* 37 (1976): 309–25.

Johnson, Charles S., *The Negro College Graduate* (1938).

241 Education / 13.11

Jones, Maxine D., and Joe M. Richardson, *Talladega College: The First Century* (1990).

Kennedy, Thomas C., "Southland College: The Society of Friends and Black Education in Arkansas," *Arkansas Historical Quarterly* 42 (1983): 207–38.

Kersey, Harry A., Jr., "St. Augustine School: Seventy-Five Years of Negro Parochial Education in Gainesville, Florida," *Florida Historical Quarterly* 51 (1972): 58–63.

Lamon, Lester C., "The Tennessee Agricultural and Industrial Normal School: Public Education for Black Tennesseans," *Tennessee Historical Quarterly* 32 (1973): 42–58.

Leavell, Ullin W., *Philanthropy in Negro Education* (1930).

Logan, Rayford W., *Howard University: The First Hundred Years, 1867–1967* (1969).

Mabee, Carleton, *Black Education in New York State: From Colonial to Modern Times* (1979).

Margo, Robert A., *Race and Schooling in the South, 1880–1950: An Economic History* (1990).

Mayberry, B. D., "The Tuskegee Movable School: A Unique Contribution to National and International Agriculture and Rural Development," *Agricultural History* 65 (1991): 85–104.

McNair, Nathaniel Clayton, Jr., *Continuing Education in a Small Historically Black Private College: A Case Study* (1980).

Morris, Gabrielle, *Head of the Class: An Oral History of African-American Achievement in Higher Education and Beyond* (1995).

Nevfelt, Harvey, and Leo McGee, *Education of the African American Adult: A Historical Overview* (1990).

Neyland, Leedell W., "State-Supported Higher Education among Negroes in the State of Florida," *Florida Historical Quarterly* 43 (1964): 105–22.

Patterson, Zella J., *Langston University: A History* (1979).

Peabody, Francis Greenwood, *Education for Life: The Story of Hampton Institute* (1922).

Plank, David N., and Marcia E. Turner, "Contrasting Patterns in Black School Politics: Atlanta and Memphis, 1865–1985," *Journal of Negro Education* 60 (1991): 203–18.

Preer, Jean L., *Lawyers v. Educators: Black Colleges and Desegregation in Public Higher Education* (1982).

Putney, Martha S., "The Black Colleges in the Maryland State College System: Quest for Equal Opportunity, 1908–1975," *Maryland Historical Magazine* 75 (1980): 335–43.

Range, Willard, *The Rise and Progress of Negro Colleges in Georgia, 1865–1949* (1951).

Richardson, Joe M., *A History of Fisk University, 1865–1946* (1980).

Russell, Lester F., *Black Baptist Secondary Schools in Virginia, 1887–1957* (1981).

Scott, J. Irving, *The Education of Black People in Florida* (1974).

Shannon, Samuel H., "Land-Grant College Education and Black Tennesseans: A Case Study in the Politics of Education," *History of Education Quarterly* 22 (1982): 139–57.

Smith, J. Owens, "The Politics of Income and Educational Differences between Blacks and West Indians," *Journal of Ethnic Studies* 13 (1985): 17–30.

Smith, Timothy L., "Native Blacks and Foreign Whites: Varying Responses to Educational Opportunity in America, 1880–1950," *Perspectives in American History* 6 (1972): 309–35.

Spivey, Donald, "Crisis on a Black Campus: Langston University and Its Struggle for Survival," *Chronicles of Oklahoma* 59 (1982): 430–47.

Summerville, James, *Educating Black Doctors: A History of Meharry Medical College* (1983).

Synott, Marcia G., "The Admissions and Assimilation of Minority Students at Harvard, Yale, and Princeton, 1900–1950," *History of Education Quarterly* 19 (1979): 285–304.

Thomas, James S., "Methodism's Splendid Mission: The Black Colleges," *Methodist History* 22 (1984): 139–57.

Walker, Vanessa Siddle, *Their Highest Potential: An African American School Community in the Segregated South* (1996).

Weatherford, W. D., ed., *A Survey of the Negro Boy in Nashville, Tennessee* (1932).

Weinberg, Meyer, *A Chance to Learn: The History of Race and Education in the United States* (1977).

Wharton, David Eugene, *A Struggle Worthy of Note: The Engineering and Technological Education of Black Americans* (1992).

White, Arthur O., "State Leadership and Black Education in Florida, 1876–1976," *Phylon* 42 (1981): 168–79.

Williams, Lawrence H., *Black Higher Education in Kentucky, 1879–1930: The History of Simmons University* (1987).

Williams, Mildred M., et al., *The Jeanes Story: A Chapter in the History of American Education, 1908–1968* (1979).

Woodson, Carter G., *The Education of the Negro prior to 1861: A History of the Education of the Colored People of the United States from the Beginning of Slavery to the Civil War* (2d ed., 1919).

——— *The Miseducation of the Negro* (1933).

Wright, Marion Thompson, *The Education of Negroes in New Jersey* (1941).

13.12 WORK AND ENTREPRENEURIAL ACTIVITY

Andrew, Mildred Gwin, *The Men and Mills: A History of the Southern Textile Industry* (1987).

Bailey, Ronald W., comp., *Black Business Enterprise: Historical and Contemporary Perspectives* (1971).

Bloch, Herman D., "Craft Unions and the Negro in Historical Perspective," *Journal of Negro History* 43 (1958): 10–33.

Bolster, W. Jeffrey, *Black Jacks: African American Seamen in the Age of Sail* (1997).

Burrows, John H., *The Necessity of Myth: A History of the National Negro Business League, 1900–1945* (1977).

Cantor, Milton, comp., *Black Labor in America* (1969).

Carnegie, Mary Elizabeth, *The Path We Tread: Blacks in Nursing Worldwide, 1854–1994* (3d ed., 1995).

Coleman, A. Lee, and Larry D. Hall, "Black Farm Operators and Farm Population, 1900–1970: Alabama and Kentucky," *Phylon* 40 (1979): 387–402.

Dickerson, Dennis C., *Out of the Crucible: Black Steelworkers in Western Pennsylvania, 1875–1980* (1986).

Durham, Philip, and Everett L. Jones, *Negro Cowboys* (1965).

Edwards, Gilbert Franklin, *The Negro Professional Class* (1959).

Fink, Gary M., and Merle Elwyn Reed, ed., *Essays in Southern Labor History: Selected Papers* (1977).

Foley, Neil, *The White Scourge: Mexicans, Blacks, and Poor Whites in Texas Cotton Culture* (1997).

Foner, Philip S., *Organized Labor and the Black Worker, 1619–1973* (1974).

Foner, Philip S., and Ronald L. Lewis, ed., *Black Workers: A Documentary History from Colonial Times to the Present* (1989).

Franklin, Charles Lionel, *The Negro Labor Unionist of New York: Problems and Conditions among Negroes in the Labor Unions in Manhattan with Special Reference to the N.R.A. and Post-N.R.A. Situations* (1936).

Greene, Lorenzo, and Carter G. Woodson, *The Negro Wage Earner* (1930).

Greer, Edward, "Racism and U.S. Steel, 1906–1974," *Radical America* 10 (1976): 45–66.

Harmon, J. H., Jr., Arnett G. Lindsay, and Carter G. Woodson, *The Negro as a Business Man* (1929).

Harris, William H., *The Harder We Run: Black Workers since the Civil War* (1982).

Haynes, Marion, "A Century of Change: Negroes in the U.S. Economy, 1860–1960," *Monthly Labor Review* (1985): 1359–65.

Henderson, Alexa Benson, *Atlanta Life Insurance Company: Guardian of Black Economic Dignity* (1990).

Hickman, Nollie W., "Black Labor in the Forest Industries of Piney Woods, 1840–1933," in Noel Polk, ed., *Mississippi's Piney Woods: A Human Perspective* (1986): 79–91.

Hill, Herbert, *Black Labor and the American Legal System* (1977).

Honey, Michael Keith, *Black Workers Remember: An Oral History of Segregation, Unionism, and the Freedom Struggle* (1999).

Jacobsen, Julius, ed., *The Negro and the American Labor Movement* (1968).

Jones, Jacqueline, *American Work: Four Centuries of Black and White Labor* (1998).

——— *Labor of Love, Labor of Sorrow: Black Women, Work, and the Family, from Slavery to the Present* (1985).

Joyce, Donald Franklin, *Black Book Publishers in the United States: A Historical Dictionary of the Presses, 1817–1990* (1991).

——— *Gatekeepers of Black Culture: Black-Owned Book Publishing in the United States, 1817–1981* (1983).

Kilson, Marion, "Black Women in the Professions, 1890–1970," *Monthly Labor Review* 100 (1977): 38–41.

Kinzer, Robert, and Edward Sagarin, *The Negro in American Business: The Conflict Between Separatism and Integration* (1950).

Lebergott, Stanley, *The American Economy: Income, Wealth, and Want* (1976).

Lewis, Ronald L., *Black Coal Miners in America: Race, Class, and Community Conflict, 1780–1980* (1987).

Light, Ivan Hubert, *Ethnic Enterprise in America: Business and Welfare among Chinese, Japanese, and Blacks* (1972).

Mandle, Jay R., *Not Slave, Not Free: The African American Economic Experience since the Civil War* (1992).

Marshall, Ray, *The Negro Worker* (1967).

McDonald, Forrest, and Grady McWhiney, "The South from Self-Sufficiency to Peonage: An Interpretation," *American Historical Review* 85 (1980): 1095–1118.

McGee, Leo, and Robert Boone, "Black Rural Land Decline in the South," *Black Scholar* 8 (1977): 8–11.

Perata, David D., *Those Pullman Blues: An Oral History of the African American Railroad Attendant* (1996).

Schweninger, Loren, *Black Property Owners in the South, 1790–1915* (1990).

Silverman, Robert Mark, "The Effects of Racism and Racial Discrimination on Minority Business Development: The Case of Black Manufacturers in Chicago's Ethnic Beauty Aids Industry," *Journal of Social History* 31 (1998): 571–97.

Spero, Sterling D., and Abram L. Harris, *The Black Worker: The Negro and the Labor Movement* (1931).

Stuart, M. S., *An Economic Detour: A History of Insurance in the Lives of American Negroes* (1940).

Trent, William J., *Development of Negro Life Insurance Enterprises* (1932).

Trotter, Joe William, Jr., "African-American Workers: New Directions in United States Labor Historiography," *Labor History* 35 (1994): 495–523.

Trueblood, Roy W., "Union Negotiations between Black Methodists in America," *Methodist History* 8 (1970): 18–29.

Tucker, Susan, "A Complex Bond: Southern Black Domestic Workers and Their White Employers," *Frontiers* 9 (1987): 6–13.

——— *Telling Memories among Southern Women: Domestic Workers and Their Employers in the Segregated South* (1988).

Walker, Juliet E. K., ed., *Encyclopedia of African American Business History* (1999).

——— *History of Black Business in America: Capitalism, Race, Entrepreneurship* (1998).

Weems, Robert E., Jr., *Black Business in Black Metropolis: The Chicago Metropolitan Assurance Company, 1925–1985* (1996).

——— *Desegregating the Dollar: African American Consumerism in the Twentieth Century* (1998).

Wesley, Charles H., *Negro Labor in the United States, 1850–1925: A Study in American Economic History* (1927).

Wiener, Jonathan M., "Class Structure and Economic Development in the American South, 1865–1955," *American Historical Review* 84 (1979): 970–92.

Wilhelm, Sidney M., "The Economic Demise of Blacks in America: A Prelude to Genocide," *Journal of Black Studies* 17 (1986): 201–54.

Woodard, Michael D., *Black Entrepreneurs in America: Stories of Struggle and Success* (1999).

Woodson, Carter G., *The Negro Professional Man and the Community* (1934).

Wright, Gavin, *Old South, New South: Revolutions in the Southern Economy since the Civil War* (1986).

13.13   SCIENCE AND TECHNOLOGY

Burt, McKinley, Jr., *Black Inventors of America* (2d ed., 1989).

Ives, Patricia Carter, *Creativity and Inventions: The Genius of Afro-Americans and Women in the United States and Their Patents* (1987).

James, Portia P., *The Real McCoy: African-American Invention and Innovation, 1619–1930* (1989).

Jenkins, Edward S., "Impact of Social Conditions: A Study of the Work of American Black Scientists and Inventors," *Journal of Black Studies* 14 (1984): 477–91.

Klein, Aaron E., *The Hidden Contributors: Black Scientists and Inventors in America* (1971).

Pearson, Willie, Jr., and H. Kenneth Bechtel, ed., *Blacks, Science, and American Education* (1989).

Van Sertima, Ivan, ed., *Blacks in Science: Ancient and Modern* (1983).

Williams, James C., *At Last Recognition in America: A Reference Handbook of Unknown Black Inventors and their Contributions to America* (1978).

Wharton, David Eugene, *A Struggle Worthy of Note: The Engineering and Technological Education of Black Americans* (1992).

13.14 MEDICINE AND HEALTH

Akiwowo, Akinsola, "Racialism and Shifts in the Mental Orientation of Black People in West Africa and the Americas, 1856–1956," *Phylon* 31 (1970): 256–64.

Beardsley, Edward H., *A History of Neglect: Health Care for Blacks and Mill Workers in the Twentieth-Century South* (1987).

Byrd, W. Michael, and Linda A. Clayton, *An American Health Dilemma: A Medical History of African Americans and the Problem of Race* (2000).

Cutright, Phillips, and Edward Shorter, "The Effects of Health on the Completed Fertility of Non-White and White U.S. Women Born from 1867 through 1935," *Journal of Social History* 13 (1979): 191–218.

Falk, Leslie A., "Black Abolitionist Doctors and Healers, 1810–1885," *Bulletin of the History of Medicine* 54 (1980): 258–72.

Hine, Darlene Clark, *Black Women in White: Racial Conflict and Cooperation in the Nursing Profession, 1890–1950* (1989).

———— "Co-Laborers in the Work of the Lord: Nineteenth-Century Black Women Physicians," in Ruth Abrams, ed., *"Send Us a Lady Physician": Women Doctors in America, 1835–1930* (1985): 107–20.

Holt, Thomas, Cassandra Smith-Parker, and Rosalyn Terborg-Penn, *A Special Mission: The Story of Freedmen's Hospital, 1862–1962* (1975).

Kiple, Kenneth F., ed., *The African Exchange: Toward a Biological History of Black People* (1987).

Kiple, Kenneth F., "A Survey of Recent Literature on the Biological Past of the Black," in Kenneth F. Kiple, ed., *The African Exchange: Toward a Biological History of Black People* (1987): 7–34.

Kiple, Kenneth F., and Virginia Himmelsteib King, *Another Dimension to the Black Diaspora: Diet, Disease, and Racism* (1981).

Kiple, Kenneth F., and Virginia H. Kiple, "Black Yellow Fever Immunities, Innate and Acquired, As Revealed in the American South," *Social Science History* 1 (1977): 419–36.

Lewis, Julien Herman, *The Biology of the Negro* (1942).

McBride, David, *Integrating the City of Medicine: Blacks in Philadelphia Health Care, 1910–1965* (1989).

McFalls, Joseph A., Jr., "Impact of VD on the Fertility of the U.S. Black Population, 1880–1950," *Social Biology* 20 (1973): 2–19.

Postell, William Dosite, *The Health of Slaves on Southern Plantations* (1951).

Rankin-Hall, Lesley M., *A Biohistory of Nineteenth Century Afro-Americans: The Burial Remains of a Philadelphia Cemetery* (1997).

Reitzes, Dietrich C., *Negroes and Medicine* (1958).

Rice, Mitchell F., "On Assessing Black Health Status: A Historical Overview," *Urban League Review* 9 (1985–86): 6–12.

Seham, Max, *Blacks and American Medical Care* (1973).

Smith, Susan L., *Sick and Tired of Being Sick and Tired: Black Women's Health Activism in America, 1890–1950* (1995).

Summerville, James, *Educating Black Doctors: A History of Meharry Medical College* (1983).

Torchia, Marion M., "Tuberculosis among American Negroes: Medical Research on a Racial Disease, 1830–1950," *Journal of the History of Medicine and Allied Sciences* 32 (1977): 252–79.
Warren, Christian, "Northern Chills, Southern Fevers: Race-Specific Mortality in American Cities, 1730–1900," *Journal of Southern History* 63 (1997): 23–56.

13.15   STUDIES IN FOREIGN LANGUAGES

Achode, Codjo S., *Appelle-moi nègre: Crise et quête d'identité noire de l'Amérique à l'Afrique, d'hier à demain* [Call Me Nigger: Crises and Questions of Black Identity from America to Africa, from Yesterday to Tomorrow] (1993). In French.
Adam, Michel, "Les origines ethniques de la population afro-americaine: incertitudes et ambiguités" [The Ethnic Origins of the Afro-American Population: Uncertainties and Ambiguities], *Cultures et Développement [Belgium]* 15 (1983): 253–94. In French.
Bacharan, Nicole, *Histoire des Noirs américains au vingtième siècle* [History of Black Americans in the Twentieth Century] (1994). In French.
Balen, Noël, *L'odyssée du jazz* [Jazz Odyssey] (1993). In French.
Bard, Patrick, and Jean-Claude Charles, *Jazz* (1990). In French.
Bergerot, Franck, and Arnaud Merlin, *L'Épopéia du jazz* [The Epic of Jazz] (2 vols., 1991). In French.
Cartosio, Bruno, "L'esperienza afroamericana e la storiografia: pregiudizi, cancellazioni, confini" [The Afro-American Experience and Historiography: Prejudices, Cancellations, Boundaries], *Rivista Internazionale di Studi Americani [International Journal of American Studies]* 1 (1994): 31–39. In Italian.
Claudio Gorlier, *Storia dei negri degli Stati Uniti* [History of Negroes in the United States] (1963). In Italian.
Daridan, Jean, *De Lincoln à Johnson: Noirs et Blancs* [From Lincoln to Johnson: Blacks and Whites] (1965). In French.
Dauer, Alfons M., *Der Jazz: Seine Ursprünge und Seine Entwicklung* [Jazz: Its Origin and Development] (1958). In German.
De Stefano, Gildo, *Trecento anni di jazz, 1619–1919: Le origini della musica afro-americana tra sociologia e antropologia* [Three Hundred Years of Jazz, 1619–1919: The Origins of Afro-American Music within Sociology and Anthropology] (1986). In Italian.
Diaz Soler, Luis M., *Historia de la esclavitud negra en Puerto Rico (1493–1890)* [History of Black Slavery in Puerto Rico, 1493–1890] (1953). In Spanish.
Dorigné, Michel, *Histoire du jazz* [The History of Jazz] (2 vols., 1968). In French.
Fabre, Geneviève, Rachel Ertel, and Elise Marienstras, *En marge: les minorités aux États-Unis* [In the Margin: The Minorities of the United States] (1977). In French.
Fabre, Michel, *La Rive noire: de Harlem à la Seine* [The Black Bank: From Harlem to the Seine] (1985). In French.
——— *Les Noirs américains* [Black Americans] (2d ed., 1970). In French.
Fléouter, Claude, *La Mémoire du peuple noir* [The Memory of Black People] (1979). In French.
Fohlen, Claude, *Histoire de l'esclavage aux États-Unis* [The History of Slavery in the United States] (1998). In French.
——— *Les Noirs aux États-Unis* [Blacks in the United States] (1994). In French.
Geiss, Immanuel, *Die Afro-Amerikaner* [The Afro-Americans] (1969). In German.
Ginzburg Migliorino, Ellen, *La marcia immobile: Storia dei neri americani dal 1770 al 1970* [The Motionless March: History of Black Americans from 1770 to 1970] (1994). In Italian.
Gladu, Andre, and Michel Brault, *Les Créoles* [The Creoles] (rev. ed., 1990). In French.
Gorlier, Claudio, *Storia dei negri degli Stati Uniti* [History of Negroes in the United States] (1963). In Italian.
Gräbener, Jürgen, "Vodou und Gesellschaft in Haiti" [Voodoo and Society in Haiti], *Internationales Jahrbuch für Religionssoziologie [International Yearbook for the Sociology of Religion]* 6 (1970): 158–76. In German.

Gracchus, Fritz, *Les lieux de la mère dans les sociétés afroaméricaines: pour une généalogie du concept de matrifocalité* [The Place of the Mother in Afro-American Society: A Geneology of the Concept of Matriarchy] (1980). In French.

Guerin, Daniel, *De l'Oncle Tom aux Panthères: le drame des Noirs américains* [From Uncle Tom to the Panthers: The Black American Drama] (rev. ed., 1973). In French.

Gundolf, Hubert, *Eines Tages Werden Wir Siegen: Von der Sklaverei zum Bürgerrecht* [One Day We Shall Win: From Slavery to Civil Rights] (1968). In German.

Hegmanns, Dirk, "Afrobrasil: von der Rassistichen Ausgrenzung zur Kulturellen Identität" [Afro-Brazil: From Racist Marginalisation to Cultural Identity], in Working Paper No. 216, *Lateinamerika-Programm* [The Latin America Program] (1994). In German.

Honda, Sozo, *Amerika Kokujin no Rekishi* [A History of African-Americans] (1964, 1991). In Japanese.

——— *Amerika Shakai to Kokujin* [Essays on Black People in American Society] (1972). In Japanese.

———, ed., *Amerika Shakai-shi no Sekai* [Perspectives in American Social History: Issues of Race and Ethnicity] (1989). In Japanese.

Ihde, Horst, *Von der Plantage zum Schwarzen Ghetto: Geschichte und Kultur der Afroamerikaner in den USA* [From the Plantation to the Black Ghetto: History and Culture of the Afro-Americans in the USA] (1975). In German.

Izzo, Carlo, *Blues e spirituals: poesie anonime e d'autore dei Negri d'America* [Blues and Spirituals: Anonymous and Authored Poetry by Negroes in America] (1963). In Italian.

Jost, Ekkehard, *Sozialgeschichte des Jazz in den USA* [Social History of Jazz in the USA] (1982). In German.

Kung, Nien-nien, *Mei Guo Hei Ren Yun Dong Shi* [History of Black Movements in the United States] (1968). In Chinese.

——— *Mei Guo Hei Ren Sheng Huo Shi* [History of the African-Americans] (vol. 2, 1968). In Chinese.

Lehmann, Theo, *Negro Spirituals: Geschichte und Theologie* [Negro Spirituals: History and Theology] (1965). In German.

Loria, Achille, "Die Sklavenwirtschaft im Modernen Amerika und im Europâischen Alterthume" [The Slave-Economy in Modern America and in Ancient Europe], *Zeitschrift für Social- und Wirtschaftsgeschichte* [Journal for Social and Economic History] 4 (1896): 67–118. In German.

Malson, Lucien, *Des musiques du jazz* [About Jazz Music] (1983). In French.

——— *Histoire du jazz et de la musique afro-américaine* [The History of Jazz and Afro-American Music] (rev. ed., 1978). In French.

Mattiello, Cristina, *Le Chiese nere negli Stati Uniti: dalla religione degli schiavi alla teologia nera della liberazione* [Black Churches in the United States: From Slave Religion to Black Liberation Theology] (1993). In Italian.

Mauro, Walter, *Jazz e universo negro* [Jazz and the Negro Universe] (1972). In Italian.

Minnella, Nando, *L'altra America: i neri, 1870–1970* [The Other America: Blacks, 1870–1970] (1980). In Italian.

Ndiaye, Pap, "L'histoire afro-américaine" [African American History and Historiography], in Jean Heffer and François Weil, ed., *Chantiers de l'histoire américaine* [The Singers of American History] (1994): 273–307. In French.

Osanai, Hiroshi, *Kuroi Amerika-jin* [Black Americans] (1968). In Japanese.

Otsuka, Hideyuki, *Amerika Gasshukoku-shi to Jinshu Sabetsu* [Racial Discrimination in United States History] (1982). In Japanese.

Paraire, Philippe, *Les Noirs américains: généalogie d'une exclusion* [African-Americans: The Geneology of an Exclusion] (1993). In French.

Paraire, Philippe, and Michael Welply, *Les Noirs américains depuis le temps de l'ésclavage* [Black Americans Since Slavery] (2d ed., 1992). In French.

Pereda Valdés, Ildefonso, *Línea de color: ensayos afro-americanos* [Color Line: Afro-American Essays] (1938). In Spanish.

Portelli, Alessandro, *Bianchi e neri nella letteratura americana: la dialettica dell'identità* [Whites and Blacks in American Literature: The Dialectic of Identity] (1976). In Italian.

——— "La filosofía y los hechos: Narracción, interpretación y significado en las evocaciones y las fuentes orales" [Philosophy and Facts: Narration, Interpretation, and Meaning in Autobiography and Oral History], *Fundamentos de Antropología* [*Fundamentals of Anthropology*] 3 (1994): 33–39. In Spanish.

——— *La linea del colore: saggi sulla cultura afroamericana* [The Color Line: Essays on African-American Culture] (1994). In Italian.

——— *Saggi sulla cultura afro-americana* [Essays on Afro-American Culture] (1979). In Italian.

——— "'The Power of Blackness': gli afroamericani e l'energia del sottosuolo" ['The Power of Blackness': African-Americans and the Energy of the Underground], *Rivista Internazionale di Studi Nordamericani* [*International Journal of North American Studies*] 1 (1994): 22–34. In Italian.

Réda, Jacques, *L'Improviste: une lecture du jazz* [Improvised: A Reading of Jazz] (rev. and expanded ed., 1990). In French.

Rie, Robert, *Das Schicksal der Neger in den Vereinigten Staaten von Amerika* [The Fate of the Negroes in the United States of America] (1956). In German.

Rodrigues, Urbano Tavares, ed., *O Problema Racial nos E. U. A. visto por Portuguêses* [The United States' Racial Problem As Viewed by the Portuguese] (1968). In Portuguese.

Rogge, Heinz, "Das Erbe Afrikas in Sprache und Kultur der Nordamerikanischen Gullahs" [The African Heritage in Language and Culture of the North American Gullahs], *Zeitschrift für Volkskunde* 61 (1965): 30–37. In German.

Rojas-Mix, Miguel, *Cultura afroamericana de esclavos a ciudadanos* [Afro-American Culture from Slaves to Citizens] (1990). In Spanish.

Rosario, José Colomban, and Justina Carrión, *El negro: Haití, Estados Unidos, Puerto Rico* [The Blacks: Haiti, the United States, and Puerto Rico] (2d ed., 1951). In Spanish.

Rüster, Bernd, *Rassenbeziehungen in den USA* [Race Relations in the USA] (1973). In German.

Sacre, Robert, *Musique cajun et musiques noires en Louisiane francophone* [Cajun Music and Black Music in French-Speaking Louisiana] (1990). In French.

Schoell, Franck Louis, *La question des Noirs aux États-Unis* [The Question of Blacks in the United States] (3d ed., 1983). In French.

Serna, Juan Manuel, *Los afronorteamericanos: historia y destino* [The Afro-Americans of the United States: History and Destiny] (1994). In Spanish.

Shi, Xianrong, "Mei Guo Hei Ren De San Ci Wen Yi Fu Xing" [Three Renaissances of Afro-American Culture], *Mei Guo Yan Jiu* 4 (1988): 73–88. In Chinese.

St. Martin, Gerard Labarre, *Écrits louisianais du dix-neuvième siècle: nouvelles, contes, et fables* [Nineteenth Century Writings from Louisiana: Reports, Stories, and Fables] (1979). In French.

Steger, Hanns-Albert, "Revolutionäre Hintergründe des Kreolischen Synkretismus" [The Revolutionary Background of Creole Syncretism], *Internationales Jahrbuch für Religionssoziologie* [*International Yearbook for the Sociology of Religion*] 6 (1970): 99–141. In German.

Steinberger, Heide, *Rassendiskriminierung und Oberster Gerichtshof in den Vereinigten Staaten von Amerika: Ein Beispiel Richterlicher Fortentwicklung von Verfassungsrecht* [Racial Discrimination and the Supreme Court in the United States of America: An Example of the Evolution of Constitutional Law] (1969). In German.

Valtz Mannucci, Loretta, *I neri nella storia degli Stati Uniti: Appunti per una storia* [Blacks in United States History: Notes toward a History] (1981). In Italian.

Wartenweiler, Fritz, *Schwarze in den USA: Von General Armstrong zu Louis Armstrong* [Blacks in the USA: From General Armstrong to Louis Armstrong] (1960). In German.

Yang, Shengmao, ed., *Mei Guo Hei Ren Yun Dong Da Shi Ji* [Chronicles of African American Movements] (1973). In Chinese.

Yourcenar, Marguerite, trans., *Fleuve profond, sombre rivière: les Negro spirituals* [Deep River, Dark River: The Negro Spirituals] (rev. ed., 1982). In French.

——— *Le problème noir aux États-Unis: 1619–1964* [The Black Problem in the United States] (1964). In French.

14   1492–1690

John Thornton

14.1.1   Africa

Ajayi, J. F. Ade, and J. E. Inikori, "An Account of Research on the Slave Trade in Nigeria," in Unesco, *The African Slave Trade from the Fifteenth to the Nineteenth Century* (1979): 247–49.

Barbot, Jean, *Barbot on Guinea: The Writings of Jean Barbot on West Africa, 1687–1712,* ed. Adam Jones, Robin Law, and P. E. H. Hair (1992).

Battel, Andrew, *Strange Adventures of Andrew Battel of Leigh, in Angola and the Adjoining Regions,* ed. E. G. Ravenstein (1901).

Bazin, Jean, "War and Servitude in Segou," *Economy and Society* 3 (1974): 107–44.

Bean, Richard, "A Note on the Relative Importance of Slaves and Gold in West African Exports," *Journal of African History* 15 (1974): 351–56.

Birmingham, David, *Trade and Conflict in Angola: The Mbundu and Their Neighbours under the Influence of the Portugese, 1483–1790* (1966).

Blake, John, *Europeans in West Africa, 1450–1560* (2 vols., 1942).

Bohannan, Paul, and Philip Curtin, *Africa and Africans* (1988).

Bosman, Willem, *A New and Accurate Description of the Coast of Guinea: Divided into the Gold, the Slave, and the Ivory Coast,* ed. John Ralph Willis, J. D. Fage, and R. E. Bradbury (4th ed., 1967).

Bradbury, R. E., *Benin Studies* (1973).

Brooks, George, *Landlords and Strangers: Ecology, Society, and Trade in Western Africa, 1000–1630* (1993).

Cooper, Frederick, "Review Article: The Problem of Slavery in African Studies," *Journal of African History* 20 (1979): 103–25.

Curtin, Philip D., *Africa Remembered: Narratives by West Africans from the Era of the Slave Trade* (1967).

——— *Economic Change in Pre-Colonial Africa: Senegambia in the Era of the Slave Trade* (2 vols., 1975).

Daaku, Kwame Yeboah, "The Slave Trade and African Society," *Emerging Themes of African History* (1968): 134–40.

——— *Trade and Politics on the Gold Coast, 1600–1720* (1970).

DeCorse, Christopher R., "Culture Contact, Continuity, and Change on the Gold Coast, AD 1400–1900," *African Archaeological Review* 10 (1992): 163–96.

Eltis, David, "The Relative Importance of Slaves and Commodities in the Atlantic Trade of Seventeenth-Century Africa," *Journal of African History* 35 (1994): 237–50.

Eltis, David, and Lawrence C. Jennings, "Trade between Western Africa and the Atlantic World in the Pre-Colonial Era," *American Historical Review* 93 (1988): 936–59.

Fage, John D., "The Effect of the Export Slave Trade on African Populations," *The Population Factor in African Studies* (1975): 15–23.

——— "Slavery and the Slave Trade in the Context of West African History," *Journal of African History* 10 (1969): 393–404.

——— "Slaves and Society in Western Africa, c.1445–c.1700," *Journal of African History* 3 (1980): 289–310.

———— "Some Remarks on Beads and Trade in Lower Guinea in the Sixteenth and Seventeenth Centuries," *Journal of African History* 3 (1962): 343–47.

Fage, John D., and Roland Oliver, ed., *The Cambridge History of Africa* (8 vols., 1975–85).

Feinberg, Harvey, *Africans and Europeans in West Africa: Elminans and Dutchmen on the Gold Coast during the Eighteenth Century* (1989).

Gates, Henry Louis, Jr., *Wonders of the African World* (1999).

Gemery, Henry A., and Jan S. Hogendorn, "Technological Change, Slavery, and the Slave Trade," in Clive Dewey, and A. G. Hopkins, ed., *Imperial Impact: Studies in the Economic History of Africa and India* (1978): 243–58.

Gleave, M. B., and R. M. Prothero, "Population Density and 'Slave Raiding': A Comment," *Journal of African History* 12 (1971): 319–27.

Gomez, Michael Angelo, *Pragmatism in the Age of Jihad: The Precolonial State of Bundu* (1992).

Goody, Jack, *Technology, Tradition, and the State in Africa* (1971).

Gray, Richard, and David Birmingham, ed., *Pre-Colonial African Trade: Essays on Trade in Central and Eastern Africa before 1800* (1970).

Hair, P. E. H., *The Founding of the Castelo de São Jorge da Mina: An Analysis of the Sources* (1994).

Hair, P. E. H., and Avelino Teixeira da Mota, *East of Mina: Afro-European Relations on the Gold Coast in the 1550s and 1560s* (1988).

Harms, Robert W., *River of Wealth, River of Sorrow: The Central Zaire Basin in the Era of the Slave and Ivory Trade, 1500–1891* (1981).

———— "Slavery Systems in Africa," *History of Africa* 5 (1978): 327–35.

Heintze, Beatrix, "Written Sources, Oral Traditions, and Oral Traditions as Written Sources: The Steep and Thorny Way to Early Angolan History," *Paideuma* 33 (1987): 263–87.

Henige, David, "John Kabes of Komenda: An Early African Entrepreneur and State Builder," *Journal of African History* 18 (1977): 1–19.

Henige, David P., and Marion Johnson, "Agaja and the Slave Trade: Another Look at the Evidence," *History in Africa* 3 (1976): 57–67.

Herskovits, Melville J., *Dahomey: An Ancient West African Kingdom* (1938).

———— "The Significance of West Africa for Negro Research," *Journal of Negro History* 21 (1936): 15–30.

Hilton, Ann, *The Kingdom of Kongo* (1985).

Hiskett, Mervyn, *The Development of Islam in West Africa* (1984).

Hopkins, Anthony G., *An Economic History of West Africa* (1973).

Iliffe, John, *The African Poor: A History* (1987).

Inikori, Joseph E., ed., *Forced Migration: The Impact of the Export Slave Trade on African Societies* (1982).

Isert, Paul Erdmann, *Letters on West Africa and the Slave Trade: Paul Erdmann Isert's Journey to Guinea and the Caribbean Islands in Columbia, 1788,* ed. and trans. Selena Winsnes (1992).

Jobson, Richard, *The Golden Trade: Or, a Description of the River Gambra and the Golden Trade of the Aethiopians, Set down as They Were Collected in Travelling Part of the Yeares 1620 and 1621* (1623; rpt. 1968).

Johnson, Marion, "Review Article: 'Polanyi, Peukert, and the Political Economy of Dahomey,'" *Journal of African History* 21 (1980): 395–98.

Jones, Adam, ed. and trans., *Brandenburg Sources for West African History, 1680–1700* (1985).

————, ed. and trans., *German Sources for West African History, 1559–1669* (1983).

———— "The Kquoja Kingdom: A Forest State in Seventeenth Century West Africa," *Paideuma* 29 (1983): 23–43.

———— *West Africa in the Mid-Seventeenth Century: An Anonymous Dutch Manuscript* (1994).

———— "Who Were the Vai?" *Journal of African History* 22 (1981): 159–78.

Kati, Mahmoud, *Tarikh El-Fettach, 1913* (2 vols., 1964).

Kea, Ray A., *Settlements, Trade, and Politics on the Seventeenth-Century Gold Coast* (1982).

Klein, A. Norman, "The Two Asantes: Competing Interpretations of 'Slavery' in Akan-Asante Culture and Society," in Paul E. Lovejoy, ed., *The Ideology of Slavery in Africa* (1981): 149–67.

—— "West African Unfree Labor before and after the Rise of the Atlantic Slave Trade," in Laura Foner, and Eugene D. Genovese, ed., *Slavery in the New World: A Reader in Comparative History* (1969): 87–95.

Klein, Martin A., "Women in Slavery in the Western Sudan," in Claire C. Robertson, and Martin A. Klein, ed., *Women and Slavery in Africa* (1965): 67–92.

Law, Robin, ed., *Contemporary Source Material for the History of the Old Oyo Empire, 1627–1824* (1993).

—— "Dahomey and the Slave Trade: Reflections on the Historiography of the Rise of Dahomey," *Journal of African History* 27 (1986): 237–67.

——, ed., *Further Correspondence of the Royal African Company of England Relating to the 'Slave Coast', 1681–1699: Selected Documents from Ms. Rawlinson C.745–47 in the Bodleian Library, Oxford* (1992).

—— "Horses, Firearms, and Political Power in Pre-Colonial West Africa," *Past and Present* 72 (1976): 112–32.

—— "Ideologies of Royal Power: The Dissolution and Reconstruction of Political Authority on the 'Slave Coast', 1680–1750," *Africa* 57 (1987): 321–44.

—— "'My Head Belongs to the King': On the Political and Ritual Significance of Decapitation in Pre-Colonial Dahomey," *Journal of African History* 30 (1989): 399–416.

—— *The Oyo Empire, c.1600-c.1836: A West African Imperialism in the Era of the Atlantic Slave Trade* (1977).

—— "Problems of Plagiarism, Harmonization, and Misunderstanding in Contemporary European Sources: Early [Pre-1680's] Sources for the 'Slave Coast' of West Africa," *Paideuma* 33 (1987): 337–58.

—— "Religion, Trade, and Politics on the 'Slave Coast': Roman Catholic Missions in Allada and Whydah in the Seventeenth Century," *Journal of Religion in Africa* 21 (1991): 42–77.

—— "Royal Monopoly and Private Enterprise in the Atlantic Trade: The Case of Dahomey," *Journal of African History* 18 (1977): 555–77.

—— *The Slave Coast of West Africa, 1550–1750: The Impact of the Atlantic Slave Trade on an African Society* (1991).

—— "Slave-Raiders and Middlemen, Monopolists and Free-Traders: The Supply of Slaves for the Atlantic Trade in Dahomey, c.1715–1850," *Journal of African History* 30 (1989): 45–68.

—— "Slaves, Trade, and Taxes: The Material Basis of Political Power in Precolonial West Africa," *Research in Economic Anthropology: An Annual Compilation of Research* 1 (1978): 37–52.

Levtzion, Nehemia, *Ancient Ghana and Mali* (1973).

Lovejoy, Paul E., ed., *The Ideology of Slavery in Africa* (1981).

—— "The Impact of the Atlantic Slave Trade on Africa: A Review of the Literature," *Journal of African History* 30 (1989): 365–94.

—— *Transformations in Slavery: A History of Slavery in Africa* (1983).

MacGaffey, Wyatt, *Religion and Society in Central Africa: The Bakongo of Lower Zaire* (1986).

Makepeace, Margaret, *Trade on the Guinea Coast, 1657–1666: The Correspondence of the English East India Company* (1991).

Manning, Patrick, "The Enslavement of Africans: A Demographic Model," *Canadian Journal of African Studies/Revue Canadienne des Études Africaines* 15 (1981): 499–526.

—— "Local Versus Regional Impact of Slave Exports on Africa: Historical Perspectives," in Dennis Cordell, and Joel Gregory, ed., *African Population and Capitalism* (1987): 35–49.

—— *Slavery, Colonialism, and Economic Growth in Dahomey, 1640–1960* (1982).

—— "Slaves, Palm Oil, and Political Power on the West African Coast," *African Historical Studies* 2 (1969): 279–88.

Marees, Pieter de, *Description and Historical Account of the Gold Kingdom of Guinea*, ed. and trans. Adam Jones, and Albert van Dantzig (1987).

Martin, Phyllis, "The Trade of Loango in the Seventeenth and Eighteenth Centuries," in *Forced Migration: The Impact of the Export Slave Trade on African Societies* (1982): 202–20.

Mason, Michael, "Population Density and 'Slave Raiding': The Case of the Middle Belt of Nigeria," *Journal of African History* 10 (1969): 551–64.

McCaskie, T. C., *State and Society in Pre-Colonial Asante* (1995).

Miers, Suzanne, and Igor Kopytoff, ed., *Slavery in Africa: Historical and Anthropological Perspectives* (1977).

Miller, Joseph C., *Kings and Kinsmen: Early Mbundu States in Angola* (1976).

———— "Lineages, Ideology, and the History of Slavery in Western Central Africa," in Paul E. Lovejoy, ed., *The Ideology of Slavery in Africa* (1981): 41–72.

———— "The Slave Trade in Congo and Angola," in Martin L. Kilson, and Robert I. Rotberg, ed., *The African Diaspora: Interpretive Essays* (1976): 75–113.

Morton-Williams, Peter, "The Oyo Yoruba and the Atlantic Trade, 1670–1830," *Journal of the Historical Society of Nigeria* 3 (1964): 25–45.

Newbury, C. W., "An Early Inquiry into Slavery and Captivity in Dahomey," *Zaire* 14 (1960): 53–67.

Northrup, David, "The Growth of Trade among the Igbo before 1800," *Journal of African History* 13 (1972): 217–36.

Obichere, Boniface I., "Women and Slavery in the Kingdom of Dahomey," *Revue Francaise d'Histoire d'Outre-Mer* 65 (1978): 5–20.

Palmer, Herbert Richmond, *Sudanese Memoirs* (1967).

Patterson, Karl David, *The Northern Gabon Coast to 1875* (1975).

Patterson, Orlando, *Slavery and Social Death: A Comparative Study* (1982).

Phillips, John, "A Journal of the Voyage in the Hannibal of London, Ann. 1693–1694," in Awnsham Churchill, *A Collection of Voyages and Travels* (6 vols., 1732).

Piot, Charles, "Of Slaves and the Gift: Kabre Sale of Kin during the Era of the Slave Trade," *Journal of African History* 37 (1996): 31–50.

Polanyi, Karl, *Dahomey and the Slave Trade: An Analysis of An Archaic Economy* (1966).

Robertson, Claire, and Martin Klein, ed., *Women and Slavery in Africa* (1983).

Roberts, Richard, "Ideology, Slavery, and Social Formation: The Evolution of Maraka Slavery in the Middle Niger Valley," in *Ideology of Slavery in Africa* (1981): 171–200.

Rodney, Walter, "African Slavery and Other Forms of Social Oppression on the Upper Guinea Coast in the Context of the Atlantic Slave-Trade," *Journal of African History* 7 (1966): 431–43.

———— "Gold and Slaves on the Gold Coast," *Transactions of the Historical Society of Ghana* 10 (1969): 13–28.

———— "Portuguese Attempts at Monopoly on the Upper Guinea Coast, 1580–1650," *Journal of African History* 6 (1965): 307–22.

———— "Upper Guinea and the Significance of the Origins of Africans Enslaved in the New World," *Journal of Negro History* 54 (1969): 327–45.

Ryder, A. F. C., "Dutch Trade on the Nigerian Coast during the Seventeenth Century," *Journal of the Historical Society of Nigeria* 3 (1965): 195–210.

———— "Missionary Activity in the Kingdom of Warri to the Early Nineteenth Century," *Journal of the Historical Society of Nigeria* 2 (1960): 1–24.

———— "The Re-Establishment of Portuguese Factories on the Costa da Mina to the Mid-Eighteenth Century," *Journal of the Historical Society of Nigeria* 1 (1958): 157–83.

Sadi, Abd al-Rahman ibn Abd Allah, *Tarikh Es-Soudan,* ed. and trans. Octave Victor Houdas, and Edmond Benoist (2 vols., 1964).

Searing, James F., "Aristocrats, Slaves, and Peasants: Power and Dependency in the Wolof States, 1700–1850," *International Journal of African Historical Studies* 21 (1988): 475–503.

———— *West African Slavery and Atlantic Commerce: The Senegal River Valley, 1700–1860* (1993).

Teixeira da Mota, Avelino, and P. E. H. Hair, *East of Mina: Afro-European Relations on the Gold Coast in the 1550s and 1560s* (1988).

Thomas, Robert P., and Richard N. Bean, "The Fishers of Men: The Profits of the Slave Trade," *Journal of Economic History* 34 (1974): 885–914.

Thornton, John K., *Africa and Africans in the Making of the Atlantic World, 1400–1800* (2d ed., 1998).

———— "The African Experience of the '20. And Odd Negroes' Arriving in Virginia in 1619," *William and Mary Quarterly* 55 (1998): 421–34.

———— "The Art of War in Angola, 1575–1680," *Comparative Studies in Society and History* 30 (1988): 360–78.

———— "Central African Names and African-American Naming Patterns," *William and Mary Quarterly* 50 (1993): 727–42.

———— "The Correspondence of the Kongo Kings, 1614–1635: Problems of Internal Written Evidence on a Central African Kingdom," *Paideuma* 33 (1987): 407–21.

———— "Demography and History in the Kingdom of Kongo, 1550–1750," *Journal of African History* 18 (1977): 507–30.

———— "The Demographic Effect of the Slave Trade on Western Africa, 1500–1850," *African Historical Demography* 2 (1981): 691–720.

———— "The Development of an African Catholic Church in the Kingdom of Kongo, 1491–1750," *Journal of African History* 25 (1984): 147–67.

———— *The Kingdom of Kongo: Civil War and Transition, 1641–1718* (1983).

———— "The Kingdom of Kokongo, ca. 1390–1678: The Development of an African Social Formation," *Cahiers d'Etudes Africaines* 22 (1983): 325–42.

———— "Legitimacy and Political Power: Queen Njinga, 1624–1663," *Journal of African History* 32 (1991): 25–40.

———— "On the Trail of Voodoo: African Christianity in Africa and the Americas," *Americas* 44 (1988): 261–78.

———— "A Resurrection for the Jaga," *Cahiers d'Etudes Africaines* 18 (1978): 223–27.

———— "Sexual Demography: The Impact of the Slave Trade on Family Structure," in Claire Robertson, and Martin Klein, ed., *Women and Slavery in Africa* (1983): 39–48.

———— "The Slave Trade in Eighteenth Century Angola: Effects on Demographic Structures," *Canadian Journal of African Studies/Revue Canadienne D'Etudes Africaines* 14 (1980): 417–27.

———— "Traditions, Documents, and the Ife-Benin Relationship," *History in Africa: A Journal of Method* 15 (1988): 351–62.

Tilleman, Erick, *A Short and Simple Account of the Country Guinea and Its Nature [1697]*, trans. Selena Axelron Winsnes (1994).

Uchendu, Victor, "Slavery in Southeast Nigeria," *Trans-Action* 4 (1967): 52–54.

———— "Slaves and Slavery in Igboland, Nigeria," in Suzanne Miers, and Igor Kopytoff, ed., *Slavery in Africa: Historical and Anthropological Perspectives* (1977): 121–32.

Uzoigwe, G. N., "The Slave Trade and African Societies," *Transactions of the Historical Society of Ghana* 14 (1973): 187–212.

van Dantzig, Albert, ed. and trans., *The Dutch and the Guinea Coast, 1674–1742: A Collection of Documents from the General State Archive at the Hague* (1978).

Villault, Nicolas, *A Relation of the Coasts of Africk Called Guinee* (1670).

Vogt, John L., "The Early Sao Tome-Principe Trade with Mina, 1500–1540," *International Journal of African Historical Studies* 6 (1973): 453–67.

———— *Portuguese Rule on the Gold Coast, 1469–1682* (1979).

Watt, James, *Journal of James Watt: Expedition to Timbo, Capital of the Fula Empire in 1794*, ed. Bruce Mouser (1994).

Webb, James A., *Desert Frontier: Ecological and Economic Change along the Western Sahel, 1600–1850* (1995).

———— "The Horse and Slave Trade between the Western Sahara and Senegambia," *Journal of African History* 34 (1993): 221–46.

Wilks, Ivor, *Forests of Gold: Essays on the Akan and the Kingdom of Asante* (1993).

Wilson, Louis, *The Krobo People of Ghana to 1892: A Political and Social History* (1991).

Wrigley, Christopher C., "Historicism in Africa: Slavery and State Formation," *African Affairs* 70 (1971): 113–24.

Yarak, Larry, *Asante and the Dutch, 1744–1873* (1990).

14.1.2   Studies in Foreign Languages (Africa)

Almeida, Pedro Ramos de, *Portugal e a Escravatura em Africa* [Portugal and Slavery in Africa] (1978). In Portuguese.

Augé, Marc, "Les faiseurs d'ombre: Servitude et structure lignagère dans la société Alladin [The Makers of Shadows: Servitude and Lineage Structure in Alladin Society]," in *L'Ésclavage en Afrique Precoloniale* [Slavery in Precolonial Africa] (1975): 455–75. In French.

Ballong-Wen-Mewuda, J. Bato'ora, *São Jorge da Mina, 1482–1637: La vie d'un comptoir portugais en Afrique Occidentale* [Sao Jorge da Mina, 1482–1637: The Life of a Portuguese Trading Post in West Africa] (1993). In French.

Bassani, Ezio, "Uno Capuccino nell'Africa nera nel Seicento: I disegni dei Manoscritti Araldi del Padre Giovanni Antonio Cavazzi da Montecuccolo [A Capuchin in Black Africa in the Seventeenth Century: The Drawings in the Araldi Manuscripts of Father Giovanni Antonio da Montecuccolo]," *Quaderni Poro* 4 (1987): 9–107. In Italian.

Bathily, Abdoulaye, *Les portes de l'or: Le Royaume de Galam (Sénégal) de l'ere musulmane au temps de négriers, VIIIe–XVIIIe siècles* [The Golden Gates: The Kingdom of Galam (Senegal) from the Muslim Era to the Time of the Slave Traders, Eighth–Eighteenth Centuries] (1989). In French.

Becker, Charles, and Victor Martin, "Kayor and Baol: Senegalese Kingdoms and the Slave Trade in the Eighteenth Century," in J. E. Inikori, ed., *Forced Migration: The Impact of the Export Slave Trade on African Societies* (1982): 100–25.

Boulegue, Jean, *Les Anciens Royaumes Wolof: Le Grand Jolof* [The Ancient Wolof Kingdoms: The Grand Jolof] (1987). In French.

——— "Un empire Peul dans le Soudan Occidental au debut du XVIIe siecle [A Peul Empire in Western Sudan in Early Seventeenth Century]," in *La Parole, le sol, l'ecrit: 2000 ans d'histoire Africaine* [The Word, The Soil, The Writing: 2000 Years of African History] (1981). In French.

Brasio, Antonio, *Monumenta Missionaria Africana: Africa Occidentale* [African Missionary Statements: West Africa] (15 vols., 1952–88). In Portuguese.

Cadornega, Antonio de Oliveria de, *Historia Geral das Guerras Angolanas, 1680* [General History of Angolan Wars, 1680] (1972). In Portuguese.

Caltanisetta, Luca da, *Il Congo agli inizi del settecento nella relazione di P. Luca da Caltanisetta* [The Congo at the Beginning of the Eighteenth Century in the Account of Father Luca Da Caltanisetta], ed. Romain Rainero (1974). In Italian.

Carli, Dionigio da Piacenza, *Il moro trasportado nell'inclita citta di Venezia* [The Moor Transported to the Inclement City of Venice] (1687). In Italian.

——— "Relation nouvelle et curieuse d'un voyage au Congo, fait en années 1666 et 1667 [New and Curious Account of a Voyage to the Congo for the Years 1666 and1667]," in Jean Baptiste Labat, ed. and trans., *Relation Historique de l'Ethiopie occidentale* [Historical Communication of Eastern Ethiopia] (5 vols., 1732). In French.

Cavazzi, Giovanni Antonio, *Descripcão Historica dos tres Reinos do Congo, Matamba e Angola* [Historical Description of the Three Kingdoms of Congo, Matamba, and Angola] (1965). In Portuguese.

Coelho, Francisco de Lemos, *Duas Descripcões Seiscentistas da Guine* [Two Sixteenth-Century Descriptions of Guinea] (1953). In Portuguese.

Daget, Serge, "Role et contribution des états-cotiers dans l'evolution des rapports entre Africains et Europeens du XVe au XIXe Siècles [Role and Contribution of Coastal States in the Growth of Relations between Africans and Europeans in the Fifteenth-Nineteenth Centuries]," *Annales de l'Université d'Abidjan* 13 (1980): 313–36. In French.

Dantzig, Albert van, "Les Hollandais sur la côte des esclaves: Parties gagnées et parties perdues [The Dutch in Slave Coastal Areas: Gains and Losses]," *Etudes Africaines Offertes à Henri Brunschwig* (1982): 79–89. In French.

Dapper, Olifert, *Naukeurige Beschrijvinge der Afrikaensche Gewesten* (1676). In Dutch.

de Thulin, Dieudonné, "Les Capucins au Congo: l'Ésclavage et la traite des noirs au Congo, 1482–1878 [The Capuchins in the Congo: Slavery and Trade of Blacks in the Congo, 1482–1878]," *Études Franciscaines [Franciscan Studies]* 35 (1923): 615–31. In French.

Deffontaine, Yann, *Guerre et société au royaume de Fetu, Ghana, 1471–1720* [War and Society in the Kingdom of Fetu, Ghana, 1471–1720] (1993). In French.

del Gaudio, Giovanni, *Il problema della schiavitu: Con particolare riferimento alle popolazionidel Sudan Occidentale e della Guinea Settentrionale* [The Question of Slavery: With Particular Reference to the Western Sudan and Southern Guinean Population] (1972). In Italian.

Dieng, Amady Aly, *Classes sociales et mode de production esclavagiste en Afrique de l'Ouest* [Social Classes and Modes of Production by Slaves of West Africa] (1974). In French.

Diop, Louise-Marie, "Méthode et calculs approximatifs pour la construction d'une courbe représentative de l'evolution de la population de l'Afrique noire, du milieu du XVIè siècle au milieu du XXè [Method and Approximate Calculations for the Determination of a Representative Curve of the Evolution of the Population of Black Africa, from the Mid-Sixteenth to Mid-Twentieth Century]," *African Historical Demography* 2 (1981): 139–50. In French.

du Jarric, Pierre, *Histoire des choses plus memorables, adventures tant des Indes Orientales que autres pays de la decouverte des portugais* [Account of the Most Memorable Incidents Befalling the Portugese, in the East Indies and Other Lands of Their Discovery] (3 vols., 1608–1614). In French.

Elwert, Georg, *Wirtschaft und Herrschaft von 'Daxome'* [Dahomey] *im 18. Jahrhundert: Okonomie des Sklavenraubs und Gesellschaftsstruktur 1724 bis 1818; Verbunden mit Untersuchungen uber Verwendung und Bestimmung der Begriffe Klasse, Macht, und Religion in diesem Kontext* [Economy and Rulership in Dahomey in the Eighteenth Century: Slave Economy and Social Structure, 1724–1818; Combined with Research on the Definition of the Terms Class, Power, and Religion in This Context] (1973). In German.

Filesi, Teobaldo, "Nazionalismo e religione nel Congo all'inizio del 1700 [Nationalism and Religion in the Congo at the Beginning of the Eighteenth Century]," *Africa* 9 (1971): 267–303, 463–508, 645–68. In Italian.

Gaeta, Antonio da, *La maravigliosa conversione alla santa fede di Cristo della Regina Singa. E del suo eegno di Matamba nell'Africa Meridionale* [The Marvelous Converison of Queen Singha to the Holy Faith of Christ in the Kingdom of Matamba in Southern Africa] (1669). In Italian.

Gaston-Martin, *Nantes au XVIIIe Siècle: L'ere des Négriers, 1714–1774* [Nantes in the XVIII Century, the Era of Slave Traders, 1714–1774] (1993). In French.

Gayibor, Nicoué, ed., *Toponymie historique et glossonymes actuals de l'ancienne côte des esclaves, XVe–XIXe siècles* [Historic Toponyms and Current Glossonyms on the Former Slave Coast, Fifteenth-Nineteenth Centuries] (1990). In French.

Girard, Jean, *L'Or du Bambouk: Une dynamique de civilization Ouest-Africaine: Du Royaume de Gabou à La Casamance* [The Gold of Bambouk: A Dynamic of a West African Civilization: From the Kingdom of Gabou to Casamance] (1992). In French.

Heintze, Beatrix, "Das Ende des Unabhangigen Staates Ndongo [Angola]: Neue Chronologie und Reinterpretation, 1617–1630 [The End of the Independent States of Angola: A New Chronology and Reinterpretation, 1617–1630]," *Paideuma* 27 (1981): 197–203. In Dutch.

———. "Die Portugiesische Besiedlungs und Wirtschaftpolitik in Angola, 1570–1607 [The Portuguese Settlement and Economic Policy in Angola, 1570–1607]," *Aufsatze zur Portugiesischen Kulturgeschichte* 17 (1981–1982): 200–19. In Dutch.

———. "Unbekanntes Angola: Der Staat Ndongo im 16. Jahrhundert [The Unknown Angola: The Angolan State in the Sixteenth Century]," *Anthropos* 72 (1977): 749–805. In Dutch.

Héritier, François, "Des cauris et des hommes: Production d'esclaves et accumulation de cauris chez les Samo [Cowries and Men: Slave Production and Accumulation of Cowries among the Samo]," in Claude Meillassoux, ed., *L'Esclavage en Afrique Precoloniale* (1975). In French.

Jadin, Louis, "Le Congo et la secte des Antoniens: Restauration du Royaume sous Pedro IV et la 'Saint Antoine' Congolaise, 1694–1718 [The Congo and the Antonine Sect: Restoration of the Kingdom under Pedro IV and Saint Anthony of the Congo, 1694–1718]," *Bulletin de l'Institut Historique Belge de Rome* 33 (1961): 411–615. In French.

———. "Rivaltes Luso-Neerlandaise au Sohio, Congo: Tentatives missionaires des récollects Flammands et tribulations des Capucins Italiens, 1670–1675 [Luso-Dutch Rivalries in Sohio, Congo: Missionary Attempts by the Dutch and the Trials of Italian Capuchins, 1670–1675]," *Bulletin de l'Institut Historique Belge de Rome* 37 (1966): 137–359. In French.

Lange, Dierick, and Silvio Berthoud, "L'Interieur de l'Afrique Occidentale d'apres Giovanni Lorenzo Anania [The Interior of Western Africa according to Giovanni Lorenzo d'Anania]," *Journal of World History* 14 (1972): 299–351. In French.

Lopes, Duarte, *Relazione del reame di Congo* [Tale of the Congo Kingdom], ed. Filippo Pigafetta, and Giorgio Raimond Cardona (1978). In Italian.

Ly, Abdoulaye, *La compagnie du Sénégal* (2d ed., 1993). In French.

Ly, Madina, "L'empire du Mali a-t-il survéçu jusqu'à la fin du XVI siècle? [Did the Mali Empire Survive until the End of the Sixteenth Century?]," *Bulletin de l'Institut Fondamental de l'Afrique Noire* 38 (1976): 234–56. In French.

Malowist, Marian, "Le commerce d'or et d'esclaves au Soudan Occidental [Commerce of Gold and Slaves in the Western Sudan]," *Africana Bulletin* 4 (1966): 49–72. In French.

Mateus, Cardoso, *Historia do Reino do Congo* [History of the Congo Kingdom], ed. Antonio Brasio (1969). In Portuguese.

Meillassoux, Claude, *L'Ésclavage en Afrique precoloniale* [Slavery in Precolonial Africa] (1975). In French.

——— "Role de l'esclavage dans l'histoire de l'Afrique Occidentale [The Role of Slavery in the History of West Africa]," *Anthropologie et societes [Anthropology and Society]* 2 (1978): 117–48. In French.

Montesarchio, Girolamo da, *La prefettura apostolica del Congo alla meta del XVII secolo: La relazione inedita di Girolamo da Montesarchio* [The Apostolic Prefecture of the Congo in the Mid-Seventeenth Century: The Unpublished Account of Girolamo da Montesarchio], ed. Calogero Piazza (1976). In Italian.

Mosto, Alvise da, *Le Navigazioni Atlantiche di Alvise da Mosto* [The Atlantic Navigation of Alvise da Mosto], ed. Tullia Gasparrini-Leporace (1929). In Italian.

Naber, S. P. L'Honoré, "Nota van Pieter Mortamer over het Gewest Angola [Notes from Pieter Mortamer on Western Angola]," *Bijdragen en Mededeelingen van het Historisch Genootschap* 54 (1933): 1–42. In Dutch.

Nooteboom, C., "Slavehandel, Levensbron Van Een Oud Koninkrijk: Economische Analyse van de Geschiedenis van het Oude Dahomey [Slave Trade: The Livelihood of an Old Kingdom: Economic Analysis of the History of Old Dahomey]," *Afrika* 4 (1967): 100–03. In Dutch.

Oliveira, Esteves Maria Luisa, ed., *Portugaliae Monumenta Africana* (2 vols., 1993). In Portuguese.

Orlova, A. S., "Institution de l'esclavage dans l'etat du Congo au Moyen Age, XVIe–XVIIe siecles [The Institution of Slavery in the Congo in the Middle Ages, Sixteenth-Seventeenth Centuries]," *VIIe Congres International des Sciences Anthropologique et Ethnologique [Seventh International Congress of Anthropological and Ethnological Sciences]* 9 (1964): 196–202. In French.

Pacheco Pereira, Duarte, *Esmeraldo de Situ Orbis* [Esmeraldo of Situ Orbis] (1905). In Spanish.

Peukert, Werner, *Der Atlantische Sklavenhandel von Dahomey, 1740–1797: Eine Untersuchung zur Wirtschafts—und Sozialgeschichte Afrikas und Wirtschaftsanthropologie* [The Atlantic Slave Trade in Dahomey, 1740–1797: An Investigation in the Economic and Social History of Africa and Economic Anthropology] (1975). In German.

Pigafetta, Filippo, and Duarte Lopes, *Description du Royaume de Congo et des contrées environnates* [Description of the Congo Kingdom and Surrounding Regions], ed. Willy Bal (1965). In French.

Rey, Pierre-Phillipe, "L'esclavage lignager chez les Tsangui, les Punu et les Kuni du Congo-Brazzaville: Sa place dans le systeme d'ensemble des rapports de production [Hereditary Enslavement among the Tsangui, Punu, and Kuni of Congo-Brazzaville: Its Role in the System of Production]," in *L'Esclavage en Afrique Precoloniale* (1975): 509–28. In French.

Rømer, Ludevig Ferdinand, *Le Golfe de Guinée, 1700–1750: Récit de L. F. Römer, marchand d'esclaves dur la Côte Ouest Africaine* [The Gulf of Guinea, 1700–1750: Account of L. F. Römer, Slave Merchant on the West Coast of Africa], ed. and trans. Mette Dige-Hess (1989). In French.

Ruyters, Dierick, *Toortse der Zee-Veart, 1623* [Torch of the Seafarer,1623], ed. S. P. L'Honore Naber (1913). In Dutch.

Saintogne, Jean Alphonse de, *Les voyages advantureux* [Voyages of Adventure] (1559). In French.

Salvadorini, Vittorio, ed., *Le missioni a Benin e Warri Nel XVII Secolo: La relazione inedita di bonaventura da Firenze* [The Missions to Benin and Warri in the Seventeenth Century: The Unpublished Tale of Bonaventura Da Firenze] (1972). In Italian.

Simonetti, Giuseppe, "Il P. Giacinto da Vetralla e la sua missione nel Congo [Father Giacinto da Vetralla and His Mission in the Congo]," *Bolletino della Societa Geografica Italiana [Bulletin of the Italian Geographical Society]* 10 (1907): 305–22, 369–81. In Italian.

Suret-Canale, Jean, "Contexte et conséquences sociales de la traite africaine [Context and Social Consequences of African Trade]," *Presence Africaine: Revue Culturelle du Monde Noir* 50 (1964): 127–50. In French.

Teixeira da Mota, Avelino, "Un document nouveau pour l'histoire des Peuls au Sénegal pendant les XVéme et XVéme siècles [A New Document for the History of the Peuls in Senegal during the Fifteenth and Sixteenth Centuries]," *Boletim Cultural da Guine Portuguesa* 24 (1969): 781–860. In French.

———— "A Viagem do Navio Santiago à Sierra Leona e Rio de S. Domingos em 1526 [Livro de Armação] [The Voyage of the Santiago to Sierra Leone and the River of San Domingo in 1526]," *Boletim Cultural da Guine Portuguese* 24 (1969): 529–79. In Portuguese.

Teixeira, Marli Geralda, "Notas sôbre o Reino do Congo no século XVI [Notes on the Kingdom of the Congo in the Sixteenth Century]," *Afro-Asia* 4–5 (1967): 77–88. In Portuguese.

Terray, Emmanuel, "La captivité dans le Royaume Abron du Gyaman [Captivity in the Abron Kingdom of Gyaman]," in Claude Meillassoux, *L'Ésclavage en Afrique Precoloniale [Slavery in Precolonial Africa]* (1975): 389–453. In French.

Turner, J. Michael, "Escravos Brasileiros no Daomé [Brazilian Slaves in Dahomey]," *Afro-Asia* 10–11 (1970): 5–24. In Portuguese.

Tymowski, Michal, *Le developpement et regression chez les peuples de la boucle du Niger a l'epoque precoloniale* [Development and Decline of the Peoples of the Niger during Pre-colonial Times] (1974). In French.

———— "Les domains des Princes du Songhay (Soudan Occidental): Comparison avec la grande propriété foncière en Europe au début de l'epoque féodale [The Dominions of the Songhay Princes (West Sudan): Comparison with Large Landownership in Europe in the Early Feudal Age]," *Annales: Economies, Societes, Civilisations* 25 (1970): 1637–58. In French.

van Dantzig, Albert, "Effects of the Atlantic Slave Trade on Some West African Societies," *Revue Française d'Histoire d'Outre-Mer* 62 (1975): 252–69. In French.

van den Broecke, Pieter, *Reizen naar West-Afrika van Pieter van den Broecke, 1605–1614* [The Travels of Pieter van den Broecke to West Africa], ed. K. Ratelband (1950). In Dutch.

14.2.1   Atlantic Slave Trade

Alden, Dauril, and Joseph C. Miller, "'Out of Africa': The Slave Trade and the Transmission of Smallpox to Brazil, ca. 1560–ca. 1830," *Journal of Interdisciplinary History* 18 (1987): 195–224.

———— "Unwanted Cargoes: The Origins and Dissemination of Smallpox via the Slave Trade from Africa to Brazil, 1560–1830," in Kenneth F. Kiple, ed., *The African Exchange: Toward a Biological History of Black People* (1988): 35–109.

Bellarosa, James M., "The Tragic Slaving Voyage of the St. John," *American Neptune* 40 (1980): 293–97.

Berlin, Ira, "The Slave Trade and the Development of Afro-American Society in English Mainland North America, 1619–1775," *Southern Studies* 20 (1981): 122–36.

Blakely, Allison, *Blacks in the Dutch World: The Evolution of Racial Imagery in a Modern Society* (1993).

Boogaart, Ernst van den, and Pieter C. Emmer, "The Dutch Participation in the Atlantic Slave Trade, 1595–1650," in Henry A. Gemery, and Jan S. Hogendorn, ed., *The Uncommon Market: Essays in the Economic History of the Atlantic Slave Trade* (1979): 353–75.

Brown, Soi-Daniel W., "From the Tongues of Africa: A Partial Translation of Oldendorps's Interviews," *Plantation Society in the Americas* 2 (1983): 37–61.

Carreira, Antonio, "Portuguese Research on the Slave Trade," in Unesco, ed., *The African Slave Trade from the Fifteenth to the Nineteenth Century* (1979): 250–64.

Cohn, Raymond L., and Richard A. Jensen, "The Determinants of Slave Mortality Rates on the Middle Passage," *Explorations in Economic History* 19 (1982): 269–82.

Conti, Luigi, "The Catholic Church and the Slave Trade," in Unesco, *The African Slave Trade from the Fifteenth to the Nineteenth Century* (1979): 265–68.

Curtin, Philip D., *Africa Remembered: Narratives by West Africans from the Era of the Slave Trade* (1967).

———— *The Atlantic Slave Trade: A Census* (1969).

———— "The Atlantic Slave Trade, 1600–1800," *History of West Africa* 1 (1972): 240–68.

———— "Epidemiology and the Slave Trade," *Political Science Quarterly* 83 (1968): 190–216.

———— "Measuring the Atlantic Slave Trade," in Stanley L. Engerman, and Eugene D. Genovese, ed., *Race and Slavery in the Western Hemisphere: Quantitative Studies*: 107–28.

———— "The Slave Trade and the Atlantic Basin: Intercontinental Perspectives," in Nathan Huggins, Martin Kilson, and Daniel M. Fox, ed., *Key Issues in the Afro-American Experience* (1971): 74–93.

———— "Supplementary Report on Slave-Trade Studies in the United States," in Unesco, *The African Slave Trade from the Fifteenth to the Nineteenth Century* (1979): 269.

Davies, K. G., *The Royal African Company* (1957).

Diouf, Sylviane A., *Servants of Allah: African Muslims Enslaved in the Americas* (1998).

Donnan, Elizabeth, *Documents Illustrative of the History of the Slave Trade to America* (1930–35).

Dow, George Francis, *Slave Ships and Slaving* (1927).

Du Bois, W. E. B., *The Suppression of the African Slave Trade to the United States of America, 1638–1870* (1970).

Duignan, Peter, and Clarence Clendenen, *The United States and the African Slave Trade, 1619–1862* (1963).

Emmer, Pieter C., "Surinam and the Decline of the Dutch Slave Trade," *Revue Française d'Histoire d'Outre-Mer* 1–2 (1975): 245–51.

Engerman, Stanley, and Eugene Genovese, ed., *Race and Slavery in the Western Hemisphere: Quantitative Studies* (1975).

Evans, William McKee, "From the Land of Canaan to the Land of Guinea: The Strange Odyssey of the 'Sons of Ham,'" *American Historical Review* 85 (1980): 15–43.

Faber, Eli, *Jews, Slaves, and the Slave Trade: Setting the Record Straight* (1998).

Fernandez-Armesto, Felipe, *The Canary Islands after the Conquest: The Making of a Colonial Society in the Early Sixteenth Century* (1982).

Forbes, Jack D., *Black Africans and Native Americans: Color, Race, and Caste in the Evolution of Red-Black Peoples* (1988).

Fyfe, Christopher, "The Dynamics of African Dispersal: The Transatlantic Slave Trade," in Martin L. Kilson, and Robert I. Rotberg, ed., *The African Diaspora: Interpretive Essays* (1976): 57–74.

———— "A Historiographical Survey of the Transatlantic Slave Trade from West Africa," in *The Transatlantic Slave Trade from West Africa* (1965): 81–92.

———— "The Impact of the Slave Trade on West Africa," in *The Transatlantic Slave Trade from West Africa* (1965): 57–74.

Gemery, Henry A., and Jan S. Hogendorn, "The Atlantic Slave Trade: A Tentative Economic Model," *Journal of African History* 15 (1974): 223–46.

———— *The Uncommon Market: Essays in the Economic History of the Atlantic Slave Trade* (1979).

Gray, Richard, "The Vatican and the Atlantic Slave Trade," *History Today* 31 (1981): 37–39.

Greenfield, Sidney M., "Madeira and the Beginnings of New World Sugar Cane Cultivation and Plantation Slavery: A Study in Institution Building," *Annals of the New York Academy of Sciences* 292 (1977): 536–52.

Hair, P. E. H., *The Atlantic Slave Trade and Black Africa* (1978).

Inikori, Joseph E., "The Origin of the Diaspora: The Slave Trade from Africa," *Tarikh* 5 (1978): 1–19.

———— "The Slave Trade and the Atlantic Economies, 1451–1870," in Unesco, *The African Slave Trade from the Fifteenth to the Nineteenth Century* (1979): 56–87.

———— "Under-Population in Nineteenth Century West Africa: The Role of the Export Slave Trade," *African History Demography: Volume II* (1981): 283–313.

Inikori, Joseph E., and Stanley L. Engerman, ed., *The African Slave Trade: Effects on Economies, Societies, and Peoples in Africa, the Americas, and Europe* (1992).

Isert, Paul Erdmann, *Letters on West Africa and the Slave Trade: Paul Erdmann Isert's Journey to Guinea and the Caribbean Islands in Columbia, 1788*, ed. and trans. Selena Winsnes (1992).

King, James F., "Descriptive Data on Negro Slaves in Spanish Importation Records and Bills of Sale," *Journal of Negro History* 2 (1943): 204–30.

Klein, Herbert S., "African Women in the Atlantic Slave Trade," in Claire C. Robertson, and Martin A. Klein, ed., *Women and Slavery in Africa* (1983): 29–38.

———— *The Middle Passage: Comparative Studies in the Atlantic Slave Trade* (1978).

Le Veen, E. Phillip, "The African Slave Supply Response," *African Studies Review* 18 (1975): 9–28.

Lovejoy, Paul, "The Volume of the Atlantic Slave Trade: A Synthesis," *Journal of African History* 23 (1982): 473–501.

Lunn, Arnold Henry Moore, *A Saint in the Slave Trade: Peter Claver, 1581–1654* (1935).

Manning, Patrick, "The Slave Trade in the Bight of Benin, 1640–1890," in Henry A. Gemery and Jan S. Hogendorn, ed., *The Uncommon Market: Essays in the Economic History of the Atlantic Slave Trade* (1979): 107–41.

Mannix, Daniel P., and Malcolm Cowley, *Black Cargoes: A History of the Atlantic Slave Trade, 1518–1865* (1962).

Maxwell, John Francis, *Slavery and the Catholic Church: The History of the Catholic Teaching concerning the Moral Legitimacy of the Institution of Slavery.* (1975).

Miller, Joseph C., "Mortality in the Atlantic Slave Trade: Statistical Evidence on Causality," *Journal of Interdisciplinary History* 11 (1980): 385–423.

Munford, Clarence, *The Black Ordeal of Slavery and Slave Trading in the French West Indies, 1625–1715* (3 vols., 1991).

Nodal, Roberto, "Black Presence in the Canary Islands [Spain]," *Journal of Black Studies* 12 (1981): 83–90.

Page, Willie F., *The Dutch Triangle: The Netherlands and the Atlantic Slave Trade, 1621–1664* (1997).

Palmer, Colin A., *Human Cargoes: The British Slave Trade to Spanish America, 1700–1739* (1981).

Pierce, Milfred C., "The Atlantic Slave Trade: A Case for Reparation," *Negro History Bulletin* 35 (1972): 44–47.

Pierson, William D., "White Cannibals, White Martyrs: Fear, Depression, and Religious Faith as Causes of Suicide among New Slaves," *Journal of Negro History* 62 (1977): 147–59.

Pollitt, Ronald, "John Hawkin's Troublesome Voyages: Merchants, Bureaucrats, and the Origins of the Slave Trade," *Journal of British History* 12 (1973): 26–40.

Postma, Johannes, "The Dimension of the Dutch Slave Trade from Western Africa," *Journal of African History* 2 (1972): 237–48.

——— *The Dutch in the Atlantic Slave Trade, 1600–1815* (1990).

——— "The Dutch Slave Trade: A Quantitative Assessment," *Revue Française d'Histoire de Outre-Mer* 1–2 (1975): 232–44.

——— "Mortality in the Dutch Slave Trade, 1675–1795," in Henry A. Gemery and Jan S. Hogendorn, ed., *The Uncommon Market: Essays in the Economic History of the Atlantic Slave Trade* (1979): 239–60.

——— "The Origins of African Slaves: The Dutch Activities on the Guinea Coast, 1675–1795," in Stanley Engerman, and Eugene Genovese, ed., *Race and Slavery in the Western Hemisphere: Quantitative Studies* (1975): 33–49.

Richardson, David, "Slave Exports from West and Central Africa, 1700–1810: New Estimates of Volume and Distribution," *Journal of African History* 30 (1989): 1–22.

Romero, Fernando, "The Slave Trade and the Negro in South America," *Hispanic American Historical Review* 3 (1944): 368–86.

Ryder, A. F. C., "An Early Portuguese Trading Voyage to the Forcados River," *Journal of the Historical Society of Nigeria* 1 (1959): 294–321.

Sanders, Ronald, *Lost Tribes and Promised Lands* (1978).

Saunders, A. C. de C. M., *A Social History of Black Slaves and Freedmen in Portugal, 1441–1555* (1982).

Scelle, Georges, "The Slave Trade in the Spanish Colonies of America: The Assiento," *American Journal of International Law* 4 (1910): 612–61.

Schroeder, Walter A., Edwin S. Munger, and Darleen R. Powars, "Sickle Cell Anaemia, Genetic Variations, and the Slave Trade to the United States," *Journal of African History* 31 (1990): 163–80.

Solow, Barbara L., ed., *Slavery and the Rise of the Atlantic System* (1991).

Thornton, Anthony P., "Spanish Slave-Ships in the English West Indies, 1660–1685," *Hispanic American Historical Review* 35 (1955): 374–85.

Thornton, John K., "The African Experience of the '20. And Odd Negroes' Arriving in Virginia in 1619," *William and Mary Quarterly* 55 (1998): 421–34.

Unesco, *The African Slave Trade from the Fifteenth to the Nineteenth Century* (1979).

Unger, W. S., "Essay on the History of the Dutch Slave Trade," in M. A. P. Meilink-Roelofsz, ed., Maria J. L. van Yperen, trans., *Dutch Authors on West Indian History: A Historiographical Selection* (1982): 46–98.

University of Edinburgh, Centre of African Studies, *The Transatlantic Slave Trade from West Africa* (1965).

Verlinden, Charles, *The Beginnings of Modern Colonization* (1970).

Vogt, John L., "The Lisbon Slave House and the African Trade, 1486–1521," *Proceedings of the American Philosophical Society* 117 (1973): 1–16.

Wax, Darold D., "Negro Resistance to the Early American Slave Trade," *Journal of Negro History* 51 (1966): 1–15.

——— "A People of Beastly Living: Europe, Africa, and the Atlantic Slave Trade," *Phylon* 41 (1980): 12–24.

Wright, I. A., "The Coymans Asiento, 1685–1689," *Bijdragen voor Vaderlandse Geschiedenis en Oudheidkunde* 6 (1924): 23–62.

14.2.2   Studies in Foreign Languages (Atlantic Slave Trade)

Aguet, Isabelle, *La Traite des Negres* [Negro Trafficking] (1971). In French.

Amitié (Frigate), *Un navire de commerce sur la côte Senegambienne en 1685* [A Merchant Ship on the Senegambian Coast in 1685] (1964). In French.

Andel, M. A. van, "Geneeskunde en Hygiene op de Slavenschpen in den Compagnietijd [Health and Hygiene aboard the Slave Ships in the Time of the Company]," *Nederlands Tijdschrift voor Geneeskunde* 1 (1931): 614–37. In Dutch.

Assadourian, Carlos Sempat, *El trafico de esclavos en Cordoba de Angola a Potosi, siglos XVI–XVII* [Slave Traffic in Cordoba, from Angola to Potosi, Sixteenth-Seventeenth Centuries] (1966). In Spanish.

Cortés Alonso, Vicenta, "La población negra de Palo de la Frontera, 1568–1579 [Negro Population of Palo de la Frontera, 1568–1579]," *Actas y Memorias del XXXVI Congreso Internacional de Americanistas* 3 (1964): 609–18. In Spanish.

——— "La trata de esclavos durante los primeros descubrimientos, 1489–1516 [Slave Trade during the First Discoveries, 1489–1516]," *Anuario de Estudios Atlanticos* 9 (1963): 23–49. In Spanish.

——— "Procedencia de los esclavos negros en Valencia, 1482–1516 [Provenance of Negro Slaves in Valencia, 1482–1516]," *Revista Española de Antropologia Americana* 7 (1972): 123–51. In Spanish.

Daget, Serge, ed., *De la traite à l'esclavage* [From Trade to Slavery] (2 vol., 1988). In French.

Dantzig, Albert van, *Het Nederlanse Aandeel in de Slavenhandel* [The Role of the Netherlands in the Slave Trade] (1968). In Dutch.

Debien, Gabriel, Marcel Delafosse, and Guy Thilmans, "Journal d'un voyage de traite en Guinée, à Cayenne et aux Antilles fait par Jean Barbot en 1678–1679 [Journal of a Trading Voyage in Guinea, to Cayenne, and to the Antilles, Led by Jean Barbot in 1678–1679]," *Bulletin de l'Institut Fondamental d'Afrique Noire* 40 (1978): 235–395. In French.

Deschamps, Hubert J., *Histoire de la traite des noirs de L'antiquite a nos jours* [History of the Slave Trade from Antiquity to Our Days] (1972). In French.

——— "La traite des noirs: Vue d'ensemble et perspectives [The Slave Trade: Overview and Perspectives]," *Comptes-Rendus Mensuels des Seances* 39 (1969): 384–98. In French.

Ducasse, Andre, *Les negriers, ou le traffic des esclaves* [Slave Ships, or Traffic in Slaves] (1948). In French.

——— "Les negriers, bières flottantes [Slave Ships, Floating Coffins]," *Historia* 37 (1978): 78–85. In French.

Eekhof, A., "Twee Ducumenten Betreffende den Slavenhadel in de 17e Eeuw [Two Documents Describing the Slave Trade in the Seventeenth Century]," *Nederlandsch Archief voor Kerkgescheidenis* 11 (1914): 271–98. In Dutch.

Emmer, Pieter C., Jean Mettas, and Jean-Claude Nardin, *La traite des noirs par l'Atlantique: Nouvelles approches* [Negro Trade in the Atlantic: New Approaches] (1976). In French.

Ferrez, Gilberto, "Diario Anonimo de uma Viagem as Costas d'Africa e as Indias Espanholas: o Trafico de Escravos, 1702–1703 [The Anonymous Diary of a Voyage to the Coast of Africa and the Spanish Indies: The Traffic of Slaves, 1702–1703]," *Revista do Instituto Historico e Geografico Brasileiro* (1965): 3–42. In Portuguese.

Franco Silva, Alfonso, *Registro Documental sobre la esclavitud sevillano, 1453–1513* [Official Documents on Sevillian Slavery, 1453–1513] (1979). In Spanish.

Groenhuis, G., "De Zonen van Cham: Gereformeerde Predikanten over de Slaverniij, van Udemans Coopmansschip [1640] tot Capitieins Godgeleerd Onderzoekschrift [1742] [The Sons of Cham: Dutch Reformed Preachers' Thoughts about Slavery from the Udemans Merchant Ship [1640] to the Captain's Theological Research Paper]," *Klio [The Hague]* 7 (1980): 221–25. In Dutch.

Kellenbenz, Hermann, "La place de l'Elbe inferieure dans le commerce triangulaire au milieu du XVIIe Siècle [The Minor Role of the Elbe in the Slave Trade in the Seventeenth Century]," *Revue Française d'Histoire d'Outre-Mer* 1–2 (975): 186–95. In French.

Kernkamp, G. W., "Een Contract tot Slavenhandel van 1657 [An Early Contract in Slave Trading from 1657]," *Bijdragen en Mededeelingen van het Historisch Genootschap* 22 (1901): 444–59. In Dutch.

Kesler, C. K., "Uit de Eerste Dagen van den West-Indischen Slavenhandel [From the First Days of the West Indian Slave Trade]," *West-Indische Gids* 22 (1940): 175–85. In Dutch.

Lapeyre, Henry, "La trata negrier avec l'Amerique Espangnole [The Slave Trade with Spanish America]," *Homenaje a Jaime Vicens Vives* 1, 2 (1938): 178–82. In French.

Lara, Oruno D., "Traite negrière et resistance africaine [Slave Traders and African Resistance]," *Presence Africaine* 94 (1975): 140–70. In French.

Leme, Luiz Antonio Padovani, "As Origens da Escravidão Negra na America: Uma Necessidade Interna," *Cadernos de Pesquisa: Tudo e Historia [The Origins of the Slaves in America: An Essential Collection of Historical Essays]* (1978): 53–57. In Portuguese.

Lopes, A. Correia, *A Escravatura: Subsidios para a sua Historia* (1944). In Portuguese.

Loth, Heinrich, *Sklaverei: Die Geschichte des Sklavenhandels zwischen Afrika und Amerika* [Slavery: History of the Slave Trade between Africa and America] (1981). In German.

Lu, Kun, "Hei Nu Mao Yi De Xing Zi Yu Fa Zhan [The Rise and Development of the Black Slave Trade]," *Liaoning Daxue Xuebao* 5 (1978): 83–89. In Chinese.

Maianga, Jose, "A luta dos escravos em Sao Tome no seculo XVI [The Struggle of the Slaves in Sao Tome in the Sixteenth Century]," *Africa: Literatura, Arte, Cultura [Africa: Literature, Art, and Culture]* 2 (1980): 437–43. In Portuguese.

Malowist, Marian, "Les debuts du systeme de plantations dans la periode des grande decouvertes [The Birth of the Plantation System in the Era of Great Discoveries]," *African Bulletin* 10 (1969): 9–30. In French.

Mauny, Raymond, "Le Livre de bord du navire *Santa Maria da Comceica* [1522] [The Log Book of the Ship *Santa Maria da Comceca*]," *Bulletin de l'Institut Fondamental d'Afrique Noire* 29 (1967): 512–35. In French.

———— "Livres de bord de navires Portugais faisant la traite sur les cotes d'Afrique Occidentale au XVIe siècle [The Log Book of Portuguese Slave Ships on the Coasts of West Africa in the Sixteenth Century]," *Provence Historique* 25 (1975): 79–85. In French.

Mauny, Raymond, and N. I. de Moraes, "Reglement du *San Christoca* allant de Sao Tome à la Mine [1535] [Timetable of the *San Christoca* for Its Journey from Sao Tome to Mina]," *Bulletin de l'Institut Fondamental d'Afrique Noire* 37 (1975): 779–83. In French.

Mauro, Frederic, *Le Portugal et l'Atlantique au XVIIe Siècle, 1570–1670: Etude economique* [The Portuguese and the Atlantic in the Seventeenth Century: A Study of Economics] (1960). In French.

Menkman, W. R., "Slavenhandel en Rechtsbedeeling op Curaco op het einde der 17e eeuw [The Slave Trade and the Legal Situation in Curacao by the End of the Seventeenth Century]," *Niewe West-Indische Gids* 17 (1935–36): 11–26. In Dutch.

Moraes, Nize Izabel de, "La campagne negriere du San-Antonio-e-as-almas [1670]," *Bulletin de l'Institut Fondamental d'Afrique Noire* 40 (1978): 708–17. In French.

Quenum, Alphonse, *Les eglises chrétienne et la traite Atlantique du XVe au XIXe Siècle* [The Christian Churches and the Atlantic Slave Trade from the Fifteenth to the Nineteenth Century] (1993). In French.

Salvador, Jose Goncalves, *Os Magnatas do Trafico Negreiro: Seculos XVI e XVII* [The Magnates of Negro Trafficking, Sixteenth and Seventeenth Centuries] (1981). In Portuguese.

Sampaio Garcia, Rosendo, "O Portugues Duarte Lopes e o Comercio Espanhol de Escravos Negros [The Portuguese Duarte Lopes and the Spanish Traffic of Black Slaves]," *Revista de historia* 31 (1957): 375–85. In Portuguese.

Sandoval, Alonso de, *De instauranda aethiopum salute: El mundo del esclavitude negra en America* (1957). In Spanish.

Scelle, Georges, *La traite negriere aux Indes de Castille, Contrats et traites d'Assiento: Etudes de droit public et d'histoire diplomatique puisee aux sources originales et accompagnee de plusieurs documents inedits* [The Slave Trade to the Indies from Castille, Contracts, and Treaties of Assent: Legal Studies of Civil Law and History of Diplomacy Retrieved by the Original Sources and Accompanied by Several Unpublished Documents] (1906). In French.

Tardieu, Jean-Pierre, "Les principales structures administratives Espagnoles de la traite des noirs vers les Indes Occidentales [The Principal Spanish Administrative Structures in the Slave Trade in the West Indies]," *Cahiers du Monde Hispanique et Luso-Bresilien* 37 (1981): 51–84. In French.

Teixeira da Mota, Avelino, "As Rotas Maritimas Portuguesas no Atlantico de Meados do Seculo XV ao Penultimo Quartal do Seculo XVI," *Do Tempo e Da Historia* 3 (1970): 13–33. In Portuguese.

van Brakel, S., "Bescheiden over den Slavenhandel der West-Indische Compagnie, Medegedeeld Door [Information on the Slave Trade of the West Indies Company]," *Economisch-Historisch Jaarboek* 4 (1918): 47–83. In Dutch.

Verger, Pierre, *Flux et reflux de la traite des negres entre le Golfe de Benin et Bahia de Todos os Santos, du XVIIIe au XIXe Siècle* (1968). In French.

——— "Mouvement de Navires entre Bahia et le Golfe du Benin, XVIIe–XIXe Siècles [The Movement of Ships between Bahia and the Gulf of Benin, Seventeenth-Nineteenth Centuries]," *Revue Francaise d'Histoire d'Outre-Mer* 55 (1968): 5–36. In French.

Verlinden, Charles, "Les debuts de la traite Portugaise en Afrique, 1433–1448 [The Beginning of Portuguese Trade with Africa, 1433–1448]," *Miscellanea Mediaevalia in Memoriam Jan Frederic Niermeyer* (1967): 365–77. In French.

Vila Vilar, Enriqueta, *Hispanoamerica y el comercio de esclavos: Los asientos Portugueses* [Hispanic America and the Commerce of Slaves: The Portuguese Agreements] (1977). In Spanish.

——— "La sublevacion de Portugal y la de negros," *Iberoamerikanisches Archiv* 2 (1976): 171–92. In Spanish.

——— "Los asientos portugueses y el contrabando de negros," *Anuario de Estudios Americanos* 30 (1975): 557–609. In Spanish.

Zavala, Silvio Arturo, *Servidumbre natural y libertad cristiana, segun los tratadistas Espanoles de los siglos XVI y XVII* (1944). In Spanish.

14.3.1 Caribbean

Agorsah E. Kofi, *Maroon Heritage: Archaeological, Ethnographical, and Historical Perspectives* (1994).

Aimes, Hubert Hillary Suffern, *A History of Slavery in Cuba, 1511 to 1868* (1907).

Beckles, Hilary, "From Land to Sea: Runaway Barbados Slaves and Servants, 1630–1700," *Slavery and Abolition* 6 (1985): 79–94.

——— *Natural Rebels: A Social History of Enslaved Black Women in Barbados* (1989).

——— *White Servitude and Black Slavery in Barbados, 1627–1715* (1989).

——— "White Women and Slavery in the Caribbean," *History Workshop Journal* (1993): 66–82.

Benzoni, Girolamo, *History of the New World*, trans. W. H. Smyth (1857).

Brace, Joan, "From Chattel to Person: Martinique, 1635–1848," *Plantation Society in the Americas* 2 (1983): 63–80.

Buisseret, David J., "Slaves Arriving in Jamaica, 1684–1692," *Revue Francaise d'Histoire d'Outre-Mer* 64 (1977): 85–88.

Bush, Barbara, *Slave Women in Caribbean Society, 1650–1838* (1990).

Campbell, Mavis C., "Maroonage in Jamaica: Its Origin in the Seventeenth Century," in Vera Rubin, and Arthur Luden, ed., *Annals of the New York Academy of Sciences: Comparative Perspectives on Slavery in the New World Plantation Societies* (1977): 389–419.

———— "The Maroons of Jamaica: Imperium in Imperio," *Pan-African Journal* 1 (1975): 45–55.

Campbell, Mavis, *The Maroons of Jamaica, 1655–1796: A History of Resistance, Collaboration and Betrayal* (1988).

Craton, Michael M., *Searching for the Invisible Man: Slaves and Plantation Life in Jamaica* (1977).

———— *Sinews of Empire: A Short History of British Slavery* (1974).

Dunn, Richard S., *Sugar and Slaves: The Rise of the Planter Class in the English West Indies, 1624–1713* (1972).

Frey, Sylvia R., and Betty Wood, *Come Shouting to Zion: African American Protestantism in the American South and Caribbean to 1830* (1998).

Galenson, David W., "The Atlantic Slave Trade and the Barbados Market, 1673–1723," *Journal of Economic History* 32 (1982): 491–511.

———— "The Slave Trade to the English West Indies, 1673–1724," *Economic History Review* 32 (1979): 241–49.

Gaspar, D. Barry, "Runaways in Seventeenth-Century Antigua, West Indies," *Boletin de Estudios Latinamericanos y del Caribe [Bulletin of Latin American and Carribean Studies]* (1979): 3–13.

Hall, Neville A. T., *Slave Society in the Danish West Indies* (1992).

Handler, Jerome S., "The Amerindian Slave Population of Barbados in the Seventeenth and Early Eighteenth Centuries," *Caribbean Studies* 4 (1969): 38–64.

———— "An Archaeological Investigation of the Domestic Life of Plantation Slaves in Barbados," *Journal of the Barbados Museum and Historical Society* 2 (1972): 64–72.

Handler, Jerome S., and Charlotte J. Frisbie, "Aspects of Slave Life in Barbados: Music and its Cultural Context," *Caribbean Studies* 4 (1972): 5–46.

Handler, Jerome S., and Frederick W. Lange, *Plantation Slavery in Barbados: An Archeological and Historical Investigation* (1978).

Handler, Jerome S., and Robert S. Corruccini, "Plantation Slave Life in Barbados: A Physical and Anthropological Analysis," *Journal of Interdisciplinary History* 1 (1983): 65–90.

Handler, Jerome S., *The Unappropriated People: Freedmen in the Slave Society of Barbados* (1974).

Handler, Jerome S., and JoAnn Jacoby, "Slave Names and Naming in Barbados, 1650–1830," *William and Mary Quarterly* 53 (1996): 685–728.

Harlow, Vincent, ed., *Colonizing Expeditions to the West Indies and Guiana, 1623–1667* (1967).

Higman, Barry W., "Economics of Circum-Caribbean Slavery," in Vera Rubin, and Arthur Luden, ed., *Annals of the New York Academy of Sciences: Comparative Perspectives on Slavery in New World Plantation Societies* (1977): 143–44.

Jesse, C., "Religion among the Early Slaves in the French Antilles," *Journal of the Barbados Museum and Historical Society* 1 (1960): 4–10.

Kiple, Kenneth F., and Virginia H. Kiple, "Deficiency Diseases in the Caribbean," *Journal of Interdisiplinary History* 2 (1980): 197–216.

Kopytoff, Barbara Klamon, "Colonial Treaty as Sacred Charter of the Jamaican Maroons," *Ethnohistory* 1 (1979): 45–64.

———— "The Development of Jamaican Maroon Ethnicity," *Caribbean Quarterly* 22 (1976): 33–50.

———— "The Early Political Development of Jamaican Maroon Societies," *William and Mary Quarterly* 2 (1978): 287–307.

———— "Guerilla Warfare in Eighteenth Century Jamaica," *Expedition* 2 (1977): 20–26.

———— "Jamaican Maroon Political Organization: The Effects of the Treaties," *Social and Economic Studies* (1976): 87–105.

Lange, Frederick W., "Slave Mortuary Practices, Barbados, West Indies," *Actas del XLI Congresso Internacionale de Americanistas* 2 (1974): 477–83.

Ligon, Richard, *A True and Exact History of the Island of Barbados* (1657).

Mathurin, Lucille, *The Rebel Woman in the British West Indies during Slavery* (1975).

Molen, Patricia A., "Population and Social Patterns in Barbados in the Early Eighteenth Century," *William and Mary Quarterly* 2 (1971): 287–300.

Munford, Clarence, *The Black Ordeal of Slavery and Slave Trading in the French West Indies, 1625–1715* (3 vols., 1991).

Packwood, Cyril Outerbridge, *Chained on the Rock: Slavery in Bermuda* (1975).

Patterson, Orlando, "From Endo-deme to Matri-deme: An Interpretation of the Development of Kinship and Social Organization among the Slaves of Jamaica, 1655–1830," in Samuel Proctor, ed., *Eighteenth-Century Florida and the Caribbean* (1976): 50–59.

———— "Slavery, Acculturation, and Social Change: The Jamaican Case," *British Journal of Sociology* 2 (1966): 151–64.

———— "Slavery and Slave Revolts: A Socio-Historical Analysis of the First Maroon War, 1655–1740," *Social and Economic Studies* 3 (1970): 289–325.

———— *The Sociology of Slavery: An Analysis of the Origins, Development, and Structure of Negro Slave Society in Jamaica* (1967).

Rath, Richard, "African Music in Seventeenth-Century Jamaica: Cultural Transit and Transmission," *William and Mary Quarterly* 50 (1993): 700–26.

Rodney, Walter, "The State of Research in Guyana," in Unesco, *The African Slave Trade from the Fifteenth to the Nineteenth Century* (1979): 298.

Schuler, Monica, "Akan Slave Rebellions in the British Caribbean," *Savacou* 1 (1970): 8–31.

———— "Ethnic Slave Rebellions in the Caribbean and the Guianas," *Journal of Social History* 3 (1970): 374–85.

Sheridan, Richard B., *Sugar and Slavery: An Economic History of the British West Indies, 1623–1775* (1974).

Sloane, Hans, *A Voyage to the Islands Madera, Barbados, Neives, S. Christopher's and Jamaica* (2 vols., 1707–25).

Thornton, Anthony P., "The Organization of the Slave Trade in the English West Indies, 1660–1685," *William and Mary Quarterly* 12 (1955): 399–409.

Thornton, John K., *Africa and Africans in the Making of the Atlantic World, 1400–1800* (2d ed., 1998).

Trapham, Thomas, *A Discourse on the State of Health of the Island of Jamaica* (1679).

Wood, Betty, *The Origins of American Slavery: Freedom and Bondage in the English Colonies* (1997).

14.3.2 Studies in Foreign Languages (Caribbean)

Adelaide, Jacques, "La colonisation Francaise aux Antilles à la fin du 17e Siècles d'apres les 'Voyage aux Isles d'Amerique' de Père Labat. Troisième partie: Les Esclaves [French Colonization in the Antilles at the End of the Seventeenth Century, according to 'The Voyage to the American Isles' by Father Labat. Third Part: The Slaves]," *Bulletin de la Societe d'Histoire de la Guadeloupe* 8 (1967): 26–41. In French.

Algería, Ricardo E., "El Rey Miguel: Héroe puertorriqueño de la lucha por la libertad de los esclavos [King Miguel: Puerto Rican Hero in the Struggle for the Freedom of Slaves]," *Revista de Historia de America* 85 (1978): 9–26. In Spanish.

———— "Los origenes de la esclavitud negra en Puerto Rico [The Origins of Black Slavery in Puerto Rico]," *Revista del Instituto de Cultura Puertorriqueña [Review of the Puerto Rican Cultural Institute]* 16 (1973): 3–7. In Spanish.

Alvarez Nazario, Manuel, "Nuevos datos sobre las procedencias de los antiguos esclavos de Puerto Rico [New Data on the Provenance of the Early Slaves in Puerto Rico]," *La Torre* 21 (1973): 23–37. In Spanish.

Andreu Ocariz, Juan Jose, "La rebelión de los esclavos de Boca Nigua [The Slave Rebellion of Boca Nigua]," *Anuario de Studios Americanos* 27 (1970): 551–81. In Spanish.

Berkel, Adriaan van, *Amerikaansche Voyagien, Behelzende en Reis na Rio de Berbice . . . Guiana* [American Voyage, including a Trip to Rio de Berbice] (1695). In Dutch.

Biet, Antoine, *Voyage de la France Equinoxiale en L'Isle de Cayenne* [Voyage of the France Equinoxiale to the Cayenne Isle] (1664). In French.

Bouton, Jacques, *Relation de l'establissment des Francais depuis l'an 1635 en L'Isle de La Martinique* [Account of the French Settlement after 1635 on the Isle of Martinique] (1640). In French.

Chatillon, Marcel, "L'evangelisation des esclaves au XVIIe siècle: Lettres du R. P. Jean Mongin [The Evangelization of the Slaves in the Seventeenth Century: Letters of R. P. Jean Mongin]," *Bulletin de la Societe d'Histoire de la Guadeloupe* 60 (1984): 1–136. In French.

Cornevin, Robert, "Note au sujet des origines des esclaves des Antilles [Note on the Subject of Slave Origin in the Antilles]," *Bulletin de l'Institut Francaise d'Afrique Noire* 1–2 (1965): 370–71. In French.

de Rochefort, Charles, *Histoire naturelle et morale des Iles Antilles de l'Amerique* [Natural and Moral History of the American Antilles] (1658). In French.

de St. Michel, Maurile, *Voyages des Isles Camercanes* [Travels to the Camercanes Islands] (1653). In French.

Debien, Gabriel, "La christianisation des esclaves des Antilles Françaises aux XVIIe et XVIIIe siècles [Christianization of Slaves in the French Antilles in the Seventeenth and Eighteenth Centuries]," *Revue d'Histoire de l'Amerique Française* 20 (1967): 525–55. In French.

————— "La nourriture des esclaves sur les Plantations des Antilles Françaises aux XVIIe et XVIIIe siècles [Nutrition of the Slaves in the French Antilles, Seventeenth and Eighteenth Centuries]," *Caribbean Studies* 2 (1964): 3–27. In French.

Debien, Gabriel, and J. Houdaille, "Les origines des esclaves aux Antilles [The Origins of the Slaves from the Antilles]," *Bulletin de l'Institut Français d'Afrique Noire* 1–2 (1964): 166–211. In French.

Deive, Carlos Esteban, *La esclavitud del negro en Santo Domingo, 1492–1844* [The Enslavement of the Blacks in Santo Domingo] (1980). In Spanish.

du Tertre, Jean-Baptiste, *Histoire generale des Antilles habitees par les Francais* [General History of the Antilles Inhabited by the French] (4 vols., 1667). In French.

Franco, Jose Luciano, "Cuatro siglos de lucha por la libertad: los palenques [Four Centuries of Struggle for Freedom: The Slave Hideouts]," *Revista de la Biblioteca Nacional Jose Marti* 1 (1967): 5–44. In Spanish.

————— *Ensayos sobre el Caribe* [Essays on the Caribbean] (1974). In Spanish.

————— *Las Palenques de los Negros Cimarrones* [The Settlements of the Runaway Blacks] (1973). In Spanish.

Gautier, Arlette, *Les soeurs de solitude: La condition feminine dans l'esclavage aux Antilles du XVIIe au XIXe siècles* [Sisters of Solitude: The Female Condition in the Antilles from the Seventeenth Century to the Nineteenth Century] (1985). In French.

Herlein, J. D., *Beschryvinge van de Volk Plantige Zuriname* [Descriptions of the Plantation Folk in Surinam] (1718). In Dutch.

Larrazabel Blanco, Carlos, *Los Negros y la esclavitud en Santo Domingo* [Negros and Slavery in Santo Domingo] (1967). In Spanish.

Macias Dominguez, *Cuba en la primera mitad de siglo XVII* [Cuba in the First Part of the Seventeenth Century] (1978). In Spanish.

Martin, Gaston, *Histoire de l'esclavage dans les colonies française* [History of Slavery in the French Colonies] (1948). In French.

Pelleprat, Pierre, *Relation des Missions des PP. de la Compagnie de Jesus dans les Isles, et dans la Terre Ferme de l'Amerique Meridionale* [Communication from the Missions of the PP of the Jesus Company in the Islands and the Continent of America] (1655). In French.

Perez Bento, Manuel, "La condicion social de los negros en la Habana durante el siglo XVI [The Social Condition of the Blacks in Havana during the Sixteenth Century]," *Revista Bimestre Cubana* (1922): 266–94. In Spanish.

14.4.1 Europe

Blackburn, Robin, "The Old World Background to European Colonial Slavery," *William and Mary Quarterly* 54 (1997): 65–102.

Blakely, Allison, *Blacks in the Dutch World: The Evolution of Racial Imagery in a Modern Society* (1993).

Edwards, Paul, and James Walvin, "Africans in Britain, 1500–1800," in Martin L. Kilson, and Robert I. Rotberg, ed., *The African Diaspora: Interpretive Essays* (1976): 173–204.

Hair, P. E. H., "Black African Slaves at Valencia, 1482–1516: An Onomastic Inquiry," *History in Africa* 7 (1980): 119–39.

Patterson, Orlando, *Slavery and Social Death: A Comparative Study* (1982).

Shyllon, Folarin O., *Black Slaves in Britain* (1974).

Vaughan, Alden T., and Virginia Mason Vaughan, "Before *Othello*: Elizabethan Representations of Sub-Saharan Africans," *William and Mary Quarterly* 54 (1997): 19–44.

Walvin, James, *Black and White: The Negro and English Society, 1555–1945* (1973).

Walvin, James, comp., *The Black Presence: A Documentary History of the Negro in England, 1555–1860* (1972).

14.4.2 Studies in Foreign Languages (Europe)

Cortés Alonso, Vicenta, *La esclavitud en Valencia durante el reinado de los reyes Catolicos, 1479–1516* [Slavery in Valencia during the Reign of the Catholic Kings, 1479–1516] (1964). In Spanish.

14.5.1 North America, British and Dutch Colonies

Berlin, Ira, "From Creole to African: Atlantic Creoles and the Origins of African-American Society in Mainland North America," *William and Mary Quarterly* 53 (1996): 251–88.

——— "Time, Space, and the Evolution of Afro-American Society on British Mainland North America," *American Historical Review* 85 (1980): 44–78.

Breen, T. H., and Stephen Innes, *"Myne Owne Ground": Race and Freedom on Virginia's Eastern Shore, 1640–1676* (1980).

Brewer, James H., "Negro Property Owners in Seventeenth-Century Virginia," *William and Mary Quarterly* 12 (1955): 575–80.

Candler, Mark Allen, "The Beginnings of Slavery in Georgia," *Magazine of History* 13 (1911): 549–54.

Cope, Robert S., *Carry Me Back: Slavery and Servitude in Seventeenth Century Virginia* (1973).

Craven, Wesley Frank, "Twenty Negroes to Jamestown in 1619?" *Virginia Quarterly Review* 47 (1971): 416–20.

Curtin, Philip D., *The Rise and Fall of the Plantation Complex: Essays on Atlantic History* (1990).

Davis, Thomas J., "New York's Long Black Line: A Note on the Growing Slave Population, 1626–1790," *Afro-Americans in New York Life and History* 2 (1978): 41–60.

De Jong, Gerald Francis, "The Dutch Reformed Church and Negro Slavery in Colonial America," *Church History* 40 (1971): 423–36.

Elkins, Stanley M., "Slavery in Capitalist and Non-Capitalist Countries," in Laura Foner, and Eugene D. Genovese, ed., *Slavery in the New World: A Reader in Comparative History* (1969): 8–26.

Frey, Sylvia R., and Betty Wood, *Come Shouting to Zion: African American Protestantism in the American South and Caribbean to 1830* (1998).

Goodfriend, Joyce D., "Burghers and Blacks: The Evolution of a Slave Society at New Amsterdam," *New York History* 59 (1978): 125–44.

Johnson, Whittington B., "The Origin and Nature of African Slavery in Seventeenth-Century Maryland," *Maryland Historical Magazine* 73 (1978): 236–45.

Jordan, Winthrop D., *White over Black: American Attitudes toward the Negro, 1550–1812* (1968).

Kimmel, Ross M., "Free Blacks in Seventeenth-Century Maryland," *Maryland Historical Magazine* 71 (1976): 19–25.

Kulikoff, Allan, "The Beginnings of the Afro-American Family in Maryland," in Aubrey C. Land, Lois Greed Carr, and Edward C. Papenfuse, ed., *Law, Society, and Politics in Early Maryland* (1977): 171–96.

Menard, Russell R., "From Servants to Slaves: The Transformation of the Chesapeake Labor System," *Southern Studies* 16 (1977): 355–90.

——— "The Maryland Slave Population, 1658 to 1730: A Demographic Profile of Blacks in Four Counties," *William and Mary Quarterly* 32 (1975): 29–54.

Morgan, Edmund S., "The First American Boom: Virginia, 1618 to 1630," *William and Mary Quarterly* 28 (1971): 169–98.

——— "The Labor Problem at Jamestown, 1607–1618," *American Historical Review* 76 (1971): 565–611.

Porter, Kenneth W., "Negroes on the Southern Frontier, 1670–1763," *Journal of Negro History* 33 (1948): 53–78.

Scherer, Lester B., *Slavery and the Churches in Early America, 1619–1819* (1975).

Sirmans, M. Eugene, "The Legal Status of the Slave in South Carolina, 1670–1740," *Journal of Southern History* 28 (1962): 462–73.

Thornton, John K., "Central African Names and African-American Naming Patterns," *William and Mary Quarterly* 50 (1993): 727–42.

———— "On the Trail of Voodoo: African Christianity in Africa and the Americas," *Americas* 44 (1988): 261–78.

Wagman, Morton, "Corporate Slavery in New Netherland," *Journal of Negro History* 65 (1980): 34–42.

Wood, Betty, *The Origins of American Slavery: Freedom and Bondage in the English Colonies* (1997).

Wood, Peter H., *Black Majority: Negroes in Colonial South Carolina from 1670 through the Stono Rebellion* (1974).

———— "'It Was a Negro Taught Them': A New Look at African Labor in Early South Carolina," in Roger D. Abrams and John F. Szwed, *Discovering Afro-America* (1975): 26–45.

14.5.2 Studies in Foreign Languages (North America, British and Dutch Colonies)

Emmer, Pieter C., "De Slavenhandel van en naar Nieuw-Nederland [The Slave Trade to and from the New Netherlands]," *Economisch-En Sociaal-Historisch Jaarboek* 35 (1972): 94–147. In Dutch.

Häbler, Konrad, "Die Anfänge der Sklaverei in Amerika [The Beginnings of Slavery in America]," *Zeitschrift für Social-und Wirtschaftsgeschichte* [*Journal for Social and Economic History*] 4 (1896): 176–223. In German.

Knapp, Georg Friedrich, "Ursprung der Sklaverei in den Kolonien [Origin of Slavery in the Colonies]," in *Die Landarbeiter in Knechtschaft und Freiheit: Gesammelte Vorträge* [Farm Workers in Bondage and in Freedom: A Collection of Lectures] (1909): 1–20. In German.

14.6.1 North America, Mexico

Aguirre Beltrán, Gonzalo, "Races in Seventeenth Century Mexico," *Phylon* 3 (1945): 212–18.

———— "The Slave Trade in Mexico," *Hispanic American Historical Review* 24 (1944): 412–31.

———— "The Tribal Origins of Slaves in Mexico," *Journal of Negro History* 31 (1946): 269–352.

Barnett, Ward J., *The Sugar Hacienda of the Marqueses del Valle* (1970).

Boyd-Bowman, Peter, "Negro Slaves in Early Colonial Mexico," *Americas* 26 (1954): 134–51.

Brady, Robert L., "The Domestic Slave Trade in Sixteenth-Century Mexico," *Americas* 24 (1968): 281–89.

Carroll, Patrick, *Blacks in Colonial Veracruz: Race, Ethnicity, and Regional Development* (1991).

Clemence, Stella Risley, "Deed of Emancipation of a Negro Woman Slave, Dated Mexico, September 14, 1585," *Hispanic American Historical Review* 10 (1930): 51–57.

Davidson, David M., "Negro Slave Control and Resistance in Colonial Mexico, 1519–1650," *Hispanic American Historical Review* 46 (1966): 235–53.

Konrad, Herman W., *A Jesuit Hacienda in Colonial Mexico: Santa Lucia, 1576–1767* (1980).

Logan, Rayford W., "Estevanico, Negro Discoverer of the Southwest: A Critical Reexamination," *Phylon* 1 (1940): 305–13.

Love, Edgar F., "Legal Restrictions on Afro-Indian Relations in Colonial Mexico," *Journal of Negro History* 55 (1970): 131–39.

———— "Marriage Patterns of Persons of African Descent in a Colonial Mexico City Parish," *Hispanic American Historical Review* 51 (1971): 79–91.

———— "Negro Resistance to Spanish Rule in Colonial Mexico," *Journal of Negro History* 52 (1967): 89–103.

Mayer, Vincent, Jr., *The Black on New Spain's Northern Frontier: San Jose de Parral, 1631 to 1641* (1974).

Palmer, Colin A., "Religion and Magic in Mexican Slave Society, 1570–1650," in Stanley L. Engerman, and Eugene D. Genovese, ed., *Race and Slavery in the Western Hemisphere: Quantitative Studies* (1975): 311–28.

———— *Slaves of the White God: Blacks in Mexico, 1570–1650* (1976).

Riley, G. Michael, "Labor in Cortesian Enterprises: The Cuernavaca Area, 1522–1549," *Americas* 28 (1972): 271–87.

Rodiles, Ignacio Márques, "The Slave Trade with America—Negroes in Mexico," *Freedomways* 1 (1961): 296–307.

Tyler, Ronnie C., "Fugitive Slaves in Mexico," *Journal of Negro History* 57 (1972): 1–12.

14.6.2 Studies in Foreign Languages (North America, Mexico)

Aguirre Beltrán, Gonzalo, "Comercio de esclavos en México por 1542 [Slave Traffic in Mexico around 1542]," *Afroamerica* 1–2 (1945): 25–40. In Spanish.

——— *Cuijla: Esbozo etnográfico de un pueblo negro* [Cuijla: Ethnographic Sketch of a Negro Village] (1958). In Spanish.

——— *La población negra de México, 1519–1810: Estudió etno-histórico* [The Negro Population of Mexico, 1519–1810: An Ethnohistorical Study] (1946). In Spanish.

——— *Medicina y magia: El proceso de acculturación en la estructura colonial* [Medicine and Magic: The Acculturation Process in the Colonial Structure] (1963). In Spanish.

Aguirre Beltrán, Miguel, "El trabajo del Indio comparado con el del Negro en Nueva España [The Work of the Indian Compared to the Negro's Work in New Spain]," *Mexico Agrario* 6 (1942): 203–07. In Spanish.

Alberro, Solange B. de, "Noirs et mulatres dans la société coloniale Mexicaine, d'apres les Archives de l'Inquisition, XVIe–XVIIe Siècles [Blacks and Mulattos in Mexican Colonial Society, According to the Archives of the Inquisition, Sixteenth-Seventeenth Centuries]," *Cahiers des Amerique Latines* [*Notes on Latin America*] 17 (1978): 57–87. In French.

Cantu Corro, Jose, *La esclavitud en el Mundo y en México* [Slavery in the World and in Mexico] (1926).

14.7.1 South America and Central America

Bowser, Frederick, *The African Slave in Colonial Peru, 1524–1650* (1974).

Brady, Robert L., "The Role of *Las Casas* in the Emergence of Negro Slavery in the New World," *Revista de Historia de America* (1966): 43–55.

Browning, James, *Negro Companions of the Spanish Explorers in the New World* (1938).

Cardoso, Geraldo da Silva, *Negro Slavery in the Sugar Plantations of Veracruz and Pernambuco, 1550–1680: A Comparative Study* (1983).

Chandler, David L., "Family Bonds and Bondsmen: The Slave Family in Colonial Colombia," *Latin America Research Review* 2 (1981): 107–31.

Cushner, Nicholas P., "Slave Mortality and Reproduction on Jesuit Haciendas in Colonial Peru," *Hispanic American Historical Review* 2 (1975): 177–99.

Earle of Berkshire, A Publication of Guiana's Plantation (1632).

Elkins, Stanley M., "Slavery in Capitalist and Non-Capitalist Countries," in Laura Foner, and Eugene D. Genovese, ed., *Slavery in the New World: A Reader in Comparative History* (1969): 8–26.

Ferry, Robert J., "Encomienda, African Slavery, and Agriculture in Seventeenth Century Caracas," *Hispanic American Historical Review* 4 (1981): 609–35.

Fiehrer, Thomas, "Slaves and Freedom in Colonial Central America: Rediscovering a Forgotten Black Past," *Journal of Negro History* 1 (1979): 39–47.

Harlow, Vincent, ed., *Colonizing Expeditions to the West Indies and Guiana, 1623–1667* (1967).

King, James F., "The Case of Jose Ponciano de Ayarza: A Document of Gracias al Sacar," *Hispanic American Historical Review* 4 (1951): 640–47.

——— "Descriptive Data on Negro Slaves in Spanish Importation Records and Bills of Sale," *Journal of Negro History* 2 (1943): 204–30.

——— "Negro History in Continental Spanish America," *Journal of Negro History* 1 (1944): 7–23.

——— "Negro Slavery in New Granada," *Greater America: Essays in Honor of H. E. Bolton* (1945): 295–318.

Kunst, J., "Notes on Negroes in Guatemala during the Seventeenth Century," *Journal of Negro History* 4 (1916): 392–98.

MacLeod, Murdo, *Spanish Central America: A Socioeconomic History* (1973).

Morner, Magnus, *Race and Class in Latin America* (1970).

——— *Race Mixture in the History of Latin America* (1967).

——— "The Theory and Practice of Racial Segregation in Colonial Spanish America," *Proceedings of the 32nd International Congress of Americanists* 1 (1956): 127–35.

Olien, Michael D., "Black and Part-Black Populations in Colonial Costa Rica: Ethnohistorical Resources and Problems," *Ethnohistory* 1 (1980): 13–29.

"Papers Bearing on the Negroes of Cuba in the Seventeenth Century," *Journal of Negro History* 12 (1927): 55–95.

Patterson, Orlando, *Slavery and Social Death: A Comparative Study* (1982).

Phelan, John L., "The Road to Esmeraldas: The Failure of a Spanish Conquest in the Seventeenth Century," *Essays in History and Literature Presented by the Fellows of the Newberry Library to Stanley Pargellis* (1965): 91–107.

Pollack-Eltz, Angelina, "Slave Revolts in Venezuela," in Vera Rubin, and Arthur Tuden, ed., *Comparative Perspectives on Slavery in New World Plantation Societies* (1977): 439–45.

Rippy, J. Fred, "The Negro and the Spanish Pioneer in the New World," *Journal of Negro History* 2 (1921): 183–99.

Romero, Fernando, "The Slave Trade and the Negro in South America," *Hispanic American Historical Review* 3 (1944): 368–86.

Rout, Leslie B., *The African Experience in Spanish America: 1502 to the Present Day* (1976).

Sater, William F., "The Black Experience in Chile," in Robert Brent Toplin, ed., *Slavery and Race Relations in Latin America* (1974): 13–50.

Schuler, Monica, "Ethnic Slave Rebellions in the Caribbean and the Guianas," *Journal of Social History* 3 (1970): 374–85.

Sharp, William F., "Manumission, Libres, and Black Resistance: The Colombian Choco, 1680–1810," in Robert Brent Toplin, ed., *Slavery and Race Relations in Latin America* (1974): 89–111.

——— "The Profitability of Slavery in the Colombian Choco, 1680–1810," *Hispanic American Historical Review* 3 (1975): 468–95.

——— *Slavery on the Spanish Frontier: The Colombian Choco, 1680–1810* (1976).

Sweet, David G., "Black Robes and 'Black Destiny': Jesuit Views of African Slavery in Seventeenth-Century Latin America," *Revista de Historia de America* (1978): 87–133.

Thornton, John K., "On the Trail of Voodoo: African Christianity in Africa and the Americas," *Americas* 44 (1988): 261–78.

Toplin, Robert Brent, ed., *Slavery and Race Relations in Latin America* (1974).

Vigil, Ralph H., "Negro Slaves and Rebels in the Spanish Possessions, 1503–1558," *Historian* 4 (1971): 637–55.

Wright, Richard, "Negro Companions of the the the Spanish Explorers," *American Anthropologist* 2 (1902): 217–28.

14.7.2   Studies in Foreign Languages (South America and Central America)

Acosta Saignes, Miguel, "Gentilicios Africanos en Venezuela [African Expression in Venezuela]," *El Movimiento Emancipador de Hispanoamerica: Actas y Ponencias* 3 (1961): 9–30. In Spanish.

——— "La etnohistoria y el estudio del negro en Mexico [The Ethnohistory and the Study on the Negro in Mexico]," *Acculturation in the Americas* (1952): 161–68. In Spanish.

——— *Vida de negros e indios en las minas de Cocorote, durante el siglo XVII: Estudios antropologicos publicados en homenaje al Dr. Manuel Gamio* [Life of the Negros and Indians in the Cocorote Mines, during the Seventeenth Century: Published Anthropological Writings in Honor of Dr. Manuel Gamio] (1956). In Spanish.

——— *Vida de los esclavos negros en Venezuela* [Life of the Black Slaves in Venezuela] (1967). In Spanish.

Alcala y Henke, Agustin, *La esclavitud de los negros en la America Espanola* [The Enslavement of Blacks in Spanish America] (1919). In Spanish.

Amunategui y Solar, Domingo, "La trata de negros en Chile [The Treatment of Negros in Chile]," *Revista Chilena de Historia y Geografia* (1922): 173–91. In Spanish.

Arenal, Celestino del, "La theoria de la servidumbre natural en el pensamiento Espanol de los siglos XVI y XVII [The Theory of Natural Servitude in Spanish Thought in the Sixteenth and Seventeenth Centuries]," *Historiografia e Bibliografia Americanistas* (1975–76): 67–126. In Spanish.

Armas, Medina Fernando de, "El santo de los esclavos [The Health of the Slaves]," *Estudios Americanos* (1955): 55–61. In Spanish.

Arrazola, Roberto, *Palenque: Primer pueblo libre de America* [Palenque, First Free American Town] (1970). In Spanish.

Assadourian, Carlos Sempat, *El trafico de esclavos en Cordoba, 1588–1610: Segun las actas de protocolos del archivo historico de Cordoba* [The Traffic of Slaves in Cordoba, 1588–1610: According to the Protocol Acts of the Historical Archives of Cordoba] (1965). In Spanish.

Borrego Pla, Maria del Carmen, "Palenques de negros cimarrones en Cartegena de India [Hide-outs of the Runaway Slaves in Cartegena de India]," *Atti del XL Congresso Internazionale degli Americanisti* 3 (1972): 429–32. In Spanish.

———— *Palenques de negros en Cartegena de Indias a fines del siglo XVII* [Hide-outs of Blacks in Cartegena de Indias at the End of the Seventeenth Century] (1973). In Spanish.

Crespo, R. Alberto, *Esclavos negros en Bolivia* [Black Slaves in Bolivia] (1977). In Spanish.

Cruz, Pedro Tobar, "La esclavitud del negro en Guatemala [Negro Slavery in Guatemala]," *Antropologia e Historia de Guatemala* [*Anthropology and History of Guatemala*] 1 (1965): 3–14. In Spanish.

Deive, Carlos Esteban, *La esclavitud del negro en Santo Domingo, 1492–1844* [The Enslavement of the Blacks in Santo Domingo, 1492–1844] (1980). In Spanish.

Eguren, Juan A., "Sandoval frente a los esclavos negros, 1607–1652 [Sandoval confronting the Black Slaves, 1607–1652]," *Montalban* 1 (1972): 405–32. In Spanish.

———— "Sandoval frente a la raza esclavizada [Sandoval confronting the Enslaved Race]," *Revista de la Academia Colombiana de Historia Eclesiastica* (1973): 57–86. In Spanish.

Escalante, Aguiles, *El negro en Colombia* [The Negro in Colombia] (1964). In Spanish.

Fortune, Armado, "Estudio sobre la insurrecion de los negros esclavos: los cimarrones de Panama [Studies on Slave Insurrections: The Runaways of Panama]," *Loteria* 1 (1956): 61–68. In Spanish.

Franco, Jose Luciano, *Esclavitud, comercio y traffico negreros* [Slavery, Commerce and the Traffic in Negros] In Spanish.

Guillot, Carlos F., *Negros rebeldes y negros cimarrones: perfil afroamericano en la historia del Nuevo Mundo durante el siglo XVI* [Rebellious and Runaway Blacks: Profile of Afro-American History in the New World during the Sixteenth Century] (1972). In Spanish.

Harth-Terre, Emilio, *Informe sobre el descubrimiento de documentos que revelan la trata y comercio de esclavos negros por los indios del comun durante el gobierno virreinal en el Peru* [Report about the Discovery of Documents that Reveal the Treatment and Commerce of the Black Slaves by the Indians in the Time during the Biannual Government in Peru] (1961). In Spanish.

Helmer, Marie, "Note sur les esclaves Indiens au Perou, XVIe siècle [Notes on the Indian Slaves in Peru, Sixteenth Century]," *Bulletin de la Faculte des Lettres de Strasbourg* 7 (1965): 683–90. In French.

Jara, Alvaro, "Importacion de trabajadores indigenas en el siglo XVII [Importation of the Indigenous Workers in the Seventeenth Century]," *Miscellanea Paulo Revet* 2 (1958): 733–63. In Spanish.

———— "Los asientos de trabajo y la provision del mano de obra para los no-encomenderos en la ciudad de Santiago, 1586–1600," *Revista Chilena de Historia y Geografia* (1957): 177–212. In Spanish.

Linde, Jan Marinus van der, *Surinaamse Suikerheren en Hun Kerk: Plantagekolonie en Handelskerk ten Tijde van Johannes Basseliers, Predikant en Planter in Suriname, 1667–1689* [Surinamese Sugar Lords and Their Church: Plantation Colony and Trade in the Times of Johannes Baesseliers, Preacher and Planter in Suriname, 1667–1689] (1966). In Dutch.

Melendez Chaverri, Carlos, "Los origenes de los esclavos africanos en Costa Rica [The Origins of African Slaves in Costa Rica]," *XXXVI Congreso Internacional de Americanistas: Actas y Antologia* 4 (1972): 387–91. In Spanish.

Melendez Chaverri, Carlos, and Quince Duncan, *El Negro en Costa Rica: Antologia* [The Negro in Costa Rica: An Anthology] (1972). In Spanish.

Mellafe, Rolando, *La introducción de la esclavitud negra en Chile: Tráfico y rutas* [The Introduction of Negro Slavery in Chile: Traffic and Routes] (1984).

Millones, Luis, "Gente negra en el Peru: esclavos y conquistadores [Blacks in Peru: Slaves and Conquistadors]," *America indiginea* 3 (1971): 593–624. In Spanish.

Molinari, Diego Luis, *La trata de negros: Datos para su estudio en el Rio de la Plata* [The Treatment of Negroes: Data for Study in Rio de la Plata] (1944). In Spanish.

Nodal, Roberto, "Estebanillo: pionero negro en la conquista de America," *Revista de historia de America* (1980): 49–55. In Spanish.

Palacios Preciado, Jorge, *La trata de negros por Cartagena de Indias, 1650–1750* (1973). In Spanish.

Pertinente Beschrijvinge van Guiana, Gelegen aen de Vaste Kust van America [Pertinent Descriptions from Guiana, Situated on the Vast Coast of America] (1676). In Dutch.

Picon-Sala, Mariano, *Pedro Claver, el santo de los esclavos* [Pedro Claver, Saint of the Slaves] (1950). In Spanish.

Porras, Troconis Gabriel, *Vida de San Pedro Claver, esclavo de los esclavos* [Life of Saint Pedro Claver, Slave of Slaves] (1954). In Spanish.

Quinter, Rodolfo, "La cultura de conquista engendra la esclavitud [The Culture of Conquest Engendered by Slavery]," *Anuario del Instituto de Antropologia e Historia* 1 (1964): 99–110. In Spanish.

Ramos Perez, Demetrio, "El negocio negrero de los Welsler y sus habilidades monopolitas," *Revista de Historia de America* 81 (1976): 7–81. In Spanish.

Romero, Fernando, "El Negro en tierra firme durante el siglo XVI [The Negro on the Mainland during the Sixteenth Century]," *Actas y memorias del XXVII Congreso Internacional de Americanistas* 2 (1939): 441–61. In Spanish.

———— "El 'rey bayano' y los negros panamenos en los mediados del siglo XVI," *Hombre y cultura* [*Man and Culture*] 1 (1975): 39. In Spanish.

Sales de Bohigas, Nuria, *Sobre esclavos reclutas, y mercaderes de quintas* (1974). In Spanish.

Sampaio Garcia, Rozendo, "Contribuicao ao Estudo do Approvisionamento de Escravos Negros na America Espanhola, 1580–1640," *Anais do Museu Paulista* (1962): 1–195. In Portuguese.

Tardieu, Jean-Pierre, "Le marronnage a Lima, 1535–1650: Atermoiements et répression [Runaway Slaves in Lima, 1535–1650: Repression and Postponements]," *Revue Historique [Historical Review]* (1987): 293–319. In French.

———— *L'Eglise et les noirs au Pérou (XVIe–XVIIe siècles)* [The Church and the Blacks in Peru (XVI–XVII Centuries)] (1993). In French.

Troconis de Veracoechea, Ermila, *Documentos para el estudio de los esclavos negros en Venezuela* [Documents for the Study of Slaves in Venezuela] (1969). In Spanish.

Vial Correa, Gonzalo, *El Africano en el reino de Chile: Ensayo historico-juridico* [The African and the Regime of Chile: Historical and Legal Essays] (1957). In Spanish.

Wolff, Inge, "Negersklaverei und Negerhandel in Hochperu, 1545–1640 [Slavery and the Slave Trade in Upper Peru, 1545–1640]," *Jahrbuch fur Geshichte con Staat, Wirtschaft und Gesellschaft Lateinamerikas* 1 (1964): 157–86. In German.

Zavala, Silvio, "Relaciones historicas entre indios y negros en Ibero-America [Historical Relations between Indians and Blacks in Ibero-America]," *Revista de Indias* (1946): 53–65. In Spanish.

Zuluaga, Rosa Mercedes, "La trata de negros en la region Cuyana durante el siglo XVII [The Treatment of Blacks in the Cuyana Region during the Seventeenth Century," *Revista de la Junta de Estudios Historicos de Mendoza* 2 (1970): 39–66. In Spanish.

14.8.1   South America, Brazil

Alden, Dauril, and Joseph C. Miller, "'Out of Africa': The Slave Trade and the Transmission of Smallpox to Brazil, ca. 1560-ca. 1830," *Journal of Interdisciplinary History* 18 (1987): 195–224.

Anderson, Robert N., "The Quilombo of Palmares: A New Overview of a Maroon State in Seventeenth-Century Brazil," *Journal of Latin American Studies* 28 (1996): 545–66.

Boxer, Charles R., *Race Relations in the Portuguese Colonial Empire, 1415–1825* (1963).

Diouf, Sylviane A., *Servants of Allah: African Muslims Enslaved in the Americas* (1998).

Elkins, Stanley M., "Slavery in Capitalist and Non-Capitalist Countries," in Laura Foner, and Eugene D. Genovese, ed., *Slavery in the New World: A Reader in Comparative History* (1969): 8–26.

Funari, Pedro Paulo, *The Archaeology of Palmares and Its Contribution to the Understanding of the History of African-American Culture* (1995).

Greenfield, Sidney M., "Entrepreneurship and Dynasty Building in the Portuguese Empire in the Seventeenth Century: The Career of Salvador Correia de Sé e Benevides," in Sidney M. Greenfield, Arnold Strickon, and Robert T. Aubey, ed., *Entrepreneurs in Cultural Context* (1979): 21–63.

Kent, R. K., "Palmares: An African State in Brazil," *Journal of African History* 6 (1965): 161–75.

Mattoso, Katia M. de Quieros, *To Be a Slave in Brazil, 1550–1888,* trans. Arthur Goldhammer (1986).

Mulvey, Patricia A., "Black Brothers and Sisters: Membership in the Black Lay Brotherhoods of Colonial Brazil," *Luso- Brazilian Review* 17 (1980): 253–79.

——— "Slave Confraternities in Brazil: Their Role in Colonial Society," *Americas* 39 (1982): 39–68.

Orser, C. E., *In Search of Zumbi* (1982).

Ribeiro, René, "Relations of the Negro with Christianity in Portuguese America: The Negro and the New Social Slavery Structure," *Americas* 14 (1958): 454–84.

Russell-Wood, A. J. R., *The Black Man in Slavery and Freedom in Colonial Brazil* (1982).

——— "Iberian Expansion and the Issue of Black Slavery: Changing Portuguese Attitudes, 1440–1770," *American Historical Review* 83 (1978): 16–42.

Schwartz, Stuart B., "Colonial Brazil: The Role of the State in a Slave Social Formation," *Essays in the Political, Economic, and Social History of Colonial Latin America* 3 (1982): 1–23.

——— "The Mocambo: Slave Resistance in Colonial Bahia," *Journal of Social History* 3 (1970): 313–33.

——— *Slaves, Peasants, and Rebels: Reconsidering Brazilian Slavery* (1992).

Verger, Pierre, *Bahia and the West African Trade, 1549–1851* (1964).

14.8.2   Studies in Foreign Languages (South America, Brazil)

Benci, Jorge, *Economia Cristá dos Senhores no Governo dos Escravos: Livro Brasiliero de 1700* [Christian Economy of the Lords Governing Slaves: A Brazilian Book from 1700] (1954). In Portuguese.

Brandão, Alfredo, "Os Negros na Historia de Alagôas [Negroes in the History of Alagôas]," *Estudos Afro-Brasileiros* 1 (1935): 55–91. In Portuguese.

Cardoso, Ciro Flammarion Santana, *Agricultura, Escravadão e Capitalismo* [Agriculture, Slavery, and Capitalism] (1979). In Portuguese.

Carneiro, Edison, *O Quilombo dos Palmares* [The Quilombo of Palmares] (1946). In Portuguese.

de Carvalho, Alfredo, "Diario da Viagem do Capitao Joao Blaer aos Palmares em 1645 [Voyage Diary of Captain João Blaer to Palmares in 1645]," *Revista do Instituto Archeologico e Geographico Pernambucano* 10 (1902): 87–96. In Portuguese.

Ennes, Ernesto, *As Guerras nos Palmares: Subsidios para a sua Historia* [The Wars in Palmares: Contributions to its History] (1938). In Portuguese.

Freitas, Decio, *Escravos e Senhores-de-Escravos* [Slaves and Slave-Lords] (1977). In Portuguese.

——— *Inserreicos Escravas* [Slave Insurrections] (1976). In Portuguese.

——— *O Escravismo Brasileiro* [Brazilian Slavery] (1980). In Portuguese.

——— *Palmares: A Guerra dos Escravos* [Palmares: The War of the Slaves] (1973). In Portuguese.

Freitas, Mario Martins de, *Reino Negro de Palmares* [Negro Kingdom of Palmares] (1954). In Portuguese.

Frietas, Octavio de, *Doencas Africanas no Brasil* [African Sicknesses in Brazil] (1935). In Portuguese.

Funari, Pedro Paulo, "A 'Republica de Palmares' e a Arqueologia da Serra da Barriga [The 'Republic of Palmares' and the Archaeology of the Serra da Barriga]," *Revista Universidad de São Paulo* 28 (1996): 6–13. In Portuguese.

Goulart, Mauricio, *Escravidão Africana no Brasil: Das Origens a Extincão do Trafico* [African Slavery in Brazil: From Origin to Extinction of Trafficking] (1949). In Portuguese.

Hell, Jürgen, "Der Brasilianische Plantagen-Komplex, 1532–1808: Ein Beitrag zur Charakteristik der Sklaverei in Amerika [The Brazilian Plantation Complex, 1532–1808: A Contribution to the Characteristics of Slavery in America]," *Asien-Afrika-Latien-Amerikaa* 6 (1978): 117–38.

Instituto do Açucar e Alçool, *Documentos para a Historia do Açucar* [Documents for a History of Sugar] (3 vols., 1954). In Portuguese.

Macedo, Sergio D. T., *Apontamentos para a Historia do Trafico Negreiro no Brasil* [Notes for the History of Negro Traffic in Brazil] (1942). In Portuguese.

——— *Palmares: A Troia Negra* [Palmares: The Black Troy] (1963). In Portuguese.

Malheiro, Perdigao, and Agostinho Marques, *A Escravidão no Brasil: Ensaio Historico, Juridico, Social* [Slavery in Brazil: A Historical, Juridical, and Social Essay] (1976). In Portuguese.

Mauro, Frédéric, "L'Atlantique Portugais et les esclaves, 1570–1670 [The Portuguese Atlantic and the Slaves, 1570–1670]," *Revista de Faculdade de Letras* 22 (1956): 5–55. In Portuguese.

Mello, Mario, "A Republica dos Palmares [The Republic of Palmares]," *Estudos Afro-Brasileiros* 32 (1934): 189–92. In Portuguese.

Mendes, M. Maia, "Escravatura no Brasil, 1500–1700 [Slavery in Brazil, 1500–1700]," *Congresso do Mundo Portugues* 10 (1940): 31–55. In Portuguese.

Moraes Filho, Evaristo de, *A Escravidão Africana no Brasil: Das Origens a Extincão* [African Slavery in Brazil: From Its Origins to Its Extinction] (1933). In Portuguese.

Moura, Clovis, *Rebelioes da Senzala: Quilombos, Inserrecioes, Guerrilhas* [Slave Rebellions: Quilombos, Insurrections, Guerrillas] (1959). In Portuguese.

Pádua, Ciro T. de, "O Negro no Planalto: Do Século XVI ao século XIX [The Negro in Planalto: From the Sixteenth Century to the Twentieth Century]," *Revista do Instituto Histórico e Geográfico de Sao Paulo* 41 (1942): 127–264. In Portuguese.

Pedreira, Pedro Tomas, *Os Quilombos Brasileiros* [The Brazilian Quilombos] (1973). In Portuguese.

Queiroz, Suely Robles reis de, "El origen de los negros brasilenos [The Origin of Brazilian Negroes]," *Revista de la Universidad de Mexico* 25 (1970): 18–24. In Spanish.

Ramos, Artur, *O Negro na Civilizacao Brasileira* [The Negro in Brazilian Civilization] (1956). In Portuguese.

"Relacao das Guerras Feitas aos Palmares de Pernambuco no tempo do Governador D. Pedro de Almeida de 1675 a 1678 [Report of Wars Waged against Palmares of Pernambuco in the Time of Governor Don Pedro de Almeida from 1675 to 1678]," *Revista do Instituto Archaeologico e Geographico Pernambucano* 10 (1859): In Portuguese.

Ribeiro, Silvia Lara, "Do Mouro Cativo ao Escravo Negro: Continuidade ou Ruptura? [From Captive Moor to Negro Slave: Continuity or Rupture?]," *Anais do Museu Paulista* 30 (1980–81): 375–98. In Portuguese.

Rios, Jose Artur, "A Fazenda de Cafe: Da Escravidao ao Trabalho Livre [The Coffee Plantation: From Slavery to Free Labor]," *Ensaios Sobre Cafe e Desenvolvimento Econimico* (1973): 3–27. In Portuguese.

Rodriques, Nina Raymundo, *Os Africanos no Brasil* [Africans in Brazil] (1945). In Portuguese.

——— "A Troia Negreo: Erros e Lacunas da Historia de Palmares [A Black Troy: Errors and Gaps in the History of Palmares]," *Revista do Instituto Historico e Geographico Brasileiro* 75 (1912): 231–58. In Portuguese.

Saraiva, Antonio Jose, "Le Père Antonio Vieira, S. J., et la question de l'esclavage des noirs au XVIIe Siècle [Father Antonio Vieira, S. J., and the Question of Negro Slavery in the Seventeenth Century]," *Añnales: Èconomies, Sociétés, Civilisations* [Annals: Economy, Society, and Civilisations] 22 (1967): 1289–1309. In French.

Willeke, Venantius, "Kirche und Negersklaven in Brasilien, 1550–1888 [Church and Negro Slaves in Brazil, 1550–1888]," *Neue Zietschrift fur Missionswissenschaft* 32 (1976): 11–29. In German.

15 _1690–1772_

Peter H. Wood

15.1 GENERAL STUDIES

Abrahams, Roger D., and John F. Szwed, ed., _After Africa: Extracts from British Travel Accounts and Journals of the Seventeenth, Eighteenth, and Nineteenth Centuries concerning the Slaves, Their Manners, and Customs in the British West Indies_ (1983).

Beckles, Hilary McD, and Verene Shepherd, ed., _Caribbean Freedom: Society and Economy from Emancipation to the Present_ (1993).

Berlin, Ira, _Many Thousands Gone: The First Two Centuries of Slavery in North America_ (1998).

——— "Time, Space, and the Evolution of Afro-American Society on Mainland British North America," _American Historical Review_ 85 (1980): 44–78.

Berlin, Ira, and Ronald Hoffman, ed., _Slavery and Freedom in the Age of the American Revolution_ (1983).

Bernhard, Virginia, "Bermuda and Virginia in the Seventeenth Century: A Comparative View," _Journal of Social History_ 19 (1985): 57–70.

Conniff, Michael L., and Thomas J. Davis, _Africans in the Americas: A History of the Black Diaspora_ (1994).

Curtin, Philip D., _The Rise and Fall of the Plantation Complex: Essays in Atlantic History_ (1990).

Davis, David Brion, _The Problem of Slavery in Western Culture_ (1966).

Eltis, David, "Europeans and the Rise and Fall of African Slavery in the Americas: An Interpretation," _American Historical Review_ 98 (1993): 1399–423.

Greene, Lorenzo Johnston, _The Negro in Colonial New England, 1620–1776_ (1942).

Hall, Gwendolyn Midlo, _Africans in Colonial Louisiana: The Development of Afro-Creole Culture in the Eighteenth Century_ (1992).

Jones, Rhett S., "Structural Differentiation and the Status of Blacks in British Colonial America, 1630–1775," _Journal of Human Relations_ 19 (1971): 322–46.

Jordan, Winthrop D., _The White Man's Burden: Historical Origins of Racism in the United States_ (1974).

Kaplan, Sidney, and Emma Nogrady Kaplan, _The Black Presence in the Era of the American Revolution_ (rev. ed., 1989).

Klingberg, Frank Joseph, _An Appraisal of the Negro in Colonial South Carolina: A Study in Americanization_ (1941).

Kobrin, David, _The Black Minority in Early New York_ (1975).

Kulikoff, Allan, "The Origins of Afro-American Society in Tidewater Maryland and Virginia, 1700 to 1790," _William and Mary Quarterly_ 35 (1978): 226–59.

——— _Tobacco and Slaves: The Development of Southern Cultures in the Chesapeake, 1680–1800_ (1986).

Landers, Jane, "African Presence in Early Spanish Colonization of the Caribbean and the Southeastern Borderlands," in David Hurst Thomas, ed., _Archaeological and Historical Perspectives on the Spanish Borderlands East_ (1990): 315–27.

Main, Gloria L., _Tobacco Colony: Life in Early Maryland, 1650–1720_ (1982).

Mintz, Sidney Wilfred, and Richard Price, _The Birth of African-American Culture: An Anthropological Perspective_ (1992).

Morgan, Edmund S., *American Slavery, American Freedom: The Ordeal of Colonial Virginia* (1975).

Morgan, Philip D., *Slave Counterpoint: Black Culture in the Eighteenth-Century Chesapeake and Lowcountry* (1998).

Nash, Gary B., *Race, Class, and Politics: Essays on American Colonial and Revolutionary Society* (1986).

Piersen, William D., *Black Yankees: The Development of an Afro-American Subculture in Eighteenth-Century New England* (1988).

———— *From Africa to America: African American History, 1600–1790* (1996).

Rippy, J. Fred, "The Negro and the Spanish Pioneer in the New World," *Journal of Negro History* 6 (1921): 183–89.

Sensbach, Jon F., "Charting a Course in Early African-American History," *William and Mary Quarterly* 50 (1993): 394–405.

Wood, Peter H., *Strange New Land: African Americans, 1617–1776* (1996).

Wright, Donald R., *African Americans in the Colonial Era: From African Origins through the American Revolution* (1990).

Wright, J. Leitch, Jr., "Blacks in British East Florida," *Florida Historical Quarterly* 54 (1976): 425–42.

15.2 HISTORIOGRAPHY

Carrington, Selwyn, "The State of the Debate on the Role of Capitalism in the Ending of the Slave System," *Journal of Caribbean History* 22 (1988): 20–41.

Greenberg, Douglas, "The Middle Colonies in Recent American Historiography," *William and Mary Quarterly* 36 (1979): 396–427.

Williams-Myers, A. J., "The African Presence in the Mid-Hudson Valley before 1800: A Preliminary Historiographical Sketch," *Afro-Americans in New York Life and History* 8 (1984): 31–39.

Wood, Peter H., "'I Did the Best I Could for My Day': The Study of Early Black History during the Second Reconstruction, 1960 to 1976," *William and Mary Quarterly* 35 (1978): 185–225.

15.3 RACE RELATIONS

15.3.1 Slave Trade

Ackerman, Robert K., "Colonial Land Policies and the Slave Problem," *South Carolina Historical Association, Proceedings* (1965): 28–35.

Anstey, Roger T., *The Atlantic Slave Trade and British Abolition, 1760–1810* (1975).

———— "The Slave Trade of the Continental Powers, 1760–1810," *Economic History Review* 30 (1977): 259–68.

———— "The Volume of the North American Slave-Carrying Trade from Africa, 1761–1810," *Revue Française d'Histoire d'Outre-Mer* 62 (1975): 47–66.

Austen, Ralph A., and Woodruff D. Smith, "Private Tooth Decay As Public Economic Virtue: The Slave-Sugar Triangle, Consumerism, and European Industrialization," *Social Science History* 14 (1990): 95–115.

Baesjou, René, "The Historical Evidence in Old Maps and Charts of Africa with Special Reference to West Africa," *History in Africa* 15 (1988): 1–83.

Bean, Richard Nelson, *The British Trans-Atlantic Slave Trade, 1650–1775* (1975).

Berlin, Ira, "The Slave Trade and the Development of Afro-American Society in English Mainland North America, 1619–1775," *Southern Studies* 20 (1981): 122–36.

Burnard, Trevor, "Who Bought Slaves in Early America?: Purchasers of Slaves from the Royal African Company in Jamaica, 1674–1708," *Slavery and Abolition* 2 (1996): 68–92.

Burnside, Madeleine, *Spirits of the Passage: The Transatlantic Slave Trade in the Seventeenth Century*, ed. Rosemarie Robotham (1997).

Cottman, Michael, *The Wreck of the Henrietta Marie: An African American's Journey to Uncover a Sunken Slave Ship's Past* (1999).

277

Coughtry, Jay, *The Notorious Triangle: Rhode Island and the African Slave Trade, 1700–1807* (1981).

Crane, Elaine F., "'The First Wheel of Commerce': Newport, Rhode Island and the Slave Trade, 1760–1776," *Slavery and Abolition* 1 (1980): 178–98.

Curtin, Philip D., *The Atlantic Slave Trade: A Census* (1969).

Darity, William, Jr., "The Numbers Game and the Profitability of the British Trade in Slaves," *Journal of Economic History* 45 (1985): 693–703.

————— "Profitability of the British Trade in Slaves Once Again," *Explorations in Economic History* 26 (1989): 380–84.

Davidson, Basil, *Black Mother: Africa and the Atlantic Slave Trade* (rev. and expanded ed., 1980).

Donnan, Elizabeth, ed., *Documents Illustrative of the History of the Slave Trade to America* (4 vols., 1930–35).

Eltis, David, *Economic Growth and the Ending of the Transatlantic Slave Trade* (1987).

————— "Free and Coerced Transatlantic Migrations: Some Comparisons," *American Historical Review* 88 (1983): 251–80.

Eltis, David, and Stanley L. Engerman, "Fluctuations in Sex and Age Ratios in the Transatlantic Slave Trade, 1663–1864," *Economic History Review* 46 (1993): 308–23.

————— "Was the Slave Trade Dominated by Men?" *Journal of Interdisciplinary History* 23 (1992): 237–57.

Evans, William McKee, "From the Land of Canaan to the Land of Guinea: The Strange Odyssey of the 'Sons of Ham,'" *American Historical Review* 85 (1980): 15–43.

Ewald, Janet J., "Slavery in Africa and the Slave Trade from Africa," *American Historical Review* 97 (1992): 465–85.

Faber, Eli, *Jews, Slaves, and the Slave Trade: Setting the Record Straight* (1998).

Frank, Andrew, and Darlene Clark Hine, ed., *The Birth of Black America: The Age of Discovery and the Slave Trade* (1996).

Fuller, John, *The Fuller Letters, 1728–1755: Guns, Slaves, and Finance,* ed. David Crossley and Richard Saville (1991).

Garland, Charles, and Herbert S. Klein, "The Allotment of Space for Slaves aboard Eighteenth-Century British Slave Ships," *William and Mary Quarterly* 42 (1985): 238–48.

Gemery, Henry A., Jan S. Hogendorn, and Marion Johnson, "Evidence on English/African Terms of Trade in the Eighteenth Century," *Explorations in Economic History* 27 (1990): 157–77.

Gemery, Henry A., and Jan S. Hogendorn, ed., *The Uncommon Market: Essays in the Economic History of the Atlantic Slave Trade* (1979).

Glausser, Wayne, "Three Approaches to Locke and the Slave Trade," *Journal of the History of Ideas* 51 (1990): 199–216.

Gragg, Larry D., "The Barbados Connection: John Parris and the Early New England Trade with the West Indies," *New England Historical and Genealogical Register* 140 (1986): 99–113.

————— "The Troubled Voyage of the Rainbow," *History Today* 39 (1989): 36–41.

Grubb, Farley, and Tony Stitt, "The Liverpool Emigrant Servant Trade and the Transition to Slave Labor in the Chesapeake, 1697–1707: Market Adjustments to War," *Explorations in Economic History* 31 (1994): 376–405.

Hair, P. E. H., "Antera Duke of Old Calabar: A Little More about an African Entrepreneur," *History in Africa* 17 (1990): 359–65.

Inikori, Joseph E., "The Credit Needs of the African Trade and the Development of the Credit Economy in England," *Explorations in Economic History* 27 (1990): 197–231.

————— "Slavery and Atlantic Commerce, 1650–1800," *American Economic Review* 82 (1992): 151–57.

————— "The Sources of Supply for the Atlantic Slave Exports from the Bight of Benin and the Bight of Bonny (Biafra)," *Odu* 31 (1987): 104–23.

Inikori, Joseph E., and Stanley L. Engerman, ed., *The Atlantic Slave Trade: Effects on Economies, Societies, and Peoples in Africa, the Americas, and Europe* (1992).

Klein, Herbert S., "African Women in the Atlantic Slave Trade," in Claire C. Robertson and Martin A. Klein, ed., *Women and Slavery in Africa* (1983): 29–48.

————— *The Middle Passage: Comparative Studies in the Atlantic Slave Trade* (1978).

———— "Slaves and Shipping in Eighteenth-Century Virginia," *Journal of Interdisciplinary History* 5 (1975): 383–412.

Law, Robin, "Between the Sea and the Lagoons: The Interaction of Maritime and Inland Navigation on the Precolonial Slave Coast," *Cahiers d'Études Africaines* 29 (1989): 209–37.

———— "Dahomey and the Slave Trade: Reflections on the Historiography of the Rise of Dahomey," *Journal of African History* 27 (1986): 237–67.

———— *The Slave Coast of West Africa, 1550–1750: The Impact of the Atlantic Slave Trade on an African Society* (1991).

———— "Slave-Raiders and Middlemen, Monopolists and Free-Traders: The Supply of Slaves for the Atlantic Trade in Dahomey, c. 1715–1850," *Journal of African History* 30 (1989): 45–68.

———— "'The Common People Were Divided': Monarchy, Aristocracy and Political Factionalism in the Kingdom of Whydah, 1671–1727," *International Journal of African Historical Studies* 23 (1990): 201–29.

Littlefield, Daniel C., *Rice and Slaves: Ethnicity and the Slave Trade in Colonial South Carolina* (1981).

———— "The Slave Trade to Colonial South Carolina: A Profile," *South Carolina Historical Magazine* 91 (1990): 68–99.

Lovejoy, Paul E., ed., *Africans in Bondage: Studies in Slavery and the Slave Trade: Essays in Honor of Philip D. Curtin on the Occasion of the Twenty-Fifth Anniversary of African Studies at the University of Wisconsin* (1986).

———— "The Volume of the Atlantic Slave Trade: A Synthesis," *Journal of African History* 23 (1982): 473–501.

Lovejoy, Paul E., and David Richardson, "Trust, Pawnship, and Atlantic History: The Institutional Foundations of the Old Calabar Slave Trade," *American Historical Review* 104 (1999): 333–55.

Manning, Patrick, "Coastal Society in the Republic of Bénin: Reproduction of a Regional System," *Cahiers d'Études Africaines* 29 (1989): 239–57.

———— "Migrations of Africans to the Americas: The Impact on Africans, Africa, and the New World," *History Teacher* 26 (1993): 279–96.

———— "The Slave Trade: The Formal Demography of a Global System," *Social Science History* 14 (1990): 255–79.

———— *Slavery and African Life: Occidental, Oriental, and African Slave Trades* (1990).

Mannix, Daniel Pratt, *Black Cargoes: A History of the Atlantic Slave Trade, 1518–1865* (1962).

McGowan, Winston, "African Resistance to the Atlantic Slave Trade in West Africa," *Slavery and Abolition* 11 (1990): 5–29.

Miller, Joseph Calder, *Way of Death: Merchant Capitalism and the Angolan Slave Trade, 1730–1830* (1988).

Minchinton, Walter E., "Characteristics of British Slaving Vessels, 1698–1775," *Journal of Interdisciplinary History* 20 (1989): 53–81.

———— "The Seaborne Slave Trade of North Carolina," *North Carolina Historical Review* 71 (1994): 1–61.

O'Callaghan, Edmund Bailey, ed., *Voyages of the Slavers St. John and Arms of Amsterdam, 1659, 1663: Together with Additional Papers Illustrative of the Slave Trade under the Dutch* (1867).

Platt, Virginia Bever, "The East India Company and the Madagascar Slave Trade," *William and Mary Quarterly* 26 (1969): 548–77.

Pope-Hennessy, James, *Sins of the Fathers: A Study of the Atlantic Slave Traders, 1441–1807* (1967).

Postma, Johannes, *The Dutch in the Atlantic Slave Trade, 1600–1815* (1990).

Price, Jacob M., "*Sheffield* vs. *Starke*: Institutional Experimentation in the London-Maryland Trade, ca. 1696–1706," *Business History* 28 (1986): 19–39.

Rawley, James A., "Richard Harris, Slave Trader Spokesman," *Albion* 23 (1991): 439–58.

———— *The Transatlantic Slave Trade: A History* (1981).

Reynolds, Edward, *Stand the Storm: A History of the Atlantic Slave Trade* (1985).

Richardson, David, "Accounting for Profits in the British Trade in Slaves: Reply to William Darity," *Explorations in Economic History* 26 (1989): 492–99.

———— "The British Slave Trade to Colonial South Carolina," *Slavery and Abolition* 12 (1991): 125–72.

———— "The Costs of Survival: The Transport of Slaves in the Middle Passage and the Profitability of the Eighteenth-Century British Slave Trade," *Explorations in Economic History* 24 (1987): 178–96.

———— "The Eighteenth-Century British Slave Trade: Estimates of Its Volume and Coastal Distribution in Africa," *Research in Economic History* 12 (1989): 151–95.

———— "Slave Exports from West and West-Central Africa, 1700–1810: New Estimates of Volume and Distribution," *Journal of African History* 30 (1989): 1–22.

———— "The Slave Trade, Sugar, and British Economic Growth, 1748–1776," *Journal of Interdisciplinary History* 17 (1987): 739–69.

Rodney, Walter, "Upper Guinea and the Significance of the Origins of Africans Enslaved in the New World," *Journal of Negro History* 54 (1969): 327–45.

Starr, J. Barton, "Slave Trading in Jamaica," *Slavery and Abolition* 10 (1989): 73–75.

Steckel, Richard H., and Richard A. Jensen, "New Evidence on the Causes of Slave and Crew Mortality in the Atlantic Slave Trade," *Journal of Economic History* 46 (1986): 57–77.

Tattersfield, Nigel, *The Forgotten Trade: Comprising the Log of the Daniel and Henry of 1700 and Accounts of the Slave Trade from the Minor Ports of England, 1698–1725* (1991).

Wax, Darold D., "Africans on the Delaware: The Pennsylvania Slave Trade, 1759–1765," *Pennsylvania History* 50 (1983): 38–49.

———— "Black Immigrants: The Slave Trade in Colonial Maryland," *Maryland Historical Magazine* 73 (1978): 30–45.

———— "The Browns of Providence and the Slaving Voyage of the Brig *Sally,* 1764–1765," *American Neptune* 32 (1972): 171–79.

———— "Negro Import Duties in Colonial Pennsylvania," *Pennsylvania Magazine of History and Biography* 97 (1973): 22–44.

———— "Negro Import Duties in Colonial Virginia: A Study of British Commercial Policy and Local Public Policy," *Virginia Magazine of History and Biography* 79 (1971): 29–44.

———— "Negro Imports into Pennsylvania, 1720–1766," *Pennsylvania History* 32 (1965): 254–87.

———— "'New Negroes Are Always in Demand': The Slave Trade in Eighteenth-Century Georgia," *Georgia Historical Quarterly* 68 (1984): 193–220.

———— "A Philadelphia Surgeon on a Slaving Voyage to Africa, 1749–1751," *Pennsylvania Magazine of History and Biography* 92 (1968): 465–93.

———— "Preferences for Slaves in Colonial America," *Journal of Negro History* 58 (1973): 371–401.

———— "Quaker Merchants and the Slave Trade in Colonial Pennsylvania," *Pennsylvania Magazine of History and Biography* 86 (1962): 143–59.

Westbury, Susan, "Analysing a Regional Slave Trade: The West Indies and Virginia, 1698–1775," *Slavery and Abolition* 7 (1986): 241–56.

15.3.2   Slavery

Abrahams, Roger D., *Singing the Master: The Emergence of African American Culture in the Plantation South* (1992).

Beckles, Hilary McD, "The Colours of Property: Brown, White and Black Chattels and Their Responses on the Caribbean Frontier," *Slavery and Abolition* 15 (1994): 36–51.

———— *White Servitude and Black Slavery in Barbados, 1627–1715* (1989).

Berlin, Ira, *Many Thousands Gone: The First Two Centuries of Slavery in North America* (1998).

Bolland, O. Nigel, "Slavery in Belize," *Journal of Belizean Affairs* 6 (1978): 3–36.

Briggs, Winstanley, "Slavery in French Colonial Illinois," *Chicago History* 18 (1989–90): 66–81.

Corbett, Theodore G., "Migration to a Spanish Imperial Frontier in the Seventeenth and Eighteenth Centuries: St. Augustine," *Hispanic American Historical Review* 54 (1974): 414–30.

Craton, Michael, *Empire, Enslavement, and Freedom in the Caribbean* (1997).

———— *Searching for the Invisible Man: Slaves and Plantation Life in Jamaica* (1978).

Deal, Joseph Douglas, *Race and Class in Colonial Virginia: Indians, Englishmen, and Africans on the Eastern Shore during the Seventeenth Century* (1993).

Domar, Evsey D., "The Causes of Slavery or Serfdom: A Hypothesis," *Journal of Economic History* 30 (1970): 18–32.

Dunn, Richard S., *Sugar and Slaves: The Rise of the Planter Class in the English West Indies, 1624–1713* (1972).

Ekberg, Carl J., "Black Slaves in the Illinois Country, 1721–1765," *Proceedings of the Annual Meeting of the French Colonial Historical Society* 11 (1987): 265–77.

Finkelman, Paul, ed., *Slavery and the Law* (1997).

Ford, Worthington Chauncey, ed., *Washington as an Employer and Importer of Labor* (1889).

Forster, Robert, "Slavery in Virginia and Saint-Domingue in the Late Eighteenth Century," *Proceedings of the Annual Meeting of the French Colonial Historical Society* (1990): 1–13.

Gaspar, David Barry, "Working the System: Antigua Slaves and Their Struggle to Live," *Slavery and Abolition* 13 (1992): 131–55.

Green, William A., "Supply versus Demand in the Barbadian Sugar Revolution," *Journal of Interdisciplinary History* 18 (1988): 403–18.

Greene, Jack P., "Colonial South Carolina and the Caribbean Connection," *South Carolina Historical Magazine* 88 (1987): 192–210.

Hall, Douglas, *In Miserable Slavery: Thomas Thistlewood in Jamaica, 1750–1786* (1989).

Handlin, Oscar, and Mary F. Handlin, "Origins of the Southern Labor System," *William and Mary Quarterly* 7 (1950): 199–222.

Harris, Norman D., *The History of Negro Servitude in Illinois, and of the Slavery Agitation in That State, 1719–1864* (1969).

Hatt, Christine, *Slavery: From Africa to the Americas* (1997).

Hill, Charles L., "Slavery and Its Aftermath in Beverly, Massachusetts: Juno Larcom and Her Family," *Essex Institute Historical Collections* 116 (1980): 111–30.

Inikori, Joseph E., "Slavery and the Development of Industrial Capitalism in England," *Journal of Interdisciplinary History* 17 (1987): 771–93.

Johnson, Whittington B., "The Origin and Nature of African Slavery in Seventeenth Century Maryland," *Maryland Historical Magazine* 73 (1978): 236–45.

Jordan, Winthrop D., "Modern Tensions and the Origins of American Slavery," *Journal of Southern History* 28 (1962): 18–30.

Kay, Marvin L. Michael, and Lorin Lee Cary, *Slavery in North Carolina, 1748–1775* (1995).

Klein, Herbert S., *Slavery in the Americas: A Comparative Study of Virginia and Cuba* (1967).

Klein, Rachel N., *Unification of a Slave State: The Rise of the Planter Class in the South Carolina Backcountry, 1760–1808* (1990).

Lee, Jean Butenhoff, "The Problem of Slave Community in the Eighteenth-Century Chesapeake," *William and Mary Quarterly* 43 (1986): 333–61.

Lewis, Ronald L., *Coal, Iron, and Slaves: Industrial Slavery in Maryland and Virginia, 1715–1865* (1979).

Littlefield, Daniel C., "Continuity and Change in Slave Culture: South Carolina and the West Indies," *Southern Studies* 26 (1987): 202–16.

——— *Rice and Slaves: Ethnicity and the Slave Trade in Colonial South Carolina* (1981).

McBurney, Christian, "The South Kingstown Planters: Country Gentry in Colonial Rhode Island," *Rhode Island History* 45 (1986): 81–93.

McKnight, Andrew N., "Lydia Broadnax, Slave and Free Women of Color," *Southern Studies* 5 (1994): 17–30.

McManus, Edgar J., *Black Bondage in the North* (1973).

Menard, Russell, "From Servants to Slaves: The Transformation of the Chesapeake Labor System," *Southern Studies* 16 (1977): 355–90.

Morgan, Edmund S., *American Slavery, American Freedom: The Ordeal of Colonial Virginia* (1975).

——— "Slavery and Freedom: The American Paradox," *Journal of American History* 59 (1972): 5–29.

Morgan, Philip D., *Slave Counterpoint: Black Culture in the Eighteenth-Century Chesapeake and Lowcountry* (1998).

Morgan, Philip D., and Michael L. Nicholls, "Slaves in Piedmont Virginia, 1720–1790," *William and Mary Quarterly* 46 (1989): 211–51.

Moss, Simeon F., "The Persistence of Slavery and Involuntary Servitude in a Free State, 1685–1866," *Journal of Negro History* 35 (1950): 289–314.

Mullin, Gerald W., "Rethinking American Negro Slavery from the Vantage Point of the Colonial Era," *Louisiana Studies* 12 (1973): 398–422.

Mullin, Michael, "Women and the Comparative Study of American Negro Slavery," *Slavery and Abolition* 6 (1985): 25–40.

Nordstrom, Carl, "Slavery in a New York County: Rockland County, 1686–1827," *Afro-Americans in New York Life and History* 1 (1977): 145–66.

Olwell, Robert, *Masters, Slaves, and Subjects: The Culture of Power in the South Carolina Low Country, 1740–1790* (1998).

Palmie, Stephan, ed., *Slave Cultures and the Cultures of Slavery* (1996).

Patterson, Orlando, *The Sociology of Slavery: An Analysis of the Origins, Development and Structure of Negro Slave Society in Jamaica* (1967).

Phillips, Ulrich B., "The Slave Labor Problem in the Charleston District," *Political Science Quarterly* 22 (1907): 416–39.

Rosivach, Vincent J., "Agricultural Slavery in the Northern Colonies and in Classical Athens: Some Comparisons," *Comparative Studies in Society and History* 35 (1993): 551–67.

Sheridan, Richard B., "The Condition of the Slaves in the Settlement and Economic Development of the British Windward Islands, 1763–1775," *Journal of Caribbean History* 24 (1990): 121–45.

——— *Sugar and Slavery: An Economic History of the British West Indies, 1623–1775* (1974).

Shuffelton, Frank, "Circumstantial Accounts, Dangerous Art: Recognizing African-American Culture in Travelers' Narratives," *Eighteenth-Century Studies* 27 (1994): 589–603.

Shyllon, Folarin, "Slave Advertisements in the British West Indies," *Caribbean Studies* 18 (1978–79): 175–99.

Siebert, Wilbur H., "Slavery and White Servitude in East Florida, 1726–1776," *Florida Historical Society Quarterly* 10 (1931): 3–23.

Smith, Mark M., *Mastered by the Clock: Time, Slavery, and Freedom in the American South* (1997).

Solow, Barbara L., "Capitalism and Slavery in the Exceedingly Long Run," *Journal of Interdisciplinary History* 17 (1987): 711–37.

———, ed., *Slavery and the Rise of the Atlantic System* (1991).

Solow, Barbara L., and Stanley L. Engerman, ed., *British Capitalism and Caribbean Slavery: The Legacy of Eric Williams* (1987).

Stinchcombe, Arthur L., "Freedom and Oppression of Slaves in the Eighteenth-Century Caribbean," *American Sociological Review* 59 (1994): 911–29.

Towner, Lawrence, *Good Master Well Served: Masters and Servants in Colonial Massachusetts* (1997).

Tully, Alan, "Patterns of Slaveholding in Colonial Pennsylvania: Chester and Lancaster Counties, 1729–1758," *Journal of Social History* 6 (1973): 285–305.

Wagman, Morton, "Corporate Slavery in New Netherland," *Journal of Negro History* 65 (1980): 34–42.

Walvin, James, *Slaves and Slavery: The British Colonial Experience* (1992).

Ward, John Robert, *British West Indian Slavery, 1750–1834: The Process of Amelioration* (1988).

Wax, Darold D., "The Demand for Slave Labor in Colonial Pennsylvania," *Pennsylvania History* 34 (1967): 331–45.

Williams, Eric Eustace, *Capitalism and Slavery* (1944, 1994).

Wood, Betty, *The Origins of American Slavery: Freedom and Bondage in the English Colonies* (1997).

——— *Slavery in Colonial Georgia, 1730–1775* (1984).

Wood, Peter H., *Black Majority: Negroes in Colonial South Carolina from 1670 through the Stono Rebellion* (1974).

Wright, Gavin, "Capitalism and Slavery on the Islands: A Lesson from the Mainland," *Journal of Interdisciplinary History* 17 (1987): 851–70.

Zafar, Rafia, "Capturing the Captivity: African Americans among the Puritans," *Melus* 17 (1991): 19–36.

15.3.3   Free Blacks

Berlin, Ira, *Slaves without Masters: The Free Negro in the Antebellum South* (1975).

Bethel, Elizabeth Rauh, *The Roots of African American Identity: Memory and History in Antebellum Free Communities* (1997).

Breen, T. H., and Stephen Innes, "Seventeenth-Century Virginia's Forgotten Yeomen: The Free Blacks," *Virginia Cavalcade* 32 (1982): 10–19.

Brewer, James H., "Negro Property Holders in Seventeenth-Century Virginia," *William and Mary Quarterly* 12 (1955): 575–80.

Carr, Lois G. and Russell R. Menard, "Immigration and Opportunity: The Freedman in Early Colonial Maryland," in Thad W. Tate, Jr. and David L. Ammerman, ed., *The Chesapeake in the Seventeenth Century: Essays on Anglo-American Society* (1979): 206–42.

Christoph, Peter R., "The Freedmen of New Amsterdam: Afro-Americans in New Netherland," *Journal of the Afro-American Historical and Genealogical Society* 5 (1984): 109–22.

Cox, Edward L., *Free Coloreds in the Slave Societies of St. Kitts and Grenada, 1763–1833* (1984).

Davidson, Thomas E., "Free Blacks in Old Somerset County, 1745–1755," *Maryland Historical Magazine* 80 (1985): 151–56.

Everett, Donald E., "Free Persons of Color in Colonial Louisiana," *Louisiana History* 7 (1966): 21–50.

Fitchett, E. Horace, "The Traditions of the Free Negro in Charleston, South Carolina," *Journal of Negro History* 25 (1940): 139–52.

Foner, Laura, "The Free People of Color in Louisiana and St. Domingue: A Comparative Portrait of Two Three-Caste Societies," *Journal of Social History* 3 (1970): 406–30.

Hanger, Kimberly S., "Patronage, Property and Persistence: The Emergence of a Free Black Elite in Spanish New Orleans," *Slavery and Abolition* 17 (1996): 44–64.

Hopkins, Leroy T., "Black Eldorado on the Susquehanna: The Emergence of Black Columbia, 1726–1861," *Journal of Lancaster County Historical Society* 89 (1985): 110–32.

Horton, James O., and Lois E. Horton, *In Hope of Liberty: Culture, Community and Protest among Northern Free Blacks, 1700–1860* (1996).

Kimmel, Ross M., "Free Blacks in Seventeenth-Century Maryland," *Maryland Historical Magazine* 71 (1976): 19–25.

Landers, Jane, "Gracia Real de Santa Teresa de Mose: A Free Black Town in Spanish Colonial Florida," *American Historical Review* 95 (1990): 9–30.

———— "Spanish Sanctuary: Fugitives in Florida, 1687–1790," *Florida Historical Quarterly* 62 (1984): 296–313.

Nicholls, Michael L., "Passing through This Troublesome World: Free Blacks in the Early Southside," *Virginia Magazine of History and Biography* 92 (1984): 50–70.

Olwell, Robert, "Becoming Free: Manumission and the Genesis of a Free Black Community in South Carolina, 1740–1790," *Slavery and Abolition* 17 (1996): 1–19.

Reitz, Elizabeth J., "Zooarchaeological Analysis of a Free African Community: Gracia Real De Santa Teresa De Mose," *Historical Archaeology* 28 (1994): 23–40.

Schwarz, Philip J., "Emancipators, Protectors, and Anomalies: Free Black Slaveowners in Virginia," *Virginia Magazine of History and Biography* 95 (1987): 317–38.

Wortis, Helen, "The Black Inhabitants of Shelter Island," *Long Island Forum* 36 (1973): 146–53.

Wright, I. A., comp., "Dispatches of Spanish Officials Bearing on the Free Negro Settlement of Gracia Real de Santa Teresa de Mose, Florida," *Journal of Negro History* 9 (1924): 144–95.

15.3.4   Resistance (Antebellum)

Aptheker, Herbert, *American Negro Slave Revolts* (1943).

Beckles, Hilary McD, *Black Rebellion in Barbados: The Struggle against Slavery, 1627–1838* (1984).

———— "From Land to Sea: Runaway Barbados Slaves and Servants, 1630–1700," *Slavery and Abolition* 6 (1985): 79–94.

———— "Rebels without Heroes: Slave Politics in Seventeenth-Century Barbados," *Journal of Caribbean History* 18 (1983): 1–21.

Beckles, Hilary McD, and Karl Watson, "Social Protest and Labour Bargaining: The Changing Nature of Slaves' Responses to Plantation Life in Eighteenth-Century Barbados," *Slavery and Abolition* 8 (1987): 272–93.

Campbell, Mavis Christine, *The Maroons of Jamaica, 1655–1796: A History of Resistance, Collaboration, and Betrayal* (1988).

Chase, Jeanne, "The 1741 Conspiracy to Burn New York: Black Plot or Black Magic?" *Social Science Information* 22 (1983): 969–81.

Copeland, David A., "The Proceedings of the Rebellious Negroes: News of Slave Insurrections and Crimes in Colonial Newspapers," *American Journalism* 12 (1995): 83–106.

Craton, Michael, and D. Gail Saunders, "Seeking a Life of Their Own: Aspects of Slave Resistance in the Bahamas," *Journal of Caribbean History* 24 (1990): 1–27.

Dadzie, Stella, "Searching for the Invisible Woman: Slavery and Resistance in Jamaica," *Race and Class* 32 (1990): 21–38.

Davis, Thomas J., *A Rumor of Revolt: The "Great Negro Plot" in Colonial New York* (1985).

———— "These Enemies of Their Own Household: A Note on the Troublesome Slave Population in Eighteenth-Century New York City," *Journal of the Afro-American Historical and Genealogical Society* 5 (1983): 133–47.

de Groot, Silvia W., "A Comparison between the History of Maroon Communities in Surinam and Jamaica," *Slavery and Abolition* 6 (1985): 173–84.

Farley, M. Foster, "The Fear of Negro Slave Revolts in South Carolina, 1690–1865," *Afro-American Studies* 3 (1972): 199–207.

Forbes, Ella, "African Resistance to Enslavement: The Nature and the Evidentiary Record," *Journal of Black Studies* 23 (1993): 39–59.

Gaspar, David Barry, *Bondmen and Rebels: A Study of Master-Slave Relations in Antigua, with Implications for Colonial British America* (1985).

———— "'To Bring Their Offending Slaves to Justice': Compensation and Slave Resistance in Antigua, 1669–1763," *Caribbean Quarterly* 30 (1984): 45–59.

Hathaway, G. G., "Fire, Fire, Scorch, Scorch: An Historical Footnote on Arson and Conspiracy," *Journal of Human Relations* 17 (1969): 526–45.

Hill, Daniel G., *The Freedom-Seekers: Blacks in Early Canada* (1981).

Hodges, Graham Russell /Brown, Alan Edward, ed., *"Pretends to Be Free": Runaway Slave Advertisements from Colonial and Revolutionary New York and New Jersey* (1994).

Katz, William Loren, *Breaking the Chains: African-American Slave Resistance* (1998).

Kay, Marvin L. Michael, and Lorin Lee Cary, "Slave Runaways in Colonial North Carolina, 1748–1775," *North Carolina Historical Review* 63 (1986): 1–39.

Lara, Oruno D., "Resistance to Slavery: From Africa to Black America," in Vera Rubin and Arthur Tuden, ed., *Comparative Perspectives on Slavery in New World Plantation Societies* (1977): 464–80.

Launitz-Schurer, Leopold S., Jr., "Slave Resistance in Colonial New York: An Interpretation of Daniel Horsmanden's New York Conspiracy," *Phylon* 41 (1980): 137–51.

Leaming, Hugo Prosper, *Hidden Americans: Maroons of Virginia and the Carolinas* (1995).

McMillan, Timothy J., "Black Magic: Witchcraft, Race, and Resistance in Colonial New England," *Journal of Black Studies* 25 (1994): 99–117.

Meaders, Daniel E., "South Carolina Fugitives As Viewed through Local Colonial Newspapers with Emphasis on Runaway Notices, 1732–1801," *Journal of Negro History* 60 (1975): 288–319.

Morgan, Philip D., and George D. Terry, "Slavery in Microcosm: A Conspiracy Scare in Colonial South Carolina," *Southern Studies* 21 (1982): 121–45.

Mullin, Gerald W., *Flight and Rebellion: Slave Resistance in Eighteenth-Century Virginia* (1972).

Nichols, Elaine, *No Easy Run to Freedom: Maroons in the Great Dismal Swamp of North Carolina and Virginia, 1677–1850* (1988).

Paquette, Robert L., "Social History Update: Slave Resistance and Social History," *Journal of Social History* 24 (1991): 681–85.

Pearson, Edward A., "'A Countryside Full of Flames': A Reconsideration of the Stono Rebellion and Slave Rebelliousness in the Early Eighteenth-Century South Carolina Lowcountry," *Slavery and Abolition* 2 (1996): 22–50.

Sidbury, James, *Ploughshares into Swords: Race, Rebellion, and Identity in Gabriel's Virginia, 1730–1810* (1997).

Sisson, Mary Barr, ed., *The Gathering Storm, 1787–1829: From the Framing of the Constitution to Walker's Appeal* (1996).

Smith, Billy G., and Richard Wojtowicz, comp., *Blacks Who Stole Themselves: Advertisements for Runaways in the Pennsylvania Gazette, 1728–1790* (1989).

Suttles, William C., Jr., "African Religious Survivals As Factors in American Slave Revolts," *Journal of Negro History* 56 (1971): 97–104.

TePaske, John J., "The Fugitive Slave: Intercolonial Rivalry and Spanish Slave Policy, 1687–1764," in Samuel Proctor, ed., *Eighteenth-Century Florida and Its Borderlands* (1975): 1–12.

Thornton, John K., "African Dimensions of the Stono Rebellion," *American Historical Review* 96 (1991): 1101–13.

Waldstreicher, David, "Reading the Runaways: Self-Fashioning, Print Culture, and Confidence in Slavery in the Eighteenth-Century Mid-Atlantic," *William and Mary Quarterly* 56 (1999): 243–72.

Watson, Alan D., "Impulse toward Independence: Resistance and Rebellion among North Carolina Slaves, 1750–1775," *Journal of Negro History* 63 (1978): 317–28.

Wax, Darold D., "Negro Resistance to the Early American Slave Trade," *Journal of Negro History* 51 (1966): 1–15.

Windley, Lathan Algerna, *A Profile of Runaway Slaves in Virginia and South Carolina from 1730 through 1787* (1995).

———— comp., *Runaway Slave Advertisements: A Documentary History from the 1730's to 1790* (4 vols., 1983).

Wood, Betty, "Some Aspects of Female Resistance to Chattel Slavery in Low Country Georgia, c.1736–1815," *Historical Journal* 30 (1987): 603–22.

Wood, Peter H., "'The Dream Deferred': Black Freedom Struggles on the Eve of White Independence," in Gary Y. Okihiro, ed., *In Resistance: Studies in African, Caribbean, and Afro-American History* (1986): 166–87.

15.3.5 Abolitionism and Emancipation

Ashworth, John, "The Relationship between Capitalism and Humanitarianism," *American Historical Review* 92 (1987): 813–28.

Baker, Frank, "The Origins, Character, and Influence of John Wesley's Thoughts upon Slavery," *Methodist History* 22 (1984): 75–86.

Carter, George E., "A Review of Slavery, Emancipation, and Abolition in South Africa and the United States in the Eighteenth Century," *American Studies International* 29 (1991): 69–75.

Craton, Michael, James Walvin, and David Wright, *Slavery, Abolition, and Emancipation: Black Slaves and the British Empire: A Thematic Documentary* (1976).

Drescher, Seymour, *Capitalism and Anti-Slavery: British Mobilization in Comparative Perspective: The Second Anstey Memorial Lectures in the University of Kent at Canterbury, 1984* (1986).

———— "The Long Goodbye: Dutch Capitalism and Anti-Slavery in Comparative Perspective," *American Historical Review* 99 (1994): 44–69.

Juhnke, William E., "Benjamin Franklin's View of the Negro and Slavery," *Pennsylvania History* 41 (1974): 375–88.

Locke, Mary Stoughton, *Anti-Slavery in America: From the Introduction of African Slaves to the Prohibition of the Slave Trade, 1619–1808* (1901).

MacKinley, Peter W., "The New England Puritan Attitude toward Black Slavery," *Old-Time New England* 63 (1973): 81–88.

Miller, John Chester, *The Wolf by the Ears: Thomas Jefferson and Slavery* (1977).

Mitchell, Virgil L., "Colonial Bondage and the Abolition of Slavery in the North," *Rendezvous* 11 (1976): 29–52.

Rosenthal, Bernard, "Puritan Conscience and New England Slavery," *New England Quarterly* 46 (1973): 62–81.

Schmidt, Leigh Eric, "'The Grand Prophet,' Hugh Bryan: Early Evangelicalism's Challenge to the Establishment and Slavery in the Colonial South," *South Carolina Historical Magazine* 87 (1986): 238–50.

Thomas, Paul, "Changing Attitudes in an Expanding Empire: The Anti-Slavery Movement, 1760–1783," *Slavery and Abolition* 5 (1984): 50–72.

Wiecek, William M., *The Sources of Anti-Slavery Constitutionalism in America, 1760–1848* (1977).

15.3.6 Black/White Relations

Allen, Theodore, "'. . . They Would Have Destroyed Me': Slavery and the Origins of Racism," *Radical America* 9 (1975): 41–64.

Breen, T. H., "A Changing Labor Force and Race Relations in Virginia, 1660–1710," *Journal of Social History* 7 (1973): 3–25.

Cantor, Milton, "The Image of the Negro in Colonial Literature," *New England Quarterly* 36 (1963): 452–78.

Chaplin, Joyce E., "Slavery and the Principle of Humanity: A Modern Idea in the Early Lower South," *Journal of Social History* 24 (1990): 299–315.

Curtin, Philip D., "The Environment beyond Europe and the European Theory of Empire," *Journal of World History* 1 (1990): 131–50.

Davidson, Basil, "Columbus: The Bones and Blood of Racism," *Race and Class* 33 (1992): 17–25.

Davis, David Brion, *The Problem of Slavery in Western Culture* (1966).

Degler, Carl N., "Slavery and the Genesis of American Race Prejudice," *Comparative Studies in Society and History* 2 (1959): 49–66.

Dinkin, Robert J., "Seating the Meeting House in Early Massachusetts," *New England Quarterly* 43 (1970): 450–64.

Drescher, Seymour, "The Ending of the Slave Trade and the Evolution of European Scientific Racism," *Social Science History* 14 (1990): 415–50.

Farr, James, "'So Vile and Miserable an Estate': The Problem of Slavery in Locke's Political Thought," *Political Theory* 14 (1986): 263–89.

Ingersoll, Thomas N., "'Releese Us out of This Cruell Bondegg': An Appeal from Virginia in 1723," *William and Mary Quarterly* 51 (1994): 777–82.

Jordan, Winthrop D., *White over Black: American Attitudes toward the Negro, 1550–1812* (1968).

Juhnke, William E., "Benjamin Franklin's View of the Negro and Slavery," *Pennsylvania History* 41 (1974): 375–88.

Kilbride, Daniel, "Slavery and Utilitarianism: Thomas Cooper and the Mind of the South," *Journal of Southern History* 59 (1993): 469–86.

Kirsch, George B., "Jeremy Belknap and the Problem of Blacks and Indians in Early America," *History of New Hampshire* 34 (1979): 202–22.

Klotter, James C., "Slavery and Race: A Family Perspective," *Southern Studies* 17 (1978): 375–97.

Kolchin, Peter, "In Defense of Servitude: American Pro-Slavery and Russian Proserfdom Arguments, 1760–1860," *American Historical Review* 85 (1980): 809–27.

Linebaugh, Peter, and Marcus Rediker, "The Many-Headed Hydra: Sailors, Slaves, and the Atlantic Working Class in the Eighteenth Century," *Journal of Historical Sociology* 3 (1990): 225–52.

Morgan, Jennifer L., "'Some Could Suckle over Their Shoulder': Male Travelers, Female Bodies, and the Gendering of Racial Ideology, 1500–1770," *William and Mary Quarterly* 54 (1997): 167–92.

Nelson, William Javier, "Racial Definition: Background for Divergence," *Phylon* 47 (1986): 318–26.

Roper, John Herbert, and Lolita G. Brockington, "Slave Revolt, Slave Debate: A Comparison," *Phylon* 45 (1984): 98–110.

Ruchames, Louis, "The Sources of Racial Thought in Colonial America," *Journal of Negro History* 52 (1967): 251–72.

Sobel, Mechal, *The World They Made Together: Black and White Values in Eighteenth-Century Virginia* (1987).

Sweet, James H., "The Iberian Roots of American Racist Thought," *William and Mary Quarterly* 54 (1997): 143–66.

Tise, Larry E., *Pro-Slavery: A History of the Defense of Slavery in America, 1701–1840* (1987).

Vassar, Rena, "William Knox's Defense of Slavery, 1768," *Proceedings of the American Philosophical Society* 114 (1970): 310–26.

Vaughan, Alden T., "The Origins Debate: Slavery and Racism in Seventeenth-Century Virginia," *Virginia Magazine of History and Biography* 97 (1989): 311–54.

Von Frank, Albert J., "John Saffin: Slavery and Racism in Colonial Massachusetts," *Early American Literature* 29 (1994): 254–72.

Wax, Darold D., "Georgia and the Negro before the American Revolution," *Georgia Historical Quarterly* 51 (1967): 63–77.

———— "The Image of the Negro in the *Maryland Gazette*, 1745–1775," *Journalism Quarterly* 46 (1969): 73–80.

Wood, Betty, "A Note on the Georgia Malcontents," *Georgia Historical Quarterly* 63 (1979): 264–78.

15.3.7 Black/Native American Relations

Bentley, Martha M., "The Slaveholding Catawbas," *South Carolina Historical Magazine* 92 (1991): 85–98.

Carew, Jan, "United We Stand!: Joint Struggles of Native Americans and African Americans in the Columbian Era," *Monthly Review* 44 (1992): 103–27.

Ellison, Mary, "Black Perceptions and Red Images: Indian and Black Literary Links," *Phylon* 44 (1983): 44–55.

Forbes, Jack D., "The Manipulation of Race, Caste and Identity: Classifying Afro-Americans, Native Americans and Red-Black People," *Journal of Ethnic Studies* 17 (1990): 1–51.

———— "Mulattoes and People of Color in Anglo-North America: Implications for Black-Indian Relations," *Journal of Ethnic Studies* 12 (1984): 17–61.

———— "Mustees, Half-Breeds and Zambos in Anglo North America: Aspects of Black-Indian Relations," *American Indian Quarterly* 7 (1983): 57–83.

———— "The Use of the Terms 'Negro' and 'Black' to Include Persons of Native American Ancestry in 'Anglo' North America," *Explorations in Ethnic Studies* 7 (1984): 11–23.

Halliburton, R., Jr., "Black Slavery among the Cherokees," *American History Illustrated* 11 (1976): 12–19.

Hann, John H., "Heathen Acuera, Murder, and a Potano Cimarrona: The St. Johns River and the Alachua Prairie in the 1670's," *Florida Historical Quarterly* 70 (1992): 451–74.

Johnson, Kenneth W., Jonathan M. Leader, and Robert C. Wilson Wilson, ed., *Indians, Colonists, and Slaves: Essays in Memory of Charles H. Fairbanks* (1985).

Katz, William Loren, "Black and Indian Cooperation and Resistance to Slavery," *Freedomways* 17 (1977): 164–74.

Landers, Jane, "Black-Indian Interaction in Spanish Florida," *Colonial Latin American Historical Review* 2 (1993): 141–62.

Lauber, Almon Wheeler, *Indian Slavery in Colonial Times within the Present Limits of the United States* (1913).

McLoughlin, William G., "Red Indians, Black Slavery and White Racism: America's Slaveholding Indians," *American Quarterly* 26 (1974): 367–85.

Mulroy, Kevin, "Ethnogenesis and Ethnohistory of the Seminole Maroons," *Journal of World History* 4 (1993): 287–305.

Perdue, Theda, "People without a Place: Aboriginal Cherokee Bondage," *Indian History* 9 (1976): 31–37.

Searcy, Martha Condray, "The Introduction of African Slavery into the Creek Indian Nation," *Georgia Historical Quarterly* 66 (1982): 21–32.

Trinkley, Michael, ed., *Indian and Freedmen Occupation at the Fish Haul Site (38BU805), Beaufort County, South Carolina* (1986).

Usner, Daniel H., Jr., *Indians, Settlers, and Slaves in a Frontier Exchange Economy: The Lower Mississippi Valley before 1783* (1992).

Webre, Stephen, "The Problem of Indian Slavery in Spanish Louisiana, 1769–1803," *Louisiana History* 25 (1984): 117–35.

Willis, William S., Jr., "Anthropology and Negroes on the Southern Colonial Frontier," in James C. Curtis and Lewis L. Gould, ed., *The Black Experience in America: Selected Essays* (1970): 33–50.

Wright, J. Leitch, Jr., *Creeks and Seminoles: The Destruction and Regeneration of the Muscogulge People* (1986).

15.3.8   Black/Ethnic Relations

Beckles, Hilary McD, "A 'Riotous and Unruly Lot': Irish Indentured Servants and Freemen in the English West Indies, 1644–1713," *William and Mary Quarterly* 47 (1990): 503–22.

15.4   GOVERNMENT

15.4.1   Law

Allain, Mathé, "Slave Policies in French Louisiana," *Louisiana History* 21 (1980): 127–37.

Alpert, Jonathan L., "The Origin of Slavery in the United States: The Maryland Precedent," *American Journal of Legal History* 14 (1970): 189–222.

Bellamy, Donnie D., "The Legal Status of Black Georgians during the Colonial and Revolutionary Eras," *Journal of Negro History* 74 (1989): 1–10.

Bernhard, Virginia, "Beyond the Chesapeake: The Contrasting Status of Blacks in Bermuda, 1616–1663," *Journal of Southern History* 54 (1988): 545–64.

Billings, Warren M., "The Cases of Fernando and Elizabeth Key: A Note on the Status of Blacks in Seventeenth-Century Virginia," *William and Mary Quarterly* 30 (1973): 467–74.

———— "The Law of Servants and Slaves in Seventeenth-Century Virginia," *Virginia Magazine of History and Biography* 99 (1991): 45–62.

Brasseaux, Carl A., "The Administration of Slave Regulations in French Louisiana, 1724–1766," *Louisiana History* 21 (1980): 139–58.

Burnard, Trevor, "Inheritance and Independence: Women's Status in Early Colonial Jamaica," *William and Mary Quarterly* 48 (1991): 93–114.

Bush, Jonathan A., "Free to Enslave: The Foundations of Colonial American Slave Law," *Yale Journal of Law and Humanities* 5 (1993): 417–70.

Crawford, Paul, "A Footnote on Courts for Trial of Negroes in Colonial Pennsylvania," *Journal of Black Studies* 5 (1974): 167–74.

De Pauw, Linda Grant, "Land of the Unfree: Legal Limitations on Liberty in Pre-Revolutionary America," *Maryland Historical Magazine* 68 (1973): 355–68.

Drescher, Seymour, "Manumission in a Society without Slave Law: Eighteenth-Century England," *Slavery and Abolition* 10 (1989): 85–101.

Ellefson, C. Ashley, "An Appeal of Murder in Maryland," *South Atlantic Quarterly* 67 (1968): 527–41.

Fede, Andrew, *People without Rights: An Interpretation of the Fundamentals of the Law of Slavery in the U.S. South* (1992).

Finkelman, Paul, ed., *Slavery and the Law* (1997).

Greenberg, Douglas, "Patterns of Criminal Prosecution in Eighteenth-Century New York," *New York History* 56 (1975): 133–53.

Higginbotham, A. Leon, Jr., *In the Matter of Color: The Colonial Period* (1978).

Klein, Mary O., "'We Shall Be Accountable to God': Some Inquiries into the Position of Blacks in Somerset Parish, Maryland, 1692–1865," *Maryland Historical Magazine* 87 (1992): 399–406.

Michals, Teresa, "'That Sole and Despotic Dominion': Slaves, Wives, and Game in Blackstone's *Commentaries*," *Eighteenth-Century Studies* 27 (1993–1994): 195–216.

Morgan, Gwenda, "Law and Social Change in Colonial Virginia: The Role of the Grand Jury in Richmond County, 1692–1776," *Virginia Magazine of History and Biography* 95 (1987): 453–80.

Palmer, Paul C., "Servant into Slave: The Evolution of the Legal Status of the Negro Laborer in Colonial Virginia," *South Atlantic Quarterly* 65 (1966): 355–70.

Schmidt, Fredrika Teute, and Barbara Ripel Wilhelm, "Early Pro-Slavery Petitions in Virginia," *William and Mary Quarterly* 30 (1973): 133–46.

Schwarz, Philip J., *Twice Condemned: Slaves and the Criminal Laws of Virginia, 1705–1865* (1988).

Snyder, Terri L., "Legal History of the Colonial South: Assessment and Suggestions," *William and Mary Quarterly* 50 (1993): 18–27.

Watson, Alan D., "North Carolina Slave Courts, 1715–1785," *North Carolina Historical Review* 60 (1983): 24–36.

Wiecek, William M., "The Statutory Law of Slavery and Race in the Thirteen Mainland Colonies of British America," *William and Mary Quarterly* 34 (1977): 258–80.

Williams, Oscar R., "The Regimentation of Blacks on the Urban Frontier in Colonial Albany, New York City, and Philadelphia," *Journal of Negro History* 63 (1978): 329–38.

15.4.2 Crime and Punishment

Kim, Hyong-In, "Slavery of the United States: The Result of Revisionism," *Studies in American History* 4 (1996): 97–134.

Slotkin, Richard, "Narratives of Negro Crime in New England, 1675–1800," *American Quarterly* 25 (1973): 3–31.

Wood, Betty, "Prisons, Workhouses, and the Control of Slave Labour in Low Country Georgia, 1763–1815," *Slavery and Abolition* 8 (1987): 247–71.

15.4.3 Military

Handler, Jerome S., Arthur C. Aufderheide, Robert S. Corrucini, Elizabeth M. Brandon, and Lorentz E. Wittmers, Jr., "Freedmen and Slaves in the Barbados Militia," *Journal of Caribbean History* 19 (1984): 1–25.

Jones, George Fenwick, "The Black Hessians: Negroes Recruited by the Hessians in South Carolina and Other Colonies," *South Carolina Historical Magazine* 83 (1982): 287–302.

Quarles, Benjamin, *The Negro in the American Revolution* (1961).

Voelz, Peter Michael, *Slave and Soldier: The Military Impact of Blacks in the Colonial Americas* (1993).

15.5 DEMOGRAPHY

Axtell, James, "The Columbian Mosaic in Colonial America," *Wisconsin Magazine of History* 76 (1992–1993): 132–44.

Burnard, Trevor, "A Failed Settler Society: Marriage and Demographic Failure in Early Jamaica," *Journal of Social History* 28 (1994): 63–82.

Butler, Mary, "Mortality and Labour on the Codrington Estates, Barbados," *Journal of Caribbean History* 19 (1984): 48–67.

Cody, Cheryll Ann, "A Note on Changing Patterns of Slave Fertility in the South Carolina Rice District, 1735–1865," *Southern Studies* 16 (1977): 457–63.

Cohn, Raymond L., "Maritime Mortality in the Eighteenth and Nineteenth Centuries: A Survey," *International Journal of Maritime History* 1 (1989): 159–91.

Corruccini, Robert S., Elizabeth M. Brandon, and Jerome S. Handler, "Inferring Fertility from Relative Mortality in Historically Controlled Cemetary Remains from Barbados," *American Antiquity* 54 (1989): 609–14.

Davis, Jack E., "Changing Places: Slave Movement in the South," *Historian* 55 (1993): 657–76.

Galenson, David W., "Population Turnover in the English West Indies in the Late Seventeenth Century: A Comparative Perspective," *Journal of Economic History* 45 (1985): 227–39.

Handler, Jerome S., and Robert S. Corruccini, "Weaning among West Indian Slaves: Historical and Bioanthropological Evidence from Barbados," *William and Mary Quarterly* 43 (1986): 111–17.

Kay, Marvin L. Michael and Lorin Lee Cary, "A Demographic Analysis of Colonial North Carolina with Special Emphasis upon the Slave and Black Populations," in Jeffery J. Crow and Flora J. Hatley, ed., *Black Americans in North Carolina and the South* (1984): 71–121.

Klein, Herbert S., and Stanley L. Engerman, "Fertility Differentials between Slaves in the United States and the British West Indies: A Note on Lactation Practices and Their Possible Implications," *William and Mary Quarterly* 35 (1978): 357–74.

Kulikoff, Allan, "A 'Prolifick' People: Black Population Growth in the Chesapeake Colonies, 1700–1790," *Southern Studies* 16 (1977): 391–428.

McKee, Jesse O., "A Geographical Analysis of the Origin, Diffusion, and Spatial Distribution of the Black American in the United States," *Southern Quarterly* 12 (1974): 203–16.

Menard, Russell R., "The Maryland Slave Population, 1658 to 1730: A Demographic Profile of Blacks in Four Counties," *William and Mary Quarterly* 32 (1975): 29–54.

———— "Slave Demography in the Lowcountry, 1670–1740: From Frontier Society to Plantation Regime," *South Carolina Historical Magazine* 96 (1995): 280–303.

Moorhouse, B-Ann, "A 1698 Census New Utrecht," *Journal of Long Island History* 14 (1977): 54–57.

Rutman, Darrett B., Charles Wetherell, and Anita H. Rutman, "Rhythms of Life: Black and White Seasonality in the Early Chesapeake," *Journal of Interdisciplinary History* 11 (1980): 29–53.

Sheridan, Richard B., *Doctors and Slaves: A Medical and Demographic History of Slavery in the British West Indies, 1680–1834* (1985).

———— "The Maroons of Jamaica, 1730–1830: Livelihood, Demography, and Health," *Slavery and Abolition* 6 (1985): 152–72.

Stevens, C. J., "Black Births and Baptisms in Mannikintown," *Journal of the Afro-American Historical and Genealogical Society* 4 (1983): 15–20.

Stewart, Roma Jones, "The Migration of a Free People," *Michigan History* 71 (1987): 34–39.

Westbury, Susan, "Slaves of Colonial Virginia: Where They Came From," *William and Mary Quarterly* 42 (1985): 228–37.

Wood, Peter H., "The Changing Population of the Colonial South: An Overview by Race and Region, 1685–1790," in Peter H. Wood, Gregory A. Waselkov and M. Thomas Hatley, ed., *Powhatan's Mantle: Indians in the Colonial Southeast* (1989): 35–103.

15.6   FAMILY

Brouwer, Merle, "Marriage and Family Life among Blacks in Colonial Pennsylvania," *Pennsylvania Magazine of History and Biography* 99 (1975): 368–72.

Callum, Agnes Kane, "Tracing a Family's Heritage through Court Records," *Journal of the Afro-American Historical and Genealogical Society* 6 (1985): 18–26.

Cody, Cheryll Ann, "Naming, Kinship, and Estate Dispersal: Notes on Slave Family Life on a South Carolina Plantation, 1786 to 1833," *William and Mary Quarterly* 39 (1982): 192–211.

———— "There Was No 'Absalom' on the Ball Plantations: Slave-Naming Practices in the South Carolina Low Country, 1720–1865," *American Historical Review* 92 (1987): 563–96.

Foster, Herbert J., "African Patterns in the Afro-American Family," *Journal of Black Studies* 14 (1983): 201–32.

Goodfriend, Joyce D., "Black Families in New Netherland, Afro-Americans in New Netherland," *Journal of the Afro-American Historical and Genealogical Society* 5 (1984): 94–107.

Hanger, Kimberly S., "Household and Community Structure among the Free Population of Spanish New Orleans," *Louisiana History* 30 (1989): 63–79.

Hoff, Henry B., "Additions and Corrections to 'A Colonial Black Family in New York and New Jersey: Pieter Santomee and His Descendants,'" *Journal of the Afro-American Historical and Genealogical Society* 10 (1989): 158–60.

———— "A Colonial Black Family in New York and New Jersey: Pieter Santomee and His Descendants," *Journal of the Afro-American Historical and Genealogical Society* 9 (1988): 101–34.

Holly, H. Hobart, "Genealogical Notes: Records of Blacks and Indians in Old Braintree, Massachusetts," *New England Historical and Genealogical Register* 140 (1986): 171–79.

Jordan, Winthrop D., and Sheila L. Skemp, ed., *Race and Family in the Colonial South: Essays* (1987).

Kulikoff, Allan, "The Beginnings of the Afro-American Family in Maryland," in Aubrey C. Land, Lois Green Carr and Edward C. Papenfuse, ed., *Law, Society, and Politics in Early Maryland* (1977): 171–96.

Paustian, P. Robert, "The Evolution of Personal Naming Practices among American Blacks," *Names* 26 (1978): 177–91.

Russell, Donna Valley, "The Abrahams of Natick and Grafton, Massachusetts," *Journal of the Afro-American Historical and Genealogical Society* 5 (1984): 47–52.

Thornton, John, "Central African Names and African-American Naming Patterns," *William and Mary Quarterly* 50 (1993): 727–42.

15.7 SOCIETY

15.7.1 Urban Life (Including Migration)

Cray, Robert E., Jr., "White Welfare and Black Strategies: The Dynamics of Race and Poor Relief in Early New York, 1700–1825," *Slavery and Abolition* 7 (1986): 273–89.

Goodfriend, Joyce D., "Burghers and Blacks: The Evolution of a Slave Society at New Amsterdam," *New York History* 59 (1978): 125–44.

Ingersoll, Thomas N., *Mammon and Manon in Early New Orleans: The First Slave Society in the Deep South, 1718–1819* (1999).

Johnson, Jerah, "New Orleans's Congo Square: An Urban Setting for Early Afro-American Culture Formation," *Louisiana History* 32 (1991): 117–57.

Lucas, Marion B., "African Americans on the Kentucky Frontier," *Register of the Kentucky Historical Society* 95 (1997): 121–34.

Morgan, Philip D., "Black Life in Eighteenth-Century Charleston," *Perspectives in American History* 1 (1984): 187–232.

Nash, Gary B., *Forging Freedom: The Formation of Philadelphia's Black Community, 1720–1840* (1988).

——— "Slaves and Slaveowners in Colonial Philadelphia," *William and Mary Quarterly* 30 (1973): 223–56.

Oedel, Howard T., "Slavery in Colonial Portsmouth," *History of New Hampshire* 21 (1966): 3–11.

Reidy, Joseph P., "'Negro Election Day' and Black Community Life in New England, 1750–1860," *Marxist Perspectives* 1 (1978): 102–17.

Tate, Thad W., *The Negro in Eighteenth-Century Williamsburg* (1965).

White, Shane, "'It Was a Proud Day': African Americans, Festivals, and Parades in the North, 1741–1834," *Journal of American History* 81 (1994): 13–50.

——— *Somewhat More Independent: The End of Slavery in New York City, 1770–1810* (1991).

15.7.2 Material Culture

Adams, Eric, "Religion and Freedom: Artifacts Indicate That African Culture Persisted Even in Slavery," *Omni* 16 (1993): 8.

Armstrong, Douglas V., "An Archaeological Study of the Afro-Jamaican Community at Drax Hall," *Jamaica Journal* 24 (1991): 3–8.

Deagan, Kathleen A., *Spanish St. Augustine: The Archaeology of a Colonial Creole Community* (1983).

DeCorse, Christopher R., "West African Archaeology and the Slave Trade," *Slavery and Abolition* 12 (1991): 92–96.

Epperson, Terrence W., "Race and the Disciplines of the Plantation," *Historical Archaeology* 24 (1990): 29–36.

Fairbanks, Charles H., "The Plantation Archaeology of the Southeastern Coast," *Historical Archaeology* 18 (1984): 1–14.

——— "Spaniards, Planters, Ships, and Slaves: Historical Archaeology in Florida and Georgia," *Archaeology* 29 (1976): 164–72.

Ferguson, Leland G., "Looking for the 'Afro' in Colono-Indian Pottery," in Robert L. Schuyler, ed., *Archaeological Perspectives on Ethnicity in America* (1980): 14–28.

——— *Uncommon Ground: Archaeology and Early African America, 1650–1800* (1992).

Gilbert, Judith A., "Esther and Her Sisters: Free Women of Color As Property Owners in Colonial St. Louis, 1765–1803," *Gateway Heritage* 17 (1996): 14–23.

Groover, Mark D., "Evidence for Folkways and Cultural Exchange in the Eighteenth-Century South Carolina Backcountry," *Historical Archaeology* 28 (1994): 41–64.

Handler, Jerome S., and Frederick W. Lange, *Plantation Slavery in Barbados: An Archaeological and Historical Investigation* (1978).

Harrington, Spencer P. M., "Bones and Bureaucrats," *Archaeology* 46 (1993): 28–38.

Higman, B. W., "The Spatial Economy of Jamaican Sugar Plantations: Cartographic Evidence from the Eighteenth and Nineteenth Centuries," *Journal of Historical Geography* 13 (1987): 17–39.

Jamieson, Ross W., "Material Culture and Social Death: African-American Burial Practices," *Historical Archaeology* 29 (1995): 39–58.

Kelso, William M., *Captain Jones's Wormslow: A Historical, Archaeological, and Architectural Study of an Eighteenth-Century Plantation Site near Savannah, Georgia* (1979).

——— *Kingsmill Plantations, 1619–1800: Archaeology of Country Life in Colonial Virginia* (1984).

Klingelhofer, Eric, "Aspects of Early Afro-American Material Culture: Artifacts from the Slave Quarters in Garrison Plantation, Maryland," *Historical Archaeology* 21 (1987): 112–19.

Lewis, Kenneth E., *Hampton: Initial Archaeological Investigations at an Eighteenth Century Rice Plantation in the Santee Delta, South Carolina* (1979).

——— "Settlement Activity and Patterning on Two Rice Plantations in the South Carolina Lowcountry," *The Conference on Historic Site Archaeology Papers, S.C. Institute of Archaeology and Anthropology, University of S.C.* 14 (1979): 1–12.

Malloy, Tom, and Brenda Malloy, "Slavery in Colonial Massachusetts As Seen through Selected Gravestones," *Markers* 11 (1994): 112–41.

Orser, Charles E., Jr., "The Past Ten Years of Plantation Archaeology in the Southeastern United States," *Southeastern Archaeology* 3 (1984): 1–12.

Posnansky, Merrick, "Toward an Archaeology of the Black Diaspora," *Journal of Black Studies* 15 (1984): 195–206.

Reitz, Elizabeth J., "Zooarchaeological Analysis of a Free African Community: Gracia Real De Santa Teresa De Mose," *Historical Archaeology* 28 (1994): 23–40.

Samford, Patricia, "The Archaeology of African-American Slavery and Material Culture," *William and Mary Quarterly* 53 (1996): 87–114.

Sanford, Douglas W., "The Archaeology of Plantation Slavery in Piedmont Virginia: Context and Process," in Paul A. Shackel and Barbara J. Little, ed., *Historical Archaeology of the Chesapeake* (1994): 115–30.

——— "Middle Range Theory and Plantation Archaeology: An Analysis of Domestic Slavery at Monticello, Albermarle County, Virginia, ca. 1770–1830," *Quarterly Bulletin of the Archeological Society of Virginia* 46 (1991): 20–30.

Singleton, Theresa Ann, ed., *The Archaeology of Slavery and Plantation Life* (1985).

Stine, Linda France, Lesley M. Drucker, Martha Zierden, and Christopher Judge, ed., *Carolina's Historical Landscapes: Archaeological Perspectives* (1997).

Upton, Dell, "White and Black Landscapes in Eighteenth-Century Virginia," in Robert Blair St. George, ed., *Material Life in America, 1600–1860* (1988): 357–69.

VanWest, Carroll, and Mary S. Hoffschwelle, "'Slumbering on Its Old Foundations': Interpretation at Colonial Williamsburg," *South Atlantic Quarterly* 83 (1984): 157–75.

Vlach, John Michael, *By the Work of Their Hands: Studies in Afro-American Folklife* (1991).

Waselkov, Gregory A., "Archaeology of Old Mobile, 1702–1711," *Gulf Coast Historical Review* 6 (1990): 6–21.

Yentsch, Anne Elizabeth, *A Chesapeake Family and Their Slaves: A Study in Historical Archaeology* (1994).

15.7.3   Color and Class

Bustamante, Adrian, "'The Matter Was Never Resolved': The Caste System in Colonial New Mexico, 1693–1823," *New Mexico Historical Review* 66 (1991): 143–63.

Deagan, Kathleen A., "Mestizaje in Colonial St. Augustine," *Ethnohistory* 20 (1973): 55–65.

Jordan, Winthrop D., "American Chiaroscuro: The Status and Definition of Mulattoes in the British Colonies," *William and Mary Quarterly* 19 (1962): 183–200.

LaFoy, D. C., "A Historical Review of Three Gulf Coast Creole Communities," *Gulf Coast Historical Review* 3 (1988): 6–19.

15.7.4 Associational Life

Dirks, Robert, *The Black Saturnalia: Conflict and Its Ritual Expression on British West Indian Slave Plantations* (1987).

Kuyk, Betty M., "The African Derivation of Black Fraternal Orders in the United States," *Comparative Studies in Society and History* 25 (1983): 559–92.

Reidy, Joseph P., "'Negro Election Day' and Black Community Life in New England, 1750–1860," *Marxist Perspectives* 1 (1978): 102–17.

Wade, Melvin, "'Shining in Borrowed Plumage': Affirmation of Community in the Black Coronation Festivals of New England, c. 1750–c. 1850," *Western Folklore* 40 (1981): 211–31.

White, Shane, "'It Was a Proud Day': African Americans, Festivals, and Parades in the North, 1741–1834," *Journal of American History* 81 (1994): 13–50.

15.8 RELIGION

Anesko, Michael, "So Discreet a Zeal: Slavery and the Anglican Church in Virginia, 1680–1730," *Virginia Magazine of History and Biography* 93 (1985): 247–78.

Austin, Allan D., ed., *African Muslims in Antebellum America: A Sourcebook* (1984).

Bradley, Michael R., "The Role of the Black Church in the Colonial Slave Society," *Louisiana Studies* 14 (1975): 413–21.

Brasseaux, Carl A., "The Moral Climate of French Colonial Louisiana, 1699–1763," *Louisiana History* 27 (1986): 27–41.

Carroll, Kenneth L., "An Eighteenth-Century Episcopalian Attack on Quaker and Methodist Manumission of Slaves," *Maryland Historical Magazine* 80 (1985): 139–50.

Curry, Mary Cuthrell, *Making the Gods in New York: The Yoruba Religion in the African American Community* (1997).

DeJong, Gerald F., "The Dutch Reformed Church and Negro Slavery in Colonial America," *Church History* 40 (1971): 423–36.

Diouf, Sylviane A., *Servants of Allah: African Muslims Enslaved in the Americas* (1998).

Frey, Sylvia R., and Betty Wood, *Come Shouting to Zion: African American Protestantism in the American South and British Caribbean to 1830* (1998).

George, Carol V. R., *Segregated Sabbaths: Richard Allen and the Emergence of Independent Black Churches, 1760–1840* (1973).

Gomez, Michael A., "Muslims in Early America," *Journal of Southern History* 60 (1994): 671–710.

Hudson, Winthrop S., "The American Context As an Area for Research in Black Church Studies," *Church History* 52 (1983): 157–71.

Jackson, Harvey H., "Hugh Bryan and the Evangelical Movement in Colonial South Carolina," *William and Mary Quarterly* 43 (1986): 594–614.

Kelly, Donald Brooks, "Joshua Evans, 1731–1798: A Study in Eighteenth Century Quaker Singularity," *Quaker History* 75 (1986): 67–82.

King, David R., "Missionary Vestryman," *Historical Magazine of the Protestant Episcopal Church* 34 (1965): 361–68.

Klein, Herbert S., and Elsa V. Goveia, "Anglicanism, Catholicism, and the Negro Slave," *Comparative Studies in Society and History* 8 (1966): 295–327.

Kopytoff, Barbara K., "Religious Change among the Jamaican Maroons: The Ascendance of the Christian God within a Traditional Cosmology," *Journal of Social History* 20 (1987): 463–84.

Levy, B. H., "Joseph Solomon Ottolenghi: Kosher Butcher in Italy, Christian Missionary in Georgia," *Georgia Historical Quarterly* 66 (1982): 119–44.

Miller, Randall M., "Black Catholics in the Slave South: Some Needs and Opportunities for Study," *Records of the American Catholic Historical Society of Philadelphia* 86 (1975): 93–106.

Pigou, Elizabeth, "A Note on Afro-Jamaican Beliefs and Rituals," *Jamaica Journal* 20 (1987): 23–26.

Raboteau, Albert J., "African-Americans, Exodus, and the American Israel," in Albert J. Raboteau, *A Fire in the Bones: Reflections of African-American Religious History* (1995): 17–36.

———— *Slave Religion: The "Invisible Institution" in the Antebellum South* (1978).

Roediger, David R., "And Die in Dixie: Funerals, Death and Heaven in the Slave Community, 1700–1865," *Massachusetts Review* 22 (1981): 163–83.

Scherer, Lester B., *Slavery and the Churches in Early America, 1619–1819* (1975).

Seeman, Erik R., "'Justise Must Take Plase': Three African Americans Speak of Religion in Eighteenth-Century New England," *William and Mary Quarterly* 56 (1999): 393–414.

Sensback, Jon F., *A Separate Canaan: The Making of an Afro-Moravian World in North Carolina, 1763–1840* (1998).

Soderlund, Jean R., *Quakers and Slavery: A Divided Spirit* (1985).

Stange, Douglas C., "'A Compassionate Mother to Her Poor Negro Slaves': The Lutheran Church and Negro Slavery in Early America," *Phylon* 29 (1968): 272–81.

Suttles, William C., Jr., "African Religious Survivals As Factors in American Slave Revolts," *Journal of Negro History* 56 (1971): 97–104.

Thornton, John K., "On the Trail of Voodoo: African Christianity in Africa and the Americas," *Americas* 44 (1988): 261–78.

Van Horne, John C., "Joseph Solomon Ottolenghe, ca. 1711–1775: Catechist to the Negroes, Superintendent of the Silk Culture, and Public Servant in Colonial Georgia," *Proceedings of the American Philosophical Society* 125 (1981): 398–409.

Van Sertima, Ivan, "African Linguistic and Mythological Structures in the New World," in Rhoda L. Goldstein, ed., *Black Life and Culture in the United States* (1971): 12–35.

15.9   THOUGHT AND EXPRESSION

15.9.1   Race, Gender, and Identity

Berlin, Ira, "From Creole to African: Atlantic Creoles and the Origins of African-American Society in Mainland North America," *William and Mary Quarterly* 53 (1996): 251–88.

Bethel, Elizabeth Rauh, *The Roots of African-American Identity: Memory and History in Free Antebellum Communities* (1997).

Bilby, Kenneth M., "'Two Sister Pikni': A Historical Tradition of Dual Ethnogenesis in Eastern Jamaica," *Caribbean Quarterly* 30 (1984): 10–25.

Gomez, Michael A., *Exchanging Our Country Marks: The Transformation of African Identities in the Colonial and Antebellum South* (1998).

Long, Richard A., "Some Backgrounds for African Continuity Studies," *Journal of African Studies* 2 (1975–76): 561–68.

Mullin, Michael, *Africa in America: Slave Acculturation and Resistance in the American South and the British Caribbean, 1736–1831* (1992).

Norton, Mary Beth, "'My Resting Reaping Times': Sarah Osborn's Defence of Her 'Unfeminine' Activities, 1767," *Signs* 2 (1976): 515–29.

Soderlund, Jean R., "Black Women in Colonial Pennsylvania," *Pennsylvania Magazine of History and Biography* 107 (1983): 49–68.

Thomas, John I., "Historical Antecedents and Impact of Blacks on the Indigenous White Populations of Brazil and the American South, 1500–1800," *Ethnohistory* 19 (1972): 147–69.

White, Shane, and Graham White, "Slave Hair and African American Culture in the Eighteenth and Nineteenth Centuries," *Journal of Southern History* 61 (1995): 45–76.

15.9.2   Emigrationism and Nationalism

Jones, Rhett S., "Structural Isolation and the Genesis of Black Nationalism in North America," *Colby Library Quarterly* 15 (1979): 252–66.

15.9.3   Language and Linguistics

Cassidy, Frederic G., "Barbadian Creole: Possibility and Probability," *American Speech* 61 (1986): 195–205.

Read, Allen Walker, "The Speech of Negroes in Colonial America," *Journal of Negro History* 24 (1939): 247–58.

15.9.4   Folklore and Humor

Cohen, David S., "In Search of Carolus Africanus Rex: Afro-Dutch Folklore in New York and New Jersey," *Journal of the Afro-American Historical and Genealogical Society* 5 (1984): 148–68.

Lalla, Barbara, "Black Laughter: Foundations of Irony in the Earliest Jamaican Literature," *Journal of Black Studies* 20 (1990): 414–25.

Pemberton, Doris Hollis, *Juneteenth at Comanche Crossing* (1983).

Stoney, Samuel Gaillard, and Gertrude Matthews Shelby, *Black Genesis: A Chronicle* (1930).

15.9.5   Literature and Poetry

Athey, Stephanie, and Daniel Cooper Alarcón, "Oroonoko's Gendered Economies of Honor/Horror: Reframing Colonial Discourse Studies in the Americas," *American Literature* 65 (1993): 415–43.

Barash, Carol, "The Character of Difference: The Creole Woman As Cultural Mediator in Narratives about Jamaica," *Eighteenth-Century Studies* 23 (1990): 406–24.

Baum, Rosalie Murphy, "Early-American Literature: Reassessing the Black Contribution," *Eighteenth-Century Studies* 27 (1994): 533–49.

Cottrol, Robert J., ed., *From African to Yankee: Narratives of Slavery and Freedom in Antebellum New England* (1998).

Fichtelberg, Joseph, "Word between Worlds: The Economy of Equiano's Narrative," *American Literary History* 5 (1993): 459–80.

Flanzbaum, Hilene, "Unprecedented Liberties: Re-Reading Phillis Wheatley," *MELUS* 18 (1993): 71–81.

Fleischner, Jennifer, *Mastering Slavery: Memory, Family, and Identity in Women's Slave Narratives* (1996).

Isani, Mukhtar Ali, "Far from 'Gambia's Golden Shore': The Black in Late Eighteenth-Century American Imaginative Literature," *William and Mary Quarterly* 36 (1979): 353–72.

Jamison, Hal, "'The Tempest' and 'Babouk': Shakespeare and the Colonial Subject," *Monthly Review* 45 (1993): 58–61.

Jordan, June, "The Difficult Miracle of Black Poetry in America or Something like a Sonnet for Phillis Wheatley," *Massachusetts Review* 27 (1986): 252–62.

Levernier, James A., "Style As Protest in the Poetry of Phillis Wheatley," *Style* 27 (1993): 172–93.

Mason, Julian, "Black Writers of the South," *Mississippi Quarterly* 31 (1978): 169–84.

Matson, R. Lynn, "Phillis Wheatley: Soul Sister?" *Phylon* 33 (1972): 222–30.

O'Neale, Sondra A., "Challenge to Wheatley's Critics: 'There Was No Other "Game" in Town,'" *Journal of Negro Education* 54 (1985): 500–11.

——— "A Slave's Subtle War: Phillis Wheatley's Use of Biblical Myth and Symbol," *Early American Literature* 21 (1986): 144–65.

Pedersen, Carl, "Middle Passages: Representations of the Slave Trade in Caribbean and African-American Literature," *Massachusetts Review* 34 (1993): 225–38.

Pendleton, Leila Amos, and Laura E. Wilkes, *A Narrative of the Negro: Missing Pages in American History, Recalling the Services of Negroes in the Early Wars in the United States of America* (1996).

Proper, David R., "Lucy Terry Prince: 'Singer of History,'" *Contributions in Black Studies* 9–10 (1990–92): 187–214.

Rawley, James A., "The World of Phillis Wheatley," *New England Quarterly* 50 (1977): 666–77.

Richards, Phillip M., "Phillis Wheatley and Literary Americanization," *American Quarterly* 44 (1992): 163–91.

Richmond, Merle A., *Bid the Vassal Soar: Interpretive Essays on the Life and Poetry of Phillis Wheatley, ca. 1753–1784, and George Moses Horton, ca. 1797–1883* (1974).

Shields, John C., "Phillis Wheatley's Subversion of Classical Stylistics," *Style* 27 (1993): 252–70.

Silvers, Anita, "Pure Historicism and the Heritage of Hero(in)es: Who Grows in Phyllis Wheatley's Garden?" *Journal of Aesthetics and Art Criticism* 51 (1993): 475–82.

Smith, Eleanor, "Phillis Wheatley: A Black Perspective," *Journal of Negro Education* 43 (1974): 401–07.

Tolson, M. B., "The Foreground of Negro Poetry," *Kansas Quarterly* 7 (1975): 30–35.

Wechselblatt, Martin, "Gender and Race in Yarico's Epistles to Inkle: Voicing the Feminine/Slave," *Studies in Eighteenth-Century Culture* 19 (1989): 197–223.

15.9.6 Music and Performing Arts

Epstein, Dena J., *Sinful Tunes and Spirituals: Black Folk Music to the Civil War* (1977).

Morgan, Michael J., "Rock and Roll Unplugged: African-American Music in Eighteenth-Century America," *Eighteenth-Century Studies* 27 (1994): 649–62.

Oldfield, J. R., "The 'Ties of Soft Humanity': Slavery and Race in British Drama, 1760–1800," *Huntington Library Quarterly* 56 (1993): 1–14.

Rath, Richard Cullen, "African Music in Seventeenth-Century Jamaica: Cultural Transit and Transition," *William and Mary Quarterly* 50 (1993): 700–26.

Shrubsall, Wayne, "Banjo As Icon," *Journal of Popular Culture* 20 (1987): 31–59.

15.9.7 Art (Drawing, Painting, Photography, Printmaking, Sculpture)

Lacey, Barbara E., "Visual Images of Blacks in Early American Imprints," *William and Mary Quarterly* 53 (1996): 137–80.

Twining, Mary, "Black American Quilts: An Artistic Craft," *Jamaica Journal* 16 (1983): 66–71.

15.9.8 Architecture and Design

Anthony, Carl, "The Big House and the Slave Quarters, Part I: Prelude to New World Architecture," *Landscape* 21 (1989): 8–19.

Carll-White, Allison, "South Carolina's Forgotten Craftsmen," *South Carolina Historical Magazine* 86 (1985): 32–38.

Cecelski, David S., "The Hidden World of Mullet Camps: African-American Architecture on the North Carolina Coast," *North Carolina Historical Review* 70 (1993): 1–13.

Kelso, William M., *Captain Jones's Wormslow: A Historical, Archaeological, and Architectural Study of an Eighteenth-Century Plantation Site near Savannah, Georgia* (1979).

Upton, Dell, "New Views of the Virginia Landscape," *Virginia Magazine of History and Biography* 96 (1988): 403–70.

Wood, Peter H., "Whetting, Setting and Laying Timbers: Black Builders in the Early South," *Southern Exposure* 8 (1980): 3–8.

15.10 EDUCATION

Hornick, Nancy Slocum, "Anthony Benezet and the Africans' School: Toward a Theory of Full Equality," *Pennsylvania Magazine of History and Biography* 99 (1975): 399–421.

Van Horne, John C., "Impediments to the Christianization and Education of Blacks in Colonial America: The Case of the Associates of Dr. Bray," *Historical Magazine of the Protestant Episcopal Church* 50 (1981): 243–69.

15.11 WORK AND ENTREPRENEURIAL ACTIVITY

Beckles, Hilary McD, "An Economic Life of Their Own: Slaves As Commodity Producers and Distributors in Barbados," *Slavery and Abolition* 12 (1991): 31–47.

Beckles, Hilary McD, and Andrew Downes, "An Economic Formalisation of the Origins of Black Slavery in the British West Indies, 1624–1645," *Social and Economic Studies* 34 (1985): 1–25.

———— "The Economics of Transition to the Black Labor System in Barbados, 1630–1680," *Journal of Interdisciplinary History* 18 (1987): 225–47.

Bennett, J. Harry, *Bondsmen and Bishops: Slavery and Apprenticeship on the Codrington Plantation of Barbados, 1710–1838* (1958).

Berlin, Ira, and Philip D. Morgan, ed., *Cultivation and Culture: Labor and the Shaping of Slave Life in the Americas* (1993).

Bolster, W. Jeffrey, *Black Jacks: African-American Seamen in the Age of Sail* (1997).

Carll, M. Allison, "'Great Neatness of Finish': Slave Carpenters in South Carolina's Charleston District, 1760–1800," *Southern Studies* 26 (1987): 89–100.

Carney, Judith A., "From Hands to Tutors: African Expertise in the South Carolina Rice Economy," *Agricultural History* 67 (1993): 1–30.

Chaplin, Joyce E., "Tidal Rice Cultivation and the Problem of Slavery in South Carolina and Georgia, 1760–1815," *William and Mary Quarterly* 49 (1992): 29–61.

Craton, Michael, "The Historical Roots of the Plantation Model," *Slavery and Abolition* 5 (1984): 189–221.

Darity, William, Jr., "British Industry and the West Indies Plantations," *Social Science History* 14 (1990): 117–49.

Emmer, Pieter C., ed., *Colonialism and Migration: Indentured Labour before and after Slavery* (1986).

Farr, James, "A Slow Boat to Nowhere: The Multi-Racial Crews of the American Whaling Industry," *Journal of Negro History* 68 (1983): 159–70.

Galenson, David W., *Traders, Planters, and Slaves: Market Behavior in Early English America* (1986).

———— "White Servitude and the Growth of Black Slavery in Colonial America," *Journal of Economic History* 41 (1981): 39–49.

Gray, Ralph, and Betty Wood, "The Transition from Indentured to Involuntary Servitude in Colonial Georgia," *Explorations in Economic History* 13 (1976): 353–70.

Hancock, Harold B., "The Indenture System in Delaware, 1681–1921," *Delaware History* 16 (1974): 47–59.

Johnson, Whittington Bernard, *The Promising Years, 1750–1830: The Emergence of Black Labor and Business* (1993).

Lewis, Ronald L., "The Use and Extent of Slave Labor in the Virginia Iron Industry: The Antebellum Era," *West Virginia History* 38 (1977): 141–56.

Marshall, Woodville K., "Provision Ground and Plantation Labour in Four Windward Islands: Competition for Resources during Slavery," *Slavery and Abolition* 12 (1991): 48–67.

Menard, Russell R., "Financing the Lowcountry Export Boom: Capital and Growth in Early South Carolina," *William and Mary Quarterly* 51 (1994): 659–76.

Morgan, Philip D., "Work and Culture: The Task System and the World of Lowcountry Blacks, 1700 to 1880," *William and Mary Quarterly* 39 (1982): 563–99.

Otto, John S., and Nain E. Anderson, "The Origins of Southern Cattle-Grazing: A Problem in West Indian History," *Journal of Caribbean History* 21 (1988): 138–53.

Perdue, Robert Eugene, *Black Laborers and Black Professionals in Early America, 1750–1830* (1975).

Shammas, Carole, "Black Women's Work and the Evolution of Plantation Society in Virginia," *Labor History* 26 (1985): 5–28.

Sheridan, Richard B., "From Chattel to Wage Slavery in Jamaica, 1740–1860," *Slavery and Abolition* 14 (1993): 13–40.

Stewart, James B., "Building a Cooperative Economy: Lessons from the Black Experience," *Review of Social Economy* 42 (1984): 360–68.

Usner, Daniel H., Jr., "The Frontier Exchange Economy of the Lower Mississippi Valley in the Eighteenth Century," *William and Mary Quarterly* 44 (1987): 165–92.

Walker, Joseph E., "Negro Labor in the Charcoal Iron Industry of Southeastern Pennsylvania," *Pennsylvania Magazine of History and Biography* 93 (1969): 466–86.

Walsh, Lorena S., "Plantation Management in the Chesapeake, 1620–1820," *Journal of Economic History* 49 (1989): 393–406.

Ward, John Robert, *British West Indian Slavery, 1750–1834: The Process of Amelioration* (1988).

Whitman, T. Stephen, "Industrial Slavery at the Margin: The Maryland Chemical Works," *Journal of Southern History* 59 (1993): 31–62.

Williams-Myers, A. J., "Hands That Picked No Cotton: An Exploratory Examination of African Slave Labor in the Colonial Economy of the Hudson River Valley to 1800," *Afro-Americans in New York Life and History* 11 (1987): 25–51.

Wood, Betty, "'White Society' and the 'Informal' Slave Economies of Low Country Georgia, c.1763–1830," *Slavery and Abolition* 11 (1990): 313–31.

Zahedieh, Nuala, "Trade, Plunder, and Economic Development in Early English Jamaica, 1655–1689," *Economic History Review* 39 (1986): 205–22.

15.12   MEDICINE AND HEALTH

Bankole, Katherine Kemi, *Slavery and Medicine: Enslavement and Medical Practices in Antebellum Louisiana* (1997).

Bougerol, C., "Medical Practices in the French West Indies: Master and Slave in the Seventeenth and Eighteenth Centuries," *History and Anthropology* 2 (1985): 125–43.

Childs, St. Julien Ravenel, "Kitchen Physick: Medical and Surgical Care of Slaves on an Eighteenth-Century Rice Plantation," *Mississippi Valley Historical Review* 20 (1934): 549–54.

Cohn, Raymond L., "Deaths of Slaves in the Middle Passage," *Journal of Economic History* 45 (1985): 685–92.

Crader, Diana C., "Slave Diet at Monticello," *American Antiquity* 55 (1990): 690–717.

Curtin, Philip D., "Epidemiology and the Slave Trade," *Political Science Quarterly* 83 (1968): 190–216.

———— "The Slavery Hypothesis for Hypertension among African Americans: The Historical Evidence," *American Journal of Public Health* 82 (1992): 1681–86.

Handler, Jerome S., Arthur C. Auferheide, Robert S. Corrucini, Elizabeth M. Brandon, and Lorentz E. Wittmers, Jr., "Lead Contact and Poisoning in Barbados Slaves: Historical, Chemical, and Biological Evidence," *Social Science History* 10 (1986): 399–425.

Handler, Jerome S., and Robert S. Corruccini, "Plantation Slave Life in Barbados: A Physical Anthropological Analysis," *Journal of Interdisciplinary History* 14 (1983): 65–90.

Jacobi, Keith P., Delia Collins Cook, and Robert S. Corruccini, "Congenital Syphilis in the Past: Slaves at Newton Plantation, Barbados, West Indies," *American Journal of Physical Anthropology* 89 (1992): 145–58.

Kiple, Kenneth F., *The Caribbean Slave: A Biological History* (1984).

———— "A Survey of Recent Literature on the Biological Past of the Black," *Social Science History* 10 (1986): 343–68.

Kiple, Kenneth F., and Brian T. Higgins, "Mortality Caused by Dehydration during the Middle Passage," *Social Science History* 13 (1989): 421–37.

Kiple, Kenneth F., and Virginia Kiple, "The African Connection: Slavery, Disease, and Racism," *Phylon* 41 (1980): 211–22.

Klepp, Susan E., "Seasoning and Society: Racial Differences in Mortality in Eighteenth-Century Philadelphia," *William and Mary Quarterly* 51 (1994): 473–506.

Laurence, B. R., "'Barbados Leg': Filariasis in Barbados, 1625–1900," *Medical History* 33 (1989): 480–88.

Puckrein, Gary, "Climate, Health and Black Labor in the English Americas," *Journal of American Studies* 13 (1979): 179–93.

Rice, Mitchell F., "On Assessing Black Health Status: A Historical Overview," *Urban League Review* 9 (1985–86): 6–12.

Schroeder, Walter A., Edwin S. Munger, and Darleen R. Powars, "Sickle Cell Anemia [sic], Genetic Variations, and the Slave Trade to the United States," *Journal of African History* 31 (1990): 163–80.

Sheridan, Richard B., "The Crisis of Slave Subsistence in the British West Indies during and after the American Revolution," *William and Mary Quarterly* 33 (1976): 615–41.

———— "Slave Medicine in Jamaica: Thomas Thistlewood's 'Receipts for a Physick,' 1750–1786," *Jamaican Historical Review* 17 (1991): 1–18.

Stewart, Larry, "The Edge of Utility: Slaves and Smallpox in the Early Eighteenth Century," *Medical History* 29 (1985): 54–70.

Voeks, Robert, "African Medicine and Magic in the Americas," *Geographical Review* 83 (1993): 66–78.

Wagner, Mark, "The Introduction and Early Use of African Plants in the New World," *Tennessee Archaeologist* 6 (1981): 112–23.

Wood, Betty, and T. R. Clayton, "Slave Birth, Death and Disease on Golden Grove Plantation, Jamaica, 1765–1810," *Slavery and Abolition* 6 (1985): 99–121.

15.13   STUDIES IN FOREIGN LANGUAGES

Andreu Ocariz, Juan José, *Movimientos rebeldes de los esclavos negros durante el dominio español en Luisiana* [Rebel Movements of Black Slaves during the Spanish Rule in Louisiana] (1977). In Spanish.

Fabre, Geneviève, "Éspaces de liberté, les loisirs des ésclaves" [Spaces of Freedom: The Moments of Leisure for the Slaves], in Elise Marienstras and Barbara Karsky, ed., *Travail et loisirs dans l'Amérique pré-industrielle* (1991). In French.

Fodde, Luisanna, *Autobiografie neri nell'America dell'Ottocento* [Black Autobiographies in Eighteenth-Century America] (1982). In Italian.

Loth, Heinrich, *Sklaverei: Die Geschichte des Sklavenhandels zwischen Afrika und Amerika* [Slavery: History of the Slave Trade between Africa and America] (1981). In German.

Mac-Lean y Estenos, Roberto, *Negros en el Nuevo Mundo* [Blacks in the New World] (1948). In Spanish.

Martin, Peter, *Das Rebellische Eigentum: Vom Kampf der Afroamerikaner gegen Ihre Versklavung* [Rebellious Property: The Struggle of the Afro-Americans against Their Enslavement] (1985). In German.

Nishide, Keiichi, "Minami Karoraina Kokujin Dorei-sei no Seiritsu" [The Formation of a Negro Slave Society in Colonial South Carolina], *The Studies in Western History* 133 (1984): 20–35. In Japanese.

Nodal, Roberto, *Pioneros negros en el suroeste Hispanico Americano* [Black Pioneers in the Hispanic-American Southwest] (1975). In Spanish.

Savigny, Carl Werner von, *Schwarze Handelsware: Soziologische und Ökonomische Aspekte des Britischen Negersklavenhandels in den Nordamerikanischen Kolonien Während des 17. und 18. Jahrhunderts* [Black Commodities: Sociological and Economic Aspects of the British Negro Slave Trade in the North American Colonies during the Seventeenth and Eighteenth Centuries] (1980). In German.

Tang, Taohua, *Mei Guo Li Shi Shang De Hei Ren Nu Li Zhi* [Black Slavery in the History of the United States] (1980). In Chinese.

16 *1772–1831*

Gary B. Nash

16.1 GENERAL STUDIES

Berlin, Ira, and Ronald Hoffman, ed., *Slavery and Freedom in the Age of the American Revolution* (1983).

Cottrol, Robert J., ed., *From African to Yankee: Narratives of Slavery and Freedom in Antebellum New England* (1998).

Franklin, John Hope, "The North, the South, and the American Revolution," *Journal of American History* 62 (1975): 5–23.

Hirsch, Leo H., Jr., "The Negro and New York, 1783–1865," *Journal of Negro History* 16 (1931): 382–473.

Kaplan, Sidney, *The Black Presence in the Era of the American Revolution, 1770–1800* (1973).

Knight, Franklin J. W., "The American Revolution and the Caribbean," in Ira Berlin and Ronald Hoffman, ed., *Slavery and Freedom in the Age of the American Revolution* (1983): 237–61.

Porter, Dorothy B., "The Black Role during the Era of the Revolution," *Smithsonian* 4 (1973): 52–57.

Quarles, Benjamin, "Black History's Antebellum Origins," *Proceedings of the American Antiquarian Society* (1989): 89–122.

Wright, Donald R., *African Americans in the Colonial Era: From African Origins through the American Revolution* (1990).

16.2 HISTORIOGRAPHY

Bethel, Elizabeth Rauh, *The Roots of African-American Identity: Memory and History in Free Antebellum Communities* (1997).

Burg, B. R., "The Rhetoric of Miscegenation: Thomas Jefferson, Sally Hemings, and Their Historians," *Phylon* 47 (1986): 128–38.

Lynd, Staughton, "On Turner, Beard, and Slavery," *Journal of Negro History* 48 (1963): 235–50.

Scarborough, William K., "The Southern Plantation Overseer: A Reevaluation," *Agricultural History* 38 (1964): 13–20.

Washington, Margaret, "African American History and the Frontier Thesis," *Journal of the Early Republic* 13 (1993): 230–41.

16.3 RACE RELATIONS

16.3.1 Slave Trade

Anstey, Roger T., "The Slave Trade of the Continental Powers, 1760–1810," *Economic History Review* 30 (1977): 259–68.

———— "The Volume of the North American Slave-Carrying Trade from Africa, 1761–1810," *Revue Française d'Histoire d'Outre-Mer* 62 (1975): 47–66.

Bailey, Ronald, "The Slave(ry) Trade and the Development of Capitalism in the United States: The Textile Industry in New England," *Social Science History* 14 (1990): 373–414.

Bancroft, Frederic, *Slave-Trading in the Old South* (1931).

Berlin, Ira, "The Slave Trade and the Development of Afro-American Society in English Mainland North America, 1619–1775," *Southern Studies* 2 (1991): 335–49.

Billias, George A., "Misadventures of a Maine Slaver," *American Neptune* 19 (1959): 114–22.

Brady, Patrick S., "The Slave Trade and Sectionalism in South Carolina, 1787–1808," *Journal of Southern History* 38 (1972): 601–20.

Brooke, George M., Jr., "The Role of the United States Navy in the Suppression of the African Slave Trade," *American Neptune* 21 (1961): 28–41.

Clark, Thomas D., "The Slave Trade between Kentucky and the Cotton Kingdom," *Mississippi Valley Historical Review* 21 (1934): 331–42.

Cohn, Raymond L., "Deaths of Slaves in the Middle Passage," *Journal of Economic History* 45 (1985): 685–92.

Cohn, Raymond L., and Richard A. Jensen, "The Determinants of Slave Mortality Rates on the Middle Passage," *Explorations in Economic History* 19 (1982): 269–82.

Collins, Winfield Hazlitt, *The Domestic Slave Trade of the Southern States* (1904).

Coughtry, Jay, *The Notorious Triangle: Rhode Island and the African Slave Trade, 1700–1807* (1981).

Coxe, Louis Osborne, *The Middle Passage* (1960).

Crane, Elaine F., "'The First Wheel of Commerce': Newport, Rhode Island and the Slave Trade, 1760–1776," *Slavery and Abolition* 1 (1980): 178–98.

Curtin, Philip D., ed., *Africa Remembered: Narratives by West Africans from the Era of the Slave Trade* (1967).

———— *The Atlantic Slave Trade: A Census* (1969).

Curtin, Philip D., Roger Anstey, and Joseph E. Inikori, "Discussion: Measuring the Atlantic Slave Trade," *Journal of African History* 17 (1976): 595–628.

Davidson, Basil, *Black Mother: The Years of the African Slave Trade* (1961).

Davies, Kenneth Gordon, *The Royal African Company* (1957).

Deyle, Steven, "The Irony of Liberty: Origins of the Domestic Slave Trade," *Journal of the Early Republic* 12 (1992): 37–62.

Donnan, Elizabeth, "The New England Slave Trade after the Revolution," *New England Quarterly* 3 (1930): 251–78.

Du Bois, William Edward Burghardt, *Suppression of the African Slave-Trade to the United States of America, 1638–1870* (1896).

Elbashir, Ahmed E., *The United States, Slavery, and the Slave Trade in the Nile Valley* (1983).

Eltis, David, "The British Contribution to the Nineteenth-Century Transatlantic Slave Trade," *Economic History Review* 32 (1979): 211–27.

———— "Mortality and Voyage Length in the Middle Passage: New Evidence from the Nineteenth Century," *Journal of Economic History* 44 (1984): 301–08.

Foster, Herbert J., "Partners or Captives in Commerce? The Role of Africans in the Slave Trade," *Journal of Black Studies* 6 (1976): 421–44.

Freudenberger, Herman, and Johnathan B. Pritchett, "The Domestic United States Slave Trade: New Evidence," *Journal of Interdisciplinary History* 21 (1991): 447–77.

Gwynn, Julian, "The Economics of the Transatlantic Slave Trade: A Review," *Histoire Sociale/Social History* 25 (1992): 151–62.

Harmon, Judd Scott, "Marriage of Convenience: The United States Navy in Africa, 1820–1843," *American Neptune* 32 (1972): 264–76.

Heffernan, William, "The Slave Trade and Abolition in Travel Literature," *Journal of the History of Ideas* 34 (1973): 185–208.

Inikori, Joseph E., "Measuring the Atlantic Slave Trade: An Assessment of Curtin and Anstey," *Journal of African History* 17 (1976): 197–223.

———— "Slavery and Atlantic Commerce, 1650–1800," *American Economic Review* 80 (1992): 151–57.

Inikori, Joseph E., and Stanley L. Engerman, ed., *The Atlantic Slave Trade: Effects on Economies, Societies, and Peoples in Africa, the Americas, and Europe* (1992).

Isert, Paul Erdmann, *Letters on West Africa and the Slave Trade: Paul Erdmann Isert's Journey to Guinea and the Caribbean Islands in Columbia,* tr. Selena Axelrod Wisnes (1788).

James, Cyril Lionel Robert, "The Atlantic Slave Trade and Slavery: Some Interpretations of Their Significance in the Development of the United States and the Western World," in John A. Williams and Charles F. Harris, ed., *Amistad One: Writings on Black History and Culture* (1970): 119–64.

Johnson, Walter, *Soul by Soul: Life Inside the Antebellum Slave Market* (1999).

Jones, Alison, "The Rhode Island Slave Trade: A Trading Advantage in Africa," *Slavery and Abolition* 2 (1981): 227–44.

Kiple, Kenneth F., "The Case against a Nineteenth-Century Cuba-Florida Slave Trade," *Florida History Quarterly* 49 (1971): 346–55.

Klein, Herbert S., "North American Competition and the Characteristics of the African Slave Trade to Cuba, 1790–1794," *William and Mary Quarterly* 28 (1971): 87–102.

————— "Slaves and Shipping in Eighteenth-Century Virginia," *Journal of Interdisciplinary History* 5 (1975): 383–412.

Lachance, Paul F., "The Politics of Fear: French Louisianans and the Slave Trade, 1786–1809," *Plantation Societies in the Americas* 1 (1979): 162–97.

Laprade, William T., "The Domestic Slave Trade in the District of Columbia," *Journal of Negro History* 11 (1926): 17–34.

Littlefield, Daniel C., *Rice and Slaves: Ethnicity and the Slave Trade in Colonial South Carolina* (1981).

Lloyd, Christopher, *The Navy and the Slave Trade: The Suppression of the African Slave Trade in the Nineteenth Century* (1949).

Lovejoy, Paul E., and David Richardson, "Trust, Pawnship, and Atlantic History: The Institutional Foundations of the Old Calabar Slave Trade," *American Historical Review* 104 (1999): 332–35.

Marable, Manning, "Death of the Quaker Slave Trade," *Quaker History* 63 (1974): 17–33.

McGowan, Winston, "African Resistance to the Atlantic Slave Trade in West Africa," *Slavery and Abolition* 11 (1990): 5–29.

Miller, Joseph C., "Mortality in the Atlantic Slave Trade: Statistical Evidence on Causality," *Journal of Interdisciplinary History* 11 (1981): 385–423.

Miller, William L., "A Note on the Importance of the Interstate Slave Trade of the Antebellum South," *Journal of Political Economy* 73 (1965): 181–87.

Mouser, Bruce L., "The Voyage of the Good Sloop Dolphin to Africa, 1795–1796," *American Neptune* 38 (1978): 249–61.

Newman, Debra L., "Slave Manifests," *Journal of the Afro-American Historical and Genealogical Society* 3 (1982): 40–44.

Pingeon, Frances D., "An Abominable Business: The New Jersey Slave Trade, 1818," *New Jersey History* 109 (1991): 15–36.

Platt, Virginia Bever, "'And Don't Forget the Guinea Voyage': The Slave Trade of Aaron Lopez of Newport," *William and Mary Quarterly* 32 (1975): 601–18.

Pope-Hennessy, James, *Sins of the Fathers: A Study of the Atlantic Slave Traders, 1441–1807* (1967).

Reynolds, Edward, *Stand the Storm: A History of the Atlantic Slave Trade* (1985).

Rodney, Walter, "African Slavery and Other Forms of Social Oppression on the Upper Guinea Coast in the Context of the Atlantic Slave Trade," *Journal of African History* 7 (1966): 219–46.

Rottenberg, Simon, "The Business of Slave Trading," *South Atlantic Quarterly* 66 (1967): 402–23.

Shingleton, Royce G., "David Brydie Mitchell and the African Importation Case of 1820," *Journal of Negro History* 58 (1973): 327–40.

Smith, Julia Floyd, "Slavetrading in Antebellum Florida," *Florida History Quarterly* 50 (1972): 252–61.

Soderlund, Jean R., "Black Importation and Migration into Southeastern Pennsylvania, 1682–1810," *Proceedings of the American Philosophical Society* 133 (1989): 144–53.

Spears, John Randolph, *The American Slave-Trade: An Account of Its Origin, Growth, and Suppression* (1900).

Stafford, Frances, "Illegal Importations: Enforcement of the Slave Trade Laws along the Florida Coast, 1810–1828," *Florida History Quarterly* 46 (1967): 124–33.

Staudenraus, P. J., "Victims of the African Slave Trade, a Document," *Journal of Negro History* 41 (1956): 148–51.

Steckel, Richard H., and Richard A. Jensen, "New Evidence on the Causes of Slave and Crew Mortality in the Atlantic Slave Trade," *Journal of Economic History* 46 (1986): 57–77.

Stein, Robert, "The Profitability of the Nantes Slave Trade, 1783–1792," *Journal of Economic History* 35 (1975): 779–93.

Stephenson, Wendell Holmes, *Isaac Franklin, Slave Trader and Planter of the Old South, with Plantation Records* (1938).

Stevens, Michael E., "'To Get As Many Slaves As You Can': An 1807 Slaving Voyage," *South Carolina Historical Magazine* 87 (1986): 187–92.

Sweig, Donald M., "Reassessing the Human Dimension of the Interstate Slave Trade," *Prologue* 12 (1980): 5–22.

Tadman, Michael, "Slave Trading in the Antebellum South: An Estimate of the Extent of the Inter-Regional Slave Trade," *Journal of American Studies* 13 (1979): 195–220.

Tansey, Richard, "Bernard King and the New Orleans Slave Trade," *Louisiana History* 23 (1982): 159–78.

Walvin, James, *Slavery and the Slave Trade: A Short Illustrated History* (1983).

Ward, William Ernest Frank, *The Royal Navy and the Slavers: The Suppression of the Atlantic Slave Trade* (1969).

Wax, Darold D., "'A People of Beastly Living': Europe, Africa, and the Atlantic Slave Trade," *Phylon* 41 (1980): 12–24.

——— "'New Negroes Are Always in Demand': The Slave Trade in Eighteenth-Century Georgia," *Georgia Historical Quarterly* 68 (1984): 193–220.

——— "Quaker Merchants and the Slave Trade in Colonial Pennsylvania," *Pennsylvania Magazine of History and Biography* 86 (1962): 143–59.

——— "Thomas Rogers and the Rhode Island Slave Trade," *American Neptune* 35 (1975): 289–301.

Wesley, Charles H., "Manifests of Slave Shipments along the Waterways, 1808–1864," *Journal of Negro History* 8 (1942): 155–74.

Weyl, Nathaniel, "Natural Selection through Slavery and the African Slave Trade," *Mankind Quarterly* 15 (1974): 3–17.

Whitridge, Arnold, "The American Slave-Trade," *History Today* 8 (1958): 462–72.

Wolff, Richard D., "British Imperialism and the East African Slave Trade," *Science and Society* 36 (1972): 443–62.

16.3.2   Slavery

Africa, Philip, "Slaveholding in the Salem Community, 1771–1851," *North Carolina Historical Review* 54 (1977): 271–307.

Agonito, Joseph, "St. Inigoes Manor: A Nineteenth Century Jesuit Plantation," *Maryland Historical Magazine* 72 (1977): 83–98.

Arena, C. Richard, "Landholding and Political Power in Spanish Louisiana," *Louisiana Historical Quarterly* 38 (1955): 23–39.

Arroyo, Elizabeth Fortson, "Poor Whites, Slaves, and Free Blacks in Tennessee, 1796–1861," *Tennessee Historical Quarterly* 55 (1996): 56–65.

Baker, T. Lindsay, and Julie P. Baker, ed., *Till Freedom Cried Out: Memories of Texas Slave Life* (1997).

Baltimore, Lester B., "Benjamin F. Stringfellow: The Fight for Slavery on the Missouri Border," *Missouri Historical Review* 62 (1967): 14–29.

Beeman, Richard R., *The Evolution of the Southern Backcountry: A Case Study of Lundenburg Country, Virginia, 1746–1832* (1984).

Bellamy, Donald D., and Diane E. Walker, "Slaveholding in Antebellum Augusta and Richmond County, Georgia," *Phylon* 48 (1987): 165–77.

Bellamy, Donnie D., "Macon, Georgia, 1823–1860: A Study in Urban Slavery," *Phylon* 45 (1984): 298–310.

————— "Slavery in Microcosm: Onslow County, North Carolina," *Journal of Negro History* 62 (1977): 339–50.

Berlin, Ira, *Many Thousands Gone: The First Two Centuries of Slavery in North America* (1998).

————— "The Slave Trade and the Development of Afro-American Society in English Mainland North America," *Southern Studies* 20 (1981): 122–36.

Berlin, Ira, and Ronald Hoffman, ed., *Slavery and Freedom in the Age of the American Revolution* (1983).

Bigham, Shauna, and Robert May, "The Time o' All Times? Masters, Slaves, and Christmas in the Old South," *Journal of the Early Republic* 18 (1998): 263–88.

Blassingame, John W., *The Slave Community: Plantation Life in the Antebellum South* (1972; rev. and expanded ed., 1979).

Brackett, Jeffrey R., *The Negro in Maryland: A Study of the Institution of Slavery* (1889).

Budziszewski, J., "A Whig View of Slavery, Development, and the World Market," *Slavery and Abolition* 4 (1983): 199–213.

Bullock, Henry Allen, "A Hidden Passage in the Slave Regime," in James C. Curtis and Lewis L. Gould, ed., *The Black Experience in America: Selected Essays* (1970): 3–32.

Burnham, Philip, "Selling Poor Steven," *American Heritage* 44 (1993): 90–97.

Cassell, Frank A., "Slaves of the Chesapeake Bay Area and the War of 1812," *Journal of Negro History* 57 (1972): 144–55.

Caulfield, Mina Davis, "Slavery and the Origins of Black Culture," in Peter I. Rose, ed., *Americans from Africa: Slavery and Its Aftermath* (1970): 171–93.

Cheung, Floyd D., "Les Cenelles and Quadroon Balls: 'Hidden Transcripts' of Resistance and Domination in New Orleans, 1803–1845," *Southern Literary Journal* 29 (1997): 5–16.

Close, Stacey K., *Elderly Slaves of the Plantation South* (1997).

Cohen, William, "Thomas Jefferson and the Problem of Slavery," *Journal of American History* 56 (1969): 503–26.

Crowe, Charles, "Slavery, Ideology, and 'Cliometrics,'" *Technology and Culture* 17 (1976): 271–85.

David, Paul A., and Peter Temin, "Slavery: The Progressive Institution?" *Journal of Economic History* 34 (1974): 739–83.

Davis, David Brion, "American Slavery and the American Revolution," in Ira Berlin and Ronald Hoffman, ed., *Slavery and Freedom in the Age of the American Revolution* (1983): 262–82.

Degler, Carl N., "Slavery in Brazil and the United States: An Essay in Comparative History," *American History Review* 75 (1970): 1004–28.

Dunne, Gerald T., "Bushrod Washington and the Mount Vernon Slaves," *Supreme Court Historical Society Yearbook* (1980): 25–29.

Dunn, Richard S., "A Tale of Two Plantations: Slave Life at Mesopotamia in Jamaica and Mount Airy in Virginia, 1799–1828," *William and Mary Quarterly* 24 (1977): 32–65.

Elkins, Stanley M., *Slavery: A Problem in American Institutional and Intellectual Life* (3d rev. ed., 1976).

————— "The Slavery Debate," *Commentary* 60 (1975): 40–54.

————— "The Social Consequences of Slavery," in Nathan I. Huggins, Martin Kilson and Daniel M. Fox, ed., *Key Issues in the Afro-American Experience* (vol. 1, 1971): 138–53.

Essig, James D., "Connecticut Ministers and Slavery, 1790–1795," *Journal of American Studies* 15 (1981): 27–44.

Feldstein, Stanley, ed., *Once a Slave: The Slave's View of Slavery* (1971).

Findlay, Ronald, "Slavery, Incentives, and Manumission: A Theoretical Model," *Journal of Political Economy* 83 (1975): 923–34.

Flanders, Ralph B., *Plantation Slavery in Georgia* (1930).

Fleischner, Jennifer, *Mastering Slavery: Memory, Family, and Identity in Women's Slave Narratives* (1996).

Foner, Philip S., "Alexander Von Humboldt on Slavery in America," *Science and Society* 47 (1983): 330–42.

Freehling, William W., "The Founding Fathers and Slavery," *American History Review* 71 (1972): 81–93.

Gallman, Robert E., "Human Capital in the 80 Years of the Republic: How Much Did America Owe the Rest of the World?" *American Economic Review* 67 (1977): 27–31.

Genovese, Eugene D., *Roll, Jordan, Roll: The World the Slaves Made* (1974).

Goveia, Elsa V., *Slave Society in the British Leeward Islands at the End of the Eighteenth Century* (1965).

Hall, Gwendolyn Midlo, *Africans in Colonial Louisiana: The Development of Afro-Creole Culture in the Eighteenth Century* (1992).

Harris, Norman D., *The History of Negro Servitude in Illinois, and of the Slavery Agitation in That State, 1719–1864* (1969).

Heath, Barbara J., *Hidden Lives: The Archaeology of Slave Life at Thomas Jefferson's Poplar Forest* (1999).

Henry, Howell Meadoes, *The Police Control of the Slave in South Carolina* (1914).

Hickey, Donald R., ed., "Slavery and the Republican Experiment: A View from Western Virginia in 1806," *West Virginia History* 39 (1978): 236–40.

Higman, B. W., *Slave Population and Economy in Jamaica, 1807–1834* (1976).

Hoetink, Harmannus, *Slavery and Race Relations in the Americas: Comparative Notes on Their Nature and Nexus* (1973).

Holman, H. T., "Slaves and Servants on Prince Edward Island: The Case of Jupiter Wise," *Acadiensis* 12 (1982): 100–04.

Holmes, Jack D. L., "The Role of Blacks in Spanish Alabama: The Mobile Districts, 1780–1813," *Alabama Historical Quarterly* 37 (1975): 5–18.

Huggins, Nathan Irvin, *Black Odyssey: The Afro-American Ordeal in Slavery* (1977).

Hunter, Lloyd A., "Slavery in St. Louis, 1808–1860," *Missouri Historical Society Bulletin* 30 (1974): 233–65.

Ireland, Ralph R., "Slavery on Long Island: A Study of Economic Motivation," *Journal of Long Island History* 6 (1966): 1–12.

Jackson, Harvey H., "'American Slavery, American Freedom,' and the Revolution of the Lower South: The Case of Lachlan McIntosh," *Southern Studies* 19 (1980): 81–93.

Johnson, Whittington B., *Black Savannah, 1788–1864* (1996).

Kendall, John, "New Orleans' 'Peculiar Institution,'" *Louisiana Historical Quarterly* 23 (1940): 864–86.

Klein, Mary O., "'We Shall Be Accountable to God': Some Inquiries into the Position of Blacks in Somerset Parish Maryland, 1692–1865," *Maryland Historical Magazine* 87 (1992): 399–406.

Kolchin, Peter, "Reevaluating the Antebellum Slave Community: A Comparative Perspective," *Journal of American History* 70 (1983): 579–601.

——— *Unfree Labor: American Slavery and Russian Serfdom* (1987).

Kulikoff, Allan, "Black Society and the Economics of Slavery," *Maryland Historical Magazine* 70 (1975): 203–10.

——— *Tobacco and Slaves: The Development of Southern Cultures in the Chesapeake, 1680–1800* (1986).

Lachance, Paul, "Use and Misuse of the Slave Community Paradigm," *Canadian Review of American Studies* 17 (1986): 449–58.

Lane, Ann J., ed., *The Debate over Slavery: Stanley Elkins and His Critics* (1971).

Lee, Jean Butenhoff, "The Problem of Slave Community in the Eighteenth-Century Chesapeake," *William and Mary Quarterly* 43 (1986): 333–61.

Lerner, Gerda, "Women and Slavery," *Slavery and Abolition* 4 (1983): 173–98.

Levesque, George A., "Slavery in the Ideology and Politics of the Revolutionary Generation," *Canadian Review of American Studies* 18 (1987): 367–81.

Lewis, Ronald L., *Coal, Iron, and Slaves: Industrial Slavery in Maryland and Virginia, 1715–1865* (1979).

Littlefield, Daniel C., "Continuity and Change in Slave Culture: South Carolina and the West Indies," *Southern Studies* 26 (1987): 202–16.

——— *Rice and Slaves: Ethnicity and the Slave Trade in Colonial South Carolina* (1981).

Logan, Gwendolyn Evans, "The Slave in Connecticut during the American Revolution," *Connecticut Historical Society Bulletin* 30 (1965): 73–80.

Lord, Donald C., "Slave Ads As Historical Evidence," *History Teacher* 5 (1972): 10–16.

Mackinley, Peter W., "The New England Puritan Attitude toward Black Slavery," *Old-Time New England* 63 (1973): 81–88.

MacLeod, Duncan J., *Slavery, Race, and the American Revolution* (1974).

Masur, Louis P., "Slavery in Eighteenth-Century Rhode Island: Evidence from the Census of 1774," *Slavery and Abolition* 6 (1985): 139–50.

Mathew, W. M., "Agricultural Adaptation and Race Control in the American South: The Failure of the Ruffin Reforms," *Slavery and Abolition* 7 (1986): 129–47.

McColley, Robert, *Slavery and Jeffersonian Virginia* (1964).

McDougle, Ivan Eugene, *Slavery in Kentucky, 1792–1865* (1918).

McKnight, Andrew N., "Lydia Broadnax, Slave and Free Women of Color," *Southern Studies* 5 (1994): 17–30.

McPherson, James M., "Slavery and Race," *Perspectives in American History* 3 (1969): 460–73.

Meaders, Daniel, "Kidnapping Blacks in Philadelphia: Isaac Hopper's Tales of Oppression," *The Journal of Negro History* 80 (1995): 47–65.

Mellon, Matthew Taylor, ed., *Early American Views on Negro Slavery* (1934).

Merrens, H. Roy, "A View of Coastal South Carolina in 1778: The Journal of Ebenezer Hazard," *South Carolina Historical Magazine* 73 (1972): 177–93.

Miller, Randall M., "The Golden Isles: Rice and Slaves along the Georgia Coast," *Georgia Historical Quarterly* 70 (1986): 81–96.

Mintz, Sidney W., *Slavery, Colonialism, and Racism: Essays* (1975).

Mohr, Clarence L., "Slavery in Oglethorpe County, Georgia, 1773–1865," *Phylon* 33 (1972): 4–21.

Mooney, Chase C., *Slavery in Tennessee* (1957).

Moore, John Hebron, *The Emergence of the Cotton Kingdom in the Old Southwest: Mississippi, 1770–1860* (1988).

———— "Two Cotton Kingdoms," *Agricultural History* 60 (1986): 1–16.

Morgan, Philip D., *Slave Counterpoint: Black Culture in the Eighteenth-Century Chesapeake and Lowcountry* (1998).

Morgan, Philip D., and Michael L. Nicholls, "Slaves in Piedmont Virginia, 1720–1790," *William and Mary Quarterly* 46 (1989): 211–51.

Moss, Simeon F., "The Persistence of Slavery and Involuntary Servitude in a Free State, 1685–1866," *Journal of Negro History* 25 (1950): 289–314.

Mullin, Gerald W., "Rethinking American Negro Slavery from the Vantage Point of the Colonial Era," *Louisiana Studies* 12 (1973): 398–422.

Mullin, Michael, *Africa in America: Slave Acculturation and Resistance in the American South and the Caribbean, 1736–1831* (1992).

———— "Women and the Comparative Study of American Negro Slavery," *Slavery and Abolition* 6 (1985): 25–40.

Nash, Gary B., "Slaves and Slaveowners in Colonial Philadelphia," *William and Mary Quarterly* 30 (1973): 223–56.

Nordstrom, Carl, "Slavery in a New York County: Rockland County, 1686–1827," *Afro-Americans in New York Life and History* 1 (1977): 145–66.

Olson, James S., "Slaves, Psyches, and History," *Journal of Ethnic Studies* 11 (1983): 95–110.

Olwell, Robert A., "'Domestick Enemies': Slavery and Political Independence in South Carolina, May 1775-March 1776," *Journal of Southern History* 55 (1989): 21–48.

———— *Masters, Slaves, and Subjects: The Culture of Power in the South Carolina Low Country, 1740–1790* (1998).

Otto, John Solomon, *Cannon's Point Plantation, 1794–1860: Living Conditions and Status Patterns in the Old South* (1984).

———— "The Case for Folk History: Slavery in the Highlands South," *Southern Studies* 20 (1981): 167–73.

———— "Slavery in a Coastal Community: Glynn County, 1790–1860," *Georgia Historical Quarterly* 64 (1979): 461–68.

Owens, Leslie Howard, *This Species of Property: Slave Life and Culture in the Old South* (1976).

Palmie, Stephan, ed., *Slave Cultures and the Cultures of Slavery* (1996).

Patterson, Orlando, *Slavery and Social Death: A Comparative Study* (1982).

———— "Slavery: The Underside of Freedom," *Slavery and Abolition* 5 (1984): 87–104.

Phifer, Edward W., "Slavery in Microcosm: Burke County, North Carolina," *Journal of Southern History* 28 (1962): 137–65.

Phillips, Christopher, *Freedom's Port: The African American Community of Baltimore, 1790–1860* (1997).

Pierce, Merrily, "Luke Decker and Slavery: His Cases with Bob and Anthony, 1817–1822," *Indiana Magazine of History* 85 (1989): 31–49.

Price, John Milton, "Slavery in Winn Parish," *Louisiana History* 8 (1967): 137–48.

Proctor, William G., Jr., "Slavery in Southwest Georgia," *Georgia Historical Quarterly* 49 (1965): 1–22.

Richter, William L., "Slavery in Baton Rouge, 1820–1860," *Louisiana History* 10 (1969): 125–45.

Robinson, Donald L., *Slavery in the Structure of American Politics, 1765–1820* (1970).

Rosenberg, Leonard B., "William Paterson and Attitudes in New Jersey on Slavery," *New Jersey History* 95 (1977): 197–206.

Rosenthal, Bernard, "Puritan Conscience and New England Slavery," *New England Quarterly* 46 (1973): 62–81.

Savannah Writers' Project, *Savannah River Plantations* (1947).

Scarborough, William K., *The Overseer: Plantation Management in the Old South* (1966).

Schaetzke, E. Anne, "Slavery in the Genessee Country (Also Known As Ontario County), 1789 to 1827," *Afro-Americans in New York Life and History* 22 (1998): 7–40.

Schantz, Mark S., "'A Very Serious Business': Managerial Relationships on the Ball Plantations, 1800–1835," *South Carolina Historical Magazine* 88 (1987): 1–22.

Schmitz, Mark, and Donald Schaefer, "Paradox Lost: Westward Expansion and Slave Prices before the Civil War," *Journal of Economic History* 41 (1981): 402–07.

Sellers, Charles G., "The Travail of Slavery," in Charles G. Sellers, ed., *The Southerner As American* (1960): 40–71.

Sellers, James Benson, *Slavery in Alabama* (1950).

Shaw, Donald Lewis, "News about Slavery from 1820–1860 in Newspapers of South, North, and West," *Journalism Quarterly* 61 (1984): 483–92.

Sheeler, J. Reuben, "The Negro on the Virginia Frontier," *Journal of Negro History* 43 (1958): 279–97.

Siebert, Wilbur H., "Slavery in East Florida, 1776–1785," *Florida Historical Society Quarterly* 10 (1932): 139–61.

Sio, Arnold A., "Interpretations of Slavery: The Slave Status in the Americas," *Comparative Studies in Society and History* 7 (1965): 289–308.

Smith, Julia Floyd, *Slavery and Rice Culture in Low Country Georgia, 1750–1860* (1985).

Smith, Mark M., *Mastered by the Clock: Time, Slavery, and Freedom in the American South* (1997).

Stampp, Kenneth M., *The Peculiar Institution: Slavery in the Antebellum South* (1956).

———— "Rebels and Sambos: The Search for the Negro's Personality in Slavery," *Journal of Southern History* 37 (1971): 367–92.

Starobin, Robert S., "Disciplining Industrial Slaves in the Old South," *Journal of Negro History* 53 (1968): 111–28.

———— "The Economics of Industrial Slavery in the Old South," *Business History Review* 44 (1970): 131–74.

———— *Industrial Slavery in the Old South* (1970).

———— "Privileged Bondsmen and the Process of Accommodation: The Role of Houseservants and Drivers As Seen in Their Own Letters," *Journal of Social History* 5 (1971): 46–70.

Stealey, John Edmund, III, "The Responsibilities and Liabilities of the Bailee of Slave Labor in Virginia," *American Journal of Legal History* 12 (1968): 336–53.

Steirer, William F., Jr., "Slavery and the Presence of Free Will," *Proceedings of the South Carolina Historical Association* (1974): 36–45.

Strickland, Arvarh E., "Aspects of Slavery in Missouri, 1821," *Missouri Historical Review* 65 (1971): 505–26.

Tate, Thad W., *The Negro in Eighteenth-Century Williamsburg* (1965).

Taylor, Joe Gray, *Negro Slavery in Louisiana* (1963).

Taylor, Rosser Howard, *Slaveholding in North Carolina: An Economic View* (1926).

Temperley, Howard, "Capitalism, Slavery, and Ideology," *Past and Present* 75 (1977): 94–118.

Tilly, Bette B., "The Spirit of Improvement: Reformism and Slavery in West Tennessee," *West Tennessee Historical Society Papers* 28 (1974): 25–42.

Towner, Lawrence, *Good Master Well Served: Masters and Servants in Colonial Massachusetts* (1997).

Trexler, Harrison Anthony, *Slavery in Missouri, 1804–1865* (1914).

True, Marshall, "Slavery in Burlington? An Historical Note," *Vermont History* 50 (1982): 227–30.

Van Deburg, William L., "Slave Drivers and Slave Narratives: A New Look at the 'Dehumanized Elite,'" *Historian* 39 (1977): 717–32.

Vedder, Richard K., "The Slave Exploitation (Expropriation) Rate," *Explorations in Economic History* 12 (1975): 453–57.

Wade, Richard C., *Slavery in the Cities: The South, 1820–1860* (1964).

Walker, Joseph E., "A Comparison of Negro and White Labor in Charcoal Iron Community," *Labor History* 10 (1969): 487–97.

Walsh, Lorena S., "Rural African Americans in the Constitutional Era in Maryland, 1776–1810," *Maryland Historical Magazine* 84 (1989): 327–41.

Wancho, Tom, "Slave Life on Plantations with a Focus on Nachitoches and the Surrounding Red River Area," *North Louisiana Historical Association Journal* 16 (1985): 79–92.

Wertz, Dorothy C., "Women and Slavery: A Cross-Cultural Perspective," *International Journal of Women's Studies* 7 (1984): 372–84.

Williams-Myers, A. J., "Hands That Picked No Cotton: An Exploratory Examination of African Slave Labor in the Colonial Economy of the Hudson River Valley to 1800," *Afro-Americans in New York Life and History* 11 (1987): 25–51.

Wood, Betty, *The Origins of American Slavery: Freedom and Bondage in the English Colonies* (1997).

———— "Prisons, Workhouses, and the Control of Slave Labour in Low Country Georgia, 1763–1815," *Slavery and Abolition* 8 (1987): 247–71.

———— "'White Society' and the 'Informal' Slave Economics of Lowcountry Georgia, c. 1763–1830," *Slavery and Abolition* 11 (1990): 313–31.

Wood, Peter H., "'Taking Care of Business' in Revolutionary South Carolina: Republicanism and the Slave Society," in Jeffrey J. Crow and Larry E. Tise, ed., *The Southern Experience in the American Revolution* (1978): 268–93.

Wood, Walter K., "Henry Edmundson, the Alleghany Turnpike, and 'Fotheringay' Plantation, 1805–1847: Planting and Trading in Montgomery County Virginia," *Virginia Magazine of History and Biography* 83 (1975): 304–20.

Woolsey, Ronald C., "The West Becomes a Problem: The Missouri Controversy and Slavery Expansion As the Southern Dilemma," *Missouri Historical Review* 77 (1983): 409–32.

Wright, Gavin, "Capitalism and Slavery on the Islands: A Lesson from the Mainland," *Journal of Interdisciplinary History* 17 (1987): 851–70.

Young, Tommy R., II, "The United States Army and the Institution of Slavery in Louisiana, 1803–1815, Part 1," *Louisiana Studies* 13 (1974): 201–22.

Zafar, Rafia, "Capturing the Captivity: African Americans among the Puritans," *Melus* 17 (1991–1992): 19–36.

16.3.3   Free Blacks

Arroyo, Elizabeth Fortson, "Poor Whites, Slaves, and Free Blacks in Tennessee, 1796–1861," *Tennessee Historical Quarterly* 55 (1996): 56–65.

Bailey, Raymond C., "Racial Discrimination against Free Blacks in Antebellum Virginia: The Case of Harry Jackson," *West Virginia History* 39 (1978): 181–86.

Baker, Pearl, and Mary B. Warren, "Registry of Free People of Colour, Columbia County, Georgia," *Journal of the Afro-American Historical and Genealogical Society* 2 (1981): 37–41.

Berlin, Ira, *Slaves without Masters: The Free Negro in the Antebellum South* (1974).

———— "The Structure of the Free Negro Caste in the Antebellum United States," *Journal of Social History* 9 (1976): 297–318.

Bethel, Elizabeth Rauh, *The Roots of African-American Identity: Memory and History in Antebellum Free Communities* (1997).

Bingham, Alfred M., "Squatter Settlements of Freed Slaves in New England," *Connecticut Historical Society Bulletin* 41 (1976): 65–80.

Bogen, David Skillen, "The Maryland Contest of *Dred Scott:* The Decline in the Legal Status of Maryland Free Blacks, 1776–1810," *American Journal of Legal History* 34 (1990): 381–411.

Bogger, Tommy L., *Free Blacks in Norfolk, Virginia, 1790–1860: The Darker Side of Freedom* (1997).

Brown, Letitia Woods, *Free Negroes in the District of Columbia, 1790–1846* (1972).

Buxbaum, Melvin H., "Cyrus Bustill Addresses the Blacks of Philadelphia, 1787," *William and Mary Quarterly* 29 (1972): 99–108.

Castle, Musette S., "A Survey of the History of African Americans in Rochester, New York, 1800–1860," *Afro-Americans in New York Life and History* 13 (1989): 7–32.

Cohen, David William, and Jack P. Greene, *Neither Slave nor Free: The Freedmen of African Descent in the Slave Societies of the New World* (1972).

Cox, Edward L., *Free Coloreds in the Slave Societies of St. Kitts and Grenada, 1763–1833* (1984).

Crow, Jeffrey J., *The Black Experience in Revolutionary North Carolina* (1977).

Curry, Leonard P., *The Free Black in Urban America, 1800–1850: The Shadow of the Dream* (1981).

Dain, Bruce, "Haiti and Egypt in Early Black Racial Discourse in the United States," *Slavery and Abolition* 14 (1993): 139–61.

Davis, Hugh, "Northern Colonizationists and Free Blacks, 1823–1837: A Case Study of Leonard Bacon," *Journal of the Early Republic* 17 (1997): 651–75.

Dunbar-Nelson, Alice, "People of Color in Louisiana," *Journal of Negro History* 1, 2 (1916, 1917): 361–76, 51–78.

England, J. Merton, "The Free Negro in Antebellum Tennessee," *Journal of Southern History* 9 (1943): 37–58.

Fitchett, E. Horace, "The Origin and Growth of the Free Negro Population of Charleston, South Carolina," *Journal of Negro History* 26 (1941): 421–37.

Flanders, Ralph B., "The Free Negro in Antebellum Georgia," *North Carolina Historical Review* 9 (1932): 250–72.

Foner, Laura, "The Free People of Color in Louisiana and St. Domingue: A Comparative Portrait of Two Three-Caste Societies," *Journal of Social History* 3 (1970): 406–30.

Foner, Philip S., "A Plea against Re-Enslavement," *Pennsylvania History* 39 (1972): 239–41.

Franklin, John Hope, *The Free Negro in North Carolina, 1790–1860* (1943).

Gammon, Tim, "Black Freedmen and the Cherokee Nation," *Journal of American Studies* 11 (1977): 357–64.

Garvin, Russell, "The Free Negro in Florida before the Civil War," *Florida Historical Quarterly* 46 (1967): 1–17.

Gould, Virginia, "In Defense of Their Creole Culture: The Free Creoles of Color of New Orleans, Mobile, and Pensacola," *Gulf Coast Historical Review* 9 (1993): 26–46.

Hall, Gwendolyn Midlo, *Africans in Colonial Louisiana: The Development of Afro-Creole Culture in the Eighteenth Century* (1992).

Halliburton, R., Jr., "Free Black Owners of Slaves: A Reappraisal of the Woodson Thesis," *South Carolina Historical Magazine* 76 (1975): 129–42.

Hanger, Kimberly S., "'Desiring Total Tranquility' and Not Getting It: Conflict Involving Free Black Women in Spanish New Orleans," *Americas* 54 (1998): 541–56.

———— "Patronage, Property, and Persistence: The Emergence of a Free Black Elite in Spanish New Orleans," *Slavery and Abolition* 17 (1996): 44–64.

Heinegg, Paul, *Free African Americans of North Carolina and Virginia* (2d ed., 1994).

Hershberg, Theodore, "Free Blacks in Antebellum Philadelphia: A Study of Ex-Slaves, Freeborn, and Socioeconomic Decline," *Journal of Social History* 5 (1971–72): 183–209.

Hickok, Charles T., *The Negro in Ohio, 1802–1870* (1896).

Hinks, Peter P., "Free Blacks and Kidnapping in Antebellum Boston," *Historical Journal of Massachusetts* 20 (1992): 16–31.

Homsey, Elizabeth Moyne, "Free Blacks in Kent County, Delaware, 1790–1830," *Working Papers from the Regional Economic History Research Center* 3 (1980): 31–57.

Hopkins, Leroy T., "Black Eldorado on the Susquehanna: The Emergence of Black Columbia, 1726–1861," *Journal of the Lancaster County Historical Society* 89 (1985): 110–32.

———— "The Negro Entry Book: A Document of Lancaster City's Antebellum Afro-American Community," *Journal of the Lancaster County Historical Society* 88 (1984): 142–80.

Horton, James Oliver, "Freedom's Yoke: Gender Conventions among (Antebellum) Free Blacks," *Feminist Studies* 12 (1986): 51–76.

———— "Weevils in the Wheat: Free Blacks and the Constitution, 1787–1860," *This Constitution* 8 (1985): 4–11.

Horton, James Oliver, and Lois E. Horton, *In Hope of Liberty: Culture, Community, and Protest among Northern Free Blacks, 1700–1860* (1997).

Ingersoll, Thomas N., "Free Blacks in a Slave Society: New Orleans, 1718–1812," *William and Mary Quarterly* 48 (1991): 173–200.

Koger, Larry, *Black Slaveowners: Free Black Slave Masters in South Carolina, 1790–1860* (1985).

Landers, Jane G., "Acquisition and Loss on a Spanish Frontier: The Free Black Homesteaders of Florida, 1784–1821," *Slavery and Abolition* 17 (1996): 85–101.

Lane, Carl, and Rhoda Freeman, "John Dipper and the Experience of the Free Black Elite, 1816–1836," *Virginia Magazine of History and Biography* 100 (1992): 485–514.

Lapsansky, Emma Jones, "Friends, Wives, and Strivings: Networks and Community Values among Nineteenth-Century Philadelphia Afro-American Elites," *Pennsylvania Magazine of History and Biography* 108 (1984): 3–24.

Lebsock, Suzanne, *The Free Women of Petersburg: Status and Culture in a Southern Town, 1784–1860* (1984).

Litwack, Leon F., *North of Slavery: The Negro in the Free States, 1790–1860* (1961).

Madden, T. O., Jr., and Ann L. Miller, *We Were Always Free: The Maddens of Culpeper County, Virginia: A Two-Hundred-Year Family History* (1992).

McGraw, Marie Tyler, "Richmond Free Blacks and African Colonization, 1816–1832," *Journal of American Studies* 21 (1987): 207–24.

Medford, Edna Greene, "'It Was a Very Comfortable Place for Poor Folks': Subsistence in a Rural Antebellum Free Black Community," *Locus* 5 (1993): 131–44.

Mills, Gary B., "Tracing Free People of Color in the Antebellum South: Methods, Sources, and Perspectives," *National Genealogical Society Quarterly* 78 (1990): 262–78.

Nash, Gary B., *Forging Freedom: The Formation of Philadelphia's Black Community, 1720–1840* (1988).

Nash, Gary B., and Jean R. Soderlund, *Freedom by Degrees: Emancipation in Pennsylvania and Its Aftermath* (1991).

Nichols, Michael L., "Passing through This Troublesome World: Free Blacks in the Early Southside," *Virginia Magazine of History and Biography* 92 (1984): 50–70.

O'Brien, John T., "Factory, Church, and Community: Blacks in Antebellum Richmond," *Journal of Southern History* 44 (1978): 509–36.

Provine, Dorothy, "The Economic Position of Free Blacks in the District of Columbia, 1800–1860," *Journal of Negro History* 58 (1973): 61–72.

Quarles, Benjamin, "Antebellum Free Blacks and the 'Spirit of '76,'" *Journal of Negro History* 61 (1976): 229–42.

Rankin, David, "Black Slaveholders: The Case of Andrew Durnford," *Southern Studies* 21 (1982): 343–47.

Reitz, Elizabeth J., "Zooarchaeological Analysis of a Free African Community: Gracia Real de Santa Teresa de Mose," *Historical Archaeology* 28 (1994): 23–40.

Robinson, Henry S., "Some Aspects of the Free Negro Population of Washington, D.C., 1800–1862," *Maryland Historical Magazine* 64 (1969): 43–64.

Rury, John L., "Philanthropy, Self-Help, and Social Control: The New York Manumission Society and Free Blacks, 1785–1810," *Phylon* 46 (1985): 231–41.

Russell, John H., "Colored Freemen As Slave Owners in Virginia," *Journal of Negro History* 1 (1916): 233–42.

———— *The Free Negro in Virginia, 1619–1865* (1913).

Schwarz, Philip J., "Emancipators, Protectors, and Anomalies: Free Black Slaveowners in Virginia," *Virginia Magazine of History and Biography* 95 (1987): 317–38.

Schweninger, Loren, "The Free-Slave Phenomenon: James P. Thomas and the Black Community in Antebellum Nashville," *Civil War History* 22 (1976): 293–307.

——— "A Negro Sojourner in Antebellum New Orleans," *Louisiana History* 20 (1979): 305–14.

Sense, Donald J., "The Free Negro and the South Carolina Courts, 1790–1860," *South Carolina Historical Magazine* 68 (1967): 140–53.

Sheeler, J. Reuben, "The Struggle of the Negro in Ohio for Freedom," *Journal of Negro History* 31 (1946): 208–26.

Spangler, Earl, "The Negro in Minnesota, 1800–1865," *Transactions of the Historical and Scientific Society of Manitoba [Canada]* 3 (1965): 13–26.

Stahl, Annie L. W., "The Free Negro in Antebellum Louisiana," *Louisiana Historical Quarterly* 25 (1942): 301–96.

Sweat, Edward F., "Social Status of the Free Negro in Antebellum Georgia," *Negro History Bulletin* 21 (1958): 129–31.

Sydnor, Charles S., "The Free Negro in Mississippi before the Civil War," *American Historical Review* 32 (1927): 769–88.

Thomas, David Y., "The Free Negro in Florida before 1865," *South Atlantic Quarterly* 10 (1911): 335–45.

Turner, Edward R., *The Negro in Pennsylvania: Slavery-Servitude-Freedom, 1639–1861* (1911).

Ulle, Robert F., "Blacks in Berks County, Pennsylvania: The Almshouse Records," *Pennsylvania Folklife* 27 (1977): 19–30.

Wade, Richard C., "The Negro in Cincinnati, 1800–1830," *Journal of Negro History* 39 (1957): 43–57.

Walker, Juilet E. K., "The Legal Status of Free Blacks in Early Kentucky, 1792–1825," *Filson Club History Quarterly* 57 (1983): 382–95.

Warner, Lee H., *Free Men in an Age of Servitude: Three Generations of a Black Family* (1992).

White, Shane, "'We Dwell in Safety and Pursue Our Honest Callings': Free Blacks in New York City, 1783–1810," *Journal of American History* 75 (1988): 445–70.

Wikramanayake, Marina, *A World in Shadow: The Free Black in Antebellum South Carolina* (1973).

Wilson, Calvin D., "Negroes Who Owned Slaves," *Popular Science Monthly* 71 (1912): 483–94.

Winch, Julie, *Philadelphia's Black Elite: Activism, Accommodation, and the Struggle for Autonomy, 1787–1848* (1988).

Winston, James E., "The Free Negro in New Orleans, 1803–1860," *Louisiana Historical Quarterly* 21 (1938): 1075–85.

Woodson, Carter Godwin, *Free Negro Heads of Families in the United States in 1830, Together with a Brief Treatment of the Free Negro* (1925).

——— *Free Negro Owners of Slaves in the United States in 1830* (1924).

——— "The Negroes of Cincinnati prior to the Civil War," *Journal of Negro History* 1 (1916): 1–22.

Woolfolk, George Ruble, *The Free Negro in Texas, 1800–1860: A Study in Cultural Compromise* (1976).

Wortis, Helen, "The Black Inhabitants of Shelter Island," *Long Island Forum* 36 (1973): 146–53.

Wright, James Martin, *The Free Negro in Maryland, 1634–1860* (1921).

Wynne, Frances Holloway, "Free Black Inhabitants of Wake County, North Carolina," *Journal of the Afro-American Historical and Genealogical Society* 1 (1980): 59–67.

16.3.4   Resistance (Antebellum)

Aptheker, Herbert, *American Negro Slave Revolts* (1943).

——— "American Negro Slave Revolts: Fifty Years Gone," *Science and Society* 51 (1987): 68–72.

——— "Maroons within the Present Limits of the United States," *Journal of Negro History* 24 (1939): 167–84.

——— "Slave Guerilla Warfare," in *To Be Free: Studies in American Negro History* (1948): 11–30.

——— "Slave Resistance in the United States," in Nathan I. Huggins, Martin Kilson and Daniel M. Fox, ed., *Key Issues in the Afro-American Experience* (vol. 1, 1971): 161–73.

Bauer, Raymond A., and Alice H. Bauer, "Day-to-Day Resistance to Slavery," *Journal of Negro History* 27 (1942): 388–419.

Baur, John E., "International Repercussions of the Haitian Revolution," *Americas* 25 (1969): 394–418.

Becton, Joseph, "Old Hickory and the Negro Fort: Exodus to Freedom," *Pensacola History Illustrated* 2 (1986): 25–32.

Boles, John B., "Tension in a Slave Society: The Trial of the Reverend Jacob Gruber," *Southern Studies* 18 (1979): 179–97.

Brown, Canter, Jr., "The 'Sarrazota, or Runaway Negro Plantations': Tampa Bay's First Black Community, 1812–1821," *Tampa Bay History* 12 (1990): 5–19.

Bush, Barbara, "Towards Emancipation: Slave Women and Resistance to Coercive Labour Regimes in the British West Indian Colonies, 1790–1838," *Slavery and Abolition* 5 (1984): 222–43.

Carroll, Joseph C., *Slave Insurrections in the United States, 1800–1865* (1938).

Cheek, William F., *Black Resistance before the Civil War* (1970).

Crow, Jeffery J., "Slave Rebelliousness and Social Conflict in North Carolina, 1775 to 1802," *William and Mary Quarterly* 37 (1980): 79–102.

Dabney, Virginius, "Gabriel's Insurrection," *American History Illustrated* 11 (1976): 24–32.

Davis, Thomas J., "Emancipation Rhetoric, Natural Rights, and Revolutionary New England: A Note on Four Black Petitions in Massachusetts, 1773–1777," *New England Quarterly* 62 (1989): 248–63.

Din, Gilbert C., "Cimarrones and the San Malo Band in Spanish Louisiana," *Louisiana History* 21 (1980): 237–62.

Dorman, James H., "The Persistent Specter: Slave Rebellion in Territorial Louisiana," *Louisiana History* 18 (1977): 389–404.

Egerton, Douglas R., "'Fly across the River': The Easter Slave Conspiracy of 1802," *North Carolina Historical Review* 68 (1991): 87–110.

——— "Gabriel's Conspiracy and the Election of 1800," *Journal of Southern History* 56 (1990): 191–214.

——— *He Shall Go out Free: The Lives of Denmark Vesey* (1999).

——— "An Upright Man: Gabriel's Virginia and the Path to Slave Rebellion," *Virginia Cavalcade* 43 (1993): 52–69.

——— *The Virginia Slave Conspiracies of 1800 and 1802* (1993).

Farley, M. Foster, "The Fear of Negro Slave Revolts in South Carolina, 1690–1865," *Afro-American Studies* 3 (1972): 199–207.

——— "A History of Negro Slave Revolts in South Carolina," *Afro-American Studies* 3 (1972): 97–102.

Foner, Philip S., "John Brown Russwurm, A Document," *Journal of Negro History* 54 (1969): 393–97.

Forbes, Ella, "African Resistance to Enslavement: The Nature and the Evidentiary Record," *Journal of Black Studies* 23 (1992): 39–59.

Franklin, John Hope, "Slavery and the Martial South," *Journal of Negro History* 37 (1952): 36–53.

Franklin, John Hope, and Loren Schweninger, *Runaway Slaves: Rebels on the Plantation* (1999).

Fredrickson, George M., and Christopher Lasch, "Resistance to Slavery," *Civil War History* 13 (1967): 315–29.

Frey, Sylvia R., "Between Slavery and Freedom: Virginia Blacks in the American Revolution," *Journal of Southern History* 49 (1983): 375–98.

——— "The British and the Black: A New Perspective," *Historian* 38 (1976): 225–38.

——— *Water from the Rock: Black Resistance in a Revolutionary Age* (1991).

Gaspar, David Barry, and David P. Geggus, ed., *A Turbulent Time: The French Revolution and the Greater Caribbean* (1997).

Geggus, David, "The Enigma of Jamaica in the 1790's: New Light on the Causes of Slave Rebellions," *William and Mary Quarterly* 44 (1987): 274–99.

Genovese, Eugene D., *From Rebellion to Revolution: Afro-American Slave Revolts in the Making of the Modern World* (1979).

——— "Rebelliousness and Docility in the Negro Slave: A Critique of the Elkins Thesis," *Civil War History* 13 (1967): 293–314.

——— "When the Slaves Left Old Master," *Civil Liberties Review* 2 (1975): 67–76.

Granade, Ray, "Slave Unrest in Florida," *Florida Historical Quarterly* 55 (1976): 18–36.

Greene, Lorenzo J., "Mutiny on the Slave Ships," *Phylon* 5 (1944): 346–54.

Halasz, Nicholas, *The Rattling Chains: Slave Unrest and Revolt in the Antebellum South* (1966).

Hall, Robert L., "Slave Resistance in Baltimore City and County, 1747–1790," *Maryland Historical Magazine* 84 (1989): 305–18.

Harding, Vincent, "Religion and Resistance among Antebellum Negroes, 1800–1860," in August Meier and Elliott Rudwick, ed., *The Making of Black America* (vol. 1, 1969): 179–97.

Hay, Robert P., "'And Ten Dollars Extra, for Every Hundred Lashes Any Person Will Give Him, to the Amount of Three Hundred': A Note on Andrew Jackson's Runaway Slave Ad of 1804 and on the Historian's Use of Evidence," *Tennessee Historical Quarterly* 36 (1977): 468–78.

Hickey, Donald R., "America's Response to the Slave Revolt in Haiti, 1791–1806," *Journal of the Early Republic* 2 (1982): 361–79.

———— "Timothy Pickering and the Haitian Slave Revolt: A Letter to Thomas Jefferson in 1806," *Essex Institute Historical Collections* 120 (1984): 149–63.

Hinks, Peter P., *To Awaken My Afflicted Brethren: David Walker and the Problem of Antebellum Slave Resistance* (1997).

Hodges, Graham Russell, and Alan Edward Brown, ed., *"Pretends to Be Free": Runaway Slave Advertisements from Colonial and Revolutionary New York and New Jersey* (1994).

Holmes, Jack D. L., "The Abortive Slave Revolt at Pointe Coupee, Louisiana, 1795," *Louisiana History* 11 (1970): 341–62.

Horsman, Reginald, "The Paradox of Dartmoor Prison," *American Heritage* 26 (1975): 12–17, 85.

Hubbard, Dolan, "David Walker's Appeal and the American Puritan Jeremiadic Tradition," *Centennial Review* 30 (1986): 331–46.

James, Cyril Lionel Robert, *The Black Jacobins: Toussaint L'Ouverture and the San Domingo Revolution* (rev. ed., 1989).

Johnson, Michael P., "Runaway Slaves and the Slave Communities in South Carolina, 1799–1830," *William and Mary Quarterly* 38 (1981): 418–41.

Jones, Howard, "The Peculiar Institution and National Honor: The Case of the *Creole* Slave Revolt," *Civil War History* 21 (1975): 28–50.

Kaplan, Sidney, "The 'Domestic Insurrections' of the Declaration of Independence," *Journal of Negro History* 61 (1976): 243–55.

Katz, William Loren, *Breaking the Chains: African-American Slave Resistance* (1998).

Kilson, Marion D. de B., "Towards Freedom: An Analysis of Slave Revolts in the United States," *Phylon* 25 (1964): 175–87.

Leaming, Hugo Prosper, *Hidden Americans: Maroons of Virginia and the Carolinas* (1995).

Lofton, John, *Insurrection in South Carolina: The Turbulent World of Denmark Vesey* (1964).

Luckingham, Bradford F., "Schoolcraft, Slavery, and Self-Emancipation," *Journal of Negro History* 50 (1965): 118–21.

McKibben, Davidson B., "Negro Slave Insurrections in Mississippi, 1800–1865," *Journal of Negro History* 34 (1949): 73–90.

McRae, Norman, "Crossing the Detroit River to Find Freedom," *Michigan History* 67 (1983): 35–39.

Meaders, Daniel, ed., *Advertisements for Runaway Slaves in Virginia, 1801–1820* (1997).

Milligan, John D., "Slave Rebelliousness and the Florida Maroons," *Prologue* 6 (1974): 4–18.

Monahan, John, and Gilbert Geis, "Controlling 'Dangerous' People," *Annals of the American Academy of Political and Social Sciences* 423 (1976): 142–51.

Mullin, Gerald W., *Flight and Rebellion: Slave Resistance in Eighteenth-Century Virginia* (1972).

———— "Gabriel's Insurrection," in Peter I. Rose, ed., *Americans from Africa, Vol. II: Old Memories, New Moods* (1970): 53–73.

Mullin, Michael, *Africa in America: Slave Acculturation and Resistance in the American South and the Caribbean, 1736–1831* (1992).

Murdoch, Richard K., "The Return of Runaway Slaves, 1790–1794," *Florida Historical Quarterly* 38 (1959): 96–113.

Mutersbaugh, Bert M., "The Background of Gabriel's Insurrection," *Journal of Negro History* 68 (1983): 209–11.

Nash, Gary B., "Slavery, Black Resistance, and the American Revolution," *Georgia Historical Quarterly* 77 (1993): 62–70.

Novak, Susan S., "Roads from Fear to Freedom: The Kansas Underground Railroad," *Kansas Heritage* 4 (1996): 9–12.

Ohline, Howard A., "Racial Anxieties and Militant Behavior, 1802," *South Carolina Historical Magazine* 73 (1972): 130–40.

Parker, Freddie L., *Running for Freedom: Slave Runaways in North Carolina, 1775–1840* (1993).

———, ed., *Stealing a Little Freedom: Advertisements for Slave Runaways in North Carolina, 1791–1840* (1994).

Parramore, Thomas C., "Aborted Takeoff: A Critique of 'Fly across the River,'" *North Carolina Historical Review* 68 (1991): 111–21.

Patterson, Orlando, "Slavery and Slave Revolts: A Socio-Historical Analysis of the First Maroon War, Jamaica, 1655–1740," *Social and Economic Studies* 19 (1970): 289–325.

Pearson, Edward A., ed., *Designs against Charleston: The Trial Record of the Denmark Vesey Slave Conspiracy of 1822* (1999).

Price, Richard, ed., *Maroon Societies: Rebel Slave Communities in the Americas* (3d ed., 1996).

Rachleff, Marshall, "Document: David Walker's Southern Agent," *Journal of Negro History* 62 (1977): 100–03.

Rawick, George, "The Historical Roots of Black Liberation," *Radical America* 2 (1968): 1–13.

Robertson, David, *Denmark Vesey: The Buried History of America's Largest Slave Rebellion and the Man Who Led It* (1999).

Rodriguez, Junius P., "Always 'En Garde': The Effects of Slave Insurrection upon the Louisiana Mentality, 1811–1815," *Louisiana History* 33 (1992): 399–416.

Roper, John Herbert, and Lolita G. Brockington, "Slave Revolt, Slave Debate: A Comparison," *Phylon* 45 (1984): 98–110.

Russel, Marion J., "American Slave Discontent in Records of the High Courts," *Journal of Negro History* 31 (1946): 411–34.

Sale, Maggie, "Critiques from Within: Antebellum Projects of Resistance," *American Literature* 64 (1992): 695–718.

Sawyer, Kem Knapp, *The Underground Railroad in American History* (1997).

Schwarz, Philip J., "Gabriel's Challenge: Slaves and Crime in Late Eighteenth Century Virginia," *Virginia Magazine of History and Biography* 90 (1982): 283–309.

Sidbury, James, *Ploughshares into Swords: Race, Rebellion, and Identity in Gabriel's Virginia, 1730–1810* (1997).

——— "Saint Domingue in Virginia: Ideology, Local Meanings, and Resistance to Slavery, 1790–1800," *Journal of Southern History* 63 (1997): 531–52.

Smith, Billy Gordon, and Richard Wojtowicz, *Blacks Who Stole Themselves: Advertisements for Runaways in the* Pennsylvania Gazette, *1728–1790* (1989).

Starobin, Robert S., ed., *Denmark Vesey: The Slave Conspiracy of 1822* (1970).

Stuckey, Sterling, "Remembering Denmark Vesey," *Negro Digest* 15 (1966): 28–41.

Suttles, William C., Jr., "African Religious Survivals As Factors in American Slave Revolts," *Journal of Negro History* 56 (1971): 97–104.

Tate, Gayle T., "Political Consciousness and Resistance among Black Antebellum Women," *Women and Politics* 13 (1993): 67–89.

Taylor, R. H., "Slave Conspiracies in North Carolina," *North Carolina Historical Review* 5 (1928): 20–34.

Toplin, Robert Brent, "The Making of Denmark Vesey's Rebellion," *Film and History* 12 (1982): 49–56.

Wade, Richard C., "The Vesey Plot: A Reconsideration," *Journal of Southern History* 30 (1964): 143–61.

Walker, David, *One Continual Cry: David Walker's Appeal to the Colored Citizens of the World, 1829–1830: Its Setting and Its Meaning: Together with the Full Text of the Third, and Last, Edition of the Appeal,* ed. Herbert Aptheker (1965).

——— *Walker's Appeal, in Four Articles, Together with a Preamble to the Colored Citizens of the World, but in Particular, and Very Expressly to Those of the United States of America. Written in Boston, in the State of Massachusetts, Sept. 28th, 1829* (1829).

Watson, Alan D., "Impulse toward Independence: Resistance and Rebellion among North Carolina Slaves, 1750–1775," *Journal of Negro History* 63 (1978): 317–28.

Windley, Lathan Algerna, *A Profile of Runaway Slaves in Virginia and South Carolina from 1730 through 1787* (1995).

———, ed., *Runaway Slave Advertisements: A Documentary History from the 1730s to 1790, Volume 1: Virginia and North Carolina; Volume 2: Maryland; Volume 3: South Carolina; Volume 4: Georgia* (1983).

Wish, Harvey, "American Slave Insurrections before 1861," *Journal of Negro History* 22 (1937): 299–320.

Wood, Betty, "Some Aspects of Female Resistance to Chattel Slavery in Low Country Georgia, 1763–1815," *Historical Journal* 30 (1987): 603–22.

Wood, Peter H., "'Impatient of Oppression': Black Freedom Struggles on the Eve of White Independence," *Southern Exposure* 12 (1984): 10–16.

16.3.5   Abolitionism and Emancipation

Adams, Alice Dana, *The Neglected Period of Anti-Slavery in America, 1808–1831* (1908).

Allen, Carlos R., Jr., ed., "David Barrow's 'Circular Letter' of 1795," *William and Mary Quarterly* 20 (1963): 440–51.

Allen, Jeffrey Brooke, "Means and Ends in Kentucky Abolitionism, 1792–1823," *Filson Club History Quarterly* 57 (1983): 365–81.

——— "The South's 'Northern Refutation' of Slavery: Pre-1830 Kentucky As a Test Case," *Southern Studies* 20 (1981): 351–60.

Anderson, Jon T., "Royall Tyler's Reaction to Slavery and the South," *Vermont History* 42 (1974): 296–310.

Aptheker, Herbert, *The Negro in the Abolitionist Movement* (1941).

Arbena, Joseph L., "Politics or Principle? Rufus King and the Opposition to Slavery, 1785–1825," *Essex Institute Historical Collections* 101 (1965): 56–77.

Ashworth, John, "The Relationship between Capitalism and Humanitarianism," *American Historical Review* 92 (1987): 813–28.

Beauregard, Erving E., "A Collegiate Outpost of Gradual Abolition," *Upper Ohio Valley Historical Review* 14 (1985): 2–9.

Bell, Mary Campbell, "Some Virginia Bills of Emancipation," *Journal of the Afro-American Historical and Genealogical Society* 5 (1984): 23–26.

Blackburn, Robin, *The Overthrow of Colonial Slavery, 1776–1848* (1988).

Blight, David W., "Perceptions of Southern Intransigence and the Rise of Radical Anti-Slavery Thought, 1816–1830," *Journal of the Early Republic* 3 (1983): 139–63.

Bogin, Ruth, "'Liberty Further Extended': A 1776 Anti-Slavery Manuscript by Lemuel Haynes," *William and Mary Quarterly* 40 (1983): 85–105.

Brown, Ira V., "Pennsylvania, 'Immediate Emancipation,' and the Birth of the American Anti-Slavery Society," *Pennsylvania History* 54 (1987): 163–78.

Bruns, Roger A., "Anthony Benezet and the Natural Rights of the Negro," *Pennsylvania Magazine of History and Biography* 96 (1972): 104–13.

Bullard, Mary Ricketson, *Black Liberation on Cumberland Island in 1815* (1983).

Carroll, Kenneth L., "The Berry Brothers of Talbot County, Maryland: Early Antislavery Leaders," *Maryland Historical Magazine* 84 (1989): 1–9.

——— "Voices of Protest: Eastern Shore Abolition Societies, 1790–1820," *Maryland Historical Magazine* 84 (1989): 350–60.

Conforti, Joseph, "Samuel Hopkins and the Revolutionary Anti-Slavery Movement," *Rhode Island History* 38 (1979): 39–49.

Craton, Michael, James Walvin, and David Wright, *Slavery, Abolition, and Emancipation: Black Slaves and the British Empire* (1976).

Davis, David Brion, "New Sidelights on Early Anti-Slavery Radicalism," *William and Mary Quarterly* 28 (1971): 585–94.

——— *The Problem of Slavery in the Age of Revolution* (1975).

——— "Reflections on Abolitionism and Ideological Hegemony," *American Historical Review* 92 (1987): 797–812.

Davis, J. Treadwell, "Nashoba: Frances Wright's Experiment in Self-Emancipation," *Southern Quarterly* 11 (1972): 63–90.

D'Elia, Donald J., "Dr. Benjamin Rush and the Negro," *Journal of the History of Ideas* 30 (1969): 413–22.

Dillon, Merton Lynn, *Slavery Attacked: Southern Slaves and Their Allies, 1619–1865* (1990).

Dumond, Dwight L., *Anti-Slavery: The Crusade for Freedom in America* (1961).

Filler, Louis, *Crusade against Slavery: Friends, Foes, and Reforms, 1820–1860* (rev. ed., 1986).

Finnie, Gordon E., "The Anti-Slavery Movement in the Upper South before 1840," *Journal of Southern History* 35 (1969): 319–42.

Fishman, George, "Taking a Stand for Freedom in Revolutionary New Jersey: Prime's Petition of 1786," *Science and Society* 56 (1992): 353–56.

Fladeland, Betty L., *Abolitionists and Working-Class Problems in the Age of Industrialization* (1984).

——— "Compensated Emancipation: A Rejected Alternative," *Journal of Southern History* 42 (1976): 169–86.

——— "Who Were the Abolitionists?" *Journal of Negro History* 49 (1964): 99–115.

Franklin, Benjamin V., "Theodore Dwight's 'African Distress': An Early Anti-Slavery Poem," *Yale University Library Gazette* 54 (1979): 26–36.

Gara, Larry, "A Southern Quaker's Plan to Abolish Slavery," *Quaker History* 58 (1969): 104–07.

Genovese, Eugene D., "In the Name of Humanity and the Cause of Reform," *Review of Radical Political Economics* 7 (1975): 365–84.

Goldin, Claudia Dale, "The Economics of Emancipation," *Journal of Economic History* 33 (1973): 66–85.

Guy, Anita Aidt, "The Maryland Abolition Society and the Promotion of the Ideals of the New Nation," *Maryland Historical Magazine* 84 (1989): 342–49.

Harwood, Thomas F., "The Abolitionist Image of Louisiana and Mississippi," *Louisiana History* 7 (1966): 281–308.

Haskell, Thomas L., "Convention and Hegemonic Interest in the Debate over Anti-Slavery: A Reply to Davis and Ashworth," *American Historical Review* 92 (1987): 829–78.

Holt, Thomas C., "Explaining Abolition," *Journal of Social History* 24 (1990): 371–78.

Jennings, Judith, "The American Revolution and the Testimony of British Quakers against the Slave Trade," *Quaker History* 70 (1981): 99–103.

Knee, Stuart E., "The Quaker Petition of 1790: A Challenge to Democracy in Early America," *Slavery and Abolition* 6 (1985): 151–59.

Levesque, George A., and Nikola A. Baumgarten, "'A Monstrous Inconsistency': Slavery, Ideology, and Politics in the Age of the American Revolution," *Contribution in Black Studies* 8 (1986–87): 20–34.

Lewitt, Robert T., "Indian Missions and Anti-Slavery Sentiment: A Conflict of Evangelical and Humanitarian Ideals," *Mississippi Valley Historical Review* 50 (1963): 39–55.

Locke, Mary Stoughton, *Anti-Slavery in America: From the Introduction of African Slaves to the Prohibition of the Slave Trade, 1619–1808* (1901).

Loveland, Anne C., "Richard Furman's 'Questions on Slavery,'" *Baptist History and Heritage* 10 (1975): 177–81.

MacEacheren, Elaine, "Emancipation of Slavery in Massachusetts: A Reexamination, 1770–1790," *Journal of Negro History* 55 (1970): 289–306.

Maclear, J. F., "The Evangelical Alliance and the Anti-Slavery Crusade," *Huntington Library Quarterly* 42 (1979): 141–64.

MacLeod, Duncan, "From Gradualism to Immediatism: Another Look," *Slavery and Abolition* 3 (1982): 140–52.

MacMaster, Richard K., "Anti-Slavery and the American Revolution," *History Today* 21 (1971): 715–23.

Matthewson, Timothy, "Abraham Bishop, 'The Rights of Black Men,' and the American Reaction to the Haitian Revolution," *Journal of Negro History* 67 (1982): 148–54.

——— "George Washington's Policy toward the Haitian Revolution," *Diplomatic History* 3 (1979): 321–36.

McManus, Edgar J., "Anti-Slavery Legislation in New York," *Journal of Negro History* 46 (1961): 207–16.

Melish, Joanne Pope, *Disowning Slavery: Gradual Emancipation and 'Race' in New England, 1780–1860* (1998).

Miller, Randall M., "The Union Humane Society," *Quaker History* 61 (1972): 91–106.

Mitchell, Virgil L., "Colonial Bondage and the Abolition of Slavery in the North," *Rendezvous* 11 (1976): 29–52.

Nash, Gary B., "From 1688 to 1799: Slavery and Freedom in Pennsylvania," in Randall M. Miller, ed., *States of Progress: Germans and Blacks in America over 300 Years* (1989): 27–37.

Payne-Gaposchkin, Cecilia Helena, "The Nashoba Plan for Removing the Evil of Slavery: Letters of Frances and Camilla Wright, 1820–1829," *Harvard Library Bulletin* 23 (1975): 221–51, 429–61.

Pease, Jane H., and William H. Pease, "The Role of Women in the Anti-Slavery Movement," *Canadian Historical Association Annual Report* (1967): 167–83.

Perry, Lewis, and Michael Fellman, ed., *Anti-Slavery Reconsidered: New Perspectives on the Abolitionists* (1979).

Quarles, Benjamin, *Black Abolitionists* (1969).

———— "Freedom's Black Vanguard," in Nathan I. Huggins, Martin Kilson and Daniel M. Fox, ed., *Key Issues in the Afro-American Experience* (vol. 1, 1971): 174–90.

———— "Lord Dunmore As Liberator," *William and Mary Quarterly* 15 (1958): 494–507.

Ratcliff, Donald J., "Captain James Riley and Anti-Slavery Sentiment in Ohio, 1819–1824," *Ohio History* 81 (1972): 76–94.

Robbins, Peggy, "Experiment at Nashoba Plantation," *American History Illustrated* 15 (1980): 12–19.

Rosen, Bruce, "Abolition and Colonization: The Years of Conflict, 1829–1834," *Phylon* 33 (1972): 177–92.

Rosswurm, Steve, "Emancipation in New York and Philadelphia," *Journal of Urban History* 21 (1995): 505–10.

Roth, Randolph A., "The First Radical Abolitionists: The Reverend James Milligan and the Reformed Presbyterians of Vermont," *New England Quarterly* 55 (1982): 540–63.

Ruchames, Louis, "Race, Marriage, and Abolitionism in Massachusetts," *Journal of Negro History* 40 (1955): 250–73.

Scarborough, Ruth, *The Opposition to Slavery in Georgia prior to 1860* (1968).

Scherer, Lester B., "A New Look at *Personal Slavery Established*," *William and Mary Quarterly* 30 (1973): 645–52.

Schwarz, Philip J., "Clark T. Moorman, Quaker Emancipator," *Quaker History* 69 (1980): 27–35.

Sowle, Patrick, "The North Carolina Manumission Society, 1816–1834," *North Carolina Historical Review* 42 (1965): 47–69.

Stanke, Michael J., "The Black Abolitionist: Saving the Past," *Afro-Americans in New York Life and History* 3 (1979): 39–44.

Steiner, Bruce E., "A Planter's Troubled Conscience," *Journal of Southern History* 28 (1962): 343–47.

Stewart, James Brewer, *Holy Warriors: The Abolitionists and American Slavery* (1976).

———— "Politics and Belief in Abolitionism: Stanley Elkins' Concept of Antiinstitutionalism and Recent Interpretations of American Anti-Slavery," *South Atlantic Quarterly* 75 (1976): 74–97.

Stouffer, Allen P., "Michael Willis and the British Roots of Canadian Anti-Slavery," *Slavery and Abolition* 8 (1987): 294–312.

Straub, Jean S., "Anthony Benezet: Teacher and Abolitionist of the Eighteenth Century," *Quaker History* 57 (1968): 3–16.

Sullivan, David K., "William Lloyd Garrison in Baltimore, 1829–1830," *Maryland Historical Magazine* 68 (1973): 64–79.

Sutherland, Daniel E., "A Special Kind of Problem: The Response of Household Slaves and Their Masters to Freedom," *Southern Studies* 20 (1981): 151–66.

Thomas, John L., "Romantic Reform in America, 1815–1865," *American Quarterly* 17 (1965): 656–81.

Thomas, Paul, "Changing Attitudes in an Expanding Empire: The Anti-Slavery Movement, 1760–1783," *Slavery and Abolition* 5 (1984): 50–72.

Thompson, Carol L., "Women and the Anti-Slavery Movement," *Current History* 70 (1976): 198–201.

Thompson, J. Earl, Jr., "Abolitionism and Theological Education at Andover," *New England Quarterly* 47 (1974): 238–61.

———— "Lyman Beecher's Long Road to Conservative Abolitionism," *Church History* 42 (1973): 89–109.

Toplin, Robert Brent, "The Specter of Crisis: Slaveholder Reactions to Abolitionism in the United States and Brazil," *Civil War History* 18 (1972): 129–38.

Troutman, Richard L., "Emancipation of Slaves by Henry Clay," *Journal of Negro History* 40 (1955): 179–81.

Turner, Wallace B., "Abolitionism in Kentucky," *Register of the Kentucky Historical Society* 69 (1971): 319–38.

Van Broekhoven, Deborah Bingham, "'A Determination to Labor . . .': Female Anti-Slavery Activity in Rhode Island," *Rhode Island History* 44 (1985): 35–46.

Wax, Darold D., "Reform and Revolution: The Movement against Slavery and the Slave Trade in Revolutionary Pennsylvania," *Western Pennsylvania Historical Magazine* 57 (1974): 403–29.

Wesley, Charles H., "The Negro in the Organization of Abolition," *Phylon* 2 (1941): 223–35.

———— "The Negroes of New York in the Emancipation Movement," *Journal of Negro History* 24 (1944): 32–74.

Whitaker, Cynthia, "The White Negro: Russian and American Abolition," *North Dakota Quarterly* 33 (1965): 32–37.

White, Shane, *Somewhat More Independent: The End of Slavery in New York City, 1770–1810* (1990).

Whitman, T. Stephen, *The Price of Freedom: Slavery and Manumission in Baltimore and Early National Maryland* (1997).

Woods, John A., "The Correspondence of Benjamin Rush and Granville Sharp, 1773–1809," *Journal of American Studies* 1 (1967): 1–38.

Young, R. J., "The Political Economy of Black Abolitionists," *Afro-Americans in New York Life and History* 18 (1994): 47–71.

Zilversmit, Arthur, "The Abolitionists: From Patience to Militance," in James C. Curtis and Lewis L. Gould, ed., *The Black Experience in America* (1970): 51–67.

———— *The First Emancipation: The Abolition of Slavery in the North* (1967).

———— "Liberty and Property: New Jersey and the Abolition of Slavery," *New Jersey History* 88 (1970): 215–26.

Zorn, Roman J., "The New England Anti-Slavery Society: Pioneer Abolition Organization," *Journal of Negro History* 42 (1957): 157–76.

16.3.6   Black/White Relations

Allen, Jeffrey Brooke, "The Origins of Proslavery Thought in Kentucky, 1792–1799," *Register of the Kentucky Historical Society* 77 (1979): 75–90.

———— "The Racial Thought of White North Carolina Opponents of Slavery, 1789–1876," *North Carolina Historical Review* 59 (1982): 49–66.

———— "Were Southern White Critics of Slavery Racists? Kentucky and the Upper South, 1791–1824," *Journal of Southern History* 44 (1978): 169–90.

Ashworth, John, "The Relationship between Capitalism and Humanitarianism," *American Historical Review* 92 (1987): 813–28.

Bailor, Keith M., "John Taylor of Caroline: Continuity, Change, and Discontinuity in Virginia's Sentiments toward Slavery, 1790–1820," *Virginia Magazine of History and Biography* 75 (1967): 290–304.

Berwanger, Eugene H., "Negrophobia in Northern Pro-Slavery and Anti-Slavery Thought," *Phylon* 33 (1972): 266–75.

Boulton, Alexander O., "The American Paradox: Jeffersonian Equality and Racial Science," *American Quarterly* 47 (1995): 467–92.

Bruce, Dickson D., Jr., "Racial Fear and the Pro-Slavery Argument: A Rhetorical Approach," *Mississippi Quarterly* 33 (1980): 461–78.

Burke, Joseph C., "The Pro-Slavery Argument and the First Congress," *Duquesne Review* 14 (1969): 3–15.

Carroll, Kenneth L., "An Eighteenth-Century Episcopalian Attack on Quaker and Methodist Manumission of Slaves," *Maryland Historical Magazine* 80 (1985): 139–50.

Collier, Eugenia, "Paradox in Paradise: The Black Image in Revolutionary America," *Black Scholar* 21 (1991): 2–9.

Davis, David Brion, *Was Thomas Jefferson an Authentic Enemy of Slavery?: An Inaugural Lecture Delivered before the University of Oxford on 18 February 1970* (1970).

Diggins, John P., "Slavery, Race, and Equality: Jefferson and the Pathos of the Enlightenment," *American Quarterly* 28 (1976): 206–28.

Drescher, Seymour, "The Ending of the Slave Trade and the Evolution of European Scientific Racism," *Social Science History* 14 (1990): 415–50.

Faust, Drew Gilpin, "A Southern Stewardship: The Intellectual and the Pro-Slavery Argument," *American Quarterly* 31 (1979): 63–80.

Fredrickson, George M., *The Black Image in the White Mind: The Debate on Afro-American Character and Destiny, 1817–1914* (1971).

——— "Toward a Social Interpretation of the Development of American Racism," in Nathan I. Huggins, Martin Kilson and Daniel M. Fox, ed., *Key Issues in the Afro-American Experience* (vol. 1, 1971): 240–54.

Gittleman, Edwin, "Jefferson's 'Slave Narrative': The Declaration of Independence As a Literary Text," *Early American Literature* 8 (1974): 239–56.

Gordon-Reed, Annette, *Thomas Jefferson and Sally Hemmings: An American Controversy* (1997).

Graffagnino, J. Kevin, "Vermont Attitudes toward Slavery: The Need for a Closer Look," *Vermont History* 45 (1977): 31–34.

Greenberg, Kenneth S., "Revolutionary Ideology and the Proslavery Argument: The Abolition of Slavery in Antebellum South Carolina," *Journal of Southern History* 42 (1976): 365–84.

Greene, John C., "The American Debate on the Negro's Place in Nature, 1780–1815," *Journal of the History of Ideas* 15 (1954): 384–96.

Gunderson, Joan R., "The Double Bonds of Race and Sex: Black and White Women in a Colonial Virginia Parish," *Journal of Southern History* 52 (1986): 351–72.

Harrington, J. Drew, "Classical Antiquity and the Pro-Slavery Argument," *Slavery and Abolition* 10 (1989): 60–72.

Howe, John R., "John Adam's Views of Slavery," *Journal of Negro History* 49 (1964): 201–06.

Ireland, Owen S., "Germans against Abolition: A Minority's View of Slavery in Revolutionary Pennsylvania," *Journal of Interdisciplinary History* 3 (1973): 685–706.

January, Alan F., "The South Carolina Association: An Agency for Race Control in Antebellum Charleston," *South Carolina Historical Magazine* 78 (1977): 191–201.

Jenkins, William Sumner, *Pro-Slavery Thought in the Old South* (1935).

Johnston, James Hugo, *Race Relations in Virginia and Miscegenation in the South, 1776–1860* (1970).

Jordan, Winthrop D., *White over Black: American Attitudes toward the Negro, 1550–1812* (1968).

Juhnke, William E., "Benjamin Franklin's View of the Negro and Slavery," *Pennsylvania History* 41 (1974): 375–88.

Kates, Don B., Jr., "Abolition, Deportation, Integration: Attitudes toward Slavery in the Early Republic," *Journal of Negro History* 53 (1968): 33–47.

Kaufman, Allen, *Capitalism, Slavery, and Republican Values: Antebellum Political Economists, 1819–1848* (1982).

Langhorne, Elizabeth, "Edward Coles, Thomas Jefferson, and the Rights of Man," *Virginia Cavalcade* 23 (1973): 30–37.

Lewis, Jan, and Peter Onuf, ed., *Sally Hemings and Thomas Jefferson: History, Memory, and Civic Culture* (1999).

Livermore, George, *An Historical Research Respecting the Opinions of the Founders of the Republic on Negroes As Slaves, As Citizens, and As Soldiers* (1862).

MacLeod, Duncan J., "Toward Caste," in Ira Berlin and Ronald Hoffman, ed., *Slavery and Freedom in the Age of the American Revolution* (1983): 217–36.

Mazyck, Walter H., *George Washington and the Negro* (1932).

McKitrick, Eric L., ed., *Slavery Defended: The Views of the Old South* (1963).

Miller, John Chester, *The Wolf by the Ears: Thomas Jefferson and Slavery* (1977).

Morrison, Larry R., "'Nearer to the Brute Creation': The Scientific Defense of American Slavery before 1830," *Southern Studies* 19 (1980): 228–42.

Nash, Gary B., "Red, White, and Black: The Origins of Racism in Colonial America," in Gary B. Nash and Richard Weiss, ed., *The Great Fear: Race in the Mind of America* (1970): 1–26.

Oakes, James, "From Republicanism to Liberalism: Ideological Change and the Crisis of the Old South," *American Quarterly* 37 (1985): 551–71.

Okoye, F. Nwabueze, "Chattel Slavery As the Nightmare of the American Revolutionaries," *William and Mary Quarterly* 37 (1980): 5–28.

Papenfuse, Eric Robert, *The Evils of Necessity: Robert Goodloe Harper and the Moral Dilemma of Slavery* (1997).

Richardson, William D., "Thomas Jefferson and Race: The *Declaration* and *Notes on the State of Virginia*," *Polity* 16 (1984): 447–66.

Robson, David W., "'An Important Question Answered': William Graham's Defense of Slavery in Post-Revolutionary Virginia," *William and Mary Quarterly* 37 (1980): 644–52.

Roediger, David R., *The Wages of Whiteness: Race and the Making of the American Working Class* (1991).

Saar, Doreen Alvarez, "Crevecoeur's Thoughts on Slavery: Letters from an American Farmer and Whig Rhetoric," *Early American Literature* 22 (1987): 192–203.

Saillant, John, "The Black Body Erotic and the Republican Body Politic, 1790–1820," *Journal of the History of Sexuality* 5 (1995): 403–28.

Sheldon, Marianne Buroff, "Black-White Relations in Richmond, Virginia, 1782–1820," *Journal of Southern History* 45 (1979): 27–44.

Solomon, Mark, and Herbert Aptheker, "Racism and Anti-Racism in U.S. History," *Science and Society* 57 (1993): 74–80.

Sparks, Randy J., "Mississippi's Apostle of Slavery: James Smylie and the Biblical Defense of Slavery," *Mississippi History* 51 (1989): 89–106.

Stanton, William Ragan, *The Leopard's Spots: Scientific Attitudes toward Race in America, 1815–1859* (1960).

Takaki, Ronald, "The Black Child-Savage in Antebellum America," in Gary B. Nash and Richard Weiss, ed., *The Great Fear: Race in the Mind of America* (1970): 27–44.

Tise, Larry E., "The Interregional Appeal of Pro-Slavery Thought: An Ideological Profile of the Antebellum American Clergy," *Plantation Society in the Americas* 1 (1979): 58–72.

——— *Pro-Slavery: A History of the Defense of Slavery in America, 1701–1840* (1987).

VanDeburg, William L., "Slave Imagery in the Literature of the Early Republic," *Mississippi Quarterly* 36 (1982–83): 53–71.

Wander, Philip C., "The Savage Child: The Image of the Negro in the Pro-Slavery Movement," *Southern Speech Communication Journal* 37 (1972): 335–60.

Weir, Robert M., "The South Carolinian As Extremist," *South Atlantic Quarterly* 74 (1975): 86–103.

Wenzel, Peter, "Pre-Modern Concepts of Society and Economy in American Pro-Slavery Thought: On the Intellectual Foundations of the Social Philosophy of George Fitzhugh," *Amerikastudien* 27 (1982): 157–76.

White, Shane, "Impious Prayers: Elite and Popular Attitudes toward Blacks and Slavery in the Middle-Atlantic States, 1783–1810," *New York History* 67 (1986): 260–83.

Winans, William, and Ray Holder, "On Slavery: Selected Letters of Parson Winans, 1820–1844," *Journal of Mississippi History* 46 (1984): 323–54.

Wish, Harvey, ed., *Antebellum Writings of George Fitzhugh and Hinton Rowan Helper on Slavery* (1960).

——— *George Fitzhugh: Propagandist of the Old South* (1943).

16.3.7   Black/Native American Relations

Braund, Kathryn E. Holland, "The Creek Indians, Blacks, and Slavery," *Journal of Southern History* 57 (1991): 601–36.

Forbes, Jack D., "The Evolution of the Term Mulatto: A Chapter in Black-Native American Relations," *Journal of Ethnic Studies* 10 (1982): 45–66.

Gammon, Tim, "Black Freedmen and the Cherokee Nation," *Journal of American Studies* 11 (1977): 357–64.

Halliburton, Janet, "Black Slavery in the Creek Nation," *Chronicles of Oklahoma* 56 (1978): 298–314.

Halliburton, R., Jr., "Black Slave Control in the Cherokee Nation," *Journal of Ethnic Studies* 3 (1975): 23–35.

———— *Red over Black: Black Slavery among the Cherokee Indians* (1977).

Katz, William Loren, "Black and Indian Cooperation and Resistance to Slavery," *Freedomways* 17 (1977): 164–74.

Klos, George E., "Black Seminoles in Territorial Florida," *Southern Historian* 10 (1989): 26–42.

———— "Blacks and the Seminole Removal Debate, 1821–1835," *Florida Historical Quarterly* 68 (1989): 55–78.

Landers, Jane, "Black-Indian Interaction in Spanish Florida," *Colonial Latin American Historical Review* 2 (1993): 141–62.

McLoughlin, William G., "Red Indians, Black Slavery, and White Racism: America's Slaveholding Indians," *American Quarterly* 26 (1974): 367–85.

Mulroy, Kevin, "Ethnogenesis and Ethnohistory of the Seminole Maroons," *Journal of World History* 4 (1993): 287–305.

Nash, Gary B., "The Forgotten Experience: Indians, Blacks, and the American Revolution," in William M. Fowler, Jr. and Wallace Coyle, ed., *The American Revolution: Changing Perspectives* (1979): 27–46.

Perdue, Theda, "Cherokee Planters, Black Slaves, and African Colonization," *Chronicles of Oklahoma* 60 (1982): 322–31.

———— *Slavery and the Evolution of Cherokee Society, 1540–1866* (1979).

Searcy, Martha Condray, "The Introduction of African Slavery into the Creek Indian Nation," *Georgia Historical Quarterly* 66 (1982): 21–32.

Usner, Daniel H., Jr., "American Indians on the Cotton Frontier: Changing Economic Relations with Citizens and Slaves in the Mississippi Territory," *Journal of American History* 72 (1985): 297–317.

Watts, Jill, "'We Do Not Live for Ourselves Only': Seminole Black Perceptions and the Second Seminole War," *UCLA Historical Journal* 7 (1986): 5–28.

Wright, James Leitch, Jr., "Blacks in British East Florida," *Florida Historical Quarterly* 54 (1976): 425–42.

———— *Creeks and Seminoles: The Destruction and Regeneration of the Muscogulge People* (1986).

———— "A Note on the First Seminole War As Seen by the Indians, Negroes, and Their British Advisors," *Journal of Southern History* 34 (1968): 565–75.

16.3.8   Black/Ethnic Relations

Hopkins, Leroy T., "Uneasy Neighbors: Germans and Blacks in Nineteenth-Century Lancaster County," in Randall M. Miller, ed., *States of Progress: Germans and Blacks in America over 300 Years* (1989): 72–88.

Korn, Bertram W., "Jews and Negro Slavery in the Old South, 1789–1865," *Publication of the American Jewish Historical Society* 50 (1961): 151–201.

16.4   GOVERNMENT

16.4.1   Law

Alpert, Jonathan L., "The Law of Slavery: It Did Happen Here," *American Bar Association Journal* 55 (1969): 544–46.

Baade, Anne E., "Slave Indemnities: A German Coast Response, 1795," *Louisiana History* 20 (1979): 102–09.

Berquist, Harold E., Jr., "Henry Middleton and the Arbitrament of the Anglo-American Slave Controversy by Tsar Alexander I," *South Carolina Historical Magazine* 82 (1981): 20–31.

Bogen, David Skillen, "The Maryland Contest of *Dred Scott:* The Decline in the Legal Status of Maryland Free Blacks, 1776–1810," *American Journal of Legal History* 34 (1990): 381–411.

Brandon, Mark E., *Free in the World: American Slavery and Constitutional Failure* (1998).

Burke, Joseph C., "Max Farrand Revisited: A New Look at Southern Sectionalism and Slavery in the Federal Convention," *Duquesne Review* 12 (1967): 1–21.

——— "What Did the Prigg Decision Really Decide?" *Pennsylvania Magazine of History and Biography* 93 (1969): 73–85.

Catterall, Helen Tunnicliff, ed., *Judicial Cases concerning American Slavery and the Negro* (5 vols. 1926–1937).

Cottrol, Robert J., "Liberalism and Paternalism: Ideology, Economic Interest, and the Business Law of Slavery," *American Journal of Legal History* 31 (1987): 359–73.

Cushing, John, "The Cushing Court and the Abolition of Slavery in Massachusetts: More Notes on the 'Quock Walker Case,'" *American Journal of Legal History* 5 (1961): 118–44.

Davis, David Brion, "The Significance of Excluding Slavery from the Old North West in 1787," *Indiana Magazine of History* 84 (1988): 75–89.

DePauw, Linda Grant, "Land of the Unfree: Legal Limitations on Liberty in Pre-Revolutionary America," *Maryland Historical Magazine* 68 (1973): 355–68.

Drake, Winbourne Magruder, "The Framing of Mississippi's First Constitution," *Journal of Mississippi History* 29 (1967): 301–27.

Eggert, Gerald G., "The Impact of the Fugitive Slave Law on Harrisburg: A Case Study," *Pennsylvania Magazine of History and Biography* 109 (1985): 537–69.

Finkelman, Paul, *An Imperfect Union: Slavery, Federalism, and Comity* (1981).

——— "The Kidnapping of John Davis and the Adoption of the Fugitive Slave Law of 1793," *Journal of Southern History* 56 (1990): 397–422.

——— "The Pennsylvania Delegation and the Peculiar Institution: The Two Faces of the Keystone State," *Pennsylvania Magazine of History and Biography* 112 (1988): 49–71.

———, ed., *Slavery and the Law* (1997).

——— "Slavery and the Northwest Ordinance: A Study in Ambiguity," *Journal of the Early Republic* 6 (1986): 343–70.

Foley, William E., "Slave Freedom Suits before Dred Scott: The Case of Marie Jean Scypion's Descendants," *Missouri Historical Review* 79 (1984): 1–23.

Greene, Jack P., "'Slavery or Independence': Some Reflections on the Relationship among Liberty, Black Bondage, and Equality in Revolutionary South Carolina," *South Carolina Historical Magazine* 80 (1979): 193–214.

Griffin, J. David, "Historians and the Sixth Article of the Ordinance of 1787," *Ohio History* 78 (1969): 252–60.

Higginbotham, A. Leon, Jr., and Barbara K. Kopytoff, "Racial Purity and Interracial Sex in the Law of Colonial and Antebellum Virginia," *Georgetown Law Journal* 77 (1989): 1967–2029.

Higginbotham, Don, and William S. Price, Jr., "Was It Murder for a White Man to Kill a Slave? Chief Justice Martin Howard Condemns the Peculiar Institution in North Carolina," *William and Mary Quarterly* 36 (1979): 593–601.

Hindus, Michael S., "Black Justice under White Law: Criminal Prosecutions of Blacks in Antebellum South Carolina," *Journal of American History* 63 (1976): 575–99.

Hollander, Barnett, *Slavery in America: Its Legal History* (1962).

Horsman, Reginald, "Thomas Jefferson and the Ordinance of 1784," *Illinois Historical Journal* 79 (1986): 99–112.

Hurd, John Codman, *The Law of Freedom and Bondage in the United States* (2 vols., 1858–1862).

Jillson, Calvin, and Thornton Anderson, "Realignments in the Convention of 1787: The Slave Trade Compromise," *Journal of Politics* 39 (1977): 712–29.

Keller, Ralph A., "Methodist Newspapers and the Fugitive Slave Law: A New Perspective for the Slavery Crisis in the North," *Church History* 43 (1974): 319–39.

Klebaner, Benjamin Joseph, "American Manumission Laws and the Responsibility for Supporting Slaves," *Virginia Magazine of History and Biography* 63 (1955): 443–53.

Kutler, Stanley I., "Pennsylvania Courts, The Abolition Act, and Negro Rights," *Pennsylvania History* 30 (1963): 14–27.

Lewis, Jan, "'Of Every Age, Sex, and Condition': The Representation of Women in the Constitution," *Journal of the Early Republic* 15 (1995): 359–87.

Lynd, Staughton, *Class Conflict, Slavery, and the United States Constitution: Ten Essays* (1967).

——— "The Compromise of 1787," *Political Science Quarterly* 81 (1966): 225–50.

Martin, Ida M., "Civil Liberties in Georgia Legislation, 1800–1830," *Georgia Historical Quarterly* 45 (1961): 329–44.

McGee, Val L., "Escape from Slavery: The Milly Walker Trials," *Alabama Review* 49 (1996): 243–52.

McGuire, Robert A., and Robert L. Ohsfeldt, "An Economic Model of Voting Behavior over Specific Issues at the Constitutional Convention of 1787," *Journal of Economic History* 46 (1986): 79–111.

Morris, Thomas D., "As If the Injury Was Effected by the Natural Elements of Air or Fire: Slave Wrongs and the Liability of Masters," *Law and Society Review* 16 (1981–82): 569–99.

——— *Free Men All: The Personal Liberty Laws of the North, 1780–1861* (1974).

Murdoch, Richard K., "The Seagrove-White Stolen Property Agreement of 1797," *Georgia Historical Quarterly* 42 (1958): 258–76.

Nadelhaft, Jerome, "The Somerset Case and Slavery: Myth, Reality, and Repercussions," *Journal of Negro History* 51 (1966): 193–208.

Noonan, John Thomas, Jr., *The Antelope: The Ordeal of the Recaptured Africans in the Administrations of James Monroe and John Quincy Adams* (1977).

O'Brien, William, "Did the Jennison Case Outlaw Slavery in Massachusetts?" *William and Mary Quarterly* 17 (1960): 219–41.

Ohline, Howard A., "Republicanism and Slavery: Origins of the Three-Fifths Clause in the United States Constitution," *William and Mary Quarterly* 28 (1971): 563–84.

Onuf, Peter S., "From Constitution to Higher Law: The Reinterpretation of the Northwest Ordinance," *Ohio History* 94 (1985): 5–33.

Post, Edward M., "Kentucky Law concerning Emancipation or Freedom of Slaves," *Filson Club History Quarterly* 59 (1985): 344–67.

Quarles, Benjamin, "'Freedom Fettered': Blacks in the Constitutional Era in Maryland, 1776–1810—An Introduction," *Maryland Historical Magazine* 84 (1989): 299–304.

Quigley, Bill, and Maha Zaki, "The Significance of Race: Legislative Racial Discrimination in Louisiana, 1803–1865," *Southern University Law Review* 24 (1997): 145–205.

Schafer, Judith K., "'Guaranteed against the Vices and Maladies Prescribed by Law': Consumer Protection, the Law of Slave Sales, and the Supreme Court in Antebellum Louisiana," *American Journal of Legal History* 31 (1987): 306–21.

——— "'Open and Notorious Concubinage': The Emancipation of Slave Mistresses by Will and the Supreme Court in Antebellum," *Louisiana History* 28 (1987): 165–82.

Sigler, Jay A., "The Rise and Fall of the Three-Fifths Clause," *Mid-American* 48 (1966): 271–77.

Silverman, Jason H., "Kentucky, Canada, and Extradition: The Jesse Happy Case," *Filson Club History Quarterly* 54 (1980): 50–60.

Spector, Robert M., "The Quock Walker Case, 1781–1783: Slavery, Its Abolition, and Negro Citizenship in Early Massachusetts," *Journal of Negro History* 53 (1968): 12–32.

Steel, Edward M., Jr., "Black Monongalians: A Judicial View of Slavery and the Negro in Monongalia County, 1776–1865," *West Virginia History* 34 (1973): 331–59.

——— "Bypath to Freedom," *West Virginia History* 31 (1969): 33–39.

Teute-Schmidt, Fredrika, and Barbara Ripel Wilhelm, "Early Pro-Slavery Petitions in Virginia," *William and Mary Quarterly* 30 (1973): 133–46.

Thurston, Helen M., "The 1802 Ohio Constitutional Convention and the Status of the Negro," *Ohio History* 81 (1972): 15–37.

Tordodash, Martin, "Constitutional Aspects of Slavery," *Georgia Historical Quarterly* 55 (1971): 234–47.

Tushnet, Mark V., "The American Law of Slavery, 1810–1860, A Study in the Persistence of Legal Autonomy," *Law and Society Review* 10 (1975): 119–84.

—— *The American Law of Slavery, 1810–1860: Considerations of Humanity and Interest* (1981).

Ulmer, S. Sidney, "Sub-Group Formation in the Constitutional Convention," *Midwest Journal of Political Science* 10 (1966): 288–303.

Wahl, Jenny Bourne, "Legal Constraints on Slave Masters: The Problem of Social Cost," *American Journal of Legal History* 41 (1997): 1–24.

Walker, Juliet E., "Legal Processes and Judicial Challenges: Black Land Ownershp in Western Illinois," *Western Illinois Regional Studies* 6 (1983): 23–48.

Watson, Alan D., "North Carolina Slave Courts, 1715–1785," *North Carolina Historical Review* 60 (1983): 24–36.

Wiecek, William M., "Slavery and Abolition before the United States Supreme Court, 1820–1860," *Journal of American History* 65 (1978): 34–59.

Wood, Betty, "'Until He Shall Be Dead, Dead, Dead': The Judicial Treatment of Slaves in Eighteenth-Century Georgia," *Georgia Historical Quarterly* 71 (1987): 377–98.

Yanuck, Julius, "Thomas Ruffin and North Carolina Slave Law," *Journal of Southern History* 21 (1955): 456–75.

Zilversmit, Arthur, "Quok Walker, Mumbet, and the Abolition of Slavery in Massachusetts," *William and Mary Quarterly* 25 (1968): 614–24.

Zuckerman, Michael, "Thermidor in America: The Aftermath of Independence in the South," *Prospects* 8 (1983): 349–68.

16.4.2   Crime and Punishment

Gerlach, Don R., "Black Arson in Albany, New York, November 1793," *Journal of Black Studies* 7 (1977): 301–12.

Kim, Hyong-In, "Slavery of the United States: The Result of Revisionism," *Studies in American History* 4 (1996): 97–134.

Patrick-Stamp, Leslie, "Numbers That Are Not New: African Americans in the Country's First Prison, 1790–1835," *Pennsylvania Magazine of History and Biography* 119 (1995): 95–128.

Rice, James D., "Insurrection at Saint Inigoes: The Three Faces of Crime and Punishment in a Slave Society," *Southern Studies* 5 (1994): 51–71.

Rowe, G. S., "Black Offenders, Criminal Courts, and Philadelphia Society in the Late Eighteenth Century," *Journal of Social History* 22 (1989): 685–712.

Saunders, Robert M., "Crime and Punishment in Early National America: Richmond, Virginia, 1784–1820," *Virginia Magazine of History and Biography* 86 (1978): 33–44.

Schwarz, Philip J., "Gabriel's Challenge: Slaves and Crime in Late Eighteenth Century Virginia," *Virginia Magazine of History and Biography* 90 (1982): 283–309.

Sellin, Johan Thorsten, *Slavery and the Penal System* (1976).

Sharpe, David F., "Patterns of Racial Imprisonment in Antebellum America," *Journal of the West Virginia Historical Association* 8 (1984): 1–11.

Singleton, Royce Gordon, "The Trial and Punishment of Slaves in Baldwin County, Georgia, 1812–1826," *Southern Humanities Review* 8 (1974): 67–73.

Waldrep, Christopher, *Roots of Disorder: Race and Criminal Justice in the American South, 1817–1880* (1998).

16.4.3   Politics and Voting

Bergman, Peter M., and Jean McCarroll, comp., *The Negro in the Congressional Record, 1789–1824* (7 vols., 1969–70).

—— *The Negro in the Continental Congress* (1969).

Bloch, Herman D., "The New York Negro's Battle for Political Rights, 1777–1865," *International Review of Social History* 9 (1964): 65–80.

Bogen, David S., "The Annapolis Poll Books of 1800 and 1804: African-American Voting in the Early Republic," *Maryland Historical Magazine* 86 (1991): 57–65.

Brown, Richard H., "The Missouri Crisis, Slavery, and the Politics of Jacksonianism," *South Atlantic Quarterly* 65 (1966): 55–72.

Cooper, William James, Jr., *Liberty and Slavery: Southern Politics to 1860* (1983).

Detweiler, Philip F., "Congressional Debate on Slavery and the Declaration of Independence, 1819–1821," *American Historical Review* 63 (1957/58): 598–616.

Durden, Robert F., *The Self-Inflicted Wound: Southern Politics in the Nineteenth Century* (1985).

Fox, Dixon Ryan, "The Negro Vote in Old New York," *Political Science Quarterly* 32 (1917): 252–75.

Freehling, William W., *Prelude to Civil War: The Nullification Controversy in South Carolina, 1816–1836* (1966).

Johnson, William R., "Prelude to the Missouri Compromise," *New York Historical Society Quarterly* 48 (1964): 31–50.

McFaul, John M., "Expediency *v.* Morality: Jacksonian Politics and Slavery," *Journal of American History* 62 (1975): 24–39.

Ochenkowski, J. P., "The Origins of Nullification in South Carolina," *South Carolina Historical Magazine* 83 (1982): 121–53.

Ohline, Howard A., "Slavery, Economics, and Congressional Politics, 1790," *Journal of Southern History* 46 (1980): 335–60.

Robinson, Donald L., *Slavery in the Structure of American Politics, 1765–1820* (1971).

Rogers, George C., Jr., "South Carolina Federalists and the Origins of the Nullification Movement," *South Carolina Historical Magazine* 71 (1970): 17–32.

Ryon, Roderick N., "Moral Reform and Democratic Politics: The Dilemma of Roberts Vaux," *Quaker History* 59 (1970): 3–14.

Shugg, Roger W., "Negro Voting in the Antebellum South," *Journal of Negro History* 21 (1936): 357–64.

Watson, Harry L., "Conflict and Collaboration: Yeomen, Slaveholders, and Politics in the Antebellum South," *Social History* 10 (1985): 273–98.

Watts, Jerry G., "Somewhere over the Rainbow: Reflections on Black Politics in the Age of Jackson," *Soundings (Knoxville, TN)* 70 (1987): 407–34.

Wesley, Charles H., "The Participation of Negroes in Anti-Slavery Political Parties," *Journal of Negro History* 29 (1944): 32–74.

Wood, Kirk, "The Central Theme of Southern History: Republicanism, Not Slavery, Race, or Romanticism," *Proceedings of the South Carolina Historical Association* (1985): 107–20.

Wright, Marian Thompson, "Negro Suffrage in New Jersey, 1776–1875," *Journal of Negro History* 32 (1948): 168–224.

16.4.4 Military

Aptheker, Herbert, *The Negro in the American Revolution* (1940).

Berlin, Ira, "The Revolution in Black Life," in Alfred F. Young, ed., *The American Revolution: Explorations in the History of American Radicalism* (1976): 349–82.

Boatner, Mark M., III, "The Negro in the Revolution," *American History Illustrated* 4 (1969): 36–44.

Brown, Wallace, "Negroes and the American Revolution," *History Today* 14 (1964): 556–63.

Clark, George P., "The Role of the Haitian Volunteers at Savannah in 1779: An Attempt at an Objective View," *Phylon* 41 (1980): 356–66.

Eno, R. D., "The Strange Fate of the Black Loyalists," *American Heritage* 34 (1983): 102–09.

Farley, M. Foster, "The South Carolina Negro in the American Revolution, 1775–1783," *South Carolina Historical Magazine* 79 (1978): 75–86.

Foner, Philip S., *Blacks in the American Revolution* (1976).

Frey, Sylvia R., "Between Slavery and Freedom: Virginia Blacks in the American Revolution," *Journal of Southern History* 49 (1983): 375–98.

Gough, Robert J., "Black Men and the Early New Jersey Militia," *New Jersey History* 88 (1970): 227–38.

Greene, Lorenzo J., "Some Observations on the Black Regiment of Rhode Island in the American Revolution," *Journal of Negro History* 37 (1952): 142–72.

Hodges, Graham Russell, ed., *The Black Loyalist Directory: African Americans in Exile after the American Revolution* (1996).

Jackson, Luther P., *Virginia Negro Soldiers and Seamen in the Revolutionary War* (1944).

Jones, George Fenwick, "The Black Hessians: Negroes Recruited by the Hessians in South Carolina and Other Colonies," *South Carolina Historical Magazine* 83 (1982): 287–302.

Kaplan, Sidney, "Blacks in Massachusetts and the Shays' Rebellion," *Contributions in Black Studies* 8 (1986–87): 5–14.

Langley, Harold D., "The Negro in the Navy and Merchant Service, 1798–1860," *Journal of Negro History* 52 (1967): 273–86.

Maslowski, Pete, "National Policy toward the Use of Black Troops in the Revolution," *South Carolina Historical Magazine* 73 (1972): 1–17.

McDonnell, Michael, "Other Loyalists: A Reconsideration of the Black Loyalist Experience in the American Revolutionay Era," *Southern Historian* 16 (1995): 5–25.

Miller, Randall M., "A Backcountry Loyalist Plan to Take Georgia and the Carolinas, 1778," *South Carolina Historical Magazine* 75 (1974): 207–14.

Moore, George Henry, *Historical Notes on the Employment of Negroes in the American Army of the Revolution* (1862).

Nell, William C., *Colored Patriots of the American Revolution* (1855).

———— *Services of Colored Americans in the Wars of 1776 and 1812* (1851).

Norton, Mary Beth, "The Fate of Some Black Loyalists of the American Revolution," *Journal of Negro History* 58 (1973): 402–26.

Quarles, Benjamin, *The Negro in the American Revolution* (1961).

Russell, Francis, "Liberty to Slaves: Black Loyalists in the American Revolution," *Timeline* 4 (1987): 2–15.

Salmon, John, "'A Mission of the Most Secret and Important Kind': James Lafayette and American Espionage in 1781," *Virginia Cavalcade* 31 (1981): 78–85.

Tyson, George F., Jr., "The Carolina Black Corps: Legacy of the Revolution, 1783–1798," *Revista Interamericana [Puerto Rico]* 5 (1975–76): 648–64.

Walker, James W. St. G., *The Black Loyalists: The Search for a Promised Land in Nova Scotia and Sierra Leone, 1783–1870* (1976).

———— "Blacks As American Loyalists: The Slaves' War for Independence," *Historical Reflections* 2 (1975): 51–67.

White, David Oliver, *Connecticut's Black Soldiers, 1775–1783* (1973).

Wilson, Ellen Gibson, *The Loyal Blacks* (1976).

Wilson, Joseph T., *The Black Phalanx: A History of the Negro Soldiers of the United States in the Wars of 1775–1812, 1861–1865* (1888).

Winks, Robin W., "Negroes in the Maritimes: An Introductory Survey," *Dalhousie Review* 48 (1968–69): 453–71.

16.5 DEMOGRAPHY

Cody, Cheryll A., "A Note on Changing Patterns of Slave Fertility in the South Carolina Rice District, 1735–1865," *Southern Studies* 16 (1977): 457–63.

Holland, C. G., "The Slave Population on the Plantation of John C. Cohoon, Jr., Nansemond County, Virginia, 1811–1863," *Virginia Magazine of History and Biography* 80 (1972): 333–40.

Klein, Herbert S., and Stanley L. Engerman, "Fertility Differentials between Sales in the United States and the British West Indies: A Note on Lactation Practices and Their Possible Implications," *William and Mary Quarterly* 35 (1978): 357–74.

Lachance, Paul F., "The 1809 Immigration of Saint-Dominigue Refugees to New Orleans: Reception, Integration, and Impact," *Louisiana History* 29 (1988): 109–41.

McDaniel, Antonio, and Carlos Grushka, "Did Africans Live Longer in the Antebellum United States? The Sensitivity of Mortality Estimates of Enslaved Africans," *Historical Methods* 28 (1995): 97–105.

Steckel, Richard H., "The Fertility of American Slaves," *Research in Economic History* 7 (1982): 239–86.

VandenBerghe, Pierre L., "The African Diaspora in Mexico, Brazil, and the United States," *Social Forces* 54 (1976): 530–45.

Vinovskis, Maris A., "The Demography of the Slave Population in Antebellum America," *Journal of Interdisciplinary History* 5 (1975): 459–67.

Zelinsky, Wilbur, "The Population Geography of the Free Negro in Antebellum America," *Population Studies* 3 (1950): 386–401.

16.6 FAMILY

Bardolph, Richard, "Social Origins of Distinguished Negroes," *Journal of Negro History* 40 (1955): 211–49.

Bendler, Bruce, "Securing One of the Blessings of Liberty: Black Families in Lower New Castle County, 1790–1850," *Delaware History* 25 (1993–1994): 237–52.

Brown, Steven E., "Sexuality and the Slave Community," *Phylon* 42 (1981): 1–10.

Carvalho, Joseph, III, *Black Families in Hampden County, Massachusetts, 1650–1855* (1984).

Cashin, Joan E., "Black Families in the Old Northwest," *Journal of the Early Republic* 15 (1995): 449–75.

Cassity, Michael J., "Slaves, Families, and 'Living Space': A Note on Evidence and Historical Context," *Southern Studies* 17 (1978): 209–15.

Cody, Cheryll A., "Naming, Kinship, and Estate Dispersal: Notes on Slave Family Life on a South Carolina Plantation, 1786 to 1833," *William and Mary Quarterly* 39 (1982): 192–211.

———. "There Was No 'Absalom' on the Ball Plantations: Slave-Naming Practices in the South Carolina Low Country, 1720–1865," *American Historical Review* 92 (1987): 563–96.

Durrill, Wayne K., "Slavery, Kinship, and Dominance: The Black Community at Somerset Place Plantation, 1786–1860," *Slavery and Abolition* 13 (1992): 1–19.

Flowers, J. Clayton, "Richard Clayton of Surrey County, Virginia, and His Descendants," *Journal of the Afro-American Historical and Genealogical Society* 6 (1985): 176–83.

Fox-Genovese, Elizabeth, "Antebellum Southern Households: A New Perspective on a Familiar Question," *Review [Fernand Braudel Center]* 7 (1983): 215–53.

Frazier, Edward Franklin, *The Free Negro Family: A Study of Family Origins before the Civil War* (1932).

Hill, Charles L., "Slavery and Its Aftermath in Beverly, Massachusetts: Juno Larcom and Her Family," *Essex Institute Historical Collections* 116 (1980): 111–30.

Holsoe, Svend E., "A Portrait of a Black Midwestern Family during the Early Nineteenth Century: Edward James Roye and His Parents," *Liberian Studies Journal* 3 (1970–71): 41–52.

Horton, James Oliver, "Generations of Protest: Black Families and Social Reform in Antebellum Boston," *New England Quarterly* 49 (1976): 242–56.

Johnson, Michael P., and James L. Roark, *Black Masters: A Free Family of Color in the Old South* (1984).

Jones, Jacqueline, "'My Mother Was Much of a Woman': Black Women, Work, and the Family under Slavery," *Feminist Studies* 8 (1982): 235–69.

Kennedy-Haflett, Cynthia, "'Moral Marriage': A Mixed-Race Relationship in Nineteenth-Century Charleston, South Carolina," *South Carolina Historical Magazine* 97 (1996): 206–26.

King, Wilma, "Within the Professional Household: Slave Children in the Antebellum South," *Historian* 59 (1997): 523–40.

Klotter, James C., "Slavery and Race: A Family Perspective," *Southern Studies* 17 (1978): 375–98.

Labinjoh, Justin, "The Sexual Life of the Oppressed: An Examination of the Family Life of Antebellum Slaves," *Phylon* 35 (1974): 375–97.

Langhorne, Elizabeth, "A Black Family at Monticello," *Magazine of Albermarle County History* 43 (1985): 1–16.

Lebsock, Suzanne, "Free Black Women and the Question of Matriarchy: Petersburg, Virginia, 1784–1820," *Feminist Studies* 8 (1982): 271–92.

Lewis, Ronald L., "Slave Families at Early Chesapeake Ironworks," *Virginia Magazine of History and Biography* 86 (1978): 169–79.

Malone, Ann Patton, "Searching for the Family and Household Structure of Rural Lousiana Slaves, 1810–1864," *Louisiana History* 28 (1987): 357–79.

———— *Sweet Chariot: Slave Family and Household Structure in Nineteenth-Century Louisiana* (1992).

Morrissey, Marietta, "Women's Work, Family Formation, and Reproduction among Caribbean Slaves," *Review* 9 (1986): 339–67.

Norton, Mary Beth, Herbert G. Gutman and Ira Berlin, "The Afro-American Family in the Age of the Revolution," in Ira Berlin and Ronald Hoffman, ed., *Slavery and Freedom in the Age of the American Revolution* (1983): 175–92.

Schweninger, Loren, "A Slave Family in the Antebellum South," *Journal of Negro History* 60 (1975): 29–44.

Steckel, Richard H., "Slave Marriage and the Family," *Journal of Family History* 5 (1980): 406–21.

Stevenson, Brenda E., *Life in Black and White: Family and Community in the Slave South* (1996).

Woodson, Carter Godwin, *Free Negro Heads of Families in the United States in 1830, Together with a Brief Treatment of the Free Negro* (1925).

16.7   SOCIETY

16.7.1   Rural Life (Including Black Settlements)

Dunn, Richard S., "Black Society in the Chesapeake, 1776–1810," in Ira Berlin and Ronald Hoffman, ed., *Slavery and Freedom in the Age of the American Revolution* (1983): 49–82.

Landers, Jane, "Black Community and Culture in the Southeastern Borderlands," *Journal of the Early Republic* 18 (1998): 117–34.

Morgan, Philip D., "Black Society in the Low Country, 1760–1810," in Ira Berlin and Ronald Hoffman, ed., *Slavery and Freedom in the Age of the American Revolution* (1983): 83–142.

Pease, Jane H., and William H. Pease, *Black Utopia: Negro Communal Experiments in America* (1963).

Pease, William H., and Jane H. Pease, "Organized Negro Communities: A North American Experiment," *Journal of Negro History* 47 (1962): 19–34.

Walsh, Lorena S., "Rural African Americans in the Constitutional Era in Maryland, 1776–1810," *Maryland Historical Magazine* 84 (1989): 327–41.

16.7.2   Urban Life (Including Migration)

Coughtry, Jamie, and Jay Coughtry, "Black Pauper Burial Records: Providence, Rhode Island, 1777–1831," *Rhode Island History* 44 (1985): 109–19.

Cray, Robert E., Jr., "White Welfare and Black Strategies: The Dynamics of Race and Poor Relief in Early New York, 1700–1825," *Slavery and Abolition* 7 (1986): 273–89.

Curry, Leonard P., *The Free Black in Urban America, 1800–1850: The Shadow of the Dream* (1981).

Goldin, Claudia Dale, *Urban Slavery in the American South, 1820–1860: A Quantitative History* (1976).

Ingersoll, Thomas N., *Mammon and Manon in Early New Orleans: The First Slave Society in the Deep South, 1718–1819* (1999).

Johnson, Jerah, "New Orleans's Congo Square: An Urban Setting for Early Afro-American Culture Formation," *Louisiana History* 32 (1991): 117–57.

Johnson, Whittington B., *Black Savannah, 1788–1864* (1996).

Kulikoff, Allan, "Uprooted Peoples: Black Migrants in the Age of the American Revolution," in Ira Berlin and Ronald Hoffman, ed., *Slavery and Freedom in the Age of the American Revolution* (1983): 143–73.

Lewis, E., "Connecting Memory, Self, and the Power of Place in African-American Urban History," *Journal of Urban History* 21 (1995): 347–71.

Lucas, Marion B., "African Americans on the Kentucky Frontier," *Register of the Kentucky Historical Society* 95 (1997): 121–34.

Nash, Gary B., *Forging Freedom: The Formation of Philadelphia's Black Community, 1720–1840* (1988).

Phillips, Christopher, *Freedom's Port: The African American Community of Baltimore, 1790–1860* (1997).

Reichard, Maximilian, "Black and White on the Urban Frontier: The St. Louis Community in Transition, 1800–1830," *Missouri Historical Society Bulletin* 33 (1976): 3–17.

Slezak, Eva, "Black Householders in the 1810 Baltimore City Directory," *Journal of the Afro-American Historical and Genealogical Society* 5 (1984): 67–70.

Taylor, Henry L., "On Slavery's Fringe: City-Building and Black Community Development in Cincinnati, 1800–1850," *Ohio History* 95 (1986): 5–33.

Wade, Richard C., *Slavery in the Cities: The South, 1820–1860* (1964).

White, Shane, "'It Was a Proud Day': African Americans, Festivals, and Parades in the North, 1741–1834," *Journal of American History* 81 (1994): 13–50.

———— "A Question of Style: Blacks in and around New York City in the Late Eighteenth Century," *Journal of American Folklore* 102 (1989): 23–44.

———— *Somewhat More Independent: The End of Slavery in New York City, 1770–1810* (1991).

———— "'We Dwell in Safety and Pursue Our Honest Callings': Free Blacks in New York City, 1783–1810," *Journal of American History* 75 (1988): 445–70.

16.7.3   Material Culture

Burrison, John A., "Afro-American Folk Pottery in the South," *Southern Folklore Quarterly* 42 (1978): 175–99.

Foster, Helen Bradley, *'New Raiments of Self': African American Clothing in the Antebellum South* (1997).

Franklin, Maria, "Rethinking the Carter's Grove Slave Quarter Reconstruction: A Proposal," *Kroeber Anthropological Society Papers* 79 (1995): 147–64.

Gilbert, Judith A., "Esther and Her Sisters: Free Women of Color As Property Owners in Colonial St. Louis, 1765–1803," *Gateway Heritage* 17 (1996): 14–23.

Jamieson, Ross W., "Material Culture and Social Death: African-American Burial Practices," *Historical Archaeology* 29 (1995): 39–58.

Klingelhofer, Eric, "Aspects of Early Afro-American Material Culture: Artifacts from the Slave Quarters in Garrison Plantation, Maryland," *Historical Archaeology* 21 (1987): 112–19.

Otto, John Solomon, and Augustus Marion Burns, III, "Black Folks and Poor Buckras: Archeological Evidence of Slave and Overseer Living Conditions on an Antebellum Plantation," *Journal of Black Studies* 14 (1983): 185–200.

Rankin-Hall, Lesley M., *A Biohistory of Nineteenth Century Afro-Americans: The Burial Remains of a Philadelphia Cemetery* (1997).

Samford, Patricia, "The Archaeology of African-American Slavery and Material Culture," *William and Mary Quarterly* 53 (1996): 87–114.

Sobel, Mechal, *The World They Made Together: Black and White Values in Eighteenth-Century Virginia* (1987).

Weik, Terry, "The Archaeology of Maroon Societies in the Americas: Resistance, Cultural Continuity, and Transformation in the African Diaspora," *Historical Archaeology* 31 (1997): 81–92.

Yentsch, Anne, "Beads As Silent Witnesses of an African-American Past: Social Identity and the Artifacts of Slavery in Annapolis, Maryland," *Kroeber Anthropological Society Papers* 79 (1995): 44–60.

16.7.4   Color and Class

Brodie, Fawn M., "The Great Jefferson Taboo," *American Heritage* 23 (1972): 49–57, 97–100.

———— "Thomas Jefferson's Unknown Grandchildren," *American Heritage* 27 (1976): 28–33, 94–99.

Burg, B. R., "The Rhetoric of Miscegenation: Thomas Jefferson, Sally Hemings, and Their Historians," *Phylon* 47 (1986): 128–38.

Forbes, Jack D., "Black Pioneers: The Spanish-Speaking Afro-American of the Southwest," *Phylon* 27 (1966): 233–46.

———— "The Evolution of the Term Mulatto: A Chapter in Black-Native American Relations," *Journal of Ethnic Studies* 10 (1982): 45–66.

Graham, Pearl M., "Thomas Jefferson and Sally Hemings," *Journal of Negro History* 46 (1961): 89–103.

Harper, C. W., "House Servants and Field Hands: Fragmentation in the Antebellum Slave Community," *North Carolina Historical Review* 55 (1978): 42–59.

Horowitz, Donald L., "Color Differentiation in the American Systems of Slavery," *Journal of Interdisciplinary History* 3 (1973): 509–41.

Johnston, James Hugo, *Race Relations in Virginia and Miscegenation in the South, 1776–1860* (1970).

Melder, Keith, "Slaves and Freedmen," *Wilson Quarterly* 13 (1989): 76–83.

Mills, Gary B., "Miscegenation and the Free Negro in Antebellum 'Anglo' Alabama: A Reexamination of Southern Race Relations," *Journal of American History* 68 (1981): 16–34.

Phillips, Stephanie L., "Claiming Our Foremothers: The Legend of Sally Hemmings and the Tasks of Black Feminist Theory," *Hastings Women's Law Journal* 8 (1997): 401–65.

Schafer, Daniel L., "'A Class of People neither Freemen nor Slaves': From Spanish to American Race Relations in Florida, 1821–1861," *Journal of Social History* 26 (1993): 587–609.

16.7.5 Associational Life

Harris, Robert L., Jr., "Early Black Benevolent Societies, 1780–1830," *Massachusetts Review* 20 (1979): 603–25.

Perlman, Daniel, "Organizations of the Free Negro in New York City, 1800–1860," *Journal of Negro History* 56 (1971): 181–97.

Roff, Sandra Shoiock, "The Brooklyn African Woolman Benevolent Society Rediscovered," *Afro-Americans in New York Life and History* 10 (1986): 55–63.

Spencer, C. A., "Black Benevolent Societies and the Development of Black Insurance Companies in Nineteenth-Century Alabama," *Phylon* 46 (1985): 251–61.

Wilder, Craig Steven, "The Rise and Influence of the New York African Society for Mutual Relief, 1808–1865," *Afro-Americans in New York Life and History* 22 (1998): 7–18.

16.7.6 Leisure and Sports

Wiggins, David D., "Good Times on the Old Plantation: Popular Recreations of the Black Slave in Antebellum South, 1810–1860," *Journal of Sport History* 4 (1977): 260–84.

——— "The Play of Slave Children in the Plantation Communities of the Old South, 1820–1860," *Journal of Sport History* 7 (1980): 21–39.

16.8 RELIGION

Andrews, Dee, "The African Methodists of Philadelphia, 1794–1802," *Pennsylvania Magazine of History and Biography* 108 (1984): 471–86.

Aptheker, Herbert, "The Challenge to Dominant Religion in the United States from the Black Experience," *Journal of Religious Thought* 41 (1984–1985): 83–90.

——— "The Quakers and Negro Slavery," *Journal of Negro History* 25 (1940): 331–62.

Bailey, David T., *Shadow on the Church: Southwestern Evangelical Religion and the Issue of Slavery, 1783–1860* (1985).

Bailey, Kenneth K., "Protestantism and Afro-Americans in the Old South: Another Look," *Journal of Southern History* 41 (1975): 451–72.

Bodo, John R., *The Protestant Clergy and Public Issues, 1812–1848* (1954).

Boller, Paul F., Jr., "Washington, The Quakers, and Slavery," *Journal of Negro History* 46 (1961): 83–88.

Bradley, David Henry, *A History of the A.M.E. Zion Church: Part I, 1796–1872* (1956).

Bradley, L. Richard, "The Lutheran Church and Slavery," *Concordia Historical Institute Quarterly* 44 (1971): 32–41.

Bradley, Patricia Hayes, "'Mark the Perfect ... Behold the Upright': Freeborn Garretson Speaks for Methodism," *Methodist History* 16 (1978): 115–27.

Brooks, Walter H., "The Evolution of the Negro Baptist Church," *Journal of Negro History* 7 (1922): 11–22.

Cadbury, Henry J., "Negro Membership in the Society of Friends," *Journal of Negro History* 21 (1936): 151–213.

Calhoon, Robert M., "The African Heritage, Slavery, and Evangelical Christianity among American Blacks," *Fides et Historia* 21 (1989): 61–66.

Carroll, Kenneth L., "Maryland Quakers and Slavery," *Quaker History* 72 (1983): 27–42.

Chireau, Yvonne, "Conjure and Christianity in the Nineteenth Century: Religious Elements in African American Magic," *Religion and American Culture* 7 (1997): 225–46.

Clarke, T. Erskine, "An Experiment in Paternalism: Presbyterians and Slaves in Charleston, South Carolina," *Journal of Presbyterian History* 53 (1975): 223–38.

Cross, Jasper W., ed., "John Miller's Missionary Journal, 1816–1817: Religious Conditions in the South and Midwest," *Journal of Presbyterian History* 47 (1969): 226–61.

Curry, Mary Cuthrell, *Making the Gods in New York: The Yoruba Religion in the African American Community* (1997).

Daniel, W. Harrison, "The Methodist Episcopal Church and the Negro in the Early National Period," *Methodist History* 11 (1973): 40–53.

———— "Southern Presbyterians and the Negro in the Early National Period," *Journal of Negro History* 58 (1973): 291–312.

———— "Virginia Baptists and the Negro in the Antebellum Era," *Journal of Negro History* 56 (1971): 1–16.

Davis, J. Treadwell, "The Presbyterians and the Sectional Conflict," *Southern Quarterly* 8 (1970): 117–33.

Dickson, D. Bruce, Jr., "Religion, Society, and Culture in the Old South: A Comparative View," *American Quarterly* 26 (1974): 399–416.

Diouf, Sylviane A., *Servants of Allah: African Muslims Enslaved in the Americas* (1998).

Doane, Gilbert H., ed., "Four Letters Pertaining to the Reverend William Levington, 1793(?)-1836," *Historical Magazine of the Protestant Episcopal Church* 32 (1963): 65–69.

Drake, Thomas Edward, *Quakers and Slavery in America* (1950).

Dumond, Dwight L., "Democracy and Christian Ethics," *Journal of Negro History* 46 (1961): 1–11.

Essig, James D., *The Bonds of Wickedness: American Evangelicals against Slavery, 1770–1808* (1982).

———— "A Very Wintry Season: Virginia Baptists and Slavery, 1785–1797," *Virginia Magazine of History and Biography* 88 (1980): 170–85.

Fordham, Monroe, *Major Themes in Northern Black Religious Thought, 1800–1860* (1975).

Frey, Sylvia R., and Betty Wood, *Come Shouting to Zion: African American Protestantism in the American South and British Caribbean to 1830* (1998).

Gallay, Alan, "The Origins of Slaveholders' Paternalism: George Whitefield, The Bryan Family, and the Great Awakening in the South," *Journal of Southern History* 53 (1987): 369–94.

Genovese, Eugene D., "Black Plantation Preachers in the Slave South," *Louisiana Studies* 11 (1972): 188–214.

Genovese, Eugene D., and Elizabeth Fox-Genovese, "The Religious Ideals of Southern Slave Society," *Georgia Historical Quarterly* 70 (1986): 1–16.

George, Carol V. R., *Segregated Sabbaths: Richard Allen and the Emergence of Independent Black Churches, 1760–1840* (1973).

Glaude, Eddie S., Jr., *Exodus! Religion, Race, and Nation in Early Nineteenth-Century Black America* (2000).

Gravely, William B., "The Rise of African Churches in America, 1786–1822: Reexamining the Contexts," *Journal of Religious Thought* 41 (1984): 58–73.

Greenberg, Michael, "Slavery and the Protestant Ethic," *Louisiana Studies* 15 (1976): 209–40.

Harding, Vincent, "Religion and Resistance among Antebellum Negroes, 1800–1860," in August Meier and Elliott Rudwick, ed., *The Making of Black America* (vol. 1, 1969): 179–97.

Hildebrand, Reginald F., "Methodist Episcopal Policy on the Ordination of Black Ministers, 1784–1864," *Methodist History* 20 (1982): 124–42.

Hilty, Hiram H., *Toward Freedom for All: North Carolina Quakers and Slavery* (1984).

Hood, R. E., "From a Headstart to a Deadstart: The Historical Basis for Black Indifference toward the Episcopal Church, 1800–1860," *Historical Magazine of the Protestant Episcopal Church* 51 (1982): 269–96.

Hopkins, Leroy, "Bethel African Methodist Church in Lancaster: Prolegomenon to a Social History," *Journal of the Lancaster County Historical Society* 90 (1986): 205–36.

Huch, Ronald K., "James Gillespie Birney and the New England Friends," *Register of the Kentucky Historical Society* 67 (1969): 350–59.

Hunter, William R., "Do Not Be Conformed unto This World: An Analysis of Religious Experience in the Nineteenth-Century African American Spiritual Narrative," *Nineteenth Century Studies* 8 (1994): 75–88.

Jackson, Luther P., "Religious Development of the Negro in Virginia from 1760–1860," *Journal of Negro History* 16 (1931): 168–239.

James, Sydney Vincent, *A People among Peoples: Quaker Benevolence in Eighteenth-Century America* (1963).

Johnson, Alonzo, and Paul T. Jersild, ed., *'Ain't Gonna Lay My 'Ligion Down': African-American Religion in the South* (1996).

Lammers, Ann C., "The Rev. Absalom Jones and the Episcopal Church: Christian Theology and Black Consciousness in a New Alliance," *Historical Magazine of the Protestant Episcopal Church* 51 (1982): 159–84.

Lapsansky, Emma Jones, "Since They Got Those Separate Churches: Afro-Americans and Racism in Jacksonian Philadelphia," *American Quarterly* 32 (1980): 54–78.

Lee, Carleton L., "Religious Roots of the Negro Protest," Arnold Rose, ed., *Assuring Freedom to the Free: A Century of Emancipation in the USA* (1964): 45–71.

Levesque, George A., "Inherent Reformers—Inherited Orthodoxy: Black Baptists in Boston, 1800–1873," *Journal of Negro History* 60 (1975): 491–519.

Little, Thomas J., "George Liele and the Rise of Independent Black Baptist Churches in the Lower South and Jamaica," *Slavery and Abolition* 16 (1995): 188–204.

Lovejoy, David S., "Samuel Hopkins: Religions, Slavery, and the Revolution," *New England Quarterly* 40 (1967): 227–43.

Luker, Ralph E., "'Under Our Own Vine and Fig Tree': From American Unionism to Black Denominationalism in Newport, Rhode Island, 1760–1876," *Slavery and Abolition* 12 (1991): 23–48.

Mathews, Donald G., "Religion in the Old South: Speculation on Methodology," *South Atlantic Quarterly* 73 (1974): 34–52.

——— *Slavery and Methodism: A Chapter in American Morality, 1780–1845* (1965).

Nash, Gary B., "'To Arise out of the Dust': Absalom Jones and the African Church of Philadelphia, 1785–1795," in Gary B. Nash, *Race, Class, and Politics: Essays on American Colonial and Revolutionary Society* (1988): 323–55.

Noon, Thomas R., "Early Black Lutherans in the South (to 1865)," *Concordia Historical Institute Quarterly* 50 (1977): 50–53.

Opper, Peter Kent, "North Carolina Quakers: Reluctant Slaveholders," *North Carolina Historical Review* 52 (1975): 37–58.

Posey, Walter B., *The Baptist Church in the Lower Mississippi Valley, 1776–1845* (1957).

——— "The Baptists and Slavery in the Lower Mississippi Valley," *Journal of Negro History* 41 (1956): 117–30.

——— "Presbyterian Church Influence in Lower Mississippi Valley," *Journal of the Presbyterian Historical Society* 33 (1955): 35–50.

Purifoy, Lewis M., "The Methodist Anti-Slavery Tradition, 1784–1844," *Methodist History* 4 (1966): 3–16.

Raboteau, Albert J., "Down at the Cross: Afro-American Spirituality," *United States Catholic Historian* 8 (1989): 33–38.

——— "Slave Autonomy and Religion," *Journal of Religious Thought* 38 (1981–82): 51–64.

——— "The Slave Church in the Era of the American Revolution," in Ira Berlin and Ronald Hoffman, ed., *Slavery and Freedom in the Age of the American Revolution* (1983): 193–215.

——— *Slave Religion: The "Invisible Institution" in the Antebellum South* (1978).

Reilly, Timothy F., "Slavery and the Southwestern Evangelist in New Orleans, 1800–1861," *Journal of Mississippi History* 41 (1979): 301–17.

Roberts, Wesley, "Rejecting the Negro Pew," *Christian History* 14 (1995): 35–37.

Roediger, David R., "And Die in Dixie: Funerals, Death, and Heaven in the Slave Community, 1700–1865," *Massachusetts Review* 22 (1981): 163–83.

Saillant, John, "Hymnody and the Persistence of an African-American Faith in Sierra Leone," *Hymn* 48 (1997): 8–17.

———— "Slavery and Divine Providence in New England Calvinism: The New Divinity and a Black Protest, 1775–1805," *New England Quarterly* 68 (1995): 584–608.

Sanders, Cheryl, "Religious Conversion, Ethics, and the Afro-American Slave: Evaluating Alternative Approaches," *Journal of Political Thought* 45 (1989): 7–20.

Sanneh, Lamin, "Prelude to African Christian Independency: The Afro-American Factor in African Christianity," *Harvard Theological Review* 77 (1984): 1–32.

Sensback, Jon F., *A Separate Canaan: The Making of an Afro-Moravian World in North Carolina, 1763–1840* (1998).

Sernett, Milton C., *Black Religion and American Evangelicalism: White Protestants, Plantation Missions, and the Flowering of Negro Christianity, 1787–1865* (1975).

Sherer, Robert Glenn, Jr., "Negro Churches in Rhode Island before 1860," *Rhode Island History* 25 (1966): 9–25.

Simpson, Robert, "The Shout and Shouting in Slave Religion of the United States," *Southern Quarterly* 23 (1985): 34–47.

Smith, Julia Floyd, "Marching to Zion: The Religion of Black Baptists in Coastal Georgia prior to 1865," *Viewpoints: Georgia Baptist History* 6 (1978): 47–54.

Smith, Timothy L., "Slavery and Theology: The Emergence of Black Christian Consciousness in Nineteeth Century America," *Church History* 41 (1972): 497–512.

Sobel, Mechal, *Trabelin' On: The Slave Journey to an Afro-Baptist Faith* (1979).

Soderlund, Jean R., *Quakers and Slavery: A Divided Spirit* (1985).

Stange, Douglas C., "'A Compassionate Mother to Her Poor Negro Slaves': The Lutheran Church and Negro Slavery in Early America," *Phylon* 29 (1968): 272–81.

Stewart, James Brewer, "Evangelicalism and the Radical Strain in Southern Anti-Slavery Thought during the 1820's," *Journal of Southern History* 39 (1973): 379–96.

Suttles, William C., Jr., "African Religious Survivals As Factors in American Slave Revolts," *Journal of Negro History* 56 (1971): 97–104.

Swaney, Charles Baumer, *Episcopal Methodism and Slavery: With Sidelights on Ecclesiastical Politics* (1926).

Swift, David E., "Black Presbyterian Attacks on Racism: Samuel Cornish, Theodore Wright, and Their Contemporaries," *Journal of Presbyterian History* 51 (1973): 433–70.

———— *Black Prophets of Justice: Activist Clergy before the Civil War* (1989).

———— "Samuel Hopkins: Calvinist Social Concern in Eighteenth-Century New England," *Journal of Presbyterian History* 47 (1969): 31–54.

Thompson, J. Earl, Jr., "Slavery and Presbyterianism in the Revolutionary Era," *Journal of Presbyterian History* 54 (1976): 121–41.

Trendel, Robert, "John Jay II: Anti-Slavery Conscience of the Episcopal Church," *Historical Magazine of the Protestant Episcopal Church* 45 (1976): 237–52.

Tyms, James Daniel, *The Rise of Religious Education among Negro Baptists: A Historical Case Study* (1965).

Weeks, Stephen Beauregard, *Southern Quakers and Slavery: A Study in Institutional History* (1896).

Williams, Delores S., "Visions, Inner Voices, Apparitions, and Defiance in Nineteenth-Century Black Women's Narratives," *Women's Studies Quarterly* 21 (1993): 81–89.

Wilson, Basil, and Charles Green, "The Black Church and the Struggle for Community Empowerment in New York City," *Afro-Americans in New York Life and History* 12 (1988): 51–79.

Wilson, Gold Refined, "The Religion of the American Negro Slave: His Attitude toward Life and Death," *Journal of Negro History* 8 (1923): 41–71.

Wingfield, Harold L., "The Historical and Changing Role of the Black Church: The Social and Political Implications," *Western Journal of Black Studies* 12 (1988): 127–34.

16.9   THOUGHT AND EXPRESSION

16.9.1   Race, Gender, and Identity

Allen, Ernest, Jr., "Afro-American Identity: Reflections on the Pre-Civil War Era," *Contributions in Black Studies* 7 (1985–86): 45–93.

Baugh, John, "The Politicization of Changing Terms of Self-Reference among American Slave Descendants," *American Speech* 66 (1991): 133–46.

Berry, Mary F., and John W. Blassingame, "Africa, Slavery, and the Roots of Contemporary Black Culture," *Massachusetts Review* 18 (1977): 501–16.

Bethel, Elizabeth Rauh, *The Roots of African-American Identity: Memory and History in Free Antebellum Communities* (1997).

Bruce, Dickson D., Jr., "National Identity and African-American Colonization, 1773–1817," *Historian* 58 (1995): 15–28.

Crahan, Margaret E., and Franklin W. Knight, ed., *Africa and the Caribbean: The Legacies of a Link* (1979).

Fordham, Monroe, "Nineteenth-Century Black Thought in the United States: Some Influences of the Santo Domingo Revolution," *Journal of Black Studies* 6 (1975): 115–26.

Gomez, Michael A., *Exchanging Our Country Marks: The Transformation of African Identities in the Colonial and Antebellum South* (1998).

Gravely, William B., "The Dialectic of Double-Consciousness in Black American Freedom Celebrations, 1808–1863," *Journal of Negro History* 67 (1982).

Huggins, Nathan Irvin, "Afro-Americans: National Character and Community," *Center Magazine* 7 (1974): 51–66.

Jennings, Paul, "A Colored Man's Reminiscences of James Madison," *White House History* 1 (1983): 46–51.

Levesque, George A., "Interpreting Early Black Ideology: A Reappraisal of Historical Consensus," *Journal of the Early Republic* 1 (1981): 269–88.

Lewis, Mary Agnes, "Slavery and Personality: A Further Comment," *American Quarterly* 19 (1967): 114–21.

Reidy, Joseph P., "'Negro Election Day' and Black Community Life in New England, 1750–1860," *Marxist Perspectives* 1 (1978): 102–17.

Roediger, David, "The Meaning of Africa for the American Slave," *Journal of Ethnic Studies* 4 (1977): 1–15.

Sterling, Dorothy, comp., *Speak Out in Thunder Tones: Letters and Other Writings by Black Northerners, 1787–1865* (1973).

Sweet, Leonard I., *Black Images of America, 1784–1870* (1976).

Wade, Melvin, "'Shining in Borrowed Plumage': Affirmation of Community in the Black Coronation Festivals of New England, c. 1750-c. 1850," *Western Folklore* 40 (1981): 211–31.

White, Shane, "'It Was a Proud Day': African Americans, Festivals, and Parades in the North, 1741–1834," *Journal of American History* 81 (1994): 13–50.

Williams-Meyers, A. J., "Pinkster Carnival: Africanisms in the Hudson River Valley," *Afro-Americans in New York Life and History* 9 (1985): 7–17.

Woodson, Carter Godwin, ed., *The Mind of the Negro As Reflected in Letters Written during the Crisis, 1800–1860* (1926).

16.9.2   Emigrationism and Nationalism

Abasiattai, Monday B., "The Search for Independence: New World Blacks in Sierra Leone and Liberia, 1787–1847," *Journal of Black Studies* 23 (1992): 107–16.

Allen, Jeffrey Brooke, "'All of Us Are Highly Pleased with the Country': Black and White Kentuckians on Liberian Colonization," *Phylon* 43 (1982): 97–109.

———— "Did Southern Colonizationists Oppose Slavery? Kentucky, 1816–1850 As a Test Case," *Register of the Kentucky Historical Society* 75 (1977): 92–111.

Blackett, Richard, "The Quest for Freedom: Colonization, Abolition, and European Immigration, 1817–1860," in Randall M. Miller, ed., *States of Progress: Germans and Blacks in America over 300 Years* (1989): 38–54.

Brooks, George E., Jr., "Bolama As a Prospective Site for American Colonization in the 1820's and 1830's," *Boletim Cultural da Guine Portuguesa [Portuguese Guinea]* 28 (1973): 5–21.

———— "The Providence African Society's Sierra Leone Emigration Scheme, 1794–1795: Prologue to the African Colonization Movement," *International Journal of African Historical Studies* 7 (1974): 183–202.

Cleve, Andrew N., "Some Plans for Colonizing Liberated Negro Slaves in Hispanic America," *Journal of Negro History* 11 (1926): 35–49.

Cox, Stephen L., "'Polluted with the Blood of Africa': Bigotry, Slavery, and the New Hampshire Colonization Society," *Historical New Hampshire* 38 (1983): 117–40.

Dixon, Chris, "An Ambivalent Black Nationalism: Haiti, Africa, and Antebellum African-American Emigrationism," *Australasian Journal of American Studies (Kensington)* 10 (1992): 10–25.

Egerton, Douglas R., "Its Origin Is Not a Little Curious: A New Look at the American Colonization Society," *Journal of the Early Republic* 5 (1985): 463–80.

Fleming, Walter L., "Deportation and Colonization: An Attempted Solution of the Race Problem," in *Studies in Southern History and Politics, Inscribed to William Archibald Dunning* (1914): 3–30.

Forbes, Ella, "African-American Resistance to Colonization," *Journal of Black Studies* 21 (1990): 210–23.

Foster, Charles I., "The Colonization of Free Negroes in Liberia, 1816–1835," *Journal of Negro History* 38 (1953): 41–66.

Fox, Early Lee, *The American Colonization Society, 1817–1840* (1919).

French, David, "Elizur Wright, Jr., and the Emergence of Anti-Colonization Sentiments on the Connecticut Western Reserve," *Ohio History* 85 (1976): 49–66.

Friedman, Lawrence J., "Purifying the White Man's Country: The American Colonization Society Reconsidered, 1816–1840," *Societas* 6 (1976): 1–24.

Gardner, Bettye J., "Opposition to Emigration: A Selected Letter of William Watkins (The Colored Baltimorean)," *Journal of Negro History* 67 (1982): 155–58.

Glaude, Eddie S., Jr., *Exodus! Religion, Race, and Nation in Early Nineteenth-Century Black America* (2000).

Grant, John N., "Black Immigrants into Nova Scotia, 1776–1815," *Journal of Negro History* 58 (1973): 253–70.

Harwood, Michael, "Better for Us to Be Separated," *American Heritage* 24 (1972): 54–57, 105–07.

Kocher, Kurt Lee, "A Duty to America and Africa: A History of the Independent African Colonization Movement in Pennsylvania," *Pennsylvania History* 51 (1984): 118–53.

Lindsay, David, "'The Land of Their Fathers,' Liberia," *American History Illustrated* 7 (1972): 26–35.

Matijasic, Thomas D., "Abolition *vs.* Colonization: The Battle for Ohio," *Queen City Heritage* 45 (1987): 27–40.

———— "African Colonization Activity at Miami University during the Administration of Robert Hamilton Bishop, 1824–1841," *Old Northwest* 12 (1986): 83–94.

———— "The Foundations of Colonization: The Peculiar Nature of Race Relations in Ohio during the Early Antebellum Period," *Queen City Heritage* 49 (1991): 23–30.

McGraw, Marie Tyler, "Richmond Free Blacks and African Colonization, 1816–1832," *Journal of American Studies* 21 (1987): 207–24.

Mehlinger, Louis R., "The Attitude of the Free Negro toward African Colonization," *Journal of Negro History* 1 (1916): 276–301.

Miller, Floyd John, *The Search for a Black Nationality: Black Emigration and Colonization, 1787–1863* (1975).

Miller, Randall M., "Georgia on Their Minds: Free Blacks and the African Colonization Movement in Georgia," *Southern Studies* 117 (1978): 349–62.

Mutunhu, Tendai, "The North Carolina Quakers and Slavery: The Emigration and Settlement of Their Former Slaves in Haiti," *Journal of African-Afro-American Affairs* 4 (1980): 54–67.

Newman, Debra L., and Marcia Eisenberg, "An Inspection Roll of Negroes Taken on Board Sundry Vessels at Staten Island Bound for Nova Scotia," *Journal of the Afro-American Historical and Genealogical Society'* 1 (1980): 72–79.

Perdue, Theda, "Cherokee Planters, Black Slaves, and African Colonization," *Chronicles of Oklahoma* 60 (1982): 322–31.

Pinkney, Alphonso, *Red, Black, and Green: Black Nationalism in the United States* (1976).

Reed, Harry A., "Financing an Early Back-to-Africa Scheme," *Massachusetts Historical Society Proceedings* 90 (1978): 103–05.

Scott, William R., "'And Ethopia Shall Stretch Forth Its Hands': The Origins of Ethiopianism in Afro-American Thought, 1767–1896," *UMOJA: A Scholarly Journal of Black Studies* 2 (1978): 1–14.

Seaton, Douglas P., "Colonizers and Reluctant Colonists: The New Jersey Colonization Society and the Black Community, 1815–1848," *New Jersey History* 96 (1978): 7–22.

Seifman, Eli, "The United Colonization Societies of New York and Pennsylvania and the Establishment of the African Colony of Bassa Cove," *Pennsylvania History* 35 (1968): 23–44.

Sherwood, Henry N., "Early Negro Deportation Projects," *Mississippi Valley Historical Review* 2 (1916): 484–508.

Smith, James Wesley, *Sojourners in Search of Freedom: The Settlement of Liberia by Black Americans* (1987).

Spray, W. A., "The Settlement of the Black Refugees in New Brunswick, 1815–1836," *Acadiensis* 6 (1977): 64–79.

Staudenraus, P. J., *The African Colonization Movement, 1816–1865* (1961).

Strange, Douglas C., "Lutheran Involvement in the American Colonization Society," *Mid-America* 49 (1967): 140–51.

Streifford, David M., "The American Colonization Society: An Application of Republican Ideology to Early Antebellum Reform," *Journal of Southern Studies History* 45 (1979): 201–20.

Strickland, Arvarh E., "Negro Colonization Movements to 1840," *Lincoln Herald* 61 (1959): 43–56.

Walker, James W. St. G., *The Black Loyalists: The Search for a Promised Land in Nova Scotia and Sierra Leone, 1783–1870* (1976).

Wander, Philip C., "Salvation through Separation: The Image of the Negro in the American Colonization Society," *Quarterly Journal of Speech* 57 (1971): 57–67.

Washington, Margaret, "African American History and the Frontier Thesis," *Journal of the Early Republic* 13 (1993): 230–41.

Weeks, Louis, III, "John Holt Rice and the American Colonization Society," *Journal of Presbyterian History* 46 (1968): 26–41.

Weisbord, Robert G., "The Back-to-Africa Idea," *History Today* 18 (1968): 30–37.

Williams, Robert J., "Blacks, Colonization, and Anti-Slavery: The Views of Methodists in New Jersey, 1816–1860," *New Jersey History* 102 (1984): 50–67.

Williamson, Douglas J., "Wilbur Fisk and African Colonization: A 'Painful Portion' of American Methodist History," *Methodist History* 23 (1985): 79–98.

16.9.3   Language and Linguistics

Inscoe, John C., "Carolina Slave Names: An Index to Acculturation," *Journal of Southern History* 49 (1983): 527–54.

Rickford, John R., and Angela E. Rickford, "Cut-Eye and Suck-Teeth: African Words and Gestures in New World Guise," *Journal of American Folklore* 89 (1976): 294–309.

16.9.4   Folklore and Humor

Cohen, David S., "In Search of Carolus Africanus Rex: Afro-Dutch Folklore in New York and New Jersey," *Journal of Afro-American Historical and Genealogical Society* 5 (1984): 148–68.

Dickson, Bruce D., Jr., "The 'John and Old Master' Stories and the World of Slavery: A Study in Folktales and History," *Phylon* 35 (1974): 418–29.

Fenn, Elizabeth A., "'A Perfect Equality Seemed to Reign': Slave Society and Jonkonnu," *North Carolina Historical Review* 65 (1988): 127–53.

Ravitz, Abe C., "John Pierpont and the Slaves' Christmas," *Phylon* 21 (1960): 383–86.

Stuckey, Sterling, "Through the Prism of Folklore: The Black Ethos in Slavery," *Massachusetts Review* 9 (1968): 417–37.

16.9.5 Literature and Poetry

Brawley, Benjamin Griffith, ed., *Early Negro American Writers: Selections with Biographical and Critical Introductions* (1935).

Collins, Terence, "Phyllis Wheatley: The Dark Side of the Poetry," *Phylon* 36 (1975): 78–88.

Davis, Leona King, "Literary Opinions on Slavery in American Literature from after the Revolution to the Civil War," *Negro History Bulletin* 23 (1960): 99–101, 104; 123–27; 147–50.

Deck, Alice A., "Whose Book Is This? Authorial *versus* Editorial Control of Harriet Brent Jacobs' *Incidents in the Life of a Slave Girl: Written by Herself,*" *Women's Studies International Forum* 10 (1987): 33–40.

Desrochers, Robert E., Jr., "'Not Fade Away': The Narrative of Venture Smith, an African American in the Early Republic," *Journal of American History* 84 (1997): 40–66.

Doherty, Thomas, "Harriet Jacobs' Narrative Strategies: *Incidents in the Life of a Slave Girl,*" *Southern Literary Journal* 19 (1986): 79–91.

Edwards, Paul, "'Master' and 'Father' in Equiano's *Interesting Narrative,*" *Slavery and Abolition* 11 (1990): 216–26.

Felker, Christopher D., "The Tongues of the Learned Are Insufficient: Phillis Wheatley, Publishing Objectives, and Personal Liberty," *Resources for American Literary Study* 20 (1994): 149–79.

Fleischner, Jennifer, "Memory, Sickness, and Slavery: One Girl's Slave Story," *American Imago* 20 (1994): 149–79.

Gates, Henry Louis, Jr., "James Gronniosaw and the Trope of the Talking Book," *Southern Review* 22 (1986): 252–72.

Gribbin, William, "A *Phylon* Document . . . Advice from a Black Philadelphia Poetess of 1813," *Phylon* 34 (1973): 49–50.

Isani, Mukhtar Ali, "The British Reception of Wheatley's Poems on Various Subjects," *Journal of Negro History* 66 (1981): 144–49.

———— "Far from 'Gambia's Golden Shore': The Black in Late Eighteenth-Century American Imaginative Literature," *William and Mary Quarterly* 36 (1979): 353–72.

O'Neale, Sondra, "A Slave's Subtle War: Phillis Wheatley's Use of Biblical Myth and Symbol," *Early American Literature* 21 (1986): 144–65.

Peters, Erskine, "Jupiter Hammon: His Engagement with Interpretation," *Journal of Ethnic Studies* 8 (1981): 1–12.

Porter, Dorothy, comp., *Early Negro Writing, 1760–1837* (1971).

Richmond, Merle A., *Bid the Vassal Soar: Interpretive Essays on the Life and Poetry of Phillis Wheatley, ca. 1753–1784, and George Moses Horton, ca. 1797–1883* (1974).

Robinson, William Henry, Jr., ed., *Early Black American Poets: Selections with Biographical and Critical Introductions* (3d ed., 1971).

Scheick, William J., "Phillis Wheatley and Oliver Goldsmith: A Fugitive Satire," *Early American Literature* 19 (1984): 82–84.

Taves, Ann, "Spiritual Purity and Sexual Shame: Religious Themes in the Writings of Harriet Jacobs," *Church History* 56 (1987): 59–72.

Winchell, Donna Haisty, "Tracing the Motherlines," *Mississippi Quarterly* 46 (1993): 625–38.

Yellin, Jean Fagan, *The Intricate Knot: Black Figures in American Literature, 1776–1863* (1972).

16.9.6 Music and Performing Arts

DeMetz, Kay, "Minstrel Dancing in New Orleans' Nineteenth-Century Theaters," *Southern Quarterly* 20 (1982): 28–40.

Eaklor, Vicki Lynn, *American Anti-Slavery Songs: A Collection and Analysis* (1988).

Fisher, Miles Mark, *Negro Slave Songs in the United States* (1953).

Green, Alan W. C., "'Jim Crow', 'Zip Coon': The Northern Origins of Negro Minstrelsy," *Massachusetts Review* 11 (1970): 385–97.

Katz, Bernard, ed., *The Social Implications of Early Negro Music in the United States: With over 150 of the Songs: Many of Them with Their Music* (1969).

Lawrence, Vera Brodsky, "Micah Hawkins, the Pied Piper of Catherine Slip," *New-York Historical Society Quarterly* 62 (1978): 138–65.

Lawrence-McIntyre, Charshee Charlotte, "The Double Meanings of the Spirituals," *Journal of Black Studies* 17 (1987): 379–401.

Lovell, John, *Black Song: The Forge and the Flame: The Story of How the Afro-American Spiritual Was Hammered Out* (1972).

Morazan, Ronald R., "'Quadroon' Balls in the Spanish Period," *Louisiana History* 14 (1973): 310–15.

Over, William, "New York's African Theatre: The Vicissitudes of the Black Actor," *Afro-Americans in New York Life and History* 3 (1979): 7–13.

Southern, Eileen, "Musical Practices in Black Churches of New York and Philadelphia, c. 1800–1844," *Afro-Americans in New York Life and History* 4 (1980): 61–77.

Thompson, George A., *A Documentary History of the African Theatre* (1998).

16.9.7   Art (Drawing, Painting, Photography, Printmaking, Sculpture)

Jones, Rhett S., "Social-Scientific Perspectives on the Afro-American Arts," *Black American Literature Forum* 20 (1986): 443–48.

Lacey, Barbara E., "Visual Images of Blacks in Early American Imprints," *William and Mary Quarterly* 53 (1996): 137–80.

Twining, Mary A., "African-Afro-American Artistic Continuity," *Journal of African Studies* 2 (1975–76): 569–78.

16.9.8   Architecture and Design

Vlach, John Michael, "The Shotgun House: An African Architectural Legacy," *Pioneer American* 8 (1976): 47–56, 57–70.

Young, Amy Lambeck, Philip J. Carr, and Joseph E. Granger, "How Historical Archaeology Works: A Case Study of Slave Houses at Locust Grove," *Register of the Kentucky Historical Society* 96 (1998): 164–94.

16.10   EDUCATION

Albanese, Anthony Gerald, *The Plantation School* (1976).

Carruthers, Iva E., "Centennials of Black Miseducation: A Study of White Educational Management," *Journal of Negro Education* 46 (1977): 291–304.

Franklin, Vincent P., "Education for Colonization: Attempts to Educate Free Blacks in the United States for Emigration to Africa, 1823–1833," *Journal of Negro Education* 43 (1974): 91–103.

Gardner, Bettye J., "Antebellum Black Education in Baltimore," *Maryland Historical Magazine* 71 (1976): 360–66.

Gersman, Elinor Mondale, "The Development of Public Education for Blacks in Nineteenth-Century St. Louis Missouri," *Journal of Negro Education* 41 (1972): 35–47.

Hornick, Nancy Slocum, "Anthony Benezet and the African School: Toward a Theory of Full Equality," *Pennsylvania Magazine of History and Biography* 99 (1975): 399–421.

Jacobs, Donald M., "The Nineteenth-Century Struggle over Segregated Education in the Boston Schools," *Journal of Negro Education* 39 (1970): 76–85.

Levesque, George A., "Before Integration: The Forgotten Years of Jim Crow Education in Boston," *Journal of Negro Education* 48 (1979): 113–25.

Mabee, Carlton, "Early Black Public Schools," *Long Island Forum* 36 (1973): 214–16, 234–36.

Mohl, Raymond A., "Education As Social Control in New York City, 1784–1825," *New York History* 51 (1970): 219–37.

Poole, Thomas G., "The Role of the Church in Black Education," *Western Journal of Black Studies* 12 (1988): 135–41.

Rury, John L., "The New York African Free School, 1827–1836: Conflict over Community of Black Education," *Phylon* 44 (1983): 187–97.

Scott, Osborne, "Pre- and Post-Emancipation Schools," *Urban Review* 9 (1976): 234–41.

Silcox, Harry C., "Delay and Neglect: Negro Public Education in Antebellum Philadelphia, 1800–1860," *Pennsylvania Magazine of History and Biography* 97 (1973): 444–64.

Steen, Ivan D., "Document: 'Education to What End?' An Englishman Comments on the Plight of Blacks in the 'Free' States, 1830," *Afro-Americans in New York Life and History* 7 (1983): 55–60.

Swan, Robert J., "Did Brooklyn (N.Y.) Blacks Have Unusual Control over Their Schools? Period I, 1815–1845," *Afro-Americans in New York Life and History* 7 (1983): 25–46.

Washington, Michael, "A New Perspective on Black Education: A Review of the Literature on the Nineteenth Century New York Experience," *Afro-Americans in New York Life and History* 17 (1993): 17–28.

White, Arthur O., "Antebellum School Reform in Boston: Integrationists and Separatists," *Phylon* 34 (1973): 203–18.

———— "The Black Leadership Class and Education in Antebellum Boston," *Journal of Negro Education* 42 (1973): 504–15.

———— "Salem's Antebellum Black Community: Seedbed of the School Integration Movement," *Essex Institute Historical Collections* 108 (1972): 99–118.

Woodson, Carter Godwin, *The Education of the Negro prior to 1861: A History of the Education of the Colored People of the United States from the Beginning of Slavery to the Civil War* (2d ed., 1919).

16.11   WORK AND ENTREPRENEURIAL ACTIVITY

Armstrong, Thomas F., "From Task Labor to Free Labor: The Transition along Georgia's Rice Coast, 1820–1880," *Georgia Historical Quarterly* 64 (1980): 432–47.

Aufhauser, R. Keith, "Slavery and Scientific Management," *Journal of Economic History* 33 (1973): 811–24.

———— "Slavery and Technological Change," *Journal of Economic History* 34 (1974): 36–50.

Berlin, Ira, and Herbert G. Gutman, "Natives and Immigrants, Free Men and Slaves: Urban Workingmen in the Antebellum American South," *American Historical Review* 88 (1983): 1175–200.

Berlin, Ira, and Philip D. Morgan, ed., *The Slaves' Economy: Independent Production by Slaves in the Americas* (1991).

Binder, Wolfgang, "'Oh Ye Daughters of Africa, Awake! Awake! Arise': The Functions of Work and Leisure in Female Slave Narratives," in *Les Etats-Unis: Images du Travail et des Loisirs* (1989): 127–41.

Bishir, Catherine W., "Black Builders in Antebellum North Carolina," *North Carolina Historical Review* 61 (1984): 422–61.

Bolster, W. Jeffrey, *Black Jacks: African-American Seamen in the Age of Sail* (1997).

Bradford, Sydney, "The Negro Ironworker in Antebellum Virginia," *Journal of Southern History* 25 (1959): 194–206.

Bruce, Kathleen, "Slave Labor in the Virginia Iron Industry," *William and Mary Quarterly* 7 (1927): 21–31.

———— *Virginia Iron Manufacture in the Slave Era* (1931).

Burgess, Norma J., and Hayward Derrick Horton, "African American Women and Work: A Socio-Historical Perspective," *Journal of Family History* 18 (1993): 53–63.

Campbell, John, "As 'a Kind of Freeman'? Slaves' Market-Related Activities in the South Carolina Upcountry, 1800–1860," *Slavery and Abolition* 12 (1991): 131–69.

Carll, Allison M., "'Great Neatness of Finish': Slave Carpenters in South Carolina's Charleston District, 1760–1800," *Southern Studies* 26 (1987): 89–100.

Carll-White, Allison M., "South Carolina's Forgotten Craftsman," *South Carolina Historical Magazine* 86 (1985): 32–38.

Chaplin, Joyce E., "Tidal Rice Cultivation and the Problem of Slavery in South Carolina and Georgia, 1760–1815," *William and Mary Quarterly* 49 (1992): 29–61.

Clifton, James M., "The Rice Driver: His Role in Slave Management," *South Carolina Historical Magazine* 82 (1981): 331–53.

Dew, Charles B., "David Ross and the Oxford Iron Works: A Study of Industrial Slavery in the Early Nineteenth Century," *William and Mary Quarterly* 31 (1974): 189–224.

——— "Disciplining Slave Ironworkers in the Antebellum South: Coercion, Conciliation, and Accommodation," *American Historical Review* 79 (1974): 393–418.

Drucker, Lesley M., "Socioeconomic Patterning at an Undocumented Late Eighteenth Century Lowcountry Site: Spiers Landing, South Carolina," *Historical Archaeology* 15 (1981): 58–68.

Eaton, Clement, "Slave-Hiring in the Upper South: A Step toward Freedom," *Mississippi Valley Historical Review* 46 (1960): 663–78.

Eisterhold, John A., "Savannah: Lumber Center of the South Atlantic," *Georgia Historical Quarterly* 57 (1973): 526–43.

Farr, James, "A Slow Boat to Nowhere: The Multi-Racial Crews of the American Whaling Industry," *Journal of Negro History* 68 (1983): 159–70.

Genovese, Eugene D., "The Negro Laborer in Africa and the Slave South," *Phylon* 21 (1960): 343–50.

Gilje, Paul, and Howard B. Rock, "'Sweep O! Sweep O!': African-American Chimney Sweeps and Citizenship in the New Nation," *William and Mary Quarterly* 51 (1994): 507–08.

Green, Barbara L., "Slave Labor at the Maramec Iron Works, 1828–1850," *Missouri Historical Review* 73 (1979): 150–64.

Green, Rodney D., "Black Tobacco Factory Workers and Social Conflict in Antebellum Richmond: Were Slavery and Urban Industry Really Compatible?" *Slavery and Abolition* 8 (1987): 183–203.

Guyette, Elise A., "The Working Lives of African Vermonters in Census and Literature, 1790–1870," *Vermont History* 61 (1993): 69–84.

Hewitt, John H., "Mr. Downing and His Oyster House: The Life and Works of an African-American Entrepreneur," *New York History* 74 (1993): 228–52.

Hughes, Sarah S., "Slaves for Hire: The Allocations of Black Labor in Elizabeth City County, Virginia, 1782–1810," *William and Mary Quarterly* 35 (1978): 260–86.

Ingham, John N., "African-American Business Leaders in the South, 1810–1945: Business Success, Community Leadership, and Racial Protest," *Business and Economic History* 22 (1993): 262–72.

Killick, John R., "The Cotton Operations of Alexander Brown and Sons in the Deep South, 1820–1860," *Journal of Southern History* 43 (1977): 169–94.

Lewis, Ronald L., "'The Darkest Abode of Man': Black Miners in the First Southern Coal Field, 1780–1865," *Virginia Magazine of History and Biography* 87 (1979): 190–202.

Luraghi, Raimondo, "Wage Labor in the 'Rice Belt' of Northern Italy and Slave Labor in the American South: A First Approach," *Southern Studies* 16 (1977): 109–27.

Marks, Bayle E., "Skilled Blacks in Antebellum St. Mary's County, Maryland," *Journal of Southern History* 53 (1987): 537–64.

McGowan, James T., "'Planters without Slaves': Origins of a New World Labor System," *Southern Studies* 16 (1977): 5–26.

Morgan, Philip D., "Work and Culture: The Task System and the World of Lowcountry Blacks, 1700–1880," *William and Mary Quarterly* 39 (1982): 563–99.

Perdue, Robert E., *Black Laborers and Black Professionals in Early America, 1750–1830* (1975).

Putney, Martha S., "Black Merchant Seamen of Newport, 1803–1865: A Case Study in Foreign Commerce," *Journal of Negro History* 57 (1972): 156–68.

Robert, Joseph Clarke, *The Tobacco Kingdom: Plantation, Market, and Factory in Virginia and North Carolina, 1800–1860* (1938).

Schmitzer, Jeanne C., "The Sable Guides of Mammoth Cave," *Filson Club History Quarterly* 67 (1993): 240–58.

Schweninger, Loren, "Black-Owned Businesses in the South, 1790–1880," *Business History Review* 63 (1989): 22–60.

——— "Prosperous Blacks in the South, 1790–1880," *American Historical Review* 95 (1990): 31–56.

——— "Slave Independence and Enterprise in South Carolina, 1780–1865," *South Carolina History Magazine* 93 (1992): 101–25.

Shammas, Carole, "Black Women's Work and the Evolution of Plantation Society in Virginia," *Labor History* 26 (1985): 5–28.

Steffen, Charles G., "Changes in the Organization of Artisan Production in Baltimore, 1790–1820," *William and Mary Quarterly* 36 (1979): 101–17.

Walker, Juliet E. K., "Pioneer Slave Entrepreneurship Patterns, Processes, and Perspectives: The Case of the Slave Free Frank on the Kentucky Pennyroyal, 1795–1819," *Journal of Negro History* 68 (1983): 289–308.

——— "Racism, Slavery, and Free Enterprise: Black Entrepreneurship in the United States before the Civil War," *Business History Review* 60 (1986): 343–82.

16.12   MEDICINE AND HEALTH

Bankole, Katherine Kemi, *Slavery and Medicine: Enslavement and Medical Practices in Antebellum Louisiana* (1998).

Campbell, John, "Work, Pregnancy, and Infant Mortality among Southern Slaves," *Journal of Interdisciplinary History* 14 (1984): 793–812.

Curtin, Philip D., "Epidemiology and the Slave Trade," *Political Science Quarterly* 83 (1968): 190–216.

Engerman, Stanley L., "The Height of Slaves," *Local Population Studies [Great Britain]* 16 (1976): 45–49.

Haller, John S., Jr., "The Negro and the Southern Physician: A Study of Medical and Racial Attitudes, 1800–1860," *Medical History [Great Britain]* 16 (1972): 238–53.

Johnson, Michael P., "Smothered Slave Infants: Were Slave Mothers at Fault?" *Journal of Southern History* 47 (1981): 493–520.

Kiple, Kenneth F., and Virginia Himmelsteib King, *Another Dimension to the Black Diaspora: Diet, Disease, and Racism* (1981).

Kiple, Kenneth F., and Virginia H. Kiple, "The African Connection: Slavery, Disease, and Racism," *Phylon* 41 (1980): 211–22.

——— "Black Tongue and Black Men: Pellagra and Slavery in the Antebellum South," *Journal of Southern History* 43 (1977): 411–28.

——— "Slave Child Mortality: Some Nutritional Answers to a Perennial Puzzle," *Journal of Social History* 10 (1977): 284–309.

Klepp, Susan E., "Seasoning and Society: Racial Differences in Mortality in Eighteenth-Century Philadelphia," *William and Mary Quarterly* 51 (1994): 473–506.

Margo, Robert A., and Richard H. Steckel, "The Heights of American Slaves: New Evidence on Slave Nutrition and Health," *Social Science History* 6 (1982): 516–38.

Moore, Stacy Gibbons, "Established and Well Cultivated: Afro-American Foodways in Early Virginia," *Virginia Cavalcade* 39 (1989): 70–83.

Plummer, Betty L., "Document: Letters of James Durham to Benjamin Rush," *Journal of Negro History* 65 (1980): 261–69.

Pollard, Leslie J., "Aging and Slavery: A Gerontological Perspective," *Journal of Negro History* 66 (1981): 228–34.

Postell, William Dosite, *The Health of Slaves on Southern Plantations* (1951).

Savitt, Todd L., "Black Health on the Plantation: Masters, Slaves, and Physicians," *Medical Heritage* 2 (1986): 368–82.

——— *Medicine and Slavery: The Diseases and Health Care of Blacks in Antebellum Virginia* (1978).

——— "Smothering and Overlaying of Virginia Slave Children: A Suggested Explanation," *Bulletin of the History of Medicine* 49 (1975): 400–04.

——— "The Use of Blacks for Medical Experimentation and Demonstration in the Old South," *Journal of Southern History* 48 (1982): 331–48.

Sikes, Lewright, "Medical Care for Slaves: A Preview of the Welfare State," *Georgia Historical Quarterly* 52 (1968): 405–13.

Steckel, Richard H., "Birth Weights and Infant Mortality among American Slaves," *Explorations in Economic History* 23 (1986): 173–98.

———— "A Dreadful Childhood: The Excess Mortality of American Slaves," *Social Science History* 10 (1986): 427–65.

———— "A Peculiar Population: The Nutrition, Health, and Mortality of American Slaves from Childhood to Maturity," *Journal of Economic History* 46 (1986): 721–41.

Whitten, David O., "Medical Care of Slaves: Louisiana Sugar Region and South Carolina Rice District," *Southern Studies* 16 (1977): 153–80.

Wilson, Mary Tolford, "Peaceful Integration: The Owner's Adoption of His Slave's Food," *Journal of Negro History* 49 (1964): 116–27.

16.13 STUDIES IN FOREIGN LANGUAGES

Boden, Quinibert Philippe, *La vie intellectuelle des Noirs de la Caroline du Nord: et la partie d'influence qu'y apperte la connaissance de la langue et de la litterature française* [Black Intellectual Life in North Carolina: The Parts of the Influence Which Appear to Be Informed by French Language and Literature] (1925). In French.

Cao, Wenjuan, "Mei Guo Shang Pin Nu Li Zhi Xing Zhi Xi" [An Analysis of Chattel Slavery in the United States], *Shi Jie Li Shi* 2 (1984): 41–9. In Chinese.

Chase, Jeanne, and Jonathan Mendelbaum, "Serviteurs Fugitifs et Police des Deplacements dans la Province de New York au XVIIIe Siecle [Fugitive Servants and the Regulation of Displacement in Eighteenth-Century New York]" *Revue d'Histoire Moderne et Contemporaine* 33 (1986): 21–39. In French.

Diedrich, Maria, *Ausbruch aus der Knechtschaft: Die Amerikanische Slave Narrative zwischen Unabhängigkeitserklärung und Bürgerkrieg* [Breaking out of Servitude: The American Slave Narrative between the Declaration of Independence and the Civil War] (1986). In German.

Endo, Yasuo, "Kakumei-ki Vâjinia ni okeru Kokujin Dorei Seido: Hito to Hito tono Kankei-shi ni Itaru Izen" [The Problems of Black Slavery in Revolutionary Virginia: Preliminary Thoughts on the Sociabilités of Black Slavery], *Studies in Language and Culture (Nagoya University)* 12 (1990): 79–94. In Japanese.

Fabre, Geneviève, "Ésclaves de la liberté: les noirs, l'Indépendance et la révolution" [The Slaves of Freedom: Blacks, Independence, and Revolution], in Bernard Vincent and Elise Marienstras, ed., *Les oubliés de la Révolution américaine* [The Forgotten of the American Revolution] (1990): 55–98. In French.

———— "Temps de fête, éspace de liberté" [Times of Celebration: The Space of Freedom], in Barbara Karsky and Elise Marienstras, ed., *Travail et loisir dans les sociétés pré-industrielles* [Work and Leisure in Pre-Industrial Societies] (1991): 161–74. In French.

Fodde, Luisanna, *Autobiografie neri nell'America dell'Ottocento* [Black Autobiographies in Eighteenth-Century America] (1982). In Italian.

Forster, Robert, *Erscheinungsformen der Plantagensklaverei im 18. Jahrhundert* [Manifestations of Plantation Slavery in the Eighteenth Century] (1990). In German.

Ginzburg Migliorino, Ellen, *Gli Afro-americani, 1773–1849* [The Afro-Americans, 1773–1849] (vol. 1, 1985). In Italian.

Hall, Gwendolyn Midlo, "Raza y Libertad: La Manumision de los Esclavos Rurales de la Luisiana bajo la Jurisdiccion del Capitan General de Cuba" [Race and Freedom: Manumission of Rural Slaves in Louisiana during the Rule of the Captain General of Cuba], *Anuario de Estudios Americanos [Spain]* 43 (1986): 365–76. In Spanish.

Isaac, Marie-Therese, "Le Probleme du 'Negre-Esclave': Le Temoignage du Marquis de Chastellux et la Polemique de 1786" [The Problem of the 'Black Slave': The Testimony of the Marquis de Chastellux and the Polemic of 1786], *University of Ottawa Quarterly* 56 (1986): 81–97. In French.

Kikuchi, Ken'ichi, *Amerika no Zen-shihon-sei* [Pre-Capitalist Regime in the United States: The Plantation System of the Post-Bellum South] (1955). In Japanese.

Li, Qing, "Shi Jiu Shi Ji Mei Guo Tao Nu Wen Ti Chu Tan" [A Preliminary Study of Fugitive Slaves in the Nineteenth Century United States], *Shi Jie Li Shi* 2 (1985): 10–17. In Chinese.

Martin, Jean-Pierre, *Une Institution particulière: aspects de l'ésclavage aux États-Unis* [A Particular Institution: Aspects of Slavery in the United States] (1986). In French.

Martin, Peter, *Das Rebellische Eigentum: Vom Kampf der Afroamerikaner gegen Ihre Versklavung* [Rebellious Property: The Struggle of the Afro-Americans against Their Enslavement] (1985). In German.

Mattiello, Cristina, "'I maschi non c'entrano per niente': predicatrici e profete nere nell'America dell'Ottocento" ['Man Have Nothing to Do with It': African-American Women Preachers and Prophets in the Nineteenth Century], *Rivista Internazionale di Studi Nordamericani [International Journal of North American Studies]* 1 (1995): 24–8. In Italian.

Molinski, Bogdan, "Liberia: Poczatki Osadnictwa Murzynsko-Amerykanskiego W Afryce" [Liberia: The Beginning of Negro-American Settlement in Africa], *Przeglad Socjologiczny* 21 (1967): 231–48. In Polish.

Nishide, Keiichi, "'Amerika' Kokujin Dorei-sei Kenkyu to Dorei-sei no Joséi-shi" [The Place of Women's History in the Study of Slavery], *The American Review* 26 (1992): 49–65. In Japanese.

Nishikawa, Susumu, "Dorei no Shûkyô to Hankô" [Slave Religion and Rebellion], *The Journal of Fukuoka University of Education (Social Studies)* 32 (1984): 31–56. In Japanese.

Rossignol, Marie-Jeanne, "La Premiere Constitution d'Haiti et la Presse Americaine: Etude de Cas" [The First Constitution of Haiti and the American Press: A Case Study], *Revue Francaise d'Etudes Americaines* 52 (1992): 149–60. In French.

Sundstral, Franz, *Aus der Schwarzen Republik: Der Neger-Aufstand auf Santo Domingo, oder die Entstehungs-geschichte des Staates Haiti* [From the Black Republic: The Negro-Insurrection in Santo Domingo, or the History of the State of Haiti's Formation] (1903). In German.

Tang, Taohua, "Mei Guo Nu Li Zhi Shi Fou Shi Ren Ci De Nu Li Zhi?" [Was American Slavery a Benevolent Slavery?], *Huanan Shiyuan Xuebao* 1 (1979): 47–54. In Chinese.

—— *Mei Guo Li Shi Shang De Hei Ren Nu Li Zhi* [Black Slavery in the History of the United States] (1980). In Chinese.

17   1831–1865 (South)

STEPHANIE SHAW

17.1   GENERAL STUDIES

Abzug, Robert H., and Stephen E. Maizlish, ed., *New Perspectives on Race and Slavery in America: Essays in Honor of Kenneth M. Stampp* (1986).

Bynum, Victoria, *Unruly Women: The Politics of Social and Sexual Control in the Old South* (1992).

Campbell, Edward D. C., Jr., and Kym S. Rice, ed., *Before Freedom Came: African-American Life in the Antebellum South, to Accompany an Exhibition Organized by the Museum of the Confederacy* (1991).

Foner, Philip S., *History of Black Americans: From the Emergence of the Cotton Kingdom to the Eve of the Compromise of 1850* (1983).

Franklin, John Hope, *The Militant South, 1800–1861* (1956).

——— "Slavery and the Martial South," *Journal of Negro History* 37 (1952): 36–53.

——— "Two Worlds of Race: A Historical View," *Daedalus* 94 (1965): 899–920.

Fredrickson, George M., *The Arrogance of Race: Historical Perspectives on Slavery, Racism, and Social Inequality* (1988).

Litwack, Leon F., "Trouble in Mind: The Bicentennial and the Afro-American Experience," *Journal of American History* 74 (1987): 315–37.

Miller, Elinor, and Eugene D. Genovese, ed., *Plantation, Town, and County: Essays on the Local History of American Slave Society* (1974).

Nelson, Alice Dunbar, "People of Color in Louisiana, Part One and Two," *Journal of Negro History* 1, 2 (1916, 1917): 361–76, 51–78.

Oakes, James, *Slavery and Freedom: An Interpretation of the Old South* (1990).

Smallwood, James, "Blacks in Antebellum Texas: A Reappraisal," *Red River Valley Historical Review* 2 (1975): 443–65.

Smith, Elbert B., *The Death of Slavery: The United States, 1837–1865* (1967).

Thorpe, Earl E., *Eros and Freedom in Southern Life and Thought* (1967).

——— *The Old South: A Psychohistory* (1972).

17.2   HISTORIOGRAPHY

Anderson, James D., "Aunt Jemima in Dialectics: Genovese on Slave Culture," *Journal of Negro History* 61 (1976): 99–114.

Aptheker, Herbert, "'Resistance and Afro-American History': Some Notes on Contemporary Historiography and Suggestions for Further Research," in Gary Y. Okihiro, ed., *In Resistance: Studies in African, Caribbean, and Afro-American History* (1986): 10–20.

Blassingame, John W., "The Planter on the Couch: Earl Thorpe and the Psychodynamics of Slavery," *Journal of Negro History* 60 (1975): 320–31.

Crowe, Charles Robert, *Slavery, Race, and American Scholarship: Explorations in Historiography* (1988).

Douglas, Robert L., "Myth or Truth: A Black and White View of Slavery," *Journal of Black Studies* 19 (1989): 343–60.

Drimmer, Melvin, "Thoughts on the Study of Slavery in the Americas and the Writing of Black History," *Phylon* 36 (1975): 125–39.

Eder, Donald G., "Time under the Southern Cross," *Agricultural History* 50 (1976): 600–14.

Engerman, Stanley L., "Slavery and Emancipation in Comparative Perspective: A Look at Some Recent Debates," *Journal of Economic History* 46 (1986): 317–39.

———— "Studying the Black Family, a Review Essay of *The Black Family* by Herbert S. Gutman," *Journal of Interdisciplinary History* 3 (1978): 78–101.

Fink, Leon, George Rawick, and Evelyn Brooks, "A Symposium on Herbert Gutman's *The Black Family in Slavery and Freedom*," *Radical History Review* 4 (1977): 76–108.

Finley, M. I., "Slavery and the Historians," *Social History* 12 (1979): 247–61.

Fogel, Robert, "Cliometrics and Culture: Some Recent Developments in the Historiography of Slavery," *Journal of Social History* 11 (1977): 34–51.

Foner, Eric, "Redefining the Past," *Labor History* 16 (1975): 127–38.

Foner, Eric, Michael Greenberg, Eric Perkins, and Fred Siegel, "Symposium on *Roll, Jordan, Roll*," *Radical History Review* 3 (1976): 26–67.

Foster, Gaines M., "Guilt over Slavery: A Historiographical Analysis," *Journal of Southern History* 56 (1990): 665–94.

Genovese, Eugene D., "Materialism and Idealism in the History of Negro Slavery in the Americas," *Journal of Social History* 1 (1968): 371–94.

Gilmore, Al-Tony, ed., *Revisiting Blassingame's* The Slave Community: *The Scholars Respond* (1978).

Gross, James A., "Historians and the Literature of the Negro Worker," *Labor History* 10 (1969): 536–46.

Gross, Seymour L., and Eileen Bender, "History, Politics, and Literature: The Myth of Nat Turner," *American Quarterly* 23 (1971): 487–518.

Gutman, Herbert G., "Persistent Myths about the Afro-American Family," *Journal of Interdisciplinary History* 6 (1975): 181–210.

Hall, Jacquelyn Dowd, "Partial Truths: Writing Southern Women's History," in Virginia Bernhard, Betty Brandon, Elizabeth Fox-Genovese and Theda Purdue, ed., *Southern Women: Histories and Identities* (1992): 11–29.

Halliburton, R., Jr., "Free Black Owners of Slaves: A Reappraisal of the Woodson Thesis," *South Carolina Historical Magazine* 76 (1975): 129–42.

Hofstadter, Richard, "U. B. Philips and the Plantation Legend," *Journal of Negro History* 29 (1944): 109–24.

Huggins, Nathan Irvin, "The Deforming Mirror of Truth: Slavery and the Master Narrative of American History," *Radical History Review* 49 (1991): 25–48.

Karras, Alan L., "Of Human Bondage: Creating an Atlantic History of Slavery," *Journal of Interdisciplinary History* 22 (1991): 285–293.

Kolchin, Peter, "American Historians and Antebellum Southern Slavery, 1959–1984," in William J. Cooper, Jr., Michael F. Holt and John McCardell, ed., *A Master's Due: Essays in Honor of David Herbert Donald* (1985): 87–111.

———— "More Time on the Cross? An Evaluation of Robert William Fogel's *Without Consent or Contract*," *Journal of Southern History* 58 (1992): 491–502.

Kugler, Ruben F., "U. B. Phillips' Use of Sources," *Journal of Negro History* 47 (1962): 153–68.

Lachance, Paul, "Use and Misuse of the Slave Community Paradigm," *Canadian Review of American Studies* 17 (1986): 449–58.

Lane, Ann J., ed., *The Debate over Slavery: Stanley Elkins and His Critics* (1971).

Lichtenstein, Alex, "Industrial Slavery and the Tragedy of Robert Starobin," *Reviews in American History* 19 (1991): 604–17.

Lynd, Staughton, "Rethinking Slavery and Reconstruction," *Journal of Negro History* 50 (1965): 198–209.

Modell, John, Stephen Gudeman, and Warren C. Sanderson, "A Colloquium on Herbert Gutman's *The Black Family in Slavery and Freedom, 1750–1925*," *Social Science History* 3 (1979): 45–85.

Mohr, Clarence L., "Southern Blacks in the Civil War: A Century of Historiography," *Journal of Negro History* 39 (1974): 177–95.

Olson, James S., *Slave Life in America: A Historiography and Selected Bibliography* (1983).

Owens, Leslie H., "The African in the Garden: Reflections about New World Slavery and Its Lifelines," in Darlene Clark Hine, ed., *The State of Afro-American History: Past, Present, and Future* (1986): 25–37.

Parish, Peter J., *Slavery: History and Historians* (1989).

Preyer, Norris W., "The Historian, the Slave, and the Antebellum Textile Industry," *Journal of Negro History* 46 (1961): 67–82.

Rankin, David C., "The Tannenbaum Thesis Reconsidered: Slavery and Race Relations in Antebellum Louisiana," *Southern Studies* 18 (1979): 5–31.

Shapiro, Herbert, "Historiography and Slave Revolt and Rebelliousness in the United States: A Class Approach," in Gary Y. Okihiro, ed., *In Resistance: Studies in African, Caribbean, and Afro-American History* (1986): 133–42.

Stampp, Kenneth M., "The Historians and Southern Negro Slavery," *American Historical Review* 57 (1952): 613–24.

Sutch, Richard, "The Treatment Received by American Slaves: A Critical Review of the Evidence Presented in *Time on the Cross*," *Explorations in Economic History* 12 (1975): 335–438.

Wesley, Charles H., "Creating and Maintaining an Historical Tradition," *Journal of Negro History* 49 (1964): 13–33.

Woodman, Harold D., "The Profitability of Slavery: A Historical Perennial," *Journal of Southern History* 29 (1963): 303–25.

17.3   SECONDARY SOURCES ON NEWSPAPERS AND PERIODICALS

Blassingame, John W., and Mae G. Henderson, ed., *Antislavery Newspapers and Periodicals: Vol. II, 1835–1865, Annotated Index of Letters in the* Liberator, Anti-Slavery Record, Human Rights, *and the* Observer (1980).

Bullock, Penelope L., *The Afro-American Periodical Press, 1838–1909* (1981).

Hutton, Frankie, *The Early Black Press in America, 1827 to 1860* (1993).

——— "Social Morality in the Antebellum Black Press," *Journal of Popular Culture* 26 (1992): 71–84.

Jacobs, Donald M., ed., *Antebellum Black Newspapers: Indices to* New York Freedom's Journal *(1827–1829),* The Rights of All *(1829),* The Weekly Advocate *(1837), and* The Colored American *(1837–1841)* (1976).

17.4   RACE RELATIONS

17.4.1   Slave Trade

Bancroft, Frederic, *Slave Trading in the Old South* (1931).

Barker, Eugene C., "The African Slave Trade in Texas," *Southwestern Historical Quarterly* 6 (1902): 145–58.

Bernstein, Barton J., "Southern Politics and Attempts to Reopen the African Slave Trade," *Journal of Negro History* 51 (1966): 16–35.

Calderhead, William, "How Extensive Was the Border State Slave Trade? A New Look," *Civil War History* 18 (1972): 42–55.

Carstensen, F. V., and S. E. Goodman, "Trouble on the Auction Block: Interregional Slave Sales and the Reliability of a Linear Equation," *Journal of Interdisciplinary History* 8 (1977): 315–18.

Clark, T. D., "The Slave Trade between Kentucky and the Cotton Kingdom," *Mississippi Valley History Review* 21 (1934): 331–42.

Collins, Winfield Hazlitt, *The Domestic Slave Trade of the Southern States* (1904).

Curtin, Philip D., *The Atlantic Slave Trade: A Census* (1969).

Davis, Jack E., "Changing Places: Slave Movements in the South," *Historian* 55 (1993): 656–76.

Davis, Robert Ralph, Jr., "Buchanian Espionage: A Report on Illegal Slave Trading in the South in 1859," *Journal of Southern History* 37 (1971): 271–78.

Dodd, Dorothy, "The Schooner Emperor: An Incident of the Illegal Slave Trade in Florida," *Florida Historical Society Quarterly* 13 (1935): 117–28.

Du Bois, William Edward Burghardt, *The Supression of the African Slave-Trade to the United States of America, 1638–1870* (1896).

Eltis, David, "Free and Coerced Transatlantic Migrations: Some Comparisons," *American Historical Review* 88 (1983): 251–80.

Eltis, David, and Stanley Engerman, "Fluctuations in Sex and Age Ratios in the Transatlantic Slave Trade, 1663–1864," *Economic History Review* 46 (1993): 308–23.

Eltis, David, and James Walvin, ed., *The Abolition of the Atlantic Slave Trade: Origins and Effects in Europe, Africa, and the Americas* (1981).

Fornell, Earl W., "The Abduction of Free Negroes and Slaves in Texas," *Southwestern Historical Quarterly* 60 (1957): 369–80.

——— "Agitation in Texas for Reopening the Slave Trade," *Southwestern Historical Quarterly* 60 (1956): 245–59.

Freudenberger, Herman and Jonathan B. Pritchett, "The Domestic United States Slave Trade: New Evidence," *Journal of Interdisciplinary History* 21 (1991): 447–77.

Fyfe, Christopher, "The Dynamics of African Dispersal: The Transatlantic Slave Trade," in Martin L. Kilson and Robert I. Rotberg, ed., *The African Diaspora: Interpretive Essays* (1976): 57–75.

"Georgia and the African Slave Trade: Justice Jones M. Wayne's Charge to the Grand Jury in 1859," *Georgia Historical Quarterly* 2 (1918): 87–114.

Goldfarb, Stephen J., "An Inquiry into the Politics of the Prohibition of the International Slave Trade," *Agriculture History* 68 (1994): 20–34.

Gutman, Herbert G. and Richard Sutch, "The Slave Family: Protected Agent of Capitalist Masters or Victim of the Slave Trade?" in Paul A. David, Herbert G. Gutman, Richard Sutch, Peter Temin and Gavin Wright, ed., *Reckoning with Slavery: A Critical Study in the Quantitative History of American Negro Slavery* (1976): 94–133.

Hendrix, James Paisley, Jr., "The Efforts to Reopen the African Slave Trade in Louisiana," *Louisiana History* 10 (1969): 97–123.

Inikori, J. E., "Measuring the Atlantic Slave Trade: An Assessment of Curtin and Anstey," *Journal of African History* 17 (1976): 197–223.

Johnson, Walter, *Soul by Soul: Life Inside the Antebellum Slave Market* (1999).

Lightner, Donald L., "The Interstate Slave Trade in Antislavery Politics," *Civil War History* 36 (1990): 119–36.

Littlefield, Daniel F., Jr., "Charleston and Internal Slave Redistribution," *South Carolina Historical Magazine* 87 (1986): 93–105.

Lowe, Richard G., and Randolph B. Campbell, "The Slave-Breeding Hypothesis: A Demographic Comment on the 'Buying' and 'Selling' States," *Journal of Southern History* 42 (1976): 401–12.

McMillan, Richard, "Savannah's Coastal Slave Trade: A Quantitative Analysis of Ship Manifests, 1840–1850," *Georgia Historical Quarterly* 78 (1994): 339–59.

Miller, William L., "A Note on the Importance of the Interstate Slave Trade of the Antebellum South," *Journal of Political Economy* 73 (1965): 181–87.

Minchinton, Walter E., "The Seaborne Slave Trade of North Carolina," *North Carolina Historical Review* 71 (1994): 1–61.

Pritchett, Jonathan B., and Richard M. Chamberlain, "Selection in the Market for Slaves: New Orleans, 1830–1860," *Quarterly Journal of Economics* 108 (1993): 461–73.

Pritchett, Jonathan B., and Herman Freudenberger, "A Peculiar Sample: The Selection of Slaves for the New Orleans Market," *Journal of Economic History* 52 (1992): 109–27.

Rawley, James A., *The Transatlantic Slave Trade: A History* (1981).

Reilly, Kevin S., "Slavers in Disguise: American Whaling and the African Slave Trade, 1845–1862," *American Neptune* 53 (1993): 177–89.

Reynolds, Edward, *Stand the Storm: A History of the Atlantic Slave Trade* (1985).

Schwarz, Philip J., "The Transportation of Slaves from Virginia, 1801–1865," *Slavery and Abolition* 7 (1986): 215–40.

Smith, Julia Floyd, "Slave Trading in Antebellum Florida," *Florida Historical Quarterly* 50 (1971): 252–61.

Stafford, Frances, "Illegal Importations: Enforcement of the Slave Trade Laws along the Florida Coast, 1810–1828," *Florida Historical Quarterly* 46 (1967): 124–33.

Sutch, Richard C., "The Breeding of Slaves for Sale and the Westward Expansion of Slavery, 1850–1860," in Stanley L. Engerman and Eugene D. Genovese, ed., *Race and Slavery in the Western Hemisphere: Quantitative Studies* (1975): 173–210.

Tadman, Michael, "Slave Trading in the Antebellum South: An Estimate of the Extent of the Inter-Regional Slave Trade," *Journal of American Studies [UK]* 13 (1979): 195–220.

——— "Slave Trading and the Mentalities of Masters and Slaves in Ante-Bellum America," in Leonie J. Archer, *Slavery and Other Forms of Unfree Labor* (1988): 188–205.

——— *Speculators and Slaves: Masters, Traders, and Slaves in the Old South* (1989).

Takaki, Ronald T., "The Movement to Reopen the African Slave Trade in South Carolina," *South Carolina Historical Magazine* 66 (1965): 38–54.

——— *A Pro-Slavery Crusade: The Agitation to Reopen the African Slave Trade* (1971).

Taylor, Alrutheus A., "The Movement of the Negroes from the East to the Gulf States from 1830 to 1850," *Journal of Negro History* 8 (1923): 367–83.

Taylor, Joe G., "The Foreign Slave Trade in Louisiana after 1808," *Louisiana History* 1 (1960): 36–43.

Trexler, Harrison Anthony, "The Value and the Sale of the Missouri Slave," *Missouri Historical Review* 8 (1914): 69–85.

Walvin, James, *Slavery and the Slave Trade: A Short Illustrated History* (1983).

Wells, Tom Henderson, *The Slave Ship Wanderer* (1967).

Wesley, Charles H., "Manifests of Slave Shipments along the Waterways, 1808–1864," *Journal of Negro History* 27 (1942): 155–74.

Wish, Harvey, "The Revival of the African Slave Trade in the United States, 1856–1860," *Mississippi Valley History Review* 27 (1941): 569–88.

17.4.2 Slavery

Abzug, Robert H., and Stephen E. Maizlish, ed., *New Perspectives on Race and Slavery in America: Essays in Honor of Kenneth M. Stampp* (1986).

Africa, Philip, "Slaveholding in the Salem Community, 1771–1851," *North Carolina Historical Review* 54 (1977): 271–307.

Andrews, William L., and Henry Louis Gates, Jr., ed., *The Civitas Anthology of African American Slave Narratives* (1999).

Archer, Leonie J., ed., *Slavery and Other Forms of Unfree Labor* (1988).

Bailey, Ronald, "The Other Side of Slavery: Black Labor, Cotton, and Textile Industrialization in Great Britain and the United States," *Agriculture History* 68 (1994): 35–50.

Baker, T. Lindsay, and Julie P. Baker, ed., *Till Freedom Cried Out: Memories of Texas Slave Life* (1997).

Ballagh, James Curtis, *A History of Slavery in Virginia* (1902).

Barker, Eugene C., "The Influence of Slavery in the Colonization of Texas," *Southwestern Historical Quarterly* 28 (1924): 1–33.

Bassett, John Spencer, *Slavery in the State of North Carolina* (1899).

Bayliss, John F., ed., *Black Slave Narratives* (1970).

Beasley, Jonathan, "Blacks—Slave and Free—Vicksburg, 1850–1860," *Journal of Mississippi History* 38 (1976): 1–32.

Bellamy, Donnie D., "Slavery in Microcosm: Onslow Court, North Carolina," *Journal of Negro History* 62 (1977): 339–50.

Bellamy, Donnie D., and Diane E. Walker, "Slaveholding in Antebellum Augusta and Richmond County, Georgia," *Phylon* 48 (1987): 165–77.

Bentley, Martha M., "The Slaveholding Catawbas," *South Carolina Historical Magazine* 92 (1991): 85–98.

Berwanger, Eugene H., comp., *As They Saw Slavery* (1973).

———— "The Case of Stirrup and Edwards, 1861–1870: The Kidnapping and Georgia Enslavement of West Indian Blacks," *Georgia Historical Quarterly* 76 (1992): 1–18.

Billington, Ray Allen, "A Social Experiment: The Port Royal Journal of Charlotte L. Forten, 1862–1863," *Journal of Negro History* 35 (1950): 233–64.

Blackford, John, *Ferry Hill Plantation Journal: January 4, 1838 to January 15, 1839*, ed. Fletcher M. Wright Green (1961).

Blassingame, John W., *The Slave Community: Plantation Life in the Antebellum South* (rev. ed., 1979).

———— "Status and Social Structure in the Slave Community: Evidence from New Sources," in Harry P. Owens, ed., *Perspectives and Irony in American Slavery* (1976): 137–51.

Brackett, Jeffrey Richardson, *The Negro in Maryland: A Study of the Institution of Slavery* (1889).

Breeden, James O., ed., *Advice among Masters: The Ideal in Slave Management in the Old South* (1980).

Brown, Richard D., Lawrence B. Goodheart, and Stephen G. Rabe, ed., *Slavery in American Society* (1993).

Bullock, Henry Allen, "A Hidden Passage in the Slave Regime," in James C. Curtis and Lewis L. Gould, ed., *The Black Experience in America: Selected Essays* (1970): 3–32.

Burnham, Dorothy, "The Life of the Afro-American Woman in Slavery," *International Journal of Womens Studies* 1 (1978): 363–77.

Cade, John B., "Out of the Mouths of Ex-Slaves," *Journal of Negro History* 20 (1935): 294–337.

Campbell, Randolph B., *An Empire for Slavery: The Peculiar Institution in Texas, 1821–1865* (1989).

———— "Human Property: The Negro Slave in Harrison County, 1850–1860," *Southwestern Historical Quarterly* 76 (1973): 384–96.

Carriere, Marius, Jr., "Blacks in Pre-Civil War Memphis," *Tennessee Historical Quarterly* 48 (1989): 3–14.

Cimprich, John, *Slavery's End in Tennessee, 1861–1865* (1985).

Clifton, James M., ed., *Life and Labor on Argyle Island: Letters and Documents of a Savannah River Rice Plantation, 1833–1867* (1978).

Coleman, J. W., Jr., *Slavery Times in Kentucky* (1940).

Corlew, Robert E., "Some Aspects of Slavery in Dickson County," *Tennessee Historical Quarterly* 10 (1951): 224–48, 344–65.

Coulter, E. Merton, "Slavery and Freedom in Athens, Georgia, 1860–1866," *Georgia Historical Quarterly* 49 (1965): 264–93.

Craton, Michael, ed., *Roots and Branches: Current Directions in Slave Studies* (1979).

David, Paul A., Herbert Gutman, Richard Sutch, Peter Temin, and Gavin Wright, ed., *Reckoning with Slavery: A Critical Study in the Quantitative History of American Negro Slavery* (1976).

Davis, Angela, "Reflections on the Black Woman's Role in the Community of Slaves," *Black Scholar* 3 (1971): 2–16.

Davis, Edwin Adams, *Plantation Life in the Florida Parishes of Louisiana, 1836–1846, As Reflected in the Diary of Bennet H. Barrow* (1943).

Degler, Carl N., *Neither Black nor White: Slavery and Race Relations in Brazil and the United States* (1971).

———— "Slavery in Brazil and the United States: An Essay in Comparative History," *American Historical Review* 75 (1970): 1004–28.

Dorsett, Lyle Wesley, "Slaveholding in Jackson County, Missouri," *Missouri Historical Society Bulletin* 20 (1963): 25–37.

Durrill, Wayne K., "Slavery, Kinship, and Dominance: The Black Community at Somerset Place Plantation, 1786–1860," *Slavery and Abolition* 13 (1992): 1–19.

Dusinberre, William, *Them Dark Days: Slavery in the American Rice Swamps* (1996).

Edwards, Gary T., "'Negroes . . . and All Other Animals': Slaves and Masters in Antebellum Madison County," *Tennessee Historical Quarterly* 57 (1998): 24–35.

Elkins, Stanley M., "The Slavery Debate," *Commentary* 60 (1975): 40–54.

———— *Slavery: A Problem in American Institutional and Intellectual Life* (3d rev. ed., 1976).

———— "The Social Consequence of Slavery," in Nathan I. Huggins, Martin Kilson and Daniel M. Fox, ed., *Key Issues in the Afro-American Experience* (vol. 1, 1971): 138–53.

Eltis, David, "Europeans and the Rise and Fall of African Slavery in the Americas: An Interpretation," *American Historical Review* 98 (1993): 1399–423.

Engerman, Stanley L., "Some Economic and Demographic Comparisons of Slavery in the United States and the British West Indies," *Economic History Review [Great Britain]* 29 (1976): 258–75.

Escott, Paul D., *Slavery Remembered: A Record of Twentieth-Century Slave Narratives* (1979).

Faust, Drew Gilpin, "Culture, Conflict and Community: The Meaning of Power on an Antebellum Plantation," *Journal of Social History* 14 (1980): 83–98.

———— *James Henry Hammond and the Old South: A Design for Mastery* (1982).

Fede, Andrew, "Legitimized Violent Slave Abuse in the American South, 1619–1865: A Case Study of Law and Social Change in Six Southern States," *American Journal of Legal History* 29 (1985): 93–150.

Feldstein, Stanley, *Once a Slave: The Slaves' View of Slavery* (1971).

Fenn, Elizabeth A., "'A Perfect Equality Seemed to Reign': Slave Society and Jonkonnu," *North Carolina Historical Review* 65 (1988): 127–53.

Finkelman, Paul, ed., *State Slavery Statutes* (1989).

Flanders, Ralph B., *Plantation Slavery in Georgia* (1933).

———— "Planters' Problems in Ante-Bellum Georgia," *Georgia Historical Quarterly* 14 (1930): 17–40.

Foner, Laura, and Eugene D. Genovese, ed., *Slavery in the New World: A Reader in Comparative History* (1969).

Franklin, John Hope, "The Enslavement of Free Negroes in North Carolina," *Journal of Negro History* 29 (1944): 401–28.

———— "Slaves Virtually Free in Antebellum North Carolina," *Journal of Negro History* 28 (1943): 284–310.

Franklin, Vincent P., "Slavery, Personality, and Black Culture: Some Theoretical Issues," *Phylon* 35 (1974): 54–63.

Freyre, Gilberto, *The Masters and the Slaves: A Study in the Development of Brazilian Civilization* (1946).

Gehrke, William Herman, "Negro Slavery among the Germans in North Carolina," *North Carolina Historical Review* 14 (1937): 307–24.

Genovese, Eugene D., *Roll, Jordan, Roll: The World the Slaves Made* (1974).

———— "The Slave States of North America," David W. Cohen and Jack P. Greene, ed., *Neither Slave nor Free: The Freedmen of African Descent in the Slave Societies of the New World* (1972): 258–77.

———— *The World the Slaveholders Made: Two Essays in Interpretation* (rev. ed., 1988).

Gutman, Herbert G. and Richard Sutch, "Victorians All? The Sexual Mores and Conduct of Slaves and Their Masters," in Paul A. David, Herbert G. Gutman, Richard Sutch, Peter Temin and Gavin Wright, ed., *Reckoning with Slavery: A Critical Study in the Quantitative History of American Negro Slavery* (1976): 134–64.

Halliburton, R., Jr., *Red over Black: Black Slavery among the Cherokee Indians* (1977).

Harris, J. William, *Plain Folk and Gentry in a Slave Society: White Liberty and Black Slavery in Augusta's Hinterlands* (1985).

Harrison, Lowell Hayes, "Recollections of Some Tennessee Slaves," *Tennessee Historical Quarterly* 33 (1974): 175–90.

Hartman, Saidiya V., *Scenes of Subjection: Terror, Slavery, and Self-Making in Nineteenth-Century America* (1997).

Henry, Howell Meadoes, *The Police Control of the Slave in South Carolina* (1914).

Hine, William C., "American Slavery and Russian Serfdom: A Preliminary Comparison," *Phylon* 36 (1975): 378–84.

Hoetink, Harmannus, "Master-Slave Relations and Race Relations," in Richard D. Brown and Stephen G. Rabe, ed., *Slavery in American Society* (1969).

Holbrook, Abigail Curlee, "A Glimpse of Life in Antebellum Slave Plantations," *Southwestern Historical Quarterly* 76 (1973): 361–83.

Huggins, Nathan Irvin, *Black Odyssey: The Afro-American Ordeal in Slavery* (1977).

Hunter, Frances L., "Slave Society on the Southern Plantation," *Journal of Negro History* 7 (1922): 1–10.

Hurt, R. Douglass, "Planters and Slavery in Little Dixie," *Missouri Historical Review* 88 (1994): 397–415.

Inscoe, John C., "Mountain Masters: Slaveholding in Western North Carolina," *North Carolina Historical Review* 61 (1984): 143–73.

—— *Mountain Masters, Slavery, and the Sectional Crisis in Western North Carolina* (1989).

Jackson, Luther P., "Manumission in Certain Virginia Cities," *Journal of Negro History* 15 (1930): 278–314.

Jacoby, Karl, "Slaves by Nature? Domestic Animals and Human Slaves," *Slavery and Abolition* 15 (1994): 89–99.

Jennings, Thelma, "'Us Colored Women Had to Go through a Plenty': Sexual Exploitation of African-American Slave Women," *Journal of Women's History* 1 (1990): 45–74.

Johnston, James Hugo, "A New Interpretation of the Domestic Slave System," *Journal of Negro History* 18 (1933): 39–45.

Jones, J. Ralph, and Tom Landess, ed., "Portraits of Georgia Slaves," *Georgia Review* 22 (1968): 125–27, 254–47.

Jones, Norrece T., Jr., *Born a Child of Freedom, Yet a Slave: Mechanisms of Control and Strategies of Resistance in Antebellum South Carolina* (1990).

Jordan, Weymouth T., *Hugh Davis and His Alabama Plantation* (1948).

Joyner, Charles W., *Down by the Riverside: A South Carolina Slave Community* (1984).

—— *Remember Me: Slave Life in Coastal Georgia* (1989).

Kemble, Frances Anne, *Journal of a Residence on a Georgian Plantation in 1838–1839* (1863).

Kendall, John Smith, "New Orleans' 'Peculiar Institution,'" *Louisiana History Quarterly* 23 (1940): 864–86.

Kerrigan, William T., "Race, Expansion, and Slavery in Eagle Pass, Texas, 1852," *Southwestern Historical Quarterly* 101 (1998): 275–302.

King, Willis J., *Stolen Childhood: Slave Youth in Nineteenth-Century America* (1995).

Klein, Herbert S., *Slavery in the Americas: A Comparative Study of Virginia and Cuba* (1967).

Kolchin, Peter, *American Slavery, 1619–1877* (1993).

—— "Reevaluating the Antebellum Slave Community: A Comparative Perspective," *Journal of American History* 70 (1983): 579–601.

—— "Toward a Reinterpretation of Slavery," *Journal of Social History* 9 (1975): 99–113.

—— *Unfree Labor: American Slavery and Russian Serfdom* (1987).

Kotlikoff, Laurence J., and Anton J. Rupert, "The Manumission of Slaves in New Orleans," *Southern Studies* 19 (1980): 172–81.

Lane, Ann J., ed., *The Debate over Slavery: Stanley Elkins and His Critics* (1971).

LeBlanc, John R., "The Context of Manumission: Imperial Rome and Antebellum Alabama," *Alabama Review* 46 (1993): 266–87.

Lee, George R., "Slavery and Emancipation in Lewis County, Missouri," *Missouri Historical Review* 65 (1971): 294–317.

Lewis, Mary Agnes, "Slavery and Personality: A Further Comment," *American Quarterly* 19 (1967): 114–21.

Lewis, Ronald L., *Coal, Iron, and Slaves: Industrial Slavery in Maryland and Virginia, 1715–1865* (1979).

McCline, John, *Slavery in the Clover Bottoms: John McCline's Narrative of His Life during Slavery and the Civil War*, ed. Jan Furman (1998).

McGary, Howard, and Bill E. Lawson, *Between Slavery and Freedom: Philosophy and American Slavery* (1992).

McGettigan, James William, "Boone County Slaves: Sales, Estate Divisions, and Families, 1820–1865," *Missouri Historical Review* 72 (1978): 176–97; 271–95.

Meltzer, Milton, *Slavery: A World History* (1993).

Michie, James L., *Richmond Hill Plantation, 1810–1868: The Discovery of Antebellum Life on a Waccamaw Rice Plantation* (1990).

Miller, Randall M., ed., *The Afro-American Slaves: Community or Chaos?* (1981).

—— "The Fabric of Control: Slavery in Antebellum Southern Textile Mills," *Business History Review* 55 (1981): 471–90.

Miller, Randall M., and John David Smith, ed., *Dictionary of Afro-American Slavery* (1988).

Mintz, Sidney, "Was the Plantation Slave a Proletarian?" *Review* 2 (1978): 81–98.

Mintz, Steven, ed., *African American Voices: The Life Cycle of Slavery* (1993).

Mohr, Clarence L., *On the Threshold of Freedom: Masters and Slaves in Civil War Georgia* (1986).

——— "Slavery in Oglethorpe County, Georgia, 1773–1865," *Phylon* 33 (1972): 4–21.

Mooney, Chase C., *Slavery in Tennessee* (1957).

——— "Some Institutional and Statistical Aspects of Slavery in Tennessee," *Tennessee Historical Quarterly* 1 (1942): 195–228.

Moore, John Hebron, *The Emergence of the Cotton Kingdom in the Old Southwest: Mississippi, 1770–1860* (1988).

Morgan, James C., *Slavery in the United States: Four Views* (1985).

Morgan, Philip D., "The Ownership of Property by Slaves in the Mid-Nineteenth-Century Low Country," *Journal of Southern History* 49 (1983): 399–420.

Mullin, Michael, ed., *American Negro Slavery: A Documentary History* (1976).

Murphy, James B., "Slaveholding in Appalachia: A Challenge to the Egalitarian Tradition," *Southern Studies* 3 (1992): 15–33.

Naglich, Dennis, "The Slave System and the Civil War in Rural Prairieville," *Missouri Historical Review* 87 (1993): 253–73.

Naragon, Michael D., "Communities in Motion: Drapetomania, Work, and the Development of African American Slave Cultures," *Slavery and Abolition* 15 (1994): 63–87.

Nicholls, Michael L., "'In the Light of Human Beings': Richard Eppes and His Land Plantation Code of Laws," *Virginia Magazine of History and Biography* 89 (1981): 67–78.

Nichols, Charles H., *Many Thousand Gone: The Ex-Slaves' Account of Their Bondage and Freedom* (1963).

Olmsted, Frederick Law, *The Cotton Kingdom: A Traveller's Observations on Cotton and Slavery in the American Slave States: Based upon Three Former Volumes of Journeys and Investigations by the Same Author* (2d ed., 1862).

Otto, John Solomon, "Slavery in a Coastal Community: Glynn County, Georgia, 1790–1860," *Georgia Historical Quarterly* 63 (1979): 261.

Owens, Harry P., ed., *Perspectives and Irony in American Slavery: Essays* (1976).

Owens, Leslie Howard, *This Species of Property: Slave Life and Culture in the Old South* (1976).

Parish, Peter J., *Slavery: The Many Faces of a Southern Institution* (1979).

Perdue, Charles L., Jr., Thomas E. Barden, and Robert K. Phillips, ed., *Weevils in the Wheat: Interviews with Virginia Ex-Slaves* (1976).

Perdue, Theda, *Slavery and the Evolution of Cherokee Society, 1540–1866* (1979).

Phifer, Edward W., "Slavery in Microcosm: Burke County, North Carolina," *Journal of Southern History* 28 (1962): 137–65.

Phillips, Ulrich B., *American Negro Slavery: A Survey of the Supply, Employment, and Control of Negro Labor As Determined by the Plantation Regime* (1918).

——— *Life and Labor in the Old South* (1929).

——— "Plantations with Slave Labor and Free," *American Historical Review* 30 (1925): 738–53.

Phillips, Ulrich B., and James David Glunt, "Florida Plantation Records from the Papers of George Noble Jones," *Publication of the Missouri Historical Society* (1927).

Piersen, William D., "White Cannibals, Black Martyrs: Fear, Depression, and Religious Faith as Causes of Suicide among New Slaves," *Journal of Negro History* 62 (1977): 147–51.

Poe, William A., "Lott Cary: Man of Purchased Freedom," *Church History* 39 (1970): 49–61.

Powell, Lawrence N., *New Masters: Northern Planters during the Civil War and Reconstruction* (1980).

Preyer, Norris W., "The Historian, the Slave, and the Antebellum Textile Industry," *Journal of Negro History* 46 (1961): 67–82.

Price, John Milton, "Slavery in Winn Parish," *Louisiana History* 8 (1967): 137–48.

Proctor, William G., Jr., "Slavery in Southwest Georgia," *Georgia Historical Quarterly* 49 (1965): 1–22.

Pryor, F. L., "A Comparative Study of Slave Societies," *Journal of Comparative Economics* 1 (1977): 25–49.

Ravitz, Abe C., "John Pierpont and the Slaves' Christmas," *Phylon* 21 (1960): 283–86.

Rawick, George, "Self-Organization under Slavery," *Radical History Review* 4 (1977): 79–91.

Reinders, Robert C., "Slavery in New Orleans in the Decade before the Civil War," *Mid-America* 44 (1962): 211–21.

Rice, C. Duncan, *The Rise and Fall of Black Slavery* (1975).

Ripley, C. Peter, *Slaves and Freedmen in Civil War Louisiana* (1976).

Rivers, Larry E., "'Dignity and Importance': Slavery in Jefferson County, Florida, 1827–1860," *Florida Historical Quarterly* 61 (1983): 404–30.

——— "Slavery in Microcosm: Leon County, Florida, 1824 to 1860," *Journal of Negro History* 66 (1981): 235–46.

Rose, Peter Isaac, ed., *Americans from Africa: Slavery and Its Aftermath* (1970).

Rose, Willie Lee, *Slavery and Freedom*, ed. William W. Freehling (1982).

Rosengarten, Theodore, and Susan W. Walker, ed., *Tombee: Portrait of a Cotton Planter, with the Journal of Thomas B. Chaplin, 1822–1890* (1986).

Rubin, Vera, and Arthur Tuden, ed., *Comparative Perspectives on Slavery in New World Plantation Societies* (1977).

Savannah Writers' Project, *Savannah River Plantations* (1947).

Scarborough, William K., *The Overseer: Plantation Management in the Old South* (1966).

Scarpino, Philip V., "Slavery in Callaway County Missouri, 1845–1855," *Missouri Historical Review* 71 (1976, 1977): 22–43, 266–83.

Schafer, Judith Kelleher, "New Orleans Slavery in 1850 As Seen in Advertisements," *Journal of Southern History* 47 (1981): 33–56.

Seip, Terry L., "Slaves and Free Negroes in Alexandria, 1850–1860," *Louisiana History* 10 (1969): 125–45.

Sellers, James Benson, *Slavery in Alabama* (1950).

Settle, E. Ophelia, "Social Attitudes during the Slave Regime: Household Servants *versus* Field Hands," in August Meier and Elliot Rudwick, ed., *The Making of Black America: Essays in Negro Life and History: The Origins of Black Americans* (1969): 148–52.

Shaw, Stephanie J., "Mothering under Slavery in the Antebellum South," in Evelyn Nakano Glenn, Grace Chang and Linda Rennie Forcey, ed., *Mothering: Ideology, Experience, and Agency* (1994): 237–58.

Silverthorne, Elizabeth, *Plantation Life in Texas* (1986).

Sio, Arnold A., "Interpretations of Slavery: The Slave Status in the Americas," *Comparative Studies in Society and History* 7 (1965): 289–308.

Smedes, Susan Dabney, *Memorials of a Southern Planter* (1887).

Smith, Julia Floyd, *Slavery and Plantation Growth in Antebellum Florida, 1821–1860* (1973).

——— *Slavery and Rice Culture in Low Country Georgia, 1750–1860* (1985).

Smith, Mark M., *Mastered by the Clock: Time, Slavery, and Freedom in the American South* (1997).

Spraggins, Tinsley Lee, "Mobilization of Negro Labor for the Department of Virginia and North Carolina, 1861–1865," *North Carolina Historical Magazine* 24 (1947): 160–97.

Stampp, Kenneth M., *The Peculiar Institution: Slavery in the Antebellum South* (1956).

——— "Rebels and Sambos: The Search for the Negro's Personality in Slavery," *Journal of Southern History* 37 (1971): 367–92.

Starobin, Robert S., ed., *Blacks in Bondage: Letters of American Slaves* (1974).

——— *Industrial Slavery in the Old South* (1970).

——— "Privileged Bondsmen and the Process of Accommodation: The Role of House Servants and Drivers As Seen in Their Letters," *Journal of Social History* 5 (1971): 46–70.

Sydnor, Charles Sackett, *Slavery in Mississippi* (1965).

Sypher, Wylie, "Hutcheson and the 'Classical' Theory of Slavery," *Journal of Negro History* 24 (1939): 263–80.

Taylor, Joe Gray, *Negro Slavery in Louisiana* (1963).

——— "Slavery in Louisiana during the Civil War," *Louisiana History* 8 (1967): 27–33.

Taylor, Orville W., *Negro Slavery in Arkansas* (1958).

Trexler, Harrison Anthony, *Slavery in Missouri, 1804–1865* (1914).

Tyler, Ronnie C., and Lawrence R. Murphy, ed., *The Slave Narratives of Texas* (1997).

Unger, Irwin, and David Reimers, comp., *The Slavery Experience in the United States* (1970).

Wade, Richard C., *Slavery in the Cities: The South, 1820–1860* (1964).

Walker, Karen Jo, "Kingsley Plantation and Subsistence Patterns of the Southeastern Coastal Slaves," in Kenneth W. Johnson, Jonathan M. Leader and Robert C. Wilson, ed., *Indians, Colonists, and Slaves: Essays in Memory of Charles F. Fairbanks* (1985): 35–56.

Wall, Bennett H., "African Slavery," in Arthur S. Link and Rembert W. Patrick, ed., *Writing Southern History: Essays in Historiography in Honor of Fletcher M. Green* (1965): 175–97.

Walvin, James, *Slavery and the Slave Trade: A Short Illustrated History* (1983).

———— "Slaves, Free Time, and the Question of Leisure," *Slavery and Abolition* 16 (1995): 1–13.

Webber, Thomas L., "The Setting: Growing Up in the Quarter Community," in Harvey J. Graff, ed., *Growing Up in America: Historical Experiences* (1987): 198–214.

Weinstein, Allen, Frank Otto Gatell, and David Sarasohn, *American Negro Slavery: A Modern Reader* (3d ed., 1979).

White, Deborah G., *Ar'n't I a Woman? Female Slaves in the Plantation South* (1985).

———— "Female Slaves: Sex Roles and Status in the Antebellum Plantation South," *Journal of Family History* 8 (1983): 248–61.

White, John, and Ralph Willett, *Slavery in the American South* (1971).

White, Shane, and Graham White, "Slave Hair and African American Culture in the Eighteenth and Nineteenth Centuries," *Journal of Southern History* 61 (1995): 45–76.

Whitten, David O., "Slave Buying in 1835 Virginia As Revealed by Letters of a Louisiana Negro Sugar Planter," *Louisiana History* 11 (1970): 231–44.

Wiley, Bell Irvin, *Southern Negroes, 1861–1865* (1938).

Williams, Edwin L., Jr., "Negro Slavery in Florida," *Florida Historical Quarterly* 28 (1949): 93–110.

———— "Negro Slavery in Florida, Part II," *Florida Historical Quarterly* 28 (1950): 182–204.

Winks, Robin W., ed., *Slavery: A Comparative Perspective: Readings on Slavery from Ancient Times to the Present* (1972).

Wood, Betty, *Women's Work, Men's Work: The Informal Slave Economies of Low Country Georgia* (1995).

Woodson, Carter Godwin, "Freedom and Slavery in Appalachian America," in William H. Turner and Edward J. Cabbell, ed., *Blacks in Appalachia* (1985): 31–42.

Woolfolk, George R., "Sources of the History of the Negro in Texas, with Special Reference to Their Implications for Research in Slavery," *Journal of Negro History* 42 (1957): 38–47.

Wyatt-Brown, Bertram, "The Mask of Obedience: Male Slave Psychology in the Old South," *American Historical Review* 93 (1988): 1228–52.

Young, Jeffery R., "Ideology and Death on a Savannah River Rice Plantation, 1833–1867: Paternalism Amidst 'a Good Supply of Disease and Pain,'" *Journal of Southern History* 59 (1993): 673–706.

17.4.3   Economics of Slavery

Aitken, Hugh G. J., ed., *Did Slavery Pay? Readings in the Economics of Black Slavery in the United States* (1971).

Barzel, Yoram, "An Economic Analysis of Slavery," *Journal of Law and Economics* 20 (1977): 87–110.

Campbell, Randolph B., "'Intermittent Slave Ownership: Texas As a Test Case;' James Oakes, 'A Response;' Randolph B. Campbell, 'A Rejoinder,'" *Journal of Southern History* 51 (1985): 15–30.

Canarella, Giorgio, and John A. Tomaske, "The Optimal Utilization of Slaves," *Journal of Economic History* 35 (1975): 621–29.

Coles, Harry L., Jr., "Some Notes on Slaveownership and Landownership in Louisiana, 1850–1860," *Journal of Southern History* 9 (1943): 381–94.

Conrad, Alfred H., Douglas Dowd, Stanley Engerman, Eli Ginzberg, Charles Kelso, John R. Meyer, Harry N. Scheiber, and Richard Sutch, "Slavery As an Obstacle to Economic Growth in the United States: A Panel Discussion," *Journal of Economic History* 27 (1967): 518–60.

Conrad, Alfred H., and John Robert Meyer, "The Economics of Slavery in the Antebellum South," *Journal of Political Economy* 66 (1958): 95–130.

———— *The Economics of Slavery: And Other Studies in Econometric History* (1964).

Cunliffe, Marcus, *Chattel Slavery and Wage Slavery: The Anglo-American Context, 1830–1860* (1979).

Engerman, Stanley L., "The Effects of Slavery upon the Southern Economy: A Review of the Recent Debate," *Explorations in Entrepreneurial History* 4 (1967): 71–97.

———— "Some Considerations Relating to Property Rights in Man, Slave Systems," *Journal of Economic History* 33 (1973): 43–85, 100–05.

———— "Some Economic and Demographic Comparisons of Slavery in the United States and the British West Indies," *Economic History Review [Great Britain]* 29 (1976): 258–75.

Fogel, Robert William, *Without Consent or Contract: The Rise and Fall of American Slavery, Conditions of Slave Life, and the Transition to Freedom* (1989).

Fogel, Robert William and Stanley L. Engerman, "The Economics of Slavery," in Robert William Fogel and Stanley L. Engerman, ed., *The Reinterpretation of American Economic History* (1971): 311–41.

———— *Time on the Cross: The Economics of American Negro Slavery* (1974).

Fox-Genovese, Elizabeth, and Eugene D. Genovese, *Fruits of Merchant Capital: Slavery and Bourgeois Property in the Rise and Expansion of Capitalism* (1983).

Gallman, Robert E., and Ralph V. Anderson, "Slaves As Fixed Capital: Slave Labor and Southern Economic Development," *Journal of American History* 64 (1977): 24–46.

Genovese, Eugene D., "Cotton, Slavery and Soil Exhaustion in the Old South," *Cotton History Review* 2 (1961): 3–17.

———— "Livestock in the Slave Economy of the Old South: A Revised View," *Agricultural History* 36 (1962): 143–49.

———— "Materialism and Idealism in the History of Negro Slavery in the Americas," *Journal of Social History* 1 (1968): 371–94.

———— "The Medical and Insurance Costs of Slaveholding in the Cotton Belt," *Journal of Negro History* 45 (1960): 141–55.

———— *The Political Economy of Slavery: Studies in the Economy and Society of the Slave South* (1965).

———— "The Significance of the Slave Plantation for Southern Economic Development," *Journal of Southern History* 28 (1962): 422–37.

————, ed., *The Slave Economies* (2 vols., 1973).

Genovese, Eugene D., and Elizabeth Fox-Genovese, "The Slave Economies in Political Perspective," *Journal of American History* 66 (1979): 7–23.

Goldin, Claudia Dale, *Urban Slavery in the American South, 1820–1860: A Quantitative History* (1976).

Govan, Thomas P., "Was Plantation Slavery Profitable?" *Journal of Southern History* 8 (1942): 513–35.

Grant, Hugh Fraser, *Planter Management and Capitalism in Antebellum Georgia: The Journal of Hugh Fraser Grant, Ricegrower* (1954).

Gray, Lewis Cecil, *History of Agriculture in the Southern United States to 1860* (2 vols., 1933).

Gutman, Herbert G., *Slavery and the Numbers Game: A Critique of* Time on the Cross (1975).

———— "The World Two Cliometricians Made: A Review Essay of *Time on the Cross: The Economics of American Negro Slavery*," *Journal of Negro History* 60 (1975): 53–227.

Hering, Julia F., "Plantation Economy in Leon County, 1830–1840," *Florida Historical Quarterly* 33 (1954): 32–47.

Hudson, Larry E., Jr., ed., *Working toward Freedom: Slave Society and Domestic Economy in the American South* (1994).

Inscoe, John C., "Mountain Masters as Confederate Opportunists: The Profitability of Slavery in Western North Carolina," *Slavery and Abolition* 16 (1995): 84–100.

Kilbourne, Richard Holcombe, Jr., *Debt, Investment, Slaves: Credit Relations in East Feliciana Parish, Louisiana, 1825–1885* (1995).

Kulikoff, Allan, "Black Society and the Economics of Slavery," *Maryland Historical Magazine* 70 (1975): 203–10.

Leff, Nathaniel, "Long-Term Viability of Slavery in a Backward Closed Economy," *Journal of Interdisciplinary History* 5 (1974): 103–08.

Linden, Fabian, "Economic Democracy in the Slave South: An Appraisal of Some Recent Views," *Journal of Negro History* 31 (1946): 140–89.

Lowe, Richard G., and Randolph B. Campbell, "Slave Property and the Distribution of Wealth in Texas, 1860," *Journal of American History* 63 (1976): 313–24.

―――― "The Slave-Breeding Hypothesis: A Demographic Comment on the 'Buying' and 'Selling' States," *Journal of Southern History* 42 (1976): 401–12.

―――― "The Slave-Breeding Hypothesis: A Demographic Comment on the 'Buying' and 'Selling' States," *Journal of Southern History* 42 (1976): 401–12.

McDonald, Roderick A., *The Economy and Material Culture of Slaves: Goods and Chattels on the Sugar Plantations of Jamaica and Louisiana* (1993).

―――― "Independent Economic Production by Slaves on Antebellum Louisiana Sugar Plantations," *Slavery and Abolition* 12 (1991): 182–208.

McDonnell, Lawrence T., "Money Knows No Master: Market Relations and the American Slave Community," in Winfred B. Moore, Jr., Joseph F. Tripp and Lyon G. Tyler, Jr., ed., *Developing Dixie: Modernization in a Traditional Society* (1988): 31–44.

Miller, Randall M., "The Golden Isles: Rice and Slaves along the Georgia Coast," *Georgia Historical Quarterly* 70 (1986): 81–96.

Morris, Richard B., "The Measure of Bondage in the Slave States," *Mississippi Valley History Review* 41 (1954): 219–40.

Nieboer, Herman Jeremias, *Slavery As an Industrial System: Ethnological Researches* (2d ed., 1910).

Niemi, Albert W., Jr., "Inequality in the Distribution of Slave Wealth: The Cotton South and Other Agricultural Regions," *Journal of Economic History* 37 (1977): 747–54.

Perlo, Victor, *The Negro in Southern Agriculture* (1953).

Phillips, Ulrich B., "The Economic Cost of Slaveholding in the Cotton Belt," *Political Science Quarterly* 20 (1905): 257–75.

―――― "The Origin and Growth of the Southern Black Belts," *American Historical Review* 11 (1906): 798–816.

―――― *The Slave Economy of the Old South: Selected Essays in Economic and Social History*, ed. Eugene D. Genovese (1968).

Ransom, Roger L., *Conflict and Compromise: The Political Economy of Slavery, Emancipation, and the American Civil War* (1989).

Reidy, Joseph P., *From Slavery to Agrarian Capitalism in the Cotton Plantation South: Central Georgia, 1800–1880* (1992).

Rivers, Larry E., "Slavery and the Political Economy of Gadsden County, Florida, 1823–1861," *Florida Historical Quarterly* 70 (1991): 1–19.

Russel, Robert R., *Antebellum Studies in Slavery, Politics, and the Railroads* (1960).

―――― "The Economic History of Negro Slavery in the United States," *Agricultural History* 11 (1937): 308–21.

―――― "The General Effects of Slavery upon Southern Economic Progress," *Journal of Southern History* 3 (1935): 34–54.

Schantz, Mark, "'A Very Serious Business': Managerial Relationships on the Ball Plantations, 1800–1835," *South Carolina Historical Magazine* 88 (1987): 1–22.

Schlotterbeck, John, "The Internal Economy of Slavery in Virginia," *Slavery and Abolition* 12 (1991): 170–81.

Schmitz, Mark, and Donald Schaefer, "Paradox Lost: Westward Expansion and Slave Prices before the Civil War," *Journal of Economic History* 41 (1981): 402–07.

Smith, Mark M., *Debating Slavery: Economy and Society in the Antebellum American South* (1998).

Starobin, Robert S., "The Economics of Industrial Slavery in the Old South," *Business History Review* 44 (1970): 131–74.

Steckel, Richard H., *The Economics of U.S. Slave and Southern White Fertility* (1985).

Sutch, Richard, "The Treatment Received by American Slaves: A Critical Review of the Evidence Presented in *Time on the Cross*," *Explorations in Economic History* 12 (1975): 335–438.

Taylor, Rosser Howard, *Slaveholding in North Carolina: An Economic View* (1926).

Trexler, Harrison Anthony, "The Value and the Sale of the Missouri Slave," *Missouri Historical Review* 8 (1914): 69–85.

Vedder, Richard K., and David C. Stockdale, "The Profitability of Slavery Revisited: A Different Approach," *Agricultural History* 49 (1975): 392–404.

Williams, Eric, *Capitalism and Slavery* (1944).

Woodman, Harold D., "The Profitability of Slavery: A Historical Perennial," *Journal of Southern History* 29 (1963): 303–25.

———, ed. and comp., *Slavery and the Southern Economy: Sources and Readings* (1966).

Woolfolk, George R., "Planter Capitalism and Slavery: The Labor Thesis," *Journal of Negro History* 41 (1956): 103–16.

Wright, Gavin, *The Political Economy of the Cotton South: Households, Markets, and Wealth in the Nineteenth Century* (1978).

17.4.4 Free Blacks

Alexander, Adele Logan, *Ambiguous Lives: Free Women of Color in Rural Georgia, 1789–1879* (1991).

Baker, Steve, "Free Blacks in Antebellum Madison County," *Tennessee Historical Quarterly* 52 (1993): 56–63.

Barr, Ruth B., and Modeste Hargis, "The Voluntary Exile of Free Negroes of Pensacola," *Florida Historical Society Quarterly* 17 (1938): 3–14.

Beasley, Jonathan, "Blacks—Slave and Free—Vicksburg, 1850–1860," *Journal of Mississippi History* 38 (1976): 1–32.

Bellamy, Donnie D., "Free Blacks in Antebellum Missouri, 1820–1860," *Missouri Historical Review* 67 (1973): 198–226.

Bergeron, Arthur W., Jr., "Louisiana's Free Men of Color in Gray," *Journal of Confederate History* 11 (1994): 37–55.

Berlin, Ira, *Slaves without Masters: The Free Negro in the Antebellum South* (1974).

——— "The Structure of the Free Negro Caste in the Antebellum United States," *Journal of Social History* 9 (1976): 297–318.

Brady, Patricia, "Florville Foy, F.M.C.: Master Marble Cutter and Tomb Builder," *Southern Quarterly* 31 (1993): 8–20.

Brimelow, Judith M., and Michael E. Stevens, ed., *State Free Negro Capitation Tax Books, Charleston South Carolina, ca. 1811–1860 [film]* (1983).

Brown, Letitia Woods, *Free Negroes in the District of Columbia, 1790–1846* (1972).

Brown, Richard C., "The Free Blacks of Boyle County, Kentucky, 1850–1860: A Research Note," *Register of the Kentucky Historical Society* 87 (1989): 426–38.

Browning, James Blackwell, "The Free Negro in Ante-bellum North Carolina," *North Carolina Historical Magazine* 15 (1938): 23–33.

Curry, Leonard P., *The Free Black in Urban America, 1800–1850: The Shadow of the Dream* (1981).

Davis, Edwin Adams, and William Ransom Hogan, *The Barber of Natchez* (1973).

Day, Judy, and M. James Kedro, "Free Blacks in St. Louis: Antebellum Conditions, Emancipation, and the Post War Era," *Missouri Historical Society Bulletin* 30 (1974): 117–35.

Doherty, Herbert J., Jr., ed., "A Free Negro Purchases His Daughter," *Florida Historical Quarterly* 29 (1950): 38–43.

England, J. Merton, "The Free Negro in Ante-Bellum Tennessee," *Journal of Southern History* 9 (1943): 37–58.

Evans, W. A., "Free Negroes in Monroe County during Slavery Days," *Journal of Mississippi History* 3 (1941): 37–43.

Fitchett, E. Horace, "The Origin and Growth of the Free Negro Population of Charleston, South Carolina," *Journal of Negro History* 26 (1941): 421–37.

——— "The Status of the Free Negro in Charleston, South Carolina, and His Descendants in Modern Society," *Journal of Negro History* 32 (1947): 430–51.

——— "The Traditions of the Free Negro in Charleston, South Carolina," *Journal of Negro History* 25 (1940): 139–52.

Flanders, Ralph B., "The Free Negro in Ante-Bellum Georgia," *North Carolina Historical Review* 9 (1932): 250–72.

Foner, Laura, "The Free People of Color in Louisiana and St. Dominque: A Comparative Portrait of Two Three-Caste Societies," *Journal of Social History [UK]* 3 (1970): 406–30.

Franklin, John Hope, "The Enslavement of Free Negroes in North Carolina," *Journal of Negro History* 29 (1944): 401–28.

——— "The Free Negro in the Economic Life of Ante-Bellum North Carolina," *North Carolina Historical Review* 19 (1942): 359–375.

——— *The Free Negro in North Carolina, 1790–1860* (1943).

Garvin, Russell, "The Free Negro in Florida before the Civil War," *Florida Historical Quarterly* 46 (1967): 1–17.

Gould, Virginia Meacham, ed., *Chained to the Rock of Adversity: To Be Free, Black, and Female in the Old South* (1998).

Halliburton, R., Jr., "Free Black Owners of Slaves: A Reappraisal of the Woodson Thesis," *South Carolina Historical Magazine* 76 (1975): 129–42.

Harris, Robert L., Jr., "Charleston's Free Afro-American Elite: The Brown Fellowship Society and the Humane Brotherhood," *South Carolina Historical Magazine* 82 (1981): 289–310.

Higginbotham, A. Leon, Jr., and Greer C. Bosworth, "'Rather Than the Free': Free Blacks in Colonial and Antebellum Virginia," *Harvard Civil Rights-Civil Liberties Law Review* 26 (1991): 17–66.

Hogan, William Ransom, and Edwin Adams Davis, ed., *William Johnson's Natchez: The Ante-Bellum Diary of a Free Negro* (1951).

Imes, William Lloyd, "The Legal Status of Free Negroes and Slaves in Tennessee," *Journal of Negro History* 4 (1919): 254–72.

Jackson, Luther P., "The Early Strivings of the Negro in Virginia," *Journal of Negro History* 25 (1940): 25–34.

——— "Free Negroes of Petersburg, Virginia," *Journal of Negro History* 12 (1927): 365–88.

——— *Free Negro Labor and Property Holding in Virginia, 1830–1860* (1942).

——— "The Virginia Free Negro Farmer and Property Owner, 1830–1860," *Journal of Negro History* 24 (1939): 390–439.

Johnson, Franklin, *The Development of State Legislation concerning the Free Negro* (1919).

Johnson, Michael P., and James L. Roark, ed., *Black Masters: A Free Family of Color in the Old South* (1984).

———, ed., *No Chariot Let Down: Charleston's Free People of Color on the Eve of the Civil War* (1984).

——— "Strategies of Survival: Free Negro Families and the Problem of Slavery," in Carol Bleser, ed., *In Joy and In Sorrow: Women, Family, and Marriage in the Victorian South, 1830–1900* (1991): 88–102.

Johnson, Whittington B., "Free African-American Women in Savannah, 1800–1860: Affluence and Autonomy amid Adversity," *Georgia Historical Quarterly* 76 (1992): 260–83.

——— "Free Blacks in Antebellum Savannah: An Economic Profile," *Georgia Historical Quarterly* 64 (1981): 418–31.

——— "Free Blacks in Antebellum Augusta, Georgia: A Demographic and Economic Profile," *Richmond County History* 14 (1982): 10–21.

Koger, Larry, *Black Slaveowners: Free Black Slave Masters in South Carolina, 1790–1860* (1985).

Lane, Carl, and Rhoda Freeman, "John Dipper and the Experience of the Free Black Elite, 1816–1836," *Virginia Magazine of History and Biography* 100 (1992): 485–514.

Lebsock, Suzanne, *The Free Women of Petersburg: Status and Culture in a Southern Town, 1784–1860* (1984).

Littlefield, Daniel F., Jr., *The Cherokee Freedmen: From Emancipation to American Citizenship* (1978).

Littlefield, Daniel F., Jr., and Ann Littlefield, "The Beams Family: Free Blacks in Indian Territory," *Journal of Negro History* 61 (1976): 16–35.

Madden, T. O., Jr., and Ann L. Miller, *We Were Always Free: The Maddens of Culpeper County Virginia, A Two Hundred Year Family History* (1992).

Medford, Edna Greene, "'I Was Always a Union Man': The Dilemma of Free Blacks in Confederate Virginia," *Slavery and Abolition* 15 (1994): 1–16.

——— "'It Was a Very Comfortable Place for Poor Folks': Subsistence in a Rural Antebellum Free Black Community," *Locus* 5 (1993): 131–44.

Mehlinger, Louis R., "The Attitude of the Free Negro toward African Colonization," *Journal of Negro History* 1 (1916): 276–301.

Mills, Gary B., "Tracing Free People of Color in the Antebellum South: Methods, Sources, and Perspectives," *National Genealogical Society Quarterly* 78 (1990): 262–78.

Muir, Andrew Forest, "The Free Negro in Harris County, Texas," *Southwestern Historical Quarterly* 46 (1943): 214–38.

——— "The Free Negro in Jefferson and Orange Counties, Texas," *Journal of Negro History* 35 (1950): 183–206.

Provine, Dorothy, "The Economic Position of Free Blacks in the District of Columbia, 1800–1860," *Journal of Negro History* 58 (1973): 61–72.

Rankin, David C., "The Impact of the Civil War on the Free Colored Community of New Orleans," *Perspectives in American History* 11 (1977–1978): 377–416.

Reinders, Robert C., "The Decline of the New Orleans Free Negro in the Decade before the Civil War," *Journal of Mississippi History* 24 (1962): 88–99.

——— "The Free Negro in the New Orleans Economy, 1850–1860," *Louisiana History* 6 (1965): 273–85.

Robinson, Henry S., "Some Aspects of the Free Negro Population of Washington, D.C., 1800–1862," *Maryland Historical Magazine* 64 (1969): 43–64.

Russell, John H., "Colored Freemen as Slave Owners in Virginia," *Journal of Negro History* 1 (1916): 233–42.

——— *The Free Negro in Virginia, 1619–1865* (1913).

Schoen, Harold, "The Free Negro in the Republic of Texas," *Southwestern Historical Quarterly* 39, 40, 41 (1936, 1937): 292–308, 26–34, 85–113, 169–99, 267–89, 83–108.

Schwarz, Philip J., "Emancipators, Protectors, and Anomalies: Free Black Slaveowners in Virginia," *Virginia Magazine of History and Biography* 95 (1987): 317–38.

Schweninger, Loren, "Antebellum Free Persons of Color in Postbellum Louisiana," *Louisiana History* 30 (1989): 345–65.

——— "John Carruthers Stanley and the Anomaly of Black Slaveholding," *North Carolina Historical Review* 67 (1990): 159–92.

——— "Property-Owning Free African-American Women in the South, 1800–1870," *Journal of Women's History* 1 (1990): 13–44.

Scott, Jean Sampson, comp., "Index to Free Negro Register, 1797–1841: Book I, Arlington, VA," *Journal of Afro-American Historical and Geneaological Society* 3 (1982): 18–27.

Seip, Terry L., "Slaves and Free Negroes in Alexandria, 1850–1860," *Louisiana History* 10 (1969): 125–45.

Sellers, James B., "Free Negroes of Tuscaloosa County before the Thirteenth Amendment," *Alabama Review* 23 (1970): 110–127.

Stahl, Annie Lee West, "The Free Negro in Ante-Bellum Louisiana," *Louisiana Historical Quarterly* 25 (1942): 301–96.

Sterkx, H. E., *The Free Negro in Antebellum Louisiana* (1972).

Stuckert, Robert P., "Free Black Populations of the Southern Appalachian Mountains: 1860," *Journal of Black Studies* 23 (1993): 358–70.

Sweig, Donald, ed., *"Registration of the Free Negroes Commencing September Court 1822, Book No. 2" and "Register of Free Blacks 1835, Book 3": Being the Full Text of the Two Extant Volumes, 1822–1861, of Registrations of Free Blacks Now in the County Courthouse, Fairfax, Virginia* (1977).

Sydnor, Charles S., "The Free Negro in Mississippi before the Civil War," *American Historical Review* 32 (1927): 769–88.

Tansey, Richard, "Out-of-State Free Blacks in Late Antebellum New Orleans," *Louisiana History* 22 (1981): 369–86.

Taylor, Rosser Howard, *The Free Negro in North Carolina* (1920).

Uzzel, Odell, "Free Negro/Slave Marriages and Family Life in Antebellum North Carolina," *Western Journal of Black Studies* 18 (1994): 64–9.

Warner, Lee H., *Free Men in an Age of Servitude: Three Generations of a Black Family* (1992).

Wikramanayake, Marina, *A World in Shadow: The Free Black in Antebellum South Carolina* (1973).

Wilson, Carol, *Freedom at Risk: The Kidnapping of Free Blacks in America, 1780–1865* (1994).

Wilson, Carol, and Calvin D. Wilson, "White Slavery: An American Paradox," *Slavery and Abolition [London]* 19 (1998): 1–23.

Winston, James E., "The Free Negro in New Orleans, 1803–1860," *Louisiana Historical Quarterly* 21 (1938): 1075–85.

Woodson, Carter Godwin, ed. and comp., *Free Negro Owners of Slaves in the United States in 1830* (1924).

———— *Free Negro Heads of Families in the United States in 1830: Together with a Brief Treatment of the Free Negro* (1925).

Woolfolk, George Ruble, *The Free Negro in Texas, 1800–1860: A Study in Cultural Compromise* (1976).

Wright, James Martin, *The Free Negro in Maryland, 1634–1860* (1921).

17.4.5   Resistance (Antebellum)

Addington, Wendell G., "Slave Insurrections in Texas," *Journal of Negro History* 35 (1950): 408–34.

Aptheker, Herbert, *American Negro Slave Revolts* (1943).

———— "Maroons within the Present Limits of the United States," *Journal of Negro History* 24 (1939): 167–84.

———— *Nat Turner's Slave Rebellion: Together with the Full Text of the So-Called "Confessions" of Nat Turner Made in Prison in 1831* (1966).

———— *Negro Slave Revolts in the United States, 1526–1860* (1939).

———— "'Resistance and Afro-American History': Some Notes on Contemporary Historiography and Suggestions for Further Research," in Gary Y. Okihiro, ed., *In Resistance: Studies in African, Caribbean, and Afro-American History* (1986): 10–20.

———— *To Be Free: Studies in American Negro History* (1948).

———— *"We Will Be Free": Advertisements for Runaways and the Reality of American Slavery* (1984).

Bauer, Raymond A., and Alice H. Bauer, "Day to Day Resistance to Slavery," *Journal of Negro History* 27 (1942): 388–419.

Bracey, John H., Jr., August Meier, and Elliott Rudwick, ed., *American Slavery: The Question of Resistance* (1971).

Cable, Mary, *Black Odyssey: The Case of the Slave Ship Amistad* (1971).

Carroll, Joseph C., *Slave Insurrections in the United States, 1800–1865* (1938).

Carter, Dan T., "The Anatomy of Fear: The Christmas Day Insurrection Scare of 1865," *Journal of Southern History* 42 (1976): 345–64.

Cecelski, David S., "The Shores of Freedom: The Maritime Underground Railroad in North Carolina, 1800–1861," *North Carolina Historical Review* 71 (1994): 174–206.

Chapman, Abraham, comp., *Steal Away: Stories of the Runaway Slaves* (1971).

Cheek, William F., *Black Resistance before the Civil War* (1970).

Collison, Gary, *Shadrach Minkins: From Fugitive Slave to Citizen* (1997).

Craft, William, and Ellen Craft, *Running a Thousand Miles for Freedom; or, the Escape of William and Ellen Craft from Slavery* (1860).

Dalzell, Frederick, "Dream Working Amistad: Representing Slavery, Revolt, and Freedom in America, 1839 and 1997," *New England Quarterly* 71 (1998): 127–33.

Davis, Mary Kemp, *Nat Turner before the Bar of Judgment: Fictional Treatments of the Southampton Slave Insurrection* (1999).

Dew, Charles B., "Black Ironworkers and the Slave Insurrection Panic of 1856," *Journal of Southern History* 41 (1975): 321–38.

Dormon, James H., "The Persistent Specter: Slave Rebellion in Territorial Louisiana," *Louisiana History* 18 (1977): 389–404.

Drewry, William Sidney, *Slave Insurrections in Virginia, 1830–1865* (1900).

———— *The Southampton Insurrection* (1900).

Duff, John B., and Peter McQuillsin Mitchell, comp., *The Nat Turner Rebellion: The Historical Event and the Modern Controversy* (1971).

Durling, Gregory B., "Female Labor, Malingering, and the Abuse of Equipment under Slavery: Evidence from the Marydale Plantation Diary," *Southern Studies* 5 (1994): 31–49.

Ellison, Mary, "Resistance to Oppression: Black Women's Response to Slavery in the United States," *Slavery and Abolition* 4 (1983): 56–63.

Forbes, Ella, "African Resistance to Enslavement: The Nature and the Evidentiary Record," *Journal of Black Studies* 23 (1992): 39–59.

Fox-Genovese, Elizabeth, "Strategies and Forms of Resistance: Focus on Slave Women in the United States," in Gary Y. Okihiro, ed., *In Resistance: Studies in African, Caribbean, and Afro-American History* (1986): 143–65.

Franklin, John Hope, and Loren Schweninger, *Runaway Slaves: Rebels on the Plantation* (1999).

Fredrickson, George M., and Christopher Lasch, "Resistance to Slavery," *Civil War History* 13 (1967): 315–29.

Freehling, William W., "Denmark Vesey's Peculiar Reality," in Robert H. Abzug and Stephen E. Maizlish, ed., *New Perspectives on Race and Slavery in America: Essays in Honor of Kenneth M. Stampp* (1986): 25–47.

Gara, Larry, *The Liberty Line: The Legend of the Underground Railroad* (1961).

——— "The Underground Railroad: A Re-Evaluation," *Ohio Historical Quarterly* 69 (1960): 217–30.

Genovese, Eugene D., *From Rebellion to Revolution: Afro-American Slave Revolts in the Making of the Modern World* (1979).

——— "Rebelliousness and Docility in the Negro Slave: A Critique of the Elkins Thesis," *Civil War History* 13 (1967): 293–314.

Goldstein, Leslie F., "Violence As an Instrument for Social Change: The Views of Frederick Douglass, 1817–1895," *Journal of Negro History* 61 (1976): 61–72.

Gordon, A. H., "The Struggle of the Negro Slaves for Physical Freedom," *Journal of Negro History* 13 (1928): 22–35.

Granade, Ray, "Slave Unrest in Florida," *Florida Historical Quarterly* 55 (1976): 18–36.

Green, Jeffrey A., Jr., "Fear, Hypocrisy, and Racial Notions: The White Response to the Nat Turner Insurrection As Revealed through the Southern Press, 1931–1932," *Griot* 13 (1994): 14–25.

Gross, Seymour L., and Eileen Bender, "History, Politics, and Literature: The Myth of Nat Turner," *American Quarterly* 23 (1971): 487–518.

Halasz, Nicholas, *The Rattling Chains: Slave Unrest and Revolt in the Antebellum South* (1966).

Hine, Darlene Clark, "Female Slave Resistance: The Economics of Sex," *Western Journal of Black Studies* 3 (1979): 123–27.

Johnson, Frank Roy, *The Nat Turner Slave Insurrection* (1966).

Jones, Howard, *Mutiny on the Amistad: The Saga of a Slave Revolt and Its Impact on American Abolition, Law, and Diplomacy* (1987).

Jones, Norrece T., Jr., *Born a Child of Freedom, Yet a Slave: Mechanisms of Control and Strategies of Resistance in Antebellum South Carolina* (1990).

Jordan, Winthrop D., *Tumult and Silence at Second Creek: An Inquiry into a Civil War Slave Conspiracy* (rev. ed., 1995).

Katz, William Loren, "Black and Indian Cooperation and Resistance to Slavery," *Freedomways* 17 (1977): 164–74.

Kelley, Donald Brooks, "Harper's Ferry: Prelude to Crisis in Mississippi," *Journal of Mississippi History* 27 (1965): 351–72.

Kilson, Marion D. de B., "Towards Freedom: An Analysis of Slave Revolts in the United States," *Phylon* 25 (1964): 175–87.

Kromer, Helen, *The Amistad Revolt, 1839: The Slave Uprising aboard the Spanish Schooner* (1997).

Logsdon, Joseph, "Diary of a Slave: Recollection and Prophecy," in William G. Shade and Roy C. Herrenkohl, ed., *Seven on Black: Reflections on the Negro Experience in America* (1969): 24–48.

Logue, Cal M., "Transcending Coercion: The Communicative Strategies of Black Slaves on Antebellum Plantations," *Quarterly Journal of Speech* 67 (1981): 31–46.

Lumpkin, Katherine DuPre, "'The General Plan Was Freedom': A Negro Secret Order on the Underground Railroad," *Phylon* 28 (1967): 63–77.

Marten, James, "Slaves and Rebels: The Peculiar Institution in Texas, 1861–1865," *East Texas Historical Journal* 28 (1991): 29–36.

Martins, Christopher, *The Amistad Affair* (1970).

May, Robert E., "John A. Quitman and His Slaves: Reconciling Slave Resistance with the Pro-Slavery Defense," *Journal of Southern History* 46 (1980): 551–70.

McKibben, Davidson Burns, "Negro Slave Insurrections in Mississippi, 1800–1865," *Journal of Negro History* 34 (1949): 73–90.

Miles, Edwin A., "The Mississippi Slave Insurrection Scare of 1835," *Journal of Negro History* 42 (1957): 38–47.

Milligan, John D., "Slave Rebelliousness and the Florida Maroons," *Prologue* 6 (1974): 4–18.

Moore, Robert, Jr., "A Ray of Hope, Extinguished: St. Louis Slave Suits for Freedom," *Gateway Heritage* 14 (1993–4): 4–15.

Moore, W. K., "An Abortive Slave Uprising," *Missouri Historical Review* 52 (1958): 123–26.

Morris, Charles Edward, "Panic and Reprisal: Reaction in North Carolina to the Nat Turner Insurrection, 1831," *North Carolina Historical Review* 62 (1985): 29–52.

Morris, Christopher, "An Event in Community Organization; The Mississippi Slave Insurrection Scare of 1853," *Journal of Social History* 22 (1988): 93–112.

Oates, Stephen B., *The Fires of Jubilee: Nat Turner's Fierce Rebellion* (1975).

Obtiko, Mary Ellen, "'Custodians of a House of Resistance': Black Women Respond to Slavery," in Dana V. Hiller and Robin Ann Sheets, ed., *Women and Men: The Consequences of Power* (1977): 256–69.

Patrick, Rembert Wallace, *Florida Fiasco: Rampant Rebels on the Georgia-Florida Border, 1810–1815* (1954).

Price, Richard, ed., *Maroon Societies: Rebel Slave Communities in the Americas* (3d ed., 1996).

Rachleff, Marshall, "Big Joe, Little Joe, Bill, and Jack: An Example of Slave-Resistance in Alabama," *Alabama Review* 32 (1979): 141–46.

Russell, Marion J., "American Slave Discontent in Records of the High Courts," *Journal of Negro History* 31 (1946): 411–34.

Schafer, Judith Kelleher, "The Immediate Impact of Nat Turner's Insurrection on New Orleans," *Louisiana History* 21 (1980): 361–76.

Sheridan, Richard B., "From Slavery in Missouri to Freedom in Kansas: The Influx of Black Fugitives and Contrabands into Kansas, 1854–1865," *Kansas History* 12 (1989): 28–47.

Shore, Laurence, "Making Mississippi Safe for Slavery: The Insurrectionary Panic of 1835," in Orville Vernon Burton and Robert C. McMath, Jr., ed., *Class, Conflict, and Consensus: Antebellum Southern Community Studies* (1982): 96–127.

Siebert, Wilbur H., *The Underground Railroad from Slavery to Freedom* (1898).

Simpson, Mark, "Nat Turner at the Limits of Travel," *Cultural Critique* 37 (1997): 31–60.

Still, William, *The Underground Railroad* (1872).

Stone, Albert E., *The Return of Nat Turner: History, Literature, and Cultural Politics in Sixties America* (1992).

Strickland, John Scott, "The Great Revival and Insurrectionary Fears in North Carolina: An Examination of Antebellum Southern Society and Slave Revolt Panics," in Orville Vernon Burton and Robert C. McMath, Jr., ed., *Class, Conflict, and Consensus: Antebellum Southern Community Studies* (1982): 57–95.

Tate, Gayle T., "Free Black Resistance in the Antebellum Era, 1830 to 1860," *Journal of Black Studies* 28 (1998): 764–82.

Taylor, R. H., "Slave Conspiracies in North Carolina," *North Carolina Historical Review* 5 (1928): 20–34.

Terborg-Penn, Rosalyn, "Black Women Freedom Fighters in Early Nineteenth Century Maryland," *Maryland Heritage* 2 (1984): 11–12.

———— "Black Women in Resistance: A Cross-Cultural Perspective," in Gary Y. Okihiro, ed., *In Resistance: Studies in African, Caribbean, and Afro-American History* (1986): 188–209.

Tomlins, Christopher L., "In Nat Turner's Shadow: Reflections on the Norfolk Dry Dock Affair of 1830–1831," *Labor History* 33 (1992): 494–508.

Toplin, Robert Brent, "Peter Still *versus* the Peculiar Institution," *Civil War History* 13 (1967): 340–49.

Tragle, Henry Irving, comp., *The Southampton Slave Revolt of 1831: A Compilation of Source Material* (1971).

Turley, David, "Slavery in the Americas: Resistance, Liberation, Emancipation," *Slavery and Abolition* 14 (1993): 109–16.

Turner, Nat, *The Confessions of Nat Turner, the Leader of the Late Insurrection in Southampton, As Fully and Voluntarily Made to Thomas R. Gray, in the Prison Where He Was Confined, and Acknowledged by Him to Be Such When Read before the Court of Southampton, with the Certificate, under the Seal of Court Convened at Jerusalem, November 5, 1831, for His Trial* (1831).

Weisenburger, Steven, *Modern Medea: A Family Story of Slavery and Child-Murder from the Old South* (1998).

White, William W., "The Texas Slave Insurrection in 1860," *Southwestern Historical Quarterly* 52 (1949): 259–85.

Wish, Harvey, "American Slave Insurrections before 1861," *Journal of Negro History* 22 (1937): 299–320.

——— "Slave Disloyalty under the Confederacy," *Journal of Negro History* 23 (1938): 435–50.

——— "The Slave Insurrection Panic of 1856," *Journal of Southern History* 5 (1939): 206–22.

17.4.6   Abolitionism and Emancipation

Alford, Terry L., "Some Manumissions Recorded in the Addams County Deed Books in Chancery Clerk's Office, Natchez, Mississippi, 1795–1835," *Journal of Mississippi History* 33 (1971): 39–50.

Belz, Herman, *A New Birth of Freedom: The Republican Party and Freedmen's Rights, 1861–1866* (1976).

Berlin, Ira, Barbara J. Fields, Thavolia Glymph, Joseph P. Reidy, and Leslie S. Rowland, ed., *The Destruction of Slavery, Series I, Vol. 1 of Freedom: A Documentary History of Emancipation, 1861–1867* (1985).

Berlin, Ira, Barbara J. Fields, Thavolia Glymph, Steven F. Miller, Joseph P. Reidy, Leslie S. Rowland, and Julie Saville, "Writing Freedom's History: The Destruction of Slavery," *Prologue* 17 (1985): 211–27.

Berlin, Ira, Thavolia Glymph, Steven F. Miller, Joseph P. Reidy, Leslie S. Rowland, and Julie Saville, ed., *The Wartime Genesis of Free Labor: The Lower South, Series I, Vol. 3 of Freedom: A Documentary History of Emancipation, 1861–1867* (1990).

Berlin, Ira, Steven F. Miller, Joseph P. Reidy, and Leslie S. Rowland, ed., *The Wartime Genesis of Free Labor: The Upper South, Series I, Vol. 2 of Freedom: A Documentary History of Emancipation, 1861–1867* (1993).

Billington, Ray Allen, "A Social Experiment: The Port Royal Journal of Charlotte L. Forten, 1862–1863," *Journal of Negro History* 35 (1950): 233–64.

Blackett, R. J. M., *Beating against the Barriers: Biographical Essays in Nineteenth-Century Afro-American History* (1986).

Blackett, Richard, "The Quest for Freedom: Colonization, Abolition, and European Immigration, 1817–1860," in Randall M. Miller, ed., *States of Progress: Germans and Blacks in America over 300 Years* (1989): 38–54.

Blassingame, John W., and Mae G. Henderson, ed., *Antislavery Newspapers and Periodicals: Vol. II, 1835–1865, Annotated Index of Letters in the* Liberator, Anti-Slavery Record, Human Rights, *and the* Observer (1980).

Brink, Dan C., "What Did Freedom Mean? The Aftermath of Slavery as Told by Former Slaves and Former Masters in Free Societies," *Organization of American Historians' Magazine of History* 4 (1989): 35–46.

Byrne, William A., "'Uncle Billy' Sherman Comes to Town: The Free Winter of Black Savannah," *Georgia Historical Quarterly* 79 (1995): 91–116.

Carroll, Kenneth, "Religious Influences on the Manumission of Slaves in Carolina, Dorchester, and Talbot Counties," *Maryland Historical Magazine* 56 (1961): 176–98.

Currie, James T., ed, "Freedmen at Davis Bend, April 1864," *Journal of Mississippi History* 46 (1984): 120–29.

Davis, David Brion, "Abolitionists and the Freedmen: An Essay Review," *Journal of Southern History* 31 (1965): 164–70.

Dillon, Merton Lynn, *Slavery Attacked: Southern Slaves and Their Allies, 1619–1865* (1990).

Duberman, Martin B., ed., *The Anti-Slavery Vanguard: New Essays on the Abolitionists* (1965).

Dumond, Dwight L., *Antislavery: The Crusade for Freedom in America* (1961).

Durden, Robert F., *The Gray and the Black: The Confederate Debate on Emancipation* (1972).

Escott, Paul D., "The Context of Freedom: Georgia's Slaves during the Civil War," *Georgia Historical Quarterly* 58 (1974): 79–104.

Faust, Drew Gilpin, "Trying to Do a Man's Business: Slavery, Violence, and Gender in the American Civil War," *Gender and History* 4 (1992): 197–214.

Fellman, Michael, "Emancipation in Missouri," *Missouri Historical Review* 83 (1988): 36–56.

Filler, Louis, *Crusade against Slavery: Friends, Foes, and Reforms, 1820–1860* (rev. ed., 1986).

——— *Slavery in the United States of America* (1972).

Foner, Eric, *Nothing but Freedom: Emancipation and Its Legacy* (1983).

Frankel, Noralee, *Freedom's Women: Black Women and Families in Civil War Era Mississippi* (1999).

Franklin, John Hope, *The Emancipation Proclamation* (1963).

Freehling, Alison Goodyear, *Drift toward Dissolution: The Virginia Slavery Debate of 1831–1832* (1982).

Gerteis, Louis S., *From Contraband to Freedman: Federal Policy towards Southern Blacks, 1861–1865* (1973).

——— "Salmon P. Chase, Radicalism and the Politics of Emancipation, 1861–1864," *Journal of American History* 60 (1973): 42–52.

Goodman, Paul, "The Manual Labor Movement and the Origins of Abolitionism," *Journal of the Early Republic* 13 (1993): 355–88.

Harrison, Lowell Hayes, *The Antislavery Movement in Kentucky* (1978).

Harrold, Stanley, "John Brown's Forerunners: Slave Rescue Attempts and the Abolitionists, 1841–1851," *Radical History Review* 55 (1993): 89–110.

Howard, Victor B., *Black Liberation in Kentucky: Emancipation and Freedom, 1862–1884* (1983).

Jackson, Luther P., "Manumission in Certain Virginia Cities," *Journal of Negro History* 15 (1930): 278–314.

Klebaner, Benjamin Joseph, "American Manumission Law and the Responsibility for Supporting Slaves," *Virginia Magazine of History and Biography* 63 (1955): 443–53.

Lee, George R., "Slavery and Emancipation in Lewis County, Missouri," *Missouri Historical Review* 65 (1971): 294–317.

Litwack, Leon F., *Been in the Storm So Long: The Aftermath of Slavery* (1979).

——— "Free at Last!" in Tamara K. Hareven, ed., *Anonymous Americans: Explorations in Nineteenth Century Social History* (1971): 131–71.

Lutz, Alma, *Crusade for Freedom: Women of the Antislavery Movement* (1968).

Mandel, Bernard, *Labor: Free and Slave: Workingmen and the Anti-Slavery Movement in the United States* (1955).

Martin, Asa Earl, *The Anti-Slavery Movement in Kentucky prior to 1850* (1918).

McPherson, James M., "Abolitionist and Negro Opposition to Colonization during the Civil War," *Phylon* 26 (1965): 391–99.

——— *The Struggle for Equality: Abolitionists and the Negro in the Civil War and Reconstruction* (1964).

Messner, William F., "Black Violence and White Response: Louisiana, 1862," *Journal of Southern History* 41 (1975): 19–38.

Morgan, Lynda J., *Emancipation in Virginia's Tobacco Belt, 1850–1870* (1992).

Nichols, Charles Harold, *Many Thousand Gone: The Ex-Slaves' Account of Their Bondage and Freedom* (1963).

Pease, Jane H., and William H. Pease, *They Who Would Be Free: Blacks' Search for Freedom, 1830–1861* (1974).

Pease, William H., and Jane H. Pease, "Antislavery Ambivalence: Immediatism, Expediency, Race," *American Quarterly* 17 (1965): 682–95.

Piacentino, Edward J., "Doesticks' Assault on Slavery: Style and Technique in 'The Great Auction Sale of Slaves at Savannah, Georgia,'" *Phylon* 48 (1987): 196–203.

Quarles, Benjamin, *Allies for Freedom: Blacks and John Brown* (1974).

——— *Black Abolitionists* (1969).

Reynolds, Donald E., "Reluctant Martyr: Anthony Bewley and the Texas Slave Insurrection Panic of 1860," *Southwestern Historical Quarterly* 96 (1993): 344–61.

Ripley, C. Peter, ed., *The Black Abolitionist Papers* (5 vols., 1985–1992).

Ripley, C. Peter, Roy E. Finkenbine, Michael F. Hembree, and Donald Yacovone, ed., *Witness for Freedom: African American Voices on Race, Slavery, and Emancipation* (1993).

Roark, James, *Masters without Slaves: Southern Planters in the Civil War and Reconstruction* (1977).

Rohrs, Richard C., "Antislavery Politics and the Pearl Incident of 1848," *Historian* 56 (1994): 711–24.

Rose, Willie Lee, *Rehearsal for Reconstruction: The Port Royal Experiment* (1964).

Saville, Julie, *The Work of Reconstruction: From Slave to Wage Laborer in South Carolina, 1860–1870* (1994).

Scarborough, Ruth, *The Opposition to Slavery in Georgia prior to 1860* (1933).

Schafer, Judith Kelleher, "'Open and Notorious Concubinage': The Emancipation of Slave Mistresses by Will and the Supreme Court in Antebellum Louisiana," *Louisiana History* 28 (1987): 165–82.

Scott, Rebecca, "Comparing Emancipations: A Review Essay," *Journal of Social History* 20 (1987): 565–83.

Sears, Richard D., *The Day of Small Things: Abolitionism in the Midst of Slavery, Berea, Kentucky, 1854–64* (1986).

Sowle, Patrick, "The North Carolina Manumission Society, 1816–1834," *North Carolina Historical Review* 42 (1965): 47–69.

Stewart, James Brewer, *Holy Warriors: The Abolitionists and American Slavery* (1976).

Turley, David, "Slavery in the Americas: Resistance, Liberation, Emancipation," *Slavery and Abolition* 14 (1993): 109–16.

Verney, Kevern J., "Trespassers in the Land of Their Birth: Black Land Ownership in South Carolina and Mississippi during the Civil War and Reconstruction, 1861–1877," *Slavery and Abolition* 4 (1983): 64–79.

Wagandt, Charles Lewis, *The Mighty Revolution: Negro Emancipation in Maryland, 1862–1864* (1965).

Walters, Ronald G., *The Antislavery Appeal: American Abolitionism after 1830* (1976).

Wesley, Charles H., "The Emancipation of the Free Coloured Population in the British Empire," *Journal of Negro History* 19 (1934): 137–70.

White, Charles, *John Brown's Raid at Harpers Ferry: An Eyewitness Account by Charles White*, ed. Rayburn S. Moore (1959).

Wiggins, William H., *O Freedom! Afro-American Emancipation Celebrations* (1987).

Wiley, Bell Irvin, *Southern Negroes, 1861–1865* (1938).

Wolf, Hazel C., "An Abolition Martyrdom in Maryland," *Maryland Historical Magazine* 47 (1952): 224–33.

Yee, Shirley, *Black Women Abolitionists: A Study in Activism, 1828–1860* (1992).

17.4.7 Black/White Relations

Boime, Albert, *The Art of Exclusion: Representing Blacks in the Nineteenth Century* (1990).

Castel, Albert, "Civil War Kansas and the Negro," *Journal of Negro History* 51 (1966): 125–38.

Clinton, Catherine, "Caught in the Web of the Big House: Women and Slavery," in Walter J. Fraser, Jr., R. Frank Saunders, Jr. and Jon L. Wakelyn, ed., *The Web of Southern Social Relations: Women, Family, and Education* (1985): 19–34.

——— *The Plantation Mistress: Women's World in the Old South* (1982).

——— "'Southern Dishonor': Flesh, Blood, Race, and Bondage," in Carol Bleser, ed., *In Joy and In Sorrow: Women, Family, and Marriage in the Victorian South, 1830–1900* (1991): 52–68.

Craven, Avery O., "Poor Whites and Negroes in the Ante-Bellum South," *Journal of Negro History* 15 (1930): 14–25.

Davis, John A., "The Influence of Africans on American Culture," *Annals of the American Academy of Political and Social Science* 354 (1964): 75–83.

Ellenberg, George B., "African Americans, Mules and the Southern Mindscape, 1850–1950," *Agricultural History* 72 (1998): 381–98.

Fahey, David M., *Temperance and Racism: John Bull, Johnny Reb, and the Good Templars* (1996).

Fox-Genovese, Elizabeth, *Within the Plantation Household: Black and White Women of the Old South* (1988).

Fredrickson, George M., *The Black Image in the White Mind: The Debate on Afro-American Character and Destiny, 1817–1914* (1971).

Haley, John, *Charles N. Hunter and Race Relations in North Carolina* (1987).

Hesseltine, William B., "Some New Aspects of the Pro-Slavery Argument," *Journal of Negro History* 1 (1936): 1–14.

Hodes, Martha, *White Women, Black Men: Illicit Sex in the Nineteenth-Century South* (1997).

January, Alan F., "The South Carolina Association: An Agency for Race Control in Antebellum South Carolina," *South Carolina Historical Magazine* 78 (1977): 191–201.

Johnston, James Hugo, *Race Relations in Virginia and Miscegenation in the South, 1776–1860* (1970).

Jordan, Ervin L., Jr., "Sleeping with the Enemy: Sex, Black Women, and the Civil War," *Western Journal of Black Studies* 18 (1994): 55–63.

McMillen, Sally Gregory, *Southern Women: Black and White in the Old South* (1992).

Morris, Christopher, "The Articulation of Two Worlds: The Master-Slave Relationship Reconsidered," *Journal of American History* 85 (1998): 982–1007.

Parkhurst, Jessie W., "The Role of the Black Mammy in the Plantation Household," *Journal of Negro History* 23 (1938): 349–69.

Schafer, Daniel L., "'A Class of People neither Freemen nor Slaves': From Spanish to American Race Relations in Florida, 1821–1861," *Journal of Social History* 26 (1993): 587–609.

Seabrook, Isaac Dubose, *Before and After; or, The Relations of the Races at the South,* ed. John Hammond Moore (1967).

Shalhope, Robert E., "Race, Class, Slavery and the Antebellum Mind," *Journal of Southern History* 37 (1971): 557–74.

Sobel, Mechal, "All Americans are Part African: Slave Influence on 'White' Values," in Leonie J. Archer, *Slavery and Other Forms of Unfree Labor* (1988): 176–87.

Takaki, Ronald T., "The Black Child-Savage in Ante-Bellum America," in Gary B. Nash and Richard Weiss, ed., *The Great Fear: Race in the Mind of America* (1970): 27–44.

Tripp, Steven Elliott, *Yankee Town, Southern City: Race and Class Relations in Civil War Lynchburg* (1996).

Wesley, Charles H., "The Concept of the Inferiority of the Negro in American Thought," *Journal of Negro History* 25 (1940): 540–56.

Wills, W. Ridley, II, "Black-White Relations in the Belle Meade Plantation," *Tennessee Historical Quarterly* 50 (1991): 17–32.

Wilson, Mary Tolford, "Peaceful Integration: The Owner's Adoption of His Slave's Food," *Journal of Negro History* 49 (1964): 116–27.

Wyllie, Irvin G., "Race and Class Conflict on Missouri's Cotton Frontier," *Journal of Southern History* 20 (1954): 183–96.

17.4.8   Black/Native American Relations

Abel, Annie Heloise, *The American Indian As Slaveholder and Secessionist: An Omitted Chapter in the Diplomatic History of the Southern Confederacy* (1915).

Bateman, Rebecca B., "Africans and Indians: A Comparative Study of the Black Carib and Black Seminole," *Ethnohistory* 37 (1990): 1–24.

Braund, Kathryn E. Holland, "The Creek Indians, Blacks, and Slavery," *Journal of Southern History* 57 (1991): 601–36.

Britten, Thomas A., *A Brief History of the Seminole-Negro Indian Scouts* (1999).

Gibson, Arrell Morgan, *The Chickasaws* (1971).

Halliburton, R., Jr., "Black Slave Control in the Cherokee Nation," *Journal of Ethnic Studies* 3 (1975): 23–35.

———— *Red over Black: Black Slavery among the Cherokee Indians* (1977).

Hoover, Dwight W., *The Red and the Black* (1976).

Katz, William Loren, "Black and Indian Cooperation and Resistance to Slavery," *Freedomways* 17 (1977): 164–74.

Klos, George, "Blacks and the Seminole Removal Debate, 1821–1835," *Florida Historical Quarterly* 68 (1989): 55–78.

Littlefield, Daniel F., Jr., *Africans and Seminoles: From Removal to Emancipation* (1977).

————— *Africans and Creeks: From the Colonial Period to the Civil War* (1979).

————— *The Cherokee Freedmen: From Emancipation to American Citizenship* (1978).

————— *The Chickasaw Freedmen: A People without a Country* (1980).

Littlefield, Daniel F., Jr., and Ann Littlefield, "The Beams Family: Free Blacks in Indian Territory," *Journal of Negro History* 61 (1976): 16–35.

McLoughlin, William G., "Red Indians, Black Slavery, and White Racism: America's Slaveholding Indians," *American Quarterly* 26 (1974): 367–85.

McReynolds, Edwin C., *The Seminoles* (1957).

Neilson, John C., "Indian Masters, Black Slaves: An Oral History of the Civil War in Indian Territory," *Panhandle-Plains Historical Review* 65 (1992): 42–54.

Perdue, Theda, *Slavery and the Evolution of Cherokee Society, 1540–1866* (1979).

Peters, Virginia Bergman, *The Florida Wars* (1979).

Porter, Kenneth W., "Florida Slaves and Free Negroes in the Seminole War, 1835–1842," *Journal of Negro History* 28 (1943): 390–421.

————— "John Caesar: Seminole Negro Partisan," *Journal of Negro History* 31 (1946): 190–207.

————— "The Negro Abraham," *Florida Historical Quarterly* 25 (1946): 1–43.

————— "Negro Guides and Interpreters in the Early Stages of the Seminole War: December 28, 1835–March 6, 1837," *Journal of Negro History* 35 (1950): 174–82.

————— "Negroes and Indians on the Texas Frontier, 1834–1874," *Southwestern Historical Quarterly* 53 (1949): 151–63.

————— "Negroes and Indians on the Texas Frontier, 1831–1876," *Journal of Negro History* 41 (1956): 185–214; 285–310.

————— "Negroes and the Seminole War, 1835–1842," *Journal of Southern History* 30 (1964): 427–50.

————— "Notes Supplementary to 'Relations between Negroes and Indians,'" *Journal of Negro History* 18 (1933): 282–321.

————— "Osceola and the Negroes," *Florida Historical Quarterly* 33 (1955): 235–39.

————— "Relations between Negroes and Indians within the Present Limits of the United States," *Journal of Negro History* 13 (1932): 287–367.

Sefton, James E., "Black Slaves, Red Masters, White Middlemen: A Congressional Debate of 1852," *Florida Historical Quarterly* 51 (1972): 113–28.

Smith, C. Calvin, "The Oppressed Oppressors: Negro Slavery among the Choctaw Indians of Oklahoma," *Red River Valley Historical Review* 2 (1975): 240–54.

Symposium on Indians in the Old South, *Red, White, and Black*, ed. Charles M. Hudson (1971).

Usner, Daniel H., Jr., "American Indians on the Cotton Frontier: Changing Economic Relations with Citizens and Slaves in the Mississippi," *Journal of American History* 72 (1985): 297–317.

Walton, George, *Fearless and Free: The Seminole Indian War, 1835–1842* (1977).

Wright, James Leitch, Jr., *Creeks and Seminoles: The Destruction and Regeneration of the Muscogulge People* (1986).

17.4.9   Black/Ethnic Relations

Brown, Canter, Jr., "Race Relations in Territorial Florida, 1821–1845," *Florida Historical Quarterly* 73 (1995): 287–307.

Dunson, A. A., "Notes on the Missouri Germans on Slavery," *Missouri Historical Review* 59 (1965): 355–66.

Korn, Bertram W., "Jews and Negro Slavery in the Old South, 1789–1865," *Publication of the American Jewish History Society* 50 (1961): 32–37.

Meyers, Arthur S., "'Come! Let Us Fly to Freedom's Sky': The Response of Irish Immigrants in the South to Slavery during the Antebellum Period," *Journal of Southwest Georgia History* 7 (1989–92): 20–39.

Rousey, Dennis C., "Aliens in the WASP Nest: Ethnocultural Diversity in the Antebellum Urban South," *Journal of American History* 79 (1992): 152–64.

Woodson, Carter Godwin, "Freedom and Slavery in Appalachian America," *Journal of Negro History* 1 (1916): 132–50.

17.4.10   Segregation/Jim Crow

Fischer, Roger A., "Racial Segregation in Ante Bellum New Orleans," *American Historical Review* 74 (1969): 926–57.

17.4.11   Violence and Racial Disturbances

Clinton, Catherine, "'With a Whip in His Hand': Rape, Memory, and African-American Women," in Geneviéve Fabre and Robert O'Meally, ed., *History and Memory in African-American Culture* (1994): 205–218.
Howington, Arthur F., "Violence in Alabama: A Study of Late Ante-Bellum Montgomery," *Alabama Review* 27 (1974): 213–31.

17.5   GOVERNMENT

17.5.1   Law

Accomondo, Christina, "'The Laws Were Laid down to Me Anew': Harriet Jacobs and the Reframing of Legal Fictions," *African American Review* 32 (1998): 229–45.
Bardaglio, Peter W., "Rape and the Law in the Old South: Calculated to Excite Indignation in Every Heart," *Journal of Southern History* 60 (1994): 749–72.
Beatty-Brown, Florence R., "Legal Status of Arkansas Negroes before Emancipation," *Arkansas Historical Quarterly* 28 (1969): 6–13.
Berry, Mary Frances, *Black Resistance/White Law: A History of Constitutional Racism in America* (rev. and expanded ed., 1995).
Binder, Guyora, "Did the Slaves Author the Thirteenth Amendment? An Essay in Redemptive History," *Yale Journal of Law and the Humanities* 5 (1993): 471–506.
Bodenhamer, David J., and James W. Ely, Jr., ed., *Ambivalent Legacy: A Legal History of the South* (1984).
Brandon, Mark E., *Free in the World: American Slavery and Constitutional Failure* (1998).
Brewer, James Howard, "Legislation Designed to Control Slavery in Wilmington and Fayetteville," *North Carolina Historical Review* 30 (1953): 155–66.
Burnham, Margaret A., "An Impossible Marriage: Slave Law and Family Law," *Law and Inequality* 5 (1987): 187–225.
Campbell, Stanley W., *The Slave Catchers: Enforcement of the Fugitive Slave Law, 1850–1860* (1970).
Catterall, Helen Tunnicliff, ed., *Judicial Cases concerning American Slavery and the Negro* (5 vols., 1926–1937).
——— "Some Antecedents of the Dred Scott Case," *American Historical Review* 30 (1924): 56–71.
Clark, Ernest James, Jr., "Aspects of the North Carolina Slave Code, 1715–1860," *North Carolina Historical Review* 39 (1962): 148–64.
Coulter, E. Merton, "Four Slave Trials in Elbert County, Georgia," *Georgia Historical Quarterly* 41 (1957): 237–46.
Crouch, Barry A., "'All the Vile Passions': The Texas Black Code of 1866," *Southwestern Historical Quarterly* 97 (1993): 13–34.
Currier, James T., "From Slavery to Freedom in Mississippi's Legal System," *Journal of Negro History* 65 (1980): 112–25.
Edwards, John E., "Slave Justice in Four Middle Georgia Counties," *Georgia Historical Quarterly* 57 (1973): 265–73.
Edwards, Laura E., "The Problem of Dependency: African Americans, Labor Relations, and the Law in the Nineteenth-Century South," *Agricultural History* 72 (1998): 313–40.
Ehrlich, Walter, *They Have No Rights: Dred Scott's Struggle for Freedom* (1979).

Elkins, Stanley, and Eric McKitrick, "Institutions and the Law of Slavery: Slavery in Capitalist and Non-Capitalist Cultures," *American Quarterly* 9 (1957): 159–89.

Fede, Andrew, "Legitimized Violent Slave Abuse in the American South, 1619–1865: A Case Study of Law and Social Change in Six Southern States," *American Journal of Legal History* 29 (1985): 93–150.

———— *People without Rights: An Interpretation of the Fundamentals of the Law of Slavery in the U.S. South* (1992).

Fehrenbacher, Don Edward, *The Dred Scott Case: Its Significance in American Law and Politics* (1978).

Finkelman, Paul, ed., *Articles on American Slavery* (18 vols., 1989).

————, ed., *Free Blacks, Slaves, and Slaveowners in Civil and Criminal Courts: The Pamphlet Literature* (1988).

———— *The Law of Freedom and Bondage: A Casebook* (1986).

———— *Slavery in the Courtroom: An Annotated Bibliography of American Cases* (1985).

————, ed., *Slavery, Race, and the American Legal System, 1700–1872* (16 vols., 1988).

————, ed., *Slavery and the Law* (1997).

————, ed., *State Slavery Statutes* (1989).

Flanigan, Daniel J., "Criminal Procedure in Slave Trials in the Antebellum South," *Journal of Southern History* 40 (1974): 537–64.

Foley, William E., "Slave Freedom Suits before Dred Scott: The Case of Marie Jean Scypion's Descendants," *Missouri Historical Review* 79 (1984): 1–23.

Forness, Norman O., "The Master, the Slave, and the Patent Laws: A Vignette of the 1850's," *Prologue* 26 (1994): 48–53.

Franklin, John Hope, *The Emancipation Proclamation* (1963).

Gerteis, Louis S., *From Contraband to Freedman: Federal Policy towards Southern Blacks, 1861–1865* (1973).

Guild, June Purcell, *Black Laws of Virginia: A Summary of the Legislative Acts of Virginia Concerning Negroes from Earliest Times to the Present* (1936).

Hamer, Philip M., "Great Britain, the United States, and the Negro Seamen Acts, 1822–1848," *Journal of Southern History* 1 (1935): 3–28.

Harris, William C., "Formulation of the First Mississippi Plan: The Black Code of 1865," *Journal of Mississippi History* 29 (1967): 181–201.

Hopkins, Vincent Charles, *Dred Scott's Case* (1951).

Howard, Warren S., *American Slavers and the Federal Law, 1837–1862* (1963).

Howington, Arthur F., *What Sayeth the Law: The Treatment of Slaves and Free Blacks in the State and Local Courts of Tennessee* (1986).

Imes, William Lloyd, "The Legal Status of Free Negroes and Slaves in Tennessee," *Journal of Negro History* 4 (1919): 254–72.

Johnson, Franklin, *The Development of State Legislation concerning the Free Negro* (1919).

Jones, Howard, *Mutiny on the Amistad: The Saga of a Slave Revolt and Its Impact on American Abolition, Law, and Diplomacy* (1987).

Jordan, Winthrop D., *Tumult and Silence at Second Creek: An Inquiry into a Civil War Slave Conspiracy* (rev. ed., 1995).

Keir, A. E., "The Texas Supreme Court and Trial Rights of Blacks, 1845–1860," *Journal of American History* 58 (1971): 622–42.

Klebaner, Benjamin Joseph, "American Manumission Law and the Responsibility for Supporting Slaves," *Virginia Magazine of History and Biography* 63 (1955): 443–53.

Kunkel, Paul A., "Modification in Louisiana Negro Legal Status under Louisiana Constitutions, 1812–1957," *Journal of Negro History* 44 (1959): 1–25.

Kutler, Stanley I., ed., *The Dred Scott Decision: Law or Politics?* (1967).

Lang, Meredith, *Defender of the Faith: The High Court of Mississippi, 1817–1875* (1977).

Lapp, Rudolph M., *Archy Lee: A California Fugitive Slave Case* (1969).

Lichtenstein, Alex, "'That Disposition to Theft, with Which They Have Been Branded': Moral Economy, Slave Management, and the Law," *Journal of Social History* 21 (1988): 413–40.

Ludlum, Robert P., "The Antislavery 'Gag-Rule': History and Argument," *Journal of Negro History* 26 (1941): 203–43.

Mathias, F. F., "John Randolph's Freedmen: The Thwarting of a Will," *Journal of Southern History* 39 (1973): 263–72.

McMillan, Malcolm Cook, *Constitutional Development in Alabama, 1798–1901: A Study in Politics, The Negro, and Sectionalism* (1955).

McPherson, Robert, ed., "Georgia Slave Trials, 1837–1849," *American Journal of Legal History* 4 (1960): 257–84, 364–77.

Mecklin, John M., "The Evolution of the Slave Status in American Democracy, Part Two," *Journal of Negro History* 2 (1917): 229–51.

Mooney, Chase Curran, "The Question of Slavery and the Free Negro in the Tennessee Constitutional Convention of 1834," *Journal of Southern History* 12 (1946): 487–509.

Morris, Richard B., "Labor Controls in Maryland in the Nineteenth Century," *Journal of Southern History* 14 (1948): 385–400.

Nash, A. E. Keir, "Fairness and Formalism in the Trials of Blacks in the State Supreme Courts of the Old South," *Virginia Law Review* 56 (1970): 64–100.

———— "A More Equitable Past? Southern Supreme Courts and the Protection of the Antebellum Negro," *North Carolina Law Review* 48 (1970): 197–242.

———— "The Texas Supreme Court and Trial Rights of Blacks, 1845–1860," *Journal of American History* 58 (1971): 622–42.

Nelson, B. H., "Some Aspects of Negro Life in North Carolina during the Civil War," *North Carolina Historical Review* 25 (1948): 143–66.

Neman, Donald G., "The Freedmen's Bureau and the Mississippi Black Code," *Journal of Mississippi History* 40 (1978): 91–118.

Nye, Russel Blaine, *Fettered Freedom: Civil Liberties and the Slavery Controversy, 1830–1860* (rev. ed., 1963).

Rogers, W. McDowell, "Free Negro Legislation in Georgia before 1865," *Georgia Historical Quarterly* 16 (32): 27–37.

Russell, Marion J., "American Slave Discontent in Records of the High Courts," *Journal of Negro History* 31 (1946): 411–34.

Schafer, Judith Kelleher, *Slavery, the Civil Law, and the Supreme Court of Louisiana* (1994).

Schmidt, James D., *Free to Work: Labor Law, Emancipation, and Reconstruction, 1815–1880* (1998).

Senese, Donald J., "The Free Negro and the South Carolina Courts, 1790–1860," *South Carolina Historical Magazine* 68 (1967): 140–53.

Shaw, Robert B., *A Legal History of Slavery in the United States* (1991).

Simpson, Albert F., "The Political Significance of Slave Representation," *Journal of Southern History* 7 (1941): 315–42.

Sommerville, Diane Miller, "The Rape Myth in the Old South Reconsidered," *Journal of Southern History* 61 (1995): 481–518.

Steel, Edward M., Jr., "Black Monongalians: A Judicial View of Slavery and the Negro in Monongalia County, 1776–1865," *West Virginia History* 34 (1973): 331–59.

Swan, Jon, "The Slave Who Sued for Freedom," *American Heritage* 41 (1990): 51–55.

Talmadge, John E., "Georgia Tests the Fugitive Slave Law," *Georgia Historical Quarterly* 49 (1965): 57–64.

Taylor, R. H., "Humanizing the Slave Code of North Carolina," *North Carolina Historical Review* 2 (1925): 323–31.

Thompson, Joseph Conan, "Toward a More Humane Oppression: Florida's Slave Codes, 1821–1861," *Florida Historical Quarterly* 71 (1993): 324–38.

Tushnet, Mark V., *The American Law of Slavery, 1810–1860: Considerations of Humanity and Interest* (1981).

Wagandt, Charles L., "The Army versus Maryland Slavery, 1862–1864," *Civil War History* 10 (1964): 141–48.

Wahl, Jenny Bourne, *The Bondsman's Burden: An Economic Analysis of the Common Law of Southern Slavery* (1998).

———— "Legal Constraints on Slave Masters: The Problem of Social Cost," *American Journal of Legal History* 41 (1997): 1–24.

Watson, Alan, *Slave Law in the Americas* (1989).

Weisenburger, Steven, *Modern Medea: A Family Story of Slavery and Child-Murder from the Old South* (1998).

Wiecek, William M., "Slavery and Abolition before the United States Supreme Court, 1820–1860," *Journal of American History* 65 (1978): 34–59.

Williams, E. Russ, Jr., "Slave Patrol Ordinances of St. Tammany Parish, Louisiana, 1835–1838," *Louisiana History* 13 (1972): 399–412.

Wilson, Theodore Brantner, *The Black Codes of the South* (1965).

Wren, J. Thomas, "A 'Two-Fold Character': The Slave As Person and Property in Virginia Court Cases, 1800–1860," *Southern Studies* 24 (1985): 417–31.

Yanuck, Julius, "The Garner Fugitive Slave Case," *Mississippi Valley Historical Review* 40 (1953): 47–66.

Younger, Richard D., "Southern Grand Juries and Slavery," *Journal of Negro History* 40 (1955): 166–78.

17.5.2   Crime and Punishment

Ayers, Edward L., *Vengeance and Justice: Crime and Punishment in the Nineteenth Century American South* (1984).

Finkelman, Paul, ed., *Free Blacks, Slaves, and Slaveowners in Civil and Criminal Courts: The Pamphlet Literature* (1988).

Hindus, Michael S., "Black Justice under White Law: Criminal Prosecution of Blacks in Antebellum South Carolina," *Journal of American History* 63 (1976): 1–17.

———— *Prison and Plantation: Crime, Justice, and Authority in Massachusetts and South Carolina, 1767–1878* (1980).

Lichtenstein, Alex, "'That Disposition to Theft, with Which They Have Been Branded': Moral Economy, Slave Management, and the Law," *Journal of Social History* 21 (1988): 413–40.

McLaurin, Melton Alonza, *Celia, A Slave* (1991).

Schwarz, Philip J., *Twice Condemned: Slaves and the Criminal Laws of Virginia, 1705–1865* (1988).

Sellin, J. Thorsten, *Slavery and the Penal System* (1976).

Waldrep, Christopher, *Roots of Disorder: Race and Criminal Justice in the American South, 1817–1880* (1998).

Ware, Lowry, "The Burning of Jerry: The Last Slave Execution by Fire in South Carolina," *South Carolina Historical Magazine* 91 (1990): 100–06.

Wyatt-Brown, Bertram, "Community, Class, and Snopesian Crime: Local Justice in the Old South," in Orville Vernon Burton and Robert C. McMath, Jr., ed., *Class, Conflict, and Consensus: Antebellum Southern Community Studies* (1982): 173–206.

17.5.3   Politics and Voting

Belz, Herman, "Origins of Negro Suffrage during the Civil War," *Southern Studies* 17 (1978): 115–30.

Cimprich, John, "The Beginning of the Black Suffrage Movement in Tennessee, 1864–1865," *Journal of Negro History* 65 (1980): 185–95.

Foner, Eric, "Politics and Prejudices: The Free Soil Party and the Negro, 1849–1852," *Journal of Negro History* 50 (1965): 239–66.

O'Donovan, Susan E., "Philip Joiner: Southwest Georgia's Black Republican," *Journal of Southwest Georgia History* 4 (1986): 56–71.

Pease, Jane H., and William H. Pease, "Negro Conventions and the Problem of Black Leadership," *Journal of Black Studies* 2 (1971): 29–44.

Quarles, Benjamin, "Frederick Douglass and the Woman's Rights Movement," *Journal of Negro History* 25 (1940): 35–44.

Shugg, Roger Wallace, "Negro Voting in the Antebellum South," *Journal of Negro History* 21 (1936): 357–64.

Tunnell, Ted, "Free Negros and the Freedmen: Black Politics in New Orleans during the Civil War," *Southern Studies* 19 (1980): 5–28.

Walker, S. Jay, "Frederick Douglass and Woman Suffrage," *Black Scholar* 4 (1973): 24–31.

17.5.4   Military

Aptheker, Herbert, "Negro Casualties in the Civil War" and "Negroes in the Union Navy," in *To Be Free: Studies in American Negro History* (1948): 75–112, 113–35.

———— "The Negro in the Civil War," in Herbert Aptheker, *Essays in the History of the American Negro* (1945): 163–205.

Bailey, Anne J., "A Texas Cavalry Raid: Reaction to Black Soldiers and Contrabands," *Civil War History* 35 (1989): 138–52.

Belz, Herman, "Law, Politics, and Race in the Struggle for Equal Pay during the Civil War," *Civil War History* 22 (1976): 197–213.

Bergeron, Arthur W., Jr., "Louisiana's Free Men of Color in Gray," *Journal of Confederate History* 11 (1994): 37–55.

Berlin, Ira, Barbara J. Fields, Joseph P. Reidy, and Leslie S. Rowland, "Writing Freedom's History," *Prologue* 14 (1982): 129–39.

Berlin, Ira, Wayne Durrill, Steven F. Miller, Leslie S. Rowland, and Leslie Schwalm, "'To Canvass the Nation': The War for Union Becomes a War for Freedom," *Prologue* 20 (1988): 227–47.

Berlin, Ira, Joseph P. Reidy, and Leslie S. Rowland, ed., *The Black Military Experience, Series II of Freedom: A Documentary History of Emancipation, 1861–1867* (1982).

Berlin, Ira, Joseph P. Reidy, and Leslie S. Rowland, ed., *Freedom's Soldiers: The Black Military Experience in the Civil War* (1998).

Berry, Mary Frances, "Negro Troops in Blue and Gray: The Louisiana Native Guards, 1861–1863," *Louisiana History* 8 (1967): 165–90.

Blackerby, H. C., *Blacks in Blue and Gray: Afro-American Service in the Civil War* (1979).

Blassingame, John W., "The Recruitment of Negro Troops in Maryland," *Maryland Historical Magazine* 58 (1963): 20–29.

———— "The Recruitment of Negro Troops in Missouri during the Civil War," *Missouri Historical Review* 58 (1964): 326–38.

———— "The Recruitment of Colored Troops in Kentucky, Maryland, and Missouri, 1863–1865," *Historian* 29 (1967): 533–45.

Brewer, James H., *The Confederate Negro: Virginia's Craftsmen and Military Laborers, 1861–1865* (1969).

Cartwright, Thomas Y., "'Better Confederates Did Not Live': Black Southerners in Nathan Bedford Forrest's Commands," in Arthur W. Bergeron, John McGlone and Richard M. Rollins, ed., *Black Southerners in Gray: Essays on Afro-Americans in Confederate Armies* (1994): 94–120.

Castel, Albert, "Fort Pillow: Victory or Massacre," *American History Illustrated* 9 (1974): 4–10, 46–48.

Chester, Thomas Morris, *Thomas Morris Chester, Black Civil War Correspondent: His Dispatches from the Virginia Front*, ed. R. J. M. Blackett (1989).

Cimprich, John, and Robert C. Mainfort, Jr., "The Fort Pillow Massacre: A Statistical Note," *Journal of American History* 76 (1989): 830–37.

Cornish, Dudley Taylor, *The Sable Arm: Negro Troops in the Union Army, 1861–1865* (1956).

Daniels, Nathan W., *Thank God My Regiment an African One: The Civil War Diary of Colonel Nathan W. Daniels*, ed. Claire P. Weaver (1998).

Davis, William C., "The Massacre at Saltville," *Civil War Times Illustrated* 9 (1971): 4–11, 43–48.

Dyer, Brainard, "The Treatment of Colored Union Troops by the Confederates, 1861–1865," *Journal of Negro History* 20 (1935): 273–86.

Ellison, Mary, "African American Music and Muskets in Civil War New Orleans," *Louisiana History* 35 (1994): 285–319.

Everett, Donald E., "Ben Butler and the Louisiana Native Guards, 1861–1862," *Journal of Southern History* 24 (1958): 202–17.

———— "Emigrés and Militiamen: Free Persons of Color in New Orleans, 1803–1815," *Journal of Negro History* 38 (1953): 377–402.

Foner, Philip S., "The First Negro Meeting in Maryland," *Maryland Historical Magazine* 66 (1971): 60–67.

Glatthaar, Joseph T., "The Civil War through the Eyes of a Sixteen-Year-Old Black Officer: The Letters of Lieutenant John H. Crowder of the First Louisiana Native Guards," *Louisiana History* 35 (1994): 201–16.

———— *Forged in Battle: The Civil War Alliance of Black Soldiers and White Officers* (1990).

Gooding, James Henry, *On the Altar of Freedom: A Black Soldier's Civil War Letters from the Front,* ed. Virginia Matzke Adams (1991).

Harrington, Fred Harvey, "The Fort Jackson Mutiny," *Journal of Negro History* 27 (1942): 420–31.

Hollandsworth, James G., Jr., *The Louisiana Native Guards: The Black Military Experience during the Civil War* (1995).

Huch, Ronald K., "Fort Pillow Massacre: The Aftermath of Paducah," *Journal of the Illinois State Historical Society* 66 (1973): 62–70.

Johnson, John Allen, "The Medal of Honor and Sergeant John Ward and Private Pompey Factor," *Arkansas Historical Quarterly* 29 (1970): 361–75.

Jordan, Ervin L., Jr., *Black Confederates and Afro-Yankees in Civil War Virginia* (1995).

Krech, Shepard, III, "The Participation of Maryland Blacks in the Civil War: Perspectives from Oral History," *Ethnohistory* 27 (1980): 67–78.

Long, E. B., "The Paducah Affair: Bloodless Action That Altered the Civil War in the Mississippi Valley," *Register of the Kentucky Historical Society* 70 (1972): 253–76.

Longacre, Edward G., "Black Troops in the Army of the James, 1863–1865," *Military Affairs* 45 (1981): 1–8.

Lovett, Bobby L., "Nashville's Fort Negley: A Symbol of Blacks' Involvement with the Union Army," *Tennessee Historical Quarterly* 41 (1982): 3–22.

———— "The Negro's Civil War in Tennessee, 1861–1865," *Journal of Negro History* 61 (1976): 36–50.

———— "The West Tennessee Colored Troops in Civil War Combat," *West Tennessee Historical Society Papers* 34 (1980): 53–70.

McCline, John, *Slavery in the Clover Bottoms: John McCline's Narrative of His Life during Slavery and the Civil War,* ed. Jan Furman (1998).

McConnell, Roland Calhoun, *Negro Troops in Antebellum Louisiana: A History of the Battalion of Free Men of Color* (1968).

McPherson, James M., *Battle Cry of Freedom: The Civil War Era* (1988).

Messner, William F., "The Vicksburg Campaign of 1862: A Case Study in the Federal Utilization of Black Labor," *Louisiana History* 16 (1975): 371–81.

Metzer, Jacob, "The Records of the U.S. Colored Troops as a Historical Source: An Exploratory Examination," *Historical Methods* 14 (1981): 123–32.

Mills, Gary B., "Patriotism Frustrated: The Native Guards of Confederate Natchitoches," *Louisiana History* 18 (1977): 437–51.

Mohr, Clarence L., "Before Sherman: Georgia Blacks and the Union War Effort, 1861–1864," *Journal of Southern History* 45 (1979): 331–52.

Neal, Diane, and Thomas W. Kremm, "'The King of Revolution Is the Bayonet': General Thomas C. Hindman's Proposal to Arm the Slaves," *Journal of Confederate History* 7 (1991): 81–96.

Nelson, Bernard H., "Confederate Slave Impressment Legislation, 1861–1865," *Journal of Negro History* 31 (1946): 392–410.

Peters, Virginia Bergman, *The Florida Wars* (1979).

Porter, Kenneth W., "Florida Slaves and Free Negroes in the Seminole War, 1835–1842," *Journal of Negro History* 28 (1943): 390–421.

———— "John Caesar: Seminole Negro Partisan," *Journal of Negro History* 31 (1946): 190–207.

———— "Negroes and the Seminole War, 1835–1842," *Journal of Southern History* 30 (1964): 427–50.

————."Three Fighters for Freedom," *Journal of Negro History* 28 (1943): 51–72.

Preisser, Thomas M., "The Virginia Decision to Use Negro Soldiers in the Civil War, 1864–1865," *Virginia Magazine of History and Biography* 83 (1975): 98–113.

Quarles, Benjamin, *The Negro in the Civil War* (1953).

Reid, Richard, "Raising the African Brigade: Early Black Recruitment in Civil War North Carolina," *North Carolina Historical Review* 70 (1993): 266–301.

Rollins, Richard, "Black Confederates at Gettysburg," in Arthur W. Bergeron, John McGlone and Richard M. Rollins, ed., *Black Southerners in Gray: Essays on Afro-Americans in Confederate Armies* (1994).

———— "Black Southerners in Gray," in Arthur W. Bergeron, John McGlone and Richard M. Rollins, ed., *Black Southerners in Gray: Essays on Afro-Americans in Confederate Armies* (1994).

———— "Servants and Soldiers: Tennessee's Black Southerners in Gray," in Arthur W. Bergeron, John McGlone and Richard M. Rollins, ed., *Black Southerners in Gray: Essays on Afro-Americans in Confederate Armies* (1994): 75–93.

Shannon, Fred A., "The Federal Government and the Negro Soldier, 1861–1865," *Journal of Negro History* 11 (1926): 563–83.

Solomon, Irvin D., "Southern Extremities: The Significance of Fort Myers in the Civil War," *Florida Historical Quarterly* 72 (1993): 129–152.

Sommers, Richard J., "The Dutch Gap Affair: Military Atrocities and Rights of Negro Soldiers," *Civil War History* 21 (1975): 51–64.

Stephens, George E., *A Voice of Thunder: The Civil War Letters of George E. Stephens,* ed. Donald Yacovone (1997).

Taylor, Susie King, *Reminiscences of My Life in Camp with the Thirty-Second United States Colored Troops Late First S. C. Volunteers* (1902).

Thompson, Erwin N., "The Negro Soldiers on the Frontier: A Fort Davis Case Study," *Journal of the West* 7 (1968): 217–35.

Walton, George, *Fearless and Free: The Seminole Indian War, 1835–1842* (1977).

Wesley, Charles H., "The Employment of Negroes As Soldiers in the Confederate Army," *Journal of Negro History* 4 (1919): 239–53.

Westwood, Howard C., "Benjamin Butler's Enlistment of Black Troops in New Orleans in 1862," *Louisiana History* 26 (1985): 5–22.

———— *Black Troops, White Commanders, and Freedmen during the Civil War* (1992).

———— "Captive Black Union Soldiers in Charleston: What to Do?" *Civil War History* 28 (1982): 28–44.

Wilson, Joseph T., *The Black Phalanx: A History of the Negro Soldiers of the United States in the Wars of 1775–1812, 1861–1865* (1888).

Wright, J. Leitch, Jr., "A Note on the First Seminole War As Seen by the Indians, Negroes, and Their British Advisers," *Journal of Southern History* 34 (1968): 565–75.

17.6 DEMOGRAPHY

Barney, William L., "Towards the Civil War: The Dynamics of Change in a Black Belt County," in Orville Vernon Burton and Robert C. McMath, Jr., ed., *Class, Conflict, and Consensus: Antebellum Southern Community Studies* (1982): 146–72.

Blackburn, George M., and Sherman L. Ricards, "A Demographic History of Slavery: Georgetown County, South Carolina, 1850," *South Carolina Historical Magazine* 76 (1975): 215–24.

Brigham, Clarence S., "Antebellum Census Enumerations in Florida," *Florida Historical Society Quarterly* 6 (1927): 42–55.

Dodd, Donald B., and Wynelle S. Dodd, *Historical Statistics of the South, 1790–1970: A Compilation of State-Level Census Statistics for the Sixteen States of Alabama, Arkansas, Delaware, Florida, Georgia, Kentucky, Louisiana, Maryland, Mississippi, North Carolina, Oklahoma, South Carolina, Tennessee, Texas, Virginia, West Virginia* (1973).

Eblen, Jack E., "New Estimates of the Vital Rates of the United States Black Population in the Nineteenth Century," *Demography* 11 (1974): 300–19.

Engerman, Stanley L., "Some Economic and Demographic Comparisons of Slavery in the United States and the British West Indies," *Economic History Review [Great Britain]* 29 (1976): 258–75.

Farrison, William Edward, "The Negro Population of Guilford County, North Carolina, before the Civil War," *North Carolina Historical Review* 21 (1944): 319–29.

Friedlander, Amy, "Establishing Historical Probabilities for Archaeological Interpretations: Slave Demography of Two Plantations in the South Carolina Lowcountry, 1740–1820," in Theresa A. Singleton, ed., *The Archaeology of Slavery and Plantation Life* (1985): 215–38.

Garonzik, Joseph, "The Racial and Ethnic Make-Up of Baltimore Neighborhoods, 1850–1870," *Maryland Historical Magazine* 71 (1976): 392–402.

Holland, C. G., "The Slave Population on the Plantation of John C. Cohoon, Jr., Nansemond County, Virginia, 1811–1863: Selected Demographic Characteristics," *Virginia Magazine of History and Biography* 80 (1972): 333–40.

Hutchinson, Janis, "The Age-Sex Structure of the Slave Population in Harris County, Texas, 1850 and 1860," *American Journal of Physical Anthropology* 74 (1987): 231–38.

Johnson, Whittington B., "Free Blacks in Antebellum Augusta, Georgia: A Demographic and Economic Profile," *Richmond County History* 14 (1982): 10–21.

Klein, Herbert S., and Stanley Engerman, "Fertility Differentials between Slaves in the United States and the British West Indies: A Note on Lactation Practices and Their Possible Implications," *William and Mary Quaterly* 35 (1978): 357–74.

Lantz, Herman, and Lewellyn Hendrix, "Black Fertility and the Black Family in the Nineteenth Century: A Re-Examination of the Past," *Journal of Family History* 3 (1978): 251–61.

Meeker, Edward, "Mortality Trends of Southern Blacks, 1850–1910: Some Preliminary Findings," *Explorations in Economic History* 13 (1976): 13–42.

Mooney, Chase C., "Some Institutional and Statistical Aspects of Slavery in Tennessee," *Tennessee Historical Quarterly* 1 (1942): 195–228.

Owsley, Douglas W., Charles E. Owsley, and Robert W. Mann, "Demography and Pathology of an Urban Slave Population from New Orleans," *American Journal of Physical Anthropology* 74 (1987): 185–97.

Steckel, Richard H., *The Economics of U.S. Slave and Southern White Fertility* (1985).

——— "The Fertility of American Slaves," *Research in Economic History* 7 (1982): 239–86.

——— "Miscegenation and the American Slave Schedules," *Journal of Interdisciplinary History* 11 (1980): 251–63.

——— "Slave Height Profiles from Coastwise Manifests," *Explorations in Economic History* 16 (1979): 363–80.

Vinovskis, Maris A., "The Demography of the Slave Population in Antebellum America," *Journal of Interdisciplinary History* 5 (1975): 459–67.

17.7 FAMILY

Berlin, Ira, Steven F. Miller, and Leslie S. Rowland, "Afro-American Families in the Transition from Slavery to Freedom," *Radical History Review* 42 (1988): 89–121.

Berlin, Ira, and Leslie S. Rowland, ed., *Families and Freedom: A Documentary History of African-American Kinship in the Civil War Era* (1997).

Blackburn, George, and Sherman L. Ricards, "The Mother-Headed Family among Free Negroes in Charleston, South Carolina, 1850–1860," *Phylon* 42 (1981): 11–25.

Blassingame, John W., "The Slave Family in America," *American History Illustrated* 7 (1972): 10–17.

Brasfield, Curtis, "'To My Daughter and the Heirs of Her Body': Slave Passages as Illustrated by the Latham-Smithwick Family," *National Genealogical Society* 81 (1993): 270–82.

Brown, Steven E., "Sexuality and the Slave Community," *Phylon* 42 (1981): 1–10.

Burnham, Dorothy, "Children of the Slave Community in the United States," *Freedomways* 19 (1979): 75–81.

Burnham, Margaret A., "An Impossible Marriage: Slave Law and Family Law," *Law and Inequality* 5 (1987): 187–225.

Burton, Orville Vernon, *In My Father's House Are Many Mansions: Family and Community in Edgefield, South Carolina* (1985).

Cassity, Michael J., "Slaves, Families, and 'Living Space': A Note on Evidence and Historical Context," *Southern Studies* 17 (1978): 209–15.

Cody, Cheryll Ann, "There Was No 'Absolom' on the Ball Plantations: Slave-Naming Practices in the South Carolina Low Country, 1720–1865," *American Historical Review* 92 (1987): 563–96.

Cornelius, Janet, "Slave Marriages in a Georgia Congregation," in Orville Vernon Burton and Robert C. McMath, Jr., ed., *Class, Conflict, and Consensus: Antebellum Southern Community Studies* (1982): 128–45.

Crowley, John, "The Importance of Kinship: Testamentary Evidence from South Carolina," *Journal of Interdisciplinary History* 16 (1986): 559–77.

Diedrich, Maria, "'My Love Is Black As Yours Is Fair': Premarital Love and Sexuality in the Antebellum Slave Narrative," *Phylon* 47 (1986): 238–47.

Doherty, Herbert J., Jr., ed., "A Free Negro Purchases His Daughter," *Florida Historical Quarterly* 29 (1950): 38–43.

Du Bois, William Edward Burghardt, ed., *The Negro American Family: Report of a Social Study Made by the College Classes of 1909 and 1910 of Atlanta University* (1908).

Durrill, Wayne K., "Slavery, Kinship, and Dominance: The Black Community at Somerset Place Plantation, 1786–1860," *Slavery and Abolition* 13 (1992): 1–19.

Engerman, Stanley L., "Studying the Black Family: A Review Essay of *The Black Family* by Herbert S. Gutman," *Journal of Interdisciplinary History* 3 (1978): 78–101.

Farnham, Christie, "Sapphire? The Issue of Dominance in the Slave Family, 1830–1865," in Carol Groneman and Mary Beth Norton, ed., *"To Toil the Livelong Day": American Women at Work, 1780–1980* (1987): 68–83.

Fink, Leon, George Rawick, and Evelyn Brooks, "A Symposium on Herbert Gutman's *The Black Family in Slavery and Freedom,*" *Radical History Review* 4 (1977): 76–108.

Frankel, Noralee, *Freedom's Women: Black Women and Families in Civil War Era Mississippi* (1999).

Frazier, Edward Franklin, *The Free Negro Family: A Study of Family Origins before the Civil War* (1932).

——— *The Negro Family in the United States* (1966).

——— "The Negro Slave Family," *Journal of Negro History* 15 (1930): 198–259.

Genovese, Eugene D., "'Our Family, White and Black': Family and Household in the Southern Slaveholder's World View," in Carol Bleser, ed., *In Joy and In Sorrow: Women, Family, and Marriage in the Victorian South, 1830–1900* (1991): 69–87.

——— "The Slave Family: Women—A Reassessment of Matriarchy, Emasculation, Weakness," *Southern Voices* 1 (1974): 9–16.

Gutman, Herbert G., *The Black Family in Slavery and Freedom, 1750–1925* (1976).

——— "Marital and Sexual Norms among Slave Women," in Nancy F. Cott and Elizabeth H. Pleck, ed., *A Heritage of Her Own: Toward a New Social History of American Women* (1979): 298–310.

——— "Persistent Myths about the Afro-American Family," *Journal of Interdisciplinary History* 6 (1975): 181–210.

——— "Slave Family and Its Legacies," *Historical Reflections* 6 (1979): 183–99.

Gutman, Herbert G. and Richard Sutch, "The Slave Family: Protected Agent of Capitalist Masters or Victim of the Slave Trade?" in Paul A. David, Herbert G. Gutman, Richard Sutch, Peter Temin and Gavin Wright, ed., *Reckoning with Slavery: A Critical Study in the Quantitative History of American Negro Slavery* (1976): 94–133.

Inscoe, John C., "Carolina Slave Names: An Index to Acculturation," *Journal of Southern History* 49 (1983): 527–54.

——— "Generation and Gender As Reflected in Carolina Slave Naming Practices: A Challenge to the Gutman Thesis," *South Carolina Historical Magazine* 94 (1993): 252–63.

Johnson, Michael P., and James L. Roark, ed., *Black Masters: A Free Family of Color in the Old South* (1984).

——— "Strategies of Survival: Free Negro Families and the Problem of Slavery," in Carol Bleser, ed., *In Joy and In Sorrow: Women, Family, and Marriage in the Victorian South, 1830–1900* (1991): 88–102.

Jones, Jacqueline, "'My Mother Was Much of a Woman': Black Women, Work, and the Family under Slavery," *Feminist Studies* 8 (1982): 235–69.

Jupiter, Del E., "From Augusta to Ester: Analyzing a Slave Household for Child-Parent Relationships," *National Genealogical Society Quarterly* 85 (1997): 245–75.

King, Wilma, *Stolen Childhood: Slave Youth in Nineteenth-Century America* (1995).

Klein, Mary O., "'We Shall Be Accountable to God': Some Inquiries into the Position of Blacks in Somerset Parish, Maryland, 1692–1865," *Maryland Historical Magazine* 87 (1992): 399–406.

Krech, Shepard, III, "Black Family Organization in the Nineteenth Century: An Ethnological Perspective," *Journal of Interdisciplinary History* 12 (1982): 429–52.

Labinjoh, Justin, "The Sexual Life of the Oppressed: An Examination of the Family Life of Ante-Bellum Slaves," *Phylon* 35 (1974): 375–97.

Lantz, Herman, "Family and Kin As Revealed in the Narratives of Ex-Slaves," *Social Science Quarterly* 60 (1980): 667–75.

Lantz, Herman, and Lewellyn Hendrix, "Black Fertility and the Black Family in the Nineteenth Century: A Re-Examination of the Past," *Journal of Family History* 3 (1978): 251–61.

Lewis, Ronald L., "Slave Families at Early Chesapeake Iron Works," *Virginia Magazine of History and Biography* 86 (1978): 169–79.

Malone, Ann Patton, "Searching for the Family and Household Structure of Rural Louisiana Slaves, 1810–1864," *Louisiana History* 28 (1987): 357–79.

——— *Sweet Chariot: Slave Family and Household Structure in Nineteenth-Century Louisiana* (1992).

McDaniel, Antonio, "The Power of Culture: A Review of the Idea of Africa's Influence on Family Structure in Antebellum America," *Journal of Family History* 15 (1990): 225–38.

McMillen, Sally Gregory, *Motherhood in the Old South: Pregnancy, Childbirth, and Infant Rearing* (1990).

Model, John, Stephen Gudeman, and Warren C. Sanderson, "A Colloquium on Herbert Gutman's *The Black Family in Slavery and Freedom, 1750–1925*," *Social Science History* 3 (1979): 45–85.

Patterson, Ruth Polk, *The Seed of Sally Good'n: A Black Family of Arkansas, 1833–1953* (1985).

Ripley, C. Peter, "The Black Family in Transition: Louisiana, 1860–1865," *Journal of Southern History* 41 (1975): 369–80.

Schweninger, Loren, "A Slave Family in the Antebellum South," *Journal of Negro History* 60 (1975): 29–44.

Sides, Sudie Duncan, "Slave Weddings and Religion," *History Today [UK]* 24 (1974): 77–87.

Staples, Robert, "The Black Family in Evolutionary Perspective," *Black Scholar* 5 (1974): 2–9.

Steckel, Richard H., "Slave Marriage and the Family," *Journal of Family History* 5 (1980): 406–21.

Stevenson, Brenda E., "Distress and Discord in Virginia Slave Families, 1830–1860," in Carol Bleser, ed., *In Joy and In Sorrow: Women, Family, and Marriage in the Victorian South, 1830–1900* (1991): 103–24.

——— *Life in Black and White: Family and Community in the Slave South* (1996).

Thornton, John, "Central African Names and African-American Naming Patterns," *William and Mary Quarterly* 50 (1993): 727–42.

Uzzel, Odell, "Free Negro/Slave Marriages and Family Life in Antebellum North Carolina," *Western Journal of Black Studies* 18 (1994): 64–9.

Warner, Lee H., *Free Men in an Age of Servitude: Three Generations of a Black Family* (1992).

Webber, Thomas L., "The Setting: Growing Up in the Quarter Community," in Harvey J. Graff, ed., *Growing Up in America: Historical Experiences* (1987): 198–214.

Wetherell, Charles, "Slave Kinship: A Case Study of the South Carolina Good Hope Plantation, 1835–1856," *Journal of Family History* 6 (1981): 294–308.

White, John, "Whatever Happened to the Slave Family in the Old South?" *Journal of American Studies [UK]* 8 (1974): 383–90.

Williams, Roger M., *The Bonds: An American Family* (1971).

Woods, C. P. D., and Sister Frances Jerome, *Marginality and Identity: A Colored Creole Family through Ten Generations* (1972).

Woodson, Carter Godwin, *Free Negro Heads of Families in the United States in 1830: Together with a Brief Treatment of the Free Negro* (1925).

17.8 SOCIETY

17.8.1 Rural Life (Including Black Settlements)

Jenkins, Robert L., "African-Americans on the Natchez Trace, 1800–1865," *Southern Quarterly* 29 (1991): 43–62.

Pease, William H., and Jane H. Pease, *Black Utopia: Negro Communal Experiments in America* (1963).

Penningroth, Dylan, "Slavery, Freedom, and Social Claims to Property among African Americans in Liberty County, Georgia, 1850–1880," *Journal of American History* 84 (1997): 405–35.

17.8.2 Urban Life (Including Migration)

Curry, Leonard P., *The Free Black in Urban America, 1800–1850: The Shadow of the Dream* (1981).

Goldin, Claudia Dale, "A Model to Explain the Relative Decline of Urban Slavery: Empirical Results," in Stanley L. Engerman and Eugene D. Genovese, ed., *Race and Slavery in the Western Hemisphere: Quantitative Studies* (1975): 427–50.

———— *Urban Slavery in the American South, 1820–1860: A Quantitative History* (1976).

Green, Rodney D., "Black Tobacco Factory Workers and Social Conflict in Antebellum Richmond: Were Slavery and Urban Industry Really Compatible?" *Slavery and Abolition* 8 (1987): 183–203.

Greenwood, Janette Thomas, *Bittersweet Legacy: The Black and White "Better Classes" in Charlotte, 1850–1910* (1994).

Johnson, Jerah, "New Orleans' Congo Square: An Urban Setting for Early Afro-American Culture Formation," *Louisiana History* 32 (1991): 117–57.

Johnson, Whittington B., *Black Savannah, 1788–1864* (1996).

O'Brien, John T., "Factory, Church, and Community: Blacks in Antebellum Richmond," *Journal of Southern History* 44 (1978): 509–36.

Owsley, Douglas W., Charles E. Owsley, and Robert W. Mann, "Demography and Pathology of an Urban Slave Population from New Orleans," *American Journal of Physical Anthropology* 74 (1987): 185–97.

Powers, Bernard Edward, Jr., *Black Charlestonians: A Social History, 1822–1885* (1994).

Reichard, Maximilian, "Black and White on the Urban Frontier: The St. Louis Community in Transition, 1800–1830," *Missouri Historical Society Bulletin* 33 (1976): 3–17.

Richter, William L., "Slavery in Baton Rouge, 1820–1860," in Theodore Kornweibel, Jr., ed., *In Search of the Promised Land: Essays in Black Urban History* (1981): 58–70.

Tripp, Steven Elliott, *Yankee Town, Southern City: Race and Class Relations in Civil War Lynchburg* (1996).

Tyler-McGraw, Marie, and Gregg Kimball, *In Bondage and in Freedom: Antebellum Black Life in Richmond, Virginia* (1988).

Wade, Richard C., *Slavery in the Cities: The South, 1820–1860* (1964).

17.8.3 Material Culture

Adams, William Hampton, ed., *Historical Archaeology of Plantations at Kings Bay, Camden County, Georgia* (1987).

Ascher, Robert, and Charles H. Fairbanks, "Excavation of a Slave Cabin: Georgia, USA," *Historical Archaeology* 5 (1971): 3–17.

Cassity, Michael J., "Slaves, Families, and 'Living Space': A Note on Evidence and Historical Context," *Southern Studies* 17 (1978): 209–15.

Catts, Wade P., and Davy McCall, "A Report of the Archaeological Investigations at the House of Thomas Cuff, a Free Black Laborer, 108 Cannon Street, Chestertown, Kent County, Maryland," *North American Archaeologist* 12 (1991): 155–81.

Friedlander, Amy, "Establishing Historical Probabilities for Archaeological Interpretations: Slave Demography of Two Plantations in the South Carolina Lowcountry, 1740–1820," in Theresa A. Singleton, ed., *The Archaeology of Slavery and Plantation Life* (1985): 215–38.

Fry, Gladys-Marie, "Harriet Powers: Portrait of a Black Quilter," *Sage* 4 (1987): 11–16.

———— *Stitched from the Soul: Slave Quilts from the Ante-Bellum South* (1990).

Lewis, Kenneth E., "Plantation Layout and Function in the South Carolina Lowcountry," in Theresa A. Singleton, ed., *The Archaeology of Slavery and Plantation Life* (1985): 35–65.

Lornell, Kip, "Black Material Folk Culture," *Southern Folklore Quarterly* 42 (1978): 287–94.

Orser, Charles E., Jr., "Beneath the Material Surface of Things: Commodities, Artifacts, and Slave Populations," *Historical Archaeology* 26 (1992): 95–104.

Reinhart, Theodore R., ed., *The Archaeology of Shirley Plantation* (1984).

Schuyler, Robert L., ed., *Archaeological Perspectives on Ethnicity in America: Afro American and Asian American Culture History* (1980).

Starke, Barbara M., "Slave Narratives: Accounts of What They Wore," in Barbara M. Starke, Lillian O. Holloman and Barbara K. Nordquist, ed., *African-American Dress and Adornment: A Cultural Perspective* (1990): 69–81.

Tandberg, Gerilyn G., "Field Hand Clothing in Louisiana and Mississippi during the Antebellum Period," *Press* 6 (1980): 89–103.

Vlach, John Michael, *By the Work of Their Hands: Studies in Afro-American Folklife* (1992).

———— "Evidence of Slave Housing in Washington," *Washington History* 5 (1993–94): 64–74.

Walston, Mark L., "A Survey of Slave Housing in Montgomery County: The Montgomery County Story," *Maryland Historical Magazine* 27 (1984): 111–26.

———— "'Uncle Tom's Cabin' Revisted: Origins and Interpretations of Slave Housing in the American South," *Southern Studies* 24 (1985): 357–73.

Warner, Patricia Campbell, and Debra Parker, "Slave Clothing and Textiles in North Carolina, 1775–1835," Barbara M. Starke, Lillian Holloman and Barbara K. Nordquist, ed., *African-American Dress and Adornment: A Cultural Perspective* (1990): 82–92.

Wheaton, Thomas R. and Patrick H. Garrow, "Acculturation and the Archaeological Record in the Carolina Lowcountry," in Theresa A. Singleton, ed., *The Archaeology of Slavery and Plantation Life* (1985): 239–59.

White, Shane, "Digging Up the African-American Past: Historical Archaeology, Photography, and Slavery," *Australasian Journal of American Studies* 11 (1992): 37–47.

Wright, Gwendolyn, *Building the Dream: A Social History of Housing in America* (1981).

17.8.4 Color and Class

Greenwood, Janette Thomas, *Bittersweet Legacy: The Black and White "Better Classes" in Charlotte, 1850–1910* (1994).

Hoetink, Harmannus, "Negro and Coloured," in Richard D. Brown and Stephen G. Rabe, ed., *Slavery in American Society* (1969): 72–77.

Horowitz, Donald L., "Color Differentiation in the American Systems of Slavery," *Journal of Interdisciplinary History* 3 (1973): 509–41.

Johnston, James Hugo, *Race Relations in Virginia and Miscegenation in the South, 1776–1860* (1970).

Joseph, J. W., "White Columns and Black Hands: Class and Classification in the Plantation Ideology of the Georgia and South Carolina Low Country," *History and Archaeology* 27 (1993): 57–73.

Kolchin, Peter, "Class Consciousness," *Reviews in American History* 20 (1992): 585–90.

Lachance, Paul F., "The Formation of a Three-Caste Society: Evidence from Wills in Antebellum New Orleans," *Social Science History* 18 (1994): 211–42.

Mills, Gary B., *The Forgotten People: Cane River's Creoles of Color* (1977).

———— "Miscegenation and the Free Negro in Antebellum 'Anglo' Alabama: A Reexamination of Southern Race Relations," *Journal of American History* 68 (1981): 16–34.

Steckel, Richard H., "Miscegenation and the American Slave Schedules," *Journal of Interdisciplinary History* 11 (1980): 251–63.

Toplin, Robert Brent, "Between Black and White: Attitudes toward Southern Mulattoes, 1830–1861," *Journal of Southern History* 45 (1979): 185–200.

Woodson, Carter Godwin, "The Beginnings of the Miscegenation of the Whites and Blacks," *Journal of Negro History* 3 (1918): 335–53.

17.8.5   Associational Life

Harris, Robert L., Jr., "Charleston's Free Afro-American Elite: The Brown Fellowship Society and the Humane Brotherhood," *South Carolina Historical Magazine* 82 (1981): 289–310.

Spencer, C. A., "Black Benevolent Societies and the Development of Black Insurance Companies in Nineteenth-Century Alabama," *Phylon* 46 (1985): 251–61.

17.8.6   Leisure and Sports

Walser, Richard, "His Worship the John Kuner," *North Carolina Folklore* 19 (1971): 160–72.

Walvin, James, "Slaves, Free Time, and the Question of Leisure," *Slavery and Abolition* 16 (1955): 1–13.

Wiggins, David, "Good Times on the Old Plantation: Popular Recreations of the Black Slave in Antebellum South, 1810–1860," *Journal of Sport History* 4 (1977): 260–84.

———— "The Play of Slave Children in the Plantation Communities of the Old South, 1820–1860," *Journal of Sport History* 7 (1980): 21–39.

———— "Sport and Popular Pastimes: Shadow of the Slavequarter," *Canadian Journal of the History of Sport and Physical Education* 11 (1980): 61–88.

17.9   RELIGION

Alho, Olli, *The Religion of the Slaves: A Study of the Religious Tradition and Behaviour of Plantation Slaves in the United States, 1830–1865* (1976).

Andrews, William L., ed., *Sisters of the Spirit: Three Black Women's Autobiographies of the Nineteenth Century* (1986).

Aptheker, Herbert, "The Quakers and Negro Slavery," *Journal of Negro History* 25 (1940): 331–62.

Austin, Allan D., ed., *African Muslims in Antebellum America: A Sourcebook* (1984).

Bailey, David T., *Shadow on the Church: Southwestern Evangelical Religion and the Issue of Slavery, 1783–1860* (1985).

Bailey, Kenneth K., "Protestantism and Afro-Americans in the Old South: Another Look," *Journal of Southern History* 41 (1975): 451–72.

Baldwin, Lewis V., *"Invisible" Strands in African Methodism: A History of the African Union Methodist Protestant and Union American Methodist Episcopal Churches, 1805–1980* (1983).

Boles, John B., ed., *Masters and Slaves in the House of the Lord: Race and Religion in the American South, 1740–1870* (1988).

———— *Religion in Antebellum Kentucky* (1976).

Bradley, David Henry, Jr., *A History of the AME Zion Church: Part I, 1796–1872* (1956).

Bringhurst, Newell G., *Saints, Slaves, and Blacks: The Changing Place of Black People within Mormonism* (1981).

Brooks, Walter H., "The Evolution of the Negro Baptist Church," *Journal of Negro History* 7 (1922): 11–22.

———— "The Priority of the Silver Bluff Church and Its Promoters," *Journal of Negro History* 7 (1922): 172–96.

Bryant, Johnathan M., "My Soul An't Yours Mas'r: The Records of the African Church at Penfield, 1848–1863," *Georgia Historical Quarterly* 75 (1994): 401–12.

Butler, Jon, *Awash in a Sea of Faith: Christianizing the American People* (1990).

Carroll, Kenneth L., "Religious Influences on the Manumission of Slaves in Carolina, Dorchester, and Talbot Counties," *Maryland Historical Magazine* 56 (1961): 176–98.

Charles, Allan D., "Black-White Relations in an Antebellum Church in the Carolina Up Country," *South Carolina Historical Magazine* 89 (1988): 218–26.

Chireau, Yvonne, "Conjure and Christianity in the Nineteenth Century: Religious Elements in African American Magic," *Religion and American Culture* 7 (1997): 225–46.

Creel, Margaret Washington, *"A Peculiar People": Slave Religion and Community-Culture among the Gullahs* (1988).

Cromwell, John W., "First Negro Churches in the District of Columbia," *Journal of Negro History* 7 (1922): 64–106.

Crowther, Edward R., "Mississippi Baptists, Slavery, and Secession, 1806–1861," *Journal of Mississippi History* 56 (1994): 129–48.

Daniel, W. Harrison, "Southern Protestantism and the Negro, 1860–1865," *North Carolina Historical Review* 41 (1964): 338–59.

——— "Virginia Baptists and the Negro in the Antebellum Era," *Journal of Negro History* 56 (1971): 1–16.

Dickson, D. Bruce, Jr., "Religion, Society and Culture in the Old South: A Comparative View," *American Quarterly* 26 (1974): 399–416.

Drake, Thomas Edward, *Quakers and Slavery in America* (1950).

Durden, Robert F., "The Establishment of Calvary Protestant Episcopal Church for Negroes in Charleston," *South Carolina Historical Magazine* 65 (1964): 63–84.

Dvorak, Katharine L., *An African-American Exodus: The Segregation of the Southern Churches* (1991).

Fisk University, Nashville Social Science Institute, *God Struck Me Dead: Religious Conversion Experiences and Autobiographies of Ex-Slaves* (1945).

Genovese, Eugene D., "Black Plantation Preachers in the Slave South," *Louisiana Studies* 11 (1972): 188–214.

——— "Black Preachers in the Slave South," *Southern Studies* 2 (1991): 203–29.

Genovese, Eugene D., and Elizabeth Fox-Genovese, "The Religious Ideals of Southern Slave Society," *Georgia Historical Quarterly* 70 (1986): 1–16.

Gomez, Michael A., "Muslims in Early America," *Journal of Southern History* 60 (1994): 671–710.

Gravely, William B., "The Afro-American Methodist Tradition: A Review of Sources in Reprint," *Methodist History* 9 (1971): 21–33.

Hall, Robert L., "'Yonder Come Day': Religious Dimensions of the Transition from Slavery to Freedom in Florida," *Florida Historical Quarterly* 65 (1987): 411–32.

Harding, Vincent, "Religion and Resistance among Antebellum Negroes, 1800–1860," in August Meier and Elliot Rudwick, ed., *The Making of Black America: Essays in Negro Life and History: The Origins of Black Americans* (1969): 179–97.

Harrison, William Pope, comp. and ed., *The Gospel among the Slaves: A Short Account of Missionary Operations among the African Slaves of the Southern States* (1893).

Hartzell, Joseph C., "Methodism and the Negro in the United States," *Journal of Negro History* 8 (1923): 301–15.

Haynes, Leonard L., Jr., *The Negro Community within American Protestantism, 1619–1844* (1953).

Hickin, Patricia, "Situation Ethics and Antislavery Attitudes in the Virginia Churches," in John B. Boles, ed., *America: The Middle Period: Essays in Honor of Bernard Mayo* (1973): 188–215.

Hicks, William, *History of Louisiana Negro Baptists from 1804 to 1914* (1915).

Holder, Ray, *William Winans: Methodist Leader in Antebellum Mississippi* (1977).

Howard, Victor B., "The Southern Aid Society and the Slavery Controversy," *Church History* 41 (1972): 208–24.

Irons, Charles F., "And All These Things Shall Be Added unto You: The First African Baptist Church, Richmond, 1841–1865," *Virginia Cavalcade* 47 (1998): 26–35.

Jackson, James Conroy, "The Religious Education of the Negro in South Carolina prior to 1850," *Historical Magazine of the Protestant Episcopal Church* 36 (1967): 35–61.

Jackson, Luther P., "Religious Instruction of Negroes, 1830–1860, with Special Reference to South Carolina," *Journal of Negro History* 15 (1930): 72–114.

——— "Religious Development of the Negro in Virginia from 1760 to 1860," *Journal of Negro History* 16 (1931): 168–239.

Jeansonne, Glen, "Southern Baptist Attitudes toward Slavery, 1856–1861," *Georgia Historical Quarterly* (1971): 510–22.

Joyner, Charles W., "'Believer I Know': The Emergence of African-American Christianity," in Paul E. Johnson, ed., *African-American Christianity: Essays in History* (1994): 18–46.

King, Willis J., "The Negro Membership of the (Former) Methodist Church in the (New) United Methodist Church," *Methodist History* 7 (1969): 32–43.

Klein, Herbert S., "Angelicism, Catholicism and the Negro Slave," *Comparative Studies in Society and History* 8 (1966): 295–327.

———— "The Negro and the Church of England in Virginia," in Richard D. Brown, ed., *Slavery in American Society* (1969): 32–37.

Lockett, James D., "The Negro and the Presbyterian Church of the South from the Antebellum through the Postbellum Period," *Griot* 10 (1992): 53–60.

Loveland, Anne C., *Southern Evangelicals and the Social Order, 1800–1860* (1980).

Maddex, Jack P., Jr., "A Paradox of Christian Amelioration: Proslavery Ideology and Church Ministries to Slaves," in Walter J. Fraser, Jr. and Winfred B. Moore, Jr., ed., *The Southern Enigma: Essays on Race, Class, and Folk Culture* (1983): 105–18.

Martin, Sandy Dwayne, "Black Churches and the Civil War: Theological and Ecclesiastical Significance of Black Methodist Involvement, 1861–1865," *Methodist History* 32 (1994): 174–86.

Mathews, Donald G., "Charles Colcock Jones and the Southern Evangelical Crusade to Form a Bi-Racial Community," *Journal of Southern History* 41 (1975): 299–320.

———— "The Methodist Mission to the Slaves, 1829–1844," *Journal of American History* 51 (1965): 615–31.

———— *Religion in the Old South* (1977).

———— *Slavery and Methodism: A Chapter in American Morality, 1780–1845* (1965).

McKinney, Richard I., "American Baptists and Black Education in Florida," *American Baptist Quarterly* 11 (1992): 309–26.

McKivigan, John R., and Mitchell Snay, ed., *Religion and the Antebellum Debate over Slavery* (1998).

Miller, Randall M., "Black Catholics in the Slave South: Some Needs and Opportunities for Study," *Records of the American Historical Society* 86 (1975): 93–106.

———— "The Failed Mission: The Catholic Church and Black Catholics in the Old South," in Edward Magdol and Jon L. Wakelyn, ed., *The Southern Common People: Studies in Nineteenth-Century Social History* (1980): 37–54.

———— "'It Is Good to Be Religious': A Loyal Slave on God, Masters, and the Civil War," *North Carolina Historical Review* 54 (1977): 66–71.

"Minutes of Old Fellowship Baptist Church, Wilcox County, in the Mt. Moriah Community," *Alabama History Quarterly* 17 (1955): 228–389.

Moore, David O., "The Withdrawal of Blacks from Southern Baptist Churches following Emancipation," *Baptist History and Heritage* 16 (1981): 12–18.

Moore, LeRoy, Jr., "The Spiritual: Soul of Black Religion," *American Quarterly* 23 (1971): 658–76.

O'Brien, John T., "Factory, Church, and Community: Blacks in Antebellum Richmond," *Journal of Southern History* 44 (1978): 509–36.

Piersen, William D., "White Cannibals, Black Martyrs: Fear, Depression, and Religious Faith as Causes of Suicide among New Slaves," *Journal of Negro History* 62 (1977): 147–51.

Poe, William A., "Lott Cary: Man of Purchased Freedom," *Church History* 39 (1970): 49–61.

Posey, Walter B., "The Baptists and Slavery in the Lower Mississippi Valley," *Journal of Negro History* 41 (1956): 117–30.

———— *The Baptist Church in the Lower Mississippi Valley, 1776–1845* (1957).

Raboteau, Albert J., "African-Americans, Exodus and the American Israel," in Paul E. Johnson, ed., *African-American Christianity: Essays in History* (1994): 1–17.

———— *Slave Religion: The "Invisible Institution" in the Antebellum South* (1978).

Reilly, Timothy F., "Slavery and the Southwestern Evangelist in New Orleans, 1800–1861," *Journal of Mississippi History* 41 (1979): 301–17.

Reinders, Robert C., "The Churches and the Negro in New Orleans, 1850–1860," *Phylon* 22 (1961): 241–48.

Sensbach, Jon F., "Culture and Conflict in the Early Black Church: A Moravian Mission Congregation in Antebellum North Carolina," *North Carolina Historical Review* 71 (1994): 401–29.

Sernett, Milton C., *Black Religion and American Evangelicalism: White Protestants, Plantation Missions, and the Flowering of Negro Christianity, 1787–1865* (1975).

Sides, Sudie Duncan, "Slave Weddings and Religion," *History Today [UK]* 24 (1974): 77–87.

Simpson, Robert, "The Shout and Shouting in Slave Religion of the United States," *Southern Quarterly* 23 (1985): 34–47.

Sloat, William A., III, "George Whitefield, African-Americans, and Slavery," *Methodist History* 33 (1994): 3–13.

Smith, Edward D., *Climbing Jacob's Ladder: The Rise of Black Churches in Eastern American Cities, 1740–1877* (1988).

Smith, Julia Floyd, "Marching to Zion: The Religion of Black Baptists in Coastal Georgia prior to 1865," *Viewpoints: Georgia Baptist History* (1978): 47–54.

Smith, Timothy L., "Slavery and Theology: The Emergence of Black Christian Consciousness in Nineteenth-Century America," *Church History* 41 (1972): 497–512.

Sobel, Mechal, "'They Can Never Both Prosper Together': Black and White Baptists in Antebellum Nashville, Tennessee," *Tennessee Historical Quarterly* 38 (1979): 296–307.

———— *Trabelin' On: The Slave Journey to an Afro-Baptist Faith* (1979).

Soderlund, Jean R., *Quakers and Slavery: A Divided Spirit* (1985).

Southall, Eugene Portlette, "The Attitude of the Methodist Episcopal Church, South, toward the Negro from 1844 to 1870," *Journal of Negro History* 16 (1931): 359–70.

Stange, Douglas C., "'A Compassionate Mother to Her Poor Negro Slaves': The Lutheran Church and Negro Slavery in Early America," *Phylon* 29 (1968): 272–81.

———— "Our Duty to Preach the Gospel to Negroes: Southern Lutherans and American Slavery," *Concordia Historical Institute Quarterly* 42 (1969): 171–82.

Stockton, Carl R., "Conflict among Evangelical Brothers: Anglo-American Churchmen and the Slavery Controversy, 1848–1853," *Anglican and Episcopal History* 62 (1993): 499–513.

Suttles, William C., Jr., "African Religious Survivals As Factors in American Slave Revolts," *Journal of Negro History* 56 (1971): 97–104.

Swift, David E., *Black Prophets of Justice: Activist Clergy before the Civil War* (1989).

Todd, Willie Grier, "North Carolina Baptists and Slavery," *North Carolina Historical Review* 24 (1947): 135–59.

Touchstone, Blake, "Voodoo in New Orleans," *Louisiana History* 13 (1972): 371–86.

Upton, Mrs. R. Chester, ed., "Minutes of the Antioch Baptist Church, Marion County, Mississippi, 1828–1850: Nathan Smart and Hosea Davis Bible Records," *Journal of Mississippi History* 27 (1965): 191–209.

Walker, Clarence E., *A Rock in a Weary Land: The African Methodist Episcopal Church during the Civil War and Reconstruction* (1982).

Wamble, Gaston Hugh, "Negroes and Missouri Protestant Churches before and after the Civil War," *Missouri Historical Review* 61 (1967): 321–47.

Washington, James Melvin, *Frustrated Fellowship: The Black Baptist Quest for Social Power* (1986).

Washington, Margaret, "Community Regulation and Cultural Specialization in Gullah Folk Religion," in Paul E. Johnson, ed., *African-American Christianity: Essays in History* (1994): 47–79.

Weeks, Stephen B., *Southern Quakers and Slavery, A Study in Institutional History* (1896).

Whatley, George C., III, "The Alabama Presbyterian and His Slave, 1830–1864," *Alabama Review* 13 (1960): 40–51.

Williams, Michael Patrick, "The Black Evangelical Ministry in the Antebellum Border States: Profiles of Elders John Berry Meachum and Noah Davis," *Foundations* 21 (1978): 225–41.

Wills, David W., and Richard Newman, ed., *Black Apostles at Home and Abroad: Afro-Americans and the Christian Mission from the Revolution to Reconstruction* (1982).

Wilson, G. R., "The Religion of the American Negro Slave: His Attitude toward Life and Death," *Journal of Negro History* 8 (1923): 41–71.

17.10   THOUGHT AND EXPRESSION

17.10.1   Race, Gender, and Identity

Abrahams, Roger D., *Singing the Master: The Emergence of African American Culture in the Plantation South* (1992).

Buckley, Thomas E., "Unfixing Race: Class, Power, and Identity in an Interracial Family," *Virginia Magazine of History and Biography* 102 (1994): 349–80.

Cooper, Frederick, "Elevating the Race: The Social Thought of Black Leaders, 1827–1850," *American Quarterly* 24 (1972): 604–25.

Gomez, Michael A., *Exchanging Our Country Marks: The Transformation of African Identities in the Colonial and Antebellum South* (1998).

Goodson, Martia Graham, "The Slave Narrative Collection: A Tool for Reconstructing Afro-American Women's History," *Western Journal of Black Studies* 3 (1979): 116–22.

Gravely, William B., "The Dialectic of Double Consciousness in Black American Freedom Celebrations, 1808–1863," *Journal of Negro History* 67 (1982): 302–17.

Greenwood, Janette Thomas, *Bittersweet Legacy: The Black and White "Better Classes" in Charlotte, 1850–1910* (1994).

Joyner, Charles W., "'If You Ain't Got Education': Slave Language and Slave Thought in Antebellum Charleston," in Michael O'Brien and David Moltke-Hansen, ed., *Intellectual Life in Antebellum Charleston* (1986): 225–78.

Levine, Lawrence W., *Black Culture and Black Consciousness: Afro-American Folk Thought from Slavery to Freedom* (1977).

———— "Slave Songs and Slave Consciousness: An Exploration in Neglected Sources," in Tamara K. Hareven, ed., *Anonymous Americans: Explorations in the Nineteenth-Century Social History* (1971): 99–130.

McPherson, James M., *The Negro's Civil War: How American Negroes Felt and Acted during the War for the Union* (1965).

Stuckey, Sterling, *Slave Culture: Nationalist Theory and the Foundations of Black America* (1987).

———— "Through the Prism of Folklore: The Black Ethos in Slavery," *Massachussetts Review* 9 (1968): 417–37.

Sweet, Leonard I., *Black Images of America, 1784–1870* (1976).

White, Shane, and Graham White, "Slave Hair and African American Culture in the Eighteenth and Nineteenth Centuries," *Journal of Southern History* 61 (1995): 45–76.

Wiggins, William H., *O Freedom! Afro-American Emancipation Celebrations* (1987).

Woods, C. P. D., and Sister Frances Jerome, *Marginality and Identity: A Colored Creole Family through Ten Generations* (1972).

Woodson, Carter Godwin, ed., *The Mind of the Negro As Reflected in Letters Written during the Crisis, 1800–1860* (1926).

Yacovone, Donald, "The Fruits of Africa: Slavery, Emancipation, and Afro-American Culture," *American Quarterly* 40 (1988): 569–76.

17.10.2   Emigrationism and Nationalism

Allen, Jeffrey B., "'All of Us Are Highly Pleased with the Country': Black and White Kentuckians on Liberian Colonization," *Phylon* 43 (1982): 97–109.

Bell, Howard H., "The Negro Emigration Movement, 1849–1854: A Phase of Negro Nationalism," *Phylon* 20 (1959): 132–42.

———— "Negro Nationalism: A Factor in Emigration Projects, 1858–1861," *Journal of Negro History* 47 (1962): 42–53.

Bellamy, Donnie D., "The Persistency of Colonization in Missouri," *Missouri Historical Review* 72 (1977): 1–24.

Harris, Robert L., Jr., "H. Ford Douglas: Afro-American Antislavery Emigrationist," *Journal of Negro History* 62 (1977): 217–34.

Mehlinger, Louis R., "The Attitude of the Free Negro toward African Colonization," *Journal of Negro History* 1 (1916): 276–301.

Miller, Floyd John, *The Search for a Black Nationality: Black Emigration and Colonization, 1787–1863* (1975).

Miller, Randall M., ed., *"Dear Master": Letters of a Slave Family* (1978).

Mitchell, Memory F., ed., "Freedom Brings Problems: Letters from the McKays and the Nelsons in Liberia," *North Carolina Historical Review* 70 (1993): 430–65.

Moses, Wilson Jeremiah, ed., *Liberian Dreams: Back-to-Africa Narratives from the 1850's* (1998).

Nicholls, Michael L., "News from Monrovia, 1834–1846: The Letters of Peyton Skipwith to John Hartwell Cocke," *Virginia Magazine of History and Biography* 85 (1977): 65–85.

Shepard, E. Lee, Frances S. Pollard, and Janet B. Schwartz, "'The Love of Liberty Brought Us Here': Virginians and the Colonization of Liberia," *Virginia Magazine of History and Biography* 102 (1994): 89–100.

Smith, James Wesley, *Sojourners in Search of Freedom: The Settlement of Liberia by Black Americans* (1987).

Stopak, Aron, "The Maryland State Colonization Society: Independent State Action in the Colonization Movement," *Maryland Historical Magazine* 63 (1968): 275–98.

Tyler-McGraw, Marie, "'The Prize I Mean Is the Prize of Liberty': A Loudoun Family in Liberia," *Virginia Magazine of History and Biography* 97 (1989): 355–74.

Wiley, Bell I., *Slaves No More: Letters from Liberia, 1833–1869* (1980).

Woodson, Carter Godwin, *A Century of Negro Migration* (1918).

Woodson, Carter Godwin, ed., "Documents: Letters to the American Colonization Society," *Journal of Negro History* 10 (1925): 154–311.

17.10.3   Folklore and Humor

Dickson, Bruce D., Jr., "'John and Old Master' Stories and the World of Slavery: A Study in Folk Tales and History," *Phylon* 35 (1974): 418–29.

Georgia Writers' Project, *Drums and Shadows: Survival Studies among the Georgia Coastal Negroes* (1940).

Gorn, Elliot J., "Black Magic: Folk Beliefs of the Slave Community," in Ronald L. Numbers and Todd L. Savitt, ed., *Science and Medicine in the Old South* (1989): 295–326.

——— "Black Spirits: The Ghostlore of Afro-American Slaves," *American Quarterly* 36 (1984): 549–65.

Oster, Harry, "Negro Humor: John and Old Marster," *Journal of the Folklore Institute* 5 (1968): 42–57.

Roberts, John W., *From Trickster to Badman: The Black Folk Hero in Slavery and Freedom* (1989).

Stuckey, Sterling, "Through the Prism of Folklore: The Black Ethos in Slavery," *Massachusetts Review* 9 (1968): 417–37.

Whiting, Helen A., *Negro Folk Tales* (1938).

17.10.4   Literature and Poetry

Accomondo, Christina, "'The Laws Were Laid down to Me Anew': Harriet Jacobs and the Reframing of Legal Fictions," *African American Review* 32 (1998): 229–45.

Fleischner, Jennifer, *Mastering Slavery: Memory, Family, and Identity in Women's Slave Narratives* (1996).

Jackson, Blyden, "George Moses Horton, North Carolinian," *North Carolina Historical Review* 53 (1976): 140–47.

Wood, Marcus, "Seeing Is Believing, or Finding the 'Truth' in Slave Narrative: The Narrative of Henry Bibb As Perfect Misrepresentation," *Slavery and Abolition [London]* 18 (1997): 174–211.

17.10.5   Music and Performing Arts

Allen, William Francis, Charles Pickard Ware, and Lucy McKim Garrison, comp., *Slave Songs of the United States* (1867).

Bailey, Ben E., "Music in Slave Era Mississippi," *Journal of Mississippi History* 54 (1992): 29–58.

Baldwin, Brooke, "The Cakewalk: A Study in Stereotype and Reality," *Journal of Social History* 15 (1981): 205–18.

Bluestein, Gene, "America's Folk Instrument: Notes on the Five-String Banjo," *Western Folklore* 23 (1964): 241–48.

Bowen, Elbert R., "Negro Minstrels in Early Rural Missouri," *Missouri Historical Review* 47 (1953): 103–09.

Cimbala, Paul A., "Fortunate Bondsmen: Black 'Musicianers' and Their Role As an Antebellum Southern Plantation Slave Elite," *Southern Studies* 18 (1979): 291–303.

Donaldson, Gary A., "A Window on Slave Culture: Dances at Congo Square in New Orleans, 1800–1862," *Journal of Negro History* 69 (1984): 63–72.

Dormon, James H., Jr., *Theater in the Ante Bellum South, 1815–1861* (1967).

Ellison, Mary, "African American Music and Muskets in Civil War New Orleans," *Louisiana History* 35 (1994): 285–319.

Epstein, Dena J. Polacheck, *Sinful Tunes and Spirituals: Black Folk Music to the Civil War* (1977).

Evans, David, "Afro-American One-Stringed Instruments," *Western Folklore* 29 (1979): 229–45.

Fisher, Miles Mark, *Negro Slave Songs in the United States* (1953).

Griffith, Benjamin W., "A Longer Version of 'Guinea Negro Song': From a Georgia Frontier Songster," *Southern Folklore* 28 (1964): 116–18.

Hansen, Chadwick, "Jenny's Toe: Negro Shaking Dances," *American Quarterly* 19 (1967): 554–63.

Katz, Bernard, ed., *The Social Implications of Early Negro Music in the United States: With over One Hundred and Fifty of the Songs, Many of Them with Their Music* (1969).

Levine, Lawrence W., *Black Culture and Black Consciousness: Afro-American Folk Thought from Slavery to Freedom* (1977).

——— "Slave Songs and Slave Consciousness: An Exploration in Neglected Sources," in Tamara K. Harevan, ed., *Anonymous Americans: Explorations in the Nineteenth-Century Social History* (1971): 99–130.

Moore, LeRoy, Jr., "The Spiritual: Soul of Black Religion," *American Quarterly* 23 (1971): 658–76.

Nathan, Hans, *Dan Emmett and the Rise of Early Negro Minstrelsy* (1962).

Parrish, Lydia Austin, *Slave Songs of the Georgia Sea Islands* (1942).

Southern, Eileen, "An Origin for the Negro Spiritual," *Black Scholar* 3 (1972): 8–13.

Whalum, Wendell Phillips, "James Weldon Johnson's Theories and Performance Practices of Afro-American Folksongs," *Phylon* 32 (1971): 383–95.

Winans, Robert B., "The Folk, the Stage, and Five-String Banjos in the Nineteenth Century," *Journal of American Folklore* 89 (1976): 407–37.

17.10.6 Art (Drawing, Painting, Photography, Printmaking, Sculpture)

Brady, Patricia, "Black Artists in Antebellum New Orleans," *Louisiana History* 32 (1991): 5–28.

Newton, James E., "Slave Artisans and Craftsmen: The Roots of Afro-American Art," *Black Scholar* 9 (1977): 35–44.

Newton, James E., and Ronald L. Lewis, ed., *The Other Slaves: Mechanics, Artisans, and Craftsmen* (1978).

Pleasants, J. Hall, "Joshua Johnston: The First American Negro Portrait Painter," *Maryland Historical Magazine* 37 (1942): 121–49.

Poesch, Jessie, *The Art of the Old South: Painting, Sculpture, Architecture and the Products of Craftsmen, 1560–1860* (1983).

Stavisky, Leonard Price, "The Origins of Negro Craftsmanship in Colonial America," *Journal of Negro History* 32 (1947): 417–29.

Vlach, John Michael, "Afro-American Folk Crafts in Nineteenth Century Texas," *Western Folklore* 40 (1981): 149–61.

17.10.7 Architecture and Design

Bishir, Catherine W., "Black Builders in Antebellum North Carolina," *North Carolina Historical Review* 61 (1984): 422–61.

Poesch, Jessie, *The Art of the Old South: Painting, Sculpture, Architecture and the Products of Craftsmen, 1560–1860* (1983).

Vlach, John Michael, *Back of the Big House: The Architecture of Plantation Slavery* (1993).

Young, Amy Lambeck, Philip J. Carr, and Joseph E. Granger, "How Historical Archaeology Works: A Case Study of Slave Houses at Locust Grove," *Register of the Kentucky Historical Society* 96 (1998): 164–94.

17.11 EDUCATION

Armstrong, Warren B., "Union Chaplains and the Education of the Freedmen," *Journal of Negro History* 52 (1967): 104–15.

Bellamy, Donnie D., "The Education of Blacks in Missouri prior to 1861," *Journal of Negro History* 59 (1974): 143–57.

Birnie, C. W., "Education of the Negro in Charleston, South Carolina, prior to the Civil War," *Journal of Negro History* 12 (1927): 13–21.

Brady, Patricia, "Trials and Tribulations: American Missionary Association Teachers and Black Education in Occupied New Orleans, 1863–1864," *Louisiana History* 31 (1990): 5–20.

Brigham, R. I., "Negro Education in Ante-Bellum Missouri," *Journal of Negro History* 30 (1945): 405–20.

Butchart, Ronald E., *Northern Schools, Southern Blacks, and Reconstruction: Freedmen's Education, 1862–1875* (1980).

Cornelius, Janet, "'We Slipped and Learned to Read': Slave Accounts of the Literacy Process, 1830–1865," *Phylon* 44 (1983): 171–86.

—— *"When I Can Read My Title Clear": Literacy, Slavery, and Religion in the Antebellum South* (1991).

Fen, Sing-Nan, "Notes on the Education of Negroes at Norfolk and Portsmouth, Virginia, during the Civil War," *Phylon* 28 (1967): 197–207.

Foner Philip S., and Josephine F. Pacheco, *Three Who Dared: Prudence Crandall, Margaret Douglass, and Myrtilla Minor—Champions of Antebellum Black Education* (1984).

Gardner, Bettye, "Ante-Bellum Black Education in Baltimore," *Maryland Historical Magazine* 71 (1976): 360–66.

Green, Fletcher M., "Northern Missionary Activities in the South, 1846–1861," *Journal of Southern History* 21 (1955): 147–72.

Jackson, James Conroy, "The Religious Education of the Negro in South Carolina prior to 1850," *Historical Magazine of the Protestant Episcopal Church* 36 (1967): 35–61.

Jackson, Luther P., "The Educational Efforts of the Freedmen's Bureau and Freedmen's Societies in South Carolina, 1862–1872," *Journal of Negro History* 8 (1923): 1–40.

—— "Religious Instruction of Negroes, 1830–1860, with Special Reference to South Carolina," *Journal of Negro History* 15 (1930): 72–114.

Lawson, Ellen NicKenzie, and Marlene D. Merrill, *The Three Sarahs: Documents of Antebellum Black College Women* (1984).

McKinney, Richard I., "American Baptists and Black Education in Florida," *American Baptist Quarterly* 11 (1992): 309–26.

Morris, Robert Charles, *Reading, 'Riting, and Reconstruction: The Education of Freedmen in the South, 1861–1870* (1981).

Nelson, Paul David, "Experiment in Interracial Education at Berea College, 1858–1908," *Journal of Negro History* 59 (1974): 13–27.

Peeps, J. M. Stephen, "Northern Philanthropy and the Emergence of Black Higher Education: Do-Gooders, Compromisers, or Co-Conspirators?" *Journal of Negro Education* 50 (1981): 251–69.

Perkins, Linda M., "The Black Female American Missionary Association Teacher in the South, 1861–1870," in Jeffrey A. Crow and Flora J. Hatley, ed., *Black Americans in North Carolina and the South* (1984): 122–36.

Porter, Betty, "The History of Negro Education in Louisiana," *Louisiana History Quarterly* 25 (1942): 728–821.

Putney, Martha S., "The Baltimore Normal School for the Education of Colored Teachers: Its Founders and Its Founding," *Maryland Historical Magazine* 72 (1977): 238–52.

Rachal, John R., "Gideonites and Freedmen: Adult Literacy Education at Port Royal, 1862–1865," *Journal of Negro Education* 55 (1986): 453–69.

Richardson, Joe M., "The American Missionary Association and Black Education in Civil War Missouri," *Missouri Historical Review* 69 (1975): 433–88.

Sparks, Randy J., "'The White People's Arms Are Longer Than Ours': Blacks, Education, and the American Missionary Association in Reconstruction Mississippi," *Journal of Mississippi History* 54 (1992): 1–28.

Tyms, James D., *The Rise of Religious Education among Negro Baptists: A Historical Case Study* (1965).

Webber, Thomas L., *Deep Like the Rivers: Education in the Slave Quarter Community, 1831–1865* (1978).

Wilson, Keith, "Education as a Vehicle of Racial Control: Major General N. P. Banks in Louisiana, 1863–1864," *Journal of Negro Education* 50 (1981): 156–70.

Woodson, Carter Godwin, *The Education of the Negro prior to 1861: A History of the Education of the Colored People of the United States from the Beginning of Slavery to the Civil War* (1915).

17.12   WORK AND ENTREPRENEURIAL ACTIVITY

Armstrong, Thomas F., "From Task Labor to Free Labor: The Transition along Georgia's Rice Coast, 1820–1880," *Georgia Historical Quarterly* 64 (1980): 432–47.

Barton, Keith C., "'Good Cooks and Washers': Slave Hiring, Domestic Labor, and the Market in Bourbon County, Kentucky," *Journal of American History* 84 (1997): 436–60.

Beirne, D. Randall, "The Impact of Black Labor on European Immigration into Baltimore's Oldtown, 1790–1910," *Maryland Historical Magazine* 83 (1988): 331–45.

Berlin, Ira, Thavolia Glymph, Steven F. Miller, Joseph P. Reidy, Leslie S. Rowland, and Julie Saville, ed., *The Wartime Genesis of Free Labor: The Lower South, Series I, Vol. 3 of Freedom: A Documentary History of Emancipation, 1861–1867* (1990).

Berlin, Ira, and Herbert G. Gutman, "Natives and Immigrants, Free Men, and Slaves: Urban Workingmen in the Antebellum South," *American Historical Review* 88 (1983): 1175–200.

Berlin, Ira, Steven F. Miller, Joseph P. Reidy, and Leslie S. Rowland, ed., *The Wartime Genesis of Free Labor: The Upper South, Series I, Vol. 2 of Freedom: A Documentary History of Emancipation, 1861–1867* (1993).

Berlin, Ira, and Philip D. Morgan, ed., *Cultivation and Culture: Labor and the Shaping of Slave Life in the Americas* (1993).

———, ed., *The Slaves' Economy: Independent Production by Slaves in the Americas* (1991).

Bigelow, Martha M., "Freedmen of the Mississippi Valley, 1862–1865," *Civil War History* 8 (1962): 38–47.

——— "Vicksburg: Experiment in Freedom," *Journal of Mississippi History* 26 (1964): 28–44.

Bonekemper, Edward H., III, "Negro Ownership of Real Property in Hampton and Elizabeth City County, Virginia, 1860–1870," *Journal of Negro History* 55 (1970): 165–81.

Bradford, S. Sydney, "The Negro Ironworker in Antebellum Virginia," *Journal of Southern History* 25 (1959): 194–206.

Brady, Patricia, "Florville Foy, F. M. C.: Master Marble Cutter and Tomb Builder," *Southern Quarterly* 31 (1993): 8–20.

Bruce, Kathleen, *Virginia Iron Manufacture in the Slave Era* (1930).

Byrne, William A., "The Hiring of Woodson, Slave Carpenter of Savannah," *Georgia Historical Quarterly* 77 (1993): 245–63.

Campbell, John, "As 'a Kind of Freeman': Slaves' Market-Related Activities in the South Carolina Upcountry, 1800–1860," *Slavery and Abolition* 12 (1991): 131–69.

Campbell, Randolph B., "Slave Hiring in Texas," *American Historical Review* 93 (1988): 107–14.

Christian, Marcus Bruce, *Negro Ironworkers in Louisiana, 1718–1900* (1972).

Clifton, James M., "The Rice Driver: His Role in Slave Management," *South Carolina Historical Magazine* 82 (1981): 331–53.

Cohen-Lack, Nancy, "A Struggle for Sovereignty: National Consolidation, Emancipation, and Free Labor in Texas, 1865," *Journal of Southern History* 58 (1992): 57–98.

Cole, Stephanie, "Changes for Mrs. Thornton's Arthur: Patterns of Domestic Service in Washington, DC, 1800–1835," *Social Science History* 15: 367–80.

Cook, Bernard A., and James R. Watson, *Louisiana Labor: From Slavery to "Right-to-Work"* (1985).

Cox, LaWanda, "The Promise of Land for the Freedmen," *Mississippi Valley Historical Review* 45 (1958): 413–40.

David, Paul A., and Peter Temin, "Capitalist Masters, Bourgeois Slaves," *Journal of Interdisciplinary History* 5 (1975): 445–57.

Della, M. Ray, Jr., "The Problems of Negro Labor in the 1850's," *Maryland Historical Magazine* 66 (1971): 1–13.

Dew, Charles B., "Black Ironworkers and the Slave Insurrection Panic of 1856," *Journal of Southern History* 41 (1975): 321–38.

———— *Bond of Iron: Master and Slave at Buffalo Forge* (1994).

———— "Disciplining Slave Ironworkers in the Antebellum South: Coercion, Conciliation, and Accommodation," *American Historical Review* 79 (1974): 393–418.

———— *Ironmaker to the Confederacy: Joseph R. Anderson and the Tredgar Iron Works* (1966).

———— "Sam Williams, Forgeman: The Life of an Industrial Slave in the Old South," in James M. McPherson and J. Morgan Kousser, ed., *Region, Race, and Reconstruction: Essays in Honor of C. Vann Woodward* (1982): 199–239.

———— "Slavery and Technology in the Antebellum Southern Iron Industry: The Case of Buffalo Forge," in Ronald L. Numbers and Todd L. Savitt, ed., *Science and Medicine in the Old South* (1989): 107–26.

Durham, Philip, and Everett L. Jones, "Slaves on Horseback," *Pacific Historical Review* 33 (1964): 405–09.

Eaton, Clement, "Slave-Hiring in the Upper South: A Step toward Freedom," *Mississippi Valley Historical Review* 46 (1960): 663–78.

Foner, Philip S., and Ronald L. Lewis, ed., *The Black Worker to 1869* (1978).

Foshee, Andrew W., "Slave Hiring in Rural Louisiana," *Louisiana History* 26 (1985): 63–73.

Franklin, John Hope, "James Boon, Free Negro Artisan," *Journal of Negro History* 30 (1945): 150–80.

Genovese, Eugene D., "The Negro Laborer in Africa and the Slave South," *Phylon* 21 (1960): 343–50.

Green, Barbara L., "Slave Labor at the Maramec Iron Works, 1828–1850," *Missouri Historical Review* 73 (1979): 150–64.

Green, Fletcher M., "Georgia's Forgotten Industry: Gold Mining," *Georgia Historical Quarterly* 19 (1935): 93–111, 210–28.

———— "Gold Mining in Antebellum Virginia," *Virginia Magazine of History and Biography* 45 (1937): 227–35, 357–66.

———— "Gold Mining: A Forgotten Industry of Antebellum North Carolina," *North Carolina Historical Review* 14 (1937): 1–19, 135–55.

Green, Rodney D., "Black Tobacco Factory Workers and Social Conflict in Antebellum Richmond: Were Slavery and Urban Industry Really Compatible?" *Slavery and Abolition* 8 (1987): 183–203.

Gross, James A., "Historians and the Literature of the Negro Worker," *Labor History* 10 (1969): 536–46.

Gutman, Herbert G. and Richard Sutch, "Sambo Makes Good, or Were Slaves Imbued with the Protestant Work Ethic?" in Paul A. David, Herbert G. Gutman, Richard Sutch, Peter Temin and Gavin Wright, ed., *Reckoning with Slavery: A Critical Study in the Quantitative History of American Negro Slavery* (1976): 55–93.

Hagy, James W., "Black Business Women in Antebellum Charleston," *Journal of Negro History* 72 (1987): 42–44.

Harper, C. W., "Black Aristocrats: Domestic Servants on the Antebellum Plantation," *Phylon* 46 (1985): 123–35.

———— "House Servants and Field Hands: Fragmentation in the Antebellum Slave Community," *North Carolina Historical Review* 55 (1978): 42–59.

House, Albert V., "Labor Management Problems on Georgia Rice Plantations, 1840–1860," *Agricultural History* 28 (1954): 149–55.

————, ed., *Planter Management and Capitalism in Ante-Bellum Georgia: The Journal of Hugh Fraser Grant, Ricegrower* (1954).

Hudson, Larry E., Jr., ed., *Working toward Freedom: Slave Society and Domestic Economy in the American South* (1994).

Jackson, Luther P., *Free Negro Labor and Property Holding in Virginia, 1830–1860* (1942).

———— "The Virginia Free Negro Farmer and Property Owner, 1830–1860," *Journal of Negro History* 24 (1939): 390–439.

Johnson, Michael P., "Work, Culture, and the Slave Community: Slave Occupations in the Cotton Belt in 1860," *Labor History* 27 (1986): 325–55.

Jones, Jacqueline, "'My Mother Was Much of a Woman': Black Women, Work, and the Family under Slavery," *Feminist Studies* 8 (1982): 235–69.

Lander, E. M., "Slave Labor in South Carolina Cotton Mills," *Journal of Negro History* 38 (1953): 161–73.

Lewis, Ronald L., *Coal, Iron, and Slaves: Industrial Slavery in Maryland and Virginia, 1715–1865* (1979).

———— "Slave Families at Early Chesapeake Iron Works," *Virginia Magazine of History and Biography* 86 (1978): 169–79.

———— "'The Darkest Abode of Man': Black Miners in the First Southern Coal Field, 1780–1865," *Virginia Magazine of History and Biography* 87 (1979): 190–202.

Mann, Susan A., "Slavery, Sharecropping, and Sexual Inequality," *Signs* 14 (1989): 774–98.

Marks, Bayly E., "Skilled Blacks in Antebellum St. Mary's County, Maryland," *Journal of Southern History* 53 (1987): 537–64.

McDonald, Roderick A., *The Economy and Material Culture of Slaves: Goods and Chattels on the Sugar Plantations of Jamaica and Louisiana* (1993).

Medford, Edna Greene, "'There Was So Many Degrees in Slavery . . .': Unfree Labor in an Antebellum Mixed Farming Community,'" *Slavery and Abolition* 14 (1993): 35–47.

Menard, Russell, "From Servants to Slaves: The Transformation of the Chesapeake Labor System," *Southern Studies* 16 (1977): 355–90.

Messner, William F., *Freedmen and the Ideology of Free Labor: Louisiana, 1862–1865* (1978).

———— "The Vicksburg Campaign of 1862: A Case Study in the Federal Utilization of Black Labor," *Louisiana History* 16 (1975): 371–81.

Moore, John Hebron, "Simon Gray, Riverman: A Slave Who Was Almost Free," *Mississippi Valley Historical Review* 49 (1962): 471–84.

Morgan, Philip D., "The Ownership of Property by Slaves in the Mid-Nineteenth-Century Low Country," *Journal of Southern History* 49 (1983): 399–420.

———— "Work and Culture: The Task System and the World of Low-Country Blacks, 1700–1880," *William and Mary Quarterly* 39 (1982): 563–99.

Morris, Richard B., "Labor Controls in Maryland in the Nineteenth Century," *Journal of Southern History* 14 (1948): 385–400.

Newton, James E., and Ronald L. Lewis, ed., *The Other Slaves: Mechanics, Artisans, and Craftsmen* (1978).

Obatala, J. K., "The Unlikely Story of Blacks Who Were Loyal to Dixie," *Smithsonian* 9 (1979): 94–101.

O'Brien, John T., "Factory, Church, and Community: Blacks in Antebellum Richmond," *Journal of Southern History* 44 (1978): 509–36.

Pease, William H., "Three Years among the Freedmen: William C. Gannett and the Port Royal Experiment," *Journal of Negro History* 42 (1957): 98–118.

Perdue, Robert Eugene, *Black Laborers and Black Professionals in Early America, 1750–1830* (1975).

Pinchback, Raymond B., *The Virginia Negro Artisan and Tradesman* (1926).

Pritchard, Walter, "Routine on a Louisiana Sugar Plantation under the Slavery Regime," *Mississippi Valley Historical Review* 14 (1927): 168–78.

Putney, Martha S., *Black Sailors: Afro-American Merchant Seamen and Whalemen prior to the Civil War* (1987).

Reese, James V., "The Early History of Labor Organizations in Texas, 1838–1876," *Southwestern Historical Quarterly* 72 (1968): 1–20.

Reid, Robert D., "The Negro in Alabama during the Civil War," *Journal of Negro History* 35 (1950): 265–88.

Rose, Willie Lee, *Rehearsal for Reconstruction: The Port Royal Experiment* (1964).

Saville, Julie, "Grassroots Reconstruction: Agricultural Labour and Collective Action in South Carolina, 1860–1868," *Slavery and Abolition* 12 (1991): 173–82.

———— *The Work of Reconstruction: From Slave to Wage Laborer in South Carolina, 1860–1870* (1994).

Schantz, Mark, "'A Very Serious Business': Managerial Relationships on the Ball Plantations, 1800–1835," *South Carolina Historical Magazine* 88 (1987): 1–22.

Schecter, Patricia A., "Free and Slave Labor in the Old South: The Tredegar Iron Worker's Strike of 1847," *Labor History* 35 (1995): 165–86.

Schmitzer, Jeanne C., "The Sable Guides of Mammoth Cave," *Filson Club History Quarterly* 67 (1993): 240–58.

Schnittman, Suzanne, "Black Workers in Antebellum Richmond," in Gary M. Fink and Merl E. Reed, ed., *Race, Class, and Community in Southern Labor History* (1994): 72–86.

Schweninger, Loren, *Black Property Owners in the South, 1790–1915* (1990).

———— "Black-Owned Businesses in the South, 1790–1880," *Business History Review* 63 (1989): 22–60.

———— "Property-Owning Free African-American Women in the South, 1800–1870," *Journal of Women's History* 1 (1990): 13–44.

———— "Prosperous Blacks in the South, 1790–1880," *American Historical Review* 95 (1990): 31–56.

———— "The Roots of Enterprise: Black-Owned Businesses in Virginia, 1830–1880," *Virginia Magazine of History and Biography* 100 (1992): 515–42.

———— "Slave Independence and Enterprise in South Carolina, 1780–1865," *South Carolina Historical Magazine* 93 (1992): 101–25.

———— "The Underside of Slavery: The Internal Economy Self-Hire, and Quasi-Freedom in Virginia, 1780–1865," *Slavery and Abolition* 12 (1991): 1–22.

———— "A Vanishing Breed: Black Farm Owners in the South, 1651–1982," *Agricultural History* 63 (1989): 41–60.

Shammas, Carole, "Black Women's Work and the Evolution of Plantation Society in Virginia," *Labor History* 26 (1985): 5–28.

Shlomowitz, Ralph, "On Punishments and Rewards in Coercive Labour Systems," *Slavery and Abolition* 12 (1991): 97–102.

Sitterson, J. Carlyle, "Hired Labor on Sugar Plantations of the Ante-Bellum South," *Journal of Southern History* 14 (1948): 192–205.

Spraggins, Tinsley Lee, "Mobilization of Negro Labor for the Department of Virginia and North Carolina, 1861–1865," *North Carolina Historical Magazine* 24 (1947): 160–97.

Starobin, Robert S., "Disciplining Industrial Slaves in the Old South," *Journal of Negro History* 53 (1968): 111–28.

———— *Industrial Slavery in the Old South* (1970).

Stealey, John E., III, *The Antebellum Kanawha Salt Business and Western Markets* (1993).

———— "Slavery and the Western Virginia Salt Industry," *Journal of Negro History* 59 (1974): 105–31.

Van Deburg, William L., "Elite Slave Behavior during the Civil War: Black Drivers and Foreman in Historical Perspective," *Southern Studies* 16 (1977): 253–69.

———— "The Slave Drivers of Arkansas: A New View from the Narratives," *Arkansas Historical Quarterly* 35 (1976): 231–45.

———— *The Slave Drivers: Black Agricultural Labor Supervisors in the Antebellum South* (1979).

Walker, Juliet E. K., "Racism, Slavery, and Free Enterprise: Black Entrepreneurship in the United States before the Civil War," *Business History Review* 60 (1986): 343–82.

Wesley, Charles H., *Negro Labor in the United States, 1850–1925: A Study in American Economic History* (1927).

Whitman, T. Stephen, "Industrial Slavery at the Margin: The Maryland Chemical Works," *Journal of Southern History* 59 (1993): 31–62.

Wood, Betty, *Women's Work, Men's Work: The Informal Slave Economies of Low Country Georgia* (1995).

17.13   MEDICINE AND HEALTH

Axelsen, Diana E., "Women As Victims of Medical Experimentation: J. Marion Sims' Surgery on Slave Women, 1845–1850," *Sage* 2 (1985): 10–12.

Boney, F. N., "Doctor Thomas Hamilton: Two Views of a Gentleman of the Old South," *Phylon* 28 (1967): 288–92.

————— "Slaves As Guinea Pigs: Georgia and Alabama Episodes," *Alabama Review* 37 (1984): 45–51.

Cadwallader, D. E., and F. J. Wilson, "Folklore Medicine among Georgia's Piedmont Negroes after the Civil War," *Georgia Historical Quarterly* 49 (1965): 217–27.

Campbell, John, "Work, Pregnancy, and Infant Mortality among Southern Slaves," *Journal of Interdisciplinary History* 14 (1984): 793–812.

Cardell, Nicholas Scott, and Mark Myron Hopkins, "The Effect of Milk Intolerance on the Consumption of Milk by Slaves in 1860," *Journal of Interdisciplinary History* 8 (1978): 507–13.

Crader, Diana C., "Slave Diet at Monticello," *American Antiquity* 55: 690–717.

Engerman, Stanley L., "The Height of Slaves," *Local Population Studies [Great Britain]* 16 (1976): 45–49.

Finley, Randy, "In War's Wake: Health Care and Arkansas Freedmen, 1863–1868," *Arkansas Historical Quarterly* 51 (1992): 135–63.

Fisher, Walter, "Physicians and Slavery in the Antebellum Southern Medical Journal," *Journal of the History of Medicine and Allied Sciences* 23 (1968): 36–49.

Georgia Writers' Project, *Drums and Shadows: Survival Studies among the Georgia Coastal Negroes* (1940).

Gibbs, Tyson, Kathleen Gargill, Leslie Sue Liberman, and Elizabeth Reitz, "Nutrition in a Slave Population: An Anthroplogical Examination," *Medical Anthropology* 4 (1980): 175–262.

Goodson, Martia Graham, "Medical-Botanical Contributions of African Slave Women to American Medicine," *Journal of Black Studies* 11 (1987): 198–203.

Goodyear, James D., "The Sugar Connection: A New Perpsective on the History of Yellow Fever," *Bulletin of the History of Medicine* 52 (1978): 5–21.

Gorn, Elliot J., "Black Magic: Folk Beliefs of the Slave Community," in Ronald L. Numbers and Todd L. Savitt, ed., *Science and Medicine in the Old South* (1989): 295–326.

Haller, John S., Jr., "The Negro and the Southern Physician: A Study of Medical and Racial Attitudes, 1800–1860," *Medical History [Great Britain]* 16 (1972): 238–53.

Harvey, Katherine A., "Practicing Medicine at the Baltimore Almshouse, 1828–1850," *Maryland Historical Magazine* 74 (1979): 223–37.

Johnson, Michael P., "Smothered Slave Infants: Were Slave Mothers at Fault?" *Journal of Southern History* 47 (1981): 493–520.

Jordan, Weymouth T., "Plantation Medicine in the Old South," *Alabama Review* 3 (1950): 83–107.

Kaufman, Martin, "*Medicine and Slavery:* An Essay Review," *Georgia Historical Quarterly* 64 (1979): 380–90.

Kiple, Kenneth F., and Virginia Himmelsteib King, *Another Dimension to the Black Diaspora: Diet, Disease, and Racism* (1981).

Kiple, Kenneth F., and Virginia H. Kiple, "The African Connection: Slavery, Disease, and Racism," *Phylon* 41 (1980): 211–22.

————— "Black Tongue and Black Men: Pellagra and Slavery in the Antebellum South," *Journal of Southern History* 43 (1977): 411–28.

————— "Slave Child Mortality: Some Nutritional Answers to a Perennial Puzzle," *Journal of Social History* 10 (1977): 284–309.

Lacy, Virginia Jane, and David Edwin Harrell, Jr., "Plantation Home Remedies: Medicinal Recipes from the Diaries of John Pope," *Tennessee Historical Quarterly* 22 (1963): 259–65.

Lee, Anne S., and Everett S. Lee, "The Health of Slaves and the Health of Freedmen: A Savannah Study," *Phylon* 38 (1977): 170–80.

Meeker, Edward, "Mortality Trends of Southern Blacks, 1850–1910: Some Preliminary Findings," *Explorations in Economic History* 13 (1976): 13–42.

Morgan, John H., "An Essay on the Production of Abortion among our Negro Population," *Nashville Journal of Medicine and Surgery* 19 (1860): 117–23.

Olsen, Jennifer, and J. Lawrence Angel, "Life Stresses of Slavery," *American Journal of Physical Anthropology* 74 (1987): 199–211.

Owsley, Douglas W., Charles E. Owsley, and Robert W. Mann, "Demography and Pathology of an Urban Slave Population from New Orleans," *American Journal of Physical Anthropology* 74 (1987): 185–97.

Pollard, Leslie J., "Aging and Slavery: A Gerontological Perspective," *Journal of Negro History* 66 (1981): 228–34.

Postell, William Dosite, *The Health of Slaves on Southern Plantations* (1951).

Rathbun, Ted A., "Health and Disease at a South Carolina Plantation: 1840–1870," *American Journal of Physical Anthropology* 74 (1987): 239–53.

Savitt, Todd L., "Black Health on the Plantation: Masters, Slaves, and Physicians," *Medical History* 2 (1986): 368–82.

——— *Medicine and Slavery: The Diseases and Health Care of Blacks in Antebellum Virginia* (1978).

——— "Slave Health and Southern Distinctiveness," in Todd L. Savitt and James Harvey Young, ed., *Disease and Distinctiveness in the American South* (1988): 120–53.

——— "Slave Life Insurance in Virginia and North Carolina," *Journal of Southern History* 43 (1977): 583–600.

——— "Smothering and Overlaying of Virginia Slave Children: A Suggested Explanation," *Bulletin of the History of Medicine* 49 (1975): 400–04.

——— "The Use of Blacks for Medical Experimentation and Demonstration in the Old South," *Journal of Southern History* 48 (1982): 331–48.

Sikes, Lewright, "Medical Care for Slaves: A Preview of the Welfare State," *Georgia Historical Quarterly* 52 (1968): 405–13.

Steckel, Richard H., "Birth Weights and Infant Mortality among American Slaves," *Explorations in Economic History* 23 (1986): 173–98.

——— "A Dreadful Childhood: The Excess Mortality of American Slaves," *Social Science History* 10 (1986): 427–66.

——— "A Peculiar Population: The Nutrition, Health, and Mortality of American Slaves from Childhood to Maturity," *Journal of Economic History* 46 (1986): 721–41.

——— "Slave Mortality: Analysis of Evidence from Plantation Records," *Social Science History* 3 (1979): 86–114.

Sutch, Richard, "The Care and Feeding of Slaves," in Paul A. David, Herbert G. Gutman, Richard Sutch, Peter Temin and Gavin Wright, ed., *Reckoning with Slavery: A Critical Study in the Quantitative History of American Negro Slavery* (1976): 231–301.

Sydnor, Charles S., "Life Span of Mississippi Slaves," *American Historical Review* 35 (1930): 566–74.

Taylor, R. H., "Feeding Slaves," *Journal of Negro History* 9 (1924): 139–43.

Torchia, Marion M., "Tuberculosis among American Negroes: Medical Research on a Racial Disease, 1830–1950," *Journal of the History of Medicine and Allied Sciences* 32 (1977): 252–79.

Trussell, James, and Richard Steckel, "The Age of Slaves at Menarche and Their First Birth," *Journal of Interdisciplinary History* 8 (1978): 477–505.

Twyman, Robert W., "The Clay Eater: A New Look at an Old Southern Enigma," *Journal of Southern History* 37 (1971): 439–48.

Walsh, Lorena S., "Fevers, Aches, and Cures: Medical Life in Old Virginia," *Journal of American History* 79 (1992): 152–64.

Whitten, David O., "Medical Care of Slaves: Louisiana Sugar Region and South Carolina Rice District," *Southern Studies* 16 (1977): 153–80.

17.14   STUDIES IN FOREIGN LANGUAGES

Accardo, Annalucia and Alessandro Portelli, "Spia nel campo o nemico: Lo schiavo domestico come nemico interno" [A Spy in the Enemy Camp: House Slave As Internal Enemy], in Enrico Pozzi, ed., *Lo straniero interno* (1993): 71–87. In Italian.

Armellin, Bruno, *La condizione dello schiavo: Autobiografie degli schiavi neri negli Stati Uniti* [The Slave Condition: Slave Autobiography in the United States] (1975). In Italian.

Carlier, Auguste, *De l'esclavage dans ses rapports avec l'union américaine* [On the Relationship of Slavery and the American Union] (1862, 1960). In French.

Diedrich, Maria, *Ausbruch aus der Knechtschaft: Die Amerikanische Slave Narrative zwischen Unabhängigkeitserklärung und Bürgerkrieg* [Breaking out of Servitude: The American Slave Narrative between the Declaration of Independence and the Civil War] (1986). In German.

Dixon, Christa, *Wesen und Wandel Geistlicher Volkslieder: Negro Spirituals* [Character and Change in Spiritual Folksongs: Negro Spirituals] (1967). In German.

Emmer, Piet C., "Die Fesseln Gebrochen? Die Abschaffung der Westindischen Sklaverei in Theorie und Praxis" [Broken Chains? The Abolition of West Indian Slavery in Theory and Practice], in *Vortage zur Wirtschafts und Überseegeschichte* [Lectures in Economic and Overseas History] (1982) In German.

Fabre, Michel, *Ésclaves et planteurs: dans le sud des États-Unis au 19ème siècle* [Slaves and Planters in the South of the United States in the Nineteenth Century] (1979). In French.

———— "La représentation du noir sur les enveloppes patriotiques pendant la Guerre de Sécession" [The Representation of Blacks on Patriotic Covers during the Civil War], *Revue Française d'Études Américains* [*The French Review of American Studies*] 7 (1979): 9–16. In French.

Fukumoto, Yasunobu, *Kokujin Dorei-hô Keisei to Sono Haikei* [The Origins and Developments of Slave Codes] (1983). In Japanese.

Ginzburg Migliorino, Ellen, "Frederick Douglass e John Brown" [Frederick Douglass and John Brown], *Annali della Facoltà di Scienze Politiche dell'Università di Milano* [*Annals of the Faculty of Political Science at the University of Milan*] 2 (1982): 555–561. In Italian.

———— *L'emancipazione degli Afro-americani: il dibattito negli Stati Uniti prima della Guerra Civile* [The Emancipation of Afro-Americans: The Pre-Civil War Debate in the United States] (1989). In Italian.

Gomes, Heloisa Toller, *As Marcas da Escravidão: o Negro e o Discurso Oitocentista no Brasil e nos Estados Unidos* [The Marks of Slavery: The Black and Nineteenth Century Discourse in Brazil and the United States] (1994). In Portuguese.

Halle, Ernst von, *Baumwollproduktion und Pflanzungswirtschaft in den Nordamerikanischen Südstaaten: Die Sklavenzeit* [Cotton Production and Plantation Economy in the North American Southern States: The Slave Era] (1897). In German.

Hirai, Yasuhiro, "Kokujin to Pâfekushonizumu: Morumon Kyôkai ni okeru Kokujin-Seisaku no Keisei" [Blacks and Perfectionism: The Formation of Negro Policy in the Mormon Church], *Area Studies (The University of Tokyo)* 2 (1991): 33–54. In Japanese.

Honda, Sozo, *Amerika Nanbu Dorei-sei Shakai no Keizai Kouzô* [The Economic Structure of Slavery in the Ante-Bellum South] (1964). In Japanese.

Huo, Guanghan, and Ningdi Guo, "Lun Mei Guo Hei Ren Yu Nei Zhan" [On Black Americans and the Civil War], *Zhengzhou Daxue Xuebao* 2 (1983): 105–113. In Chinese.

———— "Mei Guo Nei Zhan Zhong Hei Ren De Li Shi Di Wei He Zuo Yong" [The Historical Positions and Functions of Black Americans during the Civil War], in *1981–1983 Mei Guo Shi Lun Wen Ji* (1983): 172–88. In Chinese.

Kikuchi, Ken'ichi, *Amerika Dorei-seido to Kindai Shakai no Seichô* [American Slavery and the Growth of Modern Society] (1950). In Japanese.

———— *Amerika Kokujin Dorei-seido to Nanboku Sensô* [American Slavery and the Coming of the Civil War] (1954). In Japanese.

———— *Amerika no Zen-shihon-sei* [Pre-Capitalist Regime in the United States: The Plantation System of the Post-Bellum South] (1955). In Japanese.

Krüger-Charlé, Michael, *Modernisierung und Sklaverei: Die Industrialisierungsdebatte im Alten Süden der USA, 1840–1860* [Modernization and Slavery: The Industrialization Debate in the Old South of the United States, 1840–1860] (1988). In German.

Lee, Youcheng, "Yu Yue: *Dao Ge La Si Zi Zhuan Sheng Ping Xu Shu* Zhong Shi Zi De Zheng Zhi Xing" [Breakthrough: The Political Nature of Literacy in *The Narrative of Frederick Douglass*], in *Mei Guo Wen Xue, Bi Jiao Wen Xue, Sha Shi Bi Ya: Chu Li-min Jiao Shou Qi Shi Sou Qing Lun Wen Ji* (1980): 103–25. In Chinese.

Liu, Zuochang, "Dao Ge La Si Yu Mei Guo Hei Ren Jie Fang Yun Dong" [Frederick Douglass and the Emancipation of Black Americans], *Li Shi Xue* 4 (1979): 150–59. In Chinese.

——— "Mei Guo Nei Zhan Qi Jian Hei Ren Fan Dui Zhong Zu Qi Shi De Dou Zheng" [Black Americans' Struggle against Racial Discrimination during the Civil War], *Shi Xue Yue Kan* 9 (1969): 34–39. In Chinese.

Martin, Peter, *Das Rebellische Eigentum: Vom Kampf der Afroamerikaner gegen Ihre Versklavung* [Rebellious Property: The Struggle of the Afro-Americans against Their Enslavement] (1985). In German.

Mashimo, Takeshi, "Natto Tânâ no Dorei Hanran" [On Nat Turner's Slave Rebellion], *Bulletin of Osaka College of Music* 57 (1978): 109–41. In Japanese.

——— "Rivaivarizumu to Dorei Haishi Undô" [Religious Revivalism and Abolitionism: A Study on the Lane Seminary Rebellion], *Doshisha American Studies* 27 (1991): 11–22. In Japanese.

Mattiello, Cristina, "'I maschi non c'entrano per niente': predicatrici e profete nere nell'America dell'Ottocentro" ['Man Have Nothing to Do with It': African-American Women Preachers and Prophets in the Nineteenth Century], *Rivista Internazionale di Studi Nordamericani [International Journal of North American Studies]* 1 (1995): 24–8. In Italian.

Omori, Kazuteru, "Anteberamu-ki Bosuton ni okeru Kôkyôiku Tôgô Undo" [African Americans' Struggle for Quality Education in Antebellum Boston: The Massachusetts Desegregation Act of 1855 and the Limits of Abolitionist Thought], *Studies of American History* 13 (1990): 35–52. In Japanese.

——— "Masachûsettsu-shû Tôgô Kyoiku-hô (1855) no Rekishi-teki Igi" [Why Was the Massachusetts Desegregation Act of 1855 Adopted? African Americans and Irish Immigrants in an Industrializing Society], *Hitotsubashi Kenkyu* 16 (1991): 157–74. In Japanese.

Shi, Xianrong, "Mei Guo Hei Ren Nu Li Ge Qu" [The Songs of American Black Slaves], *Mei Guo Yan Jiu* 1 (1990): 128–39. In Chinese.

——— "Mei Guo Hei Ren Nu Li Ji Shi Wen Xue" [The Narrative Literature of Afro-American Slaves], *Mei Guo Yan Jiu* 2 (1990): 123–37. In Chinese.

Shimizu, Tadashige, "Amerika Shokumin Kyôkai" [The American Colonization Society], *Kobe College Studies* 40 (1993): 37–63. In Japanese.

——— "Matin R. Direnî no Iju Rosen" [Martin R. Delany's Emigrationism], *Kobe College Studies* 32 (1985): 151–60. In Japanese.

Takemoto, Yuko, "Mâtin R. Direnî no Afurika Imin Undô" [Martin R. Delany's Proposal for Colonization in Africa], *The Studies in Western History* 156 (1990): 18–35. In Japanese.

Tang, Taohua, "Mei Guo Nu Li Zhi Shi Fou Shi Ren Ci De Nu Li Zhi?" [Was American Slavery a Benevolent Slavery?], *Huanan Shiyuan Xuebao* 1 (1979): 47–54. In Chinese.

——— *Mei Guo Li Shi Shang De Hei Ren Nu Li Zhi* [Black Slavery in the History of the United States] (1980). In Chinese.

Wang, Shaowei, "Guan Yu Mei Zhou Hei Ren Nu Li Zhi De Bi Jiao Yan Jiu" [On Comparative Studies of Slavery in the Americas], *Shi Jie Shi Yan Jiu Dong Tai* 6 (1988): 2–6. In Chinese.

Yamamoto, Mikio, *Amerika Kokujin Dorei-sei* [American Negro Slavery] (1957). In Japanese.

Yang, Liwen, "Mei Gu Nei Zhan Qian Nan Bu Hei Nu Zhi De Xing Zhi" [The Nature of Slavery in the Southern United States before the Civil War], *Mei Guo Shi Lun Wen Ji* (1980): 256–277. In Chinese.

Yang, Shengmao, "Lin Ken Yu Hei Ren Nu Li De 'Jie Fang': Yi Ge Ping Jia" [Abraham Lincoln and the 'Emancipation' of Black Slaves: An Evaluation], *Nankai Daxue Xuebao* 4, 5 (1978): 168–85. In Chinese.

Yin, Xiaohuang, "Shi Jiu Shi Ji Mei Guo Hei Ren De Ju Zhu Zhuang Kuang" [The Living Conditions of Northern Blacks in the Nineteenth Century United States], *Nanjing Daxue Xuebao* 5 (1989): 53–58. In Chinese.

Zhang, Zelai, "Shi Lun Lin Ken De Hei Ren Zhi Min Zheng Ce" [On Lincoln's Black Colonization Policy], *Hebei Daxue Xuebao* 3 (1989): 134–38. In Chinese.

18   *1831–1865 (North)*

Richard J. M. Blackett

18.1   GENERAL STUDIES

Bartlett, Irving H., *From Slave to Citizen: The Story of the Negro in Rhode Island* (1954).
Bell, Howard H., ed., *Minutes of the Proceedings of the National Negro Conventions, 1830–1864* (1969).
——— "Negroes in California, 1849–1859," *Phylon* 28 (1967): 151–60.
——— *A Survey of the Negro Convention Movement, 1830–1861* (1969).
Cottrol, Robert J., ed., *From African to Yankee: Narratives of Slavery and Freedom in Antebellum New England* (1998).
Foner, Philip S., and George E. Walker, ed., *Proceedings of the Black State Conventions, 1840–1865* (2 vols., 1979).
Goode, Kenneth G., *California's Black Pioneers: A Brief Historical Survey* (1974).
Hickok, Charles T., *The Negro in Ohio, 1802–1870* (1896).
Hirsch, Leo, Jr., "The Negro and New York, 1783–1865," *Journal of Negro History* 16 (1931): 382–473.
Lapp, Rudolph M., *Blacks in Gold Rush California* (1977).
Litwack, Leon F., *North of Slavery: The Negro in the Free States, 1790–1860* (1961).
McRae, Norman, *Negroes in Michigan during the Civil War* (1966).
Sterling, Dorothy, comp., *Speak Out in Thunder Tones: Letters and Other Writings by Black Northerners, 1787–1865* (1973).
Turner, Edward R., *The Negro in Pennsylvania: Slavery–Servitude–Freedom, 1639–1861* (1911).
Voegeli, V. Jacque, *Free but Not Equal: The Midwest and the Negro during the Civil War* (1967).
Woodson, Carter Godwin, ed., *The Mind of the Negro As Reflected in Letters Written during the Crisis, 1800–1860* (1926).

18.2   HISTORIOGRAPHY

Bethel, Elizabeth Rauh, *The Roots of African-American Identity: Memory and History in Free Antebellum Communities* (1997).
Lenz, Gunter H., ed., *History and Tradition in Afro-American Culture* (1984).
Quarles, Benjamin, *Black Mosaic: Essays in Afro-American History and Historiography* (1988).
Sweet, Leonard I., *Black Images of America, 1784–1870* (1976).

18.3   SECONDARY SOURCES ON NEWSPAPERS AND PERIODICALS

Abrams, Ray H., "Copperhead Newspapers and the Negro," *Journal of Negro History* 20 (1935): 131–52.
Dann, Martin E., comp., *The Black Press, 1827–1890: The Quest for National Identity* (1971).
Gross, Bella, "*Freedom's Journal* and *The Rights of All*," *Journal of Negro History* 17 (1932): 241–86.

Jacobs, Donald M., ed., *Antebellum Black Newspapers: Indices to* New York Freedom's Journal *(1827–1829),* The Rights of All *(1829),* The Weekly Advocate *(1837), and* The Colored American *(1837–1841)* (1976).

Murray, Alexander L., "*The Provincial Freeman:* A New Source for the History of the Negro in Canada and the United States," *Journal of Negro History* 44 (1959): 123–35.

Rhodes, Jane, *Mary Ann Shadd Cary: The Black Press and Protest in the Nineteenth Century* (1998).

Tripp, Bernell, *Origins of the Black Press: New York, 1827–1847* (1992).

Williams, Gilbert Anthony, The Christian Recorder, *Newspaper of the African Methodist Episcopal Church: History of a Forum of Ideas, 1854–1902* (1996).

18.4   RACE RELATIONS

18.4.1   Slavery

Finkelman, Paul, ed., *Slavery in the North and the West* (1989).

Harris, Norman D., *The History of Negro Servitude in Illinois, and of the Slavery Agitation in That State, 1719–1864* (1904).

18.4.2   Free Blacks

Bell, Howard H., "Free Negroes in the North, 1830–1835: A Study in National Cooperation," *Journal of Negro Education* 26 (1957): 447–55.

Bethel, Elizabeth Rauh, *The Roots of African-American Identity: Memory and History in Antebellum Free Communities* (1997).

Bracey, John H., Jr., August Meier, and Elliott Rudwick, ed., *Free Blacks in America, 1800–1860* (1971).

Hinks, Peter P., "'Frequently Plunged into Slavery': Free Blacks and Kidnapping in Antebellum Boston," *Historical Journal of Massachusetts* 20 (1992): 16–31.

Horton, James Oliver, *Free People of Color: Inside the African American Community* (1993).

———— "Generations of Protest: Black Families and Social Reform in Antebellum Boston," *New England Quarterly* 49 (1976): 242–56.

Horton, James Oliver, and Lois E. Horton, *In Hope of Liberty: Culture, Community and Protest among Northern Free Blacks, 1700–1860* (1997).

Johnson, Franklin, *The Development of State Legislation concerning the Free Negro* (1919).

Quarles, Benjamin, "Antebellum Free Blacks and the 'Spirit of '76,'" *Journal of Negro History* 61 (1976): 229–42.

Smith, Gene A., "Griffin Dobson: Virginia Slave, California Freeman," *Virginia Cavalcade* 46 (1997): 278–87.

Voegeli, V. Jacque, *Free but Not Equal: The Midwest and the Negro during the Civil War* (1967).

Woodson, Carter Godwin, *Free Negro Heads of Families in the United States in 1830: Together with a Brief Treatment of the Free Negro* (1925).

Yee, Shirley J., "Finding a Place: Mary Ann Shadd Cary and the Dilemmas of Black Migration to Canada, 1850–1870," *Frontiers* 18 (1997): 1–16.

Young, R. J., *Antebellum Black Activists: Race, Gender, and Self* (1996).

18.4.3   Resistance (Antebellum)

Bell, Howard H., "Expressions of Negro Militancy in the North, 1840–1860," *Journal of Negro History* 45 (1959): 11–20.

Bigglestone, William E., *They Stopped in Oberlin: Black Residents and Visitors of the Nineteenth Century* (1981).

Blockson, Charles L., *The Underground Railroad in Pennsylvania* (1981).

Collison, Gary L., *Shadrach Minkins: From Fugitive Slave to Citizen* (1997).

Craft, William, and Ellen Craft, *Running a Thousand Miles for Freedom; or, the Escape of William and Ellen Craft from Slavery* (1860).

Drew, Benjamin, *A North-Side View of Slavery: The Refugee: Or, the Narratives of Fugitive Slaves in Canada* (1856).

Gara, Larry, *The Liberty Line: The Legend of the Underground Railroad* (1961).

———— "William Still and the Underground Railroad," *Pennsylvania History* 28 (1969): 33–44.

Garnet, Henry Highland, *An Address to the Slaves of the United States of America* (1848).

———— *The Past and the Present Condition, and the Destiny, of the Colored Race* (1848).

Goldstein, Leslie F., "Violence As an Instrument for Social Change: The Views of Frederick Douglass, 1817–1895," *Journal of Negro History* 61 (1976): 61–72.

Jones, Howard, *Mutiny on the Amistad: The Saga of a Slave Revolt and Its Impact on American Abolition, Law, and Diplomacy* (1987).

Landon, Fred, "Amherstburg, Terminus of the Underground Railroad," *Journal of Negro History* 10 (1925): 1–9.

———— "The Anderson Fugitive Case," *Journal of Negro History* 7 (1922): 233–42.

———— "Canadian Negroes and the Rebellion of 1837," *Journal of Negro History* 7 (1922): 377–79.

Lapp, Rudolph M., *Archy Lee: A California Fugitive Slave Case* (1969).

McBride, David, "Black Protest against Racial Politics: Gardner, Hinton, and the Memorial of 1838," *Pennsylvania History* 46 (1979): 149–62.

McKivigan, John R., "James Redpath, John Brown, and Abolitionist Advocacy of Slave Insurrection," *Civil War History* 37 (1991): 293–313.

Nichols, Charles Harold, *Many Thousand Gone: The Ex-Slaves' Account of Their Bondage and Freedom* (1963).

Novak, Susan S., "Roads from Fear to Freedom: The Kansas Underground Railroad," *Kansas Heritage* 4 (1996): 9–12.

Priebe, Paula J., "Central and Western New York and the Fugitive Slave Law of 1850," *Afro-Americans in New York Life and History* 16 (1992): 19–29.

Sawyer, Kem Knapp, *The Underground Railroad in American History* (1997).

Siebert, Wilbur Henry, *The Underground Railroad from Slavery to Freedom* (1898).

———— *The Underground Railroad in Massachusetts* (1936).

Smedley, Robert Clemens, *History of the Underground Railroad in Chester and the Neighboring Counties of Pennsylvania* (1883).

Still, William, *The Underground Railroad* (1872).

Strother, Horatio T., *The Underground Railroad in Connecticut* (1962).

Turner, Edward R., "The Underground Railroad in Pennsylvania," *Pennsylvania Magazine of History and Biography* 36 (1912): 309–18.

Walker, David, *Walker's Appeal in Four Articles: Together with a Preamble to the Coloured Citizens of the World, but in Particular, and Very Expressly to Those of the United States of America* (3d ed., 1830).

Winch, Julie, "Philadelphia and the Other Underground Railroad," *Pennsylvania Magazine of History and Biography* 111 (1987): 3–25.

Yanuck, Julius, "The Garner Fugitive Slave Case," *Mississippi Valley Historical Review* 40 (1953): 47–66.

Zorn, Roman J., "Criminal Extradition Menaces: The Canadian Haven for Fugitive Slaves, 1841–1861," *The Canadian Historical Review* 78 (1957): 284–314.

18.4.4   Abolitionism and Emancipation

Aptheker, Herbert, *The Negro in the Abolitionist Movement* (1941).

Armistead, Wilson, *A Tribute for the Negro: Being a Vindication of the Moral, Intellectual, and Religious Capabilities of the Coloured Portion of Mankind with Particular Reference to the African Race* (1848).

Barnes, Gilbert H., and Dwight L. Dumond, ed., *Letters of Theodore Dwight Weld, Angelina Grimke, and Sarah Grimke, 1822–1844* (2 vols., 1934).

Bell, Howard H., "The American Moral Reform Society, 1836–1841," *Journal of Negro Education* 27 (1958): 34–40.

—— "National Negro Conventions of the Middle 1840's: Moral Suasion *vs.* Political Action," *Journal of Negro History* 42 (1957): 247–60.

Blackett, Richard J. M., "' . . . Freedom, or the Martyr's Grave': Black Pittsburgh's Aid to the Fugitive Slave," *Western Pennsylvania Historical Magazine* 61 (1978): 117–34.

—— "African Americans, the British Working Class, and the American Civil War," *Slavery and Abolition* 2 (1996): 51–67.

—— *Building an Anti-Slavery Wall: Black Americans in the Atlantic Abolitionist Movement, 1830–1860* (1983).

Blight, David W., *Frederick Douglass' Civil War: Keeping Faith in Jubilee* (1989).

Bolt, Christine, *The Anti-Slavery Movement and Reconstruction: A Study in Anglo-American Cooperation, 1833–1877* (1969).

Boromé, Joseph A., "The Vigilant Committee of Philadelphia," *Pennsylvania Magazine of History and Biography* 92 (1968): 320–51.

Bracey, John H., August Meier, and Elliott Rudwick, ed., *Blacks in the Abolitionist Movement* (1971).

Brown, Ira V., "Pennsylvania, 'Immediate Emancipation,' and the Birth of the American Anti-Slavery Society," *Pennsylvania History* 54 (1987): 163–78.

—— "Racism and Sexism: The Case of Pennsylvania Hall," *Phylon* 37 (1976): 126–36.

Browne, Patrick T. J., "'To Defend Mr. Garrison': William Cooper Nell and the Personal Politics of Antislavery," *New England Quarterly* 70 (1997): 415–42.

Collison, Gary L., "Alexander Burton and Salem's 'Fugitive Riot Act' of 1851," *Essex Institute Historical Collections* 128 (1992): 17–26.

Dillon, Merton Lynn, *Benjamin Lundy and the Struggle for Negro Freedom* (1966).

Duberman, Martin B., ed., *The Anti-Slavery Vanguard: New Essays on the Abolitionists* (1965).

Dumond, Dwight L., *Anti-Slavery: The Crusade for Freedom in America* (1961).

Edelstein, Tilden G., *Strange Enthusiasm: A Life of Thomas Wentworth Higginson* (1968).

Eisan, Frances K., *Saint or Demon? The Legendary Delia Webster Opposing Slavery* (1998).

Filler, Louis, *Crusade against Slavery: Friends, Foes, and Reforms, 1820–1860* (rev. ed., 1986).

Finkelman, Paul, ed., *Abolitionists in Northern Courts: The Pamphlet Literature* (1988).

Fredrickson, George M., *The Inner Civil War: Northern Intellectuals and the Crisis of the Union* (1965).

Fulkerson, Gerald, "Exile As Emergence: Frederick Douglass in Great Britain, 1845–1847," *Quarterly Journal of Speech* 60 (1974): 69–82.

Gara, Larry, "The Professional Fugitive in the Abolition Movement," *Wisconsin Magazine of History* 48 (1965): 196–204.

Garrison, William Lloyd, *The Letters of William Lloyd Garrison,* ed. Walter M. Merrill and Louis Ruchames (6 vols., 1971–81).

George, Carol V. R., "Widening the Circle: The Black Church and the Abolitionist Crusade, 1830–1860," in Lewis Perry and Michael Fellman, ed., *Antislavery Reconsidered: New Perspectives on the Abolitionists* (1979): 75–95.

Goodman, Paul, *Of One Blood: Abolitionism and the Origins of Racial Equality* (1998).

Hembree, Michael F., "The Question of 'Begging': Fugitive Slave Relief in Canada, 1830–1865," *Civil War History* 37 (1991): 314–27.

Horton, Lois E., "Community Organization and Social Activism: Black Boston and the Anti-Slavery Movement," *Sociological Inquiry* 55 (1985): 182–99.

Jacobs, Donald M., *Courage and Conscience: Black and White Abolitionists in Boston* (1993).

—— "William Lloyd Garrison's *Liberator* and Boston's Blacks, 1830–1865," *New England Quarterly* 44 (1971): 259–77.

Katz, William Loren, "The Black/White Fight against Slavery and for Women's Rights in America," *Freedomways* 16 (1976): 230–36.

Kraditor, Aileen S., *Means and Ends in American Abolitionism: Garrison and His Critics on Strategy and Tactics, 1834–1850* (1969).

Landon, Fred, "The Anti-Slavery Society of Canada," *Journal of Negro History* 4 (1919): 33–40.

Lerner, Gerda, "The Grimke Sisters and the Struggle against Race Prejudice," *Journal of Negro History* 48 (1963): 277–91.

—— *The Grimke Sisters from South Carolina: Pioneers for Women's Rights and Abolition* (1971).

Levy, Ronald, "Bishop Hopkins and the Dilemma of Slavery," *Pennsylvania Magazine of History and Biography* 91 (1967): 56–71.

Lightner, David L., "The Door to the Slave Bastille: The Abolitionist Slave Assault upon the Interstate Slave Trade," *Civil War History* 34 (1988): 235–52.

Litwack, Leon F., "The Abolitionist Dilemma: The Antislavery Movement and the Northern Negro," *New England Quarterly* 34 (1961): 50–73.

———— "The Emancipation of the Negro Abolitionist," in Martin Duberman, ed., *The Antislavery Vanguard* (1965): 137–55.

Lutz, Alma, *Crusade for Free Women: Women of the Anti-Slavery Movement* (1968).

Mabee, Carleton, *Black Freedom: The Nonviolent Abolitionists from 1830 through the Civil War* (1970).

Mahoney, Olivia, "Black Abolitionists," *Chicago History* 20 (1991): 22–37.

McInerney, Daniel J., "'A State of Commerce': Market Power and Slave Power in Abolitionist Political Economy," *Civil War History* 37 (1991): 101–19.

McKivigan, John R., *The War against Pro-Slavery Religion: Abolitionism and the Northern Churches, 1830–1865* (1984).

McKivigan, John R., and Jason H. Silverman, "Monarchial Liberty and Republican Slavery: West Indies Emancipation Celebrations in Upstate New York and Canada West," *Afro-Americans in New York Life and History* 10 (1986): 7–18.

McManus, Michael J., *Political Abolitionism in Wisconsin, 1840–1861* (1998).

McPherson, James M., "A Brief for Equality: The Abolitionist Reply to the Racist Myth, 1860–1865," in Martin Duberman, ed., *The Antislavery Vanguard* (1965): 156–77.

———— *The Struggle for Equality: Abolitionists and the Negro in the Civil War and Reconstruction* (1995).

Meier, August, "Frederick Douglass' Vision for America: A Case Study in Nineteenth-Century Protest," in Harold M. Hyman and Leonard Levy, ed., *Freedom and Reform* (1967): 127–48.

Melish, Joanne Pope, *Disowning Slavery: Gradual Emancipation and 'Race' in New England, 1780–1860* (1998).

Middleton, Stephen, "Cincinnati and the Fight for the Law of Freedom in Ohio, 1830–1856," *Locus* 4 (1991): 59–73.

———— *Ohio and the Anti-Slavery Activities of Salmon Portland Chase, 1830–1849* (1990).

Mulderink, Earl F., III, "'The Whole Town is Ringing with It': Slave Kidnapping Charges against Nathan Johnson of New Bedford, Massachusetts, 1839," *New England Quarterly* 61 (1988): 341–57.

Oates, Stephen B., *To Purge This Land with Blood: A Biography of John Brown* (1970).

Osofsky, Gilbert, "Abolitionists, Irish Immigrants, and the Dilemmas of Romantic Nationalism," *American Historical Review* 80 (1975): 889–912.

Pease, William H., and Jane H. Pease, "Boston Garrisonians and the Problem of Frederick Douglass," *Canadian Journal of History* 2 (1967): 29–48.

———— *Bound with Them in Chains: A Biographical History of the Anti-Slavery Movement* (1972).

———— *They Who Would Be Free: Blacks' Search for Freedom, 1830–1861* (1974).

Quarles, Benjamin, *Allies for Freedom: Blacks and John Brown* (1974).

———— *Black Abolitionists* (1969).

———— comp., *Blacks on John Brown* (1972).

———— "Letters from Negro Leaders to Gerrit Smith," *Journal of Negro History* 27 (1942): 432–53.

———— "Ministers without Portfolio," *Journal of Negro History* 39 (1954): 27–42.

Reinders, Robert C., "Anglo-Canadian Abolitionism: The John Anderson Case, 1860–1861," *Renaissance and Modern Studies* 19 (1975): 72–97.

———— "The John Anderson Case, 1860–1861: A Study in Anglo-Canadian Imperial Relations," *Canadian Historical Review* 56 (1975): 393–415.

Rhodes, Jane, *Mary Ann Shadd Cary: The Black Press and Protest in the Nineteenth Century* (1998).

Rice, Charles Duncan, *The Scots Abolitionists, 1833–1861* (1981).

Riddell, William R., "The Slave in Upper Canada," *Journal of Negro History* 4 (1919): 372–95.

Ripley, C. Peter, ed., *The Black Abolitionist Papers* (5 vols., 1985).

Rogers, William B., *"We Are All Together Now": Frederick Douglass, William Lloyd Garrison, and the Prophetic Tradition* (1995).

Ruchames, Louis, "Race, Marriage, and Abolition in Massachusetts," *Journal of Negro History* 40 (1955): 250–73.

Rury, John L., "Philanthropy, Self-Help, and Social Control: The New York Manumission Society and Free Blacks, 1785–1810," *Phylon* 46 (1985): 231–41.

Schnell, Kempes, "Anti-Slavery Influences on the Status of Slaves in a Free State," *Journal of Negro History* 50 (1965): 257–73.

Schor, Joel, "The Rivalry between Frederick Douglass and Henry Highland Garnet," *Journal of Negro History* 64 (1979): 30–38.

Sernett, Milton C., *Abolition's Axe: Beriah Green, Oneida Institute, and the Black Freedom Struggle* (1986).

Shapiro, Samuel, "The Rendition of Samuel Burns," *Journal of Negro History* 44 (1959): 34–51.

Shepperson, George, "Frederick Douglass in Scotland," *Journal of Negro History* 38 (1953): 307–21.

Sheridan, Richard B., "From Slavery in Missouri to Freedom in Kansas: The Influx of Black Fugitives and Contrabands into Kansas, 1854–1865," *Kansas History* 12 (1989): 28–47.

Stirn, James R., "Urgent Gradualism: The Case of the American Union for the Relief and Improvement of the Colored Race," *Civil War History* 25 (1979): 309–28.

Stouffer, Allen P., *The Light of Nature and the Law of God: Anti-Slavery in Ontario, 1833–1877* (1992).

Sumler-Lewis, Janice, "The Forten-Purvis Women of Philadelphia and the American Anti-Slavery Crusade," *Journal of Negro History* 66 (1981): 281–88.

Swift, David Everett, *Black Prophets of Justice: Activist Clergy before the Civil War* (1989).

———— "O, This Heartless Prejudice," *Wesleyan* 67 (1984): 13–17.

Taylor, Clare, comp., *British and American Abolitionists: An Episode in Transatlantic Understanding* (1974).

Teed, Paul E., "Racial Nationalism and Its Challengers: Theodore Parker, John Rock, and the Antislavery Movement," *Civil War History* 41 (1995): 142–60.

Tobin, Jacqueline L., and Raymond G. Dobard, *Hidden in Plain View: The Secret History of Quilts and the Underground Railroad* (1999).

Toplin, Robert Brent, "Peter Still versus the Peculiar Institution," *Civil War History* 13 (1967): 340–49.

Tyler, Alice Felt, *Freedom's Ferment: Phases of American Social History from the Colonial Period to the Outbreak of the Civil War* (1944).

Usrey, Miriam L., "Charles Lenox Remond: Garrison's Ebony Echo at the World Anti-Slavery Convention, 1840," *Essex Institute Historical Collections* 106 (1970): 112–25.

Venet, Wendy Hamand, *Neither Ballots nor Bullets: Women Abolitionists and the Civil War* (1991).

Walker, Peter F., *Moral Choices: Memory, Desire, and Imagination in Nineteenth-Century American Abolition* (1978).

Wesley, Charles H., "The Negroes of New York in the Emancipation Movement," *Journal of Negro History* 24 (1939): 65–103.

———— "The Negro's Struggle for Freedom in Its Birthplace," *Journal of Negro History* 30 (1945): 62–81.

Yee, Shirley J., *Black Women Abolitionists: A Study in Activism, 1828–1860* (1992).

Yellin, Jean Fagan, *Women and Sisters: The Anti-Slavery Feminists in American Culture* (1989).

18.4.5 Black/White Relations

Berwanger, Eugene H., *The Frontier against Slavery: Western Anti-Negro Prejudice and the Slavery Extension Controversy* (1967).

Fehrenbacher, Don E., "Only His Stepchildren: Lincoln and the Negro," *Civil War History* 20 (1974): 293–310.

Franklin, John Hope, *A Southern Odyssey: Travelers in the Antebellum North* (1976).

Fredrickson, George M., *The Black Image in the White Mind: The Debate on Afro-American Character and Destiny, 1817–1914* (1971).

———— "A Man but Not a Brother: Abraham Lincoln and Racial Equality," *Journal of Southern History* 41 (1975): 39–58.

Lapsansky, Emma Jones, "Since They Got Those Separate Churches: Afro-Americans and Racism in Jacksonian Philadelphia," *American Quarterly* 32 (1980): 54–78.

Levy, David W., "Racial Stereotypes in Antislavery Fiction," *Phylon* 31 (1970): 265–79.

Lorimer, Douglas A., *Colour, Class, and the Victorians: English Attitudes to the Negro in the Mid-Nineteenth Century* (1978).

Lott, Eric, *Love and Theft: Blackface Minstrelsy and the American Working Class* (1993).

Nathan, Hans, *Dan Emmett and the Rise of Early Negro Minstrelsy* (1962).

Quillin, Frank U., *The Color Line in Ohio: A History of Race Prejudice in a Typical Northern State* (1913).

Reiss, Benjamin, "P.T. Barnum, Joice Heth, and Antebellum Spectacles of Race," *American Quarterly* 51 (1999): 78–107.

Roediger, David R., *The Wages of Whiteness: Race and the Making of the American Working Class* (1991).

Rubin, Jay, "Black Nativism: The European Immigrant in Negro Thought, 1830–1860," *Phylon* 39 (1978): 193–202.

Shaffert, Charles F., *The Editorial Attitudes of the* New York Daily Tribune *and the* New York Daily Times *towards the Negro, 1850–1859* (1969).

Silverman, Jason H., *Unwelcome Guests: Canada West's Response to American Fugitive Slaves, 1800–1865* (1985).

Stanton, William, *The Leopard's Spots: Scientific Attitudes toward Race in America, 1815–1859* (1960).

Strickland, Arvarh E., "The Illinois Background of Lincoln's Attitude toward Slavery and the Negro," *Journal of the Illinois State Historical Society* 56 (1963): 474–94.

Sweet, Leonard I., *Black Images of America, 1784–1870* (1976).

Toll, Robert C., *Blacking Up: The Minstrel Show in Nineteenth-Century America* (1974).

18.4.6   Black/Native American Relations

May, Katja, *African Americans and Native Americans in the Creek and Cherokee Nations, 1830's to 1920's: Collision and Collusion* (1996).

18.4.7   Black/Ethnic Relations

Rubin, Jay, "Black Nativism: The European Immigrant in Negro Thought, 1830–1860," *Phylon* 39 (1978): 193–202.

18.4.8   Violence and Racial Disturbances

Bernstein, Iver, *The New York City Draft Riots: Their Significance for American Society and Politics in the Age of the Civil War* (1990).

Feldberg, Michael, *The Philadelphia Riots of 1844: A Study of Ethnic Conflict* (1975).

——— *The Turbulent Era: Riot and Disorder in Jacksonian America* (1980).

Geffen, Elizabeth M., "Violence in Philadelphia in the 1840's and 1850's," *Pennsylvania History* 36 (1969): 381–410.

Goldstein, Leslie F., "Violence As an Instrument for Social Change: The Views of Frederick Douglass, 1817–1895," *Journal of Negro History* 61 (1976): 61–72.

Grimsted, David, "Rioting in Its Jacksonian Setting," *American Historical Review* 77 (1972): 361–97.

Hensel, William Uhler, *The Christiana Riot and the Treason Trials of 1851: An Historical Sketch* (rev. ed., 1911).

Kerber, Linda K., "Abolitionists and Amalgamators: The New York Race Riots of 1834," *New York History* 48 (1967): 28–39.

Montgomery, David, "The Shuttle and the Cross: Weavers and Artisans in the Kensington Riots of 1844," *Journal of Social History* 5 (1972): 411–46.

Richards, Leonard L., *Gentlemen of Property and Standing: Anti-Abolition Mobs in Jacksonian America* (1970).

Runcie, John, "'Hunting the Nigs' in Philadelphia: The Race Riot of August, 1834," *Pennsylvania History* 39 (1972): 187–218.

Shiffin, Steven H., "The Rhetoric of Black Violence in the Antebellum Period: Henry Highland Garnet," *Journal of Black Studies* 2 (1971): 45–56.

Slaughter, Thomas Paul, *Bloody Dawn: The Christiana Riot and Racial Violence in the Antebellum North* (1991).

Werner, John M., *Reaping the Bloody Harvest: Race Riots in the United States during the Age of Jackson, 1824–1849* (1986).

18.5 GOVERNMENT

18.5.1 Law

Albin, Ray R., "The *Perkins* Case: The Ordeal of Three Slaves in Gold Rush California," *California History* 67 (1988): 214–27.

Berwanger, Eugene H., "The 'Black Law' Question in Antebellum California," *Journal of the West* 6 (1967): 205–20.

Brandon, Mark E., *Free in the World: American Slavery and Constitutional Failure* (1998).

Broussard, Albert S., "Slavery in California Revisited: The Fate of a Kentucky Slave in Gold Rush California," *Pacific Historian* 29 (1985): 17–21.

Burke, Joseph C., "What Did the *Prigg* Decision Really Decide?" *Pennsylvania Magazine of History and Biography* 93 (1969): 73–85.

Cable, Mary, *Black Odyssey: The Case of the Slave Ship* Amistad (1971).

Calligaro, Lee, "The Negro's Legal Status in Pre-Civil War New Jersey," *New Jersey History* 85 (1967): 167–80.

Campbell, Stanley W., *The Slave Catchers: Enforcement of the Fugitive Slave Law, 1850–1860* (1970).

Eggert, Gerald G., "The Impact of the Fugitive Slave Law on Harrisburg: A Case Study," *Pennsylvania Magazine of History and Biography* 109 (1985): 537–70.

Erickson, Leonard, "Politics and the Repeal of Ohio's Black Laws, 1837–1849," *Ohio History* 82 (1973): 154–75.

Fehrenbacher, Don E., *The Dred Scott Case: Its Significance in American Law and Politics* (1978).

Finkelman, Paul, ed., *Abolitionists in Northern Courts: The Pamphlet Literature* (1988).

———— Dred Scott *vs.* Sandford: *A Brief History with Documents* (1997).

———— "Evading the Ordinance: The Persistance of Bondage in Indiana and Illinois," *Journal of the Early Republic* 9 (1989): 21–51.

———— "The Protection of Black Rights in Seward's New York," *Civil War History* 34 (1988): 211–34.

———— "Slavery, the 'More Perfect Union,' and the Prairie State," *Illinois Historical Journal* 80 (1987): 248–69.

Fisher, James A., "The Struggle for Negro Testimony in California, 1851–1863," *Southern California Quarterly* 51 (1969): 313–24.

Franklin, John Hope, *The Emancipation Proclamation* (1963).

Gertz, Elmer, "The Black Laws of Illinois," *Journal of the Illinois State Historical Society* 56 (1963): 454–73.

Hamer, Philip M., "Great Britain, the United States, and the Negro Seaman Acts, 1822–1848," *Journal of Southern History* 1 (1935): 3–28.

Johnson, Franklin, *The Development of State Legislation Concerning the Free Negro* (1919).

Lemons, J. Stanley, and Michael A. McKenna, "Re-Enfranchisement of Rhode Island Negroes," *Rhode Island History* 30 (1971): 3–13.

Levy, Leonard W., "Sim's Case: The Fugitive Slave Law in Boston in 1851," *Journal of Negro History* 35 (1950): 39–74.

McClure, James P., Leigh Johnsen, Kathleen Norman, and Michael Vanderlan, ed., "Circumventing the *Dred Scott* Decision: Edward Bates, Salmon P. Chase, and the Citizenship of African Americans," *Civil War History* 43 (1997): 279–309.

Middleton, Stephen, *The Black Laws in the Old Northwest: A Documentary History* (1993).

Morris, Thomas D., *Free Men All: The Personal Liberty Laws of the North, 1780–1861* (1974).

Preston, Emmett D., Jr., "The Fugitive Slave Acts in Ohio," *Journal of Negro History* 28 (1943): 422–77.

Rosenberg, Norman L., "Personal Liberty Laws and Sectional Crisis, 1850–1861," *Civil War History* 17 (1971): 25–44.

Skjeie, Sheila M., *California and the Fifteenth Amendment: A Study of Racism* (1973).

Thurston, Helen M., "The 1802 Ohio Constitutional Convention and the Status of the Negro," *Ohio History* 81 (1972): 15–37.

von Frank, Albert J., *The Trials of Anthony Burns: Freedom and Slavery in Emerson's Boston* (1998).

18.5.2   Crime and Punishment

Patrick-Stamp, Leslie, "Numbers That Are Not New: African Americans in the Country's First Prison, 1790–1835," *Pennsylvania Magazine of History and Biography* 119 (1995): 95–128.

18.5.3   Politics and Voting

Fehrenbacher, Don E., "Republicans and Black Suffrage in New York State: The Grass Roots Response," *Civil War History* 21 (1975): 136–47.

Field, Phyllis F., *The Politics of Race in New York: The Struggle for Black Suffrage in the Civil War Era* (1982).

Foner, Eric, *Free Soil, Free Labor, Free Men: The Ideology of the Republican Party before the Civil War* (1970).

———— "Politics and Prejudice: The Free Soil Party and the Negro, 1849–1852," *Journal of Negro History* 50 (1965): 239–56.

Formisano, Ronald P., "The Edge of Caste: Colored Suffrage in Michigan, 1827–1861," *Michigan History* 56 (1972): 19–41.

Fox, Dixon Ryan, "The Negro Vote in Old New York," *Political Science Quarterly* 32 (1917): 252–75.

Hill, D. G., "The Negro As a Political and Social Issue in the Oregon Country," *Journal of Negro History* 33 (1948): 130–45.

Jackson, W. Sherman, "Emancipation, Negrophobia, and Civil War Politics in Ohio, 1863–1865," *Journal of Negro History* 65 (1980): 250–60.

Mittrick, Robert, *A History of Negro Voting in Pennsylvania during the Nineteenth Century* (1985).

Olbrich, Emil, *The Development of Sentiment on Negro Suffrage to 1860* (1912).

Wesley, Charles H., "Negro Suffrage in the Period of Constitution-Making, 1787–1865," *Journal of Negro History* 32 (1947): 143–68.

———— "The Participation of Negroes in Anti-Slavery Political Parties," *Journal of Negro History* 29 (1944): 32–74.

Wright, Marion T., "Negro Suffrage in New Jersey, 1776–1875," *Journal of Negro History* 33 (1948): 168–224.

18.5.4   Military

Abbott, Richard H., "Massachusetts and the Recruitment of Southern Negroes, 1863–1865," *Civil War History* 14 (1968): 197–210.

Belz, Herman, "Law, Politics, and Race in the Struggle for Equal Pay during the Civil War," *Civil War History* 22 (1976): 197–213.

Berlin, Ira, Joseph P. Reidy, and Leslie S. Rowland, ed., *The Black Military Experience.* Volume 2 of *Freedom: A Documentary History of Emancipation, 1861–1867* (1982).

Berlin, Ira, Joseph P. Reidy, and Leslie S. Rowland, ed., *Freedom's Soldiers: The Black Military Experience in the Civil War* (1998).

Berry, Mary Frances, *Military Necessity and Civil Rights Policy: Black Citizenship and the Constitution, 1861–1868* (1977).

Binder, Frederick M., "Pennsylvania Negro Regiments in the Civil War," *Journal of Negro History* 37 (1952): 383–417.

Blackerby, H. C., *Blacks in Blue and Gray: Afro-American Service in the Civil War* (1979).

Blassingame, John W., "The Union Army As an Educational Institution for Negroes, 1861–1865," *Journal of Negro Education* 34 (1965): 152–59.

Burchard, Peter, *One Gallant Rush: Robert Gould Shaw and His Brave Black Regiment* (1965).

Califf, Joseph Mark, *Record of the Services of the Seventh Regiment: U.S. Colored Troops, from September, 1863, to November, 1866* (1878).

Chenery, William H., *The Fourteenth Regiment Rhode Island Heavy Artillery (Colored) in the War to Preserve the Union, 1861–1865* (1898).

Chester, Thomas Morris, *Thomas Morris Chester: Black Civil War Correspondent: His Dispatches from the Virginia Front*, ed. Richard J. M. Blackett (1989).

Cimprich, John, and Robert C. Mainfort, Jr., "The Fort Pillow Massacre: A Statistical Note," *Journal of American History* 76 (1989): 830–37.

Clark, Peter H., *The Black Brigade of Cincinnati: Being a Report of Its Labors and a Muster-Roll of Its Members* (1864).

Cornish, Dudley Taylor, *The Sable Arm: Negro Troops in the Union Army, 1861–1865* (1956).

Cowden, Robert, *A Brief Sketch of the Organization and Services of the Fifty-Ninth Regiment of United States Colored Infantry* (1883).

Cox, Clinton, *Undying Glory: The Story of the Massachusetts 54th Regiment* (1991).

Dyer, Brainard, "The Treatment of Colored Union Troops by the Confederates, 1861–1865," *Journal of Negro History* 20 (1935): 273–86.

Ellis, Richard N., "The Civil War Letters of an Iowa Family," *Annals of Iowa* 39 (1969): 561–86.

Emilio, Luis F., *A Brave Black Regiment: History of the Fifty-Fourth Regiment of Massachusetts Volunteer Infantry, 1863–1865* (1894).

Gladstone, William A., *United States Colored Troops, 1863–1867* (1990).

Glatthaar, Joseph T., *Forged in Battle: The Civil War Alliance of Black Soldiers and White Officers* (1990).

Goldman, Hal, "Black Citizenship and Military Self-Presentation in Antebellum Massachusetts," *Historical Journal of Massachusetts* 26 (1997): 157–83.

Gooding, James Henry, *On the Altar of Freedom: A Black Soldier's Civil War Letters from the Front*, ed. Virginia Matzke Adams (1991).

Hicken, Victor, "The Record of Illinois' Negro Soldiers in the Civil War," *Journal of the Illinois State Historical Society* 56 (1963): 529–51.

Higginson, Thomas Wentworth, *Army Life in a Black Regiment* (1870).

Hill, Isaac, *A Sketch of the Twenty-Ninth Regiment of Connecticut Colored Troops* (1867).

Hunt, Sanford B., "The Negro As a Soldier," *Journal of Psychological Medicine and Jurisprudence* 1: 161–86.

Mays, Joe H., *Black Americans and Their Contributions toward Union Victory in the American Civil War, 1861–1865* (1984).

McPherson, James M., *Marching toward Freedom: The Negro in the Civil War, 1861–1865* (1968).

——— *The Negro's Civil War: How American Negroes Felt and Acted during the War for the Union* (1965).

Metzer, Jacob, "The Records of the U.S. Colored Troops As a Historical Source: An Exploratory Examination," *Historical Methods* 14 (1981): 123–32.

Murray, Donald M., and Robert M. Rodney, "Colonel Julian E. Bryant: Champion of the Negro Soldier," *Journal of the Illinois State Historical Society* 56 (1963): 257–81.

Quarles, Benjamin, *The Negro in the Civil War* (1953).

Redkey, Edwin S., "Black Chaplains in the Union Army," *Civil War History* 33 (1987): 331–50.

——— *A Grand Army of Black Men: Letters from African-American Soldiers in the Union Army, 1861–1865* (1992).

Seraile, William, "The Struggle to Raise Black Regiments in New York State, 1861–1864," *New York Historical Society Quarterly* 58 (1974): 215–33.

Shannon, Fred A., "The Federal Government and the Negro Soldier, 1861–1865," *Journal of Negro History* 11 (1926): 563–83.

Steiner, Paul E., *Medical History of a Civil War Regiment: Disease in the Sixty-Fifth United States Colored Infantry* (1977).

Stevens, Michael E., ed., *As If It Were Glory: Robert Beecham's Civil War from the Iron Brigade to the Black Regiments* (1999).

Werstein, Irving, *The Storming of Fort Wagner: Black Valor in the Civil War* (1970).

Wesley, Charles H., and Patricia W. Romero, *Afro-Americans in the Civil War: From Slavery to Citizenship* (rev. ed., 1976).

Westwood, Howard C., *Black Troops, White Commanders, and Freedmen during the Civil War* (1992).

Williams, George Washington, *A History of the Negro Troops in the War of the Rebellion, 1861–1865* (1888).

Wilson, Keith, "Thomas Webster and the 'Free Military School for Applicants for Command of Colored Troops,'" *Civil War History* 29 (1983): 101–22.

18.6 DEMOGRAPHY

Bilotta, James D., "A Quantitative Approach to Buffalo's Black Population of 1860," *Afro-Americans in New York Life and History* 12 (1988): 19–34.

Coray, Michael S., "Negro and Mulatto in the Pacific West, 1850–1860: Changing Patterns of Black Population Growth," *Pacific Historian* 29 (1985): 18–27.

Eichholz, Alice, and James M. Rose, *Free Black Heads of Household in the New York State Federal Census, 1790–1830* (1981).

Eisenberg, Marcia, "Blacks in the 1850 Federal Census: City of Chicago, Cook County, Illinois," *Journal of the Afro-American Historical and Genealogical Society* 6 (1985): 44–46, 76–85, 112–15.

Furgal, Suzanne Kersten, "Blacks and Mulattoes in Wards Three and Four Chicago, Cook County, Illinois As Enumerated in the 1860 Federal Census," *Journal of the Afro-American Historical and Genealogical Society* 8 (1987): 79–86.

——— "Blacks Enumerated in the Federal Census of Cook County, Illinois, outside of Chicago," *Journal of the Afro-American Historical and Genealogical Society* 8 (1987): 137–39.

Zelinsky, Wilbur, "The Population Geography of the Free Negro in Antebellum America," *Population Studies* 3 (1949): 386–401.

18.7 FAMILY

Berlin, Ira, and Leslie S. Rowland, ed., *Families and Freedom: A Documentary History of African-American Kinship in the Civil War Era* (1997).

Holsoe, Svend E., "A Portrait of a Black Midwestern Family during the Early Nineteenth Century: Edward James Roye and His Parents," *Liberian Studies Journal* 3 (1970): 41–52.

Woodson, Carter Godwin, *Free Negro Heads of Families in the United States in 1830: Together with a Brief Treatment of the Free Negro* (1925).

18.8 SOCIETY

18.8.1 Rural Life (Including Black Settlements)

Caro, Edythe Quinn, *"The Hills" in the Mid-Nineteenth Century: The History of a Rural Afro-American Community in Westchester County, New York* (1988).

Fields, Harold B., "Free Negroes in Cass County before the Civil War," *Michigan History* 44 (1960): 649–58.

Lyles, Carl C., *Lyles Station, Indiana: Yesterday and Today* (1984).

Pease, William H., and Jane H. Pease, *Black Utopia: Negro Communal Experiments in America* (1963).

Stewart, Roma Jones, "The Migration of a Free People: Cass County's Black Settlers from North Carolina," *Michigan History* 7 (1987): 34–39.

Wilson, Benjamin C., *The Rural Black Heritage between Chicago and Detroit, 1850–1929: A Photograph Album and Random Thoughts* (1985).

18.8.2 Urban Life (Including Migration)

Castle, Musette S., "A Survey of the History of African Americans in Rochester, New York, 1800–1860," *Afro-Americans in New York Life and History* 13 (1989): 7–32.

Cottrol, Robert J., *The Afro-Yankees: Providence's Black Community in the Antebellum Era* (1982).

Curry, Leonard P., *The Free Black in Urban America, 1800–1850: The Shadow of the Dream* (1981).

Hershberg, Theodore, "Free Blacks in Antebellum Philadelphia: A Study of Ex-Slaves, Freeborn, and Socio-Economic Decline," *Journal of Social History* 5 (1971–1972): 183–209.

Horton, James Oliver, and Lois E. Horton, *Black Bostonians: Family Life and Community Struggle in the Antebellum North* (1979).

Levesque, George A., *Black Boston: African American Life and Culture in Urban America, 1750–1860* (1994).

Mabee, Carleton, "Charity in Travail: Two Orphan Asylums for Blacks," *New York History* 55 (1974): 55–77.

Mumford, Esther H., *Seattle's Black Victorians, 1852–1901* (1980).

Nash, Gary B., *Forging Freedom: The Formation of Philadelphia's Black Community, 1720–1840* (1988).

Needles, Edward, *Ten Years' Progress: Or, a Comparison of the State and Condition of the Colored People in the City and County of Philadelphia from 1837 to 1847* (1849).

Phillips, Christopher, *Freedom's Port: The African American Community of Baltimore, 1790–1860* (1997).

Pih, Richard W., "Negro Self-Improvement Efforts in Antebellum Cincinnati, 1836–1850," *Ohio History* 78 (1969): 179–87.

Rammelkamp, Julian, "The Providence Negro Community, 1820–1842," *Rhode Island History* 7 (1948): 20–33.

Taylor, Henry L., "On Slavery's Fringe: City-Building and Black Community Development in Cincinnati, 1800–1850," *Ohio History* 95 (1986–1987): 5–33.

——— "Spatial Organization and the Residential Experience: Black Cincinnati in 1850," *Social Science History* 10 (1986): 45–70.

Wade, Richard C., "The Negro in Cincinnati, 1800–1830," *Journal of Negro History* 39 (1954): 43–57.

Walker, George E., *The Afro-American in New York City, 1827–1860* (1993).

Warner, Robert A., *New Haven Negroes: A Social History* (1940).

Williams-Myers, A. J., "The Plight of African Americans in Ante-Bellum New York City," *Afro-Americans in New York Life and History* 22 (July 1998): 43–90.

Winch, Julie, *Philadelphia's Black Elite: Activism, Accommodation, and the Struggle for Autonomy, 1787–1848* (1988).

Woodson, Carter Godwin, "The Negroes of Cincinnati prior to the Civil War," *Journal of Negro History* 1 (1916): 1–22.

18.8.3 Material Culture

Rankin-Hall, Lesley M., *A Biohistory of Nineteenth Century Afro-Americans: The Burial Remains of a Philadelphia Cemetery* (1997).

Tobin, Jacqueline L., and Raymond G. Dobard, *Hidden in Plain View: The Secret History of Quilts and the Underground Railroad* (1999).

18.8.4 Color and Class

Bardolph, Richard, "Social Origins of Distinguished Negroes, 1776–1865," *Journal of Negro History* 40 (1955): 211–49.

Lapsansky, Emma Jones, "Friends, Wives, and Strivings: Networks and Community Values among Nineteenth-Century Philadelphia Afro-American Elites," *Pennsylvania Magazine of History and Biography* 108 (1984): 3–24.

Willson, Joseph, *Sketches of the Higher Classes of Colored Society in Philadelphia* (1841).

18.8.5   Associational Life

Griffin, Farah Jasmine, "'A Layin' on of Hands': Organizational Efforts among Black American Women, 1790–1930," *Sage* Supplement (1988): 23–29.

Lindhorst, Marie, "Politics in a Box: Sarah Mapps Douglass and the Female Literary Association, 1831–1833," *Pennsylvania History* 65 (1998): 263–78.

Yacovone, Donald, "The Transformation of the Black Temperance Movement, 1827–1854: An Interpretation," *Journal of the Early Republic* 8 (1988): 281–97.

18.9   RELIGION

Bradley, David Henry, *A History of the A.M.E. Zion Church* Vol. 1 (1956).

Bragg, George Freeman, *History of the Afro-American Group of the Episcopal Church* (1922).

Brooks, Walter H., "The Evolution of the Negro Baptist Church," *Journal of Negro History* 7 (1922): 11–22.

Cadbury, Henry J., "Negro Membership in the Society of Friends," *Journal of Negro History* 21 (1936): 151–213.

Cole, Charles Chester, Jr., *The Social Ideas of the Northern Evangelists, 1826–1860* (1954).

Curry, Mary Cuthrell, *Making the Gods in New York: The Yoruba Religion in the African American Community* (1997).

Douglass, William, *Annals of the First African Church, in the United States of America: Now Styled the African Episcopal Church of St. Thomas, Philadelphia* (1862).

Fordham, Monroe, *Major Themes in Northern Black Religious Thought, 1800–1860* (1975).

George, Carol V. R., *Segregated Sabbaths: Richard Allen and the Emergence of Independent Black Churches, 1760–1840* (1973).

———— "Widening the Circle: The Black Church and the Abolitionist Crusade, 1830–1860," in Lewis Perry and Michael Fellman, ed., *Antislavery Reconsidered: New Perspectives on the Abolitionists* (1979): 75–95.

Gerdes, M. Reginald, "To Educate and Evangelize: Black Catholic Schools of the Oblate Sisters of Providence," *U.S. Catholic Historian* 7 (1988): 183–99.

Glaude, Eddie S., Jr., *Exodus! Religion, Race, and Nation in Early Nineteenth-Century Black America* (2000).

Gravely, William B., "The Afro-American Methodist Tradition: A Review of Sources in Reprint," *Methodist History* 9 (1971): 21–33.

———— "The Dialectic of Double Consciousness in Black American Freedom Celebrations," *Journal of Negro History* 67 (1992): 302–17.

Greene, Veryl, "The Allen A.M.E. Church, Jamaica, NY, 1834–1900: The Role of the Black Church in a Developing Nineteenth Century Community," *Afro-Americans in New York Life and History* 16 (1992): 31–39.

Hartzell, J. C., "Methodism and the Negro in the United States," *Journal of Negro History* 8 (1923): 301–15.

Hayden, Robert C., *Faith, Culture, and Leadership: A History of the Black Church in Boston* (1983).

Lapsansky, Emma Jones, "Since They Got Those Separate Churches: Afro-Americans and Racism in Jacksonian Philadelphia," *American Quarterly* 32 (1980): 54–78.

Levesque, George A., "Inherent Reformers, Inherited Orthodoxy: Black Baptists in Boston, 1800–1873," *Journal of Negro History* 60 (1975): 491–519.

Lewis, James K., "Religious Nature of the Early Negro Migration to Canada and the Amherstburg Baptist Association," *Ontario History* 58 (1966): 117–32.

Luker, Ralph E., "Under Our Own Vine and Fig Tree: From American Unionism to Black Denominationalism in Newport, Rhode Island, 1760–1876," *Slavery and Abolition* 12 (1991): 23–48.

Lythgoe, Dennis L., "Negro Slavery and Mormon Doctrine," *Western Humanities Review* 21 (1967): 327–38.

McKivigan, John R., *The War against Pro-Slavery Religion: Abolitionism and the Northern Churches, 1830–1865* (1984).

Morrow, Diane Batts, "Outsiders Within: The Oblate Sisters of Providence in 1830's Church and Society," *U.S. Catholic Historian* 15 (1997): 35–54.

Newcomb, Harvey, *The "Negro Pew": Being an Inquiry concerning the Propriety of Distinctions in the House of God, on Account of Color* (1837).

Saillant, John, "Hymnody and the Persistence of an African-American Faith in Sierra Leone," *Hymn* 48 (1997): 8–17.

Sernett, Milton C., *Black Religion and American Evangelism: White Protestants, Plantation Missions, and the Flowering of Negro Christianity, 1787–1865* (1975).

Sherer, Robert Glenn, Jr., "Negro Churches in Rhode Island before 1860," *Rhode Island History* 25 (1966): 9–25.

Stanley, Alfred Knighton, *The Children Is Crying: Congregationalism among Black People* (1979).

Swift, David Everett, "Black Presbyterian Attacks on Racism," *Journal of Presbyterian History* 51 (1973): 433–70.

———— *Black Prophets of Justice: Activist Clergy before the Civil War* (1989).

Walker, Clarence E., *A Rock in a Weary Land: The African Methodist Episcopal Church during the Civil War and Reconstruction* (1981).

Washington, Joseph R., Jr., *The First Fugitive Foreign and Domestic Doctor of Divinity: Rational Race Rules of Religion and Realism Revered and Reversed or Revised by the Reverend Doctor James William Charles Pennington* (1990).

———— *Race and Religion in Mid-Nineteenth Century America, 1850–1877: Protestant Parochial Philanthropists* (1988).

Williams, Gilbert Anthony, The Christian Recorder *Newspaper of the African Methodist Episcopal Church: History of a Forum of Ideas, 1854–1902* (1996).

Wills, David W., and Richard Newman, ed., *Black Apostles at Home and Abroad: Afro-Americans and the Christian Mission from the Revolution to Reconstruction* (1982).

18.10   THOUGHT AND EXPRESSION

18.10.1   Race, Gender, and Identity

Bell, Howard H., ed., *Minutes of the Proceedings of the National Negro Conventions, 1830–1864* (1969).

———— "National Negro Conventions of the Middle 1840's: Moral Suasion *vs.* Political Action," *Journal of Negro History* 42 (1957): 247–60.

———— *A Survey of the Negro Convention Movement, 1830–1861* (1969).

Bethel, Elizabeth Rauh, *The Roots of African-American Identity: Memory and History in Antebellum Free Communities* (1997).

Blight, David W., "For Something beyond the Battlefield: Frederick Douglass and the Struggle for the Memory of the Civil War," *Journal of American History* 75 (1989): 1156–78.

———— "Frederick Douglass and the American Apocalypse," *Civil War History* 31 (1985): 309–28.

———— "In Search of Learning, Liberty, and Self-Definition: James McCune Smith and the Ordeal of the Black Intellectual," *Afro-Americans in New York Life and History* 9 (1985): 7–25.

———— "Up from 'Twoness': Frederick Douglass and the Meaning of W.E.B. Du Bois's Concept of Double Consciousness," *Canadian Review of American Studies* 21 (1990): 301–19.

Breiseth, Christopher N., "Lincoln and Frederick Douglass: Another Debate," *Journal of the Illinois Historical Society* 68 (1975): 9–26.

Crummell, Alexander, *Destiny and Race: Selected Writings, 1840–1898,* ed. Wilson Jeremiah Moses (1992).

Dill, Bonnie Thornton, "Race, Class, and Gender: Prospectives for an All-Inclusive Sisterhood," *Feminist Studies* 9 (1983): 131–50.

Easton, Hosea, *A Treatise on the Intellectual Character, and Civil and Political Condition of the Colored People of the United States: And the Prejudice Exercised towards Them: With a Sermon on the Duty of the Church to Them* (1837).

Foner, Philip S., and George E. Walker, ed., *Proceedings of the Black State Conventions, 1840–1865* (2 vols., 1979).

Gates, Henry Louis, Jr., "Frederick Douglass and the Language of the Self," *Yale Review* 70 (1981): 592–611.

Hansen, Karen V., "'No *Kisses* Is Like Yours': An Erotic Friendship between Two African-American Women during the Mid-Nineteenth Century," *Gender and History* 7 (1995): 153–82.

Howard-Pitney, David, "The Enduring Black Jeremiad: The American Jeremiad in Black Protest Rhetoric, from Frederick Douglass to W.E.B. Du Bois," *American Quarterly* 38 (1986): 481–92.

Langston, John Mercer, *Freedom and Citizenship* (1883).

Lapsansky, Emma Jones, "Feminism, Freedom, and Community: Charlotte Forten and Women Activists in Nineteenth-Century Philadelphia," *Pennsylvania Magazine of History and Biography* 113 (1989): 3–19.

Levesque, George A., "Interpreting Early Black Ideology: A Reappraisal of Historical Consensus," *Journal of the Early Republic* 1 (1981): 269–87.

Oldfield, John, ed., *Civilization and Black Progress: Selected Writings of Alexander Crummell on the South* (1995).

Pease, William H., and Jane H. Pease, "Negro Conventions and the Problem of Black Leadership," *Journal of Black Studies* 2 (1971): 29–44.

Pennington, James W. C., *A Text Book of the Origin and History of the Colored People* (1841).

Perkins, Linda, "Black Women and Racial 'Uplift' prior to Emancipation," in Filomena Chiomana Steady, ed., *The Black Woman Cross-Culturally* (1981): 317–34.

Peterson, Carla L., *Doers of the Word: African-American Women Speakers and Writers in the North, 1830–1880* (1995).

Primus, Rebecca, *Beloved Sisters and Loving Friends: Letters from Rebecca Primus of Royal Oak, Maryland and Addie Brown of Hartford,* ed. Farah Jasmine Griffin (1999).

Sweet, Leonard I., *Black Images of America, 1784–1870* (1976).

———— "The Fourth of July and Black Americans in the Nineteenth Century: Northern Leadership Opinion within the Context of the Black Experience," *Journal of Negro History* 61 (1976): 256–75.

Woodson, Carter Godwin, ed., *The Mind of the Negro As Reflected in Letters Written during the Crisis, 1800–1860* (1926).

————, ed., *Negro Orators and Their Orations* (1925).

18.10.2   Emigration and Nationalism

Abingbade, Harrison Ola, "The Settler-African Conflicts: The Case of the Maryland Colonists and the Grebo, 1840–1900," *Journal of Negro History* 66 (1981): 93–109.

Adeleke, Tunde, *Unafrican Americans: Nineteenth-Century Black Nationalists and the Civilizing Mission* (1998).

Akpan, M. B., "Black Imperialism: Americo-Liberian Rule over the Peoples of Liberia, 1841–1964," *Canadian Journal of African Studies* 7 (1973): 217–36.

Appiah, K. Anthony, "Alexander Crummell and the Invention of Africa," *Massachusetts Review* 31 (1990): 385–406.

Aptheker, Herbert, "Consciousness of Negro Nationality: An Historical Survey," *Political Affairs* 28 (1949): 88–95.

Baily, Marilyn, "From Cincinnati, Ohio to Wilberforce, Canada: A Note on Antebellum Colonization," *Journal of Negro History* 58 (1973): 427–40.

Bell, Howard H., comp., *Black Separatism and the Caribbean, 1860* (1970).

—— "The Negro Emigration Movement, 1849–1854: A Phase of Negro Nationalism," *Phylon* 30 (1969): 132–42.

—— "Negro Nationalism: A Factor in Emigration Projects, 1858–1861," *Journal of Negro History* 47 (1962): 42–53.

—— *Search for a Place: Black Separatism and Africa, 1860* (1969).

Blackett, Richard J. M., "Anglo-American Opposition to Liberian Colonization, 1831–1833," *Historian* 41 (1979): 276–94.

—— "In Search of International Support for African Colonization: Martin R. Delany's Visit to England, 1860," *Canadian Journal of History* 10 (1975): 307–24.

—— "Martin R. Delany and Robert Campbell: Black Americans in Search of an African Colony," *Journal of Negro History* 62 (1977): 1–25.

—— "The Quest for Freedom: Colonization, Abolition, and European Immigration, 1817–1860," in Randall Miller, ed., *States of Progress: Germans and Blacks in America over 300 Years* (1989): 38–54.

Boyd, Willis D., "The American Colonization Society and the Slave Recaptives of 1860–1861: An Early Example of United States-African Relations," *Journal of Negro History* 47 (1962): 108–26.

Campbell, Penelope, *Maryland in Africa: The Maryland State Colonization Society, 1831–1857* (1971).

Carlisle, Rodney, *The Roots of Black Nationalism* (1975).

Delany, Martin R., *The Condition, Elevation, Emigration, and Destiny of the Colored People of the United States, Politically Considered* (1852).

Dick, Robert Christopher, *Black Protest: Issues and Tactics* (1974).

Edgerton, Douglas R., "'Its Origin is Not a Little Curious': A New Look at the American Colonization Society," *Journal of the Early Republic* 5 (1985): 463–80.

Farrell, John K. A., "Schemes for the Transplanting of Refugee American Negroes from Upper Canada in the 1840's," *Ontario History* 52 (1960): 245–49.

Forbes, Ella, "African-American Resistance to Colonization," *Journal of Black Studies* 21 (1990): 210–23.

Foster, Charles I., "The Colonization of Free Negroes in Liberia, 1816–1835," *Journal of Negro History* 38 (1953): 41–66.

Fox, Early Lee, *The American Colonization Society, 1817–1840* (1919).

Garrison, William Lloyd, *Thoughts on African Colonization: Or, an Impartial Exhibition of the Doctrines, Principles and Purposes of the American Colonization Society* (1832).

Glaude, Eddie S., Jr., *Exodus! Religion, Race, and Nation in Early Nineteenth-Century Black America* (2000).

Griffith, Cyril E., *The African Dream: Martin R. Delany and the Emergence of Pan-African Thought* (1975).

Heriksen, Thomas H., "African Intellectual Influences on Black Americans: The Role of Edward W. Blyden," *Phylon* 36 (1975): 279–90.

Hunt, Gaillard, "William Thornton and Negro Colonization," *Proceedings of the American Antiquarian Society* 30 (1920): 32–61.

Kass, Amalie M., "Dr. Thomas Hodgkin, Dr. Martin Delany, and the 'Return to Africa,'" *Medical History* 27 (1983): 373–93.

Kinshasa, Kwando Mbiassi, *Emigration vs. Assimilation: The Debate in the African American Press, 1827–1861* (1988).

Kirk-Greene, A. H. M., "America in the Niger Valley: A Colonization Centenary," *Phylon* 23 (1962): 225–39.

Landon, Fred, "Henry Bibb: A Colonizer," *Journal of Negro History* 5 (1920): 437–77.

—— "The Negro Migration to Canada after the Fugitive Slave Act of 1850," *Journal of Negro History* 5 (1920): 22–36.

Lockett, James D., "Abraham Lincoln and Colonization: An Episode That Ends in Tragedy at L'Ile a Vache, Haiti, 1863–1864," *Journal of Black Studies* 21 (1991): 428–44.

MacMaster, Richard K., "Henry Highland Garnet and the African Civilization Society," *Journal of Presbyterian History* 48 (1970): 95–112.

Matijasic, Thomas D., "African Colonization Activity at Miami University during the Administration of Robert Hamilton Bishop," *Old Northwest* 12 (1986): 83–94.

McKivigan, John R., "James Redpath and Black Reaction to the Haitian Emigration Bureau," *Mid-America* 69 (1987): 139–53.

McPherson, James M., "Abolitionist and Negro Opposition to Colonization during the Civil War," *Phylon* 26 (1965): 391–99.

Mehlinger, Louis, "The Attitude of the Free Negro toward African Colonization," *Journal of Negro History* 1 (1916): 276–301.

Miller, Floyd J., *The Search for a Black Nationality: Black Emigration and Colonization, 1787–1863* (1975).

——— "'The Father of Black Nationalism': Another Contender," *Civil War History* 17 (1971): 310–19.

Moses, Wilson Jeremiah, ed., *Liberian Dreams: Back-to-Africa Narratives from the 1850s* (1998).

Neely, Mark E., Jr., "Abraham Lincoln and Black Colonization, Benjamin Butler's Spurious Testimony," *Civil War History* 25 (1979): 77–83.

Padgett, James A., "Ministers to Liberia and Their Diplomacy," *Journal of Negro History* 22 (1937): 50–92.

Payne, Walter A., "Lincoln's Caribbean Colonization Plan," *Pacific Historian* 7 (1963): 65–72.

Pease, William H., and Jane H. Pease, "Black Power: The Debate in 1840," *Phylon* 29 (1968): 19–26.

——— "Opposition to the Founding of the Elgin Settlement," *Canadian Historical Review* 38 (1957): 202–18.

Pinn, Anthony B., "'Double Consciousness' in Nineteenth-Century Black Nationalism: Reflections on the Teachings of Bishop Henry McNeal Turner," *Journal of Religious Thought* 52 (1995): 15–26.

Seraile, William, "Afro-American Emigration to Haiti during the American Civil War," *Americas* 35 (1978): 185–200.

Sheips, Paul J., "Lincoln and the Chiriqui Colonization Project," *Journal of Negro History* 37 (1952): 418–53.

Shick, Tom W., *Behold the Promised Land: A History of Afro-American Settler Society in Nineteenth-Century Liberia* (1980).

——— "A Quantitative Analysis of Liberian Colonization from 1820 to 1843 with Special Reference to Mortality," *Journal of African History* 12 (1971): 45–59.

Staudenraus, P. J., *The African Colonization Movement, 1816–1865* (1961).

Streifford, David M., "The American Colonization Society: An Application of Republican Ideology to Early Antebellum Reform," *Journal of Southern History* 45 (1979): 201–20.

Stuckey, Sterling, comp., *The Ideological Origins of Black Nationalism* (1972).

Uya, Okon Edet, ed., *Black Brotherhood: Afro-Americans and Africa* (1971).

Williams, Robert J., "Blacks, Colonization and Anti-Slavery: The Views of Methodists in New Jersey, 1816–1860," *New Jersey History* 102 (1984): 50–67.

Yee, Shirley J., "Finding a Place: Mary Ann Shadd Cary and the Dilemmas of Black Migration to Canada, 1850–1870," *Frontiers* 18 (1997): 1–16.

18.10.3 Literature and Poetry

Simson, Rennie, "A Community in Turmoil: Black American Writers in New York State before the Civil War," *Afro-Americans in New York Life and History* 13 (1989): 57–67.

Zanger, Jules, "The 'Tragic Octoroon' in Pre-Civil War Fiction," *American Quarterly* 18 (1966): 63–70.

18.10.4 Music and Performing Arts

Riach, Douglas C., "Blacks and Blackfaces on the Irish Stage, 1830–1860," *Journal of American Studies* 7 (1973): 231–41.

Thompson, George A., *A Documentary History of the African Theatre* (1998).

18.10.5 Art (Drawing, Painting, Photography, Printmaking, Sculpture)

Wilson, Jackie Napolean, "African Americans in Early Photography," *Historian* 57 (1995): 713–20.

18.11   EDUCATION

Andrews, Charles S., *The History of the New-York African Free-Schools, from Their Establishment in 1787, to the Present Time* (1830).

Brown, Willis L., and Janie M. McNeal-Brown, "Langston University," *Chronicles of Oklahoma* 74 (1996): 30–49.

Butchart, Ronald E., *Northern Schools, Southern Blacks, and Reconstruction: Freedmen's Education, 1862–1875* (1980).

———— "'We Best Can Instruct Our Own People': New York African Americans in the Freedmen's Schools, 1861–1875," *Afro-Americans in New York Life and History* 12 (1988): 27–49.

Byrd, Alicia D., "Adult Educational Efforts of the Black American Church, 1600–1900," *Journal of Religious Thought* 44 (1988): 83–92.

Carroll, J. C., "The Beginnings of Public Education for Negroes in Indiana," *Journal of Negro Education* 8 (1939): 649–58.

Cooper, Afua, "The Search for Mary Bibb, Black Woman Teacher in Nineteenth-Century Canada West," *Ontario History* 83 (1991): 39–54.

Cooper, Arnie, "A Stony Road: Black Education in Iowa, 1838–1860," *Annals of Iowa* 48 (1986): 113–34.

Foner, Philip S., and Josephine F. Pacheco, *Three Who Dared: Prudence Crandall, Margaret Douglass, Myrtilla Miner—Champions of Antebellum Black Education* (1984).

Fuller, Edmund, *Prudence Crandall: An Incident of Racism in Nineteenth-Century Connecticut* (1971).

Green, William D., "Race and Segregation in St. Paul's Public Schools, 1846–1869," *Minnesota History* 55 (1996–97): 138–49.

Horton, James Oliver, "Black Education at Oberlin College: A Controversial Commitment," *Journal of Negro Education* 54 (1985): 477–99.

Jacobs, Donald M., "The Nineteenth-Century Struggle over Segregated Education in the Boston Schools," *Journal of Negro Education* 39 (1970): 76–85.

Lawson, Ellen N., and Marlene Merrill, "The Antebellum 'Talented Thousandth': Black College Students at Oberlin before the Civil War," *Journal of Negro Education* 52 (1983): 142–55.

Mabee, Carleton, "Early Black Public School," *Long Island Forum* 36 (1973): 214–16.

———— "A Negro Boycott to Integrate Boston Schools," *New England Quarterly* 41 (1968): 341–61.

———— "Sojourner Truth, Bold Prophet: Why Did She Never Learn to Read?" *New York History* 69 (1988): 55–77.

McGinnis, Frederick Alphonso, *The Education of Negroes in Ohio* (1962).

Perkins, Linda Marie, "Quaker Beneficence and Black Control: The Institute for Colored Youth, 1852–1903," in Vincent P. Franklin and James D. Anderson, ed., *New Perspectives on Black Educational History* (1978): 19–43.

Porter, Dorothy B., "The Organized Educational Activities of Negro Literary Societies, 1828–1846," *Journal of Negro Education* 5 (1936): 555–76.

Price, Edward J., Jr., "School Segregation in Nineteenth-Century Pennsylvania," *Pennsylvania History* 43 (1976): 121–37.

Rury, John L., "The New York African Free School, 1827–1836: Conflict over Community Control of Black Education," *Phylon* 44 (1983): 187–97.

Savage, W. Sherman, "Early Negro Education in the Pacific Coast States," *Journal of Negro Education* 15 (1946): 134–39.

Silcox, Harry C., "Delay and Neglect: Negro Public Education in Antebellum Philadelphia, 1800–1860," *Pennsylvania Magazine of History and Biography* 97 (1973): 444–64.

St. Clair, Sadie Daniel, "Myrtilla Miner: Pioneer in Teacher Education for Negro Women," *Journal of Negro History* 34 (1949): 30–45.

White, Arthur Owen, *Blacks and Education in Antebellum Massachusetts: Strategies for Social Mobility* (1971).

———— "Salem's Antebellum Black Community: Seedbed of the School Integration Movement," *Essex Institute Historical Collections* 108 (1972): 99–118.

White, David O., "Hartford's African Free Schools, 1830–1868," *Connecticut Historical Society Bulletin* 39 (1974): 47–53.

Woodson, Carter Godwin, *The Education of the Negro Prior to 1861: A History of the Education of the Colored People of the United States from the Beginning of Slavery to the Civil War* (1915).

18.12   WORK AND ENTREPRENEURIAL ACTIVITY

Bolster, W. Jeffrey, *Black Jacks: African-American Seamen in the Age of Sail* (1997).

Coclanis, Peter A., and J. C. Marlow, "Inland Rice Production in the South Atlantic States: A Picture in Black and White," *Agricultural History* 72 (1998): 197–212.

Guyette, Elise A., "The Working Lives of African Vermonters in Census and Literature, 1790–1870," *Vermont History* 61 (1993): 69–84.

Landon, Fred, "Agriculture among the Negro Refugees in Upper Canada," *Journal of Negro History* 21 (1936): 304–12.

Lofton, Williston, "Northern Labor and the Negro during the Civil War," *Journal of Negro History* 34 (1949): 251–73.

Mabee, Carleton, "Sojourner Truth Fights Dependence on Government: Moves Freed Slaves off Welfare in Washington to Jobs in Upstate New York," *Afro-Americans in New York Life and History* 14 (1990): 7–26.

Man, Albon P., Jr., "Labor Competition and the New York Draft Riots of 1863," *Journal of Negro History* 36 (1951): 375–405.

Minton, Henry M., *Early History of Negroes in Business in Philadelphia* (1913).

Savage, W. Sherman, "The Negro on the Mining Frontier," *Journal of Negro History* 30 (1945): 30–46.

Walker, Juliet E. K., "Prejudices, Profits, Privileges: Commentaries on 'Captive Capitalists,' Antebellum Black Entrepreneurs," *Essays in Economic and Business History* 8 (1990): 399–422.

Wesley, Charles H., *Negro Labor in the United States, 1850–1925: A Study in American Economic History* (1927).

19   1865–1877

Eric Foner

19.1   GENERAL STUDIES

Allen, James S., *Reconstruction: The Battle for Democracy* (1937).
Anderson, Eric, and Alfred A. Moss, Jr., ed., *The Facts of Reconstruction: Essays in Honor of John Hope Franklin* (1991).
Andrews, Sidney, *The South Since the War* (1866).
Bennett, Lerone, *Black Power, U.S.A.: The Human Side of Reconstruction, 1867–1877* (1967).
Berwanger, Eugene H., *The West and Reconstruction* (1981).
Burton, Orville V., and Robert C. McMath, Jr., ed., *Toward a New South? Studies in Post-Civil War Southern Communities* (1982).
Carter, Dan T., *When the War Was Over: The Failure of Self-Reconstruction in the South, 1865–1867* (1985).
Cohen, William, *At Freedom's Edge: Black Mobility and the Southern White Quest for Racial Control, 1861–1915* (1991).
Cox, LaWanda, and John H. Cox, ed., *Reconstruction, the Negro, and the New South* (1973).
Craven, Avery Odelle, *Reconstruction: The Ending of the Civil War* (1969).
Cruden, Robert, *The Negro in Reconstruction* (1969).
Dennett, John Richard, *The South As It Is, 1865–1866*, ed. Henry M. Christman (1965).
Du Bois, W. E. B., *Black Reconstruction in America: An Essay toward a History of the Part Which Black Folk Played in an Attempt to Reconstruct Democracy in America, 1860–1880* (1935).
———— "Reconstruction and Its Benefits," *American History Review* 15 (1910): 781–99.
Dunning, William Archibald, *Reconstruction, Political and Economic, 1865–1877* (1907).
Fishel, Leslie H., Jr., "Repercussions of Reconstruction: The Northern Negro, 1870–1883," *Civil War History* 14 (1968): 325–45.
Foner, Eric, *Nothing but Freedom: Emancipation and Its Legacy* (1983).
———— *Reconstruction: America's Unfinished Revolution, 1863–1877* (1988).
———— "Reconstruction Revisited," *Reviews in American History* 10 (1982): 82–100.
Foner, Philip S., and George E. Walker, ed., *Proceedings of the Black National and State Conventions, 1865–1900* (1986).
Franklin, John Hope, "Public Welfare in the South during the Reconstruction Era, 1865–1880," *Social Sciences Review* 44 (1970): 379–92.
———— *Reconstruction: After the Civil War* (1961).
Gillette, William, *Retreat from Reconstruction, 1869–1879* (1979).
Hesseltine, William B., "Economic Factors in the Abandonment of Reconstruction," *Mississippi Valley Historical Review* 22 (1935): 191–210.
Hyman, Harold M., ed., *New Frontiers of the American Reconstruction* (1966).
King, Edward, *The Southern States of North America: A Record of Journeys in Louisiana, Texas, the Indian Territory, Missouri, Arkansas, Mississippi, Alabama, Georgia, Florida, South Carolina, North Carolina, Kentucky, Tennessee, Virginia, West Virginia, and Maryland* (1875).

Kousser, J. Morgan, and James M. McPherson, ed., *Region, Race, and Reconstruction: Essays in Honor of C. Vann Woodward* (1982).

Litwack, Leon F., *Been in the Storm So Long: The Aftermath of Slavery* (1979).

Lynch, John R., *The Facts of Reconstruction* (1913).

Magdol, Edward, *A Right to the Land: Essays on the Freedmen's Community* (1977).

McGlynn, Frank, and Seymour Drescher, ed., *The Meaning of Freedon: Economics, Politics, and Culture after Slavery* (1992).

McWhiney, Grady, "Reconstruction: Index of Americanism," in Charles Grier Sellers, Jr., ed., *The Southerner As American* (1960): 89–103.

Meier, August, "Negroes in the First and Second Reconstructions," *Civil War History* 13 (1967): 114–30.

Nieman, Donald G., ed., *African American Life in the Post-Emancipation South* (12 vols., 1994).

Nordhoff, Charles, *The Cotton States in the Spring and Summer of 1875* (1876).

Olsen, Otto H., ed., *Reconstruction and Redemption in the South* (1980).

Reid, Whitelaw, *After the War: A Southern Tour* (1866).

Roark, James L., *Masters without Slaves: Southern Planters in the Civil War and Reconstruction* (1977).

Sansing, David G., ed., *What Was Freedom's Price?* (1978).

Smith, Page, *Trial By Fire: A People's History of the Civil War and Reconstruction* (1982).

Somers, Robert, *The Southern States Since the War, 1870–1871* (1871).

Sproat, John G., "Blueprint for Radical Reconstruction," *Journal of Southern History* 23 (1957): 25–44.

Stampp, Kenneth M., *The Era of Reconstruction, 1865–1877* (1965).

Stampp, Kenneth M., and Leon F. Litwack, ed., *Reconstruction: An Anthology of Revisionist Writings* (1969).

Sterling, Dorothy, ed., *The Trouble They Seen: The Story of Reconstruction in the Words of African Americans* (1976).

Thornbrough, Emma Lou, comp., *Black Reconstructionists* (1972).

Trowbridge, John Townsend, *The South: A Tour of Its Battlefields and Ruined Cities* (1866).

U.S. 39th Congress, 1st Session, *Report of the Joint Committee on Reconstruction* (1866).

U.S. 42nd Congress, 2d Session, House Report 22, *Report of the Joint Select Committee to Inquire into the Condition of Affairs in the Late Insurrectionary States* (13 Vol., 1872).

Voegeli, V. Jacque, *Free but Not Equal: The Midwest and the Negro during the Civil War* (1967).

Woodman, Harold D., *King Cotton and His Retainers: Financing and Marketing the Cotton Crop of the South, 1800–1925* (1968).

Woolfolk, George Ruble, *The Cotton Regency: The Northern Merchants and Reconstruction, 1865–1880* (1958).

19.1.1 Alabama

Amos, Harriet E., "Trials of a Unionist: Gustavus Horton, Military Mayor of Mobile during Reconstruction," *Gulf Coast Historical Review* 4 (1989): 134–51.

Bailey, Richard, *Neither Carpetbaggers nor Scalawags: Black Officeholders during the Reconstruction of Alabama, 1867–1868* (1991).

Bethel, Elizabeth Rauh, "The Freedmen's Bureau in Alabama," *Journal of Southern History* 14 (1948): 49–92.

Bond, Horace Mann, *Negro Education in Alabama: A Study in Cotton and Steel* (1939).

——— "Social and Economic Forces in Alabama Reconstruction," *Journal of Negro History* 23 (1938): 290–348.

Dillard, Tom W., "Three Important Black Leaders in Phillips County History," *Phillips County Historical Quarterly* 19 (1980, 1981): 10–23.

Fitzgerald, Michael W., "Radical Republicanism and the White Yeomanry during Alabama Reconstruction, 1865–1868," *Journal of Southern History* 54 (1988): 565–96.

——— "Railroad Subsidies and Black Aspirations: The Politics of Economic Development in Reconstruction Mobile, 1865–1879," *Civil War History* 39 (1993): 240–56.

——— "'To Give Our Votes to the Party': Black Political Agitation and Agricultural Change in Alabama, 1865–1870," *Journal of American History* 76 (1989): 489–505.

Fleming, Walter Lynwood, *Civil War and Reconstruction in Alabama* (1905).

Kolchin, Peter, *First Freedom: The Responses of Alabama's Blacks to Emancipation and Reconstruction* (1972).

McNair, Cecil E., "Reconstruction in Bullock County," *Alabama Historical Quarterly* 15 (1953): 75–125.

Montgomery, Margaret L., "Alabama Freedmen: Some Reconstruction Documents," *Phylon* 13 (1952): 245–51.

Schweninger, Loren, "Black Citizenship and the Republican Party in Reconstruction Alabama," *Alabama Review* 29 (1976): 83–103.

Sterkx, H. E., "William C. Jordan and Reconstruction in Bullock County, Alabama," *Alabama Review* 15 (1962): 61–73.

White, Kenneth B., "Wager Swayne: Racist or Realist?" *Alabama Review* 31 (1978): 92–109.

Wiener, Jonathan M., *Social Origins of the New South: Alabama, 1860–1885* (1978).

Wiggins, Sarah Woolfolk, *The Scalawag in Alabama Politics, 1865–1881* (1977).

Williams, Edward C., "The Alabama Election of 1874," *Alabama Review* 17 (1964): 210–18.

19.1.2   Arkansas

Atkinson, James H., "The Arkansas Gubernatorial Campaign and Election of 1872," *Arkansas Historical Quarterly* 1 (1942): 307–21.

Boyett, Gene W., "The Black Experience in the First Decade of Reconstruction in Pope County, Arkansas," *Arkansas Historical Quarterly* 51 (1992): 119–34.

Clayton, Powell, *The Aftermath of the Civil War in Arkansas* (1915).

Driggs, Orval T., Jr., "The Issues of the Powell Clayton Regime, 1868–1871," *Arkansas Historical Quarterly* 8 (1949): 1–75.

Hume, Richard L., "The Arkansas Constitutional Convention of 1868: A Case Study in the Politics of Reconstruction," *Journal of Southern History* 39 (1973): 183–206.

Lovett, Bobby L., "African Americans, Civil War, and Aftermath in Arkansas," *Arkansas Historical Quarterly* 54 (1995): 304–58.

McCaslin, Richard B., "Reconstructing a Frontier Oligarchy: Andrew Johnson's Amnesty Proclamation and Arkansas," *Arkansas Historical Quarterly* 49 (1990): 313–29.

Moneyhon, Carl H., *The Impact of the Civil War and Reconstruction on Arkansas: Persistence in the Midst of Ruin* (1994).

Nash, Horace D., "Black Arkansas during Reconstruction: The Ex-Slave Narratives," *Arkansas Historical Quarterly* 48 (1989): 243–59.

Pearce, Larry Wesley, "The American Missionary Association and the Freedman's Bureau in Arkansas, 1866–1968," *Arkansas Historical Quarterly* 30 (1971): 242–59.

Richter, William Lee, "'A Dear Little Job': Second Lieutenant Hiram F. Willis, Freedmen's Bureau Agent in Southwestern Arkansas, 1866–1868," *Arkansas Historical Quarterly* 50 (1991): 158–200.

St. Hilaire, Joseph M., "The Negro Delegates in the Arkansas Constitutional Convention of 1868: A Group Profile," *Arkansas Historical Quarterly* 33 (1974): 38–69.

Staples, Thomas S., *Reconstruction in Arkansas, 1862–1874* (1923).

Thompson, George H., *Arkansas and Reconstruction: The Influence of Geography, Economics, and Personality* (1976).

19.1.3   California

Chandler, Robert J., "Friends in Time of Need: Republicans and the Black Civil Rights in California during the Civil War Era," *Arizona and the West* 24 (1982): 319–40.

19.1.4   Delaware

Hancock, Harold B., "The Status of the Negro in Delaware after the Civil War, 1865–1875," *Delaware History* 13 (1968): 57–66.

19.1.5 Florida

Beatty, Bess, "John Willis Menard: A Progressive Black in Post-Civil War Florida," *Florida Historical Quarterly* 59 (1980): 123–43.

Brown, Canter, Jr., "Carpetbagger Intrigues, Black Leadership, and a Southern Loyalist Triumph: Florida's Gubernatorial Election of 1872," *Florida Historical Quarterly* 72 (1994): 275–301.

Clark, James C., "John Wallace and the Writing of Reconstruction History," *Florida Historical Quarterly* 67 (1989): 409–27.

Davis, William Watson, *The Civil War and Reconstruction in Florida* (1913).

Hume, Richard L., "Membership of the Florida Constitutional Convention of 1868: A Case Study of Republican Factionalism in the Reconstruction South," *Florida Historical Quarterly* 51 (1972): 1–21.

Klingman, Peter D., "Rascal or Representative? Joe Oates of Tallahassee and the 'Election' of 1866," *Florida Historical Quarterly* 51 (1972): 52–57.

——— *Josiah Walls: Florida's Black Congressman of Reconstruction* (1976).

Richardson, Joe M., *The Negro in the Reconstruction of Florida, 1865–1877* (1965).

Shofner, Jerrell H., *Nor Is It over Yet: Florida in the Era of Reconstruction, 1863–1877* (1974).

——— "Wartime Unionists, Unreconstructed Rebels, and Andrew Johnson's Amnesty Program in the Reconstruction Debacle of Jackson County, Florida," *Gulf Coast Historical Review* 4 (1989): 162–71.

19.1.6 Georgia

Abbott, Richard H., "Jason Clarke Swayze: Republican Editor in Reconstruction Georgia, 1867–1873," *Georgia Historical Quarterly* 79 (1995): 337–66.

Bacote, Clarence A., "William Finch, Negro Councilman, and Political Activities in Atlanta during Early Reconstruction," *Journal of Negro History* 40 (1955): 341–64.

Conway, Alan, *The Reconstruction of Georgia* (1966).

Coulter, E. Merton, *Negro Legislators in Georgia during the Reconstruction Period* (1968).

Currie-McDaniel, Ruth, *Carpetbagger of Conscience: A Biography of John Emory Bryant* (1987).

Drago, Edmund L., *Black Politicians and Reconstruction in Georgia: A Splendid Failure* (1982).

——— "Georgia's First Black Voter Registrars during Reconstruction," *Georgia Historical Quarterly* 78 (1994): 760–93.

Duncan, Russell, *Entrepreneur for Equality: Governor Rufus Bullock, Commerce, and Race in Post-Civil War Georgia* (1994).

Leigh, Frances Butler, *Ten Years on a Georgia Plantation Since the War* (1883).

Matthews, John M., "Negro Republicans in the Reconstruction of Georgia," *Georgia Historical Quarterly* 60 (1976): 145–64.

McLeod, Jonathan W., *Workers and Workplace Dynamics in Reconstruction-Era Atlanta* (1989).

Mohr, Clarence L., *On the Threshold of Freedom: Masters and Slaves in Civil War Georgia* (1986).

Nathans, Elizabeth Studley, *Losing the Peace: Georgia Republicans and Reconstruction, 1865–1871* (1968).

Rapport, Sara, "The Freedmen's Bureau As a Legal Agent for Black Men and Women in Georgia, 1865–1868," *Georgia Historical Quarterly* 73 (1989): 26–53.

Taylor, Elizabeth A., "The Origins and Development of the Convict Lease System in Georgia," *Georgia Historical Quarterly* 26 (1942): 113–28.

Thompson, C. Mildred, *Reconstruction in Georgia* (1915).

19.1.7 Illinois

Bridges, Roger D., "Equality Deferred: Civil Rights for Illinois Blacks, 1865–1885," *Journal of the Illinois State Historical Society* 74 (1981): 82–108.

19.1.8 Iowa

Berrier, G. Gail, "The Negro Suffrage Issue in Iowa, 1865–1868," *Annals of Iowa* 39 (1968): 241–61.

Dykstra, Robert K., "The Issue Squarely Met: Toward an Explanation of Iowans' Racial Attitudes, 1865–1868," *Annals of Iowa* 47 (1984): 430–50.

Wubben, Hubert H., "The Uncertain Trumpet: Iowa Republicans and Black Suffrage, 1860–1868," *Annals of Iowa* 47 (1984): 409–29.

19.1.9 Kentucky

Coulter, E. Merton, *The Civil War and Readjustment in Kentucky* (1926).

Howard, Victor B., *Black Liberation in Kentucky: Emancipation and Freedom, 1862–1884* (1983).

Norris, Marjorie M., "An Early Instance of Nonviolence: The Louisville Demonstrations of 1870–1871," *Journal of Southern History* 32 (1965): 488–504.

19.1.10 Louisiana

Binning, F. Wayne, "Carpetbaggers' Triumph: The Louisiana State Election of 1868," *Louisiana History* 14 (1973): 21–39.

Blassingame, John W., *Black New Orleans, 1860–1880* (1973).

Everett, Donald E., "Demands of the New Orleans Free Colored Population for Political Equality, 1862–1865," *Louisiana History Quarterly* 38 (1955): 43–64.

Fischer, Roger A., *The Segregation Struggle in Louisiana, 1862–1877* (1974).

Highsmith, William E., "Louisiana Landholding during War and Reconstruction," *Louisiana Historical Quarterly* 37 (1955): 39–54.

——— "Some Aspects of Reconstruction in the Heart of Louisiana," *Journal of Southern History* 13 (1947): 460–91.

Jones, Howard J., "Biographical Sketches of Members of the 1868 Louisiana State Senate," *Louisiana History* 19 (1978): 65–110.

Logsdon, Joseph, "Americans and Creoles in New Orleans: The Origins of Black Citizenship in the United States," *Amerikastudien/American Studies* 34 (1990): 187–202.

Lonn, Ellen, *Reconstruction in Louisiana after 1868* (1918).

May, J. Thomas, "The Freedmen's Bureau at the Local Level: A Study of a Louisiana Agent," *Louisiana History* 9 (1968): 5–19.

McCrary, Peyton, *Abraham Lincoln and Reconstruction: The Louisiana Experiment* (1978).

Moran, Robert E., "Local Black Elected Officials in Ascension Parish, 1868–1878," *Louisiana History* 27 (1986): 273–80.

Perkins, A. E., "James Henri Burch and Oscar James Dunn in Louisiana," *Journal of Negro History* 22 (1937): 321–34.

——— "Some Negro Officers and Legislators in Louisiana," *Journal of Negro History* 14 (1929): 523–28.

Pitre, Althea D., "The Collapse of the Warmoth Regime, 1870–1872," *Louisiana History* 6 (1965): 161–87.

Rankin, David C., "The Origins of Black Leadership on New Orleans during Reconstruction," *Journal of Southern History* (1979): 417–40.

——— "The Origins of Negro Leadership in New Orleans during Reconstruction," in Howard Rabinowitz, ed., *Southern Black Leaders of the Reconstruction Era* : 155–89.

Ripley, C. Peter, *Slaves and Freedmen in Civil War Louisiana* (1976).

Sanson, Jerry P., "White Man's Failure: The Rapides Parish 1874 Election," *Louisiana History* 31 (1990): 39–58.

Shugg, Roger W., *Origins of Class Struggle in Louisiana: A Social History of White Farmers and Laborers during Slavery and After, 1840–1875* (1939).

Taylor, Joe Gray, *Louisiana Reconstructed, 1863–1877* (1974).

Tunnell, Ted, *Crucible of Reconstruction: War, Radicalism, and Race in Louisiana, 1862–1877* (1984).

——— "Free Negroes and the Freedmen: Black Politics in New Orleans during the Civil War," *Southern Studies* 19 (1980): 5–28.

Vincent, Charles, *Black Legislators in Louisiana during Reconstruction* (1976).

——— "Louisiana's Black Legislators and Their Effort to Pass a Blue Law during Reconstruction," *Journal of Black Studies* 7 (1976): 47–56.

Warmoth, Henry Clay, *War, Politics, and Reconstruction: Stormy Days in Louisiana* (1930).

White, Howard Ashley, *The Freedmen's Bureau in Louisiana* (1970).

Williams, T. Harry, "The Louisiana Unification Movement of 1873," *Journal of Southern History* 11 (1945): 349–69.

19.1.11   Maryland

Fields, Barbara Jeanne, *Slavery and Freedom on the Middle Ground: Maryland during the Nineteenth Century* (1985).

Fuke, Richard P., "A Reform Mentality: Federal Policy toward Black Marylanders, 1864–1868," *Civil War History* 22 (1976): 214–35.

Fuke, Richard Paul, *Imperfect Equality: African Americans and the Confines of White Racial Attitudes in Post-Emancipation Maryland* (1999).

Wagandt, Charles L., *The Mighty Revolution: Negro Emancipation in Maryland, 1862–1864* (1964).

19.1.12   Mississippi

Abney, M. G., "Reconstruction in Pontotoc County," *Publications of the Mississippi Historical Society* 11 (1910): 229–70.

Ames, Blanche B., *Adlebert Ames, 1835–1933* (1964).

——— comp., *Chronicles from the Nineteenth Century: Family Letters of Blanche Butler and Adelbert Ames* (2 vols., 1957).

Aptheker, Herbert, "Mississippi Reconstruction of the Negro Leader, Charles Caldwell," *Science and Society* 11 (1947): 340–71.

Blain, William T., "Banner Unionism in Mississippi, Choctaw County, 1861–1869," *Mississippi Quarterly* 29 (1976): 207–20.

Bowman, Robert, "Reconstruction in Yazoo County," *Publications of the Mississippi Historical Society* 7 (1903): 115–30.

Brown, Julia, "Reconstruction in Yalobusha and Grenada Counties," *Publications of the Mississippi Historical Society* 12 (1912): 214–82.

Browne, F. Z., "Reconstruction in Oktibbeha County," *Publications of the Mississippi Historical Society* 13 (1913): 273–98.

Coleman, E. C., Jr., "Reconstruction in Attala County," *Publications of the Mississippi Historical Society* 10 (1910): 147–62.

Donald, David H., "The Scalawag in Mississippi Reconstruction," *Journal of Southern History* 10 (1944): 447–60.

Edwards, Thomas S., "'Reconstructing' Reconstruction: Changing Historical Paradigms in Mississippi," *Journal of Mississippi History* 51 (1989): 165–80.

Ellem, Warren A., "The Overthrow of Reconstruction in Mississippi," *Journal of Mississippi History* 54 (1992): 175–201.

——— "Who Were the Mississippi Scalawags?" *Journal of Southern History* 38 (1972): 217–40.

Frankel, Noralee, *Freedom's Women: Black Women and Families in Civil War Era Mississippi* (1999).

Gardner, Bettye J., "William H. Foote and Yazoo County Politics," *Southern Studies* 21 (1982): 398–407.

Garner, James W., *Reconstruction in Mississippi* (1901).

Hardy, W. H., "Recollections of Reconstruction in East and Southeast Mississippi," *Publications of the Mississippi Historical Society* 4 (1901): 105–32.

——— "Recollections of Reconstruction in East and Southeast Mississippi," *Publications of the Mississippi Historical Society* 7 (1903): 199–215.

——— "Recollections of Reconstruction in East and Southeast Mississippi," *Publications of the Mississippi Historical Society* 8 (1904): 137–51.

Harris, William C., "The Creed of the Carpetbaggers: The Case of Mississippi," *Journal of Southern History* 40 (1974): 199–224.

——— *The Day of the Carpetbagger: Republican Reconstruction in Mississippi* (1979).

——— *Presidential Reconstruction in Mississippi* (1967).

Kendel, Julia, "Reconstruction in Lafayette County," *Publications of the Mississippi Historical Society* 12 (1913): 223–72.

Kyle, John W., "Reconstruction in Panola County," *Publications of the Mississippi Historical Society* 13 (1913): 9–98.

Lacey, Nannie, "Reconstruction in Leake County," *Publications of the Mississippi Historical Society* 11 (1910): 271–94.

Leftwich, George J., "Reconstruction in Monroe County," *Publications of the Mississippi Historical Society* 9 (1906): 53–84.

Magee, Hattie, "Reconstruction in Lawrence and Jefferson Davis Counties," *Publications of the Mississippi Historical Society* 11 (1910): 163–204.

Morgan, Albert Talmon, *Yazoo: Or, on the Picket Line of Freedom in the South, a Personal Narrative* (1884).

Nichols, Irby C., "Reconstruction in DeSoto County," *Publications of the Mississippi Historical Society* 11 (1910): 295–316.

Pereyra, Lillian A., *James Lusk Alcorn: Persistent Whig* (1966).

Puckett, R. P., "Reconstruction in Monroe County," *Publications of the Mississippi Historical Society* 11 (1910): 103–61.

Satcher, Buford, *Blacks in Mississippi Politics, 1865–1900* (1976).

Warren, Henry Waterman, *Reminiscences of a Mississippi Carpetbagger* (1914).

Watkins, Ruth, "Reconstruction in Marshall County," *Publications of the Mississippi Historical Society* 12 (1912): 155–213.

——— "Reconstruction in Newton County," *Publications of the Mississippi Historical Society* 11 (1910): 205–28.

Wells, W. Calvin, "Reconstruction and Its Destruction in Hinds County," *Publications of the Mississippi Historical Society* 9 (1906): 85–108.

Wharton, Vernon Lane, *The Negro in Mississippi, 1865–1890* (1947).

19.1.13   Missouri

DeArmond, Fred, "Reconstruction in Missouri," *Missouri Historical Review* 61 (1967): 364–77.

Parrish, William Earl, *Missouri under Radical Rule, 1865–1870* (1965).

19.1.14   New York

Field, Phyllis F., *The Politics of Race in New York: The Struggle for Black Suffrage in the Civil War Era* (1982).

Mohr, James C., *The Radical Republicans and Reform in New York during Reconstruction* (1973).

19.1.15   North Carolina

Balanoff, Elizabeth, "Negro Leaders in the North Carolina General Assembly, July 1868-Feb. 1872," *North Carolina Historical Review* 49 (1972): 22–55.

Bernstein, Leonard, "The Participation of Negro Delegates in the Constitutional Convention of 1868 in North Carolina," *Journal of Negro History* 34 (1949): 391–409.

Billings, Dwight B., Jr., *Planters and the Making of a 'New South': Class, Politics, and Development in North Carolina, 1865–1900* (1979).

Escott, Paul D., *Many Excellent People: Power and Privilege in North Carolina, 1850–1900* (1985).

Evans, William McKee, *Ballots and Fence Rails: Reconstruction on the Lower Cape Fear* (1967).

Hamilton, Joseph Gregoire de Roulhac, *Reconstruction in North Carolina* (1914).

Harris, William C., *William Woods Holden: Firebrand of North Carolina Politics* (1987).

Logan, Frenise A., "Black and Republican: Vicissitudes of a Minority Twice over in the North Carolina House of Representatives, 1876–1877," *North Carolina Review* 61 (1984): 311–46.

Price, Charles L., "John C. Barrett, Freedmen's Bureau Agent in North Carolina," *East Carolina University Papers in History* 5 (1981): 51–74.

Reid, George W., "Four in Black: North Carolina's Black Congressmen, 1874–1901," *Journal of Negro History* 64 (1979): 229–43.

Trelease, Allen W., "Republican Reconstruction in North Carolina: A Roll-Call Analysis of the State House of Representatives, 1868–1870," *Journal of Southern History* 42 (1976): 319–44.

19.1.16 Ohio

Gerber, David A., *Black Ohio and the Color Line, 1860–1915* (1976).

19.1.17 Pennsylvania

Brown, Ira V., "Pennsylvania and the Rights of the Negro, 1865–1887," *Pennsylvania History* 28 (1961): 45–57.

Montgomery, David, "Radical Republicanism in Pennsylvania, 1866–1873," *Pennsylvania Magazine of History and Biography* 85 (1961): 439–57.

19.1.18 South Carolina

Abbott, Martin, "County Officers in South Carolina in 1868," *South Carolina Historical Magazine* 60 (1959): 30–40.

————— *The Freedmen's Bureau in South Carolina, 1865–1872* (1967).

————— "Freedom's Cry: Negroes and Their Meetings in South Carolina, 1865–1869," *Phylon* 20 (1959): 263–72.

Abbott, Richard H., "A Yankee Views the Organization of the Republican Party in South Carolina, July 1867," *South Carolina Historical Magazine* 85 (1984): 244–50.

Aptheker, Herbert, "South Carolina Negro Conventions, 1865," *Journal of Negro History* 31 (1946): 91–97.

Bryant, Lawrence Chesterfield, *Negro Lawmakers in the South Carolina Legislature, 1868–1902* (1968).

————— *Negro Legislators in South Carolina, 1865–1894* (1966).

————— *Negro Senators and Representatives in the South Carolina Legislature, 1868–1902* (1968).

————— *South Carolina Negro Legislators: A Glorious Success* (1974).

Burton, Orville V., "Edgefield Reconstruction Political Black Leaders," *Proceedings of the South Carolina Historical Association* (1988): 27–38.

—————, ed., *In My Father's House Are Many Mansions: Family and Community in Edgefield, South Carolina* (1985).

————— "Race and Reconstuction: Edgefield County, South Carolina," *Journal of Social History* 12 (1978): 31–56.

Hine, William C., "Black Politicians in Reconstruction Charleston, South Carolina: A Collective Study," *Journal of Southern History* 49 (1983): 555–84.

Holt, Thomas C., *Black over White: Negro Political Leadership in South Carolina during Reconstruction* (1977).

————— "Negro State Legislators in South Carolina during Reconstruction," in Howard Rabinowitz, ed., *Southern Black Leaders of the Reconstruction Era* (1982): 223–46.

Jenkins, Wilbert L., *Seizing the New Day: African Americans in Post-Civil War Charleston* (1998).

Lamson, Peggy, *The Glorious Failure: Black Congressman Robert Brown Elliott and the Reconstruction in South Carolina* (1973).

Pike, James S., *The Prostrate State: South Carolina under Negro Government* (1874).

Reynolds, John S., *Reconstruction in South Carolina, 1865–1877* (1905).

Rose, Willie Lee Nichols, *Rehearsal for Reconstruction: The Port Royal Experiment* (1964).

Saville, Julie, *The Work of Reconstruction: From Slave to Wage Laborer in South Carolina, 1860–1870* (1994).

Schwalm, Leslie A., *A Hard Fight For We: Women's Transition from Slavery to Freedom in Lowcountry South Carolina* (1997).

Simkins, Francis Butler, and Robert Hilliard Woody, *South Carolina during Reconstruction* (1932).

Sweat, Edward F., "The Union Leagues and the South Carolina Election of 1870," *Journal of Negro History* 61 (1976): 200–14.

Taylor, Alrutheus A., *The Negro in South Carolina during the Reconstruction* (1924).

Williamson, Joel, *After Slavery: The Negro in South Carolina during Reconstruction, 1861–1877* (1965).

19.1.19   Tennessee

Alexander, Thomas Benjamin, *Political Reconstruction in Tennessee* (1950).

Ash, Stephen V., *Middle Tennessee Society Transformed, 1860–1870: War and Peace in the Upper South* (1988).

Cimprich, John, "Military Governor Johnson and Tennessee Blacks, 1862–1865," *Tennessee Historical Quarterly* 39 (1980): 459–70.

———— *Slavery's End in Tennessee, 1861–1865* (1985).

DeLozier, Mary J., "The Civil War and Its Aftermath in Putnam County," *Tennessee Historical Quarterly* 38 (1979): 436–61.

Fraser, Walter J., Jr., "Black Reconstruction in Tennessee," *Tennessee Historical Quarterly* 34 (1975): 362–82.

Jones, James B., Jr., "'If We Are Citizens by the Law, Let Us Enjoy the Fruits of This Privilege': African-American Political Struggles in a Tennessee Mountain City, 1869–1912," *West Tennessee Historical Society Papers* 49 (1995): 87–100.

Jordan, Weymouth T., "The Freedmen's Bureau in Tennessee," *East Tennessee Historical Society's Publications* 11 (1939): 47–61.

Taylor, Alrutheus A., *The Negro in Tennessee, 1865–1880* (1941).

Tucker, David M., "Black Politics in Memphis, 1865–1875," *West Tennessee Historical Society Papers* 26 (1972): 13–19.

19.1.20   Texas

Avillo, Philip J., Jr., "Phantom Radicals: Texas Republicans in Congress, 1870–1873," *Southwestern Historical Quarterly* 77 (1974): 431–44.

Barr, Alwyn, "Black Legislators of Reconstruction Texas," *Civil War History* 32 (1986): 340–52.

Brewer, John Mason, *Negro Legislators of Texas and Their Descendants: A History of the Negro in Texas Politics from Reconstruction to Disenfranchisement* (1935).

Campbell, Randolph B., "Carpetbagger Rule in Reconstruction Texas: An Endearing Myth," *Southwestern Historical Quarterly* 97 (1994): 587–96.

———— *Grass-Roots Reconstruction in Texas, 1865–1880* (1997).

———— "Reconstruction in Nueces County, 1865–1876," *Houston Review* 16 (1994): 3–26.

———— *A Southern Community in Crisis: Harrison County, Texas, 1850–1880* (1983).

Crouch, Barry A., *The Freedmen's Bureau and Black Texans* (1992).

———— "Hesitant Recognition: Texas Black Politicians, 1865–1900," *East Texas Historical Journal* 31 (1993): 41–58.

———— "Self-Determination and Local Black Leaders in Texas," *Pylon* 39 (1978): 344–55.

———— "'Unmanacling' Texas Reconstruction: A Twenty-Year Perspective," *Southwestern Historical Quarterly* 93 (1990): 275–302.

Davis, J. R., "Reconstruction in Cleveland County," *Trinity College Historical Society Historical Papers* 10 (1914): 5–31.

Elliott, Claude, "The Freedmen's Bureau in Texas," *Southwestern Historical Quarterly* 56 (1952): 1–24.

Malone, Ann Patton, "Matt Gaines: Reconstruction Politician," in Alwyn Barr and Robert A. Calvert, ed., *Black Leaders: Texans for Their Times* (1981): 49–82.

Marten, James Alan, *Texas Divided: Loyalty and Dissent in the Lone Star State, 1856–1874* (1990).

———— "'What Is to Become of the Negro?' White Reaction to Emancipation in Texas," *Mid-America* 73 (1991): 115–33.

Moneyhon, Carl H., *Republicanism in Reconstruction Texas* (1980).

Neal, Diane, and Thomas W. Kremm, "'What Shall We Do with the Negro?' The Freedmen's Bureau in Texas," *East Texas Historical Journal* 27 (1989): 23–34.

Nieman, Donald G., "African-Americans and the Meaning of Freedom: Washington County, Texas, As a Study, 1865–1886," *Chicago-Kent Law Review* 70 (1994): 541–82.

Pitrie, Merline, *Through Many Dangers, Toils, and Snares: The Black Leadership of Texas, 1868–1900* (1985).

Ramsdell, Charles W., *Reconstruction in Texas* (1910).

Richter, William Lee, "'This Blood-Thirsty Hole': The Freedmen's Bureau Agency at Clarksville, Texas, 1867–1868," *Civil War History* 38 (1992): 51–77.

Smallwood, James M., "Black Freedmen after Emancipation: The Texan Experience," *Prologue* 27 (1995): 303–17.

———— "Charles E. Culver, a Reconstruction Agent in Texas: The Work of Local Freedmen's Bureau Agents and the Black Community," *Civil War History* 27 (1981): 350–61.

———— *Time of Hope, Time of Despair: Black Texans during Reconstruction* (1981).

19.1.21   Virginia

Eckenrode, H. J., *Political History of Virginia during the Reconstruction* (1904).

Hucles, Michael, "Many Voices, Similar Concerns: Traditional Methods of African-American Political Activity in Norfolk, Virginia, 1865–1875," *Virginia Magazine of History and Biography* 100 (1992): 543–66.

Hume, Richard L., "The Membership of the Virginia Constitutional Convention of 1867–1868: A Study of the Beginnings of Congressional Reconstruction in the Upper South," *Virginia Magazine of History and Biography* 86 (1978): 461–84.

Jackson, Luther Porter, *Negro Office-Holders in Virginia, 1865–1895* (1945).

Lowe, Richard G., "Another Look at Reconstruction in Virginia," *Civil War History* 32 (1986): 56–76.

———— "Local Black Leaders during Reconstruction in Virginia," *Virginia Magazine of History and Biography* 103 (1995): 181–206.

———— *Republicans and Reconstruction in Virginia, 1856–1870* (1991).

———— "Testimony from the Old Dominion before the Joint Committee on Reconstruction," *Virginia Magazine of History and Biography* 104 (1996): 373–98.

———— "To Speak and Act As Freemen: The Emergence of Black Republicans in Postbellum Virginia," *Virginia Cavalcade* 41 (1991): 52–63.

Moore, Louis, "The Elusive Center: Virginia Politics and the General Assembly, 1869–1871," *Virginia Magazine of History and Biography* 103 (1995): 207–36.

Morgan, Lynda J., *Emancipation in Virginia's Tobacco Belt, 1850–1870* (1992).

Morton, Richard Lee, "'Contrabands' and Quakers in the Virginia Peninsula, 1862–1869," *Virginia Magazine of History and Biography* 61 (1953): 419–29.

———— *The Negro in Virginia Politics, 1865–1902* (1919).

Mugleston, William F., ed., "The Freedmen's Bureau and Reconstruction in Virginia: The Diary of Marcus Sterling Hopkins, a Union Officer," *Virginia Magazine of History and Biography* 86 (1978): 45–102.

Reidy, Joseph P., "'Coming from the Shadow of the Past': The Transition from Slavery to Freedom at Freedom's Village, 1863–1900," *Virginia Magazine of History and Biography* 95 (1987): 403–28.

Taylor, Alrutheus A., *The Negro in the Reconstruction of Virginia* (1926).

19.1.22   West Virginia

Engle, Stephen D., "Mountaineer Reconstruction: Blacks in the Political Reconstruction of West Virginia," *Journal of Negro History* 78 (1993): 137–65.

Gerofsky, Milton, "Reconstruction in West Virginia," *West Virginia History* 6 (1945): 295–360.

Stealey, John E., III, ed., "Reports of Freedmen's Bureau Operations in West Virginia: Agents in the Eastern Panhandle," *West Virginia History* 43 (1980–1981): 94–129.

19.2 HISTORIOGRAPHY

Beale, Howard K., "On Rewriting Reconstruction History," *American History Review* 45 (1940): 807–27.

Franklin, John Hope, "Whither Reconstruction Historiography?" *Journal of Negro Education* 17 (1948): 446–61.

Hamilton, Holman, "Before *The Tragic Era:* Claude Bowers's Earlier Attitudes toward Reconstruction," *Mid-America* 55 (1973): 235–44.

Hosmer, John, and Joseph Fineman, "Black Reconstruction Historiography," *Phylon* 39 (1978): 97–107.

Kyvig, David E., "History As Present Politics: Claude Bowers' *The Tragic Era,*" *Indiana Magazine of History* 73 (1977): 17–31.

Lynch, John R., "More about the Historical Errors of James Ford Rhodes [History of the United States from the Compromise of 1850 to the Final Restoration of Home Rule at the South in 1877]," *Journal of Negro History* 3 (1918): 139–57.

———— "Some Historical Errors of James Ford Rhodes [History of the United States from the Compromise of 1850 to the Final Restoration of Home Rule at the South in 1877]," *Journal of Negro History* 2 (1917): 345–68.

McKenzie, Robert H., "Reconstruction Historiography: The View from Shelby," *Historian* 36 (1974): 207–23.

Muller, Philip R., "Look Back without Anger: A Reappraisal of William A. Dunning," *Journal of American History* 61 (1974): 325–38.

Robinson, Armstead L., "Beyond the Realm of Social Consensus: New Meanings of Reconstruction for American History," *Journal of American History* 68 (1981): 276–97.

Simkins, Francis B., "New Viewpoints of Southern Reconstruction," *Journal of Southern History* 5 (1939): 49–61.

Taylor, Alrutheus A., "Historians of the Reconstruction," *Journal of Negro History* 23 (1938): 16–34.

Weisberger, Bernard A., "The Dark and Bloody Ground of Reconstruction Historiography," *Journal of Southern History* 25 (1959): 427–47.

Wharton, Vernon L., "Reconstruction," in Arthur S. Link and Rembert W. Patrick, ed., *Writing Southern History: Essays in Historiography in Honor of Fletcher M. Green* (1965): 295–315.

Woodman, Harold D., "Sequel to Slavery: The New History Views the Postbellum South," *Journal of Southern History* 43 (1977): 523–54.

19.3 SECONDARY SOURCES ON NEWSPAPERS AND PERIODICALS

Connor, William P., "Reconstruction Rebels: The *New Orleans Tribune* in Post-Civil War Louisiana," *Louisiana History* 21 (1980): 159–81.

Foner, Philip S., "A Labor Voice for Black Equality: The *Boston Daily Evening Voice,* 1864–1867," *Science and Society* 38 (1974): 304–25.

Houzeau, Jean-Charles, *My Passage at the New Orleans "Tribune": A Memoir of the Civil War Era,* ed. Gerard F. Denault and tr. David C. Rankin (1984).

Kolchin, Peter, "The Business Press and Reconstruction, 1865–1868," *Journal of Southern History* 33 (1967): 183–96.

Littlefield, Daniel F., Jr., and Patricia W. McGraw, "*The Arkansas Freeman,* 1869–1870: Birth of the Black Press in Arkansas," *Phylon* 40 (1979): 75–85.

Logue, Cal M., "Racist Reporting during Reconstruction," *Journal of Black Studies* 9 (1979): 335–49.

Neal, Diane, "Seduction, Accommodation, or Realism? Tabbs Gross and *The Arkansas Freeman,*" *Arkansas Historical Quarterly* 48 (1989): 57–64.

Rhodes, Jane, *Mary Ann Shadd Cary: The Black Press and Protest in the Nineteenth Century* (1998).

Williams, Gilbert Anthony, *The Christian Recorder, Newspaper of the African Methodist Episcopal Church: History of a Forum of Ideas, 1854–1902* (1996).

19.4 RACE RELATIONS

19.4.1 Abolitionism and Emancipation

Bentley, George R., *A History of the Freedmen's Bureau* (1955).

Berlin, Ira, Barbara J. Fields, Thavolia Glymph, Joseph P. Reidy, and Leslie S. Rowland, ed., *The Destruction of Slavery, Series I, Vol. 1 of Freedom: A Documentary History of Emancipation, 1861–1867* (1985).

Berlin, Ira, Thavolia Glymph, Steven F. Miller, Joseph P. Reidy, Leslie S. Rowland, and Julie Saville, ed., *The Wartime Genesis of Free Labor: The Lower South, Series I, Vol. 3 of Freedom: A Documentary History of Emancipation, 1861–1867* (1990).

Berlin, Ira, Steven F. Miller, Joseph P. Reidy, and Leslie S. Rowland, ed., *The Wartime Genesis of Free Labor: The Upper South, Series I, Vol. 2 of Freedom: A Documentary History of Emancipation, 1861–1867* (1993).

Cimbala, Paul A., and Randall M. Miller, ed., *The Freedmen's Bureau and Reconstruction: Reconsiderations* (1999).

Cimprich, John, "Military Governor Johnson and Tennessee Blacks, 1862–1865," *Tennessee Historical Quarterly* 39 (1980): 459–70.

———— *Slavery's End in Tennessee, 1861–1865* (1985).

Drake, Richard B., "Freedmen's Aid Societies and Sectional Compromise," *Journal of Southern History* 29 (1963): 175–86.

Eaton, John, *Grant, Lincoln, and the Freedmen: Reminiscences of the Civil War with Special References to the Work for the Contrabands and Freedmen of the Mississippi Valley* (1907).

Foner, Eric, *Nothing but Freedom: Emancipation and Its Legacy* (1983).

Frankel, Noralee, *Freedom's Women: Black Women and Families in Civil War Era Mississippi* (1999).

Gerteis, Louis S., *From Contraband to Freedman: Federal Policy toward Southern Blacks, 1861–1865* (1973).

Golay, Michael, *Reconstruction and Reaction: The Emancipation of Slaves, 1861–1913* (1996).

Lieberman, Robert C., "The Freedmen's Bureau and the Politics of Institutional Structure," *Social Science History* 18 (1994): 405–37.

Litwack, Leon F., *Been in the Storm So Long: The Aftermath of Slavery* (1979).

Magdol, Edward, "Martin R. Delany Counsels Freedmen, July 23, 1865," *Journal of Negro History* 56 (1971): 303–09.

McPherson, James M., *The Struggle for Equality: Abolitionists and the Negro in the Civil War and Reconstruction* (1964).

Mohr, Clarence L., *On the Threshold of Freedom: Masters and Slaves in Civil War Georgia* (1986).

Ripley, C. Peter, *Slaves and Freedmen in Civil War Louisiana* (1976).

Rose, Willie Lee Nichols, *Rehearsal for Reconstruction: The Port Royal Experiment* (1964).

Stanley, Amy Dru, *From Bondage to Contract: Wage Labor, Marriage, and the Market in the Age of Slave Emancipation* (1998).

Sutherland, Daniel E., "A Special Kind of Problem: The Response of Household Slaves and Their Masters to Freedom," *Southern Studies* 20 (1981): 151–66.

19.4.2 Black/White Relations

Bentley, George R., *A History of the Freedmen's Bureau* (1955).

Cimbala, Paul A., and Randall M. Miller, ed., *The Freedmen's Bureau and Reconstruction: Reconsiderations* (1999).

Cox, John H., and LaWanda Cox, "General O. O. Howard and the 'Misrepresented Bureau,'" *Journal of Southern History* 19 (1953): 427–56.

De Forest, John William, *A Union Officer in the Reconstruction,* ed. James H. Croushore and David M. Potter (1948).

Eaton, John, *Grant, Lincoln, and the Freedmen: Reminiscences of the Civil War with Special References to the Work for the Contrabands and Freedmen of the Mississippi Valley* (1907).

Fahey, David M., *Temperance and Racism: John Bull, Johnny Reb, and the Good Templars* (1996).

Hamilton, Holman, "Before *The Tragic Era:* Claude Bowers's Earlier Attitudes toward Reconstruction," *Mid-America* 55 (1973): 235–44.

Hodes, Martha, "The Sexualization of Reconstruction Politics: White Women and Black Men in the South after the Civil War," *Journal of the History of Sexuality* 3 (1993): 402–17.

———— *White Women, Black Men: Illicit Sex in the Nineteenth-Century South* (1997).

Howard, Oliver O., *Autobiography of Oliver Otis Howard, Major General, United States Army* (2 vols., 1971).

Latham, Henry, *Black and White: A Journal of a Three-Months' Tour in the United States* (1867).

Lieberman, Robert C., "The Freedmen's Bureau and the Politics of Institutional Structure," *Social Science History* 18 (1994): 405–37.

Lorini, Alessandra, *Rituals of Race: American Public Culture and the Search for Racial Democracy* (1999).

Marten, James Alan, "'What Is to Become of the Negro?' White Reaction to Emancipation in Texas," *Mid-America* 73 (1991): 115–33.

McFeely, William S., *Yankee Stepfather: General O. O. Howard and the Freedmen* (1968).

Morgan, Jo-Ann, "Mammy the Huckster: Selling the Old South for the New Century," *American Art* 9 (1995): 86–109.

Savage, Kirk, *Standing Soldiers, Kneeling Slaves: Race, War, and Monument in Nineteenth-Century America* (1997).

Sproat, John G., *"The Best Men": Liberal Reformers in the Gilded Age* (1968).

Wood, Forrest G., *Black Scare: The Racist Response to Emancipation and Reconstruction* (1968).

19.4.3   Black/Native American Relations

May, Katja, *African Americans and Native Americans in the Creek and Cherokee Nations, 1830's to 1920's: Collision and Collusion* (1996).

19.4.4   Black/Ethnic Relations

Berthoff, Rowland T., "Southern Attitudes toward Immigration, 1865–1914," *Journal of Southern History* 17 (1951): 328–60.

Hellwig, David J., "Black Attitudes toward Immigrant Labor in the South, 1865–1910," *Filson Club History Quarterly* 54 (1980): 151–68.

Johnsen, Leigh Dana, "Equal Rights and the 'Heathen "Chinee"': Black Activism in San Francisco, 1865–1875," *Western Historical Quarterly* 11 (1980): 57–68.

19.4.5   Segregation/Jim Crow

Crouch, B. A., and L. J. Schultz, "Crisis in Color: Racial Separation in Texas during Reconstruction," *Civil War History* 16 (1970): 37–49.

Erickson, Leonard, "Toledo Desegregates, 1871," *Northwest Ohio Quarterly* 41 (1968–69): 5–12.

Fischer, Roger A., *The Segregation Struggle in Louisiana, 1862–1877* (1974).

Foner, Philip S., "The Battle to End Discrimination against Negroes on Philadelphia Streetcars: Background and Beginning of the Battle," *Pennsylvania History* 40 (1973): 261–92, 355–79.

Harlan, Louis R., "Desegregation in New Orleans Public Schools during Reconstruction," *American History Review* 67 (1962): 663–75.

Hine, William C., "The 1867 Charleston Streetcar Sit-Ins: A Case of Successful Black Protest," *South Carolina Historical Review* 77 (1976): 110–14.

Kelly, A. H., "The Congressional Controversy over School Segregation, 1867–1875," *American History Review* 64 (1959): 537–63.

Rabinowitz, Howard N., "From Exclusion to Segregation: Southern Race Relations, 1865–1890," *Journal of American History* 63 (1976): 325–50.

———— *Race Relations in the Urban South, 1865–1890* (1978).

Wright, David, and David Zoby, "Ignoring Jim Crow: The Turbulent Appointment of Richard Etheridge and the Pea Island Lifesavers," *The Journal of Negro History* 80 (1995): 66–80.

19.4.6 Violence and Racial Disturbances

Cantrell, Gregg, "Racial Violence and Reconstruction Politics in Texas, 1867–1868," *Southwestern Historical Quarterly* 93 (1990): 333–55.

Carpenter, John A., "Atrocities in the Reconstruction Period," *Journal of Negro History* 47 (1962): 234–47.

Carter, Dan T., "The Anatomy of Fear: The Christmas Day Insurrection Scare of 1865," *Journal of Southern History* 42 (1976): 345–64.

Crouch, Barry A., "A Spirit of Lawlessness: White Violence, Texas Blacks, 1865–1868," *Journal of Social History* 18 (1984): 217–32.

Dauphine, James G., "The Knights of the White Camelia and the Election of 1868: Louisiana's White Terrorists, a Benighting Legacy," *Louisiana History* 30 (1989): 173–90.

Delatte, Carolyn E., "The St. Landry Riot: A Forgotten Incident of Reconstruction Violence," *Louisiana History* 17 (1976): 41–49.

Fitz Simons, Theodore B., Jr., "The Camilla Riot," *Georgia Historical Quarterly* 35 (1951): 116–25.

Formwalt, Lee W., ed., "Petitioning Congress for Protection: A Black View of Reconstruction at the Local Level," *Georgia Historical Quarterly* 73 (1989): 305–22.

Granada, Ray, "Violence: An Instrument of Policy in Reconstruction Alabama," *Alabama Historical Quarterly* 30 (1968): 181–202.

Hahn, Steven, "'Extravagant Expectations' of Freedom: Rumour, Political Struggle, and the Christmas Insurrection Scare of 1865 in the American South," *Past and Present* 157 (1997): 122–58.

Hardwick, Kevin R., "'Your Old Father Abe Lincoln Is Dead and Damned': Black Soldiers and the Memphis Race Riot of 1866," *Journal of Social History* 27 (1993): 109–28.

Hennessey, Melinda M., "Political Terrorism in the Black Belt: The Eutaw Riot," *Alabama Review* 33 (1980): 35–48.

———— "Race and Violence in Reconstruction New Orleans: The 1868 Riot," *Louisiana History* 20 (1979): 77–92.

———— "Racial Violence during Reconstruction: The 1876 Riots in Charleston and Cainhoy," *South Carolina Historical Magazine* 86 (1985): 100–12.

———— "Reconstruction Politics and the Military: The Eufaula Riot of 1874," *Alabama Historical Quarterly* 38 (1976): 112–25.

Howard, Gene L., *Death at Cross Plains: An Alabama Reconstruction Tragedy* (1984).

Johnson, Manie W., "The Colfax Riot of April, 1873," *Louisiana Historical Quarterly* 13 (1930): 391–427.

Lovett, Bobby L., "Memphis Riots: White Reaction to Blacks in Memphis, May 1865-July 1866," *Tennessee Historical Quarterly* 38 (1979): 9–33.

Olsen, Otto H., "The Ku Klux Klan: A Study in Reconstruction Politics and Propaganda," *North Carolina Historical Review* 39 (1962): 340–62.

Peek, Ralph L., "Lawlessness in Florida, 1868–1871," *Florida Historical Quarterly* 40 (1961): 164–85.

Rable, George C., *But There Was No Peace: The Role of Violence in the Politics of Reconstruction* (1984).

Richter, William Lee, "'The Revolver Rules the Day!': Colonel DeWitt C. Brown and the Freedmen's Bureau in Paris, Texas, 1867–1868," *Southwestern Historical Quarterly* 93 (1990): 303–32.

Rogers, William W., Jr., "The Eutaw Prisoners: Federal Confrontation with Violence in Reconstruction Alabama," *Alabama Review* 43 (1990): 98–121.

Ryan, James G., "The Memphis Riots of 1866: Terror in a Black Community during Reconstruction," *Journal of Negro History* 62 (1977): 243–57.

Shapiro, Herbert, "Afro-American Responses to Race Violence during Reconstruction," *Science and Society* 36 (1972): 158–70.

——— "The Ku Klux Klan during Reconstruction: The South Carolina Episode," *Journal of Negro History* 49 (1964): 34–55.

Simkins, Francis B., "Ku Klux Klan in South Carolina, 1868–1871," *Journal of Negro History* 12 (1927): 606–47.

Sloan, John Z., "The Ku Klux Klan and the Alabama Election of 1872," *Alabama Review* 18 (1965): 113–24.

Smith, Mark M., "'All Is Not Quiet in Our Hellish County': Facts, Fiction, Politics and Race—The Ellenton Riot of 1876," *South Carolina Historical Magazine* 95 (1994): 142–55.

Stagg, J. C. A., "The Problem of Klan Violence: The South Carolina Up-Country, 1868–1871," *Journal of American Studies* 8 (1974): 303–18.

Trelease, Allen W., *White Terror: The Ku Klux Klan Conspiracy and Southern Reconstruction* (1971).

U.S. 42nd Congress, 2d Session, House Report 22, *Report of the Joint Select Committee to Inquire into the Condition of Affairs in the Late Insurrectionary States* (13 Vol., 1872).

Vandal, Gilles, "'Bloody Caddo': White Violence against Blacks in a Louisiana Parish, 1865–1875," *Journal of Social History* 25 (1991): 373–88.

——— *The New Orleans Riot of 1866: Anatomy of a Tragedy* (1983).

——— "The Policy of Violence in Caddo Parish, 1865–1884," *Louisiana History* 32 (1991): 159–82.

Waller, Altina L., "Community, Class, and Race in the Memphis Riot of 1866," *Journal of Social History* 18 (1984): 233–46.

Wetta, Frank J., "'Bulldozing the Scalawags': Some Examples of the Persecution of Southern White Republicans in Louisiana during Reconstruction," *Louisiana History* 21 (1980): 43–58.

19.4.7 Civil Rights

Berwanger, Eugene H., "Hardin and Langston: Western Black Spokesmen of the Reconstruction Era," *Journal of Negro History* 64 (1979): 101–15.

Hays, Christopher K., "The African American Struggle for Equality and Justice in Cairo, Illinois, 1865–1900," *Illinois Historical Journal* 90 (1997): 265–84.

Rhodes, Jane, *Mary Ann Shadd Cary: The Black Press and Protest in the Nineteenth Century* (1998).

19.5 GOVERNMENT

19.5.1 Law

Amir, A. R., "The Bill of Rights and the Fourteenth Amendment," *Yale Law Review* 101 (1992): 1193–284.

Applethwaite, Marjorie M., "Sharecropper and Tenant in the Courts of North Carolina," *North Carolina Historical Review* 31 (1954): 134–49.

Benedict, Michael L., "Preserving the Constitution: The Conservative Basis of Radical Reconstruction," *Journal of American History* 61 (1974): 65–90.

——— "The Problem of Constitutionism and Constitutional Liberty in the Reconstruction South," in Kermit L. Hall and James W. Ely, Jr., ed., *An Uncertain Tradition: Constitutionalism and the History of the South* (1990): 225–49.

Bernstein, David E., "The Law and Economics of Post-Civil War Restrictions on Interstate Migration by African Americans," *Texas Law Review* 76 (1998): 781–847.

Blair, William A., "Justice versus Law and Order: The Battles over the Reconstruction of Virginia's Minor Judiciary, 1865–1870," *Virginia Magazine of History and Biography* 103 (1995): 157–80.

Brandon, Mark E., *Free in the World: American Slavery and Constitutional Failure* (1998).

Brandwein, Pamela, *Reconstructing Reconstruction: The Supreme Court and the Production of Historical Truth* (1999).

Buchanan, G. Sidney, *The Quest for Freedom: A Legal History of the Thirteenth Amendment* (1976).

Campbell, Randolph B., "The District Judges of Texas in 1866–1867: An Episode in the Failure of Presidential Reconstruction," *Southwestern Historical Quarterly* 93 (1990): 357–77.

Crouch, Barry A., "'All the Vile Passions': The Texas Black Code of 1866," *Southwestern Historical Quarterly* 97 (1993): 13–34.

———— "Black Dreams and White Justice," *Prologue* 6 (1974): 255–65.

Curtis Michael Kent, *No State Shall Abridge: The Fourteenth Amendment and the Bill of Rights* (1986).

Dailey, Maceo Crenshaw, Jr., "Neither 'Uncle Tom' nor 'Accommodationist': Booker T. Washington, Emmet Jay Scott, and Constructionalism," *Atlanta History* 38 (1995): 20–33.

Edwards, Laura E., "The Problem of Dependency: African Americans, Labor Relations, and the Law in the Nineteenth-Century South," *Agricultural History* 72 (1998): 313–40.

Fairman, Charles, *Reconstruction and Reunion, 1864–1888.* Vol. 6 and 7 of *The History of the Supreme Court of the United States* (1971, 1987).

Farber, D. A., and John Muench, "The Ideological Origins of the Fourteenth Amendment," *Constitutional Commentary* 1 (1984): 235–79.

Franklin, John Hope, "The Enforcement of the Civil Rights Act of 1875," *Prologue* 6 (1974): 225–35.

Guild, June Purcell, *Black Laws of Virginia: A Summary of the Legislative Acts of Virginia concerning Negroes from Earliest Times to the Present* (1936).

Halbrook, Stephen P., *Freedmen, the Fourteenth Amendment, and the Right to Bear Arms, 1866–1876* (1998).

Hall, Kermit L., "Political Power and Constitutional Legitimacy: The South Carolina Ku Klux Klan Trials, 1871–1872," *Emory Law Journal* 33 (1984): 921–51.

Harris, William C., "Formulation of the First Mississippi Plan: The Black Code of 1865," *Journal of Mississippi History* 29 (1967): 181–201.

Hyman, Harold M., *A More Perfect Union: The Impact of the Civil War and Reconstruction on the Constitution* (1973).

Hyman, Harold M., and William M. Wiecek, *Equal Justice under Law: Constitutional Development, 1835–1875* (1982).

Kaczorowski, Robert J., "To Begin the Nation Anew: Congress, Citizenship, and Civil Rights after the Civil War," *American Historical Review* 92 (1987): 45–68.

———— *The Politics of Judicial Interpretation: The Federal Courts, Department of Justice and Civil Rights, 1866–1876* (1985).

Lebsock, Suzanne, "Radical Reconstruction and the Property Rights of Southern Women," *Journal of Southern History* 43 (1977): 195–216.

Maltz, Earl M., *Civil Rights, the Constitution, and Congress, 1863–1869* (1990).

Mancuso, Luke, *The Strange Sad War Revolving: Walt Whitman, Reconstruction, and the Emergence of Black Citizenship, 1865–1876* (1997).

Miller, Steven F., Susan E. O'Donovan, John C. Rodrigue, and Leslie S. Rowland, "Between Emancipation and Enfranchisement: Law and the Political Mobilization of Black Southerners during Presidential Reconstruction, 1865–1867," *Chicago-Kent Law Review* 70 (1995): 1059–78.

Mollison, Irvin C., "Negro Lawyers in Mississippi," *Journal of Negro History* 15 (1930): 38–71.

Moreno, Paul, "Racial Classifications and Reconstruction Legislation," *Journal of Southern History* 61 (1995): 271–304.

Nelson, William E., *The Fourteenth Amendment: From Political Principle to Judicial Doctrine* (1988).

Nieman, Donald G., "Andrew Johnson, the Freedmen's Bureau, and the Problem of Equal Rights, 1865–1866," *Journal of Southern History* 44 (1978): 399–420.

———— "The Freedmen's Bureau and the Mississippi Black Code," *Journal of Mississippi History* 40 (1978): 91–118.

———— *To Set the Law in Motion: The Freedmen's Bureau and the Legal Rights of Blacks, 1865–1868* (1979).

Oldfield, J. R., "A High and Honorable Calling: Black Lawyers in South Carolina, 1868–1915," *Journal of American Studies* 23 (1989): 395–406.

Rust, Barbara, "The Right to Vote: The Enforcement Acts and Southern Courts," *Prologue* 21 (1989): 231–38.

Schmidt, James D., *Free to Work: Labor Law, Emancipation, and Reconstruction, 1815–1880* (1998).

Scroggs, Jack B., "Carpetbagger Constitutional Reform in the South Atlantic States, 1867–1868," *Journal of Southern History* 27 (1961): 475–93.

Spackman, S. G. F., "American Federalism and the Civil Rights Act of 1875," *Journal of American Studies* 10 (1976): 313–28.

Swinney, Everette, "Enforcing the Fifteenth Amendment, 1870–1877," *Journal of Southern History* 28 (1962): 202–18.

Ten Broek, Jacobus, *Equal under Law* (1965).

Vandervelde, Lea S., "The Labor Vision of the Thirteenth Amendment," *University of Pennsylvania Law Review* 138 (1989): 437–504.

Waldrep, Christopher, "Black Access to Law in Reconstruction: The Case of Warren County, Mississippi," *Chicago-Kent Law Review* 70 (1994): 583–626.

——— "Substituting Law for the Lash: Emancipation and Legal Formalism in a Mississippi County Court," *Journal of American History* 82 (1996): 1425–51.

Wang, Xi, "The Making of Federal Enforcement Laws, 1870–1872," *Chicago-Kent Law Review* 70 (1995): 1013–58.

Wiecek, William M., "The Reconstruction of Federal Judical Power, 1863–1875," *American Journal of Legal History* 13 (1968): 333–59.

Williams, Lou F., "The South Carolina Ku Klux Klan Trials and Enforcement of Federal Rights, 1871–1872," *Civil War History* 39 (1993): 47–66.

Wilson, Theodore B., *The Black Codes of the South* (1965).

Woodman, Harold D., *New South, New Law: The Legal Foundations of Credit and Labor Relations in the Postbellum Agricultural South* (1995).

——— "Post-Civil War Southern Agriculture and the Law," *Agricultural History* 53 (1979): 319–37.

Wyatt-Brown, Bertram, "The Civil Rights Act of 1875," *Western Political Quarterly* 18 (1965): 763–75.

19.5.2   Crime and Punishment

Baenziger, Ann P., "The Texas State Police during Reconstruction: A Reexamination," *Southwestern Historical Quarterly* 72 (1969): 470–91.

Blain, William T., "Challenge to the Lawless: The Mississippi Secret Service, 1870–1871," *Journal of Mississippi History* 40 (1978): 119–31.

Crouch, Barry A., "The Fetters of Justice: Black Texans and the Penitentiary during Reconstruction," *Prologue* 28 (1996): 183–93.

Hall, Kermit L., "Political Power and Constitutional Legitimacy: The South Carolina Ku Klux Klan Trials, 1871–1872," *Emory Law Journal* 33 (1984): 921–51.

Waldrep, Christopher, *Roots of Disorder: Race and Criminal Justice in the American South, 1817–1880* (1998).

19.5.3   Politics and Voting

Abbott, Richard H., *The Republican Party and the South, 1855–1877: The First Southern Strategy* (1986).

Arconti, Steven, "To Secure the Party: Henry L. Dawes and the Politics of Reconstruction," *Historical Journal of Western Massachusetts* 5 (1977): 33–45.

Baggett, James A., "Origins of Upper South Scalawag Leadership," *Civil War History* 29 (1983): 53–73.

Belz, Herman, *Emancipation and Equal Rights* (1978).

——— "Origins of Negro Suffrage during the Civil War," *Southern Studies* 17 (1978): 115–30.

——— *Reconstructing the Union: Theory and Policy during the Civil War* (1969).

Benedict, Michael L., *A Compromise of Principle: Congressional Republicans and Reconstruction, 1863–1869* (1974).

——— "Southern Democrats in the Crisis of 1876–1877: A Reconsideration of Reunion and Reaction," *Journal of Southern History* 46 (1980): 489–524.

Bowen, David Warren, *Andrew Johnson and the Negro* (1989).

Brock, William Ranulf, *An American Crisis: Congress and Reconstruction, 1865–1867* (1963).

Brown, Canter, Jr., *Florida's Black Public Officials, 1867–1924* (1998).

Brown, Elsa B., "Negotiating and Transforming the Public Sphere: African American Political Life in the Transition from Slavery to Freedom," *Public Culture* 7 (1994): 107–46.

Campbell, Randolph B., "The Burden of Local Black Leadership during Reconstruction: A Research Note," *Civil War History* 39 (1993): 148–53.

Castel, Albert E., *The Presidency of Andrew Johnson* (1979).

Clendenen, Clarence C., "President Hayes' 'Withdrawal' of the Troops: An Enduring Myth," *South Carolina Historical Magazine* 70 (1969): 240–50.

Cox, LaWanda, and C. Fenlason, *Lincoln and Black Freedom: A Study in Presidential Leadership* (1981).

Cox, LaWanda, and John H. Cox, *Politics, Principle, and Prejudice, 1865–1866: Dilemma of Reconstruction in America* (1963).

Current, Richard N., "Carpetbaggers Reconsidered," in David H. Pinkney and Theodore Ropp, ed., *A Festschrift for Frederick B. Artz* (1964): 139–57.

———— *Those Terrible Carpetbaggers: A Reinterpretation* (1988).

———— *Three Carpetbag Governors* (1967).

Curry, Richard O., ed., *Radicalism, Racism, and Party Realignment: The Border States during Reconstruction* (1969).

Donald, David H., *Charles Sumner and the Rights of Man* (1970).

———— *The Politics of Reconstruction, 1863–1867* (1965).

Durden, Robert Franklin, *James Shephard Pike: Republicanism and the American Negro, 1850–1882* (1957).

Fishel, Leslie H., Jr., "Northern Prejudice and Negro Suffrage," *Journal of Negro History* 39 (1954): 8–26.

Fitzgerald, Michael W., *The Union League Movement in the Deep South: Politics and Agricultural Change during Reconstruction* (1989).

Foner, Eric, "African Americans in Public Office during the Era of Reconstruction," *Reconstruction* 2 (1993): 20–32.

———— "Black Reconstruction Leaders at the Grass Roots," in Leon F. Litwack and August Meier, ed., *Black Leaders of the Nineteenth Century* (1988): 219–34.

———— *Freedom's Lawmakers: A Directory of Black Officeholders during Reconstruction* (1993).

Forsythe, Harold S., "'But My Friends Are Poor': Ross Hamilton and Freedpeople's Politics in Mecklenburg County, Virginia, 1869–1901," *Virginia Magazine of History and Biography* 105 (1997): 409–38.

Gillette, William, *The Right to Vote: Politics and the Passage of the Fifteenth Amendment* (1965).

Grossman, Lawrence, *The Democratic Party and the Negro: Northern and National Politics, 1868–1892* (1976).

Hume, Richard L., "Carpetbaggers in the Reconstruction South: A Group Portrait of Outside Whites in the 'Black and Tan' Constitutional Conventions," *Journal of American History* 64 (1977): 313–30.

———— "Negro Delegates to the State Constitutional Conventions of 1867–1869," in Howard Rabinowitz, ed., *Southern Black Leaders of the Reconstruction Era* (1982): 129–53.

Hyman, Harold M., ed., *The Radical Republicans and Reconstruction, 1861–1870* (1967).

Kohl, Martha, "From Freedom to Franchise: The Debate over African American Enfranchisement, 1865–1870," *Gateway Heritage* 16 (1996): 22–35.

Lowe, Richard G., "The Freedmen's Bureau and Local Black Leadership," *Journal of American History* 80 (1993): 989–98.

Lynch, John R., "More about the Historical Errors of James Ford Rhodes [History of the United States from the Compromise of 1850 to the Final Restoration of Home Rule at the South in 1877]," *Journal of Negro History* 3 (1918): 139–57.

———— "Some Historical Errors of James Ford Rhodes [History of the United States from the Compromise of 1850 to the Final Restoration of Home Rule at the South in 1877]," *Journal of Negro History* 2 (1917): 345–68.

McFarlin, Annjennette Sophie, *Black Congressional Reconstruction Orators and Their Orations* (1976).

McFeely, William S., *Grant: A Biography* (1981).

McKinney, Gordon B., *Southern Mountain Republicans, 1865–1900* (1978).

McKitrick, Eric L., *Andrew Johnson and Reconstruction* (1960).

McPherson, Edward, *The Political History of the United States of America during the Period of Reconstruction* (1871).

McPherson, James M., "Grant or Greeley? The Abolitionist Dilemma in the Election of 1872," *American History Review* 71 (1965): 43–61.

Mohr, James C., ed., *Radical Republicans in the North: State Politics during Reconstruction* (1976).

Montgomery, David, *Beyond Equality: Labor and the Radical Republicans, 1862–1872* (1967).

O'Brien, John T., "Reconstruction in Richmond: White Restoration and Black Protest, April–June 1865," *Virginia Magazine of History and Biography* 89 (1981): 259–81.

O'Donovan, Susan E., "Philip Joiner: Southwest Georgia Black Republican Leader," *Journal of Southwest Georgia History* 4 (1986): 56–71.

Olsen, Otto H., *Carpetbagger's Crusade: The Life of Albion Winegar Tourgee* (1965).

——— "Reconsidering the Scalawags," *Civil War History* 12 (1966): 304–20.

Perman, Michael, *The Road to Redemption: Southern Politics, 1869–1879* (1984).

Peskin, Allan, "Was There a Compromise of 1877?" *Journal of American History* 60 (1973): 63–75.

Pike, James S., *The Prostrate State: South Carolina under Negro Government* (1874).

Polakoff, Keith Ian, *The Politics of Inertia: The Election of 1876 and the End of Reconstruction* (1973).

Rabinowitz, Howard N., ed., *Southern Black Leaders of the Reconstruction Era* (1982).

——— "Three Reconstruction Leaders: Blanche K. Bruce, Robert Brown Elliott, and Holland Thompson," in Leon F. Litwack and August Meier, ed., *Black Leaders of the Nineteenth Century* (1988): 191–217.

Rable, George C., "Republican Albatross: The Louisiana Question, National Politics, and the Failure of Reconstruction," *Louisiana History* 23 (1982): 109–30.

——— "Southern Interests and the Election of 1876: A Reappraisal," *Civil War History* 26 (1980): 347–61.

Riddleberger, Patrick W., "The Break in the Radical Ranks: Liberals vs. Stalwarts in the Election of 1872," *Journal of Negro History* 44 (1959): 136–57.

——— *George Washington Julian, Radical Republican: A Study in Nineteenth Century Politics and Reform* (1966).

——— "The Radicals' Abandonment of the Negro during Reconstruction," *Journal of Negro History* 45 (1960): 88–102.

Sefton, James E., *Andrew Johnson and the Uses of Constitutional Power* (1980).

Seip, Terry L., *The South Returns to Congress: Men, Economic Measures, and Intersectional Relationships, 1868–1879* (1983).

Shortreed, Margaret, "The Anti-Slavery Radicals: From Crusade to Revolution, 1840–1868," *Past and Present* 16 (1959): 65–87.

Simpson, Brooks D., "Land and the Ballot: Securing the Fruits of Emancipation?" *Pennsylvania History* 60 (1993): 176–88.

——— *Let Us Have Peace: Ulysses S. Grant and the Politics of War and Reconstruction, 1861–1868* (1991).

Simpson, Brooks D., Le Roy P. Graf, and John Muldowny, ed., *Advice after Appomattox: Letters to Andrew Johnson, 1865–1866* (1987).

Smith, Samuel Denny, *The Negro in Congress, 1870–1901* (1940).

Summers, Mark W., *Railroads, Reconstruction, and the Gospel of Prosperity: Aid under the Radical Republicans, 1865–1877* (1984).

Taylor, Alrutheus A., "Negro Congressmen a Generation After," *Journal of Negro History* 7 (1922): 127–71.

Trefousse, Hans Louis, *Benjamin Franklin Wade: Radical Republican from Ohio* (1963).

——— *The Radical Republicans: Lincoln's Vanguard for Racial Justice* (1969).

Trelease, Allen W., "Who Were the Scalawags?" *Journal of Southern History* 29 (1963): 445–68.

Williams, T. Harry, "An Analysis of Some Reconstruction Attitudes," *Journal of Southern History* 12 (1946): 469–86.

Woodward, Comer Vann, *Reunion and Reaction: The Compromise of 1877 and the End of Reconstruction* (2nd ed., 1956).

Work, Monroe N., ed., "Materials from the Scrapbook of W. A. Hayne Collected in 1874," *Journal of Negro History* 7 (1922): 311–40.

19.5.4 Military

Berlin, Ira, Joseph P. Reidy, and Leslie S. Rowland, ed., *The Black Military Experience, Series II of Freedom: A Documentary History of Emancipation, 1861–1867* (1982).

Cipriani, Tim, "Negro Soldiers on the Frontier: The Ninth and Tenth U.S. Cavalry, 1866–1891," *Griot* 16 (1997): 40–49.

Dawson, Joseph G., III, *Army Generals and Reconstruction: Louisiana, 1862–1877* (1982).

Leiker, James N., "Black Soldiers at Fort Hays, Kansas, 1867–1869: A Study in Civilian and Military Violence," *Great Plains Quarterly* 17 (1997): 3–17.

Maslowski, Peter, *Treason Must Be Made Odious: Military Occupation and Wartime Reconstruction in Nashville, Tennessee, 1862–1865* (1978).

Richter, William Lee, *The Army in Texas during Reconstruction, 1865–1870* (1987).

Sefton, James E., *The United States Army and Reconstruction, 1865–1877* (1967).

Singletary, Otis A., *Negro Militia and Reconstruction* (1957).

19.6 FAMILY

Barksdale-Hall, R. C., "The Steversons: An African-American Family in Slavery and Freedom," *Journal of the Afro-American Historical and Genealogical Society* 6 (1985): 156–70.

Berlin, Ira, Steven F. Miller, and Leslie S. Rowland, "Afro-American Families in the Transition from Slavery to Freedom," *Radical History Review* 42 (1988): 89–121.

Burton, Orville V., ed., *In My Father's House Are Many Mansions: Family and Community in Edgefield, South Carolina* (1985).

Cansler, Charles W., *Three Generations: The Story of a Colored Family of Eastern Tennessee* (1939).

Cody, C. A., "Kin and Community among the Good Hope People after Emancipation," *Ethnohistory* 41 (1994): 25–72.

Crouch, Barry A., and Larry Madaras, "Reconstruction Black Families: Perspectives from the Texas Freedmen's Bureau Records," *Prologue* 18 (1986): 109–22.

Day, Kay Young, "Kinship in a Changing Economy: A View from the Sea Islands," in Robert L. Hall and Carol B. Stack, ed., *Holding on to the Land and the Lord: Kinship, Ritual, Land Tenure, and Social Policy in the Rural South* (1982): 11–24.

Frankel, Noralee, *Freedom's Women: Black Women and Families in Civil War Era Mississippi* (1999).

Fuke, Richard P., "Planters, Apprenticeship, and Forced Labor: The Black Family under Pressure in Post-Emancipation Maryland," *Agricultural History* 62 (1988): 57–74.

Jessup, Wilbur E., "The Warren Family of Marshall County, Iowa," *Journal of the Afro-American Historical and Genealogical Society* 3 (1982): 99–104.

Murray, Pauli, *Proud Shoes: The Story of an American Family* (1956).

Scott, Rebecca, "The Battle over the Child: Child Apprenticeship and the Freedmen's Bureau in North Carolina," *Prologue* 10 (1978): 101–13.

19.7 SOCIETY

19.7.1 Rural Life (Including Black Settlements)

Bethel, Elizabeth, *Promiseland: A Century of Life in a Negro Community* (1981).

Campbell, Randolph B., "Population Persistence and Social Change in Nineteenth-Century Texas: Harrison County, 1850–1880," *Journal of Southern History* 48 (1982): 185–204.

Greenberg, Kenneth G., "The Civil War and the Redistribution of Land: Adams County, Mississippi, 1860–1870," *Agricultural History* 52 (1978): 292–307.

Hartley, William G., "Reconstruction Data from the 1870 Census: Hinds County Mississippi," *Journal of Mississippi History* 35 (1973): 55–64.

Hermann, Janet Sharp, *The Pursuit of a Dream* (1981).

Huffman, Frank J., "Town and Country in the South, 1850–1880: A Comparison of Urban and Rural Social Structures," *South Atlantic Quarterly* 76 (1977): 366–81.

Morris-Crowther, Jayne, "An Economic Study of the Substantial Slaveholders of Orangeburg County, 1860–80," *South Carolina Historical Magazine* 86 (1985): 296–314.

Naglich, Dennis, "Rural Prairieville during Reconstruction," *Missouri Historical Review* 87 (1993): 387–402.

Nathans, Sidney, "Fortress without Walls: A Black Community after Slavery," in Robert L. Hall and Carol B. Stack, ed., *Holding on to the Land and the Lord: Kinship, Ritual, Land Tenure, and Social Policy in the Rural South* (1982): 55–65.

Pease, William H., and Jane H. Pease, *Black Utopia: Negro Communal Experiments in America* (1963).

Ravage, John W., *Black Pioneers: Images of the Black Experience in the North American Frontier* (1997).

Rosengarten, Theodore, "Sea Island Encounter," *Georgia Historical Quarterly* 79 (1995): 394–406.

Schlissel, Lillian, *Black Frontiers: A History of African-American Heroes in the Old West* (1995).

Townes, A. Jane, "The Effect of Emancipation on Large Landholdings, Nelson and Goochland Counties, Virginia," *Journal of Southern History* 45 (1979): 403–12.

19.7.2 Urban Life (Including Migration)

Blassingame, John W., "Before the Ghetto: The Making of the Black Community in Savannah, Georgia, 1865–1880," *Journal of Social History* 6 (1973): 463–88.

———— *Black New Orleans, 1860–1880* (1973).

Carlton, Robert L., "Blacks in San Diego County: A Social Profile, 1850–1880," *Journal of San Diego History* 21 (1975): 7–20.

Chesson, Michael Bedout, *Richmond after the War, 1865–1890* (1981).

Cohen, William, *At Freedom's Edge: Black Mobility and the Southern White Quest for Racial Control, 1861–1915* (1991).

Engs, Robert Francis, *Freedom's First Generation: Black Hampton, Virginia, 1861–1890* (1979).

Goings, Kenneth W., and Gerald L. Smith, "'Unhidden' Transcripts: Memphis and African American Agency, 1862–1920," *Journal of Urban History* 21 (1995): 372–94.

Greene, A. C., "The Durable Society: Austin in the Reconstruction," *Southwestern Historical Quarterly* 72 (1969): 492–518.

Henderson, William D., *The Unredeemed City: Reconstruction in Petersburg, Virginia: 1865–1874* (1977).

Huffman, Frank J., "Town and Country in the South, 1850–1880: A Comparison of Urban and Rural Social Structures," *South Atlantic Quarterly* 76 (1977): 366–81.

Kellogg, John, "The Formation of Black Residential Areas in Lexington, Kentucky, 1865–1887," *Journal of Southern History* 48 (1982): 21–52.

Kornell, Gary L., "Reconstruction in Nashville, 1867–1869," *Tennessee Historical Quarterly* 30 (1971): 277–87.

Logsdon, Joseph, "Americans and Creoles in New Orleans: The Origins of Black Citizenship in the United States," *Amerikastudien/American Studies* 34 (1990): 187–202.

Logsdon, Joseph and Caryn C. Bell, "The Americanization of Black New Orleans, 1850–1900," in Arnold R. Hirsch and Joseph Logsdon, ed., *Creole New Orleans: Race and Americanization* (1992): 201–61.

O'Brien, John T., "Reconstruction in Richmond: White Restoration and Black Protest, April-June 1865," *Virginia Magazine of History and Biography* 89 (1981): 259–81.

Perdue, Robert Eugene, *The Negro in Savannah, 1865–1900* (1973).

Rabinowitz, Howard N., "The Conflict between Blacks and the Police in the Urban South, 1865–1900," *Historian* 39 (1976): 62–76.

——— *Race Relations in the Urban South, 1865–1890* (1978).

Rankin, David C., "The Impact of the Civil War on the Free Colored Community of New Orleans," *Perspectives in American History* 11 (1977–1988): 377–416.

Robinson, Armstead L., "Plans Dat Comed from God: Institution Building and the Emergence of Black Leadership in Reconstruction Memphis," in Orville Vernon Burton and Robert C. McMath, Jr., ed., *Toward a New South? Studies in Post-Civil War Southern Communities* (1982): 71–102.

Rousey, Dennis C., "Black Policemen in New Orleans during Reconstruction," *Historian* 49 (1987): 223–43.

Somers, Dale A., "Black and White in New Orleans: A Study in Urban Race Relations, 1865–1900," *Journal of Southern History* 40 (1974): 19–42.

Thomas, Herbert A., Jr., "Victims of Circumstance: Negroes in a Southern Town, 1865–1880," *Register of the Kentucky Historical Society* 71 (1973): 253–71.

Tripp, Steven Elliott, *Yankee Town, Southern City: Race and Class in Civil War Lynchburg* (1996).

Vandal, Gilles, "Black Utopia in Early Reconstruction New Orleans: The People's Bakery As a Case Study," *Louisiana History* 38 (1997): 437–52.

Vedder, Richard, Lowell Gallaway, Philip E. Graves, and Robert Sexton, "Demonstrating Their Freedom: The Post-Emancipation Migration of Black Americans," *Research in Economic History* 10 (1986): 213–39.

Yee, Shirley J., "Finding a Place: Mary Ann Shadd Cary and the Dilemmas of Black Migration to Canada, 1850–1870," *Frontiers* 18 (1997): 1–16.

19.7.3   Color and Class

Greenwood, Janette Thomas, *Bittersweet Legacy: The Black and White "Better Classes" in Charlotte, 1850–1910* (1994).

Logsdon, Joseph and Caryn C. Bell, "The Americanization of Black New Orleans, 1850–1900," in Arnold R. Hirsch and Joseph Logsdon, ed., *Creole New Orleans: Race and Americanization* (1992): 201–61.

Rankin, David C., "The Impact of the Civil War on the Free Colored Community of New Orleans," *Perspectives in American History* 11 (1977–1978): 377–416.

Schweninger, Loren, "Antebellum Free Persons of Color in Postbellum Louisiana," *Louisiana History* 30 (1989): 345–64.

——— *Black Property Owners in the South, 1790–1915* (1990).

Sutherland, Daniel E., "A Special Kind of Problem: The Response of Household Slaves and Their Masters to Freedom," *Southern Studies* 20 (1981): 151–66.

19.7.4   Associational Life

Berkeley, Kathleen C., "Colored Ladies Also Contributed: Black Women's Activities from Benevolence to Social Welfare, 1866–1896," in Walter J. Fraser, Jr., R. Frank Saunders, Jr. and Jon L. Wakelyn, ed., *The Web of Southern Social Relations: Women, Family, and Education* (1985).

Fuke, Richard P., "The Baltimore Association for the Moral and Educational Improvement of the Colored People, 1864–1870," *Maryland Historical Magazine* 66 (1971): 369–404.

Kennedy, Thomas C., "The Rise and Decline of a Black Monthly Meeting: Southland, Arkansas, 1864–1925," *Arkansas Historical Quarterly* 50 (1991): 115–39.

Robinson, Armstead L., "Plans Dat Comed from God: Institution Building and the Emergence of Black Leadership in Reconstruction Memphis," in Orville Vernon Burton and Robert C. McMath, Jr., ed., *Toward a New South? Studies in Post-Civil War Southern Communities* (1982): 71–102.

19.8   RELIGION

Abbott, Richard H., "Black Ministers and the Organization of the Republican Party in the South in 1867: Letters from the Field," *Hayes Historical Journal* 6 (1986): 23–37.

Amos, Harriet E., "Religious Reconstruction in Microcosm at Faunsdale Plantation," *Alabama Review* 42 (1989): 243–69.

Angell, Stephen W., *Bishop Henry McNeal Turner and African-American Religion in the South* (1992).

Armstrong, Thomas F., "The Building of a Black Church: Community in Post Civil War Liberty County, Georgia," *Georgia Historical Quarterly* 66 (1982): 346–67.

Bell, John L., Jr., "Baptists and the Negro in North Carolina during Reconstruction," *North Carolina Historical Review* 42 (1965): 391–409.

———— "The Presbyterian Church and the Negro in North Carolina during Reconstruction," *North Carolina Historical Review* 40 (1963): 15–36.

Burkhead, L. S., "History of the Difficulties of the Pastorate of the Front Street Methodist Church, Wilmington, N.C., for the Year 1865," *Trinity College Historical Society Historical Papers* 8 (1908–1909): 35–118.

Burrow, Rufus, Jr., "The Personalism of John Wesley Edward Bowen," *The Journal of Negro History* 82 (1997): 244–56.

Dodd, Dorothy, "'Bishop' Pearce and the Reconstruction of Leon County," *Apalachee* 2 (1946): 5–12.

Dvorak, Katherine L., *An African-American Exodus: The Segregation of the Southern Churches* (1991).

Foster, John T., Jr., and Sarah W. Foster, "The Last Shall Be First: Northern Methodists in Reconstruction Jacksonville," *Florida Historical Quarterly* 70 (1992): 265–80.

Gravely, William B., "Hiram Revels Protests Racial Separation in the Methodist Episcopal Church," *Methodist History* 8 (1970): 13–20.

———— "James Lynch and the Black Christian Mission during Reconstruction," in David W. Wills and Richard Newman, ed., *Black Apostles at Home and Abroad: Afro-Americans and the Christian Mission from the Revolution to Reconstruction* (1982): 161–88.

Gravely, William B., ed., "A Black Methodist on Reconstruction in Mississippi: Three Letters by James Lynch in 1868–1969," *Methodist History* 11 (1973): 2–18.

Hall, Robert L., "Tallahassee's Black Churches, 1865–1885," *Florida Historical Quarterly* 58 (1979): 185–96.

———— "'Yonder Come Day': Religious Aspects of the Transition from Slavery to Freedom in Florida," *Florida Historical Quarterly* 65 (1987): 411–32.

Harvey, Paul, *Redeeming the South: Religious Cultures and Racial Identities among Southern Baptists, 1865–1925* (1997).

Hayden, J. Carleton, "After the War: The Mission and Growth of the Episcopal Church among Blacks in the South, 1865–1877," *Historical Magazine of the Protestant Episcopal Church* 42 (1973): 403–28.

Hildebrand, Reginald Francis, *The Times Were Strange and Stirring: Methodist Preachers and the Crisis of Emancipation* (1995).

Montgomery, William E., *Under Their Own Vine and Fig Tree: The African-American Church in the South, 1865–1900* (1993).

Pearce, Larry Wesley, "The American Missionary Association and the Freedman's Bureau in Arkansas, 1866–1968," *Arkansas Historical Quarterly* 30 (1971): 242–59.

Redkey, Edwin S., ed., *Respect Black: The Writings and Speeches of Henry McNeal Turner* (1971).

Richardson, Joe M., *Christian Reconstruction: The American Missionary Association and Southern Blacks, 1861–1890* (1986).

———— "The Failure of the American Missionary Association to Expand Congregationalism among Southern Blacks," *Southern Studies* 18 (1979): 51–73.

Storey, John W., "Southern Baptists and the Racial Controversy in the Churches and Schools during Reconstruction," *Mississippi Quarterly* 31 (1978): 211–28.

Tripp, Steven E., "Race, Class, and Religion: Lynchburgh, Virginia's 'Great Revival of 1871,'" *Mid-America* 75 (1993): 5–21.

Walker, Clarence Earl, *A Rock in a Weary Land: The African Methodist Episcopal Church during the Civil War and Reconstruction* (1981).

Washington, James Melvin, *Frustrated Fellowship: The Black Baptist Quest for Social Power* (1986).

Williams, Gilbert Anthony, *The Christian Recorder, Newspaper of the African Methodist Episcopal Church: History of a Forum of Ideas, 1854–1902* (1996).

Zipf, Katin L., "'Among These American Heathens': Congregationalist Missionaries and African American Evangelicals during Reconstruction, 1965–1878," *North Carolina Historical Review* 75 (1997): 111–34.

19.9 THOUGHT AND EXPRESSION

19.9.1 Race, Gender, and Identity

Burton, Orville V., "African-American Status and Identity in a Postbellum Community: An Analysis of the Manuscript Census Returns," *Agricultural History* 72 (1998): 213–40.

Hansen, Karen V., "'No Kisses Is like Youres': An Erotic Friendship between Two African-American Women during the Mid-Nineteenth Century," *Gender and History* 7 (1995): 153–82.

Langston, John Mercer, *Freedom and Citizenship* (1883).

Oldfield, John, ed., *Civilization and Black Progress: Selected Writings of Alexander Crummell on the South* (1995).

Peterson, Carla L., *Doers of the Word: African-American Women Speakers and Writers in the North, 1830–1880* (1995).

Primus, Rebecca, *Beloved Sisters and Loving Friends: Letters from Rebecca Primus of Royal Oak, Maryland, and Addie Brown of Hartford*, ed. Farah Jasmine Griffin (1999).

Van Tassel, Emily F., "'Only the Law Would Rule between Us': Antimiscegenation, the Moral Economy of Dependency, and the Debate over Rights after the Civil War," *Chicago-Kent Law Review* 70 (1995): 873–926.

19.9.2 Emigrationism and Nationalism

Adeleke, Tunde, *Unafrican Americans: Nineteenth-Century Black Nationalists and the Civilizing Mission* (1998).

19.9.3 Language and Linguistics

Logue, Cal M., and Thurmon Garner, "Shift in the Rhetorical Status of Blacks after Freedom," *Southern Communication Journal* 54 (1948): 1–39.

19.9.4 Literature and Poetry

Yacovone, Donald, "Sacred Land Regained: Frances Ellen Watkins Harper and 'The Massachusetts Fifty-Fourth,' a Lost Poem," *Pennsylvania History* 62 (1995): 90–110.

19.9.5 Music and Performing Arts

Pike, Gustavus D., *The Jubilee Singers and Their Campaign for Twenty Thousand Dollars* (1872).

Ward, Andrew, *Dark Midnight When I Rise: The Story of the Jubilee Singers, Who Introduced the World to the Music of Black America* (2000).

19.10 EDUCATION

Anderson, James D., *The Education of Blacks in the South, 1860–1935* (1988).

——— "Philanthropy, the State, and the Development of Historically Black Public Colleges: The Case of Mississippi," *Minerva: A Review of Science, Learning, and Policy [London]* 35 (1997): 295–309.

Armstrong, M. F., and Helen W. Ludlow, *Hampton and Its Students* (1874).

Beck, Scott A. L., "Freedmen, Friends, Common Schools and Reconstruction," *Southern Friend* 17 (1995): 5–31.

Bell, John L., "Samuel Stanford Ashley: Carpetbagger and Educator," *North Carolina Historical Review* 72 (1995): 456–83.

Blassingame, John W., "The Union Army As an Educational Institution for Negroes," *Journal of Negro Education* 34 (1965): 152–59.

Bond, Horace Mann, *Negro Education in Alabama: A Study in Cotton and Steel* (1939).

Brady, Patricia, "Trials and Tribulations: American Missionary Association Teachers and Black Education in Occupied New Orleans, 1863–1864," *Louisiana History* 31 (1990): 5–20.

Brown, Elizabeth G., "The Intitial Admission of Negro Students to the University of Michigan," *Michigan Quarterly Review* 2 (1963): 233–36.

Brown, Titus, "Origins of African American Education in Macon, Georgia, 1865–1866," *Journal of Southwest Georgia History* 11 (1996): 43–59.

Brown, Willis L., and Janie M. McNeal-Brown, "Langston University," *Chronicles of Oklahoma* 74 (1996): 30–49.

Browne, Joseph L., "'The Expenses Are Borne by Parents': Freedmen's Schools in Southern Maryland, 1865–1870," *Maryland Historical Magazine* 86 (1991): 407–22.

Butchart, Ronald E., *Northern Schools, Southern Blacks, and Reconstruction: Freedmen's Education, 1862–1875* (1980).

———— "'We Best Can Instruct Our Own People': New York African Americans in the Freedmen's Schools, 1861–1875," *Afro-Americans in New York Life and History* 12 (1988): 27–49.

Chang, Perry, "'Angels of Peace in a Smitten Land': The Northern Teachers' Crusade in the Reconstruction South Reconsidered," *Southern Historian* 16 (1995): 26–45.

Christensen, Lawrence O., "Schools for Blacks: J. Milton Turner," *Missouri Historical Review* 76 (1982): 121–35.

Coppin, Fanny Jackson, *Reminiscences of School Life and Hints on Teaching* (1913).

Deboer, Clara Merritt, *His Truth Is Marching On: African Americans Who Taught the Freedmen for the American Missionary Association, 1861–1877* (1995).

Dillard, Irving, "James Milton Turner: A Little Known Benefactor of His People," *Journal of Negro History* 19 (1934): 372–411.

Drago, Edmund L., *Initiative, Paternalism and Race Relations: Charleston's Avery Normal Institute* (1990).

Engs, Robert Francis, *Freedom's First Generation: Black Hampton, Virginia, 1861–1890* (1979).

Green, William D., "Race and Segregation in St. Paul's Public Schools, 1846–1869," *Minnesota History* 55 (1996–97): 138–49.

Gutman, Herbert G., "Schools for Freedom: The Post-Emancipation Origins of Afro-American Education," Ira Berlin, ed., *Power and Culture: Essays on the American Working Class* (1987): 260–97.

Holland, Antonio F., and Gary R. Kremer, ed., "Some Aspects of Black Education in Reconstruction Missouri: An Address by Richard B. Foster," *Missouri Historical Review* 70 (1976): 184–198.

Holland, Rupert Sargent, ed., *Letters and Diary of Laura M. Towne: Written from the Sea Islands of South Carolina, 1862–1884* (1912).

Hornsby, Alton, Jr., "The Freedmen's Bureau Schools in Texas, 1865–1870," *Southwestern Historical Quarterly* 76 (1973): 397–417.

Huddle, Mark A., "To Educate a Race: The Making of the First State Colored Normal School, Fayetteville, North Carolina, 1865–1877," *North Carolina Historical Review* 74 (1997): 135–60.

Jacoway, Elizabeth, *Yankee Missionaries in the South: The Penn School Experiment* (1980).

Johnson, Kenneth R., "Legrand Winfield Perce: A Mississippi Carpetbagger and the Fight for Federal Aid to Education," *Journal of Mississippi History* 34 (1972): 331–56.

Johnson, Washington B., "A Black Teacher and Her School in Reconstruction Darien: The Correspondence of Hettie Sabattie and J. Murray Hoag, 1868–1869," *Georgia Historical Quarterly* 75 (1991): 90–105.

Jones, Jacqueline, *Soldiers of Light and Love: Northern Teachers and Georgia Blacks, 1865–1873* (1980).

Kennan, Clara B., "The First Negro Teacher in Little Rock," *Arkansas Historical Quarterly* 9 (1950): 194–204.

Lewis, Ronald L., "Reverend T. G. Steward and the Education of Blacks in Reconstruction Delaware," *Delaware History* 19 (1981): 156–78.

McGehee, C. Stuart, "E. O. Tade, Freedmen's Education, and the Failure of Reconstruction in Tennessee," *Tennessee Historical Quarterly* 43 (1984): 376–89.

Messner, William F., "Black Education in Louisiana, 1863–1865," *Civil War History* 22 (1976): 41–59.

Mills, Joseph A., "Motives and Behaviors of Northern Teachers in the South during Reconstruction," *Negro History Bulletin* 42 (1979): 7–9, 17.

Moneyhon, Carl H., "Public Education and Texas Reconstruction Politics, 1871–1874," *Southwestern Historical Quarterly* 92 (1989): 393–416.

Morris, Robert Charles, *Reading, 'Riting, and Reconstruction: The Education of Freedmen in the South, 1861–1870* (1981).

Myers, John B., "The Education of the Alabama Freedmen during Presidential Reconstruction, 1865–1867," *Journal of Negro Education* 30 (1971): 163–76.

Nichols, Guerdon D., "Breaking the Color Barrier at the University of Arkansas," *Arkansas Historical Quarterly* 27 (1968): 3–21.

Pearson, Elizabeth Ware, ed., *Letters From Port Royal: Written at the Time of the Civil War* (1906).

Phillips, Paul D., "Education of Blacks in Tennessee during Reconstruction, 1865–1870," *Tennessee Historical Quarterly* 46 (1987): 98–109.

Rabinowitz, Howard N., "Half a Loaf: The Shift from White to Black Teachers in the Negro Schools of the Urban South, 1865–1890," *Journal of Southern History* 40 (1974): 565–94.

Reilly, Wayne E., ed., *Sarah Jane Foster, Teacher of the Freedmen: A Diary and Letters* (1990).

Richardson, Joe M., "Fisk University: The First Critical Years," *Tennessee Historical Quarterly* 29 (1970): 24–41.

———— "Francis L. Cardozo: Black Educator during Reconstruction," *Journal Negro Education* 48 (1979): 73–83.

Richardson, Joe M., ed., "'We Are Truly Doing Missionary Work': Letters from American Missionary Association Teachers in Florida, 1864–1874," *Florida Historical Quarterly* 54 (1975): 178–95.

Rosen, F. Bruce, "The Influence of the Peabody Fund on Education in Reconstruction Florida," *Florida Historical Quarterly* 55 (1977): 310–20.

Rothrock, Thomas, "Joseph Carter Corbin and Negro Education in the University of Arkansas," *Arkansas Historical Quarterly* 30 (1971): 277–314.

Sherer, Robert G., *Subordination or Liberation? The Development and Conflicting Theories of Black Education in Nineteenth Century Alabama* (1977).

Small, Sandra E., "The Yankee Schoolmarm in Freedmen's Schools: An Analysis of Attitudes," *Journal of Southern History* 45 (1979): 381–402.

Sparks, Randy J., "'The White People's Arms Are Longer Than Ours': Blacks, Education, and the American Missionary Association in Reconstruction Mississippi," *Journal of Mississippi History* 54 (1992): 1–27.

Spivey, Donald, *Schooling for the New Slavery: Black Industrial Education, 1868–1915* (1978).

Swint, Henry L., ed., *Dear Ones at Home: Letters from Contraband Camps* (1966).

———— *The Northern Teacher in the South, 1862–1870* (1941).

———— "Reports from Educational Agents of the Freedmen's Bureau in Tennessee, 1865–1870," *Tennessee Historical Quarterly* 1 (1942): 51–80, 152–70.

Vaughn, William Preston, *Schools for All: The Blacks and Public Education in the South, 1865–1877* (1974).

West, Earle H., "The Harris Brothers: Black Northern Teachers in the Reconstruction South," *Journal Negro Education* 48 (1979): 126–38.

White, Kenneth B., "The Alabama Freedmen's Bureau and Black Education: The Myth of Opportunity," *Alabama Review* 34 (1981): 107–24.

Whitener, Daniel Jay, "Public Education in North Carolina during Reconstruction, 1865–1876," in Fletcher Melvin Green, ed., *Essays in Southern History* (1949): 67–90.

Williams, Frank B., "John Eaton, Jr.: Editor, Politician, and School Administrator, 1865–1870," *Tennessee Historical Quarterly* 10 (1951): 291–319.

Wilson, Keith, "Education As a Vehicle of Racial Control: Major General N.P. Banks in Louisiana, 1863–1864," *Journal of Negro Education* 50 (1981): 156–70.

19.11   WORK AND ENTREPRENEURIAL ACTIVITY

Alston, Lee J., and Kyle D. Kauffman, "Up, Down, and Off the Agricultural Ladder: New Evidence and Implications of Agricultural Mobility for Blacks in the Postbellum South," *Agricultural History* 72 (1998): 263–79.

Arnesen, Eric, *Waterfront Workers of New Orleans: Race, Class and Politics, 1863–1923*(1991).

Berlin, Ira, "The Terrain of Freedom: The Struggle over the Meaning of Free Labor in the U.S. South," *History Workshop Journal* 22 (1986): 108–30.

Berlin, Ira, Thavolia Glymph, Steven F. Miller, Joseph P. Reidy, Leslie S. Rowland, and Julie Saville, ed., *The Wartime Genesis of Free Labor: The Lower South*, Series I, Vol. 3 of *Freedom: A Documentary History of Emancipation, 1861–1867* (1990).

Berlin, Ira, Steven F. Miller, Joseph P. Reidy, and Leslie S. Rowland, ed., *The Wartime Genesis of Free Labor: The Upper South*, Series I, Vol. 2 of *Freedom: A Documentary History of Emancipation, 1861–1867* (1993).

Bigelow, Martha M., "Plantation Lessee Problems in 1864," *Journal of Southern History* 27 (1961): 354–67.

Billings, Dwight B., Jr., *Planters and the Making of a 'New South': Class, Politics, and Development in North Carolina, 1865–1900* (1979).

Bleser, Carol K. Rothrock, *The Promised Land: The History of the South Carolina Land Commission, 1869–1890* (1969).

Bloch, H. D., "The New York City Negro and Occupational Eviction, 1860–1910," *International Review of Social History* 5 (1960): 26–38.

Bonekemper, Edward, III, "Negro Ownership of Real Property in Hampton and Elizabeth City County, Virginia, 1860–1870," *Journal of Negro History* 55 (1970): 165–81.

Cimbala, Paul A., "The Freedmen's Bureau, the Freedmen, and Sherman's Grant in Reconstruction Georgia, 1865–1867," *Journal of Southern History* 55 (1989): 597–632.

———— "The 'Talisman Power': Davis Tillson, the Freedmen's Bureau, and Free Labor in Reconstruction Georgia, 1865–1866," *Civil War History* 28 (1982): 153–71.

Clifton, James M., "A Half-Century of a Georgia Rice Plantation," *North Carolina Historical Review* 47 (1970): 388–415.

———— "Twilight Comes to the Rice Kingdom: Postbellum Rice Culture on the South Atlantic Coast," *Georgia Historical Quarterly* 62 (1978): 146–54.

Coclanis, Peter A., and J. C. Marlow, "Inland Rice Production in the South Atlantic States: A Picture in Black and White," *Agricultural History* 72 (1998): 197–212.

Cohen, William, "Black Immobility and Free Labor: The Freedmen's Bureau and the Relocation of Black Labor, 1865–1868," *Civil War History* 30 (1984): 221–34.

———— "Negro Involuntary Servitude in the South, 1865–1940: A Preliminary Analysis," *Journal of Southern History* 42 (1976): 31–60.

Cohen-Lack, Nancy, "A Struggle for Sovereignty: National Consolidation, Emancipation, and Free Labor in Texas, 1865," *Journal of Southern History* 58 (1992): 57–98.

Cox, LaWanda, "The Promise of Land for the Freedmen," *Mississippi Valley Historical Review* 45 (1958): 413–40.

Currie, James T., *Enclave: Vicksburg and Her Plantations, 1863–1870*(1980).

Daniel, Pete, "The Metamorphosis of Slavery, 1865–1900," *Journal of American History* 66 (1979): 88–99.

Davis, Ronald L. F., *Good and Faithful Labor: From Slavery to Sharecropping in the Natchez District, 1860–1890* (1982).

Eckert, Edward K., "Contract Labor in Florida during Reconstruction," *Florida Historical Quarterly* 47 (1968): 34–50.

Ellis, L. Tuffley, "The Revolutionizing of the Texas Cotton Trade, 1865–1885," *Southwestern Historical Quarterly* 73 (1970): 478–508.

Ford, Lacy K., "Rednecks and Merchants: Economic Development and Social Tensions in the South Carolina Upcountry, 1865–1900," *Journal of American History* 71 (1984): 294–318.

Fuke, Richard P., "Planters, Apprenticeship, and Forced Labor: The Black Family under Pressure in Post-Emancipation Maryland," *Agricultural History* 62 (1988): 57–74.

Gates, Paul W., "Federal Land Policy in the South, 1866–1888," *Journal of Southern History* 6 (1940): 303–30.

Glymph, Thavolia, and John J. Kushma, ed., *Essays on the Postbellum Southern Economy* (1985).

Gottlieb, Manuel, "The Land Question in Georgia during Reconstruction," *Science and Society* 3 (1939): 356–88.

Grim, Valerie, "African-American Landlords in the Rural South, 1870–1950: A Profile," *Agricultural History* 72 (1998): 399–416.

Gutman, Herbert G., "Reconstruction in Ohio: Negroes in the Hocking Valley Coal Mines in 1873 and 1874," *Labor History* 3 (1962): 243–64.

Hermann, Janet Sharp, *The Pursuit of a Dream* (1981).

Higgs, Robert, *Competition and Coercion: Blacks in the American Economy, 1865–1914* (1977).

Hine, William C., "Black Organized Labor in Reconstruction Charleston," *Labor History* 25 (1984): 504–17.

Holt, Sharon Ann, "Making Freedom Pay: Freedpeople Working for Themselves, North Carolina, 1865–1900," *Journal of Southern History* 60 (1994): 229–62.

Humphrey, George D., "The Failure of the Mississippi Freedmen's Bureau in Black Labor Relations, 1865–1867," *Journal of Mississippi History* 45 (1983): 23–27.

Hunter, Tera W., *To 'Joy My Freedom: Southern Black Women's Lives and Labors after the Civil War* (1997).

Jaynes, Gerald David, *Branches without Roots: Genesis of the Black Working Class in the American South, 1862–1882* (1986).

Kenzer, Robert C., "The Black Businessman in the Postwar South: North Carolina, 1865–1880," *Business History Review* 63 (1989): 61–87.

———— "Black Businessmen in Post-Civil War Tennessee," *Journal of East Tennessee History* 66 (1994): 59–80.

———— "Credit Ratings of Georgia Black Businessmen, 1865–1880," *Georgia Historical Quarterly* 79 (1995): 425–40.

———— *Enterprising Southerners: Black Economic Success in North Carolina, 1865–1915* (1997).

King, J. Crawford, "The Closing of the Southern Range: An Exploratory Study," *Journal of Southern History* 48 (1982): 53–70.

Krebs, Sylvia H., "John Chinaman and Reconstruction Alabama: The Debate and the Experience," *Southern Studies* 21 (1982): 369–83.

———— "Will the Freedmen Work? White Alabamans Adjust to Free Black Labor," *Alabama Historical Quarterly* 36 (1974): 151–63.

Lanza, Michael L., *Agrarianism and Reconstruction Politics: The Southern Homestead Act* (1990).

Leashore, Bogart R., "Black Female Workers: Live-in Domestics in Detroit, Michigan, 1860–1880," *Phylon* 45 (1984): 111–20.

Lerner, Eugene, "Southern Output and Agricultural Income, 1860–1880," *Agricultural History* 33 (1959): 117–25.

Loring, Francis William, and C. F. Atkinson, *Cotton Culture and the South, Considered With Reference to Emigration* (1869).

Lovett, Bobby L., "Document: Some 1871 Accounts for the Little Rock, Arkansas, Freedmen's Saving and Trust Company," *Journal of Negro History* 66 (1981–1982): 326–28.

Matison, Sumner E., "The Labor Movement and the Negro during Reconstruction," *Journal of Negro History* 33 (1948): 426–68.

May, J. Thomas, "Continuity and Change in the Labor Program of the Union Army and the Freedmen's Bureau," *Civil War History* 17 (1971): 245–54.

McDonald, Forrest and Grady McWhiney, "The South from Self-Sufficiency to Peonage: An Interpretation," *American History Review* 85 (1980): 1095–118.

McKenzie, Robert T., "Freedmen and the Soil in the Upper South: The Reorganization of Tennessee Agriculture, 1865–1880," *Journal of Southern History* 59 (1993): 63–84.

———— "Postbellum Tenancy in Fayette County, Tennessee: Its Implications for Economic Development and Persistent Black Poverty," *Agricultural History* 61 (1987): 16–33.

McLeod, Jonathan W., *Workers and Workplace Dynamics in Reconstruction-Era Atlanta: A Case Study* (1989).

Medford, Edna G., "Land and Labor: The Quest for Black Economic Independence on Virginia's Lower Peninsula, 1865–1880," *Virginia Magazine of History and Biography* 100 (1992): 567–82.

Messner, William F., *Freedmen and the Ideology of Free Labor: Louisiana, 1862–1865* (1978).

Mollison, Irvin C., "Negro Lawyers in Mississippi," *Journal of Negro History* 15 (1930): 38–71.

Moneyhon, Carl H., "From Slave to Free Labor: The Federal Plantation Experiment in Arkansas," *Arkansas Historical Quarterly* 53 (1994): 137–60.

Morgan, Lynda J., *Emancipation in Virginia's Tobacco Belt, 1850–1870* (1992).

Novak, Daniel A., *The Wheel of Servitude: Black Forced Labor after Slavery* (1978).

Oldfield, J. R., "A High and Honorable Calling: Black Lawyers in South Carolina, 1868–1915," *Journal of American Studies* 23 (1989): 395–406.

Osborn, George C., "The Life of a Southern Plantation Owner during Reconstruction As Revealed in the Clay Sharkey Papers," *Journal of Mississippi History* 6 (1944): 103–12.

Osthaus, Carl R., *Freedmen, Philanthropy, and Fraud: A History of the Freedman's Savings Bank* (1976).

Otto, John Solomon, *Southern Agriculture during the Civil War Era, 1860–1880* (1994).

Oubre, Claude F., *Forty Acres and a Mule: The Freedmen's Bureau and Black Landownership* (1978).

Pope, Christie Farnham, "Southern Homesteads for Negroes," *Agricultural History* 44 (1970): 201–12.

Porter, Kenneth O., "Negro Labor in the Western Cattle Industry, 1866–1900," *Labor History* 10 (1969): 346–74.

Powell, Lawrence N., "The American Land Company and Agency: John A. Andrew and the Northernization of the South," *Civil War History* 21 (1975): 293–308.

———— *New Masters: Northern Planters during the Civil War and Reconstruction* (1980).

Prichard, Walter, "The Effects of the Civil War on the Louisiana Sugar Industry," *Journal of Southern History* 5 (1939): 315–32.

Rachleff, Peter J., *Black Labor in the South: Richmond, Virginia, 1865–1890* (1984).

Ransom, Roger L., and Richard Sutch, *One Kind of Freedom: The Economic Consequences of Emancipation* (1977).

Reidy, Joseph Patrick, *From Slavery to Agrarian Capitalism in the Cotton Plantation South: Central Georgia, 1800–1880* (1992).

Rodrigue, John C., "'The Great Law of Demand and Supply': The Contest over Wages in Louisiana's Sugar Region, 1870–1880," *Agricultural History* 72 (1998): 159–82.

Roland, Charles Pierce, *Louisiana Sugar Plantations during the American Civil War* (1957).

Ross, Steven J., "Free Soil, Free Labor, Free Men: John Eaton and the Davis Bend Experiment," *Journal of Southern History* 44 (1978): 213–32.

Saville, Julie, "Grassroots Reconstruction: Agricultural Labour and Collective Action in South Carolina, 1860–1868," *Slavery and Abolition* 12 (1991): 173–82.

———— *The Work of Reconstruction: From Slave to Wage Laborer in South Carolina, 1860–1870* (1994).

Schmidt, James D., *Free to Work: Labor Law, Emancipation, and Reconstruction, 1815–1880* (1998).

Schwalm, Leslie A., "'Sweet Dreams of Freedom': Freedwomen's Reconstruction of Life and Labor in Lowcountry South Carolina," *Journal of Women's History* 9 (1997): 9–38.

Schweninger, Loren, *Black Property Owners in the South, 1790–1915* (1990).

Shifflett, Crandall A., *Patronage and Poverty in the Tobacco South: Louisa County, Virginia, 1860–1900* (1982).

Shlomowitz, Ralph, "'Bound' or 'Free'? Black Labor in Cotton and Sugarcane Farming, 1865–1880," *Journal of Southern History* 50 (1984): 569–96.

———— "The Origins of Southern Sharecropping," *Agricultural History* 53 (1979): 557–75.

———— "The Squad System on Postbellum Cotton Plantations," in Orville Vernon Burton and Robert C. McMath, Jr., ed., *Toward a New South? Studies in Post-Civil War Southern Communities* (1982): 265–80.

Shofner, Jerrell H., "Militant Negro Laborers in Reconstruction Florida," *Journal of Southern History* 39 (1973): 397–408.

———— "Negro Laborers and the Forest Industries in Reconstruction Florida," *Journal of Forest History* 19 (1975): 180–91.

Simkins, Francis B., "The Problems of South Carolina Agriculture after the Civil War," *North Carolina Historical Review* 7 (1930): 46–77.

Sitterson, Joseph Carlyle, *Sugar Country* (1953).

———— "The Transition from Slave to Free Economy on the William J. Minor Plantations," *Agricultural History* 17 (1943): 216–24.

Smallwood, James M., "Perpetuation of Caste: Black Agricultural Workers in Reconstruction Texas," *Mid-America* 61 (1979): 5–23.

Sowell, David, "Racial Patterns of Labor in Postbellum Florida: Gainesville, 1870–1900," *Florida Historical Quarterly* 63 (1985): 434–44.

St. Clair, Kenneth E., "Debtor Relief in North Carolina during Reconstruction," *North Carolina Historical Review* 18 (1941): 215–35.

Stanley, Amy Dru, *From Bondage to Contract: Wage Labor, Marriage, and the Market in the Age of Slave Emancipation* (1998).

Strickland, John Scott, "'No More Mud Work': The Struggle for the Control of Labor and Production in Low Country South Carolina, 1863–1880," in Walter J. Fraser, Jr. and Winfred B. Moore, Jr., ed., *The Southern Enigma: Essays on Race, Class, and Folk Culture* (1983): 43–62.

Temin, Peter, "Patterns of Cotton Agriculture in Postbellum Georgia," *Journal of Economic History* 43 (1983): 661–74.

Thomas, Bettye C., "A Nineteenth Century Black Operated Shipyard, 1866–1884: Reflections upon Its Inception and Ownership," *Journal of Negro History* 59 (1974): 1–12.

Wagstaff, Thomas, "Call Your Old Master—'Master': Southern Political Leaders and Negro Labor during Presidential Reconstruction," *Labor History* 10 (1969): 323–45.

Wayne, Michael, *The Reshaping of Plantation Society: The Natchez District, 1860–1880* (1983).

Weiman, David F., "The Economic Emancipation of the Non-Slaveholding Class: Upcountry Farmers in the Georgia Cotton Economy," *Journal of Economic History* 45 (1985): 71–93.

Westwood, Howard C., "Sherman Marched—and Proclaimed 'Land for the Landless,'" *South Carolina Historical Magazine* 85 (1984): 33–50.

Wiener, Jonathan M., *Social Origins of the New South: Alabama, 1860–1885* (1978).

Woodman, Harold D., *King Cotton and His Retainers: Financing and Marketing the Cotton Crop of the South, 1800–1925* (1968).

———— *New South, New Law: The Legal Foundations of Credit and Labor Relations in the Postbellum Agricultural South* (1995).

———— "Postbellum Social Change and Its Effects on Marketing the South's Cotton Crop," *Agricultural History* 56 (1982): 215–30.

19.12 MEDICINE AND HEALTH

Cadwallader, D. E., and F. J. Wilson, "Folklore Medicine among Georgia's Piedmont Negroes after the Civil War," *Georgia Historical Quarterly* 49 (1965): 217–27.

Finley, Randy, "In War's Wake: Health Care and Arkansas Freedmen, 1863–1868," *Arkansas Historical Quarterly* 51 (1992): 135–63.

Foster, Gaines M., "The Limitations of Federal Health Care for Freedmen, 1862–1868," *Journal of Southern History* 48 (1982): 349–72.

Hasson, Gail S., "Health and Welfare of Freedmen in Reconstruction Alabama," *Alabama Review* 35 (1982): 94–110.

Legan, Marshall Scott, "Disease and the Freedmen in Mississippi during Reconstruction," *Journal of the History of Medicine and Applied Sciences* 28 (1973): 257–67.

Savitt, Todd L., "Politics in Medicine: The Georgia Freedmen's Bureau and the Organization of Health Care, 1865–1866," *Civil War History* 28 (1982): 45–64.

19.13   STUDIES IN FOREIGN LANGUAGES

Chen, Haihong, "Nei Zhan Hou Mei Guo Hei Ren Jiao Yu Shi Ye De Fa Zhan" [The Development of Education for Black Americans after the Civil War], *Shandong Shida Xuebao* 4 (1983): 16–21. In Chinese.

———— "Nei Zhan Hou Mei Guo Hei Ren Zheng Qu Xuan Ju Quan De Dou Zheng" [Black Americans' Struggle for Suffrage after the Civil War], *Shandong Shida Xuebao* 1 (1985): 17–22. In Chinese.

Gennaro Lerda, Valeria, "Trasformazione o scomparsa del sistema della piantagione« nel sud postbellico: recenti interpretazioni della storiografia americana" [Transformation or Disappearance of the 'Plantation System' in the Postbellum South: Recent Interpretations in American Historiography], *RSA Journal* 2 (1991): 21–35. In Italian.

Halle, Ernst von, *Baumwollproduktion und Pflanzungswirtschaft in den Nordamerikanischen Südstaaten: Sezessionskrieg und Rekonstruktion* [Cotton Production and Plantation Economy in the North American Southern States: Civil War and Reconstruction] (1906). In German.

Honda, Sozo, *Nanboku Sensô Saiken no Jidai* [The Civil War and Reconstruction Considered As a Black Liberation Movement] (1974). In Japanese.

Liu, Zuochang, "Mei Guo Nan Fang Hei Ren De Tu Di Wen Ti: Mei Guo Hei Ren Jie Fang De Guang Jian Wen Ti" [The Land Issue for Black Americans in the South: A Key Issue to the Liberation of Black Americans], *Shi Xue Yue Kan* 4 (1965): 8–13. In Chinese.

Omori, Kazuteru, "Jinshu Byôdô to Nôryoku Shugi no Sôkatsu: Nanboku Sensô go no Masachûsettsu shu ni okeru Kôminken-hô no Seitei to Kokujin 'Erîto'" [Meritocracy and Racial Equality: Civil Rights Legislation and Black 'Elites' in Post-Bellum Boston], *The American Review* 32 (1998): 57–74. In Japanese.

Serment, Jacques Henri, *La Question des Nègres et la reconstruction du sud aux États-Unis* [The Question of Negroes and Southern Reconstruction in the United States] (3d ed., 1983). In French.

Shi, Meiwen, "Nan Bei Zhan Zheng Hou De Mei Guo Hei Ren" [Black Americans after the Civil War], *Wuhan Daxue Xuebao* 4 (1978): 56–70. In Chinese.

Tsujiuchi, Makoto, *Amerika no Dorei-sei to Jiyû-shugi* [Liberalism and American Slavery] (1997). In Japanese.

———— "'Dorei-nushi-Kokujin Dorei' Kankei no Saihen Seiri" [Refashioning of the Master-Slave Relationship: The Labor Policy of the Freedmen's Bureau], in Sozo Honda, ed., *Perspectives in American Social History: Issues of Race and Ethnicity* (1989): 56–87. In Japanese.

———— "Kaihômin Ginkô no Hasan" [The Bankruptcy of the Freedmen's Bank: An Inquiry into the Reconstruction of the South], *Journal of Historical Studies* 533 (October 1984): 1–17. In Japanese.

Wang, Xi, "Hei Ren Pu Xuan Quan He Mei Guo Nei Zhan Xian Fa Xiu Zheng An De Zhi Ding, 1860–1870" [Black Suffrage and the Making of the Civil War Constitutional Amendments, 1860–1870], *Shi Jie Li Shi* 6 (1990): 67–87, 118. In Chinese.

Watanabe, Shinji, *Furontia to Kokujin Jichitai no Kensetsu* [The Frontier and the Development of Black Towns] (1989). In Japanese.

20   *1877–1915*

Leon F. Litwack

20.1   GENERAL STUDIES

American Academy of Political and Social Science, *The Negro's Progress in Fifty Years* (1913).

Ayers, Edward L., *The Promise of the New South: Life after Reconstruction* (1992).

Bacote, Clarence A., "Some Aspects of Negro Life in Georgia, 1880–1908," *Journal of Negro History* 43 (1958): 186–213.

Baker, Ray Stannard, *Following the Color Line: American Negro Citizenship in the Progressive Era* (1908).

Billings, Dwight B., *Planters and the Making of a "New South": Class, Politics, and Development in North Carolina, 1865–1900* (1979).

Clowes, W. Laird, *Black America: A Study of the Ex-Slave and His Late Master* (1891).

Dittmer, John, *Black Georgia in the Progressive Era, 1900–1920* (1977).

Finley, Randy, "Black Arkansans and World War One," *Arkansas Historical Quarterly* 49 (1990): 249–77.

Fishel, Leslie H., Jr., "Repercussions of Reconstruction: The Northern Negro, 1870–1883," *Civil War History* 14 (1968): 325–45.

Foner, Philip S., and George E. Walker, ed., *Proceedings of the Black National and State Conventions, 1865–1900* (1986).

Gaines, Kevin K., *Uplifting the Race: Black Leadership, Politics, and Culture in the Twentieth Century* (1996).

Gavins, Raymond, "The Meaning of Freedom: Black North Carolina in the Nadir, 1880–1900," in Jeffrey J. Crow, Paul D. Escott, and Charles L. Flynn, Jr., ed., *Race, Class, and Politics in Southern History: Essays in Honor of Robert F. Durden* (1989).

Gilmore, Glenda Elizabeth, *Gender and Jim Crow: Women and the Politics of White Supremacy in North Carolina, 1896–1920* (1996).

Gordon, Fon Louise, *Caste and Class: The Black Experience in Arkansas, 1880–1920* (1995).

Grant, L. Donald, *The Way It Was in the South: The Black Experience in Georgia* (1993).

Hornsby, Alton, comp., *In the Cage: Eyewitness Accounts of the Freed Negro in Southern Society, 1877–1929* (1971).

Howard, Victor B., *Black Liberation in Kentucky: Emancipation and Freedom, 1862–1884* (1983).

Hunter, Tera W., *To 'Joy My Freedom: Southern Black Women's Lives and Labors after the Civil War* (1997).

Johnston, Harry H., *The Negro in the New World* (1910).

Kirwan, Albert D., *Revolt of the Rednecks: Mississippi Politics, 1876–1925* (1951).

Lamon, Lester C., *Black Tennesseans, 1900–1930* (1977).

Litwack, Leon F., *Trouble in Mind: Black Southerners in the Age of Jim Crow* (1998).

Logan, Frenise A., *The Negro in North Carolina, 1876–1894* (1964).

Logan, Rayford W., *The Negro in American Life and Thought: The Nadir, 1877–1901* (1954).

McMillen, Neil R., *Dark Journey: Black Mississippians in the Age of Jim Crow* (1989).

Mossell, Mrs. N. F., *The Work of the Afro-American Woman* (1988).

Muraskin, William A., *Middle-Class Blacks in a White Society: Prince Hall Freemasonry in White America* (1975).

Neverdon-Morton, Cynthia, *Afro-American Women of the South and the Advancement of the Race, 1895–1925* (1989).

Nieman, Donald G., ed., *African American Life in the Post-Emancipation South, 1861–1900* (12 vols., 1994).

Rabinowitz, Howard N., *The First New South, 1865–1920* (1992).

Rice, Lawrence D., *The Negro in Texas, 1874–1900* (1971).

Tindall, George B., *South Carolina Negroes, 1877–1900* (1952).

Wharton, Vernon L., *The Negro in Mississippi, 1865–1890* (1947).

Wiener, Jonathan M., *Social Origins of the New South: Alabama, 1865–1885* (1978).

Woodward, C. Vann, *Origins of the New South, 1877–1913* (1951).

20.2 HISTORIOGRAPHY

Bacote, Clarence A., "Negro Proscriptions, Protests, and Proposed Solutions in Georgia, 1880–1908," *Journal of Southern History* 25 (1959): 471–98.

Bruce, Dickson D., Jr., "Ancient Africa and the Early Black American Historians, 1883–1915," *American Quarterly* 36 (1984): 684–99.

Carter, Dan T., "Moonlight, Magnolias, and Collard Greens: Black History and the New Romanticism," *Reviews in American History* 5 (1977): 167–73.

Maffly-Kipp, Laurie F., "Mapping the World, Mapping the Race: The Negro Race History, 1874–1915," *Church History* 64 (1995): 610–26.

Rabinowitz, Howard N., "More Than the Woodward Thesis: Assessing the Strange Career of Jim Crow," *Journal of American History* 75 (1988): 842–56.

Woodward, C. Vann, "The Negro in American Life, 1865–1918," in John A. Garraty, ed., *Interpreting American History: Conversations with Historians* (1970): 43–68.

——— "Race and Rebellion," in C. Vann Woodward, *Thinking Back: The Perils of Writing History* (1986): 81–99.

——— "The Strange Career of a Historical Controversy," in C. Vann Woodward, *American Counterpoint: Slavery and Racism in the North-South Dialogue* (1971): 234–60.

20.3 SECONDARY SOURCES ON NEWSPAPERS AND PERIODICALS

Allman, Jean M., and David R. Roediger, "The Early Editorial Career of Timothy Thomas Fortune: Class, Nationalism and Consciousness of Africa," *Afro-Americans in New York Life and History* 6 (1982): 39–52.

Best, Wallace, "The *Chicago Defender* and the Realignment of Black Chicago," *Chicago History* 24 (1995): 4–21.

Blassingame, John W., "The Press and American Intervention in Haiti and the Dominican Republic, 1904–1920," *Caribbean Studies* 9 (1969): 27–43.

Brewer, James H., "Editorials from *The Damned*," *Journal of Southern History* 28 (1962): 225–33.

Crowder, Ralph L., "Frederick Douglass, Booker T. Washington, and John Edward Bruce: The Relationship of a Militant Black Journalist with the 'Father of Civil Rights' and the 'Wizard of Tuskegee,'" *Afro-Americans in New York Life and History* 22 (1998): 91–110.

Drago, Edmund L., "The Black Press and Populism, 1890–1896," *San Jose Studies* 1 (1975): 97–103.

Drake, Donald E., II, "Militancy in Fortune's *New York Age*," *Journal of Negro History* 55 (1970): 307–22.

Ellis, Mark, "America's Black Press, 1914–1918," *History Today* 41 (1991): 20–27.

Franklin, V. P., "W. E. B. Du Bois As Journalist," *Journal of Negro Education* 56 (1987): 240–44.

Gatewood, Willard B., Jr., "A Black Editor on American Imperialism: Edward E. Cooper of the *Colored American*, 1898–1901," *Mid-America* 57 (1975): 3–19.

———— "A Negro Editor on Imperialism: John Mitchell, 1898–1901," *Journalism Quarterly* 49 (1972): 43–50.

Harlan, Louis R., "Booker T. Washington and the *Voice of the Negro*, 1904–1907," *Journal of Southern History* 45 (1979): 45–62.

Hellwig, David J., "The Afro-American Press and Woodrow Wilson's Mexican Policy, 1913–1917," *Phylon* 48 (1987): 261–70.

———— "The Afro-American Press and United States Involvement in Cuba, 1902–1912," *Mid-America* 72 (1990): 135–45.

Honey, Michael, "One View of Black Life in the South during the 'Nadir': *The Richmond Planet*, 1885–1900," *Potomac Review* 21 (1981): 28–38.

Howard-Pitney, David, "Calvin Chase's *Washington Bee* and Black Middle-Class Ideology, 1882–1900," *Journalism Quarterly* 63 (1986): 89–97.

Johnson, Abby Arthur, and Ronald M. Johnson, "Away from Accommodation: Radical Editors and Protest Journalism, 1900–1910," *Journal of Negro History* 62 (1977): 325–38.

Jones, Allen W., "The Black Press in the 'New South': Jesse C. Duke's Struggle for Justice and Equality," *Journal of Negro History* 64 (1979): 215–28.

Klassen, Teresa C., and Owen V. Johnson, "Sharpening of the *Blade*: Black Consciousness in Kansas, 1892–1897," *Journalism Quarterly* 63 (1986): 298–304.

Marks, George P., ed., *The Black Press Views American Imperialism, 1898–1900* (1971).

Matthews, John M., "Black Newspapermen and the Black Community in Georgia, 1890–1930," *Georgia Historical Quarterly* 68 (1984): 356–81.

McMillen, Neil, "Black Journalism in Mississippi: The Jim Crow Years," *Journal of Mississippi History* 49 (1987): 129–38.

Meier, August, "Booker T. Washington and the Negro Press: With Special Reference to the *Colored American Magazine*," *The Journal of Negro History* 38 (1953): 67–90.

Olzak, Susan, and Elizabeth West, "Ethnic Conflict and the Rise and Fall of Ethnic Newspapers," *American Sociological Review* 56 (1991): 458–74.

Paz, D. G., "John Albert Williams and Black Journalism in Omaha, 1895–1929," *Midwest Review* 10 (1988): 14–32.

Penn, I. Garland, *The Afro-American Press and Its Editors* (1891).

Ross, Felicia G. Jones, "The Brownsville Affair and the Political Values of Cleveland Black Newspapers," *American Journalism* 12 (1995): 107–22.

Scribner, Christopher M., "Nashville Offers Opportunity: *The Nashville Globe* and Business As a Means of Uplift, 1907–1913," *Tennessee Historical Quarterly* 54 (1995): 54–67.

Slavens, George E., "The Missouri Negro Press, 1875–1920," *Missouri Historical Review* 64 (1970): 413–31.

Snorgrass, J. William, "The Black Press in the San Francisco Bay Area, 1865–1900," *California History* 60 (1981–82): 306–17.

Stovall, Mary E., "The *Chicago Defender* in the Progressive Era," *Illinois Historical Journal* 83 (1990): 159–72.

Suggs, Henry Lewis, "Black Strategy and Ideology in the Segregation Era: P. B. Young and the *Norfolk Journal and Guide*, 1910–1954," *Virginia Magazine of History and Biography* 91 (1983): 161–90.

———— *P.B. Young, Newspaperman: Race, Politics, and Journalism in the New South, 1910–1962* (1988).

Thompson, Julius E., *The Black Press in Mississippi, 1865–1985: A Directory* (1988).

Thornbrough, Emma Lou, "American Negro Newspapers, 1880–1914," *Business History Review* 40 (1966): 467–90.

Wade-Gayles, Gloria, "Black Women Journalists in the South, 1880–1905," in Darlene Clark Hine, ed., *Black Women in American History: From Colonial Times through the Nineteenth Century* (1990): 1409–24.

Williams, Gilbert A., *The* Christian Recorder, *Newspaper of the African Methodist Episcopal Church: History of a Forum of Ideas, 1854–1902* (1996).

Williams, Nudie E., "Black Newspapers and the Exodusters of 1879," *Kansas History* 8 (1985–86): 217–25.

——— "The Black Press in Oklahoma: The Formative Years, 1889–1907," *Chronicles of Oklahoma* 61 (1983): 308–19.

Wynne, Lewis N., "Brownsville: The Reaction of the Negro Press," *Phylon* 33 (1972): 153–60.

Yellin, Jean, "Du Bois' *Crisis* and Women's Suffrage," *Massachusetts Review* 14 (1973): 365–75.

20.4   RACE RELATIONS

20.4.1   Black/White Relations

Aldrich, Mark, "Progressive Economists and Scientific Racism: Walter Willcox and Black Americans, 1895–1910," *Phylon* 40 (1979): 1–14.

Bailey, Thomas P., *Race Orthodoxy in the South, and other Aspects of the Negro Question* (1914).

Baker, Ray Stannard, *Following the Color Line: American Negro Citizenship in the Progressive Era* (1908).

Baldwin, Brooke, "The Cakewalk: A Study in Stereotype and Reality," *Journal of Social History* 15 (1981): 205–18.

Berret, Anthony J., "Huckleberry Finn and the Minstrel Show," *American Studies* 27 (1986): 37–49.

Bickley, R. Bruce, Jr., *Joel Chandler Harris* (1978).

Bigham, John Alvin, ed., *Select Discussions of Race Problems* (1916).

Boime, Albert, "Blacks in Shark-Infested Waters: Visual Encodings of Racism in Copley and Homer," *Studies in American Art* 3 (1989): 18–47.

Boskin, Joseph, "The Life and Death of Sambo: Overview of an Historical Hang-Up," *Journal of Popular Culture* 4 (1971): 647–57.

——— *Sambo: The Rise and Demise of an American Jester* (1986).

Bruce, Philip A., *The Plantation Negro as a Freeman: Observations on His Character, Condition, and Prospects in Virginia* (1889).

Cable, George W., *The Negro Question* (1898).

Carroll, Charles, *"The Negro a Beast"; Or, "In the Image of God"* (1900).

Cartwright, Joseph H., *The Triumph of Jim Crow: Tennessee Race Relations in the 1880s* (1976).

Clayton, Bruce, *The Savage Ideal: Intolerance and Intellectual Leadership in the South, 1890–1914* (1972).

Cuban, Larry, "A Strategy for Racial Peace: Negro Leadership in Cleveland, 1900–1919," *Phylon* 28 (1967): 299–311.

Dethloff, Henry C., and Robert R. Jones, "Race Relations in Louisiana, 1877–1898," *Louisiana History* 9 (1968): 301–23.

Doherty, Herbert J., Jr., "Voices of Protest from the New South, 1875–1910," *Mississippi Valley Historical Review* 42 (1955): 45–66.

Donald, David Herbert, "A Generation of Defeat," in Walter J. Fraser, Jr., and Winfred B. Moore, Jr., ed., *From the Old South to the New: Essays on the Transitional South* (1981): 3–20.

Dormon, James H., "Shaping the Popular Image of Post-Reconstruction American Blacks: The 'Coon Song' Phenomenon of the Gilded Age," *American Quarterly* 40 (1988): 450–71.

Doyle, Bertram W., *The Etiquette of Race Relations in the South* (1937).

Dyer, Thomas G., *Theodore Roosevelt and the Idea of Race* (1980).

Evans, Arthur S., "The Relationship between Industrialization and White Hostility toward Blacks in Southern Cities, 1865–1910," *Urban Affairs Quarterly* 25 (1989): 322–41.

Evans, Maurice, *Black and White in the Southern States* (1915).

Fingerhut, Eugene R., "Tom Watson, Blacks, and Southern Reform," *Georgia Historical Quarterly* 60 (1976): 324–43.

Fishbein, Leslie, "Dress Rehearsal in Race Relations: Pre-World War I American Radicals and the Black Question," *Afro-Americans in New York Life and History* 6 (1982): 7–15.

Fredrickson, George M., *The Black Image in the White Mind: The Debate on Afro-American Character and Destiny, 1817–1914* (1971).

Friedman, Lawrence J., "The Search for Docility: Racial Thought in the White South, 1861–1917," *Phylon* 31 (1970): 313–23.

———— *The White Savage: Racial Fantasies in the Postbellum South* (1970).

Gallager, Brian, "Racist Ideology and Black Abnormality in 'The Birth of a Nation,'" *Phylon* 43 (1982): 68–76.

Gatewood, Willard B., Jr., "Arkansas Negroes in the 1890's: Documents," *Arkansas Historical Quarterly* 33 (1974): 293–325.

Gerber, David A., *Black Ohio and the Color Line, 1860–1915* (1976).

Giliomee, Hermann B., "The Malady of American Racism: A South African Perspective," *Canadian Review of American Studies* 5 (1974): 202–09.

Graves, John William, *Town and Country: Race Relations in an Urban-Rural Context: Arkansas, 1865–1905* (1990).

Gross, Theodore L., "Thomas Nelson Page: Creator of a Virginia Classic," *Georgia Review* 20 (1966): 338–51.

Guy-Sheftall, Beverly, *Daughters of Sorrow: Attitudes toward Black Women, 1880–1920* (1990).

Hart, Albert B., *The Southern South* (1910).

Havig, Alan, "Richard F. Outcault's 'Pore Lil' Mose': Variations on the Black Stereotype in American Comic Art," *Journal of American Culture* 11 (1988): 33–41.

Hayes, James R., "Sociology and Racism: An Analysis of the First Era of American Sociology," *Phylon* 34 (1973): 330–41.

Haygood, Atticus G., *Our Brother in Black: His Freedom and His Future* (1881).

Hodes, Martha, *White Women, Black Men: Illicit Sex in the Nineteenth-Century South* (1997).

Holmes, William F., *The White Chief: James Kimble Vardaman* (1970).

Janiewski, Dolores E., *Sisterhood Denied: Race, Gender, and Class in a New South Community* (1985).

Johnson, Guion G., "The Ideology of White Supremacy, 1876–1910," in Fletcher Melvin Green, ed., *Essays in Southern History* (1976): 124–56.

Kaplan, Sidney, "The Negro in the Art of Homer and Eakins," *Massachusetts Review* 7 (1966): 105–20.

Lamplugh, George R., "The Image of the Negro in Popular Magazine Fiction, 1875–1900," *Journal of Negro History* 57 (1972): 177–89.

Langhorne, Orra, *Southern Sketches from Virginia, 1881–1901* (1964).

Larson, Edward J., *Sex, Race, and Science: Eugenics in the Deep South* (1995).

Lemons, J. Stanley, "Black Stereotypes As Reflected in Popular Culture, 1880–1920," *American Quarterly* 29 (1977): 102–16.

Light, Kathleen, "Uncle Remus and the Folklorists," *Southern Literary Journal* 7 (1975): 88–104.

Lopez, Claira S., "James K. Vardaman and the Negro: The Foundation of Mississippi's Racial Policy," *Southern Quarterly* 3 (1965): 155–80.

Lorini, Alessandra, *Rituals of Race: American Public Culture and the Search for Racial Democracy* (1999).

Lowitt, Richard, "David M. Key Views the Legal and Political Status of the Negro in 1885," *Journal of Negro History* 54 (1969): 285–93.

Luker, Ralph E., *The Social Gospel in Black and White: American Racial Reform, 1885–1912* (1991).

Lumpkin, Katharine D., *The Making of a Southerner* (1981).

McPherson, James M., *The Abolitionist Legacy: From Reconstruction to the NAACP* (2d ed., 1995).

Mixon, Wayne, "The Ultimate Irrelevance of Race: Joel Chandler Harris and Uncle Remus in Their Time," *Journal of Southern History* 56 (1990): 457–80.

Morgan, Jo-Ann, "Mammy the Huckster: Selling the Old South for the New Century," *American Art* 9 (1995): 86–109.

Mumford, Kevin J., *Interzones: Black/White Sex Districts in Chicago and New York in the Early Twentieth Century* (1997).

Murphy, Edgar G., *The Basis of Ascendency* (1909).

Newby, I. A., *Jim Crow's Defense: Anti-Negro Thought in America, 1900–1930* (1965).

Nolen, Claude H., *The Negro's Image in the South: The Anatomy of White Supremacy* (1967).

Odum, Howard W., *Social and Mental Traits of the Negro* (1910).

Olsen, Otto H., "Albion W. Tourgee and Negro Militants of the 1890's: A Documentary Selection," *Science and Society* 28 (1964): 183–207.

—— *Carpetbagger's Crusade* (1965).

Paddon, Anna R., and Sally Turner, "African Americans and the World's Columbian Exposition," *Illinois Historical Journal* 88 (1995): 19–36.

Page, Thomas Nelson, *The Negro: The Southerner's Problem* (1904).

Parker, David B., "Bill Arp and Blacks: The Forgotten Letters," *Georgia Historical Quarterly* 67 (1983): 336–49.

Patterson, John, "From Yeoman to Beast: Images of Blackness in Caesar's Column," *American Studies* 12 (1971): 21–31.

Rainey, Kenneth T., "Race and Reunion in Nineteenth Century Reconciliation Drama," *American Theatrical Quarterly* 2 (1988): 155–69.

Reed, Ralph E., Jr., "Emory College and the Sledd Affair of 1902: A Case Study in Southern Honor and Racial Attitudes," *Georgia Historical Quarterly* 72 (1988): 463–92.

Riggio, Thomas P., "Uncle Tom Reconstructed: A Neglected Chapter in the History of a Book," *American Quarterly* 28 (1976): 56–70.

Rollo, Vera Foster, *The Black Experience in Maryland* (1980).

Rose, Willie Lee, *Race and Region in American Historical Fiction: Four Episodes in Popular Culture* (1979).

Rubin, Louis D., Jr., "Uncle Remus and the Ubiquitous Rabbit," *Southern Review* 10 (1974): 787–804.

Rudwick, Elliott M., and August Meier, "Black Man in the 'White City': Negroes and the Columbia Exposition, 1893," *Phylon* 26 (1965): 354–61.

Savage, Kirk, *Standing Soldiers, Kneeling Slaves: Race, War, and Monument in Nineteenth-Century America* (1997).

Schneider, Gilbert D., "Daniel Emmett's Negro Sermons and Hymns: An Inventory," *Ohio History* 85 (1976): 67–83.

Shufeldt, Robert W., *The Negro: A Menace to American Civilization* (1907).

Simkins, Francis Butler, *Pitchfork Ben Tillman: South Carolinian* (1944).

Simms, L. Moody, Jr., "Charles Francis Adams, Jr., and the Negro Question," *New England Quarterly* 41 (1968): 436–38.

—— "Josiah Royce and the Southern Race Question," *Mississippi Quarterly* 22 (1969): 71–74.

—— "A Note on Sidney Lanier's Attitude toward the Negro and toward Populism," *Georgia Historical Quarterly* 52 (1968): 305–07.

—— "Theodore Du Bose Bratton, Christian Principles, and the Race Question," *Journal of Mississippi History* 38 (1976): 47–52.

Sinkler, George, "Benjamin Harrison and the Matter of Race," *Indiana Magazine of History* 65 (1969): 197–214.

Smith, John David, *An Old Creed for the New South: Pro-Slavery Ideology and Historiography, 1865–1918* (1985).

Smith, William B., *The Color Line: A Brief in Behalf of the Unborn* (1905).

Smith, William H., "William Jennings Bryan and Racism," *Journal of Negro History* 54 (1969): 127–49.

Southern, David W., *The Malignant Heritage: Yankee Progressives and the Negro Question, 1901–1914* (1968).

Spriggs, William E., "The Virginia Farmers' Alliance: A Case Study of Race and Class Identity," *Journal of Negro History* 64 (1979): 191–204.

Stone, Alfred H., *Studies in the American Race Problem* (1908).

Tate, Merze, "Decadence of the Hawaiian Nation and Proposals to Import a Negro Labor Force," *Journal of Negro History* 47 (1962): 248–63.

Terborg-Penn, Rosalyn, "Discrimination against Afro-American Women in the Women's Movement," in Sharon Harley and Rosalyn Terborg-Penn, ed., *The Afro-American Woman: Struggles and Images* (1978): 17–27.

Thornbrough, Emma L., "Booker T. Washington As Seen by His White Contemporaries," *Journal of Negro History* 53 (1968): 161–82.

Thorpe, Robert K., "'Marse Henry' and the Negro: A New Perspective," *Journalism Quarterly* 46 (1969): 467–74.

Toll, William, "The Genie of 'Race': Problems in Conceptualizing the Treatment of Black Americans," *Journal of Ethnic Studies* 4 (1976): 1–20.

Vandersee, Charles, "Henry Adams and the Invisible Negro," *South Atlantic Quarterly* 66 (1967): 13–30.

White, Ronald C., Jr., *Liberty and Justice for All: Racial Reform and the Social Gospel* (1990).

Williamson, Joel, *The Crucible of Race: Black-White Relations in the American South since Emancipation* (1984).

Woodward, C. Vann, *Tom Watson: Agrarian Rebel* (1938).

Wynes, Charles E., "Bishop Thomas U. Dudley and the Uplift of the Negro," *Register of the Kentucky Historical Society* 65 (1967): 230–38.

———, ed., *Forgotten Voices: Dissenting Southerners in an Age of Conformity* (1967).

——— "Lewis Harvey Blair: Virginia Reformer," *Virginia Magazine of History and Biography* 72 (1964): 3–18.

——— "The Race Question in the South As Viewed by British Travelers, 1865–1914," *Louisiana Studies* 13 (1974): 223–40.

——— *Race Relations in Virginia, 1870–1902* (1961).

20.4.2   Black/Native American Relations

Billington, Monroe L., "Black Cavalrymen and Apache Indians in New Mexico Territory," *Fort Concho and the South Plains Journal* 22 (1990): 54–76.

Flickinger, Robert Elliot, *The Choctaw Freedmen and the Story of Oak Hill Industrial Academy* (1914).

Johnson, Charles, Jr., "Black Seminoles: Their History and Their Quest for Land," *Journal of the Afro-American Historical and Genealogical Society* 1 (1980): 47–58.

Lindsey, Donal F., *Indians at Hampton Institute, 1877–1923* (1995).

Littlefield, Daniel F., Jr., and Lonnie E. Underhill, "The 'Crazy Snake Uprising' of 1909: A Red, Black, or White Affair?" *Arizona and the West* 20 (1978): 307–24.

——— "Negro Marshals in the Indian Territory," *Journal of Negro History* 56 (1971): 77–87.

20.4.3   Black/Ethnic Relations

Betts, John R., "The Negro and the New England Conscience in the Days of John Boyle O'Reilly," *Journal of Negro History* 51 (1966): 246–61.

Bodnar, John, Roger Simon, and Michael P. Weber, *Lives of Their Own: Blacks, Italians, and Poles in Pittsburgh, 1900–1960* (1982).

Bourgois, Philippe, "If You're Not Black You're White: A History of Ethnic Relations in St. Louis," *City and Society* 3 (1989): 106–31.

Caldwell, Dan, "The Negroization of the Chinese Stereotype in California," *Southern California Quarterly* 53 (1971): 123–31.

Foner, Philip S., "Black-Jewish Relations in the Opening Years of the Twentieth Century," *Phylon* 36 (1975): 359–67.

Hellwig, David J., "Afro-American Reactions to the Japanese and the Anti-Japanese Movement, 1906–1924," *Phylon* 38 (1977): 93–104.

——— "Black Attitudes toward Irish Immigrants," *Mid-America* 59 (1977): 39–49.

——— "Black Attitudes toward Immigrant Labor in the South, 1865–1910," *Filson Club History Quarterly* 54 (1980): 151–68.

——— "Black Images of Jews from Reconstruction to the Depression," *Societas* 8 (1978): 205–23.

James, Winston, *Holding Aloft the Banner of Ethiopia: Caribbean Radicalism in Early Twentieth-Century America* (1999).

Model, Suzanne, "The Effects of Ethnicity in the Workplace on Blacks, Italians, and Jews in 1910 New York," *Journal of Urban History* 16 (1989): 29–51.

——— "Work and Family: Blacks and Immigrants from South and East Europe," in Virginia Yans-McLaughlin, ed., *Immigration Reconsidered: History, Sociology, and Politics* (1990): 130–59.

Olzak, Susan, "Labor Unrest, Immigration, and Ethnic Conflict in Urban America, 1880–1914," *American Journal of Sociology* 94 (1989): 1303–33.

Parot, Joseph, "Ethnic *versus* Black Metropolis: The Origins of Polish-Black Housing Tensions in Chicago," and Rudolph J. Vicoli, "Ethnic *versus* Black Metropolis: A Comment," *Polish American Studies* 29 (1972): 5–33, 34–39.

Perlmann, Joel, *Ethnic Differences: Schooling and Social Structure among the Irish, Italians, Jews, and Blacks in an American City, 1880–1935* (1988).

Porter, Jack N., "John Henry and Mr. Goldberg: The Relationship between Blacks and Jews," *Journal of Ethnic Studies* 7 (1979): 73–86.

Ridout, Lionel U., "The Church, the Chinese, and the Negroes in California, 1849–1893," *History Magazine of the Protestant Episcopal Church* 28 (1959): 115–38.

Schmier, Louis, "For Him the 'Schwartzers' Couldn't Do Enough: A Jewish Peddler and His Black Customers Look at Each Other," *American Jewish History* 73 (1983): 39–55.

Shankman, Arnold, *Ambivalent Friends: Afro-Americans View the Immigrant* (1982).

———— "Black on Green: Afro-American Editors on Irish Independence, 1840–1921," *Phylon* 41 (1980): 284–99.

———— "Black on Yellow: Afro-Americans View Chinese-Americans, 1850–1935," *Phylon* 39 (1978): 1–17.

———— "Brothers across the Sea: Afro-Americans on the Persecution of Russian Jews, 1881–1917," *Jewish Social Studies* 37 (1975): 114–21.

———— "Friend or Foe? Southern Blacks View the Jew, 1880–1940," in Nathan M. Kaganoff and Melvin I. Urofsky, ed., *"Turn to the South": Essays on Southern Jewry* (1979): 105–23.

———— "The Image of Mexico and the Mexican-American in the Black Press, 1890–1935," *Journal of Ethnic Studies* 3 (1975): 43–56.

———— "The Image of the Italian in the Afro-American Press, 1886–1936," *Italian Americana* 4 (1978): 30–49.

———— "The Menacing Influx: Afro-Americans on Italian Immigration to the South, 1880–1915," *Mississippi Quarterly* 31 (1977–78): 67–88.

Spoehr, Luther W., "Sambo and the Heathen Chinee: Californians' Racial Stereotypes in the Late 1870's," *Pacific Historical Review* 42 (1973): 185–204.

Taylor, Quintard, "Blacks and Asians in a White City: Japanese Americans and African Americans in Seattle, 1890–1940," *Western Historical Quarterly* 22 (1991): 401–29.

Williams, Walter L., "Ethnic Relations of African Students in the United States with Black Americans, 1870–1900," *Journal of Negro History* 65 (1980): 228–49.

20.4.4   Segregation/Jim Crow

Boyd, Robert L., "Residential Segregation by Race and the Black Merchants of Northern Cities during the Early Twentieth Century," *Sociological Forum* 13 (1998): 595–609.

Campbell, Walter E., "Profit, Prejudice, and Protest: Utility Competition and the Generation of Jim Crow Streetcars in Savannah, 1905–1907," *Georgia Historical Quarterly* 70 (1986): 197–231.

Cartwright, Joseph H., *The Triumph of Jim Crow: Tennessee Race Relations in the 1880s* (1976).

Cell, John W., *The Highest Stage of White Supremacy: The Origins of Segregation in South Africa and the American South* (1982).

Chesteen, Richard D., "Bibliographical Essay: The Legal Validity of Jim Crow," *Journal of Negro History* 54 (1971): 284–93.

Crofts, Daniel W., "The Warner-Foraker Amendment to the Hepburn Bill: Friend or Foe of Jim Crow?" *Journal of Southern History* 39 (1973): 341–58.

Crow, Jeffrey J., "An Apartheid for the South: Clarence Poe's Crusade for Rural Segregation," in Jeffrey J. Crow, Paul D. Escott, and Charles L. Flynn, Jr., ed., *Race, Class, and Politics in Southern History: Essays in Honor of Robert F. Durden* (1989): 216–59.

Dorman, James H., "The Strange Career of Jim Crow Rice," *Journal of Social History* 3 (1969–70): 109–22.

Doyle, Bertram W., *The Etiquette of Race Relations in the South* (1937).

Ebner, Michael H., "Mrs. Miller and 'The Patterson Show': A 1911 Defeat for Racial Discrimination," *New Jersey History* 86 (1968): 88–91.

Folmsbee, Stanley J., "The Origin of the First 'Jim Crow' Law," *Journal of Southern History* 15 (1949): 235–47.

Fredrickson, George, *White Supremacy: A Comparative Study in American and South African History* (1981).

Graves, John William, "The Arkansas Separate Coach Law of 1891," *Arkansas Historical Quarterly* 32 (1973): 148–65.

———— "Jim Crow in Arkansas: A Reconsideration of Urban Race Relations in the Post-Reconstruction South," *Journal of Southern History* 55 (1989): 421–48.

Hale, Grace E., *Making Whiteness: The Culture of Segregation in the South, 1890–1940* (1998).

Kaplowitz, Craig Allan, "A Breath of Fresh Air: Segregation, Parks, and Progressivism in Nashville, Tennessee, 1900–1920," *Tennessee Historical Quarterly* 57 (1998): 132–49.

Mackey, Thomas C., "Thelma Denton and Associates: Houston's Red Light Reservation and a Question of Jim Crow," *Houston Review* 14 (1992): 139–52.

Malone, Cheryl Knott, "Louisville Free Public Library's Racially Segregated Branches, 1905–1935," *Register of the Kentucky Historical Society* 93 (1995): 159–79.

Matthews, Linda M., "Keeping Down Jim Crow: The Railroads and the Separate Coach Bills in South Carolina," *South Atlantic Quarterly* 73 (1974): 117–29.

Mellinger, Philip, "Discrimination and Statehood in Oklahoma," *Chronicles of Oklahoma* 49 (1971): 340–78.

Moore, John Hammond, "Jim Crow in Georgia," *South Atlantic Quarterly* 66 (1967): 554–65.

Newby, I. A., *Jim Crow's Defense: Anti-Negro Thought in America, 1900–1930* (1965).

Palmore, Joseph R., "The Not-So-Strange Career of Interstate Jim Crow: Race, Transportation, and the Dormant Commerce Clause, 1878–1946," *Virginia Law Review* 83 (1997): 1773–817.

Power, Garrett, "Apartheid Baltimore Style: The Residential Segregation Ordinances of 1910–1913," *Maryland Law Review* 42 (1983): 289–328.

Rabinowitz, Howard N., "From Exclusion to Segregation: Southern Race Relations, 1865–1890," *Journal of American History* 63 (1976): 325–50.

———— *Race Relations in the Urban South* (1978).

Rice, Roger L., "Residential Segregation by Law, 1910–1917," *Journal of Southern History* 34 (1968): 179–99.

Roback, Jennifer, "The Political Economy of Segregation: The Case of Segregated Streetcars," *Journal of Economic History* 46 (1986): 893–917.

Schneider, Mark L., *Boston Confronts Jim Crow, 1890–1920* (1997).

Simpson, George E., *The Negro in the Philadelphia Press* (1936).

Soifer, Aviam, "The Paradox of Paternalism and Laissez Faire Constitutionalism: United States Supreme Court, 1888–1921," *Law and History Review* 5 (1987): 249–279.

Theisen, Lee Scott, "The Fight in Lincoln, NM, 1878: The Testimony of Two Negro Participants," *Arizona and the West* 12 (1970): 173–98.

Weiss, Nancy, "The Negro and the New Freedom: Fighting Wilsonian Segregation," *Political Science Quarterly* 84 (1969): 61–79.

Williamson, Joel, ed., *The Origins of Segregation* (1968).

Woodward, C. Vann, *The Strange Career of Jim Crow* (1955; 3d rev. ed., 1974).

Wright, David, and David Zoby, "Ignoring Jim Crow: The Turbulent Appointment of Richard Etheridge and the Pea Island Lifesavers," *The Journal of Negro History* 80 (1995): 66–80.

20.4.5 Violence and Racial Disturbances

Aptheker, Bettina, "The Suppression of Free Speech: Ida B. Wells and the Memphis Lynching, 1892," *San Jose Studies* 3 (1977): 34–40.

Barnard, Ami Larkin, "The Application of Critical Race Feminism to the Anti-Lynching Movement: Black Women's Fight against Race and Gender Ideology, 1892–1920," *UCLA Women's Law Journal* 3 (1993): 1–38.

Beasley, Maurine, "The Muckrakers and Lynching: A Case Study in Racism," *Journalism History* 9 (1982–83): 86–91.

Beck, E. M., and Stewart E. Tolnay, "The Killing Fields of the Deep South: The Market for Cotton and the Lynching of Blacks, 1882–1930," *American Sociological Review* 55 (1990): 526–39.

Bederman, Gail, "'Civilization,' the Decline of Middle-Class Manliness, and Ida B. Wells's Antilynching Campaign, 1892–1894," *Radical History Review* 52 (1991): 5–30.

Brundage, W. Fitzhugh, "The Darien 'Insurrection' of 1899: Black Protest during the Nadir of Race Relations," *Georgia Historical Quarterly* 74 (1990): 234–53.

——— *Lynching in the New South: Georgia and Virginia, 1880–1930* (1993).

———, ed., *Under Sentence of Death: Lynching in the South* (1997).

Capeci, Dominic J., Jr., and Jack C. Knight, "Reckoning with Violence: W.E.B. Du Bois and the 1906 Atlanta Race Riot," *Journal of Southern History* 62 (1996): 727–66.

Cecelski, David S., and Timothy B. Tyson, ed., *Democracy Betrayed: The Wilmington Race Riot of 1898 and Its Legacy* (1998).

Corzine, Jay, James Creech, and Lin Corzine, "Black Concentration and Lynchings in the South: Testing Blalock's Power-Threat Hypothesis," *Social Forces* 61 (1983): 774–96.

Crowe, Charles, "Racial Massacre in Atlanta, September 22, 1906," *Journal of Negro History* 54 (1969): 150–73.

——— "Racial Violence and Social Reform: Origins of the Atlanta Riot of 1906," *Journal of Negro History* 53 (1968): 234–56.

Crudele, Juanita W., "A Lynching Bee: Butler County Style," *Alabama Historical Quarterly* 42 (1980): 59–71.

Curriden, Mark, and Leroy Phillips, *Contempt of Court: The Turn-of-the-Century Lynching That Launched 100 Years of Federalism* (1999).

Cutler, James E., *Lynch Law* (1905).

Downey, Dennis B., and Ramond M. Hyser, *No Crooked Death: Coatesville, Pennsylvania, and the Lynching of Zachariah Walker* (1991).

Ellis, Mary Louise, "A Lynching Averted: The Ordeal of John Miller," *Georgia Historical Quarterly* 70 (1986): 306–16.

Feldman, Glenn, "Lynching in Alabama, 1889–1921," *Alabama Review* 48 (1995): 114–41.

Goings, Kenneth W., and Gerald L. Smith, "'Unhidden' Transcripts: Memphis and African American Agency, 1862–1920," *Journal of Urban History* 21 (1996): 372–94.

Grant, L. Donald, *The Anti-Lynching Movement, 1883–1932* (1975).

Hair, William I., *Carnival of Fury: Robert Charles and the New Orleans Race Riot of 1900* (1976).

Hall, Jacquelyn Dowd, *Revolt against Chivalry: Jessie Daniel Ames and the Women's Campaign against Lynching* (1979).

Harris, J. William, "Etiquette, Lynching, and Racial Boundaries in Southern History: A Mississippi Example," *American Historical Review* 100 (1995): 387–410.

Haynes, Robert V., *A Night of Violence: The Houston Riot of 1917* (1976).

Hodes, Martha, *White Women, Black Men: Illicit Sex in the Nineteenth-Century South* (1997).

Holmes, William F., "Moonshiners and Whitecaps in Alabama, 1893," *Alabama Review* 34 (1981): 31–49.

——— "Moonshining and Collective Violence: Georgia, 1889–1895," *Journal of American History* 67 (1980): 589–611.

——— "Whitecapping: Agrarian Violence in Mississippi, 1902–1906," *Journal of Southern History* 35 (1969): 165–85.

——— "Whitecapping in Georgia: Carroll and Houston Counties, 1893," *Georgia Historical Quarterly* 64 (1980): 388–404.

Huber, Patrick J., "'Caught Up in the Violent Whirlwind of Lynching': The 1885 Quadruple Lynching in Chatham County, North Carolina," *North Carolina Historical Review* 75 (1998): 135–60.

Ingalls, Robert P., "Lynching and Establishment Violence in Tampa, 1858–1935," *Journal of Southern History* 53 (1987): 613–44.

——— *The Urban Vigilantes in the New South: Tampa, 1882–1936* (1988).

Inverarity, James, "Populism and Lynching in Louisiana, 1889–1896: A Test of Erickson's Theory of the Relationship between Boundary Crises and Repressive Justice," *American Sociological Review* 41 (1976): 262–79.

Keita Cha-Jua, Sundiata, "'Join Hands and Hearts with Law and Order': The 1893 Lynching of Samuel J. Bush and the Response of Decatur's African-American Community," *Illinois Historical Journal* 83 (1990): 187–200.

Lane, Ann J., *The Brownsville Affair: National Crisis and Black Reaction* (1971).

McKinney, Gordon B., "Industrialization and Violence in Appalachia in the 1890's," *Appalachian Journal* 4 (1977): 131–44.

Moseley, Charlton, and Frederick Brogdon, "A Lynching at Statesboro: The Story of Paul Reed and Will Cato," *Georgia Historical Quarterly* 65 (1981): 104–18.

Osofsky, Gilbert, "Race Riot, 1900: A Study of Ethnic Violence," *Journal of Negro Education* 32 (1963): 16–24.

Phillips, Charles David, "Exploring Relations among Forms of Social Control: The Lynching and Execution of Blacks in North Carolina, 1889–1918," *Law and Society Review* 21 (1987): 361–74.

Pittman, Walter E., Jr., "The Mel Cheatham Affair: Interracial Murder in Mississippi in 1889," *Journal of Mississippi History* 43 (1981): 127–33.

Prather, H. Leon, *We Have Taken a City: The Wilmington Racial Massacre and Coup of 1898* (1984).

Raper, Arthur F., *The Tragedy of Lynching* (1933).

Reed, John Shelton, "Percent Black and Lynching: A Test of Blalock's Theory," *Social Forces* 50 (1972): 356–60.

Rogers, William Warren, and Robert David Ward, *August Reckoning: Jack Turner and Racism in Post-Civil War Alabama* (1973).

Royster, Jacqueline, ed., *Southern Horrors and Other Writings: The Anti-Lynching Campaign of Ida B. Wells, 1892–1900* (1997).

Schechter, Patricia A., "'All the Intensity of My Nature': Ida B. Wells, Anger, and Politics," *Radical History Review* 70 (1998): 48–77.

Schmuhl, Robert, "History, Fantasy, Memory: Ben Hecht and a Chicago Hanging," *Illinois Historical Journal* 83 (1990): 146–58.

Senechal, Roberta, *The Sociogenesis of a Race Riot: Springfield, Illinois, in 1908* (1990).

Shapiro, Herbert, *White Violence and Black Response: From Reconstruction to Montgomery* (1988).

Soule, Sarah, "Populism and Black Lynching in Georgia, 1890–1900," *Social Forces* 71 (1992): 431–49.

Tolnay, Stewart E., and E. M. Beck, "Black Flight: Lethal Violence and the Great Migration, 1900–1930," *Social Science History* 14 (1990): 347–70.

Tolnay, Stewart E., E. M. Beck, and James L. Massey, "Black Lynchings: The Power Threat Hypothesis Revisited," *Social Forces* 67 (1989): 605–23.

Tolnay, Stewart E., and James L. Massey, "Black Competition and White Vengeance: Legal Executions of Blacks As Social Control in the Cotton South, 1890 to 1929," *Social Science Quarterly* 73 (1993): 627–44.

Tucker, David M., "Miss Ida B. Wells and Memphis Lynching," *Phylon* 32 (1971): 112–22.

Vance, W. Silas, "The Marion Riot," *Mississippi Quarterly* 27 (1974): 447–66.

Vandal, Gilles, "The Policy of Violence in Caddo Parish, 1865–1884," *Louisiana History* 32 (1991): 159–82.

Weaver, John D., *The Brownsville Raid* (1970).

Wells, Ida, *Mob Rule in New Orleans* (1900).

——— *A Red Record* (1894).

——— *Southern Horrors: Lynch Law in All Its Phases* (1892).

Wiegman, Robyn, "The Anatomy of Lynching," *Journal of the History of Sexuality* 3 (1993): 445–67.

Williams, Lee E., and Lee E. Williams, II, *Anatomy of Four Race Riots: Racial Conflict in Knoxville, Elaine (Arkansas), Tulsa and Chicago, 1919–1921* (1972).

Williamson, Edward C., "Black Belt Political Crisis: The Savage-James Lynching, 1882," *Florida Historical Quarterly* 45 (1967): 402–09.

Worth, Robert F., "The Legacy of a Lynching," *American Scholar* 67 (1998): 65–77.

Wright, George C., *Racial Violence in Kentucky, 1865–1940: Lynchings, Mob Rule, and "Legal Lynchings"* (1990).

Ziglar, William, "'Community on Trial': The Coatesville Lynching of 1911," *Pennsylvania Magazine of History and Biography* 106 (1982): 245–70.

20.4.6 Civil Rights

Abramowitz, Jack, "Origins of the NAACP," *Social Education* 15 (1951): 21–23.

Aucoin, Brent J., "Thomas Goode Jones and African American Civil Rights in the New South," *Historian* 60 (1998): 257–71.

Born, Kate, "Memphis Negro Workingmen and the NAACP," *West Tennessee History Society Papers* 28 (1974): 90–107.

Cuban, Larry, "A Strategy for Racial Peace: Negro Leadership in Cleveland, 1900–1919," *Phylon* 28 (1967): 299–311.

Dillard, Tom, "Scipio A. Jones," *Arkansas Historical Quarterly* 31 (1972): 201–19.

Foner, Philip S., "Reverend George Washington Woodbey: Early Twentieth Century Black Socialist," *Journal of Negro History* 61 (1976): 136–57.

Gaines, Kevin, "Rethinking Race and Class in African-American Struggles for Equality, 1885–1941," *American Historical Review* 102 (1997): 378–87.

Hays, Christopher K., "The African American Struggle for Equality and Justice in Cairo, Illinois, 1865–1900," *Illinois Historical Journal* 90 (1997): 265–84.

Hixson, William B., Jr., "Moorfield Storey and the Struggle for Equality," *Journal of American History* 55 (1968): 533–54.

Hughes, Langston, *Fight for Freedom: The Story of the NAACP* (1962).

Jack, Robert, *History of the National Association for the Advancement of Colored People* (1943).

Kellogg, Charles Flint, *NAACP: A History of the National Association for the Advancement of Colored People, 1909–1920* (vol. 1, 1967).

Kharif, Wali R., "Black Reaction to Segregation and Discrimination in Post-Reconstruction Florida," *Florida Historical Quarterly* 64 (1985): 161–73.

Kornweibel, Theodore, Jr., "Race, Radicalism, and Rage: The Life of Joseph J. Jones," *Afro-Americans in New York Life and History* 13 (1989): 19–38.

Kousser, J. Morgan, "A Black Protest in the 'Era of Accommodation,'" *Arkansas Historical Quarterly* 34 (1975): 149–78.

Kremm, Thomas W., and Diane Neal, "Challenges to Subordination: Organized Black Agricultural Protest in South Carolina, 1886–1895," *South Atlantic Quarterly* 77 (1978): 98–112.

McPherson, James M., *The Abolitionist Legacy: From Reconstruction to the NAACP* (2d ed., 1995).

Meier, August, "Boycotts of Segregated Streetcars, 1894–1906: A Research Note," *Phylon* 18 (1957): 296–97.

Meier, August, and Elliott M. Rudwick, "The Boycott Movement against Jim Crow Streetcars in the South, 1900–1906," *Journal of American History* 55 (1969): 756–75.

———— "Negro Boycotts of Jim Crow Schools in the North, 1897–1925," *Integrated Education* 5 (1967): 57–68.

———— "Negro Boycotts of Jim Crow Streetcars in Tennessee," *American Quarterly* 21 (1969): 755–63.

Moore, James T., "Black Militancy in Readjuster, Virginia, 1879–1883," *Journal of Southern History* 41 (1975): 167–86.

Moore, Jesse Thomas, Jr., *Search for Equality: The National Urban League, 1910–1961* (1981).

Ovington, Mary White, *Black and White Sat Down Together: The Reminiscences of an NAACP Founder* (1995).

———— *How the National Association for the Advancement of Colored People Began* (1914).

Rudwick, Elliott M., "The Niagara Movement," *Journal of Negro History* 42 (1957): 177–200.

Schechter, Patricia A., "'All the Intensity of My Nature': Ida B. Wells, Anger, and Politics," *Radical History Review* 70 (1998): 48–77.

Smith, Albert C., "Southern Violence Reconsidered: Arson As Protest in Black-Belt Georgia, 1865–1910," *Journal of Southern History* 51 (1985): 527–64.

Wedin, Carolyn, *Inheritors of the Spirit: Mary White Ovington and the Founding of the NAACP* (1997).

Weiss, Nancy J., *The National Urban League, 1910–1940* (1974).

Wilson, Sondra Kathryn, ed., *In Search of Democracy: The NAACP Writings of James Weldon Johnson, Walter White, and Roy Wilkins, 1920–1977* (1999).

Woodruff, Nan Elizabeth, "African-American Struggles for Citizenship in the Arkansas and Mississippi Deltas in the Age of Jim Crow," *Radical History Review* 55 (1993): 33–51.

Zangrando, Robert L., *The NAACP Crusade against Lynching, 1909–1950* (1980).

20.5   GOVERNMENT

20.5.1   Law

Aliluna, Leo, "Statutory Means of Impeding the Emigration of the Negro," *Journal of Negro History* 22 (1937): 148–62.

Bernstein, Barton J., "Case Law in *Plessy v. Ferguson*," *Journal of Negro History* 47 (1962): 192–98.

———— "*Plessy v. Ferguson:* Conservative Sociological Jurisprudence," *Journal of Negro History* 48 (1963): 196–205.

Bishop, David W., "*Plessy v. Ferguson:* A Reinterpretation," *Journal of Negro History* 62 (1977): 125–33.

Bridges, Roger D., "Equality Deferred: Civil Rights for Illinois Blacks, 1865–1885," *Journal of the Illinois State Historical Society* 74 (1981): 82–108.

Curriden, Mark, and Leroy Phillips, *Contempt of Court: The Turn-of-the-Century Lynching That Launched 100 Years of Federalism* (1999).

Dale, Elizabeth, "'Social Equality Does Not Exist among Themselves, nor among Us': *Baylies vs. Curry* and Civil Rights in Chicago, 1888," *American Historical Review* 102 (1997): 311–39.

Edwards, Laura E., "The Problem of Dependency: African Americans, Labor Relations, and the Law in the Nineteenth-Century South," *Agricultural History* 72 (1998): 313–40.

Fishel, Leslie H., Jr., "The Genesis of the First Wisconsin Civil Rights Act," *Wisconsin Magazine of History* 49 (1966): 324–33.

Glasrud, Bruce A., "Enforcing White Supremacy in Texas, 1900–1910," *Red River Valley Historical Review* 4 (1979): 65–74.

Holt, Wythe W., Jr., "The Virginia Constitutional Convention of 1901–1902: A Reform Movement Which Lacked Substance," *Virginia Magazine of History and Biography* 76 (1968): 67–102.

Johnson, Franklin, *The Development of State Legislation concerning the Free Negro* (1919).

Kousser, J. Morgan, *Dead End: The Development of Nineteenth-Century Litigation on Racial Discrimination in Schools: An Inaugural Lecture Delivered before the University of Oxford on 28 February 1985* (1985).

Lofgren, Charles A., *The Plessy Case: A Legal-Historical Interpretation* (1987).

McBride, David, "Fourteenth Amendment Idealism: The New York State Civil Rights Law, 1873–1918," *New York History* 71 (1990): 207–33.

Mollison, Irvin C., "Negro Lawyers in Mississippi," *Journal of Negro History* 15 (1930): 38–71.

Murray, Pauli, "The Historical Development of Race Laws in the United States," *Journal of Negro Education* 22 (1952): 4–15.

Oldfield, J. R., "A High and Honorable Calling: Black Lawyers in South Carolina, 1868–1915," *Journal of American Studies* 23 (1989): 395–406.

Olsen, Otto H., ed., *The Thin Disguise: Turning Point in Negro History, Plessy v. Ferguson. A Documentary Presentation, 1864–1896* (1967).

Pincus, Samuel N., *The Virginia Supreme Court, Blacks, and the Law, 1870–1902* (1990).

Reed, Germaine A., "Race Legislation in Louisiana, 1864–1920," *Louisiana History* 6 (1965): 379–92.

Schmidt, B. C., Jr., "Principle and Prejudice: The Supreme Court and Race Relations in the Progressive Era," *Columbia Law Review* 82 (1982): 646–718.

Smith, Douglas C., "A West Virginia Dilemma: *Martin v. Board of Education,* 1896," *West Virginia History* 40 (1979): 158–63.

Stephenson, Gilbert T., *Race Distinctions in American Law* (1910).

Thomas, Brook, ed., *Plessy v. Ferguson: A Brief History with Documents* (1997).

Weaver, Valeria W., "The Failure of Civil Rights, 1875–1883, and Its Repercussions," *Journal of Negro History* 54 (1969): 368–82.

Welke, Barbara Y., "When All the Women Were White, and All the Blacks Were Men: Gender, Class, Race, and the Road to *Plessy*, 1855–1914," *Law and History Review* 13 (1995): 261–316.

20.5.2   Crime and Punishment

Adamson, Christopher R., "Punishment after Slavery: Southern State Penal Systems, 1865–1890," *Social Problems* 30 (1983): 555–69.

Ayers, Edward L., *Vengeance and Justice: Crime and Punishment in the Nineteenth-Century American South* (1984).

Bayliss, Garland, "The Arkansas State Penitentiary under Democratic Control, 1874–1896," *Arkansas Historical Quarterly* 34 (1975): 195–215.

Beck, E. M., James L. Massey, and Stewart E. Tolnay, "The Gallows, the Mob, and the Vote: Lethal Sanctioning of Blacks in North Carolina and Georgia, 1882–1930," *Law and Society Review* 23 (1989): 317–31.

Butler, Anne M., "Still in Chains: Black Women in Western Prisons, 1865–1910," *Western Historical Quarterly* 20 (1989): 18–35.

Bynum, Victoria, "On the Lowest Rung: Court Control over Poor White and Free Black Women," in Darlene Clark Hine, ed., *Black Women in American History: From Colonial Times through the Nineteenth Century* (1990): 213–24.

Cable, George W., *The Silent South, Together with the Freedman's Case in Equity and the Convict Lease System* (1885).

Carleton, Mark, *Politics and Punishment: The History of the Louisiana State Penal System* (1971).

———— "The Politics of the Convict Lease System in Louisiana, 1868–1901," *Louisiana History* 8 (1967): 5–25.

Carper, N. G., "Slavery Revisited: Peonage in the South," *Phylon* 37 (1976): 85–99.

Casey, Orben J., "Governor Lee Cruce, White Supremacy, and Capital Punishment, 1911–1915," *Chronicles of Oklahoma* 52 (1974–1975): 456–75.

Cohen, William, "Negro Involuntary Servitude in the South, 1865–1940: A Preliminary Analysis," *Journal of Southern History* 42 (1976): 31–60.

Daniel, Pete, "The Metamorphosis of Slavery, 1865–1900," *Journal of American History* 66 (1979): 88–99.

———— *The Shadow of Slavery: Peonage in the South, 1901–1969* (1972).

———— "The Tennessee Convict War," *Tennessee Historical Quarterly* 34 (1975): 273–92.

———— "Up from Slavery and Down to Peonage: The Alonzo Bailey Case," *Journal of American History* 57 (1970): 654–70.

———— "We Are Going to Do Away with These Boys," *American Heritage* 23 (1972): 42–47, 100–01.

Du Bois, W.E.B., ed., *Some Notes on Negro Crime, Particularly in Georgia* (1904).

———— "The Spawn of Slavery: The Convict Lease System in the South," *Missionary Review of the World* 14 (1901): 737–45.

George, Paul S., "Policing Miami's Black Community, 1896–1930," *Florida Historical Quarterly* 57 (1979): 434–50.

Green, Fletcher M., "Some Aspects of the Convict Lease System in the Southern States," in Fletcher M. Green, ed., *Essays in Southern History Presented to Joseph Gregoire de Roulhac Hamilton* (1949).

Griffin, James S., "Blacks in the St. Paul Police Department: An Eighty Year Survey," *Minnesota History* 44 (1975): 255–65.

Griffiths, John D. M., "A State of Servitude Worse Than Slavery: The Politics of Penal Administration in Mississippi, 1865–1900," *Journal of Mississippi History* 55 (1993): 1–18.

King, William M., *Going to Meet a Man: Denver's Last Legal Public Execution, 27 July 1886* (1990).

Lichtenstein, Alex, "Good Roads and Chain Gangs in the Progressive South: 'The Negro Convict Is a Slave,'" *Journal of Southern History* 59 (1993): 85–110.

———— *Twice the Work of Free Labor: The Political Economy of Convict Labor in the New South* (1996).

Mancini, Matthew J., *One Dies, Get Another: Convict Leasing in the American South, 1866–1928* (1996).

Massey, James L., and Martha A. Myers, "Patterns of Repressive Social Control in Post-Reconstruction Georgia, 1882–1935," *Social Forces* 68 (1989): 458–88.

Myers, Martha A., "Economic Threat and Racial Disparities in Incarceration: The Case of Postbellum Georgia," *Criminology* 28 (1990): 627–56.

———— *Race, Labor, and Punishment in the New South* (1998).

Myers, Martha A., and James L. Massy, "Race, Labor, and Punishment in Postbellum Georgia," *Social Problems* 38 (1991): 267–87.

Nieman, Donald G., "Black Political Power and Criminal Justice: Washington County, Texas, 1868–1884," *Journal of Southern History* 53 (1989): 391–420.

Nizalowski, Edward, "Murder in Newark Valley, 1879: The Murder of Elbridge Rewey and the Trial and Execution of Daniel Searles," *Afro-Americans in New York Life and History* 11 (1987): 29–47.

Novak, Daniel A., *The Wheel of Servitude: Black Forced Labor after Slavery* (1978).

Oshinsky, David M., *'Worse Than Slavery': Parchman Farm and the Ordeal of Jim Crow Justice* (1996).

Rabinowitz, Howard N., "The Conflict between Blacks and the Police in the Urban South, 1865–1900," *Historian* 39 (1976): 62–76.

Ransom, Roger, and Richard Sutch, "Debt Peonage in the Cotton South after the Civil War," *Journal of Economic History* 32 (1972): 641–69.

Rice, James D., "Insurrection at Saint Inigoes: The Three Faces of Crime and Punishment in a Slave Society," *Southern Studies* 5 (1994): 51–71.

Roberts, Darrel, "Joseph E. Brown and the Convict Lease System," *Georgia Historical Quarterly* 44 (1960): 399–410.

Shapiro, Karin A., *A New South Rebellion: The Battle against Convict Labor in the Tennessee Coalfields, 1871–1896* (1998).

Sheldon, Randall G., "From Slave to Caste Society: Penal Changes in Tennessee, 1830–1915," *Tennessee Historical Quarterly* 38 (1979): 462–78.

Sisk, Glenn N., "Crime and Justice in the Alabama Black Belt, 1875–1917," *Mid-America* 40 (1958): 106–13.

Taylor, A. Elizabeth, "The Origins and Development of the Convict Lease System in Georgia," *Georgia Historical Quarterly* 26 (1942): 113–28.

Taylor, William B., *Brokered Justice: Race, Politics, and Mississippi Prisons, 1798–1992* (1993).

Tolnay, Stewart E., E. M. Beck, and James L. Massey, "Black Competition and White Vengeance: Legal Execution of Blacks As Social Control in the Cotton South, 1890–1929," *Social Science Quarterly* 73 (1992): 627–44.

Ward, Robert D., and William W. Rogers, *Convicts, Coal, and the Banner Mine Tragedy* (1987).

———— "Racial Inferiority, Convict Labor, and Modern Medicine: A Note on the Coalburg Affair," *Alabama History Quarterly* 44 (1982): 203–10.

Williams, Nudie E., "Black Men Who Wore the 'Star,'" *Chronicles of Oklahoma* 59 (1981): 83–90.

Wright, George C., "The Billy Club and the Ballot: Police Intimidation of Blacks in Louisville, Kentucky, 1880–1930," *Southern Studies* 23 (1984): 20–41.

Zimmerman, Hilda Jane, "The Penal Reform Movement in the South during the Progressive Era, 1890–1917," *Journal of Southern History* 17 (1951): 462–92.

20.5.3   Politics and Voting

Abramowitz, Jack, "John B. Rayner—A Grass-Roots Leader," *Journal of Negro History* 36 (1951): 160–93.

Akin, Edward N., "When a Minority Becomes the Majority: Blacks in Jacksonville Politics, 1887–1907," *Florida Historical Quarterly* 53 (1974): 123–45.

Allen, Howard W., A. R. Clausen, and Jerome M. Clubb, "Political Reform and Negro Rights in the Senate, 1909–1915," *Journal of Southern History* 37 (1971): 191–212.

Anderson, Eric, *Race and Politics in North Carolina, 1872–1901: The Black Second* (1981).

Atkins, Leak R., "Populism in Alabama: Reuben F. Kolb and the Appeals to Minority Groups," *Alabama Historical Quarterly* 32 (1970): 167–80.

Bacote, Clarence A., "The Negro in Atlanta Politics," *Phylon* 16 (1955): 333–50.

———— "Negro Officeholders in Georgia under President McKinley," *Journal of Negro History* 44 (1959): 217–39.

Bagwell, David Ashley, "The 'Magical Process': The Sayre Election Law of 1893," *Alabama Review* 25 (1972): 83–104.

Baker, Riley E., "Negro Voter Registration in Louisiana, 1879–1964," *Louisiana Studies* 4 (1965): 332–50.

Beatty, Bess, *A Revolution Gone Backward: The Black Response to National Politics, 1876–1896* (1987).

Bloch, Herman D., "New York Afro-Americans' Struggle for Political Rights and the Emergence of Political Recognition, 1865–1900," *International Review of Social History* 13 (1968): 321–49.

Brewer, J. Mason, *Negro Legislators of Texas* (1935).

Buni, Andrew, *The Negro in Virginia Politics, 1902–1965* (1967).

Cantrell, Gregg, "'Dark Tactics': Black Politics in the 1887 Texas Prohibition Campaign," *Journal of American Studies* 25 (1991): 85–93.

———— "John B. Rayner: A Study in Black Populist Leadership," *Southern Studies* 24 (1985): 432–43.

Cantrell, Gregg, and D. Scott Barton, "Texas Populists and the Failure of Biracial Politics," *Journal of Southern History* 55 (1989): 659–92.

Cartwright, Joseph H., "Black Legislators in Tennessee in the 1880's: A Case Study in Black Political Leadership," *Tennessee Historical Quarterly* 32 (1973): 265–84.

Casdorph, Paul D., *Republicans, Negroes, and Progressives in the South, 1912–1916* (1981).

Chafe, William H., "The Negro and Populism: A Kansas Case Study," *Journal of Southern History* 34 (1968): 402–19.

Claude, Richard, "Constitutional Voting Rights and Early U.S. Supreme Court Doctrine," *Journal of Negro History* 51 (1966): 114–24.

Cooper, William J., *The Conservative Regime: South Carolina, 1877–1890* (1968).

Crow, Jeffrey J., "Fusion, Confusion, and Negroism: Schisms among Negro Republicans in the North Carolina Election of 1896," *North Carolina Historical Review* 53 (1976): 364–84.

Danese, Tracy E., "Disfranchisement, Women's Suffrage, and the Failure of the Florida Grandfather Clause," *Florida Historical Quarterly* 74 (1995): 117–31.

Dillard, Tom, "To the Back of the Elephant: Racial Conflict in the Arkansas Republican Party," *Arkansas Historical Quarterly* 33 (1974): 3–15.

Edmonds, Helen G., *The Negro and Fusion Politics in North Carolina, 1894–1901* (1951).

Farris, Charles D., "The Re-Enfranchisement of Negroes in Florida," *Journal of Negro History* 39 (1954): 259–83.

Fink, Leon, "'Irrespective of Party, Color, or Social Standing': The Knights of Labor and Opposition Politics in Richmond, Virginia," *Labor History* 19 (1978): 325–49.

Fishel, Leslie H., Jr., "The 1880's: Pivotal Decade for the Black Community," *Hayes Historical Journal* 3 (1980): 85–94.

———— "The Negro in Northern Politics, 1870–1900," *Mississippi Valley Historical Review* 42 (1955): 466–89.

Forsythe, Harold S., "'But My Friends Are Poor': Ross Hamilton and Freedpeople's Politics in Mecklenburg County, Virginia, 1869–1901," *Virginia Magazine of History and Biography* 105 (1997): 409–38.

Gaboury, William J., "George Washington Murray and the Fight for Political Democracy in South Carolina," *Journal of Negro History* 62 (1977): 258–69.

Gaither, Gerald H., *Blacks and the Populist Revolt: Ballots and Bigotry in the 'New South'* (1977).

———— "The Negro Alliance Movement in Tennessee, 1888–1891," *West Tennessee Historical Society Papers* 27 (1973): 50–62.

Gatewood, Willard B., Jr., "Negro Legislators in Arkansas, 1891: A Document," *Arkansas History Quarterly* 31 (1972): 220–33.

Gelston, Arthur Lewis, "Radical *versus* Straight-Out in Post-Reconstruction Beaufort County," *South Carolina Historical Magazine* 75 (1974): 225–37.

Goldstein, Michael, "Preface to the Rise of Booker T. Washington: A View from New York City of the Demise of Independent Black Politics, 1889–1902," *Journal of Negro History* 62 (1977): 81–99.

Goodwyn, Lawrence, "Populist Dreams and Negro Rights: East Texas As a Case Study," *American Historical Review* 76 (1971): 1435–56.

Grantham, Dewey W., Jr., "Georgia Politics and the Disfranchisement of the Negro," *Georgia Historical Quarterly* 32 (1948): 1–21.

Graves, John William, "Negro Disfranchisement in Arkansas," *Arkansas Historical Quarterly* 26 (1967): 199–225.

Greene, Suzanne E., "Black Republicans on the Baltimore City Council, 1890–1931," *Maryland Historical Magazine* 74 (1979): 203–22.

Hair, William I., "Henry J. Hearsey and the Politics of Race," *Louisiana History* 17 (1976): 393–400.

Haney, James E., "Blacks and the Republican Nomination of 1908," *Ohio History* 84 (1975): 207–21.

Hiller, Amy M., "The Disfranchisement of Delaware Negroes in the Late Nineteenth Century," *Delaware History* 13 (1968): 124–53.

Hirshon, Stanley P., *Farewell to the Bloody Shirt: Northern Republicans and the Southern Negro, 1873–1893* (1962).

Holder, Calvin B., "The Rise of the West Indian Politician in New York City, 1900–1952," *Afro-Americans in New York Life and History* 4 (1980): 45–59.

Holmes, William F., "The Demise of the Colored Farmers' Alliance," *Journal of Southern History* 41 (1975): 187–200.

——— "The Leflore County Massacre and the Demise of the Colored Farmers' Alliance," *Phylon* 34 (1973): 267–74.

Horgan, James J., "Hail the Passing, Guard the Tomb: How the Literacy Tests Blocked Black Voters," *Southern Exposure* 10 (1982): 62–66.

Jones, James B., Jr., "'If We Are Citizens by the Law, Let Us Enjoy the Fruits of This Privilege': African-American Political Struggles in a Tennessee Mountain City, 1869–1912," *West Tennessee Historical Society Papers* 49 (1995): 87–100.

Katz, William, "George Henry White: A Militant Negro Congressman in the Age of Booker T. Washington," *Negro History Bulletin* 29 (1966): 125–26, 134.

Klingman, Peter D., "Inside the Ring: Bisbee-Lee Correspondence, February-April 1880," *Florida Historical Quarterly* 57 (1978): 187–204.

Koribkin, Russell, "Political Disfranchisement in Georgia," *Georgia Historical Quarterly* 74 (1990): 20–58.

Kousser, J. Morgan, *The Shaping of Southern Politics: Suffrage Restriction and the Establishment of the One-Party South, 1880–1910* (1974).

Kremer, Gary R., "Background to Apostasy: James Milton Turner and the Republican Party," *Missouri Historical Review* 71 (1976): 59–75.

Lewinson, Paul, *Race, Class, and Party: A History of Negro Suffrage and White Politics in the South* (1965).

Link, Arthur S., "The Negro As a Factor in the Campaign of 1912," *Journal of Negro History* 32 (1947): 81–99.

Mabry, William A., "Disfranchisement of the Negro in Mississippi," *Journal of Southern History* 4 (1938): 318–33.

——— *Studies in the Disfranchisement of the Negro in the South* (1933).

Martin, Robert E., *Negro Disenfranchisement in Virginia* (1938).

McKinney, Gordon B., "Racism and the Electorate: Two Late Nineteenth Century Mountain Elections," *Appalachian Journal* 1 (1973): 98–110.

——— "Southern Mountain Republicans and the Negro, 1865–1900," *Journal of Southern History* 41 (1975): 493–516.

Meier, August, "The Negro and the Democratic Party, 1875–1915," *Phylon* 17 (1965): 173–91.

Meredith, H. L., "Agrarian Socialism and the Negro in Oklahoma, 1900–1918," *Labor History* 11 (1970): 277–84.

Miller, Sally M., "The Socialist Party and the Negro, 1901–1920," *Journal of Negro History* 56 (1971): 220–29.

Moneyhon, Carl H., "Black Politics in Arkansas during the Gilded Age, 1876–1900," *Arkansas Historical Quarterly* 44 (1985): 222–45.

Moore, R. Laurence, "Flawed Fraternity: American Socialist Response to the Negro, 1901–1912," *Historian* 32 (1969): 1–18.

Morton, Richard L., *The Negro in Virginia Politics, 1865–1902* (1919).

Nieman, Donald G., "Black Political Power and Criminal Justice: Washington County, Texas, 1868–1884," *Journal of Southern History* 3 (1955): 391–420.

Perkin, Allan, "President Garfield and the Southern Question: The Making of a Policy That Never Was," *Southern Quarterly* 16 (1978): 375–86.

Pruitt, Paul M., Jr., "Defender of the Voteless: Joseph C. Manning Views the Disfranchisement Era in Alabama," *Alabama Historical Quarterly* 43 (1981): 171–85.

Reed, Adolph L., Jr., *W.E.B. Du Bois and American Political Thought: Fabianism and the Color Line* (1998).

Reid, George W., "Four in Black: North Carolina's Black Congressmen, 1874–1901," *Journal of Negro History* 64 (1979): 229–43.

Satcher, Buford, *Blacks in Mississippi Politics, 1865–1900* (1978).

Saunders, Robert M., "Southern Populists and the Negro, 1893–1895," *Journal of Negro History* 54 (1969): 240–61.

Schwartz, Michael, *Radical Protest and Social Structure: The Southern Farmers' Alliance and Cotton Tenancy, 1880–1890* (1976).

Seraile, William, "A Colored Man in the Cabinet: An Idea before Its Time, 1896," *Journal of the Afro-American Historical and Genealogical Society* 11 (1990): 1–2, 79–92.

Shaw, Barton C., *The Wool-Hat Boys: Georgia's Populist Party* (1984).

Sherman, Richard B., *The Republican Party and Black America: From McKinley to Hoover, 1896–1933* (1973).

Silcox, Harry C., "The Black 'Better Class' Political Dilemma: Philadelphia Prototype Isaiah C. Wears," *Pennsylvania Magazine of History and Biography* 113 (1989): 45–66.

Simms-Brown, R. Jean, "Populism and Black Americans: Constructive or Destructive?" *Journal of Negro History* 65 (1980): 349–60.

Smith, C. Calvin, "John E. Bush: The Politician and the Man, 1880–1916," *Arkansas Historical Quarterly* 23 (1959): 115–33.

Smith, Samuel D., *The Negro in Congress, 1870–1901* (1940).

Sponholtz, Lloyd L., "Harry Smith, Negro Suffrage, and the Ohio Constitutional Convention: Black Frustration in the Progressive Era," *Phylon* 35 (1974): 165–80.

Strange, Douglas C., "The Making of a President, 1912: The Northern Negroes' View," *Negro History Bulletin* 31 (1968): 14–23.

Taylor, Joseph H., "Populism and Disfranchisement in Alabama," *Journal of Negro History* 34 (1949): 410–27.

Terborg-Penn, Rosalyn, *African-American Women in the Struggle for the Vote, 1850–1920* (1998).

———— "The Historical Treatment of the Afro-American Woman in the Woman's Suffrage Movement, 1900–1920: A Bibliographical Essay," *Current Biography on African Affairs* 7 (1974): 245–59.

Thornbrough, Emma L., "The Brownsville Episode and the Negro Vote," *Mississippi Valley Historical Review* 44 (1957): 469–93.

Tindall, George B., "The Campaign for the Disfranchisement of Negroes in South Carolina," *Journal of Southern History* 15 (1949): 212–34.

———— "The Question of Race in the South Carolina Constitutional Convention of 1895," *Journal of Negro History* 37 (1952): 277–303.

Walton, Hanes, Jr., "Another Force for Disfranchisement: Blacks and the Prohibitionists in Tennessee," *Journal of Human Relations* 18 (1970): 728–38.

Watson, Richard L., Jr., "Furniford M. Simmons and the Politics of White Supremacy," Jeffrey J. Crow, Paul D. Escott, and Charles L. Flynn, Jr., ed., *Race, Class, and Politics in Southern History: Essays in Honor of Robert F. Durden* (1989).

Wilhoit, Francis M., "An Interpretation of Populism's Impact on the Georgia Negro," *Journal of Negro History* 52 (1967): 116–27.

Williams, Nudie E., "They Fought for Votes: The White Politician and the Black Editor," *Chronicles of Oklahoma* 64 (1986): 18–35.

Williamson, Edward C., *Florida Politics in the Gilded Age, 1877–1893* (1976).

Wilson, Harold, "The Role of Carter Glass in the Disfranchisement of the Virginia Negro," *Historian* 32 (1969): 69–82.

Wiseman, John B., "Racism in Democratic Politics, 1904–1912," *Mid-America* 51 (1969): 38–58.
Yellin, Jean, "Du Bois' *Crisis* and Women's Suffrage," *Massachusetts Review* 14 (1973): 365–75.

20.5.4 Military

Amos, Preston E., *Above and Beyond in the West: Black Medal of Honor Winners, 1870–1890* (1974).
Barr, Alwyn, "The Black Militia of the New South: Texas As a Case Study," *Journal of Negro History* 63 (1978): 209–19.
———— "The Texas 'Black Uprising' Scare of 1883," *Phylon* 41 (1980): 179–86.
Billington, Monroe L., "Black Cavalrymen and Apache Indians in New Mexico Territory," *Fort Concho and the South Plains Journal* 22 (1990): 54–76.
———— "Black Soldiers at Fort Selden, New Mexico, 1866–1891," *New Mexico Historical Review* 62 (1987): 65–79.
———— "Civilians and Black Soldiers in New Mexico Territory, 1866–1900: A Cross-Cultural Experience," *Military History of the Southwest* 19 (1989): 71–82.
———— *New Mexico's Buffalo Soldiers, 1866–1900* (1991).
Bond, Horace Mann, "The Negro in the Armed Forces of the United States Prior to World War I," *Journal of Negro Education* 12 (1943): 268–87.
Buecker, Thomas R., "Confrontation at Sturgis: An Episode in Civil-Military Race Relations, 1885," *South Dakota History* 14 (1984): 238–61.
———— "The Tenth Cavalry at Fort Robinson, 1902–1907," *Military Images* 12 (1991): 6–10.
Carroll, John M., ed., *The Black Military Experience in the American West* (1971).
Cashin, Herschel V., *Under Fire with the Tenth U.S. Cavalry* (1902).
Christian, Garna L., *Black Soldiers in Jim Crow Texas, 1899–1917* (1995).
———— "The Brownsville Raid's One Hundred Sixty-Eighth Man: The Court Martial of Corporal Knowles," *Southwestern Historical Quarterly* 93 (1989): 45–59.
———— "The Twenty-Fifth Regiment at Fort McIntosh: Precursor to Retaliatory Racial Violence," *West Texas Historical Association Year Book* 55 (1979): 149–61.
Cipriani, Tim, "Negro Soldiers on the Frontier: The Ninth and Tenth U.S. Cavalry, 1866–1891," *Griot* 16 (1997): 40–49.
Diamond, B. I., and J. O. Baylen, "The Demise of the Georgia Guard Colored, 1868–1914," *Phylon* 45 (1984): 311–13.
Eppinga, Jane, "Henry O. Flipper in the Court of Private Land Claims: The Arizona Career of West Point's First Black Graduate," *Journal of Arizona History* 36 (1995): 33–54.
Finley, Randy, "Black Arkansans and World War One," *Arkansas Historical Quarterly* 49 (1990): 249–77.
Fletcher, Marvin E., *The Black Soldier and Officer in the United States Army, 1891–1917* (1974).
———— "The Black Volunteers in the Spanish-American War," *Military Affairs* 38 (1974): 48–53.
Fowler, Arlen L., *The Black Infantry in the West, 1869–1891* (1971).
Gaines, Kevin, and Penny Von Eschen, "Ambivalent Warriors: African Americans, U.S. Expansion, and the Legacies of 1898," *Culturefront* 7 (1998): 63–64, 73–75.
Gatewood, Willard B., Jr., "Alabama's 'Negro Soldier Experiment,' 1898–1899," *Journal of Negro History* 57 (1972): 333–51.
———— "Black Troops in Florida during the Spanish-American War," *Tampa Bay History* 20 (1998): 17–31.
———— "An Experiment in Color: The Eighth Illinois Volunteers, 1898–1899," *Journal of the Illinois State History Society* 65 (1972): 293–312.
———— "Indiana Negroes and the Spanish American War," *Indiana Magazine of History* 69 (1973): 115–39.
———— "Negro Troops in Florida, 1898," *Florida Historical Quarterly* 49 (1970): 1–15.
———— "North Carolina's Negro Regiment in the Spanish-American War," *North Carolina Historical Review* 48 (1971): 370–87.
———— "Ohio's Negro Battalion in the Spanish-American War," *Northwestern Ohio Quarterly* 45 (1973): 55–56.

—— *Smoked Yankees and the Struggle for Empire: Letters from Negro Soldiers, 1898–1902* (1971).

Glass, Edward L., *The History of the Tenth Cavalry* (1921).

Hurtt, Clarence M., "The Role of the Black Infantry in the Expansion of the West," *West Virginia History* 40 (1979): 123–57.

Johnson, Edward A., *History of Negro Soldiers in the Spanish American War and Other Items of Interest* (1899).

Johnson, John Allen, "The Medal of Honor and Sergeant John Ward and Private Pompey Factor," *Arkansas Historical Quarterly* 29 (1970): 361–75.

Leckie, William H., *The Buffalo Soldiers: A Narrative of the Negro Cavalry in the West* (1967).

Littlefield, Daniel F., Jr., and Lonnie E. Underhill, "Negro Marshals in the Indian Territory," *Journal of Negro History* 56 (1971): 77–87.

Marszalek, John F., Jr., "A Black Cadet at West Point," *American Heritage* 22 (1971): 31–37, 104–106.

Muskat, Beth Taylor, "The Last March: The Demise of the Black Militia in Alabama," *Alabama Review* 43 (1990): 18–34.

Schubert, Frank N., *Black Valor: Buffalo Soldiers and the Medal of Honor, 1870–1898* (1997).

—— *Buffalo Soldiers, Braves, and the Brass: The Story of Fort Robinson, Nebraska* (1993).

—— "The Fort Robinson YMCA, 1902–1907: A Social Organization in a Black Regiment," *Nebraska History* 55 (1974): 165–79.

—— "Ten Troopers: Buffalo Soldier Medal of Honor Men Who Served at Fort Robinson," *Nebraska History* 78 (1997): 151–57.

—— "The Violent World of Emanuel Stance, Fort Robinson, 1887," *Nebraska History* 55 (1974): 203–19.

Scott, Edward Van Zile, *The Unwept: Black American Soldiers and the Spanish-American War* (1996).

Seraile, William, "Theophilus G. Steward, Intellectual Chaplain, Twenty-Fifth U.S. Colored Infantry," *Nebraska History* 66 (1985): 272–93.

Stover, Earl F., "Chaplain Henry V. Plummer, His Ministry, and His Court Martial," *Nebraska History* 56 (1975): 20–50.

20.6   DEMOGRAPHY

Atlanta University, *Mortality among Negroes in Cities* (Atlanta University Publications, No. 1, 1896).

Cohen, William, *At Freedom's Edge: Black Mobility and the Southern White Quest for Racial Control, 1861–1915* (1991).

Engerman, Stanley L., "Black Fertility and Family Structure in the U.S., 1880–1940," *Journal of Family History* 2 (1977): 117–38.

Engerrand, Steven W., "Black and Mulatto Mobility and Stability in Dallas, Texas, 1880–1910," *Phylon* 39 (1978): 203–15.

Gutmann, Myron P., and Kenneth H. Fliess, "The Social Context of Child Mortality in the American Southwest," *Journal of Interdisciplinary History* 26 (1996): 589–618.

Higgs, Robert, "Participation of Blacks and Immigrants in the American Merchant Class, 1890–1910: Some Demographic Relations," *Explorations in Economic History* 13 (1976): 153–64.

McMurry, Daniel W., and John N. Burrus, "Mississippi's Population: An Analysis of a Half-Century of Demographic Change," *Southern Quarterly* 6 (1967): 45–63.

Meeker, Edward, "Mortality Trends of Southern Blacks, 1850–1910: Some Preliminary Findings," *Explorations in Economic History* 13 (1976): 13–42.

Rose, Jerome C., "Biological Consequences of Segregation and Economic Deprivation: A Post-Slavery Population from Southwest Arkansas," *Journal of Economic History* 49 (1989): 351–60.

Tolnay, Stewart E., "Black American Fertility Transition, 1880–1940," *Sociology and Social Research* 70 (1985): 2–7.

—— "The Decline of Black Marital Fertility in the Rural South, 1910–1940," *American Sociological Review* 52 (1987): 211–17.

—— "Fertility of Southern Black Farmers in 1900: Evidence and Speculation," *Journal of Family History* 8 (1983): 314–32.

20.7 FAMILY

Barksdale-Hall, R. C., "The Steversons: An African-American Family in Slavery and Freedom," *Journal of the Afro-American Historical and Genealogical Society* 6 (1985): 156–70.

Bingham, Darrel E., "The Black Family in Evansville and Vanderburgh County, Indiana, in 1880," *Indiana Magazine of History* 75 (1979): 117–46.

————— "Family Structure of Germans and Blacks in Evansville and Vanderburgh County, Indiana, in 1880: A Comparative Study," *Old Northwest* 7 (1981): 255–75.

Bogardus, Carl R., Sr., "Black Marriages, Gallatin County, Kentucky, 1866 to 1913," *Journal of the Afro-American Historical and Genealogical Society* 2 (1981): 117–22, 161–75.

Drago, Edmund L., "The Black Household in Dougherty County, Georgia, 1870–1900," *Journal of Southwest Georgia History* 1 (1983): 38–40.

————— "Sources at the National Archives for Genealogical and Local History Research: The Black Family in Dougherty County, Georgia, 1870–1900," *Prologue* 14 (1982): 81–88.

Du Bois, W.E.B., ed., *The Negro American Family* (1908).

Engerman, Stanley L., "Black Fertility and Family Structure in the U.S., 1880–1940," *Journal of Family History* 2 (1977): 117–38.

Furstenberg, Frank F., Jr., Theodore Hershberg, and John Modell, "The Origins of the Female-Headed Black Family: The Impact of the Urban Experience," *Journal of Interdisciplinary History* 6 (1975): 211–33.

Harley, Sharon, "For the Good of Family and Race: Gender, Work, and Domestic Roles in the Black Community, 1880–1930," *Signs* 15 (1990): 336–49.

Harris, William H., "Work and the Family in Black Atlanta, 1880," *Journal of Social History* 9 (1976): 319–30.

Jessup, Wilbur E., "The Warren Family of Marshall County, Iowa," *Journal of the Afro-American Historical and Genealogical Society* 3 (1982): 99–104.

Lewis, Earl, "Afro-American Adaptive Strategies: The Visiting Habits of Kith and Kin among Black Norfolkians during the First Great Migration," *Journal of Family History* 12 (1987): 407–20.

London, Andrew S., and S. Philip Morgan, "Racial Differences in First Names in 1910," *Journal of Family History* 19 (1994): 261–84.

Morgan, Kathryn L., *Children of Strangers: The Stories of a Black Family* (1980).

Paustian, P. Robert, "The Evolution of Personal Naming Practices among American Blacks," *Names* 26 (1978): 177–91.

Pleck, Elizabeth H., "The Two-Parent Household: Black Family Structure in Late Nineteenth Century Boston," in Darlene Clark Hine, ed., *Black Women in American History: From Colonial Times through the Nineteenth Century* (1990): 1095–124.

Sanders, Wiley Britton, *Negro Child Welfare in North Carolina: A Rosenwald Study* (1933).

Shifflet, Crandall A., "The Household Composition of Rural Black Families: Louisa County, Virginia, 1880," *Journal of Interdisciplinary History* 6 (1975): 235–60.

Smith, Daniel Scott, Michael Dahlin, and Mark Friedberger, "The Family Structure of the Older Black Population in the American South in 1880 and 1900," *Sociology and Social Research* 63 (1979): 544–65.

Toll, William, "Black Families and Migration to a Multiracial Society: Portland, Oregon, 1900–1924," *Journal of American Ethnic History* 17 (1998): 38–70.

Tolnay, Stewart E., "Black Family Formation and Tenancy in the Farm South, 1900," *American Journal of Sociology* 90 (1984): 305–25.

————— *The Bottom Rung: African American Family Life on Southern Farms* (1999).

White, John, "Whatever Happened to the Slave Family of the Old South?" *Journal of American Studies* 8 (1974): 383–90.

20.8 SOCIETY

20.8.1 Rural Life (Including Black Settlements)

Abramowitz, Jack, "The Repudiation of Established Negro Leadership in the Exodus of 1879," *Social Education* 32 (1968): 29–33.

Alexander, Charles, *Battles and Victories of Allen Allensworth* (1914).

Athearn, Robert G., *In Search of Canaan: Black Migration to Kansas, 1879–1880* (1978).

Beaton, Elizabeth, "An African-American Community in Cape Breton, 1901–1904," *Acadiensis* 24 (1995): 65–97.

Bittle, William E., and Gilbert L. Geis, "Racial Self-Fulfillment and the Rise of an All-Negro Community in Oklahoma," *Phylon* 28 (1957): 247–60.

Bryant, Jonathan M., *How Curious a Land: Conflict and Change in Greene County, Georgia, 1850–1885* (1996).

Bunch, Lonnie G., III, "Allensworth: The Life, Death, and Rebirth of an All-Black Community," *Californians* 5 (1987): 26–33.

Butchart, Ronald E., and Charles T. Haley, "Tracing the Masses: A Critique of Nell Irvin Painter's Exodusters," *Afro-Americans in New York Life and History* 2 (1978): 71–82.

Carlson, Shirley J., "Black Migration to Pulaski County, Illinois, 1860–1900," *Illinois Historical Journal* 80 (1987): 37–46.

Crockett, Norman L., *The Black Towns* (1979).

Dann, Martin, "From Sodom to the Promised Land: E. P. McCabe and the Movement for Oklahoma Colonization," *Kansas Historical Quarterly* 40 (1974): 370–78.

Frehill-Row, Lisa M., "Postbellum Race Relations and Rural Land Tenure: Migration of Blacks and Whites to Kansas and Nebraska, 1870–1890," *Social Forces* 72 (1993): 77–92.

Goings, Kenneth W., "Intra-Group Differences among Afro-Americans in the Rural North: Paulding County, Ohio, 1860–1900," *Ethnohistory* 27 (1980): 79–90.

Grenz, Suzanna M., "The Exodusters of 1879: St. Louis and Kansas City Reponses," *Missouri Historical Review* 73 (1978): 54–70.

Hamilton, Kenneth M., *Black Towns and Profit: Promotion and Development in the Trans-Appalachian West, 1877–1915* (1991).

——— "The Origins and Early Promotion of Nicodemus: A Pre-Exodus, All-Black Town," *Kansas History* 5 (1982): 220–42.

Haywood, C. Robert, "'No Less a Man': Blacks in Cow Town Dodge City, 1876–1886," *Western Historical Quarterly* 19 (1988): 161–82.

Higgs, Robert, "Race, Tenure, and Resource Allocation in Southern Agriculture, 1910," *Journal of Economic History* 33 (1973): 149–69.

Hill, Mozell C., "The All-Negro Communities of Oklahoma: The Natural History of a Social Movement," *Journal of Negro History* 31 (1946): 254–68.

Holmes, William F., "Labor Agents and the Georgia Exodus, 1899–1900," *South Atlantic Quarterly* 79 (1980): 436–48.

Irby, Charles L., "The Black Settlers on Saltspring Island in the Nineteenth Century," *Phylon* 35 (1974): 368–74.

Jessup, Wilbur E., "The Warren Family of Marshall County, Iowa," *Journal of the Afro-American Historical and Genealogical Society* 3 (1982): 99–104.

Jones, Allen, "Improving Rural Life for Blacks: The Tuskegee Negro Farmers' Conference, 1892–1915," *Agricultural History* 65 (1992): 105–14.

Karst, Frederick A., "A Rural Black Settlement in St. Joseph County, Indiana, before 1900," *Indiana Magazine of History* 74 (1978): 262–67.

Kiser, Clyde Vernon, *Sea Island to City: A Study of St. Helena Islanders in Harlem and Other Urban Centers* (1932).

Littlefield, Daniel F., Jr., and Lonnie E. Underhill, "Black Dreams and 'Free' Homes: The Oklahoma Territory, 1891–1894," *Phylon* 34 (1973): 342–57.

Logan, Frenise A., "The Economic Status of the Town Negro in Post-Reconstruction North Carolina," *North Carolina Historical Review* 35 (1958): 448–60.

——— "The Movement of Negroes from North Carolina, 1876–1894," *North Carolina Historical Review* 33 (1956): 45–65.

McFeely, William S., *Sapelo's People: A Long Walk into Freedom* (1994).

Nathans, Sydney, "'Gotta Mind to Move, a Mind to Settle Down': Afro-Americans and the Plantation Frontier," in William J. Cooper, Jr., Michael F. Holt, and John McCardell, ed., *A Master's Due: Essays in Honor of David Herbert Donald* (1985): 204–22.

Painter, Nell I., *Exodusters: Black Migration to Kansas after Reconstruction* (1977).

Peoples, Morgan D., "Kansas Fever in North Louisiana," *Louisiana History* 11 (1970): 121–35.

Reggio, Michael H., "Troubled Times: Homesteading in Short-Grass Country, 1892–1900," *Chronicles of Oklahoma* 57 (1979): 196–211.

Roberson, Jere W., "Edward P. McCabe and the Langston Experiment," *Chronicles of Oklahoma* 51 (1973): 343–55.

Rosengarten, Theodore, "Sea Island Encounter," *Georgia Historical Quarterly* 79 (1995): 394–406.

Rowe, Jerome C., ed., *Gone to a Better Land: A Biohistory of a Rural Black Cemetery in the Post-Reconstruction South* (1985).

Schwendemann, Glenn, "The 'Exodusters' on the Missouri," *Kansas Historical Quarterly* 29 (1963): 25–40.

——— "Nicodemus: Negro Haven on the Solomon," *Kansas Historical Quarterly* 34 (1968): 10–31.

——— "St. Louis and the 'Exodusters' of 1879," *Journal of Negro History* 46 (1961): 32–46.

——— "Wyandotte and the First 'Exodusters' of 1879," *Kansas Historical Quarterly* 26 (1960): 233–49.

Shepard, R. Bruce, "Diplomatic Racism: Canadian Government and Black Migration from Oklahoma, 1905–1912," *Great Plains Quarterly* 3 (1983): 5–16.

——— "North to the Promised Land: Black Migration to the Canadian Plains," *Chronicles of Oklahoma* 66 (1988): 306–27.

Sisk, Glenn N., "Social Aspects of the Alabama Black Belt, 1875–1917," *Mid-America* 37 (1955): 31–47.

Steinberg, Stephen, "My Day in Nicodemus: Notes from a Field Trip to Black Kansas," *Phylon* 37 (1976): 243–49.

Strickland, Arvarh E., "Toward the Promised Land: The Exodus to Kansas and Afterward," *Missouri History Review* 69 (1975): 376–412.

Taylor, Joseph H., "The Great Migration from North Carolina in 1878," *North Carolina Historical Review* 31 (1954): 18–33.

Taylor, Quintard, "The Emergence of Black Communities in the Pacific Northwest: 1865–1910," *Journal of Negro History* 64 (1979): 342–54.

Tolnay, Stewart E., *The Bottom Rung: African American Family Life on Southern Farms* (1999).

Troper, Harold Martin, "The Creek-Negroes of Oklahoma and Canadian Immigration, 1909–1911," *Canadian Historical Review* 53 (1972): 272–88.

Wayne, George H., "Negro Migration and Colonization in Colorado, 1870–1930," *Journal of the West* 15 (1976): 102–20.

Woofter, Thomas Jackson, Jr., *Black Yeomanry: Life on St. Helena Island* (1930).

——— *Negro Migration: Changes in Rural Organization and Population of the Cotton Belt* (1920).

20.8.2 Urban Life (Including Migration)

Anderson, E. Frederick, *The Development of Leadership and Organization Building in the Black Community of Los Angeles from 1900 through World War II* (1980).

Anderson, Jervis, *This Was Harlem: A Cultural Portrait, 1900–1950* (1982).

Atlanta University, *Social and Physical Condition of Negroes in Cities* (Atlanta University Publications, No. 2, 1897).

Barr, Alwyn, "Occupational and Geographic Mobility in San Antonio, 1870–1900," *Social Science Quarterly* 51 (1970): 396–403.

Blassingame, John W., "Before the Ghetto: The Making of the Black Community in Savannah, Georgia, 1865–1880," *Journal of Social History* 6 (1973): 463–88.

——— *Black New Orleans, 1860–1880* (1973).

Bloch, Herman D., "The New York City Negro and Occupational Eviction, 1860–1910," *International Review of Social History* 5 (1960): 26–38.

Bragaw, Donald H., "Status of Negroes in a Southern Port City in the Progressive Era," *Florida Historical Quarterly* 51 (1973): 281–302.

Broussard, Albert S., *Black San Francisco: The Struggle for Racial Equality in the West, 1900–1954* (1993).

Brown, Elsa Barkley, and Gregg D. Kimball, "Mapping the Terrain of Black Richmond," *Journal of Urban History* 21 (1995): 296–346.

Carter, Edward Randolph, *The Black Side: A Partial History of the Business, Religious and Educational Side of the Negro in Atlanta, GA* (1894).

Cheek, Charles D., and Amy Friedlander, "Pottery and Pig's Feet: Space, Ethnicity, and Neighborhood in Washington, D.C., 1880–1940," *Historical Archaeology* 24 (1990): 34–60.

Christensen, Lawrence O., "Race Relations in St. Louis, 1865–1916," *Missouri Historical Review* 78 (1983): 123–36.

Christian, Garna L., "Rio Grande City: Prelude to the Brownsville Raid," *West Texas Historical Association Yearbook* 57 (1981): 118–32.

Cohen, William, *At Freedom's Edge: Black Mobility and the Southern White Quests for Racial Control, 1861–1915* (1991).

Corbett, Katharine T., and Mary E. Seematter, "Black St. Louis at the Turn of the Century," *Gateway Heritage* 7 (1986): 40–48.

Cox, Thomas C., *Blacks in Topeka, Kansas, 1865–1915: A Social History* (1982).

Craig, John M., "Community Cooperation in Ruthville, Virginia, 1900–1930," *Phylon* 48 (1987): 132–40.

Dabney, Wendell P., *Cincinnati's Colored Citizens* (1926).

Daniels, John, *In Freedom's Birthplace: A Study of the Boston Negroes* (1914).

De Graaf, Lawrence B., "The City of Black Angels: Emergence of the Los Angeles Ghetto, 1890–1930," *Pacific History Review* 39 (1970): 323–52.

Diner, Steven J., "Chicago Social Workers and Blacks in the Progressive Era," *Social Service Review* 44 (1970): 393–410.

Drucker, Arthur P., Sophia Boaz, A. L. Harris, and Miriam Schaffner, *The Colored People of Chicago* (1913).

Du Bois, W.E.B., *The Philadelphia Negro* (1899).

Emlen, John T., "The Movement for the Betterment of the Negro in Philadelphia," *Annals of the American Academy of Political and Social Science* 49 (1913): 81–92.

Engs, Robert F., *Freedom's First Generation: Black Hampton, Virginia, 1861–1890* (1979).

Epstein, Abraham, *The Negro Migrant in Pittsburgh* (1918).

Evans, Arthur S., Jr., and David Lee, *Pearl City, Florida: A Black Community Remembers* (1990).

George, Paul S., "Colored Town: Miami's Black Community, 1896–1930," *Florida Historical Quarterly* 56 (1978): 432–47.

Goings, Kenneth W., and Gerald L. Smith, "'Unhidden' Transcripts: Memphis and African American Agency, 1862–1920," *Journal of Urban History* 21 (1995): 372–94.

Gottlieb, Peter, *Making Their Own Way: Southern Blacks' Migration to Pittsburgh, 1916–1930* (1987).

Gray, Dorothy A., "Crisis of Identity: The Negro Community in Raleigh, 1890–1900," *North Carolina Historical Review* 50 (1973): 121–40.

Greenwood, Janette Thomas, *Bittersweet Legacy: The Black and White "Better Classes" in Charlotte, 1850–1910* (1994).

Grossman, James R., *Land of Hope: Chicago, Black Southerners, and the Great Migration* (1989).

———— "Migration, Race, and Class," *Journal of Urban History* 15 (1989): 224–32.

Haller, Mark H., "Policy Gambling, Entertainment, and the Emergence of Black Politics: Chicago from 1900 to 1940," *Journal of Social History* 24 (1991): 719–39.

Harley, Sharon, "Black Women in a Southern City: Washington, D.C., 1890–1920," in Joanne V. Hawks, and Sheila L. Skemp, ed., *Sex, Race, and the Role of Women in the South* (1983): 59–74.

Harris, William H., "Work and the Family in Black Atlanta, 1880," *Journal of Social History* 9 (1976): 319–30.

Harvey, Diane, "The Terri, Augusta's Black Enclave," *Richmond County History* 5 (1973): 60–75.

Haynes, George E., "Conditions among Negroes in Cities," *Annals of the American Academy of Political and Social Science* 49 (1913): 105–19.

———— *The Negro at Work in New York City* (1912).

Henri, Florette, *Black Migration: Movement North, 1900–1920* (1975).

Hewitt, William L., "So Few Undesirables: Race, Residence, and Occupation in Sioux City, 1890–1925," *Annals of Iowa* 50 (1989): 158–79.

Higgs, Robert, "The Boll Weevil, the Cotton Economy, and Black Migration, 1910–1930," *Agricultural History* 50 (1976): 335–50.

Himes, J. S., Jr., "Forty Years of Negro Life in Columbus, Ohio," *Journal of Negro History* 27 (1942): 133–54.

Hirsch, Arnold R., "On the Waterfront: Race, Class, and Politics in Post-Reconstruction New Orleans," *Journal of Urban History* 21 (1995): 511–17.

Hoffecker, Carol E., "The Politics of Exclusion: Blacks in Late Nineteenth-Century Wilmington, Delaware," *Delaware History* 16 (1974): 60–72.

Hopkins, Richard J., "Status, Mobility, and the Dimensions of Change in a Southern City: Atlanta, 1870–1910," in Kenneth T. Jackson and Stanley K. Schultz, ed., *Cities in American History* (1972).

Hurst, Marsha, "Integration, Freedom of Choice, and Community Control in Nineteenth Century Brooklyn," *Journal of Ethnic Studies* 3 (1975): 33–55.

Jackson, Philip, "Black Charity in Progressive Era Chicago," *Social Service Review* 52 (1978): 400–17.

Johnson, James Weldon, *Black Manhattan* (1930).

Johnson, Ronald M., "From Romantic Suburb to Racial Enclave: LeDroit Park, Washington, D.C., 1880–1920," *Phylon* 45 (1984): 264–270.

Katz, Michael B., and Thomas J. Sugrue, ed., *W.E.B. Du Bois, Race, and the City* (1998).

Katzman, David M., *Before the Ghetto: Black Detroit in the Nineteenth Century* (1973).

Katznelson, Ira, *Black Men, White Cities: Race, Politics, and Migration in the United States, 1900–1930, and Britain, 1948–1968* (1973).

Kellogg, John, "The Formation of Black Residential Areas in Lexington, Kentucky, 1865–1887," *Journal of Southern History* 48 (1982): 21–52.

———— "Negro Urban Clusters in the Postbellum South," *Geographical Review* 67 (1977): 310–21.

Kennedy, Louise Venable, *The Negro Peasant Turns Cityward* (1930).

Kiser, Clyde Vernon, *Sea Island to City: A Study of St. Helena Islanders in Harlem and Other Urban Centers* (1932).

Kogut, Alvin B., "The Negro and the Charity Organization Society in the Progressive Era," *Social Service Review* 44 (1970): 11–21.

Kusmer, Kenneth L., ed., *Black Communities and Urban Development in America, 1720–1990. Vol. 4, Part II: From Reconstruction to the Great Migration, 1877–1917* (1991).

———— *A Ghetto Takes Shape: Black Cleveland, 1870–1930* (1978).

Kyriakoudes, Louis M., "Southern Black Rural-Urban Migration in the Era of the Great Migration: Nashville and Middle Tennessee, 1890–1930," *Agricultural History* 72 (1998): 341–51.

Lammermeier, Paul J., "Cincinnati's Black Community: The Origins of a Ghetto, 1870–1880," in John H. Bracey, August Meier, and Elliott Rudwick, ed., *The Rise of the Ghetto* (1971): 24–28.

Lane, Roger, *Roots of Violence in Black Philadelphia, 1860–1900* (1986).

———— *William Dorsey's Philadelphia and Ours: On the Past and Future of the Black City in America* (1991).

Lang, William L., "The Nearly Forgotten Blacks on Last Chance Gulch, 1900–1912," *Pacific Northwest Quarterly* 70 (1979): 50–57.

Lewis, Earl, *In Their Own Interests: Race, Class, and Power in Twentieth-Century Norfolk, Virginia* (1991).

Light, Ivan, "The Ethnic Vice Industry, 1880–1944," *American Social Review* 42 (1977): 464–79.

Logsdon, Joseph and Caryn Cosse Bell, "The Americanization of Black New Orleans, 1850–1900," in Arnold R. Hirsch and Joseph Logsdon, ed., *Creole New Orleans: Race and Americanization* (1992).

Madyun, Gail, and Larry Malone, "Black Pioneers in San Diego: 1880–1920," *Journal of San Diego History* 27 (1981): 91–109.

Martin, Asa, *Our Negro Population: A Sociological Study of the Negroes of Kansas City, Missouri* (1913).

Marullo, Sam, "The Migration of Blacks to the North, 1911–1918," *Journal of Black Studies* 15 (1985): 291–306.

McTigue, Geraldine, "Patterns of Residence: Housing Distribution by Color in Two Louisiana Towns, 1860–1880," *Louisiana Studies* 15 (1976): 345–88.

Miller, Zane L., "Race-ism and the City: The Young Du Bois and the Role of Place in Social Theory, 1893–1901," *American Studies* 30 (1989): 89–102.

———— "Urban Blacks in the South, 1865–1920: An Analysis of Some Quantitative Data on Richmond, Savannah, New Orleans, Louisville, and Birmingham," in Leo Schnore, ed., *The New Urban History: Quantitative Explorations by American Historians* (1975): 184–204.

Mobley, Joe A., "In the Shadow of White Society: Princeville, a Black Town in North Carolina, 1865–1915," *North Carolina Historical Review* 63 (1986): 340–84.

———— *James City: A Black Community in North Carolina, 1863–1900* (1981).

Mohl, Raymond A., "Black Immigrants: Bahamians in Early Twentieth-Century Miami," *Florida Historical Quarterly* 65 (1987): 271–97.

Moore, Jesse Thomas, Jr., *Search for Equality: The National Urban League, 1910–1961* (1981).

Moore, John Hammond, "The Negro and Prohibition in Atlanta, 1885–1887," *South Atlantic Quarterly* 69 (1970): 38–57.

Mumford, Esther H., *Seattle's Black Victorians, 1852–1901* (1980).

Mumford, Kevin J., *Interzones: Black/White Sex Districts in Chicago and New York in the Early Twentieth Century* (1997).

Neverdon-Morton, Cynthia, "Black Housing Patterns in Baltimore City, 1885–1953," *Maryland Historian* 16 (1985): 25–39.

Nielson, David Gordon, *Black Ethos: Northern Urban Life and Thought, 1890–1930* (1977).

Osofsky, Gilbert, "The Enduring Ghetto," *Journal of American History* 55 (1968): 243–55.

———— *Harlem, the Making of a Ghetto: Negro New York, 1890–1930* (1966).

Ovington, Mary White, *Half a Man: The Status of the Negro in New York* (1911).

Palmer, Howard, and Tamara Palmer, "Urban Blacks in Alberta," *Alberta History* 29 (1981): 8–18.

Parris, Guichard, and Lester Brooks, *Blacks in the City: A History of the National Urban League* (1971).

Perdue, Robert E., *The Negro in Savannah, 1865–1900* (1973).

Pew, Thomas W., Jr., "Boley, Oklahoma: Trial in American Apartheid," *American West* 17 (1980): 14–21; 54–56; 63.

Philpott, Thomas L., *The Slum and the Ghetto: Neighborhood Deterioration and Middle-Class Reform, Chicago, 1880–1930* (1978).

Pleck, Elizabeth Hafkin, *Black Migration and Poverty in Boston, 1865–1900* (1979).

Rabinowitz, Howard N., *Race, Ethnicity, and Urbanization: Selected Essays* (1994).

———— *Race Relations in the Urban South* (1978).

Radford, John P., "Delicate Space: Race and Residence in Charleston, South Carolina, 1860–1880," *West Georgia College Studies in the Social Sciences* 16 (1977): 17–37.

Reid, Ira de Augustine, *The Negro Immigrant: His Background, Characteristics, and Social Adjustment, 1899–1937* (1939).

Reiff, Janice L., Michael R. Dahlin, and Daniel S. Smith, "Rural Push and Urban Pull: Work and Family Experiences of Older Black Women in Southern Cities, 1880–1900," *Journal of Social History* 16 (1983): 39–48.

Ross, Edyth L., "Black Heritage in Social Welfare: A Case Study of Atlanta," *Phylon* 37 (1976): 297–307.

Rye, Stephen H., "Buxton: Black Metropolis of Iowa," *Annals of Iowa* 41 (1972): 939–57.

Scheiner, Seth M., "The Negro Church and the Northern City, 1890–1930," in William G. Shade, and Roy C. Herrenkohl, ed., *Seven on Black: Reflections of the Negro Experience in America* (1969): 92–116.

———— *Negro Mecca: A History of the Negro in New York City, 1865–1920* (1965).

———— "The New York City Negro and the Tenement, 1880–1910," *New York History* 45 (1964): 304–15.

Schutze, Jim, *The Accommodation: The Politics of Race in an American City* (1986).

Scott, Emmett J., *Negro Migration during the War* (1920).

Somers, Dale A., "Black and White in New Orleans: A Study in Urban Race Relations, 1865–1900," *Journal of Southern History* 40 (1974): 19–42.

Spear, Allan H., *Black Chicago: The Making of a Negro Ghetto, 1890–1920* (1967).

Strickland, Arvarh E., *History of the Chicago Urban League* (1966).

Summerville, James, "The City and the Slum: 'Black Bottom' and the Development of South Nashville," *Tennessee Historical Quarterly* 40 (1981): 182–92.

Taylor, Henry, "The Use of Maps in the Study of the Black Ghetto-Formation Process: Cincinnati, 1802–1910," *Historical Methods* 17 (1984): 44–58.

Thomas, Herbert A., Jr., "Victims of Circumstance: Negroes in a Southern Town, 1865–1880," *Register of the Kentucky Historical Society* 71 (1973): 253–71.

Toll, William, "Black Families and Migration to a Multiracial Society: Portland, Oregon, 1900–1924," *Journal of American Ethnic History* 17 (1998): 38–70.

Tolnay, Stewart E., and E. M. Beck, "Black Flight: Lethal Violence and the Great Migration, 1900–1930," *Social Science History* 14 (1990): 347–70.

Tritter, Thorin, "The Growth and Decline of Harlem's Housing," *Afro-Americans in New York Life and History* 22 (1998): 67–83.

U.S. Dept. of Labor, *Negro Migration in 1916–1917* (1919).

Vedder, Richard, Lowell Gallaway, Philip E. Graves, and Robert Sexton, "Demonstrating Their Freedom: The Post-Emancipation Migration of Black Americans," *Research in Economic History* 10 (1986): 213–39.

Warner, Robert A., *New Haven Negroes: A Social History* (1940).

Washington, Jack, *In Search of a Community's Past: The Story of the Black Community of Trenton, New Jersey, 1860–1900* (1990).

Watkins-Owens, Irma, *Blood Relations: Caribbean Immigrants and the Harlem Community, 1900–1930* (1996).

Watts, Eugene J., "Black Political Progress in Atlanta, 1868–1895," *Journal of Negro History* 59 (1974): 268–86.

Weiss, Nancy J., *The National Urban League, 1910–1940* (1974).

Williams, Lee, "Concentrated Residences: The Case of Black Toledo, 1890–1930," *Phylon* 43 (1982): 167–76.

Williams, Lillian S., "Afro-Americans in Buffalo, 1900–1930: A Study in Community Formation," *Afro-Americans in New York Life and History* 8 (1984): 7–35.

——— "And Still I Rise: Black Women and Reform, Buffalo, New York, 1900–1940," *Afro-Americans in New York Life and History* 14 (1990): 7–33.

——— *Strangers in the Land of Paradise: The Creation of an African American Urban Community, Buffalo, New York, 1900–1940* (1999).

Winpenny, Thomas R., "The Economic Status of Negroes in Late Nineteenth Century Lancaster," *Journal of the Lancaster County Historical Society* 77 (1973): 124–32.

Woods, E. M., *The Negro in Etiquette: A Novelty* (1899).

Wright, George C., *Life behind a Veil: Blacks in Louisville, Kentucky, 1865–1930* (1985).

20.8.3   Material Culture

Carney, George O., "Historic Resources of Oklahoma's All-Black Towns: A Preservation Profile," *Chronicles of Oklahoma* 69 (1991): 116–33.

Hunt, Patricia K., "Clothing As an Expression of History: The Dress of African-American Women in Georgia, 1880–1910," *Georgia Historical Quarterly* 76 (1993): 459–71.

McDaniel, George W., *Hearth and Home: Preserving a People's Culture* (1982).

Schneider, Gail, "A Beginning Investigation into the Afro-American Cemeteries of Ulster County, New York," *Afro-Americans in New York Life and History* 10 (1986): 61–69.

Sisk, Glenn N., "Funeral Customs in the Alabama Black Belt, 1870–1910," *Southern Folklore Quarterly* 23 (1959): 169–71.

20.8.4 Color and Class

Arbery, Glenn C., "Victims of Likeness: Quadroons and Octoroons in Southern Fiction," *Southern Review* 25 (1989): 52–71.

Du Bois, W.E.B., and Augustus G. Dill, ed., *Morals and Manners among Negro Americans* (1914).

Frankel, Noralee, and Nancy S. Dye, ed., *Gender, Class, Race, and Reform in the Progressive Era* (1991).

Fultz, Michael, "'The Morning Cometh': African-American Periodicals, Education, and the Black Middle Class, 1900–1930," *Journal of Negro History* 80 (1995): 97–112.

Gatewood, Willard B., Jr., *Aristocrats of Color: The Black Elite, 1880–1920* (1990).

Green, Dan S., "W.E.B. Du Bois' Talented Tenth: A Strategy for Racial Advancement," *Journal of Negro Education* 46 (1977): 358–66.

Greenwood, Janette Thomas, *Bittersweet Legacy: The Black and White "Better Classes" in Charlotte, 1850–1910* (1994).

Mack, Kibibi Voloria C., *Parlor Ladies and Ebony Drudges: African American Women, Class, and Work in a South Carolina Community* (1999).

Meier, August, "Negro Class Structure and Ideology in the Age of Booker T. Washington," *Phylon* 23 (1962): 258–66.

Meier, August, and David Lewis, "History of the Negro Upper Class in Atlanta, Georgia, 1890–1958," *Journal of Negro Education* 28 (1959): 128–39.

Mencke, John G., *Mulattoes and Race Mixture: American Attitudes and Images, 1865–1918* (1979).

Merritt, Carole, "The Herndons: Style and Substance of the Black Upper Middle Class in Atlanta, 1880–1930," *Atlanta History* 37 (1993): 50–64.

Moore, Jacqueline M., *Leading the Race: The Transformation of the Black Elite in the Nation's Capital, 1880–1920* (1999).

Muraskin, William A., "An Alienated Elite: Short Stories in *The Crisis*, 1910–1950," *Journal of Black Studies* 1 (1971): 282–305.

Reuter, Edward Byron, *The Mulatto in the United States* (1918).

——— *Race Mixture: Studies in Intermarriage and Miscegenation* (1931).

Williamson, Joel, *New People: Miscegenation and Mulattoes in the United States* (1980).

20.8.5 Associational Life

Adams, Cyrus F., *The National Afro-American Council* (1902).

Berkeley, Kathleen C., "'Colored Ladies Also Contributed': Black Women's Activities from Benevolence to Social Welfare, 1866–1896," in Walter J. Fraser, Jr., Frank R. Saunders, Jr., and Jon L. Wakelyn, ed., *The Web of Southern Social Relations: Women, Family, and Education* (1985).

Bolsterli, Margaret Jones, "'It Seems to Help Me Bear It Better When She Knows about It': A Network of Women Friends in Watson, Arkansas, 1890–1891," *Southern Exposure* 11 (1983): 58–61.

Brady, Marilyn Dell, "Kansas Federation of Colored Women's Clubs, 1900–1930," *Kansas History* 9 (1986): 19–30.

Burrell, W. P., *Twenty-Five Year History of the United Order of True Reformers* (1909).

Byars, Lauretta F., "Lexington's Colored Orphan Industrial Home, 1892–1913," *Register of the Kentucky Historical Society* 89 (1991): 147–78.

Davis, Elizabeth Lindsay, *Lifting As They Climb* (1933).

——— *The Story of the Illinois Federation of Colored Women's Clubs, 1900–1922* (1922).

Dickson, Lynda F., "Toward a Broader Angle of Vision in Uncovering Women's History: Black Women's Clubs Revisited," in Darlene Clark Hine, ed., *Black Women's History: Theory and Practice* (1990): 103–20.

Du Bois, W.E.B., ed., *Efforts for Social Betterment among Negro Americans* (1909).

Fahey, David M., *The Black Lodge in White America: "True Reformer" Browne and His Economic Strategy* (1994).

Ferguson, Earline Rae, "The Woman's Improvement Club of Indianapolis: Black Women Pioneers in Tuberculosis Work, 1903–1938," *Indiana Magazine of History* 84 (1988): 237–61.

Gere, Anne Ruggles, and Sarah R. Robbins, "Gendered Literacy in Black and White: Turn-of-the-Century African-American and European-American Club Women's Printed Texts," *Signs* 21 (1996): 643–78.

Hendricks, Wanda A., *Gender, Race, and Politics in the Midwest: Black Club Women in Illinois*(1998).

Hines, Linda O., and Allen W. Jones, "A Voice of Black Protest: The Savannah Men's Sunday Club, 1905–1911," *Phylon* 35 (1974): 193–202.

Jacobs, Claude F., "Benevolent Societies of New Orleans Blacks during the Late Nineteenth and Early Twentieth Centuries," *Louisiana History* 29 (1988): 21–34.

Jones, Beverly W., "Mary Church Terrell and the National Association of Colored Women, 1896 to 1901," *Journal of Negro History* 67 (1982): 20–33.

Kennedy, Thomas C., "The Rise and Decline of a Black Monthly Meeting: Southland, Arkansas, 1864–1925," *Arkansas Historical Quarterly* 50 (1991): 115–39.

Knupfer, Anne Meis, *Toward a Tenderer Humanity and a Nobler Womanhood: African American Women's Clubs in Turn-of-the-Century Chicago* (1996).

Lerner, Gerda, "Early Community Work of Black Club Women," *Journal of Negro History* 59 (1972): 158–67.

Logan, Frenise A., "The Colored Industrial Association of North Carolina and Its Fair of 1886," *North Carolina Historical Review* 34 (1957): 58–67.

Meier, August, and Elliott M. Rudwick, "The Rise of the Black Secretariat in the NAACP, 1909–1935," *Crisis* 84 (1977): 58–69.

Mihelich, Dennis N., "The Origins of the Prince Hall Mason Grand Lodge of Nebraska," *Nebraska History* 76 (1995): 10–21.

——— "A Socioeconomic Portrait of Prince Hall Masonry in Nebraska, 1900–1920," *Great Plains Quarterly* 17 (1997): 35–47.

Moses, Wilson J., "Domestic Feminism, Conservatism, Sex Roles, and Black Women's Clubs, 1893–1896," *Journal of Social and Behavioral Sciences* 24 (1987): 166–77.

Moss, Alfred A., Jr., *The American Negro Academy: Voice of the Talented Tenth* (1981).

Neverdon-Morton, Cynthia, *Afro-American Women and the Advancement of the Race, 1895–1925* (1989).

——— "Self-Help Programs As Educative Activities of Black Women in the South, 1895–1925: Focus on Four Key Areas," *Journal of Negro Education* 51 (1982): 207–21.

Pollard, Leslie J., "Black Beneficial Societies and the Home for Aged and Infirm Colored Persons: A Research Note," *Phylon* 41 (1980): 230–34.

Reed, Christopher R., "Black Chicago Civic Organizations before 1935," *Journal of Ethnic Studies* 14 (1987): 65–77.

——— "Organized Racial Reform in Chicago during the Progressive Era: The Chicago NAACP, 1910–1920," *Michigan Historical Review* 14 (1988): 75–99.

Rogers, William W., "The Negro Alliance in Alabama," *Journal of Negro History* 45 (1950): 38–44.

Salem, Dorothy, *To Better Our World: Black Women in Organized Reform, 1890–1920*(1990).

Schmidt, Alvin J., and Nicholas Babchuk, "The Unbrotherly Brotherhood: Discrimination in Fraternal Orders," *Phylon* 34 (1973): 275–82.

Scott, Anne Firor, "Most Invisible of All: Black Women's Voluntary Associations," *Journal of Southern History* 56 (1990): 3–22.

Shaw, Stephanie J., "Black Club Women and the Creation of the National Association of Colored Women," *Journal of Women's History* 3 (1991): 10–25.

Spencer, C. A., "Black Benevolent Societies and the Development of Black Insurance Companies in Nineteenth-Century Alabama," *Phylon* 46 (1988): 251–61.

Thornbrough, Emma Lou, "The National Afro-American League, 1887–1908," *Journal of Southern History* 27 (1961): 494–512.

Waring, J. H., *Work of the Colored Law and Order League* (1900).

Watkins, Ralph, "A Reappraisal of the Role of Voluntary Associations in the African American Community," *Afro-Americans in New York Life and History* 14 (1990): 51–60.

Watkinson, James D., "William Washington Browne and the True Reformers of Richmond, Virginia," *Virginia Magazine of History and Biography* 97 (1989): 375–98.

Weisenfeld, Judith, *African American Women and Christian Activism: New York's Black YWCA, 1905–1945* (1997).

Williams, E. A., S. W. Green, and Jos L. Jones, *History and Manual of the Colored Knights of Pythias* (1917).

Williams, Loretta J., *Black Freemasonry and Middle-Class Realities* (1980).

Yearwood, Lennox, "National Afro-American Organizations in Urban Communities," *Journal of Black Studies* 8 (1978): 423–38.

20.8.6 Leisure and Sports

Berryman, Jack W., "Early Black Leadership in Collegiate Football: Massachusetts As a Pioneer," *Historical Journal of Massachusetts* 9 (1981): 17–28.

Bruce, Janet, *The Kansas City Monarchs: Champions of Black Baseball* (1985).

Captain, Gwendolyn, "Enter Ladies and Gentlemen of Color: Gender, Sport, and the Ideal of African American Manhood and Womanhood during the Late Nineteenth and Early Twentieth Centuries," *Journal of Sport History* 18 (1992): 81–102.

Evans, Art, "Joe Louis As a Key Functionary: White Reactions toward a Black Champion," *Journal of Black Studies* 16 (1985): 95–111.

Fletcher, Marvin E., "The Black Bicycle Corps," *Arizona and the West* 16 (1974): 219–32.

Gilmore, Al-Tony, *Bad Nigger! The National Impact of Jack Johnson* (1975).

Haller, Mark H., "Policy Gambling, Entertainment, and the Emergence of Black Politics: Chicago from 1900 to 1940," *Journal of Social History* 24 (1991): 719–39.

Holway, John, *Voices from the Great Black Baseball Leagues* (1975).

Lomax, Michael E., "Black Entrepreneurship in the National Pastime: The Rise of Semiprofessional Baseball in Black Chicago, 1890–1915," *Journal of Sport History* 25 (1998): 43–64.

Marable, Manning, "Black Athletes in White Men's Games, 1880–1920," *Maryland Historian* 4 (1973): 143–49.

McKinney, G. B. N., "Professional Baseball Players in the Upper South in the Gilded Age," *Journal of Sport History* 3 (1976): 273–80.

Overmyer, James, *Queen of the Negro Leagues: Effa Manley and the Newark Eagles* (1998).

Peterson, Robert, *Only the Ball Was White: A History of Legendary Black Players and All-Black Professional Teams* (1970).

Riess, Steven A., "Race and Ethnicity in American Baseball, 1900–1919," *Journal of Ethnic Studies* 4 (1977): 39–55.

Roberts, Randy, *Papa Jack: Jack Johnson and the Era of White Hopes* (1983).

Rogosin, Donn, *Invisible Men: Life in Baseball's Negro Leagues* (1985).

Ruck, Rob, "Black Sandlot Baseball: The Pittsburgh Crawfords," *Western Pennsylvania Historical Magazine* 66 (1983): 49–68.

——— *Sandlot Seasons: Sport in Black Pittsburgh* (1987).

Somers, Dale A., "A City on Wheels: The Bicycle Era in New Orleans," *Louisiana History* 8 (1967): 219–38.

Westermeier, Clifford P., "Black Rodeo Cowboys," *Red River Valley Historical Review* 3 (1978): 4–26.

White, Richard, "Baseball's John Fowler: The 1887 Season in Binghamton, New York," *Afro-Americans in New York Life and History* 16 (1992): 7–17.

Wiggins, David K., "Peter Jackson and the Elusive Heavyweight Championship: A Black Athlete's Struggle against the Late Nineteenth Century Color Line," *Journal of Sport History* 12 (1985): 143–68.

20.9   RELIGION

Angell, Stephen Ward, *Bishop Henry McNeal Turner and African-American Religion in the South* (1992).

Armstrong, Thomas F., "The Building of a Black Church: Community in Post Civil War Liberty County, Georgia," *Georgia Historical Quarterly* 66 (1982): 346–67.

Ashdown, Paul G., "Samuel Ringgold: A Missionary in the Tennessee Valley, 1860–1911," *Tennessee Historical Quarterly* 38 (1979): 204–13.

Bailey, Kenneth K., "The Post Civil War Racial Separations in Southern Protestantism: Another Look," *Church History* 46 (1977): 453–75.

———— "Southern White Protestantism at the Turn of the Century," *American Historical Review* 68 (1963): 618–35.

Berry, Benjamin D., Jr., "The Plymouth Congregational Church of Louisville, Kentucky," *Phylon* 42 (1981): 224–32.

Blyden, Edward W., *Christianity, Islam, and the Negro Race* (1888).

Bringhurst, Newell G., "'Descendants of Ham' in Zion: Discrimination against Blacks along the Shifting Mormon Frontier, 1830–1920," *Nevada History Social Quarterly* 24 (1981): 298–318.

Brooks, Evelyn, "The Feminist Theology of the Black Baptist Church, 1880–1900," in Darlene Clark Hine, ed., *Black Women in American History: From Colonial Times through the Nineteenth Century* (1990): 167–96.

Burrow, Rufus, Jr., "The Personalism of John Wesley Edward Bowen," *The Journal of Negro History* 82 (1997): 244–56.

Butler, Jon, "Communities and Congregations: The Black Church in St. Paul, 1860–1900," *Journal of Negro History* 56 (1971): 118–34.

Cloyd, Daniel Lee, "Prelude to Reform: Political, Economic, and Social Thought of Alabama Baptists, 1877–1890," *Alabama Review* 31 (1978): 48–64.

Daniel, W. Harrison, "Virginia Baptists and the Negro, 1865–1902," *Virginia Magazine of History and Biography* 76 (1968): 34–63.

Dickerson, Dennis C., "The Black Church in Industrializing Western Pennsylvania, 1870–1950," *Western Pennsylvania Historical Magazine* 64 (1981): 329–44.

———— "Charles H. Trusty: Black Presbyterian Missionary and Denominational Leader," *American Presbyterian* 67 (1989): 283–96.

Du Bois, W.E.B., ed., *The Negro Church* (1903).

Eighmy, John L., "Religious Liberalism in the South during the Progressive Era," *Church History* 38 (1969): 359–72.

Eskew, Glenn T., "Black Elitism and the Failure of Paternalism in Postbellum Georgia: The Case of Bishop Lucius Henry Holsey," *Journal of Southern History* 58 (1992): 637–66.

Estes, Phoebe Beckner, "The Reverend Peter Vinegar," *Southern Folklore Quarterly* 23 (1959): 239–52.

Flynt, Wayne, "Dissent in Zion: Alabama Baptists and Social Issues, 1900–1914," *Journal of Southern History* 35 (1969): 523–42.

———— "Religion in the Urban South: The Divided Religious Mind of Birmingham, 1900–1930," *Alabama Review* 30 (1977): 108–34.

Foner, Philip S., *Black Socialist Preacher: The Teachings of Reverend George Washington Woodbey and His Disciple, Reverend G. W. Slater, Jr.* (1983).

Foster, Gaines M., "Bishop Cheshire and Black Participation in the Episcopal Church: The Limitations of Religious Paternalism," *North Carolina Historical Review* 54 (1977): 49–65.

Fulop, Timothy E., "'The Future Golden Day of the Race': Millenialism and Black Americans in the Nadir, 1877–1901," *Harvard Theological Review* 84 (1991): 75–99.

Gaines, Wesley J., *African Methodism in the South: Or Twenty-Five Years of Freedom* (1890).

Gregg, Robert, *Sparks from the Anvil of Oppression: Philadelphia's African Methodists and Southern Migrants, 1890–1940* (1993).

Hall, Robert L., "Tallahassee's Black Churches, 1865–1885," *Florida Historical Quarterly* 58 (1979): 185–96.

Harvey, Paul, *Redeeming the South: Religious Cultures and Racial Identities among Southern Baptists, 1865–1925* (1997).

Haygood, L. M., *The Colored Man in the Methodist Episcopal Church* (1922).

Higginbotham, Evelyn Brooks, *Righteous Discontent: The Women's Movement in the Black Baptist Church, 1880–1920* (1993).

Jacobs, Sylvia M., "Three Afro-American Women Missionaries in Africa, 1882–1904," in Darlene Clark Hine, ed., *Black Women in American History: From Colonial Times through the Nineteenth Century* (1990): 693–708.

Killian, Charles, "Daniel A. Payne and the A. M. E. General Conference of 1888: A Display of Contrasts," *Negro History Bulletin* 32 (1969): 11–14.

King, Willis J., "The Negro Membership of the (Former) Methodist Church in the (New) United Methodist Church," *Methodist History* 7 (1969): 32–43.

Luker, Ralph E., "Missions, Institutional Churches, and Settlement Houses: The Black Experience, 1885–1910," *Journal of Negro History* 66 (1984): 101–13.

—— *The Social Gospel in Black and White: American Racial Reform, 1885–1912* (1991).

Marable, Manning, "The Black Faith of W.E.B. Du Bois: Sociocultural and Political Dimensions of Black Religion," *Southern Quarterly* 23 (1985): 15–33.

Martin, Sandy D., "The Baptist Foreign Mission Convention, 1880–1894," *Baptist History and Heritage* 16 (1981): 13–25.

—— "Black Baptist Women and African Mission Work, 1870–1925," *Sage* 3 (1986): 16–19.

—— *Black Baptists and African Missions: The Origins of a Movement, 1880–1915* (1989).

—— "Spelman's Emma B. Delaney and the African Mission," *Journal of Religious Thought* 41 (1984): 22–37.

Mays, Benjamin E., *The Negro's God As Reflected in His Literature* (1938).

McDowell, John Patrick, *The Social Gospel in the South: The Woman's Home Mission Movement in the Methodist Episcopal Church, South, 1886–1939* (1982).

Montgomery, William E., *Under Their Own Vine and Fig Tree: The African American Church in the South, 1865–1900* (1993).

Newman, Harvey K., "Piety and Segregation: White Protestant Attitudes towards Blacks in Atlanta, 1865–1906," *Georgia Historical Quarterly* 63 (1979): 238–51.

Noon, Thomas R., "The Alpha Synod of Lutheran Freedmen, 1889–1891," *Concordia History Institute Quarterly* 50 (1977): 64–70.

—— "Black Lutherans Licensed and Ordained, 1865–1889," *Concordia Historical Institute Quarterly* 50 (1977): 54–63.

Pearson, Fred L., Jr., and Joseph A. Tomberlin, "John Doe, Alias God: A Note on Father Divine's Georgia Career," *Georgia Historical Quarterly* 60 (1976): 43–48.

Portier, William L., "John R. Slattery's Vision for the Evangelization of American Blacks," *U.S. Catholic Historian* 5 (1986): 19–44.

Reimers, David M., "Negro Leadership in the Methodist Episcopal Church, 1900–1920: A Plea for Research in Negro Church History," *Wesleyan Quarterly Review* 3 (1966): 243–51.

Richardson, Joe M., *Christian Reconstruction: The American Missionary Association and Southern Blacks, 1861–1890* (1986).

—— "The Failure of the American Missionary Association to Expand Congregationalism among Southern Blacks," *Southern Studies* 18 (1979): 51–73.

Ridout, Lionel U., "The Church, the Chinese, and the Negroes in California, 1849–1893," *History Magazine of the Protestant Episcopal Church* 28 (1959): 115–38.

Scheiner, Seth M., "The Negro Church and the Northern City, 1890–1930," in William G. Shade, and Roy C. Herrenkohl, ed., *Seven on Black: Reflections on the Negro Experience in America* (1969): 92–117.

Sisk, Glenn N., "Negro Churches in the Alabama Black Belt, 1875–1917," *Journal of the Presbyterian Historical Society* 33 (1955): 87–92.

Spain, Rufus B., *At Ease in Zion: A Social History of Southern Baptists, 1865–1900* (1967).

Spalding, David C., "The Negro Catholic Congresses, 1889–1894," *Catholic History Review* 55 (1969): 337–57.

Trotman, C. James, "Matthew Anderson: Black Pastor, Churchman, and Social Reformer," *American Presbyterians* 66 (1988): 11–21.

Vouga, Anne F., "Presbyterian Missions and Louisville Blacks: The Early Years, 1898–1910," *Filson Club Historical Quarterly* 58 (1984): 310–35.

Wahlman, Maude S., "Religious Symbols in Afro-American Folk Art," *New York Folklore* 12 (1986): 1–24.

Warnock, Henry, "Prophets of Change: Some Southern Baptist Leaders and the Problem of Race, 1900–1921," *Baptist History and Heritage* 7 (1972): 172–85.

——— "Southern Methodists, the Negro, and Unification: The First Phase," *Journal of Negro History* 52 (1967): 287–304.

Weisenfeld, Judith, *African American Women and Christian Activism: New York's Black YWCA, 1905–1945* (1997).

Wheeler, Edward L., *Uplifting the Race: The Black Minister in the New South, 1865–1902* (1986).

Williams, Gilbert A., *The* Christian Recorder *Newspaper of the African Methodist Episcopal Church: History of a Forum of Ideas, 1854–1902* (1996).

Williams, Walter L., *Black Americans and the Evangelization of Africa, 1877–1900* (1982).

Wynes, Charles E., "William Henry Heard: Politician, Diplomat, A. M. E. Churchman," *Southern Studies* 20 (1981): 384–93.

20.10 THOUGHT AND EXPRESSION

20.10.1 Race, Gender, and Identity

Abramowitz, Jack, "Crossroads of Negro Thought, 1890–1895," *Social Education* 18 (1955): 117–20.

Alexander, Elizabeth, "We Must Be about Our Father's Business: Anna Julia Cooper and the In-Corporation of the Nineteenth-Century African-American Woman Intellectual," *Signs* 20 (1995): 336–56.

American Negro Academy, *Occasional Papers* (No. 1–22, 1897–1924).

Anthony, Arthur A., "'Lost Boundaries': Racial Passing and Poverty in Segregated New Orleans," *Louisiana History* 36 (1995): 291–312.

Appiah, Anthony, "The Uncompleted Argument: Du Bois and the Illusion of Race," *Critical Inquiry* 12 (1985): 21–37.

Aptheker, Bettina, "W.E.B. Du Bois and the Struggle for Women's Rights, 1910–1920," *San Jose Studies* 1 (1975): 7–16.

Blight, David W., "'Up from Twoness': Frederick Douglass and the Meaning of W.E.B. Du Bois's Concept of Double Consciousness," *Canadian Review of American Studies* 21 (1990): 301–19.

Brotz, Howard, ed., *Negro Social and Political Thought, 1850–1920: Representative Texts* (1966).

Bruce, Dickson D., Jr., "Booker T. Washington's *The Man Farthest Down* and the Transformation of Race," *Mississippi Quarterly* 48 (1996): 239–53.

Christensen, Lawrence O., "The Racial Views of John W. Wheeler," *Missouri Historical Review* 67 (1973): 535–47.

Cooper, Anna Julia, *A Voice from the South* (1892).

Cummings, Melbourne, "Historical Setting for Booker T. Washington and the Rhetoric of Compromise, 1895," *Journal of Black Studies* 8 (1977): 75–82.

Dailey, Maceo Crenshaw, Jr., "Neither 'Uncle Tom' nor 'Accommodationist': Booker T. Washington, Emmett Jay Scott, and Constructionalism," *Atlanta History* 38 (1995): 20–33.

Du Bois, W.E.B., *The Souls of Black Folk: Essays and Sketches* (1903).

Du Bois, W.E.B., and Augustus G. Dill, ed., *Morals and Manners among Negro Americans* (1914).

Dyer, Thomas G., "An Early Black Textbook: Floyd's Flowers or Duty and Beauty for Colored Children," *Phylon* 37 (1976): 359–61.

Elder, Arlene A., "Chesnutt on Washington: An Essential Ambivalence," *Phylon* 38 (1977): 1–8.

Ferris, William Henry, *The African Abroad or His Evolution in Western Civilization* (2 vols., 1913).

Fishel, Leslie H., Jr., "The 'Negro Question' at Mohonk: Microcosm, Mirage, and Message," *New York History* 74 (1994): 277–314.

Formwalt, Lee W., "'Corner-Stone of the Cotton Kingdom': W.E.B. Du Bois's 1898 View of Dougherty County," *Georgia Historical Quarterly* 71 (1987): 693–700.

Fortune, T. Thomas, *Black and White: Land, Labor, and Politics in the South* (1884).

Frankel, Noralee, and Nancy S. Dye, ed., *Gender, Class, Race, and Reform in the Progressive Era* (1991).

Franklin, Lucy Brown, "The Negro Exhibition of the Jamestown Tercentennial Exposition of 1907," *Negro History Bulletin* 38 (1975): 408–13.

Gaines, Kevin, "Rethinking Race and Class in African-American Struggles for Equality, 1885–1941," *American Historical Review* 102 (1997): 378–87.

Gates, Henry Louis, Jr., "The Trope of a New Negro and the Reconstruction of the Image of the Black," *Representations* 24 (1988): 129–55.

Gatewood, Willard B., Jr., "Black Americans and the Quest for Empire, 1893–1903," *Journal of Southern History* 38 (1972): 545–66.

——— *Black Americans and the White Man's Burden, 1898–1903* (1975).

——— "Black Americans and the Boer War, 1899–1902," *South Atlantic Quarterly* 75 (1976): 226–44.

——— "Kansas Negroes and the Spanish-American War," *Kansas Historical Quarterly* 37 (1971): 300–13.

——— *Smoked Yankees and the Struggle for Empire: Letters from Negro Soldiers, 1898–1902* (1971).

Gianakos, Perry E., "The Spanish American War and the Double Paradox of the Negro American," *Phylon* 26 (1965): 34–49.

Gibson, J. W., and W. H. Crogman, *Progress of a Race* (1902).

Grant, Donald L., and Mildred Bricker Grant, "Some Notes on the Capital 'N,'" *Phylon* 36 (1975): 435–43.

Green, Dan S., and Edwin D. Driver, ed., *W.E.B. Du Bois on Sociology and the Black Community* (1978).

Harlan, Louis R., "Booker T. Washington and the White Man's Burden," *American Historical Review* 71 (1966): 441–67.

Heath, Robert L., "A Time for Silence: Booker T. Washington in Atlanta," *Quarterly Journal of Speech* 64 (1978): 385–99.

Hellwig, David J., "Building a Black Nation: The Role of Immigrants in the Thought and Rhetoric of Booker T. Washington," *Mississippi Quarterly* 31 (1978): 529–50.

Higginbotham, Evelyn Brooks, *Righteous Discontent: The Women's Movement in the Black Baptist Church, 1880–1920* (1993).

James, Winston, *Holding Aloft the Banner of Ethiopia: Caribbean Radicalism in Early Twentieth-Century America* (1999).

Lewis, Elsie M., "The Political Mind of the Negro, 1865–1900," *Journal of Southern History* 21 (1955): 189–202.

Marks, George P., ed., *The Black Press Views American Imperialism, 1898–1900* (1971).

Matthews, John Michael, "The Dilemma of Negro Leadership in the New South: The Case of the Negro Young People's Congress of 1902," *South Atlantic Quarterly* 73 (1974): 130–44.

Meier, August, *Negro Thought in America, 1880–1915: Racial Ideologies in the Age of Booker T. Washington* (1963).

——— "The Racial and Educational Philosophy of Kelly Miller, 1895–1915," *Journal of Negro Education* 29 (1960): 121–27.

Miller, Kelly, *The Everlasting Stain* (1924).

——— *Out of the House of Bondage* (1914).

——— *Race Adjustment: Essays on the Negro in America* (1908).

Miller, Zane L., "Race-ism and the City: The Young Du Bois and the Role of Place in Social Theory, 1893–1901," *American Studies* 30 (1989): 89–102.

Moses, Wilson J., "W.E.B. Du Bois's [1897] *The Conservation of Races* and Its Context: Idealism, Conservatism and Hero Worship," *Massachusetts Review* 34 (1993): 275–94.

Oldfield, John, ed., *Civilization and Black Progress: Selected Writings of Alexander Crummell on the South* (1995).

O'Toole, James M., "Racial Identity and the Case of Captain Michael Healy, USRCS," *Prologue* 29 (1997): 191–201.

Phillips, Glenn O., "The Response of a West Indian Activist: D. A. Straker, 1842–1908," *Journal of Negro History* 66 (1981): 128–39.

Posnock, Ross, "The Distinction of Du Bois: Aesthetics, Pragmatism, Politics," *American Literary History* 7 (1995): 500–24.

Poxpey, C. Spencer, "The Washington-Du Bois Controversy and Its Effect on the Negro Problem," *History of Education Journal* 8 (1957): 128–52.

Quarles, Benjamin, "Frederick Douglass and the Women's Rights Movement," *Journal of Negro History* 25 (1940): 35–45.

Rath, Richard Cullen, "Echo and Narcissus: The Afrocentric Pragmatism of W.E.B. Du Bois," *Journal of American History* 84 (1997): 461–95.

Robinson, Michael C., and Frank N. Schubert, "David Fagen: An Afro-American Rebel in the Philippines, 1899–1901," *Pacific History Review* 44 (1975): 68–83.

Rouse, Jacqueline Anne, "Out of the Shadow of Tuskegee: Margaret Murray Washington, Social Activism, and Race Vindication," *The Journal of Negro History* 81 (1996): 31–46.

Rudwick, Elliott M., "The National Negro Committee Conference of 1909," *Phylon* 18 (1957): 413–19.

———— "Note on a Forgotten Black Sociologist: W.E.B. Du Bois and the Sociological Profession," *The American Sociologist* 4 (1969): 303–06.

Samuels, Wilfred D., "Hubert H. Harrison and the 'New Negro Manhood Movement,'" *Afro-Americans in New York Life and History* 5 (1981): 29–41.

Scruggs, Otey M., "Two Black Patriarchs: Frederick Douglass and Alexander Crummell," *Afro-Americans in New York Life and History* 6 (1982): 17–30.

Simms, L. Moody, Jr., "Thomas Underwood Dudley: A Forgotten Voice of Dissent," *Mississippi Quarterly* 20 (1967): 217–23.

Simond, Adah DeBlanc, "The Discovery of Being Black: A Recollection," *Southwestern History Quarterly* 76 (1973): 440–47.

Smith, John David, "A Different View of Slavery: Black Historians Attack the Pro-Slavery Argument, 1890–1920," *Journal of Negro History* 65 (1980): 298–311.

Stein, Judith, "'Of Booker T. Washington and Others': The Political Economy of Racism in the United States," *Science and Society* 38 (1975): 422–63.

Stetson, Erlene, "Black Feminism in Indiana, 1893–1933," *Phylon* 44 (1983): 292–98.

Taylor, Carol M., "W.E.B. Du Bois' Challenge to Scientific Racism," *Journal of Black Studies* 11 (1981): 449–60.

Thomas, William H., *The American Negro: What He Was, What He Is, and What He May Become* (1901).

Toll, William, "Free Men, Freedmen, and Race: Black Social Theory in the Gilded Age," *Journal of Southern History* 44 (1978): 571–96.

———— *The Resurgence of Race: Black Social Theory from Reconstruction to the Pan-African Conferences* (1979).

Walden, Daniel, "The Contemporary Opposition to the Political and Educational Ideas of Booker T. Washington," *Journal of Negro History* 45 (1960): 105–15.

Washington, Booker T., *The Future of the American Negro* (1899).

———— *The Man Farthest Down: A Record of Observation and Study in Europe* (1912).

———— *The Story of the Negro: The Rise of the Race from Slavery* (2 vols., 1909).

Washington, Booker T., and W.E.B. Du Bois, *The Negro in the South: His Economic Progress in Relation to His Moral and Religious Development* (1907).

Washington, Booker T., W.E.B. Du Bois, Paul L. Dunbar, Charles W. Chesnutt, and others, *The Negro Problem: A Series of Articles by Representative American Negroes of To-Day* (1903).

Wiggins, William H., Jr., *O Freedom!: Afro-American Emancipation Celebrations* (1987).

Williams, Vernon J., Jr., "Booker T. Washington and the Political Mythology of Africa," *Griot* 11 (1992): 10–17.

Wintz, Cary D., *African American Political Thought, 1890–1930: Washington, Du Bois, Garvey, and Randolph* (1996).

Woods, E. M., *The Negro in Etiquette: A Novelty* (1899).

Wright, W. D., "The Thought and Leadership of Kelly Miller," *Phylon* 39 (1978): 180–92.

Wynes, Charles E., "Black Diplomats to Haiti, Prejudice, and Henry Watson Furniss," *Midwest Quarterly* 24 (1983): 189–98.

20.10.2   Emigration and Nationalism

Abingbade, Harrison O., "The Settler-African Conflicts: The Case of the Maryland Colonists and the Grebo, 1840–1900," *Journal of Negro History* 66 (1981): 93–109.

Adeleke, Tunde, *Unafrican Americans: Nineteenth-Century Black Nationalists and the Civilizing Mission* (1998).

Akpan, M. B., "Liberia and the Universal Negro Improvement Association: The Background to the Creation of Garvey's Scheme for African Colonization," *Journal of African History* 14 (1973): 105–27.

Bittle, William E., and Gilbert L. Geis, "Alfred Charles Sam and an African Return: A Case Study in Negro Despair," *Phylon* 23 (1962): 178–96.

——— *The Longest Way Home: Chief Alfred C. Sam's Back-to-Africa Movement* (1964).

Fierce, Milfred C., *The Pan-African Idea in the United States, 1900–1919: African-American Interest in Africa and Interaction with West Africa* (1993).

Genovese, Eugene D., "The Legacy of Slavery and the Roots of Black Nationalism (Revised)," in *In Red and Black: Marxian Explorations in Southern and Afro-American History* (1971): 129–57.

Jacobs, Sylvia M., *The African Nexus: Black American Perspectives on the European Partitioning of Africa, 1880–1920* (1981).

Langley, J. Ayo, "Chief Sam's African Movement and Race Consciousness in West Africa," *Phylon* 32 (1971): 164–78.

Martin, Michael T., and Lamont H. Yeakey, "Pan-African Asian Solidarity: A Central Theme in Du Bois' Conception of Racial Stratification and Struggle," *Phylon* 43 (1982): 202–17.

McBride, David, "Africa's Elevation and Changing Racial Thought at Lincoln University, 1854–1886," *Journal of Negro History* 62 (1977): 363–77.

Meier, August, "The Emergence of Negro Nationalism: A Study in Ideologies," *Midwest Journal* 4 (1952): 96–104, 95–111.

Moses, Wilson J., *The Golden Age of Black Nationalism, 1850–1925* (1978).

Patton, Adell, Jr., "The 'Back-to-Africa' Movement in Arkansas," *Arkansas Historical Quarterly* 51 (1992): 164–77.

Redkey, Edwin S., "Bishop Turner's African Dream," *Journal of American History* 54 (1967): 271–90.

——— *Black Exodus: Black Nationalist and Back-to-Africa Movements, 1890–1910* (1969).

Reynolds, Alfred W., "The Alabama Negro Colony in Mexico, 1894–1896," *Alabama Review* 5 (1952): 243–68.

Tindall, George B., "The Liberian Exodus of 1878," *South Carolina Historical Magazine* 53 (1952): 133–45.

Williams, Vernon J., Jr., "Monroe N. Work's Contribution to Booker T. Washington's Nationalist Legacy," *Western Journal of Black Studies* 21 (1997): 85–91.

Williams, Walter L., "Black American Attitudes toward Africa, 1877–1900," *Pan African* 4 (1971): 173–94.

Wintz, Cary D., *African American Political Thought, 1890–1930: Washington, Du Bois, Garvey, and Randolph* (1996).

Woods, Randall B., "Black America's Challenge to European Colonialism: The Waller Affair, 1891–1895," *Journal of Black Studies* 7 (1976): 57–77.

——— "C. H. J. Taylor and the Movement for Black Political Independence, 1882–1896," *Journal of Negro History* 67 (1982): 122–25.

20.10.3   Folklore and Humor

Adams, E. C. L., *Congaree Sketches: Scenes from Negro Life in the Swamps of the Congaree* (1927).

——— *Nigger to Nigger* (1928).

David, John Russell, *Tragedy in Ragtime: Black Folktales from St. Louis* (1976).

Georgia Writers' Project, *Drums and Shadows: Survival Studies among the Georgia Coastal Negroes* (1935).

Hadler, Jeffrey, "Remus Orthography: The History of the Representation of the African-American Voice," *Journal of Folklore Research* 35 (1998): 99–126.

Hemenway, Robert, "The Functions of Folklore in Charles Chesnutt's 'The Conjure Woman,'" *Journal of the Folklore Institute* 13 (1976): 283–309.

Lyons, Mary E., *Sorrow's Kitchen: The Life and Folklore of Zora Neale Hurston* (1990).

Roberts, John W., *From Trickster to Badman: The Black Folk Hero in Slavery and Freedom* (1989).

———— "'Railroad Bill' and the American Outlaw Tradition," *Western Folklore* 40 (1981): 315–28.

Smith, John David, "The Unveiling of Slave Folk Culture, 1865–1920," *Journal of Folklore Research* 21 (1984): 47–62.

Wiggins, William H., "Jack Johnson As Bad Nigger: The Folklore of His Life," *Black Scholar* 2 (1971): 34–46.

20.10.4   Literature and Poetry

Andrews, William L., *The Fiction of Charles W. Chesnutt* (1973).

———— *The Literary Career of Charles W. Chesnutt* (1980).

———— "The Significance of Charles W. Chesnutt's 'Conjure Stories,'" *Southern Literary Journal* 7 (1974): 78–99.

———— "William Dean Howells and Charles W. Chesnutt: Criticism and Race Fiction in the Age of Booker T. Washington," *American Literacy* 48 (1976): 327–39.

Bruce, Dickson D., Jr., *Black American Writing from the Nadir: The Evolution of a Literary Tradition, 1877–1915* (1989).

Carroll, Richard A., "Black Racial Spirit: An Analysis of James Weldon Johnson's Critical Perspective," *Phylon* 32 (1971): 344–64.

Collier, Eugenia, "The Endless Journey of an Ex-Coloured Man," *Phylon* 32 (1971): 365–73.

Elder, Arlene A., *The Hindered Hand: Cultural Implications of Early African-American Fiction* (1978).

Fikes, Robert, Jr., "The Persistent Allure of Universality: African American Authors of White Life Novels, 1890–1945," *Western Journal of Black Studies* 20 (1996): 221–26.

Fleming, Robert E., "Irony As a Key to Johnson's *The Autobiography of an Ex-Coloured Man*," *American Literature* 43 (1971): 83–96.

Flusche, Michael, "Paul Laurence Dunbar and the Burden of Race," *Southern Humanities Review* 11 (1977): 49–60.

Gaines, Kevin, "Assimilationist Minstrelsy As Racial Uplift Ideology: James D. Corrothers's Literary Quest for Black Leadership," *American Quarterly* 45 (1993): 341–69.

Gillman, Susan, "Pauline Hopkins and the Occult: African-American Revisions of Nineteenth-Century Sciences," *American Literary History* 8 (1996): 57–82.

Gleason, William, "Chesnutt's Piazza Tales: Architecture, Race, and Memory in the Conjure Stories," *American Quarterly* 51 (1999): 33–77.

Griffin, Farah Jasmine, *"Who Set You Flowin'?": The African-American Migration Narrative* (1996).

Gunning, Sandra, *Race, Rape, and Lynching: The Red Record of American Literature, 1890–1912* (1996).

Harris, Trudier, *Exorcising Blackness: Historical and Literary Lynching and Burning Rituals* (1985).

Hudson, Gossie Harold, "Paul Laurence Dunbar: The Regional Heritage of Dayton's First Black Poet," *Antioch Review* 34 (1976): 430–40.

Ikonne, Chidi, *From Du Bois to Van Vechten: The Early New Negro Literature, 1903–1926* (1981).

Larson, Charles R., "The Novels of Paul Laurence Dunbar," *Phylon* 29 (1968): 257–71.

Lehman, Cynthia L., "The Social and Political Views of Charles Chesnutt: Reflections on His Major Writings," *Journal of Black Studies* 26 (1996): 274–86.

Loggins, Vernon, *The Negro Author: His Development in America* (1931).

Long, Richard A., "A Weapon of My Song: The Poetry of James Weldon Johnson," *Phylon* 32 (1971): 374–82.

Moses, Wilson J., "Dark Forests and Barbarian Vigor: Paradox, Conflict, and Africanity in Black Writing before 1914," *American Literary History* 1 (1989): 637–55.

Payne, James Robert, "Griggs and Corrothers: Historical Reality and Black Fiction," *Explorations in Ethnic Studies* 6 (1983): 1–15.

Sherman, Joan R., "Daniel Webster Davis: A Black Virginia Poet in the Age of Accommodation," *Virginia Magazine of History and Biography* 81 (1973): 457–78.

Skerrett, Joseph T., Jr., "Irony and Symbolic Action in James Weldon Johnson's *The Autobiography of an Ex-Coloured Man*," *American Quarterly* 32 (1980): 540–58.

Tate, Claudia, *Domestic Allegories of Political Desire: The Black Heroine's Text at the Turn of the Century* (1992).

Teller, Walter, and John Wideman, "Reappraisals: Charles W. Chesnutt," *American Scholar* 42 (1973): 125–34.

Turner, Darwin T., "Paul Laurence Dunbar: The Rejected Symbol," *Journal of Negro History* 52 (1967): 1–13.

Wells, Ida B., Frederick Douglass, Irvine Garland Penn and Ferdinand L. Barnett, *The Reason Why the Colored American is Not in the World's Columbian Exposition: The Afro-American's Contribution to Columbian Literature*, ed. Robert W. Rydell (1999).

Wonham, Henry B., "'The Curious Pychological Spectacle of a Mind Enslaved': Charles W. Chesnutt and Dialect Fiction," *Mississippi Quarterly* 51 (1997–1998): 55–69.

20.10.5 Music and Performing Arts

Barlow, William, *"Looking Up at Down": The Emergence of Blues Culture* (1989).

Bastin, Bruce, *Red River Blues: The Blues Tradition in the Southeast* (1986).

Blood, Melanie N., "Theatre in Settlement Houses: Hull-House Players, Neighborhood Playhouse, and Karamu Theatre," *Theatre History Studies* 16 (1996): 45–69.

Boulard, Garry, "Blacks, Italians, and the Makings of New Orleans Jazz," *Journal of Ethnic Studies* 16 (1988): 53–66.

Boyd, Joe Dan, "Judge Jackson: Black Giant of White Spirituals," *Journal of American Folklore* 83 (1970): 446–51.

Brown, Sterling, "Negro Folk Expression: Spirituals, Seculars, Ballads, and Work Songs," *Phylon* 14 (1953): 45–61.

Cavin, Susan, "Missing Women: On the Voodoo Trail to Jazz," *Journal of Jazz Studies* 3 (1975): 4–27.

Charters, Samuel B., *The Blues Makers* (1991).

——— *The Country Blues* (1959).

Cohn, Lawrence, *Nothing but the Blues: The Music and the Musicians* (1993).

Cortinoris, Irene E., "Jazz on the Riverboats, the Way a Piano Player Tells It," *Journal of Jazz Studies* 1 (1974): 72–78.

Cox, Bette Yarbrough, *Central Avenue: Its Rise and Fall, 1890-c.1955, including the Musical Renaisssance of Black Los Angeles* (1996).

Cuney-Hare, Maud, *Negro Musicians and Their Music* (1996).

Curtis, Susan, *The First Black Actors on the Great White Way* (1998).

Davis, Ronald L., "Early Jazz: Another Look," *Southwest Review* 58 (1973): 1–13; 144–54.

Dixon, R. M. W., and J. Godrich, comp., *Blues and Gospel Records, 1902–1943* (1982).

Evans, David, *Big Road Blues: Tradition and Creativity in the Folk Blues* (1982).

Fenner, Thomas P., Frederick G. Rathbun, and Miss Bessie Cleaveland, arr., *Cabin and Plantation Songs As Sung by the Hampton Students* (3d ed., 1901).

Ferris, William, *Blues from the Delta* (1978).

Gavins, Raymond, "North Carolina Black Folklore and Song in the Age of Segregation," *North Carolina Historical Review* 66 (1989): 412–42.

Hennessey, Thomas J., *From Jazz to Swing: African-American Jazz Musicians and Their Music, 1890–1935* (1994).

Kenney, William Howland, *Chicago Jazz: A Cultural History, 1904–1930* (1993).

Kofsky, Frank, "Afro-American Innovation and the Folk Tradition in Jazz: Their Historical Significance," *Journal of Ethnic Studies* 7 (1979): 1–12.

Krasner, David, *Resistence, Parody, and Double Consciousness in African American Theatre, 1895–1910* (1997).

——— "'The Mirror up to Nature': Modernist Aesthetics and Racial Authenticity in African American Theatre, 1895–1900," *Theatre History Studies* 16 (1996): 117–40.

Krehbiel, H. E., *Afro-American Folksongs: A Study in Racial and National Music* (1914).

Lee, George W., *Beale Street: Where the Blues Began* (1934).

Leonard, Susan M., "An Introduction to Black Participation in the Early Recording Era, 1890–1920," *Annual Review of Jazz Studies* 4 (1988): 31–44.

Levy, Alan H., "Composers Who Happened to Be African American: Music and Memory in the Lives of R. Nathaniel Dett and Henry T. Burleigh," *Mid-American* 74 (1992): 5–16.

Levy, Eugene, "Ragtime and Race Pride: The Career of James Weldon Johnson," *Journal of Popular Culture* 1 (1968): 357–70.

Lomax, Alan, *The Land Where the Blues Began* (1993).

——— *Mister Jelly Roll: The Fortunes of Jelly Roll Morton* (1973).

Marsh, J. B. T., *The Story of the Jubilee Singers including Their Songs: With Supplement by F.J.* (1897).

Murray, Albert, *Stomping the Blues* (1976).

Niles, John J., *Singing Soldiers* (1927).

Oakley, Giles, *The Devil's Music: A History of the Blues* (1977).

O'Connor, Patrick J., "Discovering the Rich Differences in the Blues: The Rural and Urban Genres," *Midwest Quarterly* 31 (1991): 28–42.

Odum, Howard W., and Guy B. Johnson, *The Negro and His Songs: A Study of Typical Negro Songs in the South* (1925).

——— *Negro Workaday Songs* (1926).

Oliver, Paul, *Blues Fell This Morning: The Meaning of the Blues* (1960).

——— *The Story of the Blues* (1969).

Ostendorf, Berndt, "Minstrelsy and Early Jazz," *Massachusetts Review* 20 (1979): 574–602.

Oster, Harry, *Living Country Blues* (1969).

Otto, John S., and Augustus M. Burns, "Black and White Cultural Interactions in the Early Twentieth Century South: Race and Hillbilly Music," *Phylon* 35 (1974): 407–17.

Palmer, Robert, *Deep Blues* (1981).

Paris, Arthur, "Cruse and the Crisis in Black Culture: The Case of Theater, 1900–1930," *Journal of Ethnic Studies* 5 (1977): 51–68.

Reed, Tom, *The Black Music History of Los Angeles: Its Roots* (1994).

Rehin, George F., "Review Article. The Darker Image: American Negro Minstrelsy through the Historian's Lens," *Journal of American Studies* 9 (1975): 365–73.

Riss, Thomas L., *Just before Jazz: Black Musical Theater in New York, 1890–1915* (1989).

Sackheim, Eric, comp., *The Blues Line: A Collection of Blues Lyrics* (1969).

Sacre, Robert, ed., *The Voice of the Delta: Charley Patton and the Mississippi Blues Traditions, Influences, and Comparisons* (1987).

Scarborough, Dorothy, *On The Trail of Negro Folk-Songs* (1925).

Schafer, William J., "Further Thoughts on Jazz Historiography: That Robert Charles Song," *Journal of Jazz Studies* 5 (1978): 19–27.

——— "Thoughts on Jazz Historiography: 'Buddy Bolder's Blues' vs. 'Buddy Bottley's Balloon,'" *Journal of Jazz Studies* 2 (1975): 3–14.

Schafer, William J., and Johannes Riedel, *The Art of Ragtime: Form and Meaning of an Original Black American Art* (1973).

Schultz, Elizabeth, "To Be Black and Blue: The Blues Genre in Black American Autobiography," *Kansas Quarterly* 7 (1975): 81–96.

Stephens, Judith L., "Anti-Lynch Plays by African American Women: Race, Gender, and Social Protest in American Drama," *African American Review* 26 (1992): 329–39.

Taft, Michael, *Blues Lyric Poetry: An Anthology* (1983).

——— *Blues Lyric Poetry: A Concordance* (3 vols., 1984).

Thomas, W. H., *Some Current Folk-Songs of the Negro* (1912).

Tipton, C. Robert, "The Fisk Jubilee Singers," *Tennessee Historical Quarterly* 29 (1970): 42–48.

Ward, Andrew, *Dark Midnight When I Rise: The Story of the Jubilee Singers, Who Introduced the World to the Music of Black America* (2000).

Whalum, Wendell P., "James Weldon Johnson's Theories and Performance Practices of Afro-American Folksongs," *Phylon* 32 (1971): 383–95.

White, Newman I., *American Negro Folk-Songs* (1928).

Windham, Wyolene, "Huddie 'Leadbelly' Ledbetter: Some Reminiscences of His Cousin, Blare Love," *North Louisiana History Association Journal* 7 (1976): 96–100.

Work, John W., *American Negro Songs* (1940).

20.10.6 Art (Drawing, Painting, Photography, Printmaking, Sculpture)

Campbell, Edward D. C., Jr., "Black Prism, White Lens," *Southern Exposure* 23 (1996): 12–19.

Johnston, Frances Benjamin, *The Hampton Album* (1966).

Matthews, Marcia M., "Richmond Barthe: Sculptor," *South Atlantic Quarterly* 74 (1975): 324–39.

[Miner, Leigh Richmond] Edith M. Dabbs, *Face of an Island: Leigh Richmond Miner's Photographs of Saint Helena Island* (1971).

Polk, P. H., *P. H. Polk: Photographs* (1980).

Wahlman, Maude S., "Religious Symbols in Afro-American Folk Art," *New York Folklore* 12 (1986): 1–24.

20.10.7 Architecture and Design

Grandison, Kenrick Ian, "Negotiated Space: The Black College Campus As a Cultural Record of Postbellum America," *American Quarterly* 51 (1999): 529–79.

20.10.8 Film and Broadcasting

Cripps, Thomas, *Slow Fade to Black: The Negro in American Film, 1900–1942* (1977).

———— "The Unformed Image: The Negro in the Movies before 'Birth of a Nation,'" *Maryland Historian* 2 (1971): 13–26.

Leab, Daniel J., "'All-Colored'—But Not Much Different: Films Made for Negro Ghetto Audiences, 1913–1928," *Phylon* 36 (1975): 321–39.

———— *From Sambo to Superspade: The Black Experience in Motion Pictures* (1975).

———— "The Gamut from A to B: The Image of the Black in Pre-1915 Movies," *Political Science Quarterly* 88 (1973): 53–70.

Peterson, Bernard L., Jr., "The Films of Oscar Micheaux: America's First Fabulous Black Filmmaker," *Crisis* 86 (1979): 136–41.

Silverman, Joan L., "'The Birth of a Nation': Prohibition Propaganda," *Southern Quarterly* 19 (1981): 23–30.

20.11 EDUCATION

Adams, David W., "Education in Hues: Red and Black at Hampton Institute, 1878–1893," *South Atlantic Quarterly* 76 (1977): 159–76.

———— "Philanthropists, Progressives, and Southern Black Education," *History of Education Quarterly* 23 (1983): 99–111.

Anderson, Eric, and Alfred A. Moss, Jr., *Dangerous Donations: Northern Philanthropy and Southern Black Education, 1902–1930* (1999).

Anderson, James D., *The Education of Blacks in the South, 1860–1935* (1988).

———— "Northern Foundations and the Shaping of Southern Black Rural Education, 1902–1935," *History of Education Quarterly* 18 (1978): 371–96.

———— "Philanthropy, the State, and the Development of Historically Black Public Colleges: The Case of Mississippi," *Minerva: A Review of Science, Learning, and Policy [London]* 35 (1997): 295–309.

Bayleat, Frank A., "Segregation in the Public Schools of the Oklahoma Territory," *Chronicles of Oklahoma* 39 (1961): 180–92.

Belles, A. Gilbert, "The College Faculty, the Negro Scholar, and the Julius Rosenwald Fund," *Journal of Negro History* 54 (1969): 383–92.

Bond, Horace M., *Negro Education in Alabama: A Study in Cotton and Steel* (1939).

Burnside, Jacqueline G., "A 'Delicate and Difficult Duty': Interracial Education at Maryville College, Tennessee, 1868–1901," *American Presbyterians* 72 (1994): 229–40.

——— "Suspicion *versus* Faith: Negro Criticisms of Berea College in the Nineteenth Century," *Register of the Kentucky Historical Society* 83 (1985): 237–66.

Calkins, David L., "Black Education and the Nineteenth Century City: An Institutional Analysis of Cincinnati's Colored Schools, 1850–1887," *Cincinnati History Society* 33 (1975): 161–71.

Campbell, Thomas Monroe, *The Movable School Goes to the Negro Farmer* (1936).

Carter, Doris D., "Charles P. Adams and Grambling State University: The Formative Years, 1901–1928," *Louisiana History* 17 (1976): 401–12.

Clary, George E., Jr., "Southern Methodism's Unique Adventure in Race Relations: Paine College, 1882–1903," *Methodist History* 9 (1971): 22–33.

Cole, Babalola, "Appropriation Politics and Black Schools: Howard University in the U.S. Congress, 1879–1928," *Journal of Negro Education* 46 (1977): 7–23.

Cooper, Arnold, *Between Struggle and Hope: Four Black Educators in the South, 1894–1915* (1989).

——— "Booker T. Washington and William J. Edwards of Snow Hill Institute, 1893–1915," *Alabama Review* 40 (1987): 111–32.

——— "The Tuskegee Machine in Action: Booker T. Washington's Influence on Utica Institute, 1903–1915," *Journal of Mississippi History* 48 (1986): 283–95.

——— "'We Rise upon the Structure We Ourselves Have Builded': William H. Holtzclaw and Utica Institute, 1903–1915," *Journal of Mississippi History* 47 (1985).

——— "William H. Holtzclaw: A Black Educator in the Age of Booker T. Washington," *Vitae Scholasticae* 2 (1983): 123–43.

Craig, Lee A., "Constrained Resource Allocation and the Investment in the Education of Black Americans: The 1890 Land-Grant Colleges," *Agricultural History* 65 (1991): 73–84.

Crofts, Daniel W., "The Black Response to the Blair Education Bill," *Journal of Southern History* 37 (1971): 41–65.

Davis, Leroy, "An African American Dilemma: John Hope and Black Leadership in the Early Twentieth Century," *Atlanta History* 41 (1997): 27–48.

——— *A Clashing of the Soul: John Hope and the Dilemma of African American Leadership and Black Higher Education in the Early Twentieth Century* (1998).

Dennis, Rutledge M., "Du Bois and the Role of the Educated Elite," *Journal of Negro Education* 46 (1977): 388–402.

Denton, Virginia Lantz, *Booker T. Washington and the Adult Education Movement* (1993).

Department of the Interior, Bureau of Education, *Negro Education* (2 vols, 1917).

Dews, Margery, "P. F. H. Henderson and Howard Normal School," *Georgia Historical Quarterly* 63 (1979): 252–63.

Dixon, Blase, "The Catholic University of America and the Racial Question, 1914–1918," *Records of the American Catholic Historical Society of Philadelphia* 84 (1973): 221–24.

Drake, St. Clair, "The Tuskegee Connection: Booker T. Washington and Robert E. Park," *Society* 20 (1983): 82–92.

Du Bois, W.E.B., and Augustus G. Dill, ed., *The College Bred Negro* (1910).

——— *The Common School and the Negro American* (1911).

Enck, Henry S., "Black Self-Help in the Progressive Era: The Northern Campaigns of Smaller Southern Black Industrial Schools, 1900–1915," *Journal of Negro History* 6 (1976): 73–87.

Farrison, W. Edward, "Booker T. Washington: A Study in Educational Leadership," *South Atlantic Quarterly* 41 (1942): 313–19.

Finkenbine, Roy E., "'Our Little Circle': Benevolent Reformers, the Slater Fund, and the Argument for Black Industrial Education, 1882–1908," *Hayes Historical Journal* 6 (1986): 6–22.

Fisher, John E., *The John F. Slater Fund: A Nineteenth Century Affirmative Action for Negro Education* (1986).

Fleming, Cynthia G., "The Plight of Black Educators in Post-War Tennessee, 1865–1920," *Journal of Negro History* 64 (1979): 355–64.

——— "A Survey of the Beginnings of Tennessee's Black Colleges and Universities," *Tennessee Historical Quarterly* 39 (1980): 195–207.

Franklin, John Hope, "Jim Crow Goes to School: The Genesis of Legal Segregation in Southern Schools," *South Atlantic Quarterly* 58 (1959): 225–35.

Fultz, Michael, "African American Teachers in the South, 1890–1940: Powerlessness and the Ironies of Expectations and Protest," *History of Education Quarterly* 35 (1995): 401–22.

———— "African-American Teachers in the South, 1890–1940: Growth, Feminization, and Salary Discrimination," *Teachers College Record* 96 (1995): 544–68.

Gardner, Booker T., "The Educational Contributions of Booker T. Washington," *Journal of Negro Education* 44 (1975): 502–18.

Gerber, David A., "Education, Expediency, and Ideology: Race and Politics in the Desegregation of Ohio Public Schools in the Late Nineteenth Century," *Journal of Ethnic Studies* 1 (1973): 1–31.

———— "Segregation, Separatism, and Sectarianism: Ohio Blacks and Wilberforce University's Effort to Obtain Federal Funds, 1891," *Journal of Negro Education* 45 (1976): 1–20.

Gershenberg, Irving, "The Negro and the Development of White Public Education in the South: Alabama, 1880–1930," *Journal of Negro Education* 39 (1970): 50–59.

Grundman, Adolph H., "Northern Baptists and the Founding of Virginia Union University: The Perils of Paternalism," *Journal of Negro History* 63 (1978): 26–41.

Halderman, Keith, "Blanche Armwood of Tampa and the Strategy of Interracial Cooperation," *Florida Historical Quarterly* 74 (1996): 287–303.

Haley, Charles T., "A Review Essay—Tuskegee's Wizard of Oz: Booker T. Washington and Teaching History," *Teaching History: A Journal of Methods* 9 (1984): 81–86.

Hall, Robert H., "Segregation in the Public Schools of Georgia," *Georgia Bar Journal* 16 (1954): 417–46.

Hampton Institute, *Twenty-Two Years' Work of Hampton Normal and Agricultural Institute at Hampton, Virginia: Records of Negro and Indian Graduates and Ex-Students* (1891).

Hanchett, Thomas W., "The Rosenwald Schools and Black Education in North Carolina," *North Carolina Historical Review* 65 (1988): 387–444.

Harlan, Louis R., *Separate and Unequal: Public School Campaigns and Racism in the Southern Seaboard States, 1901–1915* (1968).

———— "The Southern Education Board and the Race Issue in Public Education," *Journal of Southern History* 23 (1957): 189–202.

Harley, Sharon, "Beyond the Classroom: Organizational Lives of Black Female Educators in the District of Columbia, 1890–1930," *Journal of Negro Education* 51 (1982): 254–65.

Harris, Carl V., "Stability and Change in Discrimination against Black Public Schools: Birmingham, Alabama, 1871–1931," *Journal of Southern History* 51 (1985): 375–416.

Hartshorn, William Newton, *An Era of Progress and Promise, 1863–1910* (1910).

Hendrick, Irving G., "Approaching Equality of Educational Opportunity in California: The Successful Struggle of Black Citizens, 1880–1920," *Pacific Historian* 25 (1981): 22–29.

Hine, Darlene Clark, "The Anatomy of Failure: Medical Education Reform and the Leonard Medical School of Shaw University, 1882–1920," *Journal of Negro Education* 54 (1985): 512–25.

———— "Opportunity and Fulfillment: Sex, Race, and Class in Health Care Education," in Darlene Clark Hine, ed., *Black Women's History: Theory and Practice* (1990): 219–34.

Hogan, David John, *Class and Reform: School and Society in Chicago, 1880–1930* (1985).

———— "Education and the Making of the Chicago Working Class, 1880–1930," *History of Education Quarterly* 18 (1978): 227–70.

Holland, Antonio F., "Education over Politics: Nathan B. Young at Florida A and M College, 1901–1923," *Agricultural History* 65 (1992): 131–48.

Hornsby, Alton, Jr., "The 'Colored Branch University' Issue in Texas—Prelude to *Sweatt vs. Painter*," *Journal of Negro History* 6 (1976): 51–60.

Howard, Victor B., "The Struggle for Equal Education in Kentucky, 1866–1884," *Journal of Negro Education* 46 (1977): 305–28.

Huber, Patrick J., and Gary R. Kremer, "Nathaniel C. Bruce, Black Education, and the 'Tuskegee of the Midwest,'" *Missouri Historical Review* 86 (1991): 37–54.

Hunt, Thomas C., "The Schooling of Immigrants and Black Americans: Some Similarities and Differences," *Journal of Negro Education* 45 (1976): 423–31.

Hunter, Tera, "The Correct Thing: Charlotte Hawkins Brown and the Palmer Institute," *Southern Exposure* 11 (1983): 37–43.

Jenkins, Robert L., "The Black Land-Grant Colleges in Their Formative Years, 1890–1920," *Agricultural History* 65 (1992): 63–72.

Jones, Allen W., "The Role of Tuskegee Institute in the Education of Black Farmers," *Journal of Negro History* 60 (1975): 252–67.

Jones, H. Lawrence, "Phillip Reed: Prominent Black Educator of Wheeling," *Upper Ohio Valley Historical Review* 13 (1983): 4–9.

Kelley, Don Quinn, "Ideology and Education: Uplifting the Masses in Nineteenth Century Alabama," *Phylon* 40 (1979): 147–58.

King, Wilma, "Multicultural Education at Hampton Institute: The Shawnees, A Case Study, 1900–1923," *Journal of Negro Education* 57 (1988): 524–35.

Kousser, J. Morgan, "Making Separate Equal: Integration of Black and White School Funds in Kentucky," *Journal of Interdisciplinary History* 10 (1979): 399–428.

——— "Progressivism—For Middle Class Whites Only: North Carolina Education, 1880–1910," *Journal of Southern History* 46 (1980): 169–94.

Leloudis, James L., *Schooling the New South: Pedagogy, Self, and Society in North Carolina, 1880–1920* (1996).

Levy, William, "A Jew Views Black Education: Texas, 1890," *Western States Jewish Historical Quarterly* 8 (1976): 351–60.

Lewis, Ronald L., "Reverend T. G. Stewart and 'Mixed' Schools in Delaware, 1882," *Delaware History* 19 (1980): 53–58.

Lindsay, Beverly, and J. John Harris, III, "Progressive Education and the Black College," *Journal of Black Studies* 7 (1977): 341–57.

Livingston, Thomas W., "The Exportation of American Higher Education to West Africa: Liberia College, 1850–1900," *Journal of Negro Education* 45 (1976): 246–62.

Logan, Frenise A., "Legal Status of Public School Education for Negroes in North Carolina, 1877–1894," *North Carolina Historical Review* 32 (1955): 346–57.

——— "The Movement in North Carolina to Establish a State Supported College for Negroes," *North Carolina Historical Review* 35 (1958): 167–80.

Logan, Rayford W., "The Evolution of Private Colleges for Negroes," *Journal of Negro Education* 27 (1958): 213–20.

Mabee, Carleton, "Long Island's Black School War and the Decline of Segregation in New York State," *New York History* 58 (1977): 385–411.

Margo, Robert A., "Race Differences in Public School Expenditures: Disfranchisement and School Finance in Louisiana, 1890–1910," *Social Science History* 6 (1982): 9–34.

——— "Teacher Salaries in Black and White: The South in 1910," *Explorations in Economic History* 21 (1984): 306–26.

Martin, Sandy D., "The American Baptist Home Mission Society and Black Higher Education in the South, 1865–1920," *Foundations* 24 (1981): 310–27.

McPherson, James M., "White Liberals and Black Power in Negro Education, 1865–1915," *American Historical Review* 75 (1970): 1357–86.

Mohraz, Judy Jolley, *The Separate Problem: Case Studies of Black Education in the North, 1900–1930* (1979).

Nelson, Paul David, "Experiment in Interracial Education at Berea College, 1858–1908," *Journal of Negro History* 59 (1974): 13–27.

Noble, Stuart G., *Forty Years of the Public Schools in Mississippi, with Special Reference to the Education of the Negro* (1918).

Ochs, Stephen J., "The Ordeal of the Black Priest," *U.S. Catholic Historian* 5 (1986): 45–66.

Peeps, J. M. Stephen, "Northern Philanthropy and the Emergence of Black Higher Education: Do-Gooders, Compromisers, or Co-Conspirators?" *Journal of Negro Education* 50 (1981): 251–69.

Perkins, Linda M., "Lucy Diggs Slowe: Champion of the Self-Determination of African-American Women in Higher Education," *The Journal of Negro History* 81 (1996): 89–104.

Perlmann, Joel, *Ethnic Differences: Schooling and Social Structure among the Irish, Italians, Jews, and Blacks in an American City, 1880–1935* (1988).

——— "The Schooling of Blacks in a Northern City: Providence, R.I., 1880–1925," *Perspectives in American History* 2 (1985): 125–82.

Peterson, Paul E., *The Politics of School Reform, 1870–1940* (1985).

Preer, Jean, "'Just and Equitable Division': Jim Crow and the 1890 Land-Grant College Act," *Prologue* 22 (1990): 323–37.

Pritchett, Jonathan B., "The Burden of Negro Schooling: Tax Incidence and Racial Redistribution in Postbellum North Carolina," *Journal of Economic History* 49 (1989): 966–73.

Rabinowitz, Howard N., "Half a Loaf: The Shift from White to Black Teachers in the Negro Schools of the Urban South, 1865–1890," *Journal of Southern History* 40 (1974): 565–94.

Richardson, Joe M., "To Help a Brother On: The First Decade of Talladega College," *Alabama Historical Quarterly* 37 (1975): 19–37.

Robbins, Gerald, "Rossa B. Cooley and the Penn School: Social Dynamo in a Rural Subculture, 1901–1930," *Journal of Negro Education* 33 (1964): 43–51.

Rothrock, Thomas, "Joseph Carter Corbin and Negro Education in the University of Arkansas," *Arkansas History Quarterly* 30 (1971): 277–314.

Rubin, Louis D., ed., *Teach the Freeman: The Correspondence of Rutherford B. Hayes and the Slater Fund for Negro Education, 1881–1887* (2 vols., 1959).

Rubinstein, Stanley, and Judith Farley, "Enoch Pratt Free Library and Black Patrons: Equality in Library Services, 1882–1915," *Journal of Library History* 15 (1980): 445–53.

Sawyer, R. McLaran, "The National Educational Association and Negro Education, 1865–1884," *Journal of Negro Education* 39 (1970): 341–45.

Schall, Keith L., ed., *Stony the Road: A Chapter in the History of Hampton Institute* (1977).

Sherer, Robert G., "William Burns Patterson: Pioneer As Well As Apostle of Negro Education in Alabama," *Alabama History Quarterly* 36 (1974): 121–50.

Silcox, Harry C., "Philadelphia Negro Educator: Jacob C. White, Jr., 1837–1902," *Pennsylvania Magazine of History and Biography* 97 (1973): 75–98.

Simms, L. Moody, Jr., "William Dorsey Jelks and the Problem of Negro Education," *Alabama Review* 23 (1970): 7–74.

Sisk, Glenn N., "Negro Education in the Alabama Black Belt, 1875–1900," *Journal of Negro Education* 22 (1953): 126–35.

Sloan, Patricia E., "Early Black Nursing Schools and Responses of Black Nurses to Their Educational Programs," *Western Journal of Black Studies* 9 (1985): 1–30.

Spivey, Donald, *Schooling for the New Slavery: Black Industrial Education, 1868–1915* (1978).

Storey, John W., "The Rhetoric of Paternalism: Southern Baptists and Negro Education in the Latter Nineteenth Century," *Southern Humanities Review* 12 (1978): 101–08.

Summerville, James, *Educating Black Doctors: A History of Meharry Medical College* (1983).

Taylor, A. A., "Fisk University and the Nashville Community, 1866–1900," *Journal of Negro History* 39 (1954): 111–26.

TeSelle, Eugene, "The Nashville Institute and Roger Williams University: Benevolence, Paternalism, and Black Consciousness, 1867–1910," *Tennessee Historical Quarterly* 41 (1982): 360–79.

Thomas, Bettye C., "Public Education and Black Protest in Baltimore, 1865–1900," *Maryland Historical Magazine* 71 (1976): 381–91.

Thomas, Bettye Collier, "Public Education and Black Protest in Baltimore, 1865–1900," *Maryland Historical Magazine* 71 (1976): 381–91.

Thompkins, Robert E., "Presbyterian Religious Education among Negroes, 1864–1891," *Journal of the Presbyterian Historical Society* 29 (1951): 145–71.

Timberlake, C. L., "The Early Struggle for Education of the Blacks in the Commonwealth of Kentucky," *Register of the Kentucky History Society* 71 (1973): 225–52.

United States Department of the Interior, Bureau of Education, *Negro Education: A Study of the Private and Higher Schools for Colored People in the United States* (2 vols., 1917).

Van Meter, Sondra, "Black Resistance to Segregation in the Wichita Public Schools, 1870–1912," *Midwest Quarterly* 20 (1978): 64–77.

Vincent, Charles, "Laying the Cornerstone at Southern University," *Louisiana History* 17 (1976): 335–42.

Walters, Pamela B., and David R. James, "Schooling for Some: Child Labor and School Enrollment of Black and White Children in the Early Twentieth-Century South," *American Sociological Review* 57 (1992): 635–50.

Washington, Booker T., *Tuskegee and Its People: Their Ideals and Achievements* (1906).

Wennersten, John R., "The Travail of Black Land-Grant Schools in the South, 1890–1917," *Agricultural History* 65 (1992): 54–62.

Wennersten, John R., and Ruth E. Wennersten, "Separate and Unequal: The Evolution of a Black Land Grant College in Maryland, 1890–1930," *Maryland History Magazine* 72 (1977): 110–17.

Wesley, Charles H., *The History of Alpha Phi Alpha: A Development in Negro College Life* (1939).

West, Earle H., "The Peabody Education Fund and Negro Education, 1867–1880," *History of Education Quarterly* 6 (1966): 3–21.

Wheeler, Elizabeth L., "Isaac Fisher: The Frustrations of a Negro Educator at Branch Normal College, 1902–1911," *Arkansas Historical Quarterly* 41 (1982): 3–50.

White, Arthur O., "Race, Politics, and Education: The Sheats-Holloway Election Controversy, 1903–1904," *Florida Historical Quarterly* 53 (1975): 253–72.

Williams, Lillian S., "Community Educational Activities and the Liberation of Black Buffalo, 1900–1930," *Journal of Negro Education* 54 (1985): 174–88.

Wish, Harvey, "Negro Education and the Progressive Movement," *Journal of Negro History* 49 (1964): 184–200.

Wolcott, Victoria W., "'Bible, Bath, and Broom': Nannie Helen Burroughs's National Training School and African-American Racial Uplift," *Journal of Women's History* 9 (1997): 88–110.

Wright, George C., "The Founding of Lincoln Institute," *Filson Club History Quarterly* 49 (1975): 57–70.

Young, Alfred, "The Educational Philosophy of Booker T. Washington: A Perspective for Black Liberation," *Phylon* 37 (1976): 224–35.

20.12   WORK AND ENTREPRENEURIAL ACTIVITY

Anderson, James D., "The Southern Improvement Company: Northern Reformers' Investment in Negro Cotton Tenancy, 1900–1920," *Agricultural History* 52 (1978): 111–31.

Aptheker, Bettina, "Quest for Dignity: Black Women in the Professions, 1865–1900," in Darlene Clark Hine, ed., *Black Women in American History: From Colonial Times through the Nineteenth Century* (1990).

Arnesen, Eric, "Following the Color Line of Labor: Black Workers and the Labor Movement before 1930," *Radical History Review* 55 (1993): 53–87.

——— "Up from Exclusion: Black and White Workers, Race, and the State of Labor History," *Reviews in American History* 26 (1998): 146–74.

——— *Waterfront Workers of New Orleans: Race, Class, and Politics, 1863–1923* (1991).

Bailey, Kenneth R., "A Judicious Mixture: Negroes and Immigrants in the West Virginia Mines, 1880–1917," *West Virginia History* 34 (1973): 141–61.

Bell, Leland, "Radicalism and Race: The IWW and the Black Worker," *Journal of Human Relations* 19 (1971): 48–56.

Black, Paul V., "The Knights of Labor and the South, 1873–1893," *Southern Quarterly* 1 (1963): 201–12.

Bloch, Herman D., "Labor and the Negro, 1866–1910," *Journal of Negro History* 50 (1965): 163–84.

Bodnar, John E., "The Impact of the 'New Immigration' on the Black Worker: Steelton, Pennsylvania, 1880–1920," *Labor History* 17 (1976): 214–29.

Boyd, Robert L., "Residential Segregation by Race and the Black Merchants of Northern Cities during the Early Twentieth Century," *Sociological Forum* 13 (1998): 595–609.

Brier, Stephen, "Interracial Organizing in the West Virginia Coal Industry: The Participation of Black Mine Workers in the Knights of Labor and the United Mine Workers, 1880–1894," in Gary M. Fink, and Merl E. Reed, ed., *Essays in Southern Labor History: Selected Papers, Southern Labor History Conference, 1976* (1977): 18–43.

———— "Labor, Politics, and Race: A Black Worker's Life," *Labor History* 23 (1982): 416–21.

Bristol, Doug, "The Victory of Black Barbers over Reform in Ohio, 1902–1913," *Essays in Economic and Business History* 16 (1998): 251–60.

Brown, Thomas Isaacs, *Economic Cooperation among the Negroes of Georgia* (1917).

Campbell, Robert A., "Blacks and the Coal Mines of Western Washington, 1888–1896," *Pacific Northwest Quarterly* 73 (1982): 146–55.

Cashman, John, "Slaves under Our Flag: The Navassa Island Riot of 1889," *Maryland Historian* 24 (1993): 1–21.

Chapman, Berlin B., "Freedmen and the Oklahoma Lands," *Southwestern Social Science Quarterly* 29 (1948): 150–59.

Christensen, Lawrence O., "The Popular Image of Blacks *vs.* The Birthrights," *Missouri Historical Review* 81 (1986): 37–52.

Clark-Lewis, Elizabeth, *Living in, Living Out: African American Domestics in Washington, D.C., 1910–1940* (1994).

Coclanis, Peter A., and J. C. Marlow, "Inland Rice Production in the South Atlantic States: A Picture in Black and White," *Agricultural History* 72 (1998): 197–212.

Crosby, Earl W., "The Roots of Black Agricultural Extension Work," *Historian* 39 (1977): 228–47.

DeCanio, Stephen J., *Agriculture in the Postbellum South: The Economics of Production and Supply* (1974).

Du Bois, W.E.B., ed., *Economic Cooperation among Negro Americans* (1907).

————, ed., *Efforts for Social Betterment among Negro Americans* (1909).

————, ed., *The Negro in Business* (1899).

————, ed., *Some Efforts of American Negroes for Their Own Social Betterment* (1898).

Du Bois, W.E.B., and Augustus G. Dill, ed., *The Negro American Artisan* (1912).

Durham, Philip, and Everett L. Jones, *Negro Cowboys* (1965).

Dutcher, Dean, *The Negro in Modern Industrial Society: An Analysis of Changes in the Occupations of Negro Workers, 1910–1920* (1930).

Ferguson, Karen J., "Caught in 'No Man's Land': The Negro Cooperative Demonstration Service and the Ideology of Booker T. Washington, 1900–1918," *Agricultural History* 72 (1998): 33–54.

Ferleger, Louis, "Farm Mechanization in the Southern Sugar Sector after the Civil War," *Louisiana History* 23 (1982): 21–34.

———— "The Problem of 'Labor' in the Post-Reconstruction Louisiana Sugar Industry," *Agricultural History* 72 (1998): 140–58.

Fingard, Judith, "From Sea to Rail: Black Transportation Workers and Their Families in Halifax, C., 1870–1916," *Acadiensis* 24 (1995): 49–64.

Fink, Leon, "'Irrespective of Party, Color, or Social Standing': The Knights of Labor and Opposition Politics in Richmond, Virginia," *Labor History* 19 (1978): 325–49.

Flynn, Charles L., Jr., *White Land, Black Labor: Caste and Class in Late Nineteenth-Century Georgia* (1983).

Foner, Philip S., "The IWW and the Black Worker," *Journal of Negro History* 55 (1970): 45–64.

———— "An Open Letter to John Burns, 1894," *Bulletin of the Society for the Study of Labour History* 22 (1971): 17–20.

Foster, Craig L., "Tarnished Angels: Prostitution in Storyville, New Orleans, 1900–1910," *Louisiana History* 31 (1990): 387–97.

Frisch, Paul A., "'Gibraltar of Unionism': Women, Blacks and the Anti-Chinese Movement in Butte, Montana, 1880–1900," *Southwest Economy and Society* 6 (1984): 3–13.

Fuke, Richard Paul, "Planters, Apprenticeship, and Forced Labor: The Black Family under Pressure in Post-Emancipation Maryland," *Agricultural History* 62 (1988): 57–74.

Goldin, Claudia, "Female Labor Force Participation: The Origin of Black and White Differences, 1870 and 1880," *Journal of Economic History* 37 (1977): 87–108.

Green, Thomas L., "Junius R. Lewis and the Golden Chest Mining Company," *Colorado Magazine* 50 (1973): 24–40.

Greene, Lorenzo Johnston, and Carter G. Woodson, *The Negro Wage Earner* (1930).

Grob, Gerald N., "Organized Labor and the Negro Worker, 1865–1900," *Labor History* 1 (1960): 164–76.

Grossman, Jonathan, "Black Studies in the Department of Labor, 1897–1907," *Monthly Labor Review* 97 (1974): 17–27.

Guenther, Todd R., "'Y'All Call Me Nigger Jim Now, But Someday You'll Call Me Mr. James Edwards': Black Success on the Plains of the Equality State," *Annals of Wyoming* 61 (1989): 20–40.

Gutman, Herbert G., "Black Coal Miners and the Greenback-Labor Party in Redeemer, Alabama, 1878–1879: The Letters of Warren D. Kelley, Willis Johnson Thomas, 'Dawson,' and Others," *Labor History* 10 (1969): 506–35.

——— "The Negro and the United Mine Workers of America: The Career and Letters of Richard L. Davis and Something of Their Meaning, 1890–1900," in *Work, Culture, and Society in Industrializing America: Essays in American Working-Class and Social History* (1976).

Guzda, Henry P., "Social Experiment in the Labor Department: The Division of Negro Economics," *Public History* 4 (1982): 7–37.

Haiken, Elizabeth, "'The Lord Helps Those Who Help Themselves': Black Laundresses in Little Rock, Arkansas, 1917–1921," *Arkansas Historical Quarterly* 49 (1990): 20–50.

Hamburger, Susan, "On the Land for Life: Black Tenant Farmers on Tall Timbers Plantation," *Florida Historical Quarterly* 66 (1987): 152–59.

Hamilton, Kenneth M., *Black Towns and Profit: Promotion and Development in the Trans-Appalachian West, 1877–1915* (1991).

Hammett, Hugh B., "Labor and Race: The Georgia Railroad Strike of 1909," *Labor History* 16 (1975): 470–84.

Hargis, Peggy G., "Beyond the Marginality Thesis: The Acquisition and Loss of Land by African Americans in Georgia, 1880–1930," *Agricultural History* 72 (1998): 241–62.

Harley, Sharon, "For the Good of Family and Race: Gender, Work, and Domestic Roles in the Black Community, 1880–1930," *Signs* 15 (1990): 336–49.

Harmon, J. H., Jr., Arnett G. Lindsay, and Carter G. Woodson, *The Negro As a Business Man* (1929).

Harris, Abram L., *The Negro as Capitalist: A Study of Banking and Business among American Negroes* (1936).

Henderson, Alexa Benson, "Herman E. Perry and Black Enterprise in Atlanta, 1908–1925," *Business History Review* 61 (1987): 216–42.

Higgs, Robert, *Competition and Coercion: Blacks in the American Economy, 1865–1914* (1977).

——— "Did Southern Farmers Discriminate? Interpretive Problems and Further Evidence," *Agricultural History* 46 (1972): 325–28.

——— "Racial Wage Differentials in Agriculture: Evidence from North Carolina in 1887," *Agricultural History* 52 (1978): 308–11.

Hill, Herbert, "In the Age of Gompers and After: Racial Practices of Organized Labor," *New Politics* 4 (1965): 26–46.

Holmes, William F., "The Arkansas Cotton Pickers' Strike of 1891 and the Demise of the Colored Farmers' Alliance," *Arkansas Historical Quarterly* 32 (1973): 107–19.

Holt, Hamilton, "The Life of a Negro Peon," in Hamilton Holt, ed., *The Life Stories of Undistinguished Americans* (1986).

Hopkins, Richard J., "Occupational and Geographic Mobility in Atlanta, 1870–1896," *Journal of Southern History* 34 (1968): 200–13.

Hornsby, Anne R., "The Accumulation of Wealth by Black Georgians, 1890–1915," *Journal of Negro History* 74 (1989): 11–30.

Humphreys, Hubert, "The Rise and Fall of the Shreveport ("Colored") Labor Association As Documented by the *Shreveport Daily Times*, 1880," *North Louisiana Historical Association Journal* 19 (1988): 3–17.

Hunter, Tera W., *To 'Joy My Freedom: Southern Black Women's Lives and Labors after the Civil War* (1997).

Irwin, James C., "Farmers and Laborers: A Note on Black Occupations in the Postbellum South," *Agricultural History* 64 (1900): 53–60.

Irwin, James R., and Anthony P. O'Brien, "Where Have All the Sharecroppers Gone? Black Occupations in Postbellum Mississippi," *Agricultural History* 72 (1998): 280–97.

Janiewski, Dolores E., *Sisterhood Denied: Race, Gender, and Class in a New South Community* (1985).

———— "Sisters under Their Skins: Southern Working Women, 1880–1915," in Joanne V. Hawks, and Sheila L. Skemp, ed., *Sex, Race, and the Role of Women in the South* (1983): 13–35.

Jaynes, Gerald David, *Branches without Roots: Genesis of the Black Working Class in the American South, 1862–1882* (1986).

Jones, Allen W., "The South's First Black Farm Agents," *Agriculture History* 50 (1976): 636–44.

Jones, Lewis W., "The South's Negro Farm Agent," *Journal of Negro Education* 22 (1953): 38–45.

Kann, Kenneth, "The Knights of Labor and the Southern Black Worker," *Labor History* 18 (1977): 49–70.

Katzman, David M., *Seven Days a Week: Women and Domestic Service in Industrializing America* (1978).

Keiser, John H., "Black Strikebreakers and Racism in Illinois, 1865–1900," *Journal of the Illinois State Historical Society* 65 (1972): 313–26.

Kelsey, Carl, *The Negro Farmer* (1903).

Kenzer, Robert C., *Enterprising Southerners: Black Economic Success in North Carolina, 1865–1915* (1997).

Kessler, Sidney H., "The Organization of Negroes in the Knights of Labor," *Journal of Negro History* 37 (1952): 248–76.

Kilar, Jeremy W., "Black Pioneers in the Michigan Lumber Industry," *Journal of Forest History* 24 (1980): 142–49.

Kimball, Gregg D., "The Working People of Richmond: Life and Labor in an Industrial City, 1865–1920," *Labor's Heritage* 3 (1991): 42–65.

Kremm, Thomas W., and Diane Neal, "Clandestine Black Labor Societies and White Fear: Hiram F. Hoover and the 'Cooperative Workers of America' in the South," *Labor History* 19 (1978): 226–37.

Letwin, Daniel, *The Challenge of Interracial Unionism: Alabama Coal Miners, 1878–1921* (1998).

———— "Interracial Unionism, Gender, and 'Social Equality' in the Alabama Coalfields, 1878–1908," *Journal of Southern History* 61 (1996): 519–54.

Lewis, Ronald L., "The Black Presence in the Paint-Cabin Creek Strike, 1912–1913," *West Virginia History* 46 (1985–1986): 59–71.

———— "From Peasant to Proletarian: The Migration of Southern Blacks to the Central Appalachian Coalfields," *Journal of Southern History* 55 (1989): 77–102.

———— "Job Control and Race Relations in Coal Fields, 1879–1920," *Journal of Ethnic Studies* 12 (1985): 35–64.

———— "Race and the United Mine Workers' Union in Tennessee: Selected Letters of William R. Riley, 1892–1895," *Tennessee Historical Quarterly* 36 (1977): 524–36.

Lichtenstein, Alex, "Racial Conflict and Racial Solidarity in the Alabama Coal Strike of 1894: New Evidence for the Gutman-Hill Debate," *Labor History* 36 (1995): 63–76.

Linde, Debbie, "Sawdust in Their Shoes: Black Performers in American Circuses," *American Visions* 7 (1992): 12–19.

Logan, Frenise A., "Factors Influencing the Efficiency of Negro Farm Laborers in Post-Reconstruction North Carolina," *Agricultural History* 33 (1959): 185–89.

Lomax, Michael E., "Black Entrepreneurship in the National Pastime: The Rise of Semiprofessional Baseball in Black Chicago, 1890–1915," *Journal of Sport History* 25 (1998): 43–64.

Mack, Kibibi Voloria C., *Parlor Ladies and Ebony Drudges: African American Women, Class, and Work in a South Carolina Community* (1999).

Mandel, Bernard, "Samuel Gompers and the Negro Worker, 1886–1914," *Journal of Negro History* 40 (1955): 34–60.

Mandle, Jay R., *The Roots of Black Poverty: The Southern Plantation Economy after the Civil War* (1978).

Marable, Manning, "The Politics of Land Tenure, 1877–1915," *Agricultural History* 53 (1979): 142–52.

Marks, Carole, "Split Labor Markets and Black-White Relations, 1865–1920," *Phylon* 42 (1981): 293–308.

McGirr, Lisa, "Black and White Longshoremen in the IWW: A History of the Philadelphia Marine Transport Workers Industrial Union Local Eight," *Labor History* 36 (1995): 377–402.

McKenzie, Robert T., "Postbellum Tenancy in Fayette County, Tennessee: Its Implications for Economic and Persistent Black Poverty," *Agricultural History* 61 (1987): 16–33.

McKiven, Henry M., Jr., *Iron and Steel: Class, Race, and Community in Birmingham, Alabama, 1875–1920* (1995).

McLaurin, Melton A., *The Knights of Labor in the South* (1978).

McMath, Robert C., Jr., "Southern White Farmers and the Organization of Black Farm Workers: A North Carolina Document," *Labor History* 18 (1977): 115–19.

Mergen, Bernard, "The Pullman Porter: From 'George' to Brotherhood," *South Atlantic Quarterly* 73 (1974): 224–35.

Mintz, Steven, "Sources of Variability in Rates of Black Home Ownership in 1900," *Phylon* 46 (1983): 312–31.

Model, Suzanne, "The Effects of Ethnicity in the Workplace on Blacks, Italians, and Jews in 1910 New York," *Journal of Urban History* 16 (1989): 29–51.

———— "Work and Family: Blacks and Immigrants from South and East Europe," in Virginia Yans-McLaughlin, ed., *Immigration Reconsidered: History, Sociology, and Politics* (1990): 130–59.

Mollison, Irvin C., "Negro Lawyers in Mississippi," *Journal of Negro History* 15 (1930): 38–71.

Ng, Kenneth, and Nancy Virts, "The Black-White Income Gap in 1880," *Agricultural History* 67 (1993): 1–15.

Norrell, Robert J., "Caste in Steel: Jim Crow Careers in Birmingham, Alabama," *Journal of American History* 73 (1986): 669–94.

Ochiltree, Ian D., "'A Just and Self-Respecting System?' Black Independence, Sharecropping, and Paternalistic Relations in the American South and South Africa," *Agricultural History* 72 (1998): 352–80.

Ogden, Annegret, "'Looking for Work in Every Direction': The Voice of David Brown, Secretary of the Colored Stock Quartz Mining Company, Sierra County, California," *Californians* 9 (1991): 14–17.

Oldfield, J. R., "A High and Honorable Calling: Black Lawyers in South Carolina, 1868–1915," *Journal of American Studies* 23 (1989): 395–406.

Painter, Nell Irvin, "Black Workers from Reconstruction to the Great Depression," in Paul Buhle, and Alan Dawley, ed., *Working for Democracy* (1985): 63–71.

Pleck, Elizabeth H., "A Mother's Wages: Income Earning among Married Italian and Black Women, 1896–1911," in Nancy F. Cott, and Elizabeth H. Pleck, ed., *A Heritage of Her Own: Toward a New Social History of American Women* (1979): 367–92.

Porter, Kenneth O., "Negro Labor in the Western Cattle Industry, 1866–1900," *Labor History* 10 (1969): 346–74.

Rachleff, Peter, *Black Labor in the South: Richmond, Virginia, 1865–1890* (1984).

Reid, Ira de Augustine, *Negro Membership in American Labor Unions by the Department of Research and Investigations of the National Urban League* (1930).

Reid, Joseph D., Jr., "Sharecropping As an Understandable Market Response: The Postbellum South," *Journal of Economic History* 33 (1973): 106–30.

Reidy, Joseph P., "Mules and Machines and Men: Field Labor on Louisiana Sugar Plantations, 1887–1915," *Agricultural History* 72 (1998): 183–96.

Roberts, Charles A., "Did Southern Farmers Discriminate: The Evidence Reexamined," *Agricultural History* 49 (1975): 441–47.

Rogers, William W., "Negro Knights of Labor in Arkansas: A Case Study of the 'Miscellaneous' Strike," *Labor History* 10 (1969): 498–505.

Rosenberg, Daniel, *New Orleans Dockworkers: Race, Labor, and Unionism, 1892–1923* (1988).

Schultz, Mark R., "The Dream Realized? African-American Land Ownership in Central Georgia between Reconstruction and World War Two," *Agricultural History* 72 (1998): 298–312.

Schweninger, Loren, *Black Property Owners in the South, 1790–1915* (1990).

Seraile, William, "Ben Fletcher, I.W.W. Organizer," *Pennsylvania History* 46 (1979): 213–32.

Sharpless, Rebecca, *Fertile Ground, Narrow Choices: Women on Texas Cotton Farms, 1900–1940* (1999).

Shaw, Nate, *All God's Dangers: The Life of Nate Shaw*, comp. Theodore Rosengarten (1974).

Shaw, Stephanie J., *What a Woman Ought To Be and To Do: Black Professional Women Workers during the Jim Crow Era* (1996).

Shlomowitz, R., "'Bound' or 'Free': Black Labor in Cotton and Sugarcane Farming, 1865–1880," *Journal of Southern History* 50 (1984): 569–96.

Shofner, Jerrell H., "Forced Labor in the Florida Forests, 1880–1950," *Journal of Forest History* 25 (1981): 14–25.

Simms, James N., *Simms' Blue Book and National Negro Business and Professional Directory* (1923).

Sowell, David, "Racial Patterns of Labor in Postbellum Florida: Gainesville, 1870–1900," *Florida Historical Quarterly* 63 (1985): 434–44.

Spero, Sterling D., and Abram L. Harris, *The Black Worker: The Negro and the Labor Movement* (1931).

Stern, Mark, "Black Strikebreakers in the Coal Fields: King County, Washington, 1891," *Journal of Ethnic Studies* 5 (1977): 60–70.

Tucker, Susan, "A Complex Bond: Southern Black Domestic Workers and Their White Employers," *Frontiers* 9 (1987): 6–13.

———— *Telling Memories among Southern Women: Domestic Workers and Their Employers in the Segregated South* (1988).

Tuttle, William M., "Labor Conflict and Racial Violence: The Black Worker in Chicago, 1894–1919," *Labor History* 10 (1969): 408–32.

———— "Thirty-Five Years Overdue: Note on a Belated up from Slavery," *Labor History* 15 (1974): 86–88.

Washington, Booker T., *The Negro in Business* (1907).

Weare, Walter B., *Black Business in the New South: A Social History of the North Carolina Mutual Life Insurance Company* (1975).

Weeks, Louis, "John P. Parker: Black Abolitionist Entrepreneur, 1827–1900," *Ohio History* 80 (1971): 155–62.

Wesley, Charles H., *Negro Labor in the United States, 1850–1925* (1927).

Wetherington, Mark V., "Black Workers and Technological Change in the Birmingham Iron Industry, 1881–1931," Merl E. Reed, Leslie S. Hough, and Gary M. Fink, ed., *Southern Workers and Their Unions, 1880–1975: Selected Papers. The Second Labor History Conference, 1978* (1981).

Woodman, Harold, *New South—New Law: The Legal Foundations of Credit and Labor Relations in the Postbellum Agricultural South* (1995).

Woodman, Harold, and Gilbert C. Fite, "Postbellum Social Change and Its Effects on Marketing the South's Cotton Crop," *Agriculture History* 56 (1982): 215–30, 244–48.

Worthman, Paul B., "A Black Worker and the Bricklayers and Masons Union, 1903," *Journal of Negro History* 54 (1969): 398–404.

———— "Black Workers and Labor Unions in Birmingham, Alabama, 1879–1904," *Labor History* 10 (1969): 375–407.

———— "Working Class Mobility in Birmingham, Alabama, 1860–1914," in Tamara K. Hareven, ed., *Anonymous Americans: Explorations in Nineteenth-Century Social History* (1971).

Wright, Gavin, *Old South, New South: Revolutions in the Southern Economy Since the Civil War* (1986).

Zabawa, Robert E., and Sarah T. Warren, "From Company to Community: Agricultural Community Development in Macon County, Alabama, 1881 to the New Deal," *Agricultural History* 72 (1998): 459–86.

20.13 SCIENCE AND TECHNOLOGY

Christopher, Michael C., "Granville T. Woods: The Plight of a Black Inventor," *Journal of Black Studies* 11 (1981): 269–76.

Fouche, Rayvon, "The Exploitation of an African-American Inventor on the Fringe: Granville T. Woods and the Process of Invention," *Western Journal of Black Studies* 21 (1997): 190–98.

Hines, Linda O., "George W. Carver and the Tuskegee Agricultural Experiment Station," *Agricultural History* 53 (1979): 71–83.

Mackintosh, Barry, "George Washington Carver and the Peanut: New Light on a Much-Loved Myth," *American Heritage* 28 (1977): 66–73.

20.14 MEDICINE AND HEALTH

Beardsley, Edward H., *A History of Neglect: Health Care for Blacks and Mill Workers in the Twentieth-Century South* (1987).

———— "Making Separate Equal: Black Physicians and the Problems of Medical Segregation in the Pre-World War I South," *Bulletin of the History of Medicine* 57 (1983): 382–96.

Cabak, Melanie A., Mark D. Groover, and Scott J. Wagers, "Health Care and the Wayman A.M.E. Church," *Historical Archaeology* 29 (1995): 55–76.

Cadwallader, D. E., and F. J. Wilson, "Folklore Medicine among Georgia's Piedmont Negroes after the Civil War," *Georgia Historical Quarterly* 49 (1965): 217–27.

Courtwright, David T., "The Hidden Epidemic: Opiate Addiction and Cocaine Use in the South, 1860–1920," *Journal of Southern History* 49 (1983): 57–72.

Du Bois, W.E.B., ed., *The Health and Physique of the Negro American* (1906).

Ellis, John H., "Disease and the Destiny of a City: The 1878 Yellow Fever Epidemic in Memphis," *West Tennessee Historical Society Papers* 28 (1974): 75–89.

Galishoff, Stuart, "Germs Know No Color Line: Black Health and Public Policy in Atlanta, 1900–1918," *Journal of the History of Medicine and Allied Sciences* 40 (1985): 22–41.

Gamble, Vanessa Northington, *The Black Community Hospital: Contemporary Dilemmas in Historical Perspective* (1989).

————, ed., *Germs Have No Color Line: Blacks and American Medicine, 1900–1940* (1989).

Haller, John S., Jr., "The Physician *versus* the Negro: Medical and Anthropological Concepts of Race in the Late Nineteenth Century," *Bulletin of the History of Medicine* 44 (1970): 154–67.

———— "Race, Mortality, and Life Insurance: Negro Vital Statistics in the Late Nineteenth Century," *Journal of the History of Medicine and Allied Sciences* 25 (1970): 247–61.

Hepler, Richard W., "'The World Do Marvel': Health Care for Knoxville's Black Community, 1865–1940," *Journal of East Tennessee History* 63 (1991): 51–71.

Hine, Darlene Clark, "The Anatomy of Failure: Medical Education Reform and the Leonard Medical School of Shaw University, 1882–1920," *Journal of Negro Education* 54 (1985): 512–25.

———— "Opportunity and Fulfillment: Sex, Race, and Class in Health Care Education," in Darlene Clark Hine, ed., *Black Women's History: Theory and Practice* (1990): 219–34.

Hughes, John H., "Labeling and Treating Black Mental Illness in Alabama, 1861–1910," *Journal of Southern History* 58 (1993): 435–60.

Moldow, Gloria, *Women Doctors in Gilded-Age Washington: Race, Gender, and Professionalization* (1987).

Mosley, Marie O. Pitts, "Satisfied to Carry the Bag: Three Black Community Health Nurses' Contributions to Health Care Reform, 1900–1937," *Nursing History Review* 4 (1996): 65–82.

Rabinowitz, Howard N., "From Exclusion to Segregation: Health and Welfare Services for Southern Blacks, 1865–1890," *Social Service Review* 48 (1974): 327–54.

Rousey, Dennis C., "Yellow Fever and Black Policemen in Memphis: A Post-Reconstruction Anomaly," *Journal of Southern History* 51 (1985): 357–74.

Savitt, Todd L., "'A Journal of Our Own': The Medical and Surgical Observer at the Beginnings of an African-American Medical Profession in Late Nineteenth-Century America," *Journal of the National Medical Association* Part One & Part Two, 88 (1996): 52–60, 115–22.

———— "Abraham Flexner and the Black Medical Schools," in Barbara Barzansky and Norman Gevitz, ed., *Beyond Flexner: Medical Education in the Twentieth Century* (1992).

———— "The Education of Black Physicians at Shaw University," in Jeffrey Crow and Flora J. Hatley, ed., *Black Americans in North Carolina and the South* (1984): 160–88.

———— "Entering a White Profession: Black Physicians in the New South, 1880–1920," *Bulletin of the History of Medicine* 61 (1987): 507–40.

Seraile, William, "Susan McKinney Steward: New York State's First African-American Woman Physician," *Afro-Americans in New York Life and History* 9 (1985): 27–44.

Sloan, Patricia E., "Early Black Nursing Schools and Responses of Black Nurses to Their Educational Programs," *Western Journal of Black Studies* 9 (1985): 1–30.

Wailoo, Keith, "'A Disease Sui Generis': The Origins of Sickle Cell Anemia and the Emergence of Modern Clinical Research, 1904–1924," *Bulletin of the History of Medicine* 65 (1991): 185–208.

20.15   STUDIES IN FOREIGN LANGUAGES

Charencey, Hyacinthe Comte de, *Le Folklore nègre en Amérique . . .* [Negro Folklore in America] (1901). In French.

Feng, Jixian, "Bu Ke Hua Sheng Dun Yu Mei Guo Hei Ren Yun Dong" [Booker T. Washington and the African American Movement], *Huadong Shi Da Xuebao* 5 (1982): 61–66. In Chinese.

Gumplowicz, Philippe, *Le Roman du jazz: première époque, 1893–1930* [The Romance of Jazz: Early Period, 1893–1930] (1991). In French.

Higuchi, Hayumi, "Hakujin Yûetsu-shugi to Kokujin Shakai" [The Aftermath of the White Supremacist Terror: A Black Community in North Carolina and Its Reaction], *The American Review* 18 (1984): 134–56. In Japanese.

Huang, Songkang, "Mei Guo Dui Bu Ke Huan Sheng Dun De Zai Ping Jia" [The American Reassessment of Booker T. Washington], *Shi Jie Li Shi* 4 (1981): 68–74. In Chinese.

Iwamoto, Hiroko, "Shikago Banpaku (1893) to Kokujin Jôséi" [The World's Columbian Exposition (1893) and Black Women: Ida B.Wells and Fannie B. Williams], *Journal of Historical Studies* 45 (1993): 143–66. In Japanese.

Mattiello, Cristina, "'I maschi non c'entrano per niente': predicatrici e profete nere nell'America dell'Ottocentro" ['Man Have Nothing to Do with It': African-American Women Preachers and Prophets in the Nineteenth Century], *Rivista Internazionale di Studi Nordamericani [International Journal of North American Studies]* 1 (1995): 24–8. In Italian.

Nakamura (Sasamoto), Masako, "Amerikajin dearu koto Kokujin dearu koto" [To Be an American and to Be a Negro: The Case of W.E.B. Du Bois], in Sozo Honda, ed., *Amerika Shakai-Shi no Sekai [Perspectives in American Social History: Issues of Race and Ethnicity]* (1989): 171–200. In Japanese.

Otsuka, Hideyuki, "Shoki Dyuboisu no 'Kokujin Mondai' Ninshiki" [The Young Du Bois: How He Grasped the 'Negro Question'], *The Annual Report of Kobe City University of Foreign Studies* 5 (1968): 1–50. In Japanese.

Ouellet, Nelson, "L'exclusion de la 'porte ouverte,' les préferences raciales des patrons et la chronologie de la Grande Migration, 1865–1925" ['Open Door' Exclusion: Racial Preferences of Employers and the Chronology of the Great Migration, 1865–1925], *Canadian Review of American Studies/ Revue canadienne d'études américaines* 28 (1998): 87–128. In French.

Tété-Adjalogo, Tetevi G., *Marcus Garvey: père de l'unité africaine, garveyisme et panafricainisme* [Marcus Garvey: The Father of African Unity, Garveyism, and Panafricanism] (2 vol., 1994). In French.

———— *Marcus Garvey: père de l'unité africaine des peuples* [Marcus Garvey: The Father of the Unity of African Peoples] (2 vol., 1995). In French.

Tian, Jinyu, *Pu Ke Hua Sheng Dun* [Booker T. Washington] (1935). In Chinese.

Tricoche, George Nestler, *La Question des Noirs aux États-Unis* [The Question of Blacks in the United States] (1894). In French.

Yokoyama, Ryo, "Kokujin no Shimin-teki Jiyû o Motomeru Tatakai" [The Struggle of Afro-American People for Freedom: The N.A.A.C.P. and W.E.B. Du Bois], in Akira Imazu, ed., *America in World War I: The Crisis of the Civil Liberties* (1981): 301–35. In Japanese.

21   *1915–1932*

Joe W. Trotter and Jeffrey Conrad Stewart

21.1   GENERAL STUDIES

American Academy of Political and Social Science, *The American Negro* (1928).

Collins, L. M., ed., *The Harlem Renaissance Generation: An Anthology: Chronicle, Commentary, Conversation, Graphics, Letters, Reminiscence, Verse* (2 vols., 1972).

Cruse, Harold, *The Crisis of the Negro Intellectual* (1967).

Cunard, Nancy, ed., *Negro: An Anthology* (1934).

Douglas, Ann, *Terrible Honesty: Mongrel Manhattan in the 1920s* (1995).

Hemmingway, Theodore, "Prelude to Change: Black Carolinians in the War Years, 1914–1920," *Journal of Negro History* 65 (1980): 212–27.

Lamon, Lester C., *Black Tennesseans, 1900–1930* (1977).

Locke, Alain L., *The New Negro: An Interpretation* (1925).

Logan, Rayford W., Eugene C. Holmes, and G. Franklin Edwards, ed., *The New Negro Thirty Years Afterward: Papers Contributed to the Sixteenth Annual Spring Conference of the Division of the Social Sciences, April 20, 21, and 22, 1955* (1955).

McMillen, Neil R., *Dark Journey: Black Mississippians in the Age of Jim Crow* (1989).

Myrdal, Gunnar, with Richard Sterner and Arnold Rose, *An American Dilemma: The Negro Problem and Modern Democracy* (2 vols., 20th Anniversary ed., 1962).

Nearing, Scott, *Black America* (1929).

Wacker, R. Fred, *Ethnicity, Pluralism, and Race: Race Relations Theory in America before Myrdal* (1983).

21.2   HISTORIOGRAPHY

Butchart, Ronald E., "'Outthinking and Outflanking the Owners of the World': A Historiography of the African American Struggle for Education," *History of Education Quarterly* 28 (1988): 333–66.

Cannon, Lynn Weber, Elizabeth Higginbotham, and Marianne L. A. Leung, *Race and Class Bias in Research on Women: A Methodological Note* (1987).

Gross, James A., "Historians and the Literature of the Negro Worker," *Labor History* 10 (1969): 536–46.

Hill, Herbert, "Mythmaking As Labor History: Herbert Gutman and the United Mineworkers of America," *International Journal of Political Culture and Society* 2 (1988): 132–200.

Hine, Darlene Clark, "Carter G. Woodson: White Philanthropy and Negro Historiography," *History Teacher* 19 (1986): 405–26.

Meier, August, and Elliott Rudwick, "J. Franklin Jameson, Carter G. Woodson, and the Foundations of Black Historiography," *American Historical Review* 89 (1984): 1005–15.

Smith, John David, "Du Bois and Phillips: Symbolic Antagonists of the Progressive Era," *Centennial Review* 24 (1980): 88–102.

Wilson, Francille Rusan, "Racial Consciousness and Black Scholarship: Charles H. Wesley and the Consciousness of *Negro Labor in the United States*," *Journal of Negro History* 81 (1996): 72–88.

21.3 SECONDARY SOURCES ON NEWSPAPERS AND PERIODICALS

Best, Wallace, "The *Chicago Defender* and the Realignment of Black Chicago," *Chicago History* 24 (1995): 4–21.

Grossman, James R., "Blowing the Trumpet: The *Chicago Defender* and Black Migration during World War I," *Illinois Historical Journal* 78 (1985): 82–96.

Hogan, Lawrence D., *A Black National News Service: The Associated Negro Press and Claude Barnett, 1919–1945* (1984).

Jones, Allen W., "Voices for Improving Rural Life: Alabama's Black Agricultural Press, 1890–1965," *Agricultural History* 58 (1984): 209–20.

Jones, Lester M., "The Editorial Policy of the Negro Newspapers of 1917–1918 As Compared with That of 1941–1942," *Journal of Negro History* 29 (1944): 24–31.

Kerlin, Robert T., *The Voice of the Negro, 1919* (1920).

Kornweibel, Theodore, Jr., *No Crystal Stair: Black Life and the* Messenger, *1917–1928* (1975).

Matthews, John M., "Black Newspapermen and the Black Community in Georgia, 1890–1930," *Georgia Historical Quarterly* 68 (1984): 356–81.

Olzak, Susan, and Elizabeth West, "Ethnic Conflict and the Rise and Fall of Ethnic Newspapers," *American Sociological Review* 56 (1991): 458–74.

Pride, Armistead Scott, "Negro Newspapers: Yesterday, Today, and Tomorrow," *Journalism Quarterly* 28 (1951): 179–88.

Stroman, Carolyn A., "The *Chicago Defender* and the Mass Migration of Blacks, 1916–1918," *Journal of Popular Culture* 15 (1981): 62–7.

Vincent, Theodore G., ed., *Voices of a Black Nation: Political Journalism in the Harlem Renaissance* (1973).

21.4 RACE RELATIONS

21.4.1 Black/White Relations

Alexander, Charles C., "Kleagles and Cash: The Ku Klux Klan As a Business Organization, 1915–1930," *Business History Review* 39 (1965): 348–67.

Athey, Louis L., "Florence Kelley and the Quest for Negro Equality," *Journal of Negro History* 54 (1971): 249–61.

Bagby, Laurie M. Johnson, "The Question of Jung and Racism Reconsidered," *Psychohistory Review* 23 (1995): 283–98.

Baker, Paul E., *Negro-White Adjustment: A Challenging Analysis of Race Relations* (1934).

Barkan, Elazar, *The Retreat of Scientific Racism: Changing Concepts of Race in Britain and the United States between the World Wars* (1992).

Barry, John M., *Rising Tide: The Great Mississippi Flood of 1927 and How It Changed America* (1997).

Betten, Neil, and Raymond A. Mohl, "The Evolution of Racism in an Industrial City, 1906–1940: A Case Study of Gary, Indiana," *Journal of Negro History* 59 (1974): 51–64.

Blee, Kathleen M., *Women of the Klan: Racism and Gender in the 1920s* (1991).

Chalmers, David Mark, *Hooded Americanism: The History of the Ku Klux Klan* (1981).

Dales, David G., "North Platte Racial Incident: Black-White Confrontation, 1929," *Nebraska History* 60 (1979): 424–46.

Daykin, Walter L., "Negro Types in American White Fiction," *Sociology and Social Research* 22 (1937): 45–52.

Doyle, Bertram Wilbur, *The Etiquette of Race Relations in the South: A Study in Social Control* (1937).

Du Bois, William Edward Burghardt, "Race Relations in the United States, 1917–1947," *Phylon* 9 (1948): 234–47.

Foner, Philip Sheldon, and James S. Allen, ed., *American Communism and Black Americans: A Documentary History, 1919–1929* (1987).

Goldberg, Robert Alan, *Hooded Empire: The Ku Klux Klan in Colorado* (1981).

Gordon, Linda, "Black and White Visions of Welfare: Women's Welfare Activism, 1890–1945," *Journal of American History* 78 (1991): 559–90.

Hall, Jacquelyn Dowd, *Revolt against Chivalry: Jessie Daniel Ames and the Women's Campaign against Lynching* (1976).

Haws, Robert J., and Derrick A. Bell, ed., *The Age of Segregation: Race Relations in the South, 1890–1945: Essays* (1978).

Hutchinson, George, *The Harlem Renaissance in Black and White* (1995).

Jackson, Kenneth T., *The Ku Klux Klan in the City, 1915–1930* (1967).

Jackson, Walter, "Melville Herskovits and the Search for Afro-American Culture," in George W. Stocking, Jr., ed., *Malinowski, Rivers, Benedict and Others: Essays on Culture and Personality* (1986): 95–126.

Janiewski, Dolores E., *Sisterhood Denied: Race, Gender, and Class in a New South Community* (1985).

Jenkins, Philip, "The Ku Klux Klan in Pennsylvania, 1920–1940," *Western Pennsylvania Historical Magazine* 69 (1986): 121–37.

Jenkins, William D., *Steel Valley Klan: The Ku Klux Klan in Ohio's Mahoning Valley* (1990).

Kellner, Bruce, *Carl Van Vechten and the Irreverent Decades* (1968).

——— "'Refined Racism': White Patronage in the Harlem Renaissance," in Victor A. Kramer, ed., *The Harlem Renaissance Re-Examined* (1987): 93–106.

Kneebone, John T., *Southern Liberal Journalists and the Issue of Race, 1920–1944* (1985).

Lay, Shawn, ed., *The Invisible Empire in the West: Toward a New Historical Appraisal of the Ku Klux Klan of the 1920s* (1992).

Levine, David Allen, *Internal Combustion: The Races in Detroit, 1915–1926* (1976).

Loucks, Emerson Hunsberger, *The Ku Klux Klan in Pennsylvania: A Study in Nativism* (1936).

Lueders, Edward G., *Carl Van Vechten and the Twenties* (1955).

Lyman, Stanford M., "Civilization, Culture, and Color: Changing Foundations of Robert E. Park's Sociology of Race Relations," *International Journal of Politics, Culture, and Society* 4 (1991): 285–300.

Meredith, H. L., "Agrarian Socialism and the Negro in Oklahoma, 1900–1918," *Labor History* 11 (1970): 277–84.

Moseley, Clement Charlton, "The Political Influence of the Ku Klux Klan in Georgia, 1915–1925," *Georgia Historical Quarterly* 57 (1973): 235–55.

Myrdal, Gunnar, with Richard Sterner and Arnold Rose, *An American Dilemma: The Negro Problem and Modern Democracy* (2 vols., 20th Anniversary ed., 1962).

Naison, Mark, *Communists in Harlem during the Depression* (1983).

——— "Marxism and Black Radicalism in America: Notes on a Long (and Continuing) Journey," *Radical American* 5 (1971): 3–25.

Newby, Idus A., *Jim Crow's Defense: Anti-Negro Thought in America, 1900–1930* (1965).

Record, Wilson, *The Negro and the Communist Party* (1951).

Rice, Arnold S., *The Ku Klux Klan in American Politics* (1962).

Simpson, George E., "Race Relations and the Philadelphia Press," *Journal of Negro Education* 6 (1937): 628–30.

Snell, William R., "Fiery Crosses in the Roaring Twenties: Activities of the Revised Klan in Alabama, 1915–1930," *Alabama Review* 23 (1970): 256–76.

Solomon, Mark I., *Red and Black: Communism and Afro-Americans, 1929–1935* (1988).

Stanfield, John H., *Philanthropy and Jim Crow in American Social Science* (1985).

——— "Race Relations Research and Black Americans between the Two World Wars," *Journal of Ethnic Studies* 11 (1983): 61–93.

Stocking, G. W., *Race, Culture, and Evolution: Essays in the History of Anthropology* (1968).

Williams, Vernon J., Jr., *From a Caste to a Minority: Changing Attitudes of American Sociologists toward Afro-Americans, 1896–1945* (1989).

21.4.2   Black/Ethnic Relations

Bayor, Ronald H., "Ethnic Residential Patterns in Atlanta, 1880–1940," *Georgia Historical Quarterly* 64 (1979): 435–46.

Bodnar, John E., Roger D. Simon, and Michael P. Weber, *Lives of Their Own: Blacks, Italians, and Poles in Pittsburgh, 1900–1960* (1982).

Bodnar, John, Michael Weber, and Roger Simon, "Migration, Kinship, and Urban Adjustment: Blacks and Poles in Pittsburgh, 1900–1930," *Journal of American History* 66 (1979): 548–65.

Cowett, Mark, *Birmingham's Rabbi: Morris Newfield and Alabama, 1895–1940* (1986).

Diner, Hasia, *In the Almost Promised Land: American Jews and Blacks, 1915–1935* (1995).

Dinnerstein, Leonard, "The Origins of Black Anti-Semitism in America," *American Jewish Archives* 38 (1986): 113–22.

Hellwig, David J., "Afro-American Reactions to the Japanese and the Anti-Japanese Movement, 1906–1924," *Phylon* 38 (1977): 93–104.

——— "Black Leaders and United States Immigration Policy, 1917–1929," *Journal of Negro History* 66 (1981): 110–27.

——— "Black Meets Black: Afro-American Reactions to West Indian Immigrants in the 1920's," *South Atlantic Quarterly* 77 (1978): 206–24.

James, Winston, *Holding Aloft the Banner of Ethiopia: Caribbean Radicalism in Early Twentieth-Century America* (1999).

Lewis, David Levering, "Parallels and Divergencies: Assimilationist Strategies of Afro-American and Jewish Elites from 1910 to the Early 1930's," *Journal of American History* 71 (1984): 543–64.

Olzak, Susan, and Elizabeth West, "Ethnic Conflict and the Rise and Fall of Ethnic Newspapers," *American Sociological Review* 56 (1991): 458–74.

Owens, Irma Watkins, *Blood Relations: Caribbean Immigrants in Harlem, 1900–1930* (1991).

Papanikolas, Helen Z., "Immigrants, Minorities, and the Great War," *Utah Historical Quarterly* 58 (1990): 351–70.

Perlmann, Joel, *Ethnic Differences: Schooling and Social Structure among the Irish, Italians, Jews, and Blacks in an American City, 1880–1935* (1988).

Pinderhughes, Dianne Marie, *Race and Ethnicity in Chicago Politics: A Reexamination of Pluralist Theory* (1987).

Polos, Nicholas C., "Black Anti-Semitism in Twentieth-Century America: Historical Myth or Reality?" *American Jewish Archives* 17 (1975): 8–31.

Radzialowski, Thaddus, "The Competition for Jobs and Racial Stereotypes: Poles and Blacks in Chicago," *Polish American Studies* 33 (1976): 5–18.

Shankman, Arnold, *Ambivalent Friends: Afro-Americans View the Immigrant* (1982).

——— "Black on Yellow: Afro-Americans View Chinese-Americans, 1850–1935," *Phylon* 39 (1978): 1–17.

——— "The Image of Mexico and the Mexican-American in the Black Press, 1890–1935," *Journal of Ethnic Studies* 3 (1975): 43–56.

——— "The Image of the Italian in the Afro-American Press, 1886–1936," *Italian Americana* 4 (1978): 30–49.

Taylor, Quintard, "Blacks and Asians in a White City: Japanese Americans and African Americans in Seattle, 1890–1940," *Western Historical Quarterly* 22 (1991): 401–29.

Walter, John C., "The Caribbean Immigrant Impulse in American Life, 1900–1930," *Revista/Review Interamericana [Puerto Rico]* 11 (1981–82): 522–44.

21.4.3 Segregation/Jim Crow

Bayor, Ronald H., "Roads to Racial Segregation: Atlanta in the Twentieth Century," *Journal of Urban History* 15 (1988): 3–21.

Boyd, Robert L., "Residential Segregation by Race and the Black Merchants of Northern Cities during the Early Twentieth Century," *Sociological Forum* 13 (1998): 595–609.

Hale, Grace E., *Making Whiteness: The Culture of Segregation in the South, 1890–1940* (1998).

Johnson, Charles Spurgeon, *Patterns of Negro Segregation* (1943).

Kaplowitz, Craig Allan, "A Breath of Fresh Air: Segregation, Parks, and Progressivism in Nashville, Tennessee, 1900–1920," *Tennessee Historical Quarterly* 57 (1998): 132–49.

Malone, Cheryl Knott, "Louisville Free Public Library's Racially Segregated Branches, 1905–1935," *Register of the Kentucky Historical Society* 93 (1995): 159–79.

Meier, August, and Elliott Rudwick, "The Rise of Segregation in the Federal Bureaucracy, 1900–1930," *Phylon* 28 (1967): 178–84.

Newby, Idus A., ed., *The Development of Segregationist Thought* (1968).

——— *Jim Crow's Defense: Anti-Negro Thought in America, 1900–1930* (1965).

Palmore, Joseph R., "The Not-So-Strange Career of Interstate Jim Crow: Race, Transportation, and the Dormant Commerce Clause, 1878–1946," *Virginia Law Review* 83 (1997): 1773–1817.

Schneider, Mark L., *Boston Confronts Jim Crow, 1890–1920* (1997).

Thornbrough, Emma Lou, "Segregation in Indiana during the Klan Era of the 1920's," *Mississippi Valley Historical Review* 47 (1961): 594–618.

Weiss, Nancy, "The Negro and the New Freedom: Fighting Wilsonian Segregation," *Political Science Quarterly* 84 (1969): 61–79.

21.4.4   Violence and Racial Disturbances

Brundage, W. Fitzhugh, *Lynching in the New South: Georgia and Virginia, 1880–1930* (1993).

———, ed., *Under Sentence of Death: Lynching in the South* (1997).

Chicago Commission on Race Relations, *The Negro in Chicago: Study of Race Relations and a Race Riot* (1922).

Colburn, David R., "Rosewood and America in the Early Twentieth Century," *Florida Historical Quarterly* 76 (1997): 175–92.

Cortner, Richard C., *A Mob Intent on Death: The NAACP and the Arkansas Riot Cases* (1988).

Ellsworth, Scott, *Death in a Promised Land: The Tulsa Race Riot of 1921* (1982).

Fedo, Michael W., *"They Was Just Niggers"* (1979).

Franklin, Vincent P., "The Philadelphia Race Riot of 1918," *Pennsylvania Magazine of History and Biography* 99 (1975): 336–50.

Grable, Stephen W., "Racial Violence within the Context of Community History," *Phylon* 42 (1981): 275–83.

Grant, Donald Lee, *The Anti-Lynching Movement, 1883–1932* (1975).

Hall, Jacquelyn Dowd, *Revolt against Chivalry: Jessie Daniel Ames and the Women's Campaign against Lynching* (1976).

Harris, Trudier, *Exorcising Blackness: Historical and Literary Lynching and Burning Rituals* (1984).

Haynes, Robert V., *A Night of Violence: The Houston Riot of 1917* (1976).

Hine, Darlene Clark, "Rape and the Inner Lives of Black Women in the Middle West: Preliminary Thoughts on the Culture of Dissemblance," *Signs* 14 (1989): 912–20.

Janowitz, Morris, "Patterns of Collective Racial Violence," in Hugh Davis Graham, ed., *The History of Violence in America: Historical and Comparative Perspectives* (1970): 412–44.

Jones, Maxine D., "The Rosewood Massacre and the Women Who Survived It," *Florida Historical Quarterly* 76 (1997): 193–208.

Kerlin, Robert T., *The Voice of the Negro, 1919* (1920).

Rudwick, Elliott M., *Race Riot at East St. Louis, July 2, 1917* (1964).

Schuler, Edgar A., "The Houston Race Riot, 1917," *Journal of Negro History* 29 (1944): 300–38.

Tolnay, Stewart Emory, and E. M. Beck, "Black Flight: Lethal Violence and the Great Migration, 1900–1930," *Social Science History* 14 (1990): 347–70.

——— *A Festival of Violence: An Analysis of Southern Lynchings, 1882–1930* (1995).

Tuttle, William M., *Race Riot: Chicago in the Red Summer of 1919* (1970).

Waskow, Arthur I., *From Race Riot to Sit-In, 1919 and the 1960's: A Study in the Connections between Conflict and Violence* (1966).

White, Walter Francis, *Rope and Faggot: A Biography of Judge Lynch* (1929).

Williams, Lee E., and Lee E. Williams, II, *Anatomy of Four Race Riots: Racial Conflict in Knoxville, Elaine (Arkansas), Tulsa and Chicago, 1919–1921* (1972).

Woodruff, Nan Elizabeth, "African-American Struggles for Citizenship in the Arkansas and Mississippi Deltas in the Age of Jim Crow," *Radical History Review* 55 (1993): 33–51.

Wright, George C., *Racial Violence in Kentucky, 1865–1940: Lynchings, Mob Rule, and "Legal Lynchings"* (1990).

Zangrando, Robert L., *The NAACP Crusade against Lynching, 1909–1950* (1980).

21.4.5   Civil Rights

Eisenberg, B., "'Only for the Bourgeois': James Weldon Johnson and the NAACP, 1916–1930," *Phylon* 43 (1982): 110–24.

Gaines, Kevin, "Rethinking Race and Class in African-American Struggles for Equality, 1885–1941," *American Historical Review* 102 (1997): 378–87.

Goings, Kenneth W., *The NAACP Comes of Age: The Defeat of Judge John J. Parker* (1990).

Jack, Robert L., *History of the National Association for the Advancement of Colored People* (1943).

Kelley, Robin D. G., "'We Are Not What We Seem': Towards a Black Working-Class Opposition in the Jim Crow South," *Journal of American History* 80 (1993): 75–112.

Kellogg, Charles Flint, *NAACP: A History of the National Association for the Advancement of Colored People, 1909–1920* (1967).

Kornweibel, Theodore, Jr., *"Seeing Red": Federal Campaigns against Black Militancy, 1919–1925* (1998).

Meier, August, and Elliott Rudwick, "Attorneys Black and White: A Case Study of Race Relations within the NAACP," *Journal of American History* 62 (1976): 913–46.

Moore, Jesse Thomas, Jr., *A Search for Equality: The National Urban League, 1910–1961* (1981).

Ovington, Mary White, "The National Association for the Advancement of Colored People," *Journal of Negro History* 9 (1924): 107–16.

Parris, Guichard, and Lester Brooks, *Blacks in the City: A History of the National Urban League* (1971).

Reed, Christopher Robert, *The Chicago NAACP and the Rise of Black Professional Leadership, 1910–1966* (1997).

———   "Organized Racial Reform in Chicago during the Progressive Era: The Chicago NAACP, 1910–1920," *Michigan Historical Review* 14 (1988): 75–99.

Reich, Steven A., "Soldiers of Democracy: Black Texans and the Fight for Citizenship, 1917–1921," *Journal of American History* 82 (1996): 1478–504.

Rolinson, Mary Gambrell, "Community and Leadership in the First Twenty Years of the Atlanta NAACP, 1917–1937," *Atlanta History* 42 (1998): 5–21.

Ross, Barbara Joyce, *J. E. Spingarn and the Rise of the NAACP, 1911–1939* (1972).

Thompson, Daniel C., *The Negro Leadership Class* (1963).

Wedin, Carolyn, *Inheritors of the Spirit: Mary White Ovington and the Founding of the NAACP* (1997).

Weiss, Nancy, *The National Urban League, 1910–1940* (1974).

Wright, George C., "The NAACP and Residential Segregation in Louisville, Kentucky, 1914–1917," *Register of the Kentucky Historical Society* 78 (1980): 39–54.

Zangrando, Robert L., *The NAACP Crusade against Lynching, 1909–1950* (1980).

21.5   GOVERNMENT

21.5.1   Law

Cortner, Richard C., *A Mob Intent on Death: The NAACP and the Arkansas Riot Cases* (1988).

Harris, Carl V., "Reforms in Government Control of Negroes in Birmingham, Alabama, 1890–1920," *Journal of Southern History* 38 (1972): 567–600.

King, Desmond, "A Strong or Weak State? Race and the U.S. Federal Government in the 1920's," *Ethnic and Racial Studies [London]* 21 (1998): 21–47.

Kornweibel, Theodore, Jr., ed., *Federal Surveillance of Afro-Americans, 1917–1925: The First World War, the Red Scare, and the Garvey Movement* (rev. ed., 1986).

Mangum, Charles Staples, Jr., *The Legal Status of the Negro* (1940).

McNeil, Genna Rae, *Groundwork: Charles Hamilton Houston and the Struggle for Civil Rights* (1983).

Meier, August, and Elliott Rudwick, "Attorneys Black and White: A Case Study of Race Relations within the NAACP," *Journal of American History* 62 (1976): 913–46.

Mollison, Irvin C., "Negro Lawyers in Mississippi," *Journal of Negro History* 15 (1930): 38–71.

Styles, Fitzhugh Lee, *The Negro Lawyers' Contribution to Seventy-One Years of Our Progress* (1934).

———   *Negroes and the Law in the Race's Battle for Liberty, Equality and Justice* (1937).

Tushnet, Mark, "The Politics of Equality in Constitutional Law: The Equal Protection Clause, Dr. Du Bois, and Charles Hamilton Houston," *Journal of American History* 74 (1987): 884–903.

21.5.2 Crime and Punishment

Beck, E. M., James L. Massey, and Stewart Tolnay, "The Gallows, the Mob, and the Vote: Lethal Sanctioning of Blacks in North Carolina and Georgia, 1882–1930," *Law and Society Review* 23 (1989): 317–31.

Cohen, William, "Negro Involuntary Servitude in the South, 1865–1940: A Preliminary Analysis," *Journal of Southern History* 42 (1976): 31–60.

Massey, James L., and Martha A. Myers, "Patterns of Repressive Social Control in Post-Reconstruction Georgia, 1882–1935," *Social Forces* 68 (1989): 458–88.

Oshinsky, David M., *"Worse Than Slavery": Parchman Farm and the Ordeal of Jim Crow Justice* (1996).

Rafter, Nicole Hahn, "Gender, Prisons, and Prison History," *Social Science History* 9 (1985): 233–48.

Steiner, Jesse F., and Roy M. Brown, *The North Carolina Chain Gang: A Study of Convict Road Work* (1927).

21.5.3 Politics and Voting

Allswang, John M., "The Chicago Negro Voter and the Democratic Consensus: A Case Study, 1918–1936," *Journal of the Illinois State Historical Society* 60 (1967): 145–75.

Breen, William J., "Black Women and the Great War: Mobilization and Reform in the South," *Journal of Southern History* 44 (1978): 421–40.

Burnham, Robert A., "Reform, Politics, and Race in Cincinnati: Proportional Representation and the City Charter Committee, 1924–1959," *Journal of Urban History* 23 (1997): 131–63.

Dailey, Maceo Crenshaw, Jr., "Calvin Coolidge's Afro-American Connection," *Contributions in Black Studies* 8 (1986–87): 77–100.

Du Bois, William Edward Burghardt, "The Negro Citizen: A Study of Negro Life and Race Relations in the Light of Social Research," in Charles S. Johnson, ed., *The Negro in American Civilization* (1930): 461–70.

Garcia, George F., "Black Disaffection from the Republican Party during the Presidency of Herbert Hoover, 1928–1932," *Annals of Iowa* (1980): 462–97.

——— "Herbert Hoover and the Issue of Race," *Annals of Iowa* 44 (1979): 507–15.

Gosnell, Harold F., "The Chicago 'Black Belt' As a Political Battlefield," *American Journal of Sociology* 39 (1933): 329–41.

Higginbotham, Evelyn Brooks, "In Politics to Stay: Black Women Leaders and Party Politics during the 1920's," in Louise Tilly and Patricia Gurin, ed., *Women, Politics, and Change* (1990): 199–220.

Hine, Darlene Clark, *Black Victory: The Rise and Fall of the White Primary in Texas* (1979).

Kilson, Martin, "Political Change in the Negro Ghetto, 1900–1940's," in Nathan I. Huggins, Martin Kilson and Daniel M. Fox, ed., *Key Issues in the Afro-American Experience since 1865* (vol. 2, 1971): 167–92.

Lisio, Donald J., *Hoover, Blacks, and Lily-Whites: A Study of Southern Strategies* (1985).

Maxwell, William J., *New Negro, Old Left: African-American Writing and Communism Between the Wars* (1999).

Moreland, Laurence W., Robert P. Steed, and Tod A. Baker, ed., *Blacks in Southern Politics* (1987).

Murray, Percy E., "Harry C. Smith-Joseph B. Foraker Alliance: Coalition Politics in Ohio," *Journal of Negro History* 68 (1983): 171–84.

Pinderhughes, Dianne Marie, *Race and Ethnicity in Chicago Politics: A Reexamination of Pluralist Theory* (1987).

Reed, Adolph L., Jr., *W.E.B. Du Bois and American Political Thought: Fabianism and the Color Line* (1998).

Reed, Christopher Robert, *The Chicago NAACP and the Rise of Black Professional Leadership, 1910–1966* (1997).

Schutze, Jim, *The Accommodation: The Politics of Race in an American City* (1986).

Sherman, Richard B., *The Republican Party and Black America: From McKinley to Hoover, 1896–1933* (1973).

Solomon, Mark, *The Cry Was Unity: Communists and African Americans, 1917–1936* (1998).

Terborg-Penn, Rosalyn M., "The Historical Treatment of Afro-Americans in the Women's Movement, 1900–1920: A Bibliographical Essay," *Current Bibliography on African Affairs* 7 (1974): 245–59.

Walton, Hanes, *Black Republicans: The Politics of the Black and Tans* (1975).

Weiss, Nancy, "The Negro and the New Freedom: Fighting Wilsonian Segregation," *Political Science Quarterly* 84 (1969): 61–79.

Williams, Lillian S., "And Still I Rise: Black Women and Reform, Buffalo, New York, 1900–1940," *Afro-Americans in New York Life and History* 14 (1990): 7–33.

21.5.4   Military

Barbeau, Arthur E., and Florette Henri, *The Unknown Soldiers: African-American Troops in World War I* (1974).

Bodie, Walter S., "The Black Soldier in World War I," *Social Education* 49 (1985): 129–32.

Clement, Rufus E., "Problems of Demobilization and Rehabilitation of the Negro Soldier after World Wars I and II," *Journal of Negro Education* 12 (1943): 417–28.

Douglas, Bill, "Wartime Illusions and Disillusionment: Camp Dodge and Racial Stereotyping, 1917–1918," *Annals of Iowa* 57 (1998): 111–34.

Fletcher, Marvin Edward, *The Black Soldier and Officer in the United States Army, 1891–1917* (1974).

Hwang, Hyesung, "World War I and the New Negro," *Journal of North American Studies* 1 (1995): 43–68.

Megginson, W. J., "Black South Carolinians in World War I: The Official Roster As a Resource for Local History, Mobility, and African-American History," *South Carolina Historical Magazine* 96 (1995): 153–73.

Patton, Gerald W., *War and Race: The Black Officer in the American Military, 1915–1941* (1981).

21.6   DEMOGRAPHY

Davis, Dernoral, "Toward a Socio-Historical and Demographic Portrait of Twentieth-Century African Americans," in Alferdteen Harrison, ed., *Black Exodus: The Great Migration from the American South* (1991): 1–19.

Engerman, Stanley L., "Black Fertility and Family Structure in the U.S., 1880–1940," *Journal of Family History* 2 (1977): 117–38.

Holmes, Samuel Jackson, *The Negro's Struggle for Survival: A Study in Human Ecology* (1937).

Miller, Zane, "Urban Blacks in the South, 1865–1920: An Analysis of Some Quantitative Data on Richmond, Savannah, New Orleans, Louisville, and Birmingham," in Leo F. Schnore, ed., *The New Urban History: Quantitative Explorations by American Historians* (1975): 184–204.

Tolnay, Stewart Emory, "Class, Race, and Fertility in the Rural South, 1910 and 1940," *Rural Sociology* 60 (1995): 108–28.

U.S. Bureau of the Census, *Negroes in the United States, 1920–1932* (1935).

21.7   FAMILY

Frazier, Edward Franklin, *The Negro Family in Chicago* (1932).

Lewis, Earl, "Afro-American Adaptive Strategies: The Visiting Habits of Kith and Kin among Black Norfolkians during the First Great Migration," *Journal of Family History* 12 (1987): 407–20.

McAdoo, H. P., and R. Terborg-Penn, "Historical Trends and Perspectives of Afro-American Families," *Trends in History* 3 (1985): 97–111.

Mossell, Sadie Tanner, "The Standard of Living among One Hundred Negro Migrant Families in Philadelphia," *Annals of the American Academy of Politics and Social Science* 98 (1921): 168–218.

Neckerman, Kathryn M., "Divided Households: Extended Kin in Working-Class Chicago, 1924," *Social Science History* 19 (1995): 371–98.

———— "The Emergence of 'Underclass' Family Patterns, 1900–1940," in Michael B. Katz, ed., *The 'Underclass' Debate: Views from History* (1993): 194–219.

Reed, Ruth, *Negro Illegitimacy in New York City* (1926).

Rodrique, Jessie M., "The Black Community and the Birth Control Movement," in Kathy Peiss and Christina Simmons, ed., *Passion and Power: Sexuality in History* (1989): 138–54.

Sanders, Wiley Britton, *Negro Child Welfare in North Carolina: A Rosenwald Study* (1933).

Stehno, Sandra M., "Public Responsibility for Dependent Black Children: The Advocacy of Edith Abbott and Sophonisba Breckinridge," *Social Service Review* 62 (1988): 485–503.

Tolnay, Stewart Emory, *The Bottom Rung: African American Family Life on Southern Farms* (1999).

Williams, Melvin D., "Childhood in an Urban Black Ghetto: Two Life Histories," in Joseph M. Hawes and N. Ray Hiner, ed., *Growing Up in America: Children in Historical Perspective* (1985): 221–33.

21.8   SOCIETY

21.8.1   Rural Life (Including Black Settlements)

Johnson, Charles S., *Growing Up in the Black Belt: Negro Youth in the Rural South* (1941).

———— *Shadow of the Plantation* (1934).

Jones, Allen W., "Voices for Improving Rural Life: Alabama's Black Agricultural Press, 1890–1965," *Agricultural History* 58 (1984): 209–20.

Kirby, Jack Temple, *Rural Worlds Lost: The American South, 1920–1960* (1987).

Seals, R. Grant, "The Formation of Agricultural and Rural Development Policy with Emphasis on African-Americans: The Hatch-George and Smith-Lever Acts," *Agricultural History* 65 (1991): 12–34.

Standing, T. G., "The Problem of Rural Housing in the South," *Rural Sociology* 7 (1942): 267–75.

Tolnay, Stewart Emory, *The Bottom Rung: African American Family Life on Southern Farms* (1999).

———— "Class, Race, and Fertility in the Rural South, 1910 and 1940," *Rural Sociology* 60 (1995): 108–28.

Woodson, Carter G., *The Rural Negro* (1930).

Woofter, Thomas Jackson, Jr., *Black Yeomanry: Life on St. Helena Island* (1930).

21.8.2   Urban Life (Including Migration)

Adero, Malaika, ed., *Up South: Stories, Studies, and Letters of this Century's African-American Migrations* (1993).

Alexander, J. Trent, "The Great Migration in Comparative Perspective: Interpreting the Urban Origins of Southern Black Migrants to Depression-Era Pittsburgh," *Social Science History* 22 (1998): 349–76.

Anderson, Jervis, *This Was Harlem: A Cultural Portrait, 1900–1950* (1982).

Ballard, Allen B., *One More Day's Journey: The Story of a Family and a People* (1984).

Bauman, John F., *Public Housing, Race, and Renewal: Urban Planning in Philadelphia, 1920–1974* (1987).

Bigham, Darrel E., *We Ask Only A Fair Trial: A History of the Black Community of Evansville, Indiana* (1987).

Bodnar, John, Michael Weber, and Roger Simon, "Migration, Kinship, and Urban Adjustment: Blacks and Poles in Pittsburgh, 1900–1930," *Journal of American History* 66 (1979): 548–65.

Bontemps, Arna Wendell, and Jack Conroy, *Anyplace but Here* (rev. and expanded ed., 1966).

Bragaw, Donald H., "Status of Negroes in a Southern Port City in the Progressive Era: Pensacola, 1896–1920," *Florida Historical Quarterly* 51 (1973).

Broussard, Albert S., *Black San Francisco: The Struggle for Racial Equality, 1900–1954* (1993).

———— "Organizing the Black Community in the San Francisco Bay Area, 1915–1930," *Arizona and the West* 23 (1981): 335–54.

Campbell, Agnes Horne, comp., *Negro Housing in Towns and Cities, 1927–1937* (1937).

Clarke, John Henrik, ed., *Harlem: A Community in Transition* (new expanded ed., 1969).

Clark-Lewis, Elizabeth, *Living In, Living Out: African-American Domestics in Washington, D.C., 1910–1940* (1996).

Cohen, Jon, "'Gone up North, Gone out West, Gone!,'" *Smithsonian* 18 (1987): 72–83.

Cohen, William, "The Great Migration As a Lever for Social Change," in Alferdteen Harrison, ed., *Black Exodus: The Great Migration from the American South* (1991): 72–82.

Connolly, Harold X., *A Ghetto Grows in Brooklyn* (1977).

Corbett, Katharine T., and Mary E. Seematter, "'No Crystal Stair': Black St. Louis, 1920–1940," *Gateway Heritage* 16 (1995): 82–8.

Crew, Spencer R., *Field to Factory: Afro-American Migration, 1915–1940* (1987).

Darden, Joe T., ed., *The Ghetto: Readings with Interpretations* (1981).

De Graaf, Lawrence, "The City of Black Angels: The Emergence of the Los Angeles Ghetto, 1890–1930," *Pacific Historical Review* 39 (1970): 323–52.

Duncan, Otis Dudley, and Beverly Duncan, *Negro Population of Chicago: A Study of Residential Succession* (1957).

Edwards, Paul Kenneth, *The Southern Urban Negro As a Consumer* (1932).

Epstein, Abraham, *The Negro Migrant in Pittsburgh* (1918).

Frazier, Edward Franklin, "Negro Harlem: An Ecological Study," *American Journal of Sociology* 43 (1937): 72–88.

Gavins, Raymond, "Urbanization and Segregation: Black Leadership Patterns in Richmond, Virginia, 1900–1920," *South Atlantic Quarterly* 79 (1980): 257–73.

George, Paul S., "Colored Town: Miami's Black Community, 1896–1930," *Florida Historical Quarterly* 56 (1978): 432–47.

Glasco, Laurence, "Double Burden: The Black Experience in Pittsburgh," in Samuel P. Hays, ed., *City at the Point: Essays on the Social History of Pittsburgh* (1991): 69–109.

Gottlieb, Peter, *Making Their Own Way: Southern Blacks' Migration to Pittsburgh, 1916–1930* (1987).

Grant, Robert B., *The Black Man Comes to the City: A Documentary Account from the Great Migration to the Great Depression, 1915–1930* (1972).

Greenberg, Stephanie W., "Neighborhood Change, Racial Transition, and Work Location: A Case Study of an Industrial City, Philadelphia, 1880–1930," *Journal of Urban History* 7 (1981): 267–314.

Griffin, Farah Jasmine, *"Who Set You Flowin'?" The African-American Migration Narrative* (1995).

Grossman, James R., "Blowing the Trumpet: The *Chicago Defender* and Black Migration during World War I," *Illinois Historical Journal* 78 (1985): 82–96.

———— *Land of Hope: Chicago, Black Southerners, and the Great Migration* (1989).

Hamilton, C. Horace, "The Negro Leaves the South," *Demography* 1 (1964): 273–95.

Handlin, Oscar, *The Newcomers: Negroes and Puerto Ricans in a Changing Metropolis* (1959).

Harris, Abram L., Jr., "Negro Migration to the North," *Current History* 20 (1924): 921–25.

Harrison, Alferdteen, ed., *Black Exodus: The Great Migration from the American South* (1991).

Haynes, George Edmund, *Negro Newcomers in Detroit* (1918).

Henderson, H. Donald, "The Negro Migration of 1916–1918," *Journal of Negro History* 6 (1921): 383–498.

Henri, Florette, *Black Migration: Movement North, 1900–1920* (1975).

Higgs, Robert, "The Boll Weevil, the Cotton Economy, and Black Migration, 1910–1930," *Agricultural History* 50 (1976): 335–50.

Hine, Darlene Clark, "Black Migration to the Urban Midwest: The Gender Dimension, 1915–1945," in Joe William Trotter, Jr., ed., *The Great Migration in Historical Perspective: New Dimensions of Race, Class, and Gender* (1991): 127–46.

Hogan, Lawrence, "Afro-American History As Immigration History: The Anguillians of Perth Amboy," *Social Studies* 78 (1987): 210–12.

Janiewski, Dolores E., *Sisterhood Denied: Race, Gender, and Class in a New South Community* (1985).

Johnson, Guy, "Negro Migration and Its Consequences," *Social Forces* 2 (1924): 404–08.

Johnson, James Weldon, *Black Manhattan* (1930).

Jones, William H., *The Housing of Negroes in Washington, D.C.: A Study in Human Ecology* (1929).

———— *Recreation and Amusement among Negroes in Washington, D.C.: A Sociological Analysis of the Negro in an Urban Environment* (1927).

Katz, Michael B., and Thomas J. Sugrue, ed., *W.E.B. Du Bois, Race, and the City* (1998).

Katznelson, Ira, *Black Men, White Cities: Race, Politics, and Migration in the United States, 1900–1930, and Britain, 1948–1968* (1973).

Kennedy, Louise Venable, *The Negro Peasant Turns Cityward: Effects of Recent Migrations to Northern Centers* (1930).

Kirby, Jack Temple, "The Southern Exodus, 1910–1960: A Primer for Historians," *Journal of Southern History* 49 (1983): 585–600.

Kiser, Clyde Vernon, *Sea Island to City: A Study of St. Helena Islanders in Harlem and Other Urban Centers* (1932).

Kusmer, Kenneth L., "The Black Urban Experience in American History," in Darlene Clark Hine, ed., *The State of Afro-American History: Past, Present, and Future* (1986): 91–122.

———— *A Ghetto Takes Shape: Black Cleveland, 1870–1930* (1976).

Lane, Winthrop P., "Ambushed in the City: The Grim Side of Harlem," *The Survey* 53 (1925): 692–94, 715.

Lewis, David Levering, *When Harlem Was in Vogue* (1982).

Lewis, Earl, "Expectations, Economic Opportunities, and Life in the Industrial Age: Black Migration to Norfolk, Virginia, 1910–1945," in Joe W. Trotter, ed., *The Great Migration in Historical Perspective: New Dimensions of Race, Class, and Gender* (1991): 22–45.

———— *In Their Own Interests: Race, Class, and Power in Twentieth-Century Norfolk, Virginia* (1991).

Lewis, Earl, and David Organ, "Housing, Race and Class: The Government's Creation of Truxton, Virginia, a Model Black War Worker's Town," in Jerry Lembcke and Ray Hutchinson, ed., *Race, Class, and Urban Change* (1989): 53–78.

Lewis, Earl, and Joe W. Trotter, ed., *African Americans in the Industrial Age: A Documentary History, 1915–1945* (1996).

Lewis, Edward Erwin, *The Mobility of the Negro: A Study in the American Labor Supply* (1931).

Lewis, Ronald L., "From Peasant to Proletarian: The Migration of Southern Blacks to the Central Appalachian Coalfield," *Journal of Southern History* 55 (1989): 77–102.

Marks, Carole, "Black Workers and the Great Migration North," *Phylon* 46 (1985): 148–61.

———— *Farewell—We're Good and Gone: The Great Black Migration* (1989).

Marullo, Sam, "The Migration of Blacks to the North, 1911–1918," *Journal of Black Studies* 15 (1985): 291–306.

Massa, Ann, "Black Women in the 'White City,'" *Journal of American Studies* 8 (1974): 319–37.

McKay, Claude, *Harlem: Negro Metropolis* (1940).

McMillen, Neil R., "The Migration and Black Protest in Jim Crow Mississippi," in Alferdteen Harrison, ed., *Black Exodus: The Great Migration from the American South* (1991): 83–99.

Miller, Fredric M., "The Black Migration to Philadelphia: A 1924 Profile," *Pennsylvania Magazine of History and Biography* 108 (1984): 315–50.

Miller, Fredric M., Morris J. Vogel, and Allen F. Davis, *Philadelphia Stories: A Photographic History, 1920–1960* (1988).

Miller, Zane, "Urban Blacks in the South, 1865–1920: An Analysis of Some Quantitative Data on Richmond, Savannah, New Orleans, Louisville, and Birmingham," in Leo F. Schnore, ed., *The New Urban History: Quantitative Explorations by American Historians* (1975): 184–204.

Moore, Jesse Thomas, Jr., *A Search for Equality: The National Urban League, 1910–1961* (1981).

Moore, Shirley A., "Getting There, Being There: African-American Migration to Richmond, California, 1910–1945," in Joe William Trotter, Jr., ed., *The Great Migration in Historical Perspective: New Dimensions of Race, Class, and Gender* (1991): 106–26.

Naison, Mark, *Communists in Harlem during the Depression* (1983).

Nielson, David Gordon, *Black Ethos: Northern Urban Negro Life and Thought, 1890–1930* (1977).

Osofsky, Gilbert, "A Decade of Urban Tragedy: How Harlem Became a Slum," *New York History* 46 (1965): 330–55.

———— *Harlem, The Making of a Ghetto: Negro New York, 1890–1930* (1966).

Ottley, Roi, *"New World A-Coming": Inside Black America* (1943).

Parker, Russell D., "The Black Community in a Company Town: Alcoa, Tennessee, 1919–1939," *Tennessee Historical Quarterly* 37 (1978): 203–21.

Parris, Guichard, and Lester Brooks, *Blacks in the City: A History of the National Urban League* (1971).

Phillips, Kimberley L., "'But It Is a Fine Place to Make Money': Migration and African-American Families in Cleveland, 1915–1929," *Journal of Social History* 30 (1996): 393–413.

Philpott, Thomas Lee, *The Slum and the Ghetto: Neighborhood Deterioration and Middle-Class Reform, Chicago, 1880–1930* (1978).

Reed, Ruth, *Negro Illegitimacy in New York City* (1926).

Reid, Ira de Augustine, *The Negro Immigrant: His Background, Characteristics and Social Adjustment, 1899–1937* (1939).

——— *Social Conditions of the Negro in the Hill District of Pittsburgh* (1930).

Scheiner, Seth, *Negro Mecca: A History of the Negro in New York City, 1865–1920* (1965).

Scott, Emmett J., "Letters of Negro Migrants of 1916–1918," *Journal of Negro History* 4 (1919): 290–340, 412–65.

——— *Negro Migration during the War* (1920).

Sernett, Milton C., *Bound for the Promised Land: African American Religion and the Great Migration* (1997).

Shofner, Jerrell H., "Florida and the Black Migration," *Florida Historical Quarterly* 57 (1979): 267–88.

Spear, Allan, *Black Chicago: The Making of a Negro Ghetto, 1890–1920* (1967).

Strickland, Arvarh E., *History of the Chicago Urban League* (1966).

Stroman, Carolyn A., "The *Chicago Defender* and the Mass Migration of Blacks, 1916–1918," *Journal of Popular Culture* 15 (1981): 62–7.

Sullenger, T. Earl, *The Negro in Omaha: A Social Study of Negro Development* (1931).

Taylor, Quintard, "Black Urban Development—Another View: Seattle's Central District, 1910–1940," *Pacific Historical Review* 58 (1989): 429–48.

——— "The Great Migration: The Afro-American Communities of Seattle and Portland during the 1930's," *Arizona and the West* 23 (1981): 109–26.

Thomas, Richard W., "The Detroit Urban League, 1916–1923," *Michigan History* 60 (1976): 315–38.

——— *Life for Us Is What We Make It: Building Black Community in Detroit, 1915–1945* (1992).

Thurman, Wallace, *Negro Life in New York's Harlem: A Lively Picture of a Popular and Interesting Section* (1928).

Tolnay, Stewart Emory, and E. M. Beck, "Black Flight: Lethal Violence and the Great Migration, 1900–1930," *Social Science History* 14 (1990): 347–70.

——— "Rethinking the Role of Racial Violence in the Great Migration," in Alferdteen Harrison, ed., *Black Exodus: The Great Migration from the American South* (1991): 20–35.

Trotter, Joe William, Jr., "African Americans in the City: The Industrial Era, 1900–1950," *Journal of Urban History* 21 (1995): 438–57.

——— *Black Milwaukee: The Making of an Industrial Proletariat, 1915–1945* (1985).

———, ed., *The Great Migration in Historical Perspective: New Dimensions of Class, Race, and Gender* (1991).

——— "Race, Class and Industrial Change: Black Migration to Southern West Virginia, 1915–1932," in Joe William Trotter, Jr., ed., *The Great Migration in Historical Perspective: New Dimensions of Race, Class, and Gender* (1991): 46–67.

Vickery, William, *The Economics of Negro Migration, 1900–1960* (1977).

Walls, Dwayne E., *The Chickenbone Special* (1971).

Warner, Robert M., and Francis X. Blouin, Jr., "Documenting the Great Migrations and a Century of Ethnicity in America," *American Archivist* 39 (1976): 319–28.

Watkins-Owens, Irma, *Blood Relations: Caribbean Immigrants and the Harlem Community, 1900–1930* (1996).

Wayne, George H., "Negro Migration and Colonization in Colorado, 1870–1930," *Journal of the West* 15 (1976): 102–20.

Weaver, Robert C., *The Negro Ghetto* (1948).

Weiss, Nancy, *The National Urban League, 1910–1940* (1974).

Williams, Lee, "Concentrated Residences: The Case of Black Toledo, 1890–1930," *Phylon* 43 (1982): 167–76.

———— "Newcomers to the City: A Study of Black Population Growth in Toledo, Ohio, 1910–1930," *Ohio History* 39 (1980): 5–24.

Williams, Lillian S., "Afro-Americans in Buffalo, 1900–1930: A Study in Community Formation," *Afro-Americans in New York Life and History* 8 (1984): 7–35.

———— *Strangers in the Land of Paradise: The Creation of an African American Urban Community, Buffalo, New York, 1900–1940* (1999).

Wood, L. Hollingsworth, "The Urban League Movement," *Journal of Negro History* 9 (1924): 117–26.

Woodson, Carter Godwin, *A Century of Negro Migration* (1918).

Woofter, Thomas Jackson, Jr., *Negro Migration: Changes in Rural Organization and Population of the Cotton Belt* (1920).

Wright, George C., *Life behind a Veil: Blacks in Louisville, Kentucky, 1865–1930* (1985).

Wright, Giles R., "Oral History and the Writing of Afro-American History: The Great Migration Experience," *Journal of the Afro-American Historical and Genealogical Society* 10 (1989): 6–13.

21.8.3   Color and Class

Dollard, John, *Caste and Class in a Southern Town* (1937).

Fultz, Michael, "'The Morning Cometh': African-American Periodicals, Education, and the Black Middle Class, 1900–1930," *Journal of Negro History* 80 (1995): 97–112.

Gatewood, Willard B., *Aristocrats of Color: The Black Elite, 1880–1920* (1990).

Mack, Kibibi Voloria C., *Parlor Ladies and Ebony Drudges: African American Women, Class, and Work in a South Carolina Community* (1999).

McBride David, and Monroe H. Little, "The Afro-American Elite, 1930–1940: A Historical Profile," *Phylon* 42 (1981): 105–19.

Meier, August, and David Lewis, "History of the Negro Upper Class in Atlanta, Georgia, 1890–1958," *Journal of Negro Education* 28 (1959): 128–39.

Olney, Martha L., "When Your Word Is Not Enough: Race, Collateral, and Household Credit," *Journal of Economic History* 58 (1998): 408–31.

Tolnay, Stewart Emory, "Class, Race, and Fertility in the Rural South, 1910 and 1940," *Rural Sociology* 60 (1995): 108–28.

21.8.4   Associational Life

Barnes, Annie S., "An Urban Black Volunteer Association," *Phylon* 40 (1979): 264–9.

Brady, Marilyn Dell, "Kansas Federation of Colored Women's Clubs, 1900–1930," *Kansas History* 9 (1986): 19–30.

———— "Organizing Afro-American Girls' Clubs in Kansas in the 1920's," *Frontiers* 9 (1987): 69–73.

Chateauvert, Melinda, *Marching Together: Women of the Brotherhood of Sleeping Car Porters* (1998).

Davis, Elizabeth Lindsay, *Lifting as They Climb: National Association of Colored Women* (1933).

Eisenberg, B., "'Only for the Bourgeois': James Weldon Johnson and the NAACP, 1916–1930," *Phylon* 43 (1982): 110–24.

Gordon, Linda, "Black and White Visions of Welfare: Women's Welfare Activism, 1890–1945," *Journal of American History* 78 (1991): 559–90.

Jacobs, Claude F., "Benevolent Societies of New Orleans Blacks during the Late Nineteenth and Early Twentieth Centuries," *Louisiana History* 29 (1988): 21–33.

Kennedy, Thomas C., "The Rise and Decline of a Black Monthly Meeting: Southland, Arkansas, 1864–1925," *Arkansas Historical Quarterly* 50 (1991): 115–39.

Lerner, Gerda, "Community Work of Black Club Women," in Gerda Lerner, *The Majority Finds Its Past: Placing Women in History* (1979): 83–93.

Mihelich, Dennis N., "A Socioeconomic Portrait of Prince Hall Masonry in Nebraska, 1900–1920," *Great Plains Quarterly* 17 (1997): 35–47.

———— "World War I, the Great Migration, and the Formation of the Grand Bodies of Prince Hall Masonry," *Nebraska History* 78 (1997): 28–39.

Neverdon-Morton, Cynthia, *Afro-American Women of the South and the Advancement of the Race, 1895–1925* (1989).

Reed, Christopher, "Black Chicago Civic Organizations before 1935," *Journal of Ethnic Studies* 14 (1987): 65–77.

Salem, Dorothy, *To Better Our World: Black Women in Organized Reform, 1890–1920*(1990).

Scott, Anne Firor, "Most Invisible of All: Black Women's Voluntary Associations," *Journal of Southern History* 56 (1990): 3–22.

Warren, Stanley, "The Monster Meetings at the Negro YMCA in Indianapolis," *Indiana Magazine of History* 91 (1995): 57–80.

Watkins, Ralph, "A Reappraisal of the Role of Voluntary Associations in the African American Community," *Afro-Americans in New York Life and History* 14 (1990): 51–60.

Weisenfeld, Judith, *African American Women and Christian Activism: New York's Black YWCA, 1905–1945* (1997).

White, Deborah Gray, *Too Heavy a Load: Black Women in Defense of Themselves, 1894–1994*(1999).

Work, Monroe N., "Secret Societies As Factors in the Social and Economic Life of the Negro," *Proceedings of the Southern Sociological Congress* (1916).

21.8.5   Leisure and Sports

Bak, Richard, *Turkey Stearnes and the Detroit Stars: The Negro Leagues in Detroit, 1919–1933*(1994).

Barbeau, Arthur, "Jesse Owens and the Triumph of Black Olympians," *Journal of the West Virginia Historical Association* 4 (1980): 46–59.

Brown, Tamara, "It Don't Mean a Thing If It Ain't Got That Harlem Swing: Social Dance and the Harlem Renaissance," *Afro-Americans in New York Life and History* 22 (1998): 41–66.

Bruce, Janet, *The Kansas City Monarchs: Champions of Black Baseball* (1985).

Captain, Gwendolyn, "Enter Ladies and Gentlemen of Color: Gender, Sport, and the Ideal of African American Manhood and Womanhood during the Late Nineteenth and Early Twentieth Centuries," *Journal of Sport History* 18 (1991): 81–102.

Evans, Art, "Joe Louis as a Key Functionary: White Reactions toward a Black Champion," *Journal of Black Studies* 16 (1985): 95–111.

Gems, Gerald R., "Blocked Shot: The Development of Basketball in the African-American Community of Chicago," *Journal of Sport History* 22 (1995): 135–48.

Haller, Mark H., "Policy Gambling, Entertainment, and the Emergence of Black Politics: Chicago from 1900 to 1940," *Journal of Social History* 24 (1991): 719–39.

Jones, William H., *Recreation and Amusement among Negroes in Washington, D.C.: A Sociological Analysis of the Negro in an Urban Environment* (1927).

Mathewson, Alfred Dennis, "Major League Baseball's Monopoly Power and the Negro Leagues," *American Business Law Journal* 35 (1998): 291–318.

McBee, Kurt, "The Memphis Red Sox Stadium: A Social Institution in Memphis' African American Community," *West Tennessee Historical Society Papers* 49 (1995): 149–64.

Miller, Patrick, "With the Same Traits of Courage . . . : The Early Afro-American Experience in Sports," *Proteus* 3 (1986): 60–66.

Newman, Mark, "On the Air with Jack L. Cooper: The Beginnings of Black-Appeal Radio," *Chicago History* 12 (1983): 51–58.

Overmyer, James, *Queen of the Negro Leagues: Effa Manley and the Newark Eagles* (1998).

Reiss, Steven A., "Race and Ethnicity in American Baseball, 1900–1919," *Journal of Ethnic Studies* 4 (1977): 39–55.

Robinson, Frazier "Slow," with Paul Bauer, *Catching Dreams: My Life in the Negro Baseball Leagues* (1999).

Rogosin, Donn, *Invisible Men: Life in Baseball's Negro Leagues*(1985).

Ruck, Rob, *Sandlot Seasons: Sport in Black Pittsburgh* (1987).

Scott, Emmett, "Leisure Time and the Colored Citizen," *Playground* 18 (1925): 593–96.

Watkins, Ralph, "Recreation, Leisure, and Charity in the Afro-American Community of Buffalo, New York, 1920–1925," *Afro-Americans in New York Life and History* 6 (1982): 7–19.

21.9   RELIGION

Blatnica, Dorothy Ann, *"At the Altar of Their God": African American Catholics in Cleveland, 1922–1961* (1995).

Boyd, Robert L., "The Storefront Church Ministry in African American Communities of the Urban North during the Great Migration: The Making of an Ethnic Niche," *Social Science Journal* 35 (1998): 319–32.

Brooks, Walter H., "The Evolution of the Negro Baptist Church," *Journal of Negro History* 7 (1922): 11–22.

Burkett, Randall K., *Black Redemption: Churchmen Speak for the Garvey Movement* (1978).

———— *Garveyism as a Religious Movement: The Institutionalization of a Black Civil Religion* (1978).

Burrow, Rufus, Jr., "The Personalism of John Wesley Edward Bowen," *Journal of Negro History* 82 (1997): 244–56.

Daniel, William Andrew, *The Education of Negro Ministers* (1925).

Dickerson, Dennis C., "Black Ecumenism: Efforts to Establish a United Methodist Episcopal Church, 1918–1932," *Church History* 52 (1983): 479–91.

Fauset, Arthur Huff, *Black Gods of the Metropolis: Negro Religious Cults of the Urban North* (1944).

Flynt, Wayne, "Religion in the Urban South: The Divided Religious Mind of Birmingham, 1900–1930," *Alabama Review* 30 (1977): 108–34.

Gilkes, Cheryl Townsend, "The Role of Women in the Sanctified Church," *Journal of Religious Thought* 43 (1986): 24–41.

Gillard, John Thomas, *Colored Catholics in the United States: An Investigation of Catholic Activity in Behalf of the Negroes in the United States and a Survey of the Present Condition of the Colored Missions* (1941).

Gregg, Robert, *Sparks from the Anvil of Oppression: Philadelphia's African Methodists and Southern Migrants, 1890–1940* (1993).

Higginbotham, Evelyn Brooks, "Rethinking Vernacular Culture: Black Religion and Race Records in the 1920s and 1930s," in Waheema H. Lubiano, ed., *The House that Race Built: Black Americans, U.S. Terrain* (1997): 157–77.

———— *Righteous Discontent: The Women's Movement in the Black Baptist Church, 1880–1920* (1993).

Labbe, Dolores Egger, *Jim Crow Comes to Church: The Establishment of Segregated Catholic Parishes in South Louisiana* (2d ed., 1971).

Matthews, Donald H., *Honoring the Ancestors: An African Cultural Interpretation of Black Religion and Literature* (1998).

Mays, Benjamin Elijah, *The Negro's God as Reflected in His Literature* (1938).

Mays, Benjamin Elijah, and Joseph William Nicholson, *The Negro's Church* (1933).

McDowell, John Patrick, *The Social Gospel in the South: The Woman's Home Mission Movement in the Methodist Episcopal Church, South, 1886–1939* (1982).

McGreevy, John T., *Parish Boundaries: The Catholic Encounter with Race in the Twentieth-Century Urban North* (1996).

Miller, Robert Moats, "The Protestant Churches and Lynching, 1919–1939," *Journal of Negro History* 42 (1957): 118–31.

Paris, Arthur E., *Black Pentecostalism: Southern Religion in an Urban World* (1982).

Reagon, Bernice Johnson, ed., *We'll Understand It Better By and By: Pioneering African American Gospel Composers* (1992).

Satter, Beryl, "Marcus Garvey, Father Divine, and the Gender Politics of Race Difference and Race Neutrality," *American Quarterly* 48 (1996): 43–76.

Scheiner, Seth M., "The Negro Church and the Northern City, 1890–1930," in William G. Shade and Roy C. Herrenkohl, ed., *Seven on Black: Reflections on the Negro Experience in America* (1969): 92–117.

Sernett, Milton C., *Bound for the Promised Land: African American Religion and the Great Migration* (1997).

Shelly, Cara L., "Bradby's Baptists: Second Baptist Church of Detroit, 1910–1946," *Michigan Historical Review* 17 (1991): 1–33.

Weisenfeld, Judith, *African American Women and Christian Activism: New York's Black YWCA, 1905–1945* (1997).

21.10 THOUGHT AND EXPRESSION

21.10.1 Race, Gender, and Identity

Anderson, Jervis, *This Was Harlem: A Cultural Portrait, 1900–1950* (1982).

Anthony, Arthur A., "'Lost Boundaries': Racial Passing and Poverty in Segregated New Orleans," *Louisiana History* 36 (1995): 291–312.

Barton, Rebecca Chalmers, *Race Consciousness and the American Negro: A Study of the Correlation between the Group Experience and the Fiction of 1900–1930* (1934).

Braithwaite, William Stanley, *The William Stanley Braithwaite Reader,* ed. Philip Butcher (1972).

Bronz, Stephen H., *Roots of Negro Racial Consciousness: The 1920's: Three Harlem Renaissance Authors* (1964).

Bruce, Dickson D., "W.E.B. Du Bois and the Idea of Double Consciousness," *American Literature* 64 (June 1992): 299–309.

Bunche, Ralph J., *A World View of Race* (1936).

Carby, Hazel V., "Policing the Black Woman's Body in an Urban Context," *Critical Inquiry* 18 (1992): 738–55.

Cruse, Harold, *The Crisis of the Negro Intellectual* (1967).

Cunard, Nancy, ed., *Negro: An Anthology* (1934).

Davis, Angela Y., *Blues, Legacies, and Black Feminism: Gertrude "Ma" Rainey, Bessie Smith, and Billie Holiday* (1998).

Dill, Bonnie Thornton, "Race, Class, and Gender: Prospects for an All-Inclusive Sisterhood," *Feminist Studies* 9 (1983): 131–50.

Faulkner, Audrey Olsen, comp., *When I Was Comin' Up: An Oral History of Aged Blacks* (1982).

Garber, Eric, "A Spectacle in Color: The Lesbian and Gay Subculture of Jazz Age Harlem," in Martin Bauml Duberman, Martha Vicinus and George Chauncey, Jr., ed., *Hidden from History: Reclaiming the Gay and Lesbian Past* (1989): 318–31.

Gates, Henry Louis, Jr., ed., *"Race," Writing, and Difference* (1986).

Harris, Leonard, ed., *The Philosophy of Alain Locke: Harlem Renaissance and Beyond* (1989).

Higginbotham, Evelyn Brooks, "African-American Women's History and the Metalanguage of Race," *Signs* 17 (1992): 251–74.

———— "Rethinking Vernacular Culture: Black Religion and Race Records in the 1920s and 1930s," in Wahneema Lubiano, ed., *The House That Race Built: Black Americans, U.S. Terrain* (1997): 157–77.

Huggins, Nathan I., *Harlem Renaissance* (1971).

James, Winston, *Holding Aloft the Banner of Ethiopia: Caribbean Radicalism in Early Twentieth-Century America* (1999).

Janiewski, Dolores E., *Sisterhood Denied: Race, Gender, and Class in a New South Community* (1985).

Janken, Kenneth R., "African American and Francophone Black Intellectuals during the Harlem Renaissance," *Historian* 60 (1998): 487–505.

Johnson-Feelings, Diane, ed., *The Best of the Brownies' Book* (1996).

Kornweibel, Theodore, Jr., "Apathy and Dissent: Black America's Negative Responses to World War I," *South Atlantic Quarterly* 80 (1981): 322–38.

Lewis, David Levering, *When Harlem Was in Vogue* (1982).

Locke, Alain L., "The Concept of Race As Applied to Social Culture," *Howard Review* 1 (1924): 290–99.

———— *The New Negro: An Interpretation* (1925).

Logan, Rayford W., Eugene C. Holmes, and G. Franklin Edwards, ed., *The New Negro Thirty Years Afterward: Papers Contributed to the Sixteenth Annual Spring Conference of the Division of the Social Sciences, April 20, 21, and 22, 1955* (1955).

Lubiano, Wahneema, ed., *The House That Race Built: Black Americans, U.S. Terrain* (1997).

Moton, Robert Russa, *What the Negro Thinks* (1929).

Ochillo, Yvonne, "The Race-Consciousness of Alain Locke," *Phylon* 47 (1986): 173–81.

Satter, Beryl, "Marcus Garvey, Father Divine, and the Gender Politics of Race Difference and Race Neutrality," *American Quarterly* 48 (1996): 43–76.

Shapiro, Herbert, "A Diversity of Leadership Models: Charles N. Hunter, Marcus Garvey, and A. Philip Randolph," *Journal of American Ethnic History* 9 (1989): 108–11.

Simson, Rennie, "The Afro-American Female: The Historical Context of the Construction of Sexual Identity," in Ann Snitow, Christine Stansell and Sharon Thompson, ed., *Desire: The Politics of Sexuality* (1983): 243–49.

Stack, Carol B., "The Culture of Gender: Women and Men of Color," *Signs* 11 (1986): 321–24.

Stetson, Erlene, "Black Feminism in Indiana, 1893–1933," *Phylon* 44 (1983): 292–98.

Stewart, Jeffrey C., ed., *The Critical Temper of Alain Locke: A Selection of His Essays on Art and Culture* (1983).

————, ed., *Race Contacts and Interracial Relations: Five Lectures by Alain Locke* (1992).

Stocking, G. W., *Race, Culture, and Evolution: Essays in the History of Anthropology* (1968).

Tatum, Elbert Lee, *The Changed Political Thought of the Negro, 1915–1940* (1951).

Watson, Steven, *The Harlem Renaissance: Hub of African-American Culture, 1920–1930* (1995).

Wilson, Francille Rusan, "Racial Consciousness and Black Scholarship: Charles H. Wesley and the Consciousness of *Negro Labor in the United States*," *Journal of Negro History* 81 (1996): 72–88.

Wintz, Cary D., *African American Political Thought, 1890–1930: Washington, Du Bois, Garvey, and Randolph* (1996).

———— *Black Culture and the Harlem Renaissance* (1988).

———— *The Emergence of the Harlem Renaissance* (1996).

21.10.2   Emigration and Nationalism

Burkett, Randall K., *Black Redemption: Churchmen Speak for the Garvey Movement* (1978).

Hill, Robert A., "Racial and Radical: Cyril J. Briggs, *The Crusader* Magazine, and the African Blood Brotherhood, 1918–1922," in Robert A. Hill, ed., *The Crusader* (1987): 5–66.

Jacobs, Sylvia M., *The African Nexus: Black American Perspectives on the European Partitioning of Africa, 1880–1920* (1981).

Jacques-Garvey, Amy, ed., *Philosophy and Opinions of Marcus Garvey* (2 vols., 1923, 1925).

Kahn, Robert M., "The Political Ideology of Marcus Garvey," *Midwest Quarterly* 24 (1983): 117–37.

Lively, Adam, "Continuity and Radicalism in American Black Nationalist Thought, 1914–1929," *Journal of American Studies* 18 (1984): 207–35.

Martin, Tony, *Race First: The Ideological and Organizational Struggles of Marcus Garvey and the Universal Negro Improvement Association* (1976).

Meade, Teresa, and Gregory Alonso Pirio, "In Search of the Afro-American 'Eldorado': Attempts by North American Blacks to Enter Brazil in the 1920's," *Luso-Brazilian Review* 25 (1988): 85–110.

Plummer, Brenda Gayle, "The Afro-American Response to the Occupation of Haiti, 1915–1934," *Phylon* 43 (1982): 125–43.

Stein, Judith, *The World of Marcus Garvey: Race and Class in Modern Society* (1986).

Tolbert, Emory J., "Outpost Garveyism and the UNIA Rank and File," *Journal of Black Studies* 5 (1975): 233–53.

———— *The UNIA and Black Los Angeles: Ideology and Community in the American Garvey Movement* (1980).

Toll, William, *The Resurgence of Race: Black Social Theory from Reconstruction to the Pan-African Conferences* (1979).

Watson, Elwood, "Marcus Garvey's Garveyism: Message from a Forefather," *Journal of Religious Thought* 51 (1994): 77–94.

Wintz, Cary D., *African American Political Thought, 1890–1930: Washington, Du Bois, Garvey, and Randolph* (1996).

21.10.3   Folklore and Humor

Beilke, Debra, "'Yowlin' and Jawin': Humor and the Performance of Identity in Zora Neale Hurston's *Jonah's Gourd Vine*," *Southern Quarterly* 36 (1998): 21–33.

Botkin, Benjamin Albert, *Folk-Say: A Regional Miscellany* (4 vols., 1929–32).

Dalgarno, Emily, "'Words Walking without Masters': Ethnography and the Creative Process in *Their Eyes Were Watching God*," *American Literature* 64 (1992): 519–41.

Diepeveen, Leonard, "Folktales in the Harlem Renaissance," *American Literature* 58 (1986): 64–81.

Hemenway, Robert, "Folklore Field Notes from Zora Neale Hurston," *Black Scholar* 7 (1976): 39–46.

Hill, Lynda Marion, *Social Rituals and the Verbal Art of Zora Neale Hurston* (1996).

Lomax, Alan, *The Land Where Blues Began* (1993).

Meisenhelder, Susan, "Conflict and Resistance in Zora Neale Hurston's *Mules and Men*," *Journal of American Folklore* 109 (1996): 267–88.

Odum, Howard Washington, *Rainbow Round My Shoulder: The Blue Trail of Black Ulysses* (1928).

Puckett, Newbell Niles, *Folk Beliefs of the Southern Negro* (1926).

21.10.4   Literature and Poetry

Ako, Edward O., "Langston Hughes and the Négritude Movement: A Study in Literary Influences," *CLA Journal* 28 (1984): 46–56.

Austin, Addell P., "The *Opportunity* and *Crisis* Literary Contests, 1924–1927," *CLA Journal* 32 (1988): 235–46.

Baker, Houston A., *Afro-American Poetics: Revisions of Harlem and the Black Aesthetic* (1988).

——— *Blues, Ideology, and Afro-American Literature: A Vernacular Theory* (1984).

——— *Modernism and the Harlem Renaissance* (1987).

Barbeito, Patricia Felisa, "'Making Generations' in Jacobs, Larsen, and Hurston: A Genealogy of Black Women's Writing," *American Literature* 70 (1998): 365–96.

Bascom, Lionel C., ed., *A Renaissance in Harlem: Lost Voices of an American Commmunity* (1999).

Bone, Robert A., *The Negro Novel in America* (rev. ed. 1965).

Bronz, Stephen H., *Roots of Negro Racial Consciousness: The 1920's: Three Harlem Renaissance Authors* (1964).

Brown, Sterling A., "The Negro Author and His Publisher," *Negro Quarterly* 1 (1942): 7–20.

Chapman, Abraham, "The Harlem Renaissance in Literary History," *CLA Journal* 11 (1967): 38–58.

Davis, Arthur P., "The Alien-and-Exile Theme in Countee Cullen's Racial Poems," *Phylon* 14 (1953): 390–400.

——— "The Harlem of Langston Hughes' Poetry," *Phylon* 13 (1952): 276–83.

Dean, Sharon, and Erlene Stetson, "Flower Dust and Springtime: Harlem Renaissance Women," *Radical Teacher* 18 (1980): 1–8.

Du Bois, William Edward Burghardt, "Criteria of Negro Art," *The Crisis* 32 (1926): 290, 292, 294, 296–97.

——— "The Negro in Art: How Shall He Be Portrayed: A Symposium," *The Crisis* 32 (1926): 35–36.

DuCille, Ann, "Blues Notes on Black Sexuality: Sex and the Texts of Jessie Fauset and Nella Larsen," *Journal of the History of Sexuality* 3 (1993): 418–44.

——— *The Coupling Convention: Sex, Text, and Tradition in Black Women's Fiction* (1993).

Early, Gerald, "Three Notes toward a Cultural Definition of the Harlem Renaissance," *Callaloo* 14 (1991): 136–49.

Feeney, Joseph J., "A Sardonic, Unconventional Jessie Fauset: The Double Structure and Double Vision of Her Novels," *CLA Journal* 22 (1979): 365–82.

Ferguson, Blanche E., *Countee Cullen and the Negro Renaissance* (1966).

Ford, Nick Aaron, *The Contemporary Negro Novel: A Study in Race Relations* (1936).

Foreman, P. Gabrielle, "Looking back from Zora, or Talking out Both Sides My Mouth for Those Who Have Two Ears," *Black American Literature Forum* 24 (1990): 649–66.

Gallagher, Brian, "About Us, for Us, near Us: The Irish and Harlem Renaissances," *Éire-Ireland* 16 (1981): 14–26.

Glicksberg, Charles I., "The Negro Cult of the Primitive," *Antioch Review* 4 (1944): 47–55.

Goddard, Robert, "Agricultural Worker As Archetype in West Indian and African-American Literature," *Agricultural History* 72 (1998): 509–20.

Gregory, Horace, and Marya Zaturenska, *A History of American Poetry, 1900–1940* (1946).

Griffin, Farah Jasmine, *"Who Set You Flowin'?" The African-American Migration Narrative* (1995).

Harris, Trudier, *Exorcising Blackness: Historical and Literary Lynching and Burning Rituals* (1984).

Hart, Robert C., "Black-White Literary Relations in the Harlem Renaissance," *American Literature* 44 (1973): 612–28.

Haws, Robert J., and Derrick A. Bell, ed., *The Age of Segregation: Race Relations in the South, 1890–1945: Essays* (1978).

Huggins, Nathan I., *Harlem Renaissance* (1971).

———, ed., *Voices from the Harlem Renaissance* (1976).

Hughes, Langston, "The Negro Artist and the Racial Mountain," in Nathan I. Huggins, ed., *Voices from the Harlem Renaissance* (1976): 305–09.

Hull, Gloria T., *Color, Sex, and Poetry: Three Women Writers of the Harlem Renaissance* (1987).

Hutchinson, George, *The Harlem Renaissance in Black and White* (1995).

——— "Nella Larsen and the Veil of Race," *American Literary History* 9 (1997): 329–49.

Janken, Kenneth R., "Civil Rights and Socializing in the Harlem Renaissance: Walter White and the Fictionalization of the 'New Negro' in Georgia," *Georgia Historical Quarterly* 80 (1996): 817–34.

Johnson, Abby Arthur, "Literary Midwife: Jessie Redmon Fauset and the Harlem Renaissance," *Phylon* 39 (1978): 143–53.

Johnson, Charles Spurgeon, and John McCluskey, ed., *Black Men Speaking* (1997).

Johnson, James Weldon, "The Dilemma of the Negro Author," *American Mercury* 15 (1928): 477–81.

Kaiser, Ernest, "The Literature of Harlem," *Freedomways* 3 (1963): 276–91.

——— "The Literature of Negro Revolt," *Freedomways* 3 (1963): 36–47.

Kellner, Bruce, "'Refined Racism': White Patronage in the Harlem Renaissance," in Victor A. Kramer, ed., *The Harlem Renaissance Re-Examined* (1987): 93–106.

King, Sigrid, "Naming and Power in Zora Neale Hurston's *Their Eyes Were Watching God*," *Black American Literature Forum* 24 (1990): 683–96.

Krasner, James, "The Life of Women: Zora Neale Hurston and Female Autobiography," *Black American Literature Forum* 23 (1989): 113–26.

Lauter, Paul, "Race and Gender in the Shaping of the American Literary Canon: A Case Study from the Twenties," *Feminist Studies* 9 (1983): 435–63.

Lemke, Sieglinde, *Primitivist-Modernism: Black Culture and the Origins of Transatlantic Modernism* (1998).

Lewis, Vashti Crutcher, "The Declining Significance of the Mulatto Female As Major Character in the Novels of Zora Neale Hurston," *CLA Journal* 28 (1984): 127–49.

Locke, Alain L., "American Literary Tradition and the Negro," *Modern Quarterly* 3 (1926): 215–22.

——— "Black Truth and Black Beauty," *Opportunity* 11 (1933): 14–18.

——— "The Negro Poets of the United States," William S. Braithwaite, ed., *Anthology of Magazine Verse 1926 and Yearbook of American Poetry* (1926): 143–51.

——— "The Negro's Contribution to American Art and Literature," *The Annals of the American Academy of Political and Social Science* 140 (1928): 234–47.

Logan, Rayford W., Eugene C. Holmes, and G. Franklin Edwards, ed., *The New Negro Thirty Years Afterward: Papers Contributed to the Sixteenth Annual Spring Conference of the Division of the Social Sciences, April 20, 21, and 22, 1955* (1955).

Matthews, Donald H., *Honoring the Ancestors: An African Cultural Interpretation of Black Religion and Literature* (1998).

Maxwell, William J., *New Negro, Old Left: African-American Writing and Communism Between the Wars* (1999).

McDowell, Deborah E., "The Neglected Dimension of Jessie Redmon Fauset," *Afro-Americans in New York Life and History* 5 (1981): 33–49.

——— *"The Changing Same": Black Women's Literature, Criticism, and Theory* (1995).

McKay, Claude, *The Passion of Claude McKay: Selected Poetry and Prose, 1912–1948*, ed. Wayne Cooper (1973).

Miller, Nina, *Making Love Modern: The Intimate Public Worlds of New York's Literary Women* (1998).

Nelson, John Herbert, *The Negro Character in American Literature* (1926).

Peters, Pearlie Mae Fisher, *The Assertive Woman in Zora Neale Hurston's Fiction, Folklore, and Drama* (1997).

Pondrom, Cyrena N., "The Role of Myth in Hurston's *Their Eyes Were Watching God*," *American Literature* 58 (1986): 181–202.

Rampersad, Arnold, "The Origins of Poetry in Langston Hughes," *The Southern Review* 21 (1985): 695–705.

Robey, Judith, "Generic Strategies in Zora Neale Hurston's *Dust Tracks on a Road*," *Black American Literature Forum* 24 (1990): 667–81.

Rodgers, Lawrence R., *Canaan Bound: The African American Great Migration Novel* (1997).

Rollins, Hyder E., "The Negro in the Southern Short Story," *Sewanee Review* 24 (1916): 42–60.

Rourke, Constance, "Tradition for a Negro Literature," in Van Wyck Brooks, ed., *Roots of American Culture* (1942): 262–74.

Scruggs, Charles W., "'All Dressed up but No Place to Go': The Black Writer and His Audience during the Harlem Renaissance," *American Literature* 48 (1977): 543–63.

Singh, Amritjit, *The Novels of the Harlem Renaissance: Twelve Black Writers, 1923–1933* (1976).

Singh, Amritjit, William S. Shiver, and Stanley Brodwin, ed., *The Harlem Renaissance: Revaluations* (1989).

Smith, Felipe, *American Body Politics: Race, Gender, and Black Literary Renaissance* (1998).

Tate, Claudia, *Psychoanalysis and Black Novels: Desire and the Protocols of Race* (1998).

Turner, Darwin T., *In a Minor Chord: Three Afro-American Writers and Their Search for Identity* (1971).

Wagner, Jean, *Black Poets of the United States: From Paul Laurence Dunbar to Langston Hughes*, tr. Kenneth Douglas (1973).

Wall, Cheryl A., *Women of the Harlem Renaissance* (1995).

Watson, Steven, *The Harlem Renaissance: Hub of African-American Culture, 1920–1930* (1996).

Williams, Kenny J., "An Invisible Partnership and an Unlikely Relationship: William Stanley Braithwaite and Harriet Monroe," *Callaloo* 10 (1987): 516–50.

Wintz, Cary D., *Black Culture and the Harlem Renaissance* (1988).

———, ed., *Black Writers Interpret the Harlem Renaissance* (1996).

———, ed., *The Critics and the Harlem Renaissance* (1996).

——— *The Emergence of the Harlem Renaissance* (1996).

———, ed., *The Politics and Aesthetics of 'New Negro' Literature* (1996).

21.10.5   Music and Performing Arts

Berrett, Joshua, "Louis Armstrong and Opera," *Musical Quarterly* 76 (1992): 216–41.

Blood, Melanie N., "Theatre in Settlement Houses: Hull-House Players, Neighborhood Playhouse, and Karamu Theatre," *Theatre History Studies* 16 (1996): 45–69.

Bond, Frederick Weldon, *The Negro and the Drama: The Direct and Indirect Contribution Which the American Negro Has Made to Drama and the Legitimate Stage, with the Underlying Conditions Responsible* (1940).

Cohn, Lawrence, et al., *Nothing But the Blues: The Music and the Musicians* (1993).

Davis, Angela Y., *Blues, Legacies, and Black Feminism: Gertrude "Ma" Rainey, Bessie Smith, and Billie Holiday* (1998).

Gennari, John, "'A Weapon of Integration': Frank Marshall Davis and the Politics of Jazz," *Langston Hughes Review* 14 (1996): 16–33.

Gottlieb, Robert, ed., *Reading Jazz: A Gathering of Autobiography, Reportage, and Criticism from 1919 to Now* (1996).

Grant, George C., "The Negro in Dramatic Art," *Journal of Negro History* 17 (1932): 19–29.

Harrison, Daphne Duval, *Black Pearls: Blues Queens of the 1920s* (1988).

Hudson, Theodore R., "Duke Ellington's Literary Sources," *American Music* 9 (1991): 20–42.

Kenney, William Howland, *Chicago Jazz: A Cultural History, 1904–1930* (1993).

Lemke, Sieglinde, *Primitivist-Modernism: Black Culture and the Origins of Transatlantic Modernism* (1998).

Locke, Alain, *The Negro and His Music* (1936).

Locke, Alain L., and Gregory Montgomery, ed., *Plays of Negro Life: A Source-Book of Native American Drama* (1927).

Lomax, Alan, *Brown Girl in a Ring: An Anthology of Song Games from the Eastern Caribbean* (1997).

Lomax, John A., and Alan Lomax, ed., *Negro Folk Songs: As Sung by Lead Belly, "King of the Twelve-String Guitar Players of the World," Long-Time Convict in the Penitentiaries of Texas and Louisiana* (1936).

Long, Richard A., *The Black Tradition in American Dance* (1989).

Lyttelton, Humphrey, *The Best of Jazz, Basin Street to Harlem: Jazz Masters and Masterpieces, 1917–1930* (1978).

Marx, Edward, "Forgotten Jungle Songs: Primitivist Strategies of the Harlem Renaissance," *Langston Hughes Review* 14 (1996): 79–93.

Miller, Jeanne Marie A., "Georgia Douglas Johnson and May Miller: Forgotten Playwrights of the New Negro Renaissance," *CLA Journal* 33 (1990): 349–66.

Miller, Patrick B., "To 'Bring the Race along Rapidly': Sport, Student Culture, and Educational Mission at Historically Black Colleges during the Interwar Years," *History of Education Quarterly* 35 (1995): 111–33.

Muse, Clarence, and David Arlen, *Way down South* (1932).

Ogren, Kathy J., *The Jazz Revolution: Twenties America and the Meaning of Jazz* (1989).

Oliver, Paul, *The Story of the Blues* (1969).

Otto, John S., and Augustus M. Burns, "Black and White Cultural Interaction in the Early Twentieth Century South: Race and Hillbilly Music," *Phylon* 35 (1974): 407–17.

Reagon, Bernice Johnson, ed., *We'll Understand It Better By and By: Pioneering African American Gospel Composers* (1992).

Rice, Marc, "Frompin' in the Great Plains: Listening and Dancing to the Jazz Orchestras of Alphonso Trent, 1925–1944," *Great Plains Quarterly* 16 (1996): 107–16.

Schuller, Gunther, *Early Jazz: Its Roots and Musical Development* (1968).

Scott, Freda L., "Black Drama and the Harlem Renaissance," *Theatre Journal* 37 (1985): 426–39.

Shaw, Arnold, *The Jazz Age: Popular Music in the 1920s* (1987).

Simpson, Anne Key, "Camille Lucie Nickerson: 'The Louisiana Lady,'" *Louisiana History* 36 (1995): 431–51.

Storm, William, "Reactions of a 'Highly-Strung Girl': Psychology and Dramatic Representation in Angelina W. Grimke's *Rachel*," *African American Review* 27 (1993): 461–71.

21.10.6   Art (Drawing, Painting, Photography, Printmaking, Sculpture)

Coleman, Floyd, and John Adkins Richardson, "Black Continuities in the Art of the Renaissance," *Papers on Language and Literature* 12 (1976): 402–21.

Davis, Keith F., *The Passionate Observer: Photographs by Carl Van Vechten* (1993).

Driskell, David, David Levering Lewis, and Deborah Willis Ryan, *Harlem Renaissance: Art of Black America* (1987).

Harmon Foundation, Inc., *Exhibit of Fine Arts: Productions of American Negro Artists* (1928–31, 1933).

Helbling, Mark, "African Art: Albert C. Barnes and Alain Locke," *Phylon* 43 (1982): 57–67.

Lemke, Sieglinde, *Primitivist-Modernism: Black Culture and the Origins of Transatlantic Modernism* (1998).

Myers, Walter Dean, *One More River to Cross: An African American Photograph Album* (1995).

Perkins, Kathy A., "The Genius of Meta Warrick Fuller," *Black American Literature Forum* 24 (1990): 65–74.

Powell, Richard J., *Homecoming: The Art and Life of William H. Johnson* (1991).

Powell, Richard J., and David A. Bailey, *Rhapsodies in Black: Art of the Harlem Renaissance* (1997).

Powell, Richard J., and Jock Reynolds, *James Lesesne Wells: Sixty Years in Art* (1986).

———— *To Conserve a Legacy: American Art from Historically Black Colleges and Universities* (1999).

Reynolds, Gary A., and Beryl J. Wright, *Against the Odds: African American Artists and the Harmon Foundation* (1989).

Roberts, Richard Samuel, *A True Likeness: The Black South of Richard Samuel Roberts, 1920–1936*, ed. Thomas L. Johnson and Philip C. Dunn (1986).

Robinson, Jontyle Theresa, and Wendy Greenhouse, *The Art of Archibald J. Motley, Jr.* (1991).

Rubin, William, ed., *'Primitivism' in 20th Century Art* (2 vols., 1984).

Stewart, Jeffrey C., *To Color America: Portraits by Winold Reiss* (1989).

Torgovnick, Marianna, *Gone Primitive: Savage, Intellects, Modern Lives* (1990).

Van Der Zee, James, Owen Dodson, and Camille Billops, *Harlem Book of the Dead* (1978).

Van Vechten, Carl, *Generations in Black and White: Photographs by Carl Van Vechten from the James Weldon Johnson Memorial Collection*, ed. Rudolph P. Byrd (1993).

———— *Portraits: The Photography of Carl Van Vechten*, comp. Saul Mauriber (1978).

Waring, Laura Wheeler, *In Memoriam, Laura Wheeler Waring, 1887–1948: An Exhibition of Paintings, May and June 1949* (1949).

Wright, John Samuel, and Tracy E. Smith, *A Stronger Soul within a Finer Frame: Portraying African-Americans in the Black Renaissance* (1990).

21.10.7   Film and Broadcasting

Bogle, Donald, *Toms, Coons, Mulattoes, Mammies, and Bucks: An Interpretive History of Blacks in American Films* (3d ed., 1994).

Cripps, Thomas, "The Birth of a Race Company: An Early Stride toward a Black Cinema," *Journal of Negro History* 59 (1974): 28–37.

———— *Slow Fade to Black: The Negro in American Film, 1900–1942* (1977).

Guerrero, Edward, *Framing Blackness: The African American Image in Film* (1993).

Kisch, John, and Edward Mapp, *A Separate Cinema: Fifty Years of Black-Cast Posters* (1992).

Leab, Daniel J., "'All Colored'—But Not Much Different: Films Made for Negro Ghetto Audiences, 1913–1928," *Phylon* 36 (1975): 321–39.

———— *From Sambo to Superspade: The Black Experience in Motion Pictures* (1975).

Regester, Charlene, "The Misreading and Rereading of African American Filmmaker Oscar Micheaux," *Film History* 7 (1995): 426–49.

21.11   EDUCATION

Anderson, Eric, and Alfred A. Moss, Jr., *Dangerous Donations: Northern Philanthropy and Southern Black Education, 1902–1930* (1999).

Anderson, James D., *The Education of Blacks in the South, 1860–1935* (1988).

Aptheker, Herbert, "The Negro College Student in the 1920's: Years of Preparation and Protest, an Introduction," *Science and Society* 33 (1969): 150–67.

Bond, Horace Mann, *Negro Education in Alabama: A Study in Cotton and Steel* (1939).

Cole, Bahalola, "Appropriation Politics and Black Schools: Howard University in the U.S. Congress, 1879–1928," *Journal of Negro Education* 46 (1977): 7–23.

Daniel, Philip T. K., "A History of Discrimination against Black Students in Chicago Secondary Schools," *History of Education Quarterly* 20 (1980): 147–62.

Davis, Leroy, "An African American Dilemma: John Hope and Black Leadership in the Early Twentieth Century," *Atlanta History* 41 (1997): 27–48.

Fishman, G., "Paul Robeson's Student Days and the Fight against Racism at Rutgers," *Freedomways* 9 (1969): 221–29.

Franklin, Vincent P., "Black Social Scientists and the Mental Testing Movement, 1920–1940," in Reginald L. Jones, ed., *Black Psychology* (3d ed., 1991): 207–24.

———— *The Education of Black Philadelphia: The Social and Educational History of a Minority Community, 1900–1950* (1979).

Fultz, Michael, "African-American Teachers in the South, 1890–1940: Powerlessness and the Ironies of Expectations and Protest," *History of Education Quarterly* 35 (1995): 401–22.

———— "African-American Teachers in the South, 1890–1940: Growth, Feminization, and Salary Discrimination," *Teachers College Record* 96 (1995): 544–68.

Halderman, Keith, "Blanche Armwood of Tampa and the Strategy of Interracial Cooperation," *Florida Historical Quarterly* 74 (1996): 287–303.

Harris, Carl V., "Stability and Change in Discrimination against Black Public Schools: Birmingham, Alabama, 1871–1931," *Journal of Southern History* 51 (1985): 375–416.

Hine, Darlene Clark, "The Pursuit of Professional Equality: Meharry Medical College, 1921–1938, a Case Study," in Vincent P. Franklin and James D. Anderson, ed., *New Perspectives on Black Educational History* (1978): 173–92.

Hogan, David John, *Class and Reform: School and Society in Chicago, 1880–1930* (1985).

———— "Education and the Making of the Chicago Working Class, 1880–1930," *History of Education Quarterly* 18 (1978): 227–70.

Holmes, Dwight Oliver Wendell, *The Evolution of the Negro College* (1934).

Homel, Michael W., *Down from Equality: Black Chicagoans and the Public Schools, 1920–1941* (1984).

———— "The Politics of Public Education in Black Chicago, 1910–1941," *Journal of Negro Education* 45 (1976): 179–91.

Kelso, Richard, and Debbe Heller, *Building a Dream: Mary Bethune's School* (1996).

Margo, Robert Andrew, *Race and Schooling in the South, 1880–1950: An Economic History* (1990).

Martin, Robert Sidney, and Orvin Lee Shiflett, "Hampton, Fisk, and Atlanta: The Foundations, the American Library Association, and Library Education for Blacks, 1925–1941," *Libraries and Culture* 31 (1996): 299–325.

McNeil, Genna Rae, "To Meet the Group Needs: The Transformation of Howard University School of Law, 1920–1935," in Vincent P. Franklin and James D. Anderson, ed., *New Perspectives on Black Educational History* (1978): 149–72.

Meier, August, and Elliott Rudwick, "Early Boycotts of Segregated Schools: The Case of Springfield, Ohio, 1922–1923," *American Quarterly* 20 (1968): 744–58.

Miller, Patrick B., "To 'Bring the Race along Rapidly': Sport, Student Culture, and Educational Mission at Historically Black Colleges during the Interwar Years," *History of Education Quarterly* 35 (1995): 111–33.

Mohraz, Judy Jolley, *The Separate Problem: Case Studies of Black Education in the North, 1900–1930* (1979).

Morgan, Gordon D., "Fisk University and the Intellectual Origins of the Harlem Renaissance," *Western Journal of Black Studies* 21 (1997): 214–28.

Neverdon-Morton, Cynthia, "Self-Help Programs As Educative Activities of Black Women in the South, 1895–1925: Focus on Four Key Areas," *Journal of Negro History* 51 (1982): 207–21.

Perkins, Linda M., "Lucy Diggs Slowe: Champion of the Self-Determination of African-American Women in Higher Education," *Journal of Negro History* 81 (1996): 89–104.

Perlmann, Joel, *Ethnic Differences: Schooling and Social Structure among the Irish, Italians, Jews, and Blacks in an American City, 1880–1935* (1988).

Peterson, Paul E., *The Politics of School Reform, 1870–1940* (1985).

Reid, Ira de Augustine, *Adult Education among Negroes* (1936).

Sherman, R. B., "The 'Teachings at Hampton Institute': Social Equality, Racial Integrity, and the Virginia Public Assemblage Act of 1926," *Virginia Magazine of History and Biography* 95 (1987): 275–300.

Taggart, Robert J., "Philanthropy and Black Public Education in Delaware, 1918–1930," *Pennsylvania Magazine of History and Biography* 103 (1979): 467–83.

Thomas, William B., "Schooling As a Political Instrument of Social Control: School Response to Black Migrant Youth in Buffalo, New York, 1917–1940," *Teachers College Record* 86 (1985): 579–92.

Tyack, David B., "Growing Up Black: Perspectives on the History of Education in Northern Ghettos," *History of Education Quarterly* 9 (1969): 287–97.

Wolcott, Victoria W., "'Bible, Bath, and Broom': Nannie Helen Burroughs's National Training School and African-American Racial Uplift," *Journal of Women's History* 9 (1997): 88–110.

Wolters, Raymond, *The New Negro on Campus: Black College Rebellions of the 1920s* (1975).

Wright, Arthur D., *The Negro Rural School Fund, Inc., 1907–1933* (1933).

21.12 WORK AND ENTREPRENEURIAL ACTIVITY

Alexander, R. J., "Negro Business in Atlanta," *Southern Economic Journal* 17 (1951): 451–64.

Angel, William D., Jr., "Controlling Workers: The Galveston Dock Workers' Strike of 1920 and Its Impact on Labor Relations in Texas," *East Texas Historical Journal* 23 (1985): 14–27.

Arnesen, Eric, "Following the Color Line of Labor: Black Workers and the Labor Movement before 1930," *Radical Historical Review* 55 (1992): 53–88.

———— *Waterfront Workers of New Orleans: Race, Class, and Politics, 1863–1923* (1991).

Barnum, Darold T., *The Negro in the Bituminous Coal Mining Industry* (1970).

Baron, Harold, "The Demand for Black Labor: Historical Notes on the Political Economy of Racism," *Radical America* 5 (1971): 1–46.

Barrett, James R., "Unity and Fragmentation: Class, Race, and Ethnicity on Chicago's South Side, 1900–1922," *Journal of Social History* 18 (1984): 37–55.

———— *Work and Community in the Jungle: Chicago's Packinghouse Workers, 1894–1922* (1987).

Berglund, Abraham, Frank Traver De Vyver, and George Talmage Staenes, *Labor in the Industrial South: A Survey of Wages and Living Conditions in Three Major Industries of the New Industrial South* (1930).

Bodnar, John, "The Impact of the 'New Immigration' on the Black Worker: Steelton, Pennsylvania, 1880–1920," *Labor History* 17 (1976): 214–29.

Boyd, Robert L., "Residential Segregation by Race and the Black Merchants of Northern Cities during the Early Twentieth Century," *Sociological Forum* 13 (1998): 595–609.

Brazeal, Brailsford Reese, *The Brotherhood of Sleeping Car Porters: Its Origin and Development* (1946).

Brier, Stephen, "In Defense of Gutman: The Union's Case," *International Journal of Political Culture and Society* 2 (1988): 382–95.

———— "Labor, Politics, and Race: A Black Worker's Life," *Labor History* 23 (1982): 416–21.

Chateauvert, Melinda, *Marching Together: Women of the Brotherhood of Sleeping Car Porters* (1998).

Clark-Lewis, Elizabeth, *Living in, Living Out: African American Domestics in Washington, D.C., 1910–1940* (1994).

Cohen, William, "Negro Involuntary Servitude in the South, 1865–1940: A Preliminary Analysis," *Journal of Southern History* 42 (1976): 31–60.

Crosby, Earl W., "Limited Success against Long Odds: The Black County Agent," *Agricultural History* 57 (1983): 277–88.

———— "The Roots of Black Agricultural Extension Work," *Historian* 39 (1977): 228–47.

Dabney, Thomas L., "Southern Labor and the Negro," *Opportunity* 7 (1929): 345–49.

Daniel, Pete, *Breaking the Land: The Transformation of Cotton, Tobacco, and Rice Cultures since 1880* (1985).

———— *The Shadow of Slavery: Peonage in the South, 1901–1969* (1972).

DeCanio, Stephen J., *Agriculture in the Post-Bellum South: The Economics of Production and Supply* (1974).

Dunne, William F., *Gastonia: Citadel of the Class Struggle in the New South* (1929).

Dutcher, Dean, *The Negro in Modern Industrial Society: An Analysis of Changes in the Occupations of Negro Workers, 1910–1920* (1930).

Fickle, James E., "Management Looks at the 'Labor Problem': The Southern Pine Industry during World War I and the Postwar Era," *Journal of Southern History* 40 (1974): 61–76.

Fogel, Walter A., *The Negro in the Meat Industry* (1970).

Foner, Philip Sheldon, "The IWW and the Black Worker," *Journal of Negro History* 55 (1970): 45–64.

———— *Organized Labor and the Black Worker, 1619–1981* (2d ed., 1982).

Frazier, Edward Franklin, "Occupational Classes among Negroes in Cities," *Amerian Journal of Sociology* 35 (1930): 718–38.

Fultz, Michael, "African-American Teachers in the South, 1890–1940: Growth, Feminization, and Salary Discrimination," *Teachers College Record* 96 (1995): 544–68.

Goddard, Robert, "Agricultural Worker As Archetype in West Indian and African-American Literature," *Agricultural History* 72 (1998): 509–20.

Gottlieb, Peter, "Black Miners and the 1925–1928 Bituminous Coal Strike: The Colored Committee of Non-Union Miners, Montour Mine No. 1, Pittsburgh Coal Company," *Labor History* 28 (1987): 233–41.

———— "Migration and Jobs: The New Black Workers in Pittsburgh, 1916–1930," *Western Pennsylvania Historical Magazine* 61 (1978): 1–15.

Gould, William B., *Black Workers in White Unions: Job Discrimination in the United States* (1977).

———— "Black Workers inside the House of Labor," *Annals of the American Academy of Political and Social Science* 407 (1973): 78–90.

Greenberg, Stanley B., *Race and State in Capitalist Development: Comparative Perspectives* (1980).

Greene, Lorenzo Johnston, and Carter G. Woodson, *The Negro Wage Earner* (1930).

Griffler, Keith P., *What Price Alliance: Black Radicals Confront White Labor, 1918–1938* (1995).

Gross, James A., "Historians and the Literature of the Negro Worker," *Labor History* 10 (1969): 536–46.

Grossman, James R., "Black Labor Is the Best Labor: Southern White Reactions to the Great Migration," in Alferdteen Harrison, ed., *Black Exodus: The Great Migration from the American South* (1991): 51–72.

———— "The White Man's Union: The Great Migration and the Resonance of Race and Class in Chicago, 1916–1922," in Joe W. Trotter, ed., *The Great Migration in Historical Perspective: New Dimensions of Race, Class, and Gender* (1991): 83–105.

Guzda, H. P., "Labor Department's First Program to Assist Black Workers, 1917–1922," *Monthly Labor Review* 105 (1982): 39–44.

Halker, Clark, "A History of Local 208 and the Struggle for Racial Equality in the American Federation of Musicians," *Black Music Research Journal* 8 (1988): 207–22.

Halpern, Rick, "Race, Ethnicity, and Union in the Chicago Stockyards, 1917–1922," *International Review of Social History* 37 (1992): 25–58.

Harley, Sharon, "For the Good of Family and Race: Gender, Work, and Domestic Roles in the Black Community, 1880–1930," *Signs* 15 (1990): 336–49.

Harmon, J. H., Jr., "The Negro As a Local Business Man," *Journal of Negro History* 14 (1929): 116–55.

Harris, Abram L., Jr., "The Negro and Economic Radicalism," *Modern Quarterly* 2 (1924–25): 198–208.

———— *The Negro As Capitalist: A Study of Banking and Business among American Negroes* (1936).

———— *Race, Radicalism, and Reform: Selected Papers*, ed. William Darity, Jr. (1989).

Harris, Abram L., Jr., and Sterling D. Spero, *The Black Worker: The Negro and the Labor Movement* (1931).

Harris, William Hamilton, *Keeping the Faith: A. Philip Randolph, Milton P. Webster, and the Brotherhood of Sleeping Car Porters, 1925–37* (1977).

Haynes, Elizabeth Ross, "Negroes in Domestic Service in the United States," *Journal of Negro History* 8 (1923): 384–442.

Haynes, George E., "Effects of War Conditions on Negro Labor," *Proceedings of the Academy of Political Science* 8 (1919): 165–78.

Henderson, Alexa Benson, *Atlanta Life Insurance Company: Guardian of Black Economic Dignity* (1990).

———— "Heman E. Perry and Black Enterprise in Atlanta, 1908–1925," *Business History Review* 61 (1987): 216–42.

Herbst, Alma, *The Negro in the Slaughtering and Meat-Packing Industry in Chicago* (1932).

Higginbotham, A. Leon, Jr., "Labor Union Racial Violence," in Gilbert Ware, ed., *From the Black Bar: Voices for Equal Justice* (1976): 255–61.

Hine, Darlene Clark, ed., *Black Women in the Nursing Profession: A Documentary History* (1985).

———— *Black Women in White: Racial Conflict and Cooperation in the Nursing Profession, 1890–1950* (1989).

Howard, John C., *The Negro in the Lumber Industry* (1970).

Hudson, Hosea, *Black Worker in the Deep South: A Personal Record* (2d ed., 1991).

Janiewski, Dolores E., *Subversive Sisterhood: Black Women and Unions in the Southern Tobacco Industry* (1984).

Jones, Beverly W., "Race, Sex, and Class: Black Female Tobacco Workers in Durham, North Carolina, 1920–1940, and the Development of Female Consciousness," *Feminist Studies* 10 (1984): 441–51.

Jones, Jacqueline, "Southern Diaspora: Origins of the Northern 'Underclass,'" in Michael B. Katz, ed., *The 'Underclass' Debate: Views from History* (1993): 27–54.

Jordan, Daniel P., "The Mingo War: Labor Violence in the Southern West Virginia Coal Fields, 1919–1922," in Gary M. Fink and Merl E. Reed, ed., *Essays in Southern Labor History: Selected Papers, Southern Labor History Conference, 1976* (1977): 102–43.

Karson, Marc and Ronald Radosh, "The American Federation of Labor and the Negro Worker, 1894–1949," in Julius Jacobsen, ed., *The Negro and the American Labor Movement* (1968): 155–87.

Kelley, Robin D. G., "'We Are Not What We Seem': Towards a Black Working-Class Opposition in the Jim Crow South," *Journal of American History* 80 (1993): 75–112.

Kulik, Gary, "Black Workers and Technological Change in the Birmingham Iron Industry, 1881–1931," in Merl E. Reed, Leslie S. Hough and Gary M. Fink, ed., *Southern Workers and Their Unions, 1880–1975: Selected Papers. The Second Labor History Conference, 1978* (1981): 22–42.

Lang, Jane, and Harry N. Scheiber, "The Wilson Administration and the Wartime Mobilization of Black Americans, 1917–1918," *Labor History* 10 (1969): 433–58.

Lewis, Earl, and Joe W. Trotter, ed., *African Americans in the Industrial Age: A Documentary History, 1915–1945* (1996).

Lewis, Edward E., *The Mobility of the Negro: A Study in the American Labor Supply* (1931).

Lewis, Ronald L., "Job Control and Race Relations in Coal Fields, 1870–1920," *Journal of Ethnic Studies* 12 (1985): 36–64.

Mack, Kibibi Voloria C., *Parlor Ladies and Ebony Drudges: African American Women, Class, and Work in a South Carolina Community* (1999).

Maloney, Thomas N., and Warren C. Whatley, "Making the Effort: The Contours of Racial Discrimination in Detroit's Labor Markets, 1920–1940," *Journal of Economic History* 55 (1995): 465–93.

Marks, Carole, "The Social and Economic Life of Southern Blacks during the Migration," in Alferdteen Harrison, ed., *Black Exodus: The Great Migration from the American South* (1991): 36–50.

Marshall, F. Ray, *The Negro and Organized Labor* (1965).

———— "The Negro in Southern Unions," in Julius Jacobson, ed., *The Negro and the American Labor Movement* (1968): 128–54.

———— *The Negro Worker* (1967).

McDonald, Forrest, and Grady McWhiney, "The South from Self-Sufficiency to Peonage: An Interpretation," *American Historical Review* 85 (1980): 1095–118.

Meier, August, and Ellott Rudwick, *Black Detroit and the Rise of the UAW* (1979).

Mollison, Irvin C., "Negro Lawyers in Mississippi," *Journal of Negro History* 15 (1930): 38–71.

National Urban League, *Negro Membership in American Labor Unions* (1930).

Newman, Debra L., comp., *Selected Documents Pertaining to Black Workers among the Records of the Department of Labor and Its Component Bureaus, 1902–1969* (1977).

Northrup, Herbert Roof, *The Negro in the Automobile Industry* (1968).

———— *The Negro in the Rubber Tire Industry* (1969).

———— *The Negro in the Tobacco Industry* (1970).

———— *Organized Labor and the Negro* (1944).

Painter, Nell I., "Black Workers from Reconstruction to the Great Depression," in Paul Buhle and Alan Dawley, ed., *Working for Democracy* (1985): 62–71.

Peterson, Joyce Shaw, "Black Automobile Workers in Detroit, 1910–1930," *Journal of Negro History* 64 (1979): 177–90.

Petras, Elizabeth McLean, *Jamaican Labor Migration: White Capital and Black Labor, 1850–1930* (1988).

Puth, Robert C., "Supreme Life: The History of a Negro Life Insurance Company, 1919–1962," *Business History Review* 43 (1969): 1–20.

Radzialowski, Thaddus, "The Competition for Jobs and Racial Stereotypes: Poles and Blacks in Chicago," *Polish American Studies* 33 (1976): 5–18.

Range, Willard, "Landed and the Landless: Georgia Agriculture, 1920–1940," in Harry N. Scheiber, ed., *United States Economic History: Selected Readings* (1964): 461–73.

Reed, Merle E., Leslie S. Hough, and Gary M. Fink, ed., *Workers and Their Unions, 1880–1975: Selected Papers, the Second Southern Labor History Conference, 1978* (1981).

Risher, Howard W., Jr., *The Negro in the Railroad Industry* (1971).

Rosenberg, Daniel, *New Orleans Dockworkers: Race, Labor, and Unionism, 1892–1923* (1988).

Rosengarten, Theodore, *All God's Dangers: The Life of Nate Shaw* (1974).

Rowan, Richard L., *The Negro in the Steel Industry* (1968).

Santino, Jack, *Miles of Smiles, Years of Struggle: Stories of Black Pullman Porters* (1991).

Saxton, Alexander, "Race and the House of Labor," in Gary B. Nash and Richard Weiss, ed., *The Great Fear: Race in the Mind of America* (1970).

Schwieder, Dorothy, Joseph Hraba, and Elmer Schwieder, *Buxton: Work and Racial Equality in a Coal Mining Community* (1987).

Shaw, Stephanie J., *What a Woman Ought To Be and To Do: Black Professional Women Workers during the Jim Crow Era* (1996).

Shick, Tom W., and Don H. Doyle, "The South Carolina Phosphate Boom and the Stillbirth of the New South, 1867–1920," *South Carolina Historical Magazine* 86 (1985): 1–31.

Shofner, Jerrell H., "Forced Labor in the Florida Forests, 1880–1950," *Journal of Forest History* 25 (1981): 14–25.

Simmons, Charles, John R. Rankin, and V. G. Carter, "Negro Coal Miners in West Virginia," *Midwest Journal* 6 (1954): 60–69.

Sorelle, James M., "'An de Po Cullud Man Is in de Wuss Fix uv Awl': Black Occupational Status in Houston, Texas, 1920–1940," *Houston Review* 1 (1979): 15–26.

Stewart, James B., "The Rise and Fall of Negro Economics: The Economic Thought of George Edmund Haynes," *American Economic Review* 81 (1991): 311–14.

Straw, Richard A., "The United Mine Workers of America and the 1920 Coal Strike in Alabama," *Alabama Review* 28 (1975): 104–28.

Street, Paul, "The Logic and Limits of 'Plant Loyalty': Black Workers, White Labor, and Corporate Racial Paternalism in Chicago's Stockyards, 1916–1940," *Journal of Social History* 29 (1996): 659–81.

Trotter, Joe William, Jr., "African Americans in the City: The Industrial Era, 1900–1950," *Journal of Urban History* 21 (1995): 438–57.

——— "Blacks in the Urban North: The 'Underclass Question' in Historical Perspective," in Michael B. Katz, ed., *The 'Underclass' Debate: Views from History* (1993): 55–81.

——— "Class and Racial Inequality: The Southern West Virginia Black Coal Miners' Response, 1915–1932," in Robert H. Zieger, ed., *Organized Labor in the Twentieth-Century South* (1991): 60–83.

——— *Coal, Class, and Color: Blacks in Southern West Virginia, 1915–1932* (1990).

Tucker, David M., "Black Pride and Negro Business in the 1920's: George Washington Lee of Memphis," *Business History Review* 43 (1969): 435–51.

Tuttle, William M., Jr., "Labor Conflict and Racial Violence: The Black Worker in Chicago, 1894–1919," *Labor History* 10 (1969): 408–32.

U.S. Department of Labor, Division of Negro Economics, *The Negro at Work during the World War and during Reconstruction* (1921).

Vowels, R., "Atlanta Negro Business and the New Black Bourgeoisie," *Atlanta History Bulletin* 21 (1977): 48–63.

Walker, Melissa, "Home Extension Work among African American Farm Women in East Tennessee," *Agricultural History* 70 (1996): 487–502.

Weare, Walter B., *Black Business in the New South: A Social History of the North Carolina Mutual Life Insurance Company* (1973).

Weaver, Robert C., *Negro Labor: A National Problem* (1946).

Wilson, Walter, *Forced Labor in the United States* (1933).

Wolcott, Victoria W., "The Culture of the Informal Economy: Numbers Runners in Inter-War Black Detroit," *Radical History Review* 69 (1997): 46–75.

Woodson, Carter G., *The Negro Professional Man and the Community: With Special Emphasis on the Physician and the Lawyer* (1934).

———— "The Negro Washerwoman, a Vanishing Figure," *Journal of Negro History* 15 (1930): 269–77.

Work, Monroe N., "Racial Factors and Economic Forces in Land Tenure in the South," *Social Forces* 15 (1936): 205–15.

———— "The South's Labor Problem," *South Atlantic Quarterly* 19 (1920): 1–8.

Zellar, Gary, "H. C. Ray and Racial Politics in the African American Extension Service Program in Arkansas, 1915–1929," *Agricultural History* 72 (1998): 429–45.

Zieger, Robert H., ed., *Organized Labor in the Twentieth Century South* (1991).

21.13   SCIENCE AND TECHNOLOGY

Christopher, Michael C., "Granville T. Woods: The Plight of a Black Inventor," *Journal of Black Studies* 11 (1981): 269–76.

Diggs, Irene, *Black Innovators* (1975).

Du Bois, William Edward Burghardt, "The Negro Scientist," *American Scholar* 8 (1939): 309–20.

James, Portia P., *The Real McCoy: African-American Invention and Innovation, 1619–1930* (1988).

Metress, James, "The Scientific Misuse of the Biological Concept of Race," *Social Studies* 66 (1975): 114–16.

21.14   MEDICINE AND HEALTH

Beardsley, Edward H., *A History of Neglect: Health Care for Blacks and Mill Workers in the Twentieth-Century South* (1987).

Brown, D. Clayton, "Health of Farm Children in the South, 1900–1950," *Agricultural History* 53 (1979): 170–87.

Cherniack, Martin, *The Hawk's Nest Incident: America's Worst Industrial Disaster* (1986).

Cornely, Paul B., and Virginia M. Alexander, "The Health Status of the Negro in the United States," *Journal of Negro Education* 8 (1939): 359–75.

Daniel, Pete, "Black Power in the 1920's: The Case of Tuskegee Veterans Hospital," *Journal of Southern History* 36 (1970): 368–88.

Ferguson, Earline Rae, "The Woman's Improvement Club of Indianapolis: Black Women Pioneers in Tuberculosis Work, 1903–1938," *Indiana Magazine of History* 84 (1988): 237–61.

Fox, Daniel M., "Abraham Flexner's Unpublished Report: Foundations and Medical Education, 1909–1928," *Bulletin of the History of Medicine* 54 (1980): 475–96.

Gamble, Vanessa Northington, *The Black Community Hospital: Contemporary Dilemmas in Historical Perspective* (1989).

————, ed., *Germs Have No Color Line: Blacks and American Medicine, 1900–1940* (1989).

Goldstein, Michael L., "Black Power and the Rise of Bureaucratic Autonomy in New York City Politics: The Case of Harlem Hospital, 1917–1931," *Phylon* 41 (1980): 187–201.

Hine, Darlene Clark, ed., *Black Women in the Nursing Profession: A Documentary History* (1985).

———— *Black Women in White: Racial Conflict and Cooperation in the Nursing Profession, 1890–1950* (1989).

———— "The Pursuit of Professional Equality: Meharry Medical College, 1921–1938, a Case Study," in Vincent P. Franklin and James D. Anderson, ed., *New Perspectives on Black Educational History* (1978): 173–92.

Matthews, Holly F., "Killing the Medical Self-Help Tradition among African Americans: The Case of Lay Midwifery in North Carolina, 1912–1983," in Hans A. Baer and Yvonne Jones, ed., *African-Americans in the South: Issues of Race, Class, and Gender* (1992): 60–78.

McBride, David, *Integrating the City of Medicine: Blacks in Philadelphia Health Care, 1910–1965* (1989).

Mosley, Marie O. Pitts, "Satisfied to Carry the Bag: Three Black Community Health Nurses' Contributions to Health Care Reform, 1900–1937," *Nursing History Review* 4 (1996): 65–82.

Rikard, Marlene Hunt, "An Experiment in Welfare Capitalism: The Health Care Services of the Tennessee Coal, Iron and Railroad Company," *Journal of Economic History* 45 (1985): 467–70.

Seraile, William, "Susan McKinney Steward: New York State's First African-American Woman Physician," *Afro-Americans in New York Life and History* 9 (1985): 27–44.

Wailoo, Keith, "'A Disease Sui Generis': The Origins of Sickle Cell Anemia and the Emergence of Modern Clinical Research, 1904–1924," *Bulletin of the History of Medicine* 65 (1991): 185–208.

———— "Detecting 'Negro Blood': Black and White Identities and the Reconstruction of Sickle Cell Anemia," in Keith Wailoo, *Drawing Blood* (1997): 134–61.

21.15 STUDIES IN FOREIGN LANGUAGES

Anglero, David Oritz, *El legado de Arturo Alphonso Schomburg* [The Legacy of Arthur Alphonso Schomburg] (1984). In Spanish.

Bertella Farnetti, Paolo, "'Che la danza cominci': Il mito sovietico e la 'black question' negli Stati Uniti: 1919–1931" ['Let the Dance Begin': The Soviet Myth and the 'Black Question' in the United States, 1919–1931], *Socialismo Storia [Socialism History]* 3 (1991): 158–76. In Italian.

Billard, François, and Gilles Tordjman, *Duke Ellington* (1994). In French.

Delanoe, Nelcya, *Détroit, marche noir: des Noirs dans une grande ville industrielle des États-Unis* [Detroit, the Black Market: Blacks in a Large Industrial City of the United States] (1974). In French.

Durtain, Luc, *Quelques notes d' U.S.A.* [Notes on the U.S.A.] (1928). In French.

Fabre, Michel, and Paul Oren, *Harlem: ville noire* [Harlem: Black City] (1971). In French.

Higuchi, Hayumi, "20-seiki Shotô Amerika no Kokujin Shidôsha" [Black Leaders' Response to Industrial America at the Time of the Great Migration], *The Journal of Kyoritsu Area Studies* 2 (1992): 245–72. In Japanese.

Hippenmeyer, Jean Roland, *Jazz sur films: ou, 55 années de rapports jazz-cinéma vue à travers plus de 800 films tournés entre 1917 et 1972* [Jazz in Films: Or, Fifty-Five Years of Jazz in Cinema Shown in More Than 800 Films Made between 1917 and 1972] (1973). In French.

———— *Sidney Bechet: ou, l'extraordinaire odyssée d'un musicien de jazz: de Storyville à l'Olympia, de "Wild Cat Blues" aux "Oignons"* [Sidney Bechet: Or, the Extraordinary Odyssey of a Jazz Musician: From Storyville to Olympia, from "Wild Cat Blues" to "Onions"] (1980). In French.

Iwamoto, Hiroko, "Zenbei Kokujin Joséi Kyôkai to Sôsetsu-sha tachi" [Mary C. Terrell and the National Association of Colored Women], *Journal of Historical Studies* (1994): 39–56. In Japanese.

Leduc, Jean-Marie, and Christine Mulard, *Armstrong* (1994). In French.

Lee, You-cheng, "Ha Lin Wen Yi Fu Xing Yu Kou Shu Wen Xue De Zheng Zhi" [The Harlem Renaissance and the Politics of Oral Literature], *Zhong Wai Wen Xue* 2 (1980): 55–72. In Chinese.

Meunier, Claude, *Ring noir: quand Appollinaire, Cendrars et Picabia decouvraient les boxeurs nègres* [Black Ring: When Appollinaire, Cendrars, and Picabia Discover Black Boxers] (1992). In French.

Nakamura (Sasamoto), Masako, "W.E.B. Dyuboisu no Kyôiku Shisô" [Educational Thought of W.E.B. Du Bois: Power and Self-Realization in the Emancipation of Black People], *Studies in the History of Education* 23 (1980): 80–97. In Japanese.

Otsuji, Chieko, "A. Firippu Randorufu, 1925–1935" [A. Philip Randolph: Between the Wars: His Career As a Black Labor Leader, 1925–1935], *The Study of International Relations* 11 Supplement (1985): 55–70. In Japanese.

Panassié, Hugues, *Douze années de jazz, 1927–1938: Souvenirs* [Twelve Years of Jazz, 1927–1938: Souvenirs] (1946). In French.

———— *Les Rois du jazz: notes bibliographiques et critiques sur les principaux musiciens de jazz* [Jazz Kings: Bibliographic Notes and Critiques on the Principal Jazz Musicians] (3d ed., 1945). In French.

Richet, Isabelle, ed., *Harlem, 1900–1935: De la métropole au ghetto, de la renaissance culturelle à l'exclusion* [Harlem, 1900–1935: From Metropolis to Ghetto, from Cultural Renaissance to Exclusion] (1993). In French.

Schoell, Franck Louis, *U.S.A.: du côté des Blancs et du côté des Noirs* [U.S.A.: The Side of Whites and the Side of Blacks] (1929). In French.

Takemoto, Yuko, "W.E.B. Dyuboisu to Nihon" [W.E.B. Du Bois and Japan], *Journal of Historical Studies* 54 (1994): 79–96. In Japanese.

Takenaka, Koji, "Shikago Shokuniku Sangyo ni okeru Kokujin Sabetsu" [Discrimination against Blacks in the Slaughtering and Meat-Packing Industry in Chicago, 1910's and 1920's], *Journal of Foreign Studies* 48, 49 (1982, 1983): 157–214, 213–81. In Japanese.

———— *Shikago Kokujin Gettô Seiritsu no Shakai-shi* [A Social History of the Rising Chicago Black Ghetto] (1995). In Japanese.

Tété-Adjalogo, Tetevi G., *Marcus Garvey: père de l'unité africaine, garveyisme et panafricainisme* [Marcus Garvey: The Father of African Unity, Garveyism, and Panafricanism] (2 vol., 1994). In French.

———— *Marcus Garvey: père de l'unité africaine des peuples* [Marcus Garvey: The Father of the Unity of African Peoples] (2 vol., 1995). In French.

Yokoyama, Ryo, "Kokujin no Shimin-teki Jiyû o Motomeru Tatakai" [The Struggle of Afro-American People for Freedom: N.A.A.C.P. and W.E.B. Du Bois], in Akira Imazu, ed., *America in World War I: The Crisis of the Civil Liberties* (1981): 301–35. In Japanese.

Zammarchi, Fabrice, *Sidney Bechet* (1989). In French.

22 1932–1945

Nancy L. Grant and Darlene Clark Hine

22.1 GENERAL STUDIES

Dollard, John, *Caste and Class in a Southern Town* (1937).
Honey, Maureen, ed., *Bitter Fruit: African American Women in World War II* (1999).
Ottley, Roi, *"New World A-Coming": Inside Black America* (1943).
Powdermaker, Hortense, *After Freedom: A Cultural Study in the Deep South* (1939).
Rose, Arnold M., *The Negro in America* (1948).
Silvera, John D., comp., *The Negro in World War II* (1969).
Sterner, Richard Mauritz Edvard, *The Negro's Share: A Study of Income, Consumption, Housing and Public Assistance* (1943).
Sternsher, Bernard, ed., *The Negro in Depression and War: Prelude to Revolution, 1930–1945* (1969).
Terrill, Tom E., and Jerrold Hirsch, ed., *Such As Us: Southern Voices of the Thirties* (1978).
Tindall, George Brown, *The Emergence of the New South, 1913–1945* (1967).
Wynn, Neil A., *The Afro-American and the Second World War* (1976).

22.2 HISTORIOGRAPHY

Amott, Teresa and Julie Matthaei, "We Specialize in the Wholly Impossible: African American Women," in Teresa Amott and Julie Matthaei, *Race, Gender, and Work: A Multicultural Economic History of Women in the United States* (1991): 141–91.
Aptheker, Herbert, *The Negro People in America: A Critique of Gunnar Myrdal's* An American Dilemma (1946).
Carnegie-Myrdal Study, *The Negro in America: Research Memoranda for Use in the Preparation of Dr. Gunnar Myrdal's* An American Dilemma (1945).
Gaines, Kevin, "Rethinking Race and Class in African-American Struggles for Equality, 1885–1941," *American Historical Review* 102 (1997): 378–87.
Goings, Kenneth W. and Raymond A. Mohl, "Toward a New African American Urban History," in Kenneth W. Goings and Raymond A. Mohl, ed., *The New African American Urban History* (1996): 1–16.
Kelley, Robin D. G., "Introduction: Writing Black Working-Class History from Way, Way Below," in Robin D. G. Kelley, *Race Rebels: Culture, Politics, and the Black Working Class* (1994): 1–13.
Kusmer, Kenneth L., "The Black Urban Experience in American History," in Darlene Clark Hine, ed., *The State of Afro-American History: Past, Present, and Future* (1986): 91–122.
Plummer, Brenda Gayle, and Donald R. Culverson, "Black Americans and Foreign Affairs: A Reassessment," *Sage Race Relations Abstracts* 12 (1987): 21–31.
Sammons, Jeffrey T., "A Proportionate and Measured Response to the Provocation That Is *Darwin's Athletes*," *Journal of Sport History* 24 (1997): 378–88.
Savage, Barbara Dianne, "Introduction," in Barbara Dianne Savage, *Broadcasting Freedom: Radio, War, and the Politics of Race, 1938–1948* (1999): 1–17.

Solomon, Mark, *The Cry Was Unity: Communists and African Americans, 1917–1936* (1998).
Trotter, Joe William, Jr., "African-American Workers: New Direction in U.S. Labor Historiography," *Labor History* 35 (1994): 495–523.
———— "Introduction: Black Migration in Historical Perspective, a Review of the Literature," in Joe William Trotter, Jr., ed., *The Great Migration in Historical Perspective: New Dimensions of Race, Class, and Gender* (1991): 1–21.

22.3   SECONDARY SOURCES ON NEWSPAPERS AND PERIODICALS

Anderson, James D., "Black Liberalism at the Crossroads: The Role of the *Crisis,* 1934–1953," *Crisis* 87 (1980): 339–46.
Bain, George W., "How Negro Editors Viewed the New Deal," *Journalism Quarterly* 44 (1967): 552–54.
Barnett, Claude A., "The Role of the Press, Radio, and Motion Picture and Negro Morale," *Journal of Negro Education* 12 (1943): 474–89.
Best, Wallace, "The *Chicago Defender* and the Realignment of Black Chicago," *Chicago History* 24 (1995): 4–21.
Davis, Ralph N., "The Negro Newspapers and the War," *Sociology and Social Research* 27 (1943): 373–80.
Field, Marshall, III, *The Negro Press and the Issues of Democracy* (1944).
Finkle, Lee, *Forum for Protest: The Black Press during World War II* (1975).
Fleener, Nickieann, "'Breaking Down Buyer Resistance': Marketing the 1935 *Pittsburgh Courier* to Mississippi Blacks," *Journalism History* 13 (1986): 78–85.
Johnson, Abby Arthur, and Ronald M. Johnson, "Reform and Reaction: Black Literary Magazines in the 1930's," *North Dakota Quarterly* 46 (1978): 5–18.
Jones, Lester M., "The Editorial Policy of the Negro Newspapers of 1917–1918 As Compared with That of 1941–1942," *Journal of Negro History* 29 (1944): 24–31.
Lawson, Marjorie McKenzie, "The Adult Educational Aspects of the Negro Press," *Journal of Negro Education* 14 (1945): 431–36.
Sentman, Mary Alice, and Patrick S. Washburn, "How Excess Profits Tax Brought Ads to Black Newspapers in World War II," *Journalism Quarterly* 64 (1987): 769–74, 867.
Walters, Ronald G., "The Negro Press and the Image of Success, 1920–1939," *Midcontinent American Studies Journal* 11 (1970): 36–55.
Washburn, Patrick S., *A Question of Sedition: The Federal Government's Investigation of the Black Press during World War II* (1986).
———— "J. Edgar Hoover and the Black Press in World War II," *Journalism History* 13 (1986): 26–33.

22.4   RACE RELATIONS

22.4.1   Black/White Relations

"*An American Dilemma* Revisited," *Daedalus* [special issue] 124 (1995).
Bagby, Laurie M. Johnson, "The Question of Jung and Racism Reconsidered," *Psychohistory Review* 23 (1995): 283–98.
Capeci, Dominic J., Jr., *Race Relations in Wartime Detroit: The Sojourner Truth Housing Controversy of 1942* (1984).
Clark, Kenneth B., "Morale of the Negro on the Homefront: World Wars I and II," *Journal of Negro Education* 12 (1943): 417–28.
Council for Democracy, *The Negro in America: How We Treat Him and How We Should* (1945).
Critchlow, Donald T., "Communist Unions and Racism," *Labor History* 17 (1976): 230–44.
DeGraaf, Lawrence B., "Significant Steps on an Arduous Path: The Impact of World War II on Discrimination against African Americans in the West," *Journal of the West* 35 (1996): 24–33.
Dollard, John, *Caste and Class in a Southern Town* (1937).

Doyle, Bertram Wilbur, *The Etiquette of Race Relations in the South: A Study in Social Control* (1937).

Droker, Howard A., "Seattle Race Relations during the Second World War," in G. Thomas Edwards and Carlos Schwantes, ed., *Experiences in a Promised Land: Essays in Pacific Northwest History* (1986): 353–68.

Du Bois, William Edward Burghardt, "Race Relations in the United States, 1917–1947," *Phylon* 9 (1948): 234–47.

Ely, Melvin P., *The Adventures of Amos 'n' Andy: A Social History of an American Phenomenon* (1991).

Fishel, Leslie H., Jr. and Benjamin Quarles, "In the New Deal's Wake," in Allen Weinstein and Frank Otto Gatell, ed., *The Segregation Era, 1863–1954: A Modern Reader* (1970): 218–32.

Foner, Philip S., and Herbert Shapiro, *American Communism and Black Americans: A Documentary History, 1930–1934* (1990).

Foreman, Clark, "The Decade of Hope," *Phylon* 12 (1951): 137–50.

Grant, Nancy L., "Howard Odum: Region and Racism," *Research in Social Policy* 2 (1990): 29–68.

Graves, John Temple, "The Southern Negro and the War Crisis," *Virginia Quarterly Review* 18 (1942): 500–17.

Hall, Jacquelyn Dowd, *Revolt against Chivalry: Jessie Daniel Ames and the Women's Campaign Against Lynching* (1979).

Hewes, Laurence I., Jr., and William Y. Bell, Jr., *Intergroup Relations in San Diego: Some Aspects of Community Life in San Diego which Particularly Affect Minority Groups* (1946).

Houser, George M., *Erasing the Color Line* (1945).

Johnson, Charles Spurgeon, *To Stem This Tide: A Survey of Racial Tension Areas in the United States* (1943).

——— "The Present Status of Race Relations in the South," *Social Forces* 23 (1944): 27–28.

——— "Social Changes and Their Effects on Race Relations in the South," *Social Forces* 23 (1945): 343–48.

Kneebone, John, *Southern Liberal Journalists and the Issue of Race, 1920–1944* (1985).

Krueger, Thomas A., *And Promises to Keep: The Southern Conference for Human Welfare, 1938–1948* (1967).

Lal, Barbara Ballis, "Black and Blue in Chicago: Robert E. Park's Perspective on Race Relations in Urban America, 1914–1944," *British Journal of Sociology* 38 (1987): 546–66.

Leap, William Lester, *Red Hill—Neighborhood Life and Race Relations in a Rural Section* (1933).

Lenthall, Bruce, "Outside the Panel—Race in America's Popular Imagination: Comic Strips before and after World War II," *Journal of American Studies* 32 (1998): 39–61.

Lichtenstein, Alex, "Chain Gangs, Communism, and the 'Negro Question': John L. Spivak's *Georgia Nigger*," *Georgia Historical Quarterly* 79 (1995): 633–58.

Martin, Charles H., "White Supremacy and Black Workers: Georgia's Black Shirts Combat the Great Depression," *Labor History* 18 (1977): 366–81.

Mohl, Raymond A., "The Evolution of Racism and the Industrial City, 1906–1940: A Case Study of Gary, Indiana," *Journal of Negro History* 59 (1974): 51–64.

Odum, Howard Washington, *Race and Rumors of Race: Challenge to American Crisis* (1943).

Phelps-Stokes Fund, *Negro Status and Race Relations in the United States, 1911–1946: The Thirty-Five Year Report of the Phelps-Stokes Fund* (1948).

Reddick, Lawrence D., "The New Race-Relations Frontier," *Journal of Educational Sociology* 19 (1945): 129–45.

Salmond, John, "'Aubrey Williams Remembers': A Note on Franklin D. Roosevelt's Attitudes toward Negro Rights," *Alabama Review* 25 (1972): 62–67.

Sancton, Thomas, "A Southern View of the Race Question," *Negro Quarterly* (1943): 197–206.

Schrieke, Bertram Johannes Otto, *Alien Americans: A Study of Race Relations* (1936).

Sitkoff, Harvard, "The New Deal and Race Relations," in Harvard Sitkoff, *Fifty Years Later: The New Deal Evaluated* (1985): 93–112.

——— "Racial Militancy and Interracial Violence in the Second World War," *Journal of American History* 58 (1971): 661–81.

Skates, John R., "World War II As a Watershed in Mississippi History," *Journal of Mississippi History* 37 (1975): 131–42.

Sosna, Morton Philip, *In Search of the Silent South: Southern Liberals and the Race Issue* (1977).

Stanfield, John H., *Philanthropy and Jim Crow in American Social Science* (1985).

———— "Race Relations Research and Black Americans between the Two World Wars," *Journal of Ethnic Studies* 11 (1983): 61–93.

Sullivan, Patricia, *Days of Hope: Race and Democracy in the New Deal Era* (1996).

Thomas, William B., "Conservative Currents in Howard Washington Odum's Agenda for Social Reform in Southern Race Relations," *Phylon* 45 (1984): 121–34.

Thompson, Edgar Tristam, ed., *Race Relations and the Race Problem: A Definition and an Analysis* (1939).

Weatherford, Willis Duke, and Charles Spurgeon Johnson, *Race Relations: Adjustment of Whites and Negroes in the United States* (1934).

Williams, Vernon J., Jr., *From a Caste to a Minority: Changing Attitudes of American Sociologists toward Afro-Americans, 1896–1945* (1989).

Wirth, Louis, "Morale and Minority Groups," *American Journal of Sociology* 47 (1941): 415–38.

22.4.2   Black/Ethnic Relations

Bender, Eugene, "Reflections on Negro-Jewish Relations: The Historical Dimension," *Phylon* 30 (1969): 55–56.

Bleich, J. David, "Black Jews: A Halakhic Perspective," *Tradition* 15 (1975): 48–79.

Brooks, Charlotte, "In the Twilight Zone between Black and White: Japanese American Resettlement and Community in Chicago, 1942–1945," *Journal of American History* 86 (2000): 1655–87.

Gallicchio, Marc, "Colouring the Nationalists: The African-American Construction of China in the Second World War," *International History Review* 20 (1998): 571–96.

Greenberg, Cheryl, "Black and Jewish Responses to Japanese Internment," *Journal of American Ethnic History* 14 (1995): 3–37.

James, Winston, *Holding Aloft the Banner of Ethiopa: Caribbean Radicalism in Early Twentieth-Century America* (1998).

Kearney, Reginald, *African American Views of the Japanese: Solidarity or Sedition?* (1998).

Lang, Kurt, and Gladys Lang, "Resistance to School Desegregation: A Case Study of Backlash among Jews," *Sociological Inquiry* 35 (1965): 94–106.

Schott, Matthew J., "Prisoners Like Us: German POWs Encounter Louisiana's African-Americans," *Louisiana History* 36 (1995): 277–90.

Weiss, Richard, "Ethnicity and Reform: Minorities and the Ambiance of the Depression Years," *Journal of American History* 66 (1979): 566–85.

Williams, Oscar R., "Historical Impressions of Black-Jewish Relations prior to World War II," *Negro History Bulletin* 40 (1977): 728–31.

Wise, Stephen S., "Parallel between Hitlerism and the Persecution of Negroes in America," *Crisis* 41 (1934): 127–29.

Zinberg, Len, and William D. Braithwaite, "Afro-Americans and Anti-Semitism," *Negro Digest* 1 (1940): 38–42.

22.4.3   Segregation/Jim Crow

Barnes, Catherine A., *Journey from Jim Crow: The Desegregation of Southern Transit* (1983).

Hale, Grace Elizabeth, *Making Whiteness: The Culture of Segregation in the South, 1890–1940* (1998).

Johnson, Charles Spurgeon, *Patterns of Negro Segregation* (1943).

Palmore, Joseph R., "The Not-So-Strange Career of Interstate Jim Crow: Race, Transportation, and the Dormant Commerce Clause, 1878–1946," *Virginia Law Review* 83 (1997): 1773–817.

Southern, David W., "Beyond Jim Crow Liberalism: Judge Waring's Fight against Segregation in South Carolina, 1942–1952," *Journal of Negro History* 66 (1981): 209–27.

Thornbrough, Emma Lou, "Breaking Racial Barriers to Public Accommodations in Indiana, 1935–1963," *Indiana Magazine of History* 83 (1987): 300–43.

Weaver, Robert Clifton, "Racial Policy in Public Housing," *Phylon* 1 (1940): 153–54.

22.4.4   Violence and Racial Disturbances

The Complete Report of Mayor LaGuardia's Commission on the Harlem Riot of March 19, 1935 (1969).

Capeci, Dominic J., Jr., *The Lynching of Cleo Wright: Federal Protection of Constitutional Rights during World War II* (1998).

Capeci, Dominic J., Jr., and Martha Wilkerson, *Layered Violence: The Detroit Rioters of 1943* (1991).

Du Bay, Robert W., "Mississippi and the Proposed Federal Anti-Lynching Bills of 1937–1938," *Southern Quarterly* 7 (1968): 73–89.

Greenberg, Cheryl Lynn, *"Or Does It Explode?": Black Harlem in the Great Depression* (1991).

Hall, Jacquelyn Dowd, *Revolt against Chivalry: Jessie Daniel Ames and the Women's Campaign Against Lynching* (1979).

Hixson, William B., Jr., "Moorfield Storey and the Defense of the Dyer Anti-Lynching Bill," *New England Quarterly* 42 (1969): 65–81.

Johnson, Marilynn S., "Gender, Race, and Rumours: Re-Examining the 1943 Race Riots," *Gender and History* 10 (1998): 252–77.

Lee, Alfred McClung, *Race Riot* (1943).

Miller, Robert M., "The Protestant Churches and Lynching, 1919–1939," *Journal of Negro History* 42 (1957): 118–31.

National Urban League, *Racial Conflict: A Home Front Danger: Lessons of the Detroit Riot* (1943).

Powell, Adam Clayton, Sr., *Riots and Ruins* (1945).

Rable, George C., "The South and the Politics of Anti-Lynching Legislation, 1920–1940," *Journal of Southern History* 51 (1985): 201–20.

Raper, Arthur Franklin, *The Tragedy of Lynching* (1933).

Shogan, Robert, and Tom Craig, *The Detroit Race Riot: A Study in Violence* (1964).

Sitkoff, Harvard, "The Detroit Race Riot of 1943," *Michigan History* 53 (1969): 183–206.

——— "Racial Militancy and Interracial Violence in the Second World War," *Journal of American History* 58 (1971): 661–81.

White, Walter Francis, *What Caused the Detroit Riot? An Analysis* (1943).

Zangrando, Robert L., *The NAACP Crusade against Lynching, 1909–1950* (1980).

——— "The NAACP and a Federal Anti-Lynching Bill, 1934–1940," *Journal of Negro History* 50 (1965): 106–17.

22.4.5   Civil Rights

Bunche, Ralph J., "A Critical Analysis of the Tactics and Programs of Minority Groups," *Journal of Negro Education* 4 (1935): 308–20.

Dalfiume, Richard M., *Desegregation of the U.S. Armed Forces: Fighting on Two Fronts, 1939–1953* (1969).

——— "The 'Forgotten Years' of the Negro Revolution," *Journal of American History* 55 (1968): 90–106.

Egerton, John, *Speak Now against the Day: The Generation before the Civil Rights Movement in the South* (1994).

Fairclough, Adam, *Race and Democracy: The Civil Rights Struggle in Louisiana, 1915–1972* (1995).

——— "The Civil Rights Movement in Louisiana, 1939–1954," in Brian Ward and Tony Badger, ed., *The Making of Martin Luther King and the Civil Rights Movement* (1996): 15–28.

Finkle, Lee, "The Conservative Aims of Militant Rhetoric: Black Protest during World War II," *Journal of American History* 60 (1973): 692–713.

Gaines, Kevin, "Rethinking Race and Class in African-American Struggles for Equality, 1885–1941," *American Historical Review* 102 (1997): 378–87.

Garfinkel, Herbert, *When Negroes March: The March on Washington Movement in the Organizational Politics for FEPC* (1959).

Gavins, Raymond, "The NAACP in North Carolina during the Age of Segregation," in Armstead L. Robinson and Patricia Sullivan, ed., *New Directions in Civil Rights Studies* (1991): 105–25.

Goodman, James, *Stories of Scottsboro* (1994).

Greenbaum, Fred, "The Anti-Lynching Bill of 1935: The Irony of 'Equal Justice—Under Law,'" *Journal of Human Relations* 15 (1967): 72–85.

Hamilton, Dona Cooper, and Charles V. Hamilton, *The Dual Agenda: Race and Social Welfare Policies of Civil Rights Organizations* (1997).

Hill, Robert A., ed., *The FBI's RACON: Racial Conditions in the United States during World War II* (1995).

Hixson, William B., Jr., "Moorfield Storey and the Defense of the Dyer Anti-Lynching Bill," *New England Quarterly* 42 (1969): 65–81.

Hoffman, Edwin D., "The Genesis of the Modern Movement for Equal Rights in South Carolina, 1930–1939," *Journal of Negro History* 44 (1959): 346–69.

Homel, Michael W., "The Lilydale School Campaign of 1936: Direct Action in the Verbal Protest Era," *Journal of Negro History* 59 (1974): 228–41.

Hughes, C. Alvin, "We Demand Our Rights: The Southern Negro Youth Congress, 1937–1949," *Phylon* 48 (1987): 38–50.

James, C. L. R., George Breitman, Ed Keemer, and Fred Stanton, ed., *Fighting Racism in World War II* (1980).

Kelley, Robin D. G., *Hammer and Hoe: Alabama Communists during the Great Depression* (1990).

Kellogg, Peter, "Civil Rights Consciousness in the 1940's," *Historian* (1979): 18–41.

Kirk, John, "'He Founded a Movement': W.H. Flowers, the Committee on Negro Organizations, and the Origins of Black Activism in Arkansas, 1940–1957," in Brian Ward and Tony Badger, ed., *The Making of Martin Luther King and the Civil Rights Movement* (1996): 29–44.

McCoy, Donald R., and Richard T. Ruetten, "The Civil Rights Movement, 1940–1954," *Midwest Quarterly* 11 (1969): 11–34.

McNeil, Genna Rae, *Groundwork: Charles Hamilton Houston and the Struggle for Civil Rights* (1983).

Meier, August, and John H. Bracey, Jr., "The NAACP As a Reform Movement, 1909–1965: 'To Reach the Conscience of America,'" *Journal of Southern History* 59 (1993): 3–30.

Meier, August, and Elliott M. Rudwick, *CORE: A Study in the Civil Rights Movement, 1942–1968* (1973).

———— "How CORE Began," *Social Science Quarterly* 49 (1969): 789–99.

———— "Negro Protest at the Chicago World's Fair, 1933–1934," *Illinois State Historical Society Journal* 59 (1966): 161–71.

Murray, Florence, "The Negro and Civil Liberties during World War II," *Social Forces* 24 (1945): 211–16.

Murray, Hugh T., "The NAACP versus the Communist Party: The Scottsboro Rape Cases, 1931–1932," *Phylon* 28 (1967): 276–87.

Nelson, H. Viscount, "The Philadelphia NAACP: Race versus Class Consciousness during the Thirties," *Journal of Black Studies* 5 (1975): 255–76.

Neuchterlein, James A., "The Politics of Civil Rights: The FEPC, 1941–1946," *Prologue* 10 (1978): 171–91.

Norrell, Robert J., *Reaping the Whirlwind: The Civil Rights Movement in Tuskegee* (rev. ed., 1998).

O'Reilly, Kenneth, "The Roosevelt Administration and Black America: Federal Surveillance Policy and Civil Rights during the New Deal and World War II Years," *Phylon* 48 (1987): 12–25.

Powell, Adam Clayton, Jr., *Marching Blacks: An Interpretive History of the Rise of the Black Common Man* (1945).

Reed, Merl Elwyn, *Seedtime for the Modern Civil Rights Movement: The President's Committee on Fair Employment Practice, 1941–1946* (1991).

Rolinson, Mary Gambrell, "Community and Leadership in the First Twenty Years of the Atlanta NAACP, 1917–1937," *Atlanta History* 42 (1998): 5–21.

Ross, Barbara Joyce, *J. E. Spingarn and the Rise of the NAACP, 1911–1939* (1972).

Seawright, Sally, "Desegregation at Maryland: The NAACP and the Murray Case in the 1930's," *Maryland Historian* 1 (1970): 59–73.

Segal, Geraldine R., *In Any Fight Some Fall* (1975).

Sitkoff, Harvard, *A New Deal for Blacks: The Emergence of Civil Rights as a National Issue* (1978).

Ware, Gilbert, "Lobbying As a Means of Protest: The NAACP As an Agent of Equality," *Journal of Ne-gro Education* 33 (1964): 103–10.

Wittner, Lawrence S., "The National Negro Congress: A Reassessment," *American Quarterly* 22 (1970): 883–901.

Zangrando, Joanna Schneider and Robert L. Zangrando, "ER and Black Civil Rights," in Joan Hoff-Wilson and Marjorie Lightman, ed., *Without Precedent: The Life and Career of Eleanor Roosevelt* (1984): 88–107.

Zangrando, Robert L., *The NAACP Crusade against Lynching, 1909–1950* (1980).

——— "The NAACP and a Federal Anti-Lynching Bill, 1934–1940," *Journal of Negro History* 50 (1965): 106–17.

22.5   GOVERNMENT

22.5.1   Law

Alexander, Raymond Pace, "The Upgrading of the Negro's Status by Supreme Court Decisions," *Jour-nal of Negro History* 30 (1945): 117–49.

Dublirer, Harold, "Legislation Outlawing Racial Discrimination in Employment," *Lawyers Guild Re-view* (1945): 101–09.

Elwood, William A., prod., "The Road to *Brown*," (1990).

Guzman, Jessie Parkhurst, *Twenty Years of Court Decisions Affecting Higher Education in the South, 1938–1958* (1960).

Hastie, William H., "Toward an Equalitarian Legal Order, 1930–1950," *Annals of the American Acad-emy of Political and Social Science* (1973): 18–31.

Kelleher, Daniel T., "The Case of Lloyd Lionel Gaines: The Demise of the Separate but Equal Doc-trine," *Journal of Negro History* 56 (1971): 262–71.

Konvitz, Milton R., "A Nation within a Nation: The Negro and the Supreme Court," *American Scholar* 11 (1942): 69–78.

Mangum, Charles Staples, Jr., *The Legal Status of the Negro* (1940).

McNeil, Genna Rae, *Groundwork: Charles Hamilton Houston and the Struggle for Civil Rights* (1983).

——— "Justiciable Cause: Howard University Law School and the Struggle for Civil Rights," *Howard Law Journal* 22 (1979): 283–95.

Meier, August, and Elliott M. Rudwick, "Attorneys Black and White: A Case Study of Race Relations within the NAACP," *Journal of American History* 62 (1976): 913–46.

Moreno, Paul D., *From Direct Action to Affirmative Action: Fair Employment Law and Policy in Amer-ica, 1933–1972* (1997).

Nelson, Bernard H., *The 14th Amendment and the Negro since 1920* (1946).

Rusch, Jonathan J., "William H. Hastie and the Vindication of Civil Rights," *Howard Law Journal* 21 (1978): 749–820.

Segal, Geraldine R., *In Any Fight Some Fall* (1975).

——— *Blacks in the Law: Philadelphia and the Nation* (1983).

Siegel, David M., and Felix Frankfurter, "Charles Hamilton Houston and the 'N-Word': A Case Study in the Evolution of Judicial Attitudes towards Race," *Southern California Interdisciplinary Law Journal* 7 (1998): 317–73.

——— "Charles Hamilton Houston and the 'N-Word:' A Case Study in the Evolution of Judicial Atti-tudes towards Race," *Southern California Interdisciplinary Law Journal* 7 (1998): 317–73.

Smith, C. Calvin, "The Politics of Evasion: Arkansas' Reaction to *Smith v. Allwright*, 1944," *Journal of Negro History* 67 (1982): 40–51.

Tushnet, Mark, *The NAACP Legal Strategy against Segregated Education, 1920–1950* (1984).

Tussman, Joseph, ed., *The Supreme Court on Racial Discrimination* (1963).

Vose, Clement E., *Caucasians Only: The Supreme Court, the NAACP, and the Restrictive Covenant Cases* (1959).

Weeks, Kent M., *Adam Clayton Powell and the Supreme Court* (1971).

22.5.2 Crime and Punishment

Carter, Dan T., *Scottsboro: A Tragedy of the American South* (1969).

Goodman, James, *Stories of Scottsboro* (1994).

Lightfoot, Robert Mitchell, *Negro Crime in a Small Urban Community* (1934).

Martin, Charles H., *The Angelo Herndon Case and Southern Justice* (1976).

——— "Communists and Blacks: The ILD and the Angelo Herndon Case," *Journal of Negro History* 64 (1979): 131–41.

Moore, John Hammond, "The Angelo Herndon Case, 1932–1937," *Phylon* 32 (1971): 60–71.

Oshinsky, David M., *'Worse Than Slavery': Parchman Farm and the Ordeal of Jim Crow Justice* (1996).

Phillips, Charles David, "Social Structure and Social Control: Modeling the Discriminatory Execution of Blacks in Georgia and North Carolina, 1925–1935," *Social Forces* 65 (1986): 458–75.

Weckler, Joseph Edwin, *The Police and Minority Groups: A Program to Prevent Disorder and to Improve Relations between Different Racial, Religious, and National Groups* (1944).

Williams, Lillian S., "Attica Prisoners Seek Aid from the NAACP, 1932," *Afro-Americans in New York Life and History* 1 (1977): 211–12.

22.5.3 Politics and Voting

Allswang, John M., "The Chicago Negro Voter and the Democratic Consensus: A Case Study, 1918–1936," *Journal of the Illinois State Historical Society* 60 (1967): 145–75.

Bethune, Mary McLeod, "My Secret Talks with FDR," *Ebony* (1949): 42–51.

Broussard, Albert S., "The Politics of Despair: Black San Franciscans and the Political Process, 1920–1940," *Journal of Negro History* 69 (1984): 26–37.

Bunche, Ralph Johnson, *The Political Status of the Negro in the Age of FDR* (1973).

——— "The Negro in the Political Life of the United States," *Journal of Negro Education* 10 (1941): 567–84.

Burnham, Robert A., "Reform, Politics, and Race in Cincinnati: Proportional Representation and the City Charter Committee, 1924–1959," *Journal of Urban History* 23 (1997): 131–63.

Collins, Ernest M., "Cincinnati Negroes and Presidential Politics," *Journal of Negro History* 41 (1956): 131–37.

Cook, James F., "The Georgia Gubernatorial Election of 1942," *Atlanta Historical Bulletin* 18 (1973): 7–19.

Dalfiume, Richard M., "Military Segregation and the 1940 Presidential Election," *Phylon* 30 (1969): 42–55.

Daoust, Norma Lasalle, "Building the Democratic Party: Black Voting in Providence in the 1930s," *Rhode Island History* 44 (1985): 81–88.

Dunn, Larry W., "Knoxville Negro Voting and the Roosevelt Revolution, 1928–1936," *Eastern Tennessee Historical Society Publications* 43 (1971): 71–93.

Emmons, Caroline, "'Somebody Has Got to Do That Work': Harry T. Moore and the Struggle for African-American Voting Rights in Florida," *Journal of Negro History* 82 (1997): 232–43.

Fishel, Leslie H., Jr., "The Negro in the New Deal," *Wisconsin Magazine of History* (1964–65): 111–26.

Foner, Philip S., and Herbert Shapiro, *American Communism and Black Americans: A Documentary History, 1930–1934* (1990).

Gamm, Gerald H., *The Making of New Deal Democrats: Voting Behavior and Realignment in Boston, 1920–1940* (1989).

Gordon, Rita Werner, "The Change in the Political Alignment of Chicago's Negroes during the New Deal," *Journal of American History* 56 (1969): 584–603.

Gosnell, Harold F., *Negro Politicians: The Rise of Negro Politics in Chicago* (1935).

——— "The Negro Vote in Northern Cities," *National Municipal Review* 30 (1941): 264–78.

Gower, Calvin W., "The Struggle of Blacks for Leadership Positions in the Civilian Conservation Corps, 1933–1942," *Journal of Negro History* 61 (1976): 123–35.

Grant, Nancy L., *TVA and Black Americans: Planning for the Status Quo* (1990).

Grimshaw, William J., *Bitter Fruit: Black Politics and the Chicago Machine, 1931–1991* (1992).

Harnell, James A., "Negro Leadership in the Election Year of 1936," *Journal of Southern History* 34 (1968): 546–64.

Henderson, Elmer W., "Political Changes among Negroes in Chicago during the Depression," *Social Forces* 19 (1941): 338–46.

Hine, Darlene Clark, *Black Victory: The Rise and Fall of the White Primary in Texas* (1979).

——— "Blacks and the Destruction of the Democratic White Primary, 1935–1944," *Journal of Negro History* 62 (1977): 43–59.

——— "The Elusive Ballot: The Black Struggle against the Texas Democratic White Primary, 1932–1945," *Southwestern Historical Quarterly* 81 (1978): 371–92.

Holmes, Michael S., "The New Deal and Georgia's Black Youth," *Journal of Southern History* 38 (1972): 443–60.

Jackson, Luther Porter, "Race and Suffrage in the South Since 1940," *New South* (1948): 1–26.

Kaiser, Ernest, "The Federal Government and the Negro," *Science and Society* 20 (1956): 27–58.

Kelley, Robin D. G., *Hammer and Hoe: Alabama Communists during the Great Depression* (1990).

——— "A New War in Dixie: Communists and the Unemployed in Birmingham, Alabama, 1930–1933," *Labor History* 30 (1989): 367–84.

Key, Valdimer Orlando, Jr., *Southern Politics in State and Nation* (new ed., 1984).

Kilson, Martin, "Political Change in the Negro Ghetto, 1900–1940's," in Nathan I. Huggins, Martin Kilson and Daniel M. Fox, ed., *Key Issues in the Afro-American Experience* (vol. 2, 1971): 167–92.

Kirby, John B., *Black Americans in the Roosevelt Era: Liberalism and Race* (1980).

Klehr, Harvey, and William Tompson, "Self-Determination in the Black Belt: Origins of a Communist Policy," *Labor History* 30 (1989): 354–66.

Litchfield, Edward H., "A Case Study of Negro Political Behavior in Detroit," *Public Opinion Quarterly* 5 (1941): 267–74.

Logan, Rayford Whittingham, ed., *The Attitude of the Southern White Press toward Negro Suffrage, 1932–1940* (1940).

Marshall, Thurgood, "The Rise and Collapse of the 'White Democratic Primary,'" *Journal of Negro Education* 26 (1957): 249–54.

Martin, Charles H., "Negro Leaders, the Republican Party, and the Election of 1932," *Phylon* 32 (1971): 85–93.

McCoy, Donald R., "The Good Neighbor League and the Presidential Campaign of 1936," *Western Political Quarterly* 13 (1960): 1011–21.

Moon, Henry Lee, *Balance of Power: The Negro Vote* (1948).

——— "Racial Aspects of the Federal Public Relations Program," *Phylon* 4 (1943): 66–72.

Moran, Robert E., Sr., "Public Relief in Louisiana from 1928 to 1960," *Louisiana History* 14 (1973): 369–85.

Naison, Mark D., *Communists in Harlem during the Depression* (1983).

——— "Communism and Harlem Intellectuals in the Popular Front: Anti-Fascism and the Politics of Black Culture," *Journal of Ethnic Studies* 9 (1981): 1–25.

Norrell, Robert J., *Reaping the Whirlwind: The Civil Rights Movement in Tuskegee* (rev. ed., 1998).

Painter, Nell Irvin, ed., *The Narrative of Hosea Hudson: His Life As a Negro Communist in the South* (1979).

Plummer, Brenda Gayle, *Rising Wind: Black Americans and U.S. Foreign Affairs, 1935–1960* (1996).

Potter, Barrett G., "The Civilian Conservation Corps and New York's 'Negro Question': A Case Study in Federal-State Race Relations during the Great Depression," *Afro-Americans in New York Life and History* 1 (1977): 183–200.

Price, Margaret, *The Negro and the Ballot in the South* (1959).

Raper, Arthur F., "The Southern Negro and the NRA," *Georgia Historical Quarterly* 64 (1980): 128–45.

Record, Wilson, *Race and Radicalism: The NAACP and the Communist Party in Conflict* (1964).

Reed, Adolph, Jr., *Without Justice for All: The New Liberalism and Our Retreat from Racial Equality* (1999).

Reed, Adolph L., Jr., *W.E.B. Du Bois and American Political Thought: Fabianism and the Color Line* (1998).

Reed, Christopher Robert, "Black Chicago Political Realignment during the Depression and New Deal," *Illinois Historical Journal* 78 (1985): 242–56.

Reed, Linda, *Simple Decency and Common Sense: The Southern Conference Movement, 1938–1963* (1991).

Ross, B. Joyce, "Mary McLeod Bethune and the National Youth Administration: A Case Study of Power Relationships in the Black Cabinet of Franklin D. Roosevelt," *Journal of Negro History* 60 (1975): 1–28.

Ruchames, Louis, *Race, Jobs and Politics: The Story of FEPC* (1953).

Sears, James M., "Black Americans and the New Deal," *History Teacher* 10 (1976): 89–105.

Sitkoff, Harvard, *A New Deal for Blacks: The Emergence of Civil Rights as a National Issue* (1978).

Solomon, Mark, *The Cry Was Unity: Communists and African Americans, 1917–1936* (1998).

Spencer, Thomas T., "The Good Neighbor League Colored Committee and the 1936 Democratic Presidential Campaign," *Journal of Negro History* 63 (1978): 307–16.

Strickland, Arvarh E., "The New Deal Comes to Illinois," *Journal of the Illinois State Historical Society* 63 (1970): 55–68.

Strong, Donald S., "The Rise of Negro Voting in Texas," *American Political Science Review* 42 (1948): 518–22.

Sullivan, Patricia, *Days of Hope: Race and Democracy in the New Deal Era* (1996).

Van Zanten, John W., "Communist Theory and the Negro Question," *Review of Politics* 39 (1967): 435–56.

Walker, Melissa, "African Americans and TVA Reservoir Property Removal: Race in a New Deal Program," *Agricultural History* 72 (1998): 417–28.

Weaver, Robert Clifton, "Federal Aid, Local Control, and Negro Participation," *Journal of Negro Education* 11 (1942): 47–59.

Weber, Palmer, "The Negro Vote in the South," *Virginia Spectator* (1938): 6–7, 22, 25.

Weiss, Nancy Joan, *Farewell to the Party of Lincoln: Black Politics in the Age of FDR* (1983).

Wilkerson, Doxey Alphonso, *The Negro People and the Communists* (1944).

Wye, Christopher G., "The New Deal and the Negro Community: Toward a Broader Conceptualization," *Journal of American History* 59 (1972): 621–39.

Wynn, Linda T., "Toward a Perfect Democracy: The Struggle of African Americans in Fayette County, Tennessee, to Fulfill the Unfulfilled Right of the Franchise," *Tennessee Historical Quarterly* 55 (1996): 202–23.

22.5.4 Military

Allen, Robert L., *The Port Chicago Mutiny: The Story of the Largest Mass Mutiny Trial in U.S. Naval History* (1989).

Biggs, Bradley, *The Triple Nickles: America's First All-Black Paratroop Unit* (1986).

Bolte, Charles Guy, and Louis Harris, *Our Negro Veterans* (1947).

Brown, Earl Louis, and George R. Leighton, *The Negro and the War* (1942).

Brunson, Warren T., "What a Negro Soldier Thinks About," *Social Service Review* 18 (1944): 534–35.

Buchanan, A. Russell, *Black Americans in World War II* (1977).

Clement, Rufus E., "Problems of Demobilization and Rehabilitation of the Negro Soldier after World Wars I and II," *Journal of Negro Education* 12 (1943): 417–28.

Cripps, Thomas, and David Culbert, "The Negro Soldier, 1944: Film Propaganda in Black and White," *American Quarterly* 31 (1979): 616–40.

Dalfiume, Richard M., *Desegregation of the U.S. Armed Forces: Fighting on Two Fronts, 1939–1953* (1969).

Downey, Bill, *Uncle Sam Must Be Losing the War: Black Marines of the 51st* (1982).

Dryden, Charles W., *A-Train: Memoirs of a Tuskegee Airman* (1997).

Earley, Charity Adams, *One Woman's Army: A Black Officer Remembers the WAC* (1989).

Flynn, George Q., "Selective Service and American Blacks during World War II," *Journal of Negro History* 69 (1984): 14–25.

Francis, Charles E., *The Tuskegee Airmen: The Men Who Changed a Nation* (1988).

Hachey, Thomas E., "Jim Crow with a British Accent: Attitudes of London Government Officials toward American Negro Soldiers in England during World War II," *Journal of Negro History* 59 (1974): 65–77.

Hall, E. T., Jr., "Race Prejudice and Negro-White Relations in the Army," *American Journal of Sociology* 52 (1947): 401–10.

Halliburton, Warren J., *The Fighting Red Tails: America's First Black Airmen* (1978).

Hargrove, Hondon B., *Buffalo Soldiers in Italy: Black Americans in World War II* (1985).

Hasdorff, James C., "Reflections on the Tuskegee Experiment: An Interview with Brig. Gen. Noel F. Parrish, USAF (Ret.)," *Aerospace Historian* 24 (1977): 173–80.

Hastie, William H., *On Clipped Wings: The Story of Jim Crow in the Army Air Corps* (1943).

——— "The Negro in the Army Today," *Annals of the American Academy of Political and Social Science* (1942): 55–59.

Hine, Darlene Clark, "Mabel K. Staupers and the Integration of Black Nurses into the Armed Forces," in John Hope Franklin and August Meier, ed., *Black Leaders of the Twentieth Century* (1982): 241–57.

Johnson, Charles Spurgeon, "The Army, the Negro, and the Civilian Conservation Corps, 1933–1942," *Military Affairs* 36 (1972): 82–88.

Lee, Ulysses G., *The Employment of Negro Troops* (1966).

——— "The Draft and the Negro," *Current History* (1968): 28–33.

Long, Howard H., "The Negro Soldier in the Army of the United States," *Journal of Negro Education* 12 (1943): 307–15.

MacDonald, Dwight, and Nancy MacDonald, *The War's Greatest Scandal! The Story of Jim Crow in Uniform* (1943).

MacGregor, Morris J., Jr., *Integration of the Armed Forces, 1940–1965* (1981).

McGuire, Phillip, *Taps for a Jim Crow Army: Letters from Black Soldiers in World War II* (1983).

——— *He, Too, Spoke for Democracy: Judge Hastie, World War II, and the Black Soldier* (1988).

——— "Desegregation of the Armed Forces: Black Leadership, Protest, and World War II," *Journal of Negro History* 68 (1983): 147–58.

——— "Judge Hastie, World War II, and Army Racism," *Journal of Negro History* 62 (1977): 351–62.

——— "Judge William H. Hastie and Army Recruitment, 1940–1942," *Military Affairs* 42 (1978): 75–79.

Mershon, Sherie, and Steven Schlossman, *Foxholes and Color Lines: Desegregating the U.S. Armed Forces* (1998).

Moore, Brenda L., *To Serve My Country, To Serve My Race: The Story of the Only African American WACS Stationed Overseas during World War II* (1996).

Motley, Mary Penick, ed., *The Invisible Soldier: The Experience of the Black Soldier, World War II* (1975).

Mulzac, Hugh, *A Star to Steer By* (1963).

Nelson, Dennis Denmark, *The Integration of the Negro into the U.S. Navy* (1951).

Nichols, Lee, *Breakthrough on the Color Front* (1954).

Osur, Alan M., *Blacks in the Army Air Forces during World War II: The Problems of Race Relations* (1977).

Parks, Robert J., "The Development of Segregation in U.S. Army Hospitals, 1940–1942," *Military Affairs* 37 (1973): 145–50.

Patterson, Gordon, "Hurston Goes to War: The Army Signal Corps in Saint Augustine," *Florida Historical Quarterly* 74 (1995): 166–83.

Purdon, Eric, *Black Company: The Story of Subchaser, 1264* (1972).

Reddick, Lawrence D., "The Negro in the United States Navy during World War II," *Journal of Negro History* 32 (1947): 201–19.

Rose, Arnold M., "Army Policies toward Negro Soldiers: A Report on a Success and a Failure," *Journal of Social Issues* 3 (1947): 26–31.

Rose, Robert, *Lonely Eagles: The Story of America's Black Air Force in World War II* (1976).

Sandler, Stanley, *Segregated Skies: All-Black Combat Squadrons of World War II* (1992).

Smith, Graham A., *When Jim Crow Met John Bull: Black American Soldiers in World War II Britain* (1987).

Stevens, John D., "Black Correspondents of World War II Cover the Supply Routes," *Journal of Negro History* 57 (1972): 395–406.

Weaver, Robert Clifton, "The Negro Veteran," *Annals of the American Academy of Political and Social Science* (1945): 127–32.

Werrell, Kenneth P., "Mutiny at Army Air Force Station 569: Bamber Bridge, England, June, 1943," *Aerospace Historian* 22 (1975): 202–09.

Wiley, Bell Irvin, *The Training of Negro Troops* (1946).

Wilson, Ruth Danenhower, *Jim Crow Joins Up: A Study of Negroes in the Armed Forces of the United States* (1944).

Wollenberg, Charles, "Blacks vs. Navy Blue: The Mare Island Mutiny Court Martial," *California History* 58 (1979): 62–75.

Wynn, Neil A., *The Afro-American and the Second World War* (1976).

22.6   DEMOGRAPHY

Cox, Oliver C., "Sex Ratio and Marital Status among Negroes," *American Sociological Review* 5 (1940): 937–47.

Engerman, Stanley L., "Black Fertility and Family Structure in the U.S., 1880–1940," *Journal of Family History* 2 (1977): 117–38.

Holmes, Samuel Jackson, *The Negro's Struggle for Survival: A Study in Human Ecology* (1937).

Johnson, Guy Benton, "The Negro and the Depression in North Carolina," *Social Forces* 12 (1933): 103–15.

Margo, Robert A., "Race, Educational Attainment, and the 1940 Census," *Journal of Economic History* 46 (1986): 189–98.

North Carolina State Board of Public Welfare, *The Negro Population of North Carolina, Social and Economic* (1945).

Raymond, Richard, "Mobility and Economic Progress of Negro Americans during the 1940's," *American Journal of Economics and Sociology* 28 (1969): 337–50.

Tolnay, Stewart E., "Class, Race, and Fertility in the Rural South, 1910 and 1940," *Rural Sociology* 60 (1995): 108–28.

———— "The Decline of Black Marital Fertility in the Rural South, 1910–1940," *American Sociological Review* 52 (1987): 211–17.

22.7   FAMILY

Comer, James P., *Maggie's American Dream: The Life and Times of a Black Family* (1988).

Daniel, Robert Prentiss, *A Psychological Study of Delinquent and Non-Delinquent Negro Boys* (1932).

Davis, Allison, and John Dollard, *Children of Bondage: The Personality Development of Negro Youth in the Urban South* (1940).

Dickins, Dorothy, "Food Patterns of White and Negro Families, 1936–1948," *Social Forces* 27 (1949): 425–30.

Fisk University, Department of Social Science, *Social Study of Negro Families in the Area Selected for the Nashville Negro Federal Housing Project* (1934).

Frazier, Edward Franklin, *The Negro Family in Chicago* (1932).

———— *Negro Youth at the Crossways: Their Personality Development in the Middle States* (1940).

———— "The Impact of Urban Civilization upon Negro Family Life," *American Sociological Review* 2 (1937): 609–18.

Hertz, Hilda, "Unmarried Negro Mothers in Southern Urban Communities," *Social Forces* 23 (1944): 73–79.

King, James E., *The Impact of Federal Housing Policy on Urban African-American Families, 1930–1966* (1997).

Reid, Ira De Augustine, *In a Minor Key: Negro Youth in Story and Fact* (1940).

Rodrique, Jessie M., "The Black Community and the Birth-Control Movement," in Kathy Peiss and Christina Simmons, ed., *Passion and Power: Sexuality and History* (1989): 138–54.

Tolnay, Stewart E., *The Bottom Rung: African American Family Life on Southern Farms* (1999).

22.8 SOCIETY

22.8.1 Rural Life (Including Black Settlements)

Bent, Michael J., and Ellen F. Greene, *Rural Negro Health: A Report on a Five-Year Experiment in Health Education in Rural Tennessee* (1937).

Bond, Horace Mann and Julia W. Bond, *The Star Creek Papers*, ed. Adam Fairclough (1997).

Brown, R. Clayton, "Health of Farm Children in the South, 1900–1950," *Agricultural History* 53 (1979): 170–87.

Cantor, Louis, *A Prologue to the Protest Movement: The Missouri Sharecropper Roadside Demonstration of 1939* (1969).

Conrad, David Eugene, *The Forgotten Farmers: The Story of Sharecroppers in the New Deal* (1965).

Gordon, Lawrence, "A Brief Look at Blacks in Depression Mississippi, 1929–1934: Eyewitness Accounts," *Journal of Negro History* 64 (1979): 377–90.

Greene, Lorenzo J., "Economic Conditions among Negroes in the South, 1930, As Seen by an Associate of Dr. Carter G. Woodson," *Journal of Negro History* 64 (1979): 265–73.

Grubbs, Donald H., *Cry from the Cotton: The Southern Tenant Farmers' Union and the New Deal* (1971).

Holley, Donald, "The Negro in the New Deal Resettlement Program," *Agricultural History* 45 (1971): 179–93.

Johnson, Charles Spurgeon, *Growing up in the Black Belt: Negro Youth in the Rural South* (1941).

Kester, Howard, *Revolt among the Sharecroppers* (1936).

Kirby, Jack Temple, *Rural Worlds Lost: The American South, 1920–1960* (1987).

——— "Black and White in the Rural South, 1915–1954," *Agricultural History* 58 (1984): 411–22.

Mertz, Paul E., *New Deal Policy and Southern Rural Poverty* (1978).

Mitchell, Harry Leland, *Mean Things Happening in this Land: The Life and Times of H. L. Mitchell, Co-Founder of the Southern Tenant Farmers Union* (1979).

——— "The Founding and Early History of the Southern Tenant Farmers Union," *Arkansas Historical Quarterly* 32 (1973): 342–69.

Myrdal, Gunnar, "The Croppers' Dilemma," in Allen Weinstein and Frank Otto Gatell, ed., *The Segregation Era, 1863–1954* (1970): 197–217.

Powdermaker, Hortense, *After Freedom: A Cultural Study in the Deep South* (1939).

Raper, Arthur Franklin, *Preface to Peasantry: A Tale of Two Black Belt Counties* (1936).

Shaw, Nate, *All God's Dangers: The Life of Nate Shaw*, comp. Theodore Rosengarten (1974).

Tolnay, Stewart E., *The Bottom Rung: African American Family Life on Southern Farms* (1999).

22.8.2 Urban Life (Including Migration)

Alexander, J. Trent, "The Great Migration in Comparative Perspective: Interpreting the Urban Origins of Southern Black Migrants to Depression-Era Pittsburgh," *Social Science History* 22 (1998): 349–76.

Anderson, E. Frederick, *The Development of Leadership and Organization Building in the Black Community of Los Angeles from 1900 through World War II* (1980).

Bauman, John F., "Black Slums/Black Projects: The New Deal and Negro Housing in Philadelphia," *Pennsylvania History* 41 (1974): 311–38.

Biles, Roger, *Memphis in the Great Depression* (1986).

——— "The Urban South in the Great Depression," *Journal of Southern History* 56 (1990): 71–100.

Blackwelder, Julia Kirk, "Quiet Suffering: Atlanta Women in the 1930's," *Georgia History Quarterly* 61 (1977): 112–24.

———— "Women in the Work-Force: Atlanta, New Orleans, and San Antonio, 1930–1940," *Journal of Urban History* 4 (1978): 331–58.

Brandt, Nat, *Harlem at War: The Black Experience in WWII* (1997).

Broussard, Albert S., *Black San Francisco: The Struggle for Racial Equality, 1900–1954* (1993).

———— "Oral Recollection and the Historical Reconstruction of Black San Francisco, 1915–1940," *Oral History Review* 12 (1984): 63–80.

Capeci, Dominic J., Jr., *Race Relations in Wartime Detroit: The Sojourner Truth Housing Controversy of 1942* (1984).

Cayton, Horace Roscoe, "Negro Housing in Chicago," *Social Action* 6 (1940): 1–39.

Chavis, John M. T., and William McNitt, *A Brief History of the Detroit Urban League and Description of the League's Papers in the Michigan Historical Collections* (1971).

Chicago, Illinois Mayor's Commission on Human Relations, *Race Relations in Chicago: Report of the Mayor's Commission on Race Relations for 1945* (1945).

Cowgill, Donald O., "Trends in Residential Segregation of Nonwhites in American Cities, 1940–1950," *American Sociological Review* 21 (1956): 43–47.

Drake, St. Clair, and Horace R. Cayton, *Black Metropolis: A Study of Negro Life in a Northern City* (rev. ed., 1993).

Duncan, Otis Dudley, and Beverly Duncan, *Negro Population of Chicago: A Study of Residential Succession* (1957).

Ford, James, *Slums and Housing, with Special Reference to New York City: History, Conditions, Policy* (1936).

Frazier, Edward Franklin, "Negro Harlem: An Ecological Study," *American Journal of Sociology* 43 (1937): 72–88.

———— "Some Effects of the Depression on the Negro in Northern Cities," *Science and Society* 2 (1938): 489–99.

Gilmore, Harlan, and Logan Wilson, "Negro Socioeconomic Status in a Southern City (New Orleans)," *Sociology and Social Research* (1945): 361–73.

Greenberg, Cheryl Lynn, *"Or Does It Explode?": Black Harlem in the Great Depression* (1991).

Grimshaw, William J., *Bitter Fruit: Black Politics and the Chicago Machine, 1931–1991* (1992).

Grunsfield, Mary-Jane Loeb, *Negroes in Chicago* (1944).

Haber, Carole, and Brian Gratton, "Old Age, Public Welfare, and Race: The Case of Charleston, South Carolina," *Journal of Social History* 21 (1987): 263–79.

Hamilton, Dona C., "The National Urban League and New Deal Programs," *Social Service Review* 58 (1984): 227–43.

———— "Organizational Adaptation: The National Urban League during the Great Depression," *Journal of Sociology and Social Welfare* 14 (1987): 129–51.

Hinshaw, John, and Judith Modell, "Perceiving Racism: Homestead from Depression to Deindustrialization," *Pennsylvania History* 63 (1996): 17–52.

Hirsch, Arnold Richard, *Making the Second Ghetto: Race and Housing in Chicago, 1940–1960* (rev. ed., 1998).

Housing Authority of the City of Newark (New Jersey), *The Cost of Slums in Newark* (1946).

Karger, Howard Jacob, "Phyllis Wheatley House: A History of the Minneapolis Black Settlement House, 1924 to 1940," *Phylon* 47 (1986): 79–90.

Katz, Michael B., and Thomas J. Sugrue, ed., *W.E.B. Du Bois, Race, and the City* (1998).

King, James E., *The Impact of Federal Housing Policy on Urban African-American Families, 1930–1966* (1997).

Kusmer, Kenneth L., ed., *Black Communities and Race Relations in American Cities* (1991).

Lewis, Earl, "Connecting Memory, Self, and the Power of Place in African American Urban History," *Journal of Urban History* 21 (1995): 347–71.

Lewis, Earl, and Joe W. Trotter, ed., *African Americans in the Industrial Age: A Documentary History, 1915–1945* (1996).

Long, Herman Hodge, and Charles S. Johnson, *People vs. Property: Race Restrictive Covenants in Housing* (1947).

McKay, Claude, *Harlem: Negro Metropolis* (1940).

Mihelich, Dennis N., "World War II and the Transformation of the Omaha Urban League," *Nebraska History* 60 (1979): 401–23.

Mohl, Raymond, "Trouble in Paradise: Race and Housing in Miami during the New Deal Era," *Prologue* 19 (1987): 7–21.

Moore, Shirley Ann Wilson, "Traditions from Home: African Americans in Wartime Richmond, California," in Lewis A. Erenberg and Susan E. Hirsch, ed., *The War in American Culture: Society and Consciousness during World War II* (1996): 263–83.

Naison, Mark D., *Communists in Harlem during the Depression* (1983).

———— "Communism and Black Nationalism in the Depression: The Case of Harlem," *Journal of Ethnic Studies* 2 (1974): 24–36.

Ottley, Roi, *"New World A-Coming": Inside Black America* (1943).

Parker, Russell D., "The Black Community in a Company Town: Alcoa, Tennessee, 1919–1939," *Tennessee Historical Quarterly* 37 (1978): 203–21.

President's Conference on Home Building and Home Ownership, *Negro Housing: Report of the Committee on Negro Housing* (1932).

Reid, Ira De Augustine, *The Negro Immigrant, His Background, Characteristics, and Social Adjustment, 1899–1937* (1939).

Schwartz, Joel, "The Consolidated Tenants League of Harlem: Black Self-Help vs. White, Liberal Intervention in Ghetto Housing, 1934–1944," *Afro-Americans in New York Life and History* 10 (1986): 31–51.

Smith, Alonzo N., "Blacks and the Los Angeles Municipal Transit System, 1941–1945," *Urbanism Past and Present* 6 (1980): 25–31.

Spinney, Robert G., *World War II in Nashville: Transformation of the Homefront* (1998).

Strickland, Arvarh E., *History of the Chicago Urban League* (1966).

Sugrue, Thomas J., *The Origins of the Urban Crisis: Race and Inequality in Postwar Detroit* (1996).

Thomas, Richard Walter, *Life for Us Is What We Make It: Building Black Community in Detroit, 1915–1945* (1992).

Trotter, Joe William, Jr., *Black Milwaukee: The Making of an Industrial Proletariat, 1915–1945* (1985).

———— "African Americans in the City: The Industrial Era, 1900–1950," *Journal of Urban History* 21 (1995): 438–57.

Tuck, Stephen, "A City Too Dignified to Hate: Civic Pride, Civil Rights, and Savannah in Comparative Perspective," *Georgia Historical Quarterly* 79 (1995): 539–59.

United States Department of Labor, "Annual Family and Occupational Earnings of Residents of Two Negro Housing Projects in Atlanta," *Monthly Labor Review* 61 (1945): 1061–73.

———— "Improved Conditions for Negroes in Louisville," *Monthly Labor Review* 61 (1945): 727–28.

———— "Living Conditions of Small-Wage Earners in Chicago," *Monthly Labor Review* 22 (1936): 170–73.

United States, Works Project Administration, Illinois, *The Chicago Negro Community: A Statistical Description* (1939).

Warner, William Lloyd, Buford H. Junker, and Walter A. Adams, *Color and Human Nature: Negro Personality Development in a Northern City* (1941).

Weaver, Robert Clifton, *Hemmed In: ABC's of Race Restrictive Housing Covenants* (1945).

———— *The Negro Ghetto* (1948).

Weiss, Nancy J., *The National Urban League, 1910–1940* (1974).

Wiese, Andrew, "The Other Suburbanites: African American Suburbanization in the North before 1950," *Journal of American History* 85 (1999): 1495–524.

Williams, Lillian S., *Strangers in the Land of Paradise: The Creation of an African-American Urban Community, Buffalo, New York, 1900–1940* (1999).

Wolcott, Victoria W., "The Culture of the Informal Economy: Numbers Runners in Inter-War Black Detroit," *Radical History Review* 69 (1997): 46–75.

22.8.3 Color and Class

Kalmar, Karen L., "Southern Black Elites and the New Deal: A Case Study of Savannah, Georgia," *Georgia Historical Quarterly* 65 (1981): 341–55.

McBride, David, and Monroe H. Little, "The Afro-American Elite, 1930–1940," *Phylon* 42 (1981): 105–19.

Meier, August, and David Lewis, "History of the Negro Upper Class in Atlanta, Georgia, 1890–1958," *Journal of Negro Education* 28 (1959): 128–39.

22.8.4 Associational Life

Armitage, Sue, Theresa Banfield and Sarah Jacobus, "Black Women and Their Communities in Colorado," in Darlene Clark Hine, ed., *Black Women in United States History* (vol. 9, 1990): 51–61.

Arthur, George Robert, *Life on the Negro Frontier: A Study of the Objectives and the Success of the Activities Promoted in the Young Men's Christian Associations Operating in "Rosenwald" Buildings* (1934).

Bates, Beth Tompkins, "A New Crowd Challenges the Agenda of the Old Guard in the NAACP, 1933–1941," *American Historical Review* 102 (1997): 340–77.

Brady, Marilyn Dell, "Organizing Afro-American Girls' Clubs in Kansas in the 1920's," *Frontiers* 9 (1987): 69–73.

Bunche, Ralph J., "The Programs of Organizations Devoted to the Improvement of the Status of the American Negro," *Journal of Negro Education* 8 (1939): 539–50.

Chateauvert, Melinda, *Marching Together: Women of the Brotherhood of Sleeping Car Porters* (1998).

Cochrane, Sharlene Voogd, "'And the Pressure Never Let Up': Black Women, White Women, and the Boston YWCA, 1918–1948," in Vicki L. Crawford, Jacqueline Anne Rouse and Barbara Woods, ed., *Women in the Civil Rights Movement: Trailblazers and Torchbearers, 1941–1965* (1990): 259–69.

Dickson, Lynda F., "Toward a Broader Angle of Vision in Uncovering Women's History: Black Women's Clubs Revisited," *Frontiers* 9 (1987): 62–68.

Drake, St. Clair, *Churches and Voluntary Associations in the Chicago Negro Community* (1940).

Ergood, Bruce, "The Female Protection and the Sun Light: Two Contemporary Negro Mutual Aid Societies," in Darlene Clark Hine, ed., *Black Women in United States History* (vol. 5, 1990): 303–16.

Ferguson, Earline Rae, "The Woman's Improvement Club of Indianapolis: Black Women Pioneers in Tuberculosis Work, 1903–1938," in Darlene Clark Hine, ed., *Black Women in United States History* (vol. 6, 1990): 339–63.

Lerner, Gerda, "Early Community Work of Black Club Women," *Journal of Negro History* 59 (1974): 158–67.

Loeb, Charles Harold, *The Future Is Yours: The History of the Future Outlook League, 1935–1946* (1947).

Record, Wilson, "Negro Intellectual Leadership in the National Association for the Advancement of Colored People, 1910–1940," *Phylon* 17 (1956): 375–89.

Reed, Christopher R., *The Chicago NAACP and the Rise of Black Professional Leadership, 1910–1966* (1997).

Scott, Anne Firor, "Most Invisible of All: Black Women's Voluntary Associations," *Journal of Southern History* 56 (1990): 3–22.

Warren, Stanley, "The Monster Meetings at the Negro YMCA in Indianapolis," *Indiana Magazine of History* 91 (1995): 57–80.

Weisenfeld, Judith, *African American Women and Christian Activism: New York's Black YWCA, 1905–1945* (1997).

22.8.5 Leisure and Sports

Barbeau, Arthur, "Jesse Owens and the Triumph of Black Olympians," *Journal of the West Virginia Historical Association* 4 (1980): 46–59.

Capeci, Dominic J., Jr., and Martha Wilkerson, "Multifarious Hero: Joe Louis, American Society and Race Relations during World Crisis, 1935–1945," *Journal of Sport History* 10 (1983): 5–25.

Coburn, Mark D., "America's Great Black Hope," *American Heritage* 29 (1978): 82–91.

Cox, James A., "The Day Joe Louis Fired Shots Heard 'Round the World," *Smithsonian* 19 (1988): 170–96.

Edmonds, Anthony O., "The Second Louis-Schmeling Fight: Sport, Symbol, and Culture," *Journal of Popular Culture* 7 (1973): 42–50.

Evans, Art, "Joe Louis as a Key Functionary: White Reactions toward a Black Champion," *Journal of Black Studies* 16 (1985): 95–111.

Gems, Gerald R., "Blocked Shot: The Development of Basketball in the African-American Community of Chicago," *Journal of Sport History* 22 (1995): 135–48.

Hoberman, John M., *Darwin's Athletes: How Sport Has Damaged Black America and Preserved the Myth of Race* (1997).

Mathewson, Alfred Dennis, "Major League Baseball's Monopoly Power and the Negro Leagues," *American Business Law Journal* 35 (1998): 291–318.

Naison, Mark, "Lefties and Righties: The Communist Party and Sports during the Great Depression," *Radical America* 13 (1979): 47–59.

Otto, Solomon, and John Solomon Otto, "I Played against 'Satchel' for Three Seasons: Blacks and Whites in the 'Twilight' Leagues," *Journal of Popular Culture* 7 (1974): 797–803.

Overmyer, James, *Queen of the Negro Leagues: Effa Manley and the Newark Eagles* (1998).

Robinson, Frazier "Slow," with Paul Bauer, *Catching Dreams: My Life in the Negro Baseball Leagues* (1999).

Rosengarten, Theodore, "Reading the Hops: Recollections of Lorenzo Piper Davis and the Negro Baseball League," *Southern Exposure* 5 (1977): 62–79.

Sammons, Jeffrey T., "A Proportionate and Measured Response to the Provocation That Is *Darwin's Athletes*," *Journal of Sport History* 24 (1997): 378–88.

22.9 RELIGION

Baer, Hans A., *The Black Spiritual Movement: A Religious Response to Racism* (1984).

Blatnica, Dorothy Ann, *"At the Altar of Their God": African American Catholics in Cleveland, 1922–1961* (1995).

Drake, St. Clair, *Churches and Voluntary Associations in the Chicago Negro Community* (1940).

Fauset, Arthur Huff, *Black Gods of the Metropolis: Negro Religious Cults of the Urban North* (1944).

Harris, Michael W., *The Rise of Gospel Blues: The Music of Thomas Andrew Dorsey in the Urban Church* (1992).

Higginbotham, Evelyn Brooks, "Rethinking Vernacular Culture: Black Religion and Race Records in the 1920's and 1930's," in Wahneema H. Lubiano, ed., *The House That Race Built: Black Americans, U.S. Terrain* (1997): 157–77.

Jones, Raymond Julius, *A Comparative Study of Religious Cult Behavior among Negroes, Washington, D.C.* (1939).

Lornell, Kip, *'Happy in the Service of the Lord': African-American Sacred Vocal Harmony Quartets in Memphis* (1995).

Mays, Benjamin Elijah, *The Negro's God: As Reflected in His Literature* (1938).

Mays, Benjamin Elijah, and Joseph William Nicholson, *The Negro's Church* (1933).

McGreevy, John T., *Parish Boundaries: The Catholic Encounter with Race in the Twentieth-Century Urban North* (1996).

Miller, Robert M., "The Attitudes of American Protestantism toward the Negro, 1919–1939," *Journal of Negro History* 41 (1956): 215–40.

———— "The Protestant Churches and Lynching, 1919–1939," *Journal of Negro History* 42 (1957): 118–31.

Orser, W. Edward, "Racial Attitudes in War-Time: The Protestant Churches during the Second World War," *Church History* 41 (1972): 337–53.

Reagon, Bernice Johnson, ed., *We'll Understand It Better By and By: Pioneering African American Gospel Composers* (1992).

Richardson, Harry Van Buren, *Dark Glory: A Picture of the Church among Negroes in the Rural South* (1947).

Roberts, Harry W., "The Rural Negro Minister: His Personal and Social Characteristics," *Social Forces* 27 (1949): 291–300.

Sawyer, Mary R., "The Fraternal Council of Negro Churches, 1934–1964," *Church History* 59 (1990): 51–64.

Weisenfeld, Judith, *African American Women and Christian Activism: New York's Black YWCA, 1905–1945* (1997).

Wesley, Charles H., "The Religious Attitudes of Negro Youth," *Journal of Negro History* 21 (1936): 376–93.

Works Project Administration, New Jersey, *The Negro Church in New Jersey* (1938).

22.10 THOUGHT AND EXPRESSION

22.10.1 Race, Gender, and Identity

Allen, Ernest, Jr., "Waiting for Tojo: The Pro-Japan Vigil of Black Missourians, 1932–1943," *Gateway Heritage* 16 (1995): 38–55.

Bethune, Mary McLeod, "Clarifying Our Vision with the Facts," *Journal of Negro History* 23 (1938): 10–15.

Bond, Horace Mann, "Should the Negro Care Who Wins the War?" *Annals of the American Academy of Political and Social Science* (1942): 81–84.

Davis, Angela Y., *Blues Legacies and Black Feminism: Gertrude "Ma" Rainey, Bessie Smith, and Billie Holiday* (1998).

Ford, Nick Aaron, "What Negroes Are Fighting For: 'We Love Honor More Than We Fear Death,'" *Vital Speeches of the Day* 9 (1943): 240–42.

Gaines, Kevin, "Rethinking Race and Class in African-American Struggles for Equality, 1885–1941," *American Historical Review* 102 (1997): 378–87.

James, Winston, *Holding Aloft the Banner of Ethiopa: Caribbean Radicalism in Early Twentieth-Century America* (1998).

Johnson, Guy B., "Negro Racial Movements and Leadership in the United States," *American Journal of Sociology* 43 (1937): 57–71.

Johnson, James Weldon, *Negro Americans, What Now?* (1935).

Kelley, Robin D. G., "'Comrades, Praise Gawd for Lenin and Them!': Ideology and Culture among Black Communists in Alabama, 1930–1935," *Science and Society* 52 (1988): 59–82.

Kirby, John B., "Ralph J. Bunche and Black Radical Thought in the 1930's," *Phylon* 35 (1974): 129–41.

Linnemann, Russell J., ed., *Alain Locke: Reflections on a Modern Renaissance Man* (1982).

Logan, Rayford Whittingham, ed., *What the Negro Wants* (1944).

———— *The Negro and the Post-War World: A Primer* (1945).

Odum, Howard W., *Race and Rumors of Race: The American South in the Early Forties* (1943).

Parker, Albert, *Negroes in the Post-War World* (1943).

Perry, Pettis, *The Negro's Stake in This War* (1942).

Posnock, Ross, "The Distinction of Du Bois: Aesthetics, Pragmatism, Politics," *American Literary History* 7 (1995): 500–24.

Potamianos, George P., "Visions of a Dying Africa: Ralph J. Bunche and His Second African Journey, 1936–1938," *Journal of Black Studies* 26 (1996): 447–66.

Powell, Adam Clayton, Jr., "Is This a 'White Man's War'?" *Common Sense* 11 (1942): 111–13.

Record, Wilson, *The Negro and the Communist Party* (1951).

Reddick, Lawrence D., "The New Race-Relations Frontier," *Journal of Educational Sociology* 19 (1945): 129–45.

———— "What the Northern Negro Thinks about Democracy," *Journal of Educational Sociology* 17 (1944): 296–306.

Savage, Barbara Dianne, *Broadcasting Freedom: Radio, War, and the Politics of Race, 1938–1948* (1999).

Sollors, Werner, "W.E.B. Du Bois in Nazi Germany, 1936," *Amerikastudien* 44 (1999): 207–22.

Trefzer, Annette, "'Let Us All Be Kissing-Friends?' Zora Neale Hurston and Race Politics in Dixie," *Journal of American Studies* 31 (1997): 69–78.

Walters, Ronald G., "The Negro Press and the Image of Success, 1920–1939," *Midcontinent American Studies Journal* 11 (1970): 36–55.

White, Walter Francis, *A Rising Wind* (1945).

Williams, John Henry, *A Negro Looks at War* (1940).

Wright, Richard, "With Black Radicals in Chicago," *Dissent* 24 (1977): 156–61.

Wynn, Neil A., "Black Attitudes towards Participation in the American War Effort, 1941–1945," *Afro-American Studies* 3 (1972): 13–19.

———— "The Impact of the Second World War on the American Negro," *Journal of Contemporary History* 6 (1971): 42–53.

22.10.2 Emigration and Nationalism

Collum, Danny Duncan, ed., *African Americans in the Spanish Civil War: "This Ain't Ethiopia, but It'll Do"* (1992).

Du Bois, William Edward Burghardt, "Inter-Racial Implications of the Ethiopian Crisis," *Foreign Affairs* 14 (1935): 82–92.

Harris, Joseph E., *African-American Reactions to War in Ethiopia* (1994).

Henderson, J. A., "A. Philip Randolph and the Dilemmas of Socialism and Black Nationalism in the United States, 1917–1941," *Race and Class* 20 (1978): 143–60.

Muraskin, William, "The Harlem Boycott of 1934: Black Nationalism and the Rise of Labor Union Consciousness," *Labor History* 13 (1972): 361–73.

Naison, Mark D., "Communism and Black Nationalism in the Depression: The Case of Harlem," *Journal of Ethnic Studies* 2 (1974): 24–36.

Scott, William Randolph, *The Sons of Sheba's Race: African-Americans and the Italo-Ethiopian War, 1935–1941* (1993).

Shack, William A., "Ethiopia and Afro-Americans: Some Historical Notes, 1920–1970," *Phylon* 35 (1974): 142–55.

Von Eschen, Penny M., *Race against Empire: Black Americans and Anticolonialism, 1937–1957* (1997).

Weisbord, Robert G., "Black America and the Italian-Ethiopian Crisis: An Episode in Pan-Negroism," *Historian* 34 (1972): 230–41.

22.10.3 Language and Linguistics

Blok, H. P., "Annotations to Mr. Turner's *Africanisms in the Gullah Dialect*," *Lingua* 8 (1959): 306–21.

Cassidy, Frederic G., "The Place of Gullah," *American Speech* 55 (1980): 3–16.

———— "Sources of the African Element in Gullah," in Lawrence D. Carrington, ed., *Studies in Caribbean Language* (1983): 75–81.

Johnson, Guy Benton, *Folk Culture on St. Helena Island, South Carolina* (1930).

Lieberson, Stanley, and Kelly S. Mikelson, "Distinctive African American Names: An Experimental, Historical, and Linguistic Analysis of Innovation," *American Sociological Review* 60 (1995): 928–46.

Smitherman, Geneva, *Talkin and Testifyin: The Language of Black America* (1977).

Tyler, Bruce M., "Black Jive and White Repression," *Journal of Ethnic Studies* 16 (1989): 31–66.

22.10.4 Folklore and Humor

Harris, Trudier, "Adventures in a 'Foreign Country': African American Humor and the South," *Southern Cultures* 1 (1995): 457–65.

Hemenway, Robert, "Folklore Field Notes from Zora Neale Hurston," *Black Scholar* 7 (1976): 39–46.

Shankman, Arnold, "Black Pride and Prejudice: The Amos 'n' Andy Crusade," *Journal of Popular Culture* 12 (1978): 236–52.

Sheffey, Ruthe T., "Zora Neale Hurston's *Moses, Man of the Mountain:* A Fictionalized Manifesto on the Imperatives of Black Leadership," *CLA Journal* 29 (1985): 206–20.

22.10.5   Literature and Poetry

Clayton, Ronnie W., "Federal Writers' Projects for Blacks in Louisiana," *Louisiana History* 19 (1978): 327–35.

Davis, Angela Y., *Blues Legacies and Black Feminism: Gertrude "Ma" Rainey, Bessie Smith, and Billie Holiday* (1998).

Goddard, Robert, "Agricultural Worker As Archetype in West Indian and African-American Literature," *Agricultural History* 72 (1998): 509–20.

Gordon, Eugene, "Social and Political Problems of Negro Writers," in Henry Hart, ed., *American Writers Congress* (1935): 145–53.

Maxwell, William J., *New Negro, Old Left: African-American Writing and Communism Between the Wars* (1999).

Peters, Pearlie Mae Fisher, *The Assertive Woman in Zora Neale Hurston's Fiction, Folklore, and Drama* (1997).

Smethurst, James Edward, *The New Red Negro: The Literary Left and African American Poetry, 1930–1946* (1999).

Tidwell, John Edgar, "Recasting Negro Life History: Sterling A. Brown and the Federal Writers' Project," *Langston Hughes Review* 13 (1995): 77–82.

Wall, Cheryl A., "Mules and Men and Women: Zora Neale Hurston's Strategies of Narration and Visions of Female Empowerment," *Black American Literature Forum* 23 (1989): 661–80.

Wright, Richard, "Blueprint for Negro Writing," *New Challenge* 2 (1937): 53–65.

Young, James O., *Black Writers of the Thirties* (1973).

22.10.6   Music and Performing Arts

Aschenbrenner, Joyce, *Katherine Dunham: Reflections on the Social and Political Contexts of Afro-American Dance* (1981).

Bailey, Ben E., "The Red Tops: The Orchestra That Covered the Delta," *Black Perspective in Music* 16 (1988): 177–90.

Bogle, Donald, *Brown Sugar: Eighty Years of America's Black Female Superstars* (1980).

Carmichael, Thomas, "Beneath the Underdog: Charles Mingus, Representation, and Jazz Autobiography," *Canadian Review of American Studies* 25 (1995): 29–40.

Dance, Stanley, *The World of Swing* (1974).

Daniels, Douglas Henry, "Goodbye Pork Pie Hat: Lester Young As Spiritual Figure," *Annual Review of Jazz Studies* 4 (1988): 161–77.

——— "Los Angeles Zoot: Race 'Riot,' the Pachuco, and Black Music Culture," *Journal of Negro History* 82 (1997): 201–20.

Davis, Angela Y., *Blues Legacies and Black Feminism: Gertrude "Ma" Rainey, Bessie Smith, and Billie Holiday* (1998).

DeVeaux, Scott, *The Birth of Bebop: A Social and Musical History* (1997).

Djedje, Jacqueline Cogdell, and Eddie S. Meadows, ed., *California Soul: Music of African Americans in the West* (1998).

Dunham, Katherine, *Katherine Dunham's Journey to Accompong* (1946).

Erenberg, Lewis A., *Swingin' the Dream: Big Band Jazz and the Rebirth of American Culture* (1998).

Fraden, Rena, "The Cloudy History of Big White Fog: The Federal Theatre Project, 1938," *American Studies* 29 (1988): 5–27.

Gennari, John, "'A Weapon of Integration': Frank Marshall Davis and the Politics of Jazz," *Langston Hughes Review* 14 (1996): 16–33.

Gitler, Ira, *Jazz Masters of the Forties* (1966).

Harris, Michael W., *The Rise of Gospel Blues: The Music of Thomas Andrew Dorsey in the Urban Church* (1992).

Higginbotham, Evelyn Brooks, "Rethinking Vernacular Culture: Black Religion and Race Records in the 1920's and 1930's," in Wahneema H. Lubiano, ed., *The House That Race Built: Black Americans, U.S. Terrain* (1997): 157–77.

Kukla, Barbara J., *Swing City: Newark Nightlife, 1925–1950* (1991).

Miller, Jeanne-Marie A., "Successful Federal Theatre Dramas by Black Playwriters," *Black Scholar* 10 (1970): 79–85.

Nadler, Paul, "Liberty Censored: Black Living Newspapers of the Federal Theatre Project," *African American Review* 29 (1995): 615–22.

Olaniyan, Tejumola, *Scars of Conquest/Masks of Resistance: The Invention of Cultural Identities in African, African-American, and Caribbean Drama* (1995).

Oliver, Paul, *The Story of the Blues* (1969).

Panassie, Hugues, *Hot Jazz: The Guide to Swing Music,* trans. Lyle Dowling and Eleanor Dowling (1936).

Reagon, Bernice Johnson, "World War II Reflected in Black Music: 'Uncle Sam Called Me,'" *Southern Exposure* 1 (1974): 169–84.

Reagon, Bernice Johnson, ed., *We'll Understand It Better By and By: Pioneering African American Gospel Composers* (1992).

Reed, Tom, *The Black Music History of Los Angeles: Its Roots* (1994).

Rice, Marc, "Frompin' in the Great Plains: Listening and Dancing to the Jazz Orchestras of Alphonso Trent, 1925–1944," *Great Plains Quarterly* 16 (1996): 107–16.

Ross, Ronald, "The Role of Blacks in the Federal Theatre, 1935–1939," *Journal of Negro History* 59 (1974): 38–50.

Rout, Leslie B., Jr., "Economics and Race in Jazz," in Ray B. Browne, Richard H. Crowder, Virgil L. Lokke and William T. Stafford, ed., *Frontiers of American Culture* (1968): 154–71.

Simpson, Anne Key, "Camille Lucie Nickerson: 'The Louisiana Lady,'" *Louisiana History* 36 (1995): 431–51.

Speisman, Barbara, "From 'Spears' to *The Great Day:* Zora Neale Hurston's Vision of a Real Negro Theatre," *Southern Quarterly* 36 (1998): 34–46.

Van Rijn, Guido, *Roosevelt's Blues: African American Blues and Gospel Songs for FDR* (1997).

22.10.7   Art (Drawing, Painting, Photography, Printmaking, Sculpture)

Albany Institute of History and Art, *The Negro Artist Comes of Age: A National Survey of Contemporary American Artists* (1945).

Arvey, Verna, *In One Lifetime* (1984).

Bearden, Romare, "The Negro Artist and Modern Art," *Opportunity* 12 (1934): 371–72.

Calo, Mary Ann, "African American Art and Critical Discourse between World Wars," *American Quarterly* 51 (1999): 580–621.

Davis, Donald F., "Aaron Douglas of Fisk: Molder of Black Artists," *Journal of Negro History* 69 (1984): 95–99.

——— "Hale Woodruff of Atlanta: Molder of Black Artists," *Journal of Negro History* 69 (1984): 147–54.

Freeman, Roland L., *A Communion of the Spirits: African American Quilters, Preservers, and Their Stories* (1996).

Lewis, Theophilus, "The Frustration of Negro Art," *The Catholic World* 155 (1942): 51–57.

Natanson, Nicholas, *The Black Image in the New Deal: The Politics of FSA Photography* (1992).

Smith, Morgan, and Marvin Smith, *Harlem: The Vision of Morgan and Marvin Smith,* ed. James A. Miller (1998).

Twining, Mary, "Harvesting and Heritage: A Comparison of Afro-American and African Basketry," *Southern Folklore Quarterly* 48 (1978): 159–74.

Willis-Thomas, Deborah, and Jane Lusaka, *Visual Journal: Harlem and D.C. in the Thirties and Forties* (1996).

22.10.8 Film and Broadcasting

Bogle, Donald, *Toms, Coons, Mulattoes, Mammies, and Bucks: An Interpretive History of Blacks in American Films* (3d ed., 1994).

Cripps, Thomas, *Slow Fade to Black: The Negro in American Film, 1900–1942* (1977).

———— "Paul Robeson and Black Identity in American Movies," *Massachusetts Review* 11 (1970): 468–85.

Cripps, Thomas, and David Culbert, "The Negro Soldier, 1944: Film Propaganda in Black and White," *American Quarterly* 31 (1979): 616–40.

Ely, Melvin P., *The Adventures of Amos 'n' Andy: A Social History of an American Phenomenon* (1991).

Jerome, Victor Jeremy, *The Negro in Hollywood Films* (1950).

Koppes, Clayton R., and Gregory D. Black, "Blacks, Loyalty, and Motion Picture Propaganda in World War II," *Journal of American History* 73 (1986): 383–406.

Leab, Daniel J., *From Sambo to Superspade: The Black Experience in Motion Pictures* (1975).

———— "A Pale Black Imitation: All Colored Films, 1930–1960," *Journal of Popular Film* 4 (1975): 55–76.

McManus, John T., and Louis Kronenberger, "Motion Pictures, the Theatre, and Race Relations," *Annals of the American Academy of Political and Social Science* (1946): 152–58.

Noble, Georg, "The Negro in Hollywood," *Sight and Sound* (1939).

Savage, Barbara Dianne, *Broadcasting Freedom: Radio, War, and the Politics of Race, 1938–1948* (1999).

Simpson, Donald, "Black Images in Film: The 1940s to the Early 1960s," *Black Scholar* 21 (1990): 20–29.

Weisenfeld, Judith, "For Rent, 'Cabin in the Sky': Race, Religion, and Representational Quagmires in American Film," *Semeia* (1996): 147–65.

22.11 EDUCATION

Adams, Numa P. G., "Fifth Year Training of Negro Medical Students," *Journal of the National Medical Association* 24 (1932): 25–30.

Atkins, James A., "The Participation of Negroes in Pre-School and Adult Education Programs," *Journal of Negro Education* 7 (1938): 345–56.

Baker, Scott, "Testing Equality: The National Teacher Examination and the NAACP's Legal Campaign to Equalize Teachers' Salaries in the South, 1936–1963," *History of Education Quarterly* 35 (1995): 49–64.

Bond, Horace Mann, *Negro Education in Alabama: A Study in Cotton and Steel* (1939).

Bond, Horace Mann and Julia W. Bond, *The Star Creek Papers,* ed. Adam Fairclough (1997).

Bond, J. Max, "The Educational Program for Negroes in the TVA," *Journal of Negro Education* 6 (1937): 144–51.

Caliver, Ambrose, *A Background Study of Negro College Students* (1933).

———— *Education of Negro Teachers* (1933).

Campbell, Thomas Monroe, *The Movable School Goes to the Negro Farmer* (1936).

Chappell, Eve, "Toward Universal Values: Educational Opportunities in Harlem," *Journal of Adult Education* 7 (1935): 399–404.

Chateauvert, Melinda, "The Third Step: Anna Julia Cooper and Black Education in the District of Columbia, 1910–1960," *Sage* (1988): 7–13.

Clark, Felton Grandison, *The Control of State-Supported Teacher-Training Programs for Negroes* (1934).

———— "Administrative Control of Public Negro Colleges," *Journal of Negro Education* 3 (1934): 245–56.

Davis, William Riley, *The Development and Present Status of Negro Education in East Texas* (1934).

Drew, Charles Richard, "Negro Scholars in Scientific Research," *Journal of Negro History* 35 (1950): 135–49.

Du Bois, William Edward Burghardt, "Does the Negro Need Separate Schools?" *Journal of Negro Education* 4 (1935): 328–35.

Embree, Edwin Rogers, "Our Southern Farm System and the School," *Progressive Education* 12 (1935): 302–08.

Foreman, Clark, *Environmental Factors in Negro Elementary Education* (1932).

Franklin, John Hope, "Courses concerning the Negro in Negro Colleges," *Quarterly Review of Higher Education among Negroes* 8 (1940): 138–44.

Franklin, Vincent P., *The Education of Black Philadelphia: The Social and Educational History of a Minority Community, 1900–1950* (1979).

Gallagher, Buell Gordon, *American Caste and the Negro College* (1938).

Goldsten, Moisse H., and B. C. McLean, "A Hospital That Serves As a Center of Negro Medical Education," *Modern Hospital* 39 (1932): 65–70.

Goodenow, Ronald K., "Paradox in Progressive Educator Reform: The South and the Education of Blacks during the Depression Years," *Phylon* 39 (1978): 49–65.

——— "The Progressive Educator, Race, and Ethnicity in the Depression Years: An Overview," *History of Education Quarterly* 15 (1975): 365–94.

Gore, George William, Jr., *In-Service Professional Improvement of Negro Public School Teachers in Tennessee* (1940).

Grim, Valerie, "History Shared through Memory: The Establishment and Implementation of Education in the Brooks Farm Community, 1920–1957," *Oral History Review* 23 (1996): 1–17.

Halderman, Keith, "Blanche Armwood of Tampa and the Strategy of Interracial Cooperation," *Florida Historical Quarterly* 74 (1996): 287–303.

Homel, Michael Wallace, *Down from Equality: Black Chicagoans and the Public Schools, 1920–1941* (1984).

Hunter, Tera, "The Correct Thing: Charlotte Hawkins Brown and the Palmer Institute," *Southern Exposure* 11 (1983): 37–43.

Jackson, Reid E., "The Development and Character of Permissive and Partly Segregated Schools," *Journal of Negro Education* 16 (1947): 301–10.

Johnson, Charles Spurgeon, *The Negro College Graduate* (1938).

Kelso, Richard, and Debbe Heller, *Building a Dream: Mary Bethune's School* (1996).

Kluger, Richard, *Simple Justice: The History of* Brown v. Board of Education *and Black America's Struggle for Equality* (1976).

Lane, David A., Jr., "The Development of the Present Relationship of the Federal Government to Negro Education," *Journal of Negro Education* 7 (1938): 273–81.

Lang, Kurt, and Gladys Lang, "Resistance to School Desegregation: A Case Study of Backlash among Jews," *Sociological Inquiry* 35 (1965): 94–106.

Lawson, Marjorie McKenzie, "The Adult Educational Aspects of the Negro Press," *Journal of Negro Education* 14 (1945): 431–36.

Long, Hollis Moody, *Public Secondary Education for Negroes in North Carolina* (1932).

MacLean, Malcolm S., and R. O'Hara Lanier, "Negroes, Education, and the War," *Educational Record* 23 (1942): 35–43.

Marable, Manning, "Alain Locke, W.E.B. Du Bois, and the Crisis of Black Education during the Great Depression," in Russell J. Linnemann, ed., *Alain Locke: Reflections on a Modern Renaissance Man* (1982): 63–76.

McKinney, Richard Ishmael, *Religion in Higher Education among Negroes* (1945).

McMillan, Lewis K., "Negro Higher Education As I Have Known It," *Journal of Negro Education* 8 (1939): 9–18.

McNeil, Genna Rae, "Justiciable Cause: Howard University Law School and the Struggle for Civil Rights," *Howard Law Journal* 22 (1979): 283–95.

Miller, Kelly, "The Past, Present, and Future of the Negro College," *Journal of Negro Education* 2 (1933): 411–22.

Newbold, Nathan C., *Five North Carolina Negro Educators* (1939).

Perkins, Linda M., "Lucy Diggs Slowe: Champion of the Self-Determination of African-American Women in Higher Education," *Journal of Negro History* 81 (1996): 89–104.

Pierce, Joseph Alphonso, *Negro Business and Business Education: Their Present and Perspective Development* (1947).

Redcay, Edward Edgeworth, *County Training Schools and Public Secondary Education for Negroes in the South* (1935).

———— comp., *Public Secondary Schools for Negroes in the Southern States of the United States* (1935).

Santow, Mark, "'. . . A Growing and Accumulative Restlessness': Black Schooling in Richmond, Virginia, 1930–1942," *Griot* 16 (1997): 21–32.

Schiffman, Joseph, "The Education of Negro Soldiers in World War II," *Journal of Negro Education* 18 (1949): 22–28.

Smith, Lucius, *The Status of Marking in Negro Colleges* (1935).

Thurmond, Sarah, *A Comparison of the Intelligence and Achievement of Twelve-Year-Old Negro Children in the Rural Schools of Clarke County, Georgia* (1933).

Tillman, Nathaniel P., *The Statewide Public Forum Project: An Experiment in Civic Education among Negroes in Georgia* (1939).

Turner, Thomas W., "Agricultural Education in Negro Land-Grant Colleges," *Southern Workman* 66 (1937): 188–91.

Tushnet, Mark, *The NAACP Legal Strategy against Segregated Education, 1920–1950* (1984).

United States, Office of Education, *National Survey of the Higher Education of Negroes* (1942–1943).

———— *Postwar Education of Negroes: Educational Implications of Army Data and Experiences of Negro Veterans and War Workers* (1945).

Walker, Vanessa Siddle, *Their Highest Potential: An African American School Community in the Segregated South* (1996).

Weaver, Robert Clifton, "The Public Works Administration School Building-Aid Program and Separate Negro Schools," *Journal of Negro Education* 7 (1938): 366–74.

Woodson, Carter Godwin, *The Mis-Education of the Negro* (1933).

Wright, George C., "The Faith Plan: A Black Institution Grows during the Depression," *Filson Club Historical Quarterly* 51 (1977): 336–49.

22.12   WORK AND ENTREPRENEURIAL ACTIVITY

American Management Association, *The Negro Worker: An Analysis of Management Experience and Opinion on the Employment and Integration of the Negro in Industry* (1942).

Anderson, Karen T., "Last Hired, First Fired: Black Women Workers during World War Two," *Journal of American History* 69 (1982): 82–97.

Arnesen, Eric, "Up from Exclusion: Black and White Workers, Race, and the State of Labor History," *Reviews in American History* 26 (1998): 146–74.

Auerbach, Jerold S., "Southern Tenant Farmers: Socialist Critics of the New Deal," *Labor History* (1966): 3–18.

Bailer, Lloyd H., "The Automobile Unions and Negro Labor," *Political Science Quarterly* LIX (1944): 548–77.

Bellamy, Donnie D., "Henry A. Hunt and Black Agricultural Leadership of the New South," *Journal of Negro History* 60 (1975): 475–76.

Blackwelder, Julia Kirk, "Women in the Work-Force: Atlanta, New Orleans, and San Antonio, 1930–1940," *Journal of Urban History* 4 (1978): 331–58.

Brazeal, Brailsford Reese, *The Brotherhood of Sleeping Car Porters: Its Origins and Development* (1946).

Cantor, Louis, *A Prologue to the Protest Movement: The Missouri Sharecropper Roadside Demonstration of 1939* (1969).

Capeci, Dominic J., Jr., "Wartime Fair Employment Practice Committees: The Governor's Committee and the First FEPC in New York City, 1942–1943," *Afro-Americans in New York Life and History* 9 (1985): 45–63.

Cayton, Horace Roscoe, and George S. Mitchell, *Black Workers and the New Unions* (1939).

Chateauvert, Melinda, *Marching Together: Women of the Brotherhood of Sleeping Car Porters* (1998).

Clark-Lewis, Elizabeth, *Living in, Living Out: African American Domestics in Washington, D.C., 1910–1940* (1994).

Cole, Olen, Jr., *The African-American Experience in the Civilian Conservation Corps* (1999).

Congress of Industrial Organizations, Committee to Abolish Racial Discrimination, *Working and Fighting Together Regardless of Race, Creed, Color or National Origin* (1943).

Conrad, David Eugene, *The Forgotten Farmers: The Story of Sharecroppers in the New Deal* (1965).

Daniel, Walter G., and Carroll L. Miller, "The Participation of the Negro in the National Youth Administration Program," *Journal of Negro Education* 7 (1938): 357–65.

Davis, John A., *How Management Can Integrate Negroes in War Industries* (1942).

DeMarco, Joseph P., "The Rationale and Foundation of DuBois' Theory of Economic Cooperation," *Phylon* 35 (1974): 5–15.

Denby, Charles, *Indignant Heart: A Black Worker's Journal* (1978).

Falcone, Nicholas S., *The Negro Integrated* (1945).

Fehn, Bruce, "African-American Women and the Struggle for Equality in the Meatpacking Industry, 1940–1960," *Journal of Women's History* 10 (1998): 45–69.

Franklin, Charles Lionel, *The Negro Labor Unionist of New York: Problems and Conditions among Negroes in the Labor Unions in Manhattan with Special Reference to the N. R. A. and Post-N. R. A. Situations* (1936).

Goddard, Robert, "Agricultural Worker As Archetype in West Indian and African-American Literature," *Agricultural History* 72 (1998): 509–20.

Granger, Lester B., "Negroes and War Production," *Survey Graphic* 3 (1942): 469–71.

Gray, Brenda Clegg, *Black Female Domestics during the Depression in New York City, 1930–1940* (1993).

Green, James, "Fighting on Two Fronts: Working-Class Militancy in the 1940's," *Radical America* 9 (1975): 7–48.

Gregory, Chester W., *Women in Defense Work during World War II: An Analysis of the Labor Problem and Women's Rights* (1974).

Griffler, Keith P., *What Price Alliance? Black Radicals Confront White Labor, 1918–1938* (1995).

Grubbs, Donald H., *Cry from the Cotton: The Southern Tenant Farmers' Union and the New Deal* (1971).

Guzda, Henry P., "Frances Perkins' Interest in a New Deal for Blacks," *Monthly Labor Review* 103 (1980): 31–35.

Hall, Egerton E., *The Negro Wage Earner of New Jersey, A Study of Occupational Trade in New Jersey, of the Effect of Unequal Racial Distribution in the Occupations and of the Implications for Education and Guidance* (1933).

Harris, Abram Lincoln, *The Negro as Capitalist: A Study of Banking and Business among American Negroes* (1936).

Harris, William H., *Keeping the Faith: A. Philip Randolph, Milton P. Webster, and the Brotherhood of Sleeping Car Porters, 1925–1937* (1977).

Hayes, Lawrence John Wesley, *The Negro Federal Government Worker: A Study of His Classification Status in the District of Columbia, 1883–1938* (1941).

Helmbold, Lois Rita, "Beyond the Family Economy: Black and White Working-Class Women during the Great Depression," *Feminist Studies* 13 (1987): 629–55.

———— "Downward Occupational Mobility during the Great Depression: Urban Black and White Working Class Women," *Labor History* 29 (1988): 135–72.

Henderson, Alexa B., "FEPC and the Southern Railway Case: An Investigation into the Discriminatory Practices during World War II," *Journal of Negro History* 61 (1976): 173–87.

Herbst, Alma, *The Negro in the Slaughtering and Meat-Packing Industry in Chicago* (1932).

Hill, Timothy Arnold, *The Negro and Economic Reconstruction* (1937).

Hine, Darlene Clark, *Speak Truth to Power: Black Professional Class in United States History* (1996).

Hinshaw, John, and Judith Modell, "Perceiving Racism: Homestead from Depression to Deindustrialization," *Pennsylvania History* 63 (1996): 17–52.

Hoffsommer, Harold, "The AAA and the Sharecropper," *Social Forces* 13 (1935): 494–502.

Holmes, Michael S., "The Blue Eagle As 'Jim Crow Bird': The NRA and Georgia's Black Workers," *Journal of Negro History* 57 (1972): 276–83.

Honey, Michael, *Black Workers Remember: An Oral History of Segregation, Unionism, and the Freedom Struggle* (1999).

Housing Authority of the City of Newark (N.J.), *Migrant War Workers in Newark: A Report* (1944).

Houston, Charles H., "The Need for Negro Lawyers," *Journal of Negro Education* 4 (1935): 49–52.

Hudson, Hosea, *Black Worker in the Deep South: A Personal Record* (1972).

Johnson, Charles Spurgeon, *The Economic Status of Negroes: Summary and Analysis of the Materials Presented at the Conference on the Economic Status of the Negro Held in Washington, D.C., May 11–13, 1933* (1933).

Johnson, Charles Spurgeon, Edwin R. Embree, and W. W. Alexander, *The Collapse of Cotton Tenancy: Summary of Field Studies and Statistical Surveys, 1933–1935* (1935).

Johnson, Charles Spurgeon, Herman H. Long, and Grace Jones, *The Negro War Worker in San Francisco: A Local Self-Survey* (1944).

Jones, Beverly W., "Race, Sex, and Class: Black Female Tobacco Workers in Durham, North Carolina, 1920–1940, and the Development of Female Consciousness," *Feminist Studies* 10 (1984): 441–51.

Jones, Lu Ann, "In Search of Jennie Booth Moton, Field Agent, AAA," *Agricultural History* 72 (1998): 446–58.

Kelley, Robin D. G., "A New War in Dixie: Communists and the Unemployed in Birmingham, Alabama, 1930–1933," *Labor History* 30 (1989): 367–84.

Kesselman, Louis Coleridge, *The Social Politics of FEPC: A Study in Reform Pressure Movements* (1948).

——— "The Fair Employment Practice Commission Movement in Perspective," *Journal of Negro History* 31 (1946): 30–46.

Kester, Howard, *Revolt among the Sharecroppers* (1936).

Kiser, Clyde, "Diminishing Family Income in Harlem," *Opportunity* 13 (1935): 173–74.

Krislov, Samuel, *The Negro in Federal Employment: The Quest for Equal Opportunity* (1967).

Kruman, Marc W., "Quotas for Blacks: The Public Works Administration and the Black Construction Worker," *Labor History* 16 (1975): 37–51.

Lewis, Earl, and Joe W. Trotter, ed., *African Americans in the Industrial Age: A Documentary History, 1915–1945* (1996).

Lewis, Hylan G., "The Negro Business, Professional, and White Collar Worker," *Journal of Negro Education* 8 (1939): 430–45.

Maloney, Thomas N., "Degrees of Inequality: The Advance of Black Male Workers in the Northern Meat Packing and Steel Industries before World War II," *Social Science History* 19 (1995): 31–62.

Margo, Robert A., "Explaining Black-White Wage Convergence, 1940–1950," *Industrial and Labor Relations Review* 48 (1995): 470–81.

Marshall, F. Ray, *The Negro and Organized Labor* (1965).

Martin, Charles H., "International Labor Defense and Black America," *Labor History* 26 (1985): 165–94.

——— "Southern Labor Relations in Transition: Gadsden, Alabama, 1930–1943," *Journal of Social History* 47 (1981): 545–68.

——— "White Supremacy and Black Workers: Georgia's Black Shirts Combat the Great Depression," *Labor History* 18 (1977): 366–81.

Martin, I. Maximilian, "Accounting As a Field for Colored Men," *Journal of Accountancy* 55 (1933): 112–16.

Maryland. Governor's Commission on Problems Affecting the Negro Population, *Report of the Governor's Commission on Problems Affecting the Negro Population* (1943).

McDowell, Winston, "Race and Ethnicity during the Harlem Jobs Campaign," *Journal of Negro History* 69 (1984): 134–46.

Meier, August, and Elliott M. Rudwick, *Black Detroit and the Rise of the UAW* (1979).

——— "Communist Unions and the Black Community: The Case of the Transport Workers Union, 1934–1944," *Labor History* (1982): 165–97.

Mitchell, George Sinclair, "The Negro in Southern Trade Unionism," *Southern Economic Journal* 2 (1936): 26–33.

Mitchell, Harry Leland, "The Founding and Early History of the Southern Tenant Farmers Union," *Arkansas Historical Quarterly* 32 (1973): 324–69.

Moreno, Paul, "Racial Proportionalism and the Origins of Employment Discrimination Policy, 1933–1950," *Journal of Policy History* 8 (1996): 410–39.

Muraskin, William, "The Harlem Boycott of 1934: Black Nationalism and the Rise of Labor Union Consciousness," *Labor History* 13 (1972): 361–73.

National Urban League, *The Forgotten Tenth: An Analysis of Unemployment among Negroes in the United States and Its Social Costs, 1932–1933* (1933).

National Urban League, Department of Industrial Relations, *Unemployment Status of Negroes: A Compilation of Facts and Figures Respecting Unemployment among Negroes in One Hundred and Six Cities* (1931).

National Urban League, Industrial Relations Laboratory, *Performance of Negro Workers in 300 War Plants* (1944).

Nelson, Bruce, "Organized Labor and the Struggle for Black Equality in Mobile during World War II," *Journal of American History* 80 (1993): 952–88.

Neuchterlein, James A., "The Politics of Civil Rights: The FEPC, 1941–1946," *Prologue* 10 (1978): 171–91.

Norrell, Robert, "Caste in Steel: Jim Crow Careers in Birmingham, Alabama," *Journal of American History* 73 (1986): 669–94.

Northrup, Herbert Roof, *Organized Labor and the Negro* (1944).

———— *Will Negroes Get Jobs Now?* (1945).

———— "Organized Labor and Negro Workers," *Journal of Political Economy* 51 (1943): 206–21.

Oak, Vishnu Vitthal, *The Negro's Adventure in General Business* (1949).

Olson, James S., "Organized Black Leadership and Industrial Unionism: The Racial Response, 1936–1945," *Labor History* 10 (1969): 475–86.

Palmer, Phyllis M., *Domesticity and Dirt: Housewives and Domestic Servants in the United States, 1920–1945* (1989).

Puth, Robert C., "Supreme Life: The History of a Negro Life Insurance Company, 1919–1962," *Business History Review* 43 (1969): 1–20.

Randolph, A. Philip, "The Crisis of Negro Railroad Workers," *American Federationist* 46 (1939): 807–21.

Reed, Bernice Anita, "Accommodation between Negro and White Employees in a West Coast Aircraft Industry, 1942–1944," *Social Forces* 26 (1947): 76–84.

Reed, Merl Elwyn, *Seedtime for the Modern Civil Rights Movement: The President's Committee on Fair Employment Practice, 1941–1946* (1991).

———— "FEPC and the Federal Agencies in the South," *Journal of Negro History* 65 (1980): 43–56.

———— "The FEPC, the Black Worker, and the Southern Shipyards," *South Atlantic Quarterly* 74 (1975): 446–67.

Ryon, Roderick M., "An Ambiguous Legacy: Baltimore Blacks and the CIO, 1936–1941," *Journal of Negro History* 65 (1980): 18–33.

Salmond, John A., "The Civilian Conservation Corps and the Negro," *Journal of American History* 52 (1965): 75–88.

Santino, Jack, *Miles of Smiles, Years of Struggle: Stories of Black Pullman Porters* (1989).

Schacter, Leon B., *The Migrant Worker of New Jersey* (1945).

Schmitzer, Jeanne Cannella, "CCC Camp 510: Black Participation in the Creation of Mammoth Cave National Park," *Register of the Kentucky Historical Society* 93 (1995): 446–64.

Shaw, Nate, *All God's Dangers: The Life of Nate Shaw,* comp. Theodore Rosengarten (1974).

Shaw, Stephanie J., *What a Woman Ought To Be and To Do: Black Professional Women Workers during the Jim Crow Era* (1996).

Smith, Alonzo, and Quintard Taylor, "Racial Discrimination in the Workplace: A Study of Two West Coast Cities during the 1940's," *Journal of Ethnic Studies* 8 (1980): 35–54.

Staupers, Mabel Keaton, *No Time for Prejudice: A Story of the Integration of Negroes in Nursing in the United States* (1961).

Townsend, Willard S., "Full Employment and the Negro Worker," *Journal of Negro Education* 14 (1945): 6–10.

Trend, M. G., and W. L. Lett, "Government Capital and Minority Enterprise: An Evalution of a Depression-Era Social Program," *American Anthropologist* 88 (1986): 595–609.

U.S. Advisor on Negro Affairs, *Occupational Opportunities for Negroes,* by Robert C. Weaver (1937).

United States, Committee on Fair Employment Practice, *FEPC: How It Operates* (1944).

United States Department of Labor, "Cooperative Self-Help among the Unemployed: The Harlem Mutual Exchange," *Monthly Labor Review* 36 (1933): 492–93.

——— "Postwar Trends in Negro Employment," *Monthly Labor Review* 65 (1947): 663–65.

——— "Progress toward Fair Employment Practices," *Monthly Labor Review* 60 (1945): 1003–08.

——— "Training Negroes for War Work," *Monthly Labor Review* 57 (1943): 952–53.

——— "War and Post-War Trends in Employment of Negroes," *Monthly Labor Review* 60 (1945): 1–5.

United States, Office of the Adviser on Negro Affairs, *The Urban Negro Worker in the United States, 1925–1936* (1970).

United States, Special Committee on Farm Tenancy, *Farm Tenancy: Black and White, Two Reports* (1935, 1937).

United States, Women's Bureau, *Negro Women War Workers* (1945).

Walker, Melissa, "Home Extension Work among African American Farm Women in East Tennessee," *Agricultural History* 70 (1996): 487–502.

Weaver, Robert Clifton, *Negro Labor: A National Problem* (1946).

——— "The Employment of Negroes in U.S. War Industries," *International Labor Review* (1944): 141–59.

——— "Negro Labor Since 1929," *Journal of Negro History* 35 (1950): 20–38.

——— "Racial Employment Trends in National Defense," *Phylon* 2 (1941): 337–58.

Weems, Robert E., Jr., *Black Business in the Black Metropolis: The Chicago Metropolitan Assurance Company, 1925–1985* (1996).

Wilson, Joseph F., *Tearing down the Color Bar: A Documentary History and Analysis of the Brotherhood of Sleeping Car Porters* (1989).

Winkler, Allan M., "The Philadelphia Transit Strike of 1944," *Journal of American History* 59 (1972): 73–89.

Wolters, Raymond, *Negroes and the Great Depression: The Problem of Economic Recovery* (1970).

——— "Section 7a and the Black Worker," *Labor History* 10 (1969): 459–74.

Woodson, Carter Godwin, *The Negro Professional Man and the Community: With Special Emphasis on the Physician and the Lawyer* (1934).

Wright, Marian T., "Negro Youth and the Federal Emergency Programs: CCC and NYA," *Journal of Negro Education* 9 (1940): 397–407.

22.13   MEDICINE AND HEALTH

Adams, Numa P. G., "Fifth Year Training of Negro Medical Students," *Journal of the National Medical Association* 24 (1932): 25–30.

——— "Interpretation of Significance of Homer G. Phillips Hospital," *Journal of the National Medical Association* 26 (1934): 13–17.

——— "Sources of Supply of Negro Health Personnel, Section A: Physicians," *Journal of Negro Education* 6 (1937): 468–76.

Bent, Michael J., and Ellen F. Greene, *Rural Negro Health: A Report on a Five-Year Experiment in Health Education in Rural Tennessee* (1937).

Brown, R. Clayton, "Health of Farm Children in the South, 1900–1950," *Agricultural History* 53 (1979): 170–87.

Dixon, Russell A., "Sources of Supply of Negro Health Personnel, Section B: Dentists," *Journal of Negro Education* 6 (1937): 477–82.

——— "Sources of Supply of Negro Health Personnel, Section C: Nurses," *Journal of Negro Education* 6 (1937): 483–92.

Fraser, Gertrude Jacinta, *African American Midwifery in the South: Dialogues of Birth, Race, and Memory* (1998).

Gage, Nina D., and Alma C. Hampt, "Some Observations on Negro Nursing in the South," *Public Health Nursing* 24 (1932): 674–80.

Gamble, Vanessa Northington, ed., *Germs Have No Color Line: Blacks and American Medicine, 1900–1940* (1989).

——— *The Black Community Hospital: Contemporary Dilemmas in Historical Perspective* (1989).

Goldsten, Moisse H., and B. C. McLean, "A Hospital That Serves As a Center of Negro Medical Education," *Modern Hospital* 39 (1932): 65–70.

Gover, Mary, "Negro Mortality: Course of Mortality from Specific Causes, 1920–1944," *Public Health Reports* 63 (1948): 201–13.

Green, H. M., "Our Hospital Problem," *Journal of the National Medical Association* 27 (1936): 72–74.

Hine, Darlene Clark, *Black Women in White: Racial Conflict and Cooperation in the Nursing Profession, 1890–1950* (1989).

Jones, James Howard, *Bad Blood: The Tuskegee Syphilis Experiment* (rev. ed., 1993).

Negro Health Survey, Pittsburgh, *Tuberculosis and the Negro in Pittsburgh* (1934).

Richardson, Joe M., "Albert W. Dent: A Black New Orleans Hospital and University Administrator," *Louisiana History* 37 (1996): 309–23.

Staupers, Mabel Keaton, *No Time for Prejudice: A Story of the Integration of Negroes in Nursing in the United States* (1961).

Wilkie, Laurie A., "Transforming African American Ethnomedical Traditions: A Case Study from West Feliciana," *Louisiana History* 37 (1996): 457–71.

22.14   STUDIES IN FOREIGN LANGUAGES

Alsina Thevenet, Homero, and Hugo R. Alfaro, *El negro en el cine* [Blacks in the Movies] (1951). In Spanish.

Anglero, David Oritz, *El legado de Arturo Alphonso Schomburg* [The Legacy of Arthur Alphonso Schomburg] (1984). In Spanish.

Billard, François, *La vie quotidienne des jazzmen américains jusqu'aux années 50* [The Daily Life of American Jazzmen up to the 1950's] (1980). In French.

Billard, François, and Gilles Tordjman, *Duke Ellington* (1994). In French.

Dalannoy, Luc, *Lester Young, profession: président* [Lester Young, Profession: President] (1987). In French.

Delanoe, Nelcya, *Détroit, marche noir: des Noirs dans une grande ville industrielle des États-Unis* [Detroit, the Black Market: Blacks in a Large Industrial City of the United States] (1974). In French.

Diedrich, Maria, *Kommunismus im Afroamerikanischen Roman: Das Verhältnis Afroamerikanischer Schriftsteller zur Kommunistischen Partei der USA zwischen den Weltkriegen* [Communism in the Afro-American Novel: The Relationship of Afro-American Writers to the American Communist Party between the World Wars] (1979). In German.

Fujinaga, Yasumasa, "Kokujin-Shichô no Henka to Kôminken-Rengo no Kochiku: (1) Dai-Kyôkô to A. Fillipu Randorufu no Tôjô" [The Forging of the Civil Rights Coalition: Part One, the Great Depression and the Rise of A. Philip Randolph], *Area Studies (The University of Tokyo)* 10 (1995): 51–75. In Japanese.

———— "Kokujin-Shichô no Henka to Kôminken-Rengo no Kôchiku: (2) 1943nen no Washinton-Koushin-Undo to Aikoku-shugi" [The Forging of the Civil Rights Coalition: Part Two, the March on Washington Movement of 1943 and the Problems of Patriotism], *Area Studies (The University of Tokyo)* 12 (1997): 1–23. In Japanese.

Hippenmeyer, Jean Roland, *Jazz sur films: ou, 55 années de rapports jazz-cinéma vue à travers plus de 800 films tournés entre 1917 et 1972* [Jazz in Films: Or, Fifty-Five Years of Jazz in Cinema Shown in More Than 800 Films Made between 1917 and 1972] (1973). In French.

———— *Sidney Bechet: ou, l'extraordinaire odyssée d'un musicien de jazz: de Storyville à l'Olympia, de "Wild Cat Blues" aux "Oignons"* [Sidney Bechet: Or, the Extraordinary Odyssey of a Jazz Musician: From Storyville to Olympia, from "Wild Cat Blues" to "Onions"] (1980). In French.

Hosoya, Noriko, "Jinshu Kakuri Seido to Shuken wo meguru Nanbu Hakujin Riberaru kan no Tairitsu: Nanbu Hyuman Werufea Kaigi Seiritsu Katei to 1938nen Taikai no Sai-Kento" [Southern White Liberals' Struggle for Segregation and State's Rights in the SCHW Birmingham], *The American Review* 33 (1999): 151–70. In Japanese.

Leduc, Jean-Marie, and Christine Mulard, *Armstrong* (1994). In French.

Levet, Jean-Paul, *Talkin' that talk: le langage du blues et du jazz* [Talkin' That Talk: The Language of Blues and Jazz] (rev. ed., 1992). In French.

Malson, Lucien, and Christian Bellest, *Le Jazz* [Jazz] (2d ed., 1989). In French.

Martin, Florence, *Bessie Smith* (1994). In French.

Nabe, Marc Eduoard, *L'Âme de Billie Holiday* [The Soul of Billie Holiday] (1986). In French.

Paudras, Francis, *La Danse des infidèles: Bud Powell* [The Unfaithful Ones Are Dancing: Bud Powell] (1986). In French.

Sauvage, Marcel, *Les Mémoires de Joséphine Baker* [The Memoirs of Josephine Baker] (1949). In French.

Sayama, Kazuo, *Kokujin Yakyu no Hîrô Tachi* [Heroes of Black Baseball Players: The Rise and Fall of the Negro League] (1994). In Japanese.

Springer, Robert, *Le Blues authentique: son histoire et ses thèmes* [Genuine Blues: Its History and Themes] (1985). In French.

Tété-Adjalogo, Tetevi G., *Marcus Garvey: père de l'unité africaine, garveyisme et panafricainisme* [Marcus Garvey: The Father of African Unity, Garveyism, and Panafricanism] (2 vol., 1994). In French.

Uesugi, Shinobu, "1935 nen Arabama-shu Raunzu-gun ni okeru Watatsumi Sutoraiki ni tsuite" [The Black Community and the Cotton Pickers' Strike in Lowndes County, Alabama in 1935], *Studies in Western History* 143 (1986): 1–17. In Japanese.

——— "Shéakuroppâzu Yunion no Hakujin Ôganaizâ: Kuraido Jonson no Ningen Keisei" [The Narrative of Clyde Johnson: How He Became an Organizer for the Share Croppers' Union], *Studies in Humanities* 43 (1992): 153–196. In Japanese.

Valtz Mannucci, Loretta, *I negri americani dalla depressione al dopoguerra: Esperienze sociali e documenti letterari* [Negro Americans from the Depression to the Post-War Years: Social Experiences and Literary Documents] (1974). In Italian.

Venturini, Nadia, "East Harlem negli anni Trenta: un quartiere in transizione" [East Harlem in the 1930's: A Neighborhood in Transition], *Rivista di Studi Anglo-Americani [Journal of Anglo-American Studies]* 8 (1990): 47–55. In Italian.

——— *Neri e Italiani a Harlem: gli Anni Trenta e la guerra d'Etiopia* [Blacks and Italians in Harlem: The 1930's and the Ethiopian War] (1990). In Italian.

Zagato, Lauso, *Du Bois e la Black Reconstruction* [Du Bois and Black Reconstruction] (1975). In Italian.

Zammarchi, Fabrice, *Sidney Bechet* (1989). In French.

23   1945–1968

CLAYBORNE CARSON

23.1   GENERAL STUDIES

Bartley, Numan V., *The New South, 1945–1980* (1995).

Blackside, Inc., and Corporation for Public Broadcasting, prod., *Eyes on the Prize: America's Civil Rights Years, 1954 to 1965* (6 videocassettes, 1986–1987).

—— *Eyes on the Prize II: America at the Racial Crossroads, 1965–1985* (8 videocassettes, 1989).

Branch, Taylor, *Parting the Waters: America in the King Years, 1954–1963* (1988).

—— *Pillar of Fire: America in the King Years, 1963–1965* (1998).

Brisbane, Robert H., *Black Activism: Racial Revolution in the United States, 1954–1970* (1974).

—— *The Black Vanguard: Origins of the Negro Social Revolution, 1900–1960* (1970).

Campbell, Mary Schmidt, *Tradition and Conflict: Images of a Turbulent Decade, 1963–1973* (1985).

Cruse, Harold, *Rebellion or Revolution?* (1968).

Dornfeld, Margaret, *The Turning Tide: From the Desegregation of the Armed Forces to the Montgomery Bus Boycott, 1948–1956* (1995).

Egerton, John, *Speak Now against the Day: The Generation before the Civil Rights Movement in the South* (1994).

Harding, Vincent, *The Other American Revolution* (1980).

Kelley, Robin D. G., *Race Rebels: Culture, Politics, and the Black Working Class* (1994).

Lawson, Steven F., *Running for Freedom: Civil Rights and Black Politics in America since 1941* (1991).

Marable, Manning, *Black American Politics: From the Washington Marches to Jesse Jackson* (1985).

—— *Race, Reform, and Rebellion: The Second Reconstruction in Black America, 1945–1982* (1984).

Meier, August, Elliott Rudwick, and Francis L. Broderick, ed., *Black Protest Thought in the Twentieth Century* (1971).

Pinkney, Alphonso, *Black Americans* (4th ed., 1993).

Selby, Earl, and Miriam Selby, *Odyssey: Journey through Black America* (1971).

Sitkoff, Harvard, *The Struggle for Black Equality, 1954–1980* (1981).

Van Deburg, William L., *Black Camelot: African-American Culture Heroes in Their Times, 1960–1980* (1997).

Wilson, William Julius, *The Declining Significance of Race: Blacks and Changing American Institutions* (2d ed., 1980).

23.2   HISTORIOGRAPHY

de Graaf, Lawrence B., "Recognition, Racism, and Reflections on the Writing of Western Black History," *Pacific Historical Review* 44 (1975): 22–51.

Fairclough, Adam, "Historians and the Civil Rights Movement," *Journal of American Studies* 24 (1990): 387–98.

Kuhn, Clifford M., "'There's a Footnote to History!' Memory and the History of Martin Luther King's October 1960 Arrest and Its Aftermath," *Journal of American History* 84 (1997): 583–95.

Lawson, Steven F., "Freedom Then, Freedom Now: The Historiography of the Civil Rights Movement," *American Historical Review* 96 (1991): 456–71.

Meier, August, *A White Scholar and the Black Community, 1945–1965: Essays and Reflections* (1992).

Robinson, Armstead L., and Patricia Sullivan, ed., *New Directions in Civil Rights Studies* (1991).

Sammons, Jeffrey T., "A Proportionate and Measured Response to the Provocation That Is *Darwin's Athletes*," *Journal of Sport History* 24 (1997): 378–88.

Toll, William, "The Genie of 'Race': Problems in Conceptualizing the Treatment of Black Americans," *Journal of Ethnic Studies* 4 (1976): 1–20.

23.3 SECONDARY SOURCES ON NEWSPAPERS AND PERIODICALS

Anderson, James D., "Black Liberalism at the Crossroads: The Role of the *Crisis*, 1934–1953," *Crisis* 87 (1980): 339–46.

Cripps, Thomas, "The Death of Rastus: The Negro in American Films Since 1945," *Phylon* 28 (1967): 267–75.

Humphrey, Ronald, and Howard Schuman, "The Portrayal of Blacks in Magazine Advertisements, 1950–1982," *Public Opinion Quarterly* 48 (1984): 551–63.

Leslie, Michael, "Slow Fade To? Advertising in *Ebony* Magazine, 1957–1989," *Journalism and Mass Communication Quarterly* 72 (1995): 426–35.

Petersen, Keith S., "Anglophone African, Asian, and American Black Newspaper Coverage of the United Nations, 1949–1977," *Polity* 16 (1983): 304–19.

——— "U.S. Black Newspaper Coverage of the United Nations and U.S. White Coverage, 1948–1975," *International Organization* 33 (1979): 525–39.

23.4 RACE RELATIONS

23.4.1 Black/White Relations

Bartley, Numan V., *The New South, 1945–1980: The Story of the South's Modernization* (1995).

Bennett, Lerone, Jr., *Confrontation: Black and White* (1965).

Blauner, Bob, ed., *Black Lives, White Lives: Three Decades of Race Relations in America* (1989).

Bobo, Lawrence, and James R. Kluegel, "Opposition to Race-Targeting: Self-Interest, Stratification Ideology, or Racial Attitudes?" *American Sociological Review* 58 (1993): 443–64.

Boggs, James, *Racism and the Class Struggle: Further Pages from a Black Worker's Notebook* (1970).

Brink, William, and Louis Harris, *Black and White: A Study of U.S. Racial Attitudes Today* (1967).

Chappell, David L., "Religious Ideas of the Segregationists," *Journal of American Studies* 32 (1998): 237–62.

Demerath, Nicholas Jay, III, Gerald Marwell, and Michael T. Aiken, *Dynamics of Idealism: White Activists in a Black Movement* (1971).

Durr, Virginia Foster, *Outside the Magic Circle: The Autobiography of Virginia Foster Durr*, ed. Hollinger F. Barnard (1985).

Dye, Thomas R., *The Politics of Equality* (1971).

Erikson, Erik Hamburger, *In Search of Common Ground: Conversations with Erik H. Erikson and Huey P. Newton* (1973).

Evans, Sara Margaret, *Personal Politics: The Roots of Women's Liberation in the Civil Rights Movement and the New Left* (1979).

Fager, Charles, *White Reflections on Black Power* (1967).

Goering, John M., "Changing Perceptions and Evaluations of Physical Characteristics among Blacks, 1950–1970," *Phylon* 33 (1972): 231–41.

Goldfield, David R., *Black, White, and Southern: Race Relations and Southern Culture, 1940 to the Present* (1990).

Good, Paul, *The Trouble I've Seen: White Journalist/Black Movement* (1975).

Higham, John, ed., *Civil Rights and Social Wrongs: Black-White Relations Since World War II* (1997).

Huey, Gary, *Rebel with a Cause: P.D. East, Southern Liberalism, and the Civil Rights Movement, 1953–1971* (1985).

Jenkins, McKay, *The South in Black and White: Race, Sex, and Literature in the 1940's* (1999).

Kliman, Bernice W., "The Biscuit Eater: Racial Stereotypes, 1939–1972," *Phylon* 39 (1978): 87–96.

Korstad, Robert, and Nelson Lichtenstein, "Opportunities Found and Lost: Labor, Radicals, and the Early Civil Rights Movement," *Journal of American History* 75 (1988): 786–811.

Krause, P. Allen, "Rabbis and Negro Rights in the South, 1954–1967," *American Jewish Archives* 21 (1969): 20–47.

Levy, Burton, "The Racial Bureaucracy, 1941–1971: From Prejudice to Racism to Discrimination," *Journal of Intergroup Relations* 2 (1972): 3–32.

Levy, Charles, *Voluntary Servitude: Whites in the Negro Movement* (1968).

Lyle, Jack, ed., *The Black American and the Press* (1968).

Marx, Gary T., ed., *Racial Conflict: Tension and Change in American Society* (1971).

McGreevy, John T., *Parish Boundaries: The Catholic Encounter with Race in the Twentieth Century Urban North* (1996).

Namorato, Michael V., ed., *Have We Overcome? Race Relations Since Brown* (1979).

Omi, Michael, and Howard Winant, *Racial Formation in the United States from the 1960's to the 1980's* (1986).

Pauly, Thomas H., "Black Images and White Culture during the Decade before the Civil Rights Movement," *American Studies* 31 (1990): 101–19.

Pescosolido, Bernice A., Elizabeth Grauerholz, and Melissa A. Milkie, "Culture and Conflict: The Portrayal of Blacks in U.S. Children's Picture Books through the Mid- and Late-Twentieth Century," *American Sociological Review* 62 (1997): 443–64.

Pettigrew, Thomas F., *Racially Separate or Together?* (1969).

Pinkney, Alphonso, *The Committed: White Activists in the Civil Rights Movement* (1968).

Rothschild, Mary Aickin, *A Case of Black and White: Northern Volunteers and the Southern Freedom Summers, 1964–1965* (1982).

Rowan, Carl T., *Go South to Sorrow* (1957).

Schuman, Howard, Charlotte Steeh, and Lawrence Bobo, *Racial Attitudes in America: Trends and Interpretations* (rev. ed., 1997).

Silberman, Charles E., *Crisis in Black and White* (1964).

Southern, David W., *Gunnar Myrdal and Black-White Relations: The Use and Abuse of An American Dilemma, 1944–1969* (1987).

Thernstrom, Stephan, and Abigail Thernstrom, *America in Black and White: One Nation, Indivisible* (1997).

Toll, William, "The Genie of 'Race': Problems in Conceptualizing the Treatment of Black Americans," *Journal of Ethnic Studies* 4 (1976): 1–20.

Vander Zanden, James Wilfrid, *Race Relations in Transition: The Segregation Crisis in the South* (1965).

Warren, Robert Penn, *Who Speaks for the Negro?* (1965).

23.4.2 Black/Ethnic Relations

Berman, Paul, ed., *Blacks and Jews: Alliances and Arguments* (1994).

Blumberg, Janice Rothschild, *One Voice: Rabbi Jacob M. Rothschild and the Troubled South* (1985).

Cruse, Harold, *Plural but Equal: A Critical Study of Blacks and Minorities and America's Plural Society* (1987).

Dinnerstein, Leonard, "Southern Jewry and the Desegregation Crisis, 1954–1970," *American Jewish Historical Quarterly* 62 (1973): 231–41.

Forman, Seth, *Blacks in the Jewish Mind: A Crisis of Liberalism* (1998).

Harris, Louis, and Bert E. Swanson, *Black-Jewish Relations in New York City* (1970).

Kaufman, Jonathan, "Blacks and Jews: An Historical Perspective," *Tikkun* 3 (1988): 42–44, 92–94.

Mencarelli, James, and Steve Severin, *Protest3: Red, Black, Brown Experience in America* (1975).

Pillai, Vijay, ed., *Indian Leaders on Martin Luther King, Jr.* (1968).

Polos, Nicholas C., "Black Anti-Semitism in Twentieth-Century America: Historical Myth or Reality?" *American Jewish Archives* 17 (1975): 8–31.

Salzman, Jack, and Cornel West, ed., *Struggles in the Promised Land: Toward a History of Black-Jewish Relations in the United States* (1997).

23.4.3 Segregation/Jim Crow

Akalou, W. M., and Cary D. Wintz, "The Economic Impact of Residential Desegregation on Historically Black Neighborhoods in Houston, 1950–1990," *Essays in Economic and Business History* 13 (1995): 289–304.

Barrett, Kayla, and Barbara A. Bishop, "Integration and the Alabama Library Association: Not So Black and White," *Libraries and Culture* 33 (1998): 141–61.

Black, Earl, *Southern Governors and Civil Rights: Racial Segregation As a Campaign Issue in the Second Reconstruction* (1976).

Carter, Alice E., "Segregation and Integration in the Appalachian Coalfields: McDowell County Responds to the *Brown* Decision," *West Virginia History* 54 (1995): 78–104.

Darden, Joe T., "Black Residential Segregation Since the 1948 *Shelley v. Kraemer* Decision," *Journal of Black Studies* 25 (1995): 680–91.

Fontaine, William T., *Reflections on Segregation, Desegregation, Power, and Morals* (1967).

Lassiter, Matthew D., and Andrew B. Lewis, ed., *The Moderates' Dilemma: Massive Resistance to School Desegregation in Virginia* (1998).

McGrew, Teron, "The History of Residential Segregation in the United States and Title VIII," *Black Scholar* 27 (1997): 22–30.

McMillen, Neil R., *The Citizens' Council: Organized Resistance to the Second Reconstruction, 1954–1964* (1971).

Newby, I. A., *Challenge to the Court: Social Scientists and the Defense of Segregation, 1954–1966* (rev. ed., 1969).

Orfield, Gary, "Federal Policy, Local Power, and Metropolitan Segregation," *Political Science Quarterly* 89 (1974, 1975): 777–802.

Van Valey, Thomas L., Wade Clark Roof, and Jerome E. Wilcox, "Trends in Residential Segregation, 1960–1970," *American Journal of Sociology* 82 (1977): 826–44.

Vander Zanden, James Wilfrid, *Race Relations in Transition: The Segregation Crisis in the South* (1965).

23.4.4 Violence and Racial Disturbances

Beeler, Dorothy, "Race Riot in Columbia, Tennessee: February 25–27, 1946," *Tennessee Historical Quarterly* 39 (1980): 49–61.

Belknap, Michal R., *Federal Law and Southern Order: Racial Violence and Constitutional Conflict in the Post-Brown South* (1987).

Boesel, David, and Peter Rossi, ed., *Cities under Siege: An Anatomy of the Ghetto Riots, 1964–1968* (1971).

Breitman, George, Herman Porter, and Baxter Smith, *The Assassination of Malcolm X* (1976).

Button, James W., *Black Violence: Political Impact of the 1960's Riots* (1978).

Carter, Gregg Lee, "The 1960's Black Riots Revisited: City Level Explanations of Their Severity," *Sociological Inquiry* 56 (1986): 210–28.

——— "Black Attitudes and the 1960's Black Riots: An Aggregate-Level Analysis of the Kerner Commission's '15 Cities' Data," *Sociological Quarterly* 31 (1990): 269–86.

——— "In the Narrows of the 1960's U.S. Black Rioting," *Journal of Conflict Resolution* 30 (1986): 115–27.

Conot, Robert, *Rivers of Blood, Years of Darkness: The Unforgettable Classic Account of the Watts Riots* (1967).

Dibble, Ursula, "Socially Shared Deprivation and the Approval of Violence: Another Look at the Experience of American Blacks during the 1960's," *Ethnicity* 8 (1981): 149–68.

Fine, Sidney, *Violence in the Model City: The Cavanagh Administration, Race Relations, and the Detroit Riot of 1967* (1989).

Friedly, Michael, *Malcolm X: The Assassination* (1995).

Garrow, David, ed., *St. Augustine, Florida, 1963–1964: Mass Protest and Racial Violence* (1989).

Hersey, John R., *The Algiers Motel Incident* (1968).

Hirsch, Arnold Richard, "Massive Resistance in the Urban North: Trumbull Park, Chicago, 1953–1966," *Journal of American History* 82 (1995): 522–50.

Horne, Gerald, *Fire This Time: The Watts Uprising and the 1960's* (1995).

Hudson-Weems, Clenora, "Resurrecting Emmett Till: The Catalyst of the Modern Civil Rights Movement," *Journal of Black Studies* 29 (1998): 179–88.

Huie, William Bradford, *Three Lives for Mississippi* (1965).

Karenga, Maulana Ron, *The Roots of the US-Panther Conflict: The Perverse and Deadly Games Police Play* (1976).

Liberatore, Paul, *The Road to Hell: The True Story of George Jackson, Stephen Bingham, and the San Quentin Massacre* (1996).

Melanson, Philip H., *The Martin Luther King Assassination: New Revelations on the Conspiracy and Cover-Up, 1968–1991* (1991).

Model, Paul, "The 1965 Watts Rebellion: The Self-Definition of a Community," *Radical America* 24 (1990): 74–88.

Nelson, Jack, and Jack Bass, *The Orangeburg Massacre* (1970).

Newton, Michael, *A Case of Conspiracy* (1980).

Nossiter, Adam, *Of Long Memory: Mississippi and the Murder of Medgar Evers* (1994).

O'Brien, Gail Williams, *The Color of the Law: Race, Violence, and Justice in the Post-World War II South* (1999).

Olzak, Susan, Suzanne Shanahan, and Elizabeth H. McEneaney, "Poverty, Segregation, and Race Riots, 1960 to 1993," *American Sociological Review* 61 (1996): 590–613.

O'Reilly, Kenneth, "The FBI and the Politics of the Riots, 1964–1968," *Journal of American History* 75 (1988): 91–114.

Pepper, William, *Orders to Kill: The Truth behind the Murder of Martin Luther King, Jr.* (1991).

Posner, Gerald L., *Killing the Dream: James Earl Ray and the Assassination of Martin Luther King, Jr.* (1998).

Rhodes, Joel P., "It Finally Happened Here: The 1968 Riot in Kansas City, Missouri," *Missouri Historical Review* 91 (1997): 295–315.

Sikora, Frank, *Until Justice Rolls Down: The Birmingham Church Bombing Case* (1991).

Skolnick, Jerome H., *The Politics of Protest* (1969).

Smead, Howard, *Blood Justice: The Lynching of Mack Charles Parker* (1986).

Sugrue, Thomas J., "Introduction: John Hersey and the Tragedy of Race," in John Hersey, *The Algiers Motel Incident* (1968): 9–20.

United States, Kerner Commission, *The Kerner Report: The 1968 Report of the National Advisory Commission on Civil Disorders* (1988).

Waskow, Arthur, *From Race Riot to Sit-in, 1919 and the 1960's: A Study in the Connections between Conflict and Violence* (1966).

Weisberg, Harold, *Frame-Up: The Martin Luther King/James Earl Ray Case, Containing Suppressed Evidence* (1971).

Whitfield, Stephen J., *A Death in the Delta: The Story of Emmett Till* (1988).

Williams, Lee E., II, "Alabama Moderation: The Athens Riot of 1946," *Griot* 16 (1997): 19–23.

23.4.5 Civil Rights

Aba-Mecha, Barbara W., "South Carolina Conference of NAACP: Origin and Major Accomplishments, 1939–1954," *Proceedings of the South Carolina Historical Association* (1981): 1–21.

Allen, Zita, *Black Women Leaders of the Civil Rights Movement* (1996).

American Academy of Political and Social Science, *The Negro Protest*, ed. Arnold M. Rose (1965).

Anderson, Alan B., and George W. Pickering, *Confronting the Color Line: The Broken Promise of the Civil Rights Movement in Chicago* (1987).

Anderson, Jervis, *Bayard Rustin: Troubles I've Seen* (1997).

Andrews, Kenneth T., "The Impacts of Social Movements on the Political Process: The Civil Rights Movement and Black Electoral Politics in Mississippi," *American Sociological Review* 62 (1997): 800–19.

Assensoh, Akwasi Bretuo, *Rev. Dr. Martin Luther King, Jr., and America's Quest for Racial Integration* (1987).

Baldwin, Frederick C., *"We Ain't What We Used to Be": Photographs* (1983).

Barlow, Andrew, "The Student Movement of the 1960's and the Politics of Race," *Journal of Ethnic Studies* 19 (1991): 1–22.

Barnes, Catherine A., *Journey from Jim Crow: The Desegregation of Southern Transit* (1983).

Barnett, Bernice McNair, *Sisters in Struggle: Invisible Black Women in the Civil Rights Movement, 1945–1970* (1997).

Beardslee, William R., *The Way Out Must Lead In: Life Histories in the Civil Rights Movement* (1977).

Beckles, Colin, "Black Bookstores, Black Power, and the F.B.I.: The Case of Drum and Spear," *Western Journal of Black Studies* 20 (1996): 63–71.

Beifuss, Joan Turner, *At the River I Stand: Memphis, the 1968 Strike, and Martin Luther King* (1985).

Belfrage, Sally, *Freedom Summer* (1965).

Bell, Inge P., *CORE and the Strategy of Nonviolence* (1968).

Berry, Jason, *Amazing Grace: With Charles Evers in Mississippi* (1973).

Blackside, Inc., and Corporation for Public Broadcasting, prod., *Eyes on the Prize: America's Civil Rights Years, 1954 to 1965* (6 videocassettes, 1986–1987).

——— *Eyes on the Prize II: America at the Racial Crossroads, 1965–1985* (8 videocassettes, 1989).

Blackstock, Nelson, and Cathy Perkus, ed., *COINTELPRO: The FBI's Secret War on Political Freedom* (1975).

Bloom, Jack M., *Class, Race, and the Civil Rights Movement* (1987).

Blumberg, Rhoda Lois, *Civil Rights: The 1960's Freedom Struggle* (1984).

Bracey, John H., Jr., August Meier, and Elliott Rudwick, ed., *Conflict and Competition: Studies in the Recent Black Protest Movement* (1971).

Branch, Taylor, *Parting the Waters: America in the King Years, 1954–1963* (1988).

——— *Pillar of Fire: America in the King Years, 1963–1965* (1998).

Brink, William, and Louis Harris, *Negro Revolution in America: What Negroes Want, Why and How They Are Fighting, Whom They Support, What Whites Think of Them and Their Demands* (1964).

Brooks, Thomas R., *Walls Come Tumbling Down: A History of the Civil Rights Movement, 1940–1970* (1974).

Brown, Cynthia, ed., *Ready from Within: Septima Clark and the Civil Rights Movement* (1986).

Burner, Eric R., *And Gently He Shall Lead Them: Robert Parris Moses and Civil Rights in Mississippi* (1996).

Burns, Stewart, ed., *Daybreak of Freedom: The Montgomery Bus Boycott* (1997).

Burns, W. Haywood, *The Voices of Negro Protest in America* (1963).

Buttlar, Lois, "Media Coverage of the Black Americans' Struggle for Civil Rights," *Ethnic Forum* 8 (1988): 81–87.

Button, James W., *Blacks and Social Change: Impact of the Civil Rights Movement in Southern Communities* (1989).

Campbell, Clarice T., *Civil Rights Chronicle: Letters from the South* (1997).

Caplan, Marvin, *Farther Along: A Civil Rights Memoir* (1999).

Carson, Clayborne, *In Struggle: SNCC and the Black Awakening of the 1960's* (1981).

———, ed., *The Movement, 1964–1970* (1993).

——— *Malcolm X: The FBI File*, ed. David Gallen (1991).

———, ed., *The Papers of Martin Luther King, Jr.* (4 vols., 1992–).

———, ed., *The Student Voice, 1960–1965: Periodical of the Student Nonviolent Coordinating Committee* (1990).

Carson, Clayborne, David J. Garrow, Vincent Harding, and Darlene Clark Hine, ed., *The "Eyes on the Prize" Civil Rights Reader: Documents, Speeches, and Firsthand Accounts from the Black Freedom Struggle, 1954–1990* (rev. ed., 1991).

Chafe, William H., *Civilities and Civil Rights: Greensboro, North Carolina, and the Black Struggle for Freedom* (1980).

Clark, Septima, and Cynthia Stokes Brown, ed., *Ready from Within: Septima Clark and the Civil Rights Movement* (1990).

Cluster, Dick, ed., *They Should Have Served That Cup of Coffee* (1979).

Cobb, James C., "'Somebody Done Nailed Us on the Cross': Federal Farm and Welfare Policy and the Civil Rights Movement in the Mississippi Delta," *Journal of American History* 77 (1990): 912–36.

Counts, Will, *A Life Is More Than a Moment: The Desegregation of Little Rock's Central High* (1999).

Couto, Richard A., *Ain't Gonna Let Nobody Turn Me Round: The Pursuit of Racial Justice in the Rural South* (1991).

Crawford, Vicki L., Jacqueline Anne Rouse, and Barbara Woods, ed., *Women in the Civil Rights Movement: Trailblazers and Torchbearers, 1941–1965* (1990).

Davis, Townsend, *Weary Feet, Rested Souls: A Guided History of the Civil Rights Movement* (1998).

Dent, Tom, *Southern Journey: A Return to the Civil Rights Movement* (1997).

Dittmer, John, *Local People: The Struggle for Civil Rights in Mississippi* (1994).

Dittmer, John, George C. Wright, and W. Marvin Dulaney, *Essays on the American Civil Rights Movement*, ed. W. Marvin Dulaney and Kathleen Underwood (1993).

Dorman, Michael, *We Shall Overcome* (1964).

Dulles, Foster Rhea, *The Civil Rights Commission, 1957–1965* (1968).

Durham, Michael S., *Powerful Days: The Civil Rights Photography of Charles Moore* (1991).

Eagles, Charles W., ed., *The Civil Rights Movement in America: Essays* (1986).

—— *Outside Agitator: Jon Daniels and the Civil Rights Movement in Alabama* (1993).

Edwards, William A., "The Selma Strategy," *Journal of Ethnic Studies* 9 (1981): 111–17.

Egerton, John, *Speak Now against the Day: The Generation before the Civil Rights Movement in the South* (1994).

Ehle, John, *The Free Men* (1965).

Eskew, Glenn T., "'Bombingham': Black Protest in Postwar Birmingham, Alabama," *Historian* 59 (1997): 371–90.

—— *But for Birmingham: The Local and National Movements in the Civil Rights Struggle* (1997).

Evans, Sara Margaret, *Personal Politics: The Roots of Women's Liberation in the Civil Rights Movement and the New Left* (1979).

Evers, Charles and Andrew Szanton, *Have No Fear: The Charles Evers Story* (1997).

Evers, Myrlie B., and Fred Beauford (interviewer), "Interview: Myrlie B. Evers," *Crisis* (1988): 28–36.

Evers, Myrlie B., and William Peters, *For Us, the Living* (1967).

Fager, Charles, *Selma, 1965: The March That Changed the South* (2d ed., 1985).

—— *Uncertain Resurrection: The Poor People's Washington Campaign* (1969).

Fairclough, Adam, *Race and Democracy: The Civil Rights Struggle in Louisiana, 1915–1972* (1995).

—— *To Redeem the Soul of America: The Southern Christian Leadership Conference and Martin Luther King, Jr.* (1987).

Farmer, James, *Freedom—When?* (1966).

—— *Lay Bare the Heart: An Autobiography of the Civil Rights Movement* (1985).

Fax, Elton C., *Contemporary Black Leaders* (1970).

Fendrich, James N., *Ideal Citizens: The Legacy of the Civil Rights Movement* (1993).

—— "Keeping the Faith or Pursuing the Good Life: A Study of the Consequences of Participation in the Civil Rights Movement," *American Sociological Review* 42 (1977): 144–57.

Fields, Uriah J., *The Montgomery Story: The Unhappy Effects of the Montgomery Bus Boycott* (1959).

Findlay, James F., *Church People in the Struggle: The National Council of Churches and the Black Freedom Movement, 1950–1970* (1993).

Fleming, Cynthia Griggs, *Soon We Will Not Cry: The Liberation of Ruby Doris Smith Robinson* (1998).

—— "Black Women Activists and the Student Nonviolent Coordinating Committee: The Case of Ruby Doris Smith Robinson," *Journal of Women's History* 4 (1993): 64–82.

——— "White Lunch Counters and Black Consciousness: The Story of the Knoxville Sit-Ins," *Tennessee Historical Quarterly* 49 (1990): 40–52.

Foeman, Anita K., "Gloria Richardson: Breaking the Mold," *Journal of Black Studies* 26 (1996): 604–15.

Forman, James, *The Making of Black Revolutionaries* (1972).

Friedland, Michael B., *Lift up Your Voice Like a Trumpet: White Clergy and the Civil Rights and Antiwar War Movements, 1954–1973* (1998).

Gardner, Tom, and Cynthia Stokes Brown, "The Montgomery Bus Boycott: Interviews with Rosa Parks, E. D. Nixon, Johnny Carr, and Virginia Durr," *Southern Exposure* 9 (1981): 12–21.

Garofolo, Reebe, "The Impact of the Civil Rights Movement on Popular Music," *Radical America* 21 (1987): 14–22.

Garrow, David, *Atlanta, Georgia, 1960–1961: Sit-ins and Student Activism* (1989).

——— *Bearing the Cross: Martin Luther King, Jr., and the Southern Christian Leadership Conference* (1986).

———, ed., *Birmingham, Alabama, 1956–1963: The Black Struggle for Civil Rights* (1989).

———, ed., *Chicago, 1966: Open Housing Marches, Summit Negotiations, and Operation Breadbasket* (1989).

——— *The FBI and Martin Luther King, Jr.: From "Solo" to Memphis* (1981).

———, ed., *"Martin Luther King, Jr.: Civil Rights Leader, Theologian, Orator,"* Vol. 3 of *Martin Luther King, Jr. and the Civil Rights Movement* (1989).

——— *Protest at Selma: Martin Luther King, Jr., and the Voting Rights Act of 1965* (1978).

———, ed., *The Walking City: The Montgomery Bus Boycott, 1955–1956* (1989).

———, ed., *We Shall Overcome: The Civil Rights Movement in the United States in the 1950's and 1960's* (1989).

Gentile, Thomas, *March on Washington: August 28, 1963* (1983).

Geschwender, Barbara N., and James A. Geschwender, "Relative Deprivation and Participation in the Civil Rights Movement," *Social Science Quarterly* 54 (1973): 403–11.

Glen, John M., *Highlander: No Ordinary School, 1932–1962* (1988).

Godwin, John L., "Taming a Whirlwind: Black Civil Rights Leadership in the Community Setting, Wilmington, North Carolina, 1950–1972," *Proceedings of the South Carolina Historical Association* (1992): 67–75.

Greenberg, Cheryl Lynn, ed., *A Circle of Trust: Remembering SNCC* (1998).

Gregg, Richard Bartlett, *The Power of Nonviolence* (1959).

Gyant, LaVerne, "Passing the Torch: African American Women in the Civil Rights Movement," *Journal of Black Studies* 26 (1996): 629–47.

Haines, Herbert H., *Black Radicals and the Civil Rights Mainstream, 1954–1970* (1988).

Halberstam, David, *The Children* (1998).

Halpern, Martin, "'I'm Fighting for Freedom': Coleman Young, HUAC, and the Detroit African American Community," *Journal of American Ethnic History* 17 (1997): 19–38.

Hamblin, Robert W., "The 1965 Southern Literary Festival: A Microcosm of the Civil Rights Movement," *Journal of Mississippi History* 53 (1991): 83–114.

Hamilton, Dona Cooper, and Charles V. Hamilton, *The Dual Agenda: Race and Social Welfare Policies of Civil Rights Organizations* (1997).

Hampton, Henry, and Steve Fayer, with Sarah Flynn, *Voices of Freedom: An Oral History of the Civil Rights Movement from the 1950s through the 1980s* (1990).

Hanigan, James P., *Martin Luther King, Jr., and the Foundations of Nonviolence* (1984).

Hansberry, Lorraine, *The Movement: Documentary of a Struggle for Equality* (1964).

Harding, Vincent, *Hope and History: Why We Must Share the Story of the Movement* (1990).

Hare, A. Paul, and Herbert H. Blumberg, *Nonviolent Direct Action: American Cases, Social-Psychological Analyses* (1968).

Harmon, David Andrew, *Beneath the Image of the Civil Rights Movement and Race Relations: Atlanta, Georgia, 1946–1981* (1996).

Heacock, Roland T., *Understanding the Negro Protest* (1965).

Hentoff, Nat, *The New Equality* (1964).

Hine, William C., "Civil Rights and Campus Wrongs: South Carolina State College Students Protest, 1955–1968," *South Carolina Historical Magazine* 97 (1996): 310–40.

Hoffman, Ronald, and Peter J. Albert, ed., *We Shall Overcome: Martin Luther King, Jr., and the Black Freedom Struggle* (1990).

Holt, Len, *The Summer That Didn't End* (1965).

Hughes, C. Alvin, "A New Agenda for the South: The Role and Influence of the Highlander Folk School, 1953–1961," *Phylon* 46 (1985): 242–50.

Huie, William Bradford, *Three Lives for Mississippi* (1965).

Jackson, Jesse, *Straight from the Heart,* ed. Roger D. Hatch and Frank E. Watkins (1986).

Jacoway, Elizabeth, and David R. Colburn, ed., *Southern Businessmen and Desegregation* (1982).

Janken, Kenneth R., "From Colonial Liberation to Cold War Liberalism: Walter White, the NAACP, and Foreign Affairs, 1941–1955," *Ethnic and Racial Studies* 21 (1998): 1074–95.

Johnston, Erle, *Mississippi's Defiant Years, 1953–1973: An Interpretive Documentary with Personal Experiences* (1990).

Jones, Beverly W., "Before Montgomery and Greensboro: The Desegregation Movement in the District of Columbia, 1950–1953," *Phylon* 43 (1982): 144–54.

Kasher, Steven, *The Civil Rights Movement: A Photographic History, 1954–1968* (1996).

Katz, Milton S., and Susan B. Tucker, "A Pioneer in Civil Rights: Esther Brown and the South Park Desegregation Case of 1948," *Kansas History* 18 (1995–96): 234–47.

King, Martin Luther, Jr., *The Measure of a Man* (1968).

———— *Strength to Love* (1963).

———— *Stride toward Freedom: The Montgomery Story* (1958).

———— *A Testament of Hope: The Essential Writings of Martin Luther King, Jr.,* ed. James M. Washington (1986).

———— *The Trumpet of Conscience* (1968).

———— *Where Do We Go from Here: Chaos or Community?* (1967).

———— *Why We Can't Wait* (1964).

King, Richard H., *Civil Rights and the Idea of Freedom* (1996).

Kirk, John A., "The Little Rock Crisis and Postwar Black Activism in Arkansas," *Arkansas Historical Quarterly* 56 (1997): 273–93.

Kohn, Howard, *We Had a Dream: A Tale of the Struggle for Integration in America* (1998).

Korstad, Robert, and Nelson Lichtenstein, "Opportunities Found and Lost: Labor, Radicals, and the Early Civil Rights Movement," *Journal of American History* 75 (1988): 786–811.

Kotz, Nick, and Mary Lynn Kotz, *A Passion for Equality: George Wiley and the Movement* (1977).

Laue, James H., *Direct Action and Desegregation, 1960–1962: Toward a Theory of the Rationalization of Protest* (1989).

Lawson, Steven F., *Running for Freedom: Civil Rights and Black Politics in America since 1941* (1991).

Lawson, Steven F., and Charles Payne, *Debating the Civil Rights Movement, 1945–1968* (1998).

Lee, Chana Kai, *For Freedom's Sake: The Life of Fannie Lou Hamer* (1999).

Leigh, Wilhelmina A., "The Social Preference for Fair Housing: During the Civil Rights Movement and Since," *American Economic Review* 78 (1988): 156–62.

Levy, Peter B., ed., *Let Freedom Ring: A Documentary History of the Modern Civil Rights Movement* (1992).

Lewis, John, with Michael D'Orso, *Walking with the Wind: A Memoir of the Movement* (1998).

Lincoln, C. Eric, *Sounds of the Struggle: Persons and Perspectives in Civil Rights* (1967).

Lipsitz, George, *A Life in the Struggle: Ivory Perry and the Culture of Opposition* (1988).

Locke, Mamie E., "The Role of African-American Women in the Civil Rights and Women's Movements in Hinds County and Sunflower County, Mississippi," *Journal of Mississippi History* 53 (1991): 229–39.

Lomax, Louis E., *The Negro Revolt* (1962).

Longenecker, Stephen L., *Selma's Peacemaker: Ralph Smeltzer and Civil Rights Mediation* (1987).

Louis, Debbie, *And We Are Not Saved: A History of the Movement As People* (1970).

Luker, Ralph E., *Historical Dictionary of the Civil Rights Movement* (1997).

Lyon, Danny, *Memories of the Southern Civil Rights Movement* (1992).

Manis, Andrew M., *A Fire You Can't Put Out: The Civil Rights Life of Birmingham's Reverend Fred Shuttlesworth* (1999).

McAdam, Doug, *Freedom Summer* (1988).

McCord, William, *Mississippi: The Long Hot Summer* (1965).

McCrone, Donald J., and Richard J. Hardy, "Civil Rights Policies and the Achievement of Racial Economic Equality, 1948–1975," *American Journal of Political Science* 22 (1978): 1–17.

McKnight, Gerald D., *The Last Crusade: Martin Luther King, Jr., the FBI, and the Poor People's Campaign* (1998).

Meier, August, and John H. Bracey, Jr., "The NAACP As a Reform Movement, 1909–1965: 'To Reach the Conscience of America,'" *Journal of Southern History* 59 (1993): 3–30.

Meier, August, and Elliott Rudwick, *CORE: A Study in the Civil Rights Movement, 1942–1968* (1973).

Melcher, Mary, "Black and Whites Together: Interracial Leadership in the Phoenix Civil Rights Movement," *Journal of Arizona History* 32 (1991): 195–216.

Meredith, James, *Three Years in Mississippi* (1966).

Miller, Char, "The Mississippi Summer Project Remembered: The Stephen Mitchell Bingham Letter," *Journal of Mississippi History* 47 (1985): 284–307.

Millner, Stephen Michael, *The Montgomery Bus Boycott: Case Study in the Emergence and Career of a Social Movement* (1981).

Mills, Nicolaus, *Like a Holy Crusade: Mississippi, 1964—The Turning of the Civil Rights Movement in America* (1992).

Mitchell, Glenford E., and William H. Peace, III, ed., *The Angry Black South* (1962).

Moody, Anne, *Coming of Age in Mississippi* (1968).

Morris, Aldon, "Black Southern Student Sit-in Movement: An Analysis of Internal Organization," *American Sociological Review* 46 (1981): 744–67.

———— *The Origins of the Civil Rights Movement: Black Communities Organizing for Change* (1984).

Moses, Greg, *Revolution of Conscience: Martin Luther King, Jr. and the Philosophy of Nonviolence* (1997).

Mott, Wesley T., "The Rhetoric of Martin Luther King, Jr.: *Letter from Birmingham Jail*," *Phylon* 36 (1975): 411–21.

Muse, Benjamin, *The American Negro Revolution: From Nonviolence to Black Power, 1963–1967* (1968).

Newby, Robert G., "Segregation, Desegregation, and Racial Balance: Status Implications of These Concepts," *Urban Review* 14 (1982): 17–24.

Nordhaus, R. Edward, "S.N.C.C. and the Civil Rights Movement in Mississippi, 1963–1964: A Time of Change," *History Teacher* 17 (1983): 95–102.

Norrell, Robert J., *Reaping the Whirlwind: The Civil Rights Movement in Tuskegee* (rev. ed., 1998).

Oldendorf, Sandra Brenneman, *Highlander Folk School and the South Carolina Sea Island Citizenship School* (1987).

Oppenheimer, Martin, *The Sit-in Movement of 1960* (1989).

O'Reilly, Kenneth, *Racial Matters: The FBI's Secret File on Black America, 1960–1972* (1989).

Parks, Rosa, *The Autobiography of Rosa Parks As Told to James Haskins* (1990).

Payne, Charles, *I've Got the Light of Freedom: The Organizing Tradition and the Mississippi Freedom Struggle* (1995).

Peake, Thomas R., *Keeping the Dream Alive: A History of the Southern Christian Leadership Conference from King to the Nineteen-Eighties* (1987).

Pinkney, Alphonso, *The Committed: White Activists in the Civil Rights Movement* (1968).

Powledge, Fred, *Free at Last? The Civil Rights Movement and the People Who Made It* (1991).

Proudfoot, Merrill, *Diary of a Sit-In* (1962).

Rabby, Glenda Alice, *The Pain and the Promise: The Struggle for Civil Rights in Tallahassee, Florida* (1999).

Raines, Howell, *My Soul Is Rested: Movement Days in the Deep South Remembered* (1977).

Ramachandran, G., and T. K. Mahadevan, ed., *Nonviolence after Gandhi: A Study of Martin Luther King, Jr.* (1968).

Reed, Christopher Robert, *The Chicago NAACP and the Rise of Black Professional Leadership, 1910–1966* (1997).

Robinson, Armstead L., and Patricia Sullivan, ed., *New Directions in Civil Rights Studies* (1991).

Robinson, Jo Ann Gibson, *The Montgomery Bus Boycott and the Women Who Started It: The Memoir of Jo Ann Gibson Robinson*, ed. David Garrow (1987).

Robnett, Belinda, *How Long? How Long? African American Women in the Struggle for Civil Rights* (1997).

Rogers, Kim Lacy, "'You Came Away with Some Courage': Three Lives in the Civil Rights Movement," *Mid-America* 71 (1989): 175–94.

Rollins, Judith, *All Is Never Said: The Narrative of Odette Harper Hines* (1995).

Rosenthal, Joel, "Southern Black Student Activism: Assimilation *vs.* Nationalism," *Journal of Negro Education* 44 (1975): 113–29.

Rothschild, Mary Aickin, *A Case of Black and White: Northern Volunteers and the Southern Freedom Summers, 1964–1965* (1982).

——— "The Volunteers and the Freedom Schools: Education for Social Change in Mississippi," *History of Education Quarterly* 22 (1982): 401–20.

Rudwick, Elliott, and August Meier, "Organizational Structure and Goal Succession: A Comparative Analysis of the NAACP and CORE, 1964–1968," *Social Science Quarterly* 51 (1970): 9–24.

Salter, John R., Jr., *Jackson, Mississippi: An American Chronicle of Struggle and Schism* (1987).

Sandage, Scott A., "A Marble House Divided: The Lincoln Memorial, the Civil Rights Movement, and the Politics of Memory, 1939–1963," *Journal of American History* 80 (1993): 135–67.

Schulke, Flip, and Penelope Ortner McPhee, *King Remembered* (1986).

Sellers, Cleveland, with Robert Terrell, *The River of No Return: The Autobiography of a Black Militant and the Life and Death of SNCC* (1978).

Shapiro, Herbert, "The Vietnam War and the American Civil Rights Movement," *Journal of Ethnic Studies* 16 (1989): 117–41.

Sinsheimer, Joseph A., "The Freedom Vote of 1963: New Strategies of Racial Protest in Mississippi," *Journal of Southern History* 55 (1989): 217–44.

Smith, Charles, and Lewis Killian, *The Tallahassee Bus Protest* (1958).

Stoper, Emily, *The Student Nonviolent Coordinating Committee: The Growth of Radicalism in a Civil Rights Organization* (1989).

Sugarman, Tracy, *Stranger at the Gates: A Summer in Mississippi* (1966).

Taylor, Quintard, Jr., "The Civil Rights Movement in the American West: Black Protest in Seattle, 1960–1970," *The Journal of Negro History* 80 (1995): 1–14.

Thornton, J. Mills, III, "Challenge and Response in the Montgomery Bus Boycott of 1955–1956," *Alabama Review* 33 (1980): 163–235.

Tyson, Timothy B., *Radio Free Dixie: Robert F. Williams and the Roots of Black Power* (1999).

Wadhwani, Rohit D. G., "Kodak, FIGHT, and the Definition of Civil Rights in Rochester, New York, 1966–1967," *Historian* 60 (1997): 59–75.

Walters, Ronald, "The Great Plains Sit-in Movement, 1958–1960," *Great Plains Quarterly* 16 (1996): 85–94.

Ward, Brian, and Tony Badger, *The Making of Martin Luther King Jr. and the Civil Rights Movement* (1996).

Watters, Pat, *Down to Now: Reflections on the Southern Civil Rights Movement* (1971).

Weber, Michael, *Causes and Consequences of the African-American Civil Rights Movements* (1998).

Weiss, Nancy J., *Whitney M. Young, Jr. and the Struggle for Civil Rights* (1989).

Wigginton, Eliot and Sue Thrasher, "To Make the World We Want: An Interview with Dorothy Cotton," *Southern Exposure* 10 (1982): 25–31.

Wilhoit, Francis M., *The Politics of Massive Resistance* (1973).

Williams, Juan, *Eyes on the Prize: America's Civil Rights Years, 1954–1965* (1987).

Williams, Lea E., *Servants of the People: The 1960's Legacy of African American Leadership* (1996).

Wilson, Sondra Kathryn, ed., *In Search of Democracy: The NAACP Writings of James Weldon Johnson, Walter White, and Roy Wilkins, 1920–1977* (1999).

Wolff, Miles, *Lunch at the Five and Ten, the Greensboro Sit-Ins: A Contemporary History* (1970).

Wright, Roberta Hughes, *The Birth of the Montgomery Bus Boycott* (1991).

Wrinn, Stephen M., *Civil Rights in the Whitest State: Vermont's Perceptions of Civil Rights, 1945–1968* (1998).

Wynn, Daniel W., *The Black Protest Movement* (1974).

Young, Whitney, Jr., *To Be Equal* (1964).

Youth of the Rural Organizing and Cultural Center, *Minds Stayed on Freedom: The Civil Rights Struggle in the Rural South: An Oral History* (1991).

Zepp, Ira G., Jr., *The Social Vision of Martin Luther King, Jr.* (1989).

Zinn, Howard, *SNCC: The New Abolitionists* (1964).

23.4.6   Black Power

Abron, Jonina M., "The Legacy of the Black Panther Party," *Black Scholar* 17 (1986): 33–37.

Anderson, Jervis, "The Agonies of Black Militancy," *Dissent* 18 (1971): 23–29.

Arlen, Michael J., *An American Verdict* (1973).

Barbour, Floyd B., ed., *The Black Power Revolt: A Collection of Essays* (1968).

Barksdale, Marcellus C., "Robert F. Williams and the Indigenous Civil Rights Movement in Monroe, North Carolina, 1961," *Journal of Negro History* 69 (1984): 73–89.

Baruch, Ruth-Marion, and Pirkle Jones, *The Vanguard: A Photographic Essay on the Black Panthers* (1970).

Breitman, George, Herman Porter, and Baxter Smith, *The Assassination of Malcolm X* (1976).

Brown, Elaine, *A Taste of Power: A Black Woman's Story* (1992).

Brown, H. Rap, *Die, Nigger, Die!* (1969).

Cannon, Terry, *All Power to the People: The Story of the Black Panther Party* (1970).

Carmichael, Stokely, *Stokely Speaks: Black Power Back to Pan-Africanism* (1971).

Carmichael, Stokely, and Charles V. Hamilton, *Black Power: The Politics of Liberation in America* (1967).

Carson, Clayborne, *Malcolm X: The FBI File*, ed. David Gallen (1991).

Chaberski, Stephen George, *The Strategy of Defense in a Political Trial: The Trial of the "Panther 21"* (1975).

Churchill, Ward, and Jim Vander Wall, *Agents of Repression: The FBI's Secret War against the Black Panther Party and the American Indian Movement* (1988).

———— *The COINTELPRO Papers: Documents from the FBI's Secret Wars against Domestic Dissent* (1990).

Cleaver, Eldridge, *Soul on Ice* (1968).

Commission of Inquiry into the Black Panthers and the Police, *Search and Destroy: A Report* (1973).

Cross, Theodore L., *The Black Power Imperative: Racial Inequality and the Politics of Nonviolence* (rev. ed., 1987).

Davis, Angela Y., *Angela Davis: An Autobiography* (1974).

———— *If They Come in the Morning: Voices of Resistance* (1971).

Foner, Philip S., ed., *The Black Panthers Speak* (1970).

Freed, Donald, *Agony in New Haven: The Trial of Bobby Seale, Ericka Huggins, and the Black Panther Party* (1973).

Friedly, Michael, *Malcolm X: The Assassination* (1995).

Haskins, James, *Profiles in Black Power* (1972).

Heath, G. Louis, ed., *The Black Panther Leaders Speak: Huey P. Newton, Bobby Seale, Eldridge Cleaver, and Company Speak out through the Black Panther Party's Official Newspaper* (1976).

————, ed., *Off the Pigs!: The History and Literature of the Black Panther Party* (1976).

Henderson, Errol A., "The Lumpenproletariat As Vanguard? The Black Panther Party, Social Transformation, and Pearson's Analysis of Huey Newton," *Journal of Black Studies* 28 (1997): 171–99.

Jackson, George, *Blood in My Eye* (1972).

Jones, Charles, ed., *The Black Panther Party (Reconsidered): Reflections and Scholarship* (1997).

Keating, Edward M., *Free Huey!* (1971).

Kennebeck, Edwin, *Juror Number Four: The Trial of Thirteen Black Panthers As Seen from the Jury Box* (1973).

Killian, Lewis M., *The Impossible Revolution? Black Power and the American Dream* (1968).

Major, Reginald, *A Panther Is a Black Cat* (1971).

McCormack, Donald J., "Stokely Carmichael and Pan-Africanism: Back to Black Power," *Journal of Politics* 35 (1973): 386–409.

McEvoy, James, and Abraham Miller, ed., *Black Power and Student Rebellion* (1969).

Moore, Gilbert Stuart, *A Special Rage* (1971).

Newton, Huey P., *To Die for the People: The Writings of Huey P. Newton* (1972).

Newton, Huey P., and J. Herman Blake, *Revolutionary Suicide* (1973).

Newton, Huey P., and Ericka Huggins, *Insights and Poems* (1975).

Ngozi-Brown, Scot, "The Us Organization, Maulana Karenga, and Conflict with the Black Panther Party: A Critique of Sectarian Influences on Historical Discourse," *Journal of Black Studies* 28 (1997): 157–70.

Njeri, Akua, *My Life with the Black Panther Party* (1991).

O'Reilly, Kenneth, *Racial Matters: The FBI's Secret File on Black America, 1960–1972* (1989).

Pearson, Hugh, *The Shadow of the Panther: Huey Newton and the Price of Black Power in America* (1995).

Powledge, Fred, *Black Power/White Resistance: Notes on the New Civil War* (1967).

Seale, Bobby, *Seize the Time: The Story of the Black Panther Party and Huey P. Newton* (1970).

Staub, Michael E., "Black Panthers, New Journalism, and the Rewriting of the Sixties," *Representations* 57 (1997): 52–72.

Strain, Christopher, "'We Walked Like Men': The Deacons for Defense and Justice," *Louisiana History* 38 (1997): 43–62.

Tyson, Timothy B., *Radio Free Dixie: Robert F. Williams and the Roots of Black Power* (1999).

———— "Robert F. Williams, 'Black Power,' and the Roots of the African American Freedom Struggle," *Journal of American History* 85 (1998): 540–70.

Van Deburg, William L., *New Day in Babylon: The Black Power Movement and American Culture, 1965–1975* (1992).

Walker, Jack L., and Joel D. Aberbach, "The Meanings of Black Power: A Comparison of White and Black Interpretations of a Political Slogan," *American Political Science Review* 64 (1970): 367–88.

Weber, Shirley N., "Black Power in the 1960's: A Study of Its Impact on Women's Liberation," *Journal of Black Studies* 11 (1981): 483–98.

Williams, Robert Franklin, *Negroes with Guns*, ed. Marc Schleifer (1962).

Woodard, Komozi, *A Nation Within a Nation: Amiri Baraka (LeRoi Jones) and Black Power Politics* (1999).

Wright, Nathan, *Black Power and Urban Unrest: Creative Possibilities* (1967).

23.5   GOVERNMENT

23.5.1   Law

Aarons, Dwight, "Nationwide Preclearance of Section Five of the 1965 Voting Rights Act: Implementing the Fifteenth Amendments," *National Black Law Journal* 11 (1989): 93–116.

Bass, Jack, *Taming the Storm: The Life and Times of Judge Frank M. Johnson, Jr., and the South's Fight over Civil Rights* (1993).

———— *Unlikely Heroes: The Dramatic Story of the Southern Judges of the Fifth Circuit Who Translated the Supreme Court's* Brown *Decision into a Revolution for Equality* (1981).

Belknap, Michal R., *Federal Law and Southern Order: Racial Violence and Constitutional Conflict in the Post-*Brown *South* (1987).

Bell, Derrick A., *And We Are Not Saved: The Elusive Quest for Racial Justice* (1987).

Berger, Morroe, *Equality by Statute: The Revolution in Civil Rights* (rev. ed., 1967).

Berman, Daniel M., *A Bill Becomes a Law: Congress Enacts Civil Rights Legislation* (1966).

———— *It Is So Ordered: The Supreme Court Rules on School Segregation* (1966).

Blackburn, Sara, comp., *White Justice: Black Experience Today in America's Courtrooms* (1971).

Blaustein, Albert P., and Clarence Clyde Ferguson, Jr., *Desegregation and the Law: The Meaning and Effect of the School Segregation Cases* (2d ed., 1962).

Bynum, Victoria E., "'White Negroes' in Segregated Mississippi: Miscegenation, Racial Identity, and the Law," *Journal of Southern History* 64 (1998): 247–76.

Chaberski, Stephen George, *The Strategy of Defense in a Political Trial: The Trial of the "Panther 21"* (1975).

Crusto, Mitchell F., "Federalism and Civil Rights: The *Meredith* Case," *National Black Law Journal* 11 (1989): 233–48.

Edelman, Marian Wright, "Southern Schools Desegregation, 1954–1973: A Judicial Political Overview," *Annals of the American Academy of Political and Social Science* 407 (1973): 32–42.

Freed, Donald, *Agony in New Haven: The Trial of Bobby Seale, Ericka Huggins, and the Black Panther Party* (1973).

Freyer, Tony, *The Little Rock Crisis: A Constitutional Interpretation* (1984).

Glennon, Robert Jerome, "The Role of Law in the Civil Rights Movement: The Montgomery Bus Boycott, 1955–1957," *Law and History Review* 9 (1991): 59–112.

Hall, David, and George Henderson, "*Brown* Revisited: Charting a New Direction," *The Black Law Journal* 9 (1984): 6–37.

Hamilton, Charles V., *The Bench and the Ballot: Southern Federal Judges and Black Voters* (1973).

Harding, Vincent, "Wrestling toward the Dawn: The Afro-American Freedom Movement and the Changing Constitution," *Journal of American History* 74 (1987): 718–39.

Howie, Donald L. W., "The Image of Black People in *Brown* v. *The Board of Education*," *The Black Law Journal* 3 (1973): 371–84.

Kennebeck, Edwin, *Juror Number Four: The Trial of Thirteen Black Panthers As Seen from the Jury Box* (1973).

Kluger, Richard, *Simple Justice: The Story of* Brown v. Board of Education *and Black America's Struggle for Equality* (1975).

Loevy, Robert D., ed., *The Civil Rights Act of 1964: The Passage of the Law That Ended Racial Segregation* (1997).

Marshall, Burke, *Federalism and Civil Rights* (1964).

Martin, Waldo E., Jr., ed., Brown v. Board of Education: *A Brief History with Documents* (1998).

McCain, R. Ray, "Reactions to the United States Supreme Court Segregation Decision of 1954," *Georgia Historical Quarterly* 52 (1968): 371–87.

Moreno, Paul D., *From Direct Action to Affirmative Action: Fair Employment Law and Policy in America, 1933–1972* (1997).

Motley, Constance Baker, *Equal Justice under Law: An Autobiography* (1998).

Murphy, William P., "'Reinterpreting "Person" in Section 1983': The Hidden Influence of *Brown v. Board of Education*," *Black Law Journal* 9 (1985): 97–112.

Nier, Charles Lewis, III, "Guilty As Charged: Malcolm X and His Vision of Racial Justice for African Americans through Utilization of the United Nations International Human Rights Provisions and Institutions," *Dickinson Journal of International Law* 16 (1997): 149–89.

Rieff, Burt M., "*Browder v. Gayle:* The Legal Vehicle of the Montgomery Bus Boycott," *Alabama Review* 41 (1988): 193–208.

Robbins, Louise S., "Racism and Censorship in Cold War Oklahoma: The Case of Ruth W. Brown and the Battlesville Public Library," *Southwestern Historical Quarterly* 100 (1996): 19–48.

Tushnet, Mark V., *Making Civil Rights Law: Thurgood Marshall and the Supreme Court, 1936–1961* (1994).

——— *The NAACP's Legal Strategy against Segregated Education, 1925–1950* (1989).

Walker, Anders, "Legislating Virtue: How Segregationists Disguised Racial Discrimination As Moral Reform Following *Brown v. Board of Education*," *Duke Law Journal* 47 (1997): 399–424.

Wasby, Stephen L., Anthony A. D'Amato, and Rosemary Metrailer, *Desegregation from Brown to Alexander: An Exploration of Supreme Court Strategies* (1977).

Watson, Denton, *Lion in the Lobby: Clarence Mitchell, Jr.'s Struggle for the Passage of Civil Rights Laws* (1990).

Westin, Alan F., and Barry Mahoney, *The Trial of Martin Luther King* (1974).

Whalen, Charles, and Barbara Whalen, *The Longest Debate: A Legislative History of the 1964 Civil Rights Act* (1985).

Whittaker, Charles E., and William S. Coffin, *Law, Order, and Civil Disobedience* (1967).

Wilkinson, J. Harvie, III, *From Brown to Bakke: The Supreme Court and School Integration, 1954–1978* (1979).

Williams, Juan, *Thurgood Marshall: American Revolutionary* (1998).

Wirt, Frederick M., *Politics of Southern Equality: Law and Social Change in a Mississippi County* (1970).

23.5.2   Crime and Punishment

Chevigny, Paul, *Cops and Rebels: A Study of Provocation* (1972).

Humphry, Derek, *Police Power and Black People* (1972).

Kennedy, Randall, *Race, Crime, and the Law* (1997).

LaFree, Gary, and Kriss A. Drass, "The Effect of Changes in Intraracial Income Inequality and Educational Attainment on Changes in Arrest Rates for African Americans and Whites, 1957 to 1990," *American Sociological Review* 61 (1996): 614–35.

O'Brien, Gail Williams, *The Color of the Law: Race, Violence, and Justice in the Post-World War II South* (1999).

Oshinsky, David M., *"Worse Than Slavery": Parchman Farm and the Ordeal of Jim Crow Justice* (1996).

Rise, Eric W., *The Martinsville Seven: Race, Rape, and Capital Punishment* (1995).

23.5.3   Politics and Voting

Abney, F. Glenn, "Factors Related to Negro Voter Turnout in Mississippi," *Journal of Politics* 36 (1974): 1057–63.

Agronsky, Jonathan I. Z., *Marion Barry: The Politics of Race* (1991).

Alkalimat, Abdul, *Black Power in Chicago: Harold Washington and the Crisis of the Black Middle Class: Mass Protest* (vol. 1, 1990).

Anderson, Carol, "From Hope to Disillusion: African Americans, the United Nations, and the Struggle for Human Rights, 1944–1947," *Diplomatic History* 20 (1996): 531–64.

Andrews, Kenneth T., "The Impacts of Social Movements on the Political Process: The Civil Rights Movement and Black Electoral Politics in Mississippi," *American Sociological Review* 62 (1997): 800–19.

Barker, Lucius J., *Black Americans and the Political System* (2d ed., 1980).

Bartley, Numan V., *The Rise of Massive Resistance: Race and Politics in the South during the 1950's* (1969).

Bartley, Numan V., and Hugh D. Graham, *Southern Politics and the Second Reconstruction* (1975).

Bass, Harold F., Jr., "Presidential Party Leadership and Party Reform: Lyndon B. Johnson and the MFDP Controversy," *Presidential Studies Quarterly* 21 (1991): 85–101.

Bayes, Jane H., *Minority Politics and Ideologies in the United States* (1982).

Berman, William C., *The Politics of Civil Rights in the Truman Administration* (1970).

Black, Earl, *Southern Governors and Civil Rights: Racial Segregation As a Campaign Issue in the Second Reconstruction* (1976).

Brauer, Carl M., *John F. Kennedy and the Second Reconstruction* (1977).

Burk, Robert Fredrick, *The Eisenhower Administration and Black Civil Rights* (1984).

Burnham, Robert A., "Reform, Politics, and Race in Cincinnati: Proportional Representation and the City Charter Committee, 1924–1959," *Journal of Urban History* 23 (1997): 131–63.

Carter, Dan T., *From George Wallace to Newt Gingrich: Race in the Conservative Counterrevolution, 1963–1994* (1996).

Chung, WonSub, "Theories and Practice of Black Political Participation Since the Passage of the Voting Rights Act of 1965," *Journal of American Studies* 27 (1995): 121–40.

Clark, Septima Poinsette, and Mary A. Twining, "Voting Does Count: A Brief Excerpt from a Fabulous Decade," *Journal of Black Studies* 10 (1980): 445–47.

Duckett, Alfred, *Changing of the Guard: The New Breed of Black Politicians* (1972).

Emmons, Caroline, "'Somebody Has Got to Do That Work': Harry T. Moore and the Struggle for African-American Voting Rights in Florida," *Journal of Negro History* 82 (1997): 232–43.

Farley, Reynolds, "Trends in Racial Inequalities: Have the Gains of the 1960's Disappeared in the 1970's?" *American Sociological Review* 42 (1977): 189–208.

Foster, Lorn S., "The Voting Rights Act: Black Voting and the New Southern Politics," *Western Journal of Black Studies* 7 (1983): 120–29.

Geschwender, James A., *Class, Race, and Worker Insurgency* (1997).

Gilbert, Robert E., "John F. Kennedy and Civil Rights for Black Americans," *Presidential Studies Quarterly* 12 (1982): 386–99.

Graham, Hugh Davis, *The Civil Rights Era: Origins and Development of National Policy* (1990).

Grimshaw, William J., *Bitter Fruit: Black Politics and the Chicago Machine, 1931–1991* (1992).

Haessly, Lynn interviewer, "'We're Becoming the Mayors': An Interview with Former Sit-in Leader Harvey Gantt, Now Charlotte's Mayor," *Southern Exposure* 14 (1986): 44–51.

Hall, Tomiko Brown, "The Gentleman's White Supremacist: J. Strom Thurmond, the Dixiecrat Campaign, and the Evolution of Southern Politics," *Southern Historian* 16 (1995): 61–86.

Hamilton, Charles V., *The Bench and the Ballot: Southern Federal Judges and Black Voters* (1973).

Harrison, Rosalind, "The Relationship between Black Political Participation and the Voting Rights Act," *National Black Law Journal* 11 (1989): 79–92.

Harvey, James C., *Black Civil Rights during the Johnson Administration* (1973).

——— *Civil Rights during the Kennedy Administration* (1971).

Henry, Charles P., *Culture and African American Politics* (1990).

Holden, Matthew, *The Politics of the Black "Nation"* (1973).

Holloway, Harry, *The Politics of the Southern Negro: From Exclusion to Big City Organization* (1969).

Horne, Gerald, *Black and Red: W. E. B. Du Bois and the Afro-American Response to the Cold War 1944–1963* (1986).

Joubert, Paul E., and Ben M. Crouch, "Mississippi Blacks and the Voting Rights Act of 1965," *Journal of Negro Education* 46 (1977): 157–67.

Joyce, Patrick D., "A Reversal of Fortunes: Black Empowerment, Political Machines, and City Jobs in New York City and Chicago," *Urban Affairs Review* 32 (1997): 291–318.

Katz, Milton S., "E. Frederick Morrow and Civil Rights in the Eisenhower Administration," *Phylon* 42 (1981): 133–44.

Kellog, Peter J., "The Americans for Democratic Action and Civil Rights in 1948: Conscience in Politics or Politics in Conscience?" *Midwest Quarterly* 20 (1978): 49–63.

Kousser, J. Morgan, *Colorblind Injustice: Minority Voting Rights and the Undoing of the Second Reconstruction* (1997).

Krenn, Michael L., *Black Diplomacy: African Americans and the State Department, 1945–1969* (1999).

——— "'Outstanding Negroes' and 'Appropriate Countries': Some Facts, Figures, and Thoughts on Black U.S. Ambassadors, 1949–1988," *Diplomatic History* 14 (1990): 131–41.

Landess, Thomas H., and Richard M. Quinn, *Jesse Jackson and the Politics of Race* (1985).

Laville, Helen, and Scott Lucas, "The American Way: Edith Sampson, the NAACP, and African American Identity in the Cold War," *Diplomatic History* 20 (1996): 565–90.

Lawson, Steven F., *Black Ballots: Voting Rights in the South, 1944–1969* (1976).

——— *Civil Rights during the Johnson Administration, 1963–1969* (1984).

——— *In Pursuit of Power: Southern Blacks and Electoral Politics, 1965–1982* (1985).

——— *Running for Freedom: Civil Rights and Black Politics in America since 1941* (1991).

Lawson, Steven F., and Mark I. Gelfand, "Consensus and Civil Rights: Lyndon B. Johnson and the Black Franchise," *Prologue* 8 (1976): 65–76.

Lichtman, Allan, "The Federal Assault against Voting Discrimination in the Deep South, 1957–1967," *Journal of Negro History* 54 (1969): 346–67.

Marable, Manning, *Black American Politics: From the Washington Marches to Jesse Jackson* (1985).

Martin, John Frederick, *Civil Rights and the Crisis of Liberalism: The Democratic Party, 1945–1976* (1979).

Matthews, Donald R., and James W. Prothro, *Negroes and the New Southern Politics* (1966).

McAdam, Doug, *Political Process and the Development of Black Insurgency, 1930–1970* (1982).

McMillen, Neil R., "Black Enfranchisement in Mississippi: Federal Enforcement and Black Protest in the 1960's," *Journal of Southern History* 43 (1977): 351–72.

Moreland, Laurence, Robert Steed, and Tod Baker, ed., *Blacks in Southern Politics* (1987).

Morris, Milton D., *The Politics of Black America* (1975).

Parker, Frank R., *Black Votes Count: Political Empowerment in Mississippi after 1965* (1990).

Plummer, Brenda Gayle, *Rising Wind: Black Americans and U.S. Foreign Affairs, 1935–1960* (1996).

Reed, Adolph, Jr., *Without Justice for All: The New Liberalism and Our Retreat from Racial Equality* (1999).

Reed, Christopher Robert, *The Chicago NAACP and the Rise of Black Professional Leadership, 1910–1966* (1997).

Reed, Linda, *Simple Decency and Common Sense: The Southern Conference Movement, 1938–1963* (1991).

Reichard, Gary W., "Democrats, Civil Rights, and Electoral Strategies in the 1950's," *Congress and the Presidency* 13 (1986): 59–81.

Roark, James L., "American Black Leaders: The Response to Colonialism and the Cold War, 1943–1953," *African Historical Studies* 4 (1971): 253–70.

Sitkoff, Harvard, "Harry Truman and the Election of 1948: The Coming of Age of Civil Rights in American Politics," *Journal of Southern History* 37 (1971): 597–616.

Smith, Alonzo N., "Afro-Americans and the Presidential Elections of 1948," *Western Journal of Black Studies* 8 (1984): 101–10.

Stern, Mark, *Calculating Visions: Kennedy, Johnson, and Civil Rights* (1992).

———— "John F. Kennedy and Civil Rights: From Congress to the Presidency," *Presidential Studies Quarterly* 19 (1989): 797–823.

———— "Lyndon Johnson and Richard Russell: Institutions, Ambitions, and Civil Rights," *Presidential Studies Quarterly* 21 (1991): 687–704.

———— "Presidential Strategies and Civil Rights: Eisenhower, the Early Years, 1952–1954," *Presidential Studies Quarterly* 19 (1989): 769–95.

Stone, Chuck, *Black Political Power in America* (rev. ed., 1970).

Tate, Katherine, *From Protest to Politics: The New Black Voters in American Elections* (1993).

Thomas, Norman C., and Harold L. Wolman, "Black Interests, Black Groups, and Black Influence in the Federal Policy Process: The Cases of Housing and Education," *Journal of Politics* 32 (1970): 875–97.

Thurber, Timothy N., *The Politics of Equality: Hubert Humphrey and the African American Freedom Struggle* (1998).

Vander, Harry Joseph, III, *The Political and Economic Progress of the American Negro, 1940–1963* (1968).

Vaughan, Philip H., "The Truman Administration's Fair Deal for Black America," *Missouri Historical Review* 70 (1976): 291–305.

Walton, Hanes, Jr., *When the Marching Stopped: The Politics of the Civil Rights Regulatory Agencies* (1988).

Watters, Pat, and Reese Cleghorn, *Climbing Jacob's Ladder: The Arrival of Negroes in Southern Politics* (1967).

Wright, Gerald C., Jr., "Black Voting Turnout and Education in the 1968 Presidential Election," *Journal of Politics* 37 (1975): 563–68.

Wynn, Linda T., "Toward a Perfect Democracy: The Struggle of African Americans in Fayette County, Tennessee, to Fulfill the Unfulfilled Right of the Franchise," *Tennessee Historical Quarterly* 55 (1996): 202–23.

Young, Richard P., ed., *Roots of Rebellion: The Evolution of Black Politics and Protest Since World War II* (1970).

Young, Richard P., and Jerome S. Burstein, "Federalism and the Demise of Prescriptive Racism in the United States," *Studies in American Political Development* 9 (1995): 1–54.

23.5.4   Military

Allen, Robert L., *The Port Chicago Mutiny: The Story of the Largest Mass Mutiny Trial in U.S. Naval History* (1989).

Burk, James, "Citizenship Status and Military Service: The Quest for Inclusion by Minorities and Conscientious Objectors," *Armed Forces and Society* 21 (1995): 503–29.

Dornfeld, Margaret, *The Turning Tide: From the Desegregation of the Armed Forces to the Montgomery Bus Boycott, 1948–1956* (1995).

Gropman, Alan L., *The Air Force Integrates, 1945–1964* (2d ed., 1998).

Harris, Norman, "Blacks in Vietnam: A Holistic Perspective through Fiction and Journalism," *Western Journal of Black Studies* 10 (1986): 121–31.

Johnson, Jesse J., ed., *Black Women in the Armed Forces, 1942–1974: A Pictorial History* (1974).

MacGregor, Morris J., Jr., *Defense Studies: Integration of the Armed Forces, 1940–1965* (1981).

Mazrui, Ali A., "Boxer Muhammad Ali and Soldier Idi Amin As International Political Symbols: The Bioeconomics of Sport and War," *Comparative Studies in Society and History* 19 (1977): 189–215.

Mershon, Sherie, and Steven Schlossman, *Foxholes and Color Lines: Desegregating the U.S. Armed Forces* (1998).

Onkst, David H., "'First a Negro . . . Incidentally a Veteran': Black World War Two and the G.I. Bill of Rights in the Deep South, 1944–1948," *Journal of Social History* 31 (1998): 517–43.

Osur, Alan M., "Black-White Relations in the U.S. Military, 1940–1972," *Air University Review* 33 (1981): 69–78.

Schexnider, Alvin J., "The Development of Racial Solidarity in the Armed Forces," *Journal of Black Studies* 5 (1975): 415–35.

Taylor, Clyde, comp., *Vietnam and Black America: An Anthology of Protest and Resistance* (1973).

Terry, Wallace, ed., *Bloods, an Oral History of the Vietnam War* (1984).

Westheider, James E., *Fighting on Two Fronts: African Americans and the Vietnam War* (1997).

23.6   DEMOGRAPHY

Alston, Jon P., "The Black Population in Urbanized Areas, 1960," *Journal of Black Studies* 1 (1971): 435–42.

Cahill, Edward E., "Migration and the Decline of the Black Population in Rural and Non-Metropolitan Areas," *Phylon* 35 (1974): 284–92.

Farley, Reynolds, *Growth of the Black Population: A Study of Demographic Trends* (1970).

Gee, Ellen, and Jean E. Veevers, "Increasing Sex Mortality Differentials among Black Americans, 1950–1978," *Phylon* 46 (1985): 162–75.

Stahura, John M., "Suburban Development: Black Suburbanization and the Civil Rights Movement Since World War II," *American Sociological Review* 51 (1986): 131–44.

Turner, Charles Jackson, "Changes in Age Composition of the Rural Black Population of the South, 1950 to 1970," *Phylon* 35 (1974): 268–75.

Vickery, William Edward, *The Economics of the Negro Migration, 1900–1960* (1977).

23.7   FAMILY

Billingsley, Andrew, with Amy Tate Billingsley, *Black Families in White America* (1968).

Franklin, Donna L., *Ensuring Inequality: The Structural Transformation of the African-American Family* (1997).

Markowitz, Gerald E., and David Rosner, *Children, Race, and Power: Kenneth and Mamie Clark's Northside Center* (1996).

Scott, Daryl Michael, "The Politics of Pathology: The Ideological Origins of the Moynihan Controversy," *Journal of Policy History* 8 (1996): 81–105.

Stack, Carol B., *All Our Kin: Strategies for Survival in a Black Community* (1974).

Tolnay, Stewart E., "The Great Migration and Changes in the Northern Black Family, 1940–1990," *Social Forces* 75 (1997): 1213–38.

23.8   SOCIETY

23.8.1   Rural Life (Including Black Settlements)

Cobb, James C., "'Somebody Done Nailed Us on the Cross': Federal Farm and Welfare Policy and the Civil Rights Movement in the Mississippi Delta," *Journal of American History* 77 (1990): 912–36.

Couto, Richard A., *Ain't Gonna Let Nobody Turn Me Round: The Pursuit of Racial Justice in the Rural South* (1991).

Grim, Valerie, "The Politics of Inclusion: Black Farmers and the Quest for Agribusiness Participation, 1945–1990's," *Agricultural History* 69 (1995): 257–71.

Hesslink, George K., *Black Neighbors: Negroes in a Northern Rural Community* (1968).

Kirby, Jack Temple, *Rural Worlds Lost: The American South, 1920–1960* (1987).

Whayne, Jeannie M., "Black Farmers and the Agricultural Cooperative Extension Service: The Alabama Experience, 1945–1965," *Agricultural History* 72 (1998): 523–51.

23.8.2   Urban Life (Including Migration)

Akalou, W. M., and Cary D. Wintz, "The Economic Impact of Residential Desegregation on Historically Black Neighborhoods in Houston, 1950–1990," *Essays in Economic and Business History* 13 (1995): 289–304.

Alston, Jon P., "The Black Population in Urbanized Areas, 1960," *Journal of Black Studies* 1 (1971): 435–42.

Barkan, Elliott R., "Vigilance *versus* Vigilantism: Race and Ethnicity and the Politics of Housing, 1940–1960," *Journal of Urban History* 12 (1986): 181–89.

Bayor, Ronald H., *Race and the Shaping of Twentieth-Century Atlanta* (1996).

Blair, Thomas L., *Retreat to the Ghetto: The End of a Dream?* (1977).

Bobier, Richard, "Africaville: The Test of Urban Renewal and Race in Halifax, Nova Scotia," *Past Imperfect* 4 (1995): 163–80.

Broussard, Albert S., *Black San Francisco: The Struggle for Racial Equality, 1900–1954* (1993).

Clark, Kenneth Bancroft, *Dark Ghetto: Dilemmas of Social Power* (1965).

Duncan, Otis Dudley, and Beverly Duncan, *Negro Population of Chicago: A Study of Residential Succession* (1957).

Fainstein, Norman, and Susan Nesbitt, "Did the Black Ghetto Have a Golden Age? Class Structure and Class Segregation in New York City, 1949–1970," *Journal of Urban History* 23 (1996): 3–28.

Goodwin, E. Marvin, *Black Migration in America from 1915–1960: An Uneasy Exodus* (1990).

Hirsch, Arnold Richard, *Making the Second Ghetto: Race and Housing in Chicago, 1940–1960* (rev. ed., 1998).

————— "Massive Resistance in the Urban North: Trumbull Park, Chicago, 1953–1966," *Journal of American History* 82 (1995): 522–50.

Jennings, James, *The Politics of Black Empowerment: The Transformation of Black Activism in Urban America* (1992).

King, James E., *The Impact of Federal Housing Policy on Urban African-American Families, 1930–1966* (1997).

Kusmer, Kenneth L., "African Americans in the City Since World War II: From the Industrial to the Post-Industrial Era," *Journal of Urban History* 21 (1995): 458–504.

Lemann, Nicholas, *The Promised Land: The Great Black Migration and How It Changed America* (1992).

Mohl, Raymond A., "Making the Second Ghetto in Metropolitan Miami, 1940–1960," *Journal of Urban History* 21 (1995): 395–427.

Nightingale, Carl Husemoller, *On the Edge: A History of Poor Black Children and Their American Dreams* (1993).

Rosen, Louis, *The South Side: The Racial Transformation of an American Neighborhood* (1998).

Sasaki, Yutaka, "'But Not Next Door': Housing Discrimination and the Emergence of the Second Ghetto in Newark, New Jersey, after World War II," *Japanese Journal of American Studies* 5 (1994): 113–35.

Saunders, James Robert, *Urban Renewal and the End of Black Culture in Charlottesville, Virginia: An Oral History of Vinegar Hill* (1998).

Scribner, Christopher MacGregor, "Federal Funding, Urban Renewal, and Race Relations: Birmingham in Transition, 1945–1955," *Alabama Review* 48 (1995): 269–95.

Stafford, Walter W., "Dilemmas of Civil Rights Groups in Developing Urban Strategies and Changes in American Federalism, 1933–1970," *Phylon* 37 (1976): 59–72.

Sugrue, Thomas J., *The Origins of the Urban Crisis: Race and Inequality in Postwar Detroit* (1996).

Taulbert, Clifton L., *The Last Train North* (1995).

Tolnay, Stewart E., "The Great Migration and Changes in the Northern Black Family, 1940–1990," *Social Forces* 75 (1997): 1213–38.

Tuck, Stephen, "A City Too Dignified to Hate: Civic Pride, Civil Rights, and Savannah in Comparative Perspective," *Georgia Historical Quarterly* 79 (1995): 539–59.

Wallis, Don, *All We Had Was Each Other: The Black Community of Madison, Indiana* (1998).

23.8.3   Material Culture

Cash, Floris Barnett, "Kinship and Quilting: An Examination of an African-American Tradition," *Journal of Negro History* 80 (1995): 30–41.

Landsmark, Theodore C., "Comments on African American Contributions to American Material Life," *Winterthur Portfolio* 33 (1998): 261–82.

O'Bryant-Seabrook, Marlene, "Symbiotic Stitches: The Quilts of Maggie McFarland Gillispie and John Gillispie, Jr.," *Uncoverings* 16 (1995): 175–98.

23.8.4   Color and Class

Allen, Robert L., *Black Awakening in Capitalist America: An Analytic History* (1969).

Collins, Sharon M., "The Making of the Black Middle Class," *Social Problems* 30 (1983): 369–82.

Frazier, Edward Franklin, *Black Bourgeoisie* (1957).

Kilson, Martin, "The Black Bourgeoisie Revisited: From E. Franklin Frazier to the Present," *Dissent* 30 (1983): 85–96.

———— "The New Black Intellectuals," *Dissent* 16 (1969): 305–10.

Landry, Bart, "A Reinterpretation of the Writings of Frazier on the Black Middle Class," *Social Problems* 26 (1978): 211–22.

Lieberman, Robert C., *Shifting the Color Line: Race and the American Welfare State* (1998).

Morton, Patricia, "From Invisible Man to 'New People': The Recent Discovery of American Mulattoes," *Phylon* 46 (1985): 106–22.

Sites, Paul, and Elizabeth I. Mullins, "The American Black Elite, 1930–1978," *Phylon* 46 (1985): 269–80.

23.8.5   Associational Life

Fordham, Monroe, "The Buffalo Cooperative Economic Society, Inc., 1928–1961: A Black Self-Help Organization," *Niagara Frontier* 23 (1976): 41–49.

Jenkins, J. Craig, and Craig M. Eckert, "Channeling Black Insurgency: Elite Patronage and Professional Social Movement Organizations in the Development of the Black Movement," *American Sociological Review* 51 (1986): 812–29.

23.8.6   Leisure and Sports

Adelson, Bruce, *Brushing Back Jim Crow: The Integration of Minor League Baseball in the American South* (1999).

Ashe, Arthur R., Jr., *A Hard Road to Glory: A History of the African-American Athlete Since 1946* (3 vols., 1988).

Gems, Gerald R., "Blocked Shot: The Development of Basketball in the African-American Community of Chicago," *Journal of Sport History* 22 (1995): 135–48.

Gilbert, Tom W., *Baseball and the Color Line* (1995).

Gorn, Elliott J., *Muhammad Ali: The People's Champ* (1995).

Hauser, Thomas, *Muhammad Ali: His Life and Times* (1991).

Hoberman, John M., *Darwin's Athletes: How Sport Has Damaged Black America and Preserved the Myth of Race* (1997).

Marqusee, Mike, *Redemption Song: Muhammad Ali and the Spirit of the Sixties* (1999).

——— "Sport and Stereotype: From Role Model to Muhammad Ali," *Race and Class* 36 (1995): 1–29.

Moffi, Larry, and Jonathan Kronstadt, *Crossing the Line: Black Major Leaguers, 1947–1959* (1996).

Sammons, Jeffrey T., *Beyond the Ring: The Role of Boxing in American Society* (1988).

——— "A Proportionate and Measured Response to the Provocation That Is *Darwin's Athletes*," *Journal of Sport History* 24 (1997): 378–88.

Spivey, Donald, "The Black Athlete in Big-Time Intercollegiate Sports, 1941–1968," *Phylon* 44 (1983): 116–25.

Tygiel, Jules, *Baseball's Great Experiment: Jackie Robinson and His Legacy* (1983).

23.9   RELIGION

Baer, Hans A., *The Black Spiritual Movement: A Religious Response to Racism* (1984).

Baldwin, Lewis V., *There Is a Balm in Gilead: The Cultural Roots of Martin Luther King, Jr.* (1991).

——— *To Make the Wounded Whole: The Cultural Legacy of Martin Luther King, Jr.* (1992).

Barboza, Steven, *American Jihad: Islam after Malcom X* (1994).

Blatnica, Dorothy Ann, *"At the Altar of Their God": African American Catholics in Cleveland, 1922–1961* (1995).

Brotz, Howard, *The Black Jews of Harlem: Negro Nationalism and the Dilemmas of Negro Leadership* (1964).

Calloway-Thomas, Carolyn, and John Louis Lucaites, *Martin Luther King, Jr., and the Sermonic Power of Public Discourse* (1993).

Carson, Clayborne, and Peter Holloran, "Martin Luther King, Jr., as Scholar: A Reexamination of His Theological Writings," *Journal of American History* 78 (1991): 93–105.

Carter, Lawrence Edward, Sr., ed., *Walking Integrity: Benjamin Elijah Mays, Mentor to Martin Luther King, Jr.* (1998).

Chapman, Mark L., *Christianity on Trial: African American Religious Thought before and after Black Power* (1995).

Chappell, David L., "Religious Ideas of the Segregationists," *Journal of American Studies* 32 (1998): 237–62.

Clegg, Claude, *An Original Man: The Life and Times of Elijah Muhammad* (1997).

Collins, Donald E., *When the Church Bell Rang Racist: The Methodist Church and the Civil Rights Movement in Alabama* (1998).

Cone, James H., *Black Theology and Black Power* (1969).

——— *A Black Theology of Liberation* (1970).

——— *For My People: Black Theology and the Black Church* (1984).

DeCaro, Lou, *Malcolm and the Cross: The Nation of Islam, Malcolm X, and Christianity* (1998).

Downing, Frederick L., *To See the Promised Land: The Faith Pilgrimage of Martin Luther King, Jr.* (1986).

Fairclough, Adam, "The Southern Christian Leadership Conference and the Second Reconstruction, 1957–1973," *South Atlantic Quarterly* 80 (1981): 177–94.

———— *To Redeem the Soul of America: The Southern Christian Leadership Conference and Martin Luther King, Jr.* (1987).

Findlay, James F., *Church People in the Struggle: The National Council of Churches and the Black Freedom Movement, 1950–1970* (1993).

———— "The Mainline Churches and Head Start in Mississippi: Religious Activism in the Sixties," *Church History* 64 (1995): 237–50.

Fluker, Walter E., *They Looked for a City: A Comparative Analysis of Community in the Thought of Howard Thurman and Martin Luther King, Jr.* (1989).

Friedland, Michael B., *Lift up Your Voice Like a Trumpet: White Clergy and the Civil Rights and Antiwar Movements, 1954–1973* (1998).

Gardell, Mattias, *In the Name of Elijah Muhammad: Louis Farrakhan and the Nation of Islam* (1996).

Garrow, David, *Bearing the Cross: Martin Luther King, Jr., and the Southern Christian Leadership Conference* (1986).

Hatch, Gary Layne, "Logic in the Black Folk Sermon: The Sermons of Rev. C. L. Franklin," *Journal of Black Studies* 26 (1996): 227–44.

Hedgepeth, Chester M., "Philosophical Eclecticism in the Writings of Martin Luther King, Jr.," *Western Journal of Black Studies* 8 (1984): 79–86.

Henry, Charles P., "Delivering Daniel: The Dialectic of Ideology and Theology in the Thought of Martin Luther King, Jr.," *Journal of Black Studies* 17 (1987): 327–45.

Kater, John, Jr., "Experiment in Freedom: The Episcopal Church and the Black Power Movement," *Historical Magazine of the Protestant Episcopal Church* 48 (1979): 67–81.

Keener, Craig S., and Glenn Usry, *Defending Black Faith: Answers to Tough Questions about African-American Christianity* (1997).

King, Martin Luther, Jr., *A Knock at Midnight: Inspiration from the Great Sermons of Reverend Martin Luther King, Jr.*, ed. Clayborne Carson and Peter Holloran (1998).

Krause, P. Allen, "Rabbis and Negro Rights in the South, 1954–1967," *American Jewish Archives* 21 (1969): 20–47.

Lincoln, C. Eric, *The Black Muslims in America* (1961).

Lischer, Richard, *The Preacher King: Martin Luther King Jr. and the World That Moved America* (1995).

Lomax, Louis E., *When the Word Is Given: A Report on Elijah Muhammad, Malcolm X, and the Black Muslim World* (1964).

Lornell, Kip, *'Happy in the Service of the Lord': African-American Sacred Vocal Harmony Quartets in Memphis* (1995).

Lyght, Ernest S., *The Religious and Philosophical Foundations in the Thought of Martin Luther King, Jr.* (1972).

Manis, Andrew M., *Southern Civil Religions in Conflict: Black and White Baptists and Civil Rights, 1947–1957* (1987).

Marsh, Charles, *God's Long Summer: Stories of Faith and Civil Rights* (1997).

Miller, Keith D., *Voice of Deliverance: The Language of Martin Luther King, Jr. and Its Sources* (1992).

Moellering, Ralph L., *Christian Conscience and Negro Emancipation* (1965).

Muhammad, Elijah, *Message to the Blackman in America* (1965).

Nelsen, Hart M., and Anne Kusener Nelsen, *Black Church in the Sixties* (1975).

Newman, Mark, "The Mississippi Baptist Convention and Desegregation, 1945–1980," *Journal of Mississippi History* 59 (1997): 1–32.

Paris, Peter J., *Black Religious Leaders: Conflict in Unity* (2d ed., 1991).

———— *The Social Teaching of the Black Churches* (1985).

Peake, Thomas R., *Keeping the Dream Alive: A History of the Southern Christian Leadership Conference from King to the Nineteen-Eighties* (1987).

Reagon, Bernice Johnson, ed., *We'll Understand It Better By and By: Pioneering African American Gospel Composers* (1992).

Sawyer, Mary R., *Black Ecumenism: Implementing the Demands of Justice* (1994).

———— "The Fraternal Council of Negro Churches, 1934–1964," *Church History* 59 (1990): 51–64.

Sleeper, C. Freeman, *Black Power and Christian Responsibility: Some Biblical Foundations for Social Ethics* (1969).

Smith, Ervin, *The Ethics of Martin Luther King, Jr.* (1981).

Smith, Kenneth L., and Ira G. Zepp, *Search for the Beloved Community: The Thinking of Martin Luther King, Jr.* (1974).

Steinkraus, Warren E., "Martin Luther King's Personalism and Non-Violence," *Journal of the History of Ideas* 34 (1973): 97–111.

Wade-Gayles, Gloria, ed., *My Soul Is a Witness: African-American Women's Spirituality* (1995).

Washington, Joseph R., Jr., *The Politics of God* (1967).

West, Cornel, *Prophesy Deliverance! An Afro-American Revolutionary Christianity* (1982).

Wimberly, Anne Streaty, *Honoring African American Elders: A Ministry in the Soul Community* (1997).

23.10   THOUGHT AND EXPRESSION

23.10.1   Race, Gender, and Identity

Abel, Elizabeth, ed., *Female Subjects in Black and White: Race, Psychoanalysis, Feminism* (1997).

Baldwin, James, *The Fire Next Time* (1963).

—— *Nobody Knows My Name* (1961).

—— *Notes of a Native Son* (1955).

Banks, William M., *Black Intellectuals: Race and Responsibility in American Life* (1996).

Caton, Simone M., "Birth Control and the Black Community in the 1960's: Genocide or Power Politics?" *Journal of Social History* 31 (1998): 545–69.

Childs, John Brown, *Leadership, Conflict, and Cooperation in Afro-American Social Thought* (1989).

Clark, Kenneth Bancroft, *Dark Ghetto: Dilemmas of Social Power* (1965).

—— *King, Malcolm, Baldwin: Three Interviews* (rev. ed., 1985).

—— "The Present Dilemma of the Negro," *Journal of Negro History* 53 (1968): 1–11.

Cone, James H., *Martin, Malcolm, and America: A Dream or a Nightmare?* (1991).

Cruse, Harold, *The Crisis of the Negro Intellectual* (1967).

Davis, Allison, *Leadership, Love, and Aggression* (1983).

Davis, Angela Y., *Angela Davis: An Autobiography* (1974).

Forman, James, *Self-Determination: An Examination of the Question and Its Application to the African-American People* (1984).

James, Joy, *Race, Women, and Revolution: Black Female Militancy and the Praxis of Ella Baker* (1998).

Kapur, Sudarshan, *Raising up a Prophet: The African-American Encounter with Gandhi* (1992).

Kilson, Martin, "The New Black Intellectuals," *Dissent* 16 (1969): 305–10.

—— "Politics and Identity among Black Intellectuals," *Dissent* 28 (1981): 339–49.

Little, Monroe, "Remembering Hiroshima: Cultural Politics, World War II, and American Consciousness," *Western Journal of Black Studies* 21 (1997): 37–41.

Markowitz, Gerald, and David Rosner, *Children, Race, and Power: Kenneth and Mamie Clark's Northside Center* (1996).

Marx, Gary T., *Protest and Prejudice: A Study of Belief in the Black Community* (1967).

McKissick, Floyd, *Three-Fifths of a Man* (1969).

Rajiv, Sudhi, *Forms of Black Consciousness* (1992).

Reed, Adolph, Jr., ed., *Race, Politics, and Culture: Critical Essays on the Radicalism of the 1960's* (1986).

Reid, Inez Smith, *"Together" Black Women* (1972).

Rywkin, Michael, "Black Americans, a Race or Nationality? Some Communist Viewpoints," *Canadian Review of Studies in Nationalism* 3 (1975): 89–96.

Stone, Albert E., *The Return of Nat Turner: History, Literature, and Cultural Politics in Sixties America* (1992).

Sudarkasa, Niara, *The Strength of Our Mothers: African and African American Women and Families, Essays and Speeches* (1997).

Wallace, Michele, *Black Macho and the Myth of the Superwoman* (1979).

White, E. Frances, "Africa on My Mind: Gender, Counter Discourse, and African-American National-ism," *Journal of Women's History* 2 (1990): 73–97.

Wright, Richard, *The Color Curtain: A Report on the Bandung Conference* (1956).

Wright, W. D., *Black Intellectuals, Black Cognition, and a Black Aesthetic* (1997).

Zimmerman, Jonathan, "Beyond Double Consciousness: Black Peace Corps Volunteers in Africa, 1961–1971," *Journal of American History* 82 (1995): 999–1028.

23.10.2 Emigration and Nationalism (see also Black Power)

Alkalimat, Abdul, and Preston Wilcox, *The Legacy of Malcolm X: A Living Tradition* (1990).

Allen, Ernest, Jr., and John H. Bracey, Jr., ed., *Unite or Perish: The Contours of Black Radical and Black Nationalist Thought, 1954–1975* (2 vols., 1999).

Breitman, George, *The Last Year of Malcolm X: The Evolution of a Revolutionary* (1967).

Carmichael, Stokely, *Stokely Speaks: Black Power back to Pan-Africanism* (1971).

Clarke, John Henrik, *Malcom X: The Man and His Times* (1990).

Corsino, Louis, "Malcolm X and the Black Muslim Movement: A Social Psychology of Charisma," *Psychohistory Review* 10 (1982): 165–84.

Cunnigen, Donald, "Malcolm X's Influence on the Black Nationalist Movement of Southern Black College Students," *Western Journal of Black Studies* 17 (1993): 32–43.

Davis, Thulani, *Malcolm X: The Great Photographs* (1993).

Epps, Archie, ed., *The Speeches of Malcolm X at Harvard* (1968).

Essein-Udom, Essien Udosen, *Black Nationalism: A Search for an Identity in America* (1962).

Goldman, Peter, *The Death and Life of Malcom X* (1973).

Harris, Robert L., Jr., "Malcolm X: Human Rights and the United Nations," *Western Journal of Black Studies* 17 (1993): 1–5.

Jamal, Hakim A., *From the Dead Level: Malcolm X and Me* (1972).

Karenga, Maulana Ron, "The Oppositional Logic of Malcolm X: Differentiation, Engagement, and Re-sistance," *Western Journal of Black Studies* 17 (1993): 6–16.

Karim, Benjamin, Peter Skutches, and David Gallen, *Remembering Malcolm* (1992).

McAlister, Melani, "One Black Allah: The Middle East in the Cultural Politics of African American Liberation, 1955–1970," *American Quarterly* 51 (1999): 622–56.

McCormack, Donald J., "Stokely Carmichael and Pan-Africanism: Back to Black Power," *Journal of Politics* 35 (1973): 386–409.

Meriwether, James H., "African Americans and the Mau Mau Rebellion: Militancy, Violence, and the Struggle for Freedom," *Journal of American Ethnic History* 17 (1998): 63–86.

Ofari, Earl, *Black Liberation: Cultural and Revolutionary Nationalism* (rev. ed., 1970).

Pinkney, Alphonso, *Red, Black, and Green: Black Nationalism in the United States* (1976).

Romero, Patricia W., "W.E.B. Du Bois, Pan-Africanists, and Africa, 1963–1973," *Journal of Black Studies* 6 (1976): 321–36.

Runcie, John, "The Black Culture Movement and the Black Community," *Journal of American Studies* 10 (1976): 185–214.

Sales, William W., Jr., *From Civil Rights to Black Liberation: Malcolm X and the Organization of Afro-American Unity* (1994).

Sekayi, Dia N. R., *African American Intellectual-Activists: Legacies in the Struggle* (1997).

T'Shaka, Oba, *The Political Legacy of Malcolm X* (1983).

Von Eschen, Penny M., *Race against Empire: Black Americans and Anticolonialism, 1937–1957* (1997).

Walters, Ronald W., *Pan Africanism in the African Diaspora: An Analysis of Modern Afrocentric Political Movements* (1997).

Wolfenstein, Eugene Victor, *The Victims of Democracy: Malcolm X and the Black Revolution* (1981).

23.10.3 Language and Linguistics

Borden, Karen Wells, "Black Rhetoric in the 1960's: Sociohistorical Perspectives," *Journal of Black Studies* 3 (1973): 423–31.

Lieberson, Stanley, and Kelly S. Mikelson, "Distinctive African American Names: An Experimental, Historical, and Linguistic Analysis of Innovation," *American Sociological Review* 60 (1995): 928–46.

Rickford, John R., *African American Vernacular English: Features, Evolution, Educational Implications* (1999).

23.10.4   Folklore and Humor

Abrahams, Roger D., *Deep Down in the Jungle: Negro Narrative Folklore from the Streets of Philadelphia* (1964).

Harris, Trudier, "Adventures in a 'Foreign Country': African American Humor and the South," *Southern Cultures* 1 (1995): 457–65.

Hughes, Langston, *Simple Speaks His Mind* (1950).

——— *Simple Stakes a Claim* (1957).

——— *Simple Takes a Wife* (1953).

——— *Simple's Uncle Sam* (1965).

McKinney, Don S., "Brer Rabbit and Brother Martin Luther King, Jr.: The Folktale Background of the Birmingham Protest," *Journal of Religious Thought* 46 (1989–1990): 42–52.

Presley, James, "The Birth of Jesse B. Semple," *Southwest* 58 (1973): 219–24.

Turner, Beth, "Simplifyin': Langston Hughes and Alice Childress Remember Jesse B. Semple," *Langston Hughes Review* 15 (1997): 37–48.

23.10.5   Literature and Poetry

Brown-Guillory, Elizabeth, "Images of Blacks in Plays by Black Women," *Phylon* 47 (1986): 230–37.

Butcher, Philip, "The Younger Novelists and the Urban Negro," *CLA Journal* 4 (1961): 196–203.

Carroll, Rebecca, ed., *Swing Low: Black Men Writing* (1995).

Goddard, Robert, "Agricultural Worker As Archetype in West Indian and African-American Literature," *Agricultural History* 72 (1998): 509–20.

Hogue, W. Lawrence, *Race, Modernity, Postmodernity: A Look at the History and the Literatures of Peoples of Color Since the 1960's* (1996).

Japtok, Martin, "Paule Marshall's *Brown Girl, Brownstones:* Reconciling Ethnicity and Individualism," *African American Review* 32 (1998): 305–15.

Jenkins, McKay, *The South in Black and White: Race, Sex, and Literature in the 1940's* (1999).

Kimball, Gregg D., "Expanding the Notion: The African American Presence in *Virginia Cavalcade,* 1951–1996," *Virginia Cavalcade* 46 (1996): 82–94.

Lenz, Günter H., "Symbolic Space, Communal Rituals, and the Black Surreality of the Urban Ghetto: Harlem in Black Literature from the 1920's to the 1960's," *Callaloo* 11 (1988): 309–45.

Lieber, Todd M., "Ralph Ellison and the Metaphor of Invisibility in Black Literary Tradition," *American Quarterly* 24 (1972): 86–100.

McDowell, Deborah E., *'The Changing Same': Black Women's Literature, Criticism, and Theory* (1995).

Miller, Jeanne-Marie A., "Images of Black Women in Plays by Black Playwrights," *CLA Journal* 20 (1977): 494–507.

——— "The Plays of LeRoi Jones," *CLA Journal* 14 (1971): 331–39.

Ojo-Ade, Femi, ed., *Of Dreams Deferred, Dead or Alive: African Perspectives on African-American Writers* (1996).

Palmer, R. Roderick, "The Poetry of Three Revolutionists: Don L. Lee, Sonia Sanchez, and Nikki Giovanni," *CLA Journal* 15 (1971): 25–36.

Patterson, Lindsay, ed., *A Rock against the Wind: African-American Poems and Letters of Love and Passion* (1996).

Peavy, Charles, comp., *Afro-American Literature and Culture Since World War II: A Guide to Information Sources* (1979).

Saunders, James Robert, *The Wayward Preacher in the Literature of African American Women* (1995).

Smith, David Lionel, "The Black Arts Movement and Its Critics," *American Literary History* 3 (1991): 93–110.

Sollors, Werner, "Of Mules and Mares in a Land of Difference: Or, Quadrupeds All?" *American Quarterly* 42 (1990): 167–90.

Werner, Craig, "The Economic Evolution of James Baldwin," *CLA Journal* 23 (1979): 12–31.

Wright, Derek, "African-American Tensions in Black Writing of the 1960's," *Journal of Black Studies* 19 (1989): 442–58.

23.10.6 Music and Performing Arts

Bogle, Donald, *Brown Sugar: Eighty Years of America's Black Female Superstars* (1980).

Carawan, Guy, and Candie Carawan, comp., *We Shall Overcome! Songs of the Southern Freedom Movement* (1963).

Carmichael, Thomas, "Beneath the Underdog: Charles Mingus, Representation, and Jazz Autobiography," *Canadian Review of American Studies* 25 (1995): 29–40.

Clark, Vévé, "Performing the Memory of Difference in Afro-Caribbean Dance: Katherine Dunham's Choreography, 1938–1987," in Geneviéve Fabre and Robert O'Meally, ed., *History and Memory in African-American Culture* (1994): 188–204.

Daniels, Douglas Henry, "Los Angeles Zoot: Race 'Riot,' The Pachuco, and Black Music Culture," *Journal of Negro History* 82 (1997): 201–20.

Dent, Thomas C., Richard Schechner, and Gilbert Moses, ed., *The Free Southern Theater, by the Free Southern Theater: A Documentary of the South's Radical Black Theater, with Journals, Letters, Poetry, Essays, and a Play Written by Those Who Built It* (1969).

DeVeaux, Scott, *The Birth of Bebop: A Social and Musical History* (1997).

DjeDje, Jacqueline Cogdell, and Eddie S. Meadows, ed., *California Soul: Music of African Americans in the West* (1998).

Dunham, Katherine, *Touch of Innocence* (1959).

Dunson, Josh, *Freedom in the Air: Song Movements of the Sixties* (1965).

Edet, Edna M., "One Hundred Years of Black Protest Music," *Black Scholar* 7 (1976): 38–48.

Elam, Harry J., Jr., *Taking It to the Streets: The Social Protest Theater of Luis Valdez and Amiri Baraka* (1997).

Fryer, Paul H., "'Brown-Eyed Handsome Man': Chuck Berry and the Blues Tradition," *Phylon* 42 (1981): 60–72.

Garofolo, Reebee, "The Impact of the Civil Rights Movement on Popular Music," *Radical America* 21 (1987): 14–22.

Guralnick, Peter, *Sweet Soul Music: Rhythm and Blues and the Southern Dream of Freedom* (1986).

Heilbut, Anthony, *The Gospel Sound: Good News and Bad Times* (1971).

Jeffers, Lance, "Bullins, Baraka, and Elder: The Dawn of Grandeur in Black Drama," *CLA Journal* 16 (1972): 32–48.

Kelley, Robin D. G., "Dig They Freedom: Meditations on History and the Black Avant-Garde," *Lenox Avenue* 3 (1997): 13–27.

Ling, Peter J., "Developing Freedom Songs: Guy Carawan and the African-American Traditions of the South Carolina Sea Islands," *History Workshop Journal* 44 (1997): 198–213.

Lornell, Kip, *'Happy in the Service of the Lord': African-American Sacred Vocal Harmony Quartets in Memphis* (1995).

McNeilly, Kevin, "Charles Mingus Splits, or All the Things You Could Be by Now If Sigmund Freud's Wife Was Your Mother," *Canadian Review of American Studies* 27 (1997): 45–70.

Morris, Ronald, "Themes of Protest and Criminality in American Recorded Jazz, 1945–1975," *Annual Review of Jazz Studies* 3 (1985): 147–66.

Morse, David, *Motown and the Arrival of Black Music* (1972).

Mullen, Patrick B., "The Prism of Race: Two Texas Performers," *Southern Folklore* 54 (1997): 13–25.

Olaniyan, Tejumola, *Scars of Conquest/Masks of Resistance: The Invention of Cultural Identities in African, African-American, and Caribbean Drama* (1995).

Reagon, Bernice Johnson, ed., *We'll Understand It Better By and By: Pioneering African American Gospel Composers* (1992).

Reagon, Bernice Johnson, and Sweet Honey in the Rock, *We Who Believe in Freedom: Sweet Honey in the Rock—Still on the Journey* (1993).

Reed, Tom, *The Black Music History of Los Angeles: Its Roots* (1994).

Simpson, Anne Key, "Camille Lucie Nickerson: 'The Louisiana Lady,'" *Louisiana History* 36 (1995): 431–51.

Ward, Brian, *Just My Soul Responding: Rhythm and Blues, Black Consciousness, and Race Relations* (1998).

Wells, Alan, "Black Artists in American Popular Music, 1955–1985," *Phylon* 48 (1987): 309–16.

Werner, Craig, *A Change Is Gonna Come: Music, Race, and the Soul of America* (1999).

23.10.7   Film and Broadcasting

Barlow, William, *Voice Over: The Making of Black Radio* (1999).

Cripps, Thomas, "The Death of Rastus: The Negro in American Films Since 1945," *Phylon* 28 (1967): 267–75.

———— *Making Movies Black: The Hollywood Message Movie from World War II to the Civil Rights Era* (1993).

Fisher, Paul L., and Ralph L. Lowenstein, ed., *Race and the News Media* (1967).

Leab, Daniel J., *From Sambo to Superspade: The Black Experience in Motion Pictures* (1975).

Leslie, Michael, "Slow Fade To? Advertising in *Ebony* Magazine, 1957–1989," *Journalism and Mass Communication Quarterly* 72 (1995): 426–35.

Null, Gary, *Black Hollywood: The Negro in Motion Pictures* (1975).

Oshana, Maryann, *Women of Color: A Filmography of Minority and Third World Women* (1985).

Regester, Charlene, "African-American Actors and the Communism Scare of the 1950's: Unique Responses to the Otherness Inflicted by the Hegemonic Discourse," *Studies in American Culture* 20 (1997): 1–16.

Reid, Mark, *Redefining Black Film* (1993).

Rife, Marilyn Diane, "Black Image in American TV: The First Two Decades," *Black Scholar* 6 (1974): 7–15.

Stroman, Carolyn A., "The Socialization Influence of Television on Black Children," *Journal of Black Studies* 15 (1984): 79–100.

Taylor, Henry, and Carol Dozier, "Television Violence, African-Americans, and Social Control, 1950–1976," *Journal of Black Studies* 14 (1983): 107–36.

Vaughn, Stephen, "Ronald Reagan and the Struggle for Black Dignity in Cinema, 1937–1953," *Journal of Negro History* 77 (1992): 1–16.

Zinkhan, George M., William T. Qualls, and Abhijit Biswas, "The Use of Blacks in Magazine and Television Advertising, 1946 to 1986," *Journalism Quarterly* 67 (1990): 547–53.

23.11   EDUCATION

Banks, William M., "Afro-American Scholars in the University: Roles and Conflicts," *American Behavioral Scientist* 27 (1984): 325–38.

Bass, Jack, *Unlikely Heroes: The Dramatic Story of the Southern Judges of the Fifth Circuit Who Translated the Supreme Court's Brown Decision into a Revolution for Equality* (1981).

Bates, Daisy, *The Long Shadow of Little Rock: A Memoir* (1962).

Beals, Melba Pattillo, *Warriors Don't Cry: A Searing Memoir of the Battle to Integrate Little Rock's Central High* (1994).

Bell, Derrick, "Time for Teachers: Putting Educators Back into the *Brown* Remedy," *Journal of Negro Education* 52 (1983): 290–301.

Berry, Mary Frances, "Twentieth-Century Black Women in Education," *Journal of Negro Education* 51 (1982): 288–300.

Blassingame, John W., "Black Studies: An Intellectual Crisis," *American Scholar* 38 (1969): 548–61.

Blaustein, Albert P., and Clarence Clyde Ferguson, Jr., *Desegregation and the Law: The Meaning and Effect of the School Segregation Cases* (2d ed., 1962).

Branton, Wiley A., "Little Rock Revisited: Desegregation to Resegregation," *Journal of Negro Education* 52 (1983): 250–69.

Clark, Kenneth Bancroft, "The *Brown* Decision: Racism, Education, and Human Values," *Journal of Negro Education* 57 (1988): 125–32.

Curry, Constance, *Silver Rights* (1995).

Diamond, Raymond T., "Confrontation As Rejoinder to Compromise: Reflections on the Little Rock Desegregation Crisis," *National Black Law Journal* 11 (1989): 151–76.

Diggs, Irene, "Du Bois and Children," *Phylon* 37 (1976): 370–99.

Dillon, Patricia, "Civil Rights and School Desegregation in Sanford," *Florida Historical Quarterly* 76 (1998): 310–25.

Douglas, Davison M., *Reading, Writing, and Race: The Desegregation of the Charlotte Schools* (1995).

Edwards, Harry, *Black Students* (1970).

Evans, Art, and Annette Evans, "Black Educators before and after 1960," *Phylon* 43 (1982): 254–61.

Formisano, Ronald P., *Boston against Busing: Race, Class, and Ethnicity in the 1960's and 1970's* (1991).

Grant, Twala M., "The Missed Mandate of *Brown v. Board of Education:* Educationally Effective Schools with All Deliberate Speed," *National Black Law Journal* 13 (1993): 134–46.

Gutiérrez, Henry J., "Racial Politics in Los Angeles: Black and Mexican American Challenges to Unequal Education in the 1960's," *Southern California Quarterly* 78 (1996): 51–86.

Haines, Andrew W., "Why Law Schools Should Celebrate the Contribution of Dr. Martin Luther King, Jr.," *National Black Law Journal* 10 (1987): 224–36.

Haney, James E., "The Effects of the *Brown* Decision on Black Educators," *Journal of Negro Education* 47 (1978): 88–95.

Harris, Robert L., Jr., "Segregation and Scholarship: The American Council of Learned Societies' Committee on Negro Studies, 1941–1950," *Journal of Black Studies* 12 (1982): 315–31.

Jacobs, Gregory S., *Getting around Brown: Desegregation, Development, and the Columbus Public Schools* (1998).

Jacoway, Elizabeth, and C. Fred Williams, ed., *Understanding the Little Rock Crisis: An Exercise in Remembrance and Reconciliation* (1999).

Jones, Leon, "Desegregation and Social Reform Since 1954," *Journal of Negro Education* 43 (1974): 155–71.

Kaufman, Polly Welts, "Building a Constituency for School Desegregation: African-American Women in Boston, 1962–1972," *Teachers College Record* 92 (1991): 619–31.

Kee, Ed, "The *Brown* Decision and Milford, Delaware, 1954–1965," *Delaware History* 27 (1997–1998): 205–43.

Kellar, William Henry, *Make Haste Slowly: Moderates, Conservatives, and School Desegregation in Houston* (1999).

Kluger, Richard, *Simple Justice: The History of Brown v. Board of Education and Black America's Struggle for Equality* (1975).

Kozol, Jonathan, *Death at an Early Age: The Destruction of the Hearts and Minds of Negro Children in the Boston Public Schools* (1967).

Lassiter, Matthew D., and Andrew B. Lewis, ed., *The Moderates' Dilemma: Massive Resistance to School Desegregation in Virginia* (1998).

Leone, Janice, "Integrating the American Association of University Women, 1946–1949," *Historian* 51 (1989): 423–45.

Lowery, Bruce, "Integration at Alabama's Historically Black Colleges and Universities," *Southern Historian* 19 (1998): 38–42.

Marcello, Ronald E., "Reluctance *versus* Reality: The Desegregation of North Texas State College, 1954–1956," *Southwestern Historical Quarterly* 100 (1996): 153–86.

Pratt, Robert A., *The Color of Their Skin: Education and Race in Richmond, Virginia, 1954–1989* (1992).

Richards, Pamela Spence, "Library Services and the African-American Intelligentsia before 1960," *Libraries and Culture* 33 (1998): 91–97.

Robinson, Armstead L., ed., *Black Studies in the University* (1968).

Robinson, Armstead L., Craig Foster, and Donald Ogilvie, ed., *Black Studies in the University: A Symposium* (1969).

Roche, Jeff, *Restructured Resistance: The Sibley Commission and the Politics of Desegregation in Georgia* (1998).

Rothschild, Mary Aickin, "The Volunteers and the Freedom Schools: Education for Social Change in Mississippi," *History of Education Quarterly* 22 (1982): 401–20.

Roy, Beth, *Bitters in the Honey: Tales of Hope and Disappointment Across Divides of Race and Time* (1999).

Siskar, John F., "The B.U.I.L.D. Academy: A Historical Study of Community Action and Education in Buffalo, New York," *Afro-Americans in New York Life and History* 21 (1997): 19–40.

Staples, Robert, "Racial Ideology and Intellectual Racism: Blacks in Academia," *Black Scholar* 15 (1984): 2–17.

Wesley, Dorothy Porter, and Avril Johnson Madison (interviewer), "Dorothy Burnett Porter Wesley: Enterprising Steward of Black Culture," *Public Historian* 17 (1995): 15–40.

Willie, Charles V., "Philanthropic and Foundation Support for Blacks: A Case Study from the 1960's," *Journal of Negro Education* 50 (1981): 270–84.

Young, Carlene, "The Struggle and Dream of Black Studies," *Journal of Negro Education* 53 (1984): 368–78.

23.12   WORK AND ENTREPRENEURIAL ACTIVITY

Boyle, Kevin, "The Kiss: Racial and Gender Conflict in a 1950's Automobile Factory," *Journal of American History* 84 (1997): 496–523.

———— "'There Are No Union Sorrows That the Union Can't Heal': The Struggle for Racial Equality in the United Automobile Workers, 1940–1960," *Labor History* 36 (1995): 5–23.

Calliste, Agnes, "The Struggle for Employment Equity by Blacks on American and Canadian Railroads," *Journal of Black Studies* 25 (1995): 297–317.

Denby, Charles, *Indignant Heart: A Black Worker's Journal* (rev. ed., 1978).

Elgie, Robert A., "Industrialization and Racial Inequality within the American South, 1950–1970," *Social Science Quarterly* 61 (1980): 458–72.

Fehn, Bruce, "African-American Women and the Struggle for Equality in the Meatpacking Industry, 1940–1960," *Journal of Women's History* 10 (1998): 45–69.

———— "'The Only Hope We Had': United Packinghouse Workers Local 46 and the Struggle for Racial Equality in Waterloo, Iowa, 1948–1960," *Annals of Iowa* 54 (1995): 185–216.

Frederickson, Mary, "Four Decades of Change: Black Workers in Southern Textiles, 1941–1981," *Radical America* 16 (1982): 27–44.

Geschwender, James A., "The League of Revolutionary Black Workers: Problems of Confronting Black Marxist-Leninist Organizations," *Journal of Ethnic Studies* 2 (1974): 1–23.

Goddard, Robert, "Agricultural Worker As Archetype in West Indian and African-American Literature," *Agricultural History* 72 (1998): 509–20.

Griffin, Larry J., and Robert R. Korstad, "Class As Race and Gender: Making and Breaking a Labor Union in the Jim Crow South," *Social Science History* 19 (1995): 425–54.

Grim, Valerie, "The Politics of Inclusion: Black Farmers and the Quest for Agribusiness Participation, 1945–1990's," *Agricultural History* 69 (1995): 257–71.

Halpern, Rick, and Roger Horowitz, *Meatpackers: An Oral History of Black Packinghouse Workers and Their Struggle for Racial and Economic Equality* (1996).

Honey, Michael, *Black Workers Remember: An Oral History of Segregation, Unionism, and the Freedom Struggle* (1999).

———— "Operation Dixie: Labor and Civil Rights in the Postwar South," *Mississippi Quarterly* 45 (1992): 439–52.

Joyce, Patrick D., "A Reversal of Fortunes: Black Empowerment, Political Machines, and City Jobs in New York City and Chicago," *Urban Affairs Review* 32 (1997): 291–318.

Minchin, Timothy J., *Hiring the Black Worker: The Racial Integration of the Southern Textile Industry, 1960–1980* (1999).

Moreno, Paul, "Racial Proportionalism and the Origins of Employment Discrimination Policy, 1933–1950," *Journal of Policy History* 8 (1996): 410–39.

Parsons, Donald O., "Racial Trends in Male Labor Force Participation," *American Economic Review* 70 (1980): 911–20.

Puth, Robert C., "Supreme Life: The History of a Negro Life Insurance Company, 1919–1962," *Business History Review* 43 (1969): 1–20.

Rhee, Jong Mo, "The Redistribution of the Black Work Force in the South by Industry," *Phylon* 35 (1974): 293–300.

Sexton, Brendan, "Unions and the Black Power Brokers," *Dissent* 18 (1971): 41–49.

Stein, Judith, *Running Steel, Running America: Race, Economic Policy, and the Decline of Liberalism* (1998).

Tsonc, Peter Z. W., "Changing Patterns of Labor Force Participation Rates of Nonwhites in the South," *Phylon* 35 (1974): 301–12.

Weiss, Robert J., *"We Want Jobs": A History of Affirmative Action* (1997).

Wilson, William Julius, *The Declining Significance of Race: Blacks and Changing American Institutions* (2d ed., 1980).

23.13   SCIENCE AND TECHNOLOGY

Green, Venus, "Race and Technology: African American Women in the Bell System, 1945–1980," *Technology and Culture* 36 (1995): S101–45.

23.14   MEDICINE AND HEALTH

Beardsley, Edward H., "Desegregating Southern Medicine, 1945–1970," *International Social Science Review* 71 (1996): 37–54.

Beito, David T., "Black Fraternal Hospitals in the Mississippi Delta, 1942–1967," *Journal of Southern History* 65 (1965): 109–40.

Curtis, James L., *Blacks, Medical Schools, and Society* (1971).

Davis, Robert, "Suicide among Young Blacks: Trends and Perspectives," *Phylon* 41 (1980): 223–29.

Reitzes, Dietrich C., *Negroes and Medicine* (1958).

Richardson, Joe M., "Albert W. Dent: A Black New Orleans Hospital and University Administrator," *Louisiana History* 37 (1996): 309–23.

Waddell, William H., *The Black Man in Veterinary Medicine* (1970).

23.15   STUDIES IN FOREIGN LANGUAGES

Amendt, Gerhard, "Thesen und Anmerkungen zur Amerikanischen Bürgerrechtspolitik und zur Strategie der Kulturnationalistischen Konterrevolution" [Theses and Notes on American Civil Rights Policy and the Strategy of the Cultural-Nationalist Counter-Revolution], in Gerhard Amendt, ed., *Black Power: Dokumente und Analysen* [Black Power: Documents and Analysis] (1970): 206–33. In German.

Aoyagi, Kiyotaka, *Kokujin Daigaku Ryugaku-ki* [Studying at Fisk University: Observations and Experiences with Black America] (1964). In Japanese.

Aragón, Leopoldo, *La questión racial en los Estados Unidos* [The Racial Question in the United States] (1966). In Spanish.

Asahi, Shinbunsha, ed., *Kokujin* [Black People: Beyond Oppression and Submission] (1958). In Japanese.

Astesano, Eduardo, *El nacionalismo negro en Estados Unidos* [Black Nationalism in the United States] (1972). In Spanish.

Auer, Andréas, *Les Noirs: Les écoles publiques et le système constitutionnel aux États-Unis* [The Blacks: The Public Schools and the Constitutional System of the United States] (1975). In French.

Bas-Rabérin, Philippe, *Le Blues moderne, 1945–1973* [Modern Blues, 1945–1973] (2d ed., 1986). In French.

Becker, Jörg, *Alltäglicher Rassismus: Die Afro-Amerikanischen Rassenkonflikte im Kinder und Jugendbuch der Bundesrepublik* [Everyday Racism: Afro-American Race Conflicts in Children's and Juvenile Books of the German Federal Republic] (1977). In German.

Belski Lagazzi, Ines, *Martin Luther King: Il Suo sogno è ancora lontano* [Martin Luther King: His "Dream" Is Still Far Away] (1993). In Italian.

Bergh, Hendrik van, *Die Amerikanische Krankheit: Diagnose und Konsequenzen* [The American Disease: Diagnosis and Consequences] (1968). In German.

Bertella Farnetti, Paolo, "La fase oscura della repressione" [The Dark Phase of Repression], in Bruno Cartosio, *Senza Illusioni* (1995): 69–81. In Italian.

Blight, David, *Dialogo su Malcolm X* [Dialogue on Malcolm X] (1994). In Italian.

Blumberg, Rhoda Lois, *Los derechos civiles: la lucha por la libertad en la decada de 1960* [Civil Rights: The Fight for Freedom in the Decade of the 1960's] (1988). In Spanish.

Bollinger, Klaus, *Freiheit Sofort! Die Negerbevölkerung der USA in Kampf um Demokratie* [Freedom Now! The Negro Population of the USA in the Struggles for Democracy] (1968). In German.

Boubault, Guy, *Martin Luther King: non-violence actualité* [Martin Luther King: On the Topic of Non-Violence] (1992). In French.

Brandes, Volkhard, and Joyce Burke, *USA: Vom Rassenkampf zum Klassenkampf: Die Organisierung des Schwarzen Widerstandes* [From Race Struggle to Class Struggle: Organizing the Black Resistance] (1970). In German.

Briceño-Iragorry, Mario, *Dos responsos a Emmett Till* [Two Responses to Emmett Till] (1955). In Spanish.

Brink, William J., and Louis Harris, *La revolución de los negros en los Estados Unidos: qué es lo que desean los negros: por qué y cómo están luchando: a quiénes apoyan: qué es lo que los blancos piensan de ellos y de lo que exigen* [The Black Revolution in the United States: What the Blacks Want, Why and How They Are Struggling, Whom They Support, What the Whites Think of Them, and Their Demands] (1966). In Spanish.

Buin, Yves, *Thelonious Monk* (1988). In French.

Calderazzi, Antonio Massimo, *La revolución negra en los EE.UU.* [The Black Revolution in the United States] (1970). In Spanish.

——— *La rivoluzione negra negli Stati Uniti* [The Negro Revolution in the United States] (1968). In Italian.

Cartosio, Bruno, "Martin e Malcolm e il movimento di liberazione afro-americano" [Martin and Malcolm and the African-American Liberation Movement], in AAVV, *Dialogo su Malcolm X* [Dialogue on Malcolm X] (1994): 29–53. In Italian.

Chujo, Ken, "'Burakku Nashonarizumu' no Genzai to Kokujin no Seiji Bunka" ['Black Nationalism' and Political Cultures of the Black People], *Gendai shiso* 25 (1997): 72–87. In Japanese.

Congres international des écrivains et artistes noirs, *Deuxième congres des écrivains et artistes noirs: Rome: 26 mars-1er avril, 1959* [The Second International Congress of Black Writers and Artists: Rome, March 26–April 1, 1959] (2d ed., 1959). In French.

Constant, Denis, *Aux sources du reggae* [The Sources of Reggae] (1982). In French.

Dalannoy, Luc, *Lester Young, profession: président* [Lester Young, Profession: President] (1987). In French.

Danchin, Sébastien, *B. B. King* (1993). In French.

Daverat, Xavier, *John Coltrane* (1995). In French.

Desnoes, Edmundo, comp., *Now: el movimiento negro en Estados Unidos* [Now: The Black Movement in the United States] (1967). In Spanish.

Ensslen, Klaus, "Das Getto in der Afroamerikanischen Literatur nach 1945" [The Ghetto in Afro-American Literature after 1945], in Berndt Ostendorf, ed., *Amerikanische Gettoliteratur: Zur Literatur Ethnischer, Marginaler und Unterdrückter Gruppen in Amerika* [American Ghetto Literature: Towards Literature of Ethnic, Marginal, and Oppressed Groups in America]: 234–92. In German.

Förster, Winfried, *Das Rassenproblem in den USA* [The Race-Problem in the USA] (1973). In German.

Fujioka, Atsushi, *Amerika Nanbu no Henbô* [The Changing Face of the American South: Blacks and Landlord-Tenant Relations] (1985). In Japanese.

Gambino, Ferruccio, "Due sceneggiature per un personaggio" [Two Scripts for One Character], in *Dialogo su Malcolm X* [Dialogue on Malcolm X] (1994): 55–66. In Italian.

——— "Introduzione" [Introduction], in *Malcolm X: L'ultima battaglia: discorsi inediti* [Malcolm X: The Final Battle: Unpublished Conversations] (1993) In Italian.

Gerber, Alain, *Le Cas Coltrane* [The Coltrane Case] (1985). In French.

Giammanco, Roberto, *Malcolm X: Rifiuto, sfida, messaggio* [Malcolm X: Rejection, Challenge, Message] (1994). In Italian.

Green, Nancy L., "Juifs et noirs aux États-unis: rupture d'une 'alliance naturelle'" [Jews and Blacks in the United States: The Rupture of a 'Natural Alliance'], *Annales ESC* 42 (1987): In French.

Grosse, Heinrich W., *Die Macht der Armen: Martin Luther King und der Kampf für Soziale Gerechtigkeit* [The Power of the Poor: Martin Luther King and the Struggle for Social Justice] (1971). In German.

Guerin, Daniel, *Décolonisation du Noir américain* [The Decolonization of the Black American] (1963). In French.

Haga, Takeshi, *Amerika no Kuroi Chitai* [The Black Belt in the U.S.A.] (1958). In Japanese.

Hajek, Friederike, *Selbstzeugnisse der Afroamerikaner: Black Liberation Movement und Autobiographie* [Testimonies of Afro-Americans: Black Liberation Movement and Autobiography] (1984). In German.

Helbich, Wolfgang J., "Die Krise der Bürgerrechtsbewegung in den Vereinigten Staaten: Die Zweite Phase der Negeremanzipation 1954–1966" [The Crisis of the Civil Rights Movement in the United States: The Second Half Phase of Negro Emancipation, 1954–1966], *Europa-Archiv* 22 (1967): 359–68. In German.

Hippenmeyer, Jean Roland, *Jazz sur films: ou, 55 années de rapports jazz-cinéma vue à travers plus de 800 films tournés entre 1917 et 1972* [Jazz in Films: Or, Fifty-Five Years of Jazz in Cinema Shown in More Than 800 Films Made between 1917 and 1972] (1973). In French.

——— *Sidney Bechet: ou, l'extraordinaire odyssée d'un musicien de jazz: de Storyville à l'Olympia, de "Wild Cat Blues" aux "Oignons"* [Sidney Bechet: Or, the Extraordinary Odyssey of a Jazz Musician: From Storyville to Olympia, from "Wild Cat Blues" to "Onions"] (1980). In French.

Hoffarth, Monika, *Martin Luther King und die Amerikanische Rassenfrage: Stereotypenkorrektur und Humanitäre Erziehung durch Literarische Rezeption* [Martin Luther King and the American Race Question: The Correction of Stereotypes and Humanitarian Education through Literacy Reception] (1990). In German.

Hornung, Volker, *Wirtschaftlicher Boykott als Gewaltfreies Kampfmittel in Bürgerrechtsbewegungen: Zwei Fallstudien zur Amerikanischen Bürggerrechts- und Landarbeiterbewegung* [Economic Boycott As a Non-Violent Device of Struggle in Civil Rights Movements: Two Case Studies from the American Civil Rights and Farm Workers Movements] (1979). In German.

Hu, Jinshan, "1940–1970 Mei Guo Hei Ren Da Qian Xi Gai Lun" [The Great Migration of Afro-Americans from 1940 to 1970], *Mei Guo Yan Jiu* 4 (1995): 99–120. In Chinese.

Jahn, Jahnheinz, *Muntu: Umriß der Neoafrikanischen Kultur* [Muntu: Contours of Neo-African Culture] (1958). In German.

Joachim, Sebastien, *Le Nègre dans le roman blanc: lecture semiotique et idéologique de romans français et canadiens, 1945–1977* [The Negro in the White Novel: The Semantics and Ideology of French and Canadian Novels, 1945–1977] (1980). In French.

Kajiwara, Hisashi, *Yakusoku no Chi o Motomete* [Toward the Promised Land: M. L. King and the Civil Rights Movement] (1989). In Japanese.

Kalanda, Mabika, *La Remise en question: base de la décolonisation mentale* [Calling into Question: The Basis of Mental Decolonization] (1967). In French.

Kawashima, Masaki, "1965 nen Natsu Ikô no M. L. Kingu" [Rev. M. L. King after the Summer of 1965], *Review of History* 531 (1994): 19–34. In Japanese.

Kikuchi, Ken'ichi, *Amerika Kokujin no Tatakai* [The Battle of Black Americans for Liberation] (1965). In Japanese.

Kosaka, Noboru, *Kingu Bokushi to Marukomu X* [Rev. King and Malcom X] (1994). In Japanese.

Kugai, Saburo, *Gendai Amerika no Kiretsu* [The Fragmentation of the United States Today: Vietnam, Black Liberation, and the Assassination] (1968). In Japanese.

Leduc, Jean-Marie, and Christine Mulard, *Armstrong* (1994). In French.

Lee, Erika, "Hei Quan Yun Dong Li Lun De Tan Tao" [A Study of the Theories of the Black Power Movement], in John Murtha and Lin Li Shu, ed., *Mei Guo Liang Bai Zhou Nian: Mei Guo Li Shi Lun Wen Ji* (1976): 79–113. In Chinese.

Lenz, Günter H., ed., *Afro-Amerika im Amerikanischen Dokumentarfilm* [Afro-America in American Documentary Film] (1993). In German.

Levallet, Didier, and Denis Constant-Martin, *L'Amérique de Mingus: musique et politique* [Mingus's America: Music and Politics] (1991). In French.

Liu, Xuyi, "Cong He Fa Dou Zheng Dao Fei Bao Li Qun Zhong Zhi Jie Xing Dong: Shi Shi Nian Dai Hou Qi Dao Liu Shi Nian Dai Chu Qi De Mei Guo Hei Ren Yun Dong" [From Legitimate Struggle to the Nonviolent Direct Mass Protest: Black American Movements from the Late 1940's to the Early 1960's], in *Mei Guo Shi Lun Wen Ji* (1980): 481–503. In Chinese.

———— "Er Ci Da Zhan Hou Shi Nian Mei Guo Hei Ren Yun Dong De Qi Fu" [The Development of Black American Movement during the First Decade after World War II], *Wuhan Daxue Xuebao* 2 (1981): 37–45. In Chinese.

Llarch, Joan, *Martin Luther King: una vida por la paz* [Martin Luther King: A Life for Peace] (2d ed., 1982). In Spanish.

Lorit, Sergio C., *Luther King: Il sogno finito della non violenza?* [Luther King: The End of the Dream of Non-Violence?] (2d ed., 1970). In Italian.

Maître, Hans Joachim, *Black Power: Machtanspruch Einer Minderheit* [Black Power: A Minority's Claim to Power] (1972). In German.

Malizia, Pierfranco, *Cultura e libertà: Acculturazione e disacculturazione in Africa e nell'America nera* [Culture and Freedom: Segregation and Desegregation in Africa and Black America] (1976). In Italian.

Malson, Lucien, *Histoire du jazz moderne, 1945–1960* [History of Modern Jazz, 1945–1960] (1961). In French.

Martinelli, Alberto, and Alessandro Cavalli, *Il partito della pantera nera* [The Black Panther Party] (1971). In Italian.

Masnata, François, *Pouvoir blanc, révolte noire: essai sur la tradition démocratique aux États-Unis* [White Power, Black Revolt: An Essay on the Democratic Tradition in the United States] (1968). In French.

Materassi, Mario, "Gli avvenimenti storici e le icone letterarie: Alcune osservazioni sulla roba« della letteratura nera" [Historic Events and Literary Icons: Some Observations on the 'Stuff' of Black Literature], *Rivista di Studi Anglo-Americani [Journal of Anglo-American Studies]* 4 (1986): 161–68. In Italian.

Michels, Peter M., *Aufstand in den Ghettos: Zur Organisation des Lumpenproletariats in den USA* [Insurrection in the Ghettos: Towards the Organization of the Lumpenproletariat in the USA] (1972). In German.

———— *Bericht über den Politischen Widerstand in den USA* [Report on Political Resistance in the USA] (1974). In German.

Morikawa, Masamichi, *Hi-bôryoku kara Busô e* [From Non-Violence to Bearing Arms] (1970). In Japanese.

Nabe, Marc Eduoard, *L'Âme de Billie Holiday* [The Soul of Billie Holiday] (1986). In French.

Nagata, Ei, *Kokujin wa Hangyaku suru* [Blacks in Revolt: Malcom X and His Thinking] (1966). In Japanese.

Naso, Paolo, "Martin Luther King: la radicalità di un moderno puritano" [Martin Luther King: Radicality of a Modern Puritan], in AAVV, *Dialogo su Malcolm X* [Dialogue on Malcolm X] (1994): 77–86. In Italian.

Noack, Hans Georg, *Der Gewaltlose Aufstand: Martin Luther King und der Kampf der Amerikanischen Neger* [The Non-Violent Insurrection: Martin Luther King and the Struggle of the American Negroes] (1965). In German.

Ortiz Oderigo, Nestor R., *La música afronorteamericana* [Afro-American Music of the United States] (1962). In Spanish.

Otani, Yasuo, *Byôdô eno Michi* [The Road to Equality: African-Americans and the Supreme Court] (1993). In Japanese.

Padilla, Ramón, and Joaquín Bollo, *Estados Unidos: guerras internas; negros, puertorriqueños* [The United States: Internal Wars of Blacks and Puerto Ricans] (1972). In Spanish.

Panassié, Hugues, *Histoire du vrai jazz* [A History of True Jazz] (1959). In French.

Paolantonacci, Michèle, *Les Auteurs afro-américains, 1965–1987* [Afro-American Authors, 1965–1987] (1989). In French.

Pattee, Richard, *La segregación racial en Estados Unidos* [Racial Segregation in the United States] (1955). In Spanish.

Paudras, Francis, *La Danse des infidèles: Bud Powell* [The Unfaithful Ones Are Dancing: Bud Powell] (1986). In French.

Piccioni, Leone, *Troppa morte, troppa vita: Viaggi e pensieri intorno agli USA* [Too Much Death, Too Much Life: Journeys and Thoughts around the United States] (1969). In Italian.

Pivano, Fernanda, ed., *L'altra America negli anni Sessanta* [The Other America in the Sixties] (1972). In Italian.

Portelli, Alessandro, "Malcolm e la storia" [Malcolm and History], in *Dialogo su Malcolm* [Dialogue on Malcolm] (1994): 19–28. In Italian.

Portelli, Alessando, *Veleno di piombo sul muro: Le canzoni del Black Power* [Lead Poison on the Wall: A Collection of Black Movement Songs from the 1960's] (1969). In Italian.

Presler, Gerd, *Martin Luther King, Jr.* (1984). In German.

Putschögl, Gerhard, *John Coltrane und die Afroamerikanische Oraltradition* [John Coltrane and the Afro-American Oral Tradition] (1993). In German.

Ritschl, Dietrich, *Nur Menschen: Zur Negerfrage in den Amerikanischen Südstaaten* [Just People: On the Negro Problem in the American Southern States] (1962). In German.

Robaina, Tomás Fernández, *Bibliografía sobre estudios afro-americanos* [Bibliography on Afro-American Studies] (1968). In Spanish.

Sagrera, Martín, *Poder blanco y negro: el conflicto racial estadounidense y su repercusion mundial: ensayo* [Black Power, White Power: The Racial Conflict in the United States and Its World Wide Repercussions] (1970). In Spanish.

Saint-Michel, Serge, Bruno Le Sourd, *Martin Luther King: et le journal du racisme et de la non-violence* [Martin Luther King and the Journal of Racism and Non-Violence], ed. Alphonse Ruel (1979). In French.

Saruya, Kaname, *Amerika Kokujin Kaihô-shi* [A History of Black Americans' Struggle toward Freedom] (1968). In Japanese.

——— *Kingu Bokushi to sono Jidai* [Rev. King and His Era] (1994). In Japanese.

Sato, Tadayuki, "Kominken Tosoki Nanbu no Yudayajin" [The Jews in the South during the Civil Rights Movement], *Dokkyo Eigo Kenkyu* 45 (1996): 91–115. In Japanese.

Schuhler, Conrad, *Black Panther: Zur Konsolidierung des Klassenkampfes in den USA* [Black Panther: Toward the Consolidation of the Class Struggle in the USA] (1969). In German.

Simon, Walter B., "Schwarzer Nationalismus in den USA" [Black Nationalism in the USA], *Kölner Zeitschrift für Soziologie und Sozialpsychologie* 15 (1963): 605–42. In German.

Sueyoshi, Takaaki, *Kokujin Bunka to Kokujin Iesu* [Black Culture and Black Jesus] (1986). In Japanese.

Suzuki, Jiro, *Kuroi America-jin* [Black Americans] (1957). In Japanese.

Tallet, José Z., *El problema del negro en los Estados Unidos: informe al señor Ministro* [The Black Problem in the United States: Report to the Minister] (1960). In Spanish.

Teodori, Massimo, "Vita e sconfitta del movimento nero" [Life and Defeat of the Black Movement], in *La fine del mito americano: Saggi sulla storia, la politica e la società* [The End of the American Myth: Essays on History, Politics, and Society] (1975): 77–93. In Italian.

Tercinet, Alain, *Be-Bop* (1991). In French.

Tergeist, Peter, *Schwarze Bewegung und Gettoaufstände: Strukturen Rassischer Gewalt in den USA* [Black Movement and Ghetto Insurrections: Structures of Racial Violence in the USA] (1982). In German.

Tsujiuchi, Makoto, and Ken Chujo, *Kingu Bokushi* [Rev. King: In Search of Racial Equality and Human Brotherhood] (1993). In Japanese.

Tsukamoto, Shigeyori, *Jiyû to Byodô no Genkai* [The Limits of Freedom and Equality] (1959). In Japanese.

Uekusa, Jin'ichi, *Hâremu no Kokujin Tachi* [Black People in Harlem] (1978). In Japanese.

Uesugi, Shinobu, *Amerika Nanbu Kokujin Chitai eno Tabi* [A Research Trip to the Alabama Black Belt: The Pursuit for the Root of the Black Civil Rights Movement] (1993). In Japanese.

Valtz Mannucci, Loretta, *I nuovi americani: La rivoluzione democratica* [The New Americans: The Democratic Revolution] (1968). In Italian.

Venturini, Nadia, "Nuove tendenze nella storiografia urbana afro-americana" [New Trends in the African-American Urban History-Writing], *Movimento operaio e socialista [Working-Class and Socialist Movement]* 3 (1990): 395–400. In Italian.

Waldschmidt-Nelson, Britta, *From Protest to Politics: Schwarze Frauen in der Bürgerrechstbewegung und im Kongreß der Vereinigten Staaten* [Black Women in the Civil Rights Movement and in the United States Congress] (1998). In German.

Wang, Lin, "Mei Guo Liu Shi Nian Dai Hou Qi De Hei Ren Min Quan Yun Dong" [The Black Civil Rights Movement in the Late 1960's], *Jilin Shiyuan Xuebao* 3 (1987): 27–9. In Chinese.

Wartenweiler, Fritz, *Martin Luther King* (1968). In German.

Wilhelms, Simone, *Ghetto und Staat: Der Politische Faktor Sozialwissenschaftlicher Perspektiven und Praktisch-Administrativer Lösungsstrategien in der Behandlung Gesellschaftlicher Probleme, Dargestellt am Beispiel der Schwarzen Gettos in den USA* [Ghetto and State: The Political Factor in the Perspectives of Social Sciences and Practical-Administrative Strategies of Solution in the Handling of Social Problems, Illustrated by the Example of Black Ghettos in the USA] (1976). In German.

Yanaka, Hisako, "Jôgia-shu Atoranta Kôritsu Gakkô ni okeru Jinshu Kyôgaku o Megutte" [Public Education after the *Brown* Decision in Atlanta: From Segregation to Resegregation], *The Journal of Kyoritsu Area Studies* 7 (1995): 147–68. In Japanese.

Yang, Liwen, "Lun Hei Ren Ji Xu Zhao Shou Zhong Zu Qi Shi De Zheng Jie Ji Qi Chu Lu" [The Crux and Solution of the Continued Racial Discrimination against Afro-Americans], *Mei Guo Yan Jiu* 8 (1994): 7–27. In Chinese.

Yoshida, Ruiko, *Hâremu no Atsui Hibi* [Hot Days in Harlem] (1972). In Japanese.

——— *Watashi no Hada wa Kuroi* [My Skin Is Black] (1978). In Japanese.

Yourcenar, Marguerite, *Chants noirs* [Black Songs] (1952). In French.

——— "Mort et resurrection dans les negro" [Death and Marguerite Yourcenar: The Death and Resurrection of Negroes in Easter All over the World], in *Paques par toute la terre* (1966). In French.

24   *1968–1999*

John H. Bracey, Adam Biggs, and Corey Walker

24.1   GENERAL STUDIES

Bartley, Numan V., *The New South, 1945–1980* (1995).

Blauner, Bob, *Racial Oppression in America* (1972).

Jones, Faustine C., "External Crosscurrents and Internal Diversity: An Assessment of Black Progress, 1960–1980," *Daedalus* 110 (1981): 71–101.

Lubiano, Wahneema, ed., *The House That Race Built: Black Americans, U.S. Terrain* (1997).

Myers, Samuel L., Jr., ed., *Civil Rights and Race Relations in the Post Reagan-Bush Era* (1997).

National Urban League, *The State of Black America* (1976–1999).

Pinkney, Alphonso, *Black Americans* (4th ed., 1993).

Reagon, Bernice Johnson, ed., *Black American Culture and Scholarship: Contemporary Issues* (1985).

Sitkoff, Harvard, *The Struggle for Black Equality, 1954–1992* (rev. ed., 1993).

Van Deburg, William L., *Black Camelot: African-American Culture Heroes in Their Times, 1960–1980* (1997).

——— *New Day in Babylon: The Black Power Movement and American Culture, 1965–1975* (1992).

Wilson, William Julius, *The Declining Significance of Race: Blacks and Changing American Institutions* (1978).

24.2   HISTORIOGRAPHY

Goings, Kenneth W., and R. A. Mohl, "Toward a New African-American Urban History," *Journal of Urban History* 21 (1995): 283–95.

Sammons, Jeffrey T., "A Proportionate and Measured Response to the Provocation That Is *Darwin's Athletes*," *Journal of Sport History* 24 (1997): 378–88.

Seals, Greg, "Schlesinger's Historiography, Afrocentric Conservatism, and *The Disuniting of America*," *Journal of Thought* 33 (1998): 29–40.

Stanfield, John H., II, ed., *A History of Race Relations Research: First-Generation Recollections* (1993).

Stanfield, John H., II, and M. Dennis Rutledge, ed., *Race and Ethnicity in Research Methods* (1993).

24.3   SECONDARY SOURCES ON NEWSPAPERS AND PERIODICALS

Leslie, Michael, "Slow Fade To? Advertising in *Ebony* Magazine, 1957–1989," *Journalism and Mass Communication Quarterly* 72 (1995): 426–35.

Petersen, Keith S., "Anglophone African, Asian and American Black Newspaper Coverage of the United Nations, 1949–1977," *Polity* 16 (1983): 304–19.

——— "U.S. Black Newspaper Coverage of the United Nations and U.S. White Coverage, 1948–1975," *International Organization* 33 (1979): 525–39.

24.4 RACE RELATIONS

24.4.1 Black/White Relations

Apostle, Richard A., *The Anatomy of Racial Attitudes* (1983).

Asante, Molefi, and Alice Davis, "Black and White Communication: Analyzing Work Place Encounters," *Journal of Black Studies* 16 (1985): 77–93.

Barron, Milton L., "Recent Developments in Minority and Race Relations," *Annals of the American Academy of Political and Social Science* (1975): 125–76.

Bartley, Numan V., *The New South, 1945–1980: The Story of the South's Modernization* (1995).

Blauner, Bob, *Black Lives, White Lives: Three Decades of Race Relations in America* (1989).

Bledsoe, Timothy, Michael Combs, Lee Sigelman, and Susan Welch, "Trends in Racial Attitudes in Detroit, 1968–1992," *Urban Affairs Review* 31 (1996): 508–28.

Bobo, Lawrence, and James R. Kluegel, "Opposition to Race-Targeting: Self-Interest, Stratification Ideology, or Racial Attitudes?" *American Sociological Review* 58 (1993): 443–64.

Bobo, Lawrence, and Camille L. Zubrinsky, "Attitudes on Residential Integration: Perceived Status Differences, Mere In-Group Preference, or Racial Prejudice?" *Social Forces* 74 (1996): 883–909.

Brooks, Roy L., *Integration or Separation? A Strategy for Racial Equality* (1996).

Chideya, Farai, *Don't Believe the Hype: Fighting Cultural Misinformation about African-Americans* (1995).

Clayton, Obie, Jr., ed., *An American Dilemma Revisited: Race Relations in a Changing World* (1996).

Condran, John G., "Changes in White Attitudes toward Blacks, 1963–1977," *Public Opinion Quarterly* 43 (1979): 463–76.

Cose, Ellis, ed., *The Darden Dilemma: 12 Black Writers on Justice and Race Relations in America* (1997).

DeMott, Benjamin, *The Trouble with Friendship: Why Americans Can't Think Straight about Race* (1995).

Finkenstaedt, Rose L. H., *Face to Face: Blacks in America: White Perceptions and Black Realities* (1994).

Firebaugh, Glenn, and Kenneth E. Davis, "Trends in Anti-Black Prejudice, 1972–1984: Region and Cohort Effects," *American Journal of Sociology* 94 (1988): 251–72.

Formisano, Ronald P., *Boston against Busing: Race, Class and Ethnicity in the 1960's and 1970's* (1991).

Glaser, James M., "Back to the Black Belt: Racial Environment and White Racial Attitudes in the South," *Journal of Politics* 56 (1994): 21–41.

Goldfield, David R., *Black, White, and Southern: Race Relations and Southern Culture, 1940 to the Present* (1990).

Higham, John, ed., *Civil Rights and Social Wrongs: Black-White Relations Since World War II* (1997).

Hill, Herbert, and James E. Jones, ed., *Race in America: The Struggle for Equality* (1993).

Hochschild, Jennifer L., *Facing Up to the American Dream: Race, Class, and the Soul of the Nation* (rev ed., 1996).

Hollinger, David A., "Group Preferences, Cultural Diversity, and Social Democracy: Notes toward a Theory of Affirmative Action," *Representations* 55 (1996): 31–40.

Humphrey, Ronald, and Howard Schuman, "The Portrayal of Blacks in Magazine Advertisements, 1950–1982," *Public Opinion Quarterly* 48 (1984): 551–63.

Jackman, Mary R., and Marie Crane, "'Some of My Best Friends Are Black . . .': Interracial Friendship and Whites' Racial Attitudes," *Public Opinion Quarterly* 50 (1986): 459–86.

Jackson, Walter A., *Gunnar Myrdal and America's Conscience: Social Engineering and Racial Liberalism, 1938–1987* (1990).

Jacoby, Tamar, *Someone Else's House: America's Unfinished Struggle for Integration* (1998).

Jaynes, Gerald David, and Robin M. Williams, ed., *A Common Destiny: Blacks and American Society* (1989).

Kaplan, Samuel, "'Them': Blacks in Suburbia," *New York Affairs* 3 (1976): 20–41.

Knopke, Harry J., Robert J. Norrell, and Ronald W. Rogers, ed., *Opening Doors: Perspectives on Race Relations in Contemporary America* (1991).

Kochman, Thomas, *Black and White Styles in Conflict* (1981).

Lipsitz, George, "The Possessive Investment in Whiteness: Racialized Social Democracy and the 'White' Problem in American Studies, with Responses by George J. Sanchez, Henry Louis Taylor, Jr., and Walter E. Williams," *American Quarterly* 47 (1995): 369–427.

Metzger, L. Paul, "American Sociology and Black Assimilation: Conflicting Perspectives," *American Journal of Sociology* 76 (1971): 627–47.

Patterson, Orlando, *The Ordeal of Integration: Progress and Resentment in America's "Racial" Crisis* (1997).

Pescosolido, Bernice A., Elizabeth Grauerholz, and Melissa A. Milkie, "Culture and Conflict: The Portrayal of Blacks in U.S. Children's Picture Books through the Mid- and Late-Twentieth Century," *American Sociological Review* 62 (1997): 443–64.

Pigeon, Gerard Georges, "The Representation of Black Culture in Disney," *Radical America* 26 (1997): 29–40.

Schuman, Howard, Charlotte Steeh, and Lawrence Bobo, ed., *Racial Attitudes in America: Trends and Interpretations* (1985).

Sears, David O., Jim Sidanius, and Lawrence Bobo, ed., *Racialized Politics: The Debate About Racism in America* (1999).

Smith, T. Alexander, and Lenahan O'Connell, *Black Anxiety, White Guilt, and the Politics of Status Frustration* (1997).

Sniderman, Paul M., and Edward G. Carmines, *Reaching Beyond Race* (1997).

Sniderman, Paul M., Thomas Piazza, Philip E. Tetlock, and Ann Kendrick, "The New Racism," *American Journal of Political Science* 35 (1991): 423–47.

Steele, Shelby, *The Content of Our Character* (1990).

Sundiata, I. K., "Late Twentieth Century Patterns of Race Relations in Brazil and the United States," *Phylon* 48 (1987): 62–76.

Thernstrom, Stephan, and Abigail Thernstrom, *America in Black and White: One Nation, Indivisible* (1997).

———— "Black Progress: How Far We've Come—And How Far We Have to Go," *Brookings Review* 16 (1998): 12–16.

Thibodeau, Ruth, "From Racism to Tokenism: The Changing Face of Blacks in New Yorker Cartoons," *Public Opinion Quarterly* 53 (1989): 482–94.

Wilson, William Julius, *The Bridge Over the Racial Divide: Rising Inequality and Coalition Politics* (1999).

24.4.2   Black/Ethnic Relations

Berman, Paul, ed., *Blacks and Jews: Alliances and Arguments* (1994).

Chang, Edward T., "Jewish and Korean Merchants in African American Neighborhoods: A Comparative Perspective," *Amerasia Journal* 19 (1993): 5–21.

Dunbar, Leslie W., ed., *Minority Report: What Has Happened to Blacks, Hispanics, American Indians, and Other Minorities in the Eighties* (1984).

Franklin, V. P., Nancy L. Grant, Harold M. Kletnick, and Genn Rae McNeil, ed., *African Americans and Jews in the Twentieth Century: Studies in Convergence and Conflict* (1998).

Ginsberg, Yona, "Jewish Attitudes toward Black Neighbors in Boston and London," *Ethnicity* 8 (1981): 206–18.

Guthrie, Patricia, and Janis Hutchinson, "The Impact of Perceptions on Interpersonal Interactions in an African American/Asian American Housing Project," *Journal of Black Studies* 25 (1995): 377–95.

Jo, Moon H., "Korean Merchants in the Black Community: Prejudice among the Victims of Prejudice," *Ethnic and Racial Studies* 15 (1992): 395–411.

Kasinitz, Philip, "The Minority Within: The New Black Immigrants," *New York Affairs* 10 (1987): 44–58.

Kaufman, Jonathan, *Broken Alliance: The Turbulent Times between Blacks and Jews in America* (1988).

Lee, Letha A., "International Migration and Refugee Problems: Conflict between Black Americans and Southeast Asian Refugees," *Journal of Intergroup Relations* 14 (1986–87): 38–50.

Lerner, Michael, and Cornel West, *Jews and Blacks: A Dialogue on Race, Religion, and Culture in America* (1995).

Lieberson, Stanley, and Mary C. Waters, *From Many Strands: Ethnic and Racial Groups in Contemporary America* (1988).

Mazrui, Ali A., "Negritude, the Talmudic Tradition, and the Intellectual Performance of Blacks and Jews," *Ethnic and Racial Studies* 1 (1978): 19–36.

Mohl, Raymond A., "On the Edge: Blacks and Hispanics in Metropolitan Miami Since 1959," *Florida Historical Quarterly* 69 (1990): 37–56.

Morris, Milton D., and Gary E. Rubin, "The Turbulent Friendship: Black-Jewish Relations in the 1990's," *Annals of the American Academy of Political and Social Science* (1993): 42–60.

Myers, Samuel L., Jr., ed., *Civil Rights and Race Relations in the Post Reagan-Bush Era* (1997).

Ozick, Cynthia, "Literary Blacks and Jews," *Midstream* 18 (1972): 10–24.

Parot, Joseph, "The Racial Dilemma in Chicago's Polish Neighborhoods, 1920–1970," *Polish American Studies* 32 (1975): 27–37.

Piatt, Bill, *Black and Brown in America: The Case for Cooperation* (1997).

Pincus, Fred L., and Howard J. Ehrlich, ed., *Race and Ethnic Conflict: Contending Views on Prejudice, Discrimination, and Ethnoviolence* (1994).

Pollock, Philip H., III, and M. Elliot Vittas, "Who Bears the Burdens of Environmental Pollution? Race, Ethnicity, and Environmental Equity in Florida," *Social Science Quarterly* 76 (1995): 294–310.

Raab, Earl, "Interracial Conflict and American Jews," *Patterns of Prejudice* 25 (1991): 46–61.

Rieter, Jonathan, *Canarsie: The Jews and Italians of Brooklyn against Liberalism* (1985).

Salzman, Jack, Adina Back, and Gretchen Sullivan Sorin, ed., *Bridges and Boundaries: African Americans and American Jews* (1992).

Salzman, Jack, and Cornel West, ed., *Struggles in the Promised Land: Toward a History of Black-Jewish Relations in the United States* (1997).

Sanjek, Roger, *The Future of Us All: Race and Neighborhood Politics in New York City* (1998).

Shah, Hemant, and Michael C. Thornton, "Racial Ideology in U.S. Mainstream News Magazine Coverage of Black-Latino Interaction, 1980–1992," *Critical Studies in Mass Communication* 11 (1994): 141–61.

Sowell, Thomas, *Ethnic America: A History* (1981).

Stewart, Ella, "Communication between African Americans and Korean Americans: Before and after the Los Angeles Riots," *Amerasia Journal* 19 (1993): 23–53.

van Capelleveen, Remco, "Multiculturalism and the Color Line: African Caribbeans in New York City," *European Contributions to American Studies* 23 (1993): 172–98.

Waldinger, Roger, *Still the Promised City? African-Americans and New Immigrants in Postindustrial New York* (1996).

24.4.3   Segregation/Jim Crow

Becker, Henry Jay, "Racial Segregation among Places of Employment," *Social Forces* 58 (1980): 761–76.

Bobo, Lawrence, and Camille L. Zubrinsky, "Attitudes on Residential Integration: Perceived Status Differences, Mere In-Group Preference, or Racial Prejudice?" *Social Forces* 74 (1996): 883–909.

Fainstein, Norman, "Race, Class, and Segregation: Discourses about African Americans," *International Journal of Urban and Regional Research* 17 (1993): 384–403.

Krivo, Lauren J., Ruth D. Peterson, Helen Rizzo, and John R. Reynolds, "Race, Segregation, and the Concentration of Disadvantage, 1980–1990," *Social Problems* 45 (1998): 61–80.

Massey, Douglas S., and Nancy A. Denton, *American Apartheid: Segregation and the Making of the Underclass* (1993).

——— "Suburbanization and Segregation in U.S. Metropolitan Areas," *American Journal of Sociology* 94 (1988): 592–626.

———— "Trends in the Residential Segregation of Blacks, Hispanics, and Asians, 1970–1980," *American Sociological Review* 52 (1987): 802–25.

Massey, Douglas S., and Andrew B. Gross, "Explaining Trends in Racial Segregation, 1970–1980," *Urban Affairs Quarterly* 27 (1991): 13–35.

Stearns, Linda Brewster, and John R. Logan, "The Racial Structuring of the Housing Market and Segregation in Suburban Areas," *Social Forces* 65 (1986): 28–42.

Tobin, Gary, ed., *Divided Neighborhoods: Changing Patterns of Racial Segregation* (1987).

Zubrinsky, Camille L., and Lawrence Bobo, "Prismatic Metropolis: Race and Residential Segregation in the City of the Angels," *Social Science Research* 25 (1996): 335–74.

24.4.4   Violence and Racial Disturbances

Ammons, Lila, "Consequences of Violence in the African American Community in 1991," *Western Journal of Black Studies* 21 (1997): 199–203.

Bowser, Charles W., *Let the Bunker Burn: The Final Battle with MOVE* (1989).

Carter, Gregg Lee, "In the Narrows of the 1960's U.S. Black Rioting," *Journal of Conflict Resolution* 30 (1986): 115–27.

Gale, Dennis E., *Understanding Urban Unrest: From Reverend King to Rodney King* (1996).

Gordon, Leonard, "Aftermath of a Race Riot: The Emergent Norm Process among Black and White Community Leaders," *Sociological Perspectives* 26 (1983): 115–35.

Harris, Daryl B., "The Logic of Black Urban Rebellions," *Journal of Black Studies* 28 (1998): 368–85.

Jones, Dionne J., and Monica L. Jackson, "Racism and Interracial Violence: A Clear and Present Danger," *Urban League Review* 15 (1991): 9–26.

Liberatore, Paul, *The Road to Hell: The True Story of George Jackson, Stephen Bingham and the San Quentin Massacre* (1996).

Lupo, Alan, *Liberty's Chosen Home: The Politics of Violence in Boston* (1977).

Olzak, Susan, Suzanne Shanahan, and Elizabeth H. McEneaney, "Poverty, Segregation, and Race Riots, 1960 to 1993," *American Sociological Review* 61 (1996): 590–613.

Paige, Jeffery M., "Political Orientation and Riot Participation," *American Sociological Review* 36 (1971): 810–20.

Sanders, William B., *Gangbangs and Drive-bys: Grounded Culture and Juvenile Gang Violence* (1994).

Tscheschlok, Eric, "Long Time Coming: Miami's Liberty City Riot of 1968," *Florida Historical Quarterly* 74 (1996): 440–60.

24.4.5   Civil Rights

Amaker, Norman C., *Civil Rights and the Reagan Administration* (1989).

Ashmore, Harry S., *Civil Rights and Wrongs: A Memoir of Race and Politics, 1944–1994* (1994).

Barnett, Bernice McNair, *Sisters in Struggle: Invisible Black Women in the Civil Rights Movement 1945–1970* (1997).

Bell, Derrick, *And We Are Not Saved: The Elusive Quest for Racial Justice* (1987).

Belz, Herman, *Equality Transformed: A Quarter-Century of Affirmative Action* (1991).

Blackside, Inc., and Corporation for Public Broadcasting, prod., *Eyes on the Prize II: America at the Racial Crossroads, 1965–1985* (8 videocassettes, 1989).

Bond, Julian, "Reconstruction and the Southern Movement for Civil Rights: Then and Now," *Teachers College Record* 93 (1991): 221–35.

Button, James W., *Blacks and Social Change: Impact of the Civil Rights Movement in Southern Communities* (1989).

Caplan, Marvin, *Farther Along: A Civil Rights Memoir* (1999).

Couto, Richard A., *Ain't Gonna Let Nobody Turn Me Around: The Pursuit of Racial Justice in the Rural South* (1991).

Days, Drew S., III, "Seeking a New Civil Rights Consensus," *Daedalus* 112 (1983): 197–216.

Dent, Tom, *Southern Journey: A Return to the Civil Rights Movement* (1997).

Donohue, John J., III, and James Heckman, "Continuous *versus* Episodic Change: The Impact of Civil Rights Policy on the Economic Status of Blacks," *Journal of Economic Literature* 29 (1991): 1603–43.

Freeman, Roland L., "Mule Train: A Thirty-Year Perspective on the Southern Christian Leadership Conference's Poor People's Campaign of 1968," *Southern Cultures* 4 (1998): 91–118.

Govan, Reginald C., and William L. Taylor, ed., *One Nation, Indivisible: The Civil Rights Challenge for the 1990's: Report of the Citizens' Commission on Civil Rights* (1989).

Graham, Hugh Davis, "Race, History, and Policy: African Americans and Civil Rights since 1964," *Journal of Policy History* 6 (1994): 12–39.

Hamilton, Dona Cooper, and Charles V. Hamilton, *The Dual Agenda: Race and Social Welfare Policies of Civil Rights Organizations* (1997).

Hampton, Henry, and Steve Fayer, with Sarah Flynn, *Voices of Freedom: An Oral History of the Civil Rights Movement from the 1950s through the 1980s* (1990).

Harmon, David Andrew, *Beneath the Image of the Civil Rights Movement and Race Relations: Atlanta, Georgia, 1946–1981* (1996).

Kotz, Nick, and Mary Lynn Kotz, *A Passion for Equality: George Wiley and the Movement* (1977).

Locke, Mamie E., "The Role of African-American Women in the Civil Rights and Women's Movements in Hinds County and Sunflower County, Mississippi," *Journal of Mississippi History* 53 (1991): 229–39.

Marger, Martin N., "Social Movement Organizations and Response to Environmental Change: The NAACP, 1960–1973," *Social Problems* 32 (1984): 16–30.

McCaslin, Richard B., "Steadfast in His Intent: John W. Hargis and the Integration of the University of Texas at Austin," *Southwestern Historical Quarterly* 95 (1991): 20–41.

Sekayi, Dia N. R., *African American Intellectual-Activists: Legacies in the Struggle* (1997).

Sowell, Thomas, *Civil Rights: Rhetoric or Reality?* (1984).

Weber, Michael, *Causes and Consequences of the African-American Civil Rights Movement* (1998).

Williams, Lea E., *Servants of the People: The 1960's Legacy of African American Leadership* (1996).

24.4.6   Black Power

Baskerville, John D., "Free Jazz: A Reflection of Black Power Ideology," *Journal of Black Studies* 24 (1994): 484–97.

Beckles, Colin, "Black Bookstores, Black Power, and the F.B.I.: The Case of Drum and Spear," *Western Journal of Black Studies* 20 (1996): 63–71.

Blackside, Inc., and Corporation for Public Broadcasting, prod., *Eyes on the Prize II: America at the Racial Crossroads, 1965–1985* (8 videocassettes, 1989).

Dyson, Michael Eric, *Making Malcolm: The Myth and Meaning of Malcolm X* (1995).

Elam, Harry J., Jr., *Taking It to the Streets: The Social Protest Theater of Luis Valdez and Amiri Baraka* (1997).

Guillory, Monique, and Richard C. Green, ed., *Soul: Black Power, Politics, and Pleasure* (1998).

Harper, Frederick D., "The Influence of Malcolm X on Black Militancy," *Journal of Black Studies* 1 (1971): 387–402.

Henderson, Errol A., "Black Nationalism and Rap Music," *Journal of Black Studies* 26 (1996): 308–39.

———— "The Lumpenproletariat As Vanguard? The Black Panther Party, Social Transformation, and Pearson's Analysis of Huey Newton," *Journal of Black Studies* 28 (1997): 171–99.

Henderson, William L., and Larry C. Ledebur, "Programs for the Economic Development of the American Negro Community: The Militant Approaches," *American Journal of Economics and Sociology* 29 (1970): 337–52.

Jones, Charles, ed., *The Black Panther Party (Reconsidered): Reflections and Scholarship* (1997).

McCartney, John T., *Black Power Ideologies: An Essay in African-American Political Thought* (1992).

Ngozi-Brown, Scot, "The US Organization, Maulana Karenga, and Conflict with the Black Panther Party: A Critique of Sectarian Influences on Historical Discourse," *Journal of Black Studies* 28 (1997): 157–70.

Pearson, Hugh, *The Shadow of the Panther: Huey Newton and the Price of Black Power in America* (1995).

Staub, Michael E., "Black Panthers, New Journalism, and the Rewriting of the Sixties," *Representations* 57 (1997): 52–72.

Van Deburg, William L., *New Day in Babylon: The Black Power Movement and American Culture, 1965–1975* (1992).

24.5   GOVERNMENT

24.5.1   Law

Abernathy, Charles F., *Civil Rights and Constitutional Litigation Cases and Materials* (2nd ed., 1992).

Alozie, Nicholas O., "Distribution of Women and Minority Judges: The Effects of Judicial Selection Methods," *Social Science Quarterly* 71 (1990): 315–25.

Aptheker, Bettina, *The Morning Breaks: The Trial of Angela Davis* (2d ed., 1999).

Brooks, Roy L., *Rethinking the American Race Problem* (1991).

Bullard, Robert D., ed., *Unequal Protection: Environmental Justice and Communities of Color* (1994).

Burns, Haywood, "From *Brown* to *Bakke* and Back: Race, Law, and Social Change in America," *Daedalus* 110 (1981): 219–31.

Chambers, Julius L., "Black Americans and the Courts: Has the Clock Been Turned Back Permanently?" *State of Black America* (1990): 9–24.

——— "The Law and Black Americans: Retreat from Civil Rights," *State of Black America* (1987): 15–30.

Crenshaw, Kimberlé, and Kendall Thomas, ed., *Critical Race Theory: The Key Writings That Formed the Movement* (1995).

Edley, Christopher F., *Not All Black and White: Affirmative Action, Race, and American Values* (1996).

Ezorsky, Gertrude, *Racism and Justice: The Case for Affirmative Action* (1991).

Fiscus, Ronald J., *The Constitutional Logic of Affirmative Action,* ed. Stephen L. Wasby (1992).

Gibson, James L., and Gregory A. Caldeira, "Blacks and the United States Supreme Court: Models of Diffuse Support," *Journal of Politics* 54 (1992): 1120–45.

Graham, Barbara Luck, "Do Judicial Selection Systems Matter? A Study of Black Representation on State Courts," *American Politics Quarterly* 18 (1990): 316–36.

Gryski, Gerard S., Gary Zuk, and Deborah J. Barrow, "A Bench That Looks like America? Representation of African Americans and Latinos on the Federal Courts," *Journal of Politics* 56 (1994): 1076–86.

Halpern, Stephen C., *On the Limits of the Law: The Ironic Legacy of Title VI of the 1964 Civil Rights Act* (1995).

Higginbotham, A. Leon, Jr., "An Open Letter to Justice Clarence Thomas from a Federal Judicial Colleague," *University of Pennsylvania Law Review* 140 (1992): 1005–28.

Jacobson, Cardell K., "The *Bakke* Decision: White Reactions to the U.S. Supreme Court's Test of Affirmative Action Programs," *Journal of Conflict Resolution* 27 (1983): 687–705.

Jencks, Christopher, "Affirmative Action for Blacks: Past, Present, and Future," *American Behavioral Scientist* 28 (1985): 731–60.

Kempton, Murray, *The Briar Patch: The People of the State of New York v. Lumumba Shaku* (1973).

——— *The Briar Patch: The Trial of the Panther 21* (1997).

Kim, Dongyoung, "The Role of the Supreme Court on Affirmative Action in America," *Journal of North American Studies* 1 (1995): 69–84.

Martin, Susan E., "'Outsider within' the Station House: The Impact of Race and Gender on Black Women Police," *Social Problems* 41 (1994): 383–400.

Mayer, Jane, and Jill Abramson, *Strange Justice: The Selling of Clarence Thomas* (1994).

Moreno, Paul D., *From Direct Action to Affirmative Action: Fair Employment Law and Policy in America, 1933–1972* (1997).

Morrison, Toni, ed., *Race-ing Justice, En-gendering Power: Essays on Anita Hill, Clarence Thomas, and the Construction of Social Reality* (1992).

Phelps, Timothy, and Helen Winternitz, *Capitol Games: Clarence Thomas, Anita Hill, and the Story of a Supreme Court Nomination* (1992).

Reid, Herbert O., Sr., and Frankie Foster-Davis, "State of the Art: The Law and Education Since 1954," *Journal of Negro Education* 52 (1983): 234–49.

Rosenfeld, Michel, *Affirmative Action and Justice: A Philosophical and Constitutional Inquiry* (1991).

Tuch, Steven A., and Ronald Weitzer, "Trends: Racial Differences in Attitudes toward the Police," *Public Opinion Quarterly* 61 (1997): 642–63.

Senate Committee on the Judiciary U.S. Congress, *The Complete Transcripts of the Clarence Thomas-Anita Hill Hearings: October 11, 12, 13, 1991* (1994).

Uhlman, Thomas M., "Race, Recruitment, and Representation: Background Differences between Black and White Trial Court Judges," *Western Political Quarterly* 30 (1977): 457–70.

Washington, Linn, *Black Judges on Justice: Perspectives from the Bench* (1994).

Welch, Susan, Michael Combs, and John Gruhl, "Do Black Judges Make a Difference?" *American Journal of Political Science* 32 (1988): 126–36.

Williams, Walter, *The State against Blacks* (1984).

24.5.2 Crime and Punishment

Bing, Leon, *Do or Die* (1991).

Bridges, George S., and Robert D. Crutchfield, "Law, Social Standing, and Racial Disparities in Imprisonment," *Social Forces* 66 (1988): 699–724.

Brown, Lee P., "Crime in the Black Community," *State of Black America* (1988): 95–113.

Carroll, Leo, and Margaret E. Mondrick, "Racial Bias in the Decision to Grant Parole," *Law and Society Review* 11 (1976): 93–108.

Cohn, Steven F., Steven E. Barkan, and William A. Halteman, "Punitive Attitudes toward Criminals: Racial Consensus or Racial Conflict?" *Social Problems* 38 (1991): 287–96.

Cruz, Wilfredo, "Police Brutality in African American and Latino Communities," *Latino Studies Journal* 6 (1995): 30–47.

DaCosta Nunes, Ralph, "Public Opinion, Crime, and Race: A Congressional Response to Law and Order in America," *Political Studies* 28 (1980): 420–30.

Darity, William A., Jr., and Samuel L. Myers, Jr., "Impacts of Violent Crime on Black Family Structure," *Contemporary Policy Issues* 8 (1990): 15–29.

Davis, John A., "Blacks, Crime, and American Culture," *Annals of the American Academy of Political and Social Science* 423 (1976): 89–98.

Denno, Deborah, "Psychological Factors for the Black Defendant in a Jury Trial," *Journal of Black Studies* 11 (1981): 313–26.

Dulaney, W. Marvin, "The Texas Negro Peace Officers' Association: The Origins of Black Police Unionism," *Houston Review* 12 (1990): 59–78.

Franklin, H. Bruce, "The Literature of the American Prison," *Massachusetts Review* 18 (1977): 51–78.

Frazier, Charles E., Donna M. Bishop, and John C. Henretta, "The Social Context of Race Differentials in Juvenile Justice Dispositions," *Sociological Quarterly* 33 (1992): 447–58.

Good, David H., and Maureen A. Pirog-Good, "Employment, Crime, and Race," *Contemporary Policy Issues* 5 (1987): 91–104.

Gross, Samuel R., and Robert Mauro, *Death and Discrimination: Racial Disparities in Capital Sentencing* (1989).

Hagedorn, John M., *People and Folks: Gangs, Crime, and the Underclass in a Rustbelt City* (1988).

Harer, Miles D., and Darrell Steffensmeier, "The Differing Effects of Economic Inequality on Black and White Rates of Violence," *Social Forces* 70 (1992): 1035–54.

Hawkins, Darnell F., and Kenneth A. Hardy, "Black-White Imprisonment Rates: A State-by-State Analysis," *Social Justice* 16 (1989): 75–94.

Headley, Bernard D., *The Atlanta Youth Murders and the Politics of Race* (1998).

——— "Black Political Empowerment and Urban Crime," *Phylon* 46 (1985): 193–204.

────── "Killings That Became 'Tragedy': A Different View of What Happened in Atlanta, Georgia," *Social Justice* 16 (1989): 55–74.

Holmes, Malcolm D., and Howard C. Daudistel, "Ethnicity and Justice in the Southwest: The Sentencing of Anglo, Black, and Mexican Origin Defendants," *Social Science Quarterly* 65 (1984): 265–77.

Jackson, Bruce, *Killing Time: Life in the Arkansas Penitentiary* (1977).

Jackson, George Lester, *Soledad Brother: The Prison Letters of George Jackson* (1970).

Johnson, Roberta Ann, "The Prison Birth of Black Power," *Journal of Black Studies* 5 (1975): 395–414.

Johnstone, John W. C., Darnell F. Hawkins, and Arthur Michener, "Homicide Reporting in Chicago Dailies," *Journalism Quarterly* 71 (1994): 860–72.

Kennedy, Randall, *Race, Crime, and the Law* (1997).

LaFree, Gary, and Kriss A. Drass, "The Effect of Changes in Intraracial Income Inequality and Educational Attainment on Changes in Arrest Rates for African Americans and Whites, 1957 to 1990," *American Sociological Review* 61 (1996): 614–35.

McClain, Paula D., "Urban Black Neighborhood Environment and Homicide: A Research Note on a Decade of Change in Four Cities, 1970 to 1980," *Urban Affairs Quarterly* 24 (1989): 584–96.

McKnight, Gerald D., "A Harvest of Hate: The FBI's War against Black Youth—Domestic Intelligence in Memphis, Tennessee," *South Atlantic Quarterly* 86 (1987): 1–21.

Moeller, Gertrude L., "Fear of Criminal Victimization: The Effect of Neighborhood Racial Composition," *Sociological Inquiry* 59 (1989): 208–21.

Myers, Martha A., "Symbolic Policy and the Sentencing of Drug Offenders," *Law and Society Review* 23 (1989): 295–315.

Myers, Martha A., and Susette M. Talarico, "The Social Contexts of Racial Discrimination in Sentencing," *Social Problems* 33 (1986): 236–51.

Network of Black Organizers, *Black Prison Movements USA* (1995).

Palmer, Edward, "Black Police in America," *Black Scholar* 5 (1973): 19–27.

Parker, Keith D., Anne B. Onyekwuluje, and Komanduri S. Murty, "African Americans' Attitudes toward the Local Police: A Multivariate Analysis," *Journal of Black Studies* 25 (1995): 396–410.

Pettiway, Leon E., "The Internal Structure of the Ghetto and the Criminal Commute," *Journal of Black Studies* 16 (1985): 189–211.

Primm, Beny J., "Drug Use: Special Implications for Black America," *State of Black America* (1987): 145–58.

Radelet, Michael L., and Glenn L. Pierce, "Race and Prosecutorial Discretion in Homicide Cases," *Law and Society Review* 19 (1985): 587–621.

Rice, Mitchell F., "Racial Discrimination, Capital Punishment Policy, and the Supreme Court: The Death Penalty As a Political Devaluation of Black Life," *National Political Science Review* 4 (1993): 61–79.

Rothman, Stanley, and Stephen Powers, "Execution by Quota?" *Public Interest* (1994): 3–17.

Russell, Katheryn, *The Color of Crime: Racial Hoaxes, White Fear, Black Protectionism, and Other Macroaggresions* (1998).

Sampson, Robert J., "Urban Black Violence: The Effect of Male Joblessness and Family Disruption," *American Journal of Sociology* 93 (1987): 348–82.

Sampson, Robert J., and John H. Laub, "Structural Variations in Juvenile Court Processing: Inequality, the Underclass, and Social Control," *Law and Society Review* 27 (1993): 285–311.

Schatzberg, Rufus, and Robert J. Kelly, *African-American Organized Crime: A Social History* (1996).

Sidanius, Jim, "Race and Sentence Severity: The Case of American Justice," *Journal of Black Studies* 18 (1988): 273–81.

Skogan, Wesley G., "Crime and the Racial Fears of White Americans," *Annals of the American Academy of Political and Social Science* 539 (1995): 59–71.

Smith, Damu, "The Upsurge of Police Repression: An Analysis," *Black Scholar* 12 (1981): 35–57.

Sullivan, Mercer L., *"Getting Paid": Youth Crime and Work in the Inner City* (1989).

Wicker, Tom, *A Time to Die* (1975).

Wideman, John Edgar, *Brothers and Keepers* (1984).

Zatz, Marjorie S., "Pleas, Priors, and Prison: Racial/Ethnic Differences in Sentencing," *Social Science Research* 14 (1985): 169–93.

24.5.3 Politics and Voting

Agronsky, Jonathan I. Z., *Marion Barry: The Politics of Race* (1991).

Alkalimat, Abdul, *Black Power in Chicago: Harold Washington and the Crisis of the Black Middle Class: Mass Protest* (vol. 1, 1990).

——— *Paradigms in Black Studies: Intellectual History, Cultural Meaning and Political Ideology* (1990).

Amaker, Norman C., *Civil Rights and the Reagan Administration* (1989).

Ashmore, Harry S., *Civil Rights and Wrongs: A Memoir of Race and Politics, 1944–1994* (1994).

Banks, Manley E., II, Nelson Wikstrom, Joseph Moon, and Joseph E. Andrews, "Tranformative Leadership in the Post-Civil Rights Era: The 'War on Poverty' and the Emergence of African-American Municipal Political Leadership," *Western Journal of Black Studies* 20 (1996): 173–87.

Barker, Lucius J., "Limits of Political Strategy: A Systemic View of the African American Experience," *American Political Science Review* 88 (1994): 1–13.

Barker, Lucius J., and Jesse J. McCorry, *Black Americans and the Political System* (2nd ed., 1980).

Barker, Lucius J., and Ronald W. Walters, ed., *Jesse Jackson's 1984 Presidential Campaign: Challenge and Change in American Politics* (1989).

Bauman, John F., "W. Wilson Goode: The Black Mayor As Urban Entrepreneur," *Journal of Negro History* 77 (1992): 141–58.

Bennett, Larry, "Harold Washington and the Black Urban Regime," *Urban Affairs Quarterly* 28 (1993): 423–40.

Bobo, Lawrence, and Franklin D. Gilliam, Jr., "Race, Sociopolitical Participation, and Black Empowerment," *American Political Science Review* 84 (1990): 377–93.

Bolce, Louis, Gerald DeMaio, and Douglas Muzzio, "Blacks and the Republican Party: The Twenty Percent Solution," *Political Science Quarterly* 107 (1992): 63–79.

Braxton, Gloria J., "African-American Women and Politics: Research Trends and Directions," *National Political Science Review* 4 (1993): 281–96.

Brown, Ronald E., and Monica L. Wolford, "Religious Resources and African-American Political Action," *National Political Science Review* 4 (1993): 30–48.

Calhoun-Brown, Allison, "African American Churches and Political Mobilization: The Psychological Impact of Organizational Resources," *Journal of Politics* 58 (1996): 935–53.

Callahan, Linda F., "History: A Critical Scene within Jesse Jackson's Rhetorical Vision," *Journal of Black Studies* 24 (1993): 3–15.

Canon, David T., "Redistricting and the Congressional Black Caucus," *American Politics Quarterly* 23 (1995): 159–89.

Carmines, Edward G., Robert Huckfeldt, and Carl McCurley, "Mobilization, Counter-Mobilization, and the Politics of Race," *Political Geography* 14 (1995): 601–19.

Carter, Dan T., *From George Wallace to Newt Gingrich: Race in the Conservative Counterrevolution, 1963–1994* (1996).

——— *The Politics of Rage: George Wallace, the Origins of the New Conservatism, and the Transformation of American Politics* (1995).

Cartosio, Bruno, "U.S. Black Mayors: What Next? A European Perspective," *Monthly Review* 37 (1985): 25–39.

Ciccone, James, "A Tribute to Everett Holmes: New York State's First Black Mayor," *Afro-Americans in New York Life and History* 2 (1978): 11–16.

Clavel, Pierre, and Wim Wiewel, ed., *Harold Washington and the Neighborhoods: Progressive City Government in Chicago, 1983–1987* (1991).

Cohen, Cathy J., and Michael C. Dawson, "Neighborhood Poverty and African American Politics," *American Political Science Review* 87 (1993): 286–302.

Cooper, James L., "South Side Boss," *Chicago History* 19 (1990–91): 66–81.

Danigelis, Nicholas L., "Race, Class, and Political Involvement in the U.S.," *Social Forces* 61 (1982): 532–50.

Darcy, R., and Charles D. Hadley, "Black Women in Politics: The Puzzle of Success," *Social Science Quarterly* 69 (1988): 629–45.

Darcy, R., Charles D. Hadley, and Jason F. Kirksey, "Election Systems and the Representation of Black Women in American State Legislatures," *Women and Politics* 13 (1993): 73–89.

Dawson, Michael C., *Behind the Mule: Race and Class in African-American Politics* (1994).

Dickson, David A., "American Society and the African American Foreign Policy Lobby: Constraints and Opportunities," *Journal of Black Studies* 27 (1996): 139–51.

Duster, Troy, "Individual Fairness, Group Preferences, and the California Strategy," *Representations* 55 (1996): 41–58.

Edds, Margaret, *Claiming the Dream: The Victorious Campaign of Douglas Wilder of Virginia* (1990).

Edsall, Thomas B., and Mary D. Edsall, *Chain Reaction: The Impact of Race, Rights and Taxes on American Politics* (1991).

Ellison, Christopher G., and Bruce London, "The Social and Political Participation of Black Americans: Compensatory and Ethnic Community Perspectives Revisited," *Social Forces* 70 (1992): 681–701.

Fendrich, James M., and Charles U. Smith, "Black Activists: Ten Years Later," *Journal of Negro Education* 49 (1980): 3–19.

Flax, Jane, *The American Dream in Black and White: The Clarence Thomas Hearings* (1998).

Geschwender, James A., "The League of Revolutionary Black Workers: Problems of Confronting Black Marxist-Leninist Organizations," *Journal of Ethnic Studies* 2 (1974): 1–23.

Gill, Laverne McCain, *African American Women in Congress: Forming and Transforming History* (1997).

Glaser, James M., *Race, Campaign Politics, and the Realignment in the South* (1998).

Gomes, Ralph C., and Linda Faye Williams, ed., *From Exclusion to Inclusion: The Long Struggle for African American Political Power* (1992).

Green, Charles, and Basil Wilson, "The Afro-American, Caribbean Dialectic: White Incumbents, Black Constituents, and the 1984 Election in New York City," *Afro-Americans in New York Life and History* 11 (1987): 49–65.

—— *The Struggle for Black Empowerment in New York City: Beyond the Politics of Pigmentation* (1989).

Greer, Edward, *Big Steel: Black Politics and Corporate Power in Gary, Indiana* (1979).

Grimshaw, William J., *Bitter Fruit: Black Politics and the Chicago Machine, 1931–1991* (1992).

Guinier, Lani, *The Tyranny of the Majority: Fundamental Fairness in Representative Democracy* (1995).

Gurin, Patricia, Shirley Hatchett, and James S. Jackson, *Hope and Independence: Blacks' Response to Electoral and Party Politics* (1990).

Hadley, Charles D., "Blacks in Southern Politics: An Agenda for Research," *Journal of Politics* 56 (1994): 585–600.

Hanks, Lawrence J., *The Struggle for Black Political Empowerment in Three Georgia Counties* (1987).

Headley, Bernard D., "Black Political Empowerment and Urban Crime," *Phylon* 46 (1985): 193–204.

Herring, Cedric, ed., *African Americans and the Public Agenda: The Paradoxes of Public Policy* (1996).

Higginbotham, A. Leon, Jr., Gregory A. Clarick, and Marcelle David, "*Shaw v. Reno:* A Mirage of Good Intentions with Devastating Consequences," *Fordham Law Review* 62 (1994).

Hill, Kevin A., "Does the Creation of Majority Black Districts Aid Republicans? An Analysis of the 1992 Congressional Elections in Eight Southern States," *Journal of Politics* 57 (1995): 384–401.

Hirsch, Arnold R., "Race and Politics in Modern New Orleans: The Mayoralty of Dutch Morial," *Amerikastudien/American Studies* 35 (1990): 461–84.

Holli, Melvin G., and Paul M. Green, *Bashing Chicago Traditions: Harold Washington's Last Campaign: Chicago 1987* (1989).

Howard, John R., and Robert C. Smith, ed., *Urban Black Politics* (1978).

Huckfeldt, R. Robert, *Race and the Decline of Class in American Politics* (1989).

Jackson, Bryan O., "The Effects of Racial Group Consciousness on Political Mobilization in American Cities," *Western Political Quarterly* 40 (1987): 631–46.

Jeffries, Judson L., "Douglas Wilder and the Continuing Significance of Race: An Analysis of the 1989 Gubernatorial Election," *Journal of Political Science* 23 (1995): 87–111.

Johnson, James B., and Philip E. Secret, "Focus and Style Representational Roles of Congressional Black and Hispanic Caucus Members," *Journal of Black Studies* 26 (1996): 245–73.

Jones, Charles E., "United We Stand, Divided We Fall: An Analysis of the Congressional Black Caucus' Voting Behavior, 1975–1980," *Phylon* 48 (1987): 26–37.

Karnig, Albert K., *Black Representation and Urban Policy* (1980).

Karnig, Albert K., and Paula D. McClain, "The New South and Black Economic and Political Development: Changes from 1970 to 1980," *Western Political Quarterly* 38 (1985): 539–50.

Kincaid, John, "Beyond the Voting Rights Act: White Responses to Black Political Power in Tchula, Mississippi," *Publius* 16 (1986): 155–72.

Kousser, J. Morgan, *Colorblind Injustice: Minority Voting Rights and the Undoing of the Second Reconstruction* (1999).

Krassa, Michael A., "Getting out the Black Vote: The Party Canvass and the Black Response," *National Political Science Review* 1 (1989): 58–75.

Laville, Helen, and Scott Lucas, "The American Way: Edith Sampson, the NAACP, and African American Identity in the Cold War," *Diplomatic History* 20 (1996): 565–90.

Lawson, Steven F., "Preserving the Second Reconstruction: Enforcement of the Voting Rights Act, 1965–1975," *Southern Studies* 22 (1983): 55–75.

Lieberman, Robert C., *Shifting the Color Line: Race and the American Welfare State* (1998).

Lusane, Clarence, "Rap, Race, and Politics," *Race and Class* 35 (1993): 41–56.

Marable, Manning, and Leith Mullings, "The Divided Mind of Black America: Race, Ideology and Politics in the Post Civil Rights Era," *Race and Class* 36 (1994): 61–72.

Marwell, Gerald, Michael T. Aiken, and N. J. Demerath, III, "The Persistence of Political Attitudes among 1960's Civil Rights Activists," *Public Opinion Quarterly* 51 (1987): 359–75.

McCrary, Peyton, "Racially Polarized Voting in the South: Quantitative Evidence from the Courtroom," *Social Science History* 14 (1990): 507–31.

Miller, Jake C., "Black Legislators and African-American Relations, 1970–1975," *Journal of Black Studies* 10 (1979): 245–61.

Mladenka, Kenneth R., "Blacks and Hispanics in Urban Politics," *American Political Science Review* 83 (1989): 165–91.

Moeser, John V., and Christopher Silver, "Race, Social Stratification, and Politics: The Case of Atlanta, Memphis, and Richmond," *Virginia Magazine of History and Biography* 102 (1994): 519–50.

Morrison, Minion K. C., *Black Political Mobilization: Leadership, Power, and Mass Behavior* (1987).

Nelson, William E., Jr., "Black Mayoral Leadership: A Twenty-Year Perspective," *National Political Science Review* 2 (1990): 188–95.

Nelson, William E., Jr., and Philip J. Meranto, *Electing Black Mayors: Political Action in the Black Community* (1977).

O'Loughlin, John, "The Identification and Evaluation of Racial Gerrymandering," *Annals of the Association of American Geographers* 72 (1982): 165–84.

O'Loughlin, John, and Dale A. Berg, "The Election of Black Mayors, 1969 and 1973," *Annals of the Association of American Geographers* 67 (1977): 223–38.

Orfield, Gary, and Carole Ashkinaze, *The Closing Door: Conservative Policy and Black Opportunity* (1991).

Owens, Michael Lee, "Local Party Failure and Church-Based, Black Nonparty Organizations," *Western Journal of Black Studies* 21 (1997): 162–72.

Parker, Frank R., *Black Votes Count: Political Empowerment in Mississippi after 1965* (1990).

Payne, Richard J., "Black Americans and the Demise of Constructive Engagement," *Africa Today* 33 (1986): 71–89.

Perry, Huey L., "The Political Reincorporation of Southern Blacks: The Case of Birmingham," *National Political Science Review* 3 (1992): 230–37.

Pierce, Paulette, "The Roots of the Rainbow Coalition," *Black Scholar* 19 (1988): 2–16.

Preston, Michael B., Lenneal J. Henderson, and Paul L. Puryear, ed., *The New Black Politics: The Search for Political Power* (2nd ed., 1987).

Quadagno, Jill, *The Color of Welfare: How Racism Undermined the War on Poverty* (1994).

Reed, Adolph L., Jr., *The Jesse Jackson Phenomenon: The Crisis of Purpose in Afro-American Politics* (1986).

———— *Stirrings in the Jug: Black Politics in the Post-Segregation Era* (1999).

———— *Without Justice for All: The New Liberalism and Our Retreat from Racial Equality* (1999).

Reeves, Keith, *Voting Hopes or Fears? White Voters, Black Candidates, and Racial Politics in America* (1997).

Regalado, James A., "Organized Labor and Los Angeles City Politics: An Assessment in the Bradley Years, 1973–1989," *Urban Affairs Quarterly* 27 (1991): 87–108.

Rich, Wilbur C., *Black Mayors and School Politics: The Failure of Reform in Detroit* (1996).

———— *Coleman Young and Detroit Politics: From Social Activist to Power Broker* (1989).

————, ed., *The Politics of Minority Coalitions: Race, Ethnicity, and Shared Uncertainties* (1996).

Roscigno, Vincent J., and Donald Tomaskovic-Devey, "Racial Politics in the Contemporary South: Toward a More Critical Understanding," *Social Problems* 41 (1994): 585–607.

Rush, Mark E., ed., *Voting Rights and Redistricting in the United States* (1998).

Saltzstein, Grace Hall, "Black Mayors and Police Policies," *Journal of Politics* 51 (1989): 525–44.

Sears, David O., Jim Sidanius, and Lawrence Bobo, ed., *Racialized Politics: The Debate About Racism in America* (1999).

Shull, Steven A., and Albert C. Ringelstein, "Presidential Attention, Support, and Symbolism in Civil Rights, 1953–1984," *Social Science Journal* 26 (1989): 45–54.

Singh, Robert, "The Congressional Black Caucus in the United States Congress, 1971–1990," *Parliaments, Estates, and Representation* 14 (1994): 65–91.

Skinner, Elliot P., "Black Leaders As Foreign Policymakers," *Urban League Review* 9 (1985): 112–22.

Smith, Robert C., "The Black Congressional Delegation," *Western Political Quarterly* 34 (1981): 203–21.

———— "Financing Black Politics: A Study of Congressional Elections," *Review of Black Political Economy* 17 (1988): 5–30.

Southwell, Priscilla L., "The Mobilization Hypothesis and Voter Turnout in Congressional Elections, 1974–1982," *Western Political Quarterly* 41 (1988): 273–87.

Stokes, Carl, *Promises of Power: A Political Autobiography* (1973).

Stone, Chuck, "Black Political Power in the Carter Era," *Black Scholar* 8 (1977): 6–15.

Swain, Carol, *Black Faces, Black Interests: The Representation of African Americans in Congress* (1993).

———— *Race versus Class: The New Affirmative Action Debate* (1996).

Swain, Johnnie Dee, Jr., "Black Mayors: Urban Decline and the Underclass," *Journal of Black Studies* 24 (1993): 16–28.

Tate, Katherine, "Black Political Participation in the 1984 and 1988 Presidential Elections," *American Political Science Review* 85 (1991): 1159–76.

Thernstrom, Abigail M., *Whose Votes Count? Affirmative Action and Minority Voting Rights* (1987).

Timpone, Richard J., "Mass Mobilization or Government Intervention: The Growth of Black Registration in the South," *Journal of Politics* 57 (1995): 425–42.

Wald, Kenneth D., Dennis E. Owen, and Samuel S. Hill, Jr., "Political Cohesion in Churches," *Journal of Politics* 52 (1990): 197–215.

Walshe, A. P., "Black American Thought and African Political Attitudes in South Africa," *Review of Politics* 32 (1970): 51–77.

Walton, Hanes, *Black Political Parties: An Historical and Political Analysis* (1972).

———— *When the Marching Stopped: The Politics of Civil Rights Regulatory Agencies* (1988).

Watson, Sharon M., "'The Second Time Around': A Profile of Black Mayoral Reelection Campaigns," *Phylon* 45 (1984): 165–78.

Weinberg, Kenneth G., *Black Victory: Carl Stokes and the Winning of Cleveland* (1968).

Welch, Susan, and Lorn S. Foster, "The Impact of Economic Conditions on the Voting Behavior of Blacks," *Western Political Quarterly* 45 (1992): 221–36.

Wolters, Raymond, *Right Turn: William Bradford Reynolds, the Reagan Administration, and Black Civil Rights* (1996).

Woodrum, Eric, and Arnold Bell, "Race, Politics, and Religion in Civil Religion among Blacks," *Sociological Analysis* 49 (1989): 353–67.

24.5.4 Military

Burk, James, "Citizenship Status and Military Service: The Quest for Inclusion by Minorities and Conscientious Objectors," *Armed Forces and Society* 21 (1995): 503–29.

Harris, Norman, "Blacks in Vietnam: A Holistic Perspective through Fiction and Journalism," *Western Journal of Black Studies* 10 (1986): 121–31.

King, William, "'Our Men in Vietnam': Black Media As a Source of the Afro-American Experience in Southeast Asia," *Vietnam Generation* 1 (1989): 94–117.

Miller, Laura L., and Charles Moskos, "Humanitarians or Warriors? Race, Gender, and Combat Status in Operation Restore Hope," *Armed Forces and Society* 21 (1995): 615–37.

Moore, Brenda L., "African-American Women in the U.S. Military," *Armed Forces and Society* 17 (1991): 363–84.

Moskos, Charles C., and John Sibley Butler, *All That We Can Be: Black Leadership and Racial Integration the Army Way* (1996).

Schexnider, Alvin J., "Blacks in the Military: The Victory and the Challenge," *State of Black America* (1988): 115–28.

———— "The Development of Racial Solidarity in the Armed Forces," *Journal of Black Studies* 5 (1975): 415–35.

Segal, David R., and Naomi Verdugo, "Demographic Trends and Personnel Policies As Determinants of the Racial Composition of the Volunteer Army," *Armed Forces and Society* 20 (1994): 619–32.

Smith, A. Wade, "Public Consciousness of Blacks in the Military," *Journal of Political and Military Sociology* 11 (1983): 281–300.

Terry, Wallace, ed., *Bloods, an Oral History of the Vietnam War* (1984).

Westheider, James E., *Fighting on Two Fronts: African Americans and the Vietnam War* (1997).

24.6 DEMOGRAPHY

Amin, Ruhul, and A. G. Mariam, "Racial Differences in Housing: An Analysis of Trends and Differentials, 1960–1978," *Urban Affairs Quarterly* 22 (1987): 363–76.

Bledsoe, Timothy, Susan Welch, Lee Sigelman, and Michael Combs, "Residential Context and Racial Solidarity among African Americans," *American Journal of Political Science* 39 (1995): 434–58.

Browne, Irene, "The Baby Boom and Trends in Poverty, 1967–1987," *Social Forces* 73 (1995): 1071–95.

Cohn, Samuel, and Mark Fossett, "Why Racial Employment Inequality Is Greater in Northern Labor Markets: Regional Differences in White-Black Employment Differentials," *Social Forces* 74 (1995): 511–42.

Darden, Joe T., "Black Residential Segregation Since the 1948 *Shelley v. Kraemer* Decision," *Journal of Black Studies* 25 (1995): 680–91.

Ernst, Robert T., and Lawrence Hugg, ed., *Black America: Geographic Perspectives* (1976).

Farley, Reynolds, and William H. Frey, "Changes in the Segregation of Whites from Blacks during the 1980's: Small Steps toward a More Integrated Society," *American Sociological Review* 59 (1994): 23–45.

Feins, Judith D., and Rachel G. Bratt, "Barred in Boston: Racial Discrimination in Housing," *Journal of the American Planning Association* 49 (1983): 344–57.

Fossett, Mark A., Omer R. Galle, and Jeffrey A. Burr, "Racial Occupational Inequality, 1940–1980: A Research Note on the Impact of the Changing Regional Distribution of the Black Population," *Social Forces* 68 (1989): 415–27.

Gee, Ellen M., and Jean E. Veevers, "Increasing Sex Mortality Differentials among Black Americans, 1950–1978," *Phylon* 46 (1985): 162–75.

Gregory, James N., "The Southern Diaspora and the Urban Dispossessed: Demonstrating the Census Public Use Microdata Samples," *Journal of American History* 82 (1995): 111–34.

Hogan, Dennis P., and David L. Featherman, "Racial Stratification and Socioeconomic Change in the American North and South," *American Journal of Sociology* 83 (1977): 100–26.

Johnson, James H., Jr., and Curtis C. Roseman, "Increasing Black Outmigration from Los Angeles: The Role of Household Dynamics and Kinship Systems," *Annals of the Association of American Geographers* 80 (1990): 205–22.

Kasinitz, Philip, "The Minority Within: The New Black Immigrants," *New York Affairs* 10 (1987): 44–58.

Koball, Heather, "Have African-American Men Become Less Committed to Marriage? Explaining the Twentieth-Century Racial Cross-Over in Men's Marriage Timing," *Demography* 35 (1998): 251–58.

Leigh, Wilhelmina A., "Trends in the Housing Status of Black Americans across Selected Metropolitan Areas," *Review of Black Political Economy* 19 (1991): 43–64.

Long, James E., and Steven B. Caudill, "Racial Differences in Homeownership and Housing Wealth, 1970–1986," *Economic Inquiry* 30 (1992): 83–100.

Macpherson, David, and James B. Stewart, "The Effects of Extended Families and Marital Status on Housing Consumption by Black Female-Headed Households," *Review of Black Political Economy* 19 (1991): 65–83.

Massey, Douglas S., and Mitchell L. Eggers, "The Ecology of Inequality: Minorities and the Concentration of Poverty, 1970–1980," *American Journal of Sociology* 95 (1990): 1153–88.

Massey, Douglas S., Andrew B. Gross, and Kumiko Shibuya, "Migration, Segregation, and the Geographic Concentration of Poverty," *American Sociological Review* 59 (1994): 425–45.

McHugh, Kevin E., "Black Migration Reversal in the United States," *Geographical Review* 77 (1987): 171–82.

Oehler, Kay, "Another Look at the Black-White Trend in Unemployment Rates," *American Sociological Review* 44 (1979): 339–41.

Ottensmann, John R., and Michael E. Gleeson, "The Movement of Whites and Blacks into Racially Mixed Neighborhoods: Chicago, 1960–1980," *Social Science Quarterly* 73 (1992): 645–62.

Wilson, Frank Harold, "The Changing Distribution of the African American Population in the United States, 1980–1990," *Urban League Review* 15 (1991–92): 53–74.

24.7 FAMILY

Abelman, Robert, "A Comparison of Black and White Families As Portrayed on Religious and Secular Television Programs," *Journal of Black Studies* 20 (1989): 60–79.

Berger, Alan S., "Black Families and the Moynihan Report: A Research Evaluation," *Social Problems* 22 (1974): 145–61.

Biblarz, Timothy J., and Adrian E. Raftery, "The Effects of Family Disruption on Social Mobility," *American Sociological Review* 58 (1993): 97–109.

Billingsley, Andrew, *Climbing Jacob's Ladder: The Enduring Legacy of African-American Families* (1992).

——— "Understanding African-American Family Diversity," *State of Black America* (1990): 85–108.

Bowser, Benjamin P., ed., *Black Male Adolescents: Parenting and Education in Community Context* (1991).

Darity, William A., Jr., and Samuel L. Myers, Jr., "Impacts of Violent Crime on Black Family Structure," *Contemporary Policy Issues* 8 (1990): 15–29.

Dash, Leon, *Rosa Lee: A Mother and Her Family in Urban America* (1996).

——— *When Children Want Children: The Urban Crisis of Teenage Childbearing* (1989).

Davis, Angela, and Fania Davis, "The Black Family and the Crisis of Capitalism," *Black Scholar* 17 (1986): 33–40.

Early, Gerald, *Daughters: On Family and Fatherhood* (1994).

Edelman, Marian Wright, "Black Children in America," *State of Black America* (1989): 63–76.

Ehrlich, Ira F., "The Aged Black in America: The Forgotten Person," *Journal of Negro Education* 44 (1975): 12–23.

Ellwood, David T., and Jonathan Crane, "Family Change among Black Americans: What Do We Know?" *Journal of Economic Perspectives* 4 (1990): 65–84.

Franklin, Donna L., *Ensuring Inequality: The Structural Transformation of the African-American Family* (1997).

Gadsden, Vivian L., and Ralph R. Smith, "African American Males and Fatherhood: Issues in Research and Practice," *Journal of Negro Education* 63 (1994): 634–48.

Garfinkel, Irwin, and Sara S. McLanahan, *Single Mothers and their Children: A New American Dilemma* (1986).

Gibbs, Jewelle Taylor, Ann F. Brunswick, Michael E. Connor, Richard Dembo, Tom E. Larson, Rodney J. Reed, and Barbara Solomon, ed., *Young, Black, and Male in America: An Endangered Species* (1988).

Hare, Bruce R., "Black Youth at Risk," *State of Black America* (1988): 81–93.

Hendricks, Leo E., and Annette M. Solomon, "Reaching African-American Male Adolescent Parents through Nontraditional Techniques," *Urban League Review* 12 (1988–89): 147–57.

Hill, Robert B., "Economic Forces, Structural Discrimination, and Black Family Instability," *Review of Black Political Economy* 17 (1989): 5–23.

Hudgins, John L., "The Strengths of Black Families Revisited," *Urban League Review* 15 (1991–92): 9–20.

Hunter, Andrea G., and James Earl Davis, "Hidden Voices of Black Men: The Meaning, Structure, and Complexity of Manhood," *Journal of Black Studies* 25 (1994): 20–40.

Jacobsen, R. Brooke, and Jerry J. Bigner, "Black versus White Single Parents and the Value of Children," *Journal of Black Studies* 21 (1991): 302–12.

Jarrett, Robin L., "Living Poor: Family Life among Single Parent, African-American Women," *Social Problems* 41 (1994): 30–49.

Johnson, Leanor Boulin, "The Employed Black: The Dynamics of Work-Family Tension," *Review of Black Political Economy* 17 (1989): 69–85.

Jones, Reginald L., and Yvonne Smith, "Black Children's Associations of Class-Descriptive Labels," *Journal of Black Studies* 10 (1980): 345–53.

Kotlowitz, Alex, *There Are No Children Here: The Story of Two Boys Growing Up in the Other America* (1991).

Lukas, J. Anthony, *Common Ground: A Turbulent Decade in the Lives of Three American Families* (1985).

Macpherson, David, and James B. Stewart, "The Effects of Extended Families and Marital Status on Housing Consumption by Black Female-Headed Households," *Review of Black Political Economy* 19 (1991): 65–83.

Madison, Bernice, and Michael Schapiro, "Black Adoption—Issues and Policies: Review of the Literature," *Social Service Review* 47 (1973): 531–60.

Majors, Richard, and Janet Mancini Billson, *Cool Pose: The Dilemmas of Black Manhood in America* (1993).

Nightingale, Carl Husemoller, *On the Edge: A History of Poor Black Children and Their American Dreams* (1993).

Rubin, Lillian B., *Families on the Fault Line: America's Working Class Speaks about Family, the Economy, Race, and Ethnicity* (1994).

Scott, Daryl Michael, "The Politics of Pathology: The Ideological Origins of the Moynihan Controversy," *Journal of Policy History* 8 (1996): 81–105.

Sheehan, Susan, *Life for Me Ain't Been No Crystal Stair: One Family's Passage Through the Child Welfare System* (1993).

St. Pierre, Maurice A., "Reaganomics and Its Implications for African-American Family Life," *Journal of Black Studies* 21 (1991): 325–40.

Staples, Robert, "Social Structure and Black Family Life: An Analysis of Current Trends," *Journal of Black Studies* 17 (1987): 267–86.

Strom, Robert et al., "Grandparent Education for Black Families," *Journal of Negro Education* 61 (1992): 554–69.

Sudarkasa, Niara, *The Strength of Our Mothers: African and African American Women and Families, Essays and Speeches* (1997).

Thomas, Melvin E., and Hayward Derrick Horton, "Race, Class, and Family Structure: The Case of Family Income," *Sociological Perspectives* 35 (1992): 433–50.

Tolnay, Stewart E., "The Great Migration and Changes in the Northern Black Family, 1940–1990," *Social Forces* 75 (1997): 1213–38.

Tucker, M. Belinda, and Claudia Mitchell-Kernan, ed., *The Decline in Marriage among African-Americans: Causes, Consequences, and Policy Implications* (1995).

24.8 SOCIETY

24.8.1 Rural Life (Including Black Settlements)

Allen-Smith, Joyce E., "Blacks in Rural America: Socioeconomic Status and Policies to Enhance Economic Well-Being," *Review of Black Political Economy* 22 (1994): 7–24.

Bellamy, Donald L., and Alfred L. Parks, "Economic Development in Southern Black Belt Counties: How Does It Measure Up?" *Review of Black Political Economy* 22 (1994): 85–108.

Couto, Richard A., *Ain't Gonna Let Nobody Turn Me Around: The Pursuit of Racial Justice in the Rural South* (1991).

Grim, Valerie, "The Politics of Inclusion: Black Farmers and the Quest for Agribusiness Participation, 1945–1990's," *Agricultural History* 69 (1995): 257–71.

Guthrie, Patricia, *Catching Sense: African American Communities on a South Carolina Sea Island* (1996).

Hall, Robert L., and Carol Stack, ed., *Holding on to the Land and the Lord: Kinship, Ritual, Land Tenure, and Social Policy in the Rural South* (1982).

Humphrey, Charles A., "Educational and Social Needs in Small All-Black Towns," *Journal of Negro Education* 47 (1978): 244–55.

McGee, Leo, and Robert Boone, ed., *The Black Rural Landowner—Endangered Species: Social, Political, and Economic Implications* (1979).

Stack, Carol B., *Call to Home: African Americans Reclaim the Rural South* (1996).

Swanson, Louis E., Rosalind P. Harris, Jerry R. Skees, and Lionel Williamson, "African Americans in Southern Rural Regions: The Importance of Legacy," *Review of Black Political Economy* 22 (1994): 109–24.

Tullos, Allen, "Approaching the Black Belt," *Southern Folklore* 49 (1992): 267–78.

24.8.2 Urban Life (Including Migration)

Akalou, W. M., and Cary D. Wintz, "The Economic Impact of Residential Desegregation on Historically Black Neighborhoods in Houston, 1950–1990," *Essays in Economic and Business History* 13 (1995): 289–304.

Alba, Richard D., Nancy A. Denton, Shu-yin J. Leung, and John R. Logan, "Neighborhood Change under Conditions of Mass Immigration: The New York City Region, 1970–1990," *International Migration Review* 29 (1995): 625–56.

Anderson, Elijah, *A Place on the Corner* (1978).

——— *Code of the Street: Decency, Violence, and the Moral Life of the Inner-City* (1999).

——— *Streetwise: Race, Class, and Change in an Urban Community* (1990).

Bauman, John F., "The Truly Segregated? Exploring the Urban Underclass," *Journal of Urban History* 21 (1995): 536–48.

Bullard, Robert D., ed., *In Search of the New South: The Black Urban Experience in the 1970's and 1980's* (1989).

Campbell, Anne, *The Girls in the Gang: A Report from New York City* (1984).

Campbell, Rex R., Daniel M. Johnson, and Gary Stangler, "Return Migration of Black People to the South," *Rural Sociology* 39 (1974): 514–28.

Catlin, Robert A., *Racial Politics and Urban Planning: Gary, Indiana, 1980–1989* (1993).

Clay, Phillip L., "The Process of Black Suburbanization," *Urban Affairs Quarterly* 14 (1979): 405–24.

Conforti, Joseph M., "Newark: Ghetto or City?" *Society* 9 (1972): 20–32.

Cook, Christine C., and Mickey Lauria, "Urban Regeneration and Public Housing in New Orleans," *Urban Affairs Review* 30 (1995): 538–57.

Darden, Joe T., "Afro-American Inequality within the Urban Structure of the United States, 1967–1987," *Journal of Developing Societies* 5 (1989): 1–14.

Duneier, Mitchell, *Slim's Table: Race, Respectablity, and Masculinity* (1992).

Fainstein, Norman, and Susan Fainstein, "Urban Regimes and Black Citizens: The Economic and Social Impacts of Black Political Incorporation in U.S. Cities," *International Journal of Urban and Regional Research* 20 (1996): 22–37.

Fainstein, Susan S., and Norman I. Fainstein, "The Racial Dimension in Urban Political Economy," *Urban Affairs Quarterly* 25 (1989): 187–99.

Fusfeld, Daniel R., and Timothy Bates, *The Political Economy of the Urban Ghetto* (1984).

Galster, George C., and W. Mark Keeney, "Race, Residence, Discrimination, and Economic Opportunity: Modeling the Nexus of Urban Racial Phenomena," *Urban Affairs Quarterly* 24 (1988): 87–117.

Goings, Kenneth W., and Raymond A. Mohl, "Toward a New African American Urban History," *Journal of Urban History* 21 (1995): 283–95.

Gregory, Steven, *Black Corona: Race and the Politics of Place in an Urban Community* (1998).

Hannerz, Ulf, *Soulside: Inquiries into Ghetto Culture and Community* (1969).

Henderson, William L., and Larry C. Ledebur, "Programs for the Economic Development of the American Negro Community: The Militant Approaches," *American Journal of Economics and Sociology* 29 (1970): 337–52.

Hinshaw, John, and Judith Modell, "Perceiving Racism: Homestead from Depression to Deindustrialization," *Pennsylvania History* 63 (1996): 17–52.

Hurley, Andrew, "The Social Biases of Environmental Change in Gary, Indiana, 1945–1980," *Environmental Review* 12 (1988): 1–19.

Jankowski, Martín Sánchez, *Islands in the Street: Gangs and Urban Society* (1991).

Johnson, James H., Jr., "Recent African American Migration Trends in the United States," *Urban League Review* 14 (1990): 39–55.

Johnson, James H., Jr., and Curtis C. Roseman, "Increasing Black Outmigration from Los Angeles: The Role of Household Dynamics and Kinship Systems," *Annals of the Association of American Geographers* 80 (1990): 205–22.

Johnstone, John W. C., "Youth Gangs and Black Suburbs," *Pacific Sociological Review* 24 (1981): 355–75.

Joyce, Patrick D., "A Reversal of Fortunes: Black Empowerment, Political Machines, and City Jobs in New York City and Chicago," *Urban Affairs Review* 32 (1997): 291–318.

Kerri, James Nwannukwu, "Urbanism, Voluntarism, and Afro-American Activism," *Journal of Anthropological Research* 33 (1977): 400–20.

Kusmer, Kenneth L., "African Americans in the City Since World War II: From the Industrial to the Post-Industrial Era," *Journal of Urban History* 21 (1995): 458–504.

——— "Black Urban History in the U.S.: Retrospect and Prospect," *Trends in History* 3 (1982): 57–69.

Lemann, Nicholas, *The Promised Land: The Great Black Migration and How It Changed America* (1992).

McDougall, Harold A., *Black Baltimore: A New Theory of Community* (1993).

Miller, Abraham H., and Louis H. Bolce, "The New Urban Blacks," *Ethnicity* 3 (1976): 338–67.

Mohl, Raymond A., "The Transformation of Urban America Since the Second World War," *Amerikastudien/American Studies* 33 (1988): 53–71.

Oliver, Melvin L., "The Urban Black Community As Network: Toward a Social Network Perspective," *Sociological Quarterly* 29 (1988): 623–45.

Orser, W. Edward, "Secondhand Suburbs: Black Pioneers in Baltimore's Edmondson Village, 1955–1980," *Journal of Urban History* 16 (1990): 227–62.

Phelan, Thomas J., and Mark Schneider, "Race, Ethnicity, and Class in American Suburbs," *Urban Affairs Review* 31 (1996): 659–80.

Rodriguez, Cheryl, "Activist Stories: Culture and Continuity in Black Women's Narratives of Grassroots Community Work," *Frontiers* 19 (1998): 94–112.

Sasaki, Yutaka, "'But Not Next Door': Housing Discrimination and the Emergence of the Second Ghetto in Newark, New Jersey, after World War II," *Japanese Journal of American Studies* 5 (1994): 113–35.

St. John, Craig, Mark Edwards, and DeeAnn Wenk, "Racial Differences in Intra-urban Residential Mobility," *Urban Affairs Review* 30 (1995): 709–29.

Stahura, John M., "Changing Patterns of Suburban Racial Composition, 1970–1980," *Urban Affairs Quarterly* 23 (1988): 448–60.

——— "Suburban Development, Black Suburbanization, and the Civil Rights Movement Since World War II," *American Sociological Review* 51 (1986): 131–44.

Sullivan, Mercer L., *"Getting Paid:" Youth, Crime and Work in the Inner City* (1989).

Thernstrom, Stephan, "Reflections on the New Urban History," *Daedalus* 100 (1971): 359–75.

Thompson, Heather Ann, "Rethinking the Politics of White Flight in the Postwar City: Detroit, 1945–1980," *Journal of Urban History* 25 (1999): 163–98.

Tolnay, Stewart E., "The Great Migration and Changes in the Northern Black Family, 1940–1990," *Social Forces* 75 (1997): 1213–38.

Tucker, C. Jack, and John D. Reid, "Black Urbanization and Economic Opportunity: A Look at the Nation's Large Cities," *Phylon* 38 (1977): 55–64.

Wacquant, Loïc J. D., and William Julius Wilson, "The Cost of Racial and Class Exclusion in the Inner City," *Annals of the American Academy of Political and Social Science* (1989): 8–25.

Wallis, Don, *All We Had Was Each Other: The Black Community of Madison, Indiana* (1998).

Williams, Melvin D., "Childhood in an Urban Black Ghetto: Two Life Histories," *Umoja: A Scholarly Journal of Black Studies* 2 (1978): 169–82.

24.8.3 Material Culture

Freeman, Roland L., *A Communion of the Spirits: African American Quilters, Preservers, and Their Stories* (1996).

Landsmark, Theodore C., "Comments on African American Contributions to American Material Life," *Winterthur Portfolio* 33 (1998): 261–82.

Mathews, Christy S., "Where Do We Go from Here? Researching and Interpreting the African American Experience," *Historical Archaeology* 31 (1997): 107–13.

O'Bryant-Seabrook, Marlene, "Symbiotic Stitches: The Quilts of Maggie McFarland Gillispie and John Gillispie, Jr.," *Uncoverings* 16 (1995): 175–98.

Twining, Mary, "Harvesting and Heritage: A Comparison of Afro-American and African Basketry," *Southern Folklore Quarterly* 42 (1978): 159–74.

Weems, Robert E., Jr., "The Revolution Will Be Marketed: American Corporations and Black Consumers during the 1960's," *Radical History Review* (1994): 94–107.

Westmacott, Richard, "Yards and Gardens of Rural African Americans As Vernacular Art," *Southern Quarterly* 32 (1994): 45–63.

24.8.4 Color and Class

Alex-Assensoh, Yvette, "Myths about Race and the Underclass: Concentrated Poverty and 'Underclass' Behaviors," *Urban Affairs Review* 31 (1995): 3–19.

Auletta, Ken, *The Underclass* (rev. ed., 1999).

Austin, Roy L., and Steven Stack, "Race, Class, and Opportunity: Changing Realities and Perceptions," *Sociological Quarterly* 29 (1988): 357–69.

Banner-Haley, Charles T., *The Fruits of Integration: Black Middle-Class Ideology and Culture, 1960–1990* (1994).

Barr, Kellie E. M., Michael P. Farrell, Grace M. Barnes, and John W. Welte, "Race, Class, and Gender Differences in Substance Abuse: Evidence of Middle-Class/Underclass Polarization among Black Males," *Social Problems* 40 (1993): 314–27.

Bauman, John F., "The Truly Segregated? Exploring the Urban Underclass," *Journal of Urban History* 21 (1995): 536–48.

Bell, Michael J., *The World from Brown's Lounge: An Ethnography of Black Middle-Class Play* (1983).

Cannon, Lynn Weber, "Trends in Class Identification among Black Americans from 1952 to 1978," *Social Science Quarterly* 65 (1984): 112–26.

Cohen, Cathy J., and Michael C. Dawson, "Neighborhood Poverty and African American Politics," *American Political Science Review* 87 (1993): 286–302.

Cose, Ellis, *The Rage of the Privileged Class* (1993).

Cotton, Jeremiah, "The Gap at the Top: Relative Occupational Earnings Disadvantages of the Black Middle Class," *Review of Black Political Economy* 18 (1990): 21–38.

D'Amico, Ronald, and Nan L. Maxwell, "The Continuing Significance of Race in Minority Male Joblessness," *Social Forces* 73 (1995): 969–91.

Davis, Theodore J., Jr., "Income Inequities between Black and White Populations in Southern Nonmetropolitan Counties," *Review of Black Political Economy* 22 (1994): 145–58.

Duncan, Kevin C., "Racial Disparity in Earnings and Earnings Growth: The Case of Young Men," *Social Science Journal* 31 (1994): 237–50.

Eggers, Mitchell L., and Douglas S. Massey, "The Structural Determinants of Urban Poverty: A Comparison of Whites, Blacks, and Hispanics," *Social Science Research* 20 (1991): 217–55.

Evans, Arthur S., Jr., "Black Middle Classes: The Outlook of a New Generation," *International Journal of Politics, Culture, and Society* 6 (1992): 211–28.

Fainstein, Norman, "The Underclass/Mismatch Hypothesis As an Explanation for Black Economic Deprivation," *Politics and Society* 15 (1986–87): 403–51.

Glasgow, Douglas G., "The Black Underclass in Perspective," *State of Black America* (1987): 129–44.

———— *The Black Underclass: Poverty, Unemployment, and Entrapment of Ghetto Youth* (1980).

Graham, Lawrence Otis, *Our Kind of People: Inside America's Black Upper Class* (1999).

Green, Charles, and Basil Wilson, *The Struggle for Black Empowerment in New York City: Beyond the Politics of Pigmentation* (1989).

Hochschild, Jennifer L., *Facing Up to the American Dream: Race, Class, and the Soul of the Nation* (rev. ed., 1996).

Hughes, Michael, and Bradley R. Hertel, "The Significance of Color Remains: A Study of Life Chances, Mate Selection, and Ethnic Consciousness among Black Americans," *Social Forces* 68 (1990): 1105–20.

Jackson, Pamela Braboy, Peggy A. Thoits, and Howard F. Taylor, "Composition of the Workplace and Psychological Well-Being: The Effects of Tokenism on America's Black Elite," *Social Forces* 74 (1995): 543–57.

Jargowsky, Paul A., "Ghetto Poverty among Blacks in the 1980s," *Journal of Policy Analysis and Management* 13 (1994): 288–310.

Kasarda, John D., "Urban Industrial Transition and the Underclass," *Annals of the American Academy of Political and Social Science* (1989): 26–47.

Katz, Michael, ed., *The Underclass Debate: Views from History* (1993).

Keith, Verna M., and Cedric Herring, "Skin Tone and Stratification in the Black Community," *American Journal of Sociology* 97 (1991): 760–78.

Kilson, Martin, "The Black Bourgeoisie Revisited: From E. Franklin Frazier to the Present," *Dissent* 30 (1983): 85–96.

Massey, Douglas S., and Nancy A. Denton, *American Apartheid: Segregation and the Making of the Underclass* (1993).

Phelan, Thomas J., and Mark Schneider, "Race, Ethnicity, and Class in American Suburbs," *Urban Affairs Review* 31 (1996): 659–80.

Rolison, Garry L., "An Exploration of the Term *Underclass* As It Relates to African-Americans," *Journal of Black Studies* 21 (1991): 287–301.

Singh, Vijai P., "The Underclass in the United States: Some Correlates of Economic Change," *Sociological Inquiry* 61 (1991): 505–21.

Swain, Johnnie Dee, Jr., "Black Mayors: Urban Decline and the Underclass," *Journal of Black Studies* 24 (1993): 16–28.

Thomas, Melvin E., "Race, Class, and Personal Income: An Empirical Test of the Declining Significance of Race Thesis, 1968–1988," *Social Problems* 40 (1993): 328–42.

Tidwell, Billy J., "Black Wealth: Facts and Fiction," *State of Black America* (1988): 193–210.

Wacquant, Loïc J. D., and William Julius Wilson, "The Cost of Racial and Class Exclusion in the Inner City," *Annals of the American Academy of Political and Social Science* (1989): 8–25.

Welch, Susan, and Lorn Foster, "Class and Conservatism in the Black Community," *American Politics Quarterly* 15 (1987): 445–70.

Wilson, William Julius, *The Bridge Over the Racial Divide: Rising Inequality and Coalition Politics* (1999).

———, ed., *The Ghetto Underclass: Social Science Perspectives* (1993).

——— *The Truly Disadvantaged: The Inner City, the Underclass, and Public Policy* (1987).

——— *When Work Disappears: The World of the New Urban Poor* (1996).

Zweigenhaft, Richard L., and G. William Domhoff, ed., *Blacks in the White Establishment? A Study of Race and Class in America* (1991).

24.8.5   Associational Life

Jenkins, J. Craig, and Craig M. Eckert, "Channeling Black Insurgency: Elite Patronage and Professional Social Movement Organizations in the Development of the Black Movement," *American Sociological Review* 51 (1986): 812–29.

Marger, Martin N., "Social Movement Organizations and Response to Environmental Change: The NAACP, 1960–1973," *Social Problems* 32 (1984): 16–30.

Venkatesh, Sudhir Alladi, "Gender and Outlaw Capitalism: A Historical Account of the Black Sisters United 'Girl Gang,'" *Signs* 23 (1998): 683–709.

Woodard, Michael D., "Voluntary Association Membership among Black Americans: The Post-Civil Rights Era," *Sociological Quarterly* 28 (1986): 285–301.

24.8.6   Leisure and Sports

Bullock, Clifford A., "Fired by Conscience: The 'Black 14' Incident at the University of Wyoming and Black Protest in the Western Athletic Conference, 1968–1970," *Wyoming History Journal* 68 (1996): 4–13.

Edwards, Harry, "Sport within the Veil: The Triumphs, Tragedies, and Challenges of Afro-American Involvement," *Annals of the American Academy of Political and Social Science* (1979): 116–27.

Evans, Arthur S., Jr., "Blacks As Key Functionaries: A Study of Racial Stratification in Professional Sport," *Journal of Black Studies* 28 (1997): 43–59.

Frey, Darcy, *The Last Shot: City Streets, Basketball Dreams* (1994).

George, Nelson, *Elevating the Game: Black Men and Basketball* (1992).

Hoberman, John M., *Darwin's Athletes: How Sport Has Damaged Black America and Preserved the Myth of Race* (1997).

Kahn, Lawrence M., "Discrimination in Professional Sports: A Survey of the Literature," *Industrial and Labor Relations Review* 44 (1991): 395–418.

Lapchick, Richard E., *Broken Promises: Racism in American Sports* (1984).

——— "Race and College Sport: A Long Way to Go," *Race and Class* 36 (1995): 87–94.

Lule, Jack, "The Rape of Mike Tyson: Race, the Press, and Symbolic Types," *Critical Studies in Mass Communication* 12 (1995): 176–95.

Mackler, Bernard, "Black Superstar: The Athlete in White America," *Journal of Intergroup Relations* 4 (1975): 39–53.

Martin, Charles H., "Integrating New Year's Day: The Racial Politics of College Bowl Games in the American South," *Journal of Sport History* 24 (1997): 358–77.

——— "Jim Crow in the Gymnasium: The Integration of College Basketball in the American South," *International Journal of the History of Sport* 10 (1993): 68–86.

McCabe, Robert, and Catherine Tuthill, "Women and Blacks in College Sports," *New England Journal of History* 52 (1995): 54–62.

——— "Women and Blacks in College Sports," *New England Journal of History* 52 (1995): 54–62.

Morris, Willie, *The Courting of Marcus Dupree* (1983).

Sammons, Jeffrey T., "A Proportionate and Measured Response to the Provocation That Is *Darwin's Athletes*," *Journal of Sport History* 24 (1997): 378–88.

Schollaert, Paul T., and Donald Hugh Smith, "Team Racial Composition and Sports Attendance," *Sociological Quarterly* 28 (1987): 71–87.

Shropshire, Kenneth L., *In Black and White: Race and Sports in America* (1996).

Valenti, John, *Swee' Pea and Other Playground Legends: Tales of Drugs, Violence and Basketball* (1990).

Wiggins, David K., "'The Future of College Athletics Is at Stake': Black Athletes and Racial Turmoil on Three Predominantly White University Campuses, 1968–1972," *Journal of Sport History* 15 (1988): 304–33.

24.9 RELIGION

Allen, Ray, "Shouting the Church: Narrative and Vocal Improvisation in African-American Gospel Quartet Performance," *Journal of American Folklore* 104 (1991): 295–317.

Baer, Hans A., "Black Mainstream Churches: Emancipatory or Accommodative Responses to Racism and Social Stratification in American Society?" *Review of Religious Research* 30 (1988): 162–76.

——— *The Black Spiritual Movement: A Religious Response to Racism* (1984).

Brown, Ronald E., and Monica L. Wolford, "Religious Resources and African-American Political Action," *National Political Science Review* 4 (1993): 30–48.

Calhoun-Brown, Allison, "African American Churches and Political Mobilization: The Psychological Impact of Organizational Resources," *Journal of Politics* 58 (1996): 935–53.

Cannon, Katie G., *Black Womanist Ethics* (1988).

Carpenter, Delores Causion, "The Professionalization of the Ministry of Women," *Journal of Religious Thought* 43 (1986): 59–75.

Cato, John David, "James Herman Robinson: Crossroads Africa and American Idealism, 1958–1972," *American Presbyterians* 68 (1990): 99–107.

Chapman, Mark L., *Christianity on Trial: African American Religious Thought before and after Black Power* (1995).

Ellison, Christopher G., "Identification and Separatism: Religious Involvement and Racial Orientations among Black Americans," *Sociological Quarterly* 32 (1991): 477–94.

Ellison, Christopher G., and David A. Gay, "Region, Religious Commitment, and Life Satisfaction among Black Americans," *Sociological Quarterly* 31 (1990): 123–47.

Ellison, Christopher G., and Darren E. Sherkat, "The 'Semi-Involuntary Institution' Revisited: Regional Variations in Church Participation among Black Americans," *Social Forces* 73 (1995): 1415–37.

Foley, Albert S., "Adventures in Black Catholic History: Research and Writing," *U.S. Catholic Historian* 5 (1986): 103–18.

Gaines, Wesley J., *African Methodism in the South: Or Twenty-Five Years of Freedom* (1890).

Gardell, Mattias, *In the Name of Elijah Muhammad: Louis Farrakhan and the Nation of Islam* (1996).

Gilkes, Cheryl Townsend, "Plenty Good Room: Adaptation in a Changing Black Church," *Annals of the American Academy of Political and Social Science* (1998): 101–21.

Hunt, Larry L., and Janet G. Hunt, "Religious Affiliation and Militancy among Urban Blacks: Some Catholic/Protestant Comparisons," *Social Science Quarterly* 57 (1977): 821–33.

Lincoln, C. Eric, *Race, Religion, and the Continuing American Dilemma* (rev. ed., 1999).

Lincoln, C. Eric, and Lawrence H. Mamiya, *The Black Church in the African American Experience* (1990).

Lornell, Kip, *"Happy in the Service of the Lord": African-American Sacred Vocal Harmony Quartets in Memphis* (1995).

Milobsky, David, "Power from the Pulpit: Baltimore's African-American Clergy, 1950–1970," *Maryland Historical Magazine* 89 (1994): 274–89.

Nelsen, Hart M., "Unchurched Black Americans: Patterns of Religiosity and Affiliation," *Review of Religious Research* 29 (1988): 398–412.

Newman, Mark, "The Mississippi Baptist Convention and Desegregation, 1945–1980," *Journal of Mississippi History* 59 (1997): 1–32.

Owens, Michael Lee, "Local Party Failure and Church-Based, Black Nonparty Organizations," *Western Journal of Black Studies* 21 (1997): 162–72.

Pitts, Walter, "Keep the Fire Burnin': Language and Ritual in the Afro-Baptist Church," *Journal of the American Academy of Religion* 56 (1988): 77–97.

———— "Like a Tree Planted by the Water: The Musical Cycle in the African-American Baptist Ritual," *Journal of American Folklore* 104 (1991): 318–40.

Reagon, Bernice Johnson, ed., *We'll Understand It Better By and By: Pioneering African American Gospel Composers* (1992).

Sharps, Ronald L., "Black Catholic Gifts of Faith," *U.S. Catholic Historian* 15 (1997): 29–55.

Singer, Merrill, "The Social Context of Conversion to a Black Religious Sect," *Review of Religious Research* 30 (1988): 177–92.

Smith, Sid, "Growth of Black Southern Baptist Churches in the Inner City," *Baptist History and Heritage* 16 (1981): 49–60.

Sodiq, Yushau, "A History of Islam among the African American Muslims of Richmond," *Muslim World* 84 (1994): 258–78.

Taylor, Robert Joseph, Michael C. Thornton, and Linda M. Chatters, "Black Americans' Perceptions of the Sociohistorical Role of the Church," *Journal of Black Studies* 18 (1987): 123–38.

Wade-Gayles, Gloria, ed., *My Soul Is a Witness: African-American Women's Spirituality* (1995).

Wald, Kenneth D., Dennis E. Owen, and Samuel S. Hill, Jr., "Political Cohesion in Churches," *Journal of Politics* 52 (1990): 197–215.

Wilcox, Clyde, and Leopoldo Gomez, "Religion, Group Identification, and Politics among American Blacks," *Sociological Analysis* 51 (1990): 271–85.

Wilde, Anna Day, "Mainstreaming Kwanzaa," *Public Interest* (1995): 68–79.

Woodrum, Eric, and Arnold Bell, "Race, Politics, and Religion in Civil Religion among Blacks," *Sociological Analysis* 49 (1989): 353–67.

24.10   THOUGHT AND EXPRESSION

24.10.1   Race, Gender, and Identity

Abel, Elizabeth, ed., *Female Subjects in Black and White: Race, Psychoanalysis, Feminism* (1997).

Allen, Richard L., Michael C. Dawson, and Ronald E. Brown, "A Schema-Based Approach to Modeling an African-American Racial Belief System," *American Political Science Review* 83 (1989): 421–41.

Awkward, Michael, *Negotiating Difference: Race, Gender, and the Politics of Positionality* (1995).

Azoulay, Katya Gibel, *Black, Jewish, and Interracial: It's Not the Color of Your Skin, but the Race of Your Kin, and Other Myths of Identity* (1997).

Banks, William M., *Black Intellectuals: Race and Responsibility in American Life* (1996).

Belton, Don, ed., *Speak My Name: Black Men on Masculinity and the American Dream* (1995).

Blake, Wayne M., and Carol A. Darling, "The Dilemmas of the African American Male," *Journal of Black Studies* 24 (1994): 402–15.

Broman, Clifford L., Harold W. Neighbors, and James S. Jackson, "Racial Group Identification among Black Adults," *Social Forces* 67 (1988): 146–58.

Burgess, Norma J., "Gender Roles Revisited: The Development of the 'Woman's Place' among African American Women in the United States," *Journal of Black Studies* 24 (1994): 391–401.

Cannon, Katie G., *Black Womanist Ethics* (1988).

———— *Katie's Canon: Womanism and the Soul of the Black Community* (1996).

Caponi, Gena Dagel, *Signifyin(g), Sanctifyin' and Slam Dunking: A Reader in African American Expressive Culture* (1999).

Carbado, Devon W., ed., *Black Men on Race, Gender, and Sexuality: A Critical Reader* (1999).

Carroll, Grace, *Environmental Stress and African Americans: The Other Side of the Moon* (1998).

Chrisman, Robert, and Robert Allen, ed., *Court of Appeal: The Black Community Speaks out on the Racial and Sexual Politics of Clarence Thomas vs. Anita Hill* (1992).

Cottman, Michael H., *The Million Man March* (1995).

Cross, William E., Jr., *Shades of Black: Diversity in African American Identity* (1991).

Delany, Samuel R., *Longer Views: Extended Essays* (1996).

—— *Silent Interviews: On Language, Race, Sex, Science Fiction, and Some Comics: A Collection of Interviews* (1994).

DuCille, Ann, *Skin Trade* (1996).

Dudley, William, ed., *African Americans: Opposing Viewpoints* (1997).

Dyson, Michael Eric, *Reflecting Black: African-American Cultural Criticism* (1993).

Ebron, Paulla A., "Enchanted Memories of Regional Difference in African American Culture," *American Anthropologist* 100 (1998): 94–105.

Fossett, Judith Jackson, and Jeffrey A. Tucker, ed., *Race Consciousness: African-American Studies for the New Century* (1996).

Gates, Henry Louis, Jr., and Cornel West, *The Future of the Race* (1996).

Gay, Claudine, and Katherine Tate, "Doubly Bound: The Impact of Gender and Race on the Politics of Black Women," *Political Psychology* 19 (1998): 169–84.

Gibbs, Jewelle Taylor, and et. al, ed., *Young, Black, and Male in America: An Endangered Species* (1988).

Gilroy, Paul, *The Black Atlantic: Modernity and Double Consciousness* (1993).

—— *Small Acts: Thoughts on the Politics of Black Cultures* (1993).

Goldberg, David Theo, *Racial Subjects: Writing on Race in America* (1997).

Gordon, Lewis, ed., *Existence in Black: An Anthology of Black Existential Philosophy* (1997).

Gosse, Van, "Locating the Black Intellectual: An Interview with Harold Cruse," *Radical History Review* 71 (1998): 96–120.

Gwaltney, John, *Drylongso: A Self-Portrait of Black America* (1980).

Hairston, Loyle, Joyce Ladner, Angela Davis, Carole Gregory, and Sarah Wright, "Black Writers' Views of America," *Freedomways* 19 (1979): 151–62.

Harris, David, "Exploring the Determinants of Adult Black Identity: Context and Process," *Social Forces* 74 (1995): 227–41.

Harris, Leonard, ed., *The Philosophy of Alain Locke: Harlem Renaissance and Beyond* (1989).

Hawkeswood, William G., *One of the Children: Gay Black Men in Harlem*, ed. Alex W. Costley (1996).

Hill, Anita Faye, and Emma Coleman Jordan, ed., *Race, Gender, and Power in America: The Legacy of the Hill-Thomas Hearings* (1995).

Hunter, Andrea G., and James Earl Davis, "Hidden Voices of Black Men: The Meaning, Structure, and Complexity of Manhood," *Journal of Black Studies* 25 (1994): 20–40.

James, Stanlie M., and Abena P. A. Busia, ed., *Theorizing Black Feminisms: The Visionary Pragmatism of Black Women* (1993).

Johnson, Charles, and John McCluskey, ed., *Black Men Speaking* (1997).

Jones, Jacqueline, "Race and Gender in Modern America," *Reviews in American History* 26 (1998): 220–38.

Joseph, Gloria I., and Jill Lewis, *Common Differences: Conflicts in Black and White Feminist Perspectives* (1981).

Kenan, Randall, *Walking on Water: Black American Lives at the Turn of the Twenty-First Century* (1999).

Lemelle, Sidney, and Robin D. G. Kelley, ed., *Imagining Home: Class, Culture, and Nationalism in the African Diaspora* (1994).

Levin, Michael, *Why Race Matters: Race Differences and What They Mean* (1997).

Loury, Glenn C., *One by One from the Inside Out: Essays and Reviews on Race and Responsibility in America* (1995).

Madhubuti, Haki R., and Ron Karenga, ed., *Million Man March, Day of Absence: A Commemorative Anthology* (1996).

Majors, Richard G., and Jacob V. Gordon, ed., *The American Black Male: His Present Status and His Future* (1994).

Maligalim, Timothy Abdour, *About Face: Race in Postmodern America* (1989).

Marable, Manning, *Black Liberation in Conservative America* (1997).

—— "Groundings with My Sisters: Patriarchy and the Exploitation of Black Women," *Journal of Ethnic Studies* 11 (1983): 1–39.

———— *Speaking Truth to Power: Essays on Race, Resistance, and Radicalism* (1996).

Martin, Ben L., "From Negro to Black to African American: The Power of Names and Naming," *Political Science Quarterly* 106 (1991): 83–107.

Moraga, Cherrie, and Gloria Anzaldua, ed., *This Bridge Called My Back: Writings by Radical Women of Color* (1981).

Morrison, Minion K. C., "Afro-Americans and Africa: Grass Roots Afro-American Opinion and Attitudes toward Africa," *Comparative Studies in Society and History* 29 (1987): 269–92.

Morrison, Toni, ed., *Race-ing Justice, En-gendering Power: Essays on Anita Hill, Clarence Thomas, and the Construction of Social Reality* (1992).

Outlaw, Lucius T., *On Race and Philosophy* (1996).

Perkins, William Eric, "Harold Cruse: On the Problem of Culture and Revolution," *Journal of Ethnic Studies* 5 (1977): 3–25.

Peters, Erskine, "Afrocentricity: Problems of Logic, Method, and Nomenclature," *21st Century Afro Review* 2 (1996): 1–44.

Peterson, Paul E., ed., *Classifying by Race* (1995).

Pinsker, Sanford, "The Black Intellectuals' Common Fate and Uncommon Problems," *Virginia Quarterly Review* 70 (1994): 220–38.

Pitts, James P., "The Study of Race Consciousness: Comments on New Direction," *American Journal of Sociology* 80 (1974): 665–87.

Ragon, Sandra L., ed., *The Lynching of Language: Gender, Politics, and Power in the Hill-Thomas Hearings* (1996).

Reed, Adolph L., Jr., *Class Notes: Posing as Politics and Other Thoughts on the American Scene* (2000).

Reed, Adolph L., Jr., ed., *Race, Politics, and Culture: Critical Essays on the Radicalism of the 1960's* (1986).

Reed, Ishmael, *Airing Dirty Laundry* (1993).

———— *God Made Alaska for the Indians: Selected Essays* (1982).

———— *Writin' is Fightin': Thirty-Seven Years of Boxing on Paper* (1988).

Roberts, Dorothy E., *Killing the Black Body: Race, Reproduction, and the Meaning of Liberty* (1997).

Roethler, Jacque, "Reading in Color: Children's Book Illustrations and Identity Formation for Black Children in the United States," *African American Review* 32 (1998): 95–104.

Scott, Daryl Michael, "The Politics of Pathology: The Ideological Origins of the Moynihan Controversy," *Journal of Policy History* 8 (1996): 81–105.

Sigelman, Lee, and Susan Welch, *Black Americans' Views of Racial Inequality: The Dream Deferred* (1991).

Smith, Barbara, ed., *Home Girls: A Black Feminist Anthology* (1983).

Smitherman, Geneva, ed., *African American Women Speak Out on Anita Hill-Clarence Thomas* (1995).

Spencer, Jon Michael, *The New Colored People: The Mixed-Race Movement in America* (1997).

Tarpley, Natasha, ed., *Testimony: Young African-Americans on Self-Discovery and Black Identity* (1995).

Terry, Roderick, and Cliff Giles, *One Million Strong: A Photographic Tribute of the Million Man March and Affirmations for the African-American Male* (1996).

Thornton, Michael C., and Robert J. Taylor, "Black American Perceptions of Black Africans," *Ethnic and Racial Studies* 11 (1988): 139–50.

Tuch, Steven A., and Jack K. Martin, ed., *Racial Attitudes in the 1990's: Continuity and Change* (1997).

Watts, Jerry Gafio, *Heroism and the Black Intellectual: Ralph Ellison, Politics, and Afro-American Intellectual Life* (1994).

West, Cornel, *The Cornel West Reader* (1999).

Williams, Patricia, *The Alchemy of Race and Rights* (1991).

Wing, Adrien Katherine, ed., *Critical Race Feminism: A Reader* (1997).

Witt, Doris, *Black Hunger: Food and the Politics of U.S. Identity* (1999).

Wojniusz, Helen K., "Racial Hostility among Blacks in Chicago," *Journal of Black Studies* 10 (1979): 40–59.

Zimmerman, Jonathan, "Beyond Double Consciousness: Black Peace Corps Volunteers in Africa, 1961–1971," *Journal of American History* 82 (1995): 999–1028.

24.10.2 Emigration and Nationalism

Asante, Molefi K., *Afrocentric Idea* (1987).
———— *Afrocentricity* (1988).
Baraka, Imamu Amiri, "The Congress of Afrikan People: A Position Paper," *Black Scholar* 6 (1975): 2–15.
Bush, Roderick D., *We Are Not What We Seem: Black Nationalism and Class Struggle in the American Century* (1999).
Dubey, Madhu, *Black Women Novelists and the Nationalist Aesthetic* (1994).
Henderson, Errol A., "Black Nationalism and Rap Music," *Journal of Black Studies* 26 (1996): 308–39.
Reed, W. Edward, Erma J. Lawson, and Tyson Gibbs, "Afrocentrism in the 21st Century," *Western Journal of Black Studies* 21 (1997): 173–79.
Sundiata K., Cha-Jua, and Clarence Lang, "The Rise and Decline of Louis Farrakhan," *New Politics* 6 (1997): 47–71.
Walker, Randolph Meade, "An Afrocentric View: History's Teleological Basis," *Griot* 16 (1997): 35–39.
Walters, Ronald W., *Pan Africanism in the African Diaspora: An Analysis of Modern Afrocentric Political Movements* (1993).
White, E. Frances, "Africa on My Mind: Gender, Counter Discourse and African-American Nationalism," *Journal of Women's History* 2 (1990): 73–97.

24.10.3 Language and Linguistics

Baugh, John, *Black Street Speech: Its History, Structure, and Survival* (1983).
Hill, Patricia Liggins, "'Blues for a Mississippi Black Boy': Etheridge Knight's Craft in the Black Oral Tradition," *Mississippi Quarterly* 36 (1982–83): 21–33.
Kochman, Thomas, ed., *Rappin' and Stylin' Out: Communication in Urban Black America* (1972).
Labov, William, *Language in the Inner City: Studies in the Black English Vernacular* (1998).
Lieberson, Stanley, and Kelly S. Mikelson, "Distinctive African American Names: An Experimental, Historical, and Linguistic Analysis of Innovation," *American Sociological Review* 60 (1995): 928–46.
Neilsen, Aldon Lynn, *Black Chant: Languages of African-American Postmodernism* (1997).
Smith, Riley B., "Research Perspectives on American Black English: A Brief Historical Sketch," *American Speech* 49 (1974): 24–39.

24.10.4 Folklore and Humor

Lefever, Harry G., "'Playing the Dozens': A Mechanism for Social Control," *Phylon* 42 (1981): 73–85.
Miller, Ivor, "Night Train: The Power That Man Made," *New York Folklore* 17 (1991): 21–43.

24.10.5 Literature and Poetry

Awkward, Michael, *Inspiriting Influences: Tradition, Revision, and Afro-American Women's Novels* (1989).
Baker, Houston A., *Workings of the Spirit: The Poetics of Afro-American Women's Writing* (1991).
Baker, Houston A., and Patricia Redmond, ed., *Afro-American Literary Study in the 1990's* (1990).
Bell, Roseann P., Bettye J. Parker, and Beverly Guy-Sheftall, ed., *Sturdy Black Bridges: Visions of Black Women in Literature* (1979).
Bloom, Harold, and Willing Golding, ed., *Contemporary Black American Poets and Dramatists* (1995).
Blount, Marcellus, "'A Certain Eloquence': Ralph Ellison and the Afro-American Artist," *American Literary History* 1 (1989): 675–88.
Braxton, Joanne M., and Andree Nicola McLaughlin, ed., *Wild Women in the Whirlwind: Afra-American Culture and the Contemporary Literary Renaissance* (1990).
Brown, Fahamisha Patricia, *Performing the Wind: African American Poetry As Vernacular Culture* (1999).
Carroll, Rebecca, ed., *Swing Low: Black Men Writing* (1995).

Christian, Barbara, *Black Feminist Criticism: Perspectives on Black Women Writers*(1985).

Clark, Roger, Rachel Lennon, and Leanna Morris, "Of Caldecotts and Kings: Gendered Images in Recent American Children's Books by Black and Non-Black Illustrators," *Gender and Society* 7 (1993): 227–45.

Cornwell-Giles, JoAnne, "Afro-American Criticism and Western Consciousness: The Politics of Knowing," *Black American Literature Forum* 24 (1990): 85–98.

Doyle, Laura, *Bordering on the Body: The Racial Matrix of Modern Fiction and Culture* (1994).

Dubey, Madhu, *Black Women Novelists and the Nationalist Aesthetic* (1994).

Fishkin, Shelley Fisher, "Interrogating 'Whiteness,' Complicating 'Blackness': Remapping American Culture," *American Quarterly* 47 (1995): 428–66.

Forrest, Leon, *Relocations of the Spirit: Essays* (1994).

Franklin, H. Bruce, "The Literature of the American Prison," *Massachusetts Review* 18 (1977): 51–78.

Hanshaw, Shirley A. J., "Spinning the Anansean Web: Black Vietnam War Literature, Vernacular Theory, and *Captain Blackman*," *Literary Griot* 8 (1996): 1–35.

Hogue, W. Lawrence, *Race, Modernity, Postmodernity: A Look at the History and the Literatures of Peoples of Color since the 1960's* (1996).

Holloway, Karla F. C., *Moorings and Metaphors: Figures of Culture and Gender in Black Women's Literature* (1992).

Japtok, Martin, "Paule Marshall's *Brown Girl, Brownstones:* Reconciling Ethnicity and Individualism," *African American Review* 32 (1998): 305–15.

Killens, John O., "The Image of Black Folk in American Literature," *Black Scholar* 6 (1975): 45–52.

Kimball, Gregg D., "Expanding the Notion: The African American Presence in *Virginia Cavalcade*, 1951–1996," *Virginia Cavalcade* 46 (1996): 82–94.

McDowell, Deborah E., *The Changing Same: Black Women's Literature, Criticism and Theory* (1995).

Mikkelson, Nina, "Insiders, Outsiders, and the Question of Authenticity: Who Shall Write for African American Children?" *African American Review* 32 (1998): 33–50.

Neal, Larry, *Visions of a Liberated Future: Black Arts Movement Writings: Prose and Poetry* (1989).

Ojo-Ade, Femi, ed., *Of Dreams Deferred, Dead or Alive: African Perspectives on African-American Writers* (1996).

Ozick, Cynthia, "Literary Blacks and Jews," *Midstream* 18 (1972): 10–24.

Palmer, R. Roderick, "The Poetry of Three Revolutionists: Don L. Lee, Sonia Sanchez, and Nikki Giovanni," *CLA Journal* 15 (1971): 25–36.

Patterson, Lindsay, ed., *A Rock against the Wind: African-American Poems and Letters of Love and Passion* (1996).

Pettis, Joyce, "The Black Poet As Historian," *Umoja: A Scholarly Journal of Black Studies* 4 (1980): 41–56.

Posnock, Ross, *Color and Culture: Black Writers and the Making of the Modern Intellectual* (1998).

Pryse, Majorie, and Hortense Spillers, ed., *Conjuring: Black Women, Fiction and Literary Tradition* (1985).

Smith, David Lionel, "The Black Arts Movement and Its Critics," *American Literary History* 3 (1991): 93–110.

Sollors, Werner, "Of Mules and Mares in a Land of Difference: Or, Quadrupeds All?" *American Quarterly* 42 (1990): 167–90.

Sollors, Werner, and Maria Diedrich, ed., *The Black Columbiad: Defining Moments in African American Literature and Culture* (1994).

Tate, Claudia, ed., *Black Women Writers at Work*(1983).

Wade-Gayles, Gloria, *No Crystal Stair: Visions of Race and Sex in Black Women's Fiction* (1984).

Walker, Melissa, *Down from the Mountaintop: Black Women's Novels in the Wake of the Civil Rights Movement, 1966–1989* (1991).

Wall, Cheryl A., ed., *Changing Our Own Words: Essays on Criticism, Theory, and Writing by Black Women* (1989).

Weixlmann, Joe, and Houston A. Baker, ed., *Black Feminist Criticism and Critical Theory* (1988).

Wepman, Dennis, Ronald B. Newman, and Murry B. Binderman, "Toasts: The Black Urban Folk Poetry," *Journal of American Folklore* 87 (1974): 208–24.

Willis, Susan, *Specifying: Black Women Writing the American Experience*(1987).

Wonham, Henry B., ed., *Criticism on the Color Line: Desegrating American Literary Studies* (1996).

24.10.6 Music and Performing Arts

Adjaye, Joseph K., ed., *Language, Rhythm, and Sound: Black Popular Cultures into the Twenty-first Century* (1997).

Allen, Ray, "Shouting the Church: Narrative and Vocal Improvisation in African-American Gospel Quartet Performance," *Journal of American Folklore* 104 (1991): 295–317.

Anadolu-Okur, Nilgun, *Contemporary African American Theater: Afrocentricity in the Works of Larry Neal, Amiri Baraka, and Charles Fuller* (1997).

Andrews, W. D. E., "Theater of Black Reality: The Blues Drama of Ed Bullins," *Southwest Review* 65 (1980): 178–90.

Asante, Molefi Kete, and Kariamu Walsh Asante, ed., *The Rhythms of Unity* (1985).

Backlund, Ralph, "From a Garage on West 152d Street, A Ballet Company Soars to Moscow," *Smithsonian* 19 (1988): 28–39.

Baker, David N., Lida M. Belt, and Herman C. Hudson, ed., *The Black Composer Speaks* (1978).

Baskerville, John D., "Free Jazz: A Reflection of Black Power Ideology," *Journal of Black Studies* 24 (1994): 484–97.

Berry, Venise T., "Rap Music, Self-Concept, and Low-Income Black Adolescents," *Popular Music and Society* 14 (1990): 89–107.

Blair, M. Elizabeth, "Commercialization of the Rap Music Youth Subculture," *Journal of Popular Culture* 27 (1993): 21–33.

Bogle, Donald, *Brown Sugar: Eighty Years of America's Black Female Superstars* (1980).

Brown-Guillory, Elizabeth, "Black Women Playwrights: Exorcising Myths," *Phylon* 48 (1987): 229–39.

Carmichael, Thomas, "Beneath the Underdog: Charles Mingus, Representation, and Jazz Autobiography," *Canadian Review of American Studies* 25 (1995): 29–40.

Cheatham, Wallace McClain, ed., *Dialogues on Opera and the African-American Experience* (1997).

Costello, Mark, and David Foster Wallace, *Signifying Rappers: Rap and Race in the Urban Present* (1990).

Dixon, Wheeler Wilson, "Urban Black American Music in the Late 1980's: The 'Word' As Cultural Signifier," *Midwest Quarterly* 30 (1989): 229–41.

Djedje, Jacqueline Cogdell, and Eddie S. Meadows, ed., *California Soul: Music of African Americans in the West* (1998).

Elam, Harry J., Jr., *Taking It to the Streets: The Social Protest Theater of Luis Valdez and Amiri Baraka* (1997).

Eure, Joseph D., and James G. Spady, ed., *Nation Conscious Rap* (1991).

Fernando, S. H., Jr., *The New Beats: Exploring the Music, Culture, and Attitudes of Hip-Hop* (1994).

Garofolo, Reebee, "The Impact of the Civil Rights Movement on Popular Music," *Radical America* 21 (1987): 14–22.

George, Nelson, *Hip Hop America* (1998).

Jeffries, Rhonda B., *Performance Traditions among African-American Teachers* (1997).

Kamin, Jonathan, "Musical Culture and Perceptual Learning in the Popularization of Black Music," *Journal of Jazz Studies* 3 (1975): 54–65.

Kofsky, Frank, "The Jazz Tradition," *Journal of Black Studies* 1 (1971): 403–33.

Lornell, Kip, *"Happy in the Service of the Lord": African-American Sacred Vocal Harmony Quartets in Memphis* (1995).

Lusane, Clarence, "Rap, Race, and Politics," *Race and Class* 35 (1993): 41–56.

McDonnell, Judith, "Rap Music: Its Role As an Agent of Change," *Popular Music and Society* 16 (1992): 89–107.

Morris, Ronald L., "Themes of Protest and Criminality in American Recorded Jazz, 1945–1975," *Annual Review of Jazz Studies* 3 (1985): 147–66.

Nelson, Havelock, and Michael A. Gonzales, ed., *Bring the Noise: A Guide to Rap Music and Hip-Hop Culture* (1991).

Olaniyan, Tejumola, *Scars of Conquest/Masks of Resistance: The Invention of Cultural Identities in African, African-American, and Caribbean Drama* (1995).

Pereira, Kim, *August Wilson and the African-American Odyssey* (1995).

Perkins, William Eric, ed., *Droppin' Science: Critical Essays on Rap Music and Hip Hop Culture* (1996).

Peterson, Bernard L., *Contemporary Black American Playwrights and Their Plays: A Biographical Directory and Dramatic Index* (1988).

Pitts, Walter, "Like a Tree Planted by the Water: The Musical Cycle in the African-American Baptist Ritual," *Journal of American Folklore* 104 (1991): 318–40.

Quinn, Michael, "'Never Shoulda Been Let out the Penitentiary': Gangsta Rap and the Struggle over Racial Identity," *Cultural Critique* 34 (1996): 65–90.

Reagon, Bernice Johnson, ed., *We'll Understand It Better By and By: Pioneering African American Gospel Composers* (1992).

Reagon, Bernice Johnson, and Sweet Honey in the Rock, *We Who Believe in Freedom: Sweet Honey in the Rock—Still on the Journey* (1993).

Reed, Harry A., "The Black Bar in the Making of a Jazz Musician: Bird, Mingus, and Stan Hope," *Journal of Jazz Studies* 5 (1979): 76–90.

Rose, Tricia, *Black Noise: Rap Music and Black Culture in Contemporary America* (1994).

Rotenstein, David S., "The Helena Blues: Cultural Tourism and African-American Folk Music," *Southern Folklore* 49 (1992): 133–46.

Semmes, Clovis E., "The Dialectics of Cultural Survival and the Community Artist: Phil Cohran and the Afro-Arts Theater," *Journal of Black Studies* 24 (1994): 447–61.

Sexton, Adam, ed., *Rap on Rap: Straight-Up Talk on Hip-Hop Culture* (1995).

Sidran, Ben, *Talking Jazz: An Oral History* (1992).

Slovenz, Madeline, "'Rock the House': The Aesthetic Dimensions of Rap Music in New York City," *New York Folklore* 14 (1988): 151–63.

Smith, David Lionel, "The Black Arts Movement and Its Critics," *American Literary History* 3 (1991): 93–110.

Ward, Brian, *Just My Soul Responding: Rhythm and Blues, Black Consciousness, and Race Relations* (1998).

Werner, Craig, *A Change is Gonna Come: Music, Race, and the Soul of America* (1999).

24.10.7   Art (Drawing, Painting, Photography, Printmaking, Sculpture)

Ferris, William R., ed., *Afro-American Folk Art and Crafts* (1983).

———— "Vision in Afro-American Folk Art: The Sculpture of James Thomas," *Journal of American Folklore* 88 (1975): 115–31.

Freeman, Roland L., *A Communion of the Spirits: African American Quilters, Preservers, and Their Stories* (1996).

Govenar, Alan, "The Photographs of Benny Joseph: African American Life and Community in Houston," *Folklife Annual* (1990): 82–99.

O'Bryant-Seabrook, Marlene, "Symbiotic Stitches: The Quilts of Maggie McFarland Gillispie and John Gillispie, Jr.," *Uncoverings* 16 (1995): 175–98.

Thibodeau, Ruth, "From Racism to Tokenism: The Changing Face of Blacks in New Yorker Cartoons," *Public Opinion Quarterly* 53 (1989): 482–94.

24.10.8   Film and Broadcasting

Abelman, Robert, "A Comparison of Black and White Families As Portrayed on Religious and Secular Television Programs," *Journal of Black Studies* 20 (1989): 60–79.

Cha-Jua, Sundiata K., "Mississippi Burning: The Burning of Black Self-Activity," *Radical History Review* (1989): 125–36.

Cripps, Thomas, *Black Film as Genre* (1978).

———— "The Noble Black Savages: A Problem in the Politics of Television Art," *Journal of Popular Culture* 8 (1974): 685–95.

Dates, Jannette L., and William Barlow, ed., *Split Image: African Americans in the Mass Media* (1990).

Entman, Robert M., "Blacks in the News: Television, Modern Racism, and Cultural Change," *Journalism Quarterly* 69 (1992): 341–61.

———— "Modern Racism and the Images of Blacks in Local Television News," *Critical Studies in Mass Communication* 7 (1990): 332–45.

Hartsough, Denise, "Into a New Kitchen: Lessons from Teaching a Course on African-American Women and Film," *Michigan Academician* 24 (1992): 321–32.

Inniss, Leslie B., and Joe R. Feagin, "The Cosby Show: The View from the Black Middle Class," *Journal of Black Studies* 25 (1995): 692–711.

Kevorkian, Martin, "Computers with Color Monitors: Disembodied Black Screen Images, 1988–1996," *American Quarterly* 51 (1999): 283–310.

Lee, Spike, *Five for Five: The Films of Spike Lee* (1991).

——— *Spike Lee's Gotta Have It: Inside Guerrilla Filmmaking* (1987).

——— *Uplift the Race: The Construction of School Daze* (1988).

Lee, Spike, with Lisa Jones, *Do the Right Thing: A Spike Lee Joint* (1989).

——— *Mo' Better Blues* (1990).

Lee, Spike, with Ralph Wiley, *By Any Means Necessary: The Trials and Tribulations of the Making of Malcolm X* (1992).

Licata, Jane W., and Abhijit Biswas, "Representation, Roles, and Occupational Status of Black Models in Television Advertisements," *Journalism Quarterly* 70 (1993): 868–82.

MacDonald, J. Fred, ed., *Richard Durham's Destination Freedom: Scripts from Radio's Black Legacy, 1948–1950* (1989).

Merritt, Bishetta D., "Bill Cosby: TV Auteur?" *Journal of Popular Culture* 24 (1991): 89–102.

Newman, Mark, *Entrepreneurs of Profit and Pride: From Black-Appeal to Radio Soul* (1988).

Olaniyan, Tejumola, "'Uplift the Race!' *Coming to America, Do the Right Thing,* and the Poetics and Politics of 'Othering,'" *Cultural Critique* 34 (1996): 91–114.

Oshana, Maryann, *Women of Color: A Filmography of Minority and Third World Women* (1985).

Reagon, Bernice Johnson, ed., *Black American Culture and Scholarship: Contemporary Issues* (1985).

Redd, Lawrence N., "Radio Deregulation: The Impact on Black Families and Nonprofit Social Agencies," *Journal of Black Studies* 22 (1991): 216–38.

Reid, Mark A., "The Black Action Film: The End of the Patiently Enduring Black Hero," *Film History* 2 (1988): 23–36.

Robinson, Gene S., "Television Advertising and Its Impact on Black America," *State of Black America* (1990): 157–71.

Rodgers, Curtis E., "So You Want to Be in the Movies?" *Crisis* 90 (1983): 6–18.

Tait, Alice A., "Minority Programming in Television and the Story of Detroit's 'Profiles in Black,'" *Michigan Academician* 22 (1990): 271–86.

Taylor, Henry, and Carol Dozier, "Television Violence, African-Americans, and Social Control, 1950–1976," *Journal of Black Studies* 14 (1983): 107–36.

Walker, Sheila S., and Jennifer Rasamimanana, "Tarzan in the Classroom: How 'Educational' Films Mythologize Africa and Mis-Educate Americans," *Journal of Negro Education* 62 (1993): 3–23.

Zinkhan, George M., William J. Qualls, and Abhijit Biswas, "The Use of Blacks in Magazine and Television Advertising, 1946 to 1986," *Journalism Quarterly* 67 (1990): 547–53.

Zook, Kristal Brent, *Color by Fox: The Fox Network and the Revolution in Black Television* (1999).

24.11   EDUCATION

Allen, Walter R., Edgar G. Epps, and Nesha Z. Hariff, ed., *College in Black and White: African American Students in Predominantly White and in Historically Black Public Universities* (1991).

Altbach, Philip G., and Kofi Lomotey, ed., *The Racial Crisis in American Higher Education* (1991).

Anderson, Talmadge, "Black Encounter of Racism and Elitism in White Academe: A Critique of the System," *Journal of Black Studies* 18 (1988): 259–72.

Armor, David J., "Why Is Black Educational Achievement Rising?" *Public Interest* (1992): 65–80.

Baker, Houston A., Jr., *Black Studies, Rap and the Academy* (1993).

Barrett, Lindon, "Speaking of Failure: Undergraduate Education and Intersection of African-American Literature and Critical Theory," *Callaloo* 14 (1991): 619–30.

Berry, Gordon LaVern, and Joy Keiko Asamen, ed., *Black Students: Psychological Issues and Academic Achievement* (1989).

Bowen, William G., and Derek Bok, *The Shape of the River: Long-Term Consequences of Considering Race in College and University Admissions* (1998).

Card, David, and Alan B. Krueger, "School Quality and Black-White Relative Earnings: A Direct Assessment," *Quarterly Journal of Economics* 107 (1992): 151–200.

Constantine, Jill M., "The Effect of Attending Historically Black Colleges and Universities on Future Wages of Black Students," *Industrial and Labor Relations Review* 48 (1995): 531–46.

Curry, Constance, *Silver Rights* (1995).

Dulaney, W. Marvin, "The Texas Negro Peace Officers' Association: The Origins of Black Police Unionism," *Houston Review* 12 (1990): 59–78.

Feagin, Joe R., "The Continuing Significance of Racism: Discrimination against Black Students in White Colleges," *Journal of Black Studies* 22 (1992): 546–78.

Fechter, Alan, "The Black Scholar: An Endangered Species," *Review of Black Political Economy* 19 (1990): 49–59.

Fordham, Signithia, and John U. Ogbu, "Black Students' School Success: Coping with the 'Burden of Acting White,'" *Urban Review* 18 (1986): 176–206.

Formisano, Ronald P., *Boston against Busing: Race, Class and Ethnicity in the 1960's and 1970's* (1991).

Fossett, Judith Jackson, and Jeffrey A. Tucker, ed., *Race Consciousness: African-American Studies for the New Century* (1996).

Fuerst, J. S., "Report Card: Chicago's All-Black Schools," *Public Interest* (1981): 79–91.

Gordon, Beverly M., "Implicit Assumptions of the Holmes and Carnegie Reports: A View from an African-American Perspective," *Journal of Negro Education* 57 (1988): 141–58.

Grim, Valerie, "Integrating Oral History into the Classroom Curriculum: A Tool for Helping Students Understand the American and African-American Experience," *Teaching History: A Journal of Methods* 20 (1995): 3–19.

Gruhl, John, and Susan Welch, "The Impact of the *Bakke* Decision on Black and Hispanic Enrollment in Medical and Law Schools," *Social Science Quarterly* 71 (1990): 458–73.

Hale, Janice, *Unbank the Fire: Visions for the Education of African American Children* (1994).

Harding, Vincent, "Black Students and the Impossible Revolution," *Journal of Black Studies* 1 (1970): 75–100.

Harris, John J., III, Charles J. Russo, and Frank Brown, "The Curious Case of *Missouri v. Jenkins:* The End of the Road for Court-Ordered Desegregation?" *Journal of Negro Education* 66 (1997): 43–55.

Hatton, Barbara R., "Schools and Black Community Development: A Reassessment of Community Control," *Education and Urban Society* 9 (1977): 215–33.

Holland, Spencer H., "PROJECT 2000: An Educational Mentoring and Academic Support Model for Inner-City African American Boys," *Journal of Negro Education* 65 (1996): 315–21.

Howard-Vital, Michelle R., "African-American Women in Higher Education: Struggling to Gain Identity," *Journal of Black Studies* 20 (1989): 180–91.

Hurtado, Sylvia, "Graduate School Racial Climates and Academic Self-Concept among Minority Graduate Students in the 1970's," *American Journal of Education* 102 (1994): 330–51.

James, Joy, and Ruth Farmer, ed., *Spirit, Space, and Survival: African American Women in (White) Academe* (1993).

Joseph, Janice, "School Factors and Delinquency: A Study of African American Youths," *Journal of Black Studies* 26 (1996): 341–56.

Karen, David, "The Politics of Class, Race, and Gender: Access to Higher Education in the United States, 1960–1986," *American Journal of Education* 99 (1991): 208–37.

Kellar, William Henry, *Make Haste Slowly: Moderates, Conservatives, and School Desegregation in Houston* (1999).

Kershaw, Terry, "The Effects of Educational Tracking on the Social Mobility of African Americans," *Journal of Black Studies* 23 (1992): 152–69.

Kobrak, Peter, "Black Student Retention in Predominantly White Regional Universities: The Politics of Faculty Involvement," *Journal of Negro Education* 61 (1992): 509–30.

Loury, Linda Datcher, and David Garman, "Affirmative Action in Higher Education," *American Economic Review* 83 (1993): 99–103.

Lukas, J. Anthony, *Common Ground: A Turbulent Decade in the Lives of Three American Families* (1985).

McCaslin, Richard B., "Steadfast in His Intent: John W. Hargis and the Integration of the University of Texas at Austin," *Southwestern Historical Quarterly* 95 (1991): 20–41.

Morgan, Gordon D., and Izola Preston, *The Edge of Campus: A Journal of the Black Experience at the University of Arkansas* (1990).

Neville, Helen A., and Sundiata K. Cha-Jua, "Kufundisha: Toward a Pedagogy for Black Studies," *Journal of Black Studies* 28 (1998): 447–79.

Ogbu, John U., "Racial Stratification and Education in the United States: Why Inequality Persists," *Teachers College Record* 96 (1994): 264–98.

Orfield, Gary, Susan E. Eaton, and the Harvard Project on School Desegregation, *Dismantling Desegregation: The Quiet Reversal of Brown v. Board of Education* (1996).

Orlans, Harold, "Affirmative Action in Higher Education," *Annals of the American Academy of Political and Social Science* (1992): 144–58.

Page, Jane A., and Fred M. Page, Jr., "Gaining Access into Academe: Perceptions and Experiences of African American Teachers," *Urban League Review* 15 (1991): 27–39.

Pearson, Willie, and H. Kenneth Bechtel, ed., *Blacks, Science, and American Education* (1989).

Pratt, Robert A., *The Color of Their Skin: Education and Race in Richmond, Virginia, 1954–1989* (1992).

——— "A Promise Unfulfilled: School Desegregation in Richmond, Virginia, 1956–1986," *Virginia Magazine of History and Biography* 99 (1991): 415–48.

Record, Wilson, "Response of Sociologists to Black Studies," *Journal of Higher Education* 45 (1974): 364–90.

Robinson, Armstead L., Craig Foster, and Donald Ogilvie, ed., *Black Studies in the University: A Symposium* (1969).

Rodgers, Harrell R., Jr., and Charles S. Bullock, III, "School Desegregation: Successes and Failures," *Journal of Negro Education* 43 (1974): 139–54.

Rosenbaum, James E., Marilynn J. Kulieke, and Leonard S. Rubinowitz, "White Suburban Schools' Responses to Low-Income Black Children: Sources of Successes and Problems," *Urban Review* 20 (1988): 28–41.

Rossell, Christine H., "School Desegregation and White Flight," *Political Science Quarterly* 90 (1975–76): 675–95.

Sandefur, Gary D., and Anup Pahari, "Racial and Ethnic Inequality in Earnings and Educational Attainment," *Social Service Review* 63 (1989): 199–221.

Simmons, Roberta G., Ann Black, and Yingzhi Zhou, "African-American versus White Children and the Transition into Junior High School," *American Journal of Education* 99 (1991): 481–520.

Siskar, John F., "The B.U.I.L.D. Academy: A Historical Study of Community Action and Education in Buffalo, New York," *Afro-Americans in New York Life and History* 21 (1997): 19–40.

Smith, A. Wade, "Educational Attainment As a Determinant of Social Class among Black Americans," *Journal of Negro Education* 58 (1989): 416–29.

Smith, Susan L., and Kaye W. Borgstedt, "Factors Influencing Adjustment of White Faculty in Predominantly Black Colleges," *Journal of Negro Education* 54 (1985): 148–63.

Sowell, Thomas, *Black Education: Myths and Tragedies* (1972).

——— *Education: Assumptions versus History: Collected Papers* (1986).

Stewart, Joseph, Jr., Kenneth J. Meier, and Robert E. England, "In Quest of Role Models: Change in Black Teacher Representation in Urban School Districts, 1968–1986," *Journal of Negro Education* 58 (1989): 140–52.

Warfield-Coppock, Nsenga, "The Rite of Passage Movement: A Resurgence of African-Centered Practices for Socializing African American Youth," *Journal of Negro Education* 61 (1992): 471–82.

Washington, Valora, and Joanna Newman, "Setting Our Own Agenda: Exploring the Meaning of Gender Disparities among Blacks in Higher Education," *Journal of Negro Education* 60 (1991): 19–35.

Weinberg, Meyer, *Minority Students: A Research Appraisal* (1977).

——— *The Search for Quality Integrated Education: Policy and Research on Minority Students in School and College* (1983).

Weinberg, Meyer, and Gertrude Martin, ed., *School Desegregation in America: Experiences and Explorations* (1977).

Williams, Lea E., "Public Policies and Financial Exigencies: Black Colleges Twenty Years Later, 1965–1985," *Journal of Black Studies* 19 (1988): 135–49.

Willie, Charles V., and Ronald Edmonds, ed., *Black Colleges in America: Challenge, Development, Survival* (1978).

Willie, Charles V., Antoine M. Garibaldi, and Wornie L. Reed, ed., *The Education of African-Americans* (1991).

Yeakey, Carol Camp, and Clifford T. Bennett, "Race, Schooling, and Class in American Society," *Journal of Negro Education* 59 (1990): 3–18.

24.12   WORK AND ENTERPRENEURIAL ACTIVITY

Honey, Michael, *Black Workers Remember: An Oral History of Segregation, Unionism, and the Freedom Struggle* (1999).

Bates, Timothy, "Black Economic Well-Being Since the 1950's," *Review of Black Political Economy* 12 (1984): 5–39.

——— "The Changing Nature of Minority Business: A Comparative Analysis of Asian, Non-Minority, and Black-Owned Businesses," *Review of Black Political Economy* 18 (1989): 25–42.

Blau, Zena Smith, *The Question of Discrimination: Racial Inequality in the U.S. Labor Market*, ed. Steven Shulman and William Darity (1989).

Boyd, Robert L., "A Contextual Analysis of Black Self-Employment in Large Metropolitan Areas, 1970–1980," *Social Forces* 70 (1991): 409–29.

Browne, Robert S., "The Economic Case for Reparations to Black America," *American Economic Review* 62 (1972): 39–46.

Burstein, Paul, ed., *Equal Employment Opportunity: Labor Market Discrimination and Public Policy* (1994).

Butler, John Sibley, *Entrepreneurship and Self-Help among Black Americans: A Reconsideration of Race and Economics* (1991).

Card, David, and Alan B. Krueger, "School Quality and Black-White Relative Earnings: A Direct Assessment," *Quarterly Journal of Economics* 107 (1992): 151–200.

Center on Budget and Policy Priorities, "Falling Behind: A Report on How Blacks Have Fared under Reagan," *Journal of Black Studies* 17 (1986): 148–71.

Chay, Kenneth Y., "The Impact of Federal Civil Rights Policy on Black Economic Progress: Evidence from the Equal Employment Opportunity Act of 1972," *Industrial and Labor Relations Review* 51 (1998): 608–32.

Cole, John A., Alfred L. Edwards, Earl G. Hamilton, and Lucy J. Reuben, "Black Banks: A Survey and Analysis of the Literature," *Review of Black Political Economy* 14 (1985): 29–50.

Collins, Sharon, *Black Corporate Executives: The Making and Breaking of a Black Middle Class* (1997).

Cross, Theodore L., *Black Capitalism: Strategy for Business in the Ghetto* (1971).

D'Amico, Ronald, and Nan L. Maxwell, "The Continuing Significance of Race in Minority Male Joblessness," *Social Forces* 73 (1995): 969–91.

Davis, George, and Glegg Watson, *Black Life in Corporate America: Swimming in the Mainstream* (1982).

Duncan, Kevin C., "Racial Disparity in Earnings and Earnings Growth: The Case of Young Men," *Social Science Journal* 31 (1994): 237–50.

Eggers, Mitchell L., and Douglas S. Massey, "The Structural Determinants of Urban Poverty: A Comparison of Whites, Blacks, and Hispanics," *Social Science Research* 20 (1991): 217–55.

Elgie, Robert A., "Industrialization and Racial Inequality within the American South, 1950–1970," *Social Science Quarterly* 61 (1980): 458–72.

Farley, John E., "Disproportionate Black and Hispanic Unemployment in U.S. Metropolitan Areas: The Roles of Racial Inequality, Segregation, and Discrimination in Male Joblessness," *American Journal of Economics and Sociology* 46 (1987): 129–50.

Feagin, Joe R., and Nikitah Imani, "Racial Barriers to African American Entrepreneurship: An Exploratory Study," *Social Problems* 41 (1994): 562–84.

Figart, Deborah M., and Ellen Mutari, "Gender Segmentation of Craft Workers by Race in the 1970's and 1980's," *Review of Radical Political Economics* 25 (1993): 50–66.

Fink, Leon, and Brian Greenberg, *Upheaval in the Quiet Zone: A History of Hospital Workers' Union, Local 1199* (1989).

Frederickson, Mary, "Four Decades of Change: Black Workers in Southern Textiles, 1941–1981," *Radical America* 16 (1982): 27–44.

Gill, Andrew M., "The Role of Discrimination in Determining Occupational Structure," *Industrial and Labor Relations Review* 42 (1989): 610–23.

Good, David H., and Maureen A. Pirog-Good, "Employment, Crime, and Race," *Contemporary Policy Issues* 5 (1987): 91–104.

Gould, William, *Black Workers in White Unions: Job Discrimination in the United States* (1977).

Green, Shelley, and Paul Pryde, *Black Entrepreneurship in America* (1990).

Greer, Edward, *Big Steel: Black Politics and Corporate Power in Gary, Indiana* (1979).

Harrison, Bennett, and Lucy Gorham, "Growing Inequality in Black Wages in the 1980's and the Emergence of an African-American Middle Class," *Journal of Policy Analysis and Management* 11 (1992): 235–53.

Hill, Herbert, *Labor Union Control of Job Training: A Critical Analysis of Apprenticeship Outreach Programs and the Hometown Plans* (1974).

Hinshaw, John, and Judith Modell, "Perceiving Racism: Homestead from Depression to Deindustrialization," *Pennsylvania History* 63 (1996): 17–52.

Jackson, Pamela Braboy, Peggy A. Thoits, and Howard F. Taylor, "Composition of the Workplace and Psychological Well-Being: The Effects of Tokenism on America's Black Elite," *Social Forces* 74 (1995): 543–57.

Johnson, Leanor Boulin, "The Employed Black: The Dynamics of Work-Family Tension," *Review of Black Political Economy* 17 (1989): 69–85.

Jones, Jacqueline, *American Work: Four Centuries of Black and White Labor* (1998).

Kasarda, John D., "Urban Industrial Transition and the Underclass," *Annals of the American Academy of Political and Social Science* (1989): 26–47.

Kijakazi, Kilolo, *African-American Economic Development and Small Business Ownership* (1997).

Leonard, Jonathan S., "The Impact of Affirmative Action Regulation and Equal Employment Law on Black Employment," *Journal of Economic Perspectives* 4 (1990): 47–63.

Lichter, Daniel T., "Racial Differences in Underemployment in American Cities," *American Journal of Sociology* 93 (1988): 771–92.

Marable, Manning, *How Capitalism Underdeveloped Black America: Problems in Race, Political Economy, and Society* (1983).

Oliver, Melvin L., and Thomas M. Shapiro, *Black Wealth/White Wealth: A New Perspective on Racial Inequality* (1995).

O'Neill, Dave M., and June O'Neill, "Affirmative Action in the Labor Market," *Annals of the American Academy of Political and Social Science* (1992): 88–103.

Quester, Aline O., and William H. Greene, "The Labor Market Experience of Black and White Wives in the Sixties and Seventies," *Social Science Quarterly* 66 (1985): 854–66.

Schor, Joel, "The Black Presence in the U.S. Cooperative Extension Service Since 1945: An American Quest for Service and Equity," *Agricultural History* 60 (1986): 137–53.

Shulman, Steven and William Darity, ed., *The Question of Discrimination: Racial Inequality in the U.S. Labor Market* (1989).

Smith, Elsie J., "The Career Development of Young Black Females: The Forgotten Group," *Youth and Society* 12 (1981): 277–312.

Smith, James P., and Finis R. Welch, "Black Economic Progress after Myrdal," *Journal of Economic Literature* 27 (1989): 519–64.

Smith, Shelley A., "Sources of Earnings Inequality in the Black and White Female Labor Forces," *Sociological Quarterly* 32 (1991): 117–38.

Stein, Judith, *Running Steel, Running America: Race, Economic Policy, and the Decline of Liberalism* (1998).

Steinberg, Stephen, "Up from Slavery: The Myth of Black Progress," *New Politics* 7 (1998): 69–81.

Swinton, David H., "The Economic Status of Black Americans During the 1980's: A Decade of Limited Progress," *State of Black America* (1990): 25–52.

Thomas, David A., John J. Gabarro, and Don Tapscott, *Breaking Through: The Making of Minority Executives in Corporate America* (1999).

Thompson, J. Phillip, III, "Universalism and Deconcentration: Why Race Still Matters in Poverty and Economic Development," *Politics and Society* 26 (1998): 181–219.

Watkins, Steve, *The Black O: Racism and Redemption in an American Corporate Empire* (1997).

Weiss, Robert J., *"We Want Jobs": A History of Affirmative Action* (1997).

Wilson, William Julius, ed., *The Ghetto Underclass: Social Science Perspectives* (1993).

———— *The Truly Disadvantaged: The Inner City, the Underclass, and Public Policy* (1987).

———— *When Work Disappears: The World of the New Urban Poor* (1996).

Woodard, Michael D., *Black Entrepreneurs in America: Stories of Struggle and Success* (1997).

Ziorklui, Sam Q., "The Performance of Black-owned Commercial Banks: A Comparative Analysis," *Review of Black Political Economy* 23 (1994): 5–23.

24.13   SCIENCE AND TECHNOLOGY

Green, Venus, "Race and Technology: African American Women in the Bell System, 1945–1980," *Technology and Culture* 36 (1995): S101–43.

Pearsor, Willie, and H. Kenneth Bechtel, ed., *Blacks, Science, and American Education* (1989).

Tucker, William H., *The Science and Politics of Racial Research* (1994).

24.14   MEDICINE AND HEALTH

Bailey, Eric J., *Urban African-American Health Care* (1991).

Bone, Margaret S., *Capital Crime: Black Infant Mortality in America* (1989).

Clinton, Myrtle M., "Black Psychiatric Nurses: Historical Perspectives, 1964 to 1984," *Journal of Black Studies* 24 (1993): 213–31.

Cooke, Michael A., "Sickle Cell Anemia As a Community and Public Health Issue: South Carolina, 1971–1981," *South Carolina Historical Magazine* 94 (1993): 193–209.

Dalton, Harlon L., "AIDS in Blackface," *Daedalus* 118 (1989): 205–27.

Hammonds, Evelynn, "Missing Persons: African American Women, AIDS, and the History of Disease," *Radical America* 24 (1990): 7–23.

Headen, Alvin E., Jr., and Sandra W. Headen, "General Health Conditions and Medical Insurance Issues concerning Black Women," *Review of Black Political Economy* 14 (1985–86): 183–97.

LaVeist, Thomas A., "The Political Empowerment and Health Status of African-Americans: Mapping a New Territory," *American Journal of Sociology* 97 (1992): 1080–95.

Lynxwiler, John, and David Gay, "Reconsidering Race Differences in Abortion Attitudes," *Social Science Quarterly* 75 (1994): 67–84.

Tapper, Melbourne, *In the Blood: Sickle Cell Anemia and the Politics of Race* (1999).

Thompson, Becky Wangsgaard, "'A Way Outa No Way': Eating Problems among African-American, Latina, and White Women," *Gender and Society* 6 (1992): 546–61.

Wallace, Steven P., "Race versus Class in the Health Care of African-American Elderly," *Social Problems* 37 (1990): 517–34.

Williams, David R., David T. Takeuchi, and Russell K. Adair, "Socioeconomic Status and Psychiatric Disorder among Blacks and Whites," *Social Forces* 71 (1992): 179–94.

24.15 STUDIES IN FOREIGN LANGUAGES

African-American Summit, *Le premier sommet Africain Américain: Construire un pont pour l'avenir* [The First African-African American Summit: Constructing a Bridge for the Future] (1991). In French.

Aoyagi, Kiyotaka, *Amerika no Kokujin Kazoku* [Black Family in America] (1983). In Japanese.

Armand, Laura, "Dirigeants noirs américains et masses noires face à l'enjeu électoral" [Black American Leaders and Black Masses Face the Stakes of Elections], *Revue Française de Sciences Politiques* 1 (1978): 118–39. In French.

Bader, Stasa, *Worte wie Feuer: Dance Hall Reggae und Raggamuffin* [Words Like Fire: Dance Hall Reggae and Raggamuffin] (1988). In German.

Bard, Patrick, and Patrick Raynal, *Blues Mississippi Mud* [Mississippi Mud Blues] (1993). In French.

Barrat, Martine, and Archie Moore, *Martine Barra: musée d'art moderne de la ville de Paris du 15 novembre au 9 decembre 1984: galerie du jour du 14 novembre au 7 décembre 1984* [Martine Barra: The Paris Museum of Modern Art from November 15-December 9, 1984: Today's Gallery from November 14-December 7, 1984] (1984). In French.

Bastide, Roger, *O negro na Imprensa e na Literatura Selção dos Textos: José Marques de Melo* [The Black in the Press Literature, a Selection of Texts: José Marques de Melo] (rev. ed., 1990). In Portuguese.

Bastide, Roger, and Université de Montréal, *Centre des recherches caraibes: État actuel et perspectives d'avenir des recherches afro-américaines* [The Center for Caribbean Research: The Present Condition and Future Perspectives for Afro-American Research] (1971). In French.

Benesch, Klaus, *The Threat of History: Geschichte und Erzählung im Afro-Amerikanischen Roman der Gegenwart* [The Threat of History: History and Narration in the Contemporary African-American Novel] (1990). In German.

Bernheim, Nicole, *Voyage en Amérique noire* [Journey in Black America] (1986). In French.

Bertella Farnetti, Paolo, "I neri americani dopo il Black Power" [Black Americans after Black Power], in Bruno Cartosio, *Senza Illusioni* [Without Illusions] (1995): 82–100. In Italian.

——— *Pantere nere: Storia e mito del Black Panther Party* [Black Panthers: History and Myth of the Black Panther Party] (1995). In Italian.

Body-Gendrot, Sophie, Laura Maslow-Armand, and Daniele Stewart, *Les Noirs américains aujourd'hui* [African Americans Today] (1984). In French.

Böhmert, Horst, *Gleichheits und Freiheitsbestrebungen der Schwarzen Minßorität in den USA: Geschichte Ihrer politischen Vorstellungen und Strategien* [The Black American Strivings for Freedom and Equality: History of Their Political Ideas and Strategies] (1980). In German.

Bosch Navarro, Juan, *Facultad de teología San Vicente Ferrer de la Iglesia negra: eclesiología militante de James H. Cone* [Faculty of Theology Saint Vincent Ferrer of the Black Church: Militant Ecclesiology of James H. Cone] (1986). In Spanish.

——— *James H. Cone: teólogo de la negritud* [James H. Cone: Theologian of Blackness] (1985). In Spanish.

Brandes, Volkhard, *Black Brother: Die Bedeutung Afrikas für den Freiheitskampf des Schwarzen Amerika* [Black Brother: The Significance of Africa for Black America's Freedom Struggle] (1971). In German.

Broecking, Christian, *Der Marsalis-Faktor: Gespräche über Afroamerikanische Kultur in den Neunziger Jahren* [The Marsalis Factor: Discussions about Afro-American Culture in the Nineties] (1995). In German.

Brun, Jean-Paul, and Philippe Carles, *Jazzmen, 1979–1991* [Jazz Men, 1979–1991] (1991). In French.

Carabi, Angels, *Toni Morrison: búsqueda de una identidad afro-americana* [Toni Morrison: Search for an African-American Identity] (1988). In Spanish.

Carles, Philippe, and Jean-Louis Comolli, *Free Jazz/Black Power* (1971). In French.

Cartosio, Bruno, *Dentro l'America in crisi: saggi sulle lotte sociali negli Stati Uniti degli anni Settanta* [Within America in Crisis: Essays on the Social Struggles in the United States of the 1970's] (1980). In Italian.

———— *Senza illusioni: neri negli Stati Uniti dagli anni Sessanta alla rivolta di Los Angeles* [Without Illusions: Blacks in the United States from the Sixties to the Los Angeles Rebellion] (1995). In Italian.

Chenu, Bruno, *Dieu est noir: histoire, religion et théologie des Noirs américains* [God Is Black: The History, Religion, and Theology of American Blacks] (1977). In French.

Chumu, Maya, *Salir a la luz como lesbianas de color* [Coming out Colored] (1980). In Spanish.

Clary, Françoise, *L'espoir de vivre: violence et sexualité dans le roman afro-américain de Chester Himes à
Hal Bennett* [The Hope of Life: Violence and Sexuality in the Afro-American Novel: From Chester Himes to Hal Bennett] (1988). In French.

Constant, Denis, *Aux sources du reggae* [The Sources of Reggae] (1982). In French.

Danchin, Sébastian, *B. B. King* (1993). In French.

Es justo rebelarse! lecciones en la defensa de Robert Smith obrero del auto de Detroit [It Is Just to Rebel!
Readings in Defense of Robert Smith, Detroit Auto Worker] (1978). In Spanish.

Gabillet, Jean-Paul, "Transcendance et aliénation: le musicien de jazz noir dans Bird et *Mo' Better
Blues*" [Transcendence and Alienation: The Black Musician in Bird and *Mo' Better Blues*], *Revue
Française d'Études Américaines* 57 (1993): 275–82. In French.

Gambino, Ferruccio, "Regolare i proletari, trasformarli in poveri" [Regulating Proletarians, Transforming Them into the Poor Class], *Primo Maggio* 2 (1973–1974): 47–49. In Italian.

Giammanco, Roberto, *Black Power, potere negro: analisi e testimonianze* [Black Power: Analysis and
Documents] (1968). In Italian.

Guter, Anne, *Blick vom Rand aufs Zentrum: Gangs in der Amerikanischen Großstadt-Gesellschaft* [A
View on the Center from the Margin: Gangs in American Metropolitan Society] (1994). In German.

Hajek, Friederike, *Selbstzeugnisse der Afroamerikaner: Black Liberation Movement und Autobiographie*
[Testimonies of Afro-Americans: Black Liberation Movement and Autobiography] (1984). In
German.

Hayama, Akira, *Amerika Minshu-shugi to Kokujin Mondai* [American Democracy and Black People]
(1994). In Japanese.

Hetmann, Frederik, *Das schwarze Amerika: Vom Freiheitskampf der Amerikanischen Neger* [Black
America: On the Freedom Struggle of the American Negroes] (1970). In German.

Hoffstadt, Stephan, *Black Cinema: Afroamerikanische Filmemacher der Gegenwart* [Black Cinema:
Contemporary Afro-American Film Makers] (1995). In German.

Honda, Katsuichi, *Amerika Gasshukoku* [The United States of America: The Lives of Black and Native
Americans] (1970). In Japanese.

Hündgen, Gerald, ed., *Chasin' a Dream: Die Musik des Schwarzen Amerika von Soul bis Hip Hop*
[Chasin' a Dream: The Music of Black America from Soul to Hip Hop] (1989). In German.

Jacob, Günther, *Agit-Pop: Schwarze Musik und Weiße Hörer* [Agit-Pop: Black Music and White Lis-
teners] (1993). In German.

Kawashima, Masaki, "Bosuton Skûru Basuing Ronso Saihô" [The Boston School Busing Controversy
Revisited: Toward an Examination into the Myth of 'Failure'], *The American Review* 31 (1997):
59–83. In Japanese.

Kitamura, Takao, *Mienai Amerika* [The Invisible America: My Experience with Black America] (1973).
In Japanese.

Kosaka, Noboru, *Amerika Kokujin no Jirenma* [Dilemma of American Blacks] (1987, 1992). In Japanese.

Le Dantec-Lowry, Hélène, "Familles afro-américaines en crise" [Afro-American Families in Crisis],
Revue Française d'Études Américaines [French Review of American Studies] 64 (1995): 265–74. In
French.

Lenz, Günter H., ed., *Afro-Amerika im Amerikanischen Dokumentarfilm* [Afro-America in American
Documentary Film] (1993). In German.

Maître, Hans Joachim, *Black Power: Machtanspruch Einer Minderheit* [Black Power: A Minority's
Claim to Power] (1972). In German.

Martinelli, Alberto, and Alessandro Cavalli, *Il partito della pantera nera* [The Black Panther Party] (1971). In Italian.

Materassi, Mario, *Il ponte sullo Harlem river: Saggi e note sulla cultura e la letteratura afro-americana di oggi* [The Bridge over the Harlem River: Essays and Notes on Contemporary Afro-American Culture and Literature] (1977). In Italian.

Matsuoka, Yasushi, "Kokujin 'Seijika' no Taitô" [Emerging Black 'Politicians': The Case of L. D. Wilder], *Shisô* 809 (1992): 132–53. In Japanese.

Mattiello, Cristina, "Leadership politica e leadership religiosa nella tradizione afroamericana" [Political and Religious Leadership in the African-American Tradition], in AAVV, *Dialogo su Malcolm X* [Dialogue on Malcolm X] (1994): 67–76. In Italian.

Michels, Peter M., *Aufstand in den Ghettos: Zur Organisation des Lumpenproletariats in den USA* [Insurrection in the Ghettos: Towards the Organization of the Lumpenproletariat in the USA] (1972). In German.

———— *Bericht über den Politischen Widerstand in den USA* [Report on Political Resistance in the USA] (1974). In German.

Molla, Serge, *Les idées noires de Martin Luther King* [The Black Thoughts of Martin Luther King] (1992). In French.

Mühlen, Norbert, *Die Schwarzen Amerikaner: Anatomie einer Revolution* [Black Americans: Anatomy of a Revolution] (1964). In German.

Nakajima, Yoriko, *Kokujin no Seiji Sanka to Daisan Seiki Amerika no Shuppatsu* [Black Political Participation and the New America after the Second Reconstruction] (1989). In Japanese.

Nessuna Giustizia, Nessuna Pace [Los Angeles: No Justice, No Peace] (1992). In Italian.

Ostendorf, Berndt, "Amerikas Problem mit dem Anderen-Der Preis des Multikulturalismus" [America's Problem with the Other: The Price of Multiculturalism], in Venanz Schubert, ed., *Die Beiden Amerika: Kolumbus und die Folgen* [The Two Americas: Columbus and the Consequences] (1993): 323–61. In German.

Otani, Yasuo, *Byôdô eno Michi* [The Road to Equality: African-Americans and the Supreme Court] (1993). In Japanese.

Otsuka, Hideyuki, *Gendai Amerika Gasshukoku-ron* [The State of African-Americans in U.S. Society Today] (1992). In Japanese.

———— "Kon'nichi no Kokujin Mondai to sono Kihon-teki Tokucho" [Basic Structures of Black Oppression Today: Race, Class and Affirmative Action], *Bulletin of Buraku Problem* 13 (1991): 86–116. In Japanese.

Paolantonacci, Andree, and Bibliothèque nationale-Département des livres imprimés, *Les Auteurs afro-américains, 1965–1982: inventaire du fonds imprimé conservé à la Bibliothèque nationale* [Afro-American Authors, 1965–1982: Inventory of Printed Sources Conserved in the National Library] (1985). In French.

Pouzoulet, Catherine, "Le cinéma de Spike Lee: Images d'une ville mosaïque" [The Films of Spike Lee: Images of an Urban Mosaic], *Revue Française d'Études Américaines* 57 (1993): 265–74. In French.

Reid, Mark A., et al., *Le Cinéma noir américain* [Black American Cinema] (1988). In French.

Sagrera, Martín, *Poder blanco y negro: el conflicto racial estadounidense y su repercusion mundial: ensayo* [Black Power, White Power: The Racial Conflict in the United States and Its World Wide Repercussions] (1970). In Spanish.

Sanconie, Maïca, "L'art nègre n'est plus ce qu'il était" [Negro Art Is No Longer What It Was], *Beaux-Arts [Fine Arts]* 103 (1992): 54–64. In French.

Stril-Rever, Sofia, *Chicago-Harlem: écritures de ghettos* [Chicago to Harlem: Writings from the Ghettos] (1991). In French.

Sylla, Fodé, and Signiew Kowalewski, *Qui a peur de Malcolm X?* [Who's Afraid of Malcolm X?] (1993). In French.

Takenaka, Koji, "Amerika Kokujin no Genjô" [The Present Condition of African-Americans in Northern Metropolitan Cities], *Journal of Foreign Studies* 70 (1990): 61–116. In Japanese.

Vezzosi, Elisabetta, "Donne nere, povertà, cittadinanza" [Black Women, Poverty, Citizenship], *Rivista Internazionale di Studi Nordamericani [International Journal of North American Studies]* 1 (1995): 38–49. In Italian.

Yanaka, Hisako, "Atoranta no Kokujin Komyuniti" [Black Community in Atlanta], in Nagayo Honma,
    ed., *Communities in America* (1993): 93–132. In Japanese.
Zips, Werner, "We Are at War: Schwarzer Nationalismus in den USA im 20. Jahrhundert" [Black Na-
    tionalism in Twentieth Century USA], in Thomas Fillitz, André Gingrich and Gabriele Rasuly-
    Paleczek, ed., *Kultur, Identität und Macht: Ethnologische Beiträge zu Einem Dialog der Kulturen der
    Welt* [Culture, Identity, and Power: Ethnological Contributions to a Dialogue on Cultures of the
    World] (1993): 135–60. In German.

III

HISTORIES OF
SPECIAL SUBJECTS

25 *Women*

EVELYN BROOKS HIGGINBOTHAM

25.1 GENERAL STUDIES

Baer, Hans A., and Yvonne Jones, ed., *African Americans in the South: Issues of Race, Class, and Gender* (1992).

Bernhard, Virginia, et al., ed., *Hidden Histories of Women in the New South* (1994).

Bristow, Peggy, et al., *We're Rooted Here and They Can't Pull Us Up: Essays in African Canadian Women's History* (1994).

Davis, Angela Y., *Women, Race, and Class* (1981).

Davis, Marianna W., ed., *Contributions of Black Women to America* (2 vols., 1981).

deGraaf, Lawrence B., "Race, Sex, and Region: Black Women in the American West, 1850–1920," *Pacific Historical Review* 49 (1980): 285–313.

Giddings, Paula, *When and Where I Enter: The Impact of Black Women on Race and Sex in America* (rev. ed., 1996).

Harley, Sharon and Rosalyn Terborg-Penn, ed., *The Afro-American Woman: Struggles and Images* (1978).

Harrison, Suzan, "Black Women in the Nineteenth-Century South," *Mississippi Quarterly* 46 (1993): 285–90.

Hill, Ruth ed, *The Black Women Oral History Project* (10 vols., 1991).

Hine, Darlene Clark, ed., *Black Women's History: Theory and Practice* (2 vols., 1990).

Hine, Darlene Clark, *Black Women in the Middle West: The Michigan Experience* (1990).

———, ed., *Black Women in American History: From Colonial Times through the Nineteenth Century* (4 vols., 1990).

———, ed., *Black Women in American History: The Twentieth Century* (4 vols., 1990).

Hine, Darlene Clark, Elsa Barkley Brown, and Rosalyn Terborg-Penn, ed., *Black Women in America: An Historical Encyclopedia* (2 vols., 1993).

Hine, Darlene Clark, Wilma King, and Linda Reed, ed., *"We Specialize in the Wholly Impossible": A Reader in Black Women's History* (1995).

Hine, Darlene Clark, and Kathleen Thompson, ed., *Facts on File: Encyclopedia of Black Women in America* (1997).

——— *A Shining Thread of Hope: The History of Black Women in America* (1998).

Hoggan, Frances, *American Negro Women during Their First Fifty Years of Freedom* (1913).

Honey, Maureen, ed., *Bitter Fruit: African American Women in World War II* (1999).

Ladner, Joyce A., "Racism and Tradition: Black Womanhood in Historical Perspective," in Darlene Clark Hine, ed., *Black Women's History: Theory and Practice* (1990): 363–82.

Lerner, Gerda, comp., *Black Women in White America: A Documentary History* (1972).

Loewenberg, Bert J., and Ruth Bogin, ed., *Black Women in Nineteenth-Century American Life: Their Words, Their Thoughts, Their Feelings* (1976).

Momsen, Janet, ed., *Women and Change in the Caribbean: A Pan-Caribbean Perspective* (1993).

Mossell, Mrs. N. F., *The Work of the Afro-American Woman* (1908, 1988).

Newman, Debra L., "Black Women in the Era of the American Revolution in Pennsylvania," *Journal of Negro History* 61 (1976): 276–89.

Render, Sylvia Lyons, "Afro-American Women: The Outstanding and the Obscure," *Quarterly Journal of the Library of Congress* 32 (1975): 306–21.

Sims-Wood, Janet L., *The Progress of Afro-American Women: A Selected Bibliography and Resource Guide* (1980).

Smith, Jessie Carney, ed., *Notable Black American Women* (1992).

Steady, Filomina Chioma, ed., *The Black Woman Cross-Culturally* (1981).

Sterling, Dorothy, ed., *We Are Your Sisters: Black Women in the Nineteenth Century* (1984).

Terborg-Penn, Rosalyn, and Andrea Benton Rushing, eds., *Women in Africa and the African Diaspora: A Reader* (2d ed., 1996).

Thornbrough, Emma Lou, "The History of Black Women in Indiana," *Black History News and Notes* 13–14 (1983): 1–8.

Timberlake, Andrea, et al., ed., *Women of Color and Southern Women: A Bibliography of Social Science Research, 1975 to 1988* (1988).

White, Deborah Gray, "Mining the Forgotten: Manuscript Sources for Black Women's History," *Journal of American History* 74 (1987): 237–43.

Winegarten, Ruthe, *Black Texas Women: 150 Years of Trial and Triumph* (1995).

Yellin, Jean Fagan, "Afro-American Women, 1800–1910: A Selected Bibliography," in Gloria T. Hull, Patricia Bell Scott and Barbara Smith, ed., *All the Women Are White, All the Blacks Are Men, but Some of Us Are Brave: Black Women's Studies* (1982): 221–44.

25.2   HISTORIOGRAPHY

Amott, Teresa and Julie Matthaei, "We Specialize in the Wholly Impossible: African American Women," in Teresa Amott and Julie Matthaei, *Race, Gender, and Work: A Multicultural Economic History of Women in the United States* (1991): 141–91.

Aptheker, Bettina, *Woman's Legacy: Essays on Race, Sex, and Class in American History* (1982).

Beard, Linda Susan, "Daughters of Clio and Calliope: Afro-American Women Writers as Reclamation and Revisionist Herstorians," *Psychohistory Review* 17 (1989): 301–43.

Brown, Elsa Barkley, "Afro-American Women's Quilting: A Framework for Conceptualizing and Teaching African-American's Women's History," *Signs* 14 (1989): 921–29.

———— "'What has Happened Here': The Politics of Difference in Women's History and Feminist Politics," *Feminist Studies* 18 (1992): 295–312.

Burg, B. R., "The Rhetoric of Miscegenation: Thomas Jefferson, Sally Hemings, and Their Historians," *Phylon* 47 (1986): 128–38.

Cannon, Lynn Weber, Elizabeth Higginbotham, and Marianne L. A. Leung, *Race and Class Bias in Research on Women: A Methodological Note* (1987).

Castaneda, Antonia I., "Women of Color and the Rewriting of Western History: The Discourse, Politics, and Decolonization of History," *Pacific Historical Review* 61 (1992): 501–33.

Collins, Patricia Hill, *Black Feminist Thought: Knowledge, Consciousness, and the Politics of Empowerment* (2d ed., 1999).

———— "The Social Construction of Black Feminist Thought," *Signs* 14 (1989): 745–73.

———— "What's in a Name: Womanism, Black Feminism, and Beyond," *The Black Scholar* 26 (1996): 9–18.

Dill, Bonnie Thornton, "Race, Class, and Gender: Prospects for an All-Inclusive Sisterhood," *Feminist Studies* 9 (1983): 131–50.

Engerman, Stanley L., "Studying the Black Family: A Review Essay of *The Black Family* by Herbert S. Gutman," *Journal of Interdisciplinary History* 3 (1978): 78–101.

Etter-Lewis, Gwendolyn, "Hard Times and Strong Women: African-American Women's Oral Narratives," *Oral History Review* 19 (1991): 89–97.

Fields, Karen, "What One Cannot Remember Mistakenly," in Genevieve Fabre and Robert O'Meally, ed., *History and Memory in African-American Culture* (1994): 150–63.

Fink, Leon, George Rawick, and Evelyn Brooks, "A Symposium on Herbert Gutman's *The Black Family in Slavery and Freedom*," *Radical History Review* 4 (1977): 76–108.

Friedman, Jean E., "Women's History and the Revision of Southern History," in Joanne V. Hawks and Sheila L. Skemp, ed., *Sex, Race, and the Role of Women in the South: Essays* (1983): 3–12.

Goodson, Martia Graham, "The Slave Narrative Collection: A Tool for Reconstructing Afro-American Women's History," *Western Journal of Black Studies* 3 (1979): 116–22.

Gutman, Herbert G., "Persistent Myths about the Afro-American Family," *Journal of Interdisciplinary History* 6 (1975): 181–210.

Hall, Jacquelyn Dowd, "Partial Truths: Writing Southern Women's History," in Virginia Bernhard, Betty Brandon, Elizabeth Fox-Genovese and Theda Purdue, ed., *Southern Women: Histories and Identities* (1992): 11–29.

Hammonds, Evelynn, "Black (W)holes and the Geometry of Black Female Sexuality (More Gender Trouble: Feminism Meets Queer Theory)," *Differences: A Journal of Feminist Cultural Studies* 6 (1994): 126–46.

Higginbotham, Evelyn Brooks, "African-American Women's History and the Metalanguage of Race," *Signs* 17 (1992): 251–74.

———— "Beyond the Sound of Silence: Afro-American Women in History," in Darlene Clark Hine, ed., *Black Women's History: Theory and Practice* (1990): 175–92.

Hine, Darlene Clark, "Black Women's History, White Women's History: The Juncture of Race and Class," *Journal of Women's History* 4 (1992): 125–33.

———— *Hine Sight: Black Women and the Re-Construction of American History* (1994).

Hull, Gloria T., "The 'Bridge' between Black Studies and Women's Studies: Black Women's Studies," *Women's Studies Quarterly* 25 (1997): 40–44.

Hull, Gloria T., Patricia Bell Scott, and Barbara Smith, ed., *All the Women Are White, All the Blacks Are Men, But Some of Us Are Brave: Black Women's Studies* (1982).

James, Joy, *Shadowboxing: Representations of Black Feminist Politics* (1999).

Johnson-Odim, Cheryl, and Margaret Strobel, "Conceptualizing the History of Women in Africa, Asia, Latin America and the Caribbean, and the Middle East," *Journal of Women's History* 1 (1989): 31–62.

Jones, Jacqueline, "Race and Gender in Modern America," *Reviews in American History* 26 (1998): 220–38.

Painter, Nell Irvin, "Representing Truth: Sojourner Truth's Knowing and Becoming Known," *Journal of American History* 81 (1994): 461–92.

———— "Sojourner Truth in Life and Memory: Writing the Biography of an American Exotic," *Gender and History* 2 (1990): 3–16.

Phillips, Stephanie L., "Claiming Our Foremothers: The Legend of Sally Hemings and the Tasks of Black Feminist Theory," *Hastings Women's Law Journal* 8 (1997): 401–65.

Smith, Althea, and Abigail J. Stewart, "Approaches to Studying Racism and Sexism in Black Women's Lives," *Journal of Social Issues* 39 (1983): 1–15.

Stetson, Erlene, "Studying Slavery: Some Literary and Pedagogical Considerations on the Black Female Slave," in Gloria T. Hull, Patrica Bell Scott and Barbara Smith, ed., *All the Women are White, All the Blacks are Men, But Some of Us Are Brave* (1982): 61–84.

Stevenson, Brenda E., "Historical Dimension of Black Family Structure: A Revisionist Perspective of the Black Family," in Belinda Tucker and Claudia K. Mitchell, ed., *The Decline in Marriage among African-Americans: Causes, Consequences and Policy Implications* (1995): 27–56.

Wilson, Francille Rusan, "'This Past Was Waiting for Me When I Came': The Contextualization of Black Women's History," *Feminist Studies* 22 (1996): 345–61.

25.3   SECONDARY SOURCES ON NEWSPAPERS AND PERIODICALS

Rhodes, Jane, *Mary Ann Shadd Cary: The Black Press and Protest in the Nineteenth Century* (1998).

Sealander, Judith, "Antebellum Black Press Images of Women," *Western Journal of Black Studies* 6 (1982): 159–65.

Silverman, Jason H., "Mary Ann Shadd and the Search for Equality," in Leon Litwack and August Meier, ed., *Black Leaders of the Nineteenth Century* (1988): 87–100.

Snorgrass, J. William, "Pioneer Black Women Journalists from the 1850's," *Western Journal of Black Studies* 6 (1982): 150–58.

Streitmatter, Rodger, "Delilah Beasley: A Black Woman Who Lifted As She Climbed," *American Journalism* 11 (1994): 61–75.

———— *Raising Her Voice: African-American Women Journalists Who Changed History* (1994).

Wade-Gayles, Gloria, "Black Women Journalists in the South, 1880–1905," in Darlene Clark Hine, ed., *Black Women in American History: From Colonial Times through the Nineteenth Century* (1990): 1409–24.

25.4   RACE RELATIONS

25.4.1   Slave Trade

Eltis, David, and Stanley L. Engerman, "Fluctuations in Sex and Age Ratios in the Transatlantic Slave Trade, 1663–1864," *Economic History Review* 46 (1993): 308–23.

———— "Was the Slave Trade Dominated by Men?" *Journal of Interdisciplinary History* 23 (1992): 237–57.

Gutman, Herbert G. and Richard Sutch, "The Slave Family: Protected Agent of Capitalist Masters or Victim of the Slave Trade?" in Paul A. David, Herbert G. Gutman, Richard Sutch, Peter Temin and Gavin Wright, ed., *Reckoning with Slavery: A Critical Study in the Quantitative History of American Negro Slavery* (1976): 94–133.

Klein, Herbert S., "African Women in the Atlantic Slave Trade," in Claire C. Robertson and Martin A. Klein, ed., *Women and Slavery in Africa* (1983): 29–38.

Sutch, Richard C., "The Breeding of Slaves for Sale and the Westward Expansion of Slavery, 1850–1860," in Stanley L. Engerman and Eugene D. Genovese, ed., *Race and Slavery in the Western Hemisphere: Quantitative Studies* (1975): 173–210.

25.4.2   Slavery

Alonzo, Andrea Starr, "A Study of Two Women's Slave Narratives: *Incidents in the Life of a Slave Girl* and *The History of Mary Prince*," *Women's Studies Quarterly* 17 (1989): 118–22.

Andrews, William, ed., *Six Women's Slave Narratives* (1988).

Beckles, Hilary, *Natural Rebels: A Social History of Enslaved Black Women in Barbados* (1989).

Binder, Wolfgang, "'Oh Ye Daughters of Africa, Awake! Awake! Arise': The Functions of Work and Leisure in Female Slave Narratives," in Groupe de Recherche et d'Etudes Nord-Americaines, *Les Etats-Unis: Images du Travail et des Loisirs* (1989): 127–41.

Braxton, Joanne M., "Harriet Jacobs' *Incidents in the Life of a Slave Girl*: The Re-definition of the Slave Narrative Genre," *Massachusetts Review* 27 (1986): 379–87.

Burnham, Dorothy, "The Life of the Afro-American Woman in Slavery," *International Journal of Women Studies* 1 (1978): 363–77.

Burton, Annie L., *Memories of Childhood's Slavery Days* (1909).

Bush, Barbara, *Slave Women in Caribbean Society, 1650–1838* (1990).

Campbell, John, "As 'A Kind of Freeman'? Slaves' Market-Related Activities in the South Carolina Upcountry, 1800–1860," *Slavery and Abolition* 12 (1991): 131–69.

Clinton, Catherine, "Caught in the Web of the Big House: Women and Slavery," in Walter J. Fraser, Jr., R. Frank Saunders, Jr. and Jon L. Wakelyn, ed., *The Web of Southern Social Relations: Women, Family and Education* (1985): 19–34.

———— *The Plantation Mistress: Woman's World in the Old South* (1982).

———— "'Southern Dishonor': Flesh, Blood, Race, and Bondage," in Carol Bleser, ed., *In Joy and in Sorrow: Women, Family, and Marriage in the Victorian South, 1830–1900* (1991): 52–68.

———— "'With a Whip in His Hand': Rape, Memory, and African-American Women," in Genevieve Fabre and Robert O'Meally, ed., *History and Memory in African-American Culture* (1994): 205–18.

Clinton, Catherine, and Michele Gillespie, ed., *The Devil's Lane: Sex and Race in the Early South* (1997).

Cornelius, Janet, "Slave Marriages in a Georgia Congregation," in Orville Vernon Burton and Robert C. McMath, Jr., ed., *Class, Conflict, and Consensus: Antebellum Southern Community Studies* (1982): 128–45.

Davis, Angela Y., "Reflections on the Black Woman's Role in the Community of Slaves," *Black Scholar* 3 (1971): 2–15.

Diedrich, Maria, "'My Love Is As Black As Yours Is Fair': Premarital Love and Sexuality in the Antebellum Slave Narrative," *Phylon* 47 (1986): 238–47.

Engerman, Stanley L., "Studying the Black Family: A Review Essay of *The Black Family* by Herbert S. Gutman," *Journal of Interdisciplinary History* 3 (1978): 78–101.

Fink, Leon, George Rawick, and Evelyn Brooks, "A Symposium on Herbert Gutman's *The Black Family in Slavery and Freedom*," *Radical History Review* 4 (1977): 76–108.

Fleischner, Jennifer, *Mastering Slavery: Memory, Family, and Identity in Women's Slave Narratives* (1996).

———— "Memory, Sickness, and Slavery: One Girl's Slave Story," *American Imago* 20 (1994): 149–79.

Fox-Genovese, Elizabeth, *Within the Plantation Household: Black and White Women of the Old South* (1988).

Gaspar, David Barry, and Darlene Clark Hine, ed., *More Than Chattel: Black Women and Slavery in the Americas* (1996).

Genovese, Eugene D., "The Slave Family: Women—A Reassessment of Matriarchy, Emasculation, Weakness," *Southern Voices* 1 (1974): 9–16.

Goodson, Martia Graham, "The Slave Narrative Collection: A Tool for Reconstructing Afro-American Women's History," *Western Journal of Black Studies* 3 (1979): 116–22.

Gundersen, Joan R., "The Double Bonds of Race and Sex: Black and White Women in a Colonial Virginia Parish," *Journal of Southern History* 52 (1986): 351–72.

Gutman, Herbert G., "Persistent Myths about the Afro-American Family," *Journal of Interdisciplinary History* 6 (1975): 181–210.

———— "Slave Culture and Slave Family and Kin Network: The Importance of Time," *South Atlantic Urban Studies* 2 (1978): 73–88.

Gutman, Herbert G. and Richard Sutch, "Victorians All? The Sexual Mores and Conduct of Slaves and Their Masters," in Paul A. David, Herbert G. Gutman, Richard Sutch, Peter Temin and Gavin Wright, ed., *Reckoning with Slavery: A Critical Study in the Quantitative History of American Negro Slavery* (1976): 134–64.

Higman, Barry W., "African and Creole Slave Family Patterns in Trinidad," *Journal of Family History* 3 (1978): 163–80.

———— "Household Structure and Fertility on Jamaican Slave Plantations: A Nineteenth-Century Example," *Population Studies* 27 (1973): 527–50.

———— "The Slave Family and Household in the British West Indies, 1800–1834," *Journal of Interdisciplinary History* 6 (1975): 261–87.

Hill, Charles L., "Slavery and Its Aftermath in Beverly, Massachusetts: Juno Larcom and Her Family," *Essex Institute Historical Collections* 116 (1980): 111–30.

Jennings, Thelma, "'Us Colored Women Had to Go through a Plenty': Sexual Exploitation of African-American Slave Women," *Journal of Women's History* 1 (1990): 45–74.

Kossek, Brigitte, "Racist and Patriarchal Aspects of Plantation Slavery in Grenada: 'White Ladies,' 'Black Women Slaves,' and 'Rebels,'" in Wolfgang Binder, ed., *Slavery in the Americas* (1997): 277–303.

Kulikoff, Allan, "A 'Prolifick' People: Black Population Growth in the Chesapeake Colonies, 1700–1790," *Southern Studies* 16 (1977): 391–428.

Lerner, Gerda, "Women and Slavery," *Slavery and Abolition* 4 (1983): 173–98.

Malone, Ann Patton, *Sweet Chariot: Slave Family and Household Structure in Nineteenth-Century Louisiana* (1992).

McLaurin, Melton A., *Celia, a Slave* (1991).

McMillen, Sally Gregory, *Southern Women: Black and White in the Old South* (1992).

Model, John, Stephen Gudeman, and Warren C. Sanderson, "A Colloquium on Herbert Gutman's *The Black Family in Slavery and Freedom, 1750–1925*," *Social Science History* 3 (1979): 45–85.

Morgan, Jennifer L., "'Some Could Suckle over Their Shoulder': Male Travelers, Female Bodies, and the Gendering of Racial Ideology, 1500–1770," *William and Mary Quarterly* 54 (1997): 167–92.

Morton, Patricia, ed., *Discovering the Women in Slavery: Emancipating Perspectives on the American Past* (1996).

Mullin, Michael, "Women and the Comparative Study of American Negro Slavery," *Slavery and Abolition* 6 (1985): 25–40.

Obitko, Mary Ellen, "'Custodians of a House of Resistance': Black Women Respond to Slavery," in Dana V. Hiller and Robin Ann Sheets, ed., *Women and Men: The Consequences of Power* (1977): 256–69.

Painter, Nell Irvin, "Of Lily, Linda Brent, and Freud: A Nonexceptionalist Approach to Race, Class, and Gender in the Slave South," *Georgia Historical Quarterly* 76 (1992): 241–59.

Parent, Anthony S., and Susan Brown Wallace, "Childhood and Sexual Identity under Slavery," *Journal of the History of Sexuality* 3 (1992–93): 363–401.

Parkhurst, Jessie W., "The Role of the Black Mammy in the Plantation Household," *Journal of Negro History* 23 (1938): 349–69.

Patterson, Orlando, "From Endo-deme to Matri-deme: An Interpretation of the Development of Kinship and Social Organization among the Slaves of Jamaica, 1655–1830," *Eighteenth-Century Florida and the Caribbean* (1976): 50–59.

——— "Slavery, Alienation, and the Female Discovery of Personal Freedom," in Arien Mack, ed., *Home: A Place in the World* (1993): 159–87.

Schafer, Judith K., "'Open and Notorious Concubinage': The Emancipation of Slave Mistresses by Will and the Supreme Court in Antebellum Louisiana," *Louisiana History* 28 (1987): 165–82.

Shaw, Stephanie J., "Mothering under Slavery in the Antebellum South," in Evelyn Nakano Glenn, Grace Chang and Linda Rennie Forcey, ed., *Mothering: Ideology, Experience, and Agency* (1994): 237–58.

Starobin, Robert S., "Privileged Bondsmen and the Process of Accommodation: The Role of Houseservants and Drivers As Seen in Their Own Letters," *Journal of Social History* 5 (1971): 46–70.

Stetson, Erlene, "Studying Slavery: Some Literary and Pedagogical Considerations on the Black Female Slave," in Gloria T. Hull, Patrica Bell Scott and Barbara Smith, ed., *All the Women are White, All the Blacks are Men, But Some of Us Are Brave* (1982): 61–84.

Stevenson, Brenda E., "Distress and Discord in Virginia Slave Families, 1830–1860," in Carol Bleser, ed., *In Joy and Sorrow: Women, Family and Marriage in the Victorian South, 1830–1900* (1990): 103–34.

——— *Life in Black and White: Family and Community in the Slave South* (1996).

Wertz, Dorothy C., "Women and Slavery: A Cross-Cultural Perspective," *International Journal of Women's Studies* 7 (1984): 372–84.

White, Deborah Gray, *Ar'n't I a Woman? Female Slaves in the Plantation South* (1985).

——— "Female Slaves: Sex Roles and Status in the Antebellum Plantation South," *Journal of Family History* 8 (1983): 248–61.

White, Shane, and Graham White, "Slave Hair and African American Culture in the Eighteenth and Nineteenth Centuries," *Journal of Southern History* 61 (1995): 45–76.

Wood, Betty, *Women's Work, Men's Work: The Informal Slave Economies of Lowcountry Georgia* (1995).

Young, Mary, *"All My Trials, Lord": Selections from Women's Slave Narratives* (1995).

25.4.3   Free Blacks

Cashin, Joan E., "According to His Wish and Desire: Female Kin and Female Slaves in Planter Wills," in Christie Anne Farnham, ed., *Women of the American South: A Multicultural Reader* (1997): 90–119.

Doherty, Herbert J., Jr., ed., "A Free Negro Purchases His Daughter," *Florida Historical Quarterly* 29 (1950): 38–43.

Foner, Laura, "The Free People of Color in Louisiana and St. Domingue: A Comparative Portrait of Two Three-Caste Societies," *Journal of Social History* 3 (1970): 406–30.

Gilbert, Judith A., "Esther and Her Sisters: Free Women of Color as Property Owners in Colonial St. Louis, 1765–1803," *Gateway Heritage* 17 (1996): 14–23.

Gould, Virginia Meacham, ed., *Chained to the Rock of Adversity: To Be Free, Black, and Female in the Old South* (1998).

Hanger, Kimberly S., "'Desiring Total Tranquility' and Not Getting It: Conflict Involving Free Black Women in Spanish New Orleans," *Americas* 54 (1998): 541–56.

Horton, James Oliver, "Freedom's Yoke: Gender Conventions among Antebellum Free Blacks," *Feminist Studies* 12 (1986): 51–76.

Johnson, Michael and James Roark, "Strategies of Survival: Free Negro Families and the Problem of Slavery," Carol Bleser, ed., *In Joy and in Sorrow: Women, Family, and Marriage in the Victorian South, 1830–1900* (1991): 88–102.

Johnson, Whittington B., "Free African-American Women in Savannah, 1800–1860: Affluence and Autonomy amid Adversity," *Georgia Historical Quarterly* 76 (1992): 260–83.

Lapsansky, Emma Jones, "Friends, Wives, and Strivings: Networks and Community Values among Nineteenth-Century Philadelphia Afro-American Elites," *Pennsylvania Magazine of History and Biography* 108 (1984): 3–24.

Lebsock, Suzanne, *The Free Women of Petersburg: Status and Culture in a Southern Town, 1784–1860* (1984).

McGee, Val L., "Escape from Slavery: The Milly Walker Trials," *Alabama Review* 49 (1996): 243–52.

Proper, David R., "Lucy Terry Prince: 'Singer of History,'" *Contributions in Black Studies* 9–10 (1990–92): 187–214.

Schweninger, Loren, "Property-Owning Free African-American Women in the South, 1800–1870," *Journal of Women's History* 1 (1990): 13–44.

Uzzel, Odell, "Free Negro/Slave Marriages and Family Life in Antebellum North Carolina," *Western Journal of Black Studies* 18 (1994): 64–69.

Yee, Shirley J., "Finding a Place: Mary Ann Shadd Cary and the Dilemmas of Black Migration to Canada, 1850–1870," *Frontiers* 18 (1997): 1–16.

Young, R. J., *Antebellum Black Activists: Race, Gender, and Self* (1996).

25.4.4   Resistance (Antebellum)

Beckles, Hilary, *Natural Rebels: A Social History of Enslaved Black Women in Barbados* (1989).

Bush, Barbara, "Towards Emancipation: Slave Women and Resistance to Coercive Labour Regimes in the British West Indian Colonies, 1790–1838," *Slavery and Abolition* 5 (1984): 222–43.

Bush-Slimani, B., "Hard Labor: Women, Childbirth and Resistance in British Caribbean Slave Societies," *History Workshop* 36 (1993): 83–99.

Bynum, Victoria, *Unruly Women: The Politics of Social and Sexual Control in the Old South* (1992).

Cheung, Floyd D., "Les Cenelles and Quadroon Balls: 'Hidden Transcripts' of Resistance and Domination in New Orleans, 1803–1845," *Southern Literary Journal* 29 (1997): 5–16.

Craft, William, and Ellen Craft, *Running a Thousand Miles for Freedom; or, the Escape of William and Ellen Craft from Slavery* (1860).

Dadzie, Stella, "Searching for the Invisible Woman: Slavery and Resistance in Jamaica," *Race and Class* 32 (1990): 21–38.

Durling, Gregory B., "Female Labor, Malingering, and the Abuse of Equipment under Slavery: Evidence from the Marydale Plantation Diary," *Southern Studies* 5 (1994): 31–49.

Ellison, Mary, "Resistance to Oppression: Black Women's Response to Slavery in the United States," *Slavery and Abolition* 4 (1983): 56–63.

Fox-Genovese, Elizabeth, "Strategies and Forms of Resistance: Focus on Slave Women in the United States," in Gary Y. Okihiro, ed., *In Resistance: Studies in African, Caribbean, and Afro-American History* (1986): 143–65.

Hine, Darlene Clark, "Female Slave Resistance: The Economics of Sex," *Western Journal of Black Studies* 3 (1979): 123–27.

Mathurin, Lucille, *The Rebel Woman in the British West Indies during Slavery* (1975).

McMillan, Timothy J., "Black Magic: Witchcraft, Race, and Resistance in Colonial New England," *Journal of Black Studies* 25 (1994): 99–117.

Tate, Gayle T., "Political Consciousness and Resistance among Black Antebellum Women," *Women and Politics* 13 (1993): 67–89.

Terborg-Penn, Rosalyn, "Black Women Freedom Fighters in Early Nineteenth Century Maryland," *Maryland Heritage* 2 (1984): 11–12.

——— "Black Women in Resistance: A Cross-Cultural Perspective," in Gary Y. Okihiro, ed., *In Resistance: Studies in African, Caribbean, and Afro-American History* (1986): 188–209.

Wood, Betty, "Some Aspects of Female Resistance to Chattel Slavery in Low Country Georgia, 1736–1815," *Historical Journal* 30 (1987): 603–22.

25.4.5 Abolitionism and Emancipation

Barnes, Gilbert H., and Dwight L. Dumond, ed., *Letters of Theodore Dwight Weld, Angelina Grimke, and Sarah Grimke, 1822–1844* (2 vols., 1934).

Bogin, Ruth, "Sarah Parker Redmond: Black Abolitionist from Salem," *Essex Institute Historical Collections* 110 (1974): 120–50.

Brown, Ira V., "'Am I Not a Woman and a Sister?': The Anti-Slavery Convention of American Women, 1837–1839," *Pennsylvania History* 50 (1983): 1–19.

Davis, J. Treadwell, "Nashoba: Frances Wright's Experiment in Self-Emancipation," *Southern Quarterly* 11 (1972): 63–90.

Hartgrove, W. B., "The Story of Maria Louise Moore and Fannie M. Richards," *Journal of Negro History* 1 (1916): 23–33.

Jeffrey, Julie Roy, *The Great Silent Army of Abolitionism: Ordinary Women in the Antislavery Movement* (1998).

Lapsansky, Emma Jones, "Feminism, Freedom, and Community: Charlotte Forten and Women Activists in Nineteenth-Century Philadelphia," *Pennsylvania Magazine of History and Biography* 113 (1989): 3–19.

Lutz, Alma, *Crusade for Freedom: Women of the Anti-Slavery Movement* (1968).

McKnight, Andrew Nunn, "Lydia Broadnax, Slave, and Free Woman of Color," *Southern Studies* 5 (1994): 17–30.

Payne-Gaposchkin, Cecilia Helena, "The Nashoba Plan for Removing the Evil of Slavery: Letters of Frances and Camilla Wright, 1820–1829," *Harvard Library Bulletin* 23 (1975): 221–51, 429–61.

Pease, Jane H., and William H. Pease, "The Role of Women in the Antislavery Movement," *Canadian Historical Association Annual Report* (1967): 167–83.

Perkins, Linda M., "Black Women and Racial 'Uplift' prior to Emancipation," in Filomena Chiomana Steady, ed., *The Black Woman Cross-Culturally* (1981): 317–34.

Porter, Dorothy B., "Sarah Parker Remond, Abolitionist and Physician," *Journal of Negro History* 20 (1935): 287–93.

Quarles, Benjamin, "Harriet Tubman's Unlikely Leadership," in Leon Litwack and August Meier, ed., *Black Leaders of the Nineteenth Century* (1988): 43–57.

Rhodes, Jane, *Mary Ann Shadd Cary: The Black Press and Protest in the Nineteenth Century* (1998).

Ruchames, Louis, "Race, Marriage, and Abolition in Massachusetts," *Journal of Negro History* 40 (1955): 250–73.

Schafer, Judith K., "'Open and Notorious Concubinage': The Emancipation of Slave Mistresses by Will and the Supreme Court in Antebellum Louisiana," *Louisiana History* 28 (1987): 165–82.

Schwalm, Leslie A., *A Hard Fight For We: Women's Transition from Slavery to Freedom in Lowcountry South Carolina* (1997).

———— "'Sweet Dreams of Freedom': Freedwomen's Reconstruction of Life and Labor in Lowcountry South Carolina," *Journal of Women's History* 9 (1997): 9–38.

Silverman, Jason H., "Mary Ann Shadd and the Search for Equality," in Leon Litwack and August Meier, ed., *Black Leaders of the Nineteenth Century* (1988): 87–100.

Soderlund, Jean R., "Black Women in Colonial Pennsylvania," *Pennsylvania Magazine of History and Biography* 107 (1983): 49–68.

Sumler-Lewis, Janice, "The Forten-Purvis Women of Philadelphia and the American Anti-Slavery Crusade," *Journal of Negro History* 66 (1981–1982): 281–88.

Thompson, Carol L., "Women and the Anti-Slavery Movement," *Current History* 70 (1976): 198–201.

Van Broekhoven, Deborah Bingham, "'A Determination to Labor . . .': Female Anti-Slavery Activity in Rhode Island," *Rhode Island History* 44 (1985): 35–46.

Venet, Wendy Hamand, *Neither Ballots nor Bullets: Women Abolitionists and the Civil War* (1991).

Yee, Shirley J., *Black Women Abolitionists: A Study in Activism, 1828–1860* (1992).

Yellin, Jean Fagan, *Women and Sisters: The Antislavery Feminists in American Culture* (1989).

Yellin, Jean Fagan, and John C. Van Horne, *The Abolitionist Sisterhood: Women's Political Culture in Antebellum America* (1994).

25.4.6   Black/White Relations

Andolsen, Barbara Hilkert, *"Daughters of Jefferson, Daughters of Bootblacks": Racism and American Feminism* (1986).

Ayvazian, Andrea, and Beverly Daniel Tatum, *Women, Race, and Racism: A Dialogue in Black and White* (1994).

Blee, Kathleen M., *Women of the Klan: Racism and Gender in the 1920's* (1991).

Cheung, Floyd D., "Les Cenelles and Quadroon Balls: 'Hidden Transcripts' of Resistance and Domination in New Orleans, 1803–1845," *Southern Literary Journal* 29 (1997): 5–16.

Cochrane, Sharlene Voogd, "'And the Pressure Never Let Up': Black Women, White Women, and the Boston YWCA, 1918–1948," in Vicki L. Crawford, Jacqueline Anne Rouse and Barbara Woods, ed., *Women in the Civil Rights Movement: Trailblazers and Torchbearers, 1941–1965* (1990): 259–69.

Durr, Virginia Foster, *Outside the Magic Circle: The Autobiography of Virginia Foster Durr*, ed. Hollinger F. Barnard (1985).

Farnham, Christie Anne, ed., *Women of the American South: A Multicultural Reader* (1997).

Gilman, Sander L., "Black Bodies, White Bodies: Toward an Iconography of Female Sexuality in Late Nineteenth Century Art, Medicine, and Literature," *Critical Inquiry* 12 (1985): 204–42.

Gilmore, Glenda Elizabeth, "'A Melting Time': Black Women, White Women, and the WCTU in North Carolina, 1880–1900," in Virginia Bernhard, Betty Brandon, Elizabeth Fox-Genovese, Theda Perdue and Elizabeth Hayes Turner, ed., *Hidden Histories of Women in the New South* (1994): 153–72.

———— *Gender and Jim Crow: Women and the Politics of White Supremacy in North Carolina, 1896–1920* (1996).

Gordon-Reed, Annette, *Thomas Jefferson and Sally Hemings: An American Controversy* (1997).

Guy-Sheftall, Beverly, *Daughters of Sorrow: Attitudes toward Black Women, 1880–1920* (1990).

Hartmann, Susan M., "Women's Organizations during World War II: The Interaction of Class, Race, and Feminism," in Mary Kelley, ed., *Woman's Being, Woman's Place: Female Identity and Vocation in American History* (1979): 313–28.

Hodes, Martha, ed., *Sex, Love, Race: Crossing Boundaries in North American History* (1999).

———— *White Women, Black Men: Illicit Sex in the Nineteenth-Century South* (1997).

Jewell, Karen Sue, *From Mammy to Miss America and Beyond: Cultural Images and the Shaping of U.S. Social Policy* (1993).

Johnston, James Hugo, *Race Relations in Virginia and Miscegenation in the South, 1776–1860* (1970).

Joseph, Gloria I., and Jill Lewis, *Common Differences: Conflicts in Black and White Feminist Perspectives* (1981).

Lecaudey, Helene, "Behind the Mask: Ex-Slave Women and Interracial Sexual Relations," in Patricia Morton, ed., *Discovering the Women in Slavery: Emancipating Perspectives on the American Past* (1996): 260–77.

Lewis, Jan, and Peter Onuf, ed., *Sally Hemings and Thomas Jefferson: History, Memory, and Civic Culture* (1999).

Lubiano, Wahneema, "Black Ladies, Welfare Queens, and State Minstrels," in Toni Morrison, ed., *Race-ing Justice, En-gendering Power* (1992): 323–61.

Morazan, Ronald R., "'Quadroon' Balls in the Spanish Period," *Louisiana History* 14 (1973): 310–15.

Morgan, Jennifer L., "'Some Could Suckle over Their Shoulder': Male Travelers, Female Bodies, and the Gendering of Racial Ideology, 1500–1770," *William and Mary Quarterly* 54 (1997): 167–92.

Morgan, Jo-Ann, "Mammy the Huckster: Selling the Old South for the New Century," *American Art* 9 (1995): 86–109.

Morton, Patricia, *Disfigured Images: The Historical Assault on Afro-American Women* (1991).

Nash, Gary B., *Forbidden Love: The Secret History of Mixed-Race America* (1999).

Painter, Nell Irvin, "'Social Equality,' Miscegenation, Labor, and Power," in Numan V. Bartley, ed., *The Evolution of Southern Culture* (1988): 47–67.

Terborg-Penn, Rosalyn, "Discrimination against Afro-American Women in the Women's Movement," in Sharon Harley and Rosalyn Terborg-Penn, ed., *The Afro-American Woman: Struggles and Images* (1978): 17–27.

Thomas, Mary Martha, ed., *Stepping out of the Shadows: Alabama Women, 1819–1990* (1995).

25.4.7 Segregation/Jim Crow

Gilmore, Glenda Elizabeth, *Gender and Jim Crow: Women and the Politics of White Supremacy in North Carolina, 1896–1920* (1996).

Robbins, Louise S., "Racism and Censorship in Cold War Oklahoma: The Case of Ruth W. Brown and the Bartlesville Public Library," *Southwestern Historical Quarterly* 100 (1996): 18–46.

25.4.8 Violence and Racial Disturbances

Aptheker, Bettina, "The Suppression of Free Speech: Ida B. Wells and the Memphis Lynching, 1892," *San Jose Studies* 3 (1977): 34–40.

Barnard, Ami Larkin, "The Application of Critical Race Feminism to the Anti-Lynching Movement: Black Women's Fight against Race and Gender Ideology, 1892–1920," *UCLA Women's Law Journal* 3 (1993): 1–38.

Bederman, Gail, "'The White Man's Civilization on Trial': Ida B. Wells, Representations of Lynching, and Northern Middle-Class Manhood," in Gail Bederman, *Manliness and Civilization: A Cultural History of Gender and Race in the United States, 1880–1917* (1995).

Blee, Kathleen M., *Women of the Klan: Racism and Gender in the 1920's* (1991).

Carby, Hazel V., "'On the Threshhold of Women's Era': Lynching, Empire, and Sexuality in Black Feminist Theory," *Critical Inquiry* 12 (1985): 262–77.

Clinton, Catherine, "Bloody Terrain: Freedwomen, Sexuality, and Violence during Reconstruction," *Georgia Historical Quarterly* 76 (1992): 313–32.

Gunning, Sandra, *Race, Rape, and Lynching: The Red Record of American Literature, 1890–1912* (1996).

Hall, Jacquelyn Dowd, *Revolt against Chivalry: Jessie Daniel Ames and the Women's Campaign against Lynching* (1979).

Johnson, Marilynn S., "Gender, Race, and Rumours: Re-Examining the 1943 Race Riots," *Gender and History* 10 (1998): 252–77.

Jones, Maxine D., "The Rosewood Massacre and the Women Who Survived It," *Florida Historical Quarterly* 76 (1997): 193–208.

Jordan, Ervin L., Jr., "Sleeping with the Enemy: Sex, Black Women, and the Civil War," *Western Journal of Black Studies* 18 (1994): 55–63.

Royster, Jacqueline, *Southern Horrors and Other Writings: The Anti-Lynching Campaign of Ida B. Wells, 1892–1900* (1997).

Schechter, Patricia A., "'All the Intensity of My Nature': Ida B. Wells, Anger, and Politics," *Radical History Review* 70 (1998): 48–77.

Tucker, David M., "Miss Ida B. Wells and the Memphis Lynching," *Phylon* 32 (1971): 112–22.

Wyatt, Gail Elizabeth, "The Sociocultural Context of African American and White American Women's Rape," *Journal of Social Issues* 48 (1992): 77–91.

25.4.9   Civil Rights

Allen, Zita, *Black Women Leaders of the Civil Rights Movement* (1996).

Braukman, Stacy, "Women and the Civil Rights Movement in Tampa: An Interview with Ellen H. Green," *Tampa Bay History* 14 (1992): 62–69.

Bryan, Dianetta Gail, "Her-Story Unsilenced: Black Female Activists in the Civil Rights Movement," *Sage* 5 (1988): 60–64.

Campbell, Clarice T., *Civil Rights Chronicle: Letters from the South* (1997).

Clark, Septima, and Cynthia Stokes Brown, ed., *Ready from Within: Septima Clark and the Civil Rights Movement* (1986).

Crawford, Vicki L., Jacqueline Anne Rouse, and Barbara Woods, ed., *Women in the Civil Rights Movement: Trailblazers and Torchbearers, 1941–1965* (1990).

De Hart, Jane Sherron, "Second Wave Feminism(s) and the South: The Difference that Differences Make," in Christie Anne Farnham, ed., *Women of the American South: A Multicultural Reader* (1997): 273–301.

Evans, Sara Margaret, *Personal Politics: The Roots of Women's Liberation in the Civil Rights Movement and the New Left* (1979).

Evers, Myrlie B., and Fred Beauford (interviewer), "Interview: Myrlie B. Evers," *Crisis* (1988): 28–36.

Evers, Myrlie B., and William Peters, *For Us, the Living* (1967).

Fleming, Cynthia Griggs, "Black Women Activists and the Student Nonviolent Coordinating Committee: The Case of Ruby Doris Smith Robinson," *Journal of Women's History* 4 (1993): 64–82.

———— "'More Than a Lady': Ruby Doris Smith Robinson and Black Women's Leadership in the Student Nonviolent Coordinating Committee," in Virginia Bernhard, Betty Brandon, Elizabeth Fox-Genovese, Theda Perdue and Elizabeth Hayes Turner, ed., *Hidden Histories of Women in the New South* (1994): 204–23.

———— *Soon We Will Not Cry: The Liberation of Ruby Doris Smith Robinson* (1998).

Foeman, Anita K., "Gloria Richardson: Breaking the Mold," *Journal of Black Studies* 26 (1996): 604–15.

Gardner, Tom, and Cynthia Stokes Brown, "The Montgomery Bus Boycott: Interviews with Rosa Parks, E. D. Nixon, Johnny Carr, and Virginia Durr," *Southern Exposure* 9 (1981): 12–21.

Grant, Joanne, *Ella Baker: Freedom Bound* (1998).

Greene, Christina, "'We'll Take Our Stand': Race, Class, and Gender in the Southern Student Organizing Committee," in Virginia Bernhard, Betty Brandon, Elizabeth Fox-Genovese, Theda Perdue and Elizabeth Hayes Turner, ed., *Hidden Histories of Women in the New South* (1994): 173–203.

Gyant, LaVerne, "Passing the Torch: African American Women in the Civil Rights Movement," *Journal of Black Studies* 26 (1996): 629–47.

James, Joy, *Race, Women, and Revolution: Black Female Militancy and the Praxis of Ella Baker* (1998).

Jones, Maxine D., "'Without Compromise or Fear': Florida's African American Female Activists," *Florida Historical Quarterly* 77 (1999): 475–502.

Katz, Milton S., and Susan B. Tucker, "A Pioneer in Civil Rights: Esther Brown and the South Park Desegregation Case of 1948," *Kansas History* 18 (1995–96): 234–47.

Lee, Chana Kai, *For Freedom's Sake: The Life of Fannie Lou Hamer* (1999).

Locke, Mamie E., "The Role of African-American Women in the Civil Rights and Women's Movements in Hinds County and Sunflower County, Mississippi," *Journal of Mississippi History* 53 (1991): 229–39.

Mills, Kay, *This Little Light of Mine: The Life of Fannie Lou Hamer* (1993).

Parks, Rosa, with James Haskins, *The Autobiography of Rosa Parks* (1990).

Pitre, Merline, *In Struggle against Jim Crow: Lulu B. White and the NAACP, 1900–1957* (1999).

Robbins, Louise S., "Racism and Censorship in Cold War Oklahoma: The Case of Ruth W. Brown and the Bartlesville Public Library," *Southwestern Historical Quarterly* 100 (1996): 18–46.

Robinson, Jo Ann Gibson, *The Montgomery Bus Boycott and the Women Who Started It: The Memoir of Jo Ann Gibson Robinson,* ed. David Garrow (1987).

——— "Montgomery before King: The Power of Women," *Southern Exposure* 15 (1987): 14–16.

Robnett, Belinda, *How Long? How Long? African-American Women in the Struggle for Civil Rights* (1997).

Rollins, Judith, *All Is Never Said: The Narrative of Odette Harper Hines* (1995).

Rouse, Jacqueline Anne, "Atlanta's African-American Women's Attack on Segregation, 1900–1920," in Noralee Frankel and Nancy S. Dye, ed., *Gender, Class, Race, and Reform in the Progressive Era* (1991): 10–23.

Schechter, Patricia A., "'All the Intensity of My Nature': Ida B. Wells, Anger, and Politics," *Radical History Review* 70 (1998): 48–77.

Strong, Augusta, "Negro Women in Freedom's Battles," *Freedomways* (1967): 302–15.

25.4.10 Black Power

Brown, Elaine, *A Taste of Power: A Black Woman's Story* (1992).

Davis, Angela Y., *Angela Davis: An Autobiography* (1974).

Freed, Donald, *Agony in New Haven: The Trial of Bobby Seale, Ericka Huggins, and the Black Panther Party* (1973).

Reid, Inez Smith, *"Together" Black Women* (1972).

Shakur, Assata, *Assata: An Autobiography* (1987).

Weber, Shirley N., "Black Power in the 1960's: A Study of Its Impact on Women's Liberation," *Journal of Black Studies* 11 (1981): 483–98.

25.5 GOVERNMENT

25.5.1 Law

Accomondo, Christina, "'The Laws Were Laid down to Me Anew': Harriet Jacobs and the Reframing of Legal Fictions," *African American Review* 32 (1998): 229–45.

Alozie, Nicholas O., "Distribution of Women and Minority Judges: The Effects of Judicial Selection Methods," *Social Science Quarterly* 71 (1990): 315–25.

Bardaglio, Peter W., "Rape and the Law in the Old South: Calculated to Excite Indignation in Every Heart," *Journal of Southern History* 60 (1994): 749–72.

——— *Reconstructing the Household: Families, Sex, and the Law in the Nineteenth-Century South* (1995).

Berry, Mary Frances, *The Pig Farmer's Daughter and Other Tales of American Justice: Episodes of Racism and Sexism in the Courts from 1865 to the Present* (1999).

Burnard, Trevor, "Inheritance and Independence: Women's Status in Early Colonial Jamaica," *William and Mary Quarterly* 48 (1991): 93–114.

Bynum, Victoria, "On the Lowest Rung: Court Control over Poor White and Free Black Women," in Darlene Clark Hine, ed., *Black Women in American History: From Colonial Times through the Nineteenth Century* (1990): 213–24.

Cashin, Joan E., "According to His Wish and Desire: Female Kin and Female Slaves in Planter Wills," in Christie Anne Farnham, ed., *Women of the American South: A Multicultural Reader* (1997): 90–119.

Chrisman, Robert, and Robert L. Allen, ed., *Court of Appeal: The Black Community Speaks out on the Racial and Sexual Politics of Clarence Thomas vs. Anita Hill* (1992).

Davis, Angela Y., et al., ed., *If They Come in the Morning: Voices of Resistance* (1971).

Foley, William E., "Slave Freedom Suits before Dred Scott: The Case of Marie Jean Scypion's Descendants," *Missouri Historical Review* 79 (1984): 1–23.

Franke, Katherine M., "Becoming a Citizen: Reconstruction Era Regulation of African American Marriages," *Yale Journal of Law and the Humanities* 11 (1999): 251–309.

Higginbotham, A. Leon, Jr., and Barbara K. Kopytoff, "Racial Purity and Interracial Sex in the Law of Colonial and Antebellum Virginia," *Georgetown Law Journal* 77 (1989): 1967–2029.

Hilliard, Thomas O., Harold Dent, William Hayes, William Pierce, and Ann Ashmore Pouissant, "The Angela Davis Trial: Role of Black Psychologists in Jury Selection and Court Consultations," *Journal of Black Psychology* 1 (1974): 56–60.

Hine, Darlene Clark, "An Angle of Vision: Black Women and the United States Constitution, 1787–1987," in Darlene Clark Hine, ed., *Black Women's History: Theory and Practice* (1990): 193–204.

Lebsock, Suzanne, "Radical Reconstruction and the Property Rights of Southern Women," *Journal of Southern History* 22 (1977): 195–216.

Lewis, Jan, "'Of Every Age, Sex, and Condition': The Representation of Women in the Constitution," *Journal of the Early Republic* 15 (1995): 359–87.

McGee, Val L., "Escape from Slavery: The Milly Walker Trials," *Alabama Review* 49 (1996): 243–52.

Michals, Teresa, "'That Sole and Despotic Dominion': Slaves, Wives, and Game in Blackstone's Commentaries," *Eighteenth-Century Studies* 27 (1994): 195–216.

Morrison, Toni, ed., *Race-ing Justice, En-gendering Power: Essays on Anita Hill, Clarence Thomas, and the Construction of Social Reality* (1992).

Pascoe, Peggy, "Miscegenation Law, Court Cases, and Ideologies of 'Race' in Twentieth-Century America," *Journal of American History* 83 (1996): 44–69.

Schafer, Judith K., "'Open and Notorious Concubinage': The Emancipation of Slave Mistresses by Will and the Supreme Court in Antebellum Louisiana," *Louisiana History* 28 (1987): 165–82.

Smith, J. Clay, Jr., ed., *Rebels in Law: Voices in History of Black Women Lawyers* (1998).

Sommerville, Diane Miller, "The Rape Myth in the Old South Reconsidered," *Journal of Southern History* 61 (1995): 481–518.

Welke, Barbara Y., "When All the Women Were White, and All the Blacks Were Men: Gender, Class, Race, and the Road to *Plessy*, 1855–1914," *Law and History Review* 13 (1995): 261–316.

25.5.2 Crime and Punishment

Arnold, Regina, "Black Women in Prison: The Price of Resistance," in Maxine Baca Zinn and Bonnie Thornton Dill, ed., *Women of Color in U.S. Society* (1994): 171–84.

Butler, Anne M., "Still in Chains: Black Women in Western Prisons, 1865–1910," *Western Historical Quarterly* 20 (1989): 18–35.

Curtin, Mary Ellen, "The 'Human World' of Black Women in Alabama Prisons, 1870–1900," in Virginia Bernhard, Betty Brandon, Elizabeth Fox-Genovese, Theda Perdue and Elizabeth Hayes Turner, ed., *Hidden Histories of Women in the South* (1994): 11–30.

Davis, Angela Y., et al., ed., *If They Come in the Morning: Voices of Resistance* (1971).

Rafter, Nicole Hahn, *Partial Justice: Women in State Prisons, 1800–1935* (1985).

Venkatesh, Sudhir Alladi, "Gender and Outlaw Capitalism: A Historical Account of the Black Sisters United 'Girl Gang,'" *Signs: Journal of Women in Culture and Society* 23 (1998): 683–709.

25.5.3 Politics and Voting

Bethune, Mary McLeod, "My Secret Talks with FDR," *Ebony* (1949): 42–51.

Braxton, Gloria J., "African-American Women and Politics: Research Trends and Directions," *National Political Science Review* 4 (1993): 281–96.

Clark, Septima Poinsette, "Citizenship and Gospel," *Journal of Black Studies* 10 (1980): 461–66.

Clark, Septima Poinsette, and Mary A. Twining, "Voting Does Count: A Brief Excerpt from a Fabulous Decade," *Journal of Black Studies* 10 (1980): 445–47.

Danese, Tracy E., "Disfranchisement, Women's Suffrage, and the Failure of the Florida Grandfather Clause," *Florida Historical Quarterly* 74 (1995): 117–31.

Darcy, R., and Charles D. Hadley, "Black Women in Politics: The Puzzle of Success," *Social Science Quarterly* 69 (1988): 629–45.

Darcy, R., Charles D. Hadley, and Jason F. Kirksey, "Election Systems and the Representation of Black Women in American State Legislatures," *Women and Politics* 13 (1993): 73–89.

Edwards, Laura, *Gendered Strife and Confusion: The Political Culture of Reconstruction* (1997).

Gatewood, Willard B., Jr., "'The Remarkable Misses Rollin': Black Women in Reconstruction South Carolina," *South Carolina Historical Magazine* 92 (1991): 172–88.

Gay, Claudine, and Katherine Tate, "Doubly Bound: The Impact of Gender and Race on the Politics of Black Women," *Political Psychology* 19 (1998): 169–84.

Gill, Laverne McCain, *African-American Women in Congress: Forming and Transforming History* (1997).

Gordon, Ann D., with Bettye Collier-Thomas, John H. Bracey, Arlene Voski Avakian, and Joyce Avrech Berkman, ed., *African American Women and the Vote, 1837–1965* (1997).

Hendricks, Wanda A., *Gender, Race, and Politics in the Midwest: Black Club Women in Illinois* (1998).

Hewitt, Nancy A., and Suzanne Lebsock, ed., *Visible Women: New Essays on American Activism* (1993).

Higginbotham, Evelyn Brooks, "In Politics to Stay: Black Women Leaders and Party Politics during the 1920's," in Louise Tilly and Patricia Gurin, ed., *Women, Politics, and Change* (1990): 199–220.

Hine, Darlene Clark and Christie Anne Farnham, "Black Women's Culture of Resistance and the Right to Vote," in Christie Anne Farnham, ed., *Women of the American South: A Multicultural Reader* (1997): 204–19.

Laville, Helen, and Scott Lucas, "The American Way: Edith Sampson, the NAACP, and African-American Identity in the Cold War," *Diplomatic History* 20 (1996): 565–90.

Lebsock, Suzanne, "Woman Suffrage and White Supremacy: A Virginia Case Study," in Nancy A. Hewitt and Suzanne Lebsock, ed., *Visible Women: New Essays on American Activism* (1993): 62–100.

Linsin, Christopher E., "Something More than a Creed: Mary McLeod Bethune's Aim of Integrated Autonomy as Director of Negro Affairs," *Florida Historical Quarterly* 76 (1997): 20–41.

Naples, Nancy A., "'Just What Needed to Be Done': The Political Practice of Women Community Workers in Low-Income Neighborhoods," *Gender and Society* 5 (1991): 478–94.

Perkins, Jerry, "Political Ambition among Black and White Women: An Intragender Test of the Socialization Model," *Women and Politics* 6 (1986): 27–40.

Quarles, Benjamin, "Frederick Douglass and the Women's Rights Movement," *Journal of Negro History* 25 (1940): 35–44.

Rogers, Mary Beth, *Barbara Jordan: American Hero* (1998).

Ross, Joyce B., "Mary McLeod Bethune and the National Youth Administration: A Case Study of Power Relationships in the Black Cabinet of Franklin D. Roosevelt," *Journal of Negro History* 60 (1975): 1–28.

Saillant, John, "The Black Body Erotic and the Republican Body Politic, 1790–1820," *Journal of the History of Sexuality* 5 (1995): 403–28.

Terborg-Penn, Rosalyn, *African American Women in the Struggle for the Vote, 1850–1920* (1998).

——— "Discontented Black Feminists: Prelude and Postscripts to the Nineteenth Amendment," in Lois Scharf and Joan M. Jensen, ed., *Decades of Discontent: The Women's Movement, 1920–1940* (1983): 261–78.

——— "The Historical Treatment of the Afro-American Woman in the Woman's Suffrage Movement, 1900–1920: A Bibliographical Essay," *Current Biography on African Affairs* 7 (1974): 245–59.

Walker, S. Jay, "Frederick Douglass and Woman Suffrage," *Black Scholar* 4 (1973): 24–31.

Welch, Susan, and Lee Sigelman, "A Black Gender Gap?" *Social Science Quarterly* 70 (1989): 120–33.

——— "A Gender Gap among Hispanics? A Comparison with Blacks and Anglos," *Western Political Quarterly* 45 (1992): 181–99.

Yellin, Jean Fagin, "Du Bois' *Crisis* and Women's Suffrage," *Massachusetts Review* 14 (1973): 365–75.

25.5.4   Military

Breen, William J., "Black Women and the Great War: Mobilization and Reform in the South," *Journal of Southern History* 44 (1978): 421–40.

Earley, Charity Adams, *One Woman's Army: A Black Officer Remembers the WAC* (1989).

Enloe, Cynthia, and Harold Jordan, "Black Women in the Military," *Minerva: Quarterly Report on Women and the Military* 3 (1985): 105–16.

Hine, Darlene Clark, "Mabel K. Staupers and the Integration of Black Nurses into the Armed Forces," in John Hope Franklin and August Meier, ed., *Black Leaders of the Twentieth Century* (1982): 241–57.

Johnson, Jesse J., ed., *Black Women in the Armed Forces, 1942–1974: A Pictorial History* (1974).

Miller, Laura L., and Charles Moskos, "Humanitarians or Warriors?: Race, Gender, and Combat Status in Operation Restore Hope," *Armed Forces and Society* 21 (1995): 615–37.

Moore, Brenda L., "African-American Women in the U.S. Military," *Armed Forces and Society* 17 (1991): 363–84.

Taylor, Susie King, *A Black Woman's Civil War Memoirs: Reminiscences of My Life in Camp with the 33rd U.S. Colored Troops' Late First South Carolina Volunteers,* ed. Patricia W. Romero (1988).

Yacovone, Donald, "Sacred Land Regained: Frances Ellen Watkins Harper and 'The Massachusetts Fifty-Fourth,' a Lost Poem," *Pennsylvania History* 62 (1995): 90–110.

25.6 DEMOGRAPHY

Allen, Walter R., "The Social and Economic Statuses of Black Women in the United States," *Phylon* 42 (1981): 26–40.

Burnard, Trevor, "A Failed Settler Society: Marriage and Demographic Failure in Early Jamaica," *Journal of Social History* 28 (1994): 63–82.

Cody, Cheryll Ann, "A Note on Changing Patterns of Slave Fertility in the South Carolina Rice District, 1735–1865," *Southern Studies* 16 (1977): 457–63.

Corruccini, Robert S., Elizabeth M. Brandon, and Jerome S. Handler, "Inferring Fertility from Relative Mortality in Historically Controlled Cemetery Remains from Barbados," *American Antiquity* 54 (1989): 609–14.

Engerman, Stanley L., "Black Fertility and Family Structure in the U.S., 1880–1940," *Journal of Family History* 2 (1977): 117–38.

Higman, Barry W., "Household Structure and Fertility on Jamaican Slave Plantations: A Nineteenth-Century Example," *Population Studies* 27 (1973): 527–50.

Kilbourne, Barbara, Paula England, and Kurt Beron, "Effects of Individual, Occupational, and Industrial Characteristics on Earnings: Intersections of Race and Gender," *Social Forces* 72 (1994): 1149–76.

Klein, Herbert S., and Stanley L. Engerman, "Fertility Differentials between Slaves in the United States and the British West Indies: A Note on Lactation Practices and Their Possible Implications," *William and Mary Quarterly* 35 (1978): 357–74.

Kulikoff, Allan, "A 'Prolifick' People: Black Population Growth in the Chesapeake Colonies, 1700–1790," *Southern Studies* 16 (1977): 391–428.

Lantz, Herman, and Lewellyn Hendrix, "Black Fertility and the Black Family in the Nineteenth Century: A Re-Examination of the Past," *Journal of Family History* 3 (1978): 251–61.

Macpherson, David, and James B. Stewart, "The Effects of Extended Families and Marital Status on Housing Consumption by Black Female-Headed Households," *Review of Black Political Economy* 19 (1991): 65–83.

Malone, Ann Patton, "Searching for the Family and Household Structure of Rural Louisiana Slaves, 1810–1864," *Louisiana History* 28 (1987): 357–79.

McFalls, Joseph A., Jr., and George S. Masnick, "Birth Control and the Fertility of the U.S. Black Population, 1880 to 1980," *Journal of Family History* 6 (1981): 89–106.

Steckel, Richard H., "The Fertility of American Slaves," *Research in Economic History* 7 (1982): 239–86.

——— "Miscegenation and the American Slave Schedules," *Journal of Interdisciplinary History* 11 (1980): 251–63.

Tolnay, Stewart E., "The Decline of Black Marital Fertility in the Rural South, 1910–1940," *American Sociological Review* 52 (1987): 211–17.

25.7 FAMILY

Allen, Walter R., "Family Roles, Occupational Statuses, and Achievement Orientations among Black Women in the United States," *Signs* 4 (1979): 670–86.

Baatz, Wilmer H., *The Black Family and the Black Woman: An Annotated Bibliography: Report and Journal Literature, 1872–1979* (1981).

Berlin, Ira, Steven F. Miller, and Leslie S. Rowland, "Afro-American Families in the Transition from Slavery to Freedom," *Radical History Review* 42 (1988): 89–121.

Blackburn, George, and Sherman L. Ricards, "The Mother-Headed Family among Free Negroes in Charleston, South Carolina, 1850–1860," *Phylon* 42 (1981): 11–25.

Bogardus, Carl R., Sr., "Black Marriages, Gallatin County, Kentucky, 1866 to 1913," *Journal of the Afro-American History and Genealogical Society* 2 (1981): 117–22, 161–75.

Brasfield, Curtis, "'To My Daughter and the Heirs of Her Body': Slave Passages as Illustrated by the Latham-Smithwick Family," *National Genealogical Society* 81 (1993): 270–82.

Brouwer, Merle, "Marriage and Family Life among Blacks in Colonial Pennsylvania," *Pennsylvania Magazine of History and Biography* 99 (1975): 368–72.

Brown, Steven E., "Sexuality and the Slave Community," *Phylon* 42 (1981): 1–10.

Cody, Cheryll A., "Naming, Kinship, and Estate Dispersal: Notes on Slave Family Life on a South Carolina Plantation, 1786 to 1833," *William and Mary Quarterly* 39 (1982): 192–211.

Comer, James P., *Maggie's American Dream: The Life and Times of a Black Family* (1988).

Cornelius, Janet, "Slave Marriages in a Georgia Congregation," in Orville Vernon Burton and Robert C. McMath, Jr., ed., *Class, Conflict, and Consensus: Antebellum Southern Community Studies* (1982): 128–45.

Craton, Michael, "Changing Patterns of Slave Families in the British West Indies," *Journal of Interdisciplinary History* 10 (1979): 1–35.

Dash, Leon, *Rosa Lee: A Mother and Her Family in Urban America* (1996).

———— *When Children Want Children: The Urban Crisis of Teenage Childbearing* (1989).

Davis, Angela Y., and Fania Davis, "The Black Family and the Crisis of Capitalism," *Black Scholar* 17 (1986): 33–40.

Davis, Lenwood G., "Trends in Themes of African American Family Research 1939–1989: A Synopsis," *Western Journal of Black Studies* 14 (1990): 191–95.

Eggleston, Cecelia, "What a Negro Mother Faces," *Forum* 199 (1938): 59–62.

Farnham, Christie, "Sapphire? The Issue of Dominance in the Slave Family, 1830–1865," in Carol Groneman and Mary Beth Norton, ed., *'To Toil the Livelong Day': American Women at Work, 1780–1980* (1987): 68–83.

Foster, Herbert J., "African Patterns in the Afro-American Family," *Journal of Black Studies* 14 (1983): 201–32.

Frankel, Noralee, *Freedom's Women: Black Women and Families in Civil War Era Mississippi* (1999).

Furstenberg, Frank F., Jr., Theodore Hershberg, and John Modell, "The Origins of the Female-Headed Black Family: The Impact of the Urban Experience," *Journal of Interdisciplinary History* 6 (1975): 211–33.

Garfinkel, Irwin, and Sara S. McLanahony, *Single Mothers and their Children: A New America Dilemma* (1986).

Genovese, Eugene D., "'Our Family, White and Black': Family and Household in the Southern Slaveholder's World View," in Carol Bleser, ed., *In Joy and in Sorrow: Women, Family, and Marriage in the Victorian South, 1830–1900* (1991): 69–87.

———— "The Slave Family: Women—A Reassessment of Matriarchy, Emasculation, Weakness," *Southern Voices* 1 (1974): 9–16.

Gutman, Herbert G., *The Black Family in Slavery and Freedom, 1750–1925* (1977).

—— "Marital and Sexual Norms among Slave Women," in Nancy F. Cott and Elizabeth H. Pleck, ed., *A Heritage of Her Own: Toward a New Social History of American Women* (1979): 298–310.

—— "Slave Culture and Slave Family and Kin Network: The Importance of Time," *South Atlantic Urban Studies* 2 (1978): 73–88.

Gutman, Herbert G. and Richard Sutch, "The Slave Family: Protected Agent of Capitalist Masters or Victim of the Slave Trade?" in Paul A. David, Herbert G. Gutman, Richard Sutch, Peter Temin and Gavin Wright, ed., *Reckoning with Slavery: A Critical Study in the Quantitative History of American Negro Slavery* (1976): 94–133.

Harley, Sharon, "For the Good of Family and Race: Gender, Work, and Domestic Roles in the Black Community, 1880–1930," *Signs* 15 (1990): 336–49.

Helmbold, Lois Rita, "Beyond the Family Economy: Black and White Working-Class Women during the Great Depression," *Feminist Studies* 13 (1987): 629–55.

Hertz, Hilda, "Unmarried Negro Mothers in Southern Urban Communities," *Social Forces* 23 (1944): 73–79.

Higman, Barry W., "African and Creole Slave Family Patterns in Trinidad," *Journal of Family History* 3 (1978): 163–80.

—— "The Slave Family and Household in the British West Indies, 1800–1834," *Journal of Interdisciplinary History* 6 (1975): 261–87.

Inscoe, John C., "Generation and Gender as Reflected in Carolina Slave Naming Practices: A Challenge to the Gutman Thesis," *South Carolina Historical Magazine* 94 (1993): 252–63.

Iversen, Roberta Rehner, "Transmission of Family Values, Work, and Welfare among Poor Urban Black Women," *Work and Occupations* 23 (1996): 437–61.

Jarrett, Robin L., "Living Poor: Family Life among Single Parent, African-American Women," *Social Problems* 41 (1994): 30–49.

Jones, Faustine C., "The Lofty Role of the Black Grandmother," *Crisis* 80 (1973): 19–21.

Jones, Jacqueline, *Labor of Love, Labor of Sorrow: Black Women, Work, and the Family from Slavery to the Present* (1995).

—— "'My Mother Was Much of a Woman': Black Women, Work, and the Family under Slavery," *Feminist Studies* 8 (1982): 235–69.

Kennedy-Haflett, Cynthia, "'Moral Marriage': A Mixed-Race Relationship in Nineteenth-Century Charleston, South Carolina," *South Carolina Historical Magazine* 97 (1996): 206–26.

Kulikoff, Allan, "The Beginnings of the Afro-American Family in Maryland," in Aubrey C. Land, Lois Green Carr and Edward C. Papenfuse, ed., *Law, Society, and Politics in Early Maryland* (1977): 171–96.

Labinjoh, Justin, "The Sexual Life of the Oppressed: An Examination of the Family Life of Ante-Bellum Slaves," *Phylon* 35 (1974): 375–97.

Ladner, Joyce A., *Tomorrow's Tomorrow: The Black Woman* (1971).

Lebsock, Suzanne, "Free Black Women and the Question of Matriarchy: Petersburg, Virginia, 1784–1820," *Feminist Studies* 8 (1982): 271–92.

Malone, Ann Patton, *Sweet Chariot: Slave Family and Household Structure in Nineteenth-Century Louisiana* (1992).

Marsh, Clifton E., "Sexual Assault and Domestic Violence in the African American Community," *The Western Journal of Black Studies* 17 (1993): 149–56.

McMillen, Sally Gregory, *Motherhood in the Old South: Pregnancy, Childbirth, and Infant Rearing* (1990).

Model, John, Stephen Gudeman, and Warren C. Sanderson, "A Colloquium on Herbert Gutman's *The Black Family in Slavery and Freedom, 1750–1925*," *Social Science History* 3 (1979): 45–85.

Morrissey, Marietta, "Women's Work, Family Formation, and Reproduction Among Caribbean Slaves," *Review* 9 (1986): 339–67.

Pagnini, Deanna L., and Phillip S. Morgan, "Racial Differences in Marriage and Childbearing: Oral History Evidence from the South in the Early Twentieth Century," *American Journal of Sociology* 101 (1996): 1694–718.

Patterson, Orlando, "From Endo-deme to Matri-deme: An Interpretation of the Development of Kinship and Social Organization among the Slaves of Jamaica, 1655–1830," *Eighteenth-Century Florida and the Caribbean* (1976): 50–59.

Patterson, Ruth Polk, *The Seed of Sally Good'n: A Black Family of Arkansas, 1833–1953* (1985).

Pleck, Elizabeth H., "The Two-Parent Household: Black Family Structure in Late Nineteenth Century Boston," in Darlene Clark Hine, ed., *Black Women in American History: From Colonial Times through the Nineteenth Century* (1990): 1095–124.

Rodrique, Jessie M., "The Black Community and the Birth-Control Movement," in Kathy Peiss and Christina Simmons, ed., *Passion and Power: Sexuality and History* (1989): 138–54.

Sides, Sudie Duncan, "Slave Weddings and Religion," *History Today* 24 (1974): 77–87.

Simms, Margaret C., "Black Women Who Head Families: An Economic Struggle," *The Review of Black Political Economy* 14 (1985): 141–51.

Solinger, Rickie, "Race and 'Value': Black and White Illegitimate Babies, in the U.S.A., 1945–1965," *Gender and History* 4 (1992): 343–63.

Staples, Robert, *The Black Woman in America: Sex, Marriage, and the Family* (1973).

Steckel, Richard H., "Slave Marriage and the Family," *Journal of Family History* 5 (1980): 406–21.

Stevenson, Brenda E., "Distress and Discord in Virginia Slave Families, 1830–1860," in Carol Bleser, ed., *In Joy and in Sorrow: Women, Family and Marriage in the Victorian South, 1830–1900* (1991): 103–34.

——— "Historical Dimension of Black Family Structure: A Revisionist Perspective of the Black Family," in Belinda Tucker and Claudia K. Mitchell, ed., *The Decline in Marriage among African-Americans: Causes, Consequences and Policy Implications* (1995): 27–56.

——— *Life in Black and White: Family and Community in the Slave South* (1996).

Sudarkasa, Niara, *The Strength of Our Mothers: African and African American Women and Families: Essays and Speeches* (1996).

Uzzel, Odell, "Free Negro/Slave Marriages and Family Life in Antebellum North Carolina," *Western Journal of Black Studies* 18 (1994): 64–69.

Wilkinson, Doris Y., and Aaron Thompson, ed., *Race, Gender, and the Life Cycle: The Afro-American Experience* (1991).

25.8 SOCIETY

25.8.1 Rural Life (Including Black Settlements)

Alexander, Adele Logan, *Ambiguous Lives: Free Women of Color in Rural Georgia, 1789–1879* (1991).

Armitage, Sue, Theresa Banfield, and Sarah Jacobus, "Black Women and Their Communities in Colorado," *Frontiers* 2 (1977): 45–51.

Ebron, Paulla A., "Enchanted Memories of Regional Difference in African American Culture," *American Anthropologist* 100 (1998): 94–105.

Hilton, Kathleen C., "'Both in the Field, Each with a Plow': Race and Gender in USDA Policy, 1907–1927," in Virginia Bernhard, Betty Brandon, Elizabeth Fox-Genovese, Theda Perdue and Elizabeth Hayes Turner, ed., *Hidden Histories of Women in the New South* (1994): 114–33.

Katz, William Loren, *Black Women of the Old West* (1995).

Malone, Ann Patton, *Women on the Texas Frontier: A Cross-Cultural Perspective* (1983).

Reed, Ruth, *The Negro Women of Gainsville, Georgia* (1921).

Tolnay, Stewart E., "Class, Race, and Fertility in the Rural South 1910 and 1940," *Rural Sociology* 60 (1995): 108–28.

Walker, Melissa, "Home Extension Work among African American Farm Women in East Tennessee," *Agricultural History* 70 (1996): 487–502.

25.8.2 Urban Life (Including Migration)

Baxandall, Rosalyn, and Elizabeth Ewen, "Picture Windows: The Changing Role of Women in the Suburbs, 1945–2000," *Long Island Historical Journal* 3 (1990): 89–108.

Blackwelder, Julia Kirk, "Quiet Suffering: Atlanta Women in the 1930's," *Georgia History Quarterly* 61 (1977): 112–24.

Campbell, Anne, *The Girls in the Gang: A Report from New York City* (1984).

Carby, Hazel V., "Policing the Black Woman's Body in an Urban Context," *Critical Inquiry* 18 (1992): 738–55.

Davis, Lenwood G., comp., *Black Women in the Cities, 1872–1975: A Bibliography of Published Works on the Life and Achievements of Black Women in Cities in the United States* (1975).

de Graaf, Lawrence B., "Race, Sex and Region: Black Women in the American West, 1850–1920," in Darlene Clark Hine, ed., *Black Women in American History: From Colonial Times through the Nineteenth Century* (1990): 303–32.

Harley, Sharon, "Black Women in a Southern City: Washington, D.C., 1890–1920," in Joanne V. Hawks and Sheila L. Skemp, ed., *Sex, Race, and the Role of Women in the South* (1983): 59–74.

Hine, Darlene Clark, "Black Migration to the Urban Midwest: The Gender Dimension, 1915–1945," in Joe William Trotter, Jr., ed., *The Great Migration in Historical Perspective: New Dimensions of Race, Class, and Gender* (1991): 127–46.

———— "Rape and the Inner Lives of Black Women in the Middle West: Preliminary Thoughts on the Culture of Dissemblance," *Signs* 14 (1989): 912–20.

Massa, Ann, "Black Women in the 'White City,'" *Journal of American Studies* 8 (1974): 319–37.

Reiff, Janice L., Michael R. Dahlin, and Daniel Scott Smith, "Rural Push and Urban Pull: Work and Family Experiences of Older Black Women in Southern Cities, 1880–1900," *Journal of Social History* 16 (1983): 39–48.

Rodriguez, Cheryl, "Activist Stories: Culture and Continuity in Black Women's Narratives of Grassroots Community Work," *Frontiers* 19 (1998): 94–112.

Venkatesh, Sudhir Alladi, "Gender and Outlaw Capitalism: A Historical Account of the Black Sisters United 'Girl Gang,'" *Signs: Journal of Women in Culture and Society* 23 (1998): 683–709.

25.8.3 Material Culture

Foster, Helen Bradley, *'New Raiments of Self': African American Clothing in the Antebellum South* (1997).

Hunt, Patricia K., "Clothing as an Expression of History: The Dress of African-American Women in Georgia, 1880–1915," *Georgia Historical Quarterly* 76 (1992): 459–71.

O'Bryant-Seabrook, Marlene, "Symbiotic Stitches: The Quilts of Maggie McFarland Gillispie and John Gillispie, Jr.," *Uncoverings* 16 (1995): 175–98.

25.8.4 Color and Class

Burg, B. R., "The Rhetoric of Miscegenation: Thomas Jefferson, Sally Hemings, and Their Historians," *Phylon* 47 (1986): 128–38.

Bush, Barbara, "White 'Ladies,' Coloured 'Favorites' and Black 'Wenches': Some Considerations on Sex, Race and Class Factors in Social Relations in White Creole Society in the British Caribbean," *Slavery and Abolition* 2 (1981): 245–62.

Frankel, Noralee, and Nancy S. Dye, ed., *Gender, Class, Race, and Reform in the Progressive Era* (1991).

Graham, Pearl M., "Thomas Jefferson and Sally Hemings," *Journal of Negro History* 46 (1961): 89–103.

Johnston, James Hugo, *Race Relations in Virginia and Miscegenation in the South, 1776–1860* (1970).

Mack, Kibibi Voloria C., *Parlor Ladies and Ebony Drudges: African American Women, Class, and Work in a South Carolina Community* (1999).

Mills, Gary B., "Miscegenation and the Free Negro in Antebellum 'Anglo' Alabama: A Reexamination of Southern Race Relations," *Journal of American History* 68 (1981): 16–34.

Morazan, Ronald R., "'Quadroon' Balls in the Spanish Period," *Louisiana History* 14 (1973): 310–15.

Williamson, Joel, *New People: Miscegenation and Mulattoes in the United States* (1980).

Williams, Rhonda M., and Carla L. Peterson, "The Color of Memory: Interpreting Twentieth-Century U.S. Social Policy from a Nineteenth-Century Perspective," *Feminist Studies* 24 (1998): 7–25.

25.8.5   Associational Life

Berkeley, Kathleen C., "'Colored Ladies Also Contributed': Black Women's Activities from Benevolence to Social Welfare, 1866–1896," in Walter J. Fraser, R. Frank Saunders and Jon L. Wakelyn, ed., *The Web of Southern Social Relations: Women, Family, and Education* (1985).

Blackwell-Johnson, Joyce, "African American Activists in the Women's International League for Peace and Freedom, 1920's-1950's," *Peace and Change* 23 (1998): 466–82.

Bolsterli, Margaret Jones, "'It Seems To Help Me Bear It Better When She Knows About It': A Network of Women Friends in Watson, Arkansas, 1890–1891," *Southern Exposure* 11 (1983): 58–61.

Brady, Marilyn Dell, "Kansas Federation of Colored Women's Clubs, 1900–1930," *Kansas History* 9 (1986): 19–30.

———— "Organizing Afro-American Girls' Clubs in Kansas in the 1920's," *Frontiers* 9 (1987): 69–73.

Campbell, Anne, *The Girls in the Gang: A Report from New York City* (1984).

Chateauvert, M. Melinda, *Marching Together: Women of the Brotherhood of Sleeping Car Porters* (1998).

Cochrane, Sharlene Voogd, "'And the Pressure Never Let Up': Black Women, White Women, and the Boston YWCA, 1918–1948," in Vicki L. Crawford, Jacqueline Anne Rouse and Barbara Woods, ed., *Women in the Civil Rights Movement: Trailblazers and Torchbearers, 1941–1965* (1990): 259–69.

Davis, Amy, "'Deep in my Heart': Competition and the Function of Stepping in an African American Sorority," *North Carolina Folklore Journal* 43 (1996): 82–95.

Davis, Elizabeth Lindsay, *Lifting as They Climb: National Association of Colored Women* (1933).

———— *The Story of the Illinois Federation of Colored Women's Clubs, 1900–1922* (1922).

Dickson, Lynda F., "Toward a Broader Angle of Vision in Uncovering Women's History: Black Women's Clubs Revisited," in Darlene Clark Hine, ed., *Black Women's History: Theory and Practice* (1990): 103–20.

Ergood, Bruce, "The Female Protection and Sun Light: Two Contemporary Negro Mutual Aid Societies," in Darlene Clark Hine, ed., *Black Women in United States History* (1990): 303–16.

Ferguson, Earline Rae, "The Woman's Improvement Club of Indianapolis: Black Women Pioneers in Tuberculosis Work, 1903–1938," *Indiana Magazine of History* 84 (1988): 237–61.

Gere, Anne Ruggles, and Sarah R. Robbins, "Gendered Literacy in Black and White: Turn-of-the-Century African-American and European-American Club Women's Printed Texts," *Signs* 21 (1996): 643–78.

Giddings, Paula, *In Search of Sisterhood: Delta Sigma Theta and the Challenge of the Black Sorority Movement* (1988).

Gilkes, Cheryl Townsend, "'If It Wasn't for the Women': African American Women, Community Work, and Social Change," in Maxine Baca Zinn and Bonnie Thornton Dill, ed., *Women of Color in U.S. Society* (1994): 229–46.

Gordon, Linda, "Black and White Visions of Welfare: Women's Welfare Activism," *Journal of American History* 78 (1991): 559–90.

Griffin, Farah Jasmine, "'A Layin' on of Hands': Organizational Efforts among Black American Women, 1790–1930," *Sage* Supplement (1988): 23–29.

Hartmann, Susan M., "Women's Organizations during World War II: The Interaction of Class, Race, and Feminism," in Mary Kelley, ed., *Woman's Being, Woman's Place: Female Identity and Vocation in American History* (1979): 313–28.

Hendricks, Wanda A., *Gender, Race, and Politics in the Midwest: Black Club Women in Illinois* (1998).

Hewitt, Nancy A., "Politicizing Domesticity: Anglo, Black, and Latin Women in Tampa's Progressive Movements," in Noralee Frankel and Nancy S. Dye, ed., *Gender, Class, Race, and Reform in the Progressive Era* (1991): 24–41.

Hine, Darlene Clark, "The Housewives' League of Detroit: Black Women and Economic Nationalism," in Nancy A. Hewitt and Suzanne Lebsock, ed., *Visible Women: New Essays on American Activism* (1993): 223–42.

———— *When the Truth Is Told: A History of Black Women's Culture and Community in Indiana, 1875–1950* (1981).

Jones, Beverly W., "Mary Church Terrell and the National Association of Colored Women, 1896 to 1901," *Journal of Negro History* 67 (1982): 20–33.

Karger, Howard Jacob, "Phyllis Wheatley House: A History of the Minneapolis Black Settlement House, 1924 to 1940," *Phylon* 47 (1986): 79–90.

Kendrick, Ruby M., "'They Also Serve': The National Association of Colored Women, Inc., 1895–1954," *The Negro History Bulletin* 17 (1954): 171–75.

Knupfer, Anne Meis, *Toward a Tenderer Humanity and a Nobler Womanhood: African American Women's Clubs in Turn-of-the-Century Chicago* (1996).

Lasch-Quinn, Elisabeth, *Black Neighbors: Race and the Limits of Reform in the American Settlement House Movement, 1890–1945* (1993).

Lerner, Gerda, "Community Work of Black Club Women," in Gerda Lerner, *The Majority Finds Its Past: Placing Women in History* (1979): 83–93.

———— "Early Community Work of Black Club Women," *Journal of Negro History* 59 (1972): 158–67.

Lindhorst, Marie, "Politics in a Box: Sarah Mapps Douglass and the Female Literary Association, 1831–1833," *Pennsylvania History* 65 (1998): 263–78.

Moses, Wilson Jeremiah, "Domestic Feminism, Conservatism, Sex Roles, and Black Women's Clubs, 1893–1896," *Journal of Social and Behavioral Sciences* 24 (1987): 166–77.

Neverdon-Morton, Cynthia, *Afro-American Women of the South and the Advancement of the Race, 1895–1925* (1989).

———— "Self-Help Programs As Educative Activities of Black Women in the South, 1895–1925: Focus on Four Key Areas," *Journal of Negro Education* 51 (1982): 207–21.

Perkins, Linda M., "Black Women and Racial 'Uplift' prior to Emancipation," in Filomena Chiomana Steady, ed., *The Black Woman Cross-Culturally* (1981): 317–34.

Pfeffer, Paula F., "The Women behind the Union: Halena Wilson, Rosina Tucker, and the Ladies Auxiliary to the Brotherhood of Sleeping Car Porters," *Labor History* 36 (1995): 557–78.

Rouse, Jacqueline Anne, "Atlanta's African-American Women's Attack on Segregation, 1900–1920," in Noralee Frankel and Nancy S. Dye, ed., *Gender, Class, Race, and Reform in the Progressive Era* (1991): 10–23.

———— "Out of the Shadow of Tuskegee: Margaret Murray Washington, Social Activism, and Race Vindication," *Journal of Negro History* 81 (1996): 31–46.

Roydhouse, Marion W., "Bridging Chasms: Community and the Southern YWCA," in Nancy A. Hewitt and Suzanne Lebsock, ed., *Visible Women: New Essays on American Activism* (1993): 270–95.

Salem, Dorothy, *To Better Our World: Black Women in Organized Reform, 1890–1920* (1990).

Scott, Anne Firor, "Most Invisible of All: Black Women's Voluntary Associations," *Journal of Southern History* 56 (1990): 3–22.

Shaw, Stephanie J., "Black Club Women and the Creation of the National Association of Colored Women," *Journal of Women's History* 3 (1991): 10–25.

Terborg-Penn, Rosalyn, "African-American Women's Networks in the Anti-Lynching Crusade," in Noralee Frankel and Nancy S. Dye, ed., *Gender, Class, Race, and Reform in the Progressive Era* (1991): 148–61.

Weisenfeld, Judith, *African American Women and Christian Activism: New York's Black YWCA, 1905–1945* (1997).

———— "The Harlem YWCA and the Secular City, 1904–1945," *Journal of Women's History* 6 (1994): 62–78.

White, Deborah Gray, "The Cost of Club Work, the Price of Black Feminism," in Nancy A. Hewitt and Suzanne Lebsock, ed., *Visible Women: New Essays on American Activism* (1993): 247–69.

———— *Too Heavy a Load: Black Women in Defense of Themselves, 1894–1994* (1999).

Williams, Lillian S., "And Still I Rise: Black Women and Reform, Buffalo, New York, 1900–1940," *Afro-Americans in New York Life and History* 14 (1990): 7–33.

Yacovone, Donald, "The Transformation of the Black Temperance Movement, 1827–1854: An Interpretation," *Journal of the Early Republic* 8 (1988): 281–97.

25.8.6 Leisure and Sports

Captain, Gwendolyn, "Enter Ladies and Gentlemen of Color: Gender, Sport, and the Ideal of African American Manhood and Womanhood during the Late Nineteenth and Early Twentieth Centuries," *Journal of Sport History* 18 (1991): 81–102.

Gissendanner, Cindy Himes, "African American Women Olympians: The Impact of Race, Gender, and Class Ideologies," *Research Quarterly for Exercise and Sport* 67 (1996): 172–83.

McCabe, Robert, and Catherine Tuthill, "Women and Blacks in College Sports," *New England Journal of History* 52 (1995): 54–62.

Overmyer, James, *Queen of the Negro Leagues: Effa Manley and the Newark Eagles* (1998).

Plowden, Martha Ward, *Olympic Black Women* (1996).

25.9 RELIGION

Andrews, William L., ed., *Sisters of the Spirit: Three Black Women's Autobiographies of the Nineteenth Century* (1986).

Baer, Hans A., "The Limited Empowerment of Women in Black Spiritual Churches: An Alternative Vehicle to Religious Leadership," *Sociology of Religion* 54 (1993): 65–83.

Baker-Fletcher, Karen, "'Tar Baby' and Womanist Theology," *Theology Today* 50 (1993): 29–38.

Baldwin, Lewis V., "Black Women and African Union Methodism, 1813–1983," *Methodist History* 21 (1983): 225–37.

Cannon, Katie Geneva, *Black Womanist Ethics* (1988).

——— *Katie's Canon: Womanism and the Soul of the Black Community* (1995).

Carpenter, Delores Causion, "Black Women in Religious Institutions: A Historical Summary from Slavery to the 1960's," *Journal of Religious Thought* 46 (1989–90): 7–27.

——— "The Professionalization of the Ministry of Women," *Journal of Religious Thought* 43 (1986): 59–75.

Collier-Thomas, Bettye, *Daughters of Thunder: Black Women Preachers and Their Sermons, 1850–1979* (1998).

de Groot, Silvia W., "Maroon Women as Ancestors, Priests and Mediums in Surinam," *Slavery and Abolition* 7 (1986): 160–74.

Deggs, Sister Mary Bernard, *No Cross on Earth, No Crown in Heaven,* ed. Charles E. Nolan and Virginia Meacham Gould (2000).

DeLombard, Jeannine, "Sisters, Servants, or Saviors?: National Baptist Women Missionaries in Liberia in the 1920's," *International Journal of African Historical Studies* 24 (1991): 323–48.

Dodson, Jualynne E., and Cheryl Townsend Gilkes, "'There's Nothing like Church Food': Food and the U.S. Afro-Christian Tradition: Re-Membering Community and Feeding the Embodied S/spirit(s)," *Journal of the American Academy of Religion* 63 (1995): 519–38.

Douglas, Kelly Brown, "Teaching Womanist Theology: A Case Study," *Journal of Feminist Studies in Religion* 8 (1992): 133–39.

Eugene, Toinette M., "There is a Balm in Gilead: Black Women and the Black Church as Agents of a Therapeutic Community," *Women and Therapy* 16 (1995): 55–72.

Fallin, Wilson, Jr., *The African American Church in Birmingham, Alabama, 1815–1963: A Shelter in the Storm* (1997).

Frederickson, Mary E., "'Each One Is Dependent on the Other': Southern Churchwomen, Racial Reform, and the Process of Transformation, 1880–1940," in Nancy A. Hewitt and Suzanne Lebsock, ed., *Visible Women: New Essays on American Activism* (1993): 296–324.

Gilkes, Cheryl Townsend, "The Role of Women in the Sanctified Church," *Journal of Religious Thought* 43 (1986): 24–41.

Higginbotham, Evelyn Brooks, "The Feminist Theology of the Black Baptist Church, 1880–1900," in Darlene Clark Hine, ed., *Black Women in American History: From Colonial Times through the Nineteenth Century* (1990): 167–96.

——— *Righteous Discontent: The Women's Movement in the Black Baptist Church, 1880–1920* (1993).

Jackson, Rebecca, *Gifts of Power: The Writings of Rebecca Jackson, Black Visionary, Shaker Eldress,* ed. Jean McMahon Humez (1981).

Jacobs, Sylvia M., "Three Afro-American Women Missionaries in Africa, 1882–1904," in Darlene Clark Hine, ed., *Black Women in American History: From Colonial Times through the Nineteenth Century* (1990): 693–708.

Martin, Joan, "The Notion of Difference for Emerging Womanist Ethics: The Writings of Audre Lorde and bell hooks," *Journal of Feminist Studies in Religion* 9 (1993): 39–52.

Martin, Sandy D., "Black Baptist Women and African Mission Work, 1870–1925," *Sage* 3 (1986): 16–19.

——— "Spelman's Emma B. Delaney and the African Mission," *Journal of Religious Thought* 41 (1984): 22–37.

McDowell, John Patrick, *The Social Gospel in the South: The Woman's Home Mission Movement in the Methodist Episcopal Church, South, 1886–1939* (1982).

Morrow, Diane Batts, "Outsiders Within: The Oblate Sisters of Providence in 1830's Church and Society," *U.S. Catholic Historian* 15 (1997): 35–54.

Paris, Peter J., "From Womanist Thought to Womanist Action," *Journal of Feminist Studies in Religion* 9 (1993): 115–26.

Richardson, Marilyn, *Black Women and Religion: A Bibliography* (1980).

Riggs, Marcia Y., ed., *Can I Get a Witness? Prophetic Religious Voices of African American Women: An Anthology* (1997).

Sanders, Cheryl J., Katie G. Cannon, Emilie M. Townes, M. Shawn Copeland, bell hooks, and Cheryl Townsend Gilkes, "Christian Ethics and Theology in Womanist Perspective," *Feminist Studies in Religion* 5 (1989): 83–113.

Saunders, James Robert, *The Wayward Preacher in the Literature of African American Women* (1995).

Spencer, Janet D., comp., *Black Women in the Church: Historical Highlights and Profiles,* ed. Celia T. Marcelle and Catherine J. Robinson (1986).

Stewart, Maria W., *Maria W. Stewart: America's First Black Woman Political Writer: Essays and Speeches,* ed. Marilyn Richardson (1987).

Taves, Ann, "Spiritual Purity and Sexual Shame: Religious Themes in the Writings of Harriet Jacobs," *Church History* 56 (1987): 59–72.

Wade-Gayles, Gloria, ed., *My Soul Is a Witness: African-American Women's Spirituality* (1995).

Weisenfeld, Judith, *African American Women and Christian Activism: New York's Black YWCA, 1905–1945* (1997).

Weisenfeld, Judith, and Richard Newman, ed., *This Far by Faith: Readings in African-American Religious Biography* (1996).

West, Cynthia S'thembile, "Revisiting Female Activism in the 1960's: The Newark Branch Nation of Islam," *Black Scholar* 26 (1996): 41–48.

Wilcox, Clyde, and Sue Thomas, "Religion and Feminist Attitudes among African-American Women: A View from the Nation's Capitol," *Women and Politics* 12 (1992): 19–40.

Williams, Delores S., *Black Theology in a New Key: Feminist Theology in a Different Voice* (1996).

——— *Sisters in the Wilderness: The Challenge of Womanist God-Talk* (1993).

25.10   THOUGHT AND EXPRESSION

25.10.1   Race, Gender, and Identity

Abel, Elizabeth, Barbara Christian, and Helene Moglen, ed., *Female Subjects in Black and White: Race, Psychoanalysis, Feminism* (1997).

Aptheker, Bettina, "W. E. B. Du Bois and the Struggle for Women's Rights, 1910–1920," *San Jose Studies* 1 (1975): 7–16.

Awkward, Michael, *Negotiating Difference: Race, Gender, and the Politics of Positionality* (1995).

Bilby, Kenneth M., "'Two Sister Pikni': A Historical Tradition of Dual Ethnogenesis in Eastern Jamaica," *Caribbean Quarterly* 30 (1984): 10–25.

Binion, Victoria Jackson, "Psychological Androgyny: A Black Female Perspective," *Sex Roles: A Journal of Research* 22 (1990): 487–508.

Brody, Jennifer DeVere, "Effaced into Flesh: Black Women's Subjectivity," *Genders* 24 (1996): 184–206.

Brown, Elsa Barkley, "Womanist Consciousness: Maggie Lena Walker and the Independent Order of St. Luke," *Signs* 14 (1989): 610–33.

Burgess, Norma J., "Gender Roles Revisited: The Development of the 'Woman's Place' among African-American Women in the United States," *Journal of Black Studies* 24 (1994): 391–401.

Carlson, Shirley J., "Black Ideals of Womanhood in the Late Victorian Era," *Journal of Negro History* 77 (1992): 61–73.

Caton, Simone M., "Birth Control and the Black Community in the 1960's: Genocide or Power Politics?" *Journal of Social History* 31 (1998): 545–69.

Clark, Roger, Rachel Lennon, and Leanna Morris, "Of Caldecotts and Kings: Gendered Images in Recent American Children's Books by Black and Non-Black Illustrators," *Gender and Society* 7 (1993): 227–45.

Collins, Patricia Hill, *Black Feminist Thought: Knowledge, Consciousness, and the Politics of Empowerment* (2d ed., 1999).

———— "The Social Construction of Black Feminist Thought," *Signs* 14 (1989): 745–73.

———— "What's in a Name: Womanism, Black Feminism, and Beyond," *The Black Scholar* 26 (1996): 9–18.

Crenshaw, Kimberle, "Whose Story Is It Anyway?: Feminist and Antiracist Appropriations of Anita Hill," in Toni Morrison, ed., *Race-ing Justice, Engender-ing Power* (1992): 402–36.

Davis, Angela Y., *Angela Davis: An Autobiography* (1974).

Dill, Bonnie Thornton, "Race, Class, and Gender: Prospects for an All-Inclusive Sisterhood," *Feminist Studies* 9 (1983): 131–50.

DuCille, Ann, *Skin Trade* (1996).

Frankel, Noralee, and Nancy S. Dye, ed., *Gender, Class, Race, and Reform in the Progressive Era* (1991).

Garber, Eric, "A Spectacle in Color: The Lesbian and Gay Subculture of Jazz Age Harlem," in Martin Bauml Duberman, Martha Vicinus and George Chauncey, Jr., ed., *Hidden from History: Reclaiming the Gay and Lesbian Past* (1989): 318–31.

Giddings, Paula, "The Last Taboo," in Toni Morrison, ed., *Race-ing Justice, Engender-ing Power* (1992): 441–63.

Guy-Sheftall, Beverly, ed., *Words of Fire: An Anthology of African-American Feminist Thought* (1995).

Hairston, Loyle, Joyce Ladner, Angela Davis, Carole Gregory, and Sarah Wright, "Black Writers' Views of America," *Freedomways* 19 (1979): 151–62.

Hammonds, Evelynn, "Black (W)holes and the Geometry of Black Female Sexuality (More Gender Trouble: Feminism Meets Queer Theory)," *Differences: A Journal of Feminist Cultural Studies* 6 (1994): 126–46.

Hansen, Karen V., "'No Kisses Is like Youres': An Erotic Friendship between Two African-American Women during the Mid-Nineteenth Century," *Gender and History* 7 (1995): 153–82.

Harley, Sharon, "Nannie Helen Burroughs: 'The Black Goddess of Liberty,'" *The Journal of Negro History* 81 (1996): 62–71.

Hawkins, B. Denise, "Addie and Rebecca (Letters of Free-born African American Women during the Civil War)," *Black Issues in Higher Education* 13 (1996): 12–16.

Higginbotham, Evelyn Brooks, "African-American Women's History and the Metalanguage of Race," *Signs* 17 (1992): 251–74.

hooks, bell, *Ain't I a Woman? Black Women and Feminism* (2d ed., 1984).

———— *Talking Back: Thinking Feminist, Thinking Black* (1989).

Hraba, Joseph, and Paul Yarbrough, "Gender Consciousness and Class Action for Women: A Comparison of Black and White Female Adolescents," *Youth and Society* 15 (1983): 115–31.

Hull, Gloria T., Patricia Bell Scott, and Barbara Smith, ed., *All the Women Are White, All the Blacks Are Men, But Some of Us Are Brave: Black Women's Studies* (1982).

Hunter, Andrea G., and Sherrill L. Sellers, "Feminist Attitudes among African American Women and Men," *Gender and Society* 12 (1998): 81–100.

James, Joy, *Shadowboxing: Representations of Black Feminist Politics* (1999).

James, Stanlie M., and Abena P. A. Busia, ed., *Theorizing Black Feminisms: The Visionary Pragmatism of Black Women* (1993).

Just, Roger, "Freedom, Slavery and the Female Psyche," *History of Political Thought* 6 (1985): 169–88.

Lewis, Diane K., "Response to Inequality: Black Women, Racism, and Sexism," *Signs* 3 (1977): 339–61.

Marable, Manning, "Groundings with My Sisters: Patriarchy and the Exploitation of Black Women," *Journal of Ethnic Studies* 11 (1983): 1–39.

——— *Sexism and the Struggle for Black Liberation: Two Essays* (1980).

McCluskey, Audrey Thomas, and Elaine M. Smith, ed., *Mary McLeod Bethune: Building a Better World* (1999).

McKay, Nellie Y., "The Journals of Charlotte L. Forten-Grimke: *Les Lieux de Memoire* in African-American Women's Autoboigraphy," in Genevieve Fabre and Robert O'Meally, ed., *History and Memory in African-American Culture* (1994): 261–71.

Nain, Gemma Tang, "Black Women, Sexism and Racism: Black or Antiracist Feminism," *Feminist Review* 37 (1991): 1–23.

Nance, Teresa A., "Hearing the Missing Voice," *Journal of Black Studies* 26 (1996): 543–59.

Omolade, Barbara, "Hearts of Darkness," in Ann Snitrow, Christine Stansell and Sharon Thompson, *Powers of Desire: The Politics of Sexuality* (1983): 350–67.

Peterson, Carla L., *Doers of the Word: African-American Women Speakers and Writers in the North (1830–1880)* (1995).

Primus, Rebecca, *Beloved Sisters and Loving Friends: Letters from Rebecca Primus of Royal Oak, Maryland and Addie Brown of Hartford, Connecticut, 1854–1868*, ed. Farah Jasmine Griffin (1999).

Reagon, Bernice Johnson, "My Black Mothers and Sisters, or On Beginning a Cultural Autobiography," *Feminist Studies* 8 (1982): 81–96.

Richardson, Marilyn, ed., *Maria W. Stewart, America's First Black Woman Political Writer: Essays and Speeches* (1979).

Rooks, Noliwe M., *Hair Raising: Beauty, Culture, and African American Women* (1996).

Royster, Jacqueline Jones, and Evelynn Hammonds, "A Century of Struggle in Defense of Ourselves," *Sage* 9 (1995): 7–14.

Scott, Kesho Yvonne, *The Habit of Surviving: Black Women's Strategies for Life* (1991).

Simson, Rennie, "The Afro-American Female: The Historical Context of the Construction of Sexual Identity," in Ann Snitow, Christine Stansell and Sharon Thompson, ed., *Desire: The Politics of Sexuality* (1983): 243–49.

Smith, Barbara, ed., *Home Girls: A Black Feminist Anthology* (1983).

Smitherman, Geneva, ed., *African American Women Speak out on Anita Hill-Clarence Thomas* (1995).

Stack, Carol B., "The Culture of Gender: Women and Men of Color," *Signs* 11 (1986): 321–24.

Sterling, Dorothy, *Black Foremothers* (1979).

Stetson, Erlene, "Black Feminism in Indiana, 1893–1933," *Phylon* 44 (1983): 292–98.

Wallace, Michele, *Black Macho and the Myth of the Superwoman* (2d ed., 1990).

White, E. Frances, "Listening to the Voices of Black Feminism," *Radical America* 18 (1984): 7–25.

White, Deborah Gray, *Too Heavy a Load: Black Women in Defense of Themselves, 1894–1994* (1999).

White, Shane, and Graham White, "Slave Hair and African American Culture in the Eighteenth and Nineteenth Centuries," *Journal of Southern History* 61 (1995): 45–76.

Wilcox, Clyde, "Black Women and Feminism," *Women and Politics* 10 (1990): 65–84.

——— "Racial and Gender Consciousness among African-American Women: Sources and Consequences," *Women and Politics* 17 (1997): 73–94.

Williams, Delores S., "The Color of Feminism: Or, Speaking the Black Woman's Tongue," *Journal of Religious Thought* 43 (1986): 42–58.

Williams, Patricia J., *The Alchemy of Race and Rights* (1991).

——— "On Being the Object of Property," *Signs* 14 (1988): 5–24.

Wing, Adrien Katherine, ed., *Critical Race Feminism: A Reader* (1997).

Witt, Doris, *Black Hunger: Food and the Politics of U.S. Identity* (1999).

Young, R. J., *Antebellum Black Activists: Race, Gender, and Self* (1996).

25.10.2   Emigration and Nationalism

Bair, Barbara, "Renegotiating Liberty: Garveyism, Women, and Grassroots Organizing in Virginia," in Christie Anne Farnham, ed., *Women of the American South: A Multicultural Reader* (1997): 220–40.

Dubey, Madhu, *Black Women Novelists and the Nationalist Aesthetic* (1994).

Hudson-Weems, Clenora, "From Malcolm Little to El Hajj Malik El Shabazz: Malcolm's Evolving Attitude toward the Africana Woman," *Western Journal of Black Studies* 17 (1993): 26–31.

White, E. Frances, "Africa on My Mind: Gender, Counter Discourse, and African-American Nationalism," *Journal of Women's History* 2 (1990): 73–97.

Yee, Shirley J., "Finding a Place: Mary Ann Shadd Cary and the Dilemmas of Black Migration to Canada, 1850–1870," *Frontiers* 18 (1997): 1–16.

25.10.3   Language and Linguistics

McCarthy, Nick, "Authority, Orality, and Specificity: Resisting Inscription in Sojourner Truth's 'Ar'nt I a Woman?,'" *Sage: A Scholarly Journal on Black Women* 9 (1995): 30–35.

Ragon, Sandra L., and Christina S. Beck, ed., *The Lynching of Language: Gender, Politics, and Power in the Hill-Thomas Hearings* (1996).

Walker, Robbie Jean, ed., *The Rhetoric of Struggle: Public Address by African American Women* (1992).

25.10.4   Folklore and Humor

Hemenway, Robert, "Folklore Field Notes from Zora Neale Hurston," *Black Scholar* 7 (1976): 39–46.
––––––– "The Functions of Folklore in Charles Chesnutt's *The Conjure Woman*," *Journal of the Folklore Institute* 13 (1976): 283–309.

25.10.5   Literature and Poetry

Accomondo, Christina, "'The Laws Were Laid down to Me Anew': Harriet Jacobs and the Reframing of Legal Fictions," *African American Review* 32 (1998): 229–45.

Allen, Carol, *Black Women Intellectuals: Strategies of Nation, Family and Neighborhood in the Works of Pauline Hopkins, Jessie Fauset, and Marita Bonner* (1997).

Awkward, Michael, *Inspiriting Influences: Tradition, Revision, and Afro-American Women's Novels* (1989).

Baker, Houston A., *Workings of the Spirit: The Poetics of Afro-American Women's Writing* (1991).

Barash, Carol, "The Character of Difference: The Creole Woman as Cultural Mediator in Narratives about Jamaica," *Eighteenth-Century Studies* 23 (1990): 406–24.

Beard, Linda Susan, "Daughters of Clio and Calliope: Afro-American Women Writers as Reclamation and Revisionist Herstorians," *Psychohistory Review* 17 (1989): 301–43.

Bell, Roseann P., Bettye J. Parker, and Beverly Guy-Sheftall, ed., *Sturdy Black Bridges: Visions of Black Women in Literature* (1979).

Bloom, Harold, ed., *Black American Women Fiction Writers* (1994).
–––––––, ed., *Black American Women Poets and Dramatists* (1996).

Bracks, Lean'tin L., *Writings on Black Women of the Diaspora: History, Language, and Identity* (1998).

Braxton, Joanne M., *Black Women Writing Autobiography: Tradition within a Tradition* (1989).
––––––– "Harriet Jacobs' *Incidents in the Life of a Slave Girl*: The Re-definition of the Slave Narrative Genre," *Massachusetts Review* 27 (1986): 379–87.

Braxton, Joanne M., and Andree Nicola McLaughlin, ed., *Wild Women in the Whirlwind: Afra-American Culture and the Contemporary Literary Renaissance* (1990).

Brown-Guillory, Elizabeth, "Black Women Playwrights: Exorcising Myths," *Phylon* 48 (1987): 229–39.

Caputi, Jane, "'Specifying' Fannie Hurst: Langston Hughes's 'Limitations of Life,' Zora Neale Hurston's *Their Eyes Were Watching God*, and Toni Morrison's *The Bluest Eye* as 'Answers' to Hurst's *Imitation of Life*," *Black American Literature Forum* 24 (1990): 697–716.

Carby, Hazel V., "Policing the Black Woman's Body in an Urban Context," *Critical Inquiry* 18 (1992): 738–55.

——— "The Politics of Fiction, Anthropology, and the Folk: Zora Neale Hurston," in Genevieve Fabre and Robert O'Meally, ed., *History and Memory in African-American Culture* (1994): 28–44.

——— *Reconstructing Womanhood: The Emergence of the Afro-American Woman Novelist* (1987).

Christian, Barbara, *Black Feminist Criticism: Perspectives on Black Women Writers* (1985).

——— *Black Women Novelists: The Development of a Tradition, 1892–1976* (1980).

Collins, Terence, "Phyllis Wheatley: The Dark Side of the Poetry," *Phylon* 36 (1975): 78–88.

Dandridge, Rita B., "Male Critics/Black Women's Novels," *College Language Association Journal* 23 (1979): 1–11.

Davis, Thadious M., *Nella Larsen, Novelist of the Harlem Renaissance: A Woman's Life Unveiled* (1994).

Dean, Sharon, and Erlene Stetson, "Flower Dust and Springtime: Harlem Renaissance Women," *The Radical Teacher* 18 (1980): 1–8.

Deck, Alice A., "Whose Book is This? Authorial Versus Editorial Control of Harriet Jacobs' *Incidents in the Life of a Slave Girl: Written by Herself*," *Women's Studies International Forum* 10 (1987): 33–40.

Doherty, Thomas, "Harriet Jacobs' Narrative Strategies: *Incidents in the Life of a Slave Girl*," *Southern Literary Journal* 19 (1986): 79–91.

Doriani, Beth Maclay, "Black Womanhood in Nineteenth Century America: Subversion and Self-Constuction in Two Women's Autobiographies," *American Quarterly* 43 (1991): 199–222.

Doyle, Laura, *Bordering on the Body: The Racial Matrix of Modern Fiction and Culture* (1994).

Dubey, Madhu, *Black Women Novelists and the Nationalist Aesthetic* (1994).

DuCille, Ann, *The Coupling Convention: Sex, Text, and Tradition in Black Women's Fiction* (1993).

Dunn, Margaret M., "Narrative Quilts and Quilted Narratives: The Art of Faith Ringgold and Alice Walker," *Expressions in Ethnic Studies* 15 (1992): 27–33.

Feeney, Joseph J., "A Sardonic, Unconventional Jessie Fauset: The Double Structure and Double Vision of Her Novels," *College Language Association Journal* 22 (1979): 365–82.

Felker, Christopher D., "The Tongues of the Learned Are Insufficient: Phillis Wheatley, Publishing Objectives, and Personal Liberty," *Resources for American Literary Study* 20 (1994): 149–79.

Flanzbaum, Hilene, "Unprecedented Liberties: Re-Reading Phillis Wheatley," *MELUS* 18 (1993): 71–81.

Foreman, P. Gabrielle, "Looking Back from Zora, or Talking out Both Sides My Mouth for Those Who Have Two Ears," *Black American Literature Forum* 24 (1990): 649–66.

Gates, Henry Louis, Jr., ed., *Reading Black, Reading Feminist: A Critical Anthology* (1990).

Gillman, Susan, "Pauline Hopkins and the Occult: African-American Revisions of Nineteenth-Century Sciences," *American Literary History* 8 (1996): 57–82.

Gilman, Sander L., "Black Bodies, White Bodies: Toward an Iconography of Female Sexuality in Late Nineteenth Century Art, Medicine, and Literature," *Critical Inquiry* 12 (1985): 204–42.

Giovanni, Nikki, *Conversations with Nikki Giovanni*, ed. Virginia C. Fowler (1992).

Gribbin, William, "A *Phylon* Document . . . Advice from a Black Philadelphia Poetess of 1813," *Phylon* 34 (1973): 49–50.

Gunning, Sandra, *Race, Rape, and Lynching: The Red Record of American Literature, 1890–1912* (1996).

Gwin, Minrose C., *Black and White Women of the Old South: The Peculiar Sisterhood in American Literature* (1985).

Hamilton, Cynthia S., "Revisions, Rememories, and Exorcisms: Toni Morrison and the Slave Narrative," *Journal of American Studies* 30 (1996): 429–45.

Harris, Trudier, *From Mammies to Militants: Domestics in Black American Literature* (1982).

Hemenway, Robert, "The Functions of Folklore in Charles Chesnutt's *The Conjure Woman*," *Journal of the Folklore Institute* 13 (1976): 283–309.

Holloway, Karla F. C., *The Character of the Word: The Texts of Zora Neale Hurston* (1987).

——— *Moorings and Metaphors: Figures of Culture and Gender in Black Women's Literature* (1992).

Hubbard, Dolan, ed., *Recovered Writers/Recovered Texts: Race, Class, and Gender in Black Women's Literature* (1997).

Hull, Gloria T., *Color, Sex and Poetry: Three Women Writers of the Harlem Renaissance* (1987).

Hutchinson, George, "Nella Larsen and the Veil of Race," *American Literary History* 9 (1997): 329–49.

Isani, Mukhtar Ali, "The British Reception of Wheatley's Poems on Various Subjects," *Journal of Negro History* 66 (1981): 144–49.

Japtok, Martin, "Paule Marshall's *Brown Girl, Brownstones:* Reconciling Ethnicity and Individualism," *African American Review* 32 (1998): 305–15.

Johnson, Abby Arthur, "Literary Midwife: Jessie Redmon Fauset and the Harlem Renaissance," *Phylon* 39 (1978): 143–53.

Johnson, Georgia Douglas Camp, *The Selected Works of Georgia Douglas Johnson* (1997).

Johnson, Yvonne, *The Voices of African American Women: The Use of Narrative and Authorial Voice in the Works of Harriet Jacobs, Zora Neale Hurston, and Alice Walker* (1998).

Jordan, June, "The Difficult Miracle of Black Poetry in America or Something like a Sonnet for Phillis Wheatley," *Massachusetts Review* 27 (1986): 252–62.

Krasner, James, "The Life of Women: Zora Neale Hurston and Female Autobiography," *Black American Literature Forum* 23 (1989): 113–26.

Kubitschek, Missy Dehn, *Claiming the Heritage: African-American Women Novelists and History* (1991).

Lauter, Paul, "Race and Gender in the Shaping of the American Literary Canon: A Case Study from the Twenties," *Feminist Studies* 9 (1983): 435–63.

Lee, Valerie, *Granny Midwives and Black Women Writers: Double-Dutched Readings* (1996).

Levernier, James A., "Style As Protest in the Poetry of Phillis Wheatley," *Style* 27 (1993): 172–93.

Lewis, Vashti Crutcher, "The Declining Significance of the Mulatto Female as Major Character in the Novels of Zora Neale Hurston," *College Language Association Journal* 28 (1984): 127–49.

Matson, R. Lynn, "Phillis Wheatley: Soul Sister?" *Phylon* 33 (1972): 222–30.

Matthews, Victoria Earle, "The Value of Race Literature," *Massachusetts Review* 27 (1986): 169–91.

McDowell, Deborah E., "The Neglected Dimension of Jessie Redmon Fauset," *Afro-Americans in New York Life and History* 5 (1981): 33–49.

——— *"The Changing Same": Black Women's Literature, Criticism, and Theory* (1995).

McKay, Nellie Y., comp., *Critical Essays on Toni Morrison* (1988).

McKay, Nellie Y., and Kathryn Earle, ed., *Approaches to Teaching the Novels of Toni Morrison* (1997).

Meisenhelder, Susan, "Conflict and Resistance in Zora Neale Hurston's *Mules and Men*," *Journal of American Folklore* 109 (1996): 267–88.

Miller, Jeanne-Marie A., "Images of Black Women in Plays by Black Playwrights," *College Language Association Journal* 20 (1977): 494–507.

Moody, Joycelyn K., "Ripping Away the Veil of Slavery: Literacy, Communal Love, and Self-Esteem in Three Slave Women's Narratives," *Black American Literature Forum* 24 (1990): 633–48.

Moraga, Cherrie, and Gloria Anzaldua, ed., *This Bridge Called My Back: Writings by Radical Women of Color* (1981).

O'Neale, Sondra A., "Challenge to Wheatley's Critics: 'There Was No Other "Game" in Town,'" *Journal of Negro Education* 54 (1985): 500–11.

——— "A Slave's Subtle War: Phillis Wheatley's Use of Biblical Myth and Symbol," *Early American Literature* 21 (1986): 144–65.

Otten, Terry, *The Crime of Innocence in the Fiction of Toni Morrision* (1989).

Page, Philip, *Dangerous Freedom: Fusion and Fragmentation in Toni Morrison's Novels* (1995).

Palmer, R. Roderick, "The Poetry of Three Revolutionists: Don L. Lee, Sonia Sanchez, and Nikki Giovanni," *College Language Association Journal* 15 (1971): 25–36.

Patterson, Lindsay, ed., *A Rock against the Wind: African-American Poems and Letters of Love and Passion* (1996).

Peters, Pearlie Mae Fisher, *The Assertive Woman in Zora Neale Hurston's Fiction, Folklore, and Drama* (1998).

Peterson, Carla L., *Doers of the Word: African-American Women Speakers and Writers in the North, 1830–1880* (1995).

Pratt, Louis H., and Darnell D. Pratt, *Alice Malsenior Walker: An Annotated Bibliography, 1968–1986* (1988).

Proper, David R., "Lucy Terry Prince: 'Singer of History,'" *Contributions in Black Studies* 9–10 (1990–92): 187–214.

Pryse, Marjorie, and Hortense Spillers, ed., *Conjuring: Black Women, Fiction, and Literary Tradition* (1985).

Rawley, James A., "The World of Phillis Wheatley," *New England Quarterly* 50 (1977): 666–77.

Richards, Phillip M., "Phillis Wheatley and Literary Americanization," *American Quarterly* 44 (1992): 163–91.

Richmond, Merle A., *Bid the Vassal Soar: Interpretive Essays on the Life and Poetry of Phillis Wheatley, ca. 1753–1784, and George Moses Horton, ca. 1797–1883* (1974).

Russell, Sandi, *Render Me My Song: African-American Women Writers from Slavery to the Present* (1990).

Sadoff, Dianne F., "Gender and African-American Narrative," *American Quarterly* 43 (1991): 119–27.

Saunders, James Robert, *The Wayward Preacher in the Literature of African American Women* (1995).

Scheick, William J., "Phillis Wheatley and Oliver Goldsmith: A Fugitive Satire," *Early American Literature* 19 (1984): 82–84.

Sheffey, Ruthe T., "Zora Neale Hurston's *Moses, Man of the Mountain:* A Fictionalized Manifesto on the Imperatives of Black Leadership," *College Language Association Journal* 29 (1985): 206–20.

Shields, John C., "Phillis Wheatley's Subversion of Classical Stylistics," *Style* 27 (1993): 252–70.

Shockley, Ann Allen, ed., *Afro-American Women Writers, 1746–1933: An Anthology and Critical Guide* (1988).

Silvers, Anita, "Pure Historicism and the Heritage of Hero(in)es: Who Grows in Phillis Wheatley's Garden?" *Journal of Aesthetics and Art Criticism* 51 (1993): 475–82.

Smith, Eleanor, "Phillis Wheatley: A Black Perspective," *Journal of Negro Education* 43 (1974): 401–07.

Smith, Felipe, *American Body Politics: Race, Gender, and Black Literary Renaissance* (1998).

Stephens, Judith L., "Anti-Lynch Plays by African American Women: Race, Gender, and Social Protest in American Drama," *African American Review* 26 (1992): 329–39.

Storm, William, "Reactions of a 'Highly-Strung Girl': Psychology and Dramatic Representation in Angelina W. Grimke's *Rachel*," *African American Review* 27 (1993): 461–71.

Tate, Claudia, ed., *Black Women Writers at Work* (1983).

———— *Domestic Allegories of Political Desire: The Black Heroine's Text* (1992).

Trefzer, Annette, "'Let Us All Be Kissing-Friends?': Zora Neale Hurston and Race Politics in Dixie," *Journal of American Studies* 31 (1997): 69–78.

Tucker, Sherrie, "'Where the Blues and the Truth Lay Hiding': Rememory of Jazz in Black Women's Fiction," *Frontiers* 13 (1993): 26–44.

Wade-Gayles, Gloria, *No Crystal Stair: Visions of Race and Sex in Black Women's Fiction* (1984).

Walker, Melissa, *Down from the Mountaintop: Black Women's Novels in the Wake of the Civil Rights Movement, 1966–1989* (1991).

Wall, Cheryl A., ed., *Changing Our Own Words: Essays on Criticism, Theory, and Writing by Black Women* (1989).

Wall, Cheryl A., "Mules and Men and Women: Zora Neale Hurston's Strategies of Narration and Visions of Female Empowerment," *Black American Literature Forum* 23 (1989): 661–80.

———— *Women of the Harlem Renaissance* (1995).

Washington, Mary Helen, *Invented Lives: Narratives of Black Women, 1860–1960* (1987).

Wechselblatt, Martin, "Gender and Race in Yarico's Epistles to Inkle: Voicing the Feminine/Slave," *Studies in Eighteenth-Century Culture* 19 (1989): 197–223.

Weixlmann, Joe, and Houston A. Baker, ed., *Black Feminist Criticism and Critical Theory* (1988).

Williams, Delores S., "Visions, Inner Voices, Apparitions, and Defiance in Nineteenth-Century Black Women's Narratives," *Women's Studies Quarterly* 21 (1993): 81–89.

Willis, Susan, *Specifying: Black Women Writing the American Experience* (1987).

Yacovone, Donald, "Sacred Land Regained: Frances Ellen Watkins Harper and 'The Massachusetts Fifty-Fourth,' a Lost Poem," *Pennsylvania History* 62 (1995): 90–110.

Yellin, Jean Fagan, "The Text and Contexts of Harriet Jacobs' *Incidents in the Life of a Slave Girl: Written by Herself*," in Charles T. Davis and Henry Louis Gates, Jr., ed., *The Slave's Narrative* (1985): 262–82.

25.10.6 Music and Performing Arts

Anderson, Lisa M., *Mammies No More: The Changing Image of Black Women on Stage and Screen* (1997).

Aschenbrenner, Joyce, *Katherine Dunham: Reflections on the Social and Political Contexts of Afro-American Dance* (1981).

Aschenbrenner, Joyce, and Carolyn H. Carr, "The Dance Technique of Katherine Dunham as a Community Rite de Passage," *Western Journal of Black Studies* 13 (1989): 139–43.

Bogle, Donald, *Brown Sugar: Eighty Years of America's Black Female Superstars* (1980).

Carby, Hazel V., "'It Jus Be's Dat Way Sometime': The Sexual Politics of Women's Blues," *Radical America* 20 (1986): 9–22.

Cavin, Susan, "Missing Women: On the Voodoo Trail to Jazz," *Journal of Jazz Studies* 3 (1975): 4–27.

Clark, Veve, "Performing the Memory of Difference in Afro-Caribbean Dance: Katherine Dunham's Choreography, 1938–87," in Genevieve Fabre and Robert O'Meally, ed., *History and Memory in African-American Culture* (1994): 188–204.

Daughtry, Willia Estelle, *Sissieretta Jones: A Study of the Negro's Contribution to Nineteenth Century American Concert and Theatrical Life* (1968).

Davis, Angela Y., *Blues Legacies and Black Feminism: Gertrude "Ma" Rainey, Bessie Smith, and Billie Holiday* (1998).

Dunham, Katherine, *Katherine Dunham's Journey to Accompong* (1946).

——— *Touch of Innocence* (1959).

Finn, Julio, *The Bluesman: The Musical Heritage of Black Men and Women in the Americas* (1986).

Forman, Murray, "'Movin' Closer to an Independent Funk': Black Feminist Theory, Standpoint, and Women in Rap," *Women's Studies* 23 (1994): 35–56.

George-Graves, Nadine, *The Royalty of Negro Vaudeville: The Whitman Sisters and the Negotiation of Race, Gender and Class in African American Theater, 1900–1940* (2000).

Green, Mildred D., *Black Women Composers: A Genesis* (1983).

Handy, D. Antoinette, *Black Women in American Bands and Orchestras* (1981).

Harrison, Daphne Duval, *Black Pearls: Blues Queens of the 1920's* (1988).

Lawrence, Vera Brodsky, "Micah Hawkins, the Pied Piper of Catherine Slip," *New York Historical Society Quarterly* 62 (1978): 138–65.

Perry, Imani, "It's My Thang and I'll Swing It the Way That I Feel: Sexuality and Black Women Rappers," in Gail Dines and Jean M. Humez, ed., *Gender, Race and Class in Media: A Text Reader* (1995): 524–30.

Simpson, Anne Key, "Camille Lucie Nickerson: 'The Louisiana Lady,'" *Louisiana History* 36 (1995): 431–51.

Sims-Wood, Janet L., *Marian Anderson, an Annotated Bibliography and Discography* (1981).

Speisman, Barbara, "From 'Spears' to *The Great Day*: Zora Neale Hurston's Vision of a Real Negro Theatre," *Southern Quarterly* 36 (1998): 34–46.

Stewart, James B., "Relationships between Black Males and Females in Rhythm and Blues Music of the 1960's and 1970's," *Western Journal of Black Studies* 3 (1979): 186–96.

Tucker, Iantha Elizabeth Lake, *The Role of Afro-Americans in Dance in the United States from Slavery through 1983: A Slide Presentation* (1984).

25.10.7 Art (Drawing, Painting, Photography, Printmaking, Sculpture)

Benjamin, Tritobia Hayes, *The Life and Art of Lois Mailou Jones* (1994).

Bontemps, Jacqueline Fonvielle, and Arna A. Bontemps, *Forever Free: Art by African American Women* (1980).

Broadus-Garcia, Cassandra, "Images of Home Places: Beverly Buchanan," *School Arts* 6 (1998): 31–37.

Buick, Kirsten P., "The Ideal Works of Edmonia Lewis: Invoking and Inverting Autobiography," *American Art* 9 (1995): 4–19.

Davis, Lenwood G., and Janet L. Sims, *Black Artists in the United States: An Annotated Bibliography of Books, Articles, and Dissertations on Black Artists, 1779–1979* (1980).

Dunn, Margaret M., "Narrative Quilts and Quilted Narratives: The Art of Faith Ringgold and Alice Walker," *Expressions in Ethnic Studies* 15 (1992): 27–33.

Enwezor, Okwul, "Writing Inside the Hyphen (The Work of African American Artist Carrie Mae Weems)," *Index on Censorship* 25 (1996): 161–66.

Freeman, Roland L., *A Communion of the Spirits: African American Quilters, Preservers, and Their Stories* (1996).

Fry, Gladys-Marie, "Harriet Powers: Portrait of a Black Quilter," *Sage* 4 (1987): 11–16.

Henkes, Robert, *The Art of Black American Women: Works by Twenty-four Artists of the Twentieth Century* (1993).

Herzog, Melanie, "Art and Identity: Elizabeth Catlett," *School Arts* 92 (1992): 23–27.

———— "Elizabeth Catlett in Mexico: Identity and Cross-Cultural Intersections in the Production of Artistic Meaning," *The International Review of African American Art* 11 (1994): 18–32.

Lewis, Samella, *The Art of Elizabeth Catlett* (1984).

Linker, Kate, "Went Looking for Africa: Carrie Mae Weems," *Artforum* 31 (1993): 79–83.

Moutoussamy-Ashe, Jeanne, *Viewfinders: Black Women Photographers* (1986).

O'Bryant-Seabrook, Marlene, "Symbiotic Stitches: The Quilts of Maggie McFarland Gillispie and John Gillispie, Jr.," *Uncoverings* 16 (1995): 175–98.

Richardson, Marilyn, "Edmonia Lewis' *The Death of Cleopatra*: Myth and Identity," *The International Review of African American Art* 12 (1995): 36–53.

Robinson, Jontyle Theresa, *Bearing Witness: Contemporary Works by African-American Women Artists* (1996).

Sims, Lowery S., "Race Riots, Cocktail Parties, Black Panthers, Moon Shots and Feminists: Faith Ringgold's Observations on the 1960's in America," in Norma Broude and Mary D. Garrard, ed., *The Expanding Discourse: Feminism and Art History* (1992): 467–73.

Tesfagiorgis, Frieda High W., "Afrofemcentrism and Its Fruition in the Art of Elizabeth Catlett and Faith Ringgold," in Norma Broude and Mary D. Garrard, ed., *The Expanding Discourse: Feminism and Art History* (1992): 476–85.

Thompson, Kathleen, and Hilary Mac Austin, ed., *The Face of Our Past: Images of Black Women from Colonial America to the Present* (1999).

Waring, Laura Wheeler, *In Memoriam, Laura Wheeler Waring, 1887–1948: An Exhibition of Paintings, May and June 1949* (1949).

Wolfe, Rinna Evelyn, *Edmonia Lewis: Wildfire in Marble* (1998).

25.10.8   Film and Broadcasting

Anderson, Lisa M., *Mammies No More: The Changing Image of Black Women on Stage and Screen* (1997).

Bobo, Jacqueline, *Black Women Film and Video Artists* (1998).

Bogle, Donald, *Brown Sugar: Eighty Years of America's Black Female Superstars* (1980).

———— *Dorothy Dandridge: A Biography* (1997).

Dines, Gail, and Jean M. Humez, ed., *Gender, Race, and Class in Media: A Text Reader* (1995).

Ebron, Paulla A., "Enchanted Memories of Regional Difference in African American Culture," *American Anthropologist* 100 (1998): 94–105.

Edwards, Audrey, "From Aunt Jemima to Anita Hill: Media's Split Image of Black Women," *Media Studies Quarterly* 7 (1993): 214–23.

Hartman, S. V., and Farah Jasmine Griffin, "Are You as Colored as that Negro: The Politics of Being Seen in Julie Dash's 'Illusions,'" *Black American Literature Forum* 25 (1991): 361–374.

Hartsough, Denise, "Into a New Kitchen: Lessons from Teaching a Course on African-American Women and Film," *Michigan Academician* 24 (1992): 321–32.

Oshana, Maryann, *Women of Color: A Filmography of Minority and Third World Women* (1985).

Simmonds, Felly Nkweto, "She's Gotta Have It: The Representation of Black Female Sexuality on Film," *Feminist Review* 29 (1988): 10–22.

Stephens, Lenora Clodfelter, "Black Women in Film," *Southern Quarterly* 19 (1981): 164–70.

25.11 EDUCATION

Alexander, Adele Logan, "Susannah and the Elders or Potiphar's Wife? Allegations of Sexual Misconduct at Booker T. Washington's Tuskegee Institute," in Christie Anne Farnham, ed., *Women of the American South: A Multicultural Reader* (1997): 150–64.

Alexander, Elizabeth, "'We Must Be about Our Father's Business': Anna Julia Cooper and the In-Corporation of the Nineteenth-Century African-American Woman Intellectual," *Signs* 20 (1995): 336–56.

Arnez, Nancy L., "Selected Black Female Superintendents of Public School Systems," *Journal of Negro Education* 51 (1982): 309–17.

Bell-Scott, Patricia, "Black Women's Higher Education: Our Legacy," *Sage* 1 (1984): 8–11.

——— "To Keep My Self-Respect: Dean Lucy Diggs Slowe's 1927 Memorandum on the Sexual Harassment of Black Women," *NWSA Journal* 9 (1997): 70–76.

Benjamin, Lois, ed., *Black Women in the Academy: Promises and Perils* (1997).

Berry, Mary Frances, "Black Visions of Educational Improvement," *History of Education Quarterly* 24 (1984): 597–600.

——— "Twentieth-Century Black Women in Education," *Journal of Negro Education* 51 (1982): 288–300.

Brady, Patricia, "Trials and Tribulations: American Missionary Association Teachers and Black Education in Occupied New Orleans, 1863–1864," *Louisiana History* 31 (1990): 5–20.

Casserly, Catherine M., *African-American Women and Poverty: Can Education Alone Change the Status Quo?* (1998).

Chateauvert, M. Melinda, "The Third Step: Anna Julia Cooper and Black Education in the District of Columbia, 1910–1960," *Sage* [student supplement] (1988): 7–13.

Clark, Septima Poinsette, *Echo in My Soul* (1962).

Collier-Thomas, Bettye, "The Impact of Black Women in Education: An Historical Overview," *Journal of Negro Education* 51 (1982): 173–80.

Cooper, Afua, "The Search for Mary Bibb, Black Woman Teacher in Nineteenth-Century Canada West," *Ontario History* 83 (1991): 39–54.

Cooper, Arnie, "A Stony Road: Black Education in Iowa, 1838–1860," *Annals of Iowa* 48 (1986): 113–34.

Coppin, Fanny Jackson, *Reminiscences of School Life, and Hints on Teaching* (1913).

Davis, Angela Y., "Black Women and the Academy," *Callaloo* 17 (1994): 422–32.

Davis, Hilda, and Patricia Bell-Scott, "The Association of Deans of Women and Advisers to Girls in Negro Schools, 1929–1954: A Brief Oral History," *Sage* 6 (1989): 40–44.

Deboer, Clara Merritt, *His Truth Is Marching on: African Americans Who Taught the Freedmen for the American Missionary Association, 1861–1877* (1995).

Evans, Art, and Annette M. Evans, "Black Educators before and after 1960," *Phylon* 43 (1982): 254–61.

Foner, Philip Sheldon, and Josephine F. Pacheco, *Three Who Dared: Prudence Crandall, Margaret Douglass, Myrtilla Miner—Champions of Antebellum Black Education* (1984).

Fuller, Edmund, *Prudence Crandall: An Incident of Racism in Nineteenth-Century Connecticut* (1971).

Fultz, Michael, "African-American Teachers in the South, 1890–1940: Growth, Feminization, and Salary Discrimination," *Teachers College Record* 96 (1995): 544–68.

Grant, Linda, "Helpers, Enforcers, and Go-Betweens: Black Females in Elementary School Classrooms," in Maxine Baca Zinn and Bonnie Thornton Dill, ed., *Women of Color in U.S. Society* (1994): 43–63.

Halderman, Keith, "Blanche Armwood of Tampa and the Strategy of Interracial Cooperation," *Florida Historical Quarterly* 74 (1996): 287–303.

Harley, Sharon, "Beyond the Classroom: Organizational Lives of Black Female Educators in the District of Columbia, 1890–1930," *Journal of Negro Education* 51 (1982): 254–65.

Hartman, Saidiya, "The Territory between Us: A Report on 'Black Women in the Academy: Defending Our Name: 1894–1994,'" *Callaloo* 17 (1994): 439–50.

Hill, Catherine Mary, *Black Women, Cultural Perspective, and Private Education: Two Shades of Difference* (1996).

Hine, Darlene Clark, "The Anatomy of Failure: Medical Education Reform and the Leonard Medical School of Shaw University, 1882–1920," *Journal of Negro Education* 54 (1985): 512–25.

———— "Opportunity and Fulfillment: Sex, Race, and Class in Health Care Education," in Darlene Clark Hine, ed., *Black Women's History: Theory and Practice* (1990): 219–34.

Holland, Rupert Sargent, ed., *Letters and Diary of Laura M. Towne: Written from the Sea Islands of South Carolina, 1862–1884* (1912).

Howard-Vital, Michelle R., "African-American Women in Higher Education: Struggling to Gain Identity," *Journal of Black Studies* 20 (1989): 180–91.

Hunter, Tera, "The Correct Thing: Charlotte Hawkins Brown and the Palmer Institute," *Southern Exposure* 11 (1983): 37–43.

Ihle, Elizabeth L., ed., *Black Women in Higher Education: An Anthology of Essays, Studies, and Documents* (1992).

James, Joy, and Ruth Farmer, ed., *Spirit, Space, and Survival: African American Women in (White) Academe* (1993).

Johnson, Whittington B., "A Black Teacher and Her School in Reconstruction Darien: The Correspondence of Hettie Sabattie and J. Murray Hoag, 1868–1869," *Georgia Historical Quarterly* 75 (1991): 90–105.

Karen, David, "The Politics of Class, Race, and Gender: Access to Higher Education in the United States, 1960–1986," *American Journal of Education* 99 (1991): 208–37.

Kaufman, Polly Welts, "Building a Constituency for School Desegregation: African-American Women in Boston, 1962–1972," *Teachers College Record* 92 (1991): 619–31.

Kimball, John Calvin, *Connecticut's Canterbury Tale, Its Heroine Prudence Crandall, and Its Moral for To-day* (1885).

Lawson, Ellen NicKenzie, with Marlene D. Merrill, ed., *The Three Sarahs: Documents of Antebellum Black College Women* (1984).

Leffall, Doris C., and Janet L. Sims, "Mary McLeod Bethune—The Educator, Also Including a Selected Annotated Bibliography," *Journal of Negro Education* 45 (1976): 342–59.

Leone, Janice, "Integrating the American Association of University Women, 1946–1949," *Historian* 51 (1989): 423–45.

Lines, Amelia Akehurst, *To Raise Myself a Little: The Diaries and Letters of Jennie, a Georgia Teacher, 1851–1886*, ed. Thomas Dyer (1982).

Littlefield, Valinda W., "A Yearly Contract with Everybody and his Brother: Durham County, North Carolina Black Female Public School Teachers, 1885–1927," *The Journal of Negro History* 79 (1994): 37–54.

Mabee, Carleton, "Sojourner Truth, Bold Prophet: Why Did She Never Learn to Read?" *New York History* 69 (1988): 55–77.

Margo, Robert A., "Teacher Salaries in Black and White: The South in 1910," *Explorations in Economic History* 21 (1984): 306–26.

McCandless, Amy Thompson, "The Higher Education of Black Women in the Contemporary South," *Mississippi Quarterly* 45 (1992): 453–65.

McCluskey, Audrey Thomas, "'Most Sacrificing' Service: The Educational Leadership of Lucy Craft Laney and Mary McLeod Bethune," in Christie Anne Farnham, ed., *Women of the American South: A Multicultural Reader* (1997): 189–203.

———— "'We Specialize in the Wholly Impossible': Black Women School Founders and their Mission," *Signs* 22 (1997): 403–26.

Neverdon-Morton, Cynthia, *Afro-American Women of the South and the Advancement of the Race, 1895–1925* (1989).

Omolade, Barbara, "A Black Feminist Pedagogy," *Women's Studies Quarterly* 21 (1993): 31–39.

Perkins, Linda M., "The African American Female Elite: The Early History of African American Women in the Seven Sister Colleges, 1880–1960," *Harvard Educational Review* 67 (1997): 718–57.

———— "The Black Female American Missionary Association Teacher in the South, 1861–1870," in Jeffrey A. Crow and Flora J. Hatley, ed., *Black Americans in North Carolina and the South* (1984): 122–36.

———— "Lucy Diggs Slowe: Champion of the Self-Determination of African-American Women in Higher Education," *Journal of Negro History* 81 (1996): 89–104.

———— "The National Association of College Women: Vanguard of Black Women's Leadership in Education, 1923–1954," *Journal of Education* 172 (1990): 65–75.

Philipsen, Maike, "Values-Spoken and Values-Lived: Female African Americans' Educational Experiences in Rural North Carolina," *Journal of Negro Education* 62 (1993): 419–27.

Rector, Theresa A., "Black Nuns As Educators," *Journal of Negro Education* 51 (1982): 238–53.

Reilly, Wayne E., ed., *Sarah Jane Foster, Teacher of the Freedmen: A Diary and Letters* (1990).

Revere, Amie B., "Black Women Superintendents in the United States: 1984–1985," *Journal of Negro Education* 56 (1987): 510–20.

Richardson, Joe M., ed., "'We are Truly Doing Missionary Work': Letters From American Missionary Association Teachers in Florida, 1864–1874," *Florida Historical Quarterly* 54 (1975): 178–95.

Russell, Michele, "Black-Eyed Blues Connection: Teaching Black Women," *Women's Studies Quarterly* 25 (1997): 152–61.

Sloan, Patricia E., "Early Black Nursing Schools and Responses of Black Nurses to Their Educational Programs," *Western Journal of Black Studies* 9 (1985): 1–30.

St. Clair, Sadie D., "Myrtilla Miner: Pioneer in Teacher Education for Negro Women," *Journal of Negro History* 34 (1949): 30–45.

Washington, Mary Helen, "Anna Julia Cooper: The Black Feminist Voice of the 1890's," *Legacy* 4 (1987): 3–15.

Washington, Valora, and Joanna Newman, "Setting Our Own Agenda: Exploring the Meaning of Gender Disparities among Blacks in Higher Education," *Journal of Negro Education* 60 (1991): 19–35.

Welch, Lynne Brodie, ed., *Perspectives on Minority Women in Higher Education* (1992).

Wesley, Dorothy Porter, with Avril Johnson Madison, interviewer, "Dorothy Burnett Porter Wesley: Enterprising Steward of Black Culture," *Public Historian* 17 (1995): 15–40.

Wolcott, Victoria W., "'Bible, Bath, and Broom': Nannie Helen Burroughs's National Training School and African-American," *Journal of Women's History* 9 (1997): 88–110.

25.12   WORK AND ENTREPRENEURIAL ACTIVITY

Allen, Walter R., "Family Roles, Occupational Statuses, and Achievement Orientations among Black Women in the United States," *Signs* 4 (1979): 670–86.

———— "The Social and Economic Statuses of Black Women in the United States," *Phylon* 42 (1981): 26–40.

Anderson, Karen Tucker, "Last Hired, First Fired: Black Women Workers during World War Two," *Journal of American History* 69 (1982): 82–97.

Aptheker, Bettina, "Black Women: Love, Labor, Sorrow, Struggle," *Science and Society* 51 (1987–88): 478–85.

———— "Quest for Dignity: Black Women in the Professions, 1865–1900," in Darlene Clark Hine, ed., *Black Women in American History: From Colonial Times through the Nineteenth Century* (1990): 25–50.

Barton, Keith C., "'Good Cooks and Washers': Slave Hiring, Domestic Labor, and the Market in Bourbon County, Kentucky," *Journal of American History* 84 (1997): 436–60.

Bell, Duran, "Why Participation Rates of Black and White Women Differ," *Journal of Human Resources* 9 (1974): 465–79.

Benjamin, Lois, "Black Women Achievers: An Isolated Elite," *Sociological Inquiry* 52 (1982): 141–51.

Blackwelder, Julia Kirk, "Women in the Work Force: Atlanta, New Orleans, and San Antonio, 1930 to 1940," *Journal of Urban History* 4 (1978): 331–358.

Boris, Eileen, "Black Women and Paid Labor in the Home: Industrial Homework in Chicago in the 1920s," in Eileen Boris and Cynthia R. Daniels, ed., *Homework: Historical and Contemporary Perspectives on Paid Labor at Home* (1989): 33–52.

Brown, Elsa Barkley, "Womanist Consciousness: Maggie Lena Walker and the Independent Order of St. Luke," *Signs* 14 (1989): 610–33.

Brown, Minnie Miller, "Black Women in American Agriculture," *Agricultural History* 50 (1976): 202–12.

Burbridge, Lynn C., "Black Women in Employment and Training Programs," *Review of Black Political Economy* 14 (1985–86): 97–114.

Burgess, Norma J., and Hayward Derrick Horton, "African American Women and Work: A Socio-Historical Perspective," *Journal of Family History* 18 (1993): 53–63.

Campbell, John, "As 'A Kind of Freeman'? Slaves' Market-Related Activities in the South Carolina Upcountry, 1800–1860," *Slavery and Abolition* 12 (1991): 131–69.

Carnegie, Mary Elizabeth, *The Path We Tread: Blacks in Nursing Worldwide, 1854–1994* (3d ed., 1995).

Chateauvert, M. Melinda, *Marching Together: Women of the Brotherhood of Sleeping Car Porters* (1998).

Clark-Lewis, Elizabeth, *Living in, Living Out: African American Domestics in Washington, D.C, 1910–1940* (1994).

Cole, Stephanie, "Changes for Mrs. Thornton's Arthur: Patterns of Domestic Service in Washington, DC, 1800–1835," *Social Science History* 15 (1991): 367–79.

Cottingham, Clement, "Gender Shift in Black Communities," *Dissent* 36 (1989): 521–26.

Cunningham, James S., and Nadja Zalokar, "The Economic Progress of Black Women, 1940–1980: Occupational Distribution and Relative Wages," *Industrial and Labor Relations Review* 45 (1992): 540–55.

Derby, Doris A., *Black Women Basket Makers: A Study of Domestic Economy in Charleston County, South Carolina* (1980).

Dill, Bonnie Thornton, *Across the Boundaries of Race and Class: An Exploration of Work and Family among Black Female Domestic Servants* (1994).

Etter-Lewis, Gwendolyn, "Hard Times and Strong Women: African-American Women's Oral Narratives," *Oral History Review* 19 (1991): 89–97.

Fehn, Bruce, "African-American Women and the Struggle for Equality in the Meatpacking Industry, 1940–1960," *Journal of Women's History* 10 (1998): 45–69.

Figart, Deborah M., and Ellen Mutari, "Gender Segmentation of Craft Workers by Race in the 1970's and 1980's," *Review of Radical Political Economics* 25 (1993): 50–66.

Foster, Craig L., "Tarnished Angels: Prostitution in Storyville, New Orleans, 1900–1910," *Louisiana History* 31 (1990): 387–97.

Fosu, Augustin Kwasi, "Explaining Post-1964 Earnings Gains by Black Women: Race or Sex?" *Review of Black Political Economy* 15 (1987): 41–55.

——— "Trends in Relative Earnings Gains by Black Women: Implications for the Future," *Review of Black Political Economy* 17 (1988): 31–45.

Frisch, Paul A., "'Gibraltar of Unionism': Women, Blacks, and the Anti-Chinese Movement in Butte, Montana, 1880–1900," *Southwest Economy and Society* 6 (1984): 3–13.

Fultz, Michael, "African-American Teachers in the South, 1890–1940: Growth, Feminization, and Salary Discrimination," *Teachers College Record* 96 (1995): 544–68.

Gabin, Nancy, "'They Have Placed a Penalty on Womanhood': Women Auto Workers in Detroit-Area UAW Locals, 1945–1947," *Feminist Studies* 8 (1982): 373–98.

Geschwender, James A., and Rita Carroll-Seguin, "Exploding the Myth of African-American Progress," *Signs* 15 (1990): 285–99.

Glenn, Evelyn Nakano, "From Servitude to Service Work: Historical Continuities in the Racial Division of Paid Reproductive Labor," *Signs* 18 (1992): 1–43.

Goldin, Claudia, "Female Labor Force Participation: The Origin of Black and White Differences, 1870 and 1880," *Journal of Economic History* 37 (1977): 87–108.

Gray, Brenda Clegg, *Black Female Domestics during the Depression in New York City, 1930–1940* (1993).

Green, Venus, "Race and Technology: African American Women in the Bell System, 1945–1980," *Technology and Culture* [Supplement] 36 (1995): S101-S143.

Gregory, Chester W., *Women in Defense Work during World War II: An Analysis of the Labor Problem and Women's Rights* (1974).

Griffin, Jean T., "West African and Black Working Women: Historical and Contemporary Comparisons," *Journal of Black Psychology* 8 (1982): 55–74.

Hagy, James W., "Black Business Women in Antebellum Charleston," *Journal of Negro History* 72 (1987): 42–44.

Haiken, Elizabeth, "'The Lord Helps Those Who Help Themselves': Black Laundresses in Little Rock, Arkansas, 1917–1921," *Arkansas Historical Quarterly* 49 (1990): 20–50.

Harley, Sharon, "For the Good of Family and Race: Gender, Work, and Domestic Roles in the Black Community, 1880–1930," *Signs* 15 (1990): 336–49.

——— "When Your Work is Not Who You Are: The Development of a Working-Class Consciousness among Afro-American Women," in Noralee Frankel and Nancy S. Dye, ed., *Gender, Class, Race, and Reform in the Progressive Era* (1991): 42–55.

Helmbold, Lois Rita, "Beyond the Family Economy: Black and White Working-Class Women during the Great Depression," *Feminist Studies* 13 (1987): 629–55.

——— "Downward Occupational Mobility during the Great Depression: Urban Black and White Working Class Women," *Labor History* 29 (1988): 135–72.

Higginbotham, Elizabeth, "Black Professional Women: Job Ceilings and Employment Sectors," in Maxine Baca Zinn and Bonnie Thornton Dill, ed., *Women of Color in U.S. Society* (1994): 113–31.

Hilton, Kathleen C., "'Both in the Field, Each with a Plow': Race and Gender in USDA Policy, 1907–1927," in Virginia Bernhard, Betty Brandon, Elizabeth Fox-Genovese, Theda Perdue and Elizabeth Hayes Turner, ed., *Hidden Histories of Women in the New South* (1994): 114–33.

Hine, Darlene Clark, ed., *Black Women in the Nursing Profession: A Documentary History* (1985).

Hine, Darlene Clark, *Black Women in White: Racial Conflict and Cooperation in the Nursing Profession, 1890–1950* (1989).

Hunter, Tera W., "Domination and Resistance: The Politics of Wage Household Labor in New South Atlanta," *Labor History* 34 (1993): 205–20.

——— *To 'Joy My Freedom: Southern Black Women's Lives and Labors after the Civil War* (1997).

Janiewski, Dolores E., *Sisterhood Denied: Race, Gender, and Class in a New South Community* (1985).

——— "Sisters under Their Skins: Southern Working Women, 1880–1915," in Joanne V. Hawks and Sheila L. Skemp, ed., *Sex, Race, and the Role of Women in the South* (1983): 13–35.

——— *Subversive Sisterhood: Black Women and Unions in the Southern Tobacco Industry* (1984).

John, Daphne, and Beth Anne Shelton, "The Production of Gender Among Black and White Women and Men: The Case of Household Labor," *Sex Roles: A Journal of Research* 36 (1997): 171–94.

Johnson, Whittington B., "Free African-American Women in Savannah, 1800–1860: Affluence and Autonomy amid Adversity," *Georgia Historical Quarterly* 76 (1992): 260–83.

Jones, Beverly W., "Race, Sex, and Class: Black Female Tobacco Workers in Durham, North Carolina, 1920–1940 and the Development of Female Consciousness," *Feminist Studies* 10 (1984): 441–51.

Jones, Jacqueline, *Labor of Love, Labor of Sorrow: Black Women, Work, and the Family, from Slavery to the Present* (1985).

——— "The Political Implications of Black and White Women's Work in the South, 1890–1965," in Louise A. Tilly and Patricia Gurin, ed., *Women, Politics, and Change* (1990): 108–29.

Katzman, David M., *Seven Days a Week: Women and Domestic Service in Industrializing America* (1978).

Kilson, Marion, "Black Women in the Professions, 1890–1970," *Monthly Labor Review* 100 (1977): 38–41.

King, Mary C., "Black Women's Labor Market Status: Occupational Segregation in the United States and Great Britain," *The Review of Black Political Economy* 24 (1995): 23–43.

Klaczynska, Barbara, "Why Women Work: A Comparison of Various Groups—Philadelphia, 1910–1930," *Labor History* 17 (1976): 73–87.

Langhorne, O., "Domestic Service in the South," *American Journal of Social Science* 39 (1901): 169.

Leashore, Bogart R., "Black Female Workers: Live-in Domestics in Detroit, Michigan, 1860–1880," *Phylon* 45 (1984): 111–20.

Leonard, Jonathan S., "Women and Affirmative Action," *Journal of Economic Perspectives* 3 (1989): 61–75.

Lewis, Gail, "Situated Voices: 'Black Women's Experience' and Social Work," *Feminist Review* 53 (1996): 24–57.

Mabee, Carleton, "Sojourner Truth Fights Dependence on Government: Moves Freed Slaves off Welfare in Washington to Jobs in Upstate New York," *Afro-Americans in New York Life and History* 14 (1990): 7–26.

Mack, Kibibi Voloria C., *Parlor Ladies and Ebony Drudges: African American Women, Class, and Work in a South Carolina Community* (1999).

Malveaux, Julianne, "The Economic Interests of Black and White Women: Are They Similar?" *The Review of Black Political Economy* 14 (1985): 5–27.

Mann, Susan A., "Slavery, Sharecropping, and Sexual Inequality," *Signs* 14 (1989): 774–98.

Marks, Carole C., "The Bone and Sinew of the Race: Black Women, Domestic Service and Labor Migration," *Marriage and Family Review* 19 (1993): 149–74.

Martin, Susan E., "'Outsider within' the Station House: The Impact of Race and Gender on Black Women Police," *Social Problems* 41 (1994): 383–400.

Moses, Yolanda T., "Black American Women and Work: Historical and Contemporay Strategies for Empowerment—II," *Women's Studies International Forum* 8 (1985): 351–59.

Palmer, Phyllis M., *Domesticity and Dirt: Housewives and Domestic Servants in the United States, 1920–1945* (1989).

Pleck, Elizabeth H., "A Mother's Wages: Income Earning among Married Italian and Black Women, 1896–1911," in Nancy F. Cott and Elizabeth H. Pleck, ed., *A Heritage of Her Own: Toward A New Social History of American Women* (1979): 367–92.

Quester, Aline O., and William H. Greene, "The Labor Market Experience of Black and White Wives in the Sixties and Seventies," *Social Science Quarterly* 66 (1985): 854–66.

Rapport, Sara, "The Freedmen's Bureau as a Legal Agent for Black Men and Women in Georgia: 1865–1868," *Georgia Historical Quarterly* 73 (1989): 26–53.

Rodgers, Harrell R., Jr., "Black Americans and the Feminization of Poverty: The Intervening Effects of Unemployment," *Journal of Black Studies* 17 (1987): 402–17.

Schwalm, Leslie A., *A Hard Fight For We: Women's Transition from Slavery to Freedom in Lowcountry South Carolina* (1997).

———— "'Sweet Dreams of Freedom': Freedwomen's Reconstruction of Life and Labor in Lowcountry South Carolina," *Journal of Women's History* 9 (1997): 9–38.

Schweninger, Loren, "Property-Owning Free African-American Women in the South, 1800–1870," *Journal of Women's History* 1 (1990): 13–44.

Shammas, Carole, "Black Women's Work and the Evolution of Plantation Society in Virginia," *Labor History* 26 (1985): 5–28.

Shaw, Stephanie J., *What a Woman Ought To Be and To Do: Black Professional Women Workers during the Jim Crow Era* (1996).

Sims-Wood, Janet L., *Black Women in the Employment Sector* (1979).

Smith, Eleanor, "Black American Women and Work: A Historical Review, 1619–1920," *Women's Studies International Forum* 8 (1985): 343–49.

Smith, Elsie J., "The Career Development of Young Black Females: The Forgotten Group," *Youth and Society* 12 (1981): 277–312.

Smith, Shelley A., "Sources of Earnings Inequality in the Black and White Female Labor Forces," *Sociological Quarterly* 32 (1991): 117–38.

Spaights, Ernest, and Ann Whitaker, "Black Women in the Workforce: A New Look at an Old Problem," *Journal of Black Studies* 25 (1995): 283–96.

Staupers, Mabel Keaton, *No Time for Prejudice: A Story of the Integration of Negroes in Nursing in the United States* (1961).

Swain, Martha H., "A New Deal for Women: Gender and Race in Women's Work Relief," in Christie Anne Farnham, ed., *Women of the American South: A Multicultural Reader* (1997): 241–57.

Tucker, Susan, "A Complex Bond: Southern Black Domestic Workers and Their White Employers," *Frontiers* 9 (1987): 6–13.

———— *Telling Memories among Southern Women: Domestic Workers and Their Employers in the Segregated South* (1988).

United States Women's Bureau, *Negro Women War Workers,* ed. Kathryn Blood (1945).

U.S. Department of Labor, "Negro Women in Skilled Defense Jobs," *Monthly Labor Review* 57 (1943): 1953.

Walker, Melissa, "Home Extension Work among African American Farm Women in East Tennessee," *Agricultural History* 70 (1996): 487–502.

Wallace, Phyllis Ann, *Black Women in the Labor Force* (1980).

———— *Pathways to Work: Unemployment among Black Teenage Females* (1974).

Wood, Betty, *Women's Work, Men's Work: The Informal Slave Economies of Lowcountry Georgia* (1995).

Woodson, Carter G., "The Negro Washerwoman, a Vanishing Figure," *Journal of Negro History* 15 (1930): 269–77.

Yoder, Janice D., and Patricia Aniakudo, "'Outsider Within' the Firehouse: Subordination and Difference in the Social Interaction of African American Women Firefighters," *Gender and Society* 11 (1997): 324–41.

25.13 SCIENCE AND TECHNOLOGY

Green, Venus, "Race and Technology: African American Women in the Bell System, 1945–1980," *Technology and Culture* [Supplement] 36 (1995): S101–S143.

Ives, Patricia Carter, *Creativity and Inventions: The Genius of Afro-Americans and Women in the United States and Their Patents* (1987).

Sluby, Patricia Carter, "Black Women and Inventions," *Sage* 6 (1989): 33–35.

Warren, Wini, *Black Women Scientists in the United States* (1999).

25.14 MEDICINE AND HEALTH

Axelsen, Diana E., "Women as Victims of Medical Experimentation: J. Marion Sims' Surgery on Slave Women, 1845–1850," *Sage* 2 (1985): 10–12.

Bair, Barbara, and Susan E. Cayleff, ed., *Wings of Gauze: Women of Color and the Experience of Health and Illness* (1993).

Campbell, John, "Work, Pregnancy, and Infant Mortality among Southern Slaves," *Journal of Interdisciplinary History* 14 (1984): 793–812.

Carnegie, Mary Elizabeth, *The Path We Tread: Blacks in Nursing Worldwide, 1854–1994* (3d ed., 1995).

Carson, Carolyn Leonard, "And the Results Showed Promise . . . Physicians, Childbirth, and Southern Black Migrant Women, 1916–1930: Pittsburgh as a Case Study," *Journal of American Ethnic History* 14 (1994): 32–64.

Clinton, Myrtle M., "Black Psychiatric Nurses: Historical Perspectives, 1964 to 1984," *Journal of Black Studies* 24 (1993): 213–31.

Collins, Catherine Fisher, ed., *African-American Women's Health and Social Issues* (1996).

Cutright, Phillips, and Edward Shorter, "The Effects of Health on the Completed Fertility of Non-White and White U.S. Women Born from 1867 through 1935," *Journal of Social History* 13 (1979): 191–218.

Duelberg, Sonja I., "Preventive Health Behavior among Black and White Women in Urban and Rural Areas," *Social Science and Medicine* 34 (1992): 191–99.

Ferguson, Earline Rae, "The Woman's Improvement Club of Indianapolis: Black Women Pioneers in Tuberculosis Work, 1903–1938," *Indiana Magazine of History* 84 (1988): 237–61.

Fraser, Gertrude Jacinta, *African American Midwifery in the South: Dialogues of Birth, Race, and Memory* (1998).

Gage, Nina D., and Alma C. Hampt, "Some Observations on Negro Nursing in the South," *Public Health Nursing* 24 (1932): 674–80.

Gee, Ellen M., and Jean E. Veevers, "Increasing Sex Mortality Differentials among Black Americans, 1950–1978," *Phylon* 46 (1985): 162–75.

Goodson, Martia Graham, "Medical-Botanical Contributions of African Slave Women to American Medicine," *Journal of Black Studies* 11 (1987): 198–203.

Hammonds, Evelynn, "Missing Persons: African American Women, AIDS, and the History of Disease," *Radical America* 24 (1990): 7–23.

Headen, Alvin E., Jr., and Sandra W. Headen, "General Health Conditions and Medical Insurance Issues Concerning Black Women," *Review of Black Political Economy* 14 (1985–86): 183–97.

Hine, Darlene Clark, *Black Women in White: Racial Conflict and Cooperation in the Nursing Profession, 1890–1950* (1989).

——— "Co-Laborers in the Work of the Lord: Nineteenth-Century Black Women Physicians," in Ruth Abrams, ed., *"Send Us a Lady Physician": Women Doctors in America, 1835–1930* (1985): 107–20.

Johnson, Michael P., "Smothered Slave Infants: Were Slave Mothers at Fault?" *Journal of Southern History* 47 (1981): 493–520.

Kiple, Kenneth F., and Virginia H. Kiple, "Slave Child Mortality: Some Nutritional Answers to a Perennial Puzzle," *Journal of Social History* 10 (1977): 284–309.

Larson, Edward J., *Sex, Race, and Science: Eugenics in the Deep South* (1995).

Markowitz, Gerald, and David Rosner, *Children, Race, and Power: Kenneth and Mamie Clark's Northside Center* (1996).

Matthews, Holly F., "Killing the Medical Self-Help Tradition among African Americans: The Case of Lay Midwifery in North Carolina, 1912–1983," in Hans A. Baer and Yvonne Jones, ed., *African-Americans in the South: Issues of Race, Class, and Gender* (1992): 60–78.

McFalls, Joseph A., Jr., and George S. Masnick, "Birth Control and the Fertility of the U.S. Black Population, 1880 to 1980," *Journal of Family History* 6 (1981): 89–106.

Moldow, Gloria, *Women Doctors in Gilded-Age Washington: Race, Gender, and Professionalization* (1987).

Mosley, Marie O. Pitts, "Satisfied to Carry the Bag: Three Black Community Health Nurses' Contributions to Health Care Reform, 1900–1937," *Nursing History Review* 4 (1996): 65–82.

Savitt, Todd L., "Smothering and Overlaying of Virginia Slave Children: A Suggested Explanation," *Bulletin of the History of Medicine* 49 (1975): 400–04.

——— "The Use of Blacks for Medical Experimentation and Demonstration in the Old South," *Journal of Southern History* 48 (1982): 331–48.

Seraile, William, "Susan McKinney Steward: New York State's First African-American Woman Physician," *Afro-Americans in New York Life and History* 9 (1985): 27–44.

Smith, Elsie J., "Mental Health and Service Delivery Systems for Black Women," *Journal of Black Studies* 12 (1981): 126–41.

Smith, Susan L., *Sick and Tired of Being Sick and Tired: Black Women's Health Activism in America, 1890–1950* (1995).

Steckel, Richard H., "Birth Weights and Infant Mortality among American Slaves," *Explorations in Economic History* 23 (1986): 173–98.

Thompson, Becky Wangsgaard, "'A Way Outa No Way': Eating Problems among African-American, Latina, and White Women," *Gender and Society* 6 (1992): 546–61.

Trussel, James, and Richard Steckel, "The Age of Slaves at Menarche and Their First Birth," *Journal of Interdisciplinary History* 8 (1978): 477–505.

Young, Carlene, "Psychodynamics of Coping and Survival of the African-American Female in a Changing World," *Journal of Black Studies* 20 (1989): 208–23.

26 *Geographical Areas*

26.1 REGIONAL STUDIES

26.1.1 Midwest

Cashin, Joan E., "Black Families in the Old Northwest," *Journal of the Early Republic* 15 (1995): 449–75.

Cross, Jasper W., ed., "John Miller's Missionary Journal, 1816–1817: Religious Conditions in the South and Midwest," *Journal of Presbyterian History* 47 (1969): 226–61.

Davis, David Brion, "The Significance of Excluding Slavery from the Old Northwest in 1787," *Indiana Magazine of History* 84 (1988): 75–89.

Finkelman, Paul R., "Slavery and the Northwest Ordinance: A Study in Ambiguity," *Journal of the Early Republic* 6 (1986): 343–70.

Hine, Darlene Clark, "Black Migration to the Urban Midwest: The Gender Dimension, 1915–1945," in Joe William Trotter, Jr., ed., *The Great Migration in Historical Perspective: New Dimensions of Race, Class, and Gender* (1991): 127–46.

———— "Rape and the Inner Lives of Black Women in the Middle West: Preliminary Thoughts on the Culture of Dissemblance," *Signs* 14 (1989): 912–20.

Holsoe, Svend E., "A Portrait of a Black Midwestern Family during the Early Nineteenth Century: Edward James Roye and His Parents," *Liberian Studies Journal* 3 (1970–1971): 41–52.

Middleton, Stephen, *The Black Laws in the Old Northwest: A Documentary History* (1993).

Murphy, Marjorie, "Prairie Politics: Black Life in the Midwest, 1890–1940," *Reviews in American History* 13 (1985): 251–56.

Onuf, Peter S., "From Constitution to Higher Law: The Reinterpretation of the Northwest Ordinance," *Ohio History* 94 (1985): 5–33.

Voegeli, V. Jacque, *Free But Not Equal: The Midwest and the Negro during the Civil War* (1967).

26.1.2 North

Bailey, Ronald, "The Slave(ry) Trade and the Development of Capitalism in the United States: The Textile Industry in New England," *Social Science History* 14 (1990): 373–414.

Bell, Howard Holman, "Expressions of Negro Militancy in the North, 1840–1860," *Journal of Negro History* 45 (1960): 11–20.

———— "Free Negroes in the North, 1830–1835: A Study in National Cooperation," *Journal of Negro Education* 26 (1957): 447–55.

Coben, Stanley, "Northeastern Business and Radical Reconstruction: A Re-Examination," *Mississippi Valley Historical Review* 46 (1959): 67–90.

Cottrol, Robert, ed., *From African to Yankee: Black Narratives in Antebellum New England* (1997).

Fauset, Arthur Huff, *Black Gods of the Metropolis: Negro Religious Cults of the Urban North* (1944).

Finkelman, Paul, *Slavery in the North and the West* (1989).

Fishel, Leslie H., Jr., "The Negro in Northern Politics, 1870–1900," *Mississippi Valley Historical Review* 42 (1955): 466–89.

———— "Repercussions of Reconstruction: The Northern Negro, 1870–1883," *Civil War History* 14 (1968): 325–45.

Frazier, Edward Franklin, "Some Effects of the Depression on the Negro in Northern Cities," *Science and Society* 2 (1938): 489–99.

Gosnell, Harold Foote, "The Negro Vote in Northern Cities," *National Municipal Review* 30 (1941): 264–78.

Greene, Lorenzo Johnston, *The Negro in Colonial New England, 1620–1776* (1942).

Grossman, Lawrence, *The Democratic Party and the Negro: Northern and National Politics, 1868–92* (1976).

Henri, Florette, *Black Migration: Movement North, 1900–1920* (1975).

Horton, James O., and Lois Horton, *In Hope of Liberty: Culture, Community and Protest among Northern Free Blacks, 1700–1860* (1997).

Jones, Jacqueline, "Southern Diaspora: Origins of the Northern 'Underclass,'" in Michael B. Katz, ed., *The 'Underclass' Debate: Views from History* (1993): 27–54.

Kennedy, Louise Venable, *The Negro Peasant Turns Cityward: Effects of Recent Migrations to Northern Centers* (1930).

Litwack, Leon F., "The Abolitionist Dilemma: The Anti-Slavery Movement and the Northern Negro," *New England Quarterly* 34 (1961): 50–73.

———— *North of Slavery: The Negro in the Free States, 1790–1860* (1961).

Marullo, Sam, "The Migration of Blacks to the North, 1911–1918," *Journal of Black Studies* 15 (1985): 291–306.

Miller, Kelly, "Education of the Negro in the North," *Educational Review* 62 (1921): 232–38.

Mohr, James C., ed., *Radical Republicans in the North: State Politics during Reconstruction* (1976).

Mohraz, Judy Jolley, *The Separate Problem: Case Studies of Black Education in the North, 1900–1930* (1979).

Pechstein, L. A., "The Problem of Negro Education in Northern and Border Cities," *Elementary School Journal* 30 (1929): 192–99.

Peterson, Carla L., *Doers of the Word: African-American Women Speakers and Writers in the North (1830–1880)* (1998).

Piersen, William Dillon, *Black Yankees: The Development of an Afro-American Subculture in Eighteenth-Century New England* (1988).

Reidy, Joseph P., "'Negro Election Day' and Black Community Life in New England, 1750–1860," *Marxist Perspectives* 1 (1978): 102–17.

Scheiner, Seth M., "The Negro Church and the Northern City, 1890–1930," in William G. Shade, and Roy C. Herrenkohl, ed., *Seven on Black: Reflections of the Negro Experience in America* (1969): 92–116.

Slaughter, Thomas Paul, *Bloody Dawn: The Christian Riot and Racial Violence in the Antebellum North* (1991).

Slotkin, Richard, "Narratives of Negro Crime in New England, 1675–1800," *American Quarterly* 25 (1973): 3–31.

Smith, Edward D., *Climbing Jacob's Ladder: The Rise of Black Churches in Eastern American Cities, 1740–1877* (1988).

Sterling, Dorothy, comp., *Speak Out in Thunder Tones: Letters and Other Writings by Black Northerners, 1787–1865* (1973).

Taulbert, Clifton L., *The Last Train North* (1995).

Trotter, Joe William, Jr., "Blacks in the Urban North: The 'Underclass Question' in Historical Perspective," in Michael B. Katz, ed., *The 'Underclass' Debate: Views from History* (1993): 55–81.

Tyack, David B., "Growing up Black: Perspectives on the History of Education in Northern Ghettos," *History of Education Quarterly* 9 (1969): 287–97.

Wade, Melvin, "'Shining in Borrowed Plumage': Affirmation of Community in the Black Coronation Festivals of New England (c. 1750–c. 1850)," *Western Folklore* 40 (1981): 211–31.

White, Shane, "Impious Prayers: Elite and Popular Attitudes toward Blacks and Slavery in the Middle-Atlantic States, 1783–1810," *New York History* 67 (1986): 260–83.

———— "'It Was a Proud Day': African Americans, Festivals, and Parades in the North, 1741–1834," *Journal of American History* 81 (1994): 13–50.

Zilversmit, Arthur, *The First Emancipation: The Abolition of Slavery in the North* (1967).

26.1.3 South

Abbott, Richard H., *The Republican Party and the South, 1855–1877: The First Southern Strategy* (1986).

Abrahams, Roger D., *Singing the Master: The Emergence of African American Culture in the Plantation South* (1992).

Adamson, Christopher R., "Punishment after Slavery: Southern State Penal Systems, 1865–1890," *Social Problems* 30 (1983): 555–69.

Aiken, Charles S., "New Settlement Patterns of Rural Blacks in the American South," *Geographical Review* 75 (1985): 383–404.

Alho, Olli, *The Religion of the Slaves: A Study of the Religious Tradition and Behaviour of Plantation Slaves in the United States, 1830–1865* (1976).

Anderson, James D., *The Education of Blacks in the South, 1860–1935* (1988).

———— "Northern Foundations and the Shaping of Southern Black Rural Education, 1902–1935," *History of Education Quarterly* 18 (1978): 371–96.

Anderson, Jon T., "Royall Tyler's Reaction to Slavery and the South," *Vermont History* 42 (1974): 296–310.

Andrew, Mildred Gwin, *The Men and Mills: A History of the Southern Textile Industry* (1987).

Andrews, Sidney, *The South since the War* (1866).

Angell, Stephen Ward, *Bishop Henry McNeal Turner and African-American Religion in the South* (1992).

Ayers, Edward L., *The Promise of the New South: Life After Reconstruction* (1992).

———— *Vengeance and Justice: Crime and Punishment in the Nineteenth-Century American South* (1984).

Baggett, James A., "Origins of Upper South Scalawag Leadership," *Civil War History* 29 (1983): 53–73.

Bailey, Kenneth K., "Protestantism and Afro-Americans in the Old South: Another Look," *Journal of Southern History* 41 (1975): 451–72.

Baker, Scott, "Testing Equality: The National Teacher Examination and the NAACP's Legal Campaign to Equalize Teachers' Salaries in the South, 1936–1963," *History of Education Quarterly* 35 (1995): 49–64.

Bancroft, Frederic, *Slave Trading in the Old South* (1931).

Bardaglio, Peter W., "Rape and the Law in the Old South: Calculated to Excite Indignation in Every Heart," *Journal of Southern History* 60 (1994): 749–72.

Barnes, Kenneth C., *Who Killed John Clayton?: Political Violence and the Emergence of the New South, 1861–1893* (1998).

Bartley, Numan V., *The New South, 1945–1980* (1995).

———— *The Rise of Massive Resistance: Race and Politics in the South during the 1950s* (1969).

Beardsley, Edward H., "Desegregating Southern Medicine: 1945–1970," *International Social Science Review* 71 (1996): 37–54.

———— *A History of Neglect: Health Care for Blacks and Mill Workers in the Twentieth-Century South* (1987).

Belknap, Michal R., *Federal Law and Southern Order: Racial Violence and Constitutional Conflict in the Post-Brown South* (1987).

Bellamy, Donald D., "Henry A. Hunt and Black Agricultural Leadership of the New South," *Journal of Negro History* 60 (1975): 475–76.

Benedict, Michael L., "The Problem of Constitutionism and Constitutional Liberty in the Reconstruction South," in Kermit L. Hall, and James W. Ely, Jr., ed., *An Uncertain Tradition: Constitutionalism and the History of the South* (1990): 225–49.

———— "Southern Democrats in the Crisis of 1876–1877: A Reconsideration of Reunion and Reaction," *Journal of Southern History* 46 (1980): 489–524.

Berglund, Abraham, Frank Traver De Vyver, and George Talmage Staenes, *Labor in the Industrial South: A Survey of Wages and Living Conditions in Three Major Industries of the New Industrial South* (1930).

Berlin, Ira, "The Terrain of Freedom: The Struggle over the Meaning of Free Labor in the U.S. South," *History Workshop Journal* 22 (1986): 108–30.

————, ed., *The Wartime Genesis of Free Labor: The Lower South* (1990).

Berlin, Ira, and Herbert G. Gutman, "Natives and Immigrants, Free Men and Slaves: Urban Workingmen in the Antebellum South," *American Historical Review* 88 (1983): 1175–1200.

Bernhard, Virgina, Betty Brandon, Elizabeth Fox-Genovese, Theda Perdue, and Elizabeth Hayes Turner, ed., *Hidden Histories of Women in the New South* (1994).

Biles, Roger, "The Urban South in the Great Depression," *Journal of Southern History* 56 (1990): 71–100.

Black, Earl, *Southern Governors and Civil Rights: Racial Segregation as a Campaign Issue in the Second Reconstruction* (1976).

Black, Paul V., "The Knights of Labor and the South, 1873–1893," *Southern Quarterly* 1 (1963): 201–12.

Blassingame, John W., "The Recruitment of Colored Troops in Kentucky, Maryland, and Missouri, 1863–65," *Historian* 29 (1967): 533–45.

———— *The Slave Community: Plantation Life in the Antebellum South* (1972).

Bodenhamer, David J., and James W. Ely, Jr., ed., *Ambivalent Legacy: A Legal History of the South* (1984).

Boles, John B., *Black Southerners, 1619–1869* (1983).

————, ed., *Masters and Slaves in the House of the Lord: Race and Religion in the American South, 1740–1870* (1988).

Bolsterli, Margaret Jones, "'The Very Food We Eat': A Speculation on the Nature of Southern Culture," *Southern Humanities* 16 (1982): 119–27.

Boney, F. N., "Doctor Thomas Hamilton: Two Views of a Gentleman of the Old South," *Phylon* 28 (1967): 288–92.

———— "Southern Blacks," *Centennial Review* 16 (1972): 384–93.

Breeden, James O., ed., *Advice among Masters: The Ideal in Slave Management in the Old South* (1980).

Breen, William J., "Black Women and the Great War: Mobilization and Reform in the South," *Journal of Southern History* 44 (1978): 421–40.

Brown, D. Clayton, "Health of Farm Children in the South, 1900–1950," *Agricultural History* 53 (1979): 170–87.

Brundage, W. Fitzhugh, ed., *Under Sentence of Death: Lynching in the South* (1997).

Burton, Orville Vernon, and Robert C. McMath, Jr., ed., *Toward a New South?: Studies in Post-Civil War Southern Communities* (1982).

Campbell, Clarice T., *Civil Rights Chronicle: Letters from the South* (1997).

Campbell, Edward D. C., Jr., and Kym S. Rice, ed., *Before Freedom Came: African-American Life in the Antebellum South: To Accompany an Exhibition Organized by the Museum of the Confederacy* (1991).

Campbell, Rex R., Daniel M. Johnson, and Gary Stangler, "Return Migration of Black People to the South," *Rural Sociology* 39 (1974): 514–28.

Carawan, Guy, and Candie Carawan, comp., *We Shall Overcome! Songs of the Southern Freedom Movement* (1963).

Carter, Alice E., "Segregation and Integration in the Appalachian Coalfields: McDowell County Responds to the Brown Decision," *West Virginia History* 54 (1995): 78–104.

Cartwright, Thomas Y., "'Better Confederates Did Not Live': Black Southerners in Nathan Bedford Forrest's *Commands*," *Journal of Confederate History* 11 (1994): 94–120.

Casdorph, Paul D., *Republicans, Negroes, and Progressives in the South, 1912–1916* (1981).

Cell, John W., *The Highest Stage of White Supremacy: The Origins of Segregation in South Africa and the American South* (1982).

Clifton, James M., "Twilight Comes to the Rice Kingdom: Postbellum Rice Culture on the South At-
    lantic Coast," *Georgia Historical Quarterly* 62 (1978): 146–54.

Clinton, Catherine, *The Plantation Mistress: Women's World in the Old South* (1982).

Close, Stacey K., *Elderly Slaves of the Plantation South* (1997).

Cohen, William, "Negro Involuntary Servitude in the South, 1865–1940: A Prelminary Analysis,"
    Journal of Southern History 42 (1976): 31–60.

Conway, Cecelia, *African Banjo Echoes in Appalachia: A Study of Folk Traditions* (1995).

Courtwright, David T., "The Hidden Epidemic: Opiate Addiction and Cocaine Use in the South,
    1860–1920," *Journal of Southern History* 49 (1983): 57–72.

Couto, Richard A., *Ain't Gonna Let Nobody Turn Me Round: The Pursuit of Racial Justice in the Rural
    South* (1991).

Cox, LaWanda, and John H. Cox, ed., *Reconstruction, the Negro, and the New South* (1973).

Cross, Jasper W., ed., "John Miller's Missionary Journal, 1816–1817: Religious Conditions in the
    South and Midwest," *Journal of Presbyterian History* 47 (1969): 226–61.

Dabney, Thomas L., "Southern Labor and the Negro," *Opportunity: A Journal of Negro Life* 7 (1929):
    345–46.

Daniel, Pete, *The Shadow of Slavery: Peonage in the South, 1901–1969* (1972).

Davis, Jack E., "Changing Places: Slave Movements in the South," *Historian* 55 (1993): 656–76.

Davis, Robert Ralph, Jr., "Buchanian Espionage: A Report on Illegal Slave Trading in the South in
    1859," *Journal of Southern History* 37 (1971): 271–78.

Dennett, John Richard, *The South as It Is: 1865–1866*, ed. Henry M. Christman (1965).

Dent, Thomas C., Richard Schechner, and Gilbert Moses, ed., *The Free Southern Theater by the Free
    Southern Theater* (1969).

——— *Southern Journey: A Return to the Civil Rights Movement* (1997).

Dew, Charles B., "David Ross and the Oxford Iron Works: A Study of Industrial Slavery in the Early
    Nineteenth Century South," *William and Mary Quarterly* 31 (1974): 189–224.

——— "Disciplining Slave Ironworkers in the Antebellum South: Coercion, Conciliation, and Ac-
    commodation," *American Historical Review* 79 (1974): 383–418.

Dillon, Merton Lynn, *Slavery Attacked: Southern Slaves and Their Allies, 1619–1865* (1990).

Dodd, Donald B., and Wynelle S. Dodd, *Historical Statistics of the South, 1790–1970: A Compilation of
    State-Level Census Statistics for the Sixteen States of Alabama, Arkansas, Delaware, Florida, Geor-
    gia, Kentucky, Louisiana, Maryland, Mississippi, North Carolina, Oklahoma, South Carolina, Ten-
    nessee, Texas, Virginia, West Virginia* (1973).

Doherty, Herbert J., Jr., "Voices of Protest From the New South, 1875–1910," *Mississippi Valley Histori-
    cal Review* 42 (1955): 45–66.

Dollard, John, *Caste and Class in a Southern Town* (1937).

Doyle, Bertram Wilbur, *The Etiquette of Race Relations in the South: A Study in Social Control* (1937).

Eaton, Clement, "Slave-Hiring in the Upper South: A Step toward Freedom," *Mississippi Valley Histori-
    cal Review* 46 (1960): 663–78.

Elgie, Robert A., "Industrialization and Racial Inequality within the American South, 1950–1970," *So-
    cial Science Quarterly* 61 (1980): 458–72.

Embree, Edwin Rogers, "Our Southern Farm System and the School," *Progressive Education* 12 (1935):
    302–08.

Emerson, Thomas I., "Southern Justice in the Thirties," *Civil Liberties Review* 4 (1977): 70–74.

Emery, E. B., *Letters from the South, on the Social, Intellectual, and Moral Conditions of the Colored Peo-
    ple* (1880).

Evans, Arthur S., "The Relationship between Industrialization and White Hostility toward Blacks in
    Southern Cities, 1865–1910," *Urban Affairs Quarterly* 25 (1989): 322–41.

Evans, Maurice, *Black and White in the Southern States* (1915).

Fede, Andrew, "Legitimized Violent Slave Abuse in the American South, 1619–1865: A Case Study of
    Law and Social Change in Six Southern States," *American Journal of Legal History* 29 (1985): 93–
    150.

——— *People without Rights: An Interpretation of the Fundamentals of the Law of Slavery in the U.S.
    South* (1992).

Fickle, James E., "Management Looks at the 'Labor Problem': The Southern Pine Industry during World War I and the Postwar Era," *Journal of Southern History* 40 (1974): 61–76.

Fink, Gary M., and Merle Elwyn Reed, ed., *Essays in Southern Labor History: Selected Papers* (1977).

Finnie, Gordon E., "The Antislavery Movement in the Upper South before 1840," *Journal of Southern History* 35 (1969): 319–42.

Fitzgerald, Michael W., *The Union League Movement in the Deep South: Politics and Agricultural Change during Reconstruction* (1989).

Flanigan, Daniel J., "Criminal Procedure in Slave Trials in the Antebellum South," *Journal of Southern History* 40 (1974): 537–64.

Fligstein, Neil, *Going North: Migration of Blacks and Whites From the South, 1900–1950* (1981).

Forbes, Jack D., "Black Pioneers: The Spanish-Speaking Afro-American of the Southwest," *Phylon* 27 (1966): 233–46.

Fortune, T. Thomas, *Black and White: Land, Labor, and Politics in the South* (1884).

Foster, Helen Bradley, *'New Raiments of Self': African American Clothing in the Antebellum South* (1997).

Foster, Lorn S., "The Voting Rights Act: Black Voting and the New Southern Politics," *Western Journal of Black Studies* 7 (1983): 120–9.

Fox-Genovese, Elizabeth, *Within the Plantation Household: Black and White Women of the Old South* (1988).

Franklin, John Hope, *The Militant South, 1800–1861* (1956).

——— "Slavery and the Martial South," *Journal of Negro History* 37 (1952): 36–53.

Frederickson, Mary, "Four Decades of Change: Black Workers in Southern Textiles, 1941–1981," *Radical America* 16 (1982): 27–44.

Friedman, Lawrence, *The White Savage: Racial Fantasies in the Postbellum South* (1970).

Fultz, Michael, "African-American Teachers in the South, 1890–1940: Growth, Feminization, and Salary Discrimination," *Teachers College Record* 96 (1995): 544–68.

Gage, Nina D., and Alma C. Hampt, "Some Observations on Negro Nursing in the South," *Public Health Nursing* 24 (1932): 674–80.

Garrow, David, *Bearing the Cross: Martin Luther King, Jr., and the Southern Christian Leadership Conference* (1986).

Gates, Paul W., "Federal Land Policy in the South, 1866–1888," *Journal of Southern History* 6 (1940): 303–30.

Genovese, Eugene D., "Black Plantation Preachers in the Slave South," *Louisiana Studies* 11 (1972): 188–214.

——— "Cotton, Slavery and Soil Exhaustion in the Old South," *Cotton History Review* 2 (1961): 3–17.

——— "The Negro Laborer in Africa and the Slave South," *Phylon* 21 (1960): 343–50.

——— "'Our Family, White and Black:' Family and Household in the Southern Slaveholder's World View," in Carol Bleser, ed., *In Joy and In Sorrow: Women, Family, and Marriage in the Victorian South, 1830–1900* (1991): 69–87.

——— *The Political Economy of Slavery: Studies in the Economy and Society of the Slave South* (2d ed., 1989).

——— *Roll, Jordon, Roll: The World the Slaves Made* (1974).

——— "The Significance of the Slave Plantation for Southern Economic Development," *Journal of Southern History* 28 (1962): 422–37.

Genovese, Eugene D., and Elizabeth Fox-Genovese, "The Religious Ideals of Southern Slave Society," *Georgia Historical Quarterly* 70 (1986): 1–16.

Gershenberg, Irving, "The Negro and the Development of White Public Education in the South: Alabama, 1880–1930," *Journal of Negro Education* 39 (1970): 50–59.

Gerteis, Louis S., *From Contraband to Freedman: Federal Policy towards Southern Blacks, 1861–1865* (1973).

Gill, Flora, *Economics and the Black Exodus: An Analysis of Negro Emigration from the Southern United States, 1910–70* (1979).

Glazier, Stephen D., "Mourning in the Afro-Baptist Tradition: A Comparative Study of Religion in the American South and in Trinidad," *Southern Quarterly* 23 (1985): 141–56.

Gleason, Eliza Valeria Atkins, *The Southern Negro and the Public Library: A Study of the Government and Administration of Public Library Service to Negroes in the South* (1941).

Goldfield, David R., *Black, White, and Southern: Race Relations and Southern Culture, 1940 to the Present* (1990).

Goldin, Claudia Dale, *Urban Slavery in the American South, 1820–1860: A Quantitative History* (1976).

Gomez, Michael A., *Exchanging Our Country Marks: The Transformation of African Identities in the Colonial and Antebellum South* (1998).

Goodenow, Ronald K., "Paradox in Progressive Educator Reform: The South and the Education of Blacks during the Depression Years," *Phylon* 39 (1978): 49–65.

Graves, John Temple, "The Southern Negro and the War Crisis," *The Virginia Quarterly Review* 18 (1942): 500–17.

Gray, Lewis Cecil, *History of Agriculture in the Southern United States to 1860* (2 vols., 1933).

Green, Fletcher M., "Northern Missionary Activities in the South, 1846–1861," *Journal of Southern History* 21 (1955): 147–72.

———— "Some Aspects of the Convict Lease System in the Southern States," in Fletcher M. Green, ed., *Essays in Southern History Presented to Joseph Gregoire de Roulhac Hamilton* (1949): 112–23.

Green, Fletcher M., and J. Isaac Copeland, comp., *The Old South* (1980).

Greenberg, Kenneth S., *Honor and Slavery: Lies, Duels, Noses, Masks, Dressing as a Woman, Gifts, Strangers, Humanitarianism, Death, Slave Rebellions, the Pro-Slavery Argument, Baseball, Hunting, and Gambling in the Old South* (1997).

Greene, Lorenzo J., "Economic Conditions among Negroes in the South, 1930, as Seen by an Associate of Dr. Carter G. Woodson," *Journal of Negro History* 64 (1979): 265–73.

Griffin, Larry J., and Robert R. Korstad, "Class as Race and Gender: Making and Breaking a Labor Union in the Jim Crow South," *Social Science History* 19 (1995): 425–54.

Grim, Valerie, "African-American Landlords in the Rural South, 1870–1950: A Profile," *Agricultural History* 72 (1998): 399–416.

Grubbs, Donald H., *Cry from the Cotton: The Southern Tenant Farmers' Union and the New Deal* (1971).

Gutmann, Myron P., and Kenneth H. Fliess, "The Social Context of Child Mortality in the American Southwest," *Journal of Interdisciplinary History* 26 (1996): 589–618.

Guzman, Jessie Parkhurst, *Twenty Years of Court Decisions Affecting Higher Education in the South, 1938–1958* (1960).

Gwin, Minrose C., *Black and White Women of the Old South: The Pelican Sisterhood in American Literature* (1985).

Halasz, Nicholas, *The Rattling Chains: Slave Unrest and Revolt in the Antebellum South* (1966).

Hale, Grace Elizabeth, *Making Whiteness: The Culture of Segregation in the South, 1890–1940* (1998).

Hall, Jacquelyn Dowd, "Partial Truths: Writing Southern Women's History," in Virginia Bernhard, Betty Brandon, Elizabeth Fox-Genovese, and Theda Purdue, ed., *Southern Women: Histories and Identities* (1992): 11–29.

Hall, Tomiko Brown, "The Gentleman's White Supremacist: J. Strom Thurmond, the Dixiecrat Campaign, and the Evolution of Southern Politics," *Southern Historian* 16 (1995): 61–86.

Haller, John S., Jr., "The Negro and the Southern Physician: A Study of Medical and Racial Attitudes, 1800–1860," *Medical History* 16 (1972): 238–253.

Hamblin, Robert W., "The 1965 Southern Literary Festival: A Microcosm of the Civil Rights Movement," *Journal of Mississippi History* 53 (1991): 83–114.

Hamilton, Charles V., *The Bench and the Ballot: Southern Federal Judges and Black Voters* (1973).

Hamilton, Kenneth Marvin, *Black Towns and Profit: Promotion and Development in the Trans-Appalachian West, 1877–1915* (1991).

Harlan, Louis R., *Separate and Unequal: Public School Campaigns and Racism in the Southern Seaboard States, 1901–1915* (1968).

Harris, J. William, ed., *Society and Culture in the Slave South* (1992).

Harris, Trudier, "Adventures in a 'Foreign Country': African American Humor and the South," *Southern Cultures* 1 (1995): 457–65.

Harrison, Suzan, "Black Women in the Nineteenth-Century South," *Mississippi Quarterly* 46 (1993): 285–90.

Harrison, William Pope, comp. and ed., *The Gospel among the Slaves: A Short Account of Missionary Operations among the African Slaves of the Southern States* (1893).

Hart, Albert B., *The Southern South* (1910).

Haws, Robert J., and Derrick A. Bell, ed., *The Age of Segregation: Race Relations in the South, 1890– 1945: Essays* (1978).

Hayden, J. Carleton, "After the War: The Mission and Growth of the Episcopal Church among Blacks in the South, 1865–1877," *Historical Magazine of the Protestant Episcopal Church* 42 (1973): 403– 28.

Hellwig, David J., "Black Attitudes toward Immigrant Labor in the South, 1865–1910," *Filson Club History Quarterly* 54 (1980): 151–68.

Hertz, Hilda, "Unmarried Negro Mothers in Southern Urban Communities," *Social Forces* 23 (1944): 73–79.

Hirshon, Stanley P., *Farewell to the Bloody Shirt: Northern Republicans and the Southern Negro, 1873– 1893* (1962).

Hodes, Martha, *White Women, Black Men: Illicit Sex in the Nineteenth-Century South* (1997).

Honey, Michael, "Operation Dixie: Labor and Civil Rights in the Postwar South," *Mississippi Quarterly* 45 (1992): 439–52.

Hornsby, Alton, comp., *In the Cage: Eyewitness Accounts of the Freed Negro in Southern Society, 1877– 1929* (1971).

Hudson, Hosea, *Black Worker in the Deep South: A Personal Record* (2d ed., 1991).

Hudson, Larry E., Jr., ed., *Working toward Freedom: Slave Society and Domestic Economy in the American South* (1994).

Hughes, C. Alvin, "A New Agenda for the South: The Role and Influence of the Highlander Folk School, 1953–1961," *Phylon* 46 (1985): 242–50.

——— "We Demand our Rights: The Southern Negro Youth Congress, 1937–1949," *Phylon* 48 (1987): 38–50.

Hume, Richard L., "The Membership of the Virginia Constitutional Convention of 1867–1868: A Study of the Beginnings of Congressional Reconstruction in the Upper South," *Virginia Magazine of History and Biography* 86 (1978): 461–84.

Hunter, Frances L., "Slave Society on the Southern Plantation," *Journal of Negro History* 7 (1922): 1– 10.

Ingham, John N., "African-American Business Leaders in the South, 1810–1945: Business Success, Community Leadership and Racial Protest," *Business and Economic History* 22 (1993): 262–72.

Irwin, James C., "Farmers and Laborers: A Note on Black Occupations in the Postbellum South," *Agricultural History* 64 (1900): 53–60.

Jacoway, Elizabeth, and David R. Colburn, ed., *Southern Businessmen and Desegregation* (1982).

James, John A., "Financial Underdevelopment in the Postbellum South," *Journal of Interdisciplinary History* 11 (1981): 443–54.

Jaynes, Gerald David, *Branches without Roots: Genesis of the Black Working Class in the American South, 1862–1882* (1986).

Jenkins, William Sumner, *Pro-Slavery Thought in the Old South* (1935).

Johnson, Alonzo, and Paul T. Jersild, ed., *'Ain't Gonna Lay My 'Ligion Down': African-American Religion in the South* (1996).

Johnson, Charles Spurgeon, *Growing up in the Black Belt: Negro Youth in the Rural South* (1941).

——— "The Present Status of Race Relations in the South," *Social Forces* 23 (1944): 27–8.

——— "Social Changes and Their Effects on Race Relations in the South," *Social Forces* 23 (1945): 343–48.

Johnson, Michael P., and James L. Roark, ed., *Black Masters: A Free Family of Color in the Old South* (1984).

Johnson, Michael P., and James L. Roark, "Strategies of Survival: Free Negro Families and the Problem of Slavery," Carol Bleser, ed., *In Joy and In Sorrow: Women, Family, and Marriage in the Victorian South, 1830–1900* (1991): 88–102.

Jones, Allen W., "The Black Press in the 'New South': Jesse C. Duke's Struggle for Justice and Equality," *Journal of Negro History* 64 (1979): 215–28.

————— "The South's First Black Farm Agents," *Agriculture History* 50 (1976): 636–44.

Kelley, Robin D. G., "'We Are Not What We Seem': Rethinking Black Working-Class Opposition in the Jim Crow South," *Journal of American History* 80 (1993): 75–112.

Key, Valdimer Orlando, Jr., *Southern Politics in State and Nation* (new ed., 1984).

Killick, John R., "The Cotton Operations of Alexander Brown and Sons in the Deep South, 1820–1860," *Journal of Southern History* 43 (1977): 169–94.

King, Edward, *The Southern States of North America: A Record of Journeys in Louisiana, Texas, the Indian Territory, Missouri, Arkansas, Mississippi, Alabama, Georgia, Florida, South Carolina, North Carolina, Kentucky, Tennessee, Virginia, West Virginia and Maryland* (1875).

King, J. Crawford, "The Closing of the Southern Range: An Exploratory Study," *Journal of Southern History* 48 (1982): 53–70.

King, Spencer B., Jr., *Darien: The Death and Rebirth of a Southern Town* (1981).

Kiple, Kenneth F., and Virginia H. Kiple, "Black Tongue and Black Men: Pellagra and Slavery in the Antebellum South," *Journal of Southern History* 43 (1977): 411–428.

Kirby, Jack Temple, "Black and White in the Rural South, 1915–1954," *Agricultural History* 58 (1984): 411–22.

————— *Rural Worlds Lost: The American South, 1920–1960* (1987).

————— "The Southern Exodus, 1910–1960: A Primer for Historians," *Journal of Southern History* 49 (1983): 585–600.

Korn, Bertram W., "Jews and Negro Slavery in the Old South, 1789–1865," *Publication of the American Jewish Historical Society* 50 (1961): 151–201.

Krause, P. Allen, "Rabbis and Negro Rights in the South, 1954–1967," *American Jewish Archives* 21 (1969): 20–47.

Krebs, Sylvia H., "John Chinaman and Reconstruction Alabama: The Debate and the Experience," *Southern Studies* 21 (1982): 369–83.

Kremm, Thomas W., and Diane Neal, "Clandestine Black Labor Societies and White Fear: Hiram F. Hoover and the 'Cooperative Workers of America' in the South," *Labor History* 19 (1978): 226–37.

Krueger, Thomas A., *And Promises to Keep: The Southern Conference for Human Welfare, 1938–1948* (1967).

Ladd, Everett Carll, *Negro Political Leadership in the South* (1966).

LaFoy, D. C., "A Historical Review of Three Gulf Coast Creole Communities," *Gulf Coast Historical Review* 3 (1988): 6–19.

Landers, Jane G., "African Presence in Early Spanish Colonization of the Caribbean and the Southeastern Borderlands," in David Hurst Thomas, ed., *Archaeological and Historical Perspectives on the Spanish Borderlands East* (1990): 315–27.

Langhorne, O., "Domestic Service in the South," *American Journal of Social Science* 39 (1901): 169.

Larson, Edward J., *Sex, Race, and Science: Eugenics in the Deep South* (1995).

Lawson, Steven F., *Black Ballots: Voting Rights in the South, 1944–1969* (1976).

————— *In Pursuit of Power: Southern Blacks and Electoral Politics, 1965–1982* (1985).

Lerner, Eugene, "Southern Output and Agricultural Income, 1860–1880," *Agricultural History* 33 (1959): 117–25.

Lewinson, Paul, *Race, Class, and Party: A History of Negro Suffrage and White Politics in the South* (1932).

Lewis, Ronald L., "From Peasant to Proletarian: The Migration of Southern Blacks to the Central Appalachian Coalfield," *Journal of Southern History* 55 (1989): 77–102.

Lichtman, Allan, "The Federal Assault against Voting Discrimination in the Deep South, 1957–1967," *Journal of Negro History* 54 (1969): 346–67.

Little, Thomas J., "George Liele and the Rise of Independent Black Baptist Churches in the Lower South and Jamaica," *Slavery and Abolition* 16 (1995): 188–204.

Loveland, Anne C., *Southern Evangelicals and the Social Order, 1800–1860* (1980).

Mabry, William A., *Studies in the Disfranchisement of the Negro in the South* (1933).

Manis, Andrew M., *Southern Civil Religions in Conflict: Black and White Baptists and Civil Rights, 1947–1957* (1987).

Margo, Robert A., *Race and Schooling in the South, 1880–1950: An Economic History* (1990).

——— "Teacher Salaries in Black and White: The South in 1910," *Explorations in Economic History* 21 (1984): 306–26.

Martin, Sandy D., "The American Baptist Home Mission Society and Black Higher Education in the South, 1865–1920," *Foundations* 24 (1981): 310–27.

Mason, Julian, "Black Writers of the South," *Mississippi Quarterly* 31 (1978): 169–84.

Mathews, Donald R., *Religion in the Old South* (1977).

Matthews, Donald R., and James W. Prothro, *Negroes and the New Southern Politics* (1966).

McDonald, Forrest, and Grady McWhiney, "The South from Self-Sufficiency to Peonage: An Interpretation," *American History Review* 85 (1980): 1095–118.

McGee, Leo, and Robert Boone, "Black Rural Land Decline in the South [1910–1974]," *Black Scholar* 8 (1977): 8–11.

McKinney, Gordon B., "Industrialization and Violence in Appalachia in the 1890s," *Appalachian Journal* 4 (1977): 131–44.

——— "Racism and the Electorate: Two Late Nineteenth Century Mountain Elections," *Appalachian Journal* 1 (1973): 98–110.

——— "Southern Mountain Republicans and the Negro, 1865–1900," *Journal of Southern History* 41 (1975): 493–516.

McLaurin, Melton A., *The Knights of Labor in the South* (1978).

McMillen, Sally Gregory, *Southern Women: Black and White in the Old South* (1992).

McNally, Michael J., "A Peculiar Institution: Catholic Parish Life and the Pastoral Mission to the Blacks in the Southeast, 1850–1980," *U.S. Catholic Historian* 5 (1986): 67–80.

Meier, August, "Negroes in the First and Second Reconstructions of the South," *Civil War History* 13 (1967): 114–30.

Meier, August, and Elliott M. Rudwick, "The Boycott Movement against Jim Crow Streetcars in the South, 1900–1906," *Journal of American History* 55 (1969): 756–75.

Menard, Russell R., "Slave Demography in the Lowcountry, 1670–1740: From Frontier Society to Plantation Regime," *South Carolina Historical Magazine* 96 (1995): 280–303.

Mertz, Paul E., *New Deal Policy and Southern Rural Poverty* (1978).

Miller, William L., "A Note on the Importance of the Interstate Slave Trade of the Antebellum South," *Journal of Political Economy* 73 (1965): 181–87.

Miller, Wilbur R., "The Revenue: Federal Law Enforcement in the Mountain South, 1870–1900," *Journal of Southern History* 55 (1989): 195–216.

Miller, Zane L., "Urban Blacks in the South, 1865–1920: An Analysis of Some Quantitative Data on Richmond, Savannah, New Orleans, Louisville, and Birmingham," in Leo F. Schnore, ed., *The New Urban History: Quantitative Explorations by American Historians* (1975): 184–204.

Mitchell, George Sinclair, "The Negro in Southern Trade Unionism," *Southern Economic Journal* 2 (1936): 26–33.

Mitchell, Glenford E., and William H. Peace, III, ed., *The Angry Black South* (1962).

Mitchell, Harry Leland, "The Founding and Early History of the Southern Tenant Farmers Union," *Arkansas Historical Quarterly* 32 (1973): 324–69.

——— *Mean Things Happening in this Land: The Life and Times of H. L. Mitchell, Co-founder of the Southern Tenant Farmers Union* (1979).

Montgomery, William E., *Under Their Own Vine and Fig Tree: The African-American Church in the South, 1865–1900* (1993).

Moreland, Laurence W., Robert P. Steed, and Tod A. Baker, ed., *Blacks in Southern Politics* (1987).

Morgan, Jo-Ann, "Mammy the Huckster: Selling the Old South for the New Century," *American Art* 9 (1995): 86–109.

Morgan, Philip D., "Black Society in the Low Country, 1760–1810," in Ira Berlin, and Ronald Hoffman, ed., *Slavery and Freedom in the Age of the American Revolution* (1983): 83–142.

——— "Work and Culture: The Task System and the World of Lowcountry Blacks, 1700 to 1880," *William and Mary Quarterly* 39 (1982): 563–99.

Mullin, Michael, *Africa in America: Slave Acculturation and Resistance in the American South and the British Caribbean, 1736–1831* (1992).

Murphy, James B., "Slaveholding in Appalachia: A Challenge to the Egalitarian Tradition," *Southern Studies* 3 (1992): 15–33.

Myers, Martha A., *Race, Labor, and Punishment in the New South* (1998).

Neal, Ernest E., and Lewis W. Jones, "The Place of the Negro Farmer in the Changing Economy of the Cotton South," *Rural Sociology* 15 (1950): 30–51.

Neverdon-Morton, Cynthia, *Afro-American Women of the South and the Advancement of the Race, 1895–1925* (1989).

Noon, Thomas R., "Early Black Lutherans in the South (to 1865)," *Concordia Historical Institute Quarterly* 50 (1977): 50–53.

Oakes, James, "From Republicanism to Liberalism: Ideological Change and the Crisis of the Old South," *American Quarterly* 37 (1985): 551–71.

Odum, Howard W., *Race and Rumors of Race: The American South in the Early Forties* (1997).

Oldfield, John, ed., *Civilization and Black Progress: Selected Writings of Alexander Crummell on the South* (1995).

Olsen, Otto H., ed., *Reconstruction and Redemption in the South* (1980).

Onkst, David H., "'First a Negro . . . Incidentally a Veteran': Black World War Two and the G.I. Bill of Rights in the Deep South, 1944–1948," *Journal of Social History* 31 (1998): 517–43.

Orser, Charles E., "The Past Ten Years of Plantation Archaeology in the Southeastern United States," *Southeastern Archaeology* 3 (1984): 1–12.

Otto, John Solomon, *Cannon's Point Plantation, 1794–1860: Living Conditions and Status Patterns in the Old South* (1984).

———— "The Case for Folk History: Slavery in the Highlands South," *Southern Studies* 20 (1981): 167–73.

Otto, John S., and Augustus M. Burns, "Black and White Cultural Interaction in the Early Twentieth Century South: Race and Hillbilly Music," *Phylon* 35 (1974): 407–17.

Owens, Leslie Howard, *This Species of Property: Slave Life and Culture in the Old South* (1976).

Perman, Michael, *The Road to Redemption: Southern Politics, 1869–1879* (1984).

Pope, Christie F., "Southern Homesteads for Negroes," *Agricultural History* 44 (1970): 201–12.

Powdermaker, Hortense, *After Freedom: A Cultural Study in the Deep South* (1939).

Price, Margaret, *The Negro and the Ballot in the South* (1959).

Puckett, Newbell Niles, *Folk Beliefs of the Southern Negro* (1926).

Rabinowitz, Howard N., "The Conflict between Blacks and the Police in the Urban South, 1865–1900," *Historian* 39 (1976): 62–76.

———— *The First New South, 1865–1920* (1992).

———— "From Exclusion to Segregation: Southern Race Relations, 1865–1890," *Journal of American History* 63 (1976): 325–50.

———— "Half a Loaf: The Shift from White to Black Teachers in the Negro Schools of the Urban South, 1865–1890," *Journal of Southern History* 40 (1974): 565–94.

———— *Race Relations in the Urban South.*

Ransom, Roger L., and Richard Sutch, "Debt Peonage in the Cotton South after the Civil War," *Journal of Economic History* 32 (1972): 641–69.

———— "The Ex-Slave in the Postbellum South: A Study of the Economic Impact of Racism in a Market Environment," *Journal of Economic History* 33 (1973): 131–48.

Raper, Arthur Franklin, *Preface to Peasantry: A Tale of Two Black Belt Counties* (1936).

———— "The Southern Negro and the NRA," *Georgia Historical Quarterly* 64 (1980): 128–45.

Redcay, Edward Edgeworth, *County Training Schools and Public Secondary Education for Negroes in the South* (1935).

Reed, Linda, *Simple Decency and Common Sense: The Southern Conference Movement, 1938–1963* (1991).

Reed, Merl Elwyn, "The FEPC, the Black Worker, and the Southern Shipyards," *South Atlantic Quarterly* 74 (1975): 446–67.

Reid, Joseph D., Jr., "Sharecropping as an Understandable Market Response: The Postbellum South," *Journal of Economic History* 33 (1973): 106–30.

Reiff, Janice L., Michael R. Dahlin, and Daniel Scott Smith, "Rural Push and Urban Pull: Work and Family Experiences of Older Black Women in Southern Cities, 1880–1900," *Journal of Social History* 16 (1983): 39–48.

Rhee, Jong Mo, "The Redistribution of the Black Work Force in the South by Industry," *Phylon* 35 (1974): 293–300.

Richardson, Harry Van Buren, *Dark Glory: A Picture of the Church among Negroes in the Rural South* (1947).

Richardson, Joe M., "The Failure of the American Missionary Association to Expand Congregationalism among Southern Blacks," *Southern Studies* 18 (1979): 51–73.

Riley, Carroll L., "Blacks in the Early Southwest," *Ethnohistory* 19 (1972): 247–60.

Roark, James L., *Masters without Slaves: Southern Planters in the Civil War and Reconstruction* (1977).

Roberts, Charles A., "Did Southern Farmers Discriminate? The Evidence Reexamined," *Agricultural History* 49 (1975): 441–47.

Rousey, Dennis C., "Aliens in the WASP Nest: Ethnocultural Diversity in the Antebellum Urban South," *Journal of American History* 79 (1992): 152–64.

Rowan, Carl T., *Go South to Sorrow* (1957).

Rust, Barbara, "The Right to Vote: The Enforcement Acts and Southern Courts," *Prologue* 21 (1989): 230–38.

Savitt, Todd L., "Entering a White Profession: Black Physicians in the New South, 1880–1920," *Bulletin of the History of Medicine* 61 (1987): 507–40.

———— "The Use of Blacks for Medical Experimentation and Demonstration in the Old South," *Journal of Southern History* 48 (1982): 331–48.

Scarborough, William Kauffman, *The Overseer: Plantation Management in the Old South* (1966).

Schecter, Patricia A., "Free and Slave Labor in the Old South: The Tredegar Iron Worker's Strike of 1847," *Labor History* 35 (1995): 165–86.

Schweninger, Loren, *Black Property Owners in the South, 1790–1915* (1990).

———— "Property Owning Free African-American Women in the South, 1800–1870," *Journal of Women's History* 1 (1990): 13–44.

———— "Prosperous Blacks in the South, 1790–1880," *American Historical Review* 95 (1990): 31–56.

———— "A Slave Family in the Antebellum South," *Journal of Negro History* 60 (1975): 29–44.

———— "A Vanishing Breed: Black Farm Owners in the South, 1651–1982," *Agricultural History* 63 (1989): 41–60.

Scroggs, Jack B., "Carpetbagger Constitutional Reform in the South Atlantic States, 1867–1868," *Journal of Southern History* 27 (1961): 475–93.

Seabrook, Isaac Dubose, *Before and After, or The Relations of the Races at the South*, ed. John Hammond Moore (1967).

Shlomowitz, Ralph, "The Origins of Southern Sharecropping," *Agricultural History* 53 (1979): 557–75.

Shugg, Roger W., "Negro Voting in the Ante-bellum South," *Journal of Negro History* 21 (1936): 357–64.

Singal, Daniel Joseph, *The War Within: From Victorian to Modernist Thought in the South, 1919–1945* (1982).

Smith, Daniel Scott, Michael Dahlin, and Mark Friedberger, "The Family Structure of the Older Black Population in the American South in 1880 and 1900," *Sociology and Social Research* 63 (1979): 544–65.

Smith, Mark M., *Debating Slavery: Economy and Society in the Antebellum American South* (1998).

———— *Mastered by the Clock: Time, Slavery, and Freedom in the American South* (1997).

Somers, Robert, *The Southern States since the War, 1870–71* (1871).

Sosna, Morton Philip, *In Search of the Silent South: Southern Liberals and the Race Issue* (1977).

Starobin, Robert S., "Disciplining Industrial Slaves in the Old South," *Journal of Negro History* 53 (1968): 111–28.

———— *Industrial Slavery in the Old South* (1970).

Stokes, Melvyn, and Rick Halpern, ed., *Race and Class in the American South since 1890* (1994).

Stuckert, Robert P., "Black Populations of the Southern Appalachian Mountains," *Phylon* 48 (1987): 141–51.

———— "Free Black Populations of the Southern Appalachian Mountains: 1860," *Journal of Black Studies* 23 (1993): 358–70.

Tadman, Michael, "Slave Trading in the Ante-bellum South: An Estimate of the Extent of the Inter-Regional Slave Trade," *Journal of American Studies [UK]* 13 (1979): 195–220.

———— *Speculators and Slaves: Masters, Traders, and Slaves in the Old South* (1989).

Thomas, John I., "Historical Antecedents and Impact of Blacks on the Indigenous White Populations of Brazil and the American South, 1500–1800," *Ethnohistory* 19 (1972): 147–69.

Thorpe, Earl E., *The Old South: A Psychohistory* (1972).

Tindall, George Brown, *The Emergence of the New South, 1913–1945* (1967).

Tolnay, Stewart E., "Black Family Formation and Tenancy in the Farm South, 1900," *American Journal of Sociology* 90 (1984): 305–25.

———— "Class, Race, and Fertility in the Rural South: 1910 and 1940," *Rural Sociology* 60 (1995): 108–28.

———— "The Decline of Black Marital Fertility in the Rural South, 1910–1940," *American Sociological Review* 52 (1987): 211–17.

———— "Fertility of Southern Black Farmers in 1900: Evidence and Speculation," *Journal of Family History* 8 (1983): 314–32.

Tolnay, Stewart E., E. M. Beck, and James L. Massey, "Black Competition and White Vengeance: Legal Execution of Blacks as Social Control in the Cotton South, 1890 to 1929," *Social Science Quarterly* 73 (1992): 627–44.

Tolnay, Stewart E., and E. M. Beck, *A Festival of Violence: An Analysis of Southern Lynchings, 1882–1930* (1995).

Toplin, Robert Brent, "The Specter of Crisis: Slaveholder Reactions to Abolitionism in the United States and Brazil," *Civil War History* 18 (1972): 129–38.

Trowbridge, John Townsend, *The South: A Tour of its Battlefields and Ruined Cities* (1866).

Tucker, Susan, *Telling Memories among Southern Women: Domestic Workers and Their Employers in the Segregated South* (1988).

Turner, Charles Jackson, "Changes in Age Composition of the Rural Black Population of the South, 1950 to 1970," *Phylon* 35 (1974): 268–75.

Turner, William H., and Edward J. Gabbell, ed., *Blacks in Appalachia* (1985).

Van Deburg, William L., *The Slave Drivers: Black Agricultural Labor Supervisors in the Antebellum South* (1979).

Vander Zanden, James Wilfrid, *Race Relations in Transition: The Segregation Crisis in the South* (1965).

Vaughn, William Preston, *Schools for All: The Blacks and Public Education in the South, 1865–1877* (1974).

Wade, Richard C., *Slavery in the Cities: The South, 1820–1860* (1964).

Wade-Gayles, Gloria, "Black Women Journalists in the South, 1880–1905," in Darlene Clark Hine, ed., *Black Women in American History: From Colonial Times Through the Nineteenth Century* (1990): 1409–24.

Waldrep, Christopher, *Roots of Disorder: Race and Criminal Justice in the American South, 1817–1880* (1998).

Walker, Vanessa Siddle, *Their Highest Potential: An African American School Community in the Segregated South* (1996).

Walters, Pamela Barnhouse, and David R. James, "Schooling for Some: Child Labor and School Enrollment of Black and White Children in the Early Twentieth-Century South," *American Sociological Review* 57 (1992): 635–50.

Warnock, Henry, "Prophets of Change: Some Southern Baptist Leaders and the Problem of Race, 1900–1921," *Baptist History and Heritage* 7 (1972): 172–85.

———— "Southern Methodists, the Negro, and Unification: The First Phase," *Journal of Negro History* 52 (1967): 287–304.

Watson, Harry L., "Conflict and Collaboration: Yeomen, Slaveholders, and Politics in the Antebellum South," *Social History* 10 (1985): 273–98.

Watters, Pat, *Down to Now: Reflections on the Southern Civil Rights Movement* (1971).

Watters, Pat, and Reese Cleghorn, *Climbing Jacob's Ladder: The Arrival of Negroes in Southern Politics* (1967).

Wennerstein, John R., "The Travail of Black Land-Grant Schools in the South, 1890–1917," *Agricultural History* 65 (1992): 54–62.

Wheeler, Edward L., *Uplifting the Race: The Black Minister in the New South, 1865–1902* (1986).

Wiener, Jonathan M., "Class Structure and Economic Development in the American South, 1865–1955," *American Historical Review* 84 (1979): 970–92.

Wiggins, David D., "Good Times on the Old Plantation: Popular Recreations of the Black Slave in Antebellum South, 1810–1860," *Journal of Sport History* 4 (1977): 260–84.

———— "The Play of Slave Children in the Plantation Communities of the Old South, 1820–1860," *Journal of Sport History* 7 (1980): 21–39.

Willis, William S., Jr., "Anthropology and Negroes on the Southern Colonial Frontier," in James C. Curtis, and Lewis L. Gould, ed., *The Black Experience in America: Selected Essays* (1970): 33–50.

Wood, Peter H., "The Changing Population of the Colonial South: An Overview by Race and Region, 1685–1790," in Peter H. Wood, Gregory A. Waselkov, and M. Thomas Hatley, ed., *Powhatan's Mantle: Indians in the Colonial Southeast* (1989): 35–103.

Woodman, Harold D., *King Cotton and His Retainers: Financing and Marketing the Cotton Crop of the South, 1800–1925* (1968).

———— *New South, New Law: The Legal Foundations of Credit and Labor Relations in the Postbellum Agricultural South* (1995).

———— "Post-Civil War Southern Agriculture and the Law," *Agricultural History* 53 (1979): 319–37.

————, ed., *Slavery and the Southern Economy: Sources and Readings* (1966).

Woodman, Harold, and Gilbert C. Fite, *New South, New Law: The Legal Foundations of Credit and Labor Relations in the Postbellum Agricultural South* (1995).

———— "Postbellum Social Change and Its Effects on Marketing the South's Cotton Crop," *Agriculture History* 56 (1982): 215–30, 244–48.

Woodward, C. Vann, *Origins of the New South, 1877–1913* (1951).

Work, Monroe N., "Negro Criminality in the South," *Annals of the American Academy of Political and Social Science* 49 (1913): 74–80.

———— "The South's Labor Problem," *South Atlantic Quarterly* 19 (1920): 1–8.

Wright, Gavin, "Capitalism and Slavery on the Islands: A Lesson From the Mainland," *Journal of Interdisciplinary History* 17 (1987): 851–70.

———— *Old South, New South: Revolutions in the Southern Economy since the Civil War* (1986).

Youth of the Rural Organizing and Cultural Center, *Minds Stayed on Freedom: The Civil Rights Struggle in the Rural South: An Oral History* (1991).

Zuckerman, Michael, "Thermidor in America: The Aftermath of Independence in the South," *Prospects* 8 (1983): 349–68.

26.1.4   West

Anderson, Martha A., *Black Pioneers of the Northwest, 1800–1918* (1980).

Berwanger, Eugene H., *The Frontier against Slavery: Western Anti-Negro Prejudice and the Slavery Extension Controversy* (1967).

Butler, Anne M., "Still in Chains: Black Women in Western Prisons, 1865–1910," *Western Historical Quarterly* 20 (1989): 18–35.

deGraaf, Lawrence B., "Race, Sex, and Region: Black Women in the American West, 1850–1920," *Pacific Historical Review* 49 (1980): 285–313.

———— "Race, Sex and Region: Black Women in the American West, 1850–1920," in Darlene Clark Hine, ed., *Black Women in American History: From Colonial Times Through the Nineteenth Century* (1990): 303–32.

———— "Recognition, Racism, and Reflections on the Writing of Western Black History," *Pacific Historical Review* 44 (1975): 22–51.

———— "Significant Steps on an Arduous Path: The Impact of World War II on Discrimination against African Americans in the West," *Journal of the West* 35 (1996): 24–33.

Fowler, Arlen L., *The Black Infantry in the West, 1869–1891* (1971).

Hurtt, Clarence M., "The Role of the Black Infantry in the Expansion of the West," *West Virginia History* 40 (1979): 123–57.

Katz, William Loren, *Black Women of the Old West* (1995).

Lay, Shawn, ed., *The Invisible Empire in the West: Toward a New Historical Appraisal of the Ku Klux Klan of the 1920s* (1992).

Ravage, John W., *Black Pioneers: Images of the Black Experience in the North American Frontier* (1997).

Savage, W. Sherman, *Blacks in the West* (1976).

Schlissel, Lillian, *Black Frontiers: A History of African-American Heroes in the Old West* (1995).

Smith, Alonzo, and Quintard Taylor, "Racial Discrimination in the Workplace: A Study of Two West Coast Cities during the 1940s," *Journal of Ethnic Studies* 8 (1980): 35–54.

Taylor, Quintard, "The Emergence of Black Communities in the Pacific Northwest: 1865–1910," *Journal of Negro History* 64 (1979): 342–54.

——— *In Search of the Racial Frontier: African Americans in the American West, 1528–1900* (1998).

Yount, Lisa, *Frontier of Freedom: African Americans in the West* (1997).

26.2   STATE AND LOCAL STUDIES

26.2.1   Alabama

Amos, Harriet E., "Religious Reconstruction in Microcosm at Faunsdale Plantation," *Alabama Review* 42 (1989): 243–69.

Atkins, Leak R., "Populism in Alabama: Reuben F. Kolb and the Appeals to Minority Groups," *Alabama Historical Quarterly* 32 (1970): 167–80.

Bailey, Richard, *Neither Carpetbaggers nor Scalawags: Black Officeholders during the Reconstruction of Alabama, 1867–1878* (1991).

Bethel, Elizabeth Rauh, "The Freedmen's Bureau in Alabama," *Journal of Southern History* 14 (1948): 49–92.

Bond, Horace Mann, *Negro Education in Alabama: A Study in Cotton and Steel* (1939).

——— "Social and Economic Forces in Alabama Reconstruction," *Journal of Negro History* 23 (1938): 290–348.

Boney, F. N., "Slaves as Guinea Pigs: Georgia and Alabama Episodes," *Alabama Review* 37 (1984): 45–51.

Burns, Stewart, ed., *Daybreak of Freedom: The Montgomery Bus Boycott* (1997).

Cloyd, Daniel Lee, "Prelude to Reform: Political, Economic, and Social Thought of Alabama Baptists, 1877–1890," *Alabama Review* 31 (1978): 48–64.

Collins, Donald E., *When the Church Bell Rang Racist: The Methodist Church and the Civil Rights Movement in Alabama* (1998).

Daniel, Pete, "Black Power in the 1920s: The Case of Tuskegee Veterans Hospital," *Journal of Southern History* 36 (1970): 368–88.

Dornfeld, Margaret, *The Turning Tide: From the Desegregation of the Armed Forces to the Montgomery Bus Boycott, 1948–1956* (1995).

Eagles, Charles W., *Outside Agitator: Jon Daniels and the Civil Rights Movement in Alabama* (1993).

Eskew, Glenn T., "'Bombingham': Black Protest in Postwar Birmingham, Alabama," *Historian* 59 (1997): 371–90.

——— *But for Birmingham: The Local and National Movements in the Civil Rights Struggle* (1997).

Fager, Charles, *Selma 1965: The March that Changed the South* (2d ed., 1985).

Feldman, Glenn, "Lynching in Alabama, 1889–1921," *Alabama Review* 48 (1995): 114–41.

Fields, Uriah J., *The Montgomery Story: The Unhappy Effects of the Montgomery Bus Boycott* (1959).

Fitzgerald, Michael W., "Railroad Subsidies and Black Aspirations; The Politics of Economic Development in Reconstruction Mobile, 1865–1879," *Civil War History* 39 (1993): 240–56.

——— "'To Give Our Votes to the Party': Black Political Agitation and Agricultural Change in Alabama, 1865–1870," *Journal of American History* 76 (1989): 489–505.

Flynt, Wayne, *Alabama Baptists: Southern Baptists in the Heart of Dixie* (1998).

—— "Organized Labor Reform and Alabama Politics, 1920," *Alabama Review* 23 (1970): 163–80.

—— "Religion in the Urban South: The Divided Religious Mind of Birmingham, 1900–1930," *Alabama Review* 30 (1977): 108–34.

Garrow, David, ed., *Birmingham, Alabama, 1956–1963: The Black Struggle for Civil Rights* (1989).

Garrow, David, "Origins of the Montgomery Bus Boycott," *Southern Changes* 7 (1985): 21–8.

—— *Protest at Selma: Martin Luther King, Jr., and the Voting Rights Act of 1965* (1978).

——, ed., *The Walking City: The Montgomery Bus Boycott, 1955–1956* (1989).

Gatewood, Willard B., Jr., "Alabama's 'Negro Soldier Experiment,' 1898–1899," *Journal of Negro History* 57 (1972): 333–51.

Granada, Ray, "Violence: An Instrument of Policy in Reconstruction Alabama," *Alabama Historical Quarterly* 30 (1968): 181–202.

Gutman, Herbert G., "Black Coal Miners and the Greenback-Labor Party in Redeemer Alabama, 1878–1879: The Letters of Warren D. Kelley, Willis Johnson Thomas, 'Dawson,' and Others," *Labor History* 10 (1969): 506–535.

Harris, Carl V., "Reforms in Government Control of Negroes in Birmingham, Alabama, 1890–1920," *Journal of Southern History* 38 (1972): 567–600.

—— "Stability and Change in Discrimination against Black Public Schools: Birmingham, Alabama, 1871–1931," *Journal of Southern History* 51 (1985): 375–416.

Hasson, Gail S., "Health and Welfare of Freedmen in Reconstruction Alabama," *Alabama Review* 35 (1982): 94–110.

Hoffsommer, Harold, "The Disadvantaged Farm Family in Alabama," *Rural Sociology* 2 (1937): 383–92.

Holmes, Jack D. L., "The Role of Blacks in Spanish Alabama: The Mobile Districts, 1780–1813," *Alabama Historical Quarterly* 37 (1975): 5–18.

Holmes, William F., "Moonshiners and Whitecaps in Alabama, 1893," *Alabama Review* 34 (1981): 31–49.

Howard, Gene L., *Death at Cross Plains: An Alabama Reconstruction Tragedy* (1984).

Howington, Arthur F., "Violence in Alabama: A Study of Late Antebellum Montgomery," *Alabama Review* 27 (1974): 213–31.

Hughes, John H., "Labeling and Treating Black Illness in Alabama, 1861–1910," *Journal of Southern History* 58 (1992): 435–60.

Jones, Allen W., "Voices for Improving Rural Life: Alabama's Black Agricultural Press, 1890–1965," *Agricultural History* 58 (1984): 209–220.

Jordan, Weymouth T., *Hugh Davis and His Alabama Plantation* (1948).

Kelley, Don Quinn, "Ideology and Education: Uplifting the Masses in Nineteenth Century Alabama," *Phylon* 40 (1979): 147–58.

Kelley, Robin D. G., "'Comrades, Praise Gawd for Lenin and Them!': Ideology and Culture among Black Communists in Alabama, 1930–1935," *Science and Society* 52 (1988): 59–82.

—— *Hammer and Hoe: Alabama Communists during the Great Depression* (1990).

—— "A New War in Dixie: Communists and the Unemployed in Birmingham, Alabama, 1930–1933," *Labor History* 30 (1989): 367–84.

King, Martin Luther, Jr., *Stride Toward Freedom: The Montgomery Story* (1958).

Kolchin, Peter, *First Freedom: The Responses of Alabama's Blacks to Emancipation and Reconstruction* (1972).

Kulik, Gary, "Black Workers and Technological Change in the Birmingham Iron Industry, 1881–1931," in Merl E. Reed, Leslie S. Hough, and Gary M. Fink, ed., *Southern Workers and Their Unions, 1880–1975: Selected Papers. The Second Labor History Conference, 1978* (1981): 22–42.

LeBlanc, John R., "The Context of Manumission: Imperial Rome and Antebellum Alabama," *Alabama Review* 46 (1993): 266–87.

Letwin, Daniel, *The Challenge of Interracial Unionism: Alabama Coal Miners, 1878–1921* (1998).

Lowery, Bruce, "Integration at Alabama's Historically Black Colleges and Universities," *Southern Historian* 19 (1997): 38–42.

Martin, Charles H., "Southern Labor Relations in Transition: Gadsden, Alabama, 1930–1943," *Journal of Social History* 47 (1981): 545–68.

McKinney, Don S., "Brer Rabbit and Brother Martin Luther King, Jr.: The Folktale Background of the Birmingham Protest," *Journal of Religious Thought* 46 (1989–1990): 42–52.

McKiven, Henry M., Jr., *Iron and Steel: Class, Race, and Community in Birmingham, Alabama, 1875–1920* (1995).

McMillan, Malcolm C., *Constitutional Development in Alabama, 1798–1901: A Study in Politics, the Negro, and Sectionalism* (1955).

Millner, Stephen Michael, *The Montgomery Bus Boycott: Case Study in the Emergence and Career of a Social Movement* (1981).

Mills, Gary B., "Miscegenation and the Free Negro in Antebellum 'Anglo' Alabama: A Reexamination of Southern Race Relations," *Journal of American History* 68 (1981): 16–34.

Muskat, Beth Taylor, "The Last March: The Demise of the Black Militia in Alabama," *Alabama Review* 43 (1990): 18–34.

Myers, John B., "The Education of the Alabama Freedmen during Presidential Reconstruction, 1865–1867," *Journal of Negro Education* 40 (1971): 163–71.

Norrell, Robert J., "Caste in Steel: Jim Crow Careers in Birmingham, Alabama," *Journal of American History* 73 (1986): 669–94.

———— *Reaping the Whirlwind: The Civil Rights Movement in Tuskegee* (rev. ed., 1998).

Oates, Stephen B., "The Week the World Watched Selma," *American Heritage* 33 (1982): 48–63.

Pinkard, Ophelia T., "Blacks Named Wallace in the Federal Census Reports for 1880 and 1900: Shelby County, Alabama," *Journal of the Afro-American Historical and Genealogical Society* 6 (1988): 144–55.

Pruitt, Paul M., Jr., "Defender of the Voteless: Joseph C. Manning Views the Disfranchisement Era in Alabama," *Alabama Historical Quarterly* 43 (1981): 171–85.

Rachleff, Marshall, "Big Joe, Little Joe, Bill, and Jack: An Example of Slave-Resistance in Alabama," *Alabama Review* 32 (1979): 141–46.

Reid, Robert D., "The Negro in Alabama during the Civil War," *Journal of Negro History* 35 (1950): 265–88.

Reid, Stevenson, *History of Colored Baptists in Alabama* (1949).

Robinson, Jo Ann Gibson, *The Montgomery Bus Boycott and the Women Who Started It: The Memoir of Jo Ann Gibson Robinson,* ed. David Garrow (1987).

Rodabaugh, Karl, "The Alliance in Politics: The Alabama Gubernatorial Election of 1891," *Alabama Historical Quarterly* 36 (1974): 54–80.

Rogers, William Warren, Jr., "The Eutaw Prisoners: Federal Confrontation with Violence in Reconstruction Alabama," *Alabama Review* 43 (1990): 98–122.

———— "The Negro Alliance in Alabama," *Journal of Negro History* 45 (1950): 38–44.

Schweninger, Loren, "Black Citizenship and the Republican Party in Reconstruction Alabama," *Alabama Review* 29 (1976): 83–103.

Scribner, Christopher MacGregor, "Federal Funding, Urban Renewal, and Race Relations: Birmingham in Transition, 1945–1955," *Alabama Review* 48 (1995): 269–95.

Sellers, James B., "Free Negroes of Tuscaloosa County before the Thirteenth Amendment," *Alabama Review* 23 (1970): 110–27.

———— *Slavery in Alabama* (1950).

Sikora, Frank, *Until Justice Rolls Down: The Birmingham Church Bombing Case* (1991).

Sisk, Glenn N., "Crime and Justice in the Alabama Black Belt, 1875–1917," *Mid-America* 40 (1958): 106–13.

———— "Funeral Customs in the Alabama Black Belt, 1870–1910," *Southern Folklore Quarterly* 23 (1959): 169–71.

———— "Negro Churches in the Alabama Black Belt, 1875–1917," *Journal of the Presbyterian Historical Society* 33 (1955): 87–92.

———— "Negro Education in the Alabama Black Belt, 1875–1900," *Journal of Negro Education* 22 (1953): 126–35.

———— "Negro Migration in the Alabama Black Belt, 1875–1917," *Negro History Bulletin* 17 (1953): 32–34.

———— "Social Aspects of the Alabama Black Belt, 1875–1917," *Mid-America* 37 (1955): 31–47.

Snell, William R., "Fiery Crosses in the Roaring Twenties: Activities of the Revised Klan in Alabama, 1915–1930," *Alabama Review* 23 (1970): 256–76.

Spencer, C. A., "Black Benevolent Societies and the Development of Black Insurance Companies in 19th-Century Alabama," *Phylon* 46 (1988): 251–61.

Sterkx, H. E., "William C. Jordan and Reconstruction in Bullock County, Alabama," *Alabama Review* 15 (1962): 61–73.

Straw, Richard A., "The United Mine Workers of America and the 1920 Coal Strike in Alabama," *Alabama Review* 28 (1975): 104–28.

Taylor, Joseph H., "Populism and Disfranchisement in Alabama," *Journal of Negro History* 34 (1949): 410–27.

Thomas, Mary Martha, ed., *Stepping out of the Shadows: Alabama Women, 1819–1990* (1995).

Thornton, J. Mills, III, "Challenge and Response in the Montgomery Bus Boycott of 1955–1956," *Alabama Review* 33 (1980): 163–235.

Walker, Ann Kendrick, *Tuskegee and the Black Belt: A Portrait of a Race* (1945).

Warren, Sarah T., and Robert E. Zabawa, "The Origins of the Tuskegee National Forest: Nineteenth and Twentieth Century Resettlement and Land Development Programs in the Black Belt Region of Alabama," *Agricultural History* 72 (1998): 487–508.

Waselkov, Gregory A., "Archaeology of Old Mobile, 1702–1711," *Gulf Coast Historical Review* 6 (1990): 6–21.

White, Kenneth B., "The Alabama Freedmen's Bureau and Black Education: The Myth of Opportunity," *Alabama Review* 34 (1981): 107–24.

Wiener, Jonathan M., *Social Origins of the New South: Alabama, 1865–1885* (1978).

Wiggins, Sarah Woolfolk, *The Scalawag in Alabama Politics, 1865–1881* (1977).

Williamson, Edward C., "The Alabama Election of 1874," *Alabama Review* 17 (1964): 210–18.

Williams, Lee E., II, "Alabama Moderation: The Athens Riot of 1946," *Griot* 16 (1997): 19–23.

Worthman, Paul B., "Working Class Mobility in Birmingham, Alabama, 1860–1914," in Tamara K. Hareven, ed., *Anonymous Americans: Explorations in Nineteenth-Century Social History* (1971).

Zabawa, Robert E., and Sarah T. Warren, "From Company to Community: Agricultural Community Development in Macon County, Alabama, 1881 to the New Deal," *Agricultural History* 72 (1998): 459–86.

26.2.2   Arizona

Crow, John E., *Discrimination, Poverty, and the Negro: Arizona in the National Context* (1968).

Harris, Richard E., *The First Hundred Years: A History of Arizona Blacks* (1983).

LeSeur, Geta J., *Not All Okies Are White: The Lives of Black Cotton Pickers in Arizona* (2000).

Melcher, Mary, "Blacks and Whites Together: Interracial Leadership in the Phoenix Civil Rights Movement," *Journal of Arizona History* 32 (1991): 195–216.

Smith, Gloria L., *Arizona's Black Americana* (1977).

26.2.3   Arkansas

Atkinson, James H., "The Arkansas Gubernatorial Campaign and Election of 1872," *Arkansas Historical Quarterly* 1 (1942): 307–21.

Beals, Melba Pattillo, *Warriors Don't Cry: A Searing Memoir of the Battle to Integrate Little Rock's Central High* (1994).

Beatty-Brown, Florence R., "Legal Status of Arkansas Negroes before Emancipation," *Arkansas Historical Quarterly* 28 (1969): 6–13.

Bolsterli, Margaret Jones, "'It Seems to Help Me Bear It Better When She Knows About It': A Network of Women Friends in Watson, Arkansas, 1890–1891," *Southern Exposure* 11 (1983): 58–61.

Boyett, Gene W., "The Black Experience in the First Decade of Reconstruction in Pope County, Arkansas," *Arkansas Historical Quarterly* 51 (1992): 119–34.

Branton, Wiley A., "Little Rock Revisited: Desegregation to Resegregation," *Journal of Negro Education* 52 (1983): 250–69.

Clayton, Powell, *The Aftermath of the Civil War, in Arkansas* (1915).

Cortner, Richard C., *A Mob Intent on Death: The NAACP and the Arkansas Riot Cases* (1988).

Counts, Will, *A Life Is More Than a Moment: The Desegregation of Little Rock's Central High* (1999).

Diamond, Raymond T., "Confrontation as Rejoinder to Compromise: Reflections on the Little Rock Desegregation Crisis," *National Black Law Journal* 11 (1989): 151–76.

Dillard, Tom, "To the Back of the Elephant: Racial Conflict in the Arkansas Republican Party," *Arkansas Historical Quarterly* 33 (1974): 3–15.

Finley, Randy, "Black Arkansans and World War One," *Arkansas Historical Quarterly* 49 (1990): 249–77.

———— "In War's Wake: Health Care and Arkansas Freedmen, 1863–1868," *Arkansas Historical Quarterly* 51 (1992): 135–63.

Gatewood, Willard B., Jr., "Arkansas Negroes in the 1890s: Documents," *Arkansas Historical Quarterly* 33 (1974): 293–325.

Gordon, Fon Louise, *Caste and Class: The Black Experience in Arkansas, 1880–1920* (1995).

Graves, John William, "The Arkansas Separate Coach Law of 1891," *Arkansas Historical Quarterly* 32 (1973): 148–65.

———— "Jim Crow in Arkansas: A Reconsideration of Urban Race Relations in the Post-Reconstruction South," *Journal of Southern History* 55 (1989): 421–48.

———— "Negro Disfranchisement in Arkansas," *Arkansas Historical Quarterly* 26 (1967): 199–225.

———— *Town and Country: Race Relations in an Urban-Rural Context: Arkansas, 1865–1905* (1990).

Holmes, William F., "The Arkansas Cotton Pickers' Strike of 1891 and the Demise of the Colored Farmers' Alliance," *Arkansas Historical Quarterly* 32 (1973): 107–19.

Jackson, Bruce, *Killing Time: Life in the Arkansas Penitentiary* (1977).

Jacoway, Elizabeth, and C. Fred Williams, ed., *Understanding the Little Rock Crisis: An Exercise in Remembrance and Reconciliation* (1999).

Kennan, Clara B., "The First Negro Teacher in Little Rock," *Arkansas Historical Quarterly* 9 (1950): 194–204.

Kennedy, Thomas C., "The Rise and Decline of a Black Monthly Meeting: Southland, Arkansas, 1864–1925," *Arkansas Historical Quarterly* 50 (1991): 115–39.

———— "Southland College: The Society of Friends and Black Education in Arkansas," *Arkansas Historical Quarterly* 42 (1983): 207–38.

Kirk, John A., "The Little Rock Crisis and Postwar Black Activism in Arkansas," *Arkansas Historical Quarterly* 56 (1997): 273–93.

Littlefield, Daniel F., Jr., and Patricia W. McGraw, "The Arkansas Freeman, 1869–1870—Birth of the Black Press in Arkansas," *Phylon* 40 (1979): 75–85.

Lovett, Bobby L., "African Americans, Civil War, and Aftermath in Arkansas," *Arkansas Historical Quarterly* 54 (1995): 304–58.

McCaslin, Richard B., "Reconstructing a Frontier Oligarchy: Andrew Johnson's Amnesty Proclamation and Arkansas," *Arkansas Historical Quarterly* 49 (1990): 313–29.

Moneyhon, Carl H., "Black Politics in Arkansas during the Gilded Age, 1876–1900," *Arkansas Historical Quarterly* 44 (1985): 222–45.

———— "From Slave to Free Labor: The Federal Plantation Experiment in Arkansas," *Arkansas Historical Quarterly* 53 (1994): 137–60.

———— *The Impact of the Civil War and Reconstruction on Arkansas: Persistence in the Midst of Ruin* (1994).

Morgan, Gordon D., and Peter Kunkel, "Arkansas' Ozark Mountain Blacks: An Introduction," *Phylon* 34 (1973): 283–88.

Morgan, Gordon D., and Izola Preston, *The Edge of Campus: A Journal of the Black Experience at the University of Arkansas* (1990).

Nash, Horace D., "Black Arkansas during Reconstruction: The Ex-Slave Narratives," *Arkansas Historical Quarterly* 48 (1989): 243–59.

Nichols, Guerdon D., "Breaking the Color Barrier at the University of Arkansas," *Arkansas Historical Quarterly* 27 (1968): 3–21.

Patterson, Ruth Polk, *The Seed of Sally Good'n: A Black Family of Arkansas, 1833–1953* (1985).

Patton, Adell, Jr., "The 'Back-to-Africa' Movement in Arkansas," *Arkansas Historical Quarterly* 51 (1993): 164–77.

Pearce, Larry Wesley, "The American Missionary Association and the Freedmen in Arkansas, 1863–1878," *Arkansas Historical Quarterly* 30 (1971): 123–44.

Richter, William Lee, "'A Dear Little Job': Second Lieutenant Hiram F. Willis, Freedmen's Bureau Agent in Southwestern Arkansas, 1866–1868," *Arkansas Historical Quarterly* 50 (1991): 158–200.

Rogers, William W., "Negro Knights of Labor in Arkansas: A Case Study of the 'Miscellaneous' Strike," *Labor History* 10 (1969): 498–505.

Rose, Jerome C., "Biological Consequences of Segregation and Economic Deprivation: A Post-Slavery Population from Southwest Arkansas," *Journal of Economic History* 49 (1989): 351–60.

Rothrock, Thomas, "Joseph Carter Corbin and Negro Education in the University of Arkansas," *Arkansas History Quarterly* 30 (1971): 277–314.

Smith, C. Calvin, "The Politics of Evasion: Arkansas' Reaction to *Smith v. Allwright*, 1944," *Journal of Negro History* 67 (1982): 40–51.

St. Hilaire, Joseph M., "The Negro Delegates in the Arkansas Constitutional Convention of 1868: A Group Profile," *Arkansas Historical Quarterly* 33 (1974): 38–69.

Taylor, Orville W., *Negro Slavery in Arkansas* (1958).

Van Deburg, William L., "The Slave Drivers of Arkansas: A New View from the Narratives," *Arkansas Historical Quarterly* 35 (1976): 231–45.

Williams, Lee E., and Lee E. Williams, II, *Anatomy of Four Race Riots: Racial Conflict in Knoxville, Elaine (Arkansas), Tulsa, and Chicago, 1919–1921* (1972).

Woodruff, Nan Elizabeth, "African-American Struggles for Citizenship in the Arkansas and Mississippi Deltas in the Age of Jim Crow," *Radical History Review* 55 (1993): 33–51.

Zellar, Gary, "H. C. Ray and Racial Politics in the African American Extension Service Program in Arkansas, 1915–1929," *Agricultural History* 72 (1998): 429–45.

26.2.4 California

Adler, Patricia R., *Watts: From Suburb to Black Ghetto* (1977).

Albin, Ray R., "The Perkins Case: The Ordeal of Three Slaves in Gold Rush California," *California History* 67 (1988): 214–27.

Anderson, E. Frederick, *The Development of Leadership and Organization Building in the Black Community of Los Angeles from 1900 through World War II* (1980).

Beasley, Delilah Leontium, *The Negro Trail Blazers of California: A Compilation of Records* (1919, rev. ed., 1997).

Bell, Howard H., "Negroes in California, 1849–1859," *Phylon* 28 (1967): 151–60.

Berwanger, Eugene H., "The 'Black Law' Question in Antebellum California," *Journal of the West* 6 (1967): 205–20.

Blodgett, Peter J., and Sara S. Hodson, "Worlds of Leisure, Worlds of Grace: Recreation, Entertainment, and the Arts in the California Experience," *California History* 75 (1996): 68–83, 108–9.

Broussard, Albert S., *Black San Francisco: The Struggle for Racial Equality in the West, 1900–1954* (1993).

——— "Oral Recollection and the Historical Reconstruction of Black San Francisco, 1915–1940," *Oral History Review* 12 (1984): 63–80.

——— "Organizing the Black Community in the San Francisco Bay Area, 1915–1930," *Arizona and the West* 23 (1981): 335–54.

——— "Slavery in California Revisited: The Fate of a Kentucky Slave in Gold Rush California," *Pacific Historian* 29 (1985): 17–21.

Bunch, Lonnie G., III, "Allensworth: The Life, Death, and Rebirth of an All-Black Community," *Californians* 5 (1987): 26–33.

Caldwell, Dan, "The Negroization of the Chinese Stereotype in California," *Southern California Quarterly* 53 (1971): 123–31.

Carlton, Robert L., "Blacks in San Diego County: A Social Profile, 1850–1880," *Journal of San Diego History* 21 (1975): 7–20.

Cole, Olen, Jr., *Black Youth in the Program of the Civilian Conservation Corps for California, 1933–1942* (1986).

Coray, Michael S., "Negro and Mulatto in the Pacific West, 1850–1860: Changing Patterns of Black Population Growth," *Pacific Historian* 29 (1985): 18–27.

Crouchett, Lawrence P., Lonnie O. Bunch, III, and Martha Kendall Winnacker, *Visions toward Tomorrow: The History of the East Bay Afro-American Community, 1852–1977* (1989).

Daniels, Douglas H., "Looking for a Home: The Travelcraft Skills of San Francisco's Pioneer Black Residents," *Umoja* 1 (1977): 49–70.

———— "Los Angeles Zoot: Race 'Riot,' The Pachuco, and Black Music Culture," *The Journal of Negro History* 82 (1997): 201–20.

———— *Pioneer Urbanites: A Social and Cultural History of Blacks in San Francisco* (1979).

deGraaf, Lawrence B., "The City of Black Angels: The Emergence of the Los Angeles Ghetto, 1890–1930," *Pacific Historical Review* 39 (1970): 323–52.

Dugged, Leonard, *Colonization of Free Blacks. Memorial of Leonard Dugged, George A. Bailey, and 240 Other Free Colored Persons of California* (1862).

Fisher, James A., "The Political Development of the Black Community in California, 1850–1950," *California Historical Quarterly* 50 (1971): 256–66.

———— "The Struggle for Negro Testimony in California, 1851–1863," *Southern California Quarterly* 51 (1969): 313–24.

Goode, Kenneth G., *California's Black Pioneers: A Brief Historical Survey* (1974).

Gutiérrez, Henry J., "Racial Politics in Los Angeles: Black and Mexican American Challenges to Unequal Education in the 1960s," *Southern California Quarterly* 78 (1996): 51–86.

Hendrick, Irving G., "Approaching Equality of Educational Opportunity in California: The Successful Struggle of Black Citizens, 1880–1920," *Pacific Historian* 25 (1981): 22–29.

Hewes, Laurence I., Jr., and William Y. Bell, Jr., *Intergroup Relations in San Diego: Some Aspects of Community Life in San Diego which Particularly Affect Minority Groups* (1946).

Horne, Gerald, *Fire This Time: The Watts Uprising and the 1960s* (1995).

Johnsen, Leigh Dana, "Equal Rights and the 'Heathen "Chinee"': Black Activism in San Francisco, 1865–1875," *Western Historical Quarterly* 11 (1980): 57–68.

Johnson, Charles Spurgeon, Herman H. Long, and Grace Jones, *The Negro War Worker in San Francisco: A Local Self-Survey* (1944).

Lachatanere, Diana, "Blacks in California: An Annotated Guide to the Manuscript Sources in the CHS Library," *California History* 57 (1978): 271–76.

Lapp, Rudolph M., *Afro-Americans in California* (1979).

———— *Archy Lee: A California Fugitive Slave Case* (1969).

———— *Black in Gold Rush California* (1977).

Madyun, Gail, and Larry Malone, "Black Pioneers in San Diego: 1880–1920," *Journal of San Diego History* 27 (1981): 91–109.

McBroome, Delores Nason, *Parallel Communities: African-Americans in California's East Bay, 1850–1963* (1993).

Model, Paul, "The 1965 Watts Rebellion: The Self-Definition of a Community," *Radical America* 24 (1990): 74–88.

Moore, Shirley Ann Wilson, "Getting There, Being There: African-American Migration to Richmond, California, 1910–1945," in Joe W. Trotter, ed., *The Great Migration in Historical Perspective: New Dimension of Race, Class, and Gender* (1991): 106–26.

———— "Traditions from Home: African Americans in Wartime Richmond, California," in Lewis A. Erenberg, and Susan E. Hirsch, ed., *The War in American Culture: Society and Consciousness During World War II* (1996): 263–83.

Murphy, Larry G., *Equality before the Law: The Struggle of Nineteenth Century Black Californians for Social and Political Justice* (1967).

Noble, Georg, "The Negro in Hollywood," *Sight and Sound* (1939).

Null, Gary, *Black Hollywood: The Negro in Motion Pictures* (1975).

Odell, Thurman A., "The Negro in California before 1890," *Pacific History* 19 (1975): 321–46.

Ogden, Annegret, "'Looking for Work in Every Direction': The Voice of David Brown, Secretary of the Colored Stock Quartz Mining Company, Sierra County, California," *Californias* 9 (1991): 14–17.

Ridout, Lionel U., "The Church, the Chinese and the Negroes in California, 1849–1893," *History Magazine of the Protestant Episcopal Church* 28 (1959): 115–38.

Siracusa, Ernest V., *Black 49'ers: The Negro in the California Gold Rush, 1848–60* (1969).

Skjeie, Sheila M., *California and the Fifteenth Amendment: A Study of Racism* (1973).

Smith, Alonzo N., "Blacks and the Los Angeles Municipal Transit System, 1941–1945," *Urbanism Past and Present* 6 (1980): 25–31.

Snorgrass, J. William, "The Black Press in the San Francisco Bay Area, 1865–1900," *California History* 60 (1981–82): 306–17.

Thurman, A. Odell, *The Negro in California before 1890* (1973).

Thurman, Sue Bailey, *Pioneers of Negro Origin in California* (1952).

Zubrinsky, Camille L., and Lawrence Bobo, "Prismatic Metropolis: Race and Residential Segregation in the City of the Angels," *Social Science Research* 25 (1996): 335–74.

26.2.5 Colorado

Armitage, Sue, Theresa Banfield, and Sarah Jacobus, "Black Women and Their Communities in Colorado," in Darlene Clark Hine, ed., *Black Women's History: Theory and Practice* (1990): 51–61.

Goldberg, Robert Alan, *Hooded Empire: The Ku Klux Klan in Colorado* (1981).

King, William M., *Going to Meet a Man: Denver's Last Legal Public Execution, 27 July 1886* (1990).

Norris, Melvin Edward, Jr., *Dearfield, Colorado: The Evolution of a Rural Black Settlement* (1980).

Wayne, George H., "Negro Migration and Colonization in Colorado: 1870–1930," *Journal of the West* 15 (1976): 102–20.

26.2.6 Connecticut

Bingham, Alfred M., "Squatter Settlements of Freed Slaves in New England," *Connecticut Historical Society Bulletin* 41 (1976): 65–80.

Brewster-Walker, Sandi J., and Mary McDuffie-Hare, "Bridgeport, Connecticut, Birth of Blacks: Abstracts of Records 1855–1864 and 1871–1885," *Journal of the Afro-American History and Genealogical Society* 4 (1983): 23–31.

Brown, Barbara W., and James M. Rose, *Black Roots in Southeastern Connecticut, 1650–1900* (1980).

Crandall, Prudence, *Report of the Arguments of Counsel in the Case of Prudence Crandall Plff. in Error vs. the State of Connecticut before the Supreme Court of Errors at Their Session at Brooklyn, July Term, 1834* (1834).

Essig, James D., "Connecticut Ministers and Slavery, 1790–1795," *Journal of American Studies* 15 (1981): 27–44.

Freed, Donald, *Agony in New Haven: The Trial of Bobby Seale, Ericka Huggins, and the Black Panther Party* (1973).

French, David, "Elizur Wright, Jr., and the Emergence of Anti-Colonization Sentiments on the Connecticut Western Reserve," *Ohio History* 85 (1976): 49–66.

Fuller, Edmund, *Prudence Crandall: An Incident of Racism in Nineteenth-Century Connecticut* (1971).

Hill, Isaac, *A Sketch of the 29th Regiment of Connecticut Colored Troops* (1867).

Kimball, John Calvin, *Connecticut's Canterbury Tale, Its Heroine Prudence Crandall, and Its Moral for Today* (1885).

Logan, Gwendolyn Evans, "The Slave in Connecticut during the American Revolution," *Connecticut Historical Society Bulletin* 30 (1965): 73–80.

Seeman, Erik R., "'Justise Must Take Plase': Three African Americans Speak of Religion in Eighteenth-Century New England," *William and Mary Quarterly* 56 (1999): 393–414.

Strother, Horatio T., *The Underground Railroad in Connecticut* (1962).

Warner, Robert A., *New Haven Negroes: A Social History* (1940).

White, David Oliver, *Connecticut's Black Soldiers, 1775–1783* (1973).

——— "Hartford's African Free Schools, 1830–1868," *Connecticut Historical Society Bulletin* 39 (1974): 47–53.

26.2.7   Delaware

Bendler, Bruce, "Securing One of the Blessings of Liberty: Black Families in Lower New Castle County, 1790–1850," *Delaware History* 25 (1993–1994): 237–52.

Hancock, Harold B., "The Indenture System in Delaware, 1681–1921," *Delaware History* 16 (1974): 47–59.

——— "Not Quite Men: The Free Negroes in Delaware in the 1830's," *Civil War History* 17 (1971): 320–31.

Hiller, Amy M., "The Disfranchisement of Delaware Negroes in the Late Nineteenth Century," *Delaware History* 13 (1968): 124–53.

Hoffecker, Carol E., "The Politics of Exclusion: Blacks in Late Nineteenth-Century Wilmington, Delaware," *Delaware History* 16 (1974): 60–72.

Homsey, Elizabeth Moyne, "Free Blacks in Kent County, Delaware, 1790–1830," *Working Papers from the Regional Economic History Research Center* 3 (1980): 31–57.

Kee, Ed, "The *Brown* Decision and Milford, Delaware, 1954–1965," *Delaware History* 27 (1997/1998): 205–44.

Lewis, Ronald L., "Reverend T. G. Steward and the Education of Blacks in Reconstruction Delaware," *Delaware History* 19 (1981): 156–78.

Prather, H. Leon, *We Have Taken a City: The Wilmington Massacre and Coup of 1898* (1984).

Taggart, Robert J., "Philanthropy and Black Public Education in Delaware, 1918–1930," *Pennsylvania Magazine of History and Biography* 103 (1979): 467–83.

Williams, William H., *Slavery and Freedom in Delaware, 1639–1865* (1996).

26.2.8   District of Columbia

Borchert, James, *Alley Life in Washington: Family, Community, Religion, and Folklife in the City, 1850–1970* (1982).

——— "Urban Neighborhood and Community: Informal Group Life, 1850–1970," *Journal of Interdisciplinary History* 11 (1981): 607–31.

Brown, Letitia Woods, *Free Negroes in the District of Columbia, 1790–1846* (1972).

Brown, Letitia Woods, and Elsie M. Lewis, *Washington in the New Era, 1870–1970* (1972).

Cheek, Charles D., and Amy Friedlander, "Pottery and Pig's Feet: Space, Ethnicity, and Neighborhood in Washington, D.C., 1880–1940," *Historical Archaeology* 24 (1990): 34–60.

Clarke, Nina Honemond, *History of the Nineteenth-Century Black Churches in Maryland and Washington, D.C.* (1983).

Clark-Lewis, Elizabeth, *Living In, Living Out: African American Domestics in Washington, D.C., 1910–1940* (1994).

Cobb, W. Montague, *The First Negro Medical Society: A History of the Medico-Chirurgical Society of the District of Columbia, 1884–1939* (1939).

Cole, Stephanie, "Changes for Mrs.Thornton's Arthur: Patterns of Domestic Service in Washington, D.C., 1800–1835," *Social Science History* 15 (1991): 367–79.

Cromwell, John W., "First Negro Churches in the District of Columbia," *Journal of Negro History* 7 (1922): 64–106.

Dabney, Lillian Gertrude, *The History of Schools for Negroes in the District of Columbia, 1807–1947* (1949).

Dyson, Walter, *Howard University, the Capstone of Negro Education: A History, 1867–1940* (1941).

Fitzpatrick, Michael Andrew, "'A Great Agitation for Business': Black Economic Development in Shaw," *Washington History* 2 (1990–1991): 48–73.

Frazier, Edward Franklin, *Negro Youth at the Crossways: Their Personality Development in the Middle States* (1940).

Gardner, Bettye, and Bettye Thomas, "The Cultural Impact of the Howard Theatre on the Black Community," *The Journal of Negro History* 55 (1970): 253–65.

Green, Constance McLaughlin, *The Secret City: A History of Race Relations in the Nation's Capitol* (1967).

Harley, Sharon, "Beyond the Classroom: Organizational Lives of Black Female Educators in the District of Columbia, 1890–1930," *Journal of Negro Education* 51 (1982): 254–65.

——— "Black Women in a Southern City: Washington, D.C., 1890–1920," in Joanne V. Hawks, and Sheila L. Skemp, ed., *Sex, Race, and the Role of Women in the South* (1983): 59–74.

Hayes, Lawrence John Wesley, *The Negro Federal Government Worker: A Study of His Classification Status in the District of Columbia, 1883–1938* (1941).

Holt, Thomas C., *A Special Mission: The Story of Freedmen's Hospital, 1862–1962* (1975).

Hundley, Mary Gibson, *The Dunbar Story, 1870–1955* (1965).

Johnson, Ronald M., "From Romantic Suburb to Racial Enclave: LeDroit Park, Washington, D.C., 1880–1920," *Phylon* 45 (1984): 264–270.

Johnston, Allan, Surviving Freedom: The Black Community of Washington, D.C., 1860–1880 (1993).

Jones, Beverly W., "Before Montgomery and Greensboro: The Desegregation Movement in the District of Columbia, 1950–1953," *Phylon* 43 (1982): 144–54.

Jones, William Henry, *The Housing of Negroes in Washington, D.C.: A Study in Human Ecology* (1929).

——— *Recreation and Amusement among Negroes in Washington, D.C.: A Sociological Analysis of the Negro in an Urban Environment* (1927).

Krislov, Samuel, *The Negro in Federal Employment: The Quest for Equal Opportunity* (1967).

Lamb, Daniel Smith, *The Howard University Medical Department, Washington D.C: A Historical, Biographical, and Statistical Souvenir* (1900).

Laprade, William T., "The Domestic Slave Trade in the District of Columbia," *Journal of Negro History* 11 (1926): 17–34.

Levey, Jane Freundel, "The Scurlock Studio," *Washington History* 1 (1989): 41–58.

Moldow, Gloria, *Women Doctors in Gilded-Age Washington: Race, Gender, and Professionalization* (1987).

Moss, Alfred A., Jr., *The American Negro Academy: Voice of the Talented Tenth* (1981).

Provine, Dorothy, "The Economic Position of Free Blacks in the District of Columbia, 1800–1860," *Journal of Negro History* 589 (1973): 61–72.

Robinson, Henry S., "Some Aspects of the Free Negro Population of Washington, D.C., 1800–1862," *Maryland Historical Magazine* 64 (1969): 43–64.

Rohrs, Richard C., "Antislavery Politics and the Pearl Incident of 1848," *Historian* 56 (1994): 711–24.

Shannon, A. H., *The Negro in Washington: A Study in Race Amalgamation* (1930).

Smith, Kathryn S., "Remembering U Street," *Washington History* 9 (1997/1998): 28–53, 93–94.

Terrell, Mary Church, "History of the High School for Negroes in Washington," *Journal of Negro History* 2 (1917): 252–66.

U.S. Department of Labor, "Small Dwelling Project in the District of Columbia," *Monthly Labor Review* 44 (1937): 550–58.

Vlach, John Michael, "Evidence of Slave Housing in Washington," *Washington History* 5 (1993–94): 64–74.

Willis-Thomas, Deborah, and Jane Lusaka, *Visual Journal: Harlem and D.C. in the Thirties and Forties* (1996).

Wormley, G. Smith, "Educators of the First Half Century of Public Schools of the District of Columbia," *Journal of Negro History* 17 (1932): 124–40.

26.2.9 Florida

Akin, Edward N., "When a Minority Becomes the Majority: Blacks in Jacksonville Politics, 1887–1907," *Florida Historical Quarterly* 53 (1974): 123–45.

Barr, Ruth B., and Hodeste Hargis, "The Voluntary Exile of Free Negroes of Pensacola," *Florida Historical Society Quarterly* 17 (1938): 3–14.

Beatty, Bess, "John Willis Menard: A Progressive Black in Post-Civil War Florida," *Florida Historical Quarterly* 59 (1980): 123–43.

Bragaw, Donald H., "Status of Negroes in a Southern Port City in the Progressive Era: Pensacola, 1896–1920," *Florida Historical Quarterly* 51 (1972): 281–302.

Braukman, Stacy, "Women and the Civil Rights Movement in Tampa: An Interview with Ellen H. Green," *Tampa Bay History* 14 (1992): 62–69.

Brigham, Clarence S., "Antebellum Census Enumerations in Florida," *Florida Historical Society Quarterly* 6 (1927): 42–55.

Brown, Canter, Jr., "Carpetbagger Intrigues, Black Leadership, and a Southern Loyalist Triumph: Florida's Gubernatorial Election of 1872," *Florida Historical Quarterly* 72 (1994): 275–301.

———— *Florida's Black Public Officials, 1867–1924* (1998).

———— "Race Relations in Territorial Florida, 1821–1845," *Florida Historical Quarterly* 73 (1995): 287–307.

———— "The 'Sarrazota, or Runaway Negro Plantations': Tampa Bay's First Black Community, 1812–1821," *Tampa Bay History* 12 (1990): 5–29.

Colburn, David R., *Racial Change and Community Crisis: St. Augustine, Florida, 1877–1980* (1985).

———— "Rosewood and America in the Early Twentieth Century," *Florida Historical Quarterly* 76 (1997): 175–92.

Colburn, David R., and Jane L. Landers, ed., *The African American Heritage of Florida* (1995).

Corbett, Theodore G., "Migration to a Spanish Imperial Frontier in the Seventeenth and Eighteenth Centuries: St. Augustine," *Hispanic American Historical Review* 54 (1974): 414–30.

Danese, Tracy E., "Disfranchisement, Women's Suffrage, and the Failure of the Florida Grandfather Clause," *Florida Historical Quarterly* 74 (1995): 117–31.

Deagan, Kathleen A., "Mestizaje in Colonial St. Augustine," *Ethnohistory* 20 (1973): 55–65.

———— *Spanish St. Augustine: The Archaeology of a Colonial Creole Community* (1983).

Dillon, Patricia, "Civil Rights and School Desegregation in Sanford," *Florida Historical Quarterly* 76 (1998): 310–25.

Dodd, Dorothy, "The Schooner Emperor: An Incident of the Illegal Slave Trade in Florida," *Florida Historical Society Quarterly* 13 (1935): 117–28.

Dunn, Marvin, *Black Miami in the Twentieth Century* (1997).

Eckert, Edward K., "Contract Labor in Florida during Reconstruction," *Florida Historical Quarterly* 47 (1968): 34–50.

Emmons, Caroline, "Somebody Has Got To Do That Work: Harry T. Moore and the Struggle for African-American Voting Rights in Florida," *The Journal of Negro History* 82 (1997): 232–43.

Evans, Arthus S., Jr., and David Lee, *Pearl City, Florida: A Black Community Remembers* (1990).

Farris, Charles D., "The Re-Enfranchisement of Negroes in Florida," *Journal of Negro History* 39 (1954): 259–83.

Foster, John T. , Jr.,, and Sarah W. Foster, "The Last Shall Be First: Northern Methodists in Reconstruction Jacksonville," *Florida Historical Quarterly* 70 (1992): 265–80.

Garrow, David, ed., *St. Augustine, Florida, 1963–1964: Mass Protest and Racial Violence* (1989).

Garvin, Russell, "The Free Negro in Florida before the Civil War," *Florida Hisorical Quarterly* 46 (1967): 1–17.

Gatewood, Willard B., Jr., "Black Troops in Florida during the Spanish-American War," *Tampa Bay History* 20 (1998): 17–31.

———— "Negro Troops in Florida, 1898," *Florida Historical Quarterly* 49 (1970): 1–15.

George, Paul S., "Colored Town: Miami's Black Community, 1896–1930," *Florida Historical Quarterly* 56 (1978): 432–47.

———— "Policing Miami's Black Community, 1896–1930," *Florida Historical Quarterly* 57 (1979).

Granade, Ray, "Slave Unrest in Florida," *Florida Historical Quarterly* 55 (1976): 18–36.

Greenbaum, Susan D., *Afro-Cubans in Ybor City: A Centennial History* (1986).

Halderman, Keith, "Blanche Armwood of Tampa and the Strategy of Interracial Cooperation," *Florida Historical Quarterly* 74 (1996): 287–303.

Hall, Robert L., "Tallahassee's Black Churches, 1865–1885," *Florida Historical Quarterly* 58 (1979): 185–96.

———— "'Yonder Come Day': Religious Dimensions of the Transition from Slavery to Freedom in Florida," *Florida Historical Quarterly* 65 (1987): 411–432.

Hann, John H., "Heathen Acuera, Murder, and a Potano Cimarrona: The St. Johns River and the Alachua Prairie in the 1670s," *Florida Historical Quarterly* 70 (1992): 451–74.

Hering, Julia F., "Plantation Economy in Leon County, 1830–1840," *Florida Historical Quarterly* 33 (1954): 32–47.

Holland, Antonio F., "Education over Politics: Nathan B. Young at Florida A and M College, 1901–1923," *Agricultural History* 65 (1992): 131–48.

Hume, Richard L., "Membership of the Florida Constitutional Convention of 1868: A Case Study of Republican Factionalism in the Reconstruction South," *Florida Historical Quarterly* 51 (1972): 1–21.

Ingalls, Robert P., "Lynching and Establishment Violence in Tampa, 1858–1935," *Journal of Southern History* 53 (1987): 613–44.

Jones, Maxine D., "The Rosewood Massacre and the Women Who Survived It," *Florida Historical Quarterly* 76 (1997): 193–208.

———— "'Without Compromise or Fear': Florida's African American Female Activists," *Florida Historical Quarterly* 77 (1999): 475–502.

Kersey, Harry A., Jr., "St. Augustine School: Seventy-Five Years of Negro Parochial Education in Gainesville, Florida," *Florida Historical Quarterly* 51 (1972): 58–63.

Kharif, Wali R., "Black Reaction to Segregation and Discrimination in Post-Reconstruction Florida," *Florida Historical Quarterly* 64 (1985): 161–73.

Kiple, Kenneth F., "The Case against a Nineteenth-Century Cuba-Florida Slave Trade," *Florida History Quarterly* 49 (1971): 346–55.

Klos, George E., "Black Seminoles in Territorial Florida," *Southern Historian* 10 (1989): 26–42.

Landers, Jane G., "Acquisition and Loss on a Spanish Frontier: The Free Black Homesteaders of Florida, 1784–1821," *Slavery and Abolition* 17 (1996): 85–101.

———— *Black Society in Spanish Florida* (1999).

———— "Black-Indian Interaction in Spanish Florida," *Colonial Latin American Historical Review* 2 (1993): 141–62.

———— "Gracia Real de Santa Teresa de Mose: A Free Black Town in Spanish Colonial Florida," *American Historical Review* 95 (1990): 9–30.

———— "Spanish Sanctuary: Fugitives in Florida, 1687–1790," *Florida Historical Quarterly* 62 (1984): 296–313.

Linsin, Christopher E., "Skilled Slave Labor in Florida: 1850–1860," *Florida Historical Quarterly* 75 (1996): 183–96.

Matijasic, Thomas D., "African Colonization Activity at Miami University during the Administration of Robert Hamilton Bishop," *Old Northwest* 12 (1986): 83–94.

McDonogh, Gary W., ed., *The Florida Negro: A Federal Writers' Project Legacy* (1993).

McKinney, Richard I., "American Baptists and Black Education in Florida," *American Baptist Quarterly* 11 (1992): 309–36.

Milligan, John D., "Slave Rebelliousness and the Florida Maroon," *Prologue* 6 (1974): 4–18.

Mohl, Raymond A., "Black Immigrants: Bahamians in Early Twentieth-Century Miami," *Florida Historical Quarterly* 65 (1987): 271–97.

———— "Making the Second Ghetto in Metropolitan Miami, 1940–1960," *Journal of Urban History* 21 (1995): 395–427.

———— "On the Edge: Blacks and Hispanics in Metropolitan Miami since 1959," *Florida Historical Quarterly* 69 (1990): 37–56.

———— "Shadows in the Sunshine: Race and Ethnicity in Miami," *Tequesta* 49 (1989): 63–80.

———— "Trouble in Paradise: Race and Housing in Miami during the New Deal Era," *Prologue* 19 (1987): 7–21.

Neyland, Leedell W., "State-Supported Higher Education among Negroes in the State of Florida," *Florida Historical Quarterly* 43 (1964): 105–22.

Patrick, Rembert Wallace, *Florida Fiasco: Rampant Rebels on the Georgia-Florida Border, 1810–1815* (1954).

Patterson, Gordon, "Hurston Goes to War: The Army Signal Corps in Saint Augustine," *Florida Historical Quarterly* 74 (1995): 166–83.

Peek, Ralph L., "Lawlessness in Florida, 1868–1871," *Florida Historical Quarterly* 40 (1961): 164–85.

Peters, Virginia Bergman, *The Florida Wars* (1979).

Pollock, Philip H., III, and M. Elliot Vittas, "Who Bears the Burdens of Environmental Pollution? Race, Ethnicity, and Environmental Equity in Florida," *Social Science Quarterly* 76 (1995): 294–310.

Porter, Kenneth Wiggins, "Florida Slaves and Free Negroes in the Seminole War, 1835–1842," *Journal of Negro History* 28 (1943): 390–421.

Rabby, Glenda Alice, *The Pain and the Promise: The Struggle for Civil Rights in Tallahassee, Florida* (1999).

Richardson, Joe M., *The Negro in the Reconstruction of Florida, 1865–1877* (1965).

———, ed., "'We are Truly Doing Missionary Work': Letters From American Missionary Association Teachers in Florida, 1864–1874," *Florida Historical Quarterly* 54 (1975): 178–95.

Rivers, Larry E., "'Dignity and Importance': Slavery in Jefferson County, Florida, 1827–1860," *Florida Historical Quarterly* 61 (1983): 404–30.

——— "Slavery in Microcosm: Leon County, Florida, 1824 to 1860," *Journal of Negro History* 66 (1981): 235–45.

——— "Slavery and the Political Economy of Gadsden County, Florida, 1823–1861," *Florida Historical Quarterly* 70 (1991): 1–19.

Rosen, F. Bruce, "The Influence of the Peabody Fund on Education in Reconstruction Florida," *Florida Historical Quarterly* 55 (1977): 310–20.

Schafer, Daniel L., "'A Class of People Neither Freemen Nor Slaves': From Spanish to American Race Relations in Florida, 1821–1861," *Journal of Social History* 26 (1993): 587–609.

Scott, J. Irving, *The Education of Black People in Florida* (1974).

Shofner, Jerrell H., "Florida and the Black Migration," *Florida Historical Quarterly* 57 (1979): 267–88.

——— "Forced Labor in the Florida Forests, 1880–1950," *Journal of Forest History* 25 (1981): 14–25.

——— "Militant Negro Laborers in Reconstruction Florida," *Journal of Southern History* 39 (1973): 397–408.

——— "Negro Laborers and the Forest Industries in Reconstruction Florida," *Journal of Forest History* 19 (1975): 180–91.

——— *Nor Is It over Yet: Florida in the Era of Reconstruction, 1863–1877* (1974).

——— "Wartime Unionists, Unreconstructed Rebels, and Andrew Johnson's Amnesty Program in the Reconstruction Debacle of Jackson County, Florida," *Gulf Coast Historical Review* 4 (1989): 162–71.

Siebert, Wilbur H., "Slavery and White Servitude in East Florida, 1726–1776," *Florida Historical Society Quarterly* 10 (1931): 3–23.

——— "Slavery in East Florida, 1776–1785," *Florida Historical Society Quarterly* 10 (1932): 139–61.

Smith, Charles, and Lewis Killian, *The Tallahassee Bus Protest* (1958).

Smith, Julia Floyd, *Slavery and Plantation Growth in Antebellum Florida, 1821–1860* (1973).

——— "Slavetrading in Antebellum Florida," *Florida History Quarterly* 50 (1972): 252–61.

Sowell, David, "Racial Patterns of Labor in Postbellum Florida: Gainesville, 1870–1900," *Florida Historical Quarterly* 63 (1985): 434–44.

Stafford, Frances, "Illegal Importations: Enforcement of the Slave Trade Laws along the Florida Coast, 1810–1828," *Florida Historical Quarterly* 46 (1967): 124–33.

Thomas, David Y., "The Free Negro in Florida before 1865," *South Atlantic Quarterly* 10 (1911): 335–45.

Thompson, Joseph Conan, "Toward a More Humane Oppression: Florida's Slave Codes, 1821–1861," *Florida Historical Quarterly* 71 (1993): 324–38.

Tscheschlok, Eric, "Long Time Coming: Miami's Liberty City Riot of 1968," *Florida Historical Quarterly* 74 (1996): 440–60.

White, Arthur O., "State Leadership and Black Education in Florida, 1876–1976," *Phylon* 42 (1981): 168–79.

Williamson, Edward C., *Florida Politics in the Gilded Age, 1877–1893* (1976).

Wright, I. A., comp., "Dispatches of Spanish Officials Bearing on the Free Negro Settlement of Gracia Real de Santa Teresa de Mose, Florida," *Journal of Negro History* 9 (1924): 144–95.

Wright, J. Leitch, Jr., "Blacks in British East Florida," *Florida Historical Quarterly* 54 (1976): 425–42.

26.2.10   Georgia

Abbott, Richard H., "Jason Clarke Swayze: Republican Editor in Reconstruction Georgia, 1867–1873," *Georgia Historical Quarterly* 79 (1995): 337–66.

Adams, William Hampton, ed., *Historical Archeology of Plantations at Kings Bay, Camden County, Georgia* (1987).

Alexander, Adele Logan, *Ambiguous Lives: Free Women of Color in Rural Georgia, 1789–1879* (1991).

Alexander, R. J., "Negro Business in Atlanta," *Southern Economic Journal* 17 (1951): 451–64.

Armstrong, Thomas F., "The Building of a Black Church: Community in Post Civil War Liberty County, Georgia," *Georgia Historical Quarterly* 66 (1982): 346–67.

———— "From Task Labor to Free Labor: The Transition along Georgia's Rice Coast, 1820–1880," *Georgia Historical Quarterly* 64 (1980): 432–47.

Ascher, Robert, and Charles H. Fairbanks, "Excavation of a Slave Cabin: Georgia, USA," *Historical Archaeology* 5 (1971): 3–17.

Bacote, Clarence A., "The Negro in Atlanta Politics," *Phylon* 16 (1955): 333–50.

———— "Negro Officeholders in Georgia under President McKinley," *Journal of Negro History* 44 (1959): 217–39.

———— "Negro Proscriptions, Protests and Proposed Solutions in Georgia, 1880–1908," *Journal of Southern History* 25 (1959): 471–98.

———— "Some Aspects of Negro Life in Georgia, 1880–1908," *Journal of Negro History* 43 (1958): 186–213.

———— *The Story of Atlanta University: A Century of Service, 1865–1965* (1969).

Baker, Pearl, and Mary Bondurant Warren, "Registry of Free People of Colour, Columbia County, Georgia," *Journal of the Afro-American Historical and Genealogical Society* 2 (1981): 37–41.

Banks, Enoch M., *The Economics of Land Tenure in Georgia* (1905).

Barrow, David C., Jr., "A Georgia Plantation," *Scribner's Monthly* 21 (1881): 830–36.

Bayor, Ronald H., "Ethnic Residential Patterns in Atlanta, 1880–1940," *Georgia Historical Quarterly* 64 (1979): 435–46.

———— *Race and the Shaping of Twentieth-Century Atlanta* (1996).

———— "Roads to Racial Segregation: Atlanta in the Twentieth Century," *Journal of Urban History* 15 (1988): 3–21.

Bellamy, Donnie D., and Diane E. Walker, "Slaveholding in Antebellum Augusta and Richmond County, Georgia," *Phylon* 48 (1987): 165–77.

Bellamy, Donnie D., "The Legal Status of Black Georgians during the Colonial and Revolutionary Eras," *Journal of Negro History* 74 (1989): 1–10.

———— "Macon, Georgia, 1823–1860: A Study in Urban Slavery," *Phylon* 45 (1984).

Berwanger, Eugene H., "The Case of Stirrup and Edwards, 1861–1870: The Kidnapping and Georgia Enslavement of West Indian Blacks," *Georgia Historical Quarterly* 76 (1992): 1–18.

Birnie, Cassandra M., "Race and Politics in Georgia and South Carolina," *Phylon* 13 (1952): 236–44.

Blackwelder, Julia Kirk, "Quiet Suffering: Atlanta Women in the 1930s," *Georgia History Quarterly* 61 (1977): 112–24.

Blassingame, John W., "Before the Ghetto: The Making of the Black Community in Savannah, Georgia, 1865–1880," *Journal of Social History* 6 (1973): 463–88.

Boney, F. N., "Slaves as Guinea Pigs: Georgia and Alabama Episodes," *Alabama Review* 37 (1984): 45–51.

Brown, Thomas Isaacs, *Economic Cooperation among the Negroes of Georgia* (1917).

Brown, Titus, "Origins of African American Education in Macon, Georgia, 1865–1866," *Journal of Southwest Georgia History* 11 (1996): 43–59.

Brundage, W. Fitzhugh, *Lynching in the New South: Georgia and Virginia, 1880–1930* (1993).

Bryant, Johnathan M., "My Soul An't Yours Mas'r: The Records of the African Church at Penfield, 1848–1863," *Georgia Historical Quarterly* 75 (1994): 401–12.

Byrne, William A., "The Hiring of Woodson, Slave Carpenter of Savannah," *Georgia Historical Quarterly* 77 (1993): 245–63.

——— "'Uncle Billy' Sherman Comes to Town: The Free Winter of Black Savannah," *Georgia Historical Quarterly* 79 (1995): 91–116.

Cadwallader, D. E., and F. J. Wilson, "Folklore Medicine among Georgia's Piedmont Negroes after the Civil War," *Georgia Historical Quarterly* 49 (1965): 217–27.

Campbell, Walter E., "Profit, Prejudice, and Protest: Utility Competition and the Generation of Jim Crow Streetcars in Savannah, 1905–1907," *Georgia Historical Quarterly* 70 (1986): 197–231.

Capeci, Dominic J., Jr, and Jack C. Knight, "Reckoning with Violence: W. E. B. Du Bois and the 1906 Atlanta Race Riot," *Journal of Southern History* 62 (1996): 727–66.

Carter, Edward Randolph, *The Black Side: A Partial History of the Business, Religious and Educational Side of the Negro in Atlanta, GA* (1894).

Chaplin, Joyce E., "Tidal Rice Cultivation and the Problem of Slavery in South Carolina and Georgia, 1760–1815," *William and Mary Quarterly* 49 (1992): 29–61.

Cimbala, Paul A., "The Freedmen's Bureau, the Freedmen, and Sherman's Grant in Reconstruction Georgia, 1865–1867," *Journal of Southern History* 55 (1989): 597–632.

——— "The 'Talisman Power': Davis Tillson, the Freedmen's Bureau, and Free Labor in Reconstruction Georgia, 1865–1866," *Civil War History* 28 (1982): 153–71.

Clark, George P., "The Role of the Haitian Volunteers at Savannah in 1779: An Attempt at an Objective View," *Phylon* 41 (1980): 356–66.

Clifton, James M., "A Half-Century of a Georgia Rice Plantation," *North Carolina Historical Review* 47 (1970): 388–415.

———, ed., *Life and Labor on Argyle Island: Letters and Documents of a Savannah River Rice Plantation, 1833–1867* (1978).

Conway, Alan, *The Reconstruction of Georgia* (1966).

Cook, James F., "The Georgia Gubernatorial Election of 1942," *Atlanta Historical Bulletin* 18 (1973): 7–19.

Cornelius, Janet, "Slave Marriages in a Georgia Congregation," in Orville Vernon Burton, and Robert C. McMath, Jr., ed., *Class, Conflict, and Consensus: Antebellum Southern Community Studies* (1982): 128–45.

Coulter, E. Merton, "Four Slave Trials in Elbert County, Georgia," *Georgia Historical Quarterly* 41 (1957): 237–46.

——— "Slavery and Freedom in Athens, Georgia, 1860–1866," *Georgia Historical Quarterly* 49 (1965): 264–93.

Crowe, Charles, "Racial Violence and Social Reform: Origins of the Atlanta Riot of 1906," *Journal of Negro History* 53 (1968): 234–56.

——— "Racial Massacre in Atlanta, September 22, 1906," *Journal of Negro History* 54 (1969): 150–73.

Diamond, B. I., and J. O. Baylen, "The Demise of the Georgia Guard Colored, 1868–1914," *Phylon* 45 (1984): 311–13.

Dittmer, John, *Black Georgia in the Progressive Era, 1900–1920* (1977).

Drago, Edmund L., "The Black Household in Dougherty County, Georgia, 1870–1900," *Journal of Southwest Georgia History* 1 (1983): 38–40.

——— *Black Politicians and Reconstruction in Georgia: A Splendid Failure* (1982).

——— "Georgia's First Black Voter Registrars during Reconstruction," *Georgia Historical Quarterly* 78 (1994): 760–93.

——— "Sources at the National Archives for Genealogical and Local History Research: The Black Family in Dougherty County, Georgia, 1870–1900," *Prologue* 14 (1982): 81–88.

Du Bois, W. E. B., ed., *Some Notes on Negro Crime, Particularly in Georgia* (1904).

Duncan, Russell, *Entrepreneur for Equality: Governor Rufus Bullock, Commerce, and Race in Post-Civil War Georgia* (1994).

Edwards, John E., "Slave Justice in Four Middle Georgia Counties," *Georgia Historical Quarterly* 57 (1973): 265–73.

Eisterhold, John A., "Savannah: Lumber Center of the South Atlantic," *Georgia Historical Quarterly* 57 (1973): 526–43.

Eskew, Glenn T., "Black Elitism and the Failure of Paternalism in Postbellum Georgia: The Case of Bishop Lucius Henry Holsey," *Journal of Southern History* 58 (1992): 637–66.

Fairbanks, Charles H., "Spaniards, Planters, Ships, and Slaves: Historical Archaeology in Florida and Georgia," *Archaeology* 29 (1976): 164–72.

Flanders, Ralph B., "The Free Negro in Antebellum Georgia," *North Carolina Historical Review* 9 (1932): 250–72.

———— *Plantation Slavery in Georgia* (1933).

———— "Planters' Problems in Antebellum Georgia," *Georgia Historical Quarterly* 14 (1930): 17–40.

Flynn, Charles L., Jr., *White Land, Black Labor: Caste and Class in Late Nineteenth-Century Georgia* (1983).

Formwalt, Lee W., "'Corner-Stone of the Cotton Kingdom': W. E. B. DuBois's 1898 View of Dougherty County," *Georgia Historical Quarterly* 71 (1987): 693–700.

Galishoff, Stuart, "Germs Know No Color Line: Black Health and Public Policy in Atlanta, 1900–1918," *Journal of the History of Medicine and Allied Sciences* 40 (1985): 22–41.

Garrow, David J., ed., *Atlanta, Georgia, 1960–1961: Sit-Ins and Student Activism* (1989).

Gelfand, H. Michael, "Chronicling an African American Life in Athens: James W. Davis and His Georgia Writers' Project Interview, 1939," *Georgia Historical Quarterly* 81 (1997): 713–34.

Georgia Writers' Project, *Drums and Shadows: Survival Studies among the Georgia Coastal Negroes* (1940).

Goldsmith, Peter, "Healing and Denominationalism on the Georgia Coast," *Southern Quarterly* 23 (1985): 83–102.

———— *When I Rise Cryin' Holy: African-American Denominationalism on the Georgia Coast* (1989).

Gordon, Asa H., *The Georgia Negro: A History* (1937).

Gottlieb, Manuel, "The Land Question in Georgia during Reconstruction," *Science and Society* 3 (1939): 356–88.

Grantham, Dewey W., Jr., "Georgia Politics and the Disfranchisement of the Negro," *Georgia Historical Quarterly* 32 (1948): 1–21.

Gray, Ralph, and Betty Wood, "The Transition from Indentured to Involuntary Servitude in Colonial Georgia," *Explorations in Economic History* 13 (1976): 353–70.

Green, Fletcher M., "Georgia's Forgotten Industry: Gold Mining," *Georgia Historical Quarterly* 19 (1935): 91–11.

Griffith, Benjamin W., "A Longer Version of 'Guinea Negro Song': From a Georgia Frontier Songster," *Southern Folklore* 28 (1964): 116–18.

Hahn, Steven, *The Roots of Southern Populism: Yeoman Farmers and the Transformation of the Georgia Upcountry, 1850–1890* (1983).

Hall, Robert H., "Segregation in the Public Schools of Georgia," *Georgia Bar Journal* 16 (1954): 417–46.

Hammett, Hugh B., "Labor and Race: The Georgia Railroad Strike of 1909," *Labor History* 16 (1975): 470–84.

Hanks, Lawrence J., *The Struggle for Black Political Empowerment in Three Georgia Counties* (1987).

Hargis, Peggy G., "Beyond the Marginality Thesis: The Acquisition and Loss of Land by African Americans in Georgia, 1880–1930," *Agricultural History* 72 (1998): 241–62.

Harmon, David Andrew, *Beneath the Image of the Civil Rights Movement and Race Relations: Atlanta, Georgia, 1946–1981* (1996).

Harris, J. William, *Plain Folk and Gentry in a Slave Society: White Liberty and Black Slavery in Augusta's Hinterlands* (1985).

Harris, William H., "Work and the Family in Black Atlanta, 1880," *Journal of Social History* 9 (1976): 319–30.

Harvey, Diane, "The Terri, Augusta's Black Enclave," *Richmond County History* 5 (1973): 60–75.

Henderson, Alexa Benson, *Atlanta Life Insurance Company: Guardian of Black Economic Dignity* (1990).

————— "Herman E. Perry and Black Enterprise in Atlanta, 1908–1925," *Business History Review* 61 (1987): 216–42.

Holmes, Michael S., "The Blue Eagle as 'Jim Crow Bird': The NRA and Georgia's Black Workers," *Journal of Negro History* 57 (1972): 276–83.

————— "The New Deal and Georgia's Black Youth," *Journal of Southern History* 38 (1972): 443–60.

Holmes, William F., "Labor Agents and the Georgia Exodus, 1899–1900," *South Atlantic Quarterly* 79 (1980): 436–48.

————— "Moonshining and Collective Violence: Georgia, 1889–1895," *Journal of American History* 67 (1980): 589–611.

————— "Whitecapping in Georgia: Carroll and Houston Counties, 1893," *Georgia Historical Quarterly* 64 (1980): 388–404.

Hopkins, Richard J., "Occupational and Geographic Mobility in Atlanta, 1870–1896," *Journal of Southern History* 34 (1968): 200–13.

————— "Status, Mobility, and the Dimensions of Change in a Southern City: Atlanta, 1870–1910," in Kenneth T. Jackson, and Stanley K. Schultz, ed., *Cities in American History* (1972).

Hornsby, Anne R., "The Accumulation of Wealth by Black Georgians, 1890–1915," *Journal of Negro History* 74 (1989): 11–30.

House, Albert V., "Labor Management Problems on Georgia Rice Plantations, 1840–1860," *Agricultural History* 28 (1954): 149–55.

Hunt, Patricia K., "Clothing as an Expression of History: The Dress of African-American Women in Georgia, 1880–1910," *Georgia Historical Quarterly* 76 (1993): 459–71.

Inscoe, John C., ed., *Georgia in Black and White: Explorations in the Race Relations of a Southern State, 1865–1950* (1994).

Janken, Kenneth R., "Civil Rights and Socializing in the Harlem Renaissance: Walter White and the Fictionalization of the 'New Negro' in Georgia," *Georgia Historical Quarterly* 80 (1996): 817–34.

Johnson, Whittington B., *Black Savannah, 1788–1864* (1996).

————— "Free African-American Women in Savannah, 1800–1860: Affluence and Autonomy amid Adversity," *Georgia Historical Quarterly* 76 (1992): 260–83.

————— "Free Blacks in Antebellum Augusta, Georgia: A Demographic and Economic Profile," *Richmond County History* 14 (1982): 10–21.

Jones, Jacqueline, *Soldiers of Light and Love: Northern Teachers and Georgia Blacks, 1865–1873* (1980).

Joyner, Charles W., *Remember Me: Slave Life in Coastal Georgia* (1989).

Kalmar, Karen L., "Southern Black Elites and the New Deal: A Case Study of Savannah, Georgia," *Georgia History Quarterly* 65 (1981): 341–55.

Kelso, William M., *Captain Jones's Wormslow: A Historical, Archaeological, and Architectural Study of an Eighteenth-Century Plantation Site Near Savannah, Georgia* (1979).

Kemble, Frances Anne, *Journal of a Residence on a Georgian Plantation in 1838–1839* (1863).

Kenzer, Robert C., "Credit Ratings of Georgia Black Businessmen, 1865–1880," *Georgia Historical Quarterly* 79 (1995): 425–40.

Koribkin, Russell, "Political Disfranchisement in Georgia," *Georgia Historical Quarterly* 74 (1990): 20–58.

Levy, B. H., "Joseph Solomon Ottolenghi: Kosher Butcher in Italy, Christian Missionary in Georgia," *Georgia Historical Quarterly* 66 (1982): 119–44.

Lichtenstein, Alex, "Chain Gangs, Communism, and the 'Negro Question': John L. Spivak's *Georgia Nigger*," *Georgia Historical Quarterly* 79 (1995): 633–58.

Martin, Charles H., "White Supremacy and Black Workers: Georgia's Black Shirts Combat the Great Depression," *Labor History* 18 (1977): 366–81.

Martin, Ida M., "Civil Liberties in Georgia Legislation, 1800–1830," *Georgia Historical Quarterly* 45 (1961): 329–44.

Massey, James L., and Martha A. Myers, "Patterns of Repressive Social Control in Post-Reconstruction Georgia, 1882–1935," *Social Forces* 68 (1989): 458–88.

Matthews, John M., "Black Newspapermen and the Black Community in Georgia, 1890–1930," *Georgia Historical Quarterly* 68 (1984): 356–81.

———— "Negro Republicans in the Reconstruction of Georgia," *Georgia Historical Quarterly* 60 (1976): 145–64.

McDonogh, Gary W., *Black and Catholic in Savannah, Georgia* (1993).

McLeod, Jonathan W., *Workers and Workplace Dynamics in Reconstruction-Era Atlanta: A Case Study* (1989).

McMillan, Richard, "Savannah's Coastal Slave Trade: A Quantitative Analysis of Ship Manifests, 1840–1850," *Georgia Historical Quarterly* 78 (1994): 339–59.

McPherson, Robert, ed., "Georgia Slave Trials, 1837–1849," *American Journal of Legal History* 4 (1960): 364–77.

Meier, August, and David Lewis, "History of the Negro Upper Class in Atlanta, Georgia, 1890–1958," *Journal of Negro Education* 28 (1959): 128–39.

Mensing, Raymond C., Jr., "The Rise and Fall of the Pseudo Poor Clare Nuns of Skidway Island," *Georgia Historical Quarterly* 61 (1977): 318–28.

Merritt, Carole, "The Herndons: Style and Substance of the Black Upper Class in Atlanta, 1880–1930," *Atlanta History* 37 (1994): 50–64.

Miller, Randall M., "A Backcountry Loyalist Plan to Retake Georgia and the Carolinas, 1778," *South Carolina Historical Magazine* 75 (1974): 207–14.

———— "Georgia on Their Minds: Free Blacks and the African Colonization Movement in Georgia," *Southern Studies* 17 (1978): 349–62.

———— "The Golden Isles: Rice and Slaves along the Georgia Coast," *Georgia Historical Quarterly* 70 (1986): 81–96.

Moeser, John V., and Christopher Silver, "Race, Social Stratification, and Politics: The Case of Atlanta, Memphis, and Richmond," *Virginia Magazine of History and Biography* 102 (1994): 519–50.

Mohr, Clarence L., *On the Threshold of Freedom: Masters and Slaves in Civil War Georgia* (1986).

———— "Slavery in Oglethorpe County, Georgia, 1773–1865," *Phylon* 33 (1972): 4–21.

Moore, John Hammond, "Jim Crow in Georgia," *South Atlantic Quarterly* 66 (1967): 554–65.

———— "The Negro and Prohibition in Atlanta, 1885–1887," *South Atlantic Quarterly* 69 (1970): 38–57.

Moseley, Clement Charlton, "The Political Influence of the Ku Klux Klan in Georgia, 1915–1925," *Georgia Historical Quarterly* 57 (1973): 235–55.

Myers, Martha A., "Economic Threat and Racial Disparities in Incarceration: The Case of Postbellum Georgia," *Criminology* 28 (1990): 627–56.

Nathans, Elizabeth Studley, *Losing the Peace: Georgia Republicans and Reconstuction, 1865–1871* (1968).

Newman, Harvey K., "Piety and Segregation: White Protestant Attitudes towards Blacks in Atlanta, 1865–1906," *Georgia Historical Quarterly* 63 (1979): 238–51.

Otto, John Solomon, "Slavery in a Coastal Community—Glynn County (1790–1860)," *Georgia Historical Quarterly* 64 (1979): 461–68.

Parrish, Lydia Austin, *Slave Songs of the Georgia Sea Islands* (1942).

Pearson, Fred Lamar, Jr., and Joseph Aaron Tomberlin, "John Doe, Alias God: A Note on Father Divine's Georgia Career," *Georgia Historical Quarterly* 60 (1976): 43–48.

Penningroth, Dylan, "Slavery, Freedom, and Social Claims to Property among African Americans in Liberty Country, Georgia, 1850–1880," *Journal of American History* 84 (1997): 405–35.

Perdue, Robert E., *The Negro in Savannah, 1865–1900* (1973).

Phillips, Charles David, "Social Structure and Social Control: Modeling the Discriminatory Execution of Blacks in Georgia and North Carolina, 1925–1935," *Social Forces* 65 (1986): 458–75.

Plank, David N., and Marcia E. Turner, "Contrasting Patterns in Black School Politics: Atlanta and Memphis, 1865–1985," *Journal of Negro Education* 60 (1991): 203–18.

Pollitzer, William, *The Gullah People and Their African Heritage* (1999).

Proctor, William G., Jr., "Slavery in Southwest Georgia," *Georgia Historical Quarterly* 49 (1965): 1–22.

Range, Willard, *The Rise and Progress of Negro Colleges in Georgia, 1865–1949* (1951).

Reidy, Joseph P., *From Slavery to Agrarian Capitalism in the Cotton Plantation South: Central Georgia, 1800–1880* (1992).

Roche, Jeff, *Restructured Resistance: The Sibley Commission and the Politics of Desegregation in Georgia* (1999).

Rogers, W. McDowell, "Free Negro Legislation in Georgia before 1865," *Georgia Historical Quarterly* 16 (1932): 27–37.

Rolinson, Mary Gambrell, "Community and Leadership in the First Twenty Years of the Atlanta NAACP, 1917–1937," *Atlanta History* 42 (1998): 5–21.

Rosengarten, Theodore, "Sea Island Encounter," *Georgia Historical Quarterly* 79 (1995): 394–406.

Ross, Edyth L., "Black Heritage in Social Welfare: A Case Study of Atlanta," *Phylon* 37 (1976): 297–307.

Savannah Writers' Project, *Savannah River Plantations* (1947).

Savitt, Todd L., "Politics in Medicine: The Georgia Freedmen's Bureau and the Organization of Health Care, 1865–1866," *Civil War History* 28 (1982): 45–64.

Saye, Albert B., "The Elective Franchise in Georgia," *Georgia Review* 2 (1948): 434–46.

Scarborough, Ruth, *The Opposition to Slavery in Georgia prior to 1860* (1968).

Schultz, Mark R., "The Dream Realized? African-American Land Ownership in Central Georgia Between Reconstruction and World War Two," *Agricultural History* 72 (1998): 298–312.

Shaw, Barton C., *The Wool-Hat Boys: Georgia's Populist Party* (1984).

Singleton, Royce Gordon, "The Trial and Punishment of Slaves in Baldwin County, Georgia 1812–1826," *Southern Humanities Review* 8 (1974): 67–73.

Smith, Albert C., "Southern Violence Reconsidered: Arson As Protest in Black-Belt Georgia, 1865–1910," *Journal of Southern History* 51 (1985): 527–64.

Smith, Julia Floyd, "Marching to Zion: The Religion of Black Baptists in Coastal Georgia prior to 1865," *Viewpoints: Georgia Baptist History* 6 (1978): 47–54.

——— *Slavery and Rice Culture in Low Country Georgia, 1750–1860* (1985).

Soule, Sarah, "Populism and Black Lynching in Georgia, 1890–1900," *Social Forces* 71 (1992): 431–49.

Sweat, Edward F., "Social Status of the Free Negro in Antebellum Georgia," *Negro History Bulletin* 21 (1958): 129–31.

Szwed, John F., "Africa Lies Just Off Georgia: Sea Islands Preserve Origins of Afro-American Culture," *Africa Report* 15 (1970): 29–31.

Talmadge, John E., "Georgia Tests the Fugitive Slave Law," *Georgia Historical Quarterly* 49 (1965): 57–64.

Taylor, A. Elizabeth, "The Origins and Development of the Convict Lease System in Georgia," *Georgia Historical Quarterly* 26 (1942): 113–28.

Temin, Peter, "Patterns of Cotton Agriculture in Postbellum Georgia," *Journal of Economic History* 43 (1983): 661–74.

Terrell, Lloyd R., and Marguerite Terrell, *Blacks in Augusta: A Chronology, 1741–1977* (1977).

Thurmond, Sarah, *A Comparison of the Intelligence and Achievement of Twelve-Year-Old Negro Children in the Rural Schools of Clarke County, Georgia* (1933).

Tillman, Nathaniel P., *The Statewide Public Forum Project: An Experiment in Civic Education among Negroes in Georgia* (1939).

Tolnay, Stewart, E. M. Beck, and J. L. Massey, "The Gallows, the Mob, the Vote: Lethal Sanctioning of Blacks in North Carolina and Georgia, 1882–1930," *Law and Society Review* 23 (1989): 317–31.

Tuck, Stephen, "A City Too Dignified to Hate: Civic Pride, Civil Rights, and Savannah in Comparative Perspective," *Georgia Historical Quarterly* 79 (1995): 539–59.

U.S. Department of Labor, "Annual Family and Occupational Earnings of Residents of Two Negro Housing Projects in Atlanta," *Monthly Labor Review* 61 (1945): 1061–73.

Van Horne, John C., "Joseph Solomon Ottolenghe (ca. 1711–1775): Catechist to the Negroes, Superintendent of the Silk Culture, and Public Servant in Colonial Georgia," *Proceedings of the American Philosophical Society* 125 (1981): 398–409.

Vowels, R., "Atlanta Negro Business and the New Black Bourgeoisie," *Atlanta History Bulletin* 21 (1977): 48–63.

Wallenstein, Peter, *From Slave South to New South: Public Policy in Nineteenth-Century Georgia* (1987).

Watts, Eugene J., "Black Political Progress in Atlanta, 1868–1895," *Journal of Negro History* 59 (1974): 268–86.

Wax, Darold D., "Georgia and the Negro before the American Revolution," *Georgia Historical Quarterly* 51 (1967): 63–77.

———— "'New Negroes are Always in Demand': The Slave Trade in Eighteenth-Century Georgia," *Georgia Historical Quarterly* 68 (1984): 193–220.

Wayne, Justice James M., "Georgia and the African Slave Trade: Justice Jones M. Wayne's Charge to the Grand Jury in 1859," *Georgia Historical Quarterly* 2 (1918): 87–114.

Weiman, David F., "The Economic Emancipation of the Non-Slaveholding Class: Upcountry Farmers in the Georgia Cotton Economy," *Journal of Economic History* 45 (1985): 71–93.

Wetherington, Mark V., "The Savannah Negro Laborers' Strike of 1891," in Merl E. Reed, Leslie S. Hough, and Gary M. Fink, ed., *Southern Workers and their Unions, 1880–1975: Selected Papers. The Second Labor History Conference, 1978* (1981): 3–21.

White, Dana F., "The Black Sides of Atlanta: A Geography of Expansion and Containment, 1870–1970," *Atlanta Historical Journal* 26 (1982): 199–225.

Wilhoit, Francis M., "An Interpretation of Populism's Impact on the Georgia Negro," *Journal of Negro History* 52 (1967): 116–27.

Wood, Betty, "A Note on the Georgia Malcontents," *Georgia Historical Quarterly* 63 (1979): 264–78.

———— "Prisons, Workhouses, and the Control of Slave Labour in Low Country Georgia, 1763–1815," *Slavery and Abolition* 8 (1987): 247–71.

———— *Slavery in Colonial Georgia, 1730–1775* (1984).

———— "Some Aspects of Female Resistance to Chattel Slavery in Low Country Georgia, 1763–1815," *Historical Journal* 30 (1987): 603–22.

———— "'Until He Shall Be Dead, Dead, Dead': The Judicial Treatment of Slaves in Eighteenth-Century Georgia," *Georgia Historical Quarterly* 71 (1987): 377–98.

———— "'White Society' and the 'Informal' Slave Economies of Low Country Georgia, c.1763–1830," *Slavery and Abolition* 11 (1990): 313–31.

———— *Women's Work, Men's Work: The Informal Slave Economies of Low Country Georgia* (1995).

Young, Jeffrey Robert, *Domesticating Slavery: The Master Class in Georgia and South Carolina, 1670–1837* (1999).

26.2.11 Hawaii

Tate, Merze, "Decadence of the Hawaiian Nation and Proposals to Import a Negro Labor Force," *Journal of Negro History* 47 (1962): 248–63.

26.2.12 Illinois

Alkalimat, Abdul, *Harold Washington and the Crisis of Black Power in Chicago Mass Protest* (1989).

Allen, Robert L., *The Port Chicago Mutiny: The Story of the Largest Mass Mutiny Trial in U.S. Naval History* (1989).

Allswang, John M., "The Chicago Negro Voter and the Democratic Consensus: A Case Study, 1918–1936," *Journal of the Illinois State Historical Society* 60 (1967): 145–75.

Anderson, Alan B., and George W. Pickering, *Confronting the Color Line: The Broken Promise of the Civil Rights Movement in Chicago* (1987).

Barrett, James R., "Unity and Fragmentation: Class, Race, and Ethnicity on Chicago's South Side, 1900–1922," *Journal of Social History* 18 (1984): 37–55.

———— *Work and Community in the Jungle: Chicago's Packinghouse Workers, 1894–1922* (1987).

Belles, A. Gilbert, "The Black Press in Illinois," *Journal of the Illinois State Historical Society* 68 (1975): 344–52.

Best, Wallace, "The *Chicago Defender* and the Realignment of Black Chicago," *Chicago History* 24 (1995): 4–21.

Bowen, Louise DeKoven, *The Colored People of Chicago: An Investigation Made for the Juvenile Protective Association* (1913).

Bridges, Roger D., "Equality Deferred: Civil Rights for Illinois Blacks, 1865–1885," *Journal of the Illinois State Historical Society* 74 (1981): 82–108.

———— "John Mason Peck on Illinois Slavery," *Journal of the Illinois State Historical Society* 75 (1982): 179–217.

Briggs, Winstanley, "Slavery in French Colonial Illinois," *Chicago History* 18 (1989–90): 66–81.

Carlson, Shirley J., "Black Migration to Pulaski County, Illinois, 1860–1900," *Illinois State Historical Society Journal* 80 (1987): 37–46.

Cayton, Horace Roscoe, "Negro Housing in Chicago," *Social Action* 6 (1940): 1–39.

Chicago Mayor's Commission on Human Relations, *Race Relations in Chicago: Report of the Mayor's Committee on Race Relations for 1945* (1945).

Comstock, Alzada P., "Chicago Housing Conditions, VI: The Problem of the Negro," *American Journal of Sociology* 18 (1919): 240–57.

Daniel, Philip T. K., "A History of Discrimination against Black Students in Chicago Secondary Schools," *History of Education Quarterly* 20 (1980): 147–60.

Department of Labor, "Living Conditions of Small-Wage Earners in Chicago," *Monthly Labor Review* 22 (1936): 170–173.

Diner, Steven J., "Chicago Social Workers and Blacks in the Progressive Era," *Social Service Review* 44 (1970): 393–410.

Dorsey, James W., *Up South: Blacks in Chicago's Suburbs, 1719–1983* (1986).

Drake, St. Clair, *Churches and Voluntary Associations in the Chicago Negro Community* (1940).

Drake, St. Clair, and Horace R. Cayton, *Black Metropolis: A Study of Negro Life in a Northern City* (rev. and enlarged ed., 1993).

Drucker, Arthur P., Sophia Boaz, A. L. Harris, and Miriam Schaffner, *The Colored People of Chicago* (1913).

Duncan, Otis Dudley, and Beverly Duncan, *Negro Population of Chicago: A Study of Residential Succession* (1957).

Eisenberg, Marcia, "Blacks in the 1850 Federal Census: City of Chicago, Cook County, Illinois," *Journal of the Afro-American Historical and Genealogical Society* 6 (1985): 44–46, 76–85, 112–15.

Ekberg, Carl J., "Black Slaves in the Illinois Country, 1721–1765," *Proceedings of the Annual Meeting of the French Colonial Historical Society* 11 (1987): 265–77.

Finkelman, Paul, "Evading the Ordinance: The Persistence of Bondage in Indiana and Illinois," *Journal of the Early Republic* 9 (1989): 21–51.

———— "Slavery, the 'More Perfect Union,' and the Prairie State," *Illinois Historical Journal* 80 (1987): 248–69.

Frazier, Edward Franklin, *The Negro Family in Chicago* (1932).

Furgal, Suzanne Kersten, "Blacks and Mulattoes in Wards Three and Four Chicago, Cook County, Illinois as Enumerated in the 1860 Federal Census," *Journal of the Afro-American Historical and Genealogical Society* 8 (1987): 79–86.

———— "Blacks Enumerated in the Federal Census of Cook County, Illinois, outside of Chicago," *Journal of the Afro-American Historical and Genealogical Society* 8 (1987): 137–39.

Garrow, David, ed., *Chicago 1966: Open Housing Marches, Summit Negotiations, and Operation Breadbasket* (1989).

Gatewood, Willard B., Jr., "An Experiment in Color: The Eighth Illinois Volunteers, 1898–1899," *Journal of the Illinois State History Society* 65 (1972): 293–312.

Gems, Gerald R., "Blocked Shot: The Development of Basketball in the African-American Community of Chicago," *Journal of Sport History* 22 (1995): 135–48.

Gertz, Elmer, "The Black Laws of Illinois," *Journal of the Illinois State Historical Society* 56 (1963): 454–73.

Gordon, Rita Werner, "The Change in the Political Alignment of Chicago's Negroes during the New Deal," *Journal of American History* 56 (1969): 584–603.

Gosnell, Harold Foote, "The Chicago 'Black Belt' as a Political Battlefield," *American Journal of Sociology* 39 (1933): 329–341.

———— *Negro Politicians: The Rise of Negro Politics in Chicago* (1935).

Grimshaw, William J., *Bitter Fruit: Black Politics and the Chicago Machine, 1931–1991* (1992).

Grossman, James R., *Land of Hope: Chicago, Black Southerners, and the Great Migration* (1989).

———— "The White Man's Union: The Great Migration and the Resonance of Race and Class in Chicago, 1916–1922," in Joe W. Trotter, ed., *The Great Migration in Historical Perspective: New Dimensions of Race, Class, and Gender* (1991): 83–105.

Grunsfeld, Mary-Jane Loeb, *Negroes in Chicago* (1944).

Haller, Mark H., "Policy Gambling, Entertainment, and the Emergence of Black Politics: Chicago from 1900 to 1940," *Journal of Social History* 24 (1991): 719–39.

Halpern, Rick, "Race, Ethnicity, and Union in the Chicago Stockyards, 1917–1922," *International Review of Social History* 37 (1992): 25–58.

Harris, Norman D., *The History of Negro Servitude in Illinois, and of the Slavery Agitation in That State, 1719–1864* (1969).

Hays, Christopher K., "The African American Struggle for Equality and Justice in Cairo, Illinois, 1865–1900," *Illinois Historical Journal* 90 (1997): 265–84.

Hendricks, Wanda A., *Gender, Race, and Politics in the Midwest: Black Club Women in Illinois* (1998).

Herbst, Alma, *The Negro in the Slaughtering and Meat-Packing Industry in Chicago* (1932).

Hicken, Victor, "The Record of Illinois' Negro Soldiers in the Civil War," *Journal of the Illinois State Historical Society* 56 (1963): 529–51.

Hirsch, Arnold R., *Making the Second Ghetto: Race and Housing in Chicago, 1940–1960* (1983).

———— "Massive Resistance in the Urban North: Trumbull Park, Chicago, 1953–1966," *Journal of American History* 82 (1995): 522–50.

Hodges, Carl G., and Helene H. Levene, comp., *Illinois Negro Historymakers* (1964).

Hogan, David John, *Class and Reform: School and Society in Chicago, 1880–1930* (1985).

———— "Education and the Making of the Chicago Working Class, 1880–1930," *History of Education Quarterly* 18 (1978): 227–70.

Homel, Michael W., *Down from Equality: Black Chicagoans and the Public Schools, 1920–41* (1984).

———— "The Politics of Public Education in Black Chicago, 1910–1941," *Journal of Negro Education* 45 (1976): 179–91.

Illinois, State Commission on the Condition of the Urban Colored Population, *A Report of the Illinois State Commission on the Condition of the Urban Colored Population* (1941).

Jackson, Philip, "Black Charity in Progressive Era Chicago," *Social Service Review* 52 (1978): 400–17.

Johnstone, John W. C., Darnell F. Hawkins, and Arthur Michener, "Homicide Reporting in Chicago Dailies," *Journalism Quarterly* 71 (1994): 860–72.

Keiser, John H., "Black Strikebreakers and Racism in Illinois, 1865–1900," *Journal of the Illinois State Historical Society* 65 (1972): 313–26.

Kenney, William Howland, *Chicago Jazz: A Cultural History, 1904–1930* (1993).

Knupfer, Anne Meis, *Toward a Tenderer Humanity and a Nobler Womanhood: African American Women's Clubs in Turn-of-the-Century Chicago* (1996).

Lal, Barbara Ballis, "Black and Blue in Chicago: Robert E. Park's Perspective on Race Relations in Urban America, 1914–1944," *British Journal of Sociology* 38 (1987): 546–66.

Lemann, Nicholas, *The Promised Land: The Great Black Migration and How It Changed America* (1992).

Locke, Alain, "Chicago's New Southside Arts Center," *Magazine of Art* 34 (1941): 370–74.

Lomax, Michael E., "Black Entrepreneurship in the National Pastime: The Rise of Semiprofessional Baseball in Black Chicago, 1890–1915," *Journal of Sport History* 25 (1998): 43–64.

Meier, August, and Elliott M. Rudwick, "Negro Protest at the Chicago World's Fair, 1933–1934," *Illinois State Historical Society Journal* 59 (1966): 161–71.

Mumford, Kevin J., *Interzones: Black/White Sex Districts in Chicago and New York in the Early Twentieth Century* (1997).

Neckerman, Kathryn M., "Divided Households: Extended Kin in Working-Class Chicago, 1924," *Social Science History* 19 (1995): 371–98.

Ogden, Mary Elaine, *The Chicago Negro Community: A Statistical Description* (1939).

Ottensmann, John R., and Michael E. Gleeson, "The Movement of Whites and Blacks into Racially Mixed Neighborhoods: Chicago, 1960–1980," *Social Science Quarterly* 73 (1992): 645–62.

Parot, Joseph, "Ethnic versus Black Metropolis: The Origins of Polish-Black Housing Tensions in Chicago," *Polish American Studies* 29 (1972): 5–33.

Philpott, Thomas L., *The Slum and the Ghetto: Neighborhood Deterioration and Middle-Class Reform, Chicago 1880–1930* (1978).

Pinderhughes, Dianne M., *Race and Ethnicity in Chicago Politics: A Reexamination of Pluralist Theory* (1987).

Reed, Christopher R., "Black Chicago Political Realignment during the Depression and New Deal," *Illinois Historical Journal* 78 (1985): 242–56.

———— "Black Chicago Civic Organizations before 1935," *Journal of Ethnic Studies* 14 (1987): 65–77.

———— *The Chicago NAACP and the Rise of Black Professional Leadership, 1910–1966* (1997).

———— "Organized Racial Reform in Chicago during the Progressive Era: The Chicago NAACP, 1910–1920," *Michigan Historical Review* 14 (1988): 75–99.

Schmuhl, Robert, "History, Fantasy, Memory: Ben Hecht and a Chicago Hanging," *Illinois Historical Journal* 83 (1990): 146–58.

Senechal, Roberta, *The Sociogenesis of a Race Riot: Springfield, Illinois, in 1908* (1990).

Silverman, Robert Mark, "The Effects of Racism and Racial Discrimination on Minority Business Development: The Case of Black Manufacturers in Chicago's Ethnic Beauty Aids Industry," *Journal of Social History* 31 (1998): 571–97.

Spear, Allan, *Black Chicago: The Making of a Negro Ghetto, 1890–1920* (1967).

Stovall, Mary E., "The *Chicago Defender* in the Progressive Era," *Illinois Historical Journal* 83 (1990): 159–72.

Street, Paul, "The Logic and Limits of 'Plant Loyalty': Black Workers, White Labor, and Corporate Racial Paternalism in Chicago's Stockyards, 1916–1940," *Journal of Social History* 29 (1996): 659–81.

Strickland, Arvarh E., *History of the Chicago Urban League* (1966).

———— "The Illinois Background of Lincoln's Attitude toward Slavery and the Negro," *Journal of the Illinois State Historical Society* 56 (1963): 474–94.

Stroman, Carolyn A., "The *Chicago Defender* and the Mass Migration of Blacks, 1916–1918," *Journal of Popular Culture* 15 (1981): 62–7.

Taitt, John, *The Souvenir of Negro Progress: Chicago, 1779–1925* (1925).

Travis, Dempsey J., *An Autobiography of Black Chicago* (1981).

Tuttle, William M., Jr., "Labor Conflict and Racial Violence: The Black Worker in Chicago, 1894–1919," *Labor History* 10 (1969): 408–32.

———— *Race Riot: Chicago in the Red Summer of 1919* (1970).

Walker, Juilet E. K., "Legal Processes and Judicial Challenges: Black Land Ownershp in Western Illinois," *Western Illinois Regional Studies* 6 (1983): 23–48.

Warner, William Lloyd, Buford H. Junker, and Walter A. Adams, *Color and Human Nature: Negro Personality Development in a Northern City* (1941).

Weems, Robert E., Jr., *Black Business in the Black Metropolis: The Chicago Metropolitan Assurance Company, 1925–1985* (1996).

Williams, Lee E., and Lee E. Williams, II, *Anatomy of Four Race Riots: Racial Conflict in Knoxville, Elaine (Arkansas), Tulsa, and Chicago, 1919–1921* (1972).

Wright, Richard, "With Black Radicals in Chicago," *Dissent* 24 (1977): 156–61.

26.2.13 Indiana

Betten, Neil, and Raymond A. Mohl, "The Evolution of Racism in an Industrial City, 1906–1940: A Case Study of Gary, Indiana," *Journal of Negro History* 59 (1974): 51–64.

Bingham, Darrel E., "The Black Family in Evansville and Vanderburgh County, Indiana, in 1880," *Indiana Magazine of History* 75 (1979): 117–146.

———— "Family Structure of Germans and Blacks in Evansville and Vanderburgh County, Indiana, in 1880: A Comparative Study," *Old Northwest* 7 (1981): 255–75.

———— *We Ask Only a Fair Trial: A History of the Black Community of Evansville, Indiana* (1987).

Cameron, James, *A Time of Terror* (1982).

Carroll, J. C., "The Beginnings of Public Education for Negroes in Indiana," *Journal of Negro History* 8 (1939): 649–58.

Ferguson, Earline Rae, "The Women's Improvement Club of Indianapolis: Black Women Pioneers in Tuberculosis Work, 1903–1938," in Darlene Clark Hine, ed., *Black Women in United States History* (1990): 339–63.

Finkelman, Paul, "Evading the Ordinance: The Persistence of Bondage in Indiana and Illinois," *Journal of the Early Republic* 9 (1989): 21–51.

Hine, Darlene Clark, *When the Truth Is Told: A History of Black Women's Culture and Community in Indiana, 1875–1950* (1981).

Karst, Frederick A., "A Rural Black Settlement in St. Joseph County, Indiana, before 1900," *Indiana Magazine of History* 74 (1978): 262–67.

Lyles, Carl C., *Lyles Station, Indiana: Yesterday and Today* (1984).

McDonald, Earl E., "The Negro in Indiana before 1881," *Indiana Magazine of History* 27 (1931): 291–306.

Mohl, Raymond A., "The Evolution of Racism and Industrial City, 1906–1940: A Case Study of Gary, Indiana," *Journal of Negro History* 59 (1974): 51–64.

Mohl, Raymond A., and Neil Betten, *Steel City: Urban and Ethnic Patterns in Gary, Indiana, 1906–1950* (1986).

Poinsett, Alex, *Black Power: Gary Style; The Making of Mayor Richard Gordon Hatcher* (1970).

Stetson, Erlene, "Black Feminism in Indiana, 1893–1933," *Phylon* 44 (1983): 292–98.

Thornbrough, Emma Lou, "Breaking Racial Barriers to Public Accomodations in Indiana, 1935–1963," *Indiana Magazine of History* 83 (1987): 300–43.

——— "The History of Black Women in Indiana," *Black History News and Notes* 13–14 (1983): 1–8.

——— *The Negro in Indiana: A Study of a Minority* (1957).

——— "Segregation in Indiana during the Klan Era of the 1920's," *Mississippi Valley Historical Review* 47 (1961): 594–618.

Trotter, Joe William, *River Jordan: African-American Urban Life in the Ohio Valley* (1998).

Vincent, Stephen A., *Southern Seed, Northern Soil: African-American Farm Communities in the Midwest, 1765–1900* (1999).

Wallis, Don, *All We Had Was Each Other: The Black Community of Madison, Indiana* (1998).

Warren, Stanley, "The Monster Meetings at the Negro YMCA in Indianapolis," *Indiana Magazine of History* 91 (1995): 57–80.

26.2.14 Iowa

Berrier, G. Gail, "The Negro Suffrage Issue in Iowa—1865–1868," *Annals of Iowa* 39 (1968): 241–61.

Cooper, Arnie, "A Stony Road: Black Education in Iowa, 1838–1860," *Annals of Iowa* 48 (1986): 113–34.

Douglas, Bill, "Wartime Illusions and Disillusionment: Camp Dodge and Racial Stereotyping, 1917–1918," *Annals of Iowa* 57 (1998): 111–34.

Dykstra, Robert K., "The Issue Squarely Met: Toward an Explanantion of Iowans' Racial Attitudes, 1865–1868," *Annals of Iowa* 47 (1984): 430–50.

Ellis, Richard N., "The Civil War Letters of an Iowa Family," *Annals of Iowa* 39 (1969): 561–86.

Fehn, Bruce, "'The Only Hope We Had': United Packinghouse Workers Local 46 and the Struggle for Racial Equality in Waterloo, Iowa, 1948–1960," *Annals of Iowa* 54 (1995): 185–216.

Hewitt, William L., "So Few Undesirables: Race, Residence, and Occupation in Sioux City, 1890–1925," *Annals of Iowa* 50 (1989): 158–79.

Hill, James L., "Migration of Blacks to Iowa, 1820–1960," *Journal of Negro History* 66 (1981–1982): 289–303.

Jessup, Wilbur E., "The Warren Family of Marshall County, Iowa," *Journal of the Afro-American Historical and Genealogical Society* 3 (1982): 99–104.

Rye, Stephen H., "Buxton: Black Metropolis of Iowa," *Annals of Iowa* 41 (1972): 939–57.

Wubben, Hubert H., "The Uncertain Trumpet: Iowa Republicans and Black Suffrage: 1860–1868," *Annals of Iowa* 47 (1984): 409–29.

26.2.15   Kansas

Athearn, Robert G., *In Search of Canaan: Black Migration to Kansas, 1879–1880* (1978).

Brady, Marilyn Dell, "Kansas Federation of Colored Women's Clubs, 1900–1930," *Kansas History* 9 (1986): 19–30.

———— "Organizing Afro-American Girls' Clubs in Kansas in the 1920s," *Frontiers* 9 (1987): 69–73.

Bruce, Janet, *The Kansas City Monarchs: Champions of Black Baseball* (1985).

Castel, Albert, "Civil War Kansas and the Negro," *Journal of Negro History* 51 (1966): 125–38.

Chafe, William H., "The Negro and Populism: A Kansas Case Study," *Journal of Southern History* 34 (1968): 402–19.

Chaudhuri, Nupur, "'We All Seem Like Brothers and Sisters': The African-American Community in Manhattan, Kansas, 1865–1940," *Kansas History* 14 (1992): 270–88.

Chu, Daniel, and Bill Shaw, *Going Home to Nicodemus: The Story of an African American Frontier Town and the Pioneers Who Settled It* (1995).

Cox, Thomas C., *Blacks in Topeka, Kansas, 1865–1915: A Social History* (1982).

Frehill-Row, Lisa M., "Postbellum Race Relations and Rural Land Tenure: Migration of Blacks and Whites to Kansas and Nebraska, 1870–1890," *Social Forces* 72 (1993): 77–91.

Gatewood, Willard B., Jr., "Kansas Negroes and the Spanish-American War," *Kansas Historical Quarterly* 37 (1971): 300–13.

Grenz, Suzanna M., "The Exodusters of 1879: St. Louis and Kansas City Responses," *Missouri Historical Review* 73 (1978): 54–70.

Hamilton, Kenneth M., "The Origins and Early Promotion of Nicodemus: A Pre-Exodus, All-Black Town," *Kansas History* 5 (1982): 220–42.

Haywood, C. Robert, "'No Less a Man': Blacks in Cow Town Dodge City, 1876–1886," *Western Historical Quarterly* 19 (1988): 161–82.

Katz, Milton S., and Susan B. Tucker, "A Pioneer in Civil Rights: Esther Brown and the South Park Desegregation Case of 1948," *Kansas History* 18 (1995–96): 234–47.

Klassen, Teresa C., and Owen V. Johnson, "Sharpening of the Blade: Black Consciousness in Kansas, 1892–1897," *Journalism Quarterly* 63 (1986): 298–304.

Leiker, James N., "Black Soldiers at Fort Hays, Kansas, 1867–1869: A Study in Civilian and Military Violence," *Great Plains Quarterly* 17 (1997): 3–17.

Novak, Susan S., "Roads from Fear to Freedom: The Kansas Underground Railroad," *Kansas Heritage* 4 (1996): 9–12.

Painter, Nell I., *Exodusters: Black Migration to Kansas after Reconstruction* (1977).

Schwendemann, Glenn, "The 'Exodusters' on the Missouri," *Kansas Historical Quarterly* 29 (1963): 25–40.

———— "Nicodemus: Negro Haven on the Solomon," *Kansas Historical Quarterly* 34 (1968): 10–31.

———— "Wyandotte and the First 'Exodusters' of 1879," *Kansas Historical Quarterly* 26 (1960): 233–49.

Sheridan, Richard B., "From Slavery in Missouri to Freedom in Kansas: The Influx of Black Fugitives and Contrabands into Kansas, 1854–1865," *Kansas History* 12 (1989): 28–47.

Steinberg, Stephen, "My Day in Nicodemus: Notes From a Field Trip to Black Kansas," *Phylon* 37 (1976): 243–49.

Strickland, Arvarh E., "Toward the Promised Land: The Exodus to Kansas and Afterward," *Missouri History Review* 69 (1975): 376–412.

Van Meter, Sondra, "Black Resistance to Segregation in the Wichita Public Schools, 1870–1912," *Midwest Quarterly* 20 (1978).

26.2.16   Kentucky

Allen, Jeffrey Brooke, "'All of Us Are Highly Pleased with the Country': Black and White Kentuckians on Liberian Colonization," *Phylon* 43 (1982): 97–109.

———— "Did Southern Colonizationists Oppose Slavery? Kentucky 1816–1850 as a Test Case," *Register of the Kentucky Historical Society* 75 (1977): 92–111.

———— "Means and Ends in Kentucky Abolitionism, 1792–1823," *Filson Club History Quarterly* 57 (1983): 365–81.

———— "The Origins of Proslavery Thought in Kentucky, 1792–1799," *Register of the Kentucky Historical Society* 77 (1979): 75–90.

———— "Were Southern White Critics of Slavery Racists? Kentucky and the Upper South, 1791–1824," *Journal of Southern History* 44 (1978): 169–90.

Barton, Keith C., "'Good Cooks and Washers': Slave Hiring, Domestic Labor, and the Market in Bourbon County, Kentucky," *Journal of American History* 84 (1997): 436–60.

Berry, Benjamin D., Jr., "The Plymouth Congregational Church of Louisville, Kentucky," *Phylon* 42 (1981): 224–32.

Bogardus, Carl R., Sr., "Black Marriages, Gallatin County, Kentucky, 1866 to 1913," *Journal of the Afro-American History and Genealogical Society* 2 (1981): 117–22, 161–75.

Boles, John B., *Religion in Antebellum Kentucky* (1976).

Brown, Richard C., "The Free Blacks of Boyle County, Kentucky, 1850–1860: A Research Note," *Register of the Kentucky Historical Society* 87 (1989): 426–38.

Byars, Lauretta F., "Lexington's Colored Orphan Industrial Home, 1892–1913," *Register of the Kentucky Historical Society* 89 (1991): 147–78.

Clark, Thomas D., "The Slave Trade between Kentucky and the Cotton Kingdom," *Mississippi Valley Historical Review* 21 (1934): 331–42.

Coleman, A. Lee, and Larry D. Hall, "Black Farm Operators and Farm Population, 1900–1970: Alabama and Kentucky," *Phylon* 40 (1979): 387–402.

Coleman, J. Winston, *Slavery Times in Kentucky* (1940).

Coulter, Ellis Merton, *The Civil War and Readjustment in Kentucky* (1926).

Hardin, John A., *Fifty Years of Segregation: Black Higher Education in Kentucky, 1904–1954* (1997).

Harrison, Lowell Hayes, *The Anti-Slavery Movement in Kentucky* (1978).

Howard, Victor B., *Black Liberation in Kentucky: Emancipation and Freedom, 1862–1884* (1983).

———— "Negro Politics and the Suffrage Question in Kentucky, 1866–1872," *Register of the Kentucky Historical Society* 72 (1974): 111–13.

———— "The Struggle For Equal Education in Kentucky, 1866–1884," *Journal of Negro Education* 46 (1977): 305–28.

Kellogg, John, "The Formation of Black Residential Areas in Lexington, Kentucky, 1865–1887," *Journal of Southern History* 48 (1982): 21–52.

Lucas, Marion Brunson, "African Americans on the Kentucky Frontier," *Register of the Kentucky Historical Society* 95 (1997): 121–34.

———— *A History of Blacks in Kentucky: From Slavery to Segregation, 1760–1891* (2 vols., 1992).

Malone, Cheryl Knott, "Louisville Free Public Library's Racially Segregated Branches: 1905–35," *Register of the Kentucky Historical Society* 93 (1995): 159–79.

Martin, Asa Earl, *The Anti-Slavery Movement in Kentucky prior to 1850* (1918).

McDougle, Ivan Eugene, *Slavery in Kentucky, 1792–1865* (1918).

Montell, William L., *The Saga of Coe Ridge: A Study in Oral History* (1970).

Post, Edward M., "Kentucky Law Concerning Emancipation or Freedom of Slaves," *Filson Club History Quarterly* 59 (1985): 344–67.

Silverman, Jason H., "Kentucky, Canada, and Extradition: The Jesse Happy Case," *Filson Club History Quarterly* 54 (1980): 50–60.

———— "'Meaningful Change and Unceasing Continuity': An Essay Review of a History of Blacks in Kentucky," *Register of the Kentucky Historical Society* 91 (1993): 65–75.

Thomas, Herbert A., Jr., "Victims of Circumstance: Negroes in a Southern Town, 1865–1880," *Register of the Kentucky Historical Society* 71 (1973): 253–71.

Timberlake, C. L., "The Early Struggle for Education of the Blacks in the Commonwealth of Kentucky," *Register of the Kentucky History Society* 71 (1973): 225–52.

Trotter, Joe William, *River Jordan: African-American Urban Life in the Ohio Valley* (1998).

Turner, Wallace B., "Abolitionism in Kentucky," *Register of the Kentucky Historical Society* 69 (1971): 319–38.

U.S. Department of Labor, "Improved Conditions for Negroes in Louisville," *Monthly Labor Review* 61 (1945): 727–28.

Vouga, Anne F., "Presbyterian Missions and Louisville Blacks: The Early Years, 1898–1910," *Filson Club Historical Quarterly* 58 (1984): 310–35.

Walker, Juliet E. K., "The Legal Status of Free Blacks in Early Kentucky, 1792–1825," *Filson Club History Quarterly* 57 (1983): 382–95.

———— "Pioneer Slave Entrepreneurship-Patterns, Processes, and Perspectives: The Case of the Slave Free Frank on the Kentucky Pennyroyal, 1795–1819," *Journal of Negro History* 68 (1983): 289–308.

Williams, Lawrence H., *Black Higher Education in Kentucky, 1879–1930: The History of Simmons University* (1987).

Wright, George C., "The Billy Club and the Ballot: Police Intimidation of Blacks in Louisville, Kentucky, 1880–1930," *Southern Studies* 23 (1984): 20–41.

———— *Life behind a Veil: Blacks in Louisville, Kentucky, 1865–1930* (1985).

———— "The NAACP and Residential Segregation in Louisville, Kentucky, 1914–1917," *Register of the Kentucky Historical Society* 78 (1980): 39–54.

———— *Racial Violence in Kentucky, 1865–1940: Lynchings, Mob Rule, and "Legal Lynchings"* (1990).

Young, Amy Lambeck, Philip J. Carr, and Joseph E. Granger, "How Historical Archaeology Works: A Case Study of Slave Houses at Locust Grove," *Register of the Kentucky Historical Society* 96 (1998): 164–94.

26.2.17 Louisiana

Allain, Mathé, "Slave Policies in French Louisiana," *Louisiana History* 21 (1980): 127–37.

Anthony, Arthé A., "'Lost Boundaries': Racial Passing and Poverty in Segregated New Orleans," *Louisiana History* 36 (1995): 291–312.

Arena, C. Richard, "Landholding and Political Power in Spanish Louisiana," *Louisiana Historical Quarterly* 38 (1955): 23–39.

Arnesen, Eric, *Waterfront Workers of New Orleans: Race, Class and Politics, 1863–1923* (1991).

Baker, Riley E., "Negro Voter Registration in Louisiana, 1879–1964," *Louisiana Studies* 4 (1965): 332–50.

Bankole, Katherine Kemi, *Slavery and Medicine: Enslavement and Medical Practices in Antebellum Louisiana* (1997).

Bell, Caryn Cosse, *Revolution, Romanticism, and the Afro-Creole Protest Tradition in Louisiana 1718–1868* (1996).

Bergeron, Arthur W., Jr., "Louisiana's Free Men of Color in Gray," *Journal of Confederate History* 11 (1994): 37–55.

Berry, Mary Frances, "Negro Troops in Blue and Gray: The Louisiana Native Guards, 1861–1863," *Louisiana History* 8 (1967): 165–90.

Binning, F. Wayne, "'Carpetbaggers' Triumph: The Louisiana State Election of 1868," *Louisiana History* 14 (1973): 21–39.

Blackwelder, Julia Kirk, "Women in the Work Force: Atlanta, New Orleans, and San Antonio, 1930–1940," *Journal of Urban History* 4 (1978): 331–358.

Blassingame, John W., *Black New Orleans, 1860–1880* (1973).

Brady, Patricia, "Black Artists in Antebellum New Orleans," *Louisiana History* 32 (1991): 5–28.

———— "Trials and Tribulations: American Missionary Association Teachers and Black Education in Occupied New Orleans, 1863–1864," *Louisiana History* 31 (1990): 5–20.

Brantley, Daniel, "Blacks and Louisiana Constitutional Development, 1890–Present: A Study in Southern Political Thought and Race Relations," *Phylon* 48 (1987): 51–61.

Brasseaux, Carl A., "The Administration of Slave Regulations in French Louisiana, 1724–1766," *Louisiana History* 21 (1980): 139–58.

———— "The Moral Climate of French Colonial Louisiana, 1699–1763," *Louisiana History* 27 (1986): 27–41.

Carleton, Mark, "The Politics of the Convict Lease System in Louisiana, 1868–1901," *Louisiana History* 8 (1967): 5–25.

———— *Politics and Punishment: The History of the Louisiana State Penal System* (1971).

Cheung, Floyd D., "Les Cenelles and Quadroon Balls: 'Hidden Transcripts' of Resistance and Domination in New Orleans, 1803–1845," *Southern Literary Journal* 29 (1997): 5–16.

Christian, Marcus Bruce, *Negro Ironworkers in Louisiana, 1718–1900* (1972).

Clayton, Ronnie W., "Federal Writers' Projects for Blacks in Louisiana," *Louisiana History* 19 (1978): 327–335.

Coles, Harry L., Jr., "Some Notes on Slaveownership and Landownership in Louisiana, 1850–1860," *Journal of Southern History* 9 (1943): 381–94.

Connor, William P., "Reconstruction Rebels: The New Orleans Tribune in Post-Civil War Louisiana," *Louisiana History* 21 (1980): 159–81.

Cook, Bernard A., and James R. Watson, *Louisiana Labor: From Slavery to "Right-to-Work"* (1985).

Cook, Christine C., and Mickey Lauria, "Urban Regeneration and Public Housing in New Orleans," *Urban Affairs Review* 30 (1995): 538–57.

Dauphine, James G., "The Knights of the White Camelia and the Election of 1868: Louisiana's White Terrorists; a Benighting Legacy," *Louisiana History* 30 (1989): 173–90.

Davis, Edwin Adams, *Plantation Life in the Florida Parishes of Louisiana, 1836–1846 as Reflected in the Diary of Bennet H. Barrow* (1943).

Davis, Ronald L. F., *Good and Faithful Labor: From Slavery to Sharecropping in the Natchez District, 1860–1890* (1982).

Dawson, Joseph G., III, *Army Generals and Reconstruction: Louisiana, 1862–1877* (1982).

Delatte, Carolyn E., "The St. Landry Riot: A Forgotten Incident of Reconstruction Violence," *Louisiana History* 17 (1976): 41–9.

DeMetz, Kay, "Minstrel Dancing in New Orleans' Nineteenth-Century Theaters," *Southern Quarterly* 20 (1982): 28–40.

Dethloff, Henry C., and Robert P. Jones, "Race Relations in Louisiana, 1877–1898," *Louisiana History* 9 (1968): 301–23.

Din, Gilbert C., "*Cimarrones* and the San Malo Band in Spanish Louisiana," *Louisiana History* 21 (1980): 237–62.

Dorman, James H., "The Persistent Specter: Slave Rebellion in Territorial Louisiana," *Louisiana History* 18 (1977): 389–404.

Durling, Gregory B., "Female Labor, Malingering, and the Abuse of Equipment under Slavery: Evidence from the Marydale Plantation Diary," *Southern Studies* 5 (1994): 31–49.

Ellison, Mary, "African American Music and Muskets in Civil War New Orleans," *Louisiana History* 35 (1994): 285–319.

Everett, Donald E., "Ben Butler and the Louisiana Native Guards, 1861–1862," *Journal of Southern History* 24 (1958): 202–17.

——— "Demands of the New Orleans Free Colored Population for Political Equality, 1862–1865," *Louisiana History Quarterly* 38 (1955): 43–64.

——— "Emigrés and Militiamen: Free Persons of Color in New Orleans, 1803–1815," *Journal of Negro History* 38 (1953): 377–402.

——— "Free Persons of Color in Colonial Louisiana," *Louisiana History* 7 (1966): 21–50.

Fairclough, Adam, *Race and Democracy: The Civil Rights Struggle in Louisiana, 1915–1972* (1995).

Ferleger, Louis, "The Problem of 'Labor' in the Post-Reconstruction Louisiana Sugar Industry," *Agricultural History* 72 (1998): 140–58.

Fischer, Roger A., "Racial Segregation in Antebellum New Orleans," *American Historical Review* 74 (1969): 926–57.

Foner, Laura, "The Free People of Color in Louisiana and St. Domingue: A Comparative Portrait of Two Three-Caste Societies," *Journal of Social History* 3 (1970): 406–30.

Foshee, Andrew W., "Slave Hiring in Rural Louisiana," *Louisiana History* 26 (1985): 63–73.

Foster, Craig L., "Tarnished Angels: Prostitution in Storyville, New Orleans, 1900–1910," *Louisiana History* 31 (1990): 387–97.

Gilmore, Harlan, and Logan Wilson, "Negro Socioeconomic Status in a Southern City (New Orleans)," *Sociology and Social Research* (1945): 361–73.

Glatthaar, Joseph T., "The Civil War through the Eyes of a Sixteen-Year-Old Black Officer: The Letters of Lieutenant John H. Crowder of the 1st Louisiana Native Guards," *Louisiana History* 35 (1994): 201–16.

Gould, Virginia, "In Defense of their Creole Culture: The Free Creoles of Color of New Orleans, Mobile, and Pensacola," *Gulf Coast Historical Review* 9 (1993): 26–46.

Hair, William I., *Carnival of Fury: Robert Charles and the New Orleans Race Riot of 1900* (1976).

Hall, Gwendolyn Midlo, *Africans in Colonial Louisiana: The Development of Afro-Creole Culture in the Eighteenth Century* (1992).

Hanger, Kimberly S., "Conflicting Loyalties: The French Revolution and Free People of Color in Spanish New Orleans," *Louisiana History* 34 (1993): 5–33.

——— "'Desiring Total Tranquility' and Not Getting It: Conflict Involving Free Black Women in Spanish New Orleans," *Americas* 54 (1998): 541–56.

——— "Household and Community Structure among the Free Population of Spanish New Orleans," *Louisiana History* 30 (1989): 63–79.

——— "Patronage, Property and Persistence: The Emergence of a Free Black Elite in Spanish New Orleans," *Slavery and Abolition* 17 (1996): 44–64.

Harlan, Louis R., "Desegregation in New Orleans Public Schools during Reconstruction," *American History Review* 67 (1962): 663–75.

Hendrix, James Parsley, Jr., "The Efforts to Reopen the African Slave Trade in Louisiana," *Louisiana History* 10 (1969): 97–123.

Hennesey, Melinda M., "Race and Violence in Reconstruction New Orleans: The 1868 Riot," *Louisiana History* 20 (1979): 77–92.

Hicks, William, *History of Louisiana Negro Baptists from 1804 to 1914* (1915).

Highsmith, William E., "Louisiana Landholding during War and Reconstruction," *Louisiana Historical Quarterly* 38 (1955): 39–54.

Hirsch, Arnold R., "On the Waterfront: Race, Class, and Politics in Post-Reconstruction New Orleans," *Journal of Urban History* 21 (1995): 511–17.

Hollandsworth, James G., Jr., *The Louisiana Native Guards: The Black Military Experience during the Civil War* (1995).

Holmes, Jack D. L., "The Abortive Slave Revolt at Pointe Coupee, Louisiana, 1795," *Louisiana History* 11 (1970): 341–62.

Humphreys, Hubert, "The Rise and Fall of the Shreveport ("Colored") Labor Association as Documented By the Shreveport Daily Times, 1880," *North Louisiana Historical Association Journal* 19 (1988): 3–17.

Ingersoll, Thomas N., "Free Blacks in a Slave Society: New Orleans, 1718–1812," *William and Mary Quarterly* 48 (1991): 173–200.

——— *Mammon and Manon in Early New Orleans: The First Slave Society in the Deep South, 1718–1819* (1999).

Inverarity, James, "Populism and Lynching in Louisiana: 1889–1896: A Test of Erickson's Theory of the Relationship between Boundary Crises and Repressive Justice," *American Sociological Review* 41 (1976): 262–79.

Jacobs, Claude F., "Benevolent Societies of New Orleans: Blacks during the Late Nineteenth and Early Twentieth Centuries," *Louisiana History* 29 (1988): 21–33.

Jacobs, Claude F., and Andrew Kaslow, *The Spiritual Churches of New Orleans: Origins, Beliefs, and Rituals of an African-American Religion* (1991).

Johnson, Jerah, "New Orleans's Congo Square: An Urban Setting for Early Afro-American Culture Formation," *Louisiana History* 32 (1991): 117–57.

Jones, Howard J., "Biographical Sketches of Members of the 1868 Louisiana State Senate," *Louisiana History* 19 (1978): 65–110.

Kilbourne, Richard Holcombe, Jr., *Debt, Investment, Slaves: Credit Relations in East Feliciana Parish, Louisiana, 1825–1885* (1995).

Kunkel, Paul A., "Modification in Louisiana Negro Legal Status under Louisiana Constitutions, 1812–1957," *Journal of Negro History* 44 (1959): 1–25.

Labbe, Dolores Egger, *Jim Crow Comes to Church: The Establishment of Segregated Catholic Parishes in South Louisiana* (2d ed., 1971).

Lachance, Paul F., "The 1809 Immigration of Saint-Domingue Refugees to New Orleans: Reception, Integration and Impact," *Louisiana History* 29 (1988): 109–41.

———— "The Formation of a Three-Caste Society: Evidence from Wills in Antebellum New Orleans," *Social Science History* 18 (1994): 211–42.

———— "The Limits of Privilege: Where Free Persons of Colour Stood in the Hierarchy of Wealth in Antebellum New Orleans," *Slavery and Abolition* 17 (1996): 65–84.

———— "The Politics of Fear: French Louisianans and the Slave Trade, 1786–1809," *Plantation Societies in the Americas* 1 (1979): 162–197.

Logsdon, Joseph, "Americans and Creoles in New Orleans: The Origins of Black Citizenship in the United States," *Amerikastudien/American Studies* 34 (1990): 187–202.

Logsdon, Joseph, and Caryn C. Bell, "The Americanization of Black New Orleans," in Arnold R. Hirsch, and Joseph Logsdon, *Creole New Orleans: Race and Americanization* (1992): 201–61.

MacDonald, Robert R., John R. Kemp, and Edward F. Hass, ed., *Louisiana's Black Heritage* (1979).

Malone, Ann Patton, "Searching for the Family and Household Structure of Rural Lousiana Slaves, 1810–1864," *Louisiana History* 28 (1987): 357–79.

———— *Sweet Chariot: Slave Family and Household Structure in Nineteenth-Century Louisiana* (1992).

Margo, Robert A., "Race Differences in Public School Expenditures: Disfranchisement and School Finance in Louisiana, 1890–1910," *Social Science History* 6 (1982): 9–34.

May, J. Thomas, "The Freedmen's Bureau at the Local Level: A Study of a Louisiana Agent," *Louisiana History* 9 (1968): 5–19.

McCrary, Peyton, *Abraham Lincoln and Reconstruction: The Louisiana Experiment* (1978).

McDonald, Robert R., John R. Kemp, and Edward R. Hass, ed., *Louisiana's Black Heritage* (1979).

McDonald, Roderick A., *The Economy and Material Culture of Slaves: Goods and Chattels on the Sugar Plantations of Jamaica and Louisiana* (1993).

———— "Independent Economic Production by Slaves on Antebellum Louisiana Sugar Plantations," *Slavery and Abolition* 12 (1991): 182–208.

McTigue, Geraldine, "Patterns of Residence: Housing Distribution by Color in Two Louisiana Towns, 1860–1880," *Louisiana Studies* 15 (1976): 345–88.

Messner, William F., "Black Education in Louisiana, 1863–1865," *Civil War History* 22 (1976): 41–59.

———— "Black Violence and White Response: Louisiana 1862," *Journal of Southern History* 41 (1975): 19–38.

———— *Freedmen and the Ideology of Free Labor: Louisiana, 1862–1865* (1978).

———— "The Vicksburg Campaign of 1862: A Case Study in the Federal Utilization of Black Labor," *Louisiana History* 16 (1975): 371–81.

Middleton, Ernest J., "The Louisiana Education Association, 1901–1970," *Journal of Negro History* 47 (1978): 363–78.

Moran, Robert E., "Local Black Elected Officials in Ascension Parish (1868–1878)," *Louisiana History* 27 (1986): 273–80.

———— "The Negro Dependent Child in Louisiana, 1800–1935," *Social Service Review* 45 (1971): 53–61.

———— "Public Relief in Louisiana from 1928 to 1960," *Louisiana History* 14 (1973): 369–85.

Nelson, Alice Dunbar, "People of Color in Louisiana," *Journal of Negro History* 1 (1916): 361–76.

———— "People of Color in Louisiana, Part 2," *Journal of Negro History* 2 (1917): 51–78.

Owsley, Douglas W., Charles E. Owsley, and Robert W. Mann, "Demography and Pathology of an Urban Slave Population from New Orleans," *American Journal of Physical Anthropology* 74 (1987): 185–97.

Palmer, Robert, *A Tale of Two Cities: Memphis Rock and New Orleans Roll* (1979).

Peoples, Morgan D., "Kansas Fever in North Louisiana," *Louisiana History* 11 (1970): 121–35.

Perkins, A. E., "James Henri Burch and Oscar James Dunn in Louisiana," *Journal of Negro History* 22 (1937): 321–34.

———— "Some Negro Officers and Legislators in Louisiana," *Journal of Negro History* 14 (1929): 523–28.

Price, John Milton, "Slavery in Winn Parish," *Louisiana History* 8 (1967): 137–48.

Pritchard, Walter, "The Effects of the Civil War on the Louisiana Sugar Industry," *Journal of Southern History* 5 (1939): 315–32.

———— "Routine on a Louisiana Sugar Plantation under the Slavery Regime," *Mississippi Valley Historical Review* 14 (1927): 168–78.

Pritchett, Jonathan B., and Richard M. Chamberlain, "Selection in the Market for Slaves: New Orleans, 1830–1860," *Quarterly Journal of Economics* 108 (1993): 461–73.

Quigley, Bill, and Maha Zaki, "The Significance of Race: Legislative Racial Discrimination in Louisiana, 1803–1865," *Southern University Law Review* 24 (1997): 145–205.

Randers, Robert C., "The Free Negro in the New Orleans Economy, 1850–1860," *Louisiana History* 6 (1965): 273–85.

Rankin, David C., "The Impact of the Civil War on the Free Colored Community of New Orleans," *Perspectives in American History* 11 (1977–1978): 377–416.

——— "The Origins of Black Leadership in New Orleans during Reconstruction," *Journal of Southern History* 40 (1974): 417–40.

——— "The Tannenbaum Thesis Reconsidered: Slavery and Race Relations in Antebellum Louisiana," *Southern Studies* 18 (1979): 5–31.

Reed, Germaine A., "Race Legislation in Louisiana, 1864–1920," *Louisiana History* 6 (1965): 379–92.

Reidy, Joseph P., "Mules and Machines and Men: Field Labor on Louisiana Sugar Plantations, 1887–1915," *Agricultural History* 72 (1998): 183–96.

Reilly, Timothy F., "Slavery and the Southwestern Evangelist in New Orleans (1800–61)," *Journal of Mississippi History* 41 (1978): 301–18.

Reinders, Robert C., "The Churches and the Negro in New Orleans, 1850–1860," *Phylon* 22 (1961): 241–48.

——— "The Decline of the New Orleans Free Negro in the Decade before the Civil War," *Journal of Mississippi History* 24 (1962): 88–99.

Richardson, Joe M., "Albert W. Dent: A Black New Orleans Hospital and University Administrator," *Louisiana History* 37 (1996): 309–23.

Richter, William, "Slavery in Baton Rouge, 1820–1860," *Louisiana History* 10 (1969): 125–45.

Ripley, C. Peter, "The Black Family in Transition: Louisiana 1860–1865," *Journal of Southern History* 41 (1975): 369–80.

——— *Slaves and Freedmen in Civil War Louisiana* (1976).

Rodrigue, John C., "'The Great Law of Demand and Supply': The Contest Over Wages in Louisiana's Sugar Region, 1870–1880," *Agricultural History* 72 (1998): 159–82.

Rodriguez, Junius P., "Always 'En Garde': The Effects of Slave Insurrection upon the Louisiana Mentality, 1811–1815," *Louisiana History* 33 (1992): 399–416.

——— "'We'll Hang Jeff Davis on the Sour Apple Tree': Civil War Era Slave Resistance in Louisiana," *Gulf Coast Historical Review* 10 (1995): 6–23.

Roland, Charles Pierce, *Louisiana Sugar Plantations during the American Civil War* (1957).

Rosenberg, Daniel, *New Orleans Dockworkers: Race, Labor, and Unionism, 1892–1923* (1988).

Rousey, Dennis C., "Black Policemen in New Orleans during Reconstruction," *Historian* 49 (1987): 223–43.

Rousseve, Charles Barthelemy, *The Negro in Louisiana, Aspects of History and His Literature* (1937).

Schafer, Judith K., "'Guaranteed against the Vices and Maladies Prescribed by Law': Consumer Protection, the Law of Slave Sales, and the Supreme Court in Antebellum Louisiana," *American Journal of Legal History* 31 (1987): 306–21.

——— "The Immediate Impact of Nat Turner's Insurrection on New Orleans," *Louisiana History* 21 (1980): 361–76.

——— "The Long Arm of the Law: Slave Criminals and the Supreme Court in Antebellum Louisiana," *Tulane Law Review* 60 (1986): 1247–268.

——— "New Orleans Slavery in 1850 as Seen in Advertisements," *Journal of Southern History* 47 (1981): 33–56.

——— "'Open and Notorious Concubinage': The Emancipation of Slave Mistresses By Will and the Supreme Court in Antebellum," *Louisiana History* 28 (1987): 165–82.

——— *Slavery, The Civil Law, and The Supreme Court of Louisiana* (1994).

Schott, Matthew J., "Prisoners Like Us: German POWS Encounter Louisiana's African-Americans," *Louisiana History* 36 (1995): 277–90.

Schweninger, Loren, "Antebellum Free Persons of Color in Postbellum Louisiana," *Louisiana History* 30 (1989): 345–65.

——— "A Negro Sojourner in Antebellum New Orleans," *Louisiana History* 20 (1979): 305–14.

Simpson, Anne Key, "Camille Lucie Nickerson: 'The Louisiana Lady,'" *Louisiana History* 36 (1995): 431–51.

Somers, Dale A., "Black and White in New Orleans: A Study in Urban Race Relations, 1865–1900," *Journal of Southern History* 40 (1974): 19–42.

——— "A City on Wheels: The Bicycle Era in New Orleans," *Louisiana History* 8 (1967): 219–38.

Stahl, Annie Lee West, "The Free Negro in Antebellum Louisiana," *Louisiana History Quarterly* 25 (1942): 301–96.

Sterkx, H. E., *The Free Negro in Ante-bellum Louisiana* (1972).

Strain, Christopher, "'We Walked Like Men': The Deacons for Defense and Justice," *Louisiana History* 38 (1997): 43–62.

Tandberg, Gerilyn G., "Field Hand Clothing In Louisiana and Mississippi during the Antebellum Period," *Press* 6 (1980): 89–103.

Tansey, Richard, "Bernard Kendig and the New Orleans Slave Trade," *Louisiana History* 23 (1982): 159–78.

——— "Out-of-State Free Blacks in Late Antebellum New Orleans," *Louisiana History* 22 (1981): 369–86.

Taylor, Joe G., "The Foreign Slave Trade in Louisiana after 1808," *Louisiana History* 1 (1960): 36–43.

——— *Negro Slavery in Louisiana* (1963).

——— "Slavery in Louisiana during the Civil War," *Louisiana History* 8 (1967): 27–33.

Touchstone, Blake, "Voodoo in New Orleans," *Louisiana History* 13 (1972): 371–86.

Tunnell, Ted, *Crucible of Reconstruction: War, Radicalism, and Race in Louisiana, 1862–1877* (1984).

——— "Free Negroes and the Freedmen: Black Politics in New Orleans during the Civil War," *Southern Studies* 19 (1980): 5–28.

Usner, Daniel H., Jr., "From African Captivity to American Slavery: The Introduction of Black Laborers to Colonial Louisiana," *Louisiana History* 20 (1979): 25–48.

Vandal, Gilles, "Black Utopia in Early Reconstruction New Orleans: The People's Bakery as a Case Study," *Louisiana History* 38 (1997): 437–52.

——— "'Bloody Caddo': White Violence against Blacks in a Louisiana Parish, 1865–1875," *Journal of Social History* 25 (1991): 373–88.

——— *The New Orleans Riot of 1866: Anatomy of a Tragedy* (1983).

——— "The Policy of Violence for Caddo Parish, 1865–1884," *Louisiana History* 32 (1991): 159–82.

Vincent, Charles, *Black Legislators in Louisiana during Reconstruction* (1976).

——— "Louisiana's Black Legislators and Their Effort to Pass a Blue Law during Reconstruction," *Journal of Black Studies* 7 (1976): 47–56.

Warmoth, Henry Clay, *War, Politics, and Reconstruction: Stormy Days in Louisiana* (1930).

Webre, Stephen, "The Problem of Indian Slavery in Spanish Louisiana, 1769–1803," *Louisiana History* 25 (1984): 117–35.

Wells, Ida, *Mob Rule in New Orleans* (1900).

Wetta, Frank J., "'Bulldozing the Scalawags': Some Examples of the Persecution of Southern White Republicans in Louisiana during Reconstruction," *Louisiana History* 21 (1980): 43–58.

Whitten, David O., "Medical Care of Slaves: Louisiana Sugar Region and South Carolina Rice District," *Southern Studies* 16 (1977): 153–80.

Williams, T. Harry, "The Louisiana Unification Movement of 1873," *Journal of Southern History* 11 (1945): 349–69.

Wilson, Keith, "Education as a Vehicle of Racial Control: Major General N. P. Banks in Louisiana, 1863–64," *Journal of Negro Education* 50 (1981): 156–70.

Winston, James E., "The Free Negro in New Orleans, 1803–1861," *Louisiana Historical Quarterly* 21 (1938): 1075–85.

Young, Tommy R., II, "The United States Army and the Institution of Slavery in Louisiana, 1803–1815, Part 1," *Louisiana Studies* 13 (1974): 201–22.

26.2.18 Maine

Billias, George A., "Misadventures of a Maine Slaver," *American Neptune* 19 (1959): 114–22.

26.2.19   Maryland

Abingbade, Harrison Ola, "The Settler-African Conflicts: The Case of the Maryland Colonists and the Grebo, 1840–1900," *Journal of Negro History* 66 (1981): 93–109.

Alpert, Jonathan L., "The Origin of Slavery in the United States: The Maryland Precedent," *American Journal of Legal History* 14 (1970): 189–222.

Beirne, D. Randall, "The Impact of Black Labor on European Immigration into Baltimore's Oldtown, 1790–1910," *Maryland Historical Magazine* 83 (1988): 331–45.

Blassingame, John W., "The Recruitment of Negro Troops in Maryland," *Maryland Historical Magazine* 58 (1963): 20–29.

Bogen, David S., "The Annapolis Poll Books of 1800 and 1804: African-American Voting in the Early Republic," *Maryland Historical Magazine* 86 (1991): 57–65.

——— "The Maryland Contest of *Dred Scott:* The Decline in the Legal Status of Maryland Free Blacks, 1776–1810," *American Journal of Legal History* 34 (1990): 381–411.

Brackett, Jeffrey R., *The Negro in Maryland: A Study of the Institution of Slavery* (1889).

Brown, Philip L., *A Century of "Separate but Equal" Education in Anne Arundel County* (1988).

Browne, Joseph L., "'The Expenses are Borne by Parents': Freedmen's Schools in Southern Maryland, 1865–1870," *Maryland Historical Magazine* 86 (1991): 407–22.

Campbell, Penelope, *Maryland in Africa: The Maryland State Colonization Society, 1831–1857* (1971).

Carr, Lois G., and Russell R. Menard, "Immigration and Opportunity: The Freedman in Early Colonial Maryland," in Thad W. Tate, Jr., and David L. Ammerman, ed., *The Chesapeake in the Seventeenth Century: Essays on Anglo-American Society* (1979): 206–42.

Carroll, Kenneth L., "The Berry Brothers of Talbot County, Maryland: Early Anti-Slavery Leaders," *Maryland Historical Magazine* 84 (1989): 1–9.

——— "Maryland Quakers and Slavery," *Quaker History* 72 (1983): 27–42.

——— "Religious Influences on the Manumission of Slaves in Caroline, Dorchester, and Talbot Counties," *Maryland Historical Magazine* 56 (1961): 176–98.

Cashman, John, "Slaves under Our Flag: The Navassa Island Riot of 1889," *Maryland Historian* 24 (1993): 1–21.

Cassell, Frank A., "Slaves of the Chesapeake Bay Area and the War of 1812," *Journal of Negro History* 57 (1972): 144–55.

Catts, Wade P., and Davy McCall, "A Report of the Archaeological Investigations at the House of Thomas Cuff, A Free Black Laborer, 108 Cannon Street, Chestertown, Kent County, Maryland," *North American Archaeologist* 12 (1991): 155–81.

Clarke, Nina Honemond, *History of the Nineteenth-Century Black Churches in Maryland and Washington, D.C.* (1983).

Davidson, Thomas E., "Free Blacks in Old Somerset County, 1745–1755," *Maryland Historical Magazine* 80 (1985): 151–6.

Dunn, Richard S., "Black Society in the Chesapeake, 1776–1810," in Ira Berlin, and Ronald Hoffman, ed., *Slavery and Freedom in the Age of the American Revolution* (1983): 49–82.

Ellefson, C. Ashley, "An Appeal of Murder in Maryland," *South Atlantic Quarterly* 67 (1968): 527–41.

Fields, Barbara Jeanne, *Slavery and Freedom on the Middle Ground: Maryland during the Nineteenth Century* (1985).

Foner, Philip S., "The First Negro Meeting in Maryland," *Maryland Historical Magazine* 66 (1971): 60–67.

Freeman, Roland L., *The Arabbers of Baltimore* (1989).

Fuke, Richard P., "The Baltimore Association for the Moral and Educational Improvement of the Colored People, 1864–1870," *Maryland Historical Magazine* 66 (1971): 369–404.

——— *Imperfect Equality: African Americans and the Confines of White Racial Attitudes in Post-Emancipation Maryland* (1999).

——— "Planters, Apprenticeship, and Forced Labor: The Black Family under Pressure in Post-Emancipation Maryland," *Agricultural History* 62 (1988): 57–74.

Gardner, Bettye, "Antebellum Black Education in Baltimore," *Maryland Historical Magazine* 71 (1976): 360–66.

Garonzik, Joseph, "The Racial and Ethnic Make-Up of Baltimore Neighborhoods, 1850–70," *Maryland Historical Magazine* 71 (1976): 392–402.

Graham, Leroy, *Baltimore: The Nineteenth Century Black Capital* (1982).

Greene, Suzanne E., "Black Republicans on the Baltimore City Council, 1890–1931," *Maryland Historical Magazine* 74 (1979): 203–222.

Grubb, Farley, and Tony Stitt, "The Liverpool Emigrant Servant Trade and the Transition to Slave Labor in the Chesapeake, 1697–1707 : Market Adjustments to War," *Explorations in Economic History* 31 (1994): 376–405.

Guy, Anita Aidt, "The Maryland Abolition Society and the Promotion of the Ideals of the New Nation," *Maryland Historical Magazine* 84 (1989): 342–49.

———— *Maryland's Persistent Pursuit to End Slavery, 1850–1864* (1996).

Hall, Robert L., "Slave Resistance in Baltimore City and County, 1747–1790," *Maryland Historical Magazine* 84 (1989): 305–18.

Harvey, Katherine A., "Practicing Medicine at the Baltimore Almshouse, 1828–1850," *Maryland Historical Magazine* 74 (1979): 223–37.

Johnson, Whittington B., "The Origin and Nature of African Slavery in Seventeenth Century Maryland," *Maryland Historical Magazine* 73 (1978): 236–45.

Kimmel, Ross M., "Free Blacks in Seventeenth-Century Maryland," *Maryland Historical Magazine* 71 (1976): 19–25.

Klein, Mary O., "'We Shall Be Accountable to God': Some Inquiries into the Position of Blacks in Somerset Parish, Maryland, 1692–1865," *Maryland Historical Magazine* 87 (1992): 399–406.

Klingelhofer, Eric, "Aspects of Early Afro-American Material Culture: Artifacts from the Slave Quarters in Garrison Plantation, Maryland," *Historical Archaeology* 21 (1987): 112–19.

Krech, Shepard, III, "The Participation of Maryland Blacks in the Civil War: Perspectives from Oral History," *Ethnohistory* 27 (1980): 67–78.

Kulikoff, Allan, "The Beginnings of the Afro-American Family in Maryland," in Aubrey C. Land, Lois Green Carr, and Edward C. Papenfuse, ed., *Law, Society, and Politics in Early Maryland* (1977): 171–96.

———— "The Origins of Afro-American Society in Tidewater Maryland and Virginia: 1700 to 1790," *William and Mary Quarterly* 35 (1978): 226–59.

———— "A 'Prolifick' People: Black Population Growth in the Chesapeake Colonies, 1700–1790," *Southern Studies* 16 (1977): 391–428.

———— *Tobacco and Slaves: The Development of Southern Cultures in the Chesapeake, 1680–1800* (1986).

Lee, Jean Butenhoff, "The Problem of Slave Community in the Eighteenth-Century Chesapeake," *William and Mary Quarterly* 43 (1986): 333–61.

Lewis, Ronald L., *Coal, Iron, and Slaves: Industrial Slavery in Maryland and Virginia, 1715–1865* (1979).

Main, Gloria L., *Tobacco Colony: Life in Early Maryland, 1650–1720* (1982).

Marks, Bayly E., "Skilled Blacks in Antebellum St. Mary's County, Maryland," *Journal of Southern History* 53 (1987): 537–64.

Maryland, Inter-racial Commmission, *Report with Recommendations of the Inter-racial Commission of Maryland to the Governor and General Assembly of Maryland* (1939).

Menard, Russell R., "From Servants to Slaves: The Transformation of the Chesapeake Labor System," *Southern Studies* 16 (1977): 355–90.

———— "The Maryland Slave Population, 1658 to 1730: A Demographic Profile of Blacks in Four Counties," *William and Mary Quarterly* 32 (1975): 29–54.

Milobsky, David, "Power from the Pulpit: Baltimore's African-American Clergy, 1950–1970," *Maryland Historical Magazine* 89 (1994): 274–89.

Morgan, Philip D., *Slave Counterpoint: Black Culture in the Eighteenth-Century Chesapeake and Lowcountry* (1998).

Morris, Richard B., "Labor Controls in Maryland in the Nineteenth Century," *Journal of Southern History* 14 (1948): 385–400.

Mouser, Bruce L., "Baltimore's African Experiment, 1822–1827," *Journal of Negro History* 80 (1995): 113–30.

Neverdon-Morton, Cynthia, "Black Housing Patterns in Baltimore City, 1885–1953," *Maryland Historian* 16 (1985): 25–39.

Phillips, Christopher, *Freedom's Port: The African American Community of Baltimore, 1790–1860* (1997).

Putney, Martha S., "The Baltimore Normal School for the Education of Colored Teachers: Its Founders and its Founding," *Maryland Historical Magazine* 72 (1977): 238–52.

——— "The Black Colleges in the Maryland State College System: Quest for Equal Opportunity, 1908–1975," *Maryland Historical Magazine* 75 (1980): 335–43.

Quarles, Benjamin, "'Freedom Fettered': Blacks in the Constitutional Era in Maryland, 1776–1810—An Introduction," *Maryland Historical Magazine* 84 (1989): 299–304.

Rollo, Vera F., *The Black Experience in Maryland* (1980).

Rutman, Darrett B., Charles Wetherell, and Anita H. Rutman, "Rhythms of Life: Black and White Seasonality in the Early Chesapeake," *Journal of Interdisciplinary History* 11 (1980): 29–53.

Ryon, Roderick M., "An Ambiguous Legacy: Baltimore Blacks and the CIO, 1936–1941," *Journal of Negro History* 65 (1980): 18–33.

——— "Old West Baltimore," *Maryland History Magazine* 77 (1982): 54–69.

Seawright, Sally, "Desegregation at Maryland: The NAACP and the Murray Case in the 1930s," *Maryland Historian* 1 (1970): 59–73.

Slezak, Eva, "Black Householders in the 1810 Baltimore City Directory," *Journal of the Afro-American Historical and Genealogical Society* 5 (1984): 67–70.

Steffen, Charles G., "Changes in the Organization of Artisan Production in Baltimore, 1790 to 1820," *William and Mary Quarterly* 36 (1979): 101–17.

Terborg-Penn, Rosalyn, "Black Women Freedom Fighters in Early Nineteenth Century Maryland," *Maryland Heritage* 2 (1984): 11–12.

Thomas, Bettye C., "Public Education and Black Protest in Baltimore, 1865–1900," *Maryland Historical Magazine* 71 (1976): 381–91.

Towers, Frank, "Race, Power, and Money in Antebellum Baltimore: Mary Ridgely's Thousand-Dollar Note," *Maryland Historical Magazine* 88 (1993): 317–23.

Walsh, Lorena S., "Plantation Management in the Chesapeake, 1620–1820," *Journal of Economic History* 49 (1989): 393–406.

——— "Rural African Americans in the Constitutional Era in Maryland, 1776–1810," *Maryland Historical Magazine* 84 (1989): 327–41.

Wax, Darold D., "Black Immigrants: The Slave Trade in Colonial Maryland," *Maryland Historical Magazine* 73 (1978): 30–45.

——— "The Image of the Negro in the *Maryland Gazette,* 1745–1775," *Journalism Quarterly* 46 (1969): 73–80.

Wennersten, John R., and Ruth Ellen Wennersten, "Separate and Unequal: The Evolution of a Black Land Grant College in Maryland, 1890–1930," *Maryland History Magazine* 72 (1977): 110–17.

Whitman, T. Stephen, *The Price of Freedom: Slavery and Manumission in Baltimore and Early National Maryland* (1997).

Wright, James Martin, *The Free Negro in Maryland, 1634–1860* (1921).

Yentsch, Anne Elizabeth, "Beads as Silent Witnesses of an African-American Past: Social Identity and the Artifacts of Slavery in Annapolis, Maryland," *Kroeber Anthropological Society Papers* 79 (1995): 44–60.

——— *A Chesapeake Family and Their Slaves: A Study in Historical Archaeology* (1994).

26.2.20   Massachusetts

Abbott, Richard H., "Massachusetts and the Recruitment of Southern Negroes, 1863–1865," *Civil War History* 14 (1968): 197–210.

Bearse, Austin, *Reminiscences of Fugitive-Slave Law Days in Boston* (1880).

Berryman, Jack W., "Early Black Leadership in Collegiate Football: Massachusetts as a Pioneer," *Historical Journal of Massachusetts* 9 (1981): 17–28.

Betts, John R., "The Negro and the New England Conscience in the Days of John Boyle O'Reilly," *Journal of Negro History* 51 (1966): 246–61.

Camerota, Michael, "Westfield's Black Community, 1755–1905," *Historical Journal of Western Massachusetts* 5 (1976): 17–27.

Carvalho, Joseph, III, *Black Families in Hampden County, Massachusetts, 1650–1855* (1984).

Cochrane, Sharlene Voogd, "'And the Pressure Never Let Up': Black Women, White Women, and the Boston YWCA, 1918–1948," in Vicki L. Crawford, Jacqueline Anne Rouse, and Barbara Woods, ed., *Women in the Civil Rights Movement: Trailblazers and Torchbearers, 1941–1965* (1990): 259–69.

Cox, Clinton, *Undying Glory: The Story of the Massachusetts 54th Regiment* (1991).

Cromwell, Adelaide M., *The Other Brahmins: Boston's Black Upper Class, 1750–1950* (1994).

Cushing, John, "The Cushing Court and the Abolition of Slavery in Massachusetts: More Notes on the 'Quock Walker Case,'" *American Journal of Legal History* 5 (1961): 118–44.

Daniels, John, *In Freedom's Birthplace: A Study of the Boston Negroes* (1914).

Davis, Thomas J., "Emancipation Rhetoric, Natural Rights, and Revolutionary New England: A Note on Four Black Petitions in Massachusetts, 1773–1777," *New England Quarterly* 62 (1989): 248–63.

DeVaughn, Booker Thomas, Jr., *A History of Adult Education in the Black Community of Boston from 1900 to 1965* (1975).

Dinkin, Robert J., "Seating the Meeting House in Early Massachusetts," *New England Quarterly* 43 (1970): 450–64.

Emilio, Luis F., *A Brave Black Regiment: History of the Fifty-Fourth Regiment of Massachusetts Volunteer Infantry, 1863–1865* (1894).

Formisano, Ronald P., *Boston against Busing: Race, Class and Ethnicity in the 1960s and 1970s* (1991).

Gamm, Gerald H., *The Making of New Deal Democrats: Voting Behavior and Realignment in Boston, 1920–1940* (1989).

Goldman, Hal, "Black Citizenship and Military Self-Presentation in Antebellum Massachusetts," *Historical Journal of Massachusetts* 26 (1997): 157–83.

Hayden, Robert C., *Faith, Culture, and Leadership: A History of the Black Church in Boston* (1983).

Hill, Charles L., "Slavery and Its Aftermath in Beverly, Massachusetts: Juno Larcom and Her Family," *Essex Institute Historical Collections* 116 (1980): 111–30.

Hindus, Michael S., *Prison and Plantation: Crime, Justice, and Authority in Massachusetts and South Carolina, 1767–1878* (1980).

Hinks, Peter P., "'Frequently Plunged into Slavery': Free Blacks and Kidnapping in Antebellum Boston," *Historical Journal of Massachusetts* 20 (1992): 16–31.

Holland, Jacqueline L., "The African-American Presence on Martha's Vineyard," *Dukes County Intelligencer* 33 (1991): 3–26.

Horton, James Oliver, "Generations of Protest: Black Families and Social Reform in Antebellum Boston," *New England Quarterly* 49 (1976): 242–56.

Horton, James Oliver, and Lois Horton, *Black Bostonians: Family Life and Community Struggle in the Antebellum North* (1979).

Horton, Lois E., "Community Organization and Social Activism: Black Boston and the Anti-Slavery Movement," *Sociological Inquiry* 55 (1985): 182–99.

Jacobs, Donald M., *Courage and Conscience: Black and White Abolitionists in Boston* (1993).

———— "The Nineteenth-Century Struggle over Segregated Education in the Boston Schools," *Journal of Negro Education* 39 (1970): 76–85.

———— "William Lloyd Garrison's *Liberator* and Boston's Blacks, 1830–1865," *New England Quarterly* 44 (1971): 259–77.

Kaplan, Sidney, "Blacks in Massachusetts and the Shays' Rebellion," *Contributions in Black Studies* 8 (1986–1987): 5–14.

Kaufman, Polly Welts, "Building a Constituency for School Desegregation: African-American Women in Boston, 1962–1972," *Teachers College Record* 92 (1991): 619–31.

Kozol, Jonathan, *Death at an Early Age: The Destruction of the Hearts and Minds of Negro Children in the Boston Public Schools* (1967).

Levesque, George A., "Before Integration: The Forgotten Years of Jim Crow Education in Boston," *Journal of Negro Education* 48 (1979): 113–25.

——— *Black Boston: African American Life and Culture in Urban America, 1750–1860* (1994).

——— "Inherent Reformers—Inherited Orthodoxy: Black Baptists in Boston, 1800–1873," *Journal of Negro History* 60 (1975): 491–519.

Levy, Leonard W., "Sim's Case: The Fugitive Slave Law in Boston in 1851," *Journal of Negro History* 35 (1950): 39–74.

Mabee, Carleton, "A Negro Boycott to Integrate Boston Schools," *New England Quarterly* 41 (1968): 341–61.

MacEacheren, Elaine, "Emancipation of Slavery in Massachusetts: A Reexamination, 1770–1790," *Journal of Negro History* 55 (1970): 289–306.

Malloy, Tom, and Brenda Malloy, "Slavery in Colonial Massachusetts as Seen through Selected Gravestones," *Markers* 11 (1994): 112–41.

McMillan, Timothy J., "Black Magic: Witchcraft, Race, and Resistance in Colonial New England," *Journal of Black Studies* 25 (1994): 99–117.

Mulderink, Earl F., III, "'The Whole Town is Ringing with It': Slave Kidnapping Charges against Nathan Johnson of New Bedford, Massachusetts, 1839," *New England Quarterly* 61 (1988): 341–57.

O'Brien, William, "Did the Jennison Case Outlaw Slavery in Massachusetts?" *William and Mary Quarterly* 17 (1960): 219–41.

Paris, Arthur E., *Black Pentecostalism: Southern Religion in an Urban World* (1982).

Pease, Jane H., and William H. Pease, "Boston Garrisonians and the Problem of Frederick Douglass," *Canadian Journal of History* 2 (1967): 29–48.

Pleck, Elizabeth H., *Black Migration and Poverty in Boston, 1865–1900* (1979).

——— "The Two-Parent Household: Black Family Structure in Late Nineteenth Century Boston," in Darlene Clark Hine, ed., *Black Women in American History: From Colonial Times through the Nineteenth Century* (1990): 1095–124.

Putney, Martha S., "Black Merchant Seamen of Newport, 1803–1865: A Case Study in Foreign Commerce," *Journal of Negro History* 57 (1972): 156–68.

Ruchames, Louis, "Race, Marriage, and Abolitionism in Massachusetts," *Journal of Negro History* 40 (1955): 250–73.

Russell, Donna Valley, "The Abrahams of Natick and Grafton, Massachusetts," *Journal of the Afro-American Historical and Genealogical Society* 5 (1984): 47–52.

Schneider, Mark L., *Boston Confronts Jim Crow, 1890–1920* (1997).

Seeman, Erik R., "'Justise Must Take Plase': Three African Americans Speak of Religion in Eighteenth-Century New England," *William and Mary Quarterly* 56 (1999): 393–414.

Siebert, Wilbur Henry, *The Underground Railroad in Massachusetts* (1936).

Spector, Robert M., "The Quock Walker Case (1781–83)—Slavery, Its Abolition, and Negro Citizenship in Early Massachusetts," *Journal of Negro History* 53 (1968): 12–32.

Swift, David E., "Samuel Hopkins: Calvinist Social Concern in Eighteenth-Century New England," *Journal of Presbyterian History* 47 (1969): 31–54.

Thernstrom, Stephan, *The Other Bostonians: Poverty and Progress in the American Metropolis, 1880–1970* (1973).

Towner, Lawrence, *Good Master Well Served: Masters and Servants in Colonial Massachusetts* (1997).

von Frank, Albert J., "John Saffin: Slavery and Racism in Colonial Massachusetts," *Early American Literature* 29 (1994): 254–72.

——— *The Trials of Anthony Burns: Freedom and Slavery in Emerson's Boston* (1998).

White, Arthur O., "Antebellum School Reform in Boston: Integrationists and Separatists," *Phylon* 34 (1973): 203–18.

——— "The Black Leadership Class and Education in Antebellum Boston," *Journal of Negro Education* 42 (1973): 504–15.

——— *Blacks and Education in Antebellum Massachusetts: Strategies for Social Mobility* (1971).

——— "Salem's Antebellum Black Community: Seedbed of the School Integration Movement," *Essex Institute Historical Collections* 108 (1972): 99–118.

Zilversmit, Arthur, "Quok Walker, Mumbet, and the Abolition of Slavery in Massachusetts," *William and Mary Quarterly* 25 (1968): 614–24.

26.2.21 Michigan

Bak, Richard, *Turkey Stearnes and the Detroit Stars: The Negro Leagues in Detroit, 1919–1933* (1994).

Banner, Melvin E., *The Black Pioneer in Michigan* (1973).

Behee, John, *Hail to the Victors! Black Athletes at the University of Michigan* (1974).

Bledsoe, Timothy, Michael Combs, Lee Sigelman, and Susan Welch, "Trends in Racial Attitudes in Detroit, 1968–1992," *Urban Affairs Review* 31 (1996): 508–28.

Boyle, Kevin, "The Kiss: Racial and Gender Conflict in a 1950s Automobile Factory," *Journal of American History* 84 (1997).

Brown, Earl Louis, *Why Race Riots? Lessons from Detroit* (1944).

Brown, Elizabeth G., "The Intitial Admission of Negro Students to the University of Michigan," *Michigan Quarterly Review* 2 (1963): 233–36.

Capeci, Dominic J., Jr., *Race Relations in Wartime Detroit: The Sojourner Truth Housing Controversy of 1942* (1984).

Capeci, Dominic J., Jr., and Martha Wilkerson, *Layered Violence: The Detroit Rioters of 1943* (1991).

Chavis, John M. T., and William McNitt, *A Brief History of the Detroit Urban League and Description of the League's Papers in the Michigan Historical Collections* (1971).

Claspy, Everett, *The Negro in Southwestern Michigan: Negroes in the North in a Rural Environment* (1967).

Cox, Anna-Lisa, "A Pocket of Freedom: Blacks in Covert, Michigan, in the Nineteenth Century," *Michigan Historical Review* 21 (1995): 1–18.

Dancy, John C., "The Negro People in Michigan," *Michigan History Magazine* 24 (1940): 221–40.

DeVries, James E., *Race and Kinship in a Midwestern Town: The Black Experience in Monroe, Michigan, 1900–1915* (1984).

Dorson, Richard Mercer, ed., *Negro Folktales in Michigan* (1956).

Fields, Harold B., "Free Negroes in Cass County before the Civil War," *Michigan History* 44 (1960): 649–58.

Fine, Sidney, *Violence in the Model City: The Cavanagh Administration, Race Relations, and Detroit Riot of 1967* (1989).

Formisano, Ronald P., "The Edge of Caste: Colored Suffrage in Michigan, 1827–1861," *Michigan History* 56 (1972): 19–41.

Gaston, Juanita, *The Changing Residential Pattern of Blacks in Battle Creek, Michigan: A Story in Historical Geography* (1977).

Halpern, Martin, "'I'm Fighting for Freedom': Coleman Young, HUAC, and the Detroit African American Community," *Journal of American Ethnic History* 17 (1997): 19–38.

Haynes, George Edmund, *Negro Newcomers in Detroit* (1969).

Katzman, David M., *Before the Ghetto: Black Detroit in the Nineteenth Century* (1973).

Kilar, Jeremy W., "Black Pioneers in the Michigan Lumber Industry," *Journal of Forest History* 24 (1980): 142–49.

Leashore, Bogart R., "Black Female Workers: Live-In Domestics in Detroit, Michigan, 1860–1880," *Phylon* 45 (1984): 111–20.

Levine, David Allen, *Internal Combustion: The Races in Detroit, 1915–1926* (1976).

Litchfield, Edward H., "A Case Study of Negro Political Behavior in Detroit," *Public Opinion Quarterly* 5 (1941): 267–74.

Maloney, Thomas N., and Warren C. Whatley, "Making the Effort: The Contours of Racial Discrimination in Detroit's Labor Markets, 1920–1940," *Journal of Economic History* 55 (1995): 465–93.

McRae, Norman, "Crossing the Detroit River to Find Freedom," *Michigan History* 67 (1983): 35–9.

——— *Negroes in Michigan during the Civil War* (1966).

Meier, August, and Elliott Rudwick, *Black Detroit and the Rise of the UAW* (1979).

National Urban League, *Racial Conflict: A Home Front Danger: Lessons of the Detroit Riot* (1943).

Peterson, Joyce Shaw, "Black Automobile Workers in Detroit, 1910–1930," *Journal of Negro History* 64 (1979): 177–90.

Shelly, Cara L., "Bradby's Baptists: Second Baptist Church of Detroit, 1910–1946," *Michigan Historical Review* 17 (1991): 1–33.

Sitkoff, Harvard, "The Detroit Race Riot of 1943," *Michigan History* 53 (1969): 183–206.

Sugrue, Thomas, *The Origins of the Urban Crisis: Race and Inequality in Postwar Detroit* (1996).

Thomas, Richard W., "The Detroit Urban League, 1916–1923," *Michigan History* 60 (1976): 315–38.

——— *Life for Us is What We Make It: Building Black Community in Detroit, 1915–45* (1992).

Thompson, Heather Ann, "Rethinking the Politics of White Flight in the Postwar City: Detroit, 1945–1980," *Journal of Urban History* 25 (1999): 163–98.

Wheeler, James O., and Stanley D. Brunn, "An Agricultural Ghetto: Negroes in Cass County, Michigan, 1845–1968," *Geographical Review* 59 (1969): 317–29.

White, Walter Francis, *What Caused the Detroit Riot?: An Analysis* (1943).

Wilson, Benjamin C., *The Rural Black Heritage between Chicago and Detroit, 1850–1929: A Photograph Album and Random Thoughts* (1985).

Wolcott, Victoria W., "The Culture of the Informal Economy: Numbers Runners in Inter-War Black Detroit," *Radical History Review* 69 (1997): 46–75.

26.2.22   Minnesota

Green, William D., "Race and Segregation in St. Paul's Public Schools, 1846–69," *Minnesota History* 55 (1996): 138–49.

Griffin, James S., "Blacks in the St. Paul Police Department: An Eighty Year Survey," *Minnesota History* 44 (1975): 255–65.

Karger, Howard Jacob, "Phyllis Wheatley House: A History of the Minneapolis Black Settlement House, 1924 to 1940," *Phylon* 47 (1986): 79–90.

Spangler, Earl, *The Negro in Minnesota* (1961).

——— "The Negro in Minnesota, 1800–1865," *Transactions of the Historical and Scientific Society of Manitoba* 3 (1965): 13–26.

Taylor, David Vassar, comp., *Blacks in Minnesota: A Preliminary Guide to Historical Sources* (1976).

26.2.23   Mississippi

Abney, F. Glenn, "Factors Related to Negro Voter Turnout in Mississippi," *Journal of Politics* 36 (1974): 1057–63.

Abney, M. G., "Reconstruction in Pontotoc County," *Publications of the Mississippi Historical Society* 11 (1910): 229–70.

Alford, Terry L., "Some Manumissions Recorded in the Addams County Deed Books in Chancery Clerk's Office, Natchez, Mississippi, 1795–1835," *Journal of Mississippi History* 33 (1971): 39–50.

Anderson, James D., "Philanthropy, the State, and the Development of Historically Black Public Colleges: The Case of Mississippi," *Minerva: A Review of Science, Learning, and Policy* 35 (1997): 295–309.

Andrews, Kenneth T., "The Impacts of Social Movements on the Political Process: The Civil Rights Movement and Black Electoral Politics in Mississippi," *American Sociological Review* 62 (1997): 800–19.

Aptheker, Herbert, "Mississippi Reconstruction and the Negro Leader, Charles Caldwell," *Science and Society* 11 (1947): 340–71.

Barry, John M., *Rising Tide: The Great Mississippi Flood of 1927 and How it Changed America* (1997).

Beasley, Jonathan, "Blacks—Slave and Free—Vicksburg, 1850–1860," *Journal of Mississippi History* 38 (1976): 1–32.

Berry, Jason, *Amazing Grace: With Charles Evers in Mississippi* (1970).

Bigelow, Martha Mitchell, "Freedmen of the Mississippi Valley, 1862–1865," *Civil War History* 8 (1962): 38–47.

Blain, William T., "Banner Unionism in Mississippi, Choctaw County, 1861–1869," *Mississippi Quarterly* 29 (1976): 207–20.

——— "Challenge to the Lawless: The Mississippi Secret Service, 1870–1871," *Journal of Mississippi History* 40 (1978): 119–31.

Bowman, Robert, "Reconstruction in Yazoo County," *Publications of the Mississippi Historical Society* 7 (1903): 115–30.

Brandfon, Robert L., *Cotton Kingdom of the New South: A History of the Yazoo Mississippi Delta from Reconstruction to the Twentieth Century* (1967).

Brown, Julia, "Reconstruction in Yalobusha and Grenada Counties," *Publications of the Mississippi Historical Society* 12 (1912): 214–82.

Browne, F. Z., "Reconstruction in Oktibbeha County," *Publications of the Mississippi Historical Society* 13 (1913): 273–98.

Burner, Eric R., *And Gently He Shall Lead Them: Robert Parris Moses and Civil Rights in Mississippi* (1996).

Bynum, Victoria E., "'White Negroes' in Segregated Mississippi: Miscegenation, Racial Identity, and the Law," *Journal of Southern History* 64 (1998): 247–76.

Campbell, Clarice T., and Oscar Allan Rogers, *Mississippi: The View from Tougaloo* (1979).

Cobb, James C., "'Somebody Done Nailed Us on the Cross': Federal Farm and Welfare Policy and the Civil Rights Movement in the Mississippi Delta," *Journal of American History* 77 (1990): 912–36.

Crowther, Edward R., "Mississippi Baptists, Slavery, and Secession, 1806–1861," *Journal of Mississippi History* 56 (1994): 129–48.

Currie, James T., *Enclave: Vicksburg and Her Plantations, 1863–1870* (1980).

——— "Freedmen at Davis Bend, April 1864," *Journal of Mississippi History* 46 (1984): 120–29.

——— "From Slavery to Freedom in Mississippi's Legal System," *Journal of Negro History* 65 (1980): 112–25.

Curry, Constance, *Silver Rights* (1995).

Davis, Ronald L. F., *Good and Faithful Labor: From Slavery to Sharecropping in the Natchez District, 1860–1890* (1982).

Dittmer, John, *Local People: The Struggle for Civil Rights in Mississippi* (1994).

Drake, Winbourne Magruder, "The Framing of Mississippi's First Constitution," *Journal of Mississippi History* 29 (1967): 301–27.

Dubay, Robert W., "Mississippi and the Proposed Federal Anti-Lynching Bills of 1937–1938," *Southern Quarterly* 7 (1968): 73–89.

Ellem, Warren A., "The Overthrow of Reconstruction in Mississippi," *Journal of Mississippi History* 54 (1992): 175–201.

——— "Who Were the Mississippi Scalawags?" *Journal of Southern History* 38 (1972): 217–40.

Evans, W. A., "Free Negroes in Monroe County during Slavery Days," *Journal of Mississippi History* 3 (1941): 37–43.

Findlay, James F., "The Mainline Churches and Head Start in Mississippi: Religious Activism in the Sixties," *Church History* 64 (1995): 237–50.

Fleener, Nickieann, "Breaking Down Buyer Resistance: Marketing the 1935 Pittsburgh Courier to Mississippi Blacks," *Journalism History* 13 (1986): 78–85.

Frankel, Noralee, *Freedom's Women: Black Women and Families in Civil War Era Mississippi* (1999).

Gibson, George H., "The Mississippi Market for Woolen Goods: An 1822 Analysis," *Journal of Southern History* 31 (1965): 80–90.

Gordon, Lawrence, "A Brief Look at Blacks in Depression Mississippi, 1929–1934," *Journal of Negro History* 64 (1979): 377–90.

Gravely, William B., "A Black Methodist on Reconstruction in Mississippi: The Letters by James Lynch in 1868–1869," *Methodist History* 11 (1973): 2–18.

Greenberg, Kenneth G., "The Civil War and the Redistribution of Land: Adams County, Mississippi, 1860–1870," *Agricultural History* 25 (1978): 292–307.

Griffiths, John D. M., "A State of Servitude Worse than Slavery: The Politics of Penal Administration in Mississippi, 1865–1900," *Journal of Mississippi History* 55 (1994): 1–18.

Grim, Valerie, "History Shared through Memory: The Establishment and Implementation of Education in the Brooks Farm Community, 1920–1957," *Oral History Review* 23 (1996): 1–17.

Grubbs, Kenneth R., "Selected Aspects in the Pattern of Economic Growth and Economic Development of the Mississippi Economy, 1817–1967," *Southern Quarterly* 6 (1967): 95–115.

Harris, J. William, "Etiquette, Lynching, and Racial Boundaries in Southern History: A Mississippi Example," *American Historical Review* 100 (1995): 387–410.

Harris, William C., "Formulation of the First Mississippi Plan: The Black Code of 1865," *Journal of Mississippi History* 29 (1967): 181–201.

Hartley, William G., "Reconstruction Data from the 1870 Census: Hinds County, Mississippi," *Journal of Mississippi History* 35 (1973): 55–64.

Harwood, Thomas F., "The Abolitionist Image of Louisiana and Mississippi," *Louisiana History* 7 (1966): 281–308.

Holmes, William F., "Whitecapping: Agrarian Violence in Mississippi, 1902–1906," *Journal of Southern History* 35 (1969): 165–85.

Holtzclaw, Robert F., *Black Magnolias: A Brief History of the Afro-Mississippian, 1865–1980* (1984).

Humphrey, George D., "The Failure of the Mississippi Freedmen's Bureau in Black Labor Relations, 1865–1867," *Journal of Mississippi History* 45 (1983): 23–27.

Irwin, James R., and Anthony P. O'Brien, "Where Have All the Sharecroppers Gone? Black Occupations in Postbellum Mississippi," *Agricultural History* 72 (1998): 280–97.

Johnston, Erle, *Mississippi's Defiant Years, 1953–1973: An Interpretive Documentary with Personal Experiences* (1990).

Joubert, Paul E., and Ben M. Crouch, "Mississippi Blacks and the Voting Rights Act of 1965," *Journal of Negro Education* 46 (1977): 157–67.

Kelley, Donald Brooks, "Harper's Ferry: Prelude to Crisis in Mississippi," *Journal of Mississippi History* 27 (1965): 351–72.

Lang, Meredith, *Defender of the Faith: The High Court of Mississippi, 1817–1875* (1977).

Legan, Marshall S., "Disease and the Freedmen in Mississippi during Reconstruction," *Journal of the History of Medicine and Applied Sciences* 28 (1973): 257–67.

Locke, Mamie E., "The Role of African-American Women in the Civil Rights and Women's Movements in Hinds County and Sunflower County, Mississippi," *Journal of Mississippi History* 53 (1991): 229–39.

Lopez, Claira S., "James K. Vardaman and the Negro: The Foundation of Mississippi's Racial Policy," *Southern Quarterly* 3 (1965): 155–80.

Mabry, William A., "Disfranchisement of the Negro in Mississippi," *Journal of Southern History* 4 (1938): 318–33.

McCord, William, *Mississippi: The Long Hot Summer* (1965).

McGhee, Flora Ann Caldwell, *Mississippi Black Newspapers: Their History, Content, and Future* (1985).

McKibben, Davidson B., "Negro Slave Insurrections in Mississippi, 1800–1865," *Journal of Negro History* 34 (1949): 73–90.

McMillen, Neil R., "Black Enfranchisement in Mississippi: Federal Enforcement and Black Protest in the 1960s," *Journal of Southern History* 43 (1977): 351–72.

——— "Black Journalism in Mississippi: The Jim Crow Years," *Journal of Mississippi History* 49 (1987): 129–38.

——— *Dark Journey: Black Mississippians in the Age of Jim Crow* (1989).

——— "The Migration and Black Protest in Jim Crow Mississippi," in Alferdteen Harrison, ed., *Black Exodus: The Great Migration from the American South* (1991): 83–99.

McMurry, Daniel W., and John N. Burrus, "Mississippi's Population: An Analysis of a Half-Century of Demographic Change," *Southern Quarterly* 6 (1967): 45–63.

Meredith, James, *Three Years in Mississippi* (1966).

Miller, Char, "The Mississippi Summer Project Remembered: The Stephen Mitchell Bingham Letter," *Journal of Mississippi History* 47 (1985): 284–307.

Mills, Nicolaus, *Like a Holy Crusade: Mississippi 1964—The Turning of the Civil Rights Movement in America* (1992).

Mollison, Irvin C., "Negro Lawyers in Mississippi," *Journal of Negro History* 15 (1930): 38–71.

Moore, John Hebron, *The Emergence of the Cotton Kingdom in the Old Southwest: Mississippi, 1770–1860* (1988).

Morris, Christopher, "An Event in Community Organization: The Mississippi Slave Insurrection Scare of 1835," *Journal of Social History* 22 (1988): 93–112.

Newman, Mark, "The Mississippi Baptist Convention and Desegregation, 1945–1980," *Journal of Mississippi History* 59 (1997): 1–32.

Nichols, Irby C., "Reconstruction in DeSoto County," *Publications of the Mississippi Historical Society* 11 (1910): 295–316.

Noble, Stuart G., *Forty Years of the Public Schools in Mississippi, With Special Reference to the Education of the Negro* (1918).

Nordhaus, R. Edward, "S.N.C.C. and the Civil Rights Movement in Mississippi, 1963–64: A Time of Change," *History Teacher* 17 (1983): 95–102.

Nossiter, Adam, *Of Long Memory: Mississippi and the Murder of Medgar Evers* (1994).

Ownby, Ted, *American Dreams in Mississippi: Consumers, Poverty, and Culture, 1830–1998* (1999).

Parker, Frank R., *Black Votes Count: Political Empowerment in Mississippi after 1965* (1990).

Payne, Charles M., *I've Got the Light of Freedom: The Organizing Tradition and the Mississippi Freedom Struggle* (1995).

Pittman, Walter E., Jr., "The Mel Cheatham Affair: Interracial Murder in Mississippi in 1889," *Journal of Mississippi History* 43 (1981): 127–33.

Posey, Walter B., "The Baptists and Slavery in the Lower Mississippi Valley," *Journal of Negro History* 41 (1956): 117–30.

———— *The Baptist Church in the Lower Mississippi Valley, 1776–1845* (1957).

Rothschild, Mary Aickin, "The Volunteers and the Freedom Schools: Education for Social Change in Mississippi," *History of Education Quarterly* 22 (1982): 401–20.

Salter, John R., Jr., *Jackson, Mississippi: An American Chronicle of Struggle and Schism* (1987).

Satcher, Buford, *Blacks in Mississippi Politics, 1865–1900* (1978).

Shore, Laurence, "Making Mississippi Safe for Slavery: The Insurrectionary Panic of 1835," in Orville Vernon Burton, and Robert C. McMath, Jr., ed., *Class, Conflict, and Consensus: Antebellum Southern Community Studies* (1982): 96–127.

Shostak, David A., "Crosby Smith: Forgotten Witness to a Mississippi Nightmare," *Negro History Bulletin* 38 (1974/5): 320–25.

Sinsheimer, Joseph A., "The Freedom Vote of 1963: New Strategies of Racial Protest in Mississippi," *Journal of Southern History* 55 (1989): 217–44.

Skates, John R., "World War II as a Watershed in Mississippi History," *Journal of Mississippi History* 37 (1975): 131–42.

Sparks, Randy J., "Mississippi's Apostle of Slavery: James Smylie and the Biblical Defense of Slavery," *Mississippi History* 51 (1989): 89–106.

———— "'The White People's Arms Are Longer than Ours': Blacks, Education, and the American Missionary Association in Reconstruction Mississippi," *Journal of Mississippi History* 54 (1992): 1–27.

Sugarman, Tracy, *Stranger at the Gates: A Summer in Mississippi* (1966).

Sydnor, Charles S., "The Free Negro in Mississippi before the Civil War," *American Historical Review* 32 (1927): 51–78.

———— *Slavery in Mississippi* (1933).

Taylor, William Banks, *Brokered Justice: Race, Politics, and Mississippi Prisons, 1798–1992* (1993).

Upton, Mrs. R. Chester, ed., "Minutes of the Antioch Baptist Church, Marion County, Mississippi, 1828–1850: Nathan Smart and Hosea Davis Bible Records," *Journal of Mississippi History* 27 (1965): 191–209.

Usner, Daniel H., Jr., "American Indians on the Cotton Frontier: Changing Economic Relations with Citizens and Slaves in the Mississippi Territory," *Journal of American History* 72 (1985): 297–317.

———— "The Frontier Exchange Economy of the Lower Mississippi Valley in the Eighteenth Century," *William and Mary Quarterly* 44 (1987): 165–92.

———— *Indians, Settlers, and Slaves in a Frontier Exchange Economy: The Lower Mississippi Valley before 1783* (1992).

Verney, Kevern J., "Trespassers in the Land of Their Birth: Black Land Ownership in South Carolina and Mississippi during the Civil War and Reconstruction, 1861–1877," *Slavery and Abolition* 4 (1983): 64–79.

Waldrep, Christopher, "Black Access to Law in Reconstruction: The Case of Warren County, Mississippi," *Chicago-Kent Law Review* 70 (1994): 583–626.

——— "Substituting Law for the Lash: Emancipation and Legal Formalism in a Mississippi County Court," *Journal of American History* 82 (1996): 1425–51.

Walter, Mildred Pitts, *Mississippi Challenge* (1996).

Ward, Jerry W., Jr., "Kalamu Ya Salaam: A Primary Bibliography (in Progress)," *Mississippi Quarterly* 51 (1997/1998): 105–48.

Wharton, Vernon L., *The Negro in Mississippi, 1865–1890* (1947).

Whitfield, Stephen J., *A Death in the Delta: The Story of Emmett Till* (1988).

Wirt, Frederick M., *Politics of Southern Equality: Law and Social Change in a Mississippi County* (1970).

Woodruff, Nan Elizabeth, "African-American Struggles for Citizenship in the Arkansas and Mississippi Deltas in the Age of Jim Crow," *Radical History Review* 55 (1994): 33–51.

26.2.24   Missouri

Allen, Ernest Jr, "Waiting For Tojo: The Pro-Japan Vigil of Black Missourians, 1932–1943," *Gateway Heritage* 16 (1995): 38–55.

Baltimore, Lester B., "Benjamin F. Stringfellow: The Fight for Slavery on the Missouri Border," *Missouri Historical Review* 62 (1967): 14–29.

Bellamy, Donald D., "The Education of Blacks in Missouri prior to 1861," *Journal of Negro History* 59 (1972): 143–57.

——— "Free Blacks in Antebellum Missouri, 1820–1860," *Missouri Historical Review* 67 (1973): 198–226.

——— "The Persistency of Colonization in Missouri," *Missouri Historical Review* 72 (1977): 1–24.

Blassingame, John W., "The Recruitment of Negro Troops in Missouri during the Civil War," *Missouri Historical Review* 58 (1964): 326–38.

Bourgois, Philippe, "If You're Not Black You're White: A History of Ethnic Relations in St. Louis," *City and Society* 3 (1989): 106–31.

Bowen, Elbert R., "Negro Minstrels in Early Rural Missouri," *Missouri Historical Review* 47 (1953): 103–9.

Brigham, R. I., "Negro Education in Antebellum Missouri," *Journal of Negro History* 30 (1945): 405–20.

Brown, Richard H., "The Missouri Crisis, Slavery, and the Politics of Jacksonianism," *South Atlantic Quarterly* 65 (1966): 55–72.

Cantor, Louis, *A Prologue to the Protest Movement: The Missouri Sharecropper Roadside Demonstration of 1939* (1969).

Christensen, Lawrence O., "Race Relations in St. Louis, 1865–1916," *Missouri Historical Review* 78 (1983): 123–36.

——— "Schools for Blacks: J. Milton Turner," *Missouri Historical Review* 76 (1982): 121–35.

Clamorgan, Cyprian, *The Colored Aristocracy of St. Louis*, ed. Julie Winch (1999).

Corbett, Katharine T., "Missouri's Black History: From Colonial Times to 1970," *Gateway Heritage* 4 (1983): 16–25.

Corbett, Katharine T., and Mary E. Seematter, "Black St. Louis at the Turn of the Century," *Gateway Heritage* 7 (1986): 40–48.

——— "No Crystal Stair": Black St. Louis, 1920–1940," *Gateway Heritage* 16 (1995): 82–8.

David, John Russell, *Tragedy in Ragtime: Black Folktales from St. Louis* (1976).

Day, Judy, and M. James Kedro, "Free Blacks in St. Louis: Antebellum Conditions, Emancipation, and the Post War Era," *Missouri Historical Society Bulletin* 30 (1974): 117–35.

Dorsett, Lyle Wesley, "Slaveholding in Jackson County, Missouri," *Missouri Historical Society Bulletin* 20 (1963): 25–37.

Early, Gerald, *"Ain't But a Place": An Anthology of African American Writings about St. Louis* (1998).

Fellman, Michael, "Emancipation in Missouri," *Missouri Historical Review* 83 (1988): 36–56.

Gersman, Elinor Mondale, "The Development of Public Education for Blacks in Nineteenth-Century St. Louis Missouri," *Journal of Negro Education* 41 (1972): 35–47.

Gilbert, Judith A., "Esther and Her Sisters: Free Women of Color as Property Owners in Colonial St. Louis, 1765–1803," *Gateway Heritage* 17 (1996): 14–23.

Greene, Lorenzo J., Gary R. Kremer, and Anthony F. Holland, *Missouri's Black Heritage* (1980).

Grenz, Suzanna M., "The Exodusters of 1879: St. Louis and Kansas City Responses," *Missouri Historical Review* 73 (1978): 54–70.

Harris, John J., III, Charles J. Russo, and Frank Brown, "The Curious Case of *Missouri v. Jenkins:* The End of the Road for Court-Ordered Desegregation?" *Journal of Negro Education* 66 (1997): 43–55.

Huber, Patrick J., and Gary R. Kremer, "Nathanial C. Bruce, Black Education and the 'Tuskegee of the Midwest,'" *Missouri Historical Review* 86 (1991): 37–54.

Hunter, Lloyd A., "Slavery in St. Louis 1804–1860," *Missouri Historical Society Bulletin* 30 (1974): 233–65.

Hurt, R. Douglass, "Planters and Slavery in Little Dixie," *Missouri Historical Review* 88 (1994): 397–415.

Lee, George R., "Slavery and Emancipation in Lewis County, Missouri," *Missouri Historical Review* 65 (1971): 294–317.

McKoy, Kathy, "Afro-American Cemeteries in St. Louis," *Gateway Heritage* 6 (1985–86): 30–37.

Moore, Robert, Jr., "A Ray of Hope, Extinguished: St. Louis Slave Suits for Freedom," *Gateway Heritage* 14 (1993–94): 4–15.

Naglich, Dennis, "Rural Prairieville during Reconstruction," *Missouri Historical Review* 87 (1993): 387–402.

Parrish, William Earl, *Missouri under Radical Rule, 1865–1870* (1965).

Reichard, Maximilian, "Black and White on the Urban Frontier: The St. Louis Community in Transition, 1800–1830," *Missouri Historical Society Bulletin* 33 (1976): 3–17.

Rhodes, Joel P., "It Finally Happened Here: The 1968 Riot in Kansas City, Missouri," *Missouri Historical Review* 91 (1997): 295–315.

Rudwick, Elliott M., *Race Riot at East St. Louis, July 2, 1917* (1964).

Scarpino, Philip V., "Slavery in Callaway County, Missouri: 1845–55 (Part 2)," *Missouri Historical Review* 71 (1977): 266–83.

Schoenberg, Sandra, and Charles Bailey, "The Symbolic Meaning of an Elite Black Community: The Ville in St. Louis," *Missouri Historical Society Bulletin* 33 (1977): 94–102.

Schwendemann, Glenn, "The 'Exodusters' on the Missouri," *Kansas Historical Quarterly* 29 (1963): 25–40.

——— "St. Louis and the 'Exodusters' of 1879," *Journal of Negro History* 46 (1961): 32–46.

Slavens, George Everett, "The Missouri Negro Press, 1875–1920," *Missouri Historical Review* 64 (1970): 413–31.

Strickland, Arvarh E., "Aspects of Slavery in Missouri, 1821," *Missouri Historical Review* 65 (1971): 505–26.

Trexler, Harrison Anthony, *Slavery in Missouri, 1804–1865* (1914).

——— "The Value and the Sale of the Missouri Slave," *Missouri Historical Review* 8 (1914): 69–85.

26.2.25 Montana

Frisch, Paul A., "'Gibraltar of Unionism': Women, Blacks and the Anti-Chinese Movement in Butte, Montana, 1880–1900," *Southwest Economy and Society* 6 (1984): 3–13.

Lang, William L., "The Nearly Forgotten Blacks on Last Chance Gulch, 1900–1912," *Pacific Northwest Quarterly* 70 (1979): 50–57.

26.2.26 Nebraska

Dales, David G., "North Platte Racial Incident: Black-White Confrontation, 1929," *Nebraska History* 60 (1979): 424–46.

Mihelich, Dennis N., "The Origins of the Prince Hall Mason Grand Lodge of Nebraska," *Nebraska History* 76 (1995): 10–21.

——— "A Socioeconomic Portrait of Prince Hall Masonry in Nebraska, 1900–1920," *Great Plains Quarterly* 17 (1997): 35–47.

——— "World War II and the Transformation of the Omaha Urban League," *Nebraska History* 60 (1979): 401–23.

——— "World War I, the Great Migration, and the Formation of the Grand Bodies of Prince Hall Masonry," *Nebraska History* 78 (1997): 28–39.

Paz, D. G., "John Albert Williams and Black Journalism in Omaha, 1895–1929," *Midwest Review* 10 (1988): 14–32.

Schubert, Frank N., *Buffalo Soldiers, Braves, and the Brass: The Story of Fort Robinson, Nebraska* (1993).

Sullenger, T. Earl, *The Negro in Omaha: A Social Study of Negro Development* (1931).

26.2.27   New Hampshire

Cox, Stephen L., "'Polluted With the Blood of Africa': Bigotry, Slavery, and the New Hampshire Colonization Society," *Historical New Hampshire* 38 (1983): 117–40.

Oedel, Howard T., "Slavery in Colonial Portsmouth," *History of New Hampshire* 21 (1966): 3–11.

26.2.28   New Jersey

Calligaro, Leo, "The Negro's Legal Status in Pre-Civil War New Jersey," *New Jersey History* 85 (1967): 167–80.

Cohen, David S., "In Search of Carolus Africanus Rex: Afro-Dutch Folklore in New York and New Jersey," *Journal of the Afro-American Historical and Genealogical Society* 5 (1984): 148–68.

Conforti, Joseph M., "Newark: Ghetto or City?" *Society* 9 (1972): 20–32.

Crew, Spencer, *Black Life in Secondary Cities: A Comparative Analysis of the Black Community of Camden and Elizabeth, New Jersey, 1860–1920* (1993).

Fishman, George, *The African American Struggle for Freedom and Equality: The Development of a People's Identity, New Jersey, 1624–1850* (1997).

——— "Taking a Stand for Freedom in Revolutionary New Jersey: Prime's Petition of 1786," *Science and Society* 56 (1992): 353–56.

Gough, Robert J., "Black Men and the Early New Jersey Militia," *New Jersey History* 88 (1970): 227–38.

Hall, Egerton E., *The Negro Wage Earner of New Jersey, A Study of Occupational Trends in New Jersey, of the Effect of Unequal Racial Distribution in the Occupations and of the Implications for Education and Guidance* (1935).

Hodges, Graham Russell, *Root and Branch: African Americans in New York and East Jersey, 1613–1863* (1999).

Hodges, Graham Russell, and Alan Edward Brown, ed., *"Pretends to be Free": Runaway Slave Advertisements from Colonial and Revolutionary New York and New Jersey* (1994).

Hoff, Henry B., "Additions and Corrections to 'A Colonial Black Family in New York and New Jersey: Pieter Santomee and His Descendants,'" *Journal of the Afro-American History and Genealogical Society* 10 (1989): 158–60.

Hogan, Lawrence, "Afro-American History as Immigration History: The Anguillians of Perth Amboy," *Social Studies* 78 (1987): 210–12.

Housing Authority of the City of Newark (N.J.), *Migrant War Workers in Newark: A Report* (1944).

Kukla, Barbara J., *Swing City: Newark Nightlife, 1925–50* (1991).

New Jersey, Temporary Commission on the Condition of the Urban Colored Population, *Report of the New Jersey State Temporary Commission on the Condition of the Urban Colored Population to the Legislature of the State of New Jersey* (1939).

Overmyer, James, *Queen of the Negro Leagues: Effa Manley and the Newark Eagles* (1998).

Pennington, James W. C., *An Address Delivered at Newark, N.J. at the First Anniversary of W. India Emancipation, Aug. 1, 1839* (1839).

Pingeon, Frances D., "An Abominable Business: The New Jersey Slave Trade, 1818," *New Jersey History* 109 (1991): 14–35.

Price, Clement Alexander, ed., *Freedom Not Far Distant: A Documentary History of Afro-Americans in New Jersey* (1980).

Sasaki, Yutaka, "'But Not Next Door': Housing Discrimination and the Emergence of the Second Ghetto in Newark, New Jersey, after World War II," *Japanese Journal of American Studies* 5 (1994): 113–35.

Schacter, Leon B., *The Migrant Worker of New Jersey* (1945).

Seaton, Douglas P., "Colonizers and Reluctant Colonists: The New Jersey Colonization Society and the Black Community, 1815–1848," *New Jersey History* 96 (1978): 7–22.

Spray, W. A., "The Settlement of the Black Refugees in New Brunswick, 1815–1836," *Acadiensis* 6 (1977): 64–79.

United States Works Project Administration, New Jersey, *The Negro Church in New Jersey* (1938).

Washington, Jack, *In Search of a Community's Past: The Story of the Black Community of Trenton, New Jersey, 1860–1900* (1990).

Williams, Robert J., "Blacks, Colonization and Anti-Slavery: The Views of Methodists in New Jersey, 1816–1860," *New Jersey History* 102 (1984): 50–67.

Wright, Giles R., *Afro-Americans in New Jersey: A Short History* (1988).

Wright, Marion T., *The Education of Negroes in New Jersey* (1941).

——— "Negro Suffrage in New Jersey, 1776–1875," *Journal of Negro History* 32 (1948): 168–224.

Zilversmit, Arthur, "Liberty and Property: New Jersey and the Abolition of Slavery," *New Jersey History* 88 (1970): 215–26.

26.2.29   New Mexico

Billington, Monroe L., "Black Cavalrymen and Apache Indians in New Mexico Territory," *Fort Concho and the South Plains Journal* 22 (1990): 54–76.

——— "Black Soldiers at Fort Selden, New Mexico, 1866–1891," *New Mexico Historical Review* 62 (1987): 65–79.

——— "Civilians and Black Soldiers in New Mexico Territory, 1866–1900: A Cross-Cultural Experience," *Military History of the Southwest* 19 (1989): 71–82.

——— *New Mexico's Buffalo Soldiers, 1866–1900* (1991).

——— "A Profile of Blacks in New Mexico on the Eve of Statehood," *Password* 32 (1987): 55–66.

Bustamante, Adrian, "'The Matter Was Never Resolved': The Caste System in Colonial New Mexico, 1693–1823," *New Mexico Historical Review* 66 (1991): 143–63.

Theisen, Lee Scott, "The Fight in Lincoln, NM, 1878: The Testimony of Two Negro Participants," *Arizona and the West* 12 (1970): 173–98.

26.2.30   New York

Alba, Richard D., Nancy A. Denton, Shu-yin J. Leung, and John R. Logan, "Neighborhood Change under Conditions of Mass Immigration: The New York City Region, 1970–1990," *International Migration Review* 29 (1995): 625–56.

Anderson, Jervis, *This Was Harlem: A Cultural Portrait, 1900–1950* (1982).

Andrews, Charles S., *The History of the New York African Free-Schools, from Their Establishment in 1787, to the Present Time* (1830).

Armstead, Myra B. Young, *"Lord, Please Don't Take Me in August": African Americans in Newport and Saratoga Springs, 1870–1930* (1999).

Banner-Haley, Charles T., "An Extended Community: Sketches of Afro-American History in Three Counties along New York State's Southern Tier, 1890–1980," *Afro-Americans in New York Life and History* 13 (1989): 5–18.

Bernstein, Iver, *The New York City Draft Riots: Their Significance for American Society and Politics in the Age of the Civil War* (1990).

Bilotta, James D., "A Quantitative Approach to Buffalo's Black Population of 1860," *Afro-Americans in New York Life and History* 12 (1988): 19–34.

Bloch, Herman D., "The New York City Negro and Occupational Eviction, 1860–1910," *International Review of Social History* 5 (1960): 26–38.

———— "The New York Negro's Battle for Political Rights, 1777–1865," *International Review of Social History* 9 (1964): 65–80.

———— "New York Afro-Americans' Struggle for Political Rights and the Emergence of Political Recognition, 1865–1900," *International Review of Social History* 13 (1968): 321–49.

Brandt, Nat, *Harlem at War: The Black Experience in WWII* (1997).

Brotz, Howard, *The Black Jews of Harlem: Negro Nationalism and the Dilemmas of Negro Leadership* (1964).

Brown, Tamara, "It Don't Mean a Thing if It Ain't Got That Harlem Swing: Social Dance and the Harlem Renaissance," *Afro-Americans in New York Life and History* 22 (1998): 41–66.

Butchart, Ronald E., "'We Best Can Instruct Our Own People': New York African Americans in the Freedmen's Schools, 1861–1875," *Afro-Americans in New York Life and History* 12 (1988): 27–49.

Capeci, Dominic J., Jr., "Wartime Fair Employment Practice Committees: The Governor's Committee and the First FEPC in New York City, 1942–1943," *Afro-Americans in New York Life and History* 9 (1985): 45–63.

Caro, Edythe Quinn, *"The Hills" in the Mid-Nineteenth Century: The History of a Rural Afro-American Community in Westchester County, New York* (1988).

Castle, Musette S., "A Survey of the History of African Americans in Rochester, New York, 1800–1860," *Afro-Americans in New York Life and History* 13 (1989): 7–32.

Chappell, Eve, "Toward Universal Values: Educational Opportunities in Harlem," *Journal of Adult Education* 7 (1935): 399–404.

Chase, Jeanne, "The 1741 Conspiracy to Burn New York: Black Plot or Black Magic?" *Social Science Information* 22 (1983): 969–81.

Christoph, Peter R., "The Freedmen of New Amsterdam: Afro-Americans in New Netherland," *Journal of the Afro-American Historical and Genealogical Society* 5 (1984): 109–22.

Clarke, John Henrik, ed., *Harlem: A Community in Transition* (new expanded ed., 1969).

Cohen, David S., "In Search of Carolus Africanus Rex: Afro-Dutch Folklore in New York and New Jersey," *Journal of Afro-American Historical and Genealogical Society* 5 (1984): 148–68.

Coles, Howard W., *The Cradle of Freedom: A History of the Negro in Rochester, Western New York and Canada* (2d ed., 1943).

The Complete Report of Mayor LaGuardia's Commission on the Harlem Riot of March 19, 1935 (1969).

Connolly, Harold X., *A Ghetto Grows in Brooklyn* (1977).

Cray, Robert E., Jr., "White Welfare and Black Strategies: The Dynamics of Race and Poor Relief in Early New York, 1700–1825," *Slavery and Abolition* 7 (1986): 273–89.

Curry, Mary Cuthrell, *Making the Gods in New York: The Yoruba Religion in the African American Community* (1997).

Davis, Barbara S., *A History of the Black Community of Syracuse* (1980).

Davis, Thomas J., *A Rumor of Revolt: The "Great Negro Plot" in Colonial New York* (1985).

———— "These Enemies of Their Own Household: A Note on the Troublesome Slave Population in Eighteenth-Century New York City," *Journal of the Afro-American Historical and Genealogical Society* 5 (1983): 133–47.

———— "Three Dark Centuries around Albany: A Survey of Black Life in New York's Capital City Area before World War I," *Afro-American New York Life and History* 7 (1983): 7–23.

Drake, Donald E., "Militancy in Fortune's New York Age," *Journal of Negro History* 55 (1970): 307–22.

Eichholz, Alice, and James M. Rose, *Free Black Heads of Household in the New York State Federal Census, 1790–1830* (1981).

Fainstein, Norman, and Susan Nesbitt, "Did the Black Ghetto Have a Golden Age?: Class Structure and Class Segregation in New York City, 1949–1970," *Journal of Urban History* 23 (1996): 3–28.

Farley, Ena L., "The African American Presence in the History of Western New York," *Afro-Americans in New York Life and History* 14 (1990): 27–89.

Field, Phyllis F., *The Politics of Race in New York: The Struggle for Black Suffrage in the Civil War Era* (1982).

———— "Republicans and Black Suffrage in New York State: The Grass Roots Response," *Civil War History* 21 (1975): 136–47.

Finkelman, Paul, "The Protection of Black Rights in Seward's New York," *Civil War History* 34 (1988): 211–34.

Ford, James, *Slums and Housing, with Special Reference to New York City: History, Conditions, Policy* (1936).

Fordham, Monroe, "The Buffalo Cooperative Economic Society, Inc., 1928–1961: A Black Self-Help Organization," *Niagara Frontier* 23 (1976): 41–49.

Fox, Dixon Ryan, "The Negro Vote in Old New York," *Political Science Quarterly* 32 (1917): 252–75.

Franklin, Charles Lionel, *The Negro Labor Unionist of New York: Problems and Conditions among Negroes in the Labor Unions in Manhattan with Special Reference to the N.R.A. and Post-N.R.A. Situations* (1936).

Frazier, Edward Franklin, "Negro Harlem: An Ecological Study," *American Journal of Sociology* 43 (1937): 72–88.

Garber, Eric, "A Spectacle in Color: The Lesbian and Gay Subculture of Jazz Age Harlem," Martin Duberman, et al., ed., *Hidden from History: Reclaiming the Gay and Lesbian Past* (1989): 318–31.

Gerlach, Don R., "Black Arson in Albany, New York: November 1793," *Journal of Black Studies* 7 (1977): 301–12.

Goldstein, Michael L., "Black Power and the Rise of Bureaucratic Autonomy in New York City Politics: The Case of Harlem Hospital, 1917–1931," *Phylon* 41 (1980): 187–201.

———— "Preface to the Rise of Booker T. Washington: A View from New York City of the Demise of Independent Black Politics, 1889–1902," *Journal of Negro History* 62 (1977): 81–99.

Goodfriend, Joyce D., "Black Families in New Netherland, Afro-Americans in New Netherland," *Journal of the Afro-American Historical and Genealogical Society* 5 (1984): 94–107.

———— "Burghers and Blacks: The Evolution of a Slave Society at New Amsterdam," *New York History* 59 (1978): 125–44.

Gray, Brenda Clegg, *Black Female Domestics during the Depression in New York City, 1930–1940* (1993).

Green, Charles, and Basil Wilson, *The Struggle for Black Empowerment in New York City: Beyond the Politics of Pigmentation* (1989).

Greenberg, Cheryl Lynn, *"Or Does It Explode?": Black Harlem in the Great Depression* (1991).

Greenberg, Douglas, "Patterns of Criminal Prosecution in Eighteenth-Century New York," *New York History* 56 (1975): 133–53.

Harris, Louis, and Bert E. Swanson, *Black-Jewish Relations in New York City* (1970).

Haynes, George E., *The Negro At Work in New York City* (1912).

Headley, Joel T., *The Great Riots in New York, 1712–1873: Including a Full and Complete Account of the Four Days' Draft Riot of 1863* (1873).

Hirsch, Leo, Jr., "The Negro and New York, 1783–1865," *Journal of Negro History* 16 (1931): 382–473.

Hodges, Graham Russell, *Root and Branch: African Americans in New York and East Jersey, 1613–1863* (1999).

———— *Slavery, Freedom, and Culture among Early American Workers* (1998).

Hodges, Graham Russell, and Alan Edward Brown, ed., *"Pretends to Be Free": Runaway Slave Advertisements from Colonial and Revolutionary New York and New Jersey* (1994).

Hoff, Henry B., "A Colonial Black Family in New York and New Jersey: Pieter Santomee and His Descendants," *Journal of the Afro-American Historical and Genealogical Society* 9 (1988): 101–34.

Holder, Calvin B., "The Rise of the West Indian Politician in New York City, 1900–1952," *Afro-Americans in New York Life and History* 4 (1980): 45–59.

Huggins, Nathan I., ed., *Voices from the Harlem Renaissance* (1976).

Hurst, Marsha, "Integration, Freedom of Choice and Community Control in Nineteenth Century Brooklyn," *Journal of Ethnic Studies* 3 (1975): 33–55.

Ireland, Ralph R., "Slavery on Long Island: A Study of Economic Motivation," *Journal of Long Island History* 6 (1966): 1–12.

Janken, Kenneth R., "African American and Francophone Black Intellectuals During the Harlem Renaissance," *Historian* 60 (1998): 487–505.

Johnson, James Weldon, *Black Manhattan* (1930).

Joyce, Patrick D., "A Reversal of Fortunes: Black Empowerment, Political Machines, and City Jobs in New York City and Chicago," *Urban Affairs Review* 32 (1997): 291–318.

Katz, William Loren, *Black Legacy: A History of New York's African Americans* (1997).

Kerber, Linda K., "Abolitionists and Amalgamators: The New York Race Riots of 1834," *New York History* 48 (1967): 28–39.

Kiser, Clyde Vernon, *Sea Island to City: A Study of St. Helena Islanders in Harlem and Other Urban Centers* (1932).

Kobrin, David, *The Black Minority in Early New York* (1975).

Lane, Winthrop P., "Ambushed in the City: The Grim Side of Harlem," *The Survey* 53 (1925): 692–94, 715.

Launitz-Schurer, Leopold S., Jr., "Slave Resistance in Colonial New York: An Interpretation of Daniel Horsmanden's New York Conspiracy," *Phylon* 41 (1980): 137–51.

Lemisch, Jesse, *Jack Tar vs. John Bull: The Role of New York's Seamen in Precipitating the Revolution* (1997).

Lenz, Günter H., "Symbolic Space, Communal Rituals, and the Black Surreality of the Urban Ghetto: Harlem in Black Literature from the 1920s to the 1960s," *Callaloo* 11 (1988): 309–45.

Lewinson, Edwin R., *Black Politics in New York City* (1974).

Lewis, David Levering, *When Harlem Was in Vogue* (1982).

Lindsay, Arnett G., "The Economic Condition of the Negroes of New York prior to 1861," *Journal of Negro History* 6 (1931): 190–99.

Mabee, Carleton, *Black Education in New York State: From Colonial to Modern Times* (1979).

———— "Control by Blacks over Schools in New York State, 1830–1930," *Phylon* 40 (1979): 29–40.

———— "Long Island's Black School War and the Decline of Segregation in New York State," *New York History* 58 (1977): 385–411.

———— "Sojourner Truth Fights Dependence on Government: Moves Freed Slaves off Welfare in Washington to Jobs in Upstate New York," *Afro-Americans in New York Life and History* 14 (1990): 7–26.

Mamiya, Lawrence H., and Patricia A. Raurouma, "You Never Hear About Their Struggles: Black Oral History in Poughkeepsie, New York," *Afro-Americans in New York Life and History* 4 (1980): 55–70.

Man, Albon P., Jr., "Labor Competition and the New York Draft Riots of 1863," *Journal of Negro History* 36 (1951): 375–405.

McBride, David, "The Black-White Mortality Differential in New York State, 1900–1950: A Socio-Historical Reconsideration," *Afro-Americans in New York Life and History* 14 (1990): 71–89.

———— "Fourteenth Amendment Idealism: The New York State Civil Rights Law, 1873–1918," *New York History* 71 (1990): 207–33.

McDowell, Winston, "Race and Ethnicity during the Harlem Jobs Campaign," *Journal of Negro History* 69 (1984): 134–46.

McKay, Claude, *Harlem: Negro Metropolis* (1940).

McManus, Edgar J., "Anti-Slavery Legislation in New York," *Journal of Negro History* 46 (1961): 207–16.

———— *A History of Negro Slavery in New York* (1966).

Model, Suzanne, "The Effects of Ethnicity in the Workplace on Blacks, Italians, and Jews in 1910 New York," *Journal of Urban History* 16 (1989): 29–51.

Mohl, Raymond A., "Education as Social Control in New York City, 1784–1825," *New York History* 51 (1970): 219–37.

Morgan, Gordon D., "Fisk University and the Intellectual Origins of the Harlem Renaissance," *Western Journal of Black Studies* 21 (1997): 214–18.

Morrison, K. C., "A Profile of Black Leadership in Syracuse, New York since 1965," *Afro-Americans in New York Life and History* 12 (1988): 7–18.

Mumford, Kevin J., *Interzones: Black/White Sex Districts in Chicago and New York in the Early Twentieth Century* (1997).

Muraskin, William, "The Harlem Boycott of 1934: Black Nationalism and the Rise of Labor Union Consciousness," *Labor History* 13 (1972): 361–73.

Naison, Mark D., "Communism and Black Nationalism in the Depression: The Case of Harlem," *Journal of Ethnic Studies* 2 (1974): 24–36.

———— *Communists in Harlem during the Depression* (1983).

New York (N.Y.) Mayor's Commission on Conditions in Harlem, *The Negro in Harlem: A Report on Social and Economic Conditions Responsible for the Outbreak of March 19, 1935* (1935).

Nordstrom, Carl, "Slavery in a New York County: Rockland County, 1686–1827," *Afro-Americans in New York Life and History* 1 (1977): 145–66.

Osofsky, Gilbert, "A Decade of Urban Tragedy: How Harlem Became a Slum," *New York History* 46 (1965): 330–55.

———— *Harlem, The Making of a Ghetto: Negro New York, 1890–1930* (1963).

Ottley, Roi, *"New World A-Coming": Inside Black America* (1943).

Over, William, "New York's African Theatre: The Vicissitudes of the Black Actor," *Afro-Americans in New York Life and History* 3 (1979): 7–13.

Ovington, Mary White, *Half A Man: The Status of the Negro in New York* (1911).

Owens, Irma Watkins, *Blood Relations: Caribbean Immigrants and the Harlem Community, 1900–1930* (1996).

Perlman, Daniel, "Organizations of the Free Negro in New York City, 1800–1860," *Journal of Negro History* 56 (1971): 181–97.

Potter, Barrett G., "The Civilian Conservation Corps and New York's 'Negro Question': A Case Study in Federal-State Race Relations during the Great Depression," *Afro-Americans in New York Life and History* 1 (1977): 183–200.

Powell, Richard J., and David A. Bailey, *Rhapsodies in Black: Art of the Harlem Renaissance* (1997).

Priebe, Paula J., "Central and Western New York and the Fugitive Slave Law of 1850," *Afro-Americans in New York Life and History* 16 (1992): 19–29.

Reed, Ruth, *Negro Illegitimacy in New York City* (1926).

Riis, Jacob A., *How the Other Half Lives: Studies among the Tenements of New York* (1890).

Riss, Thomas Laurence, *Just before Jazz: Black Musical Theater in New York, 1890–1915* (1989).

Roses, Lorraine, and Ruth Elizabeth Randolph, ed., *Harlem's Glory: Black Women Writing, 1900–1950* (1996).

Rury, John L., "The New York African Free School, 1827–1836: Conflict over Community Control of Black Education," *Phylon* 44 (1983): 187–97.

———— "Philanthropy, Self-Help, and Social Control: The New York Manumission Society and Free Blacks, 1785–1810," *Phylon* 46 (1985): 231–41.

Sanjek, Roger, "After Freedom in Newtown, Queens: African-Americans and the Color Line, 1828–1899," *Long Island Historical Journal* 5 (1993): 157–67.

———— *The Future of Us All: Race and Neighborhood Politics in New York City* (1998).

Schaetzke, E. Anne, "Slavery in the Genessee Country (also known as Ontario County), 1789 to 1827," *Afro-Americans in New York Life and History* 22 (1998): 7–40.

Scharer, Laura Lynne, "African-Americans in Jefferson County, New York: 1810–1910," *Afro-Americans in New York Life and History* 19 (1995): 7–16.

Scheiner, Seth M., *Negro Mecca: A History of the Negro in New York City, 1865–1920* (1965).

———— "The New York City Negro and the Tenement, 1880–1910," *New York History* 45 (1964): 304–15.

Schneider, Gail, "A Beginning Investigation Into the Afro-American Cemeteries of Ulster County, New York," *Afro-Americans in New York Life and History* 10 (1986): 61–69.

Schwartz, Joel, "The Consolidated Tenants League of Harlem: Black Self-Help vs. White, Liberal Intervention in Ghetto Housing, 1934–1944," *Afro-Americans in New York Life and History* 10 (1986): 31–51.

Seraile, William, "The Struggle to Raise Black Regiments in New York State, 1861–1864," *New York Historical Society Quarterly* 58 (1974): 215–33.

——— "Susan McKinney Steward: New York State's First African-American Woman Physician," *Afro-Americans in New York Life and History* 9 (1985): 27–44.

Sernett, Milton C., "On Freedom's Threshold: The African American Presence in Central New York, 1760–1940," *Afro-Americans in New York Life and History* 19 (1995): 43–91.

Simson, Rennie, "A Community in Turmoil: Black American Writers in New York State before the Civil War," *Afro-Americans in New York Life and History* 13 (1989): 57–67.

Siskar, John F., "The B.U.I.L.D. Academy: A Historical Study of Community Action and Education in Buffalo, New York," *Afro-Americans in New York Life and History* 21 (1997): 19–40.

Steen, Ivan D., "Document: 'Education to What End?' An Englishman Comments on the Plight of Blacks in the 'Free' States, 1830," *Afro-Americans in New York Life and History* 7 (1983): 55–60.

Swan, Robert J., "Did Brooklyn (N.Y.) Blacks Have Unusual Control Over Their Schools? Period I: 1815–1845," *Afro-Americans in New York Life and History* 7 (1983): 25–46.

Taylor, Clarence, *The Black Churches of Brooklyn* (1994).

Thomas, William B., "Schooling as a Political Instrument of Social Control: School Response to Black Migrant Youth in Buffalo, New York, 1917–1940," *Teachers College Record* 86 (1985): 579–92.

Thompson, Mary W., *Sketches of the History, Character and Dying Testimony of Beneficiaries of the Colored Home in the City of New York* (1851).

Tripp, Bernell, *Origins of the Black Press: New York, 1827–1847* (1992).

Tritter, Thorin, "The Growth and Decline of Harlem's Housing," *Afro-Americans in New York Life and History* 22 (1998): 67–83.

U.S. Department of Labor, "Cooperative Self-Help among the Unemployed: The Harlem Mutual Exchange," *Monthly Labor Review* 36 (1933): 492–93.

Van Der Zee, James, Owen Dodson, and Camille Billops, *Harlem Book of the Dead* (1978).

Wadhwani, Rohit D. G., "Kodak, FIGHT, and the Definition of Civil Rights in Rochester, New York, 1966–1967," *Historian* 60 (1997): 59–75.

Wagman, Morton, "Corporate Slavery in New Netherland," *Journal of Negro History* 65 (1980): 34–42.

Waldinger, Roger, *Still the Promised City?: African-Americans and New Immigrants in Postindustrial New York* (1996).

Walker, George E., *The Afro-American in New York City, 1827–1860* (1993).

Washington, Michael, "A New Perspective on Black Education: A Review of the Literature on the Nineteenth Century New York Experience," *Afro-Americans in New York Life and History* 17 (1993): 17–28.

Watkins-Owens, Irma, *Blood Relations: Caribbean Immigrants and the Harlem Community, 1900–1930* (1996).

Watkins, Ralph, "Recreation, Leisure and Charity in the Afro-American Community: Buffalo, New York, 1920–1925," *Afro-Americans in New York Life and History* 6 (1982): 7–19.

Watson, Steven, *The Harlem Renaissance: Hub of African-American Culture, 1920–1930* (1995).

Weisenfeld, Judith, *African American Women and Christian Activism: New York's Black YWCA, 1905–1945* (1997).

Wesley, Charles H., "The Negroes of New York in the Emancipation Movement," *Journal of Negro History* 24 (1939): 65–103.

White, Richard, "Baseball's John Fowler: The 1887 Season in Binghamton, New York," *Afro-Americans in New York Life and History* 16 (1992): 7–17.

White, Shane, "A Question of Style: Blacks in and around New York City in the Late Eighteenth Century," *Journal of American Folklore* 102 (1989): 23–44.

——— "Slavery in New York State in the Early Republic," *Australasian Journal of American Studies* 14 (1995): 1–29.

——— *Somewhat More Independent: The End of Slavery in New York City, 1770–1810* (1990).

——— "'We Dwell in Safety and Pursue Our Honest Callings': Free Blacks in New York City, 1783–1810," *Journal of American History* 75 (1988): 445–70.

Wilder, Craig Steven, "The Rise and Influence of the New York African Society for Mutual Relief, 1808–1865," *Afro-Americans in New York Life and History* 22 (1998): 7–18.

Williams-Myers, A. J., "The African Presence in the Mid-Hudson Valley before 1800: A Preliminary Historiographical Sketch," *Afro-Americans in New York Life and History* 8 (1984): 31–39.

———— "Hands that Picked No Cotton: An Exploratory Examination of African Slave Labor in the Colonial Economy of the Hudson River Valley to 1800," *Afro-Americans in New York Life and History* 11 (1987): 25–51.

———— "Pinkster Carnival: Africanisms in the Hudson River Valley," *Afro-Americans in New York Life and History* 9 (1985): 7–17.

———— "The Plight of African Americans in Ante-Bellum New York City," *Afro-Americans in New York Life and History* 22 (1998): 43–90.

Williams, Lillian S., "And Still I Rise: Black Women and Reform, Buffalo, New York, 1900–1940," *Afro-Americans in New York Life and History* 14 (1990): 7–33.

———— "Community Educational Activities and the Liberation of Black Buffalo, 1900–1930," *Journal of Negro Education* 54 (1985): 174–88.

———— *Strangers in the Land of Paradise: The Creation of an African American Urban Community, Buffalo, New York, 1900–1940* (1999).

Williams, Oscar R., "The Regimentation of Blacks on the Urban Frontier in Colonial Albany, New York City, and Philadelphia," *Journal of Negro History* 63 (1978): 329–38.

Willis-Thomas, Deborah, and Jane Lusaka, *Visual Journal: Harlem and D.C. in the Thirties and Forties* (1996).

Wilson, Basil, and Charles Green, "The Black Church and the Struggle for Community Empowerment in New York City," *Afro-Americans in New York Life and History* 12 (1988): 51–79.

Wintz, Cary D., *The Emergence of the Harlem Renaissance* (1996).

Wortis, Helen, "The Black Inhabitants of Shelter Island," *Long Island Forum* 36 (1973): 146–53.

26.2.31   North Carolina

Africa, Philip, "Slaveholding in the Salem Community, 1771–1851," *North Carolina Historical Review* 54 (1977): 271–307.

Allen, Jeffrey Brooke, "The Racial Thought of White North Carolina Opponents of Slavery, 1789–1876," *North Carolina Historical Review* 59 (1982): 49–66.

Anderson, Eric, *Race and Politics in North Carolina, 1872–1901: The Black Second* (1981).

Applethwaite, Marjorie M., "Sharecropper and Tenant in the Courts of North Carolina," *North Carolina Historical Review* 31 (1954): 134–49.

Balanoff, Elizabeth, "Negro Leaders in the North Carolina General Assembly, July, 1868–Feb., 1872," *North Carolina Historical Review* 49 (1972): 22–55.

Barksdale, Marcellus C., "Robert F. Williams and the Indigenous Civil Rights Movement in Monroe, North Carolina, 1961," *Journal of Negro History* 69 (1984): 73–89.

Bassett, John Spencer, *Slavery and Servitude in the State of North Carolina* (1899).

Beck, E. M., James L. Massey, and Stewart E. Tolnay, "The Gallows, the Mob, and the Vote: Lethal Sanctioning of Blacks in North Carolina and Georgia, 1882–1930," *Law and Society Review* 23 (1989): 317–31.

Bell, John L., Jr., "Baptists and the Negro in North Carolina during Reconstruction," *North Carolina Historical Review* 42 (1965): 391–409.

———— "The Presbyterian Church and the Negro in North Carolina during Reconstruction," *North Carolina Historical Review* 40 (1963): 15–36.

Bellamy, Donald D., "Slavery in Microcosm: Onslow County, North Carolina," *Journal of Negro History* 62 (1977): 339–50.

Bernstein, Leonard, "The Participation of Negro Delegates in the Constitutional Convention of 1868 in North Carolina," *Journal of Negro History* 34 (1949): 391–409.

Billings, Dwight B., *Planters and the Making of the 'New South': Class Politics and Development in North Carolina, 1865–1900* (1980).

Bishir, Catherine W., "Black Builders in Antebellum North Carolina," *North Carolina Historical Review* 61 (1984): 422–61.

Blackwell, G. W., "The Displaced Tenant Farm Family in North Carolina," *Social Forces* 13 (1934): 65–71.

Brewer, James Howard, "Legislation Designed to Control Slavery in Wilmington and Fayetteville," *North Carolina Historical Review* 30 (1953): 155–66.

Browning, James Blackwell, "The Free Negro in Antebellum North Carolina," *North Carolina Historical Magazine* 15 (1938): 23–33.

Burkhead, L. S., "History of the Difficulties of the Pastorate of the Front Street Methodist Church, Wilmington, N.C., for the Year 1865," *Trinity College Historical Society Historical Papers* 8 (1908–1909): 35–118.

Cecelski, David S., "The Hidden World of Mullet Camps: African-American Architecture on the North Carolina Coast," *North Carolina Historical Review* 70 (1993): 1–13.

——— "The Shores of Freedom: The Maritime Underground Railroad in North Carolina, 1800–1861," *North Carolina Historical Review* 71 (1994): 174–206.

Cecelski, David S., and Timothy B. Tyson, ed., *Democracy Betrayed: The Wilmington Race Riot of 1898 and Its Legacy* (1998).

Clark, Ernest James, Jr., "Aspects of the North Carolina Slave Code, 1715–1860," *North Carolina Historical Review* 39 (1962): 148–64.

Crow, Jeffrey J., *The Black Experience in Revolutionary North Carolina* (1977).

——— "Fusion, Confusion, and Negroism: Schisms among Negro Republicans in the North Carolina Election of 1896," *North Carolina Historical Review* 53 (1976): 364–84.

——— "Slave Rebelliousness and Social Conflict in North Carolina, 1775 to 1802," *William and Mary Quarterly* 37 (1980): 79–102.

Crow, Jeffery J., Paul D. Escott, and Flora J. Hatley, *A History of African Americans in North Carolina* (1992).

Douglas, Davison M., *Reading, Writing, and Race: The Desegregation of the Charlotte Schools* (1995).

Dunne, William F., *Gastonia: Citadel of the Class Struggle in the New South* (1929).

Edmonds, Helen G., *The Negro and Fusion Politics in North Carolina, 1894–1901* (1951).

Escott, Paul D., *Many Excellent People: Power and Privilege in North Carolina, 1850–1900* (1985).

Farrison, William Edward, "The Negro Population of Guilford County, North Carolina, before the Civil War," *North Carolina Historical Review* 21 (1944): 319–29.

Franklin, John Hope, "The Enslavement of Free Negroes in North Carolina," *Journal of Negro History* 29 (1944): 401–28.

——— "The Free Negro in the Economic Life of Antebellum North Carolina," *North Carolina Historical Review* 19 (1942): 359–75.

——— *The Free Negro in North Carolina, 1790–1860* (1995).

——— "Slaves Virtually Free in Antebellum North Carolina," *Journal of Negro History* 28 (1943): 284–310.

Gatewood, Willard B., Jr., "North Carolina's Negro Regiment in the Spanish-American War," *North Carolina Historical Review* 48 (1971): 370–87.

Gavins, Raymond, "The Meaning of Freedom: Black North Carolina in the Nadir, 1880–1900," in Jeffrey J. Crow, Paul D. Escott, and Charles L. Flynn, Jr., ed., *Race, Class, and Politics in Southern History: Essays in Honor of Robert F. Durden* (1989).

Gehrke, William Herman, "Negro Slavery among the Germans in North Carolina," *North Carolina Historical Review* 14 (1937): 307–24.

Godwin, John L., "Taming a Whirlwind: Black Civil Rights Leadership in the Community Setting, Wilmington, North Carolina, 1950–1972," *Proceedings of the South Carolina Historical Association* (1992): 67–75.

Gray, Dorothy A., "Crisis of Identity: The Negro Community in Raleigh, 1890–1900," *North Carolina Historical Review* 50 (1973): 121–40.

Green, Fletcher M., "Gold Mining: A Forgotten Industry of Antebellum North Carolina," *North Carolina Historical Review* 14 (1937): 1–19, 135–55.

Greenwood, Janette Thomas, *Bittersweet Legacy: The Black and White "Better Classes" in Charlotte, 1850–1910* (1994).

Hanchett, Thomas W., "The Rosenwald Schools and Black Education in North Carolina," *North Carolina Historical Review* 65 (1988): 387–444.

————— *Sorting Out the New South City: Race, Class, and Urban Development in Charlotte, 1875–1975* (1998).

Heinegg, Paul, *Free African Americans of North Carolina and Virginia: Including the Family Histories of More Than 80% of Those Counted as "All Other Free Persons" in the 1790 and 1800 Census* (3d ed., 1997).

Higginbotham, Don, and William S. Price, Jr., "Was it Murder for a White Man to Kill a Slave? Chief Justice Martin Howard Condemns the Peculiar Institution in North Carolina," *William and Mary Quarterly* 36 (1979): 593–601.

Higgs, Robert, "Racial Wage Differentials in Agriculture: Evidence from North Carolina in 1887," *Agricultural History* 52 (1978): 308–11.

Hilty, Hiram H., *Toward Freedom for All: North Carolina Quakers and Slavery* (1984).

Holt, Sharon Ann, "Making Freedom Pay: Freedpeople Working for Themselves, North Carolina, 1865–1900," *Journal of Southern History* 60 (1994): 229–62.

Huber, Patrick J., "'Caught Up in the Violent Whirlwind of Lynching': The 1885 Quadruple Lynching in Chatham County, North Carolina," *North Carolina Historical Review* 75 (1998): 135–60.

Huddle, Mark A., "To Educate a Race: The Making of the First State Colored Normal School, Fayetteville, North Carolina, 1865–1877," *North Carolina Historical Review* 74 (1997): 135–60.

Inscoe, John C., "Mountain Masters: Slaveholding in Western North Carolina," *North Carolina Historical Review* 61 (1984): 143–73.

————— *Mountain Masters, Slavery, and the Sectional Crisis in Western North Carolina* (1989).

————— "Mountain Masters as Confederate Opportunists: The Profitability of Slavery in Western North Carolina, 1861–1865," *Slavery and Abolition* 16 (1995): 85–100.

Janiewski, Dolores E., *Sisterhood Denied: Race, Gender, and Class in a New South Community* (1985).

Johnson, Charles, Jr., "Pea Island: The United States Coast Guard's Black Lifesaving Station, 1880–1900," *Journal of the Afro-American Historical and Genealogical Society* 3 (1982): 67–72.

Jones, Beverly W., "Race, Sex, and Class: Black Female Tobacco Workers in Durham, North Carolina, 1920–1940, and the Development of Female Consciousness," *Feminist Studies* 10 (1984): 441–51.

Kay, Marvin L. Michael, and Lorin Lee Cary, "A Demographic Analysis of Colonial North Carolina with Special Emphasis upon the Slave and Black Populations," in Jeffery J. Crow and Flora J. Hatley, ed., *Black Americans in North Carolina and the South* (1984): 71–121.

————— "Slave Runaways in Colonial North Carolina, 1748–1775," *North Carolina Historical Review* 63 (1986): 1–39.

————— *Slavery in North Carolina, 1748–1775* (1995).

Kenzer, Robert C., "The Black Businessman in the Postwar South: North Carolina, 1865–1880," *Business History Review* 63 (1989): 61–87.

————— *Enterprising Southerners: Black Economic Success in North Carolina, 1865–1915* (1997).

Kousser, J. Morgan, "Progressivism—For Middle Class Whites Only: North Carolina Education, 1880–1910," *Journal of Southern History* 46 (1980): 169–94.

Larkins, John Rodman, *The Negro Population of North Carolina, Social and Economic* (1945).

Lash, Wiley Immanuel, "Black Lutherans in Rowan County," *Concordia Historical Institute Quarterly* 61 (1988): 74–78.

Leaming, Hugo Prosper, *Hidden Americans: Maroons of Virginia and the Carolinas* (1995).

Logan, Frenise A., "Black and Republican: Vicissitudes of a Minority Twice over in the North Carolina House of Representatives, 1876–1877," *North Carolina Review* 61 (1984): 311–46.

————— "The Colored Industrial Association of North Carolina and Its Fair of 1886," *North Carolina Historical Review* 34 (1957): 58–67.

————— "Factors Influencing the Efficiency of Negro Farm Laborers in Post-Reconstruction North Carolina," *Agricultural History* 33 (1959): 185–89.

————— "Legal Status of Public School Education for Negroes in North Carolina, 1877–1894," *North Carolina Historical Review* 32 (1955): 346–57.

————— "The Movement of Negroes from North Carolina, 1876–1894," *North Carolina Historical Review* 33 (1956): 45–65.

————— "The Movement in North Carolina to Establish a State Supported College for Negroes," *North Carolina Historical Review* 35 (1958): 167–80.

———— *The Negro in North Carolina, 1876–1894* (1964).

Long, Hollis Moody, *Public Secondary Education for Negroes in North Carolina* (1932).

Mabry, William A., *The Negro in North Carolina Politics since Reconstruction* (1940).

Matthews, Holly F., "Killing the Medical Self-Help Tradition among African Americans: The Case of Lay Midwifery in North Carolina, 1912–1983," in Hans A. Baer and Yvonne Jones, ed., *African-Americans in the South: Issues of Race, Class, and Gender* (1992): 60–78.

McMath, Robert C., Jr., "Southern White Farmers and the Organization of Black Farm Workers: A North Carolina Document," *Labor History* 18 (1977): 115–19.

Minchinton, Walter E., "The Seaborne Slave Trade of North Carolina," *North Carolina Historical Review* 71 (1994): 1–61.

Mobley, Joe A., "In the Shadow of White Society: Princeville, A Black Town in North Carolina, 1865–1915," *North Carolina Historical Review* 63 (1986): 340–84.

———— *James City: A Black Community in North Carolina, 1863–1900* (1981).

Morris, Charles Edward, "Panic and Reprisal: Reaction in North Carolina to the Nat Turner Insurrection, 1831," *North Carolina Historical Review* 62 (1985): 29–52.

Mutunhu, Tendai, "The North Carolina Quakers and Slavery: The Emigration and Settlement of Their Former Slaves in Haiti," *Journal of African-Afro-American Affairs* 4 (1980): 54–67.

Nelson, B. H., "Some Aspects of Negro Life in North Carolina during the Civil War," *North Carolina Historical Review* 25 (1948): 143–66.

Newbold, Nathan C., *Five North Carolina Negro Educators* (1939).

Opper, Peter Kent, "North Carolina Quakers: Reluctant Slaveholders," *North Carolina Historical Review* 52 (1975): 37–58.

Parker, Freddie L., *Running for Freedom: Slave Runaways in North Carolina, 1775–1840* (1993).

————, ed., *Stealing a Little Freedom: Advertisements for Slave Runaways in North Carolina, 1791–1840* (1994).

Phifer, Edward W., "Slavery in Microcosm: Burke County, North Carolina," *Journal of Southern History* 28 (1962): 137–65.

Phillips, Charles David, "Exploring Relations among Forms of Social Control: The Lynching and Execution of Blacks in North Carolina, 1889–1918," *Law and Society Review* 21 (1987): 361–74.

Prather, H. Leon, *We Have Taken a City: The Wilmington Massacre and Coup of 1898* (1984).

Price, Charles L., "John C. Barrett, Freedmen's Bureau Agent in North Carolina," *East Carolina University Papers in History* 5 (1981): 51–74.

Pritchett, Jonathan B., "The Burden of Negro Schooling: Tax Incidence and Racial Redistribution in Postbellum North Carolina," *Journal of Economic History* 49 (1989): 966–73.

Reid, George W., "Four in Black: North Carolina's Black Congressmen, 1874–1901," *Journal of Negro History* 64 (1979): 229–43.

Reid, Richard, "Raising the African Brigade: Early Black Recruitment in Civil War North Carolina," *North Carolina Historical Review* 70 (1993): 266–301.

Robert, Joseph Clarke, *The Tobacco Kingdom: Plantation, Market, and Factory in Virginia and North Carolina, 1800–1860* (1965).

Sanders, Wiley B., *Negro Child Welfare in North Carolina: A Rosenwald Study* (1933).

Savitt, Todd L., "Slave Life Insurance in Virginia and North Carolina," *Journal of Southern History* 43 (1977): 583–600.

Scott, Rebecca, "The Battle Over the Child: Child Apprenticeship and the Freedmen's Bureau in North Carolina," *Prologue* 10 (1978): 101–13.

Sensbach, Jon F., "Culture and Conflict in the Early Black Church: A Moravian Mission Congregation in Antebellum North Carolina," *North Carolina Historical Review* 71 (1994): 401–29.

———— *A Separate Canaan: The Making of an Afro-Moravian World in North Carolina, 1763–1840* (1998).

Sowle, Patrick, "The North Carolina Manumission Society, 1816–34," *North Carolina Historical Review* 42 (1965): 47–69.

Spraggins, Tinsley Lee, "Mobilization of Negro Labor for the Department of Virginia and North Carolina, 1861–1865," *North Carolina Historical Magazine* 24 (1947): 160–197.

St. Clair, Kenneth E., "Debtor Relief in North Carolina during Reconstruction," *North Carolina Historical Review* 18 (1941): 215–35.

Steiner, Jesse F., and Roy M. Brown, *The North Carolina Chain Gang: A Study of Convict Road Work* (1927).

Stewart, Roma Jones, "The Migration of a Free People: Cass County's Black Settlers from North Carolina," *Michigan History* 71 (1987): 34–39.

Strickland, John Scott, "The Great Revival and Insurrectionary Fears in North Carolina: An Examination of Antebellum Southern Society and Slave Revolt Panics," in Orville Vernon Burton, and Robert C. McMath, Jr., ed., *Class, Conflict, and Consensus: Antebellum Southern Community Studies* (1982): 57–95.

Taylor, Joseph H., "The Great Migration from North Carolina in 1878," *North Carolina Historical Review* 31 (1954): 18–33.

Taylor, Rosser Howard, "Humanizing the Slave Code of North Carolina," *North Carolina Historical Review* 2 (1925): 323–31.

———— "Slave Conspiracies in North Carolina," *North Carolina Historical Review* 5 (1928): 20–34.

———— *Slaveholding in North Carolina: An Economic View* (1926).

Todd, Willie Grier, "North Carolina Baptists and Slavery," *North Carolina Historical Review* 24 (1947): 135–59.

Trelease, Allen W., "Radical Reconstruction in North Carolina: A Roll-Call Analysis of the State House of Representatives, 1868–1870," *Journal of Southern History* 42 (1976): 319–44.

Uzzel, Odell, "Free Negro/Slave Marriages and Family Life in Antebellum North Carolina," *Western Journal of Black Studies* 18 (1994): 64–9.

Watson, Alan D., "Impulse toward Independence: Resistance and Rebellion among North Carolina Slaves, 1750–1775," *Journal of Negro History* 63 (1978): 317–28.

———— "North Carolina Slave Courts, 1715–1785," *North Carolina Historical Review* 60 (1983): 24–36.

Weare, Walter B., *Black Business in the New South: A Social History of the North Carolina Mutual Life Insurance Company* (1975).

Wynne, Frances Holloway, "Free Black Inhabitants of Wake County, North Carolina," *Journal of the Afro-American Historical and Genealogical Society* 1 (1980): 59–67.

Yanuck, Julius, "Thomas Ruffin and North Carolina Slave Law," *Journal of Southern History* 21 (1955): 456–75.

26.2.32 Ohio

Baily, Marilyn, "From Cincinnati, Ohio to Wilberforce, Canada: A Note on Antebellum Colonization," *Journal of Negro History* 58 (1973): 427–40.

Bigglestone, W. E., "Oberlin College and the Negro Student, 1865–1940," *Journal of Negro History* 56 (1971): 198–219.

———— *They Stopped in Oberlin: Black Residents and Visitors of the Nineteenth Century* (1981).

Blatnica, Dorothy Ann, *"At the Altar of Their God": African American Catholics in Cleveland, 1922–1961* (1995).

Burnham, Robert A., "Reform, Politics, and Race in Cincinnati: Proportional Representation and the City Charter Committee, 1924–1959," *Journal of Urban History* 23 (1997): 131–63.

Calkins, David L., "Black Education and the 19th Century City: An Institutional Analysis of Cincinnati's Colored Schools, 1850–1887," *Cincinnati History Society* 33 (1975): 161–71.

Clark, Peter H., *The Black Brigade of Cincinnati: Being a Report of Its Labors and a Muster-Roll of Its Members* (1864).

Collins, Ernest M., "Cincinnati Negroes and Presidential Politics," *Journal of Negro History* 41 (1956): 131–37.

Cuban, Larry, "A Strategy for Racial Peace: Negro Leadership in Cleveland, 1900–1919," *Phylon* 28 (1967): 299–311.

Dabney, Wendell P., *Cincinnati's Colored Citizens* (1926).

Davis, Lenwood G., *Blacks in the State of Ohio, 1800–1976: A Preliminary Survey* (1977).

Davis, Russell H., *Black Americans in Cleveland from George Peake to Carl B. Stokes, 1796–1969* (1972).

Erickson, Leonard, "Politics and the Repeal of Ohio's Black Laws, 1837–1849," *Ohio History* 82 (1973): 154–75.

———— "Toledo Desegregates, 1871," *Northwest Ohio Quarterly* 41 (1968–69): 5–12.

Gatewood, Willard B., Jr., "Ohio's Negro Battalion in the Spanish-American War," *Northwestern Ohio Quarterly* 45 (1973): 55–56.

Gerber, David A., *Black Ohio and the Color Line, 1860–1915* (1976).

Goings, Kenneth W., "Intra-Group Differences among Afro-Americans in the Rural North: Paulding County, Ohio, 1860–1900," *Ethnohistory* 27 (1980): 79–90.

Gutman, Herbert G., "Reconstruction in Ohio: Negroes in the Hocking Valley Coal Mines in 1873 and 1874," *Labor History* 3 (1962): 243–64.

Hickok, Charles T., *The Negro in Ohio, 1802–70* (1896).

Himes, J. S., Jr., "Forty Years of Negro Life in Columbus, Ohio," *Journal of Negro History* 27 (1942): 133–54.

Jackson, W. Sherman, "Emancipation, Negrophobia, and Civil War Politics in Ohio, 1863–1865," *Journal of Negro History* 65 (1980): 250–60.

Jacobs, Gregory S., *Getting around Brown: Desegregation, Development, and the Columbus Public Schools* (1998).

Jenkins, William D., *Steel Valley Klan: The Ku Klux Klan in Ohio's Mahoning Valley* (1990).

Kusmer, Kenneth L., *A Ghetto Takes Shape: Black Cleveland, 1870–1930* (1976).

Lammermeier, Paul J., "Cincinnati's Black Community: The Origins of a Ghetto, 1870–1880," in John H. Bracey, August Meier, and Elliott Rudwick, ed., *The Rise of the Ghetto* (1971): 24–28.

Lawson, Ellen N., and Marlene Merrill, "The Antebellum 'Talented Thousandth': Black College Students at Oberlin before the Civil War," *Journal of Negro Education* 52 (1983): 142–55.

Leigh, Patricia R., "Segregation by Gerrymander: The Creation of the Lincoln Heights (Ohio) High School District," *Journal of Negro Education* 66 (1997): 121–36.

Matijasic, Thomas D., "Abolition vs. Colonization: The Battle for Ohio," *Queen City Heritage* 45 (1987): 27–40.

McGinnis, Frederick Alphonso, *The Education of Negroes in Ohio* (1962).

Middleton, Stephen, "Cincinnati and the Fight for the Law of Freedom in Ohio, 1830–1856," *Locus* 4 (1991): 59–73.

Murray, Percy E., "Harry C. Smith-Joseph B. Foraker Alliance: Coalition Politics in Ohio," *Journal of Negro History* 68 (1983): 171–84.

Phillips, Kimberley L., "'But It Is a Fine Place to Make Money': Migration and African-American Families in Cleveland, 1915–1929," *Journal of Social History* 30 (1996): 393–413.

Pih, Richard W., "Negro Self-Improvement Efforts in Antebellum Cincinnati, 1836–1850," *Ohio History* 78 (1969): 179–87.

Preston, Emmett D., Jr., "The Fugitive Slave Acts in Ohio," *Journal of Negro History* 28 (1943): 422–77.

Quillan, Frank U., *The Color Line in Ohio: A History of Race Prejudice in a Typical Northern State* (1913).

Ratcliffe, Donald J., "Captain James Riley and Anti-Slavery Sentiment in Ohio, 1819–1824," *Ohio History* 81 (1972): 76–94.

Rodabaugh, James H., "The Negro in Ohio," *Journal of Negro History* 31 (1946): 9–29.

Ross, Felecia G. Jones, "The Brownsville Affair and the Political Values of Cleveland Black Newspapers," *American Journalism* 12 (1995): 107–22.

Sheeler, J. Reuben, "The Struggle of the Negro in Ohio for Freedom," *Journal of Negro History* 31 (1946): 208–26.

Sponholtz, Lloyd L., "Harry Smith, Negro Suffrage and the Ohio Constitutional Convention: Black Frustration in the Progressive Era," *Phylon* 35 (1974): 165–80.

Taylor, Henry L., "On Slavery's Fringe: City-Building and Black Community Development in Cincinnati, 1800–1850," *Ohio History* 95 (1986): 5–33.

———— "Spatial Organization and the Residential Experience: Black Cincinnati in 1850," *Social Science History* 10 (1986): 45–70.

Taylor, Henry, "The Use of Maps in the Study of the Black Ghetto-Formation Process: Cincinnati, 1802–1910," *Historical Methods* 17 (984): 44–58.

Thurston, Helen M., "The 1802 Ohio Constitutional Convention and the Status of the Negro," *Ohio History* 81 (1972): 15–37.

Trefousse, Hans Louis, *Benjamin Franklin Wade: Radical Republican from Ohio* (1963).

Trotter, Joe William, *River Jordan: African-American Urban Life in the Ohio Valley* (1998).

Wade, Richard C., "The Negro in Cincinnati, 1800–1830," *Journal of Negro History* 39 (1954): 43–57.

Weston, Rubin F., ed., *Blacks in Ohio History: A Conference to Commemorate the Bicentennial of the American Revolution* (1976).

Wiese, Andrew, "The Other Suburbanites: African American Suburbanization in the North before 1950," *Journal of American History* 85 (1999): 1495–1524.

Williams, Lee, "Concentrated Residences: The Case of Black Toledo, 1890–1930," *Phylon* 43 (1982): 167–76.

——— "Newcomers to the City: A Study of Black Population Growth in Toledo, Ohio, 1910–1930," *Ohio History* 39 (1980): 5–24.

Woodson, Carter G., "The Negroes of Cincinnati prior to the Civil War," *Journal of Negro History* 1 (1916): 1–22.

26.2.33 Oklahoma

Baker, T. Lindsay, and Julie P. Baker, ed., *The WPA Oklahoma Slave Narratives* (1996).

Bittle, William E., and Gilbert L. Geis, "Racial Self-Fulfillment and the Rise of an All-Negro Community in Oklahoma," *Phylon* 28 (1957): 247–60.

Brown, Willis L., and Janie M. McNeal-Brown, "Langston University," *Chronicles of Oklahoma* 74 (1996): 30–49.

Carney, George O., "Historic Resources of Oklahoma's All-Black Towns: A Preservation Profile," *Chronicles of Oklahoma* 69 (1991): 116–33.

Chapman, Berlin B., "Freedmen and the Oklahoma Lands," *Southwestern Social Science Quarterly* 29 (1948): 150–59.

Dann, Martin, "From Sodom to the Promised Land: E. P. McCabe and the Movement for Oklahoma Colonization," *Kansas Historical Quarterly* 40 (1974): 370–78.

Ellsworth, Scott, *Death in a Promised Land: The Tulsa Race Riot of 1921* (1982).

Franklin, Jimmie Lewis, *Journey toward Hope: A History of Blacks in Oklahoma* (1982).

Hill, Mozell C., "The All-Negro Communities of Oklahoma: The Natural History of a Social Movement," *Journal of Negro History* 31 (1946): 254–68.

Littlefield, Daniel F., Jr., and Lonnie E. Underhill, "Black Dreams and 'Free' Homes: The Oklahoma Territory, 1891–1894," *Phylon* 34 (1973): 342–57.

Mellinger, Philip, "Discrimination and Statehood in Oklahoma," *Chronicles of Oklahoma* 49 (1971): 340–78.

Meredith, H. L., "Agrarian Socialism and the Negro in Oklahoma, 1900–1918," *Labor History* 11 (1970): 277–84.

Pew, Thomas W., Jr., "Boley, Oklahoma: Trial in American Apartheid," *American West* 17 (1980): 14–21; 54–56; 63.

Reggio, Michael H., "Troubled Times: Homesteading in Short-Grass Country, 1892–1900," *Chronicles of Oklahoma* 57 (1979): 196–211.

Robbins, Louise S., "Racism and Censorship in Cold War Oklahoma: The Case of Ruth W. Brown and the Battlesville Public Library," *Southwestern Historical Quarterly* 100 (1996): 19–48.

Savage, Rosalind, "The Black Experience in Oklahoma from Territorial Status to 1980: A Selected Bibliography," *Chronicles of Oklahoma* 58 (1981): 465–67.

Smith, C. Calvin, "The Oppressed Oppressors: Negro Slavery among the Choctaw Indians of Oklahoma," *Red River Valley Historical Review* 2 (1975): 240–54.

Tolson, Arthur L., *The Black Oklahomans: A History, 1541–1972* (1972).

Williams, Lee E., and Lee E. Williams, II, *Anatomy of Four Race Riots: Racial Conflict in Knoxville, Elaine (Arkansas), Tulsa, and Chicago, 1919–1921* (1972).

Williams, Nudie E., "The Black Press in Oklahoma: The Formative Years, 1889–1907," *Chronicles of Oklahoma* 61 (1983): 308–19.

26.2.34   Oregon

Davis, Lenwood G., *Blacks in the State of Oregon, 1788–1974* (1974).
Hill, Daniel G., "The Negro as a Political and Social Issue in the Oregon Country," *Journal of Negro History* 33 (1948): 130–45.
McLagan, Elizabeth, *A Peculiar Paradise: A History of Blacks in Oregon, 1788–1940* (1980).
Toll, William, "Black Families and Migration to a Multiracial Society: Portland, Oregon, 1900–1924," *Journal of American Ethnic History* 17 (1998): 38–70.

26.2.35   Pennsylvania

Abrahams, Roger D., *Deep Down in the Jungle: Negro Narrative Folklore from the Streets of Philadelphia* (1964).
Alexander, J. Trent, "The Great Migration in Comparative Perspective: Interpreting the Urban Origins of Southern Black Migrants to Depression-Era Pittsburgh," *Social Science History* 22 (1998): 349–76.
Andrews, Dee, "The African Methodists of Philadelphia, 1794–1802," *Pennsylvania Magazine of History and Biography* 108 (1984): 471–86.
Bacon, Benjamin C., *Statistics of the Colored People of Philadelphia* (1856).
Barbour, George Edward, "Early Black Flyers of Western Pennsylvania, 1906–1945," *Western Pennsylvania Historical Magazine* 69 (1986): 95–119.
Bauman, John F., "Black Slums/Black Projects: The New Deal and Negro Housing in Philadelphia," *Pennsylvania History* 41 (1974): 311–38.
———— *Public Housing, Race, and Renewal: Urban Planning in Philadelphia, 1920–1974* (1987).
Binder, Frederick M., "Pennsylvania Negro Regiments in the Civil War," *Journal of Negro History* 37 (1952): 383–417.
Blackett, R. J. M., "Freedom, or the Martyr's Grave: Black Pittsburgh's Aid to the Fugitive Slave," *Western Pennsylvania Historical Magazine* 61 (1978): 117–34.
Blockson, Charles L., *Pennsylvania's Black History,* ed. Louise D. Stone (1975).
———— *The Underground Railroad in Pennsylvania* (1981).
Bodnar, John E., "The Impact of the 'New Immigration' on the Black Worker: Steelton, Pennsylvania, 1880–1920," *Labor History* 17 (1976): 214–29.
Bodnar, John E., Michael Weber, and Roger Simon, "Migration, Kinship, and Urban Adjustment: Blacks and Poles in Pittsburgh, 1900–1930," *Journal of American History* 66 (1979): 548–65.
Bodnar, John, Roger Simon, and Michael P. Weber, *Lives of Their Own: Blacks, Italians and Poles in Pittsburgh, 1900–1960* (1982).
Boromé, Joseph A., "The Vigilant Committee of Philadelphia," *Pennsylvania Magazine of History and Biography* 92 (1968): 320–51.
Brouwer, Merle, "Marriage and Family Life among Blacks in Colonial Pennsylvania," *Pennsylvania Magazine of History and Biography* 99 (1975): 368–72.
Brown, Ira V., *The Negro in Pennsylvania History* (1975).
———— "Pennsylvania and the Rights of the Negro, 1865–1887," *Pennsylvania History* 28 (1961): 45–57.
———— "Pennsylvania, 'Immediate Emancipation,' and the Birth of the American Anti-Slavery Society," *Pennsylvania History* 54 (1987): 163–78.
———— "Racism and Sexism: The Case of Pennsylvania Hall," *Phylon* 37 (1976): 126–36.
Buxbaum, Melvin H., "Cyrus Bustill Addresses the Blacks of Philadelphia [1787]," *William and Mary Quarterly* 29 (1972): 99–108.
Crawford, Paul, "A Footnote on Courts for Trial of Negroes in Colonial Pennsylvania," *Journal of Black Studies* 5 (1974): 167–74.

Davis, Allen F., and Mark H. Haller, ed., *The Peoples of Philadelphia: A History of Ethnic Groups and Lower-Class Life, 1790–1940* (1973).

Dickerson, Dennis C., "The Black Church in Industrializing Western Pennsylvania, 1870–1950," *Western Pennsylvania Historical Magazine* 64 (1981): 329–44.

———— *Out of the Crucible: Black Steelworkers in Western Pennsylvania, 1875–1980* (1986).

Douglass, William, *Annals of the First African Church, in the United States of America: Now Styled the African Episcopal Church of St. Thomas, Philadelphia* (1862).

Downey, Dennis B., and Ramond M. Hyser, *No Crooked Death: Coatesville, Pennsylvania, and the Lynching of Zachariah Walker* (1991).

Du Bois, W. E. B., *The Philadelphia Negro* (1899).

Eggert, Gerald G., "The Impact of the Fugitive Slave Law on Harrisburg: A Case Study," *Pennsylvania Magazine of History and Biography* 109 (1985): 537–70.

———— "'Two Steps Forward, A Step-and-a-Half Back': Harrisburg's African American Community in the Nineteenth Century," *Pennsylvania History* 58 (1991): 1–36.

Emlen, John T., "The Movement for the Betterment of the Negro in Philadelphia," *Annals of the American Academy of Political and Social Science* 49 (1913): 81–92.

Epstein, Abraham, *The Negro Migrant in Pittsburgh* (1918).

Feldberg, Michael, *The Philadelphia Riots of 1844: A Study of Ethnic Conflict* (1975).

Foner, Philip S., "The Battle to End Discrimination against Negroes on Philadelphia Streetcars: Background and Beginning of the Battle," *Pennsylvania History* 60 (1973): 261–92, 355–79.

Franklin, Vincent P., *The Education of Black Philadelphia: The Social and Educational History of a Minority Community, 1900–1950* (1979).

———— "The Philadelphia Race Riot of 1918," *Pennsylvania Magazine of History and Biography* 99 (1975): 336–50.

Geffen, Elizabeth M., "Violence in Philadelphia in the 1840s and 1850s," *Pennsylvania History* 36 (1969): 381–410.

Glasco, Laurence, "Double Burden: The Black Experience in Pittsburgh," in Samuel P. Hays, ed., *City at the Point: Essays on the Social History of Pittsburgh* (1991): 69–109.

Gottlieb, Peter, "Black Miners and the 1925–28 Bituminous Coal Strike: The Colored Committee of Non-Union Miners, Montour Mine No. 1, Pittsburgh Coal Company," *Labor History* 28 (1987): 233–41.

———— *Making Their Own Way: Southern Blacks' Migration to Pittsburgh, 1916–30* (1987).

———— "Migration and Jobs: The New Black Workers in Pittsburgh, 1916–1930," *Western Pennsylvania History Magazine* 61 (1978): 1–15.

Greenberg, Stephanie W., "Neighborhood Change, Racial Transition, and Work Location: A Case Study of an Industrial City, Philadelphia, 1880–1930," *Journal of Urban History* 7 (1981): 267–314.

Gregg, Robert, *Sparks from the Anvil of Oppression: Philadelphia's African Methodists and Southern Migrants, 1890–1940* (1993).

Gribbin, William, "A *Phylon* Document . . . Advice from a Black Philadelphia Poetess of 1813," *Phylon* 34 (1973): 49–50.

Hershberg, Theodore, "Blacks in Philadelphia, 1850–1980: Immigrants, Opportunities, and Racism," in Theodore Hershberg, ed., *The State of Black Philadelphia* (1981): 4–29.

———— "Free Blacks in Antebellum Philadelphia: A Study of Ex-Slaves, Freeborn, and Socioeconomic Decline," *Journal of Social History* 5 (1971/1972): 183–209.

————, ed., *Philadelphia: Work, Space, Family and Group Experience in the Nineteenth Century: Essays Toward an Interdisciplinary History of the City* (1981).

———— "A Tale of Three Cities: Blacks and Immigrants in Philadelphia: 1850–1880, 1930 and 1970," *Annals of the American Academy of Political and Social Sciences* 441 (1979): 55–81.

Hopkins, Leroy T., "Black Eldorado on the Susquehanna: The Emergence of Black Columbia, 1726–1861," *Journal of Lancaster County Historical Society* 89 (1985): 110–32.

———— "The Negro Entry Book: A Document of Lancaster City's Antebellum Afro-American Community," *Journal of the Lancaster County Historical Society* 88 (1984): 142–80.

———— "Uneasy Neighbors: Germans and Blacks in Nineteenth-Century Lancaster County," in Randall M. Miller, ed., *States of Progress: Germans and Blacks in America over 300 Years* (1989): 72–88.

Ireland, Owen S., "Germans against Abolition: A Minority's View of Slavery in Revolutionary Pennsylvania," *Journal of Interdisciplinary History* 3 (1973): 685–706.

Jenkins, Philip, "The Ku Klux Klan in Pennsylvania, 1920–1940," *Western Pennsylvania Historical Magazine* 69 (1986): 121–37.

Klepp, Susan E., "Seasoning and Society: Racial Differences in Mortality in Eighteenth-Century Philadelphia," *William and Mary Quarterly* 51 (1994): 473–506.

Kutler, Stanley I., "Pennsylvania Courts, The Abolition Act, and Negro Rights," *Pennsylvania History* 30 (1963): 14–27.

Lane, Roger, *Roots of Violence in Black Philadelphia, 1860–1900* (1986).

———— *Violent Death in the City: Suicide, Accident, and Murder in a Nineteenth Century City—Philadelphia* (1979).

———— *William Dorsey's Philadelphia and Ours: On the Past and Future of the Black City in America* (1991).

Lapsansky, Emma Jones, "Feminism, Freedom, and Community: Charlotte Forten and Women Activists in Nineteenth-Century Philadelphia," *Pennsylvania Magazine of History and Biography* 113 (1989): 3–19.

———— "Since They Got Those Separate Churches: Afro-Americans and Racism in Jacksonian Philadelphia," *American Quarterly* 32 (1980): 54–78.

Lindhorst, Marie, "Politics in a Box: Sarah Mapps Douglass and the Female Literary Association, 1831–1833," *Pennsylvania History* 65 (1998): 263–78.

Loucks, Emerson Hunsberger, *The Ku Klux Klan in Pennsylvania: A Study in Nativism* (1936).

McBride, David, *Integrating the City of Medicine: Blacks in Philadelphia Health Care, 1910–1965* (1989).

McGirr, Lisa, "Black and White Longshoremen in the IWW: A History of the Philadelphia Marine Transport Workers Industrial Union Local 8," *Labor History* 36 (1995): 377–402.

Meaders, Daniel, "Kidnapping Blacks in Philadelphia: Isaac Hopper's Tales of Oppression," *The Journal of Negro History* 80 (1995): 47–65.

Miller, Fredric, "The Black Migration to Philadelphia: A 1924 Profile," *Pennsylvania Magazine of History and Biography* 108 (1984): 315–50.

Miller, Frederic M., Morris J. Vogel, and Allen F. Davis, *Philadelphia Stories: A Photographic History, 1920–1960* (1988).

Minton, Henry M., *Early History of Negroes in Business in Philadelphia* (1913).

Montgomery, David, "Radical Republicanism in Pennsylvania, 1866–1873," *Pennsylvania Magazine of History and Biography* 85 (1961): 439–57.

Mossell, Sadie Tanner, "The Standard of Living among One Hundred Negro Migrant Families in Philadelphia," *Annals of the American Academy of Politics and Social Science* 98 (1921): 168–218.

Nash, Gary B., *Forging Freedom: The Formation of Philadelphia's Black Community, 1720–1840* (1988).

———— "From 1688 to 1799: Slavery and Freedom in Pennsylvania," in Randall M. Miller, ed., *States of Progress: Germans and Blacks in America over 300 Years* (1989): 27–37.

———— "Slaves and Slaveowners in Colonial Philadelphia," *William and Mary Quarterly* 30 (1973): 223–56.

———— "'To Arise Out of the Dust': Absalom Jones and the African Church of Philadelphia, 1785–95," in Gary B. Nash, *Race, Class, and Politics: Essays on American Colonial and Revolutionary Society* (1988): 323–55.

Nash, Gary B., and Jean R. Soderlund, *Freedom by Degrees: Emancipation in Pennsylvania and Its Aftermath* (1991).

Needles, Edward, *Ten Years' Progress: Or, A Comparison of the State and Condition of the Colored People in the City and County of Philadelphia from 1837 to 1847* (1849).

Negro Health Survey, Pittsburgh, *Tuberculosis and the Negro in Pittsburgh* (1934).

Nelson, H. Viscount, "The Philadelphia NAACP: Race versus Class Consciousness during the Thirties," *Journal of Black Studies* 5 (1975): 255–76.

New York State Temporary Commission on the Condition of the Urban Colored Population, *Second Report of the New York State Temporary Commission on the Conditions of the Colored Urban Population to the General Assembly of the State of Pennsylvania* (1939).

Newman, Debra L., "Black Women in the Era of the American Revolution in Pennsylvania," *Journal of Negro History* 61 (1976): 276–89.

Oblinger, Carl D., "Ellipses, the Black Masses, and Local Elan: A Review of the Sources for a History of the Ante-bellum Negro in Southeastern Pennsylvania," *Journal of the Lancaster County Historical Society* 74 (1970): 124–131.

——— *Freedom's Foundations: Black Communities in Southeastern Pennsylvania Towns, 1780–1860* (1972).

Patrick-Stamp, Leslie, "Numbers That Are Not New: African Americans in the Country's First Prison, 1790–1835," *Pennsylvania Magazine of History and Biography* 119 (1995): 95–128.

Pennsylvania State Temporary Commission on the Conditions of the Urban Colored Population, *Final Report of the Pennsylvania State Temporary Commission on the Conditions of the Urban Colored Population to the General Assembly of the State of Pennsylvania* (1943).

Philadelphia African Americans: Color, Class, and Style, 1840–1940: An Exhibition in the Museum of the Balch Institute for Ethnic Studies, April 4–July 9, 1988 (1988).

Price, Edward, "The Black Voting Rights Issue in Pennsylvania, 1780–1900," *Pennsylvania Magazine of History and Biography* 100 (1976): 356–73.

Price, Edward J., Jr., "School Segregation in Nineteenth-Century Pennsylvania," *Pennsylvania History* 43 (1976): 121–37.

Rankin-Hall, Lesley M., *A Biohistory of Nineteenth Century Afro-Americans: The Burial Remains of a Philadelphia Cemetery* (1997).

Reid, Ira De A., *Social Conditions of the Negro in the Hill District of Pittsburgh* (1930).

Rollins, Richard, "Black Confederates at Gettysburg," in Arthur W. Bergeron, John McGlone, and Richard M. Rollins, ed., *Black Southerners in Gray: Essays on Afro-Americans in Confederate Armies* (1994).

Rosswurm, Steve, "Emancipation in New York and Philadelphia," *Journal of Urban History* 21 (1995): 505–10.

Rowe, G. S., "Black Offenders, Criminal Courts, and Philadelphia Society in the Late Eighteenth Century," *Journal of Social History* 22 (1989): 685–712.

Ruck, Rob, *Sandlot Seasons: Sport in Black Pittsburgh* (1987).

Runcie, John, "'Hunting the Nigs' in Philadelphia: The Race Riot of August, 1834," *Pennsylvania History* 39 (1972): 187–218.

Segal, Geraldine R., *Blacks in the Law: Philadelphia and the Nation* (1983).

Seifman, Eli, "The United Colonization Societies of New York and Pennsylvania and the Establishment of the African Colony of Bassa Cove," *Pennsylvania History* 35 (1968): 23–44.

Shirk, Willis L., Jr., "Testing the Limits of Tolerance: Blacks and the Social Order in Columbia, Pennsylvania, 1800–1851," *Pennsylvania History* 60 (1993): 35–50.

Silcox, Harry C., "The Black 'Better Class' Political Dilemma: Philadelphia Prototype Isaiah C. Wears," *Pennsylvania Magazine of History and Biography* 113 (1989): 45–66.

——— "Delay and Neglect: Negro Public Education in Antebellum Philadelphia, 1800–1860," *Pennsylvania Magazine of History and Biography* 97 (1973): 444–64.

——— "Philadelphia Negro Educator: Jacob C. White, Jr., 1837–1902," *Pennsylvania Magazine of History and Biography* 97 (1973): 75–98.

Simpson, George E., "Race Relations and the Philadelphia Press," *Journal of Negro Education* 6 (1937): 628–30.

Smedley, Robert Clemens, *History of the Underground Railroad in Chester and the Neighboring Counties of Pennsylvania* (1883).

Society of Friends, *A Statistical Inquiry into the Condition of the People of Colour of the City, and Districts of Philadelphia* (1849).

Soderlund, Jean R., "Black Importation and Migration into Southeastern Pennsylvania, 1682–1810," *American Philosophical Society, Proceedings* 133 (1989): 144–53.

——— "Black Women in Colonial Pennsylvania," *Pennsylvania Magazine of History and Biography* 107 (1983): 49–68.

Southern, Eileen, "Musical Practices in Black Churches of New York and Philadelphia, c. 1800–1844," *Afro-Americans in New York Life and History* 4 (1980): 61–77.

Sumler-Lewis, Janice, "The Forten-Purvis Women of Philadelphia and the American Anti-Slavery Crusade," *Journal of Negro History* 66 (1981): 281–88.

Trotter, Joe William, *River Jordan: African-American Urban Life in the Ohio Valley* (1998).

Trotter, Joe W. , Jr., and Eric Ledell Smith, ed., *African Americans in Pennsylvania: Shifting Historical Perspectives.*

Tully, Alan, "Patterns of Slaveholding in Colonial Pennsylvania: Chester and Lancaster Counties, 1729–1758," *Journal of Social History* 6 (1973): 285–305.

Turner, Edward R., *The Negro in Pennsylvania: Slavery—Servitude—Freedom, 1639–1861* (1911).

———— "The Underground Railroad in Pennsylvania," *Pennsylvania Magazine of History and Biography* 36 (1912): 309–18.

Ulle, Robert F., "Blacks in Berks County, Pennsylvania: The Almshouse Records," *Pennsylvania Folklife* 27 (1977): 19–30.

Waldstreicher, David, "Reading the Runaways: Self-Fashioning, Print Culture, and Confidence in Slavery in the Eighteenth-Century Mid-Atlantic," *William and Mary Quarterly* 56 (1999): 243–72.

Walker, Joseph E., "Negro Labor in the Charcoal Iron Industry of Southeastern Pennsylvania," *Pennsylvania Magazine of History and Biography* 93 (1969): 466–86.

Wax, Darold D., "Africans on the Delaware: The Pennsylvania Slave Trade, 1759–1765," *Pennsylvania History* 50 (1983): 38–49.

———— "The Demand for Slave Labor in Colonial Pennsylvania," *Pennsylvania History* 34 (1967): 331–45.

———— "Negro Import Duties in Colonial Pennsylvania," *Pennsylvania Magazine of History and Biography* 97 (1973): 22–44.

———— "Quaker Merchants and the Slave Trade in Colonial Pennsylvania," *Pennsylvania Magazine of History and Biography* 86 (1962): 143–59.

———— "Reform and Revolution: The Movement against Slavery and the Slave Trade in Revolutionary Pennsylvania," *Western Pennsylvania Historical Magazine* 57 (1974): 403–29.

Whipper, William, *An Address Delivered in Wesley Church on the Evening of June 12, before the Colored Reading Society of Philadelphia* (n.d.).

Williams, Oscar R., "The Regimentation of Blacks on the Urban Frontier in Colonial Albany, New York City, and Philadelphia," *Journal of Negro History* 63 (1978): 329–38.

Willson, Joseph, *Sketches of the Higher Classes of Colored Society in Philadelphia* (1841).

Winch, Julie, "Philadelphia and the Other Underground Railroad," *Pennsylvania Magazine of History and Biography* 111 (1987): 3–25.

———— *Philadelphia's Black Elite: Activism, Accommodation, and the Struggle for Autonomy, 1787–1848* (1988).

Winkler, Allan M., "The Philadelphia Transit Strike of 1944," *Journal of American History* 59 (1972): 73–89.

Winpenny, Thomas R., "The Economic Status of Negroes in Late Nineteenth Century Lancaster," *Journal of the Lancaster County Historical Society* 77 (1973): 124–32.

Worth, Robert F., "The Legacy of a Lynching, Coatesville, Pennsylvania, 1911," *American Scholar* 67 (1998): 65–77.

Wright, Richard R., Jr., *The Negro in Pennsylvania: A Study in Economic History* (1969).

26.2.36   Rhode Island

Armstead, Myra B. Young, *"Lord, Please Don't Take Me in August": African Americans in Newport and Saratoga Springs, 1870–1930* (1999).

Bartlett, Irving H., *From Slave to Citizen: The Story of the Negro in Rhode Island* (1954).

Chenery, William H., *The Fourteenth Regiment Rhode Island Heavy Artillery (Colored) in the War to Preserve the Union* (1898).

Cottrol, Robert J., *The Afro-Yankees: Providence's Black Community in the Antebellum Era* (1982).

Coughtry, Jamie, and Jay Coughtry, "Black Pauper Burial Records: Providence, Rhode Island, 1777–1831," *Rhode Island History* 44 (1985): 109–19.

Coughtry, Jay, *The Notorious Triangle: Rhode Island and the African Slave Trade, 1700–1807* (1981).

Crane, Elaine F., "'The First Wheel of Commerce': Newport, Rhode Island and the Slave Trade, 1760–1776," *Slavery and Abolition* 1 (1980): 178–98.

Daoust, Norma Lasalle, "Building the Democratic Party: Black Voting in Providence in the 1930s," *Rhode Island History* 44 (1985): 81–88.

Gerdes, M. Reginald, "To Educate and Evangelize: Black Catholic Schools of the Oblate Sisters of Providence," *U.S. Catholic Historian* 7 (1988): 183–99.

Greene, Lorenzo J., "Some Observations on the Black Regiment of Rhode Island in the American Revolution," *Journal of Negro History* 37 (1952): 142–72.

Jones, Alison, "The Rhode Island Slave Trade: A Trading Advantage in Africa," *Slavery and Abolition* 2 (1981): 227–44.

Lemons, J. Stanley, and Michael A. McKenna, "Re-Enfranchisement of Rhode Island Negroes," *Rhode Island History* 30 (1971): 3–13.

Luker, Ralph E., "'Under Our Own Vine and Fig Tree': From African Unionism to Black Denominationalism in Newport, Rhode Island, 1760–1876," *Slavery and Abolition* 12 (1991): 23–48.

Masur, Louis P., "Slavery in Eighteenth-Century Rhode Island: Evidence from the Census of 1774," *Slavery and Abolition* 6 (1985): 139–50.

McBurney, Christian, "The South Kingstown Planters: Country Gentry in Colonial Rhode Island," *Rhode Island History* 45 (1986): 81–93.

Perlmann, Joel, "The Schooling of Blacks in a Northern City: Providence, R.I., 1880–1925," *Perspectives in American History* 2 (1985): 125–82.

Platt, Virginia Bever, "'And Don't Forget the Guinea Voyage': The Slave Trade of Aaron Lopez of Newport," *William and Mary Quarterly* 32 (1975): 601–18.

Rammelkamp, Julian, "The Providence Negro Community, 1820–1842," *Rhode Island History* 7 (1948): 20–33.

Rhode Island Commission on the Employment Problems of the Negro, *Report of the Commission on the Employment Problems of the Negro* (1943).

Sherer, Robert Glenn, Jr., "Negro Churches in Rhode Island before 1860," *Rhode Island History* 25 (1966): 9–25.

VanBroekhoven, Deborah Bingham, "'A Determination to Labor . . .': Female Anti-Slavery Activity in Rhode Island," *Rhode Island History* 44 (1985): 35–44.

Wax, Darold D., "Thomas Rogers and the Rhode Island Slave Trade," *American Neptune* 35 (1975): 289–301.

26.2.37 South Carolina

Aba-Mecha, Barbara W., "South Carolina Conference of NAACP: Origin and Major Accomplishments, 1939–1954," *Proceedings of the South Carolina Historical Association* (1981): 1–21.

Abbott, Martin, "County Officers in South Carolina in 1868," *South Carolina Historical Magazine* 60 (1959): 30–40.

——— "Freedom's Cry: Negroes and Their Meetings in South Carolina, 1865–1869," *Phylon* 20 (1959): 263–72.

Abbott, Richard H., ed., "A Yankee Views the Organization of the Republican Party in South Carolina, July 1867," *South Carolina Historical Magazine* 85 (1984): 244–50.

Aptheker, Herbert, "South Carolina Negro Conventions, 1865," *Journal of Negro History* 31 (1946): 91–97.

Birnie, C. W., "Education of the Negro in Charleston, South Carolina, prior to the Civil War," *Journal of Negro History* 12 (1927): 13–21.

Birnie, Cassandra M., "Race and Politics in Georgia and South Carolina," *Phylon* 13 (1952): 236–44.

Blackburn, George, and Sherman L. Ricards, "The Mother-Headed Family among Free Negroes in Charleston, South Carolina, 1850–1860," *Phylon* 42 (1981): 11–25.

Bleser, Carol K. Rothrock, *The Promised Land: The History of the South Carolina Land Commission, 1869–1890* (1969).

Brady, Patrick S., "The Slave Trade and Sectionalism in South Carolina, 1787–1808," *Journal of Southern History* 38 (1972): 601–20.

Bryant, Lawrence Chesterfield, *Negro Legislators in South Carolina, 1865–1894* (1966).

——— *Negro Lawmakers in the South Carolina Legislature, 1868–1902* (1968).

——— *South Carolina Negro Legislators: A Glorious Success* (1974).

Burton, Orville Vernon, *In My Father's House are Many Mansions: Family and Community in Edgefield, South Carolina* (1985).

——— "Edgefield Reconstruction Political Black Leaders," *Proceedings of the South Carolina Historical Association* (1988): 27–38.

Campbell, John, "As 'A Kind of Freeman': Slaves' Market-Related Actvities in the South Carolina Upcountry, 1800–1860," *Slavery and Abolition* 12 (1991): 131–69.

Carl, M. Allison, "Great Neatness of Finish: Slave Carpenters in South Carolina's Charleston District, 1760–1800," *Southern Studies* 26 (1987): 89–100.

Carl-White, Allison, "South Carolina's Forgotten Craftsmen," *South Carolina Historical Magazine* 86 (1985): 32–8.

Carney, Judith A., "From Hands to Tutors: African Expertise in the South Carolina Rice Economy," *Agricultural History* 67 (1993): 1–30.

Cassidy, Frederic G., "The Place of Gullah," *American Speech* 55 (1980): 3–16.

——— "Sources of the African Element in Gullah," in Lawrence D. Carrington, ed., *Studies in Caribbean Language* (1983): 75–81.

Chaplin, Joyce E., "Tidal Rice Cultivation and the Problem of Slavery in South Carolina and Georgia, 1760–1815," *William and Mary Quarterly* 49 (1992): 29–61.

Charles, Allan D., "Black-White Relations in an Antebellum Church in the Carolina Up Country," *South Carolina Historical Magazine* 89 (1988): 218–26.

Clarke, T. Erskine, "An Experiment in Paternalism: Presbyterians and Slaves in Charleston, South Carolina," *Journal of Presbyterian History* 53 (1975): 223–38.

Coclanis, Peter A., and J. C. Marlow, "Inland Rice Production in the South Atlantic States: A Picture in Black and White," *Agricultural History* 72 (1998): 197–212.

Cody, Cheryll A., "Naming, Kinship, and Estate Dispersal: Notes on Slave Family Life on a South Carolina Plantation, 1786 to 1833," *William and Mary Quarterly* 39 (1982): 192–211.

——— "A Note on Changing Patterns of Slave Fertility in the South Carolina Rice District, 1735–1865," *Southern Studies* 16 (1977): 457–63.

——— "There Was No 'Absalom' on the Ball Plantations: Slave-Naming Practices in the South Carolina Low Country, 1720–1865," *American Historical Review* 92 (1987): 563–96.

Cooper, William J., Jr., *The Conservative Regime: South Carolina, 1877–1890* (1968).

Creel, Margaret Washington, *"A Peculiar People": Slave Religion and Community-Culture among the Gullahs* (1988).

Crowley, John, "The Importance of Kinship: Testamentary Evidence from South Carolina," *Journal of Interdisciplinary History* 16 (1986): 559–77.

Crum, Mason, *Gullah: Negro Life in the South Carolina Sea Islands* (1940).

Day, Kay Young, "Kinship in a Changing Economy: A View from the Sea Islands," in Robert L. Hall, and Carol B. Stack, ed., *Holding on to the Land and the Lord: Kinship, Ritual, Land Tenure, and Social Policy in the Rural South* (1982): 11–24.

Delvin, George A., *South Carolina and Black Migration, 1865–1940: In Search of the Promised Land* (1989).

Derby, Doris A., *Black Women Basket Makers: A Study of Domestic Economy in Charleston County, South Carolina* (1980).

Drago, Edmund L., *Initiative, Paternalism, and Race Relations: Charleston's Avery Normal Institute* (1990).

Drucker, Lesley M., "Socioeconomic Patterning at an Undocumented Late Eighteenth Century Lowcountry Site: Spiers Landing, South Carolina," *Historical Archaeology* 15 (1981): 58–68.

Dusinberre, William, *Them Dark Days: Slavery in the American Rice Swamps* (1996).

Farley, M. Foster, "The Fear of Negro Slave Revolts in South Carolina, 1690–1865," *Afro-American Studies* 3 (1972): 199–207.

———— "A History of Negro Slave Revolts in South Carolina," *Afro-American Studies* 3 (1972): 97–102.

———— "The South Carolina Negro in the American Revolution, 1775–1783," *South Carolina Historical Magazine* 79 (1978): 75–86.

Fitchett, E. Horace, "The Origin and Growth of the Free Negro Population of Charleston, South Carolina," *Journal of Negro History* 26 (1941): 421–37.

———— "The Traditions of the Free Negro in Charleston, South Carolina," *Journal of Negro History* 25 (1940): 139–52.

Ford, Lacy K., "Rednecks and Merchants: Economic Development and Social Tensions in the South Carolina Upcountry, 1865–1900," *Journal of American History* 71 (1984): 294–318.

Freehling, William W., *Prelude to Civil War: The Nullification Controversy in South Carolina, 1816–1836* (1966).

French, Austa Malinda, *Slavery in South Carolina and the Ex-Slaves: Or, The Port Royal Mission* (1862).

Friedlander, Amy, "Establishing Historical Probabilities for Archaeological Interpretations: Slave Demography of Two Plantations in the South Carolina Lowcountry, 1740–1820," in Theresa A. Singleton, ed., *The Archeology of Slavery and Plantation Life* (1985): 215–38.

Gaboury, William J., "George Washington Murray and the Fight for Political Democracy in South Carolina," *Journal of Negro History* 62 (1977): 258–69.

Gatewood, Willard B., Jr., "'The Remarkable Misses Rollin': Black Women in Reconstruction South Carolina," *South Carolina Historical Magazine* 92 (1991): 172–88.

Gelston, Arthur Lewis, "Radical versus Straight-Out in Post-Reconstruction Beaufort County," *South Carolina Historical Magazine* 75 (1974): 225–37.

Greenberg, Kenneth S., "Revolutionary Ideology and the Proslavery Argument: The Abolition of Slavery in Antebellum South Carolina," *Journal of Southern History* 42 (1976): 365–84.

Greene, Jack P., "Colonial South Carolina and the Caribbean Connection," *South Carolina Historical Magazine* 88 (1987): 192–210.

———— "'Slavery or Independence': Some Reflections on the Relationship Among Liberty, Black Bondage, and Equality in Revolutionary South Carolina," *South Carolina Historical Magazine* 80 (1979): 193–214.

Groover, Mark D., "Evidence for Folkways and Cultural Exchange in the 18th-Century South Carolina Backcountry," *Historical Archaeology* 28 (1994): 41–64.

Haber, Carole, and Brian Gratton, "Old Age, Public Welfare, and Race: The Case of Charleston, South Carolina," *Journal of Social History* 21 (1987): 263–79.

Hagy, James W., "Black Business Women in Antebellum Charleston," *Journal of Negro History* 72 (1987): 42–44.

Hall, Kermit L., "Political Power and Constitutional Legitimacy: The South Carolina Ku Klux Klan Trials, 1871–1872," *Emory Law Journal* 33 (1984): 921–51.

Harris, Robert L. , Jr., "Charleston's Free Afro-American Elite: The Brown Fellowship Society and the Humane Brotherhood," *South Carolina Historical Magazine* 82 (1981): 289–310.

Hemmingway, Theodore, "Prelude to Change: Black Carolinians in the War Years, 1914–1920," *Journal of Negro History* 65 (1980): 212–27.

Hennessey, Melinda M., "Racial Violence during Reconstruction: The 1876 Riots in Charleston and Cainhoy," *South Carolina Historical Magazine* 86 (1985): 100–12.

Henry, Howell Meadoes, *The Police Control of the Slave in South Carolina* (1968).

Hindus, Michael S., "Black Justice under White Law: Criminal Prosecutions of Blacks in Antebellum South Carolina," *Journal of American History* 63 (1976): 575–99.

———— *Prison and Plantation: Crime, Justice, and Authority in Massachusetts and South Carolina, 1767–1878* (1980).

Hine, William C., "Black Organized Labor in Reconstruction Charleston," *Labor History* 25 (1984): 504–17.

———— "Black Politicians in Reconstruction Charleston, South Carolina: A Collective Study," *Journal of Southern History* 49 (1983): 555–84.

———— "Civil Rights and Campus Wrongs: South Carolina State College Students Protest, 1955–68," *South Carolina Historical Magazine* 97 (1996): 310–40.

Hoffman, Edwin D., "The Genesis of the Modern Movement for Equal Rights in South Carolina, 1930–1939," *Journal of Negro History* 44 (1959): 346–69.

Holland, Rupert Sargent, ed., *Letters and Diary of Laura M. Towne: Written from the Sea Islands of South Carolina, 1862–1884* (1912).

Holt, Thomas, *Black Over White: Negro Political Leadership in South Carolina during Reconstruction* (1977).

Inscoe, John C., "Carolina Slave Names: An Index to Acculturation," *Journal of Southern History* 49 (1983): 527–54.

Jackson, Harvey H., "Hugh Bryan and the Evangelical Movement in Colonial South Carolina," *William and Mary Quarterly* 43 (1986): 594–614.

Jackson, James Conroy, "The Religious Education of the Negro in South Carolina prior to 1850," *Historical Magazine of the Protestant Episcopal Church* 36 (1967): 35–61.

Jackson, Luther Porter, "The Educational Efforts of the Freedmen's Bureau and Freedmen's Societies in South Carolina, 1862–1872," *Journal of Negro History* 8 (1923): 1–40.

———— "Religious Instruction of Negroes, 1830–1860, With Special Reference to South Carolina," *Journal of Negro History* 15 (1930): 72–114.

January, Alan F., "The South Carolina Association: An Agency for Race Control in Antebellum South Carolina," *South Carolina Historical Magazine* 78 (1977): 191–201.

Jenkins, Wilbert L., *Seizing the New Day: African Americans in Post-Civil War Charleston* (1998).

Johnson, Guion Griffis, *A Social History of the Sea Islands with Special Reference to St. Helena Island, South Carolina* (1930).

Johnson, Guy Benton, *Folk Culture on St. Helena Island, South Carolina* (1930).

Johnson, Michael P., "Runaway Slaves and the Slave Communities in South Carolina, 1799–1830," *William and Mary Quarterly* 38 (1981): 418–41.

Johnson, Michael P., and James L. Roark, ed., *No Chariot Let Down: Charleston's Free People of Color on the Eve of the Civil War* (1984).

Jones, George Fenwick, "The Black Hessians: Negroes Recruited by the Hessians in South Carolina and other Colonies," *South Carolina Historical Magazine* 83 (1982): 287–302.

Jones, Norrece T., Jr., *Born a Child of Freedom, Yet a Slave: Mechanisms of Control and Strategies of Resistance in Antebellum South Carolina* (1990).

Joyner, Charles W., *Down by the Riverside: A South Carolina Slave Community* (1984).

———— "'If You Ain't Got Education': Slave Language and Slave Thought in Antebellum Charleston," in Michael O'Brien, and David Moltke-Hansen, ed., *Intellectual Life in Antebellum Charleston* (1986): 225–78.

Kennedy-Haflett, Cynthia, "'Moral Marriage': A Mixed-Race Relationship in Nineteenth-Century Charleston, South Carolina," *South Carolina Historical Magazine* 97 (1996): 206–26.

Kiser, Clyde Vernon, *Sea Island to City: A Study of St. Helena Islanders in Harlem and Other Urban Centers* (1932).

Klein, Rachel N., *Unification of a Slave State: The Rise of the Planter Class in the South Carolina Backcountry, 1760–1808* (1990).

Knuth, Carole Brown, "African-American Children and the Case for Community: Eleanora Tate's South Carolina Trilogy," *African American Review* 32 (1998): 85–92.

Koger, Larry, *Black Slaveowners: Free Black Slave Masters in South Carolina, 1790–1860* (1985).

Kremm, Thomas W., and Diane Neal, "Challenges to Subordination: Organized Black Agricultural Protest in South Carolina, 1886–1895," *South Atlantic Quarterly* 77 (1978): 98–112.

Lander, E. M., "Slave Labor in South Carolina Cotton Mills," *Journal of Negro History* 38 (1953): 161–73.

Leaming, Hugo Prosper, *Hidden Americans: Maroons of Virginia and the Carolinas* (1995).

Lewis, Kenneth E., *Hampton: Initial Archaeological Investigations at an Eighteenth Century Rice Plantation in the Santee Delta, South Carolina* (1979).

———— "Plantation Layout and Function in the South Carolina Lowcountry," in Theresa A. Singleton, ed., *The Archeology of Slavery and Plantation Life* (1985): 35–65.

———— "Settlement Activity and Patterning on Two Rice Plantations in the South Carolina Lowcountry," *The Conference on Historic Site Archaeology Papers, S.C. Institute of Archaeology and Anthropology, University of S.C.* 14 (1979): 1–12.

Ling, Peter J., "Developing Freedom Songs: Guy Carawan and the African-American Traditions of the South Carolina Sea Islands," *History Workshop Journal* 44 (1997): 196–213.

Littlefield, Daniel C., "Continuity and Change in Slave Culture: South Carolina and the West Indies," *Southern Studies* 26 (1987): 202–16.

———— *Rice and Slaves: Ethnicity and the Slave Trade in Colonial South Carolina* (1981).

———— "The Slave Trade to Colonial South Carolina: A Profile," *South Carolina Historical Magazine* 91 (1990): 68–99.

Mack, Kibibi Voloria C., *Parlor Ladies and Ebony Drudges: African American Women, Class, and Work in a South Carolina Community* (1999).

Matthews, Linda M., "Keeping Down Jim Crow: The Railroads and the Separate Coach Bills in South Carolina," *South Atlantic Quarterly* 73 (1974): 117–29.

Meaders, Daniel E., "South Carolina Fugitives As Viewed through Local Colonial Newspapers with Emphasis on Runaway Notices 1732–1801," *Journal of Negro History* 60 (1975): 288–319.

Megginson, W. J., "Black South Carolinians in World War I: The Official Roster as a Resource for Local History, Mobility, and African-American History," *South Carolina Historical Magazine* 96 (1995): 153–73.

Menard, Russell R., "Financing the Lowcountry Export Boom: Capital and Growth in Early South Carolina," *William and Mary Quarterly* 51 (1994): 659–76.

Merrens, H. Roy, "A View of Coastal South Carolina in 1778: The Journal of Ebenezer Harzard," *South Carolina Historical Magazine* 73 (1972): 177–93.

Morgan, Philip D., "Black Life in Eighteenth-Century Charleston," *Perspectives in American History* 1 (1984): 187–232.

———— *Slave Counterpoint: Black Culture in the Eighteenth-Century Chesapeake and Lowcountry* (1998).

Morgan, Philip D., and George D. Terry, "Slavery in Microcosm: A Conspiracy Scare in Colonial South Carolina," *Southern Studies* 21 (1982): 121–45.

Morris-Crowther, Jayne, "An Economic Study of the Substantial Slaveholders of Orangeburg County, 1860–80," *South Carolina Historical Magazine* 86 (1985): 296–314.

Newby, I. A., *Black Carolinians: A History of Blacks in South Carolina from 1895–1968* (1973).

Ochenkowski, J. P., "The Origins of Nullification in South Carolina," *South Carolina Historical Magazine* 83 (1982): 121–53.

Oldendorf, Sandra Brenneman, *Highlander Folk School and the South Carolina Sea Island Citizenship School* (1987).

Oldfield, J. R., "A High and Honorable Calling: Black Lawyers in South Carolina, 1868–1915," *Journal of American Studies* 23 (1989): 395–406.

Oliphant, Albert D., *The Evolution of the Penal System of South Carolina from 1866 to 1916* (1916).

Olwell, Robert A., "Becoming Free: Manumission and the Genesis of a Free Black Community in South Carolina, 1740–90," *Slavery and Abolition* 17 (1996): 1–19.

———— "'Domestick Enemies': Slavery and Political Independence in South Carolina, May 1775–March 1776," *Journal of Southern History* 55 (1989): 21–48.

———— *Masters, Slaves, and Subjects: The Culture of Power in the South Carolina Low Country, 1740–1790* (1998).

Pearson, Edward A., "'A Countryside Full of Flames': A Reconsideration of the Stono Rebellion and Slave Rebelliousness in the Early Eighteenth-Century South Carolina Lowcountry," *Slavery and Abolition* 2 (1996): 22–50.

Phillips, Ulrich B., "The Slave Labor Problem in the Charleston District," *Political Science Quarterly* 22 (1907): 416–39.

Pike, James Shepard, *The Prostrate State: South Carolina under Negro Government* (1874).

Pollitzer, William, *The Gullah People and Their African Heritage* (1999).

Powers, Bernard Edward, Jr., *Black Charlestonians: A Social History, 1822–1885* (1994).

Radford, John P., "Delicate Space: Race and Residence in Charleston, South Carolina, 1860–1880," *West Georgia College Studies in the Social Sciences* 16 (1977): 17–37.

Rathbun, Ted A., "Health and Disease at a South Carolina Plantation: 1840–1870," *American Journal of Physical Anthropology* 74 (1987): 239–53.

Reynolds, John S., *Reconstruction in South Carolina, 1865–1877* (1905).

Ricards, Sherman L., and George M. Blackburn, "A Demographic History of Slavery: Georgetown County, South Carolina, 1850," *South Carolina Historical Magazine* 76 (1975): 215–24.

Richardson, David, "The British Slave Trade to Colonial South Carolina," *Slavery and Abolition* 12 (1991): 125–72.

Saville, Julie, "Grassroots Reconstruction: Agricultural Labour and Collective Action in South Carolina, 1860–1868," *Slavery and Abolition* 12 (1991): 173–82.

———— *The Work of Reconstruction: From Slave to Wage Laborer in South Carolina, 1860–1870* (1994).

Schwalm, Leslie A., *A Hard Fight For We: Women's Transition from Slavery to Freedom in Lowcountry South Carolina* (1997).

———— "'Sweet Dreams of Freedom': Freedwomen's Reconstruction of Life and Labor in Lowcountry South Carolina," *Journal of Women's History* 9 (1997): 9–38.

Schweninger, Loren, "Slave Independence and Enterprise in South Carolina, 1780–1865," *South Carolina History Magazine* 93 (1992): 101–125.

Senese, Donald J., "The Free Negro and the South Carolina Courts, 1790–1860," *South Carolina Historical Magazine* 68 (1967): 140–53.

Shapiro, Herbert, "The Ku Klux Klan During Reconstruction: The South Carolina Episode," *Journal of Negro History* 49 (1964): 34–55.

Shick, Tom W., and Don H. Doyle, "The South Carolina Phosphate Boom and the Stillbirth of the New South, 1867–1920," *South Carolina Historical Magazine* 86 (1985): 1–31.

Simkins, Francis B., "The Ku Klux Klan in South Carolina, 1868–1871," *Journal of Negro History* 12 (1927): 606–47.

———— "The Problems of South Carolina Agriculture after the Civil War," *North Carolina Historical Review* 7 (1930): 46–77.

Simkins, Francis Butler, and Robert Hilliard Woody, *South Carolina during Reconstruction* (1932).

Smith, Mark M., "'All Is Not Quiet in Our Hellish County': Facts, Fiction, Politics and Race—The Ellenton Riot of 1876," *South Carolina Historical Magazine* 95 (1994): 142–55.

Smyth, William D., "Blacks and the South Carolina Interstate and West Indian Exposition," *South Carolina History Magazine* 88 (1987): 211–19.

Southern, David W., "Beyond Jim Crow Liberalism: Judge Waring's Fight against Segregation in South Carolina, 1942–1952," *Journal of Negro History* 66 (1981): 209–27.

Stagg, J. C. A., "The Problem of Klan Violence: the South Carolina Up-Country, 1868–1871," *Journal of American Studies* 8 (1974): 303–18.

Stine, Linda France, Lesley M. Drucker, Martha Zierden, and Christopher Judge, ed., *Carolina's Historical Landscapes: Archaeological Perspectives* (1997).

Strickland, John Scott, "'No More Mud Work': The Struggle for the Control of Labor and Production in Low Country South Carolina, 1863–1880," in Walter J. Fraser, Jr., and Winfred B. Moore, Jr., ed., *The Southern Enigma: Essays on Race, Class, and Folk Culture* (1983): 43–62.

Sweat, Edward F., "The Union Leagues and the South Carolina Election of 1870," *Journal of Negro History* 61 (1976): 200–14.

Takaki, Ronald, "The Movement to Reopen the African Slave Trade in South Carolina," *South Carolina Historical Magazine* 66 (1965): 38–54.

Tindall, George B., "The Campaign for the Disfranchisement of Negroes in South Carolina," *Journal of Southern History* 15 (1949): 212–34.

———— "The Liberian Exodus of 1878," *South Carolina Historical Magazine* 53 (1952): 133–45.

———— "The Question of Race in the South Carolina Constitutional Convention of 1895," *Journal of Negro History* 37 (1952): 277–303.

———— *South Carolina Negroes, 1877–1900* (1952).

Trinkley, Michael, ed., *Indian and Freedmen Occupation at the Fish Haul Site (38BU805), Beaufort County, South Carolina* (1986).

Turner, Lorenzo D., *Africanisms in the Gullah Dialect* (1949).

Tyson, George F., Jr., "The Carolina Black Corps: Legacy of the Revolution (1783–1798)," *Revista Interamericana [Puerto Rico]* 5 (1975–76): 648–64.

Vernon, Amelia Wallace, *African Americans at Mars Bluff, South Carolina* (1995).

Weir, Robert M., "The South Carolinian as Extremist," *South Atlantic Quarterly* 74 (1975): 86–103.

Williams, Lou F., "The South Carolina Ku Klux Klan Trials and Enforcement of Federal Rights, 1871–1872," *Civil War History* 39 (1993): 47–66.

Windley, Lathan Algerna, *A Profile of Runaway Slaves in Virginia and South Carolina from 1730 through 1787* (1995).

Wood, Peter H., *Black Majority: Negroes in Colonial South Carolina from 1670 through the Stono Rebellion* (1974).

———— "'Taking Care of Business' in Revolutionary South Carolina: Republicanism and the Slave Society," in Jeffery J. Crow, and Larry E. Tise, ed., *The Southern Experience in the American Revolution* (1978): 268–93.

Woofter, T. J., Jr., *Black Yeomanry: Life on St. Helena Island* (1930).

Young, Jeffrey Robert, *Domesticating Slavery: The Master Class in Georgia and South Carolina, 1670–1837* (1999).

26.2.38 South Dakota

Bernson, Sarah L., and Robert J. Eggers, "Black People in South Dakota History," *South Dakota History* 7 (1977): 241–70.

Buecker, Thomas R., "Confrontation at Sturgis: An Episode in Civil-Military Race Relations, 1885," *South Dakota History* 14 (1984): 238–61.

Gatewood, Willard B., Jr., "Kate D. Chapman Reports on 'The Yankton Colored People,' 1889," *South Dakota History* 7 (1976): 28–35.

26.2.39 Tennessee

Alexander, Thomas Benjamin, *Political Reconstruction in Tennessee* (1950).

Aptheker, Bettina, "The Suppression of Free Speech: Ida B. Wells and the Memphis Lynching, 1892," *San Jose Studies* 3 (1977): 34–40.

Arroyo, Elizabeth Fortson, "Poor White, Slaves, and Free Blacks in Tennessee, 1796–1861," *Tennessee Historical Quarterly* 55 (1996): 56–65.

Ashdown, Paul G., "Samuel Ringgold: A Missionary in the Tennessee Valley, 1860–1911," *Tennessee Historical Quarterly* 38 (1979): 204–13.

Baker, Steve, "Free Blacks in Antebellum Madison County," *Tennessee Historical Quarterly* 52 (1993): 56–63.

Beeler, Dorothy, "Race Riot in Columbia, Tennessee: February 25–27, 1946," *Tennessee Historical Quarterly* 39 (1980): 49–61.

Beifuss, Joan Turner, *At the River I Stand: Memphis, the 1968 Strike, and Martin Luther King* (1985).

Biles, Roger, *Memphis in the Great Depression* (1986).

Boutelle, Paul, George Novak, Clifton DeBerry, and Joseph Hansen, *Murder in Memphis: Martin Luther King and the Future of the Black Liberation Struggle* (1968).

Bryan, Charles F., Jr., and Jo Vita Wells, "Morristown College: Education for Blacks in the Southern Highlands," *East Tennessee Historical Society's Publications* 52–53 (1980–81): 61–77.

Burnside, Jacqueline, "'A Delicate and Difficult Duty': Interracial Education at Maryville College, Tennessee, 1868–1901," *American Presbyterians* 72 (1994): 229–40.

Cansler, Charles W., *Three Generations: The Story of a Colored Family of Eastern Tennessee* (1939).

Carriere, Marius, Jr., "Blacks in Pre-Civil War Memphis," *Tennessee Historical Quarterly* 48 (1989): 3–14.

Cartwright, Joseph H., "Black Legislators in Tennessee in the 1880s: A Case Study in Black Political Leadership," *Tennessee Historical Quarterly* 32 (1973): 265–84.

———— *The Triumph of Jim Crow: Tennessee Race Relations in the 1880s* (1976).

Cimprich, John, "The Beginning of the Black Suffrage Movement in Tennessee, 1864–65," *Journal of Negro History* 65 (1980): 185–95.

———— "Military Governor Johnson and Tennessee Blacks, 1862–65," *Tennessee Historical Quarterly* 39 (1980): 459–70.

———— *Slavery's End in Tennessee, 1861–1865* (1985).

Corlew, Robert E., "Some Aspects of Slavery in Dickson County," *Tennessee Historical Quarterly* 10 (1951): 224–48.

Daniel, Pete, "The Tennessee Convict War," *Tennessee Historical Quarterly* 34 (1975): 273–92.

Davis, John P., "The Plight of the Negro in the Tennessee Valley," *Crisis* 42 (1935): 294–95, 314–15.

Doyle, Don Harrison, *Nashville in the New South, 1880–1930* (1985).

Du Bois, William Edward Burghardt, "Black Banks and White in Memphis," *Crisis* 35 (1928): 154, 173–4.

Dunn, Larry W., "Knoxville Negro Voting and the Roosevelt Revolution, 1928–1936," *Eastern Tennessee Historical Society Publications* 43 (1971): 71–93.

Edwards, Gary T., "'Negroes . . . and All other Animals': Slaves and Masters in Antebellum Madison County," *Tennessee Historical Quarterly* 57 (1998): 24–35.

Ellis, John H., "Disease and the Destiny of a City: The 1878 Yellow Fever Epidemic in Memphis," *West Tennessee Historical Society Papers* 28 (1974): 75–89.

England, J. Merton, "The Free Negro in Antebellum Tennessee," *Journal of Southern History* 9 (1943): 37–58.

Fisk University, Department of Social Science, *Social Study of Negro Families in the Area Selected for the Nashville Negro Federal Housing Project* (1934).

Fleming, Cynthia G., "The Plight of Black Educators in Post-War Tennessee, 1865–1920," *Journal of Negro History* 64 (1979): 355–64.

———— "White Lunch Counters and Black Consciousness: The Story of the Knoxville Sit-Ins," *Tennessee Historical Quarterly* 49 (1990): 40–52.

Folmsbee, Stanley J., Robert E. Corlew, and Enoch. L. Mitchell, *History of Tennessee* (4 vols., 1960).

Fraser, Walter J., Jr., "Black Reconstructionists in Tennessee," *Tennessee Historical Quarterly* 34 (1975): 362–82.

Fuller, Thomas O., *History of Negro Baptists of Tennessee* (1936).

Gaither, Gerald H., "The Negro Alliance Movement in Tennessee, 1888–1891," *West Tennessee Historical Society Papers* 27 (1973): 50–62.

Garrow, David, *The FBI and Martin Luther King, Jr.: From "Solo" to Memphis* (1981).

Goings, Kenneth W., and Gerald L. Smith, "'Duty of the Hour': African-American Communities in Memphis, Tennessee, 1862–1923," *Tennessee Historical Quarterly* 55 (1996): 130–43.

———— "'Unhidden' Transcripts: Memphis and African American Agency, 1862–1920," *Journal of Urban History* 21 (1995): 372–94.

Gore, George William, Jr., *In-Service Professional Improvement of Negro Public School Teachers in Tennessee* (1940).

Hamilton, G. P., *The Bright Side of Memphis* (1908).

Hardwick, Kevin R., "'Your Old Father Abraham is Dead and Damned': Blacks Soldiers and the Memphis Race Riot of 1866," *Journal of Social History* 27 (1993): 109–28.

Harrison, Lowell Hayes, "Recollections of Some Tennessee Slaves," *Tennessee Historical Quarterly* 33 (1974): 175–90.

Hepler, Richard W., "'The World Do Marvel': Health Care for Knoxville's Black Community, 1865–1940," *Journal of East Tennessee History* 63 (1991): 51–71.

Honey, Michael, *Southern Labor and Black Civil Rights: Organizing Memphis Workers* (1993).

Howington, Arthur F., *What Sayeth the Law: The Treatment of Slaves and Free Blacks in the State and Local Courts of Tennessee* (1986).

Imes, William Lloyd, "The Legal Status of Free Negroes and Slaves in Tennessee," *Journal of Negro History* 4 (1919): 254–72.

Jones, James B., Jr., "'If We Are Citizens by the Law, Let Us Enjoy the Fruits of This Privilege': African-American Political Struggles in a Tennessee Mountain City, 1869–1912," *West Tennessee Historical Society Papers* 49 (1995): 87–100.

Jordan, Weymouth T., "The Freedmen's Bureau in Tennessee," *East Tennessee Historical Society's Publications* 11 (1939): 47–61.

Kaplowitz, Craig Allan, "A Breath of Fresh Air: Segregation, Parks, and Progressivism in Nashville, Tennessee, 1900–1920," *Tennessee Historical Quarterly* 57 (1998): 132–49.

Kenzer, Robert C., "Black Businessmen in Post-Civil War Tennessee," *Journal of East Tennessee History* 66 (1994): 59–80.

Kornell, Gary L., "Reconstruction in Nashville, 1867–1869," *Tennessee Historical Quarterly* 30 (1971): 277–87.

Kyriakoudes, Louis M., "Southern Black Rural-Urban Migration in the Era of the Great Migration: Nashville and Middle Tennessee, 1890–1930," *Agricultural History* 72 (1998): 341–51.

Lamon, Lester C., *Black Tennesseans, 1900–1930* (1977).

———— *Blacks in Tennessee, 1791–1970* (1981).

———— "The Tennessee Agricultural and Industrial Normal School: Public Education for Black Tennesseans," *Tennessee Historical Quarterly* 32 (1973): 42–58.

Lewis, Ronald L., "Race and the United Mine Workers' Union in Tennessee: Selected Letters of William R. Riley, 1892–1895," *Tennessee Historical Quarterly* 36 (1977): 524–36.

Lornell, Kip, *'Happy in the Service of the Lord': African-American Sacred Vocal Harmony Quartets in Memphis* (1995).

Lovett, Bobby L., *The African-American History of Nashville, Tennessee, 1780–1930: Elites and Dilemmas* (1999).

———— "Memphis Riots: White Reactions to Blacks in Memphis, May 1865-July 1866," *Tennessee Historical Quarterly* 38 (1979): 9–33.

———— "The Negro's Civil War in Tennessee, 1861–1865," *Journal of Negro History* 61 (1976): 36–50.

———— "The West Tennessee Colored Troops in Civil War Combat," *West Tennessee Historical Society Papers* 34 (1980): 53–70.

Maslowski, Peter, *Treason Must Be Made Odious: Military Occupation and Wartime Reconstruction in Nashville, Tennessee, 1862–1865* (1978).

McGehee, C. Stuart, "E. O. Tade, Freedmen's Education, and the Failure of Reconstruction in Tennessee," *Tennessee Historical Quarterly* 43 (1984): 376–89.

McKenzie, Robert Tracy, "Freedmen and the Soil in the Upper South: The Reorganization of Tennessee Agriculture, 1865–1880," *Journal of Southern History* 59 (1993): 63–84.

———— "Postbellum Tenancy in Fayette County, Tennessee: Its Implications for Economic Development and Persistent Black Poverty," *Agricultural History* 61 (1987): 16–33.

Meier, August, and Elliott M. Rudwick, "Negro Boycotts of Jim Crow Streetcars in Tennessee," *American Quarterly* 21 (1969): 755–63.

Moeser, John V., and Christopher Silver, "Race, Social Stratification, and Politics: The Case of Atlanta, Memphis, and Richmond," *Virginia Magazine of History and Biography* 102 (1994): 519–50.

Mooney, Chase Curran, "The Question of Slavery and the Free Negro in the Tennessee Constitutional Convention of 1834," *Journal of Southern History* 12 (1946): 487–509.

———— *Slavery in Tennessee* (1957).

———— "Some Institutional and Statistical Aspects of Slavery in Tennessee," *Tennessee Historical Quarterly* 1 (1942): 195–228.

Morgan, Gordon D., "Fisk University and the Intellectual Origins of the Harlem Renaissance," *Western Journal of Black Studies* 21 (1997): 214–18.

Olsson, Bengt, *Memphis Blues and Jug Bands* (1970).

Palmer, Robert, *A Tale of Two Cities: Memphis Rock and New Orleans Roll* (1979).

Parker, Russell D., "The Black Community in a Company Town: Alcoa, Tennessee, 1919–1939," *Tennessee Historical Quarterly* 37 (1978): 203–21.

Phillips, Paul D., "Education of Blacks in Tennessee during Reconstruction, 1865–1870," *Tennessee Historical Quarterly* 46 (1987): 98–109.

Plank, David N., and Marcia E. Turner, "Contrasting Patterns in Black School Politics: Atlanta and Memphis, 1865–1985," *Journal of Negro Education* 60 (1991): 203–18.

Robinson, Armstead L., "Plans Dat Comed from God: Institution Building and the Emergence of Black Leadership in Reconstruction Memphis," in Orville Vernon Burton, and Robert C. McMath, Jr., ed., *Toward a New South?: Studies in Post-Civil War Southern Communities* (1982): 71–102.

Rollins, Richard, "Servants and Soldiers: Tennessee's Black Southerners in Gray," *Journal of Confederate History* 11 (1994): 75–93.

Rousey, Dennis C., "Yellow Fever and Black Policemen in Memphis: A Post-Reconstruction Anomaly," *Journal of Southern History* 51 (1985): 357–74.

Ryan, James G., "The Memphis Riot of 1866: Terror in a Black Community during Reconstruction," *Journal of Negro History* 62 (1977): 243–57.

Schweninger, Loren, "The Free-Slave Phenomenon: James P. Thomas and the Black Community in Antebellum Nashville," *Civil War History* 22 (1976): 293–307.

Scribner, Christopher MacGregor, "Nashville Offers Opportunity: The Nashville Globe and Business as a Means of Uplift, 1907–1913," *Tennessee Historical Quarterly* 54 (1995): 54–67.

Shannon, Samuel H., "Land-Grant College Education and Black Tennesseans: A Case Study in the Politics of Education," *History of Education Quarterly* 22 (1982): 139–57.

Shapiro, Karin A., *A New South Rebellion: The Battle Against Convict Labor in the Tennessee Coalfields, 1871–1896* (1998).

Sheldon, Randall G., "From Slave to Caste Society: Penal Changes in Tennessee, 1830–1915," *Tennessee Historical Quarterly* 38 (1979): 462–78.

Sobel, Mechal, "'They Can Never Both Prosper Together:' Black and White Baptists in Antebellum Nashville, Tennessee," *Tennessee Historical Quarterly* 38 (1979): 296–307.

Spinney, Robert G., *World War II in Nashville: Transformation of the Homefront* (1998).

Summerville, James, "The City and the Slum: 'Black Bottom' and the Development of South Nashville," *Tennessee Historical Quarterly* 40 (1981): 182–92.

Sumner, David E., "The Nashville Student Movement," *American History Illustrated* 23 (1988): 28–31.

Swint, Henry L., ed, "Reports from Educational Agents of the Freedmen's Bureau in Tennessee, 1865–1870," *Tennessee Historical Quarterly* 1 (1942): 51–80, 152–70.

Taylor, Alrutheus A., "Fisk University and the Nashville Community, 1866–1990," *Journal of Negro History* 39 (1954): 111–26.

————— *The Negro in Tennessee, 1865–1880* (1941).

TeSelle, Eugene, "The Nashville Institute and Roger Williams University: Benevolence, Paternalism, and Black Consciousness, 1867–1910," *Tennessee Historical Quarterly* 41 (1982): 360–79.

Tilly, Bette B., "The Spirit of Improvement: Reformism and Slavery in West Tennessee," *West Tennessee Historical Society Papers* (1974): 25–42.

Tucker, David M., "Black Pride and Negro Business in the 1920's: George Washington Lee of Memphis," *Business History Review* 43 (1969): 435–51.

————— "Black Politics in Memphis, 1865–1875," *West Tennessee Historical Society Papers* 26 (1972): 13–19.

————— *Black Pastors and Leaders: The Memphis Clergy, 1819–1972* (1975).

————— "Miss Ida B. Wells and the Memphis Lynching," *Phylon* 32 (1971): 112–22.

Walker, Melissa, "Home Extension Work among African American Farm Women in East Tennessee," *Agricultural History* 70 (1996): 487–502.

Waller, Altina L., "Community, Class and Race in the Memphis Riot of 1866," *Journal of Social History* 18 (1984): 233–46.

Walton, Hanes, Jr., "Another Force For Disfranchisement: Blacks and the Prohibitionists in Tennessee," *Journal of Human Relations* 18 (1970): 728–38.

Williams, Lee E., and Lee E. Williams, II, *Anatomy of Four Race Riots: Racial Conflict in Knoxville, Elaine (Arkansas), Tulsa, and Chicago, 1919–1921* (1972).

Wynn, Linda T., "Toward a Perfect Democracy: The Struggle of African Americans in Fayette County, Tennessee, to Fulfill the Unfulfilled Right of the Franchise," *Tennessee Historical Quarterly* 55 (1996): 202–23.

26.2.40 Texas

Addington, Wendell G., "Slave Insurrections in Texas," *Journal of Negro History* 35 (1950): 408–34.

Akalou, W. M., and Cary D. Wintz, "The Economic Impact of Residential Desegregation on Historically Black Neighborhoods in Houston, 1950–1990," *Essays in Economic and Business History* 13 (1995): 289–304.

Angel, William D., Jr., "Controlling Workers: The Galveston Dock Workers' Strike of 1920 and its Impact on Labor Relations in Texas," *East Texas Historical Journal* 23 (1985): 14–27.

Avillo, Philip J., Jr., "Phantom Radicals: Texas Republicans in Congress, 1870–1873," *Southwestern Historical Quarterly* 77 (1974): 431–44.

Baenziger, Ann P., "The Texas State Police during Reconstruction: A Reexamination," *Southwestern Historical Quarterly* 72 (1969): 470–91.

Baker, T. Lindsay, and Julie P. Baker, ed., *Till Freedom Cried Out: Memories of Texas Slave Life* (1997).

Barker, Eugene C., "The African Slave Trade in Texas," *Southwestern Historical Quarterly* 6 (1902): 145–58.

———— "The Influence of Slavery in the Colonization of Texas," *Southwestern Historical Quarterly* 28 (1924): 1–33.

Barr, Alwyn, "Black Legislators of Reconstruction Texas," *Civil War History* 32 (1986): 340–52.

———— "The Black Militia of the New South: Texas as a Case Study," *Journal of Negro History* 63 (1978): 209–19.

———— *Black Texans: A History of Negroes in Texas, 1528–1971* (1973).

———— "Occupational and Geographic Mobility in San Antonio, 1870–1900," *Social Science Quarterly* 51 (1970): 396–403.

———— "The Texas 'Black Uprising' Scare of 1883," *Phylon* 41 (1980): 179–86.

Botson, Michael, "No Gold Watch for Jim Crow's Retirement: The Abolition of Segregated Unionism at Houston's Hughes Tool Company," *Southwestern Historical Quarterly* 101 (1998): 497–521.

Brewer, John Mason, *Negro Legislators of Texas and Their Descendants: A History of the Negro in Texas Politics from Reconstruction to Disenfranchisement* (1935).

———— *The Word on the Brazos: Negro Preacher Tales from the Brazos Bottoms of Texas* (1953).

Brophy, William J., "Black Business Development in Texas Cities, 1900–1950," *Red River Valley Historical Review* 6 (1981): 42–55.

Campbell, Randolph B., "Carpetbagger Rule in Reconstruction Texas: An Enduring Myth," *Southwestern Historical Quarterly* 97 (1994): 587–96.

———— "The District Judges of Texas in 1866–1867: An Episode in the Failure of Presidential Reconstruction," *Southwestern Historical Quarterly* 93 (1990): 357–77.

———— *An Empire for Slavery: The Peculiar Institution in Texas, 1821–1865* (1989).

———— "Grass Roots Reconstruction: The Personnel of County Government in Texas, 1865–1876," *Journal of Southern History* 58 (1992): 99–116.

———— *Grass-Roots Reconstruction in Texas, 1865–1880* (1997).

———— "'Intermittent Slave Ownership: Texas as a Test Case'; James Oakes, 'A Response'; Randolph B. Campbell, 'A Rejoinder,'" *Journal of Southern History* 51 (1985): 15–30.

———— "Population Persistence and Social Change in Nineteenth-Century Texas: Harrison County, 1850–1880," *Journal of Southern History* 48 (1982): 185–204.

———— "Reconstruction in Nueces County, 1865–1876," *Houston Review* 16 (1994): 3–26.

———— "Slave Hiring in Texas," *American Historical Review* 93 (1988): 107–14.

Cantrell, Gregg, "'Dark Tactics': Black Politics in the 1887 Texas Prohibition Campaign," *Journal of American Studies* 25 (1991): 85–93.

———— "Racial Violence and Reconstruction Politics in Texas, 1867–1868," *Southwestern Historical Quarterly* 93 (1990): 333–55.

Cantrell, Gregg, and D. Scott Barton, "Texas Populists and the Failure of Biracial Politics," *Journal of Southern History* 55 (1989): 659–92.

Christian, Garna L., *Black Soldiers in Jim Crow Texas, 1899–1917* (1995).

———— "Rio Grande City: Prelude to the Brownsville Raid," *West Texas Historical Association Yearbook* 57 (1981): 118–32.

Cohen-Lack, Nancy, "A Struggle for Sovereignty: National Consolidation, Emancipation, and Free Labor in Texas, 1865," *Journal of Southern History* 58 (1992): 57–98.

Crouch, B. A., and L. J. Schultz, "Crisis in Color: Racial Separation in Texas during Reconstruction," *Civil War History* 16 (1970): 37–49.

Crouch, Barry A., "'All the Vile Passions': The Texas Black Code of 1866," *Southwestern Historical Quarterly* 97 (1993): 13–34.

———— "The Fetters of Justice: Black Texans and the Penitentiary during Reconstruction," *Prologue* 28 (1996): 183–93.

———— *The Freedmen's Bureau and Black Texans* (1992).

———— "Hesitant Recognition: Texas Black Politicians, 1865–1900," *East Texas Historical Journal* 31 (1993): 41–58.

———— "Self-Determination and Local Black Leaders in Texas," *Phylon* 39 (1978): 344–55.

———— "A Spirit of Lawlessness: White Violence, Texas Blacks, 1865–1868," *Journal of Social History* 18 (1984): 217–32.

———— "'Unmanacling' Texas Reconstruction: A Twenty-Year Perspective," *Southwestern Historical Quarterly* 93 (1990): 275–302.

Davis, William Riley, *The Development and Present Status of Negro Education in East Texas* (1934).

Elliott, Claude, "The Freedmen's Bureau in Texas," *Southwestern Historical Quarterly* 56 (1952): 1–24.

Ellis, L. Tuffley, "The Revolutionizing of the Texas Cotton Trade, 1865–1885," *Southwestern Historical Quarterly* 73 (1970): 478–508.

Engerrand, Steven W., "Black and Mulatto Mobility and Stability in Dallas, Texas, 1880–1910," *Phylon* 39 (1978): 203–15.

Foley, Neil, *The White Scourge: Mexicans, Blacks, and Poor Whites in Texas Cotton Culture* (1997).

Fornell, Earl W., "The Abduction of Free Negroes and Slaves in Texas," *Southwestern Historical Quarterly* 60 (1957): 369–80.

———— "Agitation in Texas for Reopening the Slave Trade," *Southwestern Historical Quarterly* 60 (1956): 245–59.

Glasrud, Bruce A., "Enforcing White Supremacy in Texas, 1900–1910," *Red River Valley Historical Review* 4 (1979): 65–74.

Goodwyn, Lawrence, "Populist Dreams and Negro Rights: East Texas As A Case Study," *American Historical Review* 76 (1971): 1435–56.

Haynes, Robert V., *A Night of Violence: The Houston Riot of 1917* (1976).

Heintze, Michael R., *Private Black Colleges in Texas, 1865–1954* (1985).

Hine, Darlene Clark, *Black Victory: The Rise and Fall of the White Primary in Texas* (1979).

———— "The Elusive Ballot: The Black Struggle against the Texas Democratic White Primary, 1932–1945," *Southwest Historical Quarterly* 81 (1978).

Hornsby, Alton, Jr., "The 'Colored Branch University' Issue in Texas—Prelude to *Sweatt vs. Painter,*" *Journal of Negro History* 6 (1976): 51–60.

———— "The Freedmen's Bureau Schools in Texas, 1865–1870," *Southwestern Historical Quarterly* 76 (1973): 397–417.

Hutchinson, Janis, "The Age-Sex Structure of the Slave Population in Harris County, Texas, 1850 and 1860," *American Journal of Physical Anthropology* 74 (1987): 231–38.

Kellar, William Henry, *Make Haste Slowly: Moderates, Conservatives, and School Desegregation in Houston* (1999).

Kerrigan, William T., "Race Expansion, and Slavery in Eagle Pass, Texas, 1852," *Southwestern Historical Quarterly* 101 (1998): 275–302.

Lowe, Richard, and Randolph Campbell, "Slave Property and the Distribution of Wealth in Texas, 1860," *Journal of American History* 63 (1976): 313–24.

Mackey, Thomas C., "Thelma Denton and Associates: Houston's Red Light Reservation and a Question of Jim Crow," *Houston Review* 14 (1992): 139–52.

Malone, Ann Patton, *Women on the Texas Frontier: A Cross-Cultural Perspective* (1983).

Marcello, Ronald E., "Reluctance versus Reality: The Desegregation of North Texas State College, 1954–1956," *Southwestern Historical Quarterly* 100 (1996): 153–86.

Marten, James, "Slaves and Rebels: The Peculiar Institution in Texas, 1861–1865," *East Texas Historical Journal* 28 (1991): 29–36.

———— *Texas Divided: Loyalty and Dissent in the Lone Star State, 1856–1874* (1990).

———— "'What is to Become of the Negro?' White Reactions to Emancipation in Texas," *Mid-America* 73 (1991): 115–33.

Moneyhon, Carl H., "Public Education and Texas Reconstruction Politics, 1871–1874," *Southwestern Historical Quarterly* 92 (1989): 393–416.

—— *Republicanism in Reconstruction Texas* (1980).

Muir, Andrew Forest, "The Free Negro in Harris County, Texas," *Southwestern Historical Quarterly* 46 (1943): 214–38.

—— "The Free Negro in Jefferson and Orange Counties, Texas," *Journal of Negro History* 35.? (1950): 183–206.

Mullen, Patrick B., "The Prism of Race: Two Texas Performers," *Southern Folklore* 54 (1997): 13–25.

Nash, A. E. Keir, "The Texas Supreme Court and Trial Rights of Blacks, 1845–1860," *Journal of American History* 58 (1971): 622–42.

Neal, Diane, and Thomas W. Kremm, "'What Shall We Do with the Negro?': The Freedmen's Bureau in Texas," *East Texas Historical Journal* 27 (1989): 23–34.

Nieman, Donald G., "African-Americans and the Meaning of Freedom: Washington County, Texas as a Study, 1865–1886," *Chicago-Kent Law Review* 70 (1994): 541–82.

—— "Black Political Power and Criminal Justice: Washington County, Texas, 1868–1884," *Journal of Southern History* 3 (1955): 391–420.

Pitre, Merline, *In Struggle Against Jim Crow: Lulu B. White and the NAACP, 1900–1957* (1999).

—— *Through Many Dangers, Toils, and Snares: The Black Leadership of Texas, 1868–1900* (1985).

Porter, David, "The Battle of the Texas Giants: Halton Summers, Sam Rayburn, and the Logan-Walter Bill of 1939," *Texana* 12 (1974): 349–61.

Porter, Kenneth W., "Negroes and Indians on the Texas Frontier, 1834–1874," *Southwestern Historical Quarterly* 53 (1949): 151–63.

Reese, James V., "The Early History of Labor Organizations in Texas, 1838–1876," *Southwestern Historical Quarterly* 72 (1968): 1–20.

Reich, Steven A., "Soldiers of Democracy: Black Texans and the Fight for Citizenship, 1917–1921," *Journal of American History* 82 (1996): 1478–504.

Rice, Lawrence D., *The Negro in Texas, 1874–1900* (1971).

Richter, William Lee, *The Army in Texas during Reconstruction, 1865–1870* (1987).

—— "'The Revolver Rules the Day!': Colonel DeWitt C. Brown and the Freedmen's Bureau in Paris, Texas, 1867–1868," *Southwestern Historical Quarterly* 93 (1990): 303–32.

—— "'This Blood-Thirsty Hole': The Freedmen's Bureau Agency at Clarksville, Texas, 1867–1868," *Civil War History* 38 (1992): 51–77.

Schoen, Harold, "The Free Negro in the Republic of Texas," *Southwestern Historical Quarterly* 39–41 (6 parts, 1936): 26–308.

Schuler, Edgar A., "The Houston Race Riot, 1917," *Journal of Negro History* 29 (1944): 300–38.

Sharpless, Rebecca, *Fertile Ground, Narrow Choices: Women on Texas Cotton Farms, 1900–1940* (1999).

Silverthorne, Elizabeth, *Plantation Life in Texas* (1986).

Smallwood, James M., "Black Freedmen after Emancipation: The Texan Experience," *Prologue* 27 (1995): 303–17.

—— "Blacks in Antebellum Texas, A Reappraisal," *Red River Valley Historical Review* 2 (1975): 443–65.

—— "Perpetuation of Caste: Black Agricultural Workers in Reconstruction Texas," *Mid-America* 61 (1979): 5–23.

—— *Time of Hope, Time of Despair: Black Texans during Reconstruction* (1981).

Sorelle, James M., "'An de Po Cullud Man is in the Wuss Fix ux Awl': Black Occupational Status in Houston, Texas, 1920–40," *Houston Review* 1 (1979): 15–26.

Strong, Donald S., "The Rise of Negro Voting in Texas," *American Political Science Review* 42 (1948): 518–22.

Tyler, Ronnie C., and Lawrence R. Murphy, ed., *The Slave Narratives of Texas* (1997).

Winegarten, Ruthe, *Black Texas Women: 150 Years of Trial and Triumph* (1995).

Woolfolk, George Ruble, *The Free Negro in Texas, 1800–1860: A Study in Cultural Compromise* (1976).

26.2.41　Utah

Coleman, Ronald G., *A History of Blacks in Utah, 1825–1910* (1980).

Davis, Lenwood G., *Blacks in the State of Utah: A Working Bibliography* (1974).

26.2.42   Vermont

Guyette, Elise A., "The Working Lives of African Vermonters in Census and Literature, 1790–1870," *Vermont History* 61 (1993): 69–84.

Roth, Randolph A., "The First Radical Abolitionists: The Reverend James Milligan and the Reformed Presbyterians of Vermont," *New England Quarterly* 55 (1982): 540–63.

True, Marshall M., "Slavery in Burlington? An Historical Note," *Vermont History* 50 (1982): 227–31.

Wrinn, Stephen M., *Civil Rights in the Whitest State: Vermont's Perceptions of Civil Rigbts, 1945–1968* (1998).

26.2.43   Virginia

Anesko, Michael, "So Discreet a Zeal: Slavery and the Anglican Church in Virginia 1680–1730," *Virginia Magazine of History and Biography* 93 (1985): 247–78.

Bailey, Raymond C., "Racial Discrimination Against Free Blacks in Antebellum Virginia: The Case of Harry Jackson," *West Virginia History* 39 (1978): 181–86.

Bailor, Keith M., "John Taylor of Caroline: Continuity, Change, and Discontinuity in Virginia's Sentiments toward Slavery, 1790–1820," *Virginia Magazine of History and Biography* 75 (1967): 290–304.

Ballagh, James Curtis, *A History of Slavery in Virginia* (1902).

Beeman, Richard R., *The Evolution of the Southern Backcountry: A Case Study of Lundenburg Country, Virginia, 1746–1832* (1984).

Bell, Mary Campbell, "Some Virginia Bills of Emancipation," *Journal of the Afro-American Historical and Genealogical Society* 5 (1984): 23–26.

Bernhard, Virginia, "Bermuda and Virginia in the Seventeenth Century: A Comparative View," *Journal of Social History* 19 (1985): 57–70.

Billings, Warren M., "The Cases of Fernando and Elizabeth Key: A Note on the Status of Blacks in Seventeenth-Century Virginia," *William and Mary Quarterly* 30 (1973): 467–74.

———— "The Law of Servants and Slaves in Seventeenth-Century Virginia," *Virginia Magazine of History and Biography* 99 (1991): 45–62.

Blair, William A., "Justice versus Law and Order: The Battles over the Reconstruction of Virginia's Minor Judiciary, 1865–1870," *Virginia Magazine of History and Biography* 103 (1995): 157–80.

Bogger, Tommy L., *Free Blacks in Norfolk, Virginia, 1790–1860: The Darker Side of Freedom* (1997).

Bonekemper, Edward H., III, "Negro Ownership of Real Property in Hampton and Elizabeth City County, Virginia, 1860–1870," *Journal of Negro History* 55 (1970): 165–81.

Bradford, Sydney, "The Negro Ironworker in Antebellum Virginia," *Journal of Southern History* 25 (1959): 194–206.

Breen, T. H., "A Changing Labor Force and Race Relations in Virginia 1660–1710," *Journal of Social History* 7 (1973): 3–25.

———— *'Myne Owne Ground': Race and Freedom on Virginia's Eastern Shore, 1640–1676* (1980).

Breen, T. H., and Stephen Innes, "Seventeenth-Century Virginia's Forgotten Yeomen: The Free Blacks," *Virginia Cavalcade* 32 (1982): 10–19.

Brewer, James H., *The Confederate Negro: Virginia' s Craftsmen and Military Laborers, 1861–1865* (1965).

———— "Negro Property Holders in Seventeenth-Century Virginia," *William and Mary Quarterly* 12 (1955): 575–80.

Brown, Elsa Barkley, and Gregg D. Kimball, "Mapping the Terrain of Black Richmond," *Journal of Urban History* 21 (1995): 296–346.

Bruce, Kathleen, "Slave Labor in the Virginia Iron Industry," *William and Mary Quarterly* 7 (1927): 21–31.

———— *Virginia Iron Manufacture in the Slave Era* (1930).

Bruce, Philip A., *The Plantation Negro as a Freeman: Observations on His Character, Condition, and Prospects in Virginia* (1889).

Brundage, W. Fitzhugh, *Lynching in the New South: Georgia and Virginia, 1880–1930* (1993).

Chesson, Michael Bedout, *Richmond after the War, 1865–1890* (1981).

Chester, Thomas Morris, *Thomas Morris Chester: Black Civil War Correspondent: His Dispatches from the Virginia Front*, ed. R. J. M. Blackett (1989).

Craig, John M., "Community Cooperation in Ruthville, Virginia, 1900–1930," *Phylon* 48 (1987): 132–40.

Daniel, W. Harrison, "Virginia Baptists and the Negro, 1865–1902," *Virginia Magazine of History and Biography* 76 (1968): 34–63.

——— "Virginia Baptists and the Negro in the Antebellum Era," *Journal of Negro History* 56 (1971): 1–16.

Davis, Mary Kemp, *Nat Turner Before the Bar of Judgment: Fictional Treatments of the Southampton Slave Insurrection* (1999).

Deal, Joseph Douglas, *Race and Class in Colonial Virginia: Indians, Englishmen, and Africans on the Eastern Shore during the Seventeenth Century* (1993).

Deetz, James, *Flowerdew Hundred: The Archaeology of a Virginia Plantation, 1619–1864* (1993).

Dew, Charles B., *Bond of Iron: Master and Slave at Buffalo Forge* (1994).

Drewry, William Sidney, *Slave Insurrections in Virginia (1820–1865)* (1900).

Dunn, Richard S., "A Tale of Two Plantations: Slave Life at Mesopotamia in Jamaica and Mount Airy in Virginia, 1799 to 1828," *William and Mary Quarterly* 24 (1977): 32–65.

Earnest, Joseph B., Jr., *The Religious Development of the Negro in Virginia* (1914).

Egerton, Douglas R., *Gabriel's Rebellion: The Virginia Slave Conspiracies of 1800 and 1802* (1993).

——— "An Upright Man: Gabriel's Virginia and the Path to Slave Rebellion," *Virginia Cavalcade* 43 (1993): 52–69.

Engs, Robert F., *Freedom's First Generation: Black Hampton, Virginia, 1861–1890* (1979).

Essig, James D., "A Very Wintry Season: Virginia Baptists and Slavery, 1785–1797," *Virginia Magazine of History and Biography* 88 (1980): 170–85.

Fen, Sing-Nan, "Notes on the Education of Negroes at Norfolk and Portsmouth, Virginia, during the Civil War," *Phylon* 28 (1967): 197–207.

Fink, Leon, "'Irrespective of Party, Color, or Social Standing': The Knights of Labor and Opposition Politics in Richmond, Virginia," *Labor History* 19 (1978): 325–49.

Flowers, J. Clayton, "Richard Clayton of Surrey County, Virginia, and His Descendants," *Journal of the Afro-American Historical and Genealogical Society* 6 (1985): 176–83.

Forsythe, Harold S., "'But My Friends Are Poor': Ross Hamilton and Freedpeople's Politics in Macklenburg County, Virginia, 1869–1901," *Virginia Magazine of History and Biography* 105 (1997): 409–38.

Freehling, Alison Goodyear, *Drift toward Dissolution: The Virginia Slavery Debate of 1831–1832* (1982).

Frey, Sylvia R., "Between Slavery and Freedom: Virginia Blacks in the American Revolution," *Journal of Southern History* 49 (1983): 375–98.

Gavins, Raymond, "Urbanization and Segregation: Black Leadership Patterns in Richmond, Virginia, 1900–1920," *South Atlantic Quarterly* 79 (1980): 257–73.

Green, Rodney D., "Black Tobacco Factory Workers and Social Conflict in Antebellum Richmond: Were Slavery and Urban Industry Really Compatible?" *Slavery and Abolition* 8 (1987): 183–203.

Grundman, Adolph H., "Northern Baptists and the Founding of Virginia Union University: The Perils of Paternalism," *Journal of Negro History* 63 (1978): 26–41.

Guild, June Purcell, *Black Laws of Virginia: A Summary of the Legislative Acts of Virginia Concerning Negroes from Earliest Times to the Present* (1936).

Gunderson, Joan R., "The Double Bonds of Race and Sex: Black and White Women in a Colonial Virginia Parrish," *Journal of Southern History* 52 (1986): 351–72.

Hampton Institute, *Twenty-two Years' Work of Hampton Normal and Agricultural Institute at Hampton, Virginia: Records of Negro and Indian Graduates and Ex-students* (1893).

Heath, Barbara J., *Hidden Lives: The Archaeology of Slave Life at Thomas Jefferson's Poplar Forest* (1999).

Heinegg, Paul, *Free African Americans of North Carolina and Virginia: Including the Family Histories of More Than 80% of Those Counted as "All Other Free Persons" in the 1790 and 1800 Census* (3d ed., 1997).

Henderson, William D., *The Unredeemed City: Reconstruction in Petersburg, Virginia: 1865–1874* (1977).

Hickey, Jo Ann S., and Anthony Andrew Hickey, "Black Farmers in Virginia, 1930–1978: An Analysis of the Social Organization of Agriculture," *Rural Sociology* 52 (1987): 75–88.

Hickin, Patricia, "Situation Ethics and Anti-Slavery Attitudes in the Virginia Churches," in John B. Boles, ed., *America: The Middle Period: Essays in Honor of Bernard Mayo* (1973): 188–215.

Higginbotham, A. Leon, Jr., and Greer C. Bosworth, "'Rather than the Free': Free Blacks in Colonial and Antebellum Virginia," *Harvard Civil Rights-Civil Liberties Law Review* 26 (1991): 17–66.

Holland, C. G., "The Slave Population on the Plantation of John C. Cohoon, Jr., Nansemond County, Virginia, 1811–1863: Selected Demographic Characteristics," *Virginia Magazine of History and Biography* 80 (1972): 333–40.

Holt, Wythe W., Jr., "The Virginia Constitutional Convention of 1901–1902: A Reform Movement Which Lacked Substance," *Virginia Magazine of History and Biography* 76 (1968): 67–102.

Honey, Michael, "One View of Black Life in the South during the 'Nadir': The Richmond Planet, 1885–1900," *Potomac Review* 21 (1981): 28–38.

Hucles, Michael, "Many Voices, Similar Concerns: Traditional Methods of African-American Political Activity in Norfolk, Virginia, 1865–1875," *Virginia Magazine of History and Biography* 100 (1992): 543–66.

Hughes, Sarah S., "Slaves for Hire: The Allocations of Black Labor in Elizabeth City County, Virginia, 1782–1810," *William and Mary Quarterly* 35 (1978): 260–86.

Ingersoll, Thomas N., "'Releese Us out of This Cruell Bondegg': An Appeal from Virginia in 1723," *William and Mary Quarterly* 51 (1994): 777–82.

Irons, Charles F., "And All These Things Shall Be Added unto You: The First African Baptist Church, Richmond, 1841–1865," *Virginia Cavalcade* 47 (1998): 26–35.

Irwin, Marjorie F., *The Negro in Charlottesville and Albermarle County: An Explanatory Study* (1929).

Jackson, Luther Porter, "The Early Strivings of the Negro in Virginia," *Journal of Negro History* 25 (1940): 25–34.

———— "Free Negroes of Petersburg, Virginia," *Journal of Negro History* 12 (1927): 365–88.

———— *Free Negro Labor and Property Holding in Virginia, 1830–1860* (1942).

———— "Manumission in Certain Virginia Cities," *Journal of Negro History* 15 (1930): 278–314.

———— *Negro Office-Holders in Virginia, 1865–1895* (1945).

———— "Religious Development of the Negro in Virginia from 1760–1860," *Journal of Negro History* 16 (1931): 168–239.

———— "The Virginia Free Negro Farmer and Property Owner, 1830–1860," *Journal of Negro History* 24 (1939): 390–439.

———— *Virginia Negro Soldiers and Seamen in the Revolutionary War* (1944).

Johnson, Whittington B., "Free Blacks in Antebellum Savannah: An Economic Profile," *Richmond County History* 64 (1980): 418–31.

Johnston, James Hugo, *Race Relations in Virginia and Miscegenation in the South, 1776–1860* (1970).

Jordan, Ervin L., Jr., *Black Confederates and Afro-Yankees in Civil War Virginia* (1995).

Kelso, William M., *Kingsmill Plantations, 1619–1800: Archaeology of Country Life in Colonial Virginia* (1984).

Kimball, Gregg D., "Expanding the Notion: The African American Presence in *Virginia Cavalcade,* 1951–1996," *Virginia Cavalcade* 46 (1996): 82–94.

———— "The Working People of Richmond: Life and Labor in an Industrial City, 1865–1920," *Labor's Heritage* 3 (1991): 42–65.

Klein, Herbert S., "The Negro and the Church of England in Virginia," in Richard D. Brown, ed., *Slavery in American Society* (1969): 32–37.

———— *Slavery in the Americas: A Comparative Study of Virginia and Cuba* (1967).

———— "Slaves and Shipping in Eighteenth-Century Virginia," *Journal of Interdisciplinary History* 5 (1975): 383–412.

Kulikoff, Allan, "The Origins of Afro-American Society in Tidewater Maryland and Virginia: 1700 to 1790," *William and Mary Quarterly* 35 (1978): 226–59.

Langhorne, Orra, *Southern Sketches From Virginia, 1881–1901* (1964).

Lassiter, Matthew D., and Andrew B. Lewis, ed., *The Moderates' Dilemma: Massive Resistance to School Desegregation in Virginia* (1998).

Leaming, Hugo Prosper, *Hidden Americans: Maroons of Virginia and the Carolinas* (1995).

Lebsock, Suzanne, "Free Black Women and the Question of Matriarchy: Petersburg, Virginia, 1784–1820," *Feminist Studies* 8 (1982): 271–92.

———— *The Free Women of Petersburg: Status and Culture in a Southern Town, 1784–1860* (1984).

Lewis, Earl, "Afro-American Adaptive Strategies: The Visiting Habits of Kith and Kin among Black Norfolkians during the First Great Migration," *Journal of Family History* 12 (1987): 407–20.

———— "Expectations, Economic Opportunities, and Life in the Industrial Age: Black Migration to Norfolk, Virginia, 1910–1945," in Joe W. Trotter, ed., *The Great Migration in Historical Perspective: New Dimensions of Race, Class, and Gender* (1991): 22–45.

———— *In Their Own Interests: Race, Class, and Power in Twentieth-Century Norfolk, Virginia* (1991).

Lewis, Earl, and David Organ, "Housing, Race and Class: The Government's Creation of Truxton, Virginia, A Model Black War Worker's Town," in Jerry Lembcke and Ray Hutchinson, ed., *Race, Class, and Urban Change* (1989): 53–78.

Lewis, Ronald L., *Coal, Iron, and Slaves: Industrial Slavery in Maryland and Virginia, 1715–1865* (1979).

———— "The Use and Extent of Slave Labor in the Virginia Iron Industry: The Antebellum Era," *West Virginia History* 38 (1977): 141–56.

Lowe, Richard L., "Another Look at Reconstruction in Virginia," *Civil War History* 32 (1986): 56–76.

———— "Local Black Leaders during Reconstruction in Virginia," *Virginia Magazine of History and Biography* 103 (1995): 181–206.

———— "To Speak and Act as Freemen: The Emergence of Black Republicans in Postbellum Virginia," *Virginia Cavalcade* 41 (1991): 52–63.

Madden, T. O., Jr., and Ann L. Miller, *We Were Always Free: The Maddens of Culpeper County Virginia; A 200-year Family History* (1992).

Martin, Robert E., *Negro Disenfranchisement in Virginia* (1938).

McColley, Robert, *Slavery and Jeffersonian Virginia* (1964).

McGraw, Marie Tyler, "Richmond Free Blacks and African Colonization, 1816–1832," *Journal of American Studies* 21 (1987): 207–224.

Meaders, Daniel, ed., *Advertisements for Runaway Slaves in Virginia, 1801–1820* (1997).

Medford, Edna Greene, "'I Was Always a Union Man': The Dilemma of Free Blacks in Confederate Virginia," *Slavery and Abolition* 15 (1994): 1–16.

———— "Land and Labor: The Quest for Black Economic Independence on Virginia's Lower Peninsula, 1865–1880," *Virginia Magazine of History and Biography* 100 (1992): 567–82.

Moeser, John V., and Christopher Silver, "Race, Social Stratification, and Politics: The Case of Atlanta, Memphis, and Richmond," *Virginia Magazine of History and Biography* 102 (1994): 519–50.

Moore, Jacqueline M., *Leading the Race: The Transformation of the Black Elite in the Nation's Capital, 1880–1920* (1999).

Moore, James T., "Black Militancy in Readjuster Virginia, 1879–1883," *Journal of Southern History* 41 (1975): 167–86.

Moore, Louis, "The Elusive Center: Virginia Politics and the General Assembly, 1869–1871," *Virginia Magazine of History and Biography* 103 (1995): 207–36.

Morgan, Edmund Sears, *American Slavery, American Freedom: The Ordeal of Colonial Virginia* (1975).

Morgan, Gwenda, "Law and Social Change in Colonial Virginia: The Role of the Grand Jury in Richmond County, 1692–1776," *Virginia Magazine of History and Biography* 95 (1987): 453–80.

Morgan, Lynda J., *Emancipation in Virginia's Tobacco Belt, 1850–1870* (1992).

Morgan, Philip D., ed., *"Don't Grieve after Me": The Black Experience in Virginia, 1619–1986* (1986).

———— *Slave Counterpoint: Black Culture in the Eighteenth-Century Chesapeake and Lowcountry* (1998).

Morgan, Philip D., and Michael L. Nicholls, "Slaves in Piedmont Viriginia, 1720–1790," *William and Mary Quarterly* 46 (1989): 211–51.

Morton, Richard L., "'Contrabands' and Quakers in the Virginia Peninsula, 1862–1869," *Virginia Magazine of History and Biography* 61 (1953): 419–29.

Morton, Richard Lee, *The Negro in Virginia Politics, 1865–1902* (1919).

Mugleston, William F., ed., "The Freedmen's Bureau and Reconstruction in Virginia: The Diary of Marcus Sterling Hopkins, a Union Officer," *Virginia Magazine of History and Biography* 86 (1978): 45–102.

Mullin, Gerald W., *Flight and Rebellion: Slave Resistance in Eighteenth-Century Virginia* (1972).

O'Brien, John Thomas, Jr., *From Bondage to Citizenship: The Richmond Black Community, 1865–1867* (1990).

———— "Factory, Church, and Community: Blacks in Antebellum Richmond," *Journal of Southern History* 44 (1978): 509–36.

———— "Reconstruction in Richmond: White Restoration and Black Protest, April–June 1865," *Virginia Magazine of History and Biography* 89 (1981): 259–81.

Palmer, Paul C., "Servant into Slave: The Evolution of the Legal Status of the Negro Laborer in Colonial Virginia," *South Atlantic Quarterly* 65 (1966): 355–70.

Palmore, Joseph R., "The Not-So-Strange Career of Interstate Jim Crow: Race, Transportation, and the Dormant Commerce Clause, 1878–1946," *Virginia Law Review* 83 (1997): 1773–817.

Perdue, Charles L., Jr., Thomas E. Barden, and Robert K. Phillips, ed., *Weevils in the Wheat: Interviews with Virginia Ex-Slaves* (1976).

Pinchback, Raymond B., *The Virginia Negro Artisan and Tradesman* (1926).

Pincus, Samuel N., *The Virginia Supreme Court, Blacks, and the Law, 1870–1902* (1990).

Pratt, Robert A., *The Color of Their Skin: Education and Race in Richmond, Virginia, 1954–89* (1992).

Preisser, Thomas M., "The Virginia Decision to Use Negro Soldiers in the Civil War, 1864–1865," *Virginia Magazine of History and Biography* 83 (1975): 98–113.

Rachleff, Peter J., *Black Labor in the South: Richmond, Virginia, 1865–1890* (1984).

Richardson, William D., "Thomas Jefferson and Race: The Declaration and Notes on the State of Virginia," *Polity* 16 (1984): 447–66.

Robert, Joseph Clarke, *The Tobacco Kingdom: Plantation, Market, and Factory in Virginia and North Carolina, 1800–1860* (1965).

Robson, David W., "'An Important Question Answered': William Graham's Defense of Slavery in Post-Revolutionary Virginia," *William and Mary Quarterly* 37 (1980): 644–52.

Russell, John H., "Colored Freemen as Slave Owners in Virginia," *Journal of Negro History* 1 (1916): 233–42.

———— *The Free Negro in Virginia, 1619–1865* (1913).

Russell, Lester F., *Black Baptist Secondary Schools in Virginia, 1887–1957* (1981).

Rutman, Darrett B., and Anita H. Rutman, *A Place in Time: Middlesex County Virginia, 1650–1750* (1984).

Sanford, Douglas W., "The Archaeology of Plantation Slavery in Piedmont Virginia: Context and Process," in Paul A. Shackel, and Barbara J. Little, ed., *Historical Archaeology of the Chesapeake* (1994): 115–30.

———— "Middle Range Theory and Plantation Archaeology: An Analysis of Domestic Slavery at Monticello, Albermarle County, Virginia, ca. 1770–1830," *Quarterly Bulletin of the Archeological Society of Virginia* 46 (1991): 20–30.

Santow, Mark, "'. . . A Growing and Accumulative Restlessness': Black Schooling in Richmond, Virginia, 1930–1942," *Griot* 16 (1997): 21–32.

Saunders, James Robert, *Urban Renewal and the End of Black Culture in Charlottesville, Virginia: An Oral History of Vinegar Hill* (1998).

Saunders, Robert M., "Crime and Punishment in Early National America: Richmond, Virginia, 1784–1820," *Virginia Magazine of History and Biography* 86 (1978): 33–44.

Savitt, Todd L., *Medicine and Slavery: The Diseases and Health Care of Blacks in Antebellum Virginia* (1978).

———— "Smothering and Overlaying of Virginia Slave Children: A Suggested Explanation," *Bulletin of the History of Medicine* 49 (1975): 400–404.

Schlotterbeck, John T., "The Internal Economy of Slavery in Rural Piedmont Virginia," *Slavery and Abolition* 12 (1991): 170–81.

Schmidt, Fredrika Teute, and Barbara Ripel Wilhelm, "Early Pro-Slavery Petitions in Virginia," *William and Mary Quarterly* 30 (1973): 133–46.

Schnittman, Suzanne, "Black Workers in Antebellum Richmond," in Gary M. Fink, and Merl E. Reed, ed., *Race, Class, and Community in Southern Labor History* (1994): 72–86.

Schwarz, Philip J., "Emancipators, Protectors, and Anomalies: Free Black Slaveowners in Virginia," *Virginia Magazine of History and Biography* 95 (1987): 317–38.

———— "Gabriel's Challenge: Slaves and Crime in Late Eighteenth Century Virginia," *Virginia Magazine of History and Biography* 90 (1982): 283–309.

———— *Twice Condemned: Slaves and the Criminal Laws of Virginia, 1705–1865* (1988).

Schweninger, Loren, "The Roots of Enterprise: Black-Owned Businesses in Virginia, 1830–1880," *Virginia Magazine of History and Biography* 100 (1992): 515–42.

———— "The Underside of Slavery: The Internal Economy Self-Hire, and Quasi-Freedom in Virginia, 1780–1865," *Slavery and Abolition* 12 (1991): 1–22.

Scott, Jean Sampson, comp., "Index to Free Negro Register, 1797–1841, Book I, Arlington, VA," *Journal of the Afro-American Historical and Genealogical Society* 3 (1982): 18–27.

Seip, Terry L., "Slaves and Free Negroes in Alexandria, 1850–1860," *Louisiana History* 10 (1969): 125–45.

Shammas, Carole, "Black Women's Work and the Evolution of Plantation Society in Virginia," *Labor History* 26 (1985): 5–28.

Sheeler, J. Reuben, "The Negro on the Virginia Frontier," *Journal of Negro History* 43 (1958): 279–97.

Sheldon, Marianne Buroff, "Black-White Relations in Richmond, Virginia, 1782–1820," *Journal of Southern History* 45 (1979): 27–44.

Shepard, E. Lee, Frances S. Pollard, and Janet B. Schwartz, "'The Love of Liberty Brought Us Here': Virginians and the Colonization of Liberia," *Virginia Magazine of History and Biography* 102 (1994): 89–100.

Sherman, R. B., "The 'Teachings at Hampton Institute': Social Equality, Racial Integrity, and the Virginia Public Assemblage Act of 1926," *Virginia Magazine of History and Biography* 95 (1987): 275–300.

Shifflet, Crandall A., "The Household Composition of Rural Black Families: Louisa County, Virginia, 1880," *Journal of Interdisciplinary History* 6 (1975): 235–60.

———— *Patronage and Poverty in the Tobacco South: Louisa County, Virginia, 1860–1900* (1982).

Sidbury, James, *Ploughshares into Swords: Race, Rebellion, and Identity in Gabriel's Virginia, 1730–1810* (1997).

———— "Saint Domingue in Virginia: Ideology, Local Meanings, and Resistance to Slavery, 1790–1800," *Journal of Southern History* 63 (1997): 531–52.

Sobel, Mechal, *The World They Made Together: Black and White Values in Eighteenth-Century Virginia* (1987).

Sodiq, Yushau, "A History of Islam among the African American Muslims of Richmond," *Muslim World* 84 (1994): 258–78.

Spriggs, William Edward, "The Virginia Farmers' Alliance: A Case Study of Race and Class Identity," *Journal of Negro History* 64 (1979): 191–204.

Stealey, John Edmund, III, "The Responsibilities and Liabilities of the Bailee of Slave Labor in Virginia," *American Journal of Legal History* 12 (1968): 336–53.

Stevenson, Brenda, "Distress and Discord in Virginia Slave Families, 1830–1860," in Carol Bleser, ed., *In Joy and In Sorrow: Women, Family, and Marriage in the Victorian South, 1830–1900* (1991): 103–24.

———— *Life in Black and White: Family and Community in the Slave South* (1996).

Stevens, C. J., "Black Births and Baptisms in Mannikintown," *Journal of the Afro-American Historical and Genealogical Society* 4 (1983): 15–20.

Sweig, Donald, ed., *"Registration of the Free Negroes Commencing September Court 1822, Book No. 2" and "Register of Free Blacks 1835, Book 3": Being the Full Text of the Two Extant Volumes, 1822–1861, of Registrations of Free Blacks Now in the County Courthouse, Fairfax, Virginia* (1977).

Tate, Thad W., *The Negro in Eighteenth-Century Williamsburg* (1965).

Thornton, John, "The African Experience of the '20 and Odd Negroes' Arriving in Virginia in 1619," *William and Mary Quarterly* 55 (1998): 421–34.

Townes, A. Jane, "The Effect of Emancipation on Large Landholdings, Nelson and Goochland Counties, Virginia," *Journal of Southern History* 45 (1979): 403–12.

Tripp, Steven Elliott, *Yankee Town, Southern City: Race and Class Relations in Civil War Lynchburg* (1996).

Tucker, St. George, *A Dissertation on Slavery: With a Proposal for the Gradual Abolition of It, in the State of Virginia* (1796).

Tyler-McGraw, Marie, and Gregg D. Kimball, *In Bondage and Freedom: Antebellum Black Life in Richmond, Virginia* (1988).

United States Writers' Program: Virginia, *The Negro in Virginia* (1940).

Upton, Dell, "New Views of the Virginia Landscape," *Virginia Magazine of History and Biography* 96 (1988): 403–70.

——— "White and Black Landscapes in Eighteenth-Century Virginia," in Robert Blair St. George, ed., *Material Life in America, 1600–1860* (1988): 357–69.

Vance, Joseph C., "'Contrabands' and Quakers in the Virginia Peninsula, 1862–1869," *Virginia Magazine of History and Biography* 61 (1953): 430–38.

VanWest, Carroll, and Mary S. Hoffschwelle, "'Slumbering on Its Old Foundations': Interpretation at Colonial Williamsburg," *South Atlantic Quarterly* 83 (1984): 157–75.

Vaughan, Alden T., "The Origins Debate: Slavery and Racism in Seventeenth-Century Virginia," *Virginia Magazine of History and Biography* 97 (1989): 311–54.

Watkinson, James D., "William Washington Browne and the True Reformers of Richmond, Virginia," *Virginia Magazine of History and Biography* 97 (1989): 375–98.

Wax, Donald D., "Negro Import Duties in Colonial Virginia: A Study of British Commercial Policy and Local Public Policy," *Virginia Magazine of History and Biography* 79 (1971): 29–44.

Westbury, Susan, "Analysing a Regional Slave Trade: The West Indies and Virginia, 1698–1775," *Slavery and Abolition* 7 (1986): 241–56.

——— "Slaves of Colonial Virginia: Where They Came from," *William and Mary Quarterly* 42 (1985): 228–37.

William, Blair A., "Justice versus Law and Order: The Battle over the Reconstruction of Virginia's Minor Judiciary, 1865–1870," *Virginia Magazine of History and Biography* 103 (1995): 157–80.

Wilson, Harold, "The Role of Carter Glass in the Disfranchisement of the Virginia Negro," *Historian* 32 (1969): 69–82.

Windley, Lathan Algerna, *A Profile of Runaway Slaves in Virginia and South Carolina from 1730 through 1787* (1995).

Wood, Walter K., "Henry Edmundson, The Alleghany Turnpike, and 'Fotheringay' Plantation, 1805–1847: Planting and Trading in Montgomery County Virginia," *Virginia Magazine of History and Biography* 83 (1975): 304–20.

Wynes, Charles E., *Race Relations in Virginia, 1870–1902* (1961).

26.2.44   Washington

Campbell, Robert A., "Blacks and the Coal Mines of Western Washington, 1888–1896," *Pacific Northwest Quarterly* 73 (1982): 146–55.

Droker, Howard A., "Seattle Race Relations during the Second World War," in G. Thomas Edwards, and Carlos Schwantes, ed., *Experiences in a Promised Land: Essays in Pacific Northwest History* (1986): 353–68.

Franklin, Joseph, *All through the Night: The History of Spokane Black Americans, 1860–1940* (1989).

Mumford, Esther H., *Seattle's Black Victorians, 1852–1901* (1980).

Stern, Mark, "Black Strikebreakers in the Coal Fields: King County, Washington, 1891," *Journal of Ethnic Studies* 5 (1977): 60–70.

Taylor, Quintard, "Black Urban Development—Another View: Seattle's Central District, 1910–1940," *Pacific Historical Review* 58 (1989): 429–48.

——— "Blacks and Asians in a White City: Japanese Americans and African Americans in Seattle, 1890–1940," *Western Historical Quarterly* 22 (1991): 401–29.

——— "The Civil Rights Movement in the American West: Black Protest in Seattle, 1960–1970," *The Journal of Negro History* 80 (1995): 1–14.

——— *The Forging of a Black Community: Seattle's Central District, from 1870 through the Civil Rights Era* (1994).

26.2.45 West Virginia

Bailey, Kenneth R., "A Judicious Mixture: Negroes and Immigrants in the West Virginia Mines, 1880–1917," *West Virginia History* 34 (1973): 141–61.

Engle, Stephen D., "Mountaineer Reconstruction: Blacks in the Political Reconstruction of West Virginia," *Journal of Negro History* 78 (1993): 137–65.

Hickey, Donald R., "Slavery and the Republican Experiment: A View from Western Virginia in 1806," *West Virginia History* 39 (1978): 236–40.

Jackameit, William P., "A Short History of Negro Public Higher Education in West Virginia, 1890–1965," *West Virginia History* 37 (1976): 309–25.

Jordan, Daniel P., "The Mingo War: Labor Violence in the Southern West Virginia Coal Fields, 1919–1922," in Gary M. Fink and Merl E. Reed, ed., *Essays in Southern Labor History: Selected Papers, Southern Labor History Conference, 1976* (1977): 102–43.

Simmons, Charles, et al., "Negro Coal Miners in West Virginia," *Midwest Journal* 6 (1954): 60–69.

Smith, Douglas C., "A West Virginia Dilemma: Martin v. Board of Education, 1896," *West Virginia History* 40 (1979): 158–63.

Stealey, John Edmund, III, ed., "Reports of Freedmen's Bureau Operations in West Virginia: Agents in the Eastern Panhandle," *West Virginia History* 43 (1980–1981): 94–129.

——— "Slavery and the Western Virginia Salt Industry," *Journal of Negro History* 59 (1974): 105–31.

Steel, Edward M., Jr., "Black Monongalians: A Judicial View of Slavery and The Negro in Monongalia County, 1776–1865," *West Virginia History* 34 (1973): 331–59.

Trotter, Joe William, Jr., "Class and Racial Inequality: The Southern West Virginia Black Coal Miners' Response, 1915–1932," in Robert H. Zieger, ed., *Organized Labor in the Twentieth-Century South* (1991): 60–83.

——— *Coal, Class, and Color: Blacks in Southern West Virginia, 1915–32* (1990).

——— "Race, Class and Industrial Change: Black Migration to Southern West Virginia, 1915–32," in Joe William Trotter, Jr., ed., *The Great Migration in Historical Perspective: New Dimensions of Race, Class, and Gender* (1991): 46–67.

United States Department of Labor, "Negro Work and Welfare in West Virginia," *Monthly Labor Review* 38 (1934): 75–77.

26.2.46 Wisconsin

Cooper, Zachary L., *Black Settlers in Rural Wisconsin* (1977).

Fishel, Leslie H., Jr., "The Genesis of the First Wisconsin Civil Rights Act," *Wisconsin Magazine of History* 49 (1966): 324–33.

McManus, Michael J., *Political Abolitionism in Wisconsin, 1840–1861* (1998).

Trotter, Joe William, Jr., *Black Milwaukee: The Making of an Industrial Proletariat, 1915–45* (1985).

26.2.47 Wyoming

Bullock, Clifford A., "Fired by Conscience: The 'Black 14' Incident at the University of Wyoming and Black Protest in the Western Athletic Conference, 1968–1970," *Wyoming History Journal* 68 (1996): 4–13.

Occupation Categories

This list is adapted from the thesaurus of occupations created for Randall K. Burkett, Nancy H. Burkett, and Henry Louis Gates, Jr., ed., *Black Biography, 1790–1950: A Cumulative Index* (3 vols., 1991), a reference work prepared under the auspices of the W. E. B. Du Bois Institute for Afro-American Research. Occupations are grouped under general headings, which are used to identify subjects of biographies and autobiographies. This list gives the occupations covered by each general heading.

Abolitionist

Agriculturalist
Cowboy
Farmer or rancher
Grain inspector
Miller
Teamster
Veterinarian

Artist
Architect
Art collector or patron
Art critic or historian
Illustrator
Painter
Photographer
Printmaker
Sculptor

Athlete

Author
Editor
Poet
Writer
Aviator

Blacksmith

Businessperson (usually owner of business)
Banker
Caterer
Entrepreneur
Hairdresser, or barber
Housing authority or real estate manager
Insurance agent
Restaurant or shop owner
Shoemaker
Tailor or dressmaker
Traveling salesman or peddler

Club leader

Construction worker
Bricklayer
Carpenter
Contractor
Electrician
Housepainter
Machinery operator
Mason
Plumber

Domestic
Cook
Dishwasher
Gardener
Knitter or quilter
Servant
Shoemaker
Tailor or dressmaker

Educator
Anthropologist
Archaeologist
Classicist
College administrator
Educational reformer
Educator of the handicapped
Folklorist
Historian

Home economist
Literary scholar
Philosopher
Psychologist
Religious educator
School or college founder or administrator
Sociologist
Teacher
Explorer/Traveler
Factory worker

Government worker
Civil servant
Fire or police employee
Postal employee

Homemaker

Journalist
Editor of magazines or newspapers
Newspaper reporter
Radio producer
Radio writer
Labor leader

Lawyer
Judge
Justice of the peace

Lecturer

Librarian/Book Collector

Medical Worker
Chiropractor

Dentist
Doctor (Physician)
Midwife
Nurse
Nutritionist
Psychiatrist
Psychologist (clinical)
Public health worker
Researcher

Military person

Miner

Office Worker
Accountant
Bookkeeper
Clerk
Secretary

Performing artist
Actor or actress
Composer
Dancer
Film actor or actress
Musician
Singer

Political figure
Adviser or appointee
Party worker
Politician

Printer

Railroad employee
Conductor
Construction worker
Dining car worker
Engineer
Expressman
Porter

Reformer
Civil rights activist
Community activist
Feminist
Housing reformer
Labor reformer
NAACP worker
Black Nationalist
Prison reformer
Protest Leader
Race leader
Settlement house leader
Social worker

Socialist or radical
Suffragist
Temperance or prohibition advocate
YMCA or YWCA worker
Welfare work leader

Religious worker
Church worker
Clergy
Deacon
Evangelist
Minister
Missionary
Preacher
Religion founder or leader
Sunday school teacher

Scientist
Astronomer
Biologist
Botanist or horticulturist
Chemist
Engineer
Geographer or geologist
Inventor
Mathematician
Physicist

Seaman
Cabin boy
Marine seaman
Merchant seaman
Navigator
Pilot
Sailor
Steamboat captain
Steamboat foreman

Service industry employee
Bartender
Charwoman or cleaner
Chimney sweeper
Custodian
Hairdresser or barber
Janitor
Sexton
Waiter

Slave

Undertaker

27 *Autobiography and Biography*

Randall K. Burkett, Leon F. Litwack, and Richard Newman

27.1 AUTOBIOGRAPHICAL AND BIOGRAPHICAL WRITINGS

Aaron (?). Slave
Aaron, *The Light and Truth of Slavery: Aaron's History* (1843).

Aaron, Henry Louis "Hank" (1934–). Athlete
Aaron, Hank, *Aaron, R.F.* (1968).

Abbott, Robert Sengstacke (1870–1940). Journalist, Business Person, Political Figure, Reformer, Author
Ottley, Roi, *The Lonely Warrior: The Life and Times of Robert S. Abbott* (1955).

Abernathy, Ralph (1926–1990). Reformer, Religious Worker
Abernathy, Ralph, *And the Walls Came Tumbling Down: An Autobiography* (1989).

Abubadika, Mwlina Imiri [Robert "Sonny" Carson] (1935–). Reformer
Abubadika, Mwlina Imiri, *The Education of Sonny Carson* (1972).

Ace, Johnny [John Marshall Alexander, Jr.] (1929–1954). Performing Artist
Salem, James M., *The Late, Great Johnny Ace and the Transition from R&B to Rock 'n' Roll* (1999).

Adams, Elizabeth Laura (1909–?). Author, Artist, Journalist, Religious Worker
Adams, Elizabeth Laura, *Dark Symphony* (1942).

Adams, John Quincy (1845–1922). Domestic Worker, Author, Business Person, Religious Worker
Adams, John Quincy, *Narrative of the Life of John Quincy Adams: When in Slavery, and Now as a Freeman* (1872).

Ailey, Alvin (1931–1989). Performing Artist
Ailey, Alvin, with A. Peter Bailey, *Revelations: The Autobiography of Alvin Ailey* (1995).
Dunning, Jennifer, *Alvin Ailey: A Life in Dance* (1996).

Aldridge, Ira Frederick (1807–1867). Performing Artist
Marshall, Herbert, and Mildred Stock, *Ira Aldridge: The Negro Tragedian* (1958).
Mortimer, Owen, *Speak of Me As I Am: The Study of Ira Aldridge* (1995).

Alexander, Archer (1813–?). Slave
Eliot, William Greenleaf, *The Story of Archer Alexander from Slavery to Freedom, March 30, 1863* (1885).

Ali, Muhammad [Cassius Marcellus Clay, Jr.] (1942–). Athlete
Ali, Muhammad, and Richard Durham, *The Greatest: My Own Story* (1975).
Gorn, Elliott J., *Muhammad Ali: The People's Champ* (1995).
Hauser, Thomas, *Muhammad Ali: His Life and Times* (1991).
Marqusee, Mike, *Redemption Song: Muhammad Ali and the Spirit of the Sixties* (1999).
Remnick, David, *King of the World: Muhammad Ali and the Rise of an American Hero* (1998).

Allen, Mary Rice Hayes (1875–1935). Educator, Reformer
McCray, Carrie Allen, Freedom's Child: The Life of a Confederate General's Black Daughter (1998).

Allen, Richard (1760–1831). Religious Worker

Allen, Richard, *The Life Experience and Gospel Labors of the Rt. Rev. Richard Allen* (1960).

George, Carol V. R., *Segregated Sabbaths: Richard Allen and the Emergence of Independent Black Churches, 1760–1840* (1973).

Raboteau, Albert J., "Richard Allen and the African Church Movement," in Leon Litwack and August Meier, ed., *Black Leaders of the Nineteenth Century* (1988): 1–18.

Wesley, Charles H., *Richard Allen: Apostle of Freedom* (1935).

Allen, William G. (1820–?). Slave

Allen, William G., *The American Prejudice Against Color* (1853).

———— *A Short Personal Narrative* (1860).

Anderson, Garland (1886–1939). Author, Domestic

Anderson, Garland, *From Newsboy and Bellhop to Playwright* (1925?).

Anderson, Marian (1902–1993). Performing Artist

Anderson, Marian, *My Lord, What a Morning: An Autobiography* (1956).

Keiler, Allan, *Marian Anderson: A Singer's Journey* (2000).

Newman, Shirlee Petkin, *Marian Anderson: Lady from Philadelphia* (1965).

Patterson, Charles, *Marian Anderson* (1988).

Anderson, Robert (1819–?). Religious Worker

Anderson, Robert, *The Anderson Surpriser. Written after He Was Seventy-Five Years of Age* (1895).

———— *The Life of Rev. Robert Anderson. Born the 22d day of February, in the Year of Our Lord, 1819, and Joined the Methodist Episcopal Church in 1839. This Book Shall be Called the Young Men's Guide, Or, the Brother in White* (1892).

Anderson, Robert Ball (1843–1930). Slave, Religious Worker, Military Person, Manual Laborer, Agriculturalist

Anderson, Robert Ball, *From Slavery to Affluence: Memoirs of Robert Anderson, Ex-Slave* (1927).

Wax, Darold D., "The Odyssey of an Ex-Slave: Robert Ball Anderson's Pursuit of the American Dream," *Phylon* 45 (1984): 67–79.

Anderson, Thomas (1785–?). Slave

Anderson, Thomas, *Interesting Account of Thomas Anderson, A Slave, Taken from His Own Lips,* ed. J. P. Clark (1854).

Anderson, William J. (1811–?). Slave

Anderson, William J., *Life and Narrative of William J. Anderson, Twenty-Four Years a Slave: Or, The Dark Deeds of American Slavery Revealed. Written by Himself* (1857).

Andrews, Raymond (1934–1991). Author

Andrews, Raymond, *The Last Radio Baby: A Memoir* (1990).

———— "Once Upon a Time in Atlanta: A Memoir," *Chattahoochee Review* 18 (1998): 1–181.

Angelou, Maya [Marguerite A. Johnson] (1928–). Author

Angelou, Maya, *All God's Children Need Traveling Shoes* (1986).

———— *Gather Together in My Name* (1974).

———— *The Heart of a Woman* (1981).

———— *I Know Why the Caged Bird Sings* (1969).

———— *Singin' and Swingin' and Gettin' Merry like Christmas* (1976).

Annamaboe (?). Slave

Annamaboe, Prince of, *Royal African: Or, Memoirs of the Young Prince of Annamaboe. Comprehending a Distinct Account of His Country and Family: His Elder Brother's Voyage to France, and Reception There; the Manner in Which Himself Was Confided by his Father to the Captain Who Sold Him; His Condition While a Slave in Barbados; the True Cause of His Being Redeemed; His Voyage from Thence; and Reception Here in England* (1749?).

Archer, Chalmers, Jr. (1928–). Educator

Archer, Chalmers, *Growing Up Black in Rural Mississippi: Memories of a Family, Heritage of a Place* (1992).

Armstrong, Archer (?). Slave

Archer, Armstrong, *Compendium of Slavery: As It Exists in the Present Day in the United States* (1844).

Armstrong, Henry [Henry Jackson] (1912–). Athlete

Armstrong, Henry, *Gloves, Glory, and God: An Autobiography* (1956).

Armstrong, Louis (1898–1971). Performing Artist

Armstrong, Louis, *Louis Armstrong, In His Own Words: Selected Writings,* ed. Thomas David Brothers (1999).

———— *Satchmo: My Life in New Orleans* (1954).

———— *Swing that Music* (1936).

Armstrong, Louis, and Richard Meryman, *Louis Armstrong: A Self-Portrait* (1971).

Bergreen, Laurence, *Louis Armstrong: An Extravagant Life* (1997).

Collier, James Lincoln, *Louis Armstrong: An American Genius* (1983).

Giddins, Gary, *Satchmo* (1988).

Jones, Max, and John Chilton, *Louis: The Louis Armstrong Story, 1900–1971* (1971).

Storb, Ilse, *Louis Armstrong: The Definitive Biography* (1996).

Arnett, Benjamin William, Sr. (1838–1906). Religious Worker

Coleman, Lucretia H. Newman, *Poor Ben: A Story of Real Life* (1890).

Arter, Jared Maurice (1850–1928). Educator, Religious Worker

Arter, Jared Maurice, *Echoes from a Pioneer Life* (1922).

Ashe, Arthur Robert, Jr. (1943–1993). Athlete

Ashe, Arthur R., *Advantage Ashe* (1967).

Ashe, Arthur R., with Arnold Rampersad, *Days of Grace* (1993).

Ashe, Arthur R., with Neil Amdur, *Off the Court* (1981).

Asher, Jeremiah (1812–?). Religious Worker

Asher, Jeremiah, *An Autobiography, with Details of a Visit to England, and Some Account of the History of the Meeting Street Baptist Church, Providence, R.I., and of the Shiloh Baptist Church, Philadelphia* (1862).

———— *Incidents in the Life of the Rev. J. Asher, Pastor of Shiloh (Coloured) Baptist Church, Philadelphia, U.S.* (1850).

Atkins, James A. (1890–1969). Educator, Government Worker, Journalist

Atkins, James A., *The Age of Jim Crow* (1964).

Bailey, Pearl Mae (1918–1990). Performing Artist, Author

Bailey, Pearl, *The Raw Pearl* (1968).

Baker, Ella (1903–1986). Community Organizer, Reformer, Educator

Grant, Joanne, *Ella Baker: Freedom Bound* (1998).

Baker, Josephine (1906–1975). Performing Artist

Baker, Jean-Claude, and Chris Chase, *Josephine: The Hungry Heart* (1993).

Baker, Josephine, and Jo Bouillon, *Josephine* (1976).

Hammond, Bryan, comp., and Patrick O'Connor, *Josephine Baker* (1988).

Haney, Lynn, *Naked at the Feast: A Biography of Josephine Baker* (1981).

Rose, Phyllis, *Jazz Cleopatra: Josephine Baker in Her Time* (1989).

Baldwin, James Arthur (1924–1987). Author

Baldwin, James, *The Fire Next Time* (1963).

———— *No Name in the Street* (1972).

———— *Nobody Knows My Name: More Notes of a Native Son* (1961).

———— *Notes of a Native Son* (1955).

Campbell, James, *Talking at the Gates: A Life of James Baldwin* (1991).

Leeming, David, *James Baldwin: A Biography* (1994).

Weatherby, William J., *James Baldwin, Artist on Fire: A Portrait* (1989).

Ball, Charles (?). Slave

Ball, Charles, *Fifty Years in Chains: Or, The Life of an American Slave* (1859).

———— *Slavery in the United States: A Narrative of the Life and Adventures of Charles Ball, a Black Man, Who Lived Forty Years in Maryland, South Carolina, and Georgia, as a Slave* (1836).

Banks, J. H. (1833–?). Slave

Banks, J. H., *A Narrative of Events of the Life of J. H. Banks, an Escaped Slave, from the Cotton States Alabama, in America* (1861).

Pennington, James W. C., *A Narrative of Events of the Life of J. H. Banks, An Escaped Slave* (1861).

Banneker, Benjamin (1731–1806). Scientist

Bedini, Silvio A., *The Life of Benjamin Banneker: The First African American Man of Science* (rev. ed., 1999).

Latrobe, John H. B., *Memoir of Benjamin Banneker* (1845).

Baquaqua, Mahommah G. (?). Slave

Moore, Samuel, *Biography of Mahommah G. Baquaqua, a Native of Zoogoo, in the Interior of Africa* (1854).

Baraka, Imamu Amiri [Everett Leroi Jones] (1934–). Author, Performing Artist

Baraka, Imamu Amiri, *The Autobiography of LeRoi Jones* (1997).

Jones, LeRoi, *Home: Social Essays* (1966).

Barlow, Leila Mae (?). Educator

Barlow, Leila Mae, *Across the Years: Memoirs* (1959).

Barry, Marion Shepilov, Jr. (1936–). Political Figure, Reformer

Agronsky, Jonathan I. Z., *Marion Barry: The Politcs of Race* (1991).

Barras, Jonetta Rose, *The Last of the Black Emperors: The Hollow Comeback of Marion Barry in the New Age of Black Leaders* (1998).

Basie, Count [William James Basie] (1904–1984). Performing Artist

Basie, Count, as told to Albert Murray, *Good Morning Blues: The Autobiography of Count Basie* (1985).

Dance, Stanley, *The World of Count Basie* (1980).

Bass, Charlotta A. (1880–1969). Reformer, Journalist

Bass, Charlotta A., *Forty Years: Memoirs from the Pages of a Newspaper* (1960).

Bass, Thomas (1833–1934). Agriculturalist

Downey, Bill, *Tom Bass: Black Horseman* (1975).

Bassett, Ebenezer Don Carlos (1833–1908). Educator, Political Figure, Religious Worker

Wynes, Charles E., "Ebenezer Don Carlos Bassett: America's First Black Diplomat," *Pennsylvania History* 51 (1984): 232–40.

Bates, Daisy Gatson (1920–1999). Journalist, Reformer

Bates, Daisy, *The Long Shadow of Little Rock: A Memoir* (1962).

Battle, Augustus Allen (1864–1928). Educator, Religious Worker

Battle, Augustus Allen, *A Synopsis of the Autobiography of Rev. Augustus A. Battle* (1927).

Baxter, Freddie Mae (1923–). Domestic

Baxter, Freddie Mae, *The Seventh Child: A Lucky Life*, ed. Gloria Bley Miller (1999).

Bayley, Solomon (?). Slave

Bayley, Solomon, *A Narrative of Some Remarkable Incidents in the Life of Solomon Bayley, Formerly a Slave, in the State of Delaware, North America: Written by Himself* (2d ed., 1825).

Beals, Melba Pattillo (1942–). Author

Beals, Melba Pattillo, *Warriors Don't Cry: A Searing Memoir of the Battle to Integrate Little Rock's Central High* (1994).

———— *White Is a State of Mind: A Memoir* (1999).

Bearden, Romare (1911–1988). Artist

Schwartzman, Myron, *Romare Bearden: His Life and Art* (1990).

Beasley, Delilah Leontium (1872–1934). Educator, Reformer, Journalist

Crouchett, Lorraine Jacobs, *Delilah Leontium Beasley: Oakland's Crusading Journalist* (1990).

Bechet, Sidney Joseph (1897–1959). Performing Artist

Bechet, Sidney, *Treat It Gentle* (1960).

Chilton, John, *Sidney Bechet: The Wizard of Jazz* (1987).

Beck, Robert [Iceberg Slim] (1918–). Author

Beck, Robert, *The Naked Soul of Iceberg Slim* (1971).

———— *Pimp: The Story of My Life* (1967).

Beckwourth, James Pierson (1798–1866). Explorer/Traveler

Beckwourth, James Pierson, *The Life and Adventures of James P. Beckwourth, Mountaineer, Scout, and Pioneer, and Chief of the Crow Nation of Indians . . . Written from His Own Dictation*, ed. T. D. Bonner (1856).

Belafonte, Harry [Harold George] (1927–). Performing Artist
Shaw, Arnold, *Belafonte: An Unauthorized Biography* (1960).

Ben Solomon, Job (1702?–1773?). Slave, Educator, Political Figure, Author
Bluett, Thomas, *Some Memories of the Life of Job, The Son of Solomon the High Priest of Boonda in Africa* (1734).
Grant, Douglas, *The Fortunate Slave: An Illustration of African Slavery in the Early Eighteenth Century* (1968).

Bennett, George Washington (1898–?). Military Person
Bennett, George Washington, *Life Behind the Walls of My Self-Made Fate* (1964).

Berry, Chuck (1926–). Performing Artist
Reese, Krista, *Chuck Berry: Mr. Rock N' Roll* (1982).

Betsch, Mavynee (?). Performing Artist
Rymer, Russ, *American Beach: A Saga of Race, Wealth, and Memory* (1998).

Bethune, Mary Jane McLeod (1875–1955). Educator, Religious Worker, Club Leader, Business Person, Political Figure
Leffall, Doris C., and Janet L. Sims, "Mary McLeod Bethune the Educator, Also Including a Selected Annotated Bibliography," *Journal of Negro Education* 45 (1976): 342–59.
McCluskey, Audrey Thomas, and Elaine M. Smith, ed., *Mary McLeod Bethune: Building a Better World* (1999).
Peare, Catherine Owens, *Mary McLeod Bethune* (1951).
Rackham, Holt, *Mary McLeod Bethune: A Biography* (1964).
Ross, B. Joyce, "Mary McLeod Bethune and the National Youth Administration: A Case Study of Power Relationships in the Black Cabinet of Franklin D. Roosevelt," in John Hope Franklin and August Meier, ed., *Black Leaders of the Twentieth Century* (1982): 191–219.
Sterne, Emma Gelders, *Mary McLeod Bethune* (1957).

Bethune, Thomas Green [Blind Tom] (1849–1908). Performing Artist
Bethune, Thomas Green, *Sketch of the Life of Thomas Green Bethune (Blind Tom)* (1865).
Southall, Geneva H., *Blind Tom: The Post-Civil War Enslavement of a Black Musical Genius* (1979).
——— *Blind Tom, the Black Pianist-Composer (1849–1908): Continually Enslaved* (1999).
——— *The Continuing Enslavement of Blind Tom, the Black Pianist-Composer (1865–1887)* (1983).

Bettis, Alexander (1836–1895). Religious Worker, Educator
Nicholson, Alfred W., *Brief Sketch of the Life and Labors of Rev. Alexander Bettis* (1913).

Beverly, John William (1858–1924). Educator, Agriculturalist
Sherer, Robert G., Jr., "John William Beverly: Alabama's First Negro Historian," *Alabama Review* 26 (1973): 194–208.

Bibb, Henry (1814–1854). Author, Journalist, Abolitionist
Bibb, Henry, *Narrative of the Life and Adventures of Henry Bibb: An American Slave, Written by Himself* (1849).

Black, Leonard (1822–1883). Slave, Seaman, Religious Worker
Black, Leonard, *The Life and Sufferings of Leonard Black, a Fugitive from Slavery, Written by Himself* (1847).

Blair, Norvel (1825–?)
Blair, Norvel, *Life of Norvel Blair: A Negro Citizen of Morris, Grundy County, Illinois* (1880).

Blake, Eubie [James Hubert] (1883–1983). Performing Artist
Carter, Lawrence T., *Eubie Blake: Keys of Memory* (1979).
Kimball, Robert, and William Bolcom, *Reminiscing with Sissle and Blake* (1973).
Rose, Al, *Eubie Blake* (1979).

Blake, Margaret Jane (?). Slave
Blake, Jane, *Memoirs of Margaret Jane Blake* (1834).

Bland, James A. (1854–1911). Performing Artist
Daly, John Jay, *A Song in His Heart* (1951).

Blyden, Edward Wilmot (1832–1912). Educator, Religious Worker, Political Figure
Blyden, Edward Wilmot, *Selected Letters of Edward Wilmot Blyden*, ed. Hollis R. Lynch (1978).
Lynch, Hollis R., *Edward Wilmot Blyden: Pan-Negro Patriot, 1832–1912* (1967).

Boddie, Jacob Benjamin (1872–1936). Religious Worker
Boddie, Charles Emerson, *"Giant in the Earth": A Biography of Dr. J. B. Boddie* (1944).

Boen, William (1735–1825). Slave
Boen, William, *Anecdotes and Memoirs of William Boen, A Coloured Man, Who Lived and Died Near Mount Holly, New Jersey. To Which Is Added, the Testimony of Friends of Mount Holly Monthly Meeting Concerning Him* (1834).

Bolden, Charles Joseph ["Buddy"] (1879–1931). Performing Artist
Marquis, Donald M., *In Search of Buddy Bolden: First Man of Jazz* (1978).

Bond, Horace Mann (1904–1972). Educator
Fultz, Michael, "A 'Quintessential American': Horace Mann Bond, 1924–1939," *Harvard Education Review* 55 (1985): 416–42.
Urban, Wayne J., *Black Scholar: Horace Mann Bond, 1904–1972* (1992).

Bond, Julian (1940–). Reformer, Author, Educator
Neary, John, *Julian Bond: Black Rebel* (1971).

Bond, Scott (1852–?). Slave, Agriculturalist, Business Person, Reformer
Rudd, Daniel Arthur, and Theophilus Bond, *From Slavery to Wealth: The Life of Scott Bond* (1917).

Bonner, Cleon Richard (1911–). Educator
Bonner, Cleon Richard, *A Black Principal's Struggle to Survive* (1982).

Bontemps, Arna Wendell (1902–1973). Author
Jones, Kirkland C., *Renaissance Man from Louisiana: A Biography of Arna Wendell Bontemps* (1992).
Nichols, Charles H., ed., *Arna Bontemps–Langston Hughes Letters 1925–1967* (1980).

Booker, Simeon Saunders (1918–). Journalist
Booker, Simeon, *Black Man's America* (1964).

Boone, John William (1864–1927). Performing Artist
Fuell, Melissa, *Blind Boone: His Early Life and His Achievements* (1915).

Boothe, Charles Octavius (1845–1924). Religious Worker
Crowther, Edward R., "Charles Octavius Boothe: An Alabama Apostle of 'Uplift,'" *Journal of Negro History* 78 (1993): 110–116.

Borders, William Holmes (1905–1993). Religious Worker
English, James W., *Handyman of the Lord: The Life and Ministry of the Rev. William Holmes Borders* (1967).

Boseman, Benjamin A. (1840–1881). Physician, Political Figure
Hine, William C., "Dr. Benjamin A. Boseman, Jr.: Charleston's Black Physician-Politician," in Howard Rabinowitz, ed., *Southern Black Leaders of the Reconstruction Era* (1982): 335–62.

Bowles, Charles (1761–1843). Religious Worker
Lewis, John W., *The Life, Labors, and Travels of Elder Charles Bowles, of the Free Will Baptist Denomination* (1852).

Boyd, Richard Henry, Sr. (1843–1922). Religious Worker, Business Person
Lovett, Bobby L., *A Black Man's Dream: The First One Hundred Years: Richard Henry Boyd and the National Baptist Publishing Board* (1993).

Bradden, William S. (1871–?). Religious Worker, Military Person, Government Worker
Bradden, William S., *Under Three Banners: An Autobiography* (1940).

Bradford, John Henry Perry (1895–1961). Performing Artist
Bradford, Perry, *Born with the Blues: Perry Bradford's Own Story* (1965).

Bradley, Aaron A. (1815–1881). Political Figure
Reidy, Joseph P., "Aaron A. Bradley: Voice of Black Labor in the Georgia Lowcounty," in Howard Rabinowitz, ed., *Southern Black Leaders of the Reconstruction Era* (1982): 281–308.

Bragg, Janet Harmon (1907–1993). Aviator
Bragg, Janet Harmon, as told to Marjorie M. Kriz, *Soaring above Setbacks: The Autobiography of Janet Harmon Bragg, African American Aviator* (1996).

Braithwaite, William Stanley Beaumont (1878–1962). Author, Educator, Publisher
Braithwaite, William Stanley, *The William Stanley Braithwaite Reader,* ed. Philip Butcher (1972).

Branham, Levi (1852– ?). Slave, Educator, Blacksmith, Agriculturalist
Branham, Levi, *My Life and Travels* (1929).

Bray, Rosemary L. (1955–). Journalist
Bray, Rosemary L., *Unafraid of the Dark: A Memoir* (1998).

Bricktop [Ada Beatrice Queen Victoria Louise Smith Ducong] (1894–1984). Performing Artist
Bricktop, and James Haskins, *Bricktop* (1983).

Brooks, Gwendolyn Elizabeth (1917–). Author
Brooks, Gwendolyn, *Report from Part One* (1972).
——— *Report from Part Two* (1996).
Kent, George E., *A Life of Gwendolyn Brooks* (1990).

Brooks, Sara (1911–). Household Worker
Brooks, Sara, *You May Plow Here: The Narrative of Sara Brooks*, ed. Thordis Simonsen (1986).

Brooks, William Sampson (1865–1934). Religious Worker
Brooks, William Sampson, *Footprints of a Black Man: The Holy Land* (1915).
——— *What a Black Man Saw in a White Man's Country: Some Accounts of a Trip to the Land of the Midnight Sun* (1899).

Brookter, Marie Zachary (1931–). Government Worker
Brookter, Marie Zachary, with Jean Curtis, *Here I Am—Take My Hand* (1974).

Broonzy, William Lee Conley (1893–1958). Performing Artist
Broonzy, William Lee Conley, *Big Bill Blues: William Broonzy's Story as Told to Yannick Bruynoghe* (1955).

Broughton, Virginia Walker (1856?–1934). Religious Worker
Broughton, Virginia W., *Twenty Years' Experience of a Missionary* (1907).

Brown, Cecil (1943–). Author
Brown, Cecil, *Coming Up Down Home: A Memoir of a Southern Childhood* (1993).

Brown, Charlotte Hawkins (1883–1961). Educator
Wadelington, Charles W., and Richard F. Knapp, *Charlotte Hawkins Brown and Palmer Memorial Institute: What One Young African American Woman Could Do* (1999).

Brown, Claude (1927–). Author
Brown, Claude, *Manchild in the Promised Land* (1965).

Brown, Ed (1908–). Agriculturalist
Brown, Ed, and Jane Maguire, ed., *On Shares: Ed Brown's Story* (1975).

Brown, Elaine (1943–). Reformer, Political Figure
Brown, Elaine, *A Taste of Power: A Black Woman's Story* (1992).

Brown, George S. (1801–?). Religious Worker
Brown, George S., *Brown's Abridged Journal, Containing a Brief Account of the Life, Trials and Travels of George S. Brown, Six Years a Missionary in Liberia, West Africa* (1849).

Brown, Henry Box (1815–?). Slave, Abolitionist
Brown, Henry Box, *Narrative of the Life of Henry Box Brown, Written by Himself* (1851).

Brown, Hubert Gerald "Rap" (1943–). Reformer, Political Figure
Brown, H. Rap, *Die Nigger Die!* (1969).

Brown, Isaac (?). Slave
Brown, Isaac, *Case of the Slave Isaac Brown: An Outrage Exposed!* (1847).

Brown, Jane (?). Slave
Brown, Jane, "Narrative of the Life of Jane Brown and Her Two Children. Related to the Reverend G. W. Offley," in Greensbury Washington Offley, *A Narrative of the Life and Labors of the Rev. G. W. Offley, a Colored Man and Local Preacher* (1860).

Brown, Jesse Leroy (1926–1950). Military Person
Taylor, Theodore, *The Flight of Jesse Leroy Brown* (1998).

Brown, Jimmy [James Nathaniel] (1936–). Athlete
Brown, Jimmy, and Myron Cope, *Off My Chest* (1964).

Brown, John (1815–1877). Slave
Brown, John, *Slave Life in Georgia: A Narrative of the Life, Sufferings, and Escape of John Brown, a Fugitive Slave, Now in England*, ed. F. N. Boney (1991).

Brown, Sterling Allen (1901–1989). Author, Educator
Gabbin, Joanne V., *Sterling A. Brown: Building the Black Aesthetic Tradtion* (1985).
Brown, Sterling Nelson, Sr. (1858–1929). Religious Worker, Educator
Brown, Sterling Nelson, *My Own Life Story* (1924).
Brown, William J. (1814–1885). Religious Worker, Business Person, Political Figure, Club Leader
Brown, William J., *The Life of William J. Brown, of Providence, R.I.: With Personal Recollections of Incidents in Rhode Island* (1883).
Brown, William Wells (1815–1884). Author, Lecturer
Brown, Josephine, *Biography of an American Bondman, by His Daughter* (1856).
Brown, William Wells, *The American Fugitive in Europe: Sketches of Places and People Abroad* (1855).
——— *A Description of William Wells Brown's Original Panoramic Views of the Scenes in the Life of an American Slave: From His Birth in Slavery to His Death, or His Escape to His First Home of Freedom on British Soil* (1849).
——— *My Southern Home: Or, the South and Its People* (1852).
——— *Narrative of William W. Brown, a Fugitive Slave: Written by Himself* (1847).
Farrison, William Edward, *William Wells Brown: Author and Reformer* (1969).
Brown, Willis W. (1858 ?). Religious Worker
Phillips, Porter W., *W. W. Brown, Host* (1941).
Browne, Dinah Hope (?). Slave
Simpson, John Hawkins, *Horrors of the Virginia Slave Trade and of the Slave-Rearing Plantations. The True Story of Dinah, an Escaped Virginian Slave, Now in London* (1863).
Browne, Martha Griffith (?–1906). Slave
Browne, Martha G., *Autobiography of a Female Slave* (1857).
Browne, Rose Butler (1897–?). Educator
Browne, Rose Butler, and James W. English, *Love My Children: An Autobiography* (1969).
Browne, William Washington (1849–1897). Religious Worker, Educator, Slave, Military Person
Davis, Daniel Webster, *The Life and Public Services of Rev. Wm. Washington Browne* (1910).
Bruce, Blanche Kelso (1841–1898). Political Figure, Educator, Journalist, Military Person
Harris, William C., "Blanch K. Bruce of Mississippi: Conservative Assimilationist," in Howard Rabinowitz, ed., *Southern Black Leaders of the Reconstruction Era* (1982): 3–38.
Mann, Kenneth Eugene, "Blanche Kelso Bruce: United States Senator without a Constituency," *Journal of Mississippi History* 38 (1976): 183–98.
Shapiro, Samuel, "A Black Senator from Mississippi, Blanche K. Bruce (1841–1898)," *Review of Politics* 44 (1982): 83–109.
Urofsky, Melvin I., "Blanche K. Bruce: United States Senator, 1875–1881," *Journal of Mississippi History* 29 (1967): 118–41.
Bruce, Henry Clay (1836–1902). Religious Worker
Bruce, Henry Clay, *The New Man: Twenty-Nine Years a Slave, Twenty-Nine Years a Free Man: Recollections of H. C. Bruce* (1895).
Bruce, John Edward "Grit" (1856–1924). Journalist, Educator, Reformer, Book Collector
Gilbert, Peter, ed., *The Selected Writings of John Edward Bruce: Militant Black Journalist* (1971).
Bruner, Peter (1845–1938). Military Person, Service Industry Employee
Bruner, Peter, *A Slave's Adventures toward Freedom: Not Fiction, but the True Story of a Struggle* (1925).
Buccau, Quamino (?). Slave
Allinson, William J., *Memoir of Quamino Buccau: A Pious Methodist* (1851).
Bunche, Ralph J. (1904–1971). Educator, Author, Government Worker, Political Figure
Henry, Charles P., *Ralph Bunche: Selected Speeches and Writings* (1995).
——— *Ralph Bunche: Model Negro or American Other?* (1999).
Rivlin, Benjamin, ed., *Ralph Bunche: The Man and His Times* (1990).
Urquhart, Brian, *Ralph Bunche: An American Life* (1993).

Bundy, James F. (1862–1914). Lawyer, Educator, Business Person
Thomas, Charles M., *James F. Bundy 1862–1914: A Biography* (1944).
Burns, Anthony (1834–1862). Slave, Religious Worker
Burns, Anthony, *Narrative* (1858).
Von Frank, Albert J., *The Trials of Anthony Burns: Freedom and Slavery in Emerson's Boston* (1998).
Burroughs, Nannie Helen (1878–1961). Educator, Religious Worker, Author, Journalist
Easter, Opal V., *Nannie Helen Burroughs* (1995).
Harley, Sharon, "Nannie Helen Burroughs: 'The Black Goddess of Liberty,'" *The Journal of Negro History* 81 (1996): 62–71.
Burton, Annie L. (1858?–?). Business Person, Domestic
Burton, Annie L., *Memories of Childhood's Slavery Days* (1909).
Burton, Thomas William (1860–1939). Medical Worker
Burton, Thomas William, *What Experience Has Taught Me: An Autobiography of Thomas William Burton* (1910).
Calderon, Erma (1912– ?). Domestic Worker
Calderon, Erma, with Leonard Ray Teel, *Erma* (1981).
Callis, Henry Arthur (1887–1974)
Wesley, Charles H., *Henry Arthur Callis: Life and Legacy* (1977).
Calloway, Cab [Cabell] (1907–1994). Performing Artist
Calloway, Cab, and Bryant Rollins, *Of Minnie the Moocher and Me* (1976).
Campanella, Roy (1921–1993). Athlete
Campanella, Roy, *It's Good to Be Alive* (1959).
Campbell, Dugald (?). Slave
Campbell, Dugald, *Ten Times a Slave but Free at Last* (1916).
Campbell, Israel (?). Slave
Campbell, Israel, *Bond and Free: Or, Yearnings for Freedom, from My Green Briar House. Being the Story of My Life in Bondage, and My Life in Freedom* (1861).
Campbell, Thomas Monroe (1883–1956). Educator, Government Worker, Agriculturalist
Campbell, Thomas Monroe, *The Movable School Goes to the Negro Farmer* (1936).
Jones, Allen W., "Thomas M. Campbell: Black Agricultural Leader of the New South," *Agricultural History* 53 (1979): 42–59.
Campbell, Tunis G. (1812–1891). Political Figure, Religious Worker
Duncan, Russell, *Freedom's Shore: Tunis Campbell and the Georgia Freedmen* (1986).
Campbell-Beckett, Catherine S. (?)
Coppin, L. J., *In Memoriam: Catherine S. Campbell-Beckett* (1888).
Cannon, George Epps (1869–?). Medical Worker, Reformer, Educator, Religious Worker
Dickerson, Dennis C., "George E. Cannon: Black Churchman, Physician, and Republican Politician," *Journal of Presbyterian History* 51 (1973): 411–32.
Cansler, Charles Warner (1871–1953). Educator, Lawyer, Journalist, Political Figure, Scientist
Cansler, Charles Warner, *Three Generations: The Story of a Colored Family of Eastern Tennessee* (1939).
Cardozo, Francis Louis (1837–1903). Political Figure, Educator, Lecturer, Religious Worker
Sweat, Edward F., "Francis L. Cardozo: Profile of Integrity in Reconstruction Politics," *Journal of Negro History* 61 (1976): 200–14.
Cardozo, Thomas W. (1838–1881). Educator, Political Figure
Brock, Euline W., "Thomas W. Cardozo: Fallible Black Reconstruction Leader," *Journal of Southern History* 47 (1981): 183–206.
Carey, Lott (1780–1828). Religious Worker, Slave, Political Figure
Carey, Lott, *Biography of Elder Lott Carey, Late Missionary to Africa*, ed. James B. Taylor (1837).
Fisher, Miles Mark, *Lott Carey* (1921).
Fitts, Leroy, *Lott Carey: First Black Missionary to Africa* (1978).
Poe, William, "Lott Cary: Man of Purchased Freedom," *Church History* 39 (1970): 49–61.

Carnegie, Amos Hubert (1885–?). Religious Worker, Educator

Carnegie, Amos Hubert, *Faith Moves Mountains: An Autobiography* (1950).

Carter, Bennett Lester [Benny] (1907–). Performing Artist

Berger, Morroe, Edward Berger, and James Patrick, *Benny Carter: A Life in American Music* (2 vols., 1982).

Carter, Eugene, J. (1861–?). Religious Worker

Carter, Eugene J., *Once a Methodist, Now a Baptist: Why?* (1905).

Carter, Rubin "Hurricane" (1937–). Athlete, Reformer

Carter, Rubin "Hurricane", *The Sixteenth Round: From Number 1 Contender to #45472* (1974).

Hirsch, James S., *Hurricane: The Miraculous Journey of Rubin Carter* (2000).

Carter, Stephen L. (1954–). Lawyer, Educator

Carter, Stephen L., *Reflections of an Affirmative Action Baby* (1991).

Carver, George Washington (1860?–1943). Educator, Scientist, Agriculturalist, Artist

Carver, George Washington, *George Washington Carver in His Own Words,* ed. Gary R. Kremer (1987).

Mackintosh, Barry, "George Washington Carver: The Making of a Myth," *Journal of Southern History* 42 (1976): 507–28.

McMurry, Linda O., *George Washington Carver: Scientist and Symbol* (1981).

Cary, Lorene (1956–). Author

Cary, Lorene, *Black Ice* (1991).

Cary, Mary Ann Shadd (1823–1893). Educator, Journalist, Lawyer, Reformer

Beardin, Jim, and Linda Jean Butler, *Shadd: The Life and Times of Mary Shadd Cary* (1977).

Hancock, Harold B., "Mary Ann Shadd: Negro Editor, Educator, and Lawyer," *Delaware History* 15 (1973): 187–94.

Rhodes, Jane, *Mary Ann Shadd Cary: The Black Press and Protest in the Nineteenth Century* (1998).

Silverman, Jason H., "Mary Ann Shadd and the Search for Equality," in Leon Litwack and August Meier, ed., *Black Leaders of the Nineteenth Century* (1988): 87–100.

Catto, Octavius V. (1840–1871). Reformer, Educator, Political Figure

Silcox, Harry C., "Nineteenth Century Philadelphia Black Militant: Octavius V. Catto (1839–1871)," *Pennsylvania History* 44 (1977): 53–76.

Cayton, Horace Roscoe, Jr. (1903–1970). Educator, Journalist, Goverment Worker, Political Figure

Cayton, Horace Roscoe, *Long Old Road* (1965).

Celia (1836?–1855). Slave

McLaurin, Melton Alonza, *Celia, A Slave* (1991).

Chamberlain, Wilt [Wilton Norman] (1936–1999). Athlete

Chamberlain, Wilt, *A View from Above: Sports, Sex, and Controversy* (1991).

Chamberlain, Wilt, and David Shaw, *Wilt: Just Like Any Other 7-Foot Black Millionaire Who Lives Next Door* (1973).

Champion, Jackson Richard (1923–). Political Figure

Champion, Jackson Richard, *Blacks in the Republican Party? One Man's Experiences, a Revolutionary, Conservative Black Republican* (1975).

Charles, Ray [Ray Charles Robinson] (1930–). Performing Artist

Charles, Ray, and David Ritz, *Brother Ray: Ray Charles' Own Story* (1978).

Lydon, Michael, *Ray Charles: Man and Music* (1998).

Charles, Robert (1865/66?–1900). Reformer

Hair, William Ivy, *Carnival of Fury: Robert Charles and the New Orleans Race Riot of 1900* (1976).

Charlton, Dimmock (1801–?). Slave

Cox, Mary L., *Narrative of Dimmock Charlton: A British Subject, Taken from the Brig "Peacock" by the U.S. Sloop "Hornet," Enslaved While a Prisoner of War, and Retained Forty-Five Years in Bondage* (1859).

Chelor, Ceasor (?). Toolmaker

DeAvila, Richard T., "Ceasor Chelor and the World He Lived In: Part I," *Chronicle of the Early American Industries Association* 46 (1993): 39–42.

Chesney, Jackson (?). Slave

Webster, J. C., *Last of the Pioneers, Or, Old Times in East Tenn. Being the Life and Reminiscences of Pharoah Jackson Chesney (Aged 120 Years)* (1902).

Chesnutt, Charles Waddell (1858–1932). Author, Lawyer, Educator, Journalist

Andrews, William L., *The Literary Career of Charles W. Chesnutt* (1980).

Chesnutt, Charles W., *Charles W. Chesnutt: Essays and Speeches,* ed. Joseph R. McElrath, Jr., Robert C. Leitz, III, and Jesse S. Crisler (1999).

————— *The Journals of Charles W. Chesnutt,* ed. Richard H. Brodhead (1993).

————— *To Be an Author: Letters of Charles W. Chesnutt, 1889–1905,* ed. Joseph R. McElrath Jr. and Robert C. Leitz III (1997).

Chesnutt, Helen M., *Charles W. Chesnutt: Pioneer of the Color Line* (1952).

Heermance, J. Noel, *Charles W. Chesnutt: America's First Great Black Novelist* (1974).

Keller, Frances Richardson, *An American Crusade: The Life of Charles Waddell Chesnutt* (1978).

Render, Sylvia Lions, *Charles W. Chesnutt* (1980).

Chester, Henry L. (1896–?). Railroad Employee, Military Person, Government Worker, Labor Leader

Chester, Henry L., *Memoirs* (1978).

Chestnut, J. L., Jr. (1885–1928). Journalist, Educator, Business Person

Chestnut, J. L., and Julia Cass, *Black in Selma: The Uncommon Life of J. L. Chestnut, Jr.* (1990).

Chisholm, Shirley Anita (1924–). Political Figure

Chisholm, Shirley, *The Good Fight* (1973).

————— *Unbought and Unbossed* (1970).

Christian, Malcolm Henry (1904–?). Office Worker, Author, Performing Artist

Christian, Malcolm Henry, *My Country and I: The Interracial Experiences of an American Negro* (1963).

Church, Robert Reed, Jr. (1885–1952). Reformer, Business Person, Political Figure

Biles, Roger, "Robert R. Church, Jr., of Memphis: Black Republican Leader in the Age of Democratic Ascendancy, 1928–1940," *Tennessee Historical Quarterly* 42 (1983): 362–82.

Clark, Peter Humphries (1827–1925). Journalist, Political Figure, Educator

Foner, Philip S., "Peter H. Clark: Pioneer Black Socialist," *Journal of Ethnic Studies* 5 (1977): 17–35.

Gerber, David A., "Peter Humphries Clark: The Dialogue of Hope and Despair," in Leon Litwack and August Meier, ed., *Black Leaders of the Nineteenth Century* (1988): 173–90.

Grossman, Lawrence, "In His Veins Coursed No Bootlicking Blood: The Career of Peter H. Clark," *Ohio History* 86 (1977): 79–95.

Gutman, Herbert G., "Peter H. Clark: Pioneer Negro Socialist," *Journal of Negro Education* 34 (1965): 413–18.

Clark, Septima Poinsette (1898–1987). Educator, Reformer

Clark, Septima Poinsette, *Ready from Within: Septima Clark and the Civil Rights Movement,* ed. Cynthia Brown (1986).

Clark, Septima Poinsette, and LeGette Blythe, *Echo in My Soul* (1962).

Clarke, Lewis Garrard (1815–1897). Abolitionist, Author, Lecturer, Slave

Clarke, Lewis Garrard, *Narrative of the Sufferings of Lewis Clarke, During a Captivity of More Than Twenty-Five Years, among the Algerines of Kentucky: One of the So-Called Christian States of North America. Dictated by Himself* (1845).

Clarke, Milton (1817?–1901). Slave, Abolitionist

Clarke, Milton, *Narratives of the Sufferings of Lewis and Milton Clarke, Sons of a Soldier of the Revolution, During a Captivity of More than Twenty Years among the Slaveholders of Kentucky, One of the So Called Christian States of North America. Dictated by Themselves,* ed. Joseph C. Lovejoy (1845).

Cleaver, Eldridge [Leroy] (1935–1998). Reformer, Political Figure

Cleaver, Eldridge, *Eldridge Cleaver: Post-Prison Writings and Speeches,* ed. Robert Scheer (1969).

————— *Soul on Ice* (1968).

————— *Soul on Fire* (1978).

Rout, Kathleen, *Eldridge Cleaver* (1991).

Clement, Samuel Spottford (1861–?). Slave
> Clement, Samuel Spottford, *Memoirs of Samuel Spottford Clement: Relating Interesting Experiences in Days of Slavery and Freedom* (1908).

Clytus, John (1929–). Reformer
> Clytus, John, with Jane Rieker, *Black Men in Red Cuba* (1970).

Cobb, Ned [Nate Shaw] (1885–1973). Agriculturalist, Labor Leader
> Shaw, Nate, *All God's Dangers: The Life of Nate Shaw*, comp. Theodore Rosengarten (1974).

Cochran, Johnnie L., Jr. (1937–). Lawyer
> Cochran, Johnnie L., Jr., with Tim Rutten, *Journey to Justice* (1996).

Coker, Daniel (1780–1846). Religious Worker
> Coker, Daniel, *Journal of Daniel Coker: A Descendant of Africa, from the Time of Leaving New York, in the Ship Elizabeth, Capt. Sebor: On a Voyage for Sherbro, in Africa, in Company with Three Agents, and About Ninety Persons of Colour* (1820).

Cole, Nat "King" (1917–1965). Performing Artist
> Cole, Maria Ellington, and Louie Robinson, *Nat King Cole: An Intimate Biography* (1971).
> Epstein, Daniel Mark, *Nat King Cole* (1999).

Coleman, Bessie (1896–1926). Aviator
> Freydberg, Elizabeth Hadley, *Bessie Coleman: The Brownskin Lady Bird* (1994).
> Rich, Doris L., *Queen Bess: Daredevil Aviator* (1993).

Coleridge-Taylor, Samuel (1875–1912). Performing Aritist
> Coleridge-Taylor, Avril, *The Heritage of Samuel Coleridge-Taylor* (1979).
> Sayers, W. C. Berwick, *Samuel Coleridge-Taylor: His Life and Letters* (1915).

Coles, Samuel B. (1888–1957). Religious Worker
> Coles, Samuel B., *Preacher with a Plow* (1957).

Collins, Lee (1901–1960). Performing Artist
> Collins, Lee, *Oh, Didn't He Ramble: The Life Story of Lee Collins, as Told to Mary Collins*, ed. Frank J. Gillis and John W. Miner (1974).

Coltrane, John (1926–1967). Performing Artist
> Cole, Bill, *John Coltrane* (1976).
> Nisenson, Eric, *Ascension: John Coltrane and His Quest* (1993).
> Porter, Lewis, *John Coltrane: His Life and Music* (1998).
> Simpkins, Cuthbert Ormond, *Coltrane: A Biography* (1975).

Connerly, Ward (1939–). Edcuator, Reformer
> Connerly, Ward, *Creating Equal: My Fight against Race Preferences* (2000).

Conyou, David (1791–1847). Religious Worker
> Green, Augustus R., *The Life of the Rev. Dandridge F. Davis of the African M.E. Church. . . Also a Brief Sketch of the Life of the Rev. David Conyou of the A.M.E.C., and His Ministerial Labors* (1850).

Cooke, Samuel "Sam" (1935–1964). Performing Artist
> Wolff, Daniel, with S. R. Crain, Clifton White, and David Tenenbaum, *You Send Me: The Life And Times of Sam Cooke* (1995).

Cooper, Anna Julia Haywood (1858–1964). Educator, Club Leader, Reformer
> Cooper, Anna Julia, *The Third Step* (1950?).
> ———— *A Voice from the South, by a Black Woman From the South* (1892).
> ———— *The Voice of Anna Julia Cooper: Including A Voice from the South and Other Important Essays, Papers, and Letters*, ed. Charles Lemert and Esme Bhan (1997).
> Hutchinson, Louise Daniel, *Anna J. Cooper: A Voice from the South* (1981).

Cooper, Thomas (1775–1820). Slave
> Hopper, Isaac T., *Narrative of the Life of Thomas Cooper* (1832).

Coppin, Fanny Muriel Jackson (1836?–1913). Educator, Religious Worker, Performing Artist, Journalist, Club Leader
> Coppin, Fanny M. Jackson, *Reminiscences of School Life, and Hints on Teaching* (1913).

Coppin, Levi Jenkins (1848–1924). Educator, Religious Worker, Journalist, Business Person, Reformer
> Coppin, Levi Jenkins, *Observations of Persons and Things in South Africa, 1900–1904* (1905).

———— *Unwritten History: An Autobiography* (1913).

Corrothers, James David (1869–1917). Religious Worker
Corrothers, James David, *In Spite of the Handicap* (1919).

Cotton, Ella Earls (?). Educator
Cotton, Ella Earls, *A Spark for My People: The Sociological Autobiography of a Negro Teacher* (1954).

Craft, Ellen (1826–1891). Slave, Abolitionist, Lecturer, Agriculturalist
Craft, William, *Running a Thousand Miles for Freedom; Or, the Escape of William and Ellen Craft from Slavery* (1860).

Craft, William (1824–1900). Slave, Abolitionist, Lecturer, Author, Agriculturalist
Craft, William, *Running a Thousand Miles for Freedom; Or, the Escape of William and Ellen Craft from Slavery* (1860).

Crouch, Andrae (1942–). Performing Artist
Crouch, Andrae, and Nina Ball, *Through It All* (1974).

Crouch, Hubert Branch (1906–1980). Scientist
King, William M., "Hubert Branch Crouch and the Origins of the National Institute of Science," *Journal of Negro History* 79 (1994): 18–33.

Crum, William Darius (1859–1912). Medical Worker, Political Figure, Educator
Gatewood, Willard B., "William D. Crum: A Negro in Politics," *Journal of Negro History* 53 (1968): 301–20.

Crumes, Cole, Sr. (1906–1968)
Crumes, Cole, Sr., *My Life Is an Open Book* (1965).

Crummell, Alexander (1819–1898). Religious Worker, Educator, Reformer, Author
Crummell, Alexander, *Civilization and Black Progress: Selected Writings of Alexander Crummell on the South,* ed. J. R. Oldfield (1995).
———— *Destiny and Race: Selected Writings, 1840–1898,* ed. Wilson Jeremiah Moses (1992).
Moses, Wilson Jeremiah, *Alexander Crummell: A Study of Civilization and Discontent* (1992).
Moss, Alfred, "Alexander Crummell: Black Nationalist and Apostle of Western Civilization," in Leon Litwack and August Meier, ed., *Black Leaders of the Nineteenth Century* (1988): 237–51.
Rigsby, Gregory U., *Alexander Crummell: Pioneer in Nineteenth Century Pan-African Thought* (1987).
Scruggs, Otey, "We the Children of Africa in this Land: Alexander Crummell," in Lorraine W. Williams, ed., *Africa and the Afro-American Experience* (1977): 77–95.

Cuffe, Paul, Jr. (1786?–?)
Cuffe, Paul, *Narrative of the Life and Adventures of Paul Cuffe, A Pequot Indian: During Thirty Years Spent at Sea, and in Travelling in Foreign Lands* (1839).

Cuffe, Paul Sr. (1759–1817). Seaman, Educator, Reformer, Political Figure, Slave, Abolitionist
Alexander, William, *Memoir of Captain Paul Cuffe, A Man of Colour: To Which is Subjoined the Epistle of the Society of Sierra Leone in Africa, &c.* (1811).
Cuffe, Paul, *Captain Paul Cuffe's Logs and Letters, 1808–1817: A Black Quaker's "Voice within the Veil",* ed. Rosalind Cobb Wiggins (1996).
Harris, Sheldon H., *Paul Cuffe: Black America and the African Return* (1972).
Thomas, Lamont D., *Rise To Be a People: A Biography of Paul Cuffe* (1986).

Cuney, Norris Wright (1846–1896). Political Figure, Business Person
Hare, Maud Cuney, *Norris Wright Cuney: A Tribune of the Black People* (1913).

Dabney, Wendell Phillips (1865–1952). Journalist, Performing Artist
Beaver, Joseph T., Jr, *I Want You to Know Wendell Phillips Dabney* (1958).

Dancy, John Campbell, Jr. (1888–1967). Educator, Reformer, Business Person, Government Worker
Dancy, John Campbell, *Sand against the Wind: The Memoirs of John C. Dancy* (1966).

Dandridge, Dorothy (1924–1965). Performing Artist
Bogle, Donald, *Dorothy Dandridge: A Biography* (1997).
Dandridge, Dorothy, and Earl Conrad, *Everything and Nothing: The Dorothy Dandridge Tragedy* (1970).

Davidson, Henry Damon (1869–?). Educator, Religious Worker, Journalist, Political Figure
Davidson, Henry Damon, *"Inching Along": Or, the Life and Work of an Alabama Farm Boy, An Autobiography by Henry Damon Davidson* (1944).

Davidson, Jack (1825–1881). Military Person
Davidson, Homer K., *Black Jack Davidson: A Cavalry Commander on the Western Frontier* (1974).

Davis, Angela Yvonne (1944–). Reformer, Political Figure, Author
Davis, Angela Y., *Angela Davis: An Autobiography* (1974).

Davis, Benjamin Jefferson, Jr. (1903–1964). Political Figure, Author
Davis, Benjamin Jefferson, Jr., *Communist Councilman from Harlem: Autobiographical Notes Written in a Federal Penitentiary* (1969).

Davis, Benjamin Oliver, Jr. (1912–). Aviator, Military Person
Davis, Benjamin O., Jr., *Benjamin O. Davis, Jr., American: An Autobiography* (1991).

Davis, Benjamin Oliver, Sr. (1880–1970). Military Person, Educator, Political Figure
Fletcher, Marvin E., *America's First Black General: Benjamin O. Davis, Sr., 1880–1970* (1989).

Davis, Dandridge Fayette (1807–1847). Religious Worker
Green, Augustus R., *The Life of the Rev. Dandridge F. Davis of the African M.E. Church. . . Also a Brief Sketch of the Life of the Rev. David Conyou of the A.M.E.C., and His Ministerial Labors* (1850).

Davis, Edward (1914–). Business Person
Davis, Ed, *One Man's Way* (1979).

Davis, Frank Marshall (1907–1997). Poet, Journalist
Davis, Frank Marshall, *Livin' the Blues: Memoirs of a Black Journalist and Poet*, ed. John Edgar Tidwell (1992).

Davis, Miles Dewey, III (1926–1991). Performing Artist
Carr, Ian, *Miles Davis: A Biography* (1982).
Chambers, Jack, *Milestones I: The Music and Times of Miles Davis to 1960* (1983).
——— *Milestones II* (1985).
Cole, Bill, *Miles Davis: A Musical Biography* (1974).
Nisenson, Eric, *'Round about Midnight: A Portrait of Miles Davis* (1982).

Davis, Noah (1804–1867). Religious Worker, Author
Davis, Noah, *A Narrative of the Life of Rev. Noah Davis, a Colored Man, Written by Himself, at the Age of Fifty-Four* (1859).
Williams, Michael Patrick, "The Black Evangelical Ministry in the Antebellum Border States: Profiles of Elders John Berry Meachum and Noah Davis," *Foundations* 21 (1978): 225–41.

Davis, Ossie (1917–). Performing Artist, Author, Reformer
Davis, Ossie, and Ruby Dee, *With Ossie and Ruby: In This Life Together* (1998).

Davis, Sammy, Jr. (1925–1990). Performing Artist
Davis, Sammy, Jr., and Jane and Burt Boyar, *Yes I Can: The Story of Sammy Davis, Jr.* (1965).

Day, Helen Caldwell (1926–). Medical Worker, Journalist
Day, Helen Caldwell, *Color, Ebony* (1951).
——— *Not without Tears* (1954).

Dean, Harry (1864–1935). Seaman, Explorer/Traveler, Lecturer
Dean, Harry, with Sterling North, *The Pedro Gorino: The Adventures of a Negro Sea-Captain in Africa and on the Seven Seas in His Attempts to Found an Ethiopian Empire* (1929).

Dean, Jennie (1852?–1913). Educator, Religious Worker
Lewis, Stephen Johnson, *Undaunted Faith: The Life Story of Jennie Dean: Missionary, Teacher, Crusader, Builder, Founder of Manassas Industrial School* (1942).

Deane, Joseph (1829–?)
Deane, Joseph, *Sketch of the Life and Travels of Joseph Deane, Written by Himself* (1857).

Dee, Ruby [Ruby Ann Wallace] (1924–). Performing Artist, Author, Reformer
Davis, Ossie, and Ruby Dee, *With Ossie and Ruby: In This Life Together* (1998).

Delaney, Beauford (1902–1979). Artist
Leeming, David, *Amazing Grace: A Life of Beauford Delaney* (1998).

Delaney, Lucy A. Berry (1830–?). Reformer
Delaney, Lucy A. Berry, *From Darkness Cometh the Light: Or, Struggles for Freedom* (1891).

Delany, Annie Elizabeth (1891–1995). Writer

Delany, Sarah Louise, and Annie Elizabeth Delany, with Amy Hill Hearth, *Having Our Say: The Delany Sisters' First One Hundred Years* (1993).

Delany, Martin (1812–1885). Reformer, Medical Worker, Author, Lecturer

Griffith, Cyril E., *The African Dream: Martin R. Delany and the Emergence of Pan-African Thought* (1975).

Levine, Robert S., *Martin Delany, Frederick Douglass, and the Politics of Representative Identity* (1997).

Painter, Nell Irvin, "Martin R. Delany: Elitism and Black Nationalism," in Leon Litwack and August Meier, ed., *Black Leaders of the Nineteenth Century* (1988): 149–71.

Rollin, Frank A. [Frances E. Rollin Whipper], *Life and Public Services of Martin R. Delany* (1868).

Ullmann, Victor, *Martin Delany: The Beginnings of Black Nationalism* (1971).

Delany, Samuel R. (1942–). Author

Delany, Samuel R., *The Motion of Light in Water: Sex and Science Fiction Writing in the East Village, 1957–1965* (1988).

Delany, Sarah Louise (1889–1999). Writer

Delany, Sarah Louise, and Annie Elizabeth Delany, with Amy Hill Hearth, *Having Our Say: The Delany Sisters' First One Hundred Years* (1993).

Dellums, Ronald V. (1935–). Political Figure

Dellums, Ronald V., and H. Lee Halterman, *Lying Down with the Lions: A Public Life from the Streets of Oakland to the Halls of Power* (2000).

Denby, Charles (1907–?). Labor Leader, Factory Worker, Reformer

Denby, Charles, *Indignant Heart: A Black Worker's Journal* (1978).

Ward, Matthew [Charles Denby], *Indignant Heart* (1952).

Derricotte, Juliette (1897–1931). Educator, Religious Worker

Cuthbert, Marion, *Juliette Derricotte* (1933).

Derricotte, Toi (1941–). Poet, Educator

Derricotte, Toi, *The Black Notebooks: An Interior Journey* (1997).

Dett, Robert Nathaniel (1882–1943). Peforming Artist, Religious Worker

McBrien, Vivian Flagg, *R. Nathaniel Dett: His Life and Works* (1977).

Diallo, Ayuba Suleiman (?). Slave

Ayuba Suleiman Diallo, a Muslim Fulani of Futa Toro (Bondu), Was Kidnapped in 1730 on the Gambia and Sold as a Slave but Was Freed in America and Returned to His Homeland (1750).

Dickson, Amanda America (1849–1893)

Leslie, Kent Anderson, *Woman of Color, Daughter of Privilege: Amanda America Dickson, 1849–1893* (1995).

Dipper, John (1778–1836). Religious Worker, Business Person, Slave

Lane, Carl, and Rhoda Freeman, "John Dipper and the Experience of the Free Black Elite, 1816–1836," *Virginia Magazine of History and Biography* 87 (1992): 399–406.

Divine, Father [George Baker] (1879–1965). Religious Worker, Service Industry Employee, Author

Burnham, Kenneth E., *God Comes to America: Father Divine and the Peace Mission Movement* (1979).

Watts, Jill, *God, Harlem, U.S.A.: The Father Divine Story* (1992).

Weisbrot, Robert, *Father Divine and the Struggle for Racial Equality* (1980).

Dixon, George "Little Chocolate" (1870–1909). Athlete, Author

Dixon, George, *A Lesson in Boxing* (1893).

Dixon, Willie (1915–). Performing Artist

Dixon, Willie, with Don Snowden, *I Am the Blues: The Willie Dixon Story* (1989).

Dodds, Warren "Baby" (1898–1959). Performing Artist

Dodds, Warren, as told to Larry Gara, *The Baby Dodds Story* (1959).

Dodson, Owen (1914–1983). Writer, Educator

Hatch, James V., *Sorrow is the Only Faithful One: The Life of Owen Dodson* (1993).

Dormigold, Kate (?). Slave

Dormigold, Kate, *A Slave Girl's Story: Being an Autobiography of Kate Dormigold* (1898).

Dorsey, Thomas Andrew (1899–1993). Performing Artist, Religious Worker

Harris, Michael W., *The Rise of Gospel Blues: The Music of Thomas Andrew Dorsey in the Urban Church* (1992).

Douglass, Frederick (1817?–1895). Reformer, Lecturer, Abolitionist, Journalist, Government Worker, Political Figure

Blassingame, John, et al., ed., *The Frederick Douglass Papers, Series I: Speeches, Debates, and Interviews* (5 vols., 1979–1992).

Blassingame, John W., John R. McKivigan, Peter P. Hinks, and Gerald Fulkerson, ed., *The Frederick Douglass Papers, Series II: Autobiographical Writings* (1999-).

Blight, David W., *Frederick Douglass' Civil War: Keeping Faith in Jubilee* (1989).

Burke, Ronald K., *Frederick Douglass: Crusading Orator for Human Rights* (1996).

Chesnutt, Charles W., *Frederick Douglass* (1899).

Diedrich, Maria, *Love Across Color Lines: Ottilie Assing and Frederick Douglass* (1999).

Douglass, Frederick, *Frederick Douglass on Women's Rights*, ed. Philip Foner (1976).

———— *Life and Times of Frederick Douglass, Written by Himself: His Early Life as a Slave, His Escape from Bondage, and His Complete History to the Present Time* (1881).

———— *The Life and Writings of Frederick Douglass*, ed. Philip S. Foner (5 vols., 1950–55).

———— *My Bondage and My Freedom* (1855).

———— *Narrative of the Life of Frederick Douglass, an American Slave. Written by Himself* (1845).

Gregory, James M., *Frederick Douglass the Orator: Containing an Account of His Life; His Eminent Public Services; His Brilliant Career as Orator; Selections from His Speeches and Writings* (1893).

Huggins, Nathan I., *Slave and Citizen: The Life of Frederick Douglass* (1980).

Levine, Robert S., *Martin Delany, Frederick Douglass, and the Politics of Representative Identity* (1997).

Martin, Waldo E., Jr., "Frederick Douglass: Humanist as Race Leader," in Leon Litwack and August Meier, ed., *Black Leaders of the Nineteenth Century* (1988): 59–84.

———— *The Mind of Frederick Douglass* (1984).

McFeely, William S., *Frederick Douglass* (1991).

Preston, Dickson J., *Young Frederick Douglass: The Maryland Years* (1980).

Quarles, Benjamin, *Frederick Douglass* (1948).

Scruggs, Otey, "Two Black Patriarchs: Frederick Douglass and Alexander Crummell," *Afro-Americans in New York Life and History* 6 (1982): 17–30.

Washington, Booker T., *Frederick Douglass* (1907).

Douglass, H. Ford (1831?–1865). Abolitionist

Harris, Robert L., Jr., "H. Ford Douglass: Afro-American Anti-Slavery Emigrationist," *Journal of Negro History* 62 (1977): 217–34.

Douglass, Sarah Mapps (1806–1882). Educator, Reformer, Author, Abolitionist

Lindhorst, Marie, "Politics in a Box: Sarah Mapps Douglass and the Female Literary Association, 1831–1833," *Pennsylvania History* 65 (1998): 263–78.

Downing, George Thomas (1819–1903). Businessperson, Reformer

Washington, S. A. M., *George Thomas Downing: Sketch of His Life and Times* (1910).

Drayton, Daniel (1802–?). Slave

Drayton, Daniel, *Personal Memoir of Daniel Drayton: For Four Years and Four Months a Prisoner (For Charity's Sake) in Washington Jail. Including a Narrative of the Voyage and Capture of the Schooner Pearl* (1853).

Drew, Charles Richard (1904–1950). Athlete, Medical Worker, Scientist, Educator, Military Person, Author

Love, Spencie, *One Blood: The Death and Resurrection of Charles R. Drew* (1996).

Dryden, Charles Walter (1920–). Aviator, Military Person

Dryden, Charles W., *A-Train: Memoirs of a Tuskegee Airman* (1997).

Du Bois, William Edward Burghardt (1868–1963). Educator, Author, Reformer, Political Figure

Broderick, Francis L., *W. E. B. Du Bois: Negro Leader in a Time of Crisis* (1959).

Drake, St Clair, "Dr. W. E. B. Du Bois: A Life Lived Experimentally and Self-Documented," *Contributions in Black Studies* 8 (1987): 111–34.

Du Bois, Shirley Graham, *His Day is Marching On: A Memoir of W. E. B. Du Bois* (1971).

Du Bois, William Edward Burghardt, *The Autobiography of W. E. B. Du Bois: A Soliloquy on Viewing My Life from the Last Decade of Its First Century* (1968).

——— *The Complete Published Works of W. E. B. Du Bois,* ed. Herbert Aptheker (37 vols., 1980).

——— *The Correspondence of W. E. B. Du Bois,* ed. Herbert Aptheker (3 vols., 1973, 1976, 1978).

——— *Darkwater: Voices from within the Veil* (1920).

——— *Dusk of Dawn: An Essay toward an Autobiography of a Race Concept* (1940).

——— *In Battle For Peace: The Story of My 83rd Birthday* (1952).

——— *The Seventh Son: The Thought and Writings of W. E. B. Du Bois,* ed. Julius Lester (2 vols., 1971).

——— *The Souls of Black Folk: Essays and Sketches* (1903).

Holt, Thomas C., "The Political Uses of Alienation: W. E. B. Du Bois on Politics, Race, and Culture, 1903–1940," *American Quarterly* 42 (1990): 301–23.

Huggins, Nathan I., "W. E. B. Du Bois and Heroes," *American Studies [West Germany]* 34 (1989): 167–74.

Lewis, David Levering, *W. E. B. Du Bois: Biography of a Race, 1868–1919* (1993).

——— *W. E. B. Du Bois: The Fight for Equality and the American Century, 1919–1963* (2000).

———, ed., *W. E. B. Du Bois: A Reader* (1995).

Marable, Manning, *W. E. B.: Black Radical Democrat* (1986).

Posnock, Ross, "The Distinction of Du Bois: Aesthetics, Pragmatism, Politics," *American Literary History* 7 (1995): 500–24.

Rampersad, Arnold, *The Art and Imagination of W. E. B. Du Bois* (1976).

Reed, Adolph L., Jr., *W. E. B. Du Bois and American Political Thought: Fabianism and the Color Line* (1997).

Rudwick, Elliot, *W. E. B. Du Bois: A Study in Minority Group Leadership* (1960).

——— "W. E. B. Du Bois: Protagonist of the Afro-American Protest," in John Hope Franklin and August Meier, ed., *Black Leaders of the Twentieth Century* (1982): 63–83.

Taylor, Carol M., "W. E. B. Du Bois's Challenge to Scientific Racism," *Journal of Black Studies* 11 (1981): 449–460.

Dubois, Silvia (1768–1889). Slave

Larison, Cornelius Wilson, *Silvia Dubois: A Biografy of the Slav Who Whipt Her Mistres and Gand Her Fredom* (1883).

Dunbar, Paul Laurence (1872–1906). Author, Service Industry Employee, Journalist

Brawley, Benjamin, *Paul Laurence Dunbar: Poet of His People* (1936).

Turner, Darwin T., "Paul Laurence Dunbar: The Rejected Symbol," *Journal of Negro History* 52 (1967): 1–13.

Wiggins, Lida Keck, *The Life and Works of Paul Lawrence Dunbar* (1907).

Dunbar-Nelson, Alice Ruth Moore (1875–1935). Author, Journalist, Reformer, Club Leader

Dunbar-Nelson, Alice, *Give Us Each Day: The Diary of Alice Dunbar-Nelson,* ed. Gloria T. Hull (1984).

——— *The Works of Alice Dunbar-Nelson,* ed. Gloria T. Hull (1988).

Hull, Gloria T., "Alice Dunbar-Nelson: Delaware Writer and Woman of Affairs," *Delaware History* 17 (1976): 87–103.

Dungy, John A. (?). Slave

Dungy, J. A., *A Narrative of the Rev. John Dungy, Who Was Born a Slave* (1866).

Dunham, Katherine (1909–). Performing Artist, Anthropologist

Beckford, Ruth, *Katherine Dunham: A Biography* (1979).

Dunham, Katherine, *A Touch of Innocence* (1959).

Dunn, Oscar James (1820?–1871). Slave, Political Figure

Perkins, A. E., "Oscar James Dunn," *Phylon* 4 (1943): 105–21.

Dunnigan, Alice Allison (1906–1983). Journalist
Dunnigan, Alice Allison, *A Black Woman's Experience: From Schoolhouse to White House*(1974).

Durham, John Stephens (1861–1919). Business Person, Lawyer
Wynes, Charles E., "John Stephens Durham, Black Philadelphian: At Home and Abroad," *Pennsylvania Magazine of History and Biography* 106 (1982): 527–38.

Durnford, Andrew (1800–1859). Agriculturalist
Whitten, David O., *Andrew Durnford: A Black Sugar Planter in Antebellum Louisiana* (1981).

Earley, Charity Adams (1918–). Military Person
Earley, Charity Adams, *One Woman's Army: A Black Officer Remembers the WAC*(1989).

Early, Gerald (1952–). Author, Educator
Early, Gerald, *Daughters: On Family and Fatherhood* (1994).

Early, Jordan Winston (1814– 189?). Slave, Religious Worker
Early, Sarah J. W., *Life and Labors of Rev. Jordan W. Early, One of the Pioneers of African Methodism in the West and South* (1894).

Edelman, Marian Wright (1939–). Lawyer, Reformer
Edelman, Marian Wright, *Lanterns: A Memoir of Mentors* (1999).

Edwards, David "Honeyboy" (1915–). Performing Artist
Edwards, David "Honeyboy", *The World Don't Owe Me Nothing: The Life and Times of Delta Bluesman Honeyboy Edwards* (1997).

Edwards, Harry (1942–). Athlete, Educator, Reformer
Edwards, Harry, *The Struggle That Must Be: An Autobiography* (1980).

Edwards, William James (1869–1950). Journalist, Business Person, Educator, Reformer
Edwards, William James, *Twenty-Five Years in the Black Belt* (1918).
Stone, Donald P., *Fallen Prince: William James Edwards, Black Education and the Quest for Afro-American Nationality* (1990).

Elaw, Zilpha (1790?–1845). Religious Worker, Author
Elaw, Zilpha, *Memoirs of the Life, Religious Experience, Ministerial Travels and Labours, of Mrs Zilpha Elaw, an American Female of Colour; Together with Some Account of the Great Religious Revivals in America. Written by Herself* (1846).

Eldridge, Elleanor (1784–1845?). Slave
Green, Frances H., *Elleanor's Second Book* (1841).
———— *Memoirs of Elleanor Eldridge* (1838).

Elizabeth (?). Slave
Elizabeth, *Memoir of Old Elizabeth, a Coloured Woman* (1866).

Ellington, Edward Kennedy "Duke" (1899–1974). Performing Artist, Journalist
Collier, James Lincoln, *Duke Ellington* (1987).
Ellington, Edward Kennedy, *Music Is My Mistress* (1973).
Ellington, Mercer, *Duke Ellington in Person: An Intimate Memoir* (1978).
George, Don R., *Sweet Man: The Real Duke Ellington* (1981).
Hasse, John E., *Beyond Category: The Life and Genuis of Duke Ellington* (1993).
Lambert, G. E., *Duke Ellington* (1961).
Rattenbury, Ken, *Duke Ellington, Jazz Composer* (1990).
Tucker, Mark, *Ellington: The Early Years* (1991).

Elliott, Robert Brown (1842–1884). Political Figure, Lawyer, Explorer/Traveler
Lamson, Peggy, *The Glorious Failure: Black Congressman Robert Brown Elliott and the Reconstruction in South Carolina* (1973).

Ellison, Ralph Waldo (1914–1994). Author
Ellison, Ralph Waldo, *Shadow and Act* (1964).

Equiano, Olaudah [Gustavus Vassa] (1745?–1797). Seaman, Traveler, Explorer, Abolitionist
Equiano, Olaudah, *The Interesting Narrative of the Life of Olaudah Equiano, or Gustavus Vassa, the African. Written by Himself* (1789).

Europe, James Reese (1881–1919). Performing Artist
Badger, Reid, *A Life in Ragtime: A Biography of James Reese Europe* (1995).

Everett, Syble Ethel Byrd (1903?–). Educator, Performing Artist
    Everett, Syble Ethel Byrd, *Adventures with Life: An Autobiography of a Distinguished Negro Citizen* (1945).

Evers, James Charles (1922–). Reformer, Political Figure
    Evers, Charles, *Evers* (1971).

Evers, Medgar Wylie (1925–1963). Reformer
    Evers, Mrs. Medgar, with William Peters, *For Us, The Living* (1967).

Evers-Williams, Myrlie Beasley (1933 –). Reformer
    Evers, Mrs. Medgar, with William Peters, *For Us, The Living* (1967).
    Evers-Williams, Myrlie, with Melinda Blau, *Watch Me Fly: What I Learned on the Way to Becoming the Woman I Was Meant to Be* (1999).

Farmer, James (1920–1999). Reformer
    Farmer, James, *Lay Bare the Heart: An Autobiography of the Civil Rights Movement* (1985).

Farrakhan, Louis Abdul (1933–). Religious Leader
    Alexander, Amy, ed., *The Farrakhan Factor: African-American Writers on Leadership, Nationhood, and Minister Louis Farrakhan* (1998).
    Gardell, Mattias, *In the Name of Elijah Muhammad: Louis Farrakhan and the Nation of Islam* (1996).
    Magida, Arthur J., *Prophet of Rage: A Life of Louis Farrakhan and His Nation* (1996).

Fauset, Jessie Redmon (1882–1961). Educator, Author, Lecturer, Journalist
    Sylvander, Carolyn Wedin, *Jessie Redmon Fauset, Black American Writer* (1976).

Fedric, Francis (?). Slave
    Fedric, Francis, *Slave Life in Virginia and Kentucky: Or, Fifty Years of Slavery in the Southern States of America* (1863).

Ferebee, London R. (1849–?). Religious Worker, Slave
    Ferebee, London R., *A Brief History of the Slave Life of Rev. L. R. Ferebee, and the Battles of Life, and Four Years of His Ministerial Life* (1882).

Ferguson, Ira Lunan (1904–?). Educator
    Ferguson, Ira Lunan, *I Dug Graves at Night to Attend College by Day: The Story of a West Indian Negro American's First 30 Years in the United States: An Autobiography* (vol.1., 1968).
    ———— *I Dug Graves at Night to Attend College by Day: My Later Years as a Naturalized West-Indian American: An Autobiography* (vol. 2., 1969).
    ———— *I Dug Graves at Night to Attend College by Day: Reflections: This West Indian-American Looks Back Over 50 Years of Life in America: Humor-Pathos-Rewards: An Autobiography* (vol. 3., 1970).

Ferrill, London (1789–1854). Slave, Religious Worker
    Biography of London Ferrill, Pastor of the First Baptist Church of Colored Persons, Lexington, Ky (1854).

Fields, Alonzo (1900–?). Political Figure
    Fields, Alonzo, *My Twenty-One Years in the White House* (1961).

Fields, Mamie Garvin (1888–1987). Domestic, Educator
    Fields, Mamie Garvin, and Karen Fields, *Lemon Swamp and Other Places: A Carolina Memoir* (1983).

Finch, William (1832–1911). Political Figure
    Russell, James, and Jerry Thornberry, "William Finch of Atlanta: The Black Politician as Civic Leader," in Howard Rabinowitz, ed., *Southern Black Leaders of the Reconstruction Era* (1982): 309–34.

Fisher, Elijah John (1858–1915). Religious Worker, Business Person, Lecturer, Educator
    Fisher, Miles Mark, *The Master's Slave, Elijah John Fisher* (1922).

Fletcher, Tom [Thomas] (1873–1954). Performing Artist
    Fletcher, Tom, *100 Years of the Negro in Show Business: The Tom Fletcher Story* (1954).

Flipper, Henry Ossian (1856–1940). Military Person, Miner, Government Worker
    Black, Lowell D., and Sara H. Black, *An Officer and a Gentleman: The Military Career of Lieutenant Henry O. Flipper* (1985).
    Eppinga, Jane, *Henry Ossian Flipper: West Point's First Black Graduate* (1996).
    Flipper, Henry Ossian, *The Colored Cadet at West Point* (1878).

—— *Negro Frontiersman: The Western Memoirs of Henry O. Flipper, First Negro Graduate of West Point,* ed. Theodore D. Harris (1963).

Flood, Curt [Curtis Charles] (1938–). Athlete

Flood, Curt, with Richard Carter, *The Way It Is* (1971).

Foote, Julia A. J. (1823–1900). Religious Worker

Foote, Julia A. J., *A Brand Plucked from the Fire: An Autobiographical Sketch* (1886).

Forman, James (1928–). Reformer

Forman, James, *The Making of Black Revolutionaries: A Personal Account* (1972).

—— *The Political Thought of James Forman* (1970).

Forten, Charlotte. *See* Grimké, Charlotte Forten

Forten, James (1766–1842). Business Person, Reformer

Billington, Ray Allen, "James Forten—Forgotten Abolitionist," *Negro History Bulletin* 13 (1949): 31–36. 45.

Forten, James, *Remarks on the Life and Character of James Forten,* ed. Robert Purvis (1842).

Fortune, Timothy Thomas (1856–1928). Author, Journalist, Political Figure

Thornbrough, Emma Lou, *T. Thomas Fortune: Militant Journalist* (1972).

—— "T. Thomas Fortune: Militant Editor in the Age of Accommodation," in John Hope Franklin and August Meier, ed., *Black Leaders of the Twentieth Century* (1982): 19–37.

Foster, Pops [George Murphy] (1892–1969). Performing Artist

Foster, Pops, *Pops Foster: The Autobiography of a New Orleans Jazzman* (1971).

Frank, Free (1777–1854). Business Person, Slave

Walker, Juliet E. K., *Free Frank: A Black Pioneer on the Antebellum Frontier* (1983).

Franklin, Aretha (1942–). Performing Artist

Franklin, Aretha, and David Ritz, *Aretha: From These Roots* (1999).

Franklin, Buck Colbert (1879–1960). Lawyer

Franklin, Buck Colbert, *My Life and An Era: The Autobiography of Buck Colbert Franklin,* ed. John Hope Franklin and John Whittington Franklin (1997).

Franklin, Clarence Lavaughn (1915–1984). Religious Worker

Franklin, C. L., *Give Me This Mountain: Life and History and Selected Sermons,* ed. Jeff Todd Titon (1989).

Franklin, Henry (1843–?). Slave

Franklin, Henry, *A Sketch of Henry Franklin and Family* (1887).

Franklin, John Hope (1915–). Educator, Political Figure

Franklin, John Hope, "John Hope Franklin: A Life of Learning," in John Hope Franklin, ed., *Race and History: Selected Essays, 1938–1988* (1989): 277–291.

Franks, Gary (1953–). Political Figure

Franks, Gary, *Searching for the Promised Land: An African American's Optimistic Odyssey* (1996).

Frazier, Edward Franklin (1894–1962). Educator, Reformer, Journalist

Platt, Anthony M., *E. Franklin Frazier Reconsidered* (1991).

Frederick, Francis (1809?–?). Religious Worker

Frederick, Francis, *Autobiography of Rev. Francis Frederick, of Virginia* (1869).

Fuller, Thomas Oscar (1867–1942). Educator, Religious Worker, Political Figure, Business Person

Fuller, Thomas O., *Twenty Years in Public Life, 1890–1910* (1910).

Fulwood, Sam, III (1956–). Journalist

Fulwood, Sam, III, *Waking from the Dream: My Life in the Black Middle Class* (1996).

Gadsden, Sam (1882–?). Agriculturalist

Gadsden, Sam, *An Oral History of Edisto Island: Sam Gadsden Tells the Story* (1974).

Gaines, Patrice (1949?–). Journalist

Gaines, Patrice, *Laughing in the Dark: From Colored Girl to Woman of Color—A Journey from Prison to Power* (1994).

Garner, Errol (1921–1977). Performing Artist

Doran, James M., *Erroll Garner: The Most Happy Piano* (1985).

Garnet, Henry Highland (1815–1882). Religious Worker, Political Figure, Reformer, Journalist, Government Worker

Ofari, Earl, *"Let Your Motto Be Resistance": The Life and Thought of Henry Highland Garnet* (1972).

Schor, Joel, *Henry Highland Garnet: A Voice of Black Radicalism in the Nineteenth Century* (1977).

Smith, James McCune, "Sketch of the Life and Labors of Rev. Henry Highland Garnet," in Henry Highland Garnet, *A Memorial Discourse. . .Delivered in the Hall of the House of Representatives, Washington D.C., on Sabbath, February 12, 1865* (1865): 17–34.

Stuckey, Sterling, "A Last Stern Struggle: Henry Highland Garnet and Liberation Theory," in Leon Litwack and August Meier, ed., *Black Leaders of the Nineteenth Century* (1988): 129–47.

Garvey, Marcus (1887–1940). Journalist, Reformer, Lecturer

Cronon, E. David, *Black Moses: The Story of Marcus Garvey and the Universal Negro Improvement Association* (1955).

Garvey, Marcus, *Philosophy and Opinions of Marcus Garvey,* ed. Amy Jacques-Garvey (2 vols., 1923, 1925).

Hill, Robert A., ed., *The Marcus Garvey and Universal Negro Improvement Association Papers* (9 vols., 1983).

Levine, Lawrence W., "Marcus Garvey and the Politics of Revitalization," in John Hope Franklin and August Meier, ed., *Black Leaders of the Twentieth Century* (1982): 105–38.

Stein, Judith, *The World of Marcus Garvey: Race and Class in Modern Society* (1986).

Gaston, Arthur George (1892–1996). Business Person, Undertaker

Gaston, Arthur George, *Green Power: The Successful Way of A. G. Gaston* (1968).

Gates, Henry Louis, Jr. (1950–). Author, Educator

Gates, Henry Louis, Jr., *Colored People: A Memoir* (1994).

Gaudet, Frances Joseph (1861–1934). Educator, Homemaker, Religious Worker, Reformer, Domestic

Gaudet, Frances Joseph, *"He Leadeth Me"* (1913).

Gaye, Marvin (1939–1984). Performing Artist

Ritz, David, *Divided Soul: The Life of Marvin Gaye* (1985).

Gayle, Addison, Jr. (1932–). Educator

Gayle, Addison, Jr., *Wayward Child: A Personal Odyssey* (1977).

Gibbs, Mifflin Wistar (1823–1915). Lawyer, Political Figure, Journalist, Business Person

Dillard, Tom W., "'Golden Prospects and Fraternal Amenities': Mifflin W. Gibbs' Arkansas Years," *Arkansas Historical Quarterly* 25 (1976): 307–33.

Gibbs, Mifflin Wistar, *Shadow and Light: An Autobiography with Reminiscences of the Last and Present Century* (1902).

Gibson, Althea (1927–). Athlete

Gibson, Althea, *I Always Wanted to Be Somebody* (1958).

Gibson, Bob (1935–). Athlete

Gibson, Bob, with Lonnie Wheeler, *Stranger to the Game* (1994).

Gibson, Joshua (1911–1947). Athlete

Brashler, William, *Josh Gibson: A Life in the Negro Leagues* (1978).

Gilbert, John Wesley (1864?–1923). Religious Worker

Colclough, Joseph C., *The Spirit of John Wesley Gilbert* (1925).

Gillespie, Dizzy [John Birks] (1917–1993). Performing Artist

Gillespie, Dizzy, *To Be, or Not. . .to BOP: Memoirs* (1979).

Shipton, Alyn, *Groovin' High: The Life of Dizzy Gillespie* (1999).

Gilliam, Alice Spindle (1908–). Religious Worker, Government Worker

Gilliam, Alice Spindle, *Memoirs—An Octogenarian Speaks* (1995).

Giovanni, Nikki [Yolande Cornelis, Jr.] (1943–). Author

Giovanni, Nikki, *Gemini: An Extended Autobiographical Statement on My Twenty-Five Years of Being a Black Poet* (1971).

Gomez, Joseph (1890–1979). Religious Worker

Gomez-Jefferson, Annetta L., *In Darkness with God: The Life of Joseph Gomez, a Bishop in the African Methodist Episcopal Church* (1998).

Goodwin, Ruby Berkley (1903–?). Educator, Office Worker, Club Leader
Goodwin, Ruby Berkley, *It's Good to Be Black* (1953).
Gordon, Taylor (1893–1971). Performing Artist
Gordon, Taylor, *Born To Be* (1929).
Gordy, Berry, Jr. (1929–). Business Person, Performing Artist
Gordy, Berry, Jr., *To Be Loved: The Music, the Magic, the Memories of Motown: An Autobiography* (1994).
Gordy, Berry, Sr. (1888–1978). Business Person, Performing Artist
Gordy, Berry, Sr., *Movin' Up: Pop Gordy Tells His Story* (1979).
Grandy, Moses (1786?–?). Slave
Grandy, Moses, *Narrative of the Life of Moses Grandy: Late a Slave in the United States of America* (1843).
Grant, Robert Lee (1938–). Educator
Grant, Robert Lee, with Carl Gardner, *The Star Spangled Hustle* (1972).
Green, Elisha Winfield (1818?–1889). Religious Worker
Green, Elisha Winfield, *Life of the Rev. Elisha W. Green, One of the Founders of the Kentucky Normal and Theological Institute* (1888).
Green, Ely [Elisha] (1893–1968). Domestic, Author, Military Person
Green, Ely, *Ely: An Autobiography* (1966).
——— *Ely: Too Black, Too White*, ed. Elizabeth N. Chitty and Arthur Ben Chitty (1970).
Green, Jacob D. (1813–?). Slave
Green, Jacob D., *Narrative of the Life of J. D. Green, a Runaway Slave from Kentucky, Containing an Account of His Three Escapes, in 1839, 1846, 1848* (1864).
Green, John Paterson (1845–1940). Lawyer, Political Figure, Government Worker, Religious Worker
Green, John Paterson, *Fact Stranger Than Fiction: Seventy-Five Years of a Busy Life* (1920).
Green, William (?). Slave
Green, William, *Narrative of Events in the Life of William Green (Formerly a Slave), Written by Himself* (1853).
Greene, Lorenzo Johnston (1899–1988). Educator
Greene, Lorenzo J., *Selling Black History for Carter G. Woodson: A Diary, 1930–1933,* ed. Arvarh E. Strickland (1996).
——— *Working with Carter G. Woodson, the Father of Black History: A Diary, 1928–1930,* ed. Arvarh E. Strickland (1989).
Greene, Percy (1897–1997). Journalist
Thompson, Julius E., *Percy Greene and the* Jackson Advocate*: The Life and Times of a Radical Conservative Black Newspaperman, 1897–1977* (1994).
Gregory, Dick [Richard Claxton] (1932–). Performing Artist, Reformer
Gregory, Dick, with Robert Lipsyte, *Nigger: An Autobiography* (1964).
Gregory, Dick, *Up From Nigger* (1976).
Gregory, Louis G. (1874–1951). Religious Worker
Morrison, Gayle, *To Move the World: Louis G. Gregory and the Advancement of Racial Unity in America* (1982).
Grey, Fred D. (1930–). Lawyer, Religious Worker, Reformer
Gray, Fred D., *Bus Ride to Justice: Changing the System by the System: The Life and Works of Fred D. Gray, Preacher, Attorney, Politician* (1995).
Griggs, Richard (?). Slave
Griggs, Richard, *The Life of Richard Griggs, of Issaquena County, Mississippi, Written by Himself* (1872).
Grimes, William (1784–?). Slave
Grimes, William, *Life of William Grimes, the Runaway Slave, Written by Himself* (1825).
——— *Life of William Grimes, the Runaway Slave, Brought Down to the Present Time. Written by Himself* (1855).

Grimes, William W. (1824–?). Religious Worker, Educator

Grimes, William W., *Thirty-Three Years' Experience of an Itinerant Minister of the A.M.E. Church* (1887).

Grimké, Archibald Henry (1849–1930). Lawyer, Political Figure, Government Worker, Educator, Journalist

Bruce, Dickson D., *Archibald Grimké: Portrait of a Black Independent* (1993).

Grimké, Charlotte L. Forten (1837–1914). Abolitionist, Educator, Author, Performing Artist

Forten, Charlotte L., *The Journals of Charlotte Forten Grimke*, ed. Brenda Stevenson (1988).

Grimké, Francis James (1850–1937). Religious Worker, Educator, Reformer

Grimké, Francis James, *The Works of Francis Grimké: Addresses, Sermons, Thoughts and Meditations, Letters*, ed. Carter G. Woodson (4 vols., 1942).

Gronniosaw, James Albert Ukawsaw (1714?–1775). Author

Gates, Henry Louis, Jr., "James Gronniosaw and the Trope of the Talking Book," *Southern Review* 22 (1986): 252–72.

Gronniosaw, James Albert Ukawsaw, *A Narrative of the Most Remarkable Particulars in the Life of James Albert Ukawsaw Gronniosaw* (1770).

Guffy, Ossie (1931–). Author

Guffy, Ossie, *Ossie: The Autobiography of a Black Woman* (1971).

Haizlip, Shirlee Taylor (1937–). Author

Haizlip, Shirlee Taylor, *The Sweeter the Juice* (1994).

Haizlip, Shirlee Taylor, and Harold C. Haizlip, *In the Garden of Our Dreams: Memoirs of a Marriage* (1998).

Hall, Elder Samuel (?). Slave

Hall, Elder Samuel, *Forty-Seven Years a Slave: A Brief Story of His Life as a Slave and after Freedom* (1912).

Hall, Mansel Phillip (1859–1922). Educator, Religious Worker, Journalist

Hall, Mansel Phillip, *An Autobiography of Mansel P. Hall* (1905).

Hall, Prince (1748–1807). Reformer, Club Leader

Bruce, John E., *Prince Hall, the Pioneer of Negro Masonry* (1921).

Coil, Henry Wilson, *A Documentary Account of Prince Hall and Other Black Fraternal Orders* (1982).

Wesley, Charles H., *Prince Hall: Life and Legacy* (1977).

Hall, Samuel Daniel (1864–?). Club Leader, Slave

Elder, Orville, and Samuel Hall, *The Life of Samuel Hall, Washington, Iowa: A Slave for Forty-Seven Years* (1912).

Hamer, Fannie Lou (1917–1977). Reformer

Hamer, Fannie Lou, *To Praise Our Bridges: An Autobiography* (1967).

Kling, Susan, *Fannie Lou Hamer: A Biography* (1979).

Lee, Chana Kai, *For Freedom's Sake: The Life of Fannie Lou Hamer* (1999).

Mills, Kay, *This Little Light of Mine: The Life of Fannie Lou Hamer* (1993).

Hamilton, Grace Towns (1907–1992). Political Figure, Reformer

Spritzer, Lorraine Nelson, and Jean B. Bergmark, *Grace Towns Hamilton and the Politics of Southern Change: An African American Woman's Struggle for Racial Equality* (1997).

Hammon, Briton (?). Domestic

Hammon, Briton, *Narrative of the Uncommon Sufferings, and Surprising Deliverance of Briton Hammon, a Negro Man* (1760).

Hancock, Gordon Blaine (1884–1970). Religious Worker, Educator, Author, Reformer

Gavins, Raymond, *The Perils and Prospects of Southern Black Leadership: Gordon Blaine Hancock, 1884–1970* (1977).

Handy, William Christopher (1873–1958). Author, Performing Artist, Business Person

Handy, W. C., *Father of the Blues: An Autobiography*, ed. Arna Bontemps (1941).

Hansberry, Lorraine (1930–1965). Author

Nemiroff, Robert, *To Be Young, Gifted, and Black: Lorraine Hansberry in Her Own Words* (1969).

Harrington, Oliver W. (1913–). Artist, Author

Harrington, Oliver W., *Why I Left America and Other Essays*, ed. M. Thomas Inge (1993).

Harris, Eddy L. (1956–). Author
Harris, Eddy L., *South of Haunted Dreams, A Ride through Slavery's Old Black Yard* (1993).
——— *Still Life in Harlem* (1996).

Harrison, Bob [Robert Emanuel] (1928–). Religious Worker
Harrison, Bob, with James Montgomery, *When God Was Black* (1971).

Harrison, Hazel (1883–1969). Performing Artist
Cazort, Jean E., and Constance Tibbs Hobson, *Born to Play: The Life and Career of Hazel Harrison* (1983).

Harrison, Juanita (1891–?). Explorer
Harrison, Juanita, *My Great, Wide, Beautiful World* (1936).

Harrison, Samuel (1818–1900). Religious Worker
Harrison, Samuel, *Rev. Samuel Harrison: His Life Story as Told by Himself* (1899).

Hastie, William (1904–1976). Lawyer, Reformer, Educator, Political Reformer
Ware, Gilbert, *William Hastie: Grace under Pressure* (1984).

Hawes, Hampton (1928–1977). Performing Artist
Hawes, Hampton, and Don Asher, *Raise Up Off Me: A Portrait of Hampton Hawes* (1974).

Hawkins, Coleman (1904–1969). Performing Artist
McCarthy, Albert J., *Coleman Hawkins* (1963).

Hawkins, Walter (1809?–?). Religious Worker
Edward, S. J. Celestine, *From Slavery to a Bishopric, or the Life of Bishop Walter Hawkins of the British Methodist Episcopal Church Canada* (1891).

Hayden, William (1785–?). Slave
Hayden, William, *Narrative of William Hayden, Containing a Faithful Account of His Travels for a Number of Years, Whilst a Slave, in the South, Written by Himself* (1846).

Hayes, Roland (1887–1977). Performing Artist, Factory Worker, Religious Worker
Helm, MacKinley, *Angel Mo' and Her Son, Roland Hayes* (1942).

Haynes, Lemuel (1753–1833). Religious Worker
Cooley, Timothy Mather, *Sketches of the Life and Character of the Rev. Lemuel Haynes, A.M., for Many Years Pastor of a Church in Rutland, VT., and in Granville, New York* (1837).
Haynes, Lemuel, *Black Preacher to White America: The Collected Writings of Lemuel Haynes, 1774–1833*, ed. Richard Newman (1990).

Haywood, Harry [Harry Harwood Hall] (1898–1985). Reformer, Political Figure
Haywood, Harry, *Black Bolshevik: The Autobiography of an Afro-American Communist* (1978).

Healy, James Augustine (1830–1900). Religious Worker
Foley, Albert Sidney, *Bishop Healy: Beloved Outcaste; The Story of a Great Priest Whose Life Has Become a Legend* (1954).

Heard, William Henry (1850–1937). Educator, Religious Worker, Political Figure
Heard, William Henry, *From Slavery to the Bishopric in the A.M.E. Church: An Autobiography* (1924).

Heath, Gordon (1918–1991). Performing Artist
Heath, Gordon, *Deep Are The Roots: Memoirs of a Black Expatriate* (1992).

Hedgeman, Anna Arnold (1899–1990). Government Worker, Reformer, Political Figure, Journalist
Hedgeman, Anna Arnold, *The Gift of Chaos: Decades of American Discontent* (1977).
——— *The Trumpet Sounds: A Memoir of Negro Leadership* (1964).

Henry, George (1819–?). Religious Worker
Henry, George, *Life of George Henry; Together with a Brief History of the Colored People of America* (1894).

Henry, Thomas W. (1794–1877). Religious Worker, Slave
Henry, Thomas W., *From Slavery to Salvation: Autobiography of Rev. Thomas W. Henry of the A.M.E. Church* (1872).

Henson, Josiah (1789–1883). Slave, Religious Worker, Educator, Author, Abolitionist
Henson, Josiah, *The Life of Josiah Henson, Formerly a Slave, Now an Inhabitant of Canada, as Narrated by Himself*, ed. Samuel A. Eliot (1849).

——— *Truth Stranger than Fiction: Father Henson's Story of His Own Life*, ed. Samuel A. Eliot (1858).

Henson, Matthew Alexander (1866–1955). Explorer/Traveler, Government Worker, Seaman
Counter, S. Allen, *North Pole Legacy: Black, White, and Eskimo* (1991).
Henson, Matthew Alexander, *A Negro Explorer at the North Pole* (1912).
Robinson, Bradley, *Dark Companion* (1947).

Herndon, Angelo (1913–). Domestic, Political Figure, Reformer
Herndon, Angelo, *Let Me Live* (1937).

Heth, Joice (?). Medical Worker
The Life of Joice Heth, the Nurse of Gen. George Washington (1835).

Hicks, Estelle Bell (1891–1971). Educator
Hicks, Estelle Bell, *The Golden Apples: Memoirs of a Retired Teacher* (1959).

Hill, Anita Faye (1956–). Lawyer, Government Worker, Educator
Hill, Anita, *Speaking Truth to Power* (1997).

Hill, Hugh Morgan [Brother Blue] (1921–). Performing Artist
Lehrer, Warren, *Brother Blue: A Narrative of Brother Blue, a.k.a. Hugh Morgan Hill* (1995).

Hilliard, David (1942–). Reformer
Hilliard, David, and Lewis Cole, *This Side of Glory: The Autobiography of David Hilliard and the Story of the Black Panther Party* (1993).

Himes, Chester Bomar (1909–1984). Writer
Himes, Chester Bomar, *My Life of Absurdity: The Autobiography of Chester Himes* (1976).
——— *The Quality of Hurt: The Autobiography of Chester Himes* (1972).
Margolies, Edward, and Michel Fabre, *The Several Lives of Chester Himes* (1997).

Hines, Earl (1903–1983). Performing Artist
Dance, Stanley, *The World of Earl Hines* (1977).

Hines, Odette Harper (1914–). Reformer
Rollins, Judith, *All Is Never Said: The Narrative of Odette Harper Hines* (1995).

Hodges, Jacob (1763?–1842). Seaman, Religious Worker
Eddy, Ansel Doane, *"Black Jacob," A Monument of Grace: The Life of Jacob Hodges, an African Negro Who Died in Canadaigua, N.Y., February 1842* (1842).

Hodges, Willis Augustus (1815–1890). Political Figure, Religious Worker, Journalist
Hodges, Willis Augustus, *Free Man of Color: The Autobiography of Willis Augustus Hodges*, ed. Willard B. Gatewood, Jr. (1982).

Holiday, Billie [Eleanora Fagan; Eleanora Gough] (1915–1959). Performing Artist
Chilton, John, *Billie's Blues: Billie Holiday's Story, 1933–1959* (1975).
Clarke, Donald, *Wishing on the Moon: The Life and Times of Billie Holiday* (1994).
Holiday, Billie, with William Dufty, *Lady Sings the Blues* (1956).
Nicholson, Stuart, *Billie Holiday* (1995).
O'Meally, Robert G., *Lady Day: The Many Faces of Billie Holiday* (1991).

Holland, Endesha Ida Mae (1944–). Reformer, Educator
Holland, Endesha Ida Mae, *From the Mississippi Delta: A Memoir* (1997).

Holley, Joseph Winthrop (1874–1958). Religious Worker, Educator
Holley, Joseph Winthrop, *You Can't Build a Chimney from the Top: The South through the Life of a Negro Educator* (1948).

Holly, James Theodore (1829–1911). Religious Worker, Educator, Journalist, Business Person
Dean, David M., *Defender of the Race: James Theodore Holly, Black Nationalist Bishop* (1979).

Holsey, Lucius Henry (1842–1920). Religious Worker, Journalist, Agriculturalist, Educator
Holsey, Lucius Henry, *Autobiography, Sermons, Addresses, and Essays of Bishop L. H. Holsey* (1898).

Holtzclaw, William Henry (1874?–1943). Agriculturalist, Educator, Business Person
Holtzclaw, William Henry, *The Black Man's Burden* (1919).

Hood, James Walker (1831–1918). Religious Worker, Political Figure
Martin, Sandy Dwayne, *For God and Race: The Religious and Political Leadership of AMEZ Bishop James Walker Hood* (1999).

Hooks, Bell [Gloria Watkins] (1955–). Educator, Author, Reformer
hooks, bell, *Bone Black: Memories of Girlhood* (1996).

Hooks, Julia Ann Amanda Morehead Britton Werles (1852–1942). Educator, Performing Artist
Lewis, Selma S., and Marjean G. Kremer, *The Angel of Beale Street: A Biography of Julia Ann Hooks* (1986).

Hope, John (1868–1936). Educator, Religious Worker, Journalist, Reformer
Davis, Leroy, *A Clashing of the Soul: John Hope and the Dilemma of African American Leadership and Black Higher Education in the Early Twentieth Century* (1998).
Torrence, Frederick R., *The Story of John Hope* (1948).

Hope, Lugenia Burns (1871–1947). Reformer, Club Leader
Rouse, Jacqueline A., *Lugenia Burns Hope: Black Southern Reformer* (1989).

Horne, Lena (1917–). Performing Artist
Buckley, Gail Lumet, *The Hornes: An American Family* (1986).
Horne, Lena, *In Person: Lena Horne* (1950).
Horne, Lena, and Richard Schickel, *Lena* (1965).

Horton, Eliza (?). Author
Horton, Eliza, *My Visions: From Eliza Horton (Colored Lady)* (1916).

Houston, Charles Hamilton (1895–1950). Lawyer, Reformer, Educator
McNeil, Genna Rae, "Charles Hamilton Houston: Social Engineer for Civil Rights," in John Hope Franklin and August Meier, ed., *Black Leaders of the Twentieth Century* (1982): 221–40.
——— *Groundwork: Charles Hamilton Houston and the Struggle for Civil Rights* (1983).

Houston, Joshua (1822–1902). Political Figure
Prather, Patricia Smith, *From Slave to Statesman: The Legacy of Joshua Houston, Servant to Sam Houston* (1993).

Howard, Oscar C. (1913–). Business Person
Howard, Oscar C., *Oscar C. Howard, Master of Challenges: An Autobiography* (1974).

Hudson, Hosea (1898–1988). Labor Leader, Reformer, Agriculturalist
Hudson, Hosea, *Black Worker in the Deep South: A Personal Record* (1972).
Painter, Nell Irvin, *The Narrative of Hosea Hudson: His Life as a Negro Communist in the South* (1979).

Huggins, Nathan Irvin (1927–1989). Educator, Author
Blight, David W., "Nathan Irvin Huggins, the Art of History, and the Irony of the American Dream," *Reviews in American History* 22 (1994): 174–90.
Huggins, Nathan I., *Revelations: American History, American Myths,* ed. Brenda Smith Huggins (1989).
Levine, Lawrence W., "The Historical Odyssey of Nathan Irvin Huggins," *Radical History Review* 55 (1993): 113–32.

Hughes, Langston Mercer (1902–1967). Author, Lecturer, Journalist
Hughes, Langston Mercer, *The Big Sea: An Autobiography* (1940).
——— *I Wonder as I Wander* (1956).
Rampersad, Arnold, *The Life of Langston Hughes* (2 vols., 1986, 1988).

Hughes, Louis B. (1832–1913). Business Person, Medical Worker
Hughes, Louis, *Thirty Years a Slave, from Bondage to Freedom: The Institution of Slavery as Seen on the Plantation and in the Home of the Planter: Autobiography of Louis Hughes* (1897).

Hunt, Gilbert (?). Blacksmith
Barrett, Philip, *Gilbert Hunt, the City Blacksmith* (1859).

Hunter, Charles N. (1851–1931). Slave, Educator, Political Figure
Haley, John, *Charles N. Hunter and Race Relations in North Carolina* (1987).

Hunter, Jane Edna Harris (1882–1971). Club Leader, Reformer, Medical Worker, Educator, Lawyer
Hunter, Jane Edna Harris, *A Nickel and a Prayer: An Autobiography* (1940).
Jones, Adrienne Lash, *Jane Edna Hunter: A Case Study of Black Leadership, 1910–1950* (1990).

Hunter-Gault, Charlayne (1942–). Journalist
Hunter-Gault, Charlayne, *In My Place* (1992).
Hunton, William Alphaeus (1863–1916). Reformer, Political Figure, Lawyer
Hunton, Addie D. Waites, *William Alphaeus Hunton: A Pioneer Prophet of Young Men* (1938).
Hunton, William Alphaeus, Jr. (1903–1970). Educator, Reformer
Hunton, Dorothy, *Alphaeus Hunton: The Unsung Valiant* (1986).
Hurston, Zora Neale (1891–1960). Anthropologist, Author, Educator, Journalist
Hemenway, Robert, *Zora Neale Hurston: A Literary Biography* (1977).
Hurston, Zora Neale, *Dust Tracks on a Road: An Autobiography* (1942).
Trefzer, Annette, "'Let Us All Be Kissing-Friends?': Zora Neale Hurston and Race Politics in Dixie," *Journal of American Studies* 31 (1997): 69–78.
Jackson, Andrew (1814–?). Slave
Jackson, Andrew, *Narrative and Writings of Andrew Jackson, of Kentucky: Containing an Account of His Birth, and Twenty-Six Years of His Life While a Slave; His Escape; Five Years of Freedom, Together with Anecdotes Relating to Slavery; Journal of One Year's Travels; Sketches, etc. Narrated by Himself; Written by a Friend* (1847).
Jackson, George Lester (1941–1971). Reformer
Jackson, George Lester, *Soledad Brother: The Prison Letters of George Jackson* (1970).
Jackson, George Washington (1860–1940). Educator, Author, Club Leader, Religious Worker
Jackson, George Washington, *A Brief History of the Life and Works of G. W. Jackson* (1938).
Jackson, James (1826–1833). Slave
Paul, Susan, *Memoir of James Jackson, the Attentive and Obedient Scholar* (1835).
Jackson, James Thomas (1925–1985). Laborer, Author
Jackson, James Thomas, *Waiting in Line at the Drugstore and Other Writings of James Thomas Jackson*, comp. June Acosta (1993).
Jackson, Jesse (1941–). Religious Worker, Reformer
Frady, Marshall, *Jesse: The Life and Pilgrimage of Jesse Jackson* (1996).
Henry, Charles P., *Jesse Jackson: The Search for Common Ground* (1991).
Kosof, Anna, *Jesse Jackson* (1987).
Reynolds, Barbara A., *Jesse Jackson: The Man, the Movement, the Myth* (1975).
Jackson, Mahalia (1911–1972). Performing Artist, Religious Worker
Goreau, Laurraine, *Just Mahalia, Baby* (1975).
Jackson, Mahalia, with Evan McLeod Wylie, *Movin' on Up* (1966).
Schwerin, Jules Victor, *Got to Tell It: Mahalia Jackson, Queen of Gospel* (1992).
Jackson, Mattie (?). Slave
Jackson, Mattie, *The Story of Mattie J. Jackson: Her Parentage—Experience of Eighteen Years in Slavery—Incidents during the War—Her Escape from Slavery,* ed. L. S. Thompson (1866).
Jackson, Rebecca Cox (1795–1871). Religious Worker
Jackson, Rebecca Cox, *Gifts of Power: The Writings of Rebecca Jackson, Black Visionary, Shaker Eldress,* ed. Jean McMahon Humez (1981).
Williams, Richard E., *Called and Chosen: The Story of Mother Rebecca Jackson and The Philadelphia Shakers* (1981).
Jacobs, Harriet Ann [Linda Brent] (1813–1897). Slave, Author
Jacobs, Harriet Ann, *Incidents in the Life of a Slave Girl, Written by Herself,* ed. L. Maria Child (1861).
Jacobs, Phebe Ann (?). Slave
Jacobs, Phebe Ann, *Narrative of Phebe Ann Jacobs,* ed. Mrs T. C. Upham (1850?).
Jamal, Hakim Abdullah [Allen Donaldson] (1931–). Military Person
Jamal, Hakim Abdullah, *From the Dead Level: Malcolm X and Me* (1971).
James, Daniel "Chappie," Jr. (1920–1978). Aviator, Military Person
McGovern, James R., *Black Eagle: General Daniel "Chappie" James, Jr.* (1985).
James, Nehemiah "Skip" (1902–1969). Performing Artist
Calt, Stephen, *I'd Rather Be the Devil: Skip James and the Blues* (1994).
James, Thomas (1804–1891). Religious Worker, Abolitionist
James, Thomas, *Life of Reverend Thomas James, by Himself* (1886).

Jamison, Judith (1944–). Performing Artist

Jamison, Judith, with Howard Kaplan, *Dancing Spirit: An Autobiography* (1993).

Jamison, Monroe Franklin (1848–1918). Religious Worker, Journalist

Jamison, Monroe Franklin, *Autobiography and Work of Bishop M. F. Jamison* (1912).

Jasper, John (1812–1901). Religious Worker, Educator

Hatcher, William E., *John Jasper, the Unmatched Negro Philosopher and Preacher* (1908).

Jefferson, Isaac (1775–c.1853). Blacksmith, Slave

Jefferson, Isaac, *Memories of a Monticello Slave: As Dictated to Charles Campbell in the 1840's by Isaac, One of Thomas Jefferson's Slaves,* ed. Rayford W. Logan (1951).

Jenkins, Edmund Thornton (1894–1926). Performing Artist

Green, Jeffrey P., *Edmund Thornton Jenkins: The Life and Times of an American Black Composer, 1894–1926* (1982).

Jeter, Henry Norval (1851–1938). Religious Worker, Educator

Jeter, Henry Norval, *Forty-Two Years' Experience as a Pastor: Evangelical, Humane and Reform Activities: Brief Fifty Years' History of the New England Baptist Missionary Convention* (1918).

———— *Pastor Henry N. Jeter's Twenty-Five Years' Experience with the Shiloh Baptist Church and Her History* (1901).

Johnson, Charles Richard (1948–). Author

Byrd, Rudolph P., *I Call Myself an Artist: Writings by and about Charles Johnson* (1999).

Johnson, Charles Spurgeon (1893–1956). Political Figure, Educator, Author, Journalist, Reformer

Dunne, Matthew William, "Next Steps: Charles S. Johnson and Southern Liberalism," *Journal of Negro History* 83 (1998): 1–34.

Robbins, Richard, *Sidelines Activist: Charles S. Johnson and the Struggle for Civil Rights* (1996).

Johnson, Francis (1792–1844). Performing Artist, Military Person

LaBrew, Arthur R., *Selected Works of Francis Johnson: A Study in Military and Terpsichorean History* (1977).

Johnson, James E. "Johnny" (1926–). Military Person, Government Worker

Johnson, James E., with David W. Balsiger, *Beyond Defeat* (1978).

Johnson, James Weldon (1871–1938). Author, Educator, Reformer, Business Person, Lawyer

Johnson, James Weldon, *Along This Way: The Autobiography of James Weldon Johnson* (1933).

———— *The Selected Writings of James Weldon Johnson,* ed. Sondra Kathryn Wilson (2 vols., 1995).

Levy, Eugene, *James Weldon Johnson: Black Leader, Black Voice* (1973).

———— "James Weldon Johnson and the Development of the NAACP," in John Hope Franklin and August Meier, ed., *Black Leaders of the Twentieth Century* (1982): 85–103.

Johnson, Jesse J. (1914–). Military Worker

Johnson, Jesse J., *Ebony Brass: An Autobiography of Negro Frustration amid Aspiration* (1967).

Johnson, John Arthur "Jack" (1878–1946). Athlete, Author

Batchelor, Denzil, *Jack Johnson and His Times* (1956).

Farr, Finis, *Black Champion: The Life and Times of Jack Johnson* (1964).

Gilmore, Al-Tony, *Bad Nigger: The National Impact of Jack Johnson* (1975).

Johnson, Jack, *Jack Johnson, In the Ring and Out* (1927).

Roberts, Randy, *Papa Jack: Jack Johnson and the Era of White Hopes* (1983).

Johnson, Robert L. (1912?–1938). Performing Artist

Guralnick, Peter, *Searching for Robert Johnson* (1989).

Johnson, Thomas Lewis (1836–?). Explorer/Traveler, Religious Worker

Johnson, Thomas Lewis, *Africa for Christ: Twenty-Eight Years a Slave* (1892).

———— *Twenty-Eight Years a Slave: Or, the Story of My Life in Three Continents* (1909).

Johnson, Tommy (1896?–1956). Performing Artist

Evans, David, *Tommy Johnson* (1971).

Johnson, William (1809?–1851). Business Person

Davis, Edwin Adams, and William Ranson Hogan, *The Barber of Natchez* (1954).

Johnson, William, *William Johnson's Natchez: The Ante-Bellum Diary of a Free Negro,* ed. William Ransom Hogan and Edwin Adams Davis (1951).

———— *William Johnson's Natchez: The Ante-Bellum Diary of a Free Negro,* ed. William Ransom Hogan and Edwin Adams Davis (1951).

Johnson, William Gary "Bunk" (1879–1949). Performing Artist

Hillman, Christopher, *Bunk Johnson: His Life and Times* (1988).

Johnson, William H. (1901–1970). Artist

Powell, Richard J., *Homecoming: The Art and Life of William H. Johnson* (1991).

Johnson, William H. H. (?). Slave

Johnson, William H. H., *Life of Wm. H. H. Johnson from 1839 to 1900 and the New Race* (1904?).

Johnson, William Henry (1833–1901). Medical Worker

Johnson, William Henry, *Autobiography of Dr. William Henry Johnson: Respectfully Dedicated to His Adopted Home, The Capital City of the Empire State* (1900).

Jones, Bessie (1902–). Laborer, Folklorist, Performing Artist

Jones, Bessie, *For the Ancestors: Autobiographical Memories,* ed. John Stewart (1983).

Jones, Bill T. (1952–). Performing Artist

Jones, Bill T., with Peggy Gillespie, *Last Night on Earth* (1995).

Jones, Laurence Clifton (1884–1975). Educator, Journalist, Reformer, Lecturer

Jones, Laurence Clifton, *Piney Woods and Its Story* (1922).

———— *Up through Difficulties* (1913).

Jones, Singleton Thomas Webster (1825–1891). Religious Worker

Smith, J. W., *Sermons and Addresses of the Late Rev. Bishop Singleton T. Jones, D. D. of the A.M.E. Church, with a Memoir of His Life and Character* (1892).

Jones, Thomas H. (1803–?). Slave, Religious Worker

Jones, Thomas H., *The Experience of Tom Jones, Who Was a Slave for Forty-Three Years: Written by a Friend, as Given to Him by Brother Jones* (1854).

Joplin, Scott (1868–1917). Composer, Performing Artist

Berlin, Edward A., *King of Ragtime: Scott Joplin and His Era* (1994).

Curtis, Susan, *Dancing to a Black Man's Tune: A Life of Scott Joplin* (1994).

Gammond, Peter, *Scott Joplin and the Ragtime Era* (1975).

Reed, Addison Walker, *The Life and Works of Scott Joplin* (1973).

Jordan, Barbara Charline (1936–1996). Lawyer, Political Figure, Educator

Jordan, Barbara Charline, and Shelby Hearon, *Barbara Jordan: A Self-Portrait* (1979).

Rogers, Mary Beth, *Barbara Jordan: American Hero* (1998).

Jordan, June (1936–). Author, Reformer

Jordan, June, *Civil Wars* (1981).

Jordan, Lewis Garnett (1854–1939). Religious Worker, Slave, Reformer

Jordan, Lewis Garnett, *On Two Hemispheres: Bits from the Life Story of Lewis G. Jordan, As Told by Himself* (1935).

Joseph, John (?). Slave

Joseph, John, *The Life and Sufferings of John Joseph, a Native of Ashantee, in West Africa: Who Was Stolen from His Parents at the Age of Three Years, and Sold to Mr. Johnstone, a Cotton Planter in New Orleans, South America* (1848).

Joseph, Pleasant "Cousin Joe" (1907–?). Performing Artist

Joseph, Pleasant, and Harriet J. Ottenheimer, *Cousin Joe: Blues from New Orleans* (1987).

Julian, Hubert Fauntleroy (1897–1983). Aviator, Military Person

Julian, Hubert Fauntleroy, *Black Eagle: Colonel Hubert Julian* (1964).

Nugent, John Peer, *The Black Eagle* (1971).

Juno, Maumer (?). Slave

Juno, Maumer, *Life of Maumer Juno of Charleston, South Carolina,* ed. Seymour (1892).

Just, Ernest Everett (1883–1941). Educator, Scientist, Club Leader

Manning, Kenneth R., *Black Apollo of Science: The Life of Ernest Everett Just* (1983).

Keckley, Elizabeth Hobbs (1818–1907). Slave, Domestic Worker

Keckley, Elizabeth, *Behind the Scenes: Or, Thirty Years a Slave, and Four Years in the White House* (1868).

Keeble, Marshall (1878–?). Religious Worker

Choate, J. E., *Roll Jordan Roll: A Biography of Marshall Keeble* (1968).

Keene, Royal D. (1895–?)

Keene, Royal D., *The Light Still Shines* (1961).

Kelley, Edmond (?). Slave, Religious Worker

Kelley, Edmond, *A Family Redeemed from Bondage: Being Rev. Edmond Kelley (The Author), His Wife, and Four Children* (1851).

Kennedy, Florynce R. (1916–). Lawyer

Kennedy, Florynce R., *Color Me Flo: My Hard Life and Good Times* (1976).

Kenoly, Jacob (1876–1911). Religious Worker

Smith, C. C., *The Life and Work of Jacob Kenoly* (1912).

Killens, John Oliver (1916–1987). Author

Killens, John Oliver, *Black Man's Burden* (1965).

King, B.B. [Riley B.] (1925–). Performing Artist

Danchin, Sebastian, *"Blues Boy": The Life and Music of B. B. King* (1998).

King, B. B., and David Ritz, *Blues All Around Me: The Autobiography of B. B. King* (1996).

Sawyer, Charles, *The Arrival of B. B. King: The Authorized Biography* (1980).

King, Coretta Scott (1927–). Reformer

Henry, Sondra, and Emily Taitz, *Coretta Scott King: Keeper of the Dream* (1993).

King, Coretta Scott, *My Life with Martin Luther King, Jr.* (1969).

King, Martin Luther, Jr. (1929–1968). Religious Worker, Reformer

Albert, Peter J., and Ronald Hoffman, ed., *We Shall Overcome: Martin Luther King, Jr., and the Black Freedom Struggle* (1990).

Ansbro, John J., *Martin Luther King, Jr.: The Making of a Mind* (1982).

Bennett, Lerone, *What Manner of Man: A Biography of Martin Luther King, Jr.* (1964).

Carson, Clayborne, ed., *The Autobiography of Martin Luther King, Jr.* (1998).

———, ed., *The Papers of Martin Luther King, Jr.* (4 vols., 1992–).

Colaiaco, James A., *Martin Luther King, Jr.: Apostle of Militant Nonviolence* (1988).

Dyson, Michael Eric, *I May Not Get There with You: The True Martin Luther King, Jr.* (1999).

Garrow, David J., *Bearing the Cross: Martin Luther King, Jr., and the Southern Christian Leadership Conference* (1986).

———, ed., *Martin Luther King, Jr.: Civil Rights Leader, Theologian, Orator* (3 vols., 1989).

King, Martin Luther, Jr., *Stride toward Freedom: The Montgomery Story* (1958).

——— *Where Do We Go from Here: Chaos or Community?* (1967).

——— *Why We Can't Wait* (1964).

Lewis, David Levering, *King: A Biography* (2d ed., 1978).

——— "Martin Luther King, Jr., and the Promise of Nonviolent Populism," in John Hope Franklin and August Meier, ed., *Black Leaders of the Twentieth Century* (1982): 277–303.

Lincoln, C. Eric, ed., *Martin Luther King, Jr.: A Profile* (1970).

Miller, William R., *Martin Luther King, Jr.: His Life, Martyrdom and Meaning for the World* (1968).

Oates, Stephen B., *Let the Trumpet Sound: The Life of Martin Luther King, Jr.* (rev. ed., 1993).

Reddick, Lawrence D., *Crusader without Violence: A Biography of Martin Luther King, Jr.* (1959).

Vaughn, Wally G., and Richard W. Wills, ed., *Reflections on Our Pastor: Dr. Martin Luther King, Jr. at Dexter Avenue Baptist Church, 1954–1960* (1998).

King, Martin Luther, Sr. (1899–1984). Religious Worker, Reformer

King, Martin Luther, Sr., *Daddy King: An Autobiography* (1980).

Kitt, Eartha Mae (1928–). Performing Artist

Kitt, Eartha, *Alone with Me: A New Autobiography* (1976).

——— *Confessions of a Sex Kitten* (1991).

——— *Thursday's Child* (1956).

Knox, George L. (1841–1927). Journalist, Military Person, Political Figure, Business Person

Knox, George L., *Slave and Freeman: The Autobiography of George L. Knox*, ed. Willard B. Gatewood, Jr. (1979).

Lacy, Leslie Alexander (1937–). Educator

Lacy, Leslie Alexander, *Native Daughter* (1974).

———— *The Rise and Fall of a Proper Negro: An Autobiography* (1970).

Lamar, Jake (1961–). Journalist

Lamar, Jake, *Bourgeois Blues: An American Memoir* (1991).

Lane, Isaac (1834–1937). Religious Worker, Educator, Business Person

Lane, Isaac, *Autobiography of Bishop Isaac Lane, LL.D.; with a Short History of the A.M.E. Church in America and of Methodism* (1916).

Savage, Horace C., *Life and Times of Bishop Isaac Lane* (1958).

Lane, Lunsford (1803–?). Slave

Hawkins, William G., *Lunsford Lane; Or, Another Helper from North Carolina* (1863).

Langston, John Mercer (1829–1897). Lawyer, Educator, Political Figure, Government Worker

Cheek, William F., and Aimee Lee Cheek, *John Mercer Langston and the Fight for Black Freedom, 1829–65* (1989).

———— "John Mercer Langston: Principle and Politics," in Leon Litwack and August Meier, ed., *Black Leaders of the Nineteenth Century* (1988): 103–26.

Langston, John Mercer, *From the Virginia Plantation to the National Capitol: Or, the First and Only Negro Representative in Congress from the Old Dominion* (1894).

Larsen, Nella (1891–1964). Author, Medical Worker, Librarian/Book Collector

Davis, Thadious M., *Nella Larsen, Novelist of the Harlem Renaissance: A Woman's Life Unveiled* (1994).

Latta, Morgan London (1853–?). Religious Worker, Educator, Reformer, Agriculturalist

Latta, M. L., *The History of My Life and Work: Autobiography* (1903).

Lawrence, Margaret (1914–). Medical Worker

Lawrence-Lightfoot, Sara, *Balm in Gilead: Journey of a Healer* (1988).

Ledbetter, Leadbelly [Hudson William] (1889–1949). Performing Artist

Lomax, John A., and Alan Lomax, *Negro Folk Songs as Sung by Lead Belly* (1988).

Wolfe, Charles, and Kip Lornell, *The Life and Legend of LeadBelly* (1992).

Lee, George Washington (1894–?). Military Person, Author, Business Person, Political Figure, Reformer, Club Leader

Tucker, David M., *Lieutenant Lee of Beale Street* (1971).

Lee, Helen Corrine Jackson (1908– ?). Government Worker

Lee, Helen Corrine Jackson, *Nigger in the Window* (1978).

Lee, Jarena (1783–?). Religious Worker

Lee, Jarena, *Religious Experience and Journal of Mrs. Jarena Lee, A Coloured Lady, Giving an Account of Her Call to Preach the Gospel, Written by Herself* (1849).

Lester, Julius (1939–). Journalist, Educator

Lester, Julius, *All Is Well* (1976).

———— *Lovesong: Becoming a Jew* (1988).

———— *Search for the New Land: History as Subjective Experience* (1969).

Levington, William (1793–1836). Religious Worker

Bragg, George F., *The First Negro Priest on Southern Soil* (1909).

Lewis, George (1900–1968). Performing Artist

Bethell, Tom, *George Lewis: A Jazzman from New Orleans* (1977).

Lewis, Henry Harrison (1840–?). Religious Worker

Lewis, Henry Harrison, *Life of Rev. H. H. Lewis: Giving a History of His Early Life and Services in the Ministry. Written and Compiled by Himself* (1877).

Lewis, John (1940–). Political Figure, Reformer

Lewis, John, with Micheal D'Orso, *Walking with the Wind: A Memoir of the Movement* (1998).

Lewis, Joseph Vance (?–1923). Lawyer, Educator

Lewis, Joseph Vance, *Out of the Ditch: A True Story of an Ex-Slave* (1910).

Lincoln, C. Eric (1924–2000). Educator, Religious Worker

Lincoln, C. Eric, *Coming through the Fire: Surviving Race and Place in America* (1996).

Lipscomb, Mance (1895–1976). Performing Artist

Lipscomb, Mance, *I Say Me for a Parable: The Oral Autobiography of Mance Lipscomb, Texan Bluesman*, comp. Glen Alyn (1993).

Little Richard [Richard Wayne Penniman] (1932–). Performing Artist

White, Charles, *The Life and Times of Little Richard: The Quasar of Rock* (1984).

Locke, Alain Leroy (1886–1954). Educator, Reformer

Crane, Clare Bloodgood, *Alain Locke and the Negro Renaissance* (1971).

Locke, Alain LeRoy, *The Critical Temper of Alain Locke: A Selection of His Essays on Art and Culture,* ed. Jeffrey C. Stewart (1983).

Washington, Johnny, *Alain Locke and Philosophy: A Quest for Cultural Pluralism* (1986).

Logan, Rayford Whittingham (1897–1982). Reformer, Educator

Janken, Kenneth Robert, *Rayford W. Logan and the Dilemma of the African-American Intellectual* (1993).

Loguen, Jermain Wesley (1814–1872). Slave, Religious Worker

Loguen, Jermain Wesley, *The Rev. J. W. Loguen, as a Slave and as a Freeman: A Narrative of Real Life* (1859).

Long, Jefferson Franklin (1836–1900). Political Figure, Business Person

Matthews, John M., "Jefferson Franklin Long: The Public Career of Georgia's First Black Congressman," *Phylon* 42 (1981): 145–56.

Louis, Joe [Joseph Louis Barrow] (1914–1981). Athlete

Louis, Joe, *My Life Story* (1947).

Louis, Joe, with Edna and Art Rust, Jr., *Joe Louis, My Life* (1978).

Love, Nat (1854–1921). Agriculturalist, Railroad Employee

Love, Nat, *The Life and Adventures of Nat Love, Better Known in the Cattle Country as "Deadwood Dick," By Himself* (1907).

Loving, Neal V. (1916–1998). Aviator

Loving, Neal V., *Loving's Love: A Black American's Experience in Aviation* (1994).

Lowery, Irving E. (1850–?). Slave, Religious Worker

Lowery, Irving E., *Life on the Old Plantation in Antebellum Days: Or, a Story Based on Facts* (1911).

Lynch, James (1839–1872). Religious Worker, Journalist, Political Figure, Reformer, Agriculturalist

Harris, William C., "James Lynch: Black Leader in Southern Reconstruction," *Historian* 34 (1971): 40–61.

Lynch, John Roy (1847–1939). Lawyer, Political Figure, Reformer, Military Person

Bell, Frank C., "The Life and Times of John R. Lynch: A Case Study, 1847–1939," *Journal of Mississippi History* 38 (1976): 53–67.

Franklin, John Hope, "John Roy Lynch: Republican Stalwart from Mississippi," in Howard N. Rabinowitz, ed., *Southern Black Leaders of the Reconstruction Era* (1982): 39–58.

Lynch, John Roy, *Reminiscences of an Active Life: The Autobiography of John Roy Lynch,* ed. John Hope Franklin (1970).

Lynk, Miles Vandahurst (1871–1957). Medical Worker, Educator, Lawyer, Business Person

Lynk, Miles Vandahurst, *Sixty Years of Medicine: Or, the Life and Times of Dr. Miles V. Lynk* (1951).

Lynn, Conrad (1908–1995). Lawyer, Reformer

Lynn, Conrad, *There is a Fountain: The Autobiography of a Civil Rights Lawyer* (1979).

Mabry, Marcus (1967–). Journalist

Mabry, Marcus, *White Bucks and Black-Eyed Peas: Coming of Age Black in White America* (1995).

Magee, James H. (1839–?). Religious Worker, Educator, Author, Political Figure

Magee, James H., *The Night of Affliction and Morning of Recovery: An Autobiography* (1873).

Majozo, Estella Conwill (?–). Artist

Majozo, Estella Conwill, *Come Out the Wilderness: Memoir of a Black Woman Artist* (1999).

Malcolm X [Malcolm Little, El-Hajj Malik El-Shabazz] (1925–1965). Religious Worker, Reformer

Clarke, John Henrik, ed., *Malcolm X: The Man and His Times* (1969).

Collins, Rodnell P., with Peter Bailey, *Seventh Child: A Family Memoir of Malcolm X* (1998).

Davis, Thulani, *Malcolm X: The Great Photographs* (1993).

DeCaro, Louis A., *Malcolm and the Cross: The Nation of Islam, Malcolm X, and Christianity* (1998).

——— *On the Side of My People: A Religious Life of Malcolm X* (1996).

Dyson, Michael Eric, *Making Malcolm: The Myth and Meaning of Malcolm X* (1995).

Gallen, David, *Malcolm X: As They Knew Him* (1992).

Goldman, Peter, *The Death and Life of Malcolm X* (1979).

———— "Malcolm X: Witness for the Prosecution," in John Hope Franklin and August Meier, ed., *Black Leaders of the Twentieth Century* (1982): 305–30.

Malcolm X, with the assistance of Alex Haley, *The Autobiography of Malcom X* (1965).

Perry, Bruce, *Malcolm: The Life of a Man Who Changed Black America* (1991).

Strickland, William, *Malcolm X: Make It Plain* (1994).

Mallory, William (1826–1905?). Religious Worker

Mallory, William, *Old Plantation Days* (1902?).

Maloney, Arnold Hamilton (1888–1955). Religious Worker, Educator, Medical Worker, Scientist

Maloney, Arnold Hamilton, *Amber Gold: An Adventure in Autobiography* (1946).

Malvin, John (1795–1880). Reformer

Malvin, John, *Autobiography of John Malvin: A Narrative, Containing an Authentic Account of His Fifty Years' Struggle in the State of Ohio in Behalf of the American Slave, and the Equal Rights of All Men Before the Law Without Reference to Race or Color; Forty-Seven Years of Said Time Being Expended in the City of Cleveland* (1879).

Marrant, John (1755–1791). Religious Worker

Marrant, John, *A Narrative of the Life of John Marrant of New York, in North America: Giving an Account of His Conversion When Only Fourteen Years of Age; His Leaving His Mother's House from Religious Motives, Wandering Several Days in the Desert without Food, and Being at Last Taken by an Indian Hunter among the Cherokees, Where He Was Condemned to Die* (1815).

Marrs, Elijah Preston (1840–1910). Religious Worker, Educator, Political Figure

Marrs, Elijah Preston, *Life and History of the Rev. Elijah P. Marrs* (1885).

Mars, James (1790– ?). Slave

Mars, James, *Life of James Mars: A Slave Born and Sold in Connecticut, Written by Himself* (1866).

Marsalis, Wynton (1961–). Performing Artist

Gourse, Leslie, *Wynton Marsalis: Skain's Domain: A Biography* (1999).

Marshall, Thurgood (1908–1993). Lawyer, Reformer

Ball, Howard, *A Defiant Life: Thurgood Marshall and the Persistence of Racism in America* (1998).

Bland, Randall W., *Private Pressure on Public Law: The Legal Career of Justice Thurgood Marshall, 1934–1991* (rev. ed., 1993).

Davis, Michael D., and Hunter R. Clark, *Thurgood Marshall: Warrior at the Bar, Rebel on the Bench* (Updated and rev. ed., 1994).

Goldman, Roger L., with David Gallen, *Thurgood Marshall: Justice for All* (1992).

Rowan, Carl T., *Dream Makers, Dream Breakers: The World of Justice Thurgood Marshall* (1993).

Tushnet, Mark V., *Making Civil Rights Law: Thurgood Marshall and the Supreme Court, 1936–1961* (1994).

———— *Making Constitutional Law: Thurgood Marshall and the Supreme Court, 1961–1991* (1997).

Williams, Juan, *Thurgood Marshall: American Revolutionary* (1998).

Mason, Isaac (1822–?). Slave

Mason, Isaac, *Life of Isaac Mason as a Slave* (1893).

Mason, William Alfred Madison (1898–?). Medical Worker, Educator

Mason, William Alfred Madison, *An Odyssey in Black and White* (1978).

Matson, George (?). Religious Worker, Business Person

Scrimsher, Lila Gravatt, "The Diaries and Writings of George A. Matson, Black Citizen of Lincoln, Nebraska, 1901–1913," *Nebraska History* 52 (1971): 133–68.

Matthews, Vincent Edward (1947–). Athlete

Matthews, Vincent Edward, with Neil Amdur, *My Race Be Won* (1974).

May, Lee (1941–). Journalist

May, Lee, *In My Father's Garden* (1995).

Mays, Benjamin Elijah (1894–1984). Religious Worker, Educator, Reformer

Mays, Benjamin Elijah, *Born to Rebel: An Autobiography* (1971).

—— *Lord, The People Have Driven Me On* (1981).
Mays, Willie [William Howard] (1931–). Athlete
Mays, Willie, *Born to Play Ball* (1955).
—— *Willie Mays: My Life In and Out of Baseball* (1966).
McCall, Nathan (1954–). Author, Journalist
McCall, Nathan, *Makes Me Wanna Holler: A Young Black Man in America* (1994).
McCline, John (1852–1948). Slave, Military Person, Author
McCline, John, *Slavery in the Clover Bottoms: John McCline's Narrative of His Life during Slavery and the Civil War*, ed. Jan Furman (1998).
McCray, Mary F. (?). Slave
McCray, S. J., *Life of Mary F. McCray, Born and Raised a Slave in the State of Kentucky. By Her Husband and Son* (1898).
McDaniel, Hattie (1895–1952). Performing Artist
Jackson, Carlton, *Hattie: The Life of Hattie McDaniel* (1990).
McDonald, Emanuel B. "Sam" (1884–1957). Agriculturalist
McDonald, Emanuel B., *Sam McDonald's Farm: Stanford Reminiscences* (1954).
McDonald, William Madison (1866–1938)
Bundy, William O., *Life of William Madison McDonald, Ph.D.* (1925).
McDowell, Deborah E. (1951–). Educator
McDowell, Deborah E., *Leaving Pipe Shop: Memories of Kin* (1996).
McGregor, Charles [Charles McGregor Gordon] (1922–). Performing Artist
McGregor, Charles, with Sharon Sopher, *Up from the Walking Dead: The Charles McGregor Story* (1978).
McKay, Claude (1890–1948). Author, Government Worker, Journalist
Cooper, Wayne F., *Claude McKay: Rebel Sojourner in the Harlem Renaissance* (1987).
McKay, Claude, *A Long Way from Home* (1937).
McMillan, Terry (1951–). Author
Patrick, Diane, *Terry McMillan: The Unauthorized Biography* (1999).
McPherson, Christopher [Pherson] (1763?–1817). Religious Worker
McPherson, Christopher, *A Short History of the Life of Christopher McPherson, Alias Pherson, Son of Christ, King of Kings and Lord of Lords* (1811).
Meacham, Robert (1837–1902). Religious Worker, Political Figure
Brown, Canter, Jr., "'Where Are Now the Hopes I Cherished?': The Life and Times of Robert Meacham," *Florida Historical Quarterly* 69 (1990): 1–36.
Meachum, John B. (?). Slave
Meachum, John B., *An Address to the Colored Citizens of the United States, Prefaced by a Narrative of the Author as a Slave in Virginia* (1846).
Mebane, Mary Elizabeth (1933–). Educator
Mebane, Mary E., *Mary: An Autobiography* (1981).
—— *Mary, Wayfarer* (1983).
Medford, Hampton Thomas (1888–1964). Religious Worker
Medford, Booker T., and W. J. Walls, *From the Depths* (1948).
Melden, Charles M. (?). Slave
Melden, Charles M., *From Slave to Citizen* (1921).
Memphis Minnie [Lizzie Douglas McCoy Lawlars] (1897?–1973). Performing Artist
Garon, Paul, and Beth Garon, *Woman With Guitar: Memphis Minnie's Blues* (1992).
Menken, Adah Isaacs (1835–1868). Author, Performing Artist
Falk, Bernard, *The Naked Lady, or, Storm over Adah: A Biography of Adah Isaacs Menken* (1934).
Gershon, Noel Bertram, *Queen of the Plaza: A Biography of Adah Isaacs Menken* (1964).
Lesser, Allen, *Enchanting Rebel: The Secret of Adah Isaacs Menken* (1947).
Mankowitz, Wolf, *Mazeppa: The Lives, Loves, and Legends of Adah Isaacs Menken: A Biographical Quest* (1982).
Meredith, James Howard (1933–). Reformer
Meredith, James, *Three Years in Mississippi* (1966).

Merrick, John (1859–1919). Business Person

Andrews, Robert McCants, *John Merrick: A Biographical Sketch* (1920).

Michaux, Lightfoot Solomon (1884–1968). Religious Worker

Webb, Lillian Ashcraft, *About My Father's Business: The Life of Elder Michaux* (1981).

Micheaux, Oscar (1884–1948). Filmmaker, Author, Business Person, Railroad Employee

Bowser, Pearl, and Louise Spence, *Writing Himself into History: Oscar Micheaux, His Silent Films, and His Audiences* (2000).

Elder, Arlene, "Oscar Micheaux: The Melting Pot in the Plains," *Old North West* 2 (1976): 299–307.

Micheaux, Oscar, *The Conquest: The Story of a Negro Pioneer* (1913).

Mingus, Charles (1922–1979). Performing Artist

Mingus, Charles, *Beneath the Underdog: His World as Composed by Mingus,* ed. Nel King (1971).

Priestly, Brian, *Mingus: A Critical Biography* (1982).

Minkins, Shadrach (?). Slave, Reformer, Business Person

Collison, Gary L., *Shadrach Minkins: From Fugitive Slave to Citizen* (1997).

Mitchell, Arthur Wergs (1883–1968). Political Figure

Nordin, Dennis S., *The New Deal's Black Congressman: A Life of Arthur Wergs Mitchell* (1997).

Mitchell, Clarence Maurice, Jr. (1911–1984). Reformer

Denton, Watson, *"Lion in the Lobby": Clarence Mitchell, Jr.'s Struggle for the Passage of Civil Rights Laws* (1990).

Mix, Sarah A. (?). Religious Worker

Mix, Mrs. Edward [Sarah A. Mix], *In Memory of Departed Worth: The Life of Mrs. Edward Mix, Written by Herself in 1880* (1884).

Montejo, Esteban (1860–1973). Slave

Barnet, Miguel, ed., *The Autobiography of a Runaway Slave: Esteban Montejo* (1966).

Montgomery, Isaiah Thornton (1847–1924). Religious Worker, Military Person, Agriculturalist, Business Person, Political Figure

Hermann, Janet Sharp, "Isaiah T. Montgomery's Balancing Act," in Leon Litwack and August Meier, ed., *Black Leaders of the Nineteenth Century* (1988): 291–304.

———— *The Pursuit of a Dream* (1981).

Moody, Anne (1940–). Reformer

Moody, Anne, *Coming of Age in Mississippi* (1968).

Moore, Archie Lee (1916–). Athlete

Moore, Archie Lee, *The Archie Moore Story* (1960).

Moore, Archie Lee, and Leonard B. Pearl, *Any Boy Can: The Archie Moore Story* (1971).

Moore, Harry Tyson (1905–1951). Reformer, Educator

Green, Ben, *Before His Time: The Untold Story of Harry T. Moore, America's First Civil Rights Martyr* (1999).

Moore, Richard Benjamin (1893–1978). Political Figure, Reformer, Author

Turner, W. Burghardt, and Joyce Moore Turner, ed., *Richard B. Moore, Caribbean Militant in Harlem: Collected Writings, 1920–1972* (1988).

Morant, John James (1870–1961). Religious Worker, Educator, Journalist

Morant, John J., *Mississippi Minister* (1958).

Morgan, Joe (1943–). Athlete

Morgan, Joe, with David Falkner, *Joe Morgan: A Life in Baseball* (1993).

Morrow, Curtis James (1933–). Military Person

Morrow, Curtis James, *What's a Commie Ever Done to Black People? A Korean War Memoir of Fighting in the U.S. Army's Last All Negro Unit* (1997).

Morrow, Everett Frederic (1909–). Reformer, Military Person, Business Person

Morrow, Everett Frederic, *Black Man in the White House: A Diary of the Eisenhower Years by the Administrative Officer for Special Projects, the White House, 1955–1961* (1963).

———— *Forty Years a Guinea Pig* (1980).

———— *Way Down South up North* (1973).

Morton, Jelly Roll [Ferdinand Joseph] (1890–1941). Performing Artist

Lomax, Alan, *Mister Jelly Roll: The Fortunes of Jelly Roll Morton, New Orleans Creole and Inventor of Jazz* (1993).

Morton, Lena Beatrice (1901–?). Educator, Author

Morton, Lena Beatrice, *My First Sixty Years: Passion for Wisdom* (1965).

Moses, Robert Parris (1935–). Reformer, Educator

Burner, Eric R., *And Gently He Shall Lead Them: Robert Parris Moses and Civil Rights in Mississippi* (1996).

Motley, Constance Baker (1921–). Judge, Political Figure, Reformer

Motley, Constance Baker, *Equal Justice under Law: An Autobiography* (1998).

Motley, Willard Francis (1909–1965). Author

Motley, Willard Francis, *The Diaries of Willard Motley*, ed. Jerome Klinkowitz (1979).

Moton, Robert Russa (1867–1940). Educator, Lecturer, Government Worker, Lawyer, Club Leader

Hughes, William Hardin, *Robert Russa Moton of Hampton and Tuskegee*, ed. Frederick D. Patterson (1956).

Moton, Robert Russa, *Finding a Way Out: An Autobiography* (1920).

Muhammad, Elijah (1897–1975). Religious Worker, Political Figure, Reformer

Clegg, Claude A., *An Original Man: The Life and Times of Elijah Muhammad* (1997).

Evanzz, Karl, *The Messenger: The Rise and Fall of Elijah Muhammad* (1999).

Mulzac, Hugh N. (1886–1971). Military Person, Seaman, Business Person

Mulzac, Hugh N., *A Star to Steer By* (1965).

Mungin, Lawrence Dwayne (1957–). Lawyer

Barrett, Paul M., *The Good Black: A True Story of Race in America* (1999).

Murray, Albert L. (1916–). Author

Murray, Albert L., *South to a Very Old Place* (1971).

Murray, Jackson (?). Slave

Murray, Jackson, *Memoirs of Jackson Murray, Former Slave of the Hennen Family. Written When He Was Ninety-Two Years of Age* (1908).

Murray, Pauli (1910–1985). Reformer, Religious Worker, Educator, Lawyer, Author

Murray, Pauli, *Pauli Murray: The Autobiography of a Black Activist, Lawyer, Priest, and Poet* (1987).

———— *Proud Shoes: The Story of an American Family* (1956).

———— *Song in a Weary Throat: An American Pilgrimage* (1987).

Myers, George A. (1859–1930). Reformer, Service Industry Employee, Political Figure

Myers, George A. and James Ford Rhodes, *The Barber and the Historian: The Correspondence of George A. Myers and James Ford Rhodes, 1910–1923*, ed. John A. Garraty (1956).

Napier, James Carroll (1845–1940). Politician

Clark, Herbert L., "James Carroll Napier: National Negro Leader," *Tennessee Historical Quarterly* 49 (1990): 243–52.

Nash, Ide D. (1872–?). Author

Nash, Ide D., *Bootlegging a Failure and a Lecture to Young Men: My Prison Experience in Oklahoma* (1918).

Nelson, Jill (1952–). Author, Journalist

Nelson, Jill, *Straight, No Chaser: How I Became a Grown-Up Black Woman* (1997).

———— *Volunteer Slavery: My Authentic Negro Experience* (1993).

Nelson, Rachel West (1957–). Reformer

Webb, Sheyann, and Rachel West Nelson, as told to Frank Sikora, *Selma, Lord, Selma: Girlhood Memories of the Civil-Rights Days* (1980).

Newton, Alexander Herritage (1837–?). Construction Worker, Religious Worker, Military Person, Club Leader

Newton, Alexander Herritage, *Out of the Briars: An Autobiography and Sketch of the Twenty-Ninth Regiment, Connecticut Volunteers* (1910).

Newton, Huey Percy (1942–1989). Reformer

Newton, Huey Percy, *Revolutionary Suicide* (1973).

Norris, Clarence (1912–1989)

Norris, Clarence, and Sybil D. Washington, *The Last of the Scottsboro Boys: An Autobiography* (1979).

Northup, Solomon (1808?–1863?). Slave, Performing Artist, Author

Northup, Solomon, *Twelve Years a Slave: Narrative of Solomon Northup, a Citizen of New-York, Kidnapped in Washington City in 1841 and Rescued in 1853, from a Cotton Plantation near the Red River, in Louisiana* (1853).

Nunn, James (1882–1975). Business Person

Nunn, James, *The Oral History of James Nunn: A Unique North Carolinian*, ed. W. Wilder Towle (1977).

O'Hara, James (1844–1905). Political Figure

Anderson, Eric, "James O'Hara of North Carolina: Black Leadership and Local Government," in Howard N. Rabinowitz, ed., *Southern Black Leaders of the Reconstruction Era* (1982): 101–125.

Offley, Greensbury Washington (1808–1859). Slave, Religious Worker

Offley, Greensbury Washington, *A Narrative of the Life and Labors of the Rev. G. W. Offley, a Colored Man and Local Preacher* (1860).

O'Neal, Frederick Douglass (1905–1992). Performing Artist, Author

Simmons, Renée A., *Frederick Douglass O'Neal: Pioneer of the Actor's Equity Association* (1996).

O'Neal, William (?). Slave

O'Neal, William, *Life and History of William O'Neal: Or, the Man Who Sold His Wife* (1896).

Owens, Jesse [James Cleveland] (1913–1980). Athlete

Baker, William Joseph, *Jesse Owens: An American Life* (1986).

Owens, Jesse, *Blackthink: My Life as Black Man and White Man* (1970).

———— *I Have Changed* (1972).

———— *Jesse: A Spiritual Autobiography* (1978).

Paige, C. F. (?). Slave

Paige, C. F., *Twenty-Two Years of Freedom* (1876?).

Paige, Leroy Robert "Satchel" (1906–1982). Athlete

Paige, LeRoy (Satchel), *Maybe I'll Pitch Forever: A Great Baseball Player Tells the Hilarious Story Behind the Legend* (1962).

Paige, Leroy (Satchel), as told to Hal Lebovitz, *Pitchin' Man* (1948).

Parker, Allen (1837–?). Slave, Seaman, Laborer

Parker, Allen, *Recollections of Slavery Times* (1895).

Parker, Jamie (?). Slave

Pierson, Emily Catharine, *Jamie Parker, the Fugitive* (1851).

Parks, David (1944–). Military Person

Parks, David, *GI Diary* (1968).

Parks, Gordon Alexander Buchanan (1912–). Artist, Journalist

Parks, Gordon, *Born Black* (1971).

———— *A Choice of Weapons* (1966).

———— *To Smile in Autumn: A Memoir* (1979).

———— *Voices in the Mirror: An Autobiography* (1990).

Parks, Henry Blanton (1856?–1936). Religious Worker

Haigler, T. W., *The Life and Times of Rt. Rev. H. B. Parks* (1892).

Parks, Lillian Rogers (1897–). Domestic Worker

Parks, Lillian Rogers, with Frances Spatz Leighton, *My Thirty Years Backstairs at the White House* (1961).

Parks, Rosa (1913–). Reformer

Parks, Rosa, as Told to James Haskins, *The Autobiography of Rosa Parks* (1990).

Parks, Rosa, with Gregory Reed, *Quiet Strength: The Faith, the Hope, and the Heart of a Woman Who Changed a Nation* (1994).

Patterson, Frederick Douglass (1901–1988). Educator

Patterson, Frederick D., *Chronicles of Faith: The Autobiography of Frederick D. Patterson*, ed. Martia Graham Goodson (1991).

Patterson, Haywood (1913?–1952)

Patterson, Haywood, and Earl Conrad, *Scottsboro Boy* (1950).

Patterson, Louis H., Jr. (?). Government Worker

Patterson, Louis H., Jr., *Life and Works of a Negro Detective* (1918).

Patterson, William Lorenzo (1891–1980). Lawyer, Educator, Reformer, Journalist

Patterson, William L., *The Man Who Cried Genocide: An Autobiography* (1971).

Patton, Charley [Charlie] (1887–1934). Performing Artist

Calt, Stephen, and Gayle Wardlow, *King of the Delta Blues: The Life and Music of Charlie Patton* (1988).

Fahey, John, *Charley Patton* (1970).

Sacre, Robert, ed., *The Voice of the Delta: Charley Patton and the Mississippi Blues Traditions* (1987).

Paul, Robert Austin (1846–?). Political Figure

Williams, D. B., *A Sketch of the Life and Times of Capt. R. A. Paul* (1885).

Payne, Daniel Alexander (1811–1893). Educator, Religious Worker, Reformer, Journalist

Payne, Daniel Alexander, *Recollections of Seventy Years* (1888).

Wills, David W., "Womanhood and Domesticity in the A.M.E. Tradition: The Influence of Daniel Alexander Payne," in David W. Wills and Richard Newman, ed., *Black Apostles at Home and Abroad: Afro-Americans and the Christian Mission from the Revolution to Reconstruction* (1982): 133–46.

Paynter, John Henry (1862–1947). Military Person

Paynter, John Henry, *Fifty Years After* (1940).

———— *Horse and Buggy Days with Uncle Sam* (1943).

———— *Joining the Navy* (1895).

Peake, Mary Smith Kelsey (1823–1862). Educator

Lockwood, Lewis C., *Mary S. Peake, The Colored Teacher at Fortress Monroe* (1863).

Peery, Nelson (1925–). Reformer

Peery, Nelson, *Black Fire: The Making of an American Revolutionary* (1994).

Pelham, Benjamin B. (1862–1948). Government Worker, Journalist

Mallas, Aris A., Jr., Rea McCain, and Margaret K. Hedden, *Forty Years in Politics: The Story of Ben Pelham* (1957).

Pemberton, Gayle (1948–). Educator

Pemberton, Gayle, *The Hottest Water in Chicago: On Family, Race, Time, and American Culture* (1992).

Pennington, James William Charles (1807?–1870). Religious Worker, Abolitionist, Educator

Pennington, James W. C., *The Fugitive Blacksmith: Or Events in the History of James W. C. Pennington, Pastor of a Presbyterian Church, New York, Former Slave in the State of Maryland, U.S.* (1849).

Thomas, Herman E., *James W. C. Pennington: African American Churchman and Abolitionist* (1995).

Perry, Ivory (1930–). Reformer

Lipsitz, George, *A Life in the Struggle: Ivory Perry and the Culture of Opposition* (1988).

Perry, John Edward (1870–1962). Medical Worker, Educator, Business Person

Perry, John Edward, *Forty Cords of Wood: Memoirs of a Medical Doctor* (1947).

Petersen, Frank E. (1932–). Aviator, Military Person

Petersen, Frank E., with J. Alfred Phelps, *Into the Tiger's Jaw: America's First Black Marine Aviator* (1998).

Peterson, Daniel H. (1805?–?). Religious Worker

Peterson, Daniel H., *The Looking-Glass: Being a True Report and Narrative of the Life, Travels, and Labors of the Rev. Daniel H. Peterson* (1854).

Petry, Ann Lane (1908–1997). Author, Medical Worker, Journalist

Isaacs, Diane Scharfeld, *Ann Petry's Life and Art: Piercing Stereotypes* (1982).

Peyton, Thomas Roy (1897–1969). Medical Worker, Educator

Peyton, Thomas Roy, *Quest for Dignity: An Autobiography of a Negro Doctor* (1950).

Phillips, Charles Henry (1858–1951). Religious Worker, Agriculturalist, Railroad Employee

Phillips, Charles H., *From the Farm to the Bishopric: An Autobiography* (1932).

Pickens, William (1881–1954). Educator, Author, Lecturer, Journalist, Reformer, Government Worker

Avery, Sheldon, *Up from Washington: William Pickens and the Negro Struggle for Equality, 1900–1954* (1970).

Pickens, William, *Bursting Bonds* (1923).

————— *The Heir of Slaves: An Autobiography* (1911).

Pickett, Bill (1870–1932). Agriculturalist, Performing Artist

Hanes, Bailey C., *Bill Pickett, Bulldogger: The Biography of a Black Cowboy* (1977).

Pittman, Portia Marshall Washington (1883–1978). Performing Artist

Hill, Roy L., *Booker T.'s Child: The Life and Times of Portia Marshall Washington Pittman* (1993).

Stewart, Ruth Ann, *Portia: The Life of Portia Washington Pittman, the Daughter of Booker T. Washington* (1977).

Poindexter, Hildrus Augustus (1901–?). Military Person, Medical Worker, Educator, Political Figure, Author, Reformer, Journalist

Poindexter, Hildrus Augustus, *My World of Reality (An Autobiography)* (1973).

Poitier, Sidney (1927–). Performing Artist

Poitier, Sidney, *This Life* (1980).

Pollard, Frederick Douglass "Fritz" (1894–1986). Athlete, Business Person

Carroll, John M., *Fritz Pollard: An American Pioneer* (1991).

Pope, Oliver R. (1876–?). Educator

Pope, Oliver R., *Chalk Dust* (1967).

Porter, James Amos (1905–1970). Artist, Educator

James A. Porter, Artist and Historian: The Memory of the Legacy (1992).

Poston, Ted (1906–1974). Journalist

Hauke, Kathleen A., *Ted Poston: Pioneer American Journalist* (1998).

Potter, Eliza (?). Slave

Potter, Eliza, *A Hairdresser's Experience in High Life* (1859).

Potter, Richard J. (1843–?). Slave

Potter, Richard J., *A Narrative of the Experience, Adventures, and Escape of Richard J. Potter* (1866).

Powell, Adam Clayton, Jr. (1908–1972). Political Figure, Religious Worker

Coleman, Emmett [Ishmael Reed], *The Rise, Fall and. . .? of Adam Clayton Powell* (1967).

Hamilton, Charles V., *Adam Clayton Powell, Jr.: The Political Biography of an American Dilemma* (1991).

Haygood, Wil, *King of the Cats: The Life and Times of Adam Clayton Powell, Jr.* (1993).

Kilson, Martin, "Adam Clayton Powell, Jr.: The Militant as Politician," in John Hope Franklin and August Meier, ed., *Black Leaders of the Twentieth Century* (1982): 259–75.

Powell, Adam Clayton, Jr., *Adam by Adam: The Autobiography of Adam Clayton Powell, Jr.* (1971).

————— *Keep the Faith, Baby!* (1967).

Powell, Adam Clayton, Sr. (1865–1953). Religious Worker, Reformer, Educator, Political Figure

Powell, Adam Clayton, Sr., *Against the Tide: An Autobiography* (1938).

Powell, Colin L. (1937–). Military Person, Political Figure

Powell, Colin L., *In His Own Words: Colin L. Powell*, ed. Lisa Shaw (1995).

Powell, Colin L., with Joseph E. Persico, *My American Journey* (1995).

Powell, William Jenifer (1899–1942). Aviator, Journalist, Business Person, Military Person

Powell, William Jenifer, *Black Wings* (1934).

Powers, Tyrone (1961–). Government Worker

Powers, Tyrone, *Eyes to My Soul: The Rise or Decline of a Black FBI Agent* (1996).

Price, Joseph Charles (1854–1893). Educator, Religious Worker

Walls, William Jacob, *Joseph Charles Price: Educator and Race Leader* (1943).

Yates, Walter L., *He Spoke, Now They Speak: A Collection of Speeches and Writings of and on the Life and Works of J. C. Price* (1952).

Prince, Mary (?). Slave

Prince, Mary, *The History of Mary Prince, A West Indian Slave. Related by Herself. With a Supplement by the Author. To Which Is Added, the Narrative of Asa-Asa, a Captured African* (1831).

Prince, Nancy Gardener (1799–1856?). Domestic, Religious Worker, Author
Prince, Nancy, *A Narrative of the Life and Travels of Mrs. Nancy Prince* (1850).

Proctor, Henry Hugh, Sr. (1868–1933). Religious Worker, Reformer, Lecturer, Journalist
Proctor, Henry Hugh, Sr., *Between Black and White: Autobiographical Sketches* (1925).

Proctor, Samuel Dewitt (1921–1997). Religious Worker, Educator, Political Figure
Proctor, Samuel DeWitt, *Samuel Proctor: My Moral Odyssey* (1989).
————— *The Substance of Things Hoped For: A Memoir of African American Faith* (1995).

Rainey, Gertrude "Ma" (1886–1939). Performing Artist
Lieb, Sandra, *Mother of the Blues: A Study of Ma Rainey* (1981).
Stewart-Baxter, Derrick, *Ma Rainey and the Classic Blues Singers* (1970).

Randall, Dudley (1914–). Author
Thompson, Julius E., *Dudley Randall, Broadside Press, and the Black Arts Movement in Detroit, 1960–1995* (1999).

Randolph, Asa Philip (1889–1979). Labor Leader, Journalist, Reformer, Railroad Employee, Political Figure
Anderson, Jervis, *A. Philip Randolph: A Biographical Portrait* (1973).
Davis, Daniel S., *Mr. Black Labor: The Story of A. Philip Randolph, Father of the Civil Rights Movement* (1972).
Pfeffer, Paula F., *A. Philip Randolph: Pioneer of the Civil Rights Movement* (1990).
Quarles, Benjamin, "A. Philip Randolph: Labor Leader at Large," in John Hope Franklin and August Meier, ed., *Black Leaders of the Twentieth Century* (1982): 139–65.

Randolph, Paschal Beverly (1825–1875). Writer, Religious Worker
Deveney, John Patrick, *Paschal Beverly Randolph: A Nineteenth-Century Black American Spiritualist, Rosicrucian, and Sex Magician* (1997).

Randolph, Peter (1825–1897). Religious Worker, Reformer
Randolph, Peter, *From Slave Cabin to the Pulpit: The Autobiography of Rev. Peter Randolph* (1893).
————— *Sketches of Slave Life; or Illustrations of the Peculiar Institution* (1855).

Ransom, Reverdy Cassius (1861–1959). Religious Worker, Journalist, Reformer, Educator
Morris, Calvin S., *Reverdy C. Ransom: Black Advocate of the Social Gospel* (1990).
Ransom, Reverdy Cassius, *The Pilgrimage of Harriet Ransom's Son* (1949).
————— *School Days at Wilberforce* (1892).
Wills, David W., "Reverdy C. Ransom: The Making of an A.M.E. Bishop," in Randall K. Burkett and Richard Newman, ed., *Black Apostles: Afro-American Clergy Confront the Twentieth Century* (1978): 181–212.

Rapier, James Thomas (1839–1883). Political Figure
Schweninger, Loren, *James T. Rapier and Reconstruction* (1978).
————— "James T. Rapier of Alabama and the Noble Cause of Reconstruction," in Howard Rabinowitz, ed., *Southern Black Leaders of the Reconstruction Era* (1982): 79–99.

Ray, Charles Bennett (1807–1886). Reformer, Religious Worker
Ray, Charlotte A. B., *Sketch of the Life of the Rev. Charles B. Ray* (1887).

Ray, Emma J. Smith (1859–1930). Religious Worker, Medical Worker, Reformer
Ray, Emma J. Smith, *Twice Sold, Twice Ransomed: Autobiography of Mr. and Mrs. L. P. Ray* (1926).

Razaf, Andy (1895–1973). Performing Artist
Singer, Barry, *Black and Blue: The Life and Lyrics of Andy Razaf* (1992).

Redding, Jay Saunders (1906–1988). Author, Educator
Redding, J. Saunders, *No Day of Triumph* (1942).
————— *On Being a Negro in America* (1951).

Reddix, Jacob L. (1897–?). Educator, Religious Worker
Reddix, Jacob L., *A Voice Crying in the Wilderness: The Memoirs of Jacob L. Reddix* (1974).

Redmond, Sidney Dillon (?–1948). Medical Worker, Lawyer, Business Person, Educator
Wilson, Charles H., Sr., *God! Make Me a Man: A Biographical Sketch of Dr. Sidney Dillon Redmond* (1950).

Reed, Ishmael (1938–). Author
McGee, Patrick, *Ishmael Reed and the Ends of Race* (1997).

Reeves, Donald (1952–). Author

Reeves, Donald, *Notes of a Processed Brother* (1971).

Revels, Hiram Rhodes (1827–1901). Political Figure, Religious Worker, Lecturer, Educator

Borome, Joseph A., "The Autobiography of Hiram Rhodes Revels Together with Some Letters by and about Him," *Midwest Journal* 5 (1952–1953): 79–92.

Rice, Sarah (1909–?). Reformer, Religious Worker, Domestic

Rice, Sarah, *He Included Me: The Autobiography of Sarah Rice*, ed. Louise Westling (1989).

Richardson, George C. (1929–). Military Person

Richardson, George C., and Ingrid Frank, *Get Up, You're Not Dead!* (1975).

Ringgold, Faith (1934–). Artist

Ringgold, Faith, *We Flew over the Bridge: The Memoirs of Faith Ringgold* (1995).

Ritchie, Lionel (1949–). Performing Artist

Plutzik, Roberta, *Lionel Ritchie* (1985).

Roberts, Bari-Ellen (1953–). Business Person

Roberts, Bari-Ellen, with Jack E. White, *Roberts vs. Texaco: A True Story of Race and Corporate America* (1998).

Roberts, James (1753–?). Slave

Roberts, James, *The Narrative of James Roberts, Soldier in the Revolutionary War and at the Battle of New Orleans* (1858).

Robeson, Paul Leroy (1898–1976). Performing Artist, Athlete, Lawyer, Reformer, Political Figure

Brown, Lloyd L., *The Young Paul Robeson: On My Journey Now* (1997).

Duberman, Martin Baum, *Paul Robeson* (1989).

Editors of Freedomways, *Paul Robeson: The Great Forerunner* (1978).

Foner, Philip, ed., *Paul Robeson Speaks: Writings, Speeches, Interviews, 1918–1974* (1978).

Gilliam, Dorothy Butler, *Paul Robeson: All American* (1976).

Robeson, Eslanda Goode, *Paul Robeson, Negro* (1930).

Robeson, Paul, *Here I Stand* (1958).

Robeson, Susan, *The Whole World in His Hands: A Pictorial Biography of Paul Robeson* (1981).

Stewart, Jeffrey C., ed., *Paul Robeson: Artist and Citizen* (1998).

Robinson, Jackie [John Roosevelt] (1919–1972). Athlete

Rampersad, Arnold, *Jackie Robinson: A Biography* (1997).

Robinson, Jackie, *I Never Had It Made* (1972).

———— *Jackie Robinson: My Own Story* (1948).

Robinson, Sharon, *Stealing Home: An Intimate Family Portrait by the Daughter of Jackie Robinson* (1996).

Tygiel, Jules, *Baseball's Great Experiment: Jackie Robinson and His Legacy* (1983).

————, ed., *The Jackie Robinson Reader: Perspectives on an American Hero* (1997).

Robinson, James Herman (1907–?). Religious Worker, Educator

Cato, John David, "James Herman Robinson: Crossroads Africa and American Idealism, 1958– 1972," *American Presbyterians* 68 (1990): 99–107.

Robinson, James Herman, *Road without Turning: The Story of Reverend James H. Robinson: An Autobiography* (1950).

Robinson, John Charles (1903–1954). Aviator, Military Person

Simmons, Thomas E., *The Brown Condor: The True Adventures of John C. Robinson* (1988).

Robinson, Joseph J. (?)

Robinson, Joseph J., *Growing Up in Chi-Town: A Story of the 1960s* (1980).

Robinson, Lewis Green (1929–). Lawyer

Robinson, Lewis G., *The Making of a Man: An Autobiography* (1970).

Robinson, Randall (1941–). Lawyer, Political Figure, Reformer

Robinson, Randall, *Defending the Spirit: A Black Life in America* (1998).

Robinson, Ruby Doris Smith (1941–1967). Reformer

Fleming, Cynthia Griggs, *Soon We Will Not Cry: The Liberation of Ruby Doris Smith Robinson* (1998).

Robinson, Sugar Ray [Walker Smith, Jr.] (1921–1989). Athlete
Robinson, Sugar Ray, with Dave Anderson, *Sugar Ray* (1970).
Robinson, William Henry (1848–?). Religious Worker
Robinson, William Henry, *From Log Cabin to Pulpit; or Fifteen Years in Slavery* (1913).
Rollins, Sonny [Walter Theodore] (1930–). Performing Artist
Blancq, Charles, *Sonny Rollins: Journey of a Jazzman* (1983).
Roper, Moses (?). Slave
Roper, Moses, *A Narrative of the Adventures and Escape of Moses Roper, from American Slavery* (1838).
Rowan, Carl Thomas (1925–). Journalist
Rowan, Carl Thomas, *Breaking Barriers: A Memoir* (1991).
Ruby, George T. (1841–1882)
Moneyhon, Carl H., "George T. Ruby and the Politics of Expediency in Texas," in Howard Rabinowitz, ed., *Southern Black Leaders of the Reconstruction Era* (1982): 363–92.
Rudolph, Wilma Glodean (1940–1994). Athlete, Government Worker
Rudolph, Wilma, *Wilma* (1977).
Russell, Bill [William Felton] (1934–). Athlete
Russell, Bill, *Go up for Glory* (1966).
Russell, Bill, and Taylor Branch, *Second Wind: The Memoirs of an Opinionated Man* (1979).
Rustin, Bayard (1910–1987). Reformer
Anderson, Jervis, *Bayard Rustin: Troubles I've Seen* (1997).
Levine, Daniel, *Bayard Rustin and the Civil Rights Movement* (2000).
Rustin, Bayard, *Down the Line: The Collected Writings of Bayard Rustin* (1971).
Sadler, Robert (1911–). Religious Worker
Sadler, Robert, with Marie Chapian, *The Emancipation of Robert Sadler* (1975).
Sam, Alfred Charles (?). Reformer
Bittle, William E., and Gilbert Geis, *The Longest Way Home: Chief Alfred C. Sam's Back-to-Africa Movement* (1964).
Sayers, Gayle (1943–). Athlete
Sayers, Gayle, with Al Silverman, *I Am Third* (1972).
Scarborough, William Sanders (1852–1926). Educator
Weisenberger, Frances P., "William Sanders Scarborough: Early Life and Years at Wilberforce," *Ohio History* 71 (1962): 203–26, 287–89.
——— "William Sanders Scarborough: Scholarship, the Negro, Religion, and Politics," *Ohio History* 72 (1963): 25–50, 85–88.
Schomburg, Arthur Alfonso (1874–1938). Librarian, Book Collector, Reformer, Club Leader
Sinnette, Eleanor Des Verney, *Arthur Alfonso Schomburg, Black Bibliophile and Collector: A Biography* (1989).
Schuyler, George Samuel (1895–1977). Journalist, Author, Lecturer, Political Figure
Schuyler, George Samuel, *Black and Conservative: The Autobiography of George S. Schuyler* (1966).
Williams, Oscar R., "From Black Liberal to Black Conservative: George S. Schuyler, 1923–1935," *Afro-Americans in New York Life and History* 21 (1997): 59–68.
Schuyler, Philippa Duke (1932–1967). Performing Artist, Reformer
Schuyler, Philippa, *Adventures in Black and White* (1960).
Talalay, Kathryn M., *Composition in Black and White: The Life of Philippa Schuyler* (1995).
Seale, Bobby George (1936–). Reformer, Political Figure
Seale, Bobby, *A Lonely Rage: The Autobiography of Bobby Seale* (1978).
——— *Seize the Time: The Story of the Black Panther Party and Huey P. Newton* (1970).
Sellers, Cleveland (1944–). Reformer, Educator
Sellers, Cleveland, with Robert Terrell, *The River of No Return: The Autobiography of a Black Militant and the Life and Death of SNCC* (1973).
Sewing, Henry Warren (1891–?). Business Person
Sewing, Henry Warren, *Henry Warren Sewing, Founder of the Douglass State Bank: An Autobiography* (1971).

Seymour, William Joesph (1870–1922). Religious Worker

Tinney, James S., "William J. Seymour: Father of Modern-Day Pentacostalism," in Randall K. Burkett and Richard Newman, ed., *Black Apostles: Afro-American Clergy Confront the Twentieth Century* (1978): 213–25.

Shabazz, Hajj Bahiya [Betty] (1936–1997). Educator

Brown, Jamie Foster, *Betty Shabazz: A Sisterfriends' Tribute in Words and Pictures* (1998).

Shackelford, Otis M. (1871–?). Educator, Journalist, Author

Shackelford, Otis M., *Seeking the Best* (1909).

Shakur, Assata (1947–). Reformer, Political Figure

Shakur, Assata, *Assata: An Autobiography* (1987).

Shakur, Sanyika (1964–). Author

Shakur, Sanyika, *Monster: The Autobiography of an L.A. Gang Member* (1993).

Shakur, Tupac (1971–1996). Performing Artist

Scott, Cathy, *The Killing of Tupac Shakur* (1999).

White, Armond, *Rebel for the Hell of It: The Life of Tupac Shakur* (1997).

Sharpton, Al [Alfred, Jr.] (1954–). Religious Worker, Political Figure, Reformer

Sharpton, Al, with Anthony Walton, *Go and Tell Pharaoh: The Autobiography of Reverend Al Sharpton* (1996).

Shaw, Nate See COBB, NED

Short, Bobby [Robert Waltrip] (1924–). Performing Artist

Short, Bobby, *Black and White Baby* (1971).

Shorter, James Alexander (1817–1887). Religious Worker

Wayman, Alexander W., *The Life and Times of Rev. James Alexander Shorter, One of the Bishops of the A.M.E. Church* (1890).

Shuttlesworth, Fred L. (1922–). Religious Worker, Reformer

Manis, Andrew M., *A Fire You Can't Put Out: The Civil Rights Life of Birmingham's Reverend Fred Shuttlesworth* (1999).

Simpson, Orenthal James (1948–). Athlete

Simpson, O. J., with Pete Axthelm, *O. J.: The Education of a Rich Rookie* (1970).

Singleton, Benjamin "Pap" (1809–1892). Slave, Abolitionist, Reformer, Political Figure

Fleming, Walter L., "'Pap' Singleton, the Moses of the Colored Exodus," *American Journal of Sociology* 15 (1909): 61–95.

Singleton, George Arnett (1896–1970). Religious Worker, Educator

Singleton, George A., *The Autobiography of George A. Singleton* (1964).

Singleton, William Henry (?). Slave

Singleton, William Henry, *Recollections of My Slavery Days* (1922).

Smalls, Robert (1839–1915). Political Figure, Government Worker

Miller, Edward A., Jr., *Gullah Statesman: Robert Smalls from Slavery to Congress, 1839–1915* (1994).

Uya, Okon E., *From Slavery to Public Service: Robert Smalls, 1839–1915* (1971).

Smallwood, Thomas (?). Slave

Smallwood, Thomas, *A Narrative of Thomas Smallwood (Coloured Man) Giving an Account of His Birth—The General Period He was Held in Slavery—His Release—and Removal to Canada, etc.: Together with an Account of the Underground Railroad.* (1851).

Smith, Amanda Berry (1837–1915). Author, Reformer, Lecturer, Religious Worker

Smith, Amanda Berry, *An Autobiography: The Story of the Lord's Dealings with Mrs. Amanda Smith, the Colored Evangelist: Containing an Account of Her Life Work of Faith, and Her Travels in America, England, Ireland, Scotland, India and Africa, as an Independent Missionary* (1893).

Taylor, Marshall W., *The Life, Travels, Labors, and Helpers of Mrs. Amanda Smith, the Famous Negro Missionary Evangelist* (1886).

Smith, Bessie (1894–1937). Performing Artist

Albertson, Chris, *Bessie* (1972).

Kay, Jackie, *Bessie Smith* (1997).

Smith, Charles Spencer (1852–1923). Religious Worker, Political Figure, Educator, Journalist

Smith, C. S., *Glimpses of Africa, West, and Southwest Coast Containing the Author's Impressions and Observations during a Voyage of Six Thousand Miles from Sierra Leone to St. Paul de Loanda and Return, Including the Rio del Ray and Cameroons Rivers, and the Congo River, from Its Mouth to Matadi* (1895).

Smith, Charlie (?). Slave

Byrd, Sherman Clifton, *The Transplant: The Biography of 135-Year-Old Charlie Smith, a Former Slave* (1978).

Smith, David (1784–?). Religious Worker

Smith, David, *Biography of Rev. David Smith, of the A.M.E. Church: Being a Complete History Embracing Over Sixty Years' Labor in the Advancement of the Redeemer's Kingdom on Earth. Including "The History of the Origin and Development of Wilberforce University"* (1881).

Smith, Harry (1815–?). Business Person

Smith, Harry, *Fifty Years of Slavery in the United States of America* (1891).

Smith, Homer (1908–). Journalist

Smith, Homer, *Black Man in Red Russia: A Memoir* (1964).

Smith, James Lindsey (?–1883?). Religious Worker

Smith, James Lindsey, *Autobiography of James L. Smith* (1881).

Smith, Venture (1729?–1805)

Selden, Henry M., *Traditions of Venture! Known as Venture Smith* (1897).

Smith, Venture, *A Narrative of the Life and Adventures of Venture: A Native of Africa, but Resident Some Sixty Years in the United States of America. Related by Himself* (1798).

Smith, Willie the Lion [William Henry Joseph Bonaparte Bertholoff] (1897–1973). Performing Artist

Smith, Willie the Lion, *Music on My Mind: The Memoirs of an American Pianist* (1964).

Snow, Valaida (1900–1956). Performing Artist

Charles, Mario A., "The Age of a Jazz Woman: Valaida Snow, 1900–1956," *Journal of Negro History* 4 (1995): 183–91.

Snowden, John Baptist (1801–1885). Religious Worker

Snowden, John Baptist, and Houston Snowden, *From Whence Cometh* (1980).

Solomon, Franklin Delano Roosevelt (1934–). Reformer

Solomon, Franklin Delano Roosevelt, *A Hell of a Life*, ed. A. Peter Bailey (1976).

Somerville, John Alexander (1882–1973). Medical Worker, Religious Worker, Educator

Somerville, John Alexander, *Man of Color, an Autobiography: A Factual Report on the Status of the American Negro Today* (1949).

Soulds, Edward H. (1917–). Military Worker

Soulds, Edward H., *Black Shavetail in Whitey's Army* (1971).

Spaulding, Charles Clinton (1874–1952). Business Person, Agriculturalist, Religious Worker

Weare, Walter, "Charles Clinton Spaulding: Middle-Class Leadership in the Age of Segregation," in John Hope Franklin and August Meier, ed., *Black Leaders of the Twentieth Century* (1982): 167–90.

Spear, Chloe (1750?–1815). Slave

Spear, Chloe, *A Lady of Boston: Memoir of Mrs. Chloe Spear, a Native of Africa, Who Was Enslaved in Childhood, and Died in Boston, January 3, 1815* (1832).

Spellman, Cecil Lloyd (1906–). Educator

Spellman, Cecil Lloyd, *Rough Steps on My Stairway: The Life History of a Negro Educator* (1953).

Spencer, Anne (1882–1975). Author

Green, J. Lee, *Time's Unfading Garden: Anne Spencer's Life and Poetry* (1977).

Spencer, Chauncey Edward (1906–). Aviator, Government Worker, Political Figure

Spencer, Chauncey Edward, *Who Is Chauncey Spencer?* (1975).

Staples, Brent (1951–). Journalist

Staples, Brent, *Parallel Time: Growing Up in Black and White* (1994).

Starks, John Jacob (1876–1944). Educator, Religious Worker, Author

Starks, John Jacob, *Lo These Many Years: An Autobiographical Sketch* (1941).

Staupers, Mabel K. (1890–1989) Nurse, Reformer

Hine, Darlene Clark, "Mabel K. Staupers and the Integration of Black Nurses into the Armed Forces," in John Hope Franklin and August Meier, ed., *Black Leaders of the Twentieth Century* (1982): 241–57.

Stephens, Charlotte (1854–1951). Educator, Librarian/Book Collector

Terry, Adolphine Fletcher, *Charlotte Stephens: Little Rock's First Black Teacher* (1973).

Stephens, George E. (?). Military Person

Stephens, George E., *A Voice of Thunder: The Civil War Letters of George E. Stephens*, ed. Donald Yacovone (1997).

Stevens, Walter James (1877–?). Author, Lecturer, Government Worker, Reformer

Stevens, Walter James, *Chip on My Shoulder: Autobiography of Walter J. Stevens* (1946).

Steward, Rebecca Gould (1820–1877). Religious Worker

Steward, Theophilus Gould, *Memoirs of Mrs. Rebecca Steward, Containing: A Full Sketch of Her Life, with Various Selections from Her Writings and Letters; Also Contributions from Bishop Campbell and Others* (1877).

Steward, Austin (1794–1860). Slave

Steward, Austin, *Twenty-Two Years a Slave and Forty Years a Freeman: Embracing a Correspondence of Several Years While Resident of Wilberforce Colony, London, Canada West* (1857).

Steward, Theophilus Gould (1843–1924). Educator, Religious Worker, Military Person, Journalist

Steward, Theophilus Gould, *From 1864 to 1914: Fifty Years in the Gospel Ministry* (1914?).

Steward, William Henry (1850–?). Educator, Construction Worker

Wright, George C., "William Henry Steward: Moderate Approach to Black Leadership," in Leon Litwack and August Meier, ed., *Black Leaders of the Nineteenth Century* (1988): 275–89.

Stewart, John (1786–1823). Religious Worker

Mitchell, Joseph, *The Missionary Pioneer, or a Brief Memoir of the Life, Labours, and Death of John Stewart (Man of Colour), Founder, Under God, of the Mission Among the Wyandotts, at Upper Sandusky, Ohio* (1827).

Stewart, Maria W. (1803–1879). Author, Political Figure

Stewart, Maria W., *Maria W. Stewart, America's First Black Woman Political Writer: Essays and Speeches*, ed. Marilyn Richardson (1987).

Stewart, Thomas McCants (1854?–1923). Lawyer, Religious Worker, Author, Educator

Broussard, Albert S., *African-American Odyssey: The Stewarts, 1853–1963* (1998).

Still, James (1812–1885). Medical Worker

Still, James, *Early Recollections and Life of Dr. James Still* (1877).

Still, Peter (1801–?). Slave

Pickard, Kate E. R., *The Kidnapped and the Ransomed. Being the Personal Recollections of Peter Still and His Wife "Vina," After Forty Years of Slavery* (1856).

Still, William Grant (1895–1978). Performing Artist

Arvey, Verna, *In One Lifetime* (1984).

Smith, Catherine Parsons, *William Grant Still: A Study in Contradictions* (2000).

Still, Judith Anne, Celeste Anne Headlee, and Lisa M. Headlee-Huffman, ed., *William Grant Still and the Fusion of Cultures in American Music* (2d rev. ed., 1995).

Still, William Grant, *William Grant Still and the Fusion of Cultures in American Music*, ed. Robert Bartlett Haas (1972).

Stokes, Carl Burton (1927–1996). Political Figure

Stokes, Carl B., *Promises of Power: A Political Autobiography* (1973).

Stringer, Lee (1950–). Author

Stringer, Lee, *Grand Central Winter: Stories from the Street* (1998).

Stroyer, Jacob (1849–1908). Religious Worker

Stroyer, Jacob, *Sketches of My Life in the South* (1879).

Sullivan, Leon H. (1922–). Religious Worker, Business Person

Sullivan, Leon H., *Build, Brother, Build* (1969).

Sun Ra [Herman Blount] (1914–1993). Performing Artist
Szwed, John F., *Space is the Place: The Lives and Times of Sun Ra* (1997).
Sutton, Joseph L. (1885–1980). Agriculturalist
Krech, Shephard, *Praise the Bridge That Carries You Over: The Life of Joseph L. Sutton* (1981).
Tanner, Benjamin Tucker (1835–1923). Religious Worker
Seraile, William, *Fire in His Heart: Bishop Benjamin Tucker Tanner and the A.M.E. Church* (1998).
Tanner, Henry Ossawa (1859–1937). Artist
Matthews, Marcia M., *Henry Ossawa Tanner: American Artist* (1969).
Mosby, Dewey F., ed., *Henry Ossawa Tanner* (1991).
Tarry, Ellen (1906–). Journalist, Educator, Reformer
Tarry, Ellen, *The Third Door: The Autobiography of an American Negro Woman* (1955).
Taulbert, Clifton L. (1945–). Business Person, Military Person, Author
Taulbert, Clifton L., *The Last Train North* (1992).
———— *Once Upon a Time When We Were Colored* (1989).
———— *Watching Our Crops Come In* (1997).
Taylor, Lawrence (1959–). Athlete
Taylor, Lawrence, with David Falkner, *LT, Living on the Edge* (1987).
Taylor, Marshall William "Major" (1878–1932). Athlete
Ritchie, Andrew, *Major Taylor: The Extraordinary Career of a Champion Bicycle Racer* (1988).
Taylor, Marshall William, *The Fastest Bicycle Rider in the World: The Story of a Colored Boy's Indomitable Courage and Success against Great Odds* (1928).
Taylor, Susie King (1848–1912). Medical Worker, Reformer
Taylor, Susie King, *Reminiscences of My Life in Camp with the 33d United States Colored Troops, Late 1st S.C. Volunteers* (1902).
Teamoh, George (1818–1883?). Political Figure
Teamoh, George, *God Made Man, Man Made the Slave: The Autobiography of George Teamoh,* ed. Nash Boney, Rafia Zafar and Richard L. Hume (1990).
Teer, Barbara Ann (1937–). Performing Artist
Thomas, Lundeana Marie, *Barbara Ann Teer and the National Black Theatre* (1997).
Terrell, Mary Eliza Church (1863–1954). Lecturer, Club Leader, Political Figure, Reformer
Harley, Sharon, "Mary Church Terrell: Genteel Militant," in Leon Litwack and August Meier, ed., *Black Leaders of the Nineteenth Century* (1988): 307–21.
Jones, Beverly W., *Quest for Equality: The Life and Writings of Mary Church Terrell, 1863–1954* (1990).
Terrell, Mary Church, *A Colored Woman in a White World* (1940).
Thomas, James (1827–1913). Business Person
Thomas, James, *From Tennessee Slave to St. Louis Entrepreneur: The Autobiography of James Thomas,* ed. Loren Schweninger (1984).
Thomas, Jessie Oda (1885–?). Reformer, Educator, Government Worker
Thomas, Jesse O., *My Story in Black and White: The Autobiography of Jesse O. Thomas* (1967).
Thomas, Matt (1888–?). Service Industry Employee
Thomas, Matt, *Hopping on the Border: The Life Story of a Bellboy* (1951).
Thomas, Piri [John Peter] (1928–). Author, Reformer
Thomas, Piri, *Down These Mean Streets* (1967).
———— *Savior, Savior, Hold My Hand* (1972).
———— *Seven Long Times* (1974).
Thomas, Vivien (1910–). Medical Worker, Scientist
Thomas, Vivien, *Partners of the Heart: Vivien Thomas and His Work with Alfred Blalock* (1998).
Thomas, Will [Will Smith] (1905–?). Author, Journalist, Agriculturalist, Lecturer
Thomas, Will, *The Seeking* (1953).
Thomas, William Hannibal (1843–1935). Educator, Lawyer, Political Figure, Author
Smith, John David, *Black Judas: William Hannibal Thomas and The American Negro* (1999).
Thompson, Era Bell (1906–1986). Author, Government Worker, Journalist, Reformer
Thompson, Era Bell, *American Daughter* (1946).

Thompson, Holland (1840–1887). Political Figure

Rabinowitz, Howard N., "Holland Thompson and Black Political Participation in Montgomery, Alabama," in Howard Rabinowitz, ed., *Southern Black Leaders of the Reconstruction Era* (1982): 249–80.

Thompson, John (1812–?). Slave

Thompson, John, *The Life of John Thompson, a Fugitive Slave; Containing His History of 25 Years in Bondage, and His Providential Escape* (1856).

Thorne, Jack [David Bryant Fulton] (1861?–1941). Author, Club Leader, Railroad Employee

Thorne, Jack, *Recollections of a Sleeping Car Porter* (1892).

Thurman, Howard Washington (1900–1981). Religious Worker, Educator, Author, Lecturer

Thurman, Howard, *With Head and Heart: The Autobiography of Howard Thurman* (1979).

Yates, Elizabeth, *Howard Thurman, Portrait of a Practical Dreamer* (1964).

Tilmon, Levin (1807–1863). Religious Worker

Tilmon, Levin, *A Brief Miscellaneous Narrative of the More Early Part of the Life of L. Tilmon, Pastor of a Colored Methodist Congregational Church in the City of New York* (1853).

Tolson, Melvin Beaunorus (1899–1966). Author, Journalist, Educator

Farnsworth, Robert M., *Melvin B. Tolson 1898–1966: Plain Talk and Poetic Prophecy* (1984).

Flasch, Joy, *Melvin B. Tolson* (1972).

Tolson, Melvin Beaunorus, *Caviar and Cabbage: Selected Columns by Melvin B. Tolson from the Washington Tribune, 1937–1944*, ed. Robert M. Farnsworth (1982).

Tolton, Augustine (1854?–1897). Religious Worker

Hemesath, Caroline, *From Slave to Priest: A Biography of the Reverend Augustine Tolton (1854–1897), First Afro-American Priest of the United States* (1973).

Toomer, Jean [Nathan] (1894–1967). Author, Educator

Kerman, Cynthia E., and Richard Eldridge, *The Lives of Jean Toomer: A Hunger for Wholeness* (1987).

McKay, Nellie, *Jean Toomer, Artist: A Study of His Literary Life and Work* (1984).

Toomer, Jean, *The Wayward and the Seeking: A Collection of Writings by Jean Toomer*, ed. Darwin T. Turner (1980).

Toussaint, Pierre (1766–1853?). Slave, Business Person

Lee, Hannah Farnham Sawyer, *Memoir of Pierre Toussaint, Born a Slave in St. Domingo* (1854).

Townsend, Henry (1909–). Performing Artist

Townsend, Henry, as told to Bill Greensmith, *A Blues Life* (1999).

Traylor, Bill (1854–1947). Artist

Lyons, Mary E., and Bill Traylor, *Deep Blues: Bill Traylor, Self-Taught Artist* (1994).

Trotter, William Monroe (1872–1934). Journalist, Political Figure

Fox, Stephen R., *The Guardian of Boston: William Monroe Trotter* (1970).

Trouppe, Quincy Thomas (1912–). Athlete

Trouppe, Quincy, *Twenty Years Too Soon: Prelude to Major-League Integrated Baseball* (rev. ed., 1995).

Truth, Sojourner (1800 -1883). Religious Worker, Reformer, Abolitionist, Lecturer, Author

Fauset, Arthur H., *Sojourner Truth: God's Faithful Pilgrim* (1938).

Fitch, Suzanne Pullon, and Roseann M. Mandziuk, *Sojourner Truth as Orator: Wit, Story, and Song* (1997).

Gilbert, Olive, *Narrative of Sojourner Truth: A Bondswoman of Olden Time (Emancipated by the New York Legislature in the Early Part of the Present Century; With a History of Her Last Sickness and Death)* (1875).

Mabee, Carleton, with Susan Mabee Newhouse, *Sojourner Truth: Slave, Prophet, Legend* (1993).

Painter, Nell Irvin, *Sojourner Truth: A Life, a Symbol* (1996).

Stetson, Erlene, and Linda David, *Glorying in Tribulation: The Lifework of Sojourner Truth* (1994).

Tubman, Harriet (1820?–1913). Abolitionist, Reformer

Bradford, Sarah Elizabeth Hopkins, *Harriet, the Moses of Her People* (1886).

———— *Scenes in the Life of Harriet Tubman* (1869).

Conrad, Earl, *Harriet Tubman* (1943).

Quarles, Benjamin, "Harriet Tubman's Unlikely Leadership," in Leon Litwack and August Meier, ed., *Black Leaders of the Nineteenth Century* (1988): 43–57.

Tucker, Lorenzo (?). Performing Artist

Grupenhoff, Richard, *The Black Valentino: The Stage and Screen Career of Lorenzo Tucker* (1988).

Turner, Bridges Alfred (1908–). Educator

Turner, Bridges Alfred, *From a Plow to a Doctorate: So What!* (1945).

Turner, Henry McNeal (1834–1915). Religious Worker, Military Person, Educator, Political Figure, Abolitionist

Angell, Stephen Ward, *Bishop Henry McNeal Turner and African-American Religion in the South* (1992).

Dittmer, John, "The Education of Henry McNeal Turner," in Leon Litwack and August Meier, ed., *Black Leaders of the Nineteenth Century* (1988): 253–72.

Ponton, Mungo M., *The Life and Times of Henry M. Turner* (1917).

Redkey, Edwin S., "Bishop Turner's African Dream," *Journal of American History* 54 (1967): 271–90.

Turner, Henry McNeal, *Respect Black: The Writings and Speeches of Henry McNeal Turner*, ed. Edwin S. Redkey (1971).

Turner, James Milton (1840–1915). Slave, Political Figure, Lawyer

Christensen, Lawrence O., "J. Milton Turner: An Appraisal," *Missouri Historical Review* 70 (1975): 1–19.

Kremer, Gary R., *James Milton Turner and the Promise of America: The Public Life of a Post-Civil War Black Leader* (1991).

Turner, Nat (1800–1831). Reformer, Slave, Agriculturalist, Abolitionist

Foner, Eric, ed., *Nat Turner* (1971).

Johnson, F. Roy, *The Nat Turner Story: History of the South's Most Important Slave Revolt, with New Material Provided by Black Tradition and White Tradition* (1970).

Oates, Stephen B., *The Fires of Jubilee: Nat Turner's Fierce Rebellion* (1975).

Wood, Peter H., "Nat Turner: The Unknown Slave as Visionary Leader," in Leon Litwack and August Meier, ed., *Black Leaders of the Nineteenth Century* (1988): 21–40.

Turner, Robert Emanuel (1875–?). Railroad Employee

Turner, Robert Emanuel, *Memories of a Retired Pullman Porter* (1954).

Turpeau, David Dewitt, Sr. (1874–1947). Religious Worker, Reformer, Club Leader, Political Figure

Turpeau, David Dewitt, Sr., *Up from the Cane-Brakes: An Autobiography* (1942?).

Ugwu-Oju, Dympna (1956–). Author

Ugwu-Oju, Dympna, *What Will My Mother Say? A Tribal African Girl Comes of Age in America* (1995).

Uncle Jack (1747?–1842). Slave

White, William S., *The African Preacher, an Authentic Narrative by the Reverend William S. White, Pastor Prebyterian Church, Lexington, Virginia* (1849).

Van Der Zee, James (1886–1983). Artist

Haskins, Jim, *James Van Der Zee: The Picture-Takin' Man* (1979).

Willis, Deborah, and Rodger C. Birt, *VanDerZee: Photographer 1886–1983* (1998).

Vann, Robert Lee (1879?–1940). Lawyer, Journalist, Business Person, Political Figure

Buni, Andrew, *Robert L. Vann of the* Pittsburgh Courier: *Politics and Black Journalism* (1974).

Veney, Bethany (1815–?). Slave

Veney, Bethany, *The Narrative of Bethany Veney: A Slave Woman* (1889).

Vesey, Denmark (1767?–1822). Reformer, Slave, Abolitionist

Robertson, David, *Denmark Vesey: The Buried History of America's Largest Slave Rebellion and the Man Who Led It* (1999).

Voorhis, Robert (?). Slave

Voorhis, Robert, *Life and Adventures of Robert, the Hermit of Massachusetts, Who Has Lived 14 Years in a Cave, Secluded from Human Society. Comprising, an Account of His Birth, Parentage, Sufferings, and Providential Escape from Unjust and Cruel Bondage in Early Life—and His Reasons for Becoming a Recluse,* ed. Henry Trumbell (1829).

Waddell, William H., IV (?). Veterinarian, Educator

Waddell, William H., *People Are the Funniest Animals* (1978).

Wade-Gayles, Gloria Jean (?–). Educator, Author

Wade-Gayles, Gloria, *Pushed Back To Strength: A Black Woman's Journey Home* (1993).

———— *Rooted against the Wind: Personal Essays* (1996).

Waite, Morrison Remick (1816–1888). Political Figure, Lawyer

Magrath, C. Peter, *Morrison R. Waite: The Triumph of Character* (1963).

Walker, Aaron Thibeaux "T-Bone" (1910–1975). Performing Artist

Dance, Helen Oakley, *Stormy Monday: The T-Bone Walker Story* (1987).

Walker, Charles Thomas (1858–1921) Religious Worker

Floyd, Silas Xavier, *Life of Charles T. Walker, D. D., ("The Black Spurgeon") Pastor Mt. Olivet Baptist Church, New York City* (1902).

Walker, David (1785–1830). Business Person, Abolitionist, Author, Journalist

Hinks, Peter P., *To Awaken My Afflicted Brethren: David Walker and the Problem of Antebellum Slave Resistance* (1997).

Walker, Madam C. J. [Sarah Breedlove] (1867–1919). Business Person, Educator, Reformer, Club Leader

Bundles, A'Lelia Perry, *Madam C. J. Walker* (1991).

Walker, Maggie Lena Mitchell (1867?–1934). Journalist, Club Leader, Business Person

Brown, Elsa Barkley, "Womanist Consciousness: Maggie Lena Walker and the Independent Order of Saint Luke," *Signs* 14 (1989): 610–33.

Dabney, Wendell Phillips, *Maggie L. Walker and the I. O. of Saint Luke: The Woman and Her Work* (1927).

Walker, Margaret Abigail (1915–1998). Author

Walker, Margaret, *How I Wrote Jubilee* (1972).

Walker, Moses Fleetwood (1857–1924). Athlete

Zang, David W., *Fleet Walker's Divided Heart: The Life of Baseball's First Black Major Leaguer* (1995).

Walker, Thomas Calhoun (1862–1953). Business Person, Political Figure, Educator, Lawyer

Walker, Thomas Calhoun, *The Honey-Pod Tree: The Life Story of Thomas Calhoun Walker* (1958).

Walker, William (1819?–?). Agriculturalist

Gaines, Thomas S., *Buried Alive (Behind Prison Walls) for a Quarter of a Century* (1892).

Waller, Fats [Thomas Wright] (1904–1943). Performing Artist

Kirkeby, W. T. Ed, with Duncan P. Schiedt and Sinclair Traill, *Ain't Misbehavin': The Story of Fats Waller* (1960).

Vance, Joel, *Fats Waller: His Life and Times* (1977).

Waller, Maurice, and Anthony Calabrese, *Fats Waller* (1977).

Waller, John Lewis (1850–1907). Lawyer, Political Figure, Journalist

Woods, Randall B., *A Black Odyssey: John Lewis Waller and the Promise of American Life, 1878–1900* (1981).

Walls, Josiah (1842–1905). Political Figure, Agriculturalist

Klingman, Peter D., *Josiah Walls: Florida's Black Congressman of Reconstruction* (1976).

———— "Race and Faction in the Public Career of Florida's Josiah T. Walls," in Howard N. Rabinowitz, ed., *Southern Black Leaders of the Reconstruction Era* (1982): 59–78.

Walters, Alexander (1858–1917). Religious Worker, Seaman, Journalist, Reformer

Walters, Alexander, *My Life and Work* (1917).

Ward, Samuel Ringgold (1817–1866?). Abolitionist, Religious Worker

Burke, Ronald K., *Samuel Ringgold Ward: Christian Abolitionist* (1995).

Ward, Samuel Ringgold, *Autobiography of a Fugitive Negro: His Anti-Slavery Labours in the United States, Canada, and England* (1855).

Warfield, Bernis, Sr. (?). Religious Worker

Johnson, Lois Phelps, *I'm Gonna Fly: The Biography of Bernis Warfield* (1959).

Warfield, William (1920–). Performing Artist, Educator

Warfield, William, with Alton Miller, *William Warfield: My Music and My Life* (1991).

Warner, Ashton (?). Slave

Warner, Ashton, *Negro Slavery Described by a Negro: Being the Narrative of Ashton Warner, a Native of St. Vincent's*, ed. Simon Strickland (1831).

Washington, Booker Taliaferro (1856–1915). Educator, Political Figure, Business Person

Harlan, Louis R., "Booker T. Washington and the White Man's Burden," *American Historical Review* 71 (1966): 441–67.

———— *Booker T. Washington: The Making of a Black Leader, 1856–1901* (1972).

———— "Booker T. Washington and the Politics of Accommodation," in John Hope Franklin and August Meier, ed., *Black Leaders of the Twentieth Century* (1982): 1–18.

———— *Booker T. Washington: The Wizard of Tuskegee, 1901–1915* (1983).

Harlan, Louis R., and Raymond W. Smock, ed., *Booker T. Washington in Perspective* (1988).

Spencer, Samuel R., Jr., *Booker T. Washington and the Negro's Place in American Life* (1955).

Washington, Booker T., *The Booker T. Washington Papers*, ed. Louis R. Harlan and Raymond W. Smock (14 vols., 1972–1989).

———— *My Larger Education: Being Chapters from My Experience* (1911).

———— *The Story of My Life and Work* (1900).

———— *Up From Slavery: An Autobiography* (1901).

———— *Working with the Hands: Being a Sequel to "Up from Slavery," Covering the Author's Experiences in Industrial Training at Tuskegee* (1904).

Waters, Ethel (1896–1977). Performing Artist

Waters, Ethel, *His Eye Is on the Sparrow: An Autobiography* (1951).

———— *To Me It's Wonderful* (1972).

Waters, Muddy [McKinley Morganfield] (1915–1983). Performing Artist

Tooze, Sandra, *Muddy Waters: The Mojo Man* (1996).

Watkins, James (1823–?). Slave

Watkins, James, *Narrative of the Life of James Watkins, Formerly a Chattel in Maryland, U.S.* (1852).

Watkins, Mel (1940–). Author, Editor, Journalist

Watkins, Mel, *Dancing With Strangers: A Memoir* (1984).

Watson, Deek (?). Performing Artist

Watson, Deek, with Lee Stephenson, *The Story of the "Ink Spots"* (1967).

Watson, Henry (1813–?). Slave

Watson, Henry, *Narrative of Henry Watson, a Fugitive Slave. Written by Himself* (1849).

Wayman, Alexander Walker (1821–1895). Religious Worker

Wayman, Alexander W., *My Recollections of African M. E. Ministers: Or Forty Years' Experience in the African Methodist Episcopal Church* (1881).

Webb, John L. (1877–?). Author

Griggs, Sutton E., *Triumph of the Simple Virtues; or The Life Story of John L. Webb* (1926).

Webb, Sheyann (1957–). Reformer

Webb, Sheyann, and Rachel West Nelson, as told to Frank Sikora, *Selma, Lord, Selma: Girlhood Memories of the Civil Rights Days* (1980).

Webb, William (1836–?). Business Person, Religious Worker

Webb, William, *The History of William Webb, Composed by Himself* (1873).

Webber, Amos (1826–1904). Reformer, Military Person, Service Industry Employee

Salvatore, Nick, *We All Got History: The Memory Books of Amos Webber* (1996).

Webster, Delia (1817–1904). Abolitionist, Educator, Reformer

Eisan, Frances K., *Saint or Demon? The Legendary Delia Webster Opposing Slavery* (1998).

Runyon, Randolph Paul, *Delia Webster and the Underground Railroad* (1996).

Weir, Samuel (1812–1884). Religious Worker

West, Landon, *Life of Elder Samuel Weir (Colored)* (1913).

Wells-Barnett, Ida Bell (1869–1931). Journalist, Lecturer, Reformer, Club Leader, Political Figure, Educator

Holt, Thomas C., "The Lonely Warrior: Ida B. Wells-Barnett and the Struggle for Black Leadership," in John Hope Franklin and August Meier, ed., *Black Leaders of the Twentieth Century* (1982): 39–61.

McMurry, Linda O., *To Keep the Waters Troubled: The Life of Ida B. Wells* (1998).

Schechter, Patricia A., "'All the Intensity of My Nature': Ida B. Wells, Anger, and Politics," *Radical History Review* 70 (1998): 48–77.

Thompson, Mildred I., *Ida B. Wells-Barnett: An Exploratory Study of an American Black Woman, 1893–1930* (1990).

Wells-Barnett, Ida B., *Crusade for Justice: The Autobiography of Ida B. Wells,* ed. Alfreda M. Duster (1970).

——— *Memphis Diary of Ida B. Wells,* ed. Miriam DeCosta-Willis (1995).

Wesley, Charles Harris (1891–1987). Historian, Educator, Club Leader

Wesley, Charles H., *Charles H. Wesley: The Intellectual Tradition of a Black Historian,* ed. James L. Conyers, Jr. (1997).

Wilson, Francille Rusan, "Racial Consciousness and Black Scholarship: Charles H. Wesley and the Consciousness of *Negro Labor in the United States,*" *Journal of Negro History* 81 (1996): 72–88.

Westberry, Ransom William (1871–?)

Westberry, Ransom W., *Life and Speeches of Ransom William Westberry,* ed. John R. Wilson (1921).

Wheatley, Phillis (1753?–1784). Slave, Author

Renfro, G. Herbert, *Life and Works of Phillis Wheatley* (1916).

Robinson, William Henry, *Phillis Wheatley and Her Writings* (1984).

Wheatley, Phillis, *Memoir of Phillis Wheatley, a Native of Africa and a Slave,* ed. Benjamin Bussey Thatcher (1834).

Wheatstraw, Peetie [William Bunch] (1902–1941). Performing Artist

Garon, Paul, *The Devil's Son-in-Law: The Story of Peetie Wheatstraw and His Songs* (1971).

Wheeler, Peter (1789–?). Seaman, Slave

Lester, C. Edwards, *Chains and Freedom: Or, the Life and Adventures of Peter Wheeler, a Colored Man Yet Living* (1839).

White, Charley C. (1885–1974). Religious Worker, Agriculturalist

White, C. C., and Ada Morehead Holland, *No Quittin' Sense* (1969).

White, George (1764–?). Slave

White, George, *A Brief Account of the Life, Experiences, Travels and Gospel Labours of George White, an African: Written by Himself, and Revised by a Friend* (1810).

White, Lulu Belle Madison (1900–1957). Reformer

Pitre, Merline, *In Struggle against Jim Crow: Lulu B. White and the NAACP, 1900–1957* (1999).

White, Walter Francis (1893–1955). Reformer, Political Figure, Journalist

White, Walter Francis, *A Man Called White: The Autobiography of Walter White* (1948).

Whitmore, Terry (1947–). Military Person

Whitmore, Terry, as told to Richard Weber, *Memphis, Nam, Sweden: The Autobiography of a Black American Exile* (1971).

Wideman, John Edgar (1941–). Author, Educator

Wideman, John Edgar, *Brothers and Keepers* (1984).

——— *Fatheralong: A Meditation on Fathers and Sons, Race and Society* (1994).

Wier, Robert (1886–1974). Business Person

Wier, Sadye H., and John F. Marszalek, *A Black Businessman in White Mississippi, 1886–1974* (1977).

Wilkerson, James (?). Slave

Wilkerson, James, *Wilkerson's History of His Travels and Labors, in the United States, as a Missionary, in Particular, that of the Union Seminary, Located in Franklin Co., Ohio, Since He Purchased His Liberty in New Orleans, La., &c.* (1861).

Wilkins, Roger W. (1932–). Lawyer, Government Worker
Wilkins, Roger W., *A Man's Life: An Autobiography* (1982).
Wilkins, Roy (1901–1981). Reformer, Journalist
Wilkins, Roy, "Roy Wilkins Anthology," *Crisis* 84 (1977): 205–330.
Wilkins, Roy, with Tom Matthews, *Standing Fast: The Autobiography of Roy Wilkins* (1982).
Williams, Bert (1873–1922). Performing Artist
Charters, Ann, *Nobody: The Story of Bert Williams* (1970).
Smith, Eric Ledell, *Bert Williams: A Biography of the Pioneer Black Comedian* (1992).
Williams, Cecil (1929–). Religious Worker
Williams, Cecil, *I'm Alive! An Autobiography* (1980).
Williams, Clarence (1898–1964). Performing Artist, Business Person
Lord, Tom, *Clarence Williams* (1976).
Williams, Daniel Hale (1856?–1931). Medical Worker, Author, Educator, Reformer, Military Person, Lecturer
Buckler, Helen, *Doctor Dan: Pioneer in American Surgery* (1954).
Williams, George Washington (1849–1891). Educator, Reformer
Franklin, John Hope, *George Washington Williams: A Biography* (1985).
Williams, Gladnil Bernell (1893–?)
Williams, G. Bernell, *Look Not upon Me Because I Am Black* (1970).
Williams, Gregory Howard (1943–). Educator
Williams, Gregory Howard, *Life on the Color Line: The True Story of a White Boy Who Discovered He Was Black* (1995).
Williams, Henry Sylvester (1869–1911). Reformer
Mathurin, Owen C., *Henry Sylvester Williams and the Origins of the Pan-African Movement, 1869–1911* (1976).
Williams, Isaac D. (1821–1898). Business Person, Lecturer
Williams, Isaac D., *Sunshine and Shadow of Slave Life: Reminiscences* (1885).
Williams, James (1805–?). Slave
Williams, James, *Narrative of James Williams, an American Slave; Who Was for Several Years a Driver on a Cotton Plantation in Alabama*, ed. John Greenleaf Whittier (1838).
Williams, James H. (1864–1927). Educator, Government Worker, Business Person, Service Industry Employee
Williams, James H., *Blow the Man Down! An Autobiographical Narrative Based upon the Writings of James H. Williams*, ed. Warren F. Kuehl (1959).
Williams, James [John Thomas Evans] (1825–?). Slave
Williams, James, *Life and Adventures of James Williams, a Fugitive Slave, with a Full Description of the Underground Railroad* (1873).
Williams, John Alfred (1925–). Journalist
Williams, John Alfred, *Flashbacks: A Twenty-Year Diary of Article Writing* (1973).
Williams, Lacey Kirk (1871–1940). Religious Worker
Horace, Lillian B., *"Crowned with Glory and Honor": The Life of Rev. Lacey Kirk Williams*, ed. L. Venchael Booth (1978).
Williams, Maria P. (?). Journalist
Williams, Maria P., *My Work and Public Sentiment* (1916).
Williams, Robert Franklin (1925–1996). Reformer
Cohen, Robert Carl, *Black Crusader: A Biography of Robert Franklin Williams* (1972).
Tyson, Timothy B., *Radio Free Dixie: Robert F. Williams and the Roots of Black Power* (1999).
Williams, Sally [Aunt Sally] (1796?–?). Slave
Williams, Sally, *Aunt Sally, or The Cross the Way of Freedom: A Narrative of the Slave-Life and Purchase of the Mother of Rev. Isaac Williams, of Detroit, Michigan* (1858).
Williams, Samuel (1813–?). Religious Worker
Williams, Samuel, *Four Years in Liberia: A Sketch of the Life of the Rev. Samuel Williams* (1857).

Wilson, Harriet E. Adams (1808–1876?). Slave

Wilson, Harriet E. Adams, *Our Nig; Or, Sketches from the Life of a Free Black, in a Two-Storey White House, North. Showing that Slavery's Shadows Fall Even There* (1859).

Wilson, Sunnie (1908–1999). Business Person

Wilson, Sunnie, with John Cohassey, *Toast of the Town: The Life and Times of Sunnie Wilson* (1998).

Winfrey, Oprah (1954–). Performing Artist, Business Person

Mair, George, *Oprah Winfrey: The Real Story* (1994).

Wise, Namon (1897?–). Government Worker

Wise, Namon, *The Namon Wise Story* (1963).

Woodson, Carter Godwin (1875–1950). Educator, Reformer, Author

Durden, Robert Franklin, *Carter G. Woodson: The Father of African American History* (1998).

Goggin, Jacqueline A., *Carter G. Woodson: A Life in Black History* (1993).

Logan, Rayford W., "Carter G. Woodson: Mirror and Molder of His Time, 1875–1950," *Journal of Negro History* 58 (1973): 1–17.

Work, Monroe Nathan (1866–1945). Educator, Librarian, Book Collector, Religious Worker

McMurry, Linda O., *Recorder of the Black Experience: A Biography of Monroe Nathan Work* (1985).

Workman, Willie Mae (?). Domestic

Kytle, Elizabeth, *Willie Mae* (1958).

Wright, Arthur (1927–). Performing Artist

Wright, Arthur, *Color Me White: The Autobiography of a Black Dancer Who Turned White* (1980).

Wright, Elizabeth Evelyn (1872–1906). Educator

Morris, J. Kenneth, *Elizabeth Evelyn Wright, 1872–1906: Founder of Voorhees College* (1983).

Wright, Jonathan Jasper (1839?–1885). Lawyer, Political Figure, Educator

Woody, Robert H., "Jonathan Jasper Wright, Associate Justice of the Supreme Court of South Carolina, 1870–1877," *Journal of Negro History* 18 (1933): 114–31.

Wright, Richard Nathaniel (1908–1960). Author, Journalist

Fabre, Michel, *The Unfinished Quest of Richard Wright* (1973).

Farnsworth, Robert M., and David Ray, "The Life and Work of Richard Wright," *New Letter* 38 (1971): 5–204.

Gayle, Addison, *Richard Wright: Ordeal of a Native Son* (1980).

Walker, Margaret, *Richard Wright, Daemonic Genius: A Portrait of the Man, a Critical Look at His Work* (1988).

Webb, Constance, *Richard Wright: A Biography* (1968).

Williams, John A., *The Most Native of Sons: A Biography of Richard Wright* (1970).

Wright, Richard, *American Hunger* (1977).

——— *Black Boy: A Record of Childhood and Youth* (1937).

Wright, Richard Robert, Jr. (1878–1967). Religious Worker, Journalist, Educator, Business Person, Reformer

Wright, Richard R., Jr., *Eighty-Seven Years behind the Black Curtain: An Autobiography* (1965).

Wright, Richard Robert, Sr. (1855–1947). Educator, Business Person

Haynes, Elizabeth Ross, *The Black Boy of Atlanta* (1952).

Lemon, Harriet Beecher Stowe Wright, *Radio Speeches of Major R. R. Wright, Sr.* (1949).

Patton, June O., "'And the Truth Shall Make You Free': Richard Robert Wright, Sr., Black Intellectual and Iconoclast, 1877–1897," *Journal of Negro History* 81 (1996): 17–30.

Yancey, Arthur Asa Henry (1881–?). Government Worker

Yancey, Arthur Henry, *Interpositionulification: What the Negro May Expect* (1959).

Yates, James (1906–). Reformer

Yates, James, *Mississippi to Madrid: Memoir of a Black American in the Abraham Lincoln Brigade* (1989).

Young, Andrew (1932–). Reformer, Political Figure, Religious Worker

Young, Andrew, *An Easy Burden: The Civil Rights Movement and the Transformation of America* (1996).

———— *A Way Out of No Way: The Spiritual Memoirs of Andrew Young* (1994).

Young, Charles (1864–1922). Military Person

Chew, Abraham, *A Biography of Colonel Charles Young* (1923).

Young, Coleman Alexander (1919–1997). Political Figure, Labor Leader

Rich, Wilbur C., *Coleman Young and Detroit Politics: From Social Activist to Power Broker*(1989).

Young, Coleman A., and Lonnie Wheeler, *Hard Stuff: The Autobiography of Coleman Young* (1994).

Young, Plummer Bernard, Sr. (1884–1962). Journalist, Business Person, Club Leader, Reformer

Suggs, Henry Lewis, *P. B. Young, Newspaperman: Race, Politics, and Journalism in the New South, 1910–1962* (1988).

Young, Rosa J. (1890–?). Educator

Young, Rosa, *Light in the Dark Belt: The Story of Rosa Young as Told by Herself* (1929).

Young, Whitney Moore, Jr. (1921–1971). Reformer, Business Person, Educator, Athlete, Author

Dickerson, Dennis C., *Militant Mediator—Whitney M. Young, Jr.*(1998).

Weiss, Nancy Joan, "Whitney M. Young, Jr.: Committing the Power Structure to the Cause of Civil Rights," in John Hope Franklin and August Meier, ed., *Black Leaders of the Twentieth Century* (1982): 351–58.

———— *Whitney M. Young, Jr. and the Struggle for Civil Rights*(1989).

Younge, Sammy, Jr. (1944–1966). Reformer, Military Person

Forman, James, *Sammy Younge, Jr.: The First Black College Student to Die in the Black Liberation Movement* (1968).

Zamba (?). Slave

Zamba, *The Life and Adventures of Zamba, an African Negro King; and His Experiences of Slavery in South Carolina*, ed. Peter Neilson (1847).

27.2 COLLECTED AUTOBIOGRAPHY AND BIOGRAPHY (Including Family Histories)

Adams, H. G., *God's Image in Ebony: Being a Series of Biographical Sketches, Facts, Anecdotes, Etc.* (1854).

Adams, Revels A., *Cyclopedia of African Methodism in Mississippi* (1902).

Albany Institute of History and Art, *The Negro Artist Comes of Age: A National Survey of Contemporary American Artists* (1945).

Alexander, Adele Logan, *Homelands and Waterways: The American Journey of the Bond Family, 1846–1926* (1999).

Alexander, Charles, *One Hundred Distinguished Leaders* (1899).

Alexander, Sadie T. M., *Who's Who among Negro Lawyers* (1945).

Anderson, J. Harvey, *Biographical Souvenir Volume of the Twenty-Third Quadrennial Session of the General Conference of the African Methodist Episcopal Zion Church* (1908).

Andrews, William L., and Henry Louis Gates, Jr., ed., *The Civitas Anthology of African American Slave Narratives* (1999).

Armistead, Wilson, *A Tribute for the Negro* (1848).

Armstrong, Orland Kay, *Old Massa's People: The Old Slaves Tell Their Story* (1931).

Arnett, B. W., *Proceedings of the Semi-Centenary Celebration of the African Methodist Episcopal Church of Cincinnati* (1874).

Arnett, Benjamin W., *The Budget: Containing Biographical Sketches, Quadrennial and Annual Reports of the General Officers of the African Methodist Episcopal Church of America* (1884).

Bacote, Samuel William, *Who's Who Among the Colored Baptists of the United States, Vol. 1* (1913).

Balagoon, Kuwasi, *Look for Me in the Whirlwind: The Collective Autobiography of the New York Twenty-One* (1971).

Ballard, Allen B., *One More Day's Journey: The Story of a Family and a People* (1984).

Barber, John Warner, *A History of the Amistad Captives: Being a Circumstantial Account of the Capture of the Spanish Schooner Amistad, by the Africans on Board . . . With Biographical Sketches of Each of the Surviving Africans* (1840).

Bardolph, Richard, *The Negro Vanguard* (1959).

Battle, Charles A., *Negroes on the Island of Rhode Island* (1932).

Beardslee, William R., *The Way Out Must Lead In: Life Histories in the Civil Rights Movement* (1977).

Beasley, Delilah L., *The Negro Trail Blazers of California* (1919).

Blackett, R. J. M., *Beating against the Barriers: Biographical Essays in Nineteenth-Century Afro-American History* (1986).

Blackwell, George L., *Who Is Who in the Fifth Episcopal District in the African Methodist Episcopal Zion Church . . . May, 1920* (1920).

Blassingame, John W., ed., *Slave Testimony: Two Centuries of Letters, Speeches, Interviews, and Autobiographies* (1977).

Bontemps, Arna, *We Have Tomorrow* (1945).

Boone, R. Irving, *Directory, Negro Business and Professional Men and Women: A Survey of Negro Progress in Varied Sections of North Carolina* (1946).

Boone, Theodore S., *From George Lisle to L. K. Williams: Visits to the Tombs of Negro Baptists* (1941).

————— *Negro Baptist Chief Executives in National Places* (1948).

Boothe, Charles Octavius, *The Cyclopedia of Colored Baptists of Alabama: Their Leaders and Their Work* (1895).

Boykin, Ulysses W., *A Hand Book on the Detroit Negro* (1943).

Bragg, George F., *The Colored Harvest in the Old Virginia Diocese* (1901).

————— *Heroes of the Eastern Shore* (1939).

————— *Men of Maryland* (1925).

————— *A Race with a History and a Country* (1930).

Bratton, Mary J., ed., "Fields's Observations: The Slave Narrative of a Nineteenth Century Virginian," *Virginia Magazine of History and Biography* 88 (1980): 75–93.

Brawley, Benjamin, *Early Negro American Writers* (1935).

————— *Negro Builders and Heroes* (1937).

————— *The Negro Genius: A New Appraisal of the Achievement of the American Negro in Literature and the Fine Arts* (1937).

————— *The Negro in Literature and Art in the United States* (rev. ed., 1929).

————— *Women of Achievement: Written for the Fireside Schools* (1919).

Brewer, J. Mason, *An Historical Outline of the Negro in Travis County* (1940).

————— *Negro Legislators of Texas and Their Descendants* (1935).

Broussard, Albert S., *African-American Odyssey: The Stewarts, 1853–1963* (1998).

Brown, Hallie Q., *Homespun Heroines and Other Women of Distinction* (1926).

————— *Pen Pictures of Pioneers of Wilberforce* (1937).

Brown, James Seay, ed., *Up before Daylight: Life Histories from the Alabama Writers' Project, 1938–1939* (1982).

Brown, Virginia Pounds, and Laurella Owens, *Toting the Lead Row: Ruby Pickens Tartt, Alabama Folklorist* (1981).

Brown, William Wells, *The Black Man: His Antecedents, His Genuis, and His Achievements* (2d ed., 1863).

————— *The Rising Son, or, The Antecedents and Advancement of the Colored Race* (1874).

Bruce, John E., comp., *Short Biographical Sketches of Eminent Negro Men and Women in Europe and the United States* (1910).

Buck, D. D., *The Progression of the Race in the United States and Canada* (1907).

Bullock, Ralph W., *In Spite of Handicaps* (1927).

Burkett, Randall K., and Richard Newman, ed., *Black Apostles: Afro-American Clergy Confront the Twentieth Century* (1978).

Burrell, W. P., and D. E. Johnson, Sr., *Twenty-Five Years History of the Grand Fountain of the United Order of True Reformers, 1881–1905* (1909).

Bush, A. E., and P. L. Dorman, *History of the Mosaic Templars of America: Its Founders and Officials* (1924).

Butt, Israel L., *History of African Methodism in Virginia, or Four Decades in the Old Dominion* (1908).

Caldwell, A. B., *History of the American Negro and His Instituions, Georgia Edition, Vol. I and II* (2 vols., 1917, 1920).

——— *History of the American Negro, South Carolina Edition, Vol. III* (1919).

——— *History of the American Negro, North Carolina Edition, Vol. IV* (1921).

——— *History of the American Negro, Virginia Edition, Vol. V* (1921).

——— *History of the American Negro, Washington, D.C., Edition, Vol. VI* (1922).

——— *History of the American Negro, West Virginia Edition, Vol. VII* (1923).

Carter, Edward R., *Biographical Sketches of Our Pulpit* (1888).

——— *The Black Side: A Partial History of the Business, Religious, and Educational Side of the Negro in Atlanta, Ga.* (1894).

Cashin, Herschel V., et al., *Under Fire with the Tenth U.S. Cavalry: Being a Brief, Comprehensive Review of the Negro's Participation in the Wars of the United States* (1902).

Cayton, Horace R., *Cayton's Year Book: Seattle's Colored Citizens* (1923).

Chapman, Abraham, ed., *Steal Away: Stories of the Runaway Slaves* (1971).

Chesson, Michael B., "Richmond's Black Councilmen, 1871–1896," in Howard Rabinowitz, ed., *Southern Black Leaders of the Reconstruction Era* (1982): 191–222.

Child, L. Maria, *The Freedmen's Book* (1865).

Clayton, Ronnie W., *Mother Wit: The Ex-Slave Narratives of the Louisiana Writers' Project* (1990).

Coles, Howard W., *The Cradle of Freedom: A History of the Negro in Rochester, Western New York and Canada* (1942).

Columbia Civic Library Association, *A Directory of Negro Graduates of Accredited Library Schools, 1900–1936* (1937).

Comer, James P., *Maggie's American Dream: The Life and Times of a Black Family* (1988).

Contemporary Black Biography: Profiles from the International Black Community (1992–).

Conyers, James L., ed., *Black Lives: Essays in African-American Biography* (1999).

Cooper, Arnold, *Between Struggle and Hope: Four Black Educators in the South, 1894–1915* (1989).

Cooper, William M., *Virginia's Contribution to Negro Leadership: Biographies of Outstanding Negroes Born in Virginia* (1936).

Cox, Lewis Y., *Pioneer Footsteps* (1917).

Crawford, I. W., and P. H. Thompson, *Multum in Parvo: An Authenticated History of Progressive Negroes in Pleasing and Graphic Biographical Style* (2d ed., 1912).

Cromwell, John W., *The Negro in American History: Men and Women Eminent in the Evolution of the American of African Descent* (1914).

Culp, D. W., ed., *Twentieth Century Negro Literature: A Cyclopedia of Thought on the Vital Topics Relating to the American Negro* (1902).

Cuney-Hare, Maud, *Negro Musicians and Their Music* (1936).

Dabney, Wendell Phillips, *Cincinnati's Colored Citizens: Historical, Sociological and Biographical* (1926).

Daniel, Sadie Iola, *Women Builders* (1931).

Davis, Elizabeth Lindsay, *Lifting as They Climb* (1933).

——— *The Story of the Illinois Federation of Colored Women's Clubs, 1900–1922* (1922).

Davis, Thadious M., and Trudier Harris, ed., *Afro-American Poets since 1955 (Dictionary of Literary Biography, vol. 41)* (1985).

——— *Afro-American Writers after 1955: Dramatists and Prose Writers (Dictionary of Literary Biography, vol. 38)* (1985).

Davis, W. Milan, *Pushing Forward: A History of Alcorn A. & M. College and Portraits of Some of Its Successful Graduates* (1938).

Dawson, Charles C., *ABC's of Great Negroes* (1933).

Diggs, James Robert Lincoln, *Our Portrait Gallery* (n.d.).

Dorman, Franklin A., *Twenty Families of Color in Masschusetts: 1742–1998* (1998).

Downs, Karl E., *Meet the Negro* (2d ed., 1943).

Drew, Benjamin, *The Refugee: Or the Narratives of Fugitive Slaves in Canada. Related by Themselves, with an Account of the History and Condition of the Colored Population of Upper Canada* (1856).

Drewes, Christopher F., *Half a Century of Lutheranism among Our Colored People: A Jubilee Book, 1877–1927* (1927).

Duncan, Sara J., *Progressive Missions in the South: And Addresses with Illustrations and Sketches of Missionary Workers and Ministers and Bishops' Wives* (1906).

DuPree, Sherry Sherrod, comp. and ed., *Biographical Dictionary of African-American Holiness-Pentecostals, 1880–1990* (1989).

Earnest, Joseph B., Jr., *The Religious Development of the Negro in Virginia* (1914).

Edwards, J. Passmore, *Uncle Tom's Companions: Or, Facts Stranger than Fiction. . .Being Startling Incidents in the Lives of Celebrated Fugitive Slaves* (1852).

Ehrmann, Bess V., *"Thenceforward and Forever Free"* (1945).

Embree, Edwin R., *Thirteen Against the Odds* (1944).

Federal Writers' Project, *Lay My Burden Down: A Folk History of Slavery*, ed. B. A. Botkin (1945).

———— *These Are Our Lives* (1939).

Felps, Jettie I., *The Lost Tongues* (1945).

Fisk University, Social Science Institute, *God Struck Me Dead: Religious Conversion Experiences and Autobiographies of Negro Ex-Slaves* (1945).

———— *Unwritten History of Slavery: Autobiographical Accounts of Negro Ex-Slaves* (1945).

Fleischer, Nathaniel S., *Black Dynamite: The Story of the Negro in the Prize Ring from 1782 to 1938* (5 vols., 1938–39, 1947).

Fleming, Beatrice J., and Marion J. Pryde, *Distinguished Negroes Abroad* (1946).

Flickinger, Robert Elliott, *The Choctaw Freedmen and the Story of Oak Hill Industrial Academy* (1914).

Foner, Eric, "Black Reconstruction Leaders at the Grass Roots," in Leon Litwack and August Meier, ed., *Black Leaders of the Nineteenth Century* (1988): 219–34.

———— *Freedom's Lawmakers: A Directory of Black Officeholders during Reconstruction* (2d ed., 1996).

Fonvielle, William F., *Reminiscences of College Days* (1903).

Foster, Mamie Marie Booth, comp., *Southern Black Creative Writers, 1829–1953: Biobibliographies* (1988).

Franklin, John Hope, and August Meier, ed., *Black Leaders of the Twentieth Century* (1982).

Franklin, V. P., and Bettye Collier-Thomas, "Biography, Race Vindication, and African-American Intellectuals: Introductory Essay," *Journal of Negro History* 81 (1996): 1–16.

Fuller, Thomas O., *History of the Negro Baptists of Tennessee* (1936).

———— *Pictorial History of the American Negro* (1933).

Gaines, Wesley J., *African Methodism in the South: Or Twenty-Five Years of Freedom* (1890).

General Association of Colored Baptists, *Diamond Jubilee of the General Association of Colored Baptists in Kentucky* (1943).

Gilbert, Don, *Negro City Directory: Dallas, Tx., 1947–48* (1947?).

Goode, W. T., *The "Eighth Illinois"* (1899).

Grant, R. C., comp., *The Nashville Colored Directory: 1925 Biographical Statistical* (1925).

Greene, Harry Washington, *Holders of Doctorates among American Negroes* (1946).

Grégoire, Henri, *An Enquiry Concerning the Intellectual and Moral Faculties, and Literature of Negroes; Followed with an Account of the Life and Works of Fifteen Negroes and Mulattoes* (1810).

Gullins, W. R., *The Heroes of the Virginia Annual Conference of the A.M.E. Church* (1899).

Halberstam, David, *The Children* (1998).

Haley, James T., *Afro-American Encyclopaedia: Or, the Thoughts, Doings, and Sayings of the Race* (1896).

———— *Sparkling Gems of Race Knowledge Worth Reading* (1897).

Hall, A. L., *The Ancient, Mediaeval, and Modern Greatness of the Negro* (1907).

Hamilton, G. P., *Beacon Lights of the Race* (1911).

———— *The Bright Side of Memphis* (1908).

Hammond, L. H., *In the Vanguard of a Race* (1922).

Hampton Normal and Agricultural Institute, *Twenty-Two Years' Work of the Hampton Normal and Agricultural Institute at Hampton, Virginia* (1890).

Handy, James A., *Scraps of African Methodist Episcopal History* (1901).

Handy, W. C., *Negro Authors and Composers of the United States* (1938?).

——— *Unsung Americans Sung* (1944).

Harris, Lawrence, *Negro Population of Lexington in the Professions, Business, Education, and Religion* (1907).

Harris, Sheldon, *Blues Who's Who: A Biographical Dictionary of Blues Singers* (1979).

Harris, Trudier, ed., *Afro-American Writers from the Harlem Renaissance to 1940 (Dictionary of Literary Biography, vol. 51)* (1987).

Harris, Trudier, and Thadious M. Davis, ed., *Afro-American Fiction Writers after 1955 (Dictionary of Literary Biography, vol. 33)* (1984).

——— *Afro-American Writers before the Harlem Renaissance (Dictionary of Literary Biography, vol. 50)* (1986).

——— *Afro-American Writers, 1940–1955 (Dictionary of Literary Biography, vol. 76)* (1988).

Hartshorn, W. N., *An Era of Progress and Promise, 1863–1910* (1910).

Haynes, Elizabeth Ross, *Unsung Heroes* (1921).

Henderson, Edwin Bancroft, *The Negro in Sports* (rev. ed., 1939).

Hicks, William, *History of Louisiana Negro Baptists from 1804 to 1914* (1915).

Hine, Darlene, Elsa Barkley Brown, and Rosalyn Terborg-Penn, *Black Women in America: An Historical Encyclopedia* (2 vols., 1993).

Hodges, Graham Russell, ed., *The Black Loyalist Directory: African Americans in Exile after the American Revolution* (1995).

Holt, Thomas C., "Negro State Legislators in South Carolina during Reconstruction," in Howard Rabinowitz, ed., *Southern Black Leaders of the Reconstruction Era* (1982).

Hotaling, Edward, *The Great Black Jockeys: The Lives and Times of the Men Who Dominated America's First National Sport* (1999).

Howard University, School of Medicine, *Howard University Medical Department, Washington, D.C.: A Historical, Biographical and Statistical Souvenir* (1900).

Hume, Richard L., "Negro Delegates to the State Constitutional Conventions of 1867–1869," in Howard Rabinowitz, ed., *Southern Black Leaders of the Reconstruction Era* (1982).

Hurt, A. D., and T. J. Searcy, *The Beacon Lights of Tennessee Baptists* (1900).

Ione, Carole, *Pride of Family: Four Generations of American Women of Color* (1991).

Jackson, A. W., *A Sure Foundation* (1939).

Jackson, Luther Porter, *Negro Office-Holders in Virginia, 1865–1895* (1945).

——— *Virginia Negro Soldiers and Seamen in the Revolutionary War* (1944).

Jenness, Mary, *Twelve Negro Americans* (1936).

Johnson, William Decker, *Biographical Sketches of Prominent Negro Men and Women of Kentucky* (1897).

Jones, Edward P., *The Cayugan Baptist: Sermons, Rock-Ribbed Fundamentals, Facts and Truths and Brief Biographies of Eminent Preachers* (1922).

Jones, Maxine D., "'Without Compromise or Fear': Florida's African American Female Activists," *Florida Historical Quarterly* 77 (1999): 475–502.

Kealing, H. T., *History of African Methodism in Texas* (1885).

Keene, Josephine Bond, *Directory of Negro Business and Professional Women of Philadelphia and Vicinity* (1939).

Kenney, John A., *The Negro in Medicine* (1912).

Kentucky General Association of Colored Baptists, *Diamond Jubilee of the General Association of Colored Baptists in Kentucky* (1943).

Kerlin, Robert T., *Negro Poets and Their Poems* (1923).

Kessler, James H., *Distinguished African American Scientists of the Twentieth Century* (1996).

Koger, A. Briscoe, *Negro Baptists of Maryland* (1946).

Kotlowitz, Alex, *There Are No Children Here: The Story of Two Boys Growing up in the Other America* (1991).

Lewis, R. B., *Light and Truth: Collected from the Bible and Ancient and Modern History, Containing the Universal History of the Colored and Indian Races* (1844).

Lincoln University, *Biographical Catalogue* (1918).

Litwack, Leon, and August Meier, ed., *Black Leaders of the Nineteenth Century* (1988).

Loewenberg, Bert James, and Ruth Bogin, ed., *Black Women in Nineteenth-Century American Life: Their Words, Their Thoughts, Their Feelings* (1976).

Logan, Rayford W., and Michael R. Winston, ed., *Dictionary of American Negro Biography* (1982).

Long, Charles Sumner, *History of the A.M.E. Church in Florida* (1939).

Lovinggood, Penman, *Famous Modern Negro Musicians* (1921).

MacKerrow, P. E., *A Brief History of the Coloured Baptists of Nova Scotia* (1895).

Majors, Monroe A., *Noted Negro Women: Their Triumphs and Activities* (1893).

Mather, Frank L., ed., *Who's Who of the Colored Race: A General Biographical Dictionary of Men and Women of African Descent, Vol 1* (1915).

McWilliams, William A., comp., *Columbus Illustrated Record* (1920).

Michigan Freedmen's Progress Committee, *Michigan Manual of Freedmen's Progress,* ed. Francis H. Warren (1915).

Miller, Harriet Parks, *Pioneer Colored Christians* (1911).

Mixon, Winfield H., *History of the African Methodist Episcopal Church in Alabama, with Biographical Sketches* (1902).

Mollison, W. E., *The Leading Afro-Americans of Vicksburg, Miss., Their Enterprises, Churches, Schools, Lodges and Societies* (1908).

Monroe, Sylvester, and Peter Goldman, *Brothers, Black and Poor: A True Story of Courage and Survival* (1988).

Moorman, J. H., and E. L. Barrett, ed., *Leaders of the Colored Race in Alabama* (1928).

Morgan, Joseph H., *Morgan's History of the New Jersey Conference of the A.M.E. Church from 1872 to 1887* (1887).

Morgan, Kathryn L., *Children of Strangers: The Stories of a Black Family* (1980).

Morris, E. C., *Sermons, Addresses and Reminiscences and Important Correspondence, with a Picture Gallery of Eminent Ministers and Scholars* (1901).

Morris, O. M., *Negro Progress since Slavery* (1940).

Moseley, J. H., *Sixty Years in Congress and Twenty-Eight Out* (1960).

Mott, Abigail, comp., *Biographical Sketches and Interesting Anecdotes of Persons of Color* (1826).

Mott, Abigail, and Mary Sutton Wood, comp., *Narratives of Colored Americans* (1877).

Nell, William Cooper, *The Colored Patriots of the American Revolution* (1855).

New York, Emancipation Proclamation Commission, *A Memento of the Emancipation Proclamation Exposition of the State of New York* (1913).

Newbold, N. C., *Five North Carolina Negro Educators* (1939).

Nichols, Charles H., ed., *Black Men in Chains: Narratives by Escaped Slaves* (1972).

Nichols, J. L., and William H. Crogman, ed., *Progress of a Race, Or, the Remarkable Advancement of the American Negro, from the Bondage of Slavery, Ignorance, and Poverty to the Freedom of Citizenship, Intelligence, Affluence, Honor and Trust* (rev. ed., 1920).

Northrop, Henry Davenport, Joseph R. Gay, and I. Garland Penn, *The College of Life, Or, Practical Self-Educator: A Manual of Self-Improvement for the Colored Race . . . Giving Examples and Achievements of Successful Men and Women of the Race . . . Including Afro-American Progress* (1900).

O'Neil, Michael J., *Some Outstanding Colored People: Interesting Facts in the Lives of Representative Negroes* (1943).

Organ, Claude H., Jr., and Margaret M. Kosiba, ed., *A Century of Black Surgeons: The U.S.A. Experience* (2 vols., 1987).

Osofsky, Gilbert, ed., *Puttin' on Ole Massa: The Slave Narratives of Henry Bibb, William Wells Brown, and Solomon Northup* (1969).

Ovington, Mary White, *Portraits in Color* (1927).

Parham, William Hartwell, comp., *An Official History of the Most Worshipful Grand Lodge Free and Accepted Masons for the State of Ohio* (1906).

Parrish, C. H., *Golden Jubilee of the General Association of Colored Baptists in Kentucky. . .From 1865–1915* (1915).

Patterson, A. E., *The Possibilities of the American Negro: With Illustrations and Biographies of Some of the Leading Negroes in America* (1903).

Patterson, Ruth Polk, *The Seed of Sally Good'n: A Black Family of Arkansas, 1833–1953* (1985).

Pegues, A. W., *Our Baptist Ministers and Schools* (1892).

Penn, I. Garland, *The Afro-American Press, and Its Editors* (1891).

Pennsylvania Negro Business Directory, Illustrated, 1910: Industrial and Material Growth of the Negroes of Pennsylvania (1909).

Perdue, Charles L., Jr., Thomas E. Barden, and Robert K. Phillips, ed., *Weevils in the Wheat: Interviews with Virginia Ex-Slaves* (1976).

Perkins, A. E., ed., *Who's Who in Colored Louisiana* (1930).

Peterson, Bernard L., Jr., *Contemporary Black American Playwrights and Their Plays: A Biographical Directory and Dramatic Index* (1988).

———— *Early Black American Playwrights and Dramatic Writers: A Biographical Directory and Catalog of Plays, Films, and Broadcasting Scripts* (1990).

Phelps, Shirelle, ed., *Who's Who among African Americans* (10th ed., 1998/99).

Pipkin, J. J., *The Story of a Rising Race: The Negro in Revelation, in History and in Citizenship* (1902).

Plato, Ann, *Essays: Including Biographies and Miscellaneous Pieces, In Prose and Poetry* (1841).

Porters, David L., ed., *African-American Sports Greats: A Biographical Dictionary* (1995).

Posey, Thomas E., *The Negro Citizen of West Virginia* (1934).

Powell, Raphael P., *Human Side of a People and the Right Name: The Great Book of New Education* (1937).

Powell, Sanford Bell, *Colored American Biography Post Register* (1941).

Prince, W. H., *The Stars of the Century of African Methodism* (1916).

Quick, William H., *Negro Stars in All Ages of the World* (1898).

Rabinowitz, Howard N., ed., *Southern Black Leaders of the Reconstruction Era* (1982).

Rabinowitz, Howard N., "Three Reconstruction Leaders: Blanche K. Bruce, Robert Brown Elliott, and Holland Thompson," in Leon Litwack and August Meier, ed., *Black Leaders of the Nineteenth Century* (1988): 191–217.

Ragsdale, Bruce A., and Joel D. Treese, *Black Americans in Congress, 1870–1989* (1990).

Rankin, David C., "The Origins of Negro Leadership in New Orleans during Reconstruction," in Howard Rabinowitz, ed., *Southern Black Leaders of the Reconstruction Era* (1982): 155–189.

Rankin-Hall, Lesley M., *A Biohistory of Nineteenth Century Afro-Americans: The Burial Remains of a Philadelphia Cemetery* (1997).

Rawick, George P., ed., *The American Slave: A Composite Autobiography* (19 vols., 1973–76).

Rawick, George P., ed., *The American Slave: A Composite Autobiography: Supplement, Series 2* (10 vols., 1979).

Rawick, George P., Jan Hillegas, and Ken Lawrence, ed., *The American Slave: A Composite Autobiography: Supplement, Series 1* (12 vols., 1977).

Reagon, Bernice Johnson, and Sweet Honey in the Rock, *We Who Believe in Freedom: Sweet Honey in the Rock—Still on the Journey* (1993).

The Red Book of Houston: A Compendium of Social, Professional, Religious, Educational and Industrial Interests of Houston's Colored Population (1915).

Richardson, Ben, *Great American Negroes* (1945).

Richardson, Clement B., ed., *The National Cyclopedia of the Colored Race* (1919).

Richings, G. F., *An Album of Negro Educators* (1900).

———— *Evidences of Progress among Colored People* (1904).

Riley, James A., *The Biographical Encyclopedia of the Negro Baseball Leagues* (1994).

Robb, Frederick H. Hammurabi, *1927 Intercollegian Wonder Book; Or 1799—The Negro in Chicago—1927* (vol. 1, 1927).

———— *Intercollegian Wonder Book: Or, The Negro in Chicago, 1928–29* (vol. 2, 1929).

Rogers, J. A., *World's Greatest Men and Women of African Descent* (1931).

———— *World's Great Men of Color* (1946–47).

Rogers, William H., *Senator John P. Green, and Sketches of Prominent Men of Ohio* (1893).

Roses, Lorraine Elena, and Ruth Elizabeth Randolph, *Harlem Renaissance and Beyond: Literary Biographies of 100 Black Women Writers, 1900–1945* (1990).

Russell, Dick, *Black Genius* (1998).

Russell, Lester F., *Profile of a Black Heritage* (1977).

Salem, Dorothy C., ed., *African American Women: A Biographical Dictionary* (1993).

Sammons, Vivian Ovelton, *Blacks in Science and Medicine* (1990).

Scally, Mary Anthony, *Negro Catholic Writers, 1900–1943: A Bio-Bibliography* (1945).

Scruggs, Lawson A., *Women of Distinction: Remarkable in Works and Invincible in Character* (1892).

Shorter, Susan I., *The Heroines of African Methodism* (1891).

Simmons, William J., *Men of Mark: Eminent, Progressive and Rising* (1887).

Simms, James N., *Simms' Blue Book and National Negro Business and Professional Directory* (1923).

Smith, Anna Amelia, *Reminiscences of Colored People of Princeton, N.J.* (1913).

Smith, J. Clay, Jr., *Emancipation: The Making of the Black Lawyer, 1844–1944* (1993).

Smith, James H., *Vital Facts Concerning the African Methodist Episcopal Church* (1939).

Smith, Jessie Carney, ed., *Notable Black American Women* (1992).

————, ed., *Notable Black American Women, Book II* (1996).

————, ed., *Notable Black American Men* (1999).

Spencer, Gerald A., *Medical Symphony: A Study of the Contributions of the Negro to Medical Progress in New York* (1947).

Still, William, *The Underground Railroad* (1872).

Styles, Fitzhugh Lee, *The Negro Lawyers' Contribution to Seventy-One Years of Our Progress* (1934).

———— *Negroes and the Law in the Race's Battle for Liberty, Equality and Justice* (1937).

Taitt, John, *The Souvenir of Negro Progress: Chicago, 1779–1925* (1925).

Talbert, Horace, *The Sons of Allen* (1906).

Tanner, Benjamin T., *An Apology for African Methodism* (1867).

Terrill, Tom E., and Jerrold Hirsch, ed., *Such as Us: Southern Voices of the Thirties* (1978).

Thompson, John L., *History and Views of Colored Officers Training Camp for 1917 at Fort Des Moines, Iowa* (1917).

Thompson, Patrick H., *The History of Negro Baptists in Mississippi* (1898).

Thoms, Adah B., *Pathfinders: A History of the Progress of Colored Graduate Nurses* (1929).

Thorp, Daniel B., "Chattel With a Soul: The Autobiography of a Moravian Slave," *Pennsylvania Magazine* 112 (1988): 433–51.

Toppin, Edgar A., *A Biographical History of Blacks in America since 1528* (1971).

Trotter, James M., *Music and Some Highly Musical People* (1878).

Trottman, Beresford Sylvester Briggs, *Who's Who In Harlem: The 1949–1950 Biographical Register of a Group of Distinguished Persons of New York's Harlem, First Edition* (1950).

Tyler, Ron, and Lawrence R. Murphy, ed., *The Slave Narratives of Texas* (1997).

Vaughan, Walter R., *Vaughan's "Freedmen's Pension Bill"* (1891).

Warren, Francis H., *Michigan Manual of Freedmen's Progress* (1915).

Washington, Booker T., et al., *Tuskegee and Its People: Their Ideals and Achievements* (1906).

Washington, Booker T., N. B. Wood, and Fannie Barrier Williams, *A New Negro for a New Century* (1900).

Watkins, Sylvestre C., *The Pocket Book of Negro Facts* (1946).

Wayman, Alexander W., *Cyclopaedia of African Methodism* (1882).

———— *My Recollections of African M.E. Ministers: Or Forty Years' Experience in the African Methodist Episcopal Church* (1881).

Weeden, H. C., *Weeden's History of the Colored People of Louisville* (1897).

Weisenfeld, Judith, and Richard Newman, ed., *This Far by Faith: Readings in African-American Women's Religious Biography* (1996).

Welding, Pete, and Toby Byron, ed., *Bluesland: Portraits of Twelve Major American Blues Masters* (1991).

White, Charles Frederick, et al., *Who's Who in Philadelphia; a Collection of Thirty Biographical Sketches of Philadelphia Colored People* (1912).

White, J. Bliss, comp., *Biography and Achievements of the Colored Citizens of Chattanooga* (1904).

Whitted, J. A., *A History of the Negro Baptists of North Carolina* (1908).

Who's Who in Colored America (7 vols., 1927–1950).

Wiencek, Henry, The Hairstons: An American Family in Black and White (1999).

Williams, James, *Life and Adventures of James Williams, a Fugitive Slave, with a Full Description of the Underground Railroad* (1873).

Williams, M. W., and George W. Watkins, *Who's Who Among North Carolina Negro Baptists* (1940).

Williams, Roger M., *The Bonds: An American Family* (1971).

Wills, David W., and Richard Newman, ed., *Black Apostles at Home and Abroad: Afro-Americans and the Christian Mission from the Revolution to Reconstruction* (1982).

Woodson, Carter G., *Negro Makers of History* (1945).

Wright, Richard R., Jr., *Centennial Encyclopaedia of the African Methodist Episcopal Church* (1916).

——— *Encyclopaedia of the African Methodist Episcopal Church* (2d ed., 1947).

Wright, Richard R., Jr., *Who's Who in the General Conference 1924* (1924).

Wright, Richard R., Jr., et al., comp., *The Philadelphia Colored Business Directory* (1914).

Wynn, Commodore, *Negro Who's Who in California* (1948).

Young, Mary, and Gerald Horne, *Testaments of Courage: Selections from Men's Slave Narratives* (1995).

27.3 CRITICAL STUDIES OF AUTOBIOGRAPHY AND BIOGRAPHY

Andrews, William L., *To Tell a Free Story: The First Century of Afro-American Autobiography, 1760–1865* (1986).

Bailey, David Thomas, "A Divided Prism: Two Sources of Black Testimony on Slavery," *Journal of Southern History* 46 (1980): 381–404.

Bardolph, Richard, "The Distinguished Negro in America, 1770–1936," *American Historical Review* 60 (1955): 527–47.

Barton, Rebecca Chalmers, *Witnesses for Freedom: Negro Americans in Autobiography* (1948).

Blassingame, John W., ed., *Slave Testimony: Two Centuries of Letters, Speeches, Interviews, and Autobiographies* (1977).

——— "Using the Testimony of Ex-Slaves: Approaches and Problems," *Journal of Southern History* 41 (1975): 473–92.

Botkin, Benjamin, "The Slave as His Own Interpreter," *Library of Congress Quarterly Journal of Acquisitions* 2 (1944): 37–63.

Butterfield, Stephen, *Black Autobiography in America* (1974).

Davis, Allison, *Leadership, Love, and Aggression* (1983).

Davis, Charles T., and Henry Louis Gates, Jr., ed., *The Slave's Narrative* (1985).

D'Costa, Jean, and Barbara Lalla, *Voices in Exile: Jamaican Texts of the Eighteenth and Nineteenth Centuries* (1989).

Dyson, Michael Eric, *Making Malcolm: The Myth and Meaning of Malcolm X* (1995).

Foster, Frances Smith, *Witnessing Slavery: The Development of Antebellum Slave Narratives* (1979).

——— *Written by Herself: Literary Production by African American Women, 1746–1892* (1993).

Franklin, V. P., *Living Our Stories, Telling Our Truths: Autobiography and the Making of the African-American Intellectual Tradition* (1995).

Goodson, Martia Graham, "The Slave Narrative Collection: A Tool for Reconstructing Afro-American Women's History," *Western Journal of Black Studies* 3 (1979): 116–22.

Matlock, James, "The Autobiographies of Frederick Douglass," *Phylon* 40 (1979): 15–28.

Morgan, Winifred, "Gender-Related Difference in the Slave Narratives of Harriet Jacobs and Frederick Douglass," *Florida Historical Quarterly* 73 (1994): 147–65.

Morneno, Gary R., "Florida Slave Narratives," *Florida Historical Quarterly* 66 (1988): 399–419.

Nichols, Charles H., "Slave Narratives and the Plantation Legend," *Phylon* 10 (1949): 201–10.

O'Brien, Michael, "Old Myths/New Insights: History and Dr. King," *History Teacher* 22 (1988): 49–66.

Pinckney, Darryl, "Promisory Notes, Professionals, and Aristocrats," *New York Review of Books* (1995).

Rampersad, Arnold, "Psychology and Afro-American Biography," *Yale Review* 78 (1989): 1–18.

Samra, Matthew K., "Shadow and Substance: The Two Narratives of Sojourner Truth," *Midwest Quarterly* 38 (1997): 158–71.

Sartwell, Crispin, *Act Like You Know: African American Autobiography and White Identity* (1998).

Schultz, Elizabeth, "To Be Black and Blue: The Blues Genre in Black American Autobiography," *Kansas Quarterly* 7 (1975): 81–96.

Smith, Sidonie, *Where I'm Bound: Patterns of Slavery and Freedom in Black American Autobiography* (1974).

Smith, Valerie, *Self-Discovery and Authority in the Afro-American Narrative* (1987).

Starling, Marion Wilson, *The Slave Narrative: Its Place in American History* (1978).

Stepto, Robert Burns, *From Behind the Veil: A Study of Afro-American Narrative* (1979).

Williams, Ronald L., Jr., *African American Autobiography and the Quest for Freedom* (2000).

Woodward, C. Vann, "History from Slave Sources: A Review Essay," *American Historical Review* 79 (1974): 470–81.

Yetman, Norman R., "The Background of the Slave Narrative Collection," *American Quarterly* 19 (1967): 534–53.

——— "Ex-Slave Interviews and the Historiography of Slavery," *American Quarterly* 36 (1984): 181–210.

Contributors

Adam Biggs is a Ph.D. candidate in the History of American Civilization program at Harvard University. He is writing his dissertation on the contribution of black physicians to racial equality in late 19th- and early 20th-century America.

Richard J. M. Blackett is Moores Professor of History and African American Studies at the University of Houston. He has published in the area of Anglo-American abolitionism.

John H. Bracey has been a member of the W. E. B. Du Bois Department of Afro-American Studies at the University of Massachusetts at Amherst since 1972. Among his many publications are the manuscript microfilm series *Black Studies Research Sources* (University Publications of America) and the recent coedited volume, with Marianne Adams, *Strangers and Neighbors: Relations between Blacks and Jews in the United States* (1999).

Nathaniel Bunker was the Charles Warren Bibliographer for American History in the Harvard College Library, Harvard University.

Barbara A. Burg is Research Librarian in the Research Services Department at Widener Library, Harvard University, and liaison to the departments of Afro-American Studies and History.

Randall K. Burkett is African-American Studies Bibliographer in the Special Collections Department, Robert W. Woodruff Library, Emory University. The author of two books on Marcus Garvey, he is coeditor with Nancy H. Burkett and Henry Louis Gates, Jr., of *Black Biography, 1790–1950: A Cumulative Index* (3 vols., 1990). This was the first reference work created under the auspices of the W. E. B. Du Bois Institute for Afro-American Research at Harvard, compiled during the years he served as Associate Director of the Institute (1985–1995).

Clayborne Carson is Professor of History at Stanford University and Editor and Director of the Martin Luther King, Jr., Papers Project. He has written and edited many books on the civil rights movement, including *The Autobiography of Martin*

Luther King, Jr. (1998), *Malcolm X: The FBI File* (1991), and *In Struggle: SNCC and the Black Awakening of the 1960s* (1981).

Raquel Von Cogell is Reference Librarian at Emory University. She has previously held librarian positions at Yale University and the Schomburg Center for Research in Black Culture, New York Public Library.

Thomas Cripps, recently retired as University Distinguished Professor at Morgan State University, is the author of five books and numerous articles on film. He is also a film producer and the scriptwriter for the prizewinning film *Black Shadows on a Silver Screen* (1976). His most recent book is *Hollywood's High Noon: Movie Making and Society before Television* (1997).

James P. Danky, Newspapers and Periodicals Librarian, State Historical Society of Wisconsin Library, has published more than thirty volumes. A former Fulbright Scholar at the British Library and Fellow of the W. E. B. Du Bois Institute, he is the author of *African-American Newspapers and Periodicals: A National Bibliography* (1998).

Eric Foner is DeWitt Clinton Professor of History at Columbia University. He is the author of numerous books including *Reconstruction: America's Unfinished Revolution, 1863–1877* (1988) and *The Story of American Freedom* (1998).

John Gennari is Assistant Professor of American Studies and History at Penn State, Harrisburg. His research interests include African-American music and culture, 20th-century American cultural history, and Italian American culture.

Nancy L. Grant was Associate Professor of History at Washington University, St. Louis, until her death in 1995. She was the author of *TVA and Black Americans: Planning for the Status Quo.*

Betty Kaplan Gubert was for many years the head of reference service at the Schomburg Center for Research in Black Culture, New York Public Library. She is the author of *Invisible Wings: An Annotated Bibliography on Blacks in Aviation, 1916–1993* (1994).

Debra Newman Ham, currently Professor of History at Morgan State University, served from 1986 to 1995 as the Specialist in Afro-American History and Culture in the Manuscript Division at the Library of Congress, and from 1972 to 1986 as an archivist and Black History Specialist at the National Archives. She was the curator of a 1998 three-building Library of Congress exhibit and editor of the exhibit catalog, *The African American Odyssey* (1998); editor and senior author of *The African-American Mosaic: A Library of Congress Resource Guide for the Study of Black History and Culture* (1993); and the author of *Black History: A Guide to Civilian Records in the National Archives* (1984).

Evelyn Brooks Higginbotham is Professor of History and Afro-American Studies at Harvard University. She has published in the fields of African-American women's history, feminist theory, and African-American religion. She is the author of the prizewinning book *Righteous Discontent: The Women's Movement in the Black Baptist Church, 1880–1920* (1993).

Darlene Clark Hine is John A. Hannah Professor of American History at Michigan State University. Her most recent books are *The African-American Odyssey* (2000), coauthored with Stanley Harrold and William C. Hine, and *A Shining Thread of Hope: The History of Black Women in America* (1998), coauthored with Kathleen Thompson. Her earlier books include *Hine Sight: Black Women and the Re-Construction of American History* (1994) and *Black Women in White: Racial Conflict and Cooperation in the Nursing Profession, 1890–1950* (1989). She is editor of *The State of Afro-American History, Past, Present, and Future* (1986) and coeditor with Elsa Barkley Brown and Rosalyn Terborg-Penn of *Black Women in America: An Historical Encyclopedia* (2 vols., 1993). Hine is president-elect of the Organization of American Historians.

Earl Lewis is Professor of History and Afro-American and African Studies, Vice Provost for Academic Affairs–Graduate Studies, and Dean of the Graduate School at the University of Michigan. He is the author, coauthor, or editor of four books, and with Robin D. G. Kelley, is general editor of an 11-volume history of African-Americans for young adults.

Leon F. Litwack, the A. F. and May T. Morrison Professor of History at the University of California, Berkeley, is the author of *North of Slavery: The Negro in the Free States, 1790–1860* (1961), *Trouble in Mind: Black Southerners in the Age of Jim Crow* (1998), and *Been in the Storm So Long: The Aftermath of Slavery* (1979), which won the Pulitzer Prize in History and the Parkman Prize. He is also the coeditor of *Black Leaders of the Nineteenth Century* (1988). Litwack is the recipient of a Guggenheim Fellowship, two Distinguished Teaching Awards, and a National Endowment for the Humanities Film Grant (with which he produced *To Look for America: From Hiroshima to Woodstock*). In 1986–87 he was President of the Organization of American Historians, and in 1987 he was elected to the American Academy of Arts and Sciences.

Portia K. Maultsby is Professor of Ethnomusicology and the Director of the Archives of African American Music and Culture at Indiana University. A specialist in African-American music, her current research and publications are on the popular music tradition. She is editor of the series *Black Music and Expressive Culture,* published by Indiana University Press.

Marya McQuirter is completing a Ph.D. in History at the University of Michigan. Her research focuses on African-American urbanization in the first half of the 20th century. She is the author of two books.

Gary B. Nash is Professor of History at UCLA and director of the National Center for History in the Schools. A former president of the Organization of American Historians, he has published widely on African-American history, including *Forging Freedom: The Formation of Philadelphia's Black Community, 1720–1840* (1988); *Race and Revolution* (1990); *Freedom by Degrees: Emancipation in Pennsylvania and Its Aftermath* (1991); and *Forbidden Love: The Secret History of Mixed-Race America* (1999).

Richard Newman is Research and Fellows Officer at the W. E. B. Du Bois Institute for Afro-American Research at Harvard University. He is the author of several books including *Go Down, Moses: Celebrating the African American Spiritual* (1998) and *African American Quotations* (1998).

Stephanie Shaw is Associate Professor of History at Ohio State University. Her research and teaching interests include African-American history and the history of American women and African-American women. She has published *What a Woman Ought to Be and to Do: Black Professional Women Workers During the Jim Crow Era* (1996).

Elinor Des Verney Sinnette established the oral history department at the Moorland-Spingarn Research Center of Howard University in 1980, after a lengthy career as a librarian. After her retirement from Howard University in 1991, Dr. Sinnette has continued to serve as an oral history consultant to various academic and community constituencies.

Jeffrey Conrad Stewart is Associate Professor of History and Director of African American Studies at George Mason University. He is the author of *To Color America: Portraits by Winold Reiss* (1989), and *Paul Robeson: Artist and Citizen* (1998).

John Thornton is a specialist in the history of Africa and the African diaspora. He has published several books and many articles, among them *Africa and Africans in the Making of the Atlantic World, 1400–1800* (1998), and *The Kongolese Saint Anthony* (1998).

Joe W. Trotter is Mellon Professor of History and Director of the Center for Africanamerican Urban Studies and the Economy at Carnegie Mellon University in Pittsburgh. His publications include *River Jordan: African American Urban Life in the Ohio Valley* (1998), *Coal, Class, and Color* (1990), and *Black Milwaukee* (1985). He is currently completing a textbook on the African-American experience and conducting research on African-Americans in the urban Deep South.

Corey Walker is a Ford Foundation Fellow and Ph.D. candidate in American Studies at the College of William and Mary in Virginia. He is currently a Visiting Scholar at the Carter G. Woodson Institute at the University of Virginia, where he is completing a dissertation on African-American freemasonry in Virginia between 1866 and 1902.

Deborah Willis is a Curator of Exhibitions at the Smithsonian Institution's Center for African American History and Culture. A MacArthur Fellow in 2000, she is the author of *Reflections in Black: A History of Black Photographers, 1840 to the Present* (2000) and *Picturing Us: African American Identity in Photography* (1994).

Peter H. Wood, a former Rhodes Scholar, published a prizewinning book on slavery in colonial South Carolina entitled *Black Majority* (1974). In 1988 he coauthored with Karen Dalton *Winslow Homer's Images of Blacks: The Civil War and Reconstruction Years.* Professor Wood has been an advisor on numerous television projects, including the PBS series *Africans in America,* and has taught in the History Department at Duke University since 1975.

Author Index

References to Part I are by page number, those to Parts II and III by section number. The notation *ja* indicates joint authorship, followed by the name of the primary author. The notation *ed.* indicates editor of papers, followed by the name of the papers' subject; a name in parentheses following a citation indicates that the work is a biography and is listed under the subject's name.